"Hardy and McAffee have smartly employed a textbook-style format to produce a second-year grammar for students of biblical Hebrew. Rather than using the fully deductive or strictly inductive methods most often employed in a second year of instruction, they have successfully navigated to a mediating approach, giving us a pedagogically helpful textbook for the classroom. The volume can be used to good effect with intermediate students, but it also provides abundant and up-to-date discussion of many technical details that often seem baffling to students. This volume will immediately become a classic in the list of resources available to students of the Old Testament."

—**Bill T. Arnold,** Paul S. Amos Professor of Old Testament
Interpretation, Asbury Theological Seminary

"In *Going Deeper with Biblical Hebrew*, Hardy and McAffee provide a well-researched study of the grammar and syntax of the Hebrew Bible. In addition, they introduce students to the history of the Hebrew language and to the Masoretic text. This volume will be an excellent next step for students who have completed their study of the basics of Hebrew."

—**Mark Futato,** Robert L. Maclelland Professor of Old
Testament, Reformed Theological Seminary

"In *Going Deeper*, McAffee and Hardy have done a great service for the study of biblical Hebrew, combining solid research and thoughtful pedagogy. Finding a textbook that aids both teacher and student is a rare jewel, and this volume is a treasure trove—with grammar explanations, integrated translation exercises, vocabulary, and guided lessons on textual criticism, semantics, and syntactical analysis. In my teaching, this comprehensive resource will always be close at hand!"

—**Brian P. Gault,** professor of Old Testament, Dallas Theological Seminary

"In *Going Deeper with Biblical Hebrew*, Hardy and McAffee present fresh, pedagogically sensitive lessons in a manner applicable to all interested readers yet nuanced for Christians desirous of applying the idiosyncratic points of the biblical text to their lives. This volume creatively embodies the transitional space between beginner grammars and advanced texts that sometimes relate frivolous minutiae. Hardy and McAffee have greatly served the academy and the church by producing a scholarly yet accessible resource for all those serious about going deeper with biblical Hebrew!"

—**Dominick S. Hernández,** associate professor of Old Testament
and Semitics, Talbot School of Theology, Biola University

"Both practically accessible and linguistically rigorous, Hardy and McAffee's valuable resource meets the needs of students and professors. Though not shying away from the technical details, the authors carefully balance the technical semantic information with the important pragmatic implications. Using famously complex passages (such as the *Nephilim*) as examples both draws students in and illustrates the importance of the issues. Overall, the authors make the technical relatable and, most of all, practical to second-year Hebrew students."

—**JoAnna M. Hoyt,** associate professor of applied
linguistics, Dallas International *University*

"Hardy and McAffee give students a gift. This book offers accessible, linguistically informed details of biblical Hebrew. It brings students in contact with the rich complexity of the language. Yet *Going Deeper with Biblical Hebrew* is a steady guide. Hardy and McAffee demonstrate their pedagogical acumen throughout the book, particularly in their directed lessons on semantics and syntax. This volume is a welcome addition for students and professors alike."

—**Ethan C. Jones,** associate professor of Old Testament and Hebrew, Don and Helen Bryant Chair of Old Testament, New Orleans Baptist Theological Seminary

"Going Deeper with Biblical Hebrew combines traditional grammatical methods with the best of current cognitive linguistic approaches to illustrate, convincingly and repeatedly, how a deeper, more mature grasp of Hebrew grammar enriches our understanding of God's Word. Through clear explanations and copious examples, Hardy and McAffee demonstrate in practical terms the relationship between grammar, exegesis, and application. If you have studied biblical Hebrew, get this book, and take your interpretive skills to the next level."

—**Catherine L. McDowell,** associate professor of Old Testament, Gordon-Conwell Theological Seminary

"Going Deeper with Biblical Hebrew is a detailed exposition of biblical Hebrew intended for an intermediate or advanced seminary student. By focusing attention on the intricate details of Hebrew—phonological, morphological, syntactic, discourse, text-critical, and especially semantic —the authors integrate an intimate knowledge of the meaning-making processes of the Hebrew text with its exegetical value within a Christian context."

—**Cynthia L. Miller-Naudé** and **Jacobus A. Naudé,** senior professors of Hebrew, University of the Free State (Bloemfontein, South Africa)

"Hardy and McAffee's *Going Deeper with Biblical Hebrew* is an outstanding resource for teaching intermediate biblical Hebrew grammar. It presents grammatical concepts in an accessible way while being well-grounded in both linguistic and comparative Semitic scholarship. Along the way, Hardy and McAffee give significant attention to exegesis and how knowledge of biblical Hebrew grammar can be applied practically to the biblical text. Because of these distinctives, this volume is arguably the most useful and effective intermediate biblical Hebrew teaching grammar on the market today. Both instructors and students will profit greatly from it."

—**Benjamin J. Noonan,** associate professor of Old Testament and Hebrew, Columbia International University

"One of the main reasons Hebrew students fail to progress in long-term proficiency is due to the fact that the path from beginning Hebrew to using more advanced resources is largely uncharted and daunting. *Going Deeper with Biblical Hebrew* now provides students with a guided tour of the more advanced wonders of biblical Hebrew. The authors are to be commended for their excellent work, and students will be grateful for this tremendous resource as it 'deepens' their ability to read, study, and teach the Old Testament."

—**Miles V. Van Pelt,** Alan Hayes Belcher, Jr. Professor of Old Testament and Biblical Languages, and director, Summer Institute for Biblical Languages, Reformed Theological Seminary, Jackson

GOING
DEEPER

////////////

WITH
BIBLICAL

HEBREW

GOING
DEEPER
WITH
BIBLICAL
HEBREW

An **Intermediate** Study of the Grammar
and Syntax of the Old Testament

H. H. **Hardy II** and Matthew **McAffee**

with contributions from John D. **Meade**

B&H ACADEMIC
BRENTWOOD, TENNESSEE

To our parents,
Rocky and Joan Hardy
Oral and Susan McAffee

CONTENTS

///////////////

Preface   xi
Abbreviations   xvii
Transliteration   xxii
Linguistic Abbreviations   xxv

PART A
  1. Hebrew Language   3
  2. Retrieving the Text of the Hebrew Bible   45

PART B
  3. The Verbal System   77
  4. Verbal Stems   115
  5. Prefix and Suffix Conjugations   173
  6. Volitives   223

PART C
  7. Nouns and Noun Phrases   271
  8. Pronouns, Adjectives, and Participles   351
  9. Infinitives and Temporal Clauses   409
 10. Conjunctions, Adverbs, and Other Particles   453
 11. Prepositions   515

Guided Lesson א: Textual Criticism   577
Guided Lesson ב: Semantic Analysis   589
Guided Lesson ג: Syntactic Analysis   601
Appendix A: Continuing with Hebrew   609
Appendix B: Biblical Hebrew Vocabulary   619
Appendix C: English to Hebrew Catalogue   655
Appendix D: Glossary   659
Bibliography   675
Name Index   709
Subject Index   717
Scripture Index   725

PREFACE

//////////////

כי קרוב אליך הדבר מאד בפיך ובלבבך לעשתו

"Assuredly the word is exceedingly close to you—even in your mouth
and your heart—so that you might do it."

—Deuteronomy 30:14

INTRODUCTION

The Word of God speaks, acts, and lives. Little should invigorate the believer more.
Divine expression spoke creation into existence and sustains the world today. That
same word is light to a world full of darkness and brings hope to the oppressed,
burdened, marginalized, and weary. His verbal acts fashion, uphold, liberate, and
restore.

The Israelites knew of God's pronouncement firsthand. Those receiving it were
declared the children of God. The decree thundered from Sinai as a dark cloud
encompassed it. The Israelites heard the word on the lips of Yahweh's chosen servants. They saw it written on tablets and stone monuments. They listened as it was
recited from inscribed scrolls. They learned, memorized, and invoked it. They repeated it to their children (Deut 6:4–9). They voiced it every moment of their lives.
The word marked their entrances and their exits. It reverberated at nightfall and
intoned their waking at first light. It formed who they were—their work and rest,
their prayers and worship, their society and humanity.

The word is intended to be spoken aloud and heard. The sacred Scriptures do
not reside as static letters merely inked on a page and stored in a sacrosanct box.
One of the earliest descriptions is מִקְרָא (miqra). It is the word for "oral reading"
in Neh 8:8. This word shares a root with the verb קרא "proclaim, read aloud" and
is connected to the notion of "convocation" as part of the religious service enacted
during an assembly (see, e.g., Deut 31:11 and Josh 8:34–35). While the word of
God could be inscripturated (i.e., written), Scriptures require oration! No evidence
exists for silent reading in ancient Judaism.

The word is never meant to be far off and unknowable. As Deut 30:14 says, it
is not distant—that is foreign and unfamiliar—but resides "in your mouth and on

your heart." The spoken word inhabits the believer. The "mouth" evokes metaphors for speaking and action, and the "heart" educes the will and desires. This embodied word, we are told, enacts doing. The word is meant to be spoken, understood, and lived!

This notion and practice of holding the word near is echoed in the Christian tradition. The word of God is incarnate in the person of Jesus Christ. His words and work are the lived Word. The word made alive. Love and sacrifice covenant to create new life. And Christians speak of God's indwelling presence in their lives. The apostle Paul urges, "Let the word of Christ dwell richly among you" (Col 3:16). Christians savor the very word of God. But all too often we treat it as mundane or foreign. We have not taken seriously the admonition to abide in the word. Rather it is unknown, distant, and dead. May we not be satisfied with such complacency. Let us turn to the "words of light" (Ps 119:130) and the "words of eternal life" (John 6:68).

What does it mean to embody the Scriptures? Deuteronomy provides the pattern. God's word must be in our mouths and in our hearts. This practice certainly looks different for different folks. It might mean listening and repeating the words if you cannot read. You may recite the Scriptures in morning and evening prayer. It could entail joining others in a Bible study. And it might mean learning to read, speak, and meditate on Hebrew. One approach exercised from the earliest days of the synagogue and taken up by the early church was the daily and weekly public reading and praying of the Scriptures. Eugene Peterson described his entire ministry simply as "Scripture and prayer, prayer and Scripture."[1] These simple means of grace have always embodied the word of God for believers.

THE PURPOSE OF THIS BOOK

This book is intended to help Christians read the Hebrew Scriptures. Not everyone will have the time, opportunity, and ability to undertake such a virtuous task. For those who try, however, they need all the help they can get! Learning any language is no small task—not least one that sounds as unusual as Hebrew does to most English speakers' ears. Yet, sometimes in our search for knowledge and truth, we must set our sights on the impossible.

The primary focus of this text is grammar and interpretation. The grammatical descriptions appraise both modern linguistic methods and long-held approaches to the language. Historical, functional, and cognitive linguistic approaches are prominent in the explanations. The conclusions of other linguistic methodologies are beneficial and variously discussed, but ultimately these predilections drive our assessment.

---

[1] This modest but captivating vision is found in the epilogue of Eugene Peterson, *A Long Obedience in the Same Direction: Discipleship in an Instant Society*, rev. ed. (Downers Grove, IL: IVP, 2000), 201–3.

While the grammatical aspects reflect linguistic notions shared by believers and nonbelievers alike, the exegetical application is distinctly Christian. We have not aimed to offend in this outcome. And we hope that this work will be valuable for anyone interested in reading Hebrew. Nevertheless, we would consider it dishonest to fain ignorance of our own religious reading tradition and interpretive proclivities. Perhaps this approach is most evident in the introductory "Going Deeper" sections of each chapter and in the concluding and supplemental materials (Guided Lessons and Appendix A: Continuing with Hebrew). In these sections we explore acutely what it would mean for Christians to benefit from the study of the Hebrew Scriptures as God's Word.

WHO WILL BENEFIT?

Our primary audience includes students of Hebrew who have completed an introductory grammar. A customary pattern is for a student to begin with a one-year course in Hebrew taught from one of many entry-level textbooks currently available.[2] For many students, thirty weeks of intense memorization of forms, vocabulary, and grammatical rules allow for a rudimentary ability to read from the Hebrew Bible. The student might even have read a short book or narrative sequence, such as Ruth, Jonah, the Abrahamic narratives, or the Joseph story.

Quickly, however, most students find that the grammar learned in these short weeks of instruction becomes insufficient for the task of reading. They encounter unfamiliar words and constructions. Like a child learning to color with crayons, the basic skills of drawing and applying color to a page are the first steps. A grand universe of methods and visual mediums can be used to represent the world. The coloring book page may be displayed proudly on a parent's refrigerator, but it is a far cry from the gallery of the Art Institute of Chicago or the Musée d'Orsay. Students realize that reading Hebrew is considerably more complicated than merely mastering the presentation of a beginning grammar.

This stark and hard reality produces a quandary for even seasoned instructors. What comes next after working through an introductory textbook? Two basic approaches are common. In classic pedagogical fashion, they follow inductive and deductive methodological preferences. The first approach gives preference to reading texts. You might read a lot of texts or read texts in their smallest detail. The grammatical particulars are discussed as you go. From time to time, you review the beginning grammar or perhaps look at sections of a reference grammar, but most of the student's knowledge is formed through on-the-job training. The second approach focuses on more advanced grammars. The fine-grained details are presented and reviewed. Students examine closely the examples provided in the discussion. Then they apply that knowledge of grammar as they read individual texts.

---

[2] See "Appendix A: Continuing with Hebrew" for examples of first-year Hebrew grammars.

This resource attempts to offer a different, mediating approach. We continue the pedagogical pattern of a beginning textbook but present the material at an intermediate (or, at times, admittedly advanced) level. We do not attempt to give full coverage to introductory matters; instead, we assume the student has some familiarity with basic morphology, vocabulary, and syntax. In so doing, we move from the sterile and controlled environment of beginning Hebrew grammar to the wily and uncalibrated world of the language found in the Hebrew Bible. For the most part, our discussions are focused on general formations of grammar instead of itemized representations of all formal and functional variations. They guide the student into the next steps required to read more and more.

For the teacher interested in trying this approach, we suggest several ways to use the material.

HOW TO USE THIS MATERIAL

This volume contains ten chapters, three guided lessons, and four appendices. The material can be divided in several ways and effectively used in various instructional settings. The two most common classroom formats are a one semester course or two semester courses. In these organizations, a semester represents fifteen instructional sessions or weeks.

For a one semester course in intermediate Hebrew, the entire book can be assigned. To do this, the longest chapter may be partitioned into two parts: nouns (§7.1–8) and determiners with numerals (§7.9–10). In twelve weeks, the teacher could cover the other eleven chapters, and three weeks could be dedicated to the Guided Lessons. We suggest spreading these lessons throughout the semester and assigning an exegetical exercise related to each lesson. The assignments could be integrated into a larger exegetical paper or be assigned as independent projects. This strategy has been very effective in our own classes. It has the added benefit of allowing for some distance between the assessments rather than crowding all three at the end of the term.

For a year-long format (or two semesters), each chapter could be read over two weeks or paired with other readings. In the first semester, we would recommend covering Parts A and B (chapters 1–6), and the first Guided Lesson (text criticism). These chapters focus on understanding the text of the Hebrew Bible and the complicated issues related to Hebrew finite verbs. The second semester would comprise Part C (chapters 6–11) and the other two Guided Lessons (lexical and syntactic analyses).

CHAPTER DESCRIPTIONS

This collaborative project stands as a testament to the fact that the body is not one part but many (1 Cor 12:14). Chapters 1, 3, 4, and 9 were drafted and written jointly by both authors. McAffee was the primary author of chapters 5, 6, and 8. Hardy authored chapters 7, 10, and 11. All the chapters were greatly improved through years of collaboration and discussion. John Meade graciously agreed to contribute the material on the ancient sources (chapter 2) and Guided Lesson א: Textual Criticism. The final two exegetical exercises (Guided Lesson ב and Guided Lesson ג) represent the collaborative efforts of the two main authors. The guided lessons direct students into the vast worlds of textual criticism, word studies, and syntactic analysis. The three lessons supplement the grammatical chapters with detailed descriptions, strategies, guidelines, and models of how to accomplish important exegetical tasks. Four appendices provide additional resources for students: how to continue learning Hebrew beyond this textbook (Appendix A), vocabulary lists including words occurring 40× or more (Appendix B), an English to Hebrew catalogue (Appendix C), and a glossary of the underlined grammatical terms (Appendix D).

CHAPTER BREAKDOWN

Each chapter begins with a section highlighting a significant and expanded example of the grammar discussed. These sections are labeled "Going Deeper." The grammar of each topic is explained with biblical examples. Guided practice exercises and suggested readings end chapters 3–11.

Going Deeper

These brief discussions focus on a particular text and its interpretation. Each example is meant to connect with the grammar covered in the chapter.

Discussion

The arrangement of each chapter varies depending on the topic. Generally, the discussion moves from issues of morphology to syntax and pragmatics. Our goal is to present a broad description of the grammatical topic, represent apposite positions, and specify our understanding. We fully recognize that not every reader, teacher, or scholar will agree with our decisions, assumptions, or theoretical frameworks. At times, the two authors do not completely agree on these matters, and we frequently modified our own views while researching these topics. Ultimately, we intended to represent accurately the scholarly conversation and present clearly, albeit briefly, our conclusions.

Each grammatical topic is accompanied by Hebrew examples and translations. Translations are the authors' own unless otherwise notated. The translations are specifically rendered to focus on the grammatical topic at hand. The text may be translated in a woodenly literal manner to highlight or represent the Hebrew grammar more clearly. Most examples are provided with limited context. A copy of the Hebrew Bible would be helpful to consult (see Appendix A: Continuing with

Hebrew). The verse reference designates where the example may be found even when only part of the verse is represented. When the complete verse is included, the *sop pasuq* (the colon-like cantillation mark at the end of the verse) is included at the end of the line.

Supplementary Resources

Additional resources are available at www.deeperhebrew.com. We plan to make available various materials, such as lesson plans, suggested readings, exegetical assignments, quizzes, exams, worksheets, and answer keys.

ACKNOWLEDGMENTS

A work of this extent and scale would never be completed without countless individuals. The problem with naming anyone is that enviably others will be omitted. We offer our apologies and sincere thanks to those we fail to name here.

We first and foremost express our deepest gratitude to our wives, Anna McAffee and Amy Warren Hardy, as well as our children: Abigail, Lydia, Samuel, Marianne, and John Isaac McAffee and Samuel Lewis Hardy.

We owe a great debt to our Hebrew teachers (Dennis G. Pardee, Peter J. Gentry, Daniel I. Block), our colleagues and friends (John Meade, Tracy McKenzie, Ben Merkle, Matt Mullins, Adrianne Miles, Heath Thomas, Brian Gault, Chris Fresch, Young Bok Kim, Daniel Rodriguez, Cathy McDowell, Samuel Boyd, Drayton Benner, Mike Aubrey, Ethan Jones, Kim Phillips, Kaspars Ozolins, Fausto Liriano, Elizabeth Robar, Caleb Howard, Zach Vickery, Daniel Webster, Amy Hardy, and Billie Goodenough), our many students (particularly Seth Ellington, Dougald McLaurin, Robb Colman, Devin Moncada, Anna Marie Gedeon, Alejandro Johnson, Ryan Payne, Josh Hunter, and Dustin Walters), and our academic institutions (Southeastern Baptist Theological Seminary and Welch College).

Lastly, we appreciate the patience and encouragement of the good people at B&H Academic and the thoughtful interaction of Brian Cribb.

ABBREVIATIONS

/////////////////

𝔐	Masoretic Text
𝔰𝔪	Samaritan Pentateuch
𝔔	Dead Sea Scrolls from Qumran
𝔊	Old Greek (or popularly Septuagint, LXX)
θ′	Theodotion
α′	Aquila
σ′	Symmachus
ε′	Quinta
ς′	Sexta
𝔳	Latin Vulgate
𝔰	Syriac Peshitta
𝔗	Aramaic Targums
AB	Anchor Bible
ABD	*Anchor Yale Bible Dictionary*. 6 vols. Edited by David Noel Freedman. New York: Doubleday, 1992.
ABH	Archaic Biblical Hebrew
Akk	Akkadian
ANEM	Ancient Near Eastern Monographs
AnOr	Analecta Orientalia
AOAT	Alter Orient und Altes Testament
ArOr	*Archiv orientální*
BASOR	*Bulletin of the American Schools of Oriental Research*
BBR	*Bulletin of Biblical Research*
BDB	Francis Brown, Samuel Rolles Driver, and Charles Augustus Briggs, *A Hebrew and English Lexicon of the Old Testament*. Oxford: Clarendon, 1906.

ABBREVIATIONS	
BDF	F. Blass, A. Debrunner, and Robert W. Funk, *Greek Grammar of the New Testament and Other Early Christian Literature*. Rev. ed. Chicago: University of Chicago Press, 1961.
BH	Biblical Hebrew
BHQ	*Biblia Hebraica Quinta*. Edited by Adrian Schenker et al. Stuttgart: Deutsche Bibelgesellschaft, 2004–.
BHRG	Christo H. J. van der Merwe, Jacobus A. Naudé, and Jan H. Kroeze, *A Biblical Hebrew Reference Grammar*. 2nd ed. London: Bloomsbury Academic, 2017.
BHS	*Biblia Hebraica Stuttgartensia*. 5th ed. Edited by Karl Elliger and Wilhelm Rudolph. Stuttgart: Deutsche Bibelgesellschaft, 1997.
BL	Hans Bauer and Pontus Leander, *Historische Grammatik der hebräischen Sprache des Alten Testamentes*. Halle: Niemeyer, 1922.
Blau	Joshua Blau, *Phonology and Morphology of Biblical Hebrew*. LSAWS 2. Winona Lake, IN: Eisenbrauns, 2010.
BN	*Biblische Notizen*
BSOAS	*Bulletin of the School of Oriental and African Studies*
CAD	*The Assyrian Dictionary of the Oriental Institute of the University of Chicago*. Edited by Ignace J. Gelb et al. 21 vols. Chicago: The Oriental Institute, 1956–2010.
CBET	Contributions to Biblical Exegesis & Theology
CBH	Classical Biblical Hebrew
CBQ	*Catholic Biblical Quarterly*
CTAT	Dominique Barthélemy, *Critique textuelle de l'Ancien Testament*. 5 vols. Göttingen: Vandenhoeck & Ruprecht, 1982–2015.
DCH	*The Dictionary of Classical Hebrew*. Edited by David J. A. Clines. 6 vols. Sheffield: Sheffield Academic, 1993–2011.
DJD	*Discoveries in the Judaean Desert*. 40 vols. Oxford: Clarendon, 1955–2010.
SI	De Septuaginta Investigationes
DSS	Dead Sea Scrolls (𝔔 + Other Sites)
EA	El-Amarna tablets. According to the edition of Jörgen A. Knudtzon, *Die el-Amarna-Tafeln*. Leipzig: Hinrichs, 1908–1915. Repr., Aalen: Zeller, 1964.
EANEC	Explorations in Ancient Near Eastern Civilizations
EH	Epigraphic Hebrew

ABBREVIATIONS

EHLL	*Encyclopedia of Hebrew Language and Linguistics.* Edited by Geoffrey Khan. Leiden: Brill, 2013.
FAT	Forschungen zum Alten Testament
GKC	Friedrich Wilhelm Gesenius, *Gesenius' Hebrew Grammar.* Edited by E. Kautzsch and Sir Arthur Ernest Cowley. 2nd ed. Oxford: Clarendon, 1910.
HALOT	Ludwig Koehler and Walter Baumgartner, *The Hebrew and Aramaic Lexicon of the Old Testament.* 2 vols. Leiden: Brill, 1994–2000.
HS	*Hebrew Studies*
HSM	*Harvard Semitic Monographs*
HSS	Harvard Semitic Studies
HTR	*Harvard Theological Review*
HUCA	*Hebrew Union College Annual*
IBHS	Bruce K. Waltke and Michael Patrick O'Connor, *An Introduction to Biblical Hebrew Syntax.* Winona Lake, IN: Eisenbrauns, 1990.
IEJ	*Israel Exploration Journal*
IF	*Indogermanische Forschungen*
JANES	*Journal of Ancient Near Eastern Studies*
JAOS	*Journal of the American Oriental Society*
JBL	*Journal of Biblical Literature*
JBLMS	Journal of Biblical Literature Monograph Series
JETS	*Journal of the Evangelical Theological Society*
JHS	*Journal of Hebrew Scriptures*
JJS	*Journal of Jewish Studies*
JNES	*Journal of Near Eastern Studies*
JNSL	*Journal of Northwest Semitic Linguistics*
Joüon-Muraoka	Paul Joüon and Takamitsu Muraoka, *A Grammar of Biblical Hebrew.* 2nd ed. Rome: Pontifical Biblical Institute, 2006.
JQR	*Jewish Quarterly Review*
JSOT	*Journal for the Study of the Old Testament*
JSOTSup	*Journal for the Study of the Old Testament Supplement Series*
JSS	*Journal of Semitic Studies*
KAI	*Kanaanäische und aramäische Inschriften.* Edited by Herbert Donner and Wolfgang Röllig. 5th rev. ed. Wiesbaden: Harrassowitz, 2002.

ABBREVIATIONS

KTU	*Die keilalphabetischen Texte aus Ugarit, Ras Ibn Hani und anderen Orten* [The cuneiform alphabetic texts from Ugarit, Ras Ibn Hani and other places]. Edited by Dietrich, Manfried, Oswald Loretz, and Joaquín Sanmartín. 3rd, enl. ed. AOAT 360/1. Münster: Ugarit-Verlag, 2013.
KUSATU	*Kleine Untersuchungen zur Sprache des Alten Testaments und seiner Umwelt*
Lambdin	Thomas O. Lambdin, *Introduction to Biblical Hebrew*. New York: Scribner, 1971.
LBH	Late Biblical Hebrew
lit.	literally
LSAWS	Linguistic Studies in Ancient West Semitic
LXX	Septuagint/Old Greek (𝔊)
M^L	Leningrad Codex
Mm	Masorah magna
Mp	Masorah parva
MS(S)	Manuscript(s)
MT	Masoretic Text
NAC	New American Commentary
NAWG	*Nachrichten der Akademie der Wissenschaften in Göttingen*
NICOT	New International Commentary on the Old Testament
NIDOTTE	*New International Dictionary of Old Testament Theology and Exegesis*. Edited by Willem VanGemeran. 5 vols. Grand Rapids: Zondervan, 1997.
NOM	nominative
OLA	*Orientalia Lovaniensia Analecta*
OTL	*Old Testament Library*
Or	*Orientalia*
RevQ	*Revue de Qumran*
RS	Ras Shamra
SAOC	Studies in Ancient Oriental Civilizations
SBH	Standard Biblical Hebrew
SBLMS	Society of Biblical Literature Monograph Series
SSLL	Studies in Semitic Languages and Linguistics
SSN	Studia Semitica Neerlandica
STDJ	Studies on the Texts of the Desert of Judah

ABBREVIATIONS

SVTG	Septuaginta Vetus Testamentum Graecum
TDOT	*Theological Dictionary of the Old Testament.* Edited by G. Johannes Botterweck. 17 vols. Grand Rapids: Eerdmans, 1974–2021.
THB	*The Textual History of the Bible. Edited by Armin Lange et al. 10 vols. Leiden: Brill, 2016–.*
TLOT	*Theological Lexicon of the Old Testament.* Edited by Ernst Jenni and Claus Westermann. Translated by Mark E. Biddle. 3 vols. Peabody, MA: Hendrickson, 1997.
TrBH	Transitional Biblical Hebrew
TSAJ	Texts and Studies in Ancient Judaism
TWOT	*Theological Wordbook of the Old Testament.* Edited by R. Laird Harris et al. Chicago: Moody, 2003.
UF	*Ugarit-Forschungen*
VT	*Vetus Testamentum*
VTSup	Supplements to Vetus Testamentum
WBC	Word Biblical Commentary
Williams	R. J. Williams, *Williams' Hebrew Syntax.* Edited by John C. Beckman. 3rd ed. Toronto: University of Toronto Press, 2007.
ZAH	Zeitschrift für Althebräistik
ZAW	*Zeitschrift für die alttestamentliche Wissenschaft*
ZDMG	*Zeitschrift der Deutschen Morgenländischen Gesellschaft*

TRANSLITERATION

/////////////////

CONSONANTS		VOWELS	
ʾ	א	a	אֲ
b	בּ or ב	ā or o	אָ
g	גּ or ג	e	אֶ
d	דּ or ד	ē	אֵ
h	הּ or ה	i	אִ
w	ו	ō	אֹ
z	ז	u	אֻ
ḥ	ח	ə or Ø (silent shewa)	אְ
ṭ	ט	ĕ	אֱ
y	י	ă	אֲ
k	כּ, כ, or ך	ŏ	אֳ
l	ל	î	אִי
m	מ or ם	ê	אֵי or אֶי
n	נ or ן	ô	וֹ
s	ס	û	וּ
ʿ	ע	â	הָ
p	פּ, פ, or ף	āyw	יוָ
ṣ	צ or ץ		
q	ק		
r	ר		
š	שׁ		

xxii

CONSONANTS		VOWELS	
ś	שׂ		
t	ת or תּ		

NOTES

* For non-contextual Hebrew words, ◌ֺ (*ôlê*) is used as a generic accent mark to indicate nonfinal stress (e.g., תָּבֹ֫אנָה).
* Transcription of the consonantal text renders the letters in italicized Roman script without vowels (e.g., תָּבֹ֫אנָה transcribed as *tbʾnh*).
* Although rarely used in this volume, transliteration renders the consonants and Tiberian vowels in italicized Roman script (e.g., תָּבֹ֫אנָה transliterated as *tābōʾnâ*), adapted from *SBL Handbook of Style*, 2nd ed. (Atlanta: SBL Press, 2014).
* The symbol * means a reconstructed (and unattested) earlier Semitic form, > signifies "develops into," and < indicates "derived from."
* The historic forms are rendered in italicized Roman script with historic phonemes (e.g., **kablu* > כֶּ֫לֶב; **yaqtulū* > יִקְטְלוּ; and כֹּהֵן < **kāhinu*).
* Proto-Semitic contained at least 29 consonantal phonemes of which ancient Hebrew includes 25 historic consonants. The historic vowels are limited to three quantitatively (short or long) vowels: **a*, **i*, **u*, **ā*, **ī*, and **ū*. Diphthongs derive from a vowel and consonantal glide (e.g., **ay*, **aw*, **iy*, and **uw*). For details, see Gary A. Rendsburg, "Phonology: Biblical Hebrew," in *EHLL*, 3:100–109.
* The historic phonemes are not equivalent to the Tiberian Biblical Hebrew inventory. For a full description of the latter, see Geoffrey Khan, *The Tiberian Pronunciation Tradition of Biblical Hebrew*, vol. I, *Description of the Tiberian Pronunciation Tradition*, Cambridge Semitic Languages and Cultures 1 (Cambridge, UK: Open Book, 2020).
* Phonemic realizations are enclosed in forward slashes (e.g., שִׁבֹּלֶת /ʃɪˈbolɛθ/) using the standard symbols of International Phonetic Association (IPA) (see https://www.internationalphoneticassociation.org /content/full-ipa-chart).

LINGUISTIC ABBREVIATIONS

//////////////

*	unattested form
**	ungrammatical form
>	develops into
<	develops from
[ ]	insertion
{}	orthographic representation
/ /	phonemic realization
√	root
1	first person
2	second person
3	third person
ABS	absolute
ACC	accusative
ADJ	adjective
ADV	adverb(ial)
C	common gender
C stem	Semitic causative stem (Hebrew *Hiphil*)
CJ	conjunction
COP	copula
CP	consecutive preterite (i.e., *wayyiqtol*)
Cp stem	Semitic causative passive stem (Hebrew *Hophal*)
CSTR	construct
CV	consonant-vowel
CVC	consonant-vowel-consonant
D	dual
D stem	Semitic doubled stem (Hebrew *Piel*)

LINGUISTIC ABBREVIATIONS

DEM	demonstrative
DO	direct object
DOM	direct object marker
Dp stem	Semitic doubled passive stem (Hebrew *Pual*)
F	feminine gender
G stem	Semitic *Grund* or base stem (Hebrew *Qal*)
GEN	genitive
IMPV	imperative
INF	infinitive
IO	indirect object
JUSS	jussive
ketiv	Aramaic: "what is written"
LBH	Late Biblical Hebrew
LM	Landmark
LOC	locative
M	masculine gender
N	noun
N stem	Semitic prefixed N stem (Hebrew *Niphal*)
NEG	negation *or* negative
NOM	nominative
NP	noun phrase
OBJ	object
OC	object complement
P	plural
PC	prefix conjugation (i.e., *yiqtol*)
PN	proper name
PP	prepositional phrase
PRED	predicate
PREP	preposition
PRO	pronoun *or* pronominal
PTCL	particle
PTCP	participle
qere	Aramaic: "what is read"
REL	relative

LINGUISTIC ABBREVIATIONS

S	singular
SBH	Standard Biblical Hebrew
SC	suffix conjugation (i.e., *qātal*)
SF	suffix
SUBJ	subject
TAM	tense-aspect-mood
tD stem	Semitic prefixed-*t* doubled stem (Hebrew *Hitpael*)
TR	Trajector
V	verb
VP	verb phrase

//

PART A

//

CHAPTER 1

///////////////

HEBREW LANGUAGE

The history of the Hebrew language starts around the beginning of the first millennium BC and continues until the present. The evidence for ancient Hebrew in its earliest stages is slight and piecemeal, but we do know that it emerged within the broader linguistic setting of the ancient Near East (ANE). From this vantage point, the student encounters the ever-changing spoken and written languages of the ancient inhabitants of the Middle East. Ancient Near Eastern literatures survived because of innovation in graphic representation and historical happenstance. Many of these ancient languages remain unknown to us, as they either were not written down or have yet to be rediscovered. Hebrew, in many ways, played a minor role in this larger ancient world of language and writing. It was never the most dominant language, and its speakers did not pioneer advanced scribal technologies. But their theological writings—the collection that we today call the Hebrew Bible—endured through the labors of generations of unnamed individuals. The Bible narrates the tenacity of a people in preserving their language and writings that they understood to communicate the very words of God.

"Biblical Hebrew" is not a uniform spoken idiom but represents multiple dialects found in the texts referred to variously as the Hebrew Bible, Tanakh, and the Old Testament. Some of these instances of linguistic variation are more obvious than others. Prominently, half of the book of Daniel and the epistolary material in Ezra were written in forms of Aramaic from the second half of the first millennium. Certain northern Israelite language features are evident in the Elijah-Elisha narratives in Kings. And demonstrably later biblical writings, such as the book of Chronicles, Esther, and the Hebrew portions of Ezra-Nehemiah, reflect the complex and variable idioms of postexilic Jewish communities. These differences witness to a range of vernaculars from different interrelated locales and periods. When assessed properly, one discovers a diversity of linguistic communities, despite being found in what might appear to be a uniform corpus.

1.1 GOING DEEPER WITH HEBREW LANGUAGE

Linguistic diversity, at times, plays a key role in the biblical narrative. Judges 12 provides an infamous illustration. Upon the incursion of an Ephraimite force into Gilead—east of the Jordan River—Jephthah led his fellow Gileadites against the invading Ephraimites. The Gileadites defended their land and defeated the raiding army. Before the Ephraimites could flee back to their territory, the Gileadites outflanked them and captured the shallow crossing points of the river. A spoken challenge was established to distinguish friend from foe, insider from outsider, for anyone hoping to escape. Instead of a secret password or countersign, the authentication involved saying the appropriate passphrase correctly. Mispronunciation meant death on sight.

While both groups spoke Hebrew, distinctions in speech revealed the outsider status of the Ephraimite intruders. The account culminates with the narrative interchange in verses 5–6.

Judg 12:5b–6

וְהָיָה כִּי יֹאמְרוּ פְּלִיטֵי אֶפְרַ֫יִם אֶעֱבֹ֫רָה וַיֹּאמְרוּ לוֹ אַנְשֵׁי־גִלְעָד הַאֶפְרָתִי אַתָּה
וַיֹּ֫אמֶר ׀ לֹא: וַיֹּאמְרוּ לוֹ אֱמָר־נָא שִׁבֹּ֫לֶת וַיֹּ֫אמֶר סִבֹּ֫לֶת וְלֹא יָכִין לְדַבֵּר כֵּן וַיֹּאחֲזוּ
אוֹתוֹ וַיִּשְׁחָטֻ֫הוּ אֶל־מַעְבְּרוֹת הַיַּרְדֵּן וַיִּפֹּל בָּעֵת הַהִיא מֵאֶפְרַ֫יִם אַרְבָּעִים וּשְׁנַ֫יִם
אָֽלֶף:

When the Ephraimite deserters would say, "Let me cross," the Gileadites asked him, "Are you an Ephraimite?" He said, "No." They said to him: "Say the word ***stream***." But he responded ***steam***—he was not competent to say it similarly. They seized him and slaughtered him in the shoals of the Jordan. Forty-two thousand from Ephraim fell at that time.

The Gileadite sentries expected a response in kind. Their challenge word שִׁבֹּ֫לֶת /ʃiˈbolɛθ/ likely refers to a flowing body of water, as in the final clause of Ps 69:3: וְשִׁבֹּ֫לֶת שְׁטָפָ֫תְנִי "a stream overwhelms me."[1] In Masoretic Hebrew, the initial sound was the <u>postalveolar</u> /ʃ/, akin to English *sh*. This passcode is borrowed into English as *shibboleth* thanks to its transcription in the King James Bible.

Failing the response, the infelicitous pronunciation of the Ephraimites exposed their denied identity. The doomed impostors incompetently lisped סִבֹּ֫לֶת /siˈbolɛθ/. The exact original phonetic value is debated,[2] but the spelling with *samek* suggests

---

[1] Another less transparent option is the homophonous word meaning "an ear of grain" (Gen 41:5, 6, 17, 22, 23, 24, 26, 27, etc.). See R. Woodhouse, "Hebrew Šibbōleṯ 'Ear of Grain; (Olive) Branch' and 'Stream, Torrent, Flood': An Etymological Appraisal," *Studia Etymologica Cracoviensia* 7 (2002): 172–89.

[2] See Gary A. Rendsburg, "More on Hebrew Šibbōlet," *JSS* 33 (1988): 255–58. A. Faber, "Second Harvest: šibbolet Revisited (Yet Again)," *JSS* 37 (1992): 1–10; Ronald S. Hendel, "Sibilants and šibbōlet (Judges 12:6)," *BASOR* 301 (1996): 69–75; R. Woodhouse, "The Biblical Shibboleth Story in the Light of Late Egyptian Perceptions of Semitic Sibilants: Reconciling Divergent Views," *JAOS* 123 (2003): 271–90.

that the westerners mistakenly articulated the first sound as a voiceless <u>alveolar</u> /s/.[3] To imitate the subtle phonological difference, the English translation above employs two similar but distinguishable initial blends *str* and *st* (*stream* ~ *steam*), or if one understands it to refer to "ear of grain," possibly *sheave* ~ *sieve* would be a similar comparison. English speakers may think of various identifiable regional accent differences, such as the Standard American English (SAE) pronunciations of *car* compared with the Bostonian *cah* /ka/, *sorry* with the Canadian *sore-y* /ˈsɔɹi/, or the merger of *pin* and *pen* as /pɪn/ in various dialects. In any case, the Ephraimites paid dearly for their gaffe.

Hebrew did not require linguistic uniformity. While every difference in dialect does not have the grave consequences of Judges 12, variation in <u>phonation</u> can signal important linguistic, cultural, and sociological qualities. An accent may indicate a particular geographic origin (provincial source), socioeconomic status (high/low caste), or even first language influence (foreign accent). Group speech and writing patterns distinguish vital aspects in understanding ancient cultural perceptions. Dialects ultimately signal in-group or out-group social identification, resulting in positive and negative assumptions, which motivate respect, prestige, stereotypes, or even discrimination. Attention to perceived linguistic dissimilarities is, at times, key to interpreting the Hebrew narratives.

The people of Ephraim and Gilead had drastically different backgrounds. The patriarch Jacob favored Ephraim over the elder grandson Manasseh (Gen 48; Deut 33:13–17). The Ephraimite tribe held a prized and important inheritance in the northern hill country of Israel (Josh 16:5–17:18). During the conquest, Joshua commanded Israel as a member of Ephraim (Josh 19:49–50; Judg 2:9). Despite this leadership, the tribe failed to drive out the Canaanites (Judg 1:29). They were strong but proved impotent and petulant when not called on to act (Judg 8:1–3). The Transjordanian territory of Gilead, on the other hand, was settled by the two and half tribes of Reuben, Gad, and Manasseh. Their outsider status is demonstrated in multiple texts (Joshua 22). From the Ephraimites' perspective in particular, Gilead represented those living on the "wrong side of the tracks" (Judg 5:17).[4] And yet, God appointed one of their own to deliver them from Midianite oppression (Judges 6–8) as well as an Ammonite threat (Judg 10:6–12:7).

In this sardonic episode, Ephraim functioned like an incompetent foreign invader. The tribe stood against God's deliverer. They mocked Jephthah's compatriots as פְּלִיטֵי אֶפְרַיִם "Ephraimite fugitives," but they were thoroughly routed (12:4), and in a satirical twist they themselves became Ephraimite fugitives (12:5). As those challenging divine protection, Ephraim obtained outsider status and was driven from the land. The geographic boundary of the Jordan River on this occasion was

---

[3] Hendel, "Sibilants" argues, based on an analogous spelling variation of *š* ~ *s* with the name *Baʿliša/Baʿalis*, that the Gileadite Hebrew pronunciation was more like the Transjordanian Canaanite dialect of Ammonite than Cisjordanian Hebrew. See also Gary A. Rendsburg, "The Ammonite Phoneme /T/," *BASOR* 269 (1988): 73–79.

[4] See Daniel I. Block, *Judges, Ruth*, NAC 6 (Nashville: B&H, 1999), 385–88.

a disadvantage in retreat (cf. 3:26–29; 7:24–25).[5] The Ephraimite forces were for-eigners in the land, opponents of God's purposes, alienated from their brothers, and condemned like the Ammonites (11:32–33). Summing up their otherness, the Ephraimites mangled a basic Hebrew word and paid for it with their lives.

This foreign nature of the Ephraimite speech in Judges 12 points to the broader problem of Israel's alienation from Yahweh. The book of Judges represents an entirely downside-up world. Nothing is right. Israel is fragmented and fallen and fated for destruction. Evil is ubiquitous. God's people emulate the Canaanites. Righteousness is absent. Oppression is pervasive. Tribe battles tribe. Hebrew kills Hebrew. Redemption is partial and short-lived. Peace is only accomplished through sordid proxies, and it lasts barely a generation. The judges would deliver some from oppression, but overall they judged the Israelite tribes for their rebel-lion against God's commands. Israel had become indistinguishable from their pa-gan neighbors.

This episode illustrates the complexity of the Hebrew language. Many of these details are only visible to readers of the Bible with a keen understanding of its linguistic setting. This chapter will orient the reader to key aspects of the language within its Northwest Semitic setting. It provides details about the development of the Hebrew language and locates its place in the interpretation of the Scriptures.

1.2 CHAPTER OBJECTIVES

The following sections provide brief overviews for a wide range of language top-ics, including the Northwest Semitic setting of Hebrew, its genetic relationships within the Semitic language family, Hebrew variation through time and dialect, script innovation, and the textual and reading traditions of the Hebrew Bible.

1.3 INTRODUCTION

The Semitic language family is the linguistic context of Hebrew. Ancient speakers of Semitic languages were principally located in the Middle East as well as North and East Africa, though written evidence of Semitic has also been discovered in Southern Europe and India. This material represents some of the oldest known methods of communicating through graphic representation. Three different Se-mitic languages have served as the *linguae francae* (i.e., the common transnational languages) in the Middle East and northern Africa: Akkadian in the second millen-nium BC, Aramaic in the first millennium BC (2 Kgs 18:26; Ezra 4:7; Dan 2:4), and Arabic in modern times.

---

[5] Some have suggested that they went the wrong way home! See David Marcus, "Ridiculing the Ephraimites: The Shibboleth Incident (Judg 12:6)," *Maarav* 8 (1992): 95–105, esp. 104 n. 46.

1.4 NORTHWEST SEMITIC SETTING

The Hebrew language is described geopolitically in the biblical texts as "the lip of Canaan" (Isa 19:18) and "the language of Judah" (2 Kgs 18:26, 28; 2 Chr 32:18; Neh 13:24). Linguists group Hebrew according to its language features into the Canaanite branch along with Phoenician and the Transjordanian dialects—Ammonite, Edomite, and Moabite. Canaanite is a part of the larger language group known as Northwest Semitic, including Aramaic and Ugaritic. Northwest Semitic is a subgroup of West Semitic, which can be divided into three subgroups: Central Semitic (which included Northwest Semitic, Arabic dialects, and Old South Arabian), Ethiopian, and Modern South Arabian. West Semitic is to be distinguished from the East Semitic languages of Akkadian (and its main dialects of Assyrian and Babylonian) and Eblaite.

1.4.1 Genetic Relationship of Hebrew within Semitic

The following diagram illustrates the genetic or genealogical relationships within the Semitic languages. The arrangement is based on shared linguistic features. It represents subgroupings of related languages organized in a branching tree model.[6]

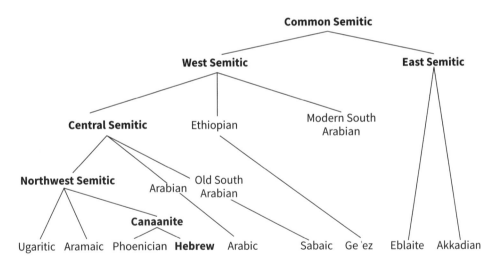

1.4.2 The Northwest Semitic Languages and their Scripts

While written language dates to the third millennium BC, the attestation of the Northwest Semitic languages begins as early as the middle of the second millennium BC. One hallmark of this group of languages is their development and

---

[6] Adapted from John Huehnergard, *A Grammar of Akkadian*, 3rd ed., HSS 45 (Winona Lake, IN: Eisenbrauns, 2011), xxiii.

adaptation of the <u>alphabetic script</u>.[7] Nearly all modern alphabetic writing systems may be traced to this invention.

The origins of the Semitic alphabet are rather mysterious and have fostered no small disagreement among scholars. Much of the controversy has centered upon a collection of early alphabetic inscriptions first discovered by W. M. Flinders Petrie in 1905 at Serabit El-Khadim in Sinai.[8] The complete decipherment and interpretation of these inscriptions continues to evade scholars. The dating of the inscriptions is particularly problematic and highly controversial, with proposed dates ranging from the nineteenth or eighteenth centuries BC to sometime between the fifteenth and twelfth centuries BC.[9] Two additional alphabetic inscriptions were recently discovered from Wadi el-Ḥôl (located on the edge of the western desert of ancient Egypt) dating from the latter portion of the Egyptian Middle Kingdom. In light of this find, John C. Darnell et al. assert: "We may now, more confidently than at any time in the past century, push the origins of alphabetic writing back to the beginning of the second millennium."[10] Yet speculation about these inscriptions and their relation to the origin of writing continues.

Scholars have identified several correspondences between signs attested in the Sinaitic inscriptions and known Egyptian <u>hieroglyphs</u>. The symbols also resemble letters from the early Phoenician script attested centuries later. The following chart outlines the correspondences.[11]

---

[7] Christopher Woods with Emily Teeter and Geoff Emberling, eds., *Visible Language: Inventions of Writing in the Ancient Middle East and Beyond*, Oriental Institute Museum Publications 32 (Chicago: The Oriental Institute, 2015).

[8] W. M. Flinders Petrie, *Seventy Years of Archaeology* (New York: Holt, 1932), 210–12. See also William F. Albright, "The Early Alphabetic Inscriptions from Sinai and Their Decipherment," *BASOR* 110 (1948): 6–22; Frank Moore Cross, "The Evolution of the Proto-Canaanite Alphabet," *BASOR* 134 (1954): 15–24.

[9] Egyptologist Alan Gardiner once proposed the Sinai inscriptions were composed toward the end of the Middle Kingdom Twelfth Dynasty (i.e., 18th cent.). See "Sinai Script and the Origin of the Alphabet," *Palestine Exploration Fund Quarterly Statement* (1929): 48–55. In contrast, Orly Goldwasser argues for composition toward the beginning of the Twelfth Dynasty (i.e., 19th–18th cent.). See "Canaanites Reading Hieroglyphs: Horus is Hathor? The Invention of the Alphabet in Sinai," *Ägypten und Levante* 16 (2006): 133; Goldwasser, "The Miners who Invented the Alphabet: A Response to Christopher Rollston," *Journal of Ancient Egyptian Interconnections* 4 (2012): 12. William F. Albright rejected Gardiner's dating and lowered it to approximately the 15th century ("Early Alphabetic Inscriptions," 12). Similarly, Benjamin Sass argued for yet a later date of the 13th century. See "The Genesis of the Alphabet and Its Development in the Second Millennium B.C.— Twenty Years Later," *De Kêmi à Birīt Nāri* 2 (2005): 157.

[10] John C. Darnell et al., "Two Early Alphabetic Inscriptions from the Wadi el-Ḥôl: New Evidence for the Origin of the Alphabet from the Western Desert of Egypt," *Annual of the American Schools of Oriental Research* 59 (2005): 90.

[11] All Semitic signs traced from photographs by Matthew McAffee and digitized by Daniel Webster.

EGYPTIAN HIEROGLYPH (GARDINER)	SERABIT L-KHADIM	WADI EL-HÔL	SIGN MEANING	AHIRAM (PHOENICIAN)	TELL FEKHERYE (ARAMAIC)	SILOAM TUNNEL (HEBREW)	HEBREW NAME
(F1)	(349)	(Inscr. 1)	"Ox" head				אָלֶף ʾalep
(O1) '12 (O4) (O6)	(349) (346)	(Inscr. 1)	House				bet
(A28)	(353)	(Inscr. 1)	Man with arms raised				he
(T3) (S38) (O30) (O29)¹³	(351)	(Inscr. 2)	Crook/ mace/ tent pole?				waw

---

[12] Gardiner initially proposed the West Semitic sign derived from the Egyptian hieroglyph for house (Gardiner O1; see table in Gardiner, "Origin of the Alphabet"). The *bet* sign attested in the Wadi el-Ḥôl inscriptions, however, is more akin to the Egyptian courtyard house sign (Gardiner O4); see Darnell et al., "Two Early Alphabetic Inscriptions," 77. Frank Moore Cross made this suggestion earlier; see "An Old Canaanite Inscription Recently Found at Lachish," *Tel Aviv* 11 (1984): 72. Goldwasser finds the courtyard proposal problematic, arguing instead for the house sign (Gardiner O1); see "Miners Who Invented the Alphabet," 16–17.

[13] Gardiner originally proposed the supporting pole (O30) as the origin of the Semitic *waw* (see table in Gardiner, "Origin of the Alphabet"). The Egyptian sign for a crook (Gardiner S38) was suggested by Goldwasser ("Miners Who Invented the Alphabet," 16). Others have traditionally argued that the Semitic *waw* originated from the Egyptian sign for mace (Gardiner T3; see G. J. Hamilton, "The Development of the Early Alphabet," [PhD diss., Harvard University, 1985], 65–69). The

EGYPTIAN HIEROGLYPH (GARDINER)	SERABIT L-KHADIM	WADI EL-HÔL	SIGN MEANING	AHIRAM (PHOENICIAN)	TELL FEKHERYE (ARAMAIC)	SILOAM TUNNEL (HEBREW)	HEBREW NAME
(O42)[14]	(362)	—	Fence?				*ḥet*
(D46) / (D47)	(349) / (353)	—	Hand				*kap*
(V1)	(346)	(Inscr. 2, 1)	Coil of Rope				*lamed*
(N35)	(349)	(Inscr. 1, 2)	Water				*mem* (cf. *mayim* "sea")
(I10)	(349)	(Inscr. 1)	Snake				*nun* (Ethiopic name: *naḥaš* "serpent")
(D4)	(354)	(Inscr. 2)	Eye				*ʿayin*

Wadi el-Ḥôl symbol appears to resemble a mace, but Darnell et al. rather argue that the most likely Egyptian origin for the sign is the tent pole (O29), since it routinely appears with either horizontal or vertical orientation ("Two Early Alphabetic Inscriptions," 85–85).

[14] Egyptian sign for a fence, as proposed by Joseph Lam, "The Invention and Development of the Alphabet," in *Visible Language: Inventions of Writing in the Ancient Middle East and Beyond*, ed. Christopher Woods with Emily Teeter and Geoff Emberling, Oriental Institute Museum Publications 32 (Chicago: The Oriental Institute, 2010), 190.

EGYPTIAN HIEROGLYPH (GARDINER)	SERABIT L-KHADIM	WADI EL-HÔL	SIGN MEANING	AHIRAM (PHOENICIAN)	TELL FEKHERYE (ARAMAIC)	SILOAM TUNNEL (HEBREW)	HEBREW NAME
(O38)	(357)	(Inscr. 2)	Corner[15]				*pe* (cf. *pēʾâ* "corner, side")
(D1) (D2)	(349) (349)	(Inscr. 1, 2)	Head				*reš* (cf. *rōʾš* "head")
(Aa32)	(349) (357)	—	Bow?[16]				*šin*

The symbols represented in the Sinaitic inscriptions show striking affinities to Egyptian hieroglyphs and later alphabetic scripts. Scholars argue that the West Semitic alphabetic script originally developed from pictographic representations of sounds. This theory is called <u>acrophony</u>, which refers to the practice of associating the name of a letter with the initial letter of its name. Alan H. Gardiner espoused this theory as a means of explaining the development of the Semitic alphabet, and the evidence from the Sinaitic inscriptions appears to support such a theory.[17]

---

[15] Gardiner originally interpreted the Proto-Sinaitic symbol ▯ (inscription 346) as a picture of a mouth resembling the corresponding Egyptian sign ⬭ (Gardiner D21); see Gardiner, "The Egyptian Origin of the Semitic Alphabet," *Journal of Egyptian Archaeology* 3 (1916): 4, plate II. Martin Sprengling, however, identified the symbol ⬡ (inscription 357) as "a *pēʾah*, 'boundary, edge, corner,' i.e., the letter *p*." See *The Alphabet: Its Rise and Development from the Sinai Inscriptions*, Oriental Institute Communications 12 (Chicago: University of Chicago Press, 1931), 22. Albright followed this interpretation, although he identifies the sign as "throw stick;" see "Early Alphabetic Inscriptions," 14, fig. 1. Albright's interpretation is further supported by the inscriptions from the Wadi el-Hôl; see Darnell et al., "Two Early Alphabetic Inscriptions," 80.

[16] Goldwasser has proposed this sign represents a bow; see "Miners Who Invented the Alphabet," 13. Gardiner suggested the sign represented a tooth; see "Egyptian Origin," 4, plate II.

[17] See Gardiner, "Egyptian Origin," 6; Cross, "Proto-Canaanite Alphabet," 24.

ACROPHONY THEORY

The table above illustrates the acrophony theory, especially as it relates to the letters *'alep, bet, kap, 'ayin,* and *reš.* The first letter (*'alep*) symbolizes the head of an ox ($\forall$), and its name אָלֶף means "cattle" (< *ʾalp-*). Its sound (the glottal stop /ʾ/) corresponds to the first consonant of its name. The similarity between the Semitic symbol for *'alep* and the Egyptian hieroglyph for ox is rather striking. Even though the meaning is similar, the sound represented by the ox-head in Egyptian does not correspond to that of *'alep.* Likewise, the symbol for the first letter of the Semitic word *bêt* "house" depicts the floorplan of a walled structure, with or without partitions ($\square$) and sometimes with an open door ($\square$) as attested in Egyptian symbols for "house." The name of the letter *kap* in Hebrew means "palm (of the hand)," symbolized in the form of a hand ($\forall$). The name of the letter *'ayin* means "eye," originally represented with the picture of an eye (∞). The pictograph for *reš* is a head ($\nearrow$), also the first letter of the Hebrew word for "head."

Orly Goldwasser theorizes that the Sinaitic inscriptions were the creation of Semitic miners during the Twelfth Dynasty of the Egyptian Middle Kingdom. She believes these miners who invented the alphabet were illiterate in the sense that they did not know how to read or write Egyptian.[18] She furthermore observes that the Sinaitic materials are "acrophonically pure," having eschewed the complexities of the Egyptian system, and therefore they suggest that "the inventors and writers had access only to the pictorial level of the Egyptian hieroglyphic script."[19] Darnell et al. have instead proposed that the alphabet originated within the confines of Egypt at the hands of individuals having a high level of literacy in Egyptian.[20] They also point to the known presence of Asiatics (the so-called Hyksos) in the early Dynastic periods and beyond, who may have adapted aspects of Egyptian writing in the service of their own Semitic language.

The debate over the earliest Semitic alphabet has been reinvigorated with the recent discovery of four incised clay cylinders from a mortuary complex at Umm el-Marra, Syria, dating from the Early Bronze Age (third millennium BC). The signs found on these cylinders have been shown to correspond to the early alphabetic symbols attested elsewhere. If this dating is maintained, it would push the development of the Semitic alphabet much earlier than has been previously recognized.[21] A short inscription was recently discovered at Lachish in a Late Bronze

---

[18] She notes the following reasons for this conclusion: (1) the Sinaitic signs differ in direction from the Egyptian prototypes; (2) a single inscription shows multiple orientations of a given sign; (3) there appears to be no order in the writing of the signs; and (4) sometimes the Sinaitic signs are invested with meaning different from the Egyptian prototype. See "Miners Who Invented the Alphabet," 12.

[19] Goldwasser, "Miners Who Invented the Alphabet," 13–14.

[20] Darnell et al., "Two Early Alphabetic Inscriptions," 90–91.

[21] See Glenn M. Schwartz, "Non-Cuneiform Writing at Third-Millennium Umm el-Marra, Syria: Evidence of an Early Alphabetic Tradition?," *Pasiphae: rivista di filologia e antichità egee* 15 (2021): 255–66.

Age context (ca. 15th century BC).[22] It bridges the gap between the early material from Egypt and later Levantine evidence.

For our purposes here, it is sufficient to conclude that alphabetic writing was developed by Semitic speaking peoples in and around Egypt toward the beginning of the second millennium BC (or perhaps even earlier). The symbolic representations of the letters were informed by Egyptian hieroglyphic prototypes. These early pictographs were "Semiticized," however, and did not necessarily adhere to the phonetic values of their counterparts in Egyptian. They were invented to write ancient Semitic.

As the Semitic script subsequently developed from its pictographic emergence in the proto-Sinaitic inscriptions, the symbols became more stylized (see table above). The characters eventually lost visual correspondence to their pictorial archetypes— although they kept their names—and developed into pure phonological symbols. For instance, the water image (𝔐) was schematized as 𝓎, representing the sound /m/. The facing stance of the letters was also formalized and oriented in the direction of the reading. For instance, in a right-to-left writing the letters faced the left (𝕂 as in the Aḥiram inscription) instead of the left-to-right orientation of 𝟁 elsewhere. Some inscriptions, such as those from Wadi el-Ḥôl, attest both right-to-left (inscription 1) and even vertical orientations (inscription 2).[23] Inscription 1 orients the signs to the left in the direction of the writing (e.g., 𝄃), whereas inscription 2 orients the signs downward, also in the direction of the writing (e.g., 𝄖). The Khirbet Qeiyafa ostracon, purportedly one of the earliest extant Hebrew inscriptions from the early first millennium BC, attests letters with several differing orientations (𝄢, 𝄙, 𝄡). Nevertheless, some scholars consider this document to be a scribal exercise—a fact that warrants appropriate caution from drawing too many conclusions regarding its arrangement.[24]

An important step along the way in the alphabet's development occurred along the northeastern coast of the Mediterranean in the ancient city-state of Ugarit during the Late Bronze Age. Ugaritic provides a remarkable bridge between the cuneiform practices of ancient Mesopotamia and the burgeoning alphabetic scripts of the Canaanite languages. The practice of writing cuneiform involved incising wedges into soft clay tablets with a square or triangle-shaped stylus. The resulting impressions give a triangular or pyramidal appearance. Varying combinations of the incised wedges represented syllables or even whole words. The practice was originally used for writing the Sumerian language, but it was adapted to write

---

[22] Felix Höflmayer et al., "Early Alphabetic Writing in the Ancient Near East: the 'Missing Link' from Tel Lachish," *Antiquity* 95 (2021): 705–19.

[23] Darnell et al., "Two Early Alphabetic Inscriptions," 75, 83.

[24] See Alan R. Millard, "The Ostracon from the Days of David Found at Khirbet Qeiyafa," *Tyndale Bulletin* 62 (2011): 1–13; Aaron Demsky, "An Iron Age IIA Alphabetic Writing Exercise from Khirbet Qeiyafa," *IEJ* 62 (2012): 186–99. For initial impressions as to this text's historical context and interpretation, see G. Galil, "The Hebrew Inscription from Khirbet Qeiyafa/Netaʿim," *UF* 41 (2009): 193–242. Brian Donnelly-Lewis, however, has produced a collation based on new high-definition images that permits a coherent reading. See "The Khirbet Qeiyafa Ostracon: A New Collation Based on the Multispectral Images, with Translation and Commentary," *BASOR* 388 (2022): 181–210.

Akkadian, an East Semitic language. Under the influence of Akkadian, cuneiform signs were used to represent numerous other languages, such as Eblaite, Hittite, Hurrian, Urartian, Elamite, and Old Persian. Cuneiform writing was a sign-based system, whereby hundreds of signs were used to convey various phonological values or words. Moreover, one sign could convey multiple values. For example, the Neo-Assyrian sign could represent the sound /an/, but it also functioned as the Sumerian <u>logogram</u> for deity, DINGIR, or even the Akkadian word *ilu(m)* "god."[25]

UGARITIC CUNEIFORM

The Ugaritians developed a unique repertoire of cuneiform signs to represent the West Semitic alphabet. Instead of adapting the hundreds of existing signs used for writing Akkadian, Ugaritic speakers developed thirty new cuneiform symbols to represent their own Northwest Semitic language. This alphabetic cuneiform was constructed using the cuneiform wedges, written left-to-right, and inscribed on clay tablets, but the forms corresponded to the linear shape of the Canaanite alphabetic letters.[26] The connection to the proto-Sinaitic script is further verified based on the parallel orders of the alphabets.

UGARITIC CUNEIFORM

à	b	g	ḫ	d	h	w	z	ḥ	ṭ	y	k	š	l
א	ב	ג		ד	ה	ו	ז	ח	ט	׳	כ		ל

m	d̠	n	ẓ	s	ʿ	p	ṣ	q	r	t̠
מ		נ		ס	ע	פ	צ	ק	ר	ש

ġ	t	ỉ	ủ	ś
	ת			

---

[25] René Labat, *Manuel d'Épigraphie Akkadiene: Signes, Syllabaire, Idéogrammes*, 6th ed. (Paris: Geuthner, 1995), 49. For a general introduction, see Dominique Charpin, *Reading and Writing in Babylon*, trans. Jane Marie Todd (Cambridge: Harvard University Press, 2011).

[26] Dennis G. Pardee, "The Ugaritic Alphabetic Cuneiform Writing System in the Context of Other Alphabetic Systems," in *Studies in Semitic and Afroasiatic Linguistics Presented to Gene B. Gragg*, ed. Cynthia L. Miller, SAOC 60 (Chicago: Oriental Institute, 2007), 181–200.

UGARITIC ABECEDARY

The order of the Ugaritic alphabet is attested on several abecedaries. The following text provides one example, listing each letter of the alphabet in order.[27]

RS 12.063 Abecedary[28]

Recto   Right Edge

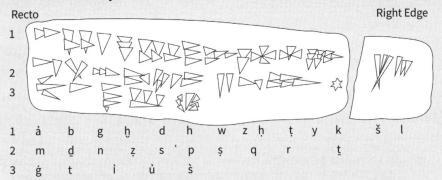

1	à	b	g	ḫ		d	h	w	z	ḥ		ṭ	y	k		š	l
2	m	ḏ	n	ẓ		s	ʿ	p	ṣ		q	r		ṯ			
3	ġ	t	i	ù		ś											

Scholars have noted that the number of signs attested in the Ugaritic alphabet corresponds to the earliest proposed phonology of Semitic.

The Ugaritic writing system shares considerable overlap with the Old South Arabian alphabet from the first millennium BC, which contains twenty-nine distinct characters. The order, however, for Old South Arabian is different. It uses a *halaḥam* sequence (i.e., h l ḥ m) which developed into the Geʿez *abugida* (alphasyllabary) that was widely used in Christian traditions in Ethiopia and Eritrea.[29] The full series is:

h l ḥ m q w š r b t s k n ḫ ṣ ś f ʾ ʿ ḍ g d ġ ṭ z d y ṯ ẓ

This alternative early alphabetic order is similar to an Ugaritic abecedary (RS 88.2215). It employs the short alphabet of twenty-seven signs.[30]

h l ḥ m q w ṯ r b t ḍ š k n ḫ ṣ s p ʾ ʿ ḍ g d ġ ṭ z y

The twenty-eight consonants of Arabic are comparable to the Ugaritic phonological inventory. The script, written right-to-left, reflects a development from several varieties of Aramaic, in particular Syriac cursive writing. The oldest Arabic sequence is likely derived from the West Semitic order.[31] This alphabetic arrangement is called an *abjad*. The letters are provided with a common Latin transcription and IPA phonetic values.

---

[27] For a full list and discussion of the eighteen abecedaries attested at Ugarit, see Robert Hawley, "Apprendre à écrire à Ougarit: une typologie des abécédaires," in *D'Ougarit à Jérusalem: Recueil d'études épigraphiques et archéologiques offert à Pierre Bordreuil*, ed. Carole Roche, Orient & Méditerranée 2 (Paris: De Boccard, 2008), 215–32.

[28] Hand copy traced by Matthew McAffee from a photograph in Pierre Bordreuil and Dennis Pardee, *A Manuel of Ugaritic*, LSAWS 3 (Winona Lake, IN: Eisenbrauns, 2009), plate 53.

[29] See Reinhard G. Lehmann, "27–30–22–26—How Many Letters Needs an Alphabet? The Case of Semitic," in *The Idea of Writing: Writing Across Borders*, ed. Alex de Voogt and Joachim Friedrich Quack (Leiden: Brill, 2012), 14–16.

[30] Pierre Bordreuil and Dennis G. Pardee, "Textes alphabétiques en ougaritique," in *Études ougaritiques 1: Travaux 1985–1995*, ed. M. Yon and D. Arnaud, Ras Shamra-Ougarit 14 (Paris: Éditions Recherche sur les Civilisations, 2001), 341–48. Compare this order to the partially attested alphabetic Ugaritic inscription from Beth-Shemesh.

[31] As with the expanded three final letters of the long alphabet in Ugaritic (see the discussion below), the twenty-two letter Arabic *abjad* is supplemented by the addition of six letters at the end.

Most modern alphabetic arrangements of Arabic are based on grouping similar letter shapes.

ش	غ	ظ	ذ	خ	ث	ت	س	ر	ق	ض	ف	ع	ص	ن	م	ل	ك	ي	ط	ح	ج	ز	و	ه	د	ج	ب	أ
š	ġ	ẓ	ḏ	ḫ	ṯ	t	s	r	q	ḍ	f	ʿ	ṣ	n	m	l	k	y	ṭ	ḥ	z	w	h	d	j	b	ʾ	
ʃ	ɣ	ðˤ	ð	x	θ	t	s	r	q	dˤ	f	ʕ	sˤ	n	m	l	k	y	tˤ	ħ	z	w	h	d	dʒ	b	ʔ	
			ת	ש	ר	ק	צ	פ	ע	ס	נ	מ	ל	כ	י	ט	ח	ז	ו	ה	ד	ג	ב	א				

ي	و	ه	ن	م	ل	ك	ق	ف	غ	ع	ظ	ط	ض	ص	ش	س	ز	ر	ذ	د	خ	ح	ج	ث	ت	ب	ا
y	w	h	n	m	l	k	q	f	ġ	ʿ	ẓ	ṭ	ḍ	ṣ	š	s	z	r	ḏ	d	ḫ	ḥ	j	ṯ	t	b	ʾ

The correspondence between the late second millennium Ugaritic alphabet and the consonants attested in Arabic is striking. It demonstrates the close correspondence of the spoken varieties of Semitic, even with large expanses of time and place separating these languages. Furthermore, comparing the relationship between related languages allows for a better understanding of difficult and rare linguistic features.[32]

The Ugaritic alphabet possesses several innovative characters that are not known from elsewhere in the West Semitic inventory. Namely, the last three symbols appear to be add-ons. These include two additional *'alep* signs (i.e., *i̇, u̇*). They are placed at the end of the alphabet and leave the impression that they supplemented an existing list of consonants. Scholars believe that the West Semitic languages originally only had one glottal stop, as in Hebrew *'alep*, but in Ugaritic the two additional *'aleps* were expanded to represent either pure vowels (i.e., *i, u*) or syllables with the glottal stop plus a different vowel (i.e., *' + i*, and *' + u*).[33] The initial letter was used for *à*, then *i* and *u̇* were innovated and placed at the end of the alphabetic sequence. With these three signs, the primary vowel qualities of Ugaritic could be represented (*a, i, u*). This symbolic enlargement may have arisen out of the need to write other languages which represented vowels (e.g., Akkadian) or contained words with initial vowels (e.g., Hittite, Hurrian).[34] As for the origin of the final character *ṡ*, it may represent an affricated sibilant (i.e., /ts/, similar to the original Hebrew *samek* ס), perhaps because the sound represented by *s* was becoming a fricative.[35] Given these considerations, Ugaritic writing resembles a cuneiform version of an earlier West Semitic alphabet consisting of thirty signs.

Individual languages adapted the twenty-two graphemes of early Canaanite in different ways. The Ugaritic attestation of a 27 + 3 alphabet suggests that the twenty-two-sign alphabet could have been a simplification of an earlier longer West

---

[32] See H. H. Hardy II, "Comparative-Historical Linguistics," in *Linguistics for Hebraists*, ed. R. Holmstedt and J. Cook, LSAWS (Winona Lake, IN: Eisenbrauns, forthcoming).

[33] Pardee, "Ugaritic Alphabetic Cuneiform," 183.

[34] Pardee, 183.

[35] See Pardee, "Ugaritic Alphabetic Cuneiform," 183 and Josef Tropper, "Das letzte Zeichen des ugaritischen Alphabets," *UF* 27 (1995): 505–28; Tropper, *Ugaritische Grammatik*, 2nd ed., AOAT 273 (Münster: Ugarit-Verlag, 2012), 42–44.

Semitic version (see above Ugaritic Cuneiform).[36] Hebrew scribes adopted the twenty-two signs to their existing phonetic system. Old Aramaic script was also developed from a similar system. Unlike Old South Arabian's almost one-to-one correspondence between consonant and symbol, the Phoenician letter inventory had fewer signs than Hebrew and Aramaic had sounds. This meant that Hebrew and Aramaic speakers had to use some of the symbols to represent more than one sound.

WHY DO LETTERS MATTER?

The "Phoenician" alphabet should be connected to Canaanite speakers more broadly. While the Phoenicians deserve credit for bringing this writing system to the Greek world, they did not invent it. The different adaptations of the Canaanite alphabet are important to keep in mind when considering potential homonyms. Homonyms are distinct words which are similar in pronunciation or spelling. Homophones are different lexemes that are pronounced equivalently—they may or may not be spelled identically (e.g., the English verb and noun, *write/right* or *see/sea*). One such example is Biblical Hebrew אִי which may represent a noun "island; coast," an interjection "alas," a negation, and even a small wild animal, perhaps a "jackal." Not every similarly written word would have been pronounced in identical ways though. Homographs are different lexemes that are written similarly to each other but are not necessarily pronounced identically (e.g., the verb *wind* and the noun *wind*). This aspect of the language confuses students since oftentimes multiple, unrelated meanings derive from what appear to be an identical root. For instance, BDB lists the root עָפָר as having two roots. The meaning of the noun עָפָר under root I is "dust," but the noun עֹפֶר from the meagerly attested root II means "young hart, stag."[37] In this instance, these two words go back to two distinct lexemes with dissimilar initial consonants. The meaning "dust" comes from the root ʿpr with the voiced pharyngeal fricative, but "stag" comes from ġpr with the voiced uvular fricative. We can support these proposed etymologies from Arabic, which does distinguish these two consonants in its sign inventory (ع /ʕ/ as compared to غ /ɣ/), and which likewise attests the roots ʿpr and ġrp.[38] Even though both lexemes are written with the same Hebrew letter (ע), the pronunciation was differentiated through at least the end of the second century BC.[39] In addition to ע, it is important to note the differences in phonemes associated with ח (/ħ/ and /x/), שׁ (/ʃ/ and /s/, differentiated in Tiberian Hebrew as שׁ and שׂ, the latter phoneme merged with ס), and the aspirated counterparts to בגד־כפת (/b/ and /bʰ/, /g/ and /gʰ/, /d/ and /dʰ/, /k/ and /kʰ/, /p/ and /pʰ/, /t/ and /tʰ/). Heterographs are different lexemes that are spelled differently but pronounced similarly. The sound merger of שׂ with ס led to such situations. Both סִיג "dross" and שִׂיג "defecation; privy" are pronounced /sigʰ/; סַר "discouraged" and שַׂר "ruler" are also pronounced in the same way. It also leads to interesting antonyms, like שֵׂכֶל "prudence, insight" and סֶכֶל "folly." Such words are sometime called contronyms or auto-antonyms.

---

[36] As argued in Pardee, "Ugaritic Alphabetic Cuneiform," 184.

[37] BDB, 779–80.

[38] Keep in mind that not every such example in Hebrew arises from distinct underlying consonantal roots.

[39] Richard L. Steiner, "On the Dating of Hebrew Sound Changes (*ḥ > ḥ and *ġ > ʿ) and Greek Translations (2 Esdras and Judith)," *JBL* 124 (2005): 229–67.

A somewhat different but related phenomenon is when languages represent different phonemes with distinctive symbols. We can illustrate this feature with Hebrew and Aramaic. In Hebrew, the proto-Semitic sound /θ/ has been combined with /s/ and represented as שׁ /ʃ/, whereas in Aramaic it is resolved as ת /t/. The word for "three" in both languages demonstrates this difference: Hebrew שָׁלֹשׁ and Aramaic תְּלָת. Similarly, Hebrew utilized the Phoenician letter {š} (Hebrew שׁ) to represent both /ʃ/ and /s/. We can see this feature in the Kuntillet ʿAjrud inscription 4, line 1 where the verb is written יׁשׂבעו "they will be satisfied."[40] In other words, the Hebrew *śin* sound /s/ is represented by the Phoenician *šin* sign. Much later the Masoretes devised a means of distinguishing these consonants in the square script—a dot on the top left side of the letter for /s/ (שׂ) and a dot on the top right side for /ʃ/ (שׁ). Before this development, however, no graphic distinction existed for the letters *śin* and *šin*.

Whereas Hebrew and Aramaic writing developed independently for nearly one half of the first millennium BC, Hebrew scribes eventually adopted the Aramaic square script to write the Hebrew language. Starting in at least the ninth century BC, scribes wrote Hebrew using the so-called Old Hebrew script derived directly from the Canaanite letters.[41] Old Aramaic is known from a similar time frame and the same Canaanite source.[42] By the fifth century BC, the Aramaic script and language was being used by the Jewish diaspora at Elephantine in Egypt.[43] The Elephantine papyri come from the time in which Aramaic became the *lingua franca* of the Babylonian and Persian Empires from 600 to 300 BC.[44] The dominance of the Aramaic language throughout the ancient world as well as widespread bilingualism and scribal training among the Jewish diaspora likely contributed to the adaptation of its script for writing Hebrew as well. Scholars argue that the change from the Old Hebrew script (sometimes called Paleo-Hebrew) to the Aramaic square script must have taken place sometime between the composition of Classical Biblical Hebrew texts and the composition of the Dead Sea Scrolls during the middle of the third century BC. A small number of the Dead Sea Scrolls were written entirely in the Old Hebrew script, however, and several others contain individual words written in Paleo-Hebrew, notably the divine name (*YHWH*). The Samaritan tradition preserved a distinct but related script while Rabbinic Judaism wholly embraced the

---

[40] For more on this text, see F. W. Dobbs-Allsopp et al., *Hebrew Inscriptions: Texts from the Biblical Period of the Monarchy with Concordance* (New Haven, CT: Yale University Press, 2005), 283.

[41] Christopher A. Rollston, "Scribal Education in Ancient Israel: The Old Hebrew Epigraphic Evidence," *BASOR* 344 (2006): 47–74. See also Seth L. Sanders, *The Invention of Hebrew* (Urbana: University of Illinois, 2011).

[42] Christopher A. Rollston, *Writing and Literacy in the World of Ancient Israel: Epigraphic Evidence from the Iron Age* (Atlanta: SBL, 2010).

[43] See GKC §25.

[44] Frank Moore Cross placed the emergence of the earliest iteration of the Jewish script toward the end of the Persian period during the fourth century BC. See "The Development of the Jewish Scripts," in *The Bible and the Ancient Near East: Essays in Honor of William Foxwell Albright*, ed. G. Ernest Wright (Winona Lake, IN: Eisenbrauns, 1979), 136. See further Samuel L. Boyd, *Language Contact, Colonial Administration, and the Construction of Identity in Ancient Israel: Constructing the Context for Contact*, HSS 66 (Leiden: Brill, 2021).

Aramaic writing.[45] This viewpoint assumes that the earliest written biblical texts must have been composed in the distinctive Hebrew writing.

The shift to writing Hebrew using the Aramaic square script seems to have been gradual. According to Joseph Naveh, the Old Hebrew script was reserved for texts of religious and national significance, while texts of a secular nature employed the Aramaic square script.[46] Eventually, the older script fell out of use in Judah, though it continued as the preferred writing system of the Samaritans.[47] The Judeans adapted the square script to their own needs, so much so that scholars have labeled it the Jewish script, which Israeli Hebrews still use today.[48]

This scribal transformation is evidenced by a textual problem from 1 Kgs 3:16. Compare the MT and LXX readings:

MT	LXX
אָז תָּבֹאנָה שְׁתַּיִם נָשִׁים זֹנוֹת אֶל־הַמֶּלֶךְ	Τότε ὤφθησαν δύο γυναῖκες πόρναι τῷ βασιλεῖ
Then two prostitutes **entered** to the king.	Then two prostitutes **saw** the king.

The LXX reading involves the confusion of a *reš* for a *bet*—the root ראה "see" compared to בוא "enter."[49] This discrepancy only makes sense in light of the Old Hebrew orthography, given the visual similarity of *reš* (𐤓) and *bet* (𐤁), as compared to the later Aramaic square script (ר and ב).[50] Sometimes the tail of the *bet* was not curved as far to the left, making it harder to distinguish it from the downward stroke of the *reš*. Textual variants like this one indicate that the variation likely occurred in a source text originally written in the Old Hebrew script.

As the above survey of Semitic scripts demonstrates, language and script are not one and the same. Spoken languages can adapt to different writing systems over time. And sometimes writing is more conservative than speech, reflecting earlier stages of the language.

1.5 DEVELOPMENT OF BIBLICAL HEBREW THROUGH TIME

Biblical Hebrew represents nearly a millennium of language history. Three periods distinguish linguistic differences reflected in these texts: Archaic Biblical Hebrew [ABH], Classical/Standard Biblical Hebrew [CBH/SBH], and Late Biblical Hebrew [LBH]. An intermediate period between the second and third phase is labeled

---

[45] See m. Yad. 4.5.

[46] Joseph Naveh, "Scripts and Inscriptions in Ancient Samaria," *IEJ* 48 (1998): 92.

[47] Naveh, "Ancient Samaria," 95.

[48] As identified by Frank Moore Cross, "The Oldest Manuscripts from Qumran," *JBL* 74 (1955): 147 n. 1.

[49] Ronald Hendel and Jan Joosten, *How Old Is the Hebrew Bible? A Linguistic, Historical, and Textual Study* (New Haven: Yale University Press, 2018), 61–62.

[50] A similar consonant confusion is found with *dalet* and *reš* in the square script (ד vs. ר).

Transitional Biblical Hebrew [TrBH].[51] Scholars attempt to map these periods using biblical textual evidence.[52]

BIBLICAL HEBREW PERIODIZATION		
PERIOD	APPROXIMATE DATES	EXAMPLE TEXTS
ABH	1200–1000 BC	Patriarch Blessing (Gen 49:2–27) Song of the Sea (Exod 15:1–18) Balaam Oracles (Num 23:7–10, 18–24; 24:3–9, 16–19) Song of Moses (Deut 32:1–43) Song of Deborah (Judg 5:1–30) Song of Hannah (1 Sam 2:1–10)
CBH/ SBH	850–586 BC	Pentateuch; Deuteronomistic History; early Prophets; numerous Psalms
TrBH	600–450 BC	Isaiah 40–66; Jeremiah; Ezekiel; Haggai; Zechariah; Lamentations
LBH	550–200 BC	Ezra-Nehemiah; Esther; Chronicles; Daniel; Ecclesiastes

Recent criticisms suggest that this periodization should not be understood as absolute and rigid. Those making these criticisms assert that these Hebrew-speaking communities possessed more than one spoken dialect or coexisting dialectal registers (i.e., <u>diglossia</u>).[53] And the phonological, orthographic, morphological, syntactic, and lexical features of each period exist on continuums rather than as distinct boundaries. As an example, scholars have pointed to the "long form" of certain prepositions, כְּמוֹ "like, as" (Exod 15:5, 8, 11) and עֲלֵי "on, upon" (Gen 49:17, 22), as a characteristic of ABH, but these same texts evidence the short forms (-כְּ in Exod 15:7, 10, 16; עַל in Gen 49:13, 26) and other non-ABH poetic texts use the expanded forms (Lam 4:5; Zech 10:8).[54] Spoken and written varieties of Hebrew were dynamic and overlapped considerably, especially in the later biblical periods.[55] With the passage of time and the influence of other languages on the

---

[51] Aaron D. Hornkohl, "Transitional Biblical Hebrew," in *Periods, Corpora, and Reading Traditions*, vol. 1 of *A Handbook of Biblical Hebrew*, ed. W. Randall Garr and Steven E. Fassberg (Winona Lake, IN: Eisenbrauns, 2016), 31–42.

[52] For a general description of each period, features, and texts, see the essays in W. Randall Garr and Steven E. Fassberg, eds., *Periods, Corpora, and Reading Traditions*, vol. 1 of *A Handbook of Biblical Hebrew* (Winona Lake, IN: Eisenbrauns, 2016) and the entries in the four volumes of *EHLL*.

[53] Gary A. Rendsburg identifies a distinct northern Israelite dialect. See *Diglossia in Ancient Hebrew*, American Oriental Series 72 (New Haven: American Oriental Society, 1990); Rendsburg, *Linguistic Evidence for the Northern Origin of Selected Psalms*, SBLMS 43 (Atlanta: Scholars Press, 1990); Rendsburg, *Israelian Hebrew in the Book of Kings*, Occasional Publications of the Department of Near Eastern Studies and the Program of Jewish Studies, Cornell University 5 (Bethesda, MD: CDL, 2002).

[54] For the origin of so-called enclitic *mem*, see Chaim Cohen, "The Enclitic *mem* in Biblical Hebrew: Its Existence and Initial Discovery," in *Sefer Moshe: The Moshe Weinfeld Jubilee Volume*, ed. Chaim Cohen, Avi Hurvitz, and Shalom M. Paul (Winona Lake, IN: Eisenbrauns, 2004), 231–60.

[55] Ian Young, Robert Rezetko, and Martin Ehrensvärd, *Linguistic Dating of Biblical Texts*, 2 vols. (London: Equinox, 2008). Also, see Dong-Hyuk Kim, *Early Biblical Hebrew, Late Biblical Hebrew,*

Hebrew-speaking community, the classical literary language of the Hebrew Bible was eventually replaced by the contemporary spoken dialect(s). Notably, a number of constructions and lexemes were borrowed through contact-induced change from Aramaic,[56] and even more distantly from Akkadian and Persian.[57] In addition, later strata of Biblical Hebrew begin to reflect changes in the verbal system—notably by the rabbinic period the "consecutive" verb conjugations (i.e., *wayyiqtol* and *wəqātal*) have essentially disappeared.[58] Examples of linguistic substitution are reflected in the synoptic material of Samuel-Kings and Chronicles. In 2 Sam 24:2, the *wəqātal* volitive (וְיָדַעְתִּי) is replaced by the prefix conjugation (וְאֵדְעָה) in 1 Chr 21:2.[59]

2 SAM 24:2	1 CHR 21:2
וּפִקְדוּ אֶת־הָעָם וְיָדַעְתִּי אֵת מִסְפַּר הָעָם	וְהָבִיאוּ אֵלַי וְאֵדְעָה אֶת־מִסְפָּרָם
"Muster the people **so that I might know** the number of the people."	"Report back to me **so that I might know** their number."

Young et al. point to "non-classical" uses of the *qātal* (e.g., עָנָה דוֹדִי וְאָמַר לִי, "my beloved answered and said to me," Song 2:10) as evidence of the language shifting from the more common *wayyiqtol* in SBH (e.g., וַיַּעַן הַמֶּלֶךְ וַיֹּאמֶר "the king answered and said," 1 Kgs 3:27).[60] Many of these developments are shared by later postbiblical Hebrew texts, including Ben Sira, the Dead Sea Scrolls, and the early rabbinic literature.

Extrabiblical sources provide a valuable but limited framework for the history of the Hebrew language. While copyists preserved the biblical texts on perishable material like papyrus and animal skins, only a small number of ancient Hebrew inscriptions are contemporaneous with the biblical literature. Generally called Epigraphic Hebrew [EH], these writings are inscribed or inked on a variety of hard surfaces, such as stone, metal, and clay. Although many of these objects (e.g., seals,

---

and Linguistic Variability: A Sociolinguistic Evaluation of the Linguistic Dating of Biblical Texts, VTSup 156 (Leiden: Brill, 2013).

[56] See, e.g., Samuel Boyd and H. H. Hardy II, "Hebrew Adverbialization, Aramaic Language Contact, and *mpny 'šr* in Exodus 19:18," in *Studies in Semitic Language Contact*, ed. Aaron Butts, SSLL 82 (Leiden: Brill, 2015), 33–51.

[57] Paul V. Mankowski, *Akkadian Loanwords in Biblical Hebrew*, HSS 47 (Leiden: Brill, 2000); Hayim Tawil, *Akkadian Lexicon Companion for Biblical Hebrew* (Brooklyn: Ktav, 2009); Benjamin J. Noonan, *Non-Semitic Loanwords in the Hebrew Bible: A Lexicon of Language Contact*, LSAWS 14 (University Park, PA: Eisenbrauns, 2019); Aren Wilson-Wright, "From Persepolis to Jerusalem: A Reevaluation of Old-Persian-Hebrew Contact in the Achaemenid Period," *VT* 65 (2015): 152–67.

[58] Moses H. Segal, "Mišnaic Hebrew and Its Relation to Biblical Hebrew and to Aramaic," *JQR* 20 (1908): 647–737, especially 682–84.

[59] For a full comparison of verbs, see Arian J. C. Verheij, *Verbs and Numbers: A Study of the Frequencies of the Hebrew Verbal Tense Forms in the Books of Samuel, Kings, and Chronicles*, SSN 28 (Assen: Van Gorcum, 1990). Robert Polzin suggests the cohortative has lost its modal semantics and is simply an archaic lengthened form. See *Late Biblical Hebrew: Toward an Historical Typology of Biblical Hebrew Prose*, HSM 12 (Missoula, MT: Scholars Press, 1976), 55.

[60] Young et al., *Linguistic Dating*, 1:244–45.

bullae, pithoi) contain only one or two words, some longer texts do exist from the earliest periods—comprised mostly of monumental and epistolary inscriptions.[61] Among these, northern and southern Hebrew dialects are distinguishable based on orthographic/phonological features.[62] In general, the phonology and morphology of EH aligns with that of BH. Nearly all of the dissimilarities are reflected as marginal examples in the Hebrew Bible. For example, the EH 3MS pronominal suffix on singular nouns -*h* is found in the *ketiv* of Gen 35:21 as אהלה "his tent" (*qere* אָהֳלוֹ), and the EH 3MS pronominal suffix with plural nouns -*w* is used with בְּנָו in 1 Sam 30:6 rather than the more common form בָּנָיו (see §1.6.3). Few epigraphic writings of much length are known from the LBH period. Later still, Ben Sira and the Dead Sea Scrolls—notably the letters of Simon bar Kokhba—reveal a clear shift toward many of the grammatical features of postbiblical Hebrew.[63]

1.6 TEXT OF THE HEBREW BIBLE

The Hebrew Bible did not materialize spontaneously as a complete work. Multiple, mostly unacknowledged, individuals wrote its compositional units over a period of several centuries. And countless more people played a role in bringing the texts into their current state of preservation. Examining this textual history provides insight into how and in what form(s) the Hebrew Bible survived for millennia. These accountings center on the ways ancient scribes constructed, collected, and copied the biblical materials. The evidence varies widely and includes early references to writing, Second Temple scroll fragments, palimpsests, and medieval manuscripts. Data also come from various early translations and citations in other writings.[64] The purpose of the following sections is to understand this basic history of the text based on textual evidence.

---

[61] See the text editions of Johannes Renz and Wolfgang Röllig, *Handbuch der althebräischen Epigraphik*, 3 vols. (Darmstadt: Wissenschaftliche, 1995–2003); Graham I. Davies, ed., *Ancient Hebrew Inscriptions: Corpus and Concordance*, 2 vols. (Cambridge: Cambridge University Press, 1991–2004); F. W. Dobbs-Allsopp et al., *Hebrew Inscriptions*; Shmuel Aḥituv, *Echoes from the Past: Hebrew and Cognate Inscriptions from the Biblical Period* (Jerusalem: Carta, 2008). For Hebrew seals, see Nahman Avigad and Benjamin Sass, *Corpus of West Semitic Stamp Seals* (Jerusalem: Israel Exploration Society, 1997); Oded Lipschits and David S. Vanderhooft, *The Yehud Stamp Impressions: A Corpus of Inscribed Impressions from the Persian and Hellenistic Periods in Judah* (Winona Lake, IN: Eisenbrauns, 2011).

[62] Widely noted differences include the phonology of Hebrew diphthongs (/ay/ becomes /e/ in northern texts, e.g., יֵן "wine," but it is retained in the south, e.g., יַיִן "wine") and the spelling of the Yahwistic elements of proper names (-*yw* in the northern texts, e.g., שמעיו and ידעיו, compared with -*yhw* in the south, e.g., שמעיהו and ידעיהו).

[63] Eric D. Reymond, *Qumran Hebrew: An Overview of Orthography, Phonology, and Morphology*, Resources for Biblical Study 76 (Atlanta: SBL, 2014). See also the essays in T. Muraoka and J. F. Elwolde, eds., *The Hebrew of the Dead Sea Scrolls and Ben Sira, Proceedings of a Symposium Held at Leiden University, 11–14 December 1995*, STDJ 26 (Leiden: Brill, 1997).

[64] See Guided Lesson א: Textual Criticism in this volume.

1.6.1 Ancient Scripture and the Modern Bible

It is important to state at the outset that many of our modern conceptions of publication are radically different from the norms of ancient writing and reproduction. The book format (i.e., the *codex*)—bound pages, written on both sides—is ubiquitous in contemporary literary works and is even carried over into digital layouts.[65] Contemporary authorship is overt. Anonymity comprises a special class of writing, and we consider it suspicious. Ownership is implicit. For copyrighted works, legal requirements necessitate authorial attribution. Moreover, modern publication assumes exact replication. Advances in technology allow for this unprecedented standard for both the writing and reproduction of the written word. Barring human error or machine malfunction, a page of text written in Kenya may be displayed *exactly* on a computer screen in Nepal and *simultaneously* printed in Peru and Indonesia.

But these conventions were unknown to ancient audiences, and until recently many were unthinkable. The codex did not begin to achieve prominence over the medium of the scroll—one continuous rolled page, written on one side—until nearly the fourth century AD in the Mediterranean world. From late antiquity until the present, scrolls have continued to be employed for many religious texts and other antiquarian purposes.[66] Furthermore, in ancient writing, authorship could be ascribed but most of the time is not claimed. No conception of copyright existed for ancient literature. Stories were borrowed and modified without concern for proprietary ownership. In addition, replication was an arduous task requiring painstaking and specialized labor, and copies were anything but impeccable. Without modern technologies, the dissemination of exact copies was essentially impossible.

Although this literary world sounds unusual, modern observers have a range of readymade metaphors that can help better envision the ancient situation. Most assume the Bible is one discrete work, like Toni Morrison's *Beloved* or Charles Dickens's *A Tale of Two Cities*, likely because modern readers engage with its text as a single volume. But the Bible is, in fact, the result of uniting together numerous individual literary texts. Each new section title is not a chapter, as in a typical book, but is itself a complete book (i.e., the book of Genesis, the book of Exodus, and so forth).[67] As such,

---

[65] For more comparison of "long-form reading," Kindle ebooks, and screen scrolling, see Conor Friedersdorf, "Reading, Writing, and Thinking Online: An Interview with Alan Jacobs," *The Atlantic*, June 8, 2010, https://www.theatlantic.com/projects/ideas-2010/archive/2010/06/reading-writing-and-thinking-online-an-interview-with-alan-jacobs/57807/.

[66] Thomas Forrest Kelly, *The Role of the Scroll: An Illustrated Introduction to Scrolls in the Middle Ages* (New York: Norton, 2019).

[67] The oldest Hebrew texts include divisions marking liturgical, content-based, and physical reading divisions, see Daniel Picus, "Reading Regularly: The Liturgical Reading of Torah in its Late Antique Material World," in *Material Aspects of Reading in Ancient and Medieval Cultures: Materiality, Presence and Performance*, ed. Anna Krauß, Jonas Leipziger, and Friederike Schücking-Jungblut, Materiale Textkulturen 26 (Berlin: de Gruyter, 2020), 217–32. However, modern chapters were not standard until the advent of modern printing. See Ernst Würthwein, *The Text of the Old Testament: An Introduction to the* Biblica Hebraica, 3rd ed., rev. and exp. Alexander Achilles Fischer, trans. Erroll F. Rhodes (Grand Rapids: Eerdmans, 2014), 30–35.

the Scriptures compare to a freshman English literature anthology or textbook as a compilation of literary works—poems, stories, chronicles, etc.—by various authors.

A better way to think about the originating literary and textual situation is like a bookshelf of your public library. As with a library shelf, separate books may be organized in a variety of ways and for several purposes.[68] Some are arranged by similarities in topic, writer, genre, publication date, language, size, or even color. These strategies answer various questions, such as: Where did these books come from? How are they related? Who thought they were important? What were they used for? One might even organize the same books on a shelf in more than one way with different purposes.[69] Such is the case because sequential arrangement is not an essential quality of scrolls.[70] Individual works only require a standardized order when collected into larger format book-scrolls or later codices.[71] We should not view organization, however, as neutral or haphazard. Different orders tell their own story. Certain communities make connections between the Scriptures based on their understandings of how these texts should be read.[72] While some texts demonstrate strong internal chronological connections (e.g., Samuel-Kings, Ezra-Nehemiah, the Torah), others subvert temporal proximity for a variety of other purposes (e.g., Ruth within the Megilloth, i.e., the five festal scrolls).[73] These ordered bookshelves provide helpful insights into how ancient readers organized and interacted with their scriptural archive and in what ways they envisaged the overarching tableau of authoritative writings.

1.6.2 The History of the Hebrew Bible

Four periods are outlined in considering the written evidence for the Hebrew Bible: (1) the period before about 250 BC, encompassing the initial composition of most biblical texts with almost no documentary evidence; (2) the period between 250 BC and AD 135, represented largely by the texts found in and around the

---

[68] The technical description is an *archive*, see Charpin, *Reading and Writing in Babylon*.

[69] Nahum Sarna suggests that the fixed order found in the early rabbinic literature (b. Baba Bathra 14b) indicates how the books were read, studied, and stored in the synagogue. See "The Order of the Books," in *Studies in Jewish Bibliography, History and Literature in Honor of I. Edward Kiev*, ed. Charles Berlin (New York: Ktav, 1971), 407–13.

[70] Menahem Haran, "Archives, Libraries, and the Order of the Biblical Books," *JANES* 22 (1993): 51–61.

[71] Menahem Haran, "Book-Scrolls at the Beginning of the Second Temple Period: The Transitions from Papyrus to Skins," *HUCA* 54 (1983): 111–22; Haran, "Book-Size and the Device of Catch-Lines in the Biblical Canon," *JJS* 36 (1985): 1–11.

[72] Starting with the landmark work of Brevard Childs (*Introduction to the Old Testament as Scripture* [Philadelphia: Fortress, 1979]), scholars have attempted to provide canonical frameworks to explain the meaning of the various extant scriptural arrangements in the context of their use in different religious communities. See further Mary C. Callaway, "Canonical Criticism," in *To Each Its Own Meaning: An Introduction to Biblical Criticisms and Their Application*, ed. Stephen R. Haynes and Steven L. McKenzie (Philadelphia: WJK, 1999), 142–55.

[73] Rolf Rendtorff, *The Old Testament: An Introduction* (Philadelphia: Fortress, 1989), 258–59; T. C. Vriezen and A. S. van der Woude, *Ancient Israelite and Early Jewish Literature*, trans. Brian Doyle (Leiden: Brill, 2005), 67–70, 446–51.

Judean desert until the Bar Kokhba revolt;[74] (3) the period between AD 135 and 800, characterized by continued standardization and consolidation around the proto-Masoretic Text; and (4) the period from about AD 800 to the end of the Middle Ages, dominated by the proliferation of the Tiberian tradition.

Before 250 BC. Little direct material evidence exists for the written form of the Scriptures before 250 BC. Excepting inscribed personal and place names as well as the reference from an ostracon at Meṣad Ḥashavyahu to a Torah regulation (Exod 22:26–27), the only certain external biblical citation comes from an inscription on two silver amulets that were excavated in 1979 within rock-cut burial caves near the Scottish Church of St. Andrew in Jerusalem.[75] The Ketef Hinnom Silver Plaques were discovered "rolled up like miniature scrolls"[76] and have been dated to at least the early sixth century BC.[77] The use of these objects was religious and likely apotropaic.[78] Each is inscribed in Paleo-Hebrew script. The plaques include several divine epithets (inscriptions I and II) and some traces of a blessing with the owner's name (inscription II). The inscriptions appear to end similarly with a text corresponding to the Aaronic blessing (Num 6:24–26): The first inscription begins with a prayer addressed to God, which is similar to texts from Dan 9:4, Neh 1:5, and Deut 7:9.

KETEF HINNOM I	KETEF HINNOM II[79]	NUM 6:24-26
יברך יהוה [4A][5A][6A] [וי]שמר [יא]ר יהוה פנ[יו]	יברך יהוה ישמרך יאר יה[ו]ה פניו [אל]יך וישם לך ש[ל]ם	יברכך יהוה וישמרך יאר יהוה פניו אליך ויחנך ישא יהוה פניו אליך וישם לך שלום
May Yahweh bless you [and] keep you, May Yahweh [make his] face shine . . .	May Yahweh bless you, keep you, May Yah[we]h make his face shine [on] you, And may he give you pe[a]ce . . .	May Yahweh bless you and keep you, May Yahweh make his face shine on you and be gracious to you, May Yahweh set his face on you and give you peace.

---

[74] Moshe Goshen-Gottstein divides this period into two separate phases for mainly historical reasons. See "Hebrew Biblical Manuscripts: Their History and Their Place in the HUBP Edition," *Biblica* 48 (1967): 246–48.

[75] Dennis G. Pardee, "Judicial Plea from Meṣad Ḥashavyahu (Yavneh-Yam): A New Philological Study," *Maarav* 1 (1978): 33–66.

[76] Gabriel Barkay, "The Priestly Benediction on Silver Plaques from Ketef Hinnom in Jerusalem," *Tel Aviv* 19 (1992): 148

[77] For an evaluation of the most recent evidence of dating these inscriptions, see Jeremy D. Smoak, *The Priestly Blessing in Inscription and Scripture* (New York: Oxford University Press, 2016).

[78] Smoak, *Priestly Blessing*.

[79] The reading follows Gabriel Barkay, Marilyn J. Lundberg, Andrew G. Vaughn, and Bruce Zuckerman, "The Amulets from Ketef Hinnom: A New Edition and Evaluation," *BASOR* 334 (2004): 41–71.

KETEF HINNOM I	DAN 9:4	NEH 1:5	DEUT 7:9
גד[ל שמר] הברית ו[ה]חסד לאהב[יו] ושמרי [מצותיו]	האל הגדול והנורא שמר הברית והחסד לאהביו ולשמרי מצותיו	האל הגדול והנורא שמר הברית וחסד לאהביו ולשמרי מצותיו	האל הנאמן שמר הברית והחסד לאהביו ולשמרי מצותו
[The] grea[t God who keeps] the covenant and [the] fidelity for those who love [him] and keep [his commandments]	The great and fearsome God who keeps the covenant and the fidelity for those who love him and keep his commandments	The great and fearsome God who keeps the covenant and fidelity for those who love him and keep his commandments	The faithful God who keeps the covenant and the fidelity for those who love him and keep his commandments

While the inscriptions are not strictly speaking biblical manuscripts, they evidence written material from a very early period conforming to biblical texts. Some lacunae and spelling differences are evident, but the Ketef Hinnom inscriptions generally represent what is found in manuscripts copied nearly a millennium later.

The biblical compositions themselves provide internal evidence glimpsing their earliest histories. A mixture of unnamed and named sources are evident. Comparing the shared passages from several the historical writings—such as Samuel-Kings, Chronicles, Psalms, Isaiah, and Jeremiah—reveals shared documentary materials.[80] Also, many biblical texts acknowledge the inclusion of their sources. These documents include letters between groups (Neh 6:17, 19) and individuals (2 Kgs 10:1–7), as well as international missives (2 Kgs 19:8–14; 2 Chr 2:3–16; 32:17)

---

[80] See e.g., Werner Lemke, "The Synoptic Problem in the Chronicler's History," *HTR* 58 (1965): 349–63; James D. Newsome, *A Synoptic Harmony of Samuel, Kings, and Chronicles: With Related Passages from Psalms, Isaiah, Jeremiah, and Ezra* (Eugene, OR: Wipf & Stock, 1986); Baruch Halpern, "Sacred History and Ideology: Chronicles' Thematic Structure-Indications of an Earlier Source," in *The Creation of Sacred Literature*, ed. Richard E. Friedman, Near Eastern Studies 22 (Berkeley: University of California Press, 1981), 35–54; P. S. F. van Keulen, Two Versions of the Solomon Narrative: An Inquiry into the Relationship between MT 1 Kgs. 2–11 and LXX 3 Reg. 2–11. VTSup 104 (Leiden: Brill, 2005); Julio Trebolle Barrera, "Kings (MT/LXX) and Chronicles: The Double and Triple Textual Tradition," in *Reflection and Refraction: Studies in Biblical Historiography in Honour of A. Graeme Auld*, ed. Robert Rezetko, Timothy H. Lim, and W. Brian Aucker, VTSup 113 (Leiden: Brill, 2007), 483–501; Gary Knoppers, "The Synoptic Problem? An Old Testament Perspective," *BBR* 19 (2009): 11–34; John Van Seters, "The Chronicler's Account of the Temple-Building: A Continuity Theme," in Changing Perspectives I: Studies in the History, Literature and Religion of Biblical Israel (London: Routledge, 2011), 99–114; Christophe Nihan, "Textual Fluidity and Rewriting in Parallel Traditions: The Case of Samuel and Chronicles," *Journal of Ancient Judaism* 4 (2013): 186–209.

As for other reconstructed sources, such as the so-called Priestly Source, biblical scholars continue to debate the particulars, their historical conditions and development, and the degree to which these academic models provide viable conclusions. See respectively Konrad Schmid, *The Old Testament: A Literary History* (Minneapolis: Fortress, 2012); Alexander Rofé, *Introduction to the Literature of the Hebrew Bible* (Jerusalem: Simor, 2009); David M. Carr, *The Formation of the Hebrew Bible: A New Reconstruction* (Oxford: Oxford University Press, 2011).

reproducing, at times, entire Hebrew and Aramaic texts (Hebrew: 2 Sam 11:15; 1 Kgs 21:9–10; 2 Kgs 5:6; 10:2–3, 6; 19:10–13; 2 Chr 2:11–15; 21:12–15; Neh 6:6–7; Jer 29:4–23, 26–28; Aramaic: Ezra 4:11–16, 17–22; 5:7–17; 7:12–26).[81] Earlier written prophetic oracles (Exod 17:14; Isa 65:6; Jer 25:13; 22:30; 51:60–64; Ezek 2:9–10), letters (2 Chr 21:12; Jer 29:1–29), and biographies (2 Chr 13:22) are credited. Various legal sources are incorporated, such as royal decrees (2 Chr 35:4; Esth 1:19; 3:9, 12; 4:8; 8:5, 8, 9) and treaties (Exod 24:7; Deut 31:26; Josh 24:16; 2 Chr 34:30–31; Neh 10:1–2). Administrative texts incorporate descriptions of land boundaries (Num 21:14; Josh 18:4–9), the sealed purchase of goods (Jer 32:10–12), census lists (Num 1:2; 26:2; 1 Chr 21), and genealogies (Gen 5:1; 1 Chr 9:1; Neh 7:5). Priestly catalogues include ritual lists (1 Chr 24:6; Neh 12:22–23), indices of cultic items (Ezra 8:31), and regulations for the Passover celebration (2 Kgs 23:21; 2 Chr 30:5). Other named historical documents are referenced as originating from the "Scroll of the Acts of Solomon" (1 Kgs 11:41), the "Annals of the King of Persia" (Esth 2:23; 6:1–2), and the edict of Cyrus (2 Chr 36:22–23; Ezra 1:1–4). Annals of the ascension narratives (1 Kgs 16:20; 2 Kgs 15:15) and the mighty acts of the kings (1 Kgs 16:27) are mentioned alongside other source material from the books of Kings and Chronicles. These books reference the military exploits of Jeroboam (1 Kgs 14:19), Jehoshaphat (1 Kgs 22:45), Jehoash (2 Kgs 13:12; 14:15), Jeroboam (2 Kgs 14:28), and Jotham (2 Chr 27:7). Records of Ahab's building ventures, such as an ivory house, are documented in the "Book of the Annals of the Israelite Kings" (1 Kgs 22:39), and the "Annals of the Judahite Kings" (2 Kgs 20:20) describes the construction of the pool and conduit of Hezekiah. Other texts include: the Decalogue (Exod 20:2–17; Deut 5:6–21; see the documentary references at Exod 34:28 and Deut 4:13), the "Scroll of the Covenant" (Exod 24:7; 2 Kgs 23:21), the "Scroll of the Wars of the Lord" (Num 21:14), and the "Scroll of the Torah (of God/Moses)" (Deut 17:18; 28:58, 61; 29:20, 21, 27; 30:10; 31:24, 26).[82] In sum, overt sources and redactional composition reveal a robust pre-history for most biblical texts, even though the documentary evidence appears to be lost.

Between 250 BC and AD 135. With the discovery of the Dead Sea Scrolls, we can glimpse a distinct moment in the textual life of ancient Jewish libraries. While scholars continue to debate the precise functions of these various texts, it is evident that a vast collection of biblical and nonbiblical documents warranted collection and were deposited for the purpose of safekeeping. Nine hundred thirty documents were discovered in eleven caves near Khirbet Qumran. The biblical materials were interspersed with retold scripture, commentaries, sectarian works, and other writings.[83] The fortress of Masada and the caves near En-Gedi, Naḥal Ḥever, Wadi

---

[81] James M. Lindenberger, *Ancient Aramaic and Hebrew Letters*, 2nd ed., Writings from the Ancient World 14 (Atlanta: Society of Biblical Literature, 2003).

[82] See similar descriptions in Josh 1:8; 8:31, 34; 23:6; 24:26; 1 Sam 10:25; 2 Kgs 14:6; 22:8, 11; Neh 8:1–18; 9:3; 13:1.

[83] See, among others, Joseph A. Fitzmyer, *A Guide to the Dead Sea Scrolls and Related Literature*, rev. ed. (Grand Rapids: Eerdmans, 2008); Harold P. Scanlin, *The Dead Sea Scrolls & Modern*

Murabbaʿat, Naḥal Sdeir, and Naḥal Ṣeʿelim yielded additional biblical writings.[84] In total, more than 200 fragmentary biblical scrolls are known from the Qumran caves and another 24 from other Judean desert sites.[85] Most of these are individual manuscripts comprising single compositions. Larger book-scrolls of the Torah and Minor Prophets are supported by several fragments containing the end and beginning of sequential books (Gen to Exod [4Q1; 4Q11], Exod to Lev [4Q17], Lev to Num [1Q3; 4Q23], Gen, Exod, Num [Mur 1], and the Twelve [4Q76; 4Q77; 4Q78; 4Q80; 4Q81; 4Q82; Mur 88]). Only the Great Isaiah Scroll (1QIsaᵃ) is preserved completely.

The DSS biblical scrolls support the antiquity of the MT tradition and confirm the coexistence of alternate editions of those same works. Before the discovery and decipherment of the scrolls, most scholars gave favored status to the earliest medieval Hebrew documents.[86] Other competing non-Hebrew sources (i.e., the Ancient Versions)—even when they represented older manuscripts—were deemed to have inferior value in textual reconstruction, based simply on account of their being translations.[87] The scrolls from the Qumran caves, however, continue to revolutionize the scholarly assumptions of textual criticism. On the one hand, the documents provide ample evidence of a textual tradition in line with the later MT consonants. These are the so-called proto-Masoretic or proto-rabbinic texts.[88] On the other hand, they provide evidence of a textual variety aligning with the Greek translations, the later Samaritan Pentateuch [SP], or even an amalgamation of several traditions. Each manuscript may be classified by its degree of similarity to one of the three main text-types[89] or as non-aligned (i.e., not conforming to these three text-types).[90] By Emanuel Tov's reckoning, the 121 most complete Qumran texts correspond as follows:[91]

Translations of the Old Testament (Wheaton, IL: Tyndale, 1993); James C. VanderKam, *The Dead Sea Scrolls and the Bible* (Grand Rapids: Eerdmans, 2012).

[84] Martin Abegg, Peter Flint, and Eugene Ulrich. *The Dead Sea Scrolls Bible: The Oldest Known Bible Translated for the First Time into English* (New York: HarperCollins, 1999), i–xvi.

[85] These numbers represent biblical texts, such as 1QIsaᵃ, 11QPsaᵇ, and so on. See Emanuel Tov, "The Biblical Texts from the Judean Desert—An Overview and Assessment," in *Hebrew Bible, Greek Bible and Qumran: Collected Essays*, TSAJ 121 (Tübingen: Mohr Siebeck, 2008), 128–54, originally published in E. D. Herbert and Emanuel Tov, eds., *The Bible as Book: The Hebrew Bible and the Judean Desert Discoveries* (London: British Library, 2002).

[86] For a general assessment of the history of scholarship, see Goshen-Gottstein, "Hebrew Biblical Manuscripts."

[87] See "Old Testament Textual Criticism: Retrieving the Text for Exegesis" in this volume.

[88] For the various terminology used to refer to these texts, see Emanuel Tov, "'Proto-Masoretic,' 'Pre-Masoretic,' 'Semi-Masoretic,' and 'Masoretic': A Study in Terminology and Textual Theory," in *Found in Translation: Essays on Jewish Biblical Translation in Honor of Leonard J. Greenspoon*, ed. James W. Barker et al. (West Lafayette, IN: Purdue University Press, 2018), 31–52.

[89] J. R. Davila, "Text-Type and Terminology: Genesis and Exodus as Test Cases," *RevQ* 16 (1993): 3–37.

[90] See the evaluation of Emanuel Tov, "A Modern Textual Outlook Based on the Qumran Scrolls," *HUCA* 53 (1982): 11–27. See further Bruno Chiesa, "Textual History and Textual Criticism of the Hebrew Old Testament," in *The Madrid Qumran Congress. Proceeding of the International Congress on the Dead Sea Scrolls Madrid 18–21 March, 1991*, ed. Julio Trebolle Barrerra and Luis Vegas Montaner, STDJ 11 (Leiden: Brill, 1992), 1:257–72.

[91] Tov, "Biblical Texts from the Judean Desert."

	TORAH (46)	PROPHETS & HAGIOGRAPHY (75)	TOTAL (121)
MT	22 (47.8%)	33 (44%)	55 (45.5%)
Non-aligned	19 (41.3%)	40 (53.3%)	59 (48.8 %)
SP	3 (6.5%)	N/A	3 (2.5%)
Greek	2 (4.4%)	2 (2.7%)	4 (3.3%)

In contrast to these scrolls found in the caves near Qumran, several other manuscripts from this period align more closely with the MT and possess a very small number of divergences.[92]

While it is tempting to assume that each of these documents is an equal witness to a biblical text (*Urtext*), such a supposition is too broad of a generalization. First, the origins of the manuscripts continue to be debated. The question of the textual diversity of the scrolls and their relationship to the site of Khirbet Qumran remains open.[93] And difficulty remains in identifying the nature of the basic sectarian groups in Second Temple Judaism and their relationship to the manuscript evidence. Even if a consensus is reached on these issues, the overarching question remains: Do the scrolls provide evidence for how authoritative scripture was viewed by just one sect or by Judaism as a whole during this time? Second, the paucity of evidence provides an uneven assessment. Famously, all the books known from the later rabbinic Bible are attested at Qumran except for Esther.[94] Should this lack of evidence signal the absence of Esther from the Qumran "bible"? On the other hand, the book of Enoch (*1 Enoch*) is known from several DSS copies. Does this mean that the community considered the book of Enoch to be canonical? The presence or absence of a document at Qumran may be connected to its perceived prestige or authority in the community, but it may also be connected to the happenstance of preservation. In the end, there remains no description of how each of these different texts were used or understood by these communities. Imagine going to a ransacked Christian bookstore and examining the range of ways that biblical passages are represented in the various books on its shelves. It would be nearly impossible to reconstruct such a disorganized amalgamation of different translations, Bible study curricula, printed liturgies, devotional guides, scripture calendars, commentaries, and even historical fiction. Each one of these could be seen as dissimilar or even competing textual evidence. On the other hand, each could be understood as complementary and useful in different settings and for various reasons. Without a store map or a very good understanding of contemporary Christian bookstores, our assessment of the data would take widely different forms.

---

[92] Ian Young, "The Biblical Scrolls from Qumran and the Masoretic Text: A Statistical Approach," in *Feasts and Fasts: A Festschrift in Honour of Alan David Crown*, ed. Marianne Dacy, Jennifer Dowling, and Suzanne Faigan, Mandelbaum Studies in Judaica 11 (Sydney: Mandelbaum, 2005), 81–139.

[93] Tov, "Biblical Texts from the Judean Desert," 145–46.

[94] Textual evidence for an independent book of Nehemiah is also lacking; however, the assumption is that the small fragment of Ezra (4Q117) would have represented a scroll containing both compositions (i.e., the combined book of Ezra-Nehemiah).

In this same period, the biblical material is referenced in historical accounts and citations. Famous passages mention the existence of scrolls and possibly even early authoritative collections.[95] The ancient Greek translator's prologue to the book of Ben Sira (also known as Sirach, ca. 132 BC) identifies this composition of Jesus ben Sira as a pedagogical enterprise supporting "the many great matters given through the Law, the Prophets, and the others that accompanied them" (Πολλῶν καὶ μεγάλων ἡμῖν διὰ τοῦ νόμου καὶ τῶν προφητῶν καὶ τῶν ἄλλων τῶν κατ' αὐτοὺς ἠκολουθηκότων δεδομένων, Sir Pro:1). This devotion came from his "reading of the Law, the Prophets, and the ancestral books" (τε τὴν τοῦ νόμου καὶ τῶν προφητῶν καὶ τῶν ἄλλων πατρίων βιβλίων ἀνάγνωσιν, Sir Pro:8–10).[96] These references bring to mind the later threefold division of the Law, the Prophets, and the Writings, but the specific scrolls are admittedly unidentified.[97] In the nearly contemporaneous book of 2 Maccabees, a letter claims that the "records" (ἀναγραφή) and "memorandum" (ὑπομνηματισμός) of Nehemiah were collected into a "library" (βιβλιοθήκη) by Judas Maccabee along with several other compositions (τὰ περὶ τῶν βασιλέων βιβλία καὶ προφητῶν καὶ τὰ τοῦ Δαυιδ καὶ ἐπιστολὰς βασιλέων περὶ ἀναθημάτων "the books concerning the kings and prophets, and those of David, and kings' letters about votive offerings," 2 Macc 2:13–15).[98] Reference to the Torah is noticeably outstanding, although τὸ βιβλίον τοῦ νόμου "the book of the law" is referenced elsewhere (1 Macc 3:48). In the time of Jesus, Philo of Alexandria wrote about Jewish commitment to the "laws, words prophesied through the prophets, religious songs, and others which produce and accomplish knowledge and piety" (νόμους καὶ λόγια θεσπισθέντα διὰ προφητῶν καὶ ὕμνους καὶ τὰ ἄλλα οἷς ἐπιστήμη καὶ εὐσέβεια συναύξονται καὶ τελειοῦνται, *De vita contemplativa* 3). The New Testament references "the Law and the Prophets" (Matt 5:17; 7:12; 11:13; 22:40; Luke 16:16, [29, 31]; Acts 13:15; 24:14; 28:23; Rom 3:21, see also 2 Macc 15:9; Diogn. 11:6), but a threefold division may be in view with reference to "everything that was written in the Law of Moses, the Prophets and Psalms" (πάντα τὰ γεγραμμένα ἐν τῷ νόμῳ Μωϋσέως καὶ τοῖς προφήταις καὶ ψαλμοῖς, Luke 24:44). Finally, Josephus in the late first century AD numbers twenty-two compositions of the Jewish scriptures (δύο δὲ μόνα πρὸς τοῖς εἴκοσι βιβλία): five books of Moses (τούτων πέντε μέν ἐστι Μωυσέως), thirteen books of the prophets after Moses (οἱ μετὰ Μωυσῆν προφῆται τὰ κατ' αὐτοὺς πραχθέντα συνέγραψαν ἐν τρισὶ καὶ δέκα βιβλίοις), and four books of religious songs and didactic poems (αἱ δὲ λοιπαὶ τέσσαρες ὕμνους εἰς τὸν θεὸν καὶ τοῖς ἀνθρώποις ὑποθήκας τοῦ βίου περιέχουσιν, *C. Ap.*, 1.38–40). Each of these descriptions point, at the very minimum, to the growing

---

[95] Haran, "Archives."

[96] Joseph Ziegler, ed., *Sapientia Iesu Filii Sirach*, SVTG 12.2 (Göttingen: Vandenhoeck & Ruprecht, 1980).

[97] The text of Ben Sira references several characters after whom various biblical books are named: Moses (Sir 45:1), Joshua (46:1), Samuel (46:13), David, Nathan (47:1), Solomon (47:13), Elijah (48:1), Jeremiah (49:6), Ezekiel (49:8), and the twelve prophets ([שנים עשר הנביאים], 49:10).

[98] Greek text cited from Werner Kappler, ed., *Maccabaeorum Liber II*, SVTG 9.2 (Göttingen: Vandenhoeck & Ruprecht, 2008).

understanding in Second Temple Judaism that some texts were recognized as having a special authoritative status for these religious communities.[99]

During this time, the biblical texts are cited in other literary sources and translated. The earliest translation is the Septuagint, dated to around the middle of the third century BC.[100] The initial translation of the Hebrew Bible into Greek included only the Pentateuch, but the entire biblical corpus was completed within about a century. Later recensions produced other versions highlighting various theological and textual differences.[101] Citations of the Hebrew Bible are found in a broad number of compositions. Some, like the Qumran scrolls and early Tannaitic literature (Mishnah, Tosefta), directly quote the Hebrew text. Others, like the NT or the early church fathers, translate the references into a common language (mostly Greek).

Between AD 135 and 800. Only a small number of Hebrew manuscripts are known from this era, so it is sometimes referred to as the "Silent Period." The Nash Papyrus provides evidence of the Hebrew text of the Decalogue and the Shema from the beginning of this period.[102] The documents from the Cairo Fustat Genizah include palimpsests of the (Greek) Bible from as early as the fifth century.[103] Other documents include Hebrew biblical manuscripts, translations, and commentaries dating to a century later.[104] The vast majority of biblical evidence comes from citations in early rabbinic and Christian literature. Many are quite substantial and even, at times, include commentaries on entire biblical books. Translations of the Hebrew and Greek texts proliferated during this period, comprising Syriac, Armenian, Ethiopic, Coptic, Latin, Aramaic, Georgian, Old Church Slavonic, and Arabic versions.[105] Several Greek recensions may also be dated to the earlier centuries AD. And the first widely known works of text criticism were initiated by Origen, Jerome, and Paul of Tella.[106] Lastly, the earliest complete biblical codices including the Hebrew Scriptures are known from the fourth and fifth centuries.[107]

---

[99] For a larger discussion of these and other sources as they relate to the notion of canon, see Stephen G. Dempster, "The Old Testament Canon, Josephus, and Cognitive Environment," in *The Enduring Authority of the Christian Scriptures*, ed. D. A. Carson (Grand Rapids: Eerdmans, 2016), 321–61.

[100] See Karen H. Jobes, *Invitation to the Septuagint*, 2nd ed. (Grand Rapids: Baker Academic, 2015); Jennifer M. Dines, *The Septuagint* (London: T&T Clark, 2004); Natalio Fernández Marcos, *The Septuagint in Context: Introduction to the Greek Version of the Bible*, trans. Wilfred G. E. Watson (Leiden: Brill, 2000).

[101] See e.g., the essays in Alison Salvesen, ed., *Origen's Hexapla and Fragments* (Tübingen: Mohr Siebeck, 1998).

[102] F. C. Burkitt, "The Hebrew Papyrus of the Ten Commandments," *JQR* 15 (1903): 392–408.

[103] For a general introduction, see Adina Hoffman and Peter Cole, *Sacred Trash: The Lost and Found World of the Cairo Geniza* (New York: Schocken, 2011).

[104] The Genizah Research Unit at Cambridge University Library houses a large number of these texts as part of the Taylor-Schechter Genizah Collection (https://www.lib.cam.ac.uk/collections/departments/taylor-schechter-genizah-research-unit). Many of these may be accessed through the Penn/Cambridge Genizah Fragment Project (http://sceti.library.upenn.edu/genizah/).

[105] See the essays in *THB* 1C.

[106] For a review of the history of the disciple of textual criticism, see Moshe Goshen-Gottstein, "The Textual Criticism of the Old Testament: Rise, Decline, Rebirth," *JBL* 102 (1983): 365–99.

[107] Bruce Metzger and Bart D. Ehrman, *The Text of the New Testament: Its Transmission, Corruption, and Restoration*, 4th ed. (New York: Oxford University Press, 2005).

After AD 800. By the end of the first millennium AD, an exclusive Hebrew textual tradition emerged, representing the authoritative scriptures for most of Judaism. This textualization is called the Masoretic Text (MT or מ‎). Marginal notations and independent treatises enumerate the exact textual nature.[108] Further, a wide-ranging reading strategy is encoded within the texts indicating their cantillation, vocalization (*niqqud*), versification, and paragraph structure. While no single manuscript embodies the MT completely, two major codices are understood as both early and faithful witnesses to this tradition. The Aleppo Codex (A) is the older exemplar, having been copied about AD 920, but the most complete text is the Leningrad Codex (Firkovitch B19A or M^L) dating to a century later (ca. AD 1008–1009).[109] Both of these codices follow the Tiberian textualization system of the Ben Asher family and the colophon of the latter claims to have been written in Cairo. All later Hebrew scrolls and codices may be traced back to this early textual tradition. While other reading traditions—notably the Babylonian and Palestinian vocalizations— are encoded using a variety of differing symbolic systems, these are all eclipsed by the MT by the early centuries of the second millennium.

The Leningrad Codex (M^L) is the basis for most modern Hebrew Bibles. The various imprints of *Biblia Hebraica*, starting with the third edition (*BHK* or *BH3*), are facsimiles of the consonants, cantillations, and vowels of M^L.[110] The fourth edition is the basis of most academic study and modern English translations. This edition is *Biblia Hebraica Stuttgartensia* or *BHS*.[111] Completed by J. Alan Groves in 1987, the *Michigan-Claremont-Westminster Electronic Hebrew Bible* is a transcription of M^L and is the basis of most digital editions.[112] The fifth edition is called *Biblia Hebraica Quinta* (*BHQ* or *BH5*) and is currently in production.[113] Aron Dotan created another printed edition, *Biblia Hebraica Leningradensia*.[114] Before the M^L editions, the Bomberg Rabbinic Bible (*Mikraot Gedolot*, 1517/1525), was

---

[108] Geoffrey Khan, *The Tiberian Pronunciation Tradition of Biblical Hebrew*, vol. 1, *Description of the Tiberian Pronunciation Tradition*, Cambridge Semitic Languages and Cultures 1 (Cambridge: Open Book, 2020).

[109] Moshe Goshen-Gottstein, *The Aleppo Codex* (Jerusalem: Magnes, 1976). Matti Friedman, *The Aleppo Codex: A True Story of Obsession, Faith, and the Pursuit of an Ancient Bible* (Chapel Hill, NC: Algonquin, 2012). Firkovich B 19A is not to be confused with the older Prophets manuscript (B 3) also catalogued in the Russian National Library.

[110] Rudolf Kittel, ed., *Biblia Hebraica*, 3rd ed. (Stuttgart: Württembergische Bibelanstalt, 1937).

[111] Karl Elliger and Wilhelm Rudolph, eds. *Biblica Hebraica Stuttgartensia*, 5th ed. (Stuttgart: Deutsche Bibelgesellschaft, 1997). Also, Donald R. Vance et al., *Biblia Hebraica Stuttgartensia: A Reader's Edition* (Peabody, MA: Hendrickson, 2014).

[112] See the project description for the *J. Alan Groves Center for Advanced Biblical Research* at Westminster Theological Seminary (https://students.wts.edu/resources/alangroves.html). Also, the *eBHS* provides the text of A. Philip Brown II and Bryan W. Smith, *A Reader's Hebrew Bible* (Grand Rapids: Zondervan, 2008); and *The Hebrew Old Testament, Reader's Edition*. Wheaton, IL: Crossway, 2021.

[113] Adrian Schenker et al., *Biblia Hebraica Quinta*, 5th ed. (Stuttgart: Deutsche Bibelgesellschaft, 2004–).

[114] Aron Dotan, ed., *Biblia Hebraica Leningradensia* (Peabody, MA: Hendrickson, 2001).

the most commonly used Hebrew text.[115] Alternatively, a number of printed editions of the Aleppo Codex have been undertaken.[116]

1.6.3 Reading Traditions

Oral Transmission. The MT combines at least two trajectories of development: the Hebrew letters and the rabbinic reading (i.e., the vowels and cantillation). Evidence for both may be traced as far back as the Second Temple period. Following the earliest tradition of copying Hebrew codices, *BHS* layers the letters, vowels, and cantillation into one text. The reading traditions were handed down from generation to generation through oral recitation and rote memorization. These traditions predate the inscriptional work of the Masoretic scribes and may be traced to early synagogue worship and education.

While these practices are arguably much older, references to the earliest reading tradition occur in the Babylonian Talmud (compiled about AD 500). Rabbi Isaac remarks on four facets of the oral recitation of Scripture as authoritative:[117]

מקרא סופרים ועטור סופרים וקריין ולא כתיבן וכתיבן ולא קריין הלכה למשה מסיני

> The reading aloud of the scribes, the dividing of the scribes, those things read but not written, and those things written but not read are *halakah* [i.e., given] to Moses from Sinai.
> (b. Ned. 37b)

In this passage, R. Isaac first identifies the appropriate reading tradition or vocalization of the Hebrew consonants (מקרא סופרים) as established by the scribes (סופרים). Examples include changes from *segol* to *qameṣ* in אֶרֶץ (see Deut 32:13), *pataḥ* to *qameṣ* in שָׁמָיִם, and *pataḥ* to *qameṣ* in מִצְרָיִם in pause. Second, he discusses the scribal crowning or separation (עטור "that which is cut off or separated" from the verb עטר "to cut off; distinguish; adorn; wreathe"), perhaps denoting the otherwise unmarked oral divisions or pauses between clauses that are created when reading. Five examples are listed. The first involves the separation in Gen 18:5. After ואקחה פת לחם וסעדו לבבכם "I will bring some bread so that you may strengthen your heart," the following two words are understood as a separate clause, אחר תעברו "Then you may pass on," even though an expected conjunction

---

[115] See Moshe H. Goshen-Gottstein, *Mikraot Gedolot. Biblia Rabbinica: A Reprint of the 1525 Venice Edition* (Jerusalem: Makor, 1972).

[116] *Jerusalem Crown, The Bible of the Hebrew University of Jerusalem* (Jerusalem: Ben-Zvi Printing, 2000). The Hebrew University Bible Project (HUBP) at the Hebrew University of Jerusalem produced a scholarly edition of this text with a critical apparatus. However, only three volumes have been produced to date: Moshe Goshen-Gottstein, ed., *The Hebrew University Bible. The Book of Isaiah* (Jerusalem: Magnus, 1995); Chaim Rabin, Shemaryahu Talmon, and Emanuel Tov, eds., *The Hebrew University Bible. The Book of Jeremiah* (Jerusalem: Magnus, 1989); Moshe H. Goshen-Gottstein and Shemaryahu Talmon, eds., *The Hebrew University Bible. The Book of Ezekiel* (Jerusalem: Magnus, 2004).

[117] Aron Dotan, "Masorah," in *Encyclopedia Judaica*, 13:609.

waw (וְאחר) is absent.[118] Third, for those words that were read but not written (וקריין ולא כתיבן), the Masoretes inserted the vocalization of the omitted word without adding their consonants. Seven such examples are listed in the Talmud, including the omission of פרת "Euphrates" in 2 Sam 8:3. The text reads בִּנְהַר־ ֹ֯, with the siglum ֹ inserted above, and points the reader to the consonants provided in the *Masorah parva* of the side margin: פרת (see further §1.6.3). Below the consonants the *Masorah parva* explains: קרֹ ולא כת, an abbreviation for קרי ולא כתב "read but not written."[119] Fourth, the Talmud lists examples of words written but not read (וכתיבן ולא קריין). One instance is 2 Kgs 5:18, where the MT leaves נא unvocalized: יִסְלַח־נָא יְהוָה "may Yahweh (please) forgive." The *Masorah parva* references נֹא with the accompanying note: כת ולא קרֹ, an abbreviation for כתב ולא קרי "written but not read."[120] These comments exemplified the importance of attending to proper reading in this early period.

Although the exact setting of the transmission is inaccessible to us, the Masoretic scribal tradition has preserved many of the details of its oral transmission in what is known as the <u>Masorah</u>.

Masorah. In the broadest sense of the term, Masorah refers to the various scribal activities of the Masoretes. In a more limited sense, it refers to the Masoretic notes themselves, whereby the Masoretes combined oral and written traditions that we find preserved in codices such as M[L] (11th cent.) or the Aleppo Codex (10th cent.).[121] This narrow definition of Masorah is divided into two groups: *Masorah finalis* and *Masorah marginalis*. Some scholars identify the *Masorah finalis* with the arrangement of the *Masorah magna* (see below) as they appeared in the Ben Chayim Rabbinic Bible, produced by Jacob ben Chayim and published in 1524/25. Ben Chayim included the *Masorah magna* in full in the margins of the text, arranging the material in alphabetical order. This feature was peculiar to Ben Chayim and did not appear in the Hebrew manuscripts.[122] *Masorah finalis* more commonly refers to the lists appearing within the manuscripts at the end of each book or section. These lists record the number of verses (פסוקים) and reading sections/divisions (סדרים) as well as the halfway point of the book. The lists in books marking the end of each of the threefold divisions in the Hebrew Bible (i.e., תורה, נביאים, or כתובים) record that information for the larger collections. For example, the *Masorah finalis* for Malachi lists information for Malachi, the Book of the Twelve, and the entire Nevi'im:

---

[118] The other four examples are: אחר תלכו in Gen 24:55 (note that *BHS* reads תלך), אחר תאסף in Num 31:2, קדמו שרים אחר נוגנים in Ps 68:26 (*BHS* reads the last word defectively as נגנים), and צדקתך כהררי אל in Ps 36:7. Each of these is read as a separate clause from what comes before.

[119] The Talmud lists six more examples: Ruth 2:11; 3:4–5; 3:17; 2 Sam 16:23; Jer 31:37; 50:29.

[120] The Talmud lists four more examples: Deut 6:1; Ruth 3:12; Jer 51:3; Ezek 48:16.

[121] Page H. Kelley et al., *The Masorah of Biblia Hebraica Stuttgartensia: Introduction and Annotated Glossary* (Grand Rapids: Eerdmans, 1998), 1.

[122] William R. Scott, *A Simplified Guide to BHS: Critical Apparatus, Masora, Accents, Unusual Letters, and Other Markings*, 3rd ed. (Richland Hills, TX: BIBAL, 1987), 10, 18; Kelley et al., *Masorah*, 24–25.

סכום הפסוקים
חמשים
וחמשה
סכום הפסוקים של שנים עשר
אלף וחמשים
וחציו לכן בגללכם ציון שדה
וסדרים כֹֿא
סכום הפסוקים של נביאים
תשעת אלפים ומאתים
ושמונים וחמשה:
טֹ ר פֿ הֹ
כל סדרי הנביאים
מאתים וארבעה:
ק ק טֹ
חצי המקרא כהקיר
בור מימיה כן

The sum of verses (פסוקים) is fifty-five. The sum of verses belonging to the Twelve (שנים עשר) are one thousand and fifty. Its halfway point is "Therefore, on account of you, Zion as a field . . ." (i.e., Mic 3:12). The sections (סדרים) include 21. The sum of the verses belonging to the Prophets (נביאים) are nine thousand, two hundred and eighty-five: i.e., 9,285. All the sections of the Prophets are two hundred and four, i.e., 204. The halfway of the reading (מקרא) is "When the well keeps its waters fresh, thus . . ." (i.e., Jer 6:7).

The *Masorah marginalis* can be further subdivided into (1) the *Masorah parva* (Mp) and (2) the *Masorah magna* (Mm). As we saw earlier, the Mp provide detailed textual and philological notes, which, in M[L], are found abbreviated in the outside margins of the text. These notes are aligned with the line of text being commented on and include a circellus (small ring, e.g., Gen 1:1 בְּרֵאשִׁית) situated above or alongside the vocalized text. The Mp notes are separated by period-like dots and ordered from right-to-left corresponding to the sequence found in the text. A few of the more common Mp abbreviations are חס ("defective spelling"), ק ("to be read") and the aggregated sums לֹ ("once"), בֹ ("twice"), גֹ ("thrice"), etc.[123] The *ketiv-qere* notes also occur within the Mp.

---

[123] For more details, see Christian D. Ginsburg, *The Massorah Compiled from Manuscripts. Alphabetically and Lexically Arranged*, 4 vols. (London, 1880–1905); Mordechai Breuer, *The Biblical Text in the Jerusalem Crown Edition and Its Sources in the Masora and Manuscripts* (Jerusalem: Keren Ha-Masora, 2003); Israel Yeivin, *Introduction to the Tiberian Masorah*, Masoretic Studies 5 (Missoula, MT: Scholars Press, 1980); Aron Dotan and Nurit Reich, *Masora Thesaurus: A Complete Alphabetic Collection of the Masora Notes in the Leningrad Codex* (Altamonte Springs: Oak Tree Software, 2014). See the extremely valuable six volume series by David Marcus, *The Masorah of the Former Prophets in the Leningrad Codex*, Texts and Studies 3 (Piscataway, NJ: Gorgias, 2017–20).

Hebrew Judges 1 in the ***Biblia Hebraica Stuttgartensia (BHS)***. This page shows a facsimile of the text of the Leningrad Codex, ***Masorah Parva, Masorah Magna,*** and the Critical Apparatus.

Book Title	JUDICES שפטים

Masora *Parva*

יא׳ זוגין דמטע בטע׳ ד. ב	1 וַיְהִ֗י אַחֲרֵי֙ מ֣וֹת יְהוֹשֻׁ֔עַ וַֽיִּשְׁאֲלוּ֙ בְּנֵ֣י יִשְׂרָאֵ֔ל בַּיהוָ֖ה לֵאמֹ֑ר ‖ס‖
ל	2 מִ֣י יַעֲלֶה־לָּ֧נוּ אֶל־הַֽכְּנַעֲנִ֛י בַּתְּחִלָּ֖ה לְהִלָּ֣חֶם בּ֑וֹ וַיֹּ֣אמֶר יְהוָ֔ה
ל	3 יְהוּדָ֣ה יַעֲלֶ֔ה הִנֵּ֛ה נָתַ֥תִּי אֶת־הָאָ֖רֶץ בְּיָד֑וֹ וַיֹּ֣אמֶר יְהוּדָה֩ לְשִׁמְע֨וֹן אָחִ֜יו
ל. ד.	עֲלֵ֧ה אִתִּ֣י בְגוֹרָלִ֗י וְנִֽלָּחֲמָה֙ בַּֽכְּנַעֲנִ֔י וְהָלַכְתִּ֧י גַם־אֲנִ֛י אִתְּךָ֖ בְּגוֹרָלֶ֑ךָ
ל	4 וַיֵּ֖לֶךְ אִתּ֥וֹ שִׁמְעֽוֹן׃ וַיַּ֣עַל יְהוּדָ֔ה וַיִּתֵּ֧ן יְהוָ֛ה אֶת־הַֽכְּנַעֲנִ֥י וְהַפְּרִזִּ֖י
יא׳	בְּיָדָ֑ם וַיַּכּ֣וּם בְּבֶ֔זֶק עֲשֶׂ֥רֶת אֲלָפִ֖ים אִֽישׁ׃ 5 וַֽיִּמְצְא֞וּ אֶת־אֲדֹנִ֤י בֶ֙זֶק֙
ב בטע׳	בְּבֶ֔זֶק וַיִּֽלָּחֲמ֖וּ בּ֑וֹ וַיַּכּ֕וּ אֶת־הַֽכְּנַעֲנִ֖י וְאֶת־הַפְּרִזִּֽי׃ 6 וַיָּ֙נָס֙ אֲדֹנִ֣י בֶ֔זֶק
ב. ב.	וַֽיִּרְדְּפ֖וּ אַחֲרָ֑יו וַיֹּאחֲז֣וּ אֹת֔וֹ וַֽיְקַצְּצ֔וּ אֶת־בְּהֹנ֥וֹת יָדָ֖יו וְרַגְלָֽיו׃ 7 וַיֹּ֣אמֶר
ל. ב.	אֲדֹֽנִי־בֶ֗זֶק שִׁבְעִ֣ים ׀ מְלָכִ֡ים בְּהֹנוֹת֩ יְדֵיהֶ֨ם וְרַגְלֵיהֶ֜ם מְקֻצָּצִ֗ים הָי֤וּ
ב׳. ד. יא׳. ל	מְלַקְּטִים֙ תַּ֣חַת שֻׁלְחָנִ֔י כַּאֲשֶׁ֣ר עָשִׂ֔יתִי כֵּ֥ן שִׁלַּם־לִ֖י אֱלֹהִ֑ים וַיְבִיאֻ֥הוּ
ד. ח׳. ל	יְרוּשָׁלַ֖͏ִם וַיָּ֥מָת שָֽׁם׃ פ 8 וַיִּלָּחֲמ֤וּ בְנֵֽי־יְהוּדָה֙ בִּיר֣וּשָׁלִַ֔ם וַיִּלְכְּד֣וּ
ר. ח׳. ל	אוֹתָ֔הּ וַיַּכּ֖וּהָ לְפִי־חָ֑רֶב וְאֶת־הָעִ֖יר שִׁלְּח֥וּ בָאֵֽשׁ׃ 9 וְאַחַ֗ר יָֽרְדוּ֙ בְּנֵ֣י
מֵֽס מל בכבֵיא ר׳ʹ מנה בסיפ	10 יְהוּדָ֔ה לְהִלָּחֵ֖ם בַּֽכְּנַעֲנִ֑י יוֹשֵׁ֣ב הָהָ֔ר וְהַנֶּ֖גֶב וְהַשְּׁפֵלָֽה׃ וַיֵּ֣לֶךְ יְהוּדָה֮
	אֶל־הַֽכְּנַעֲנִי֮ הַיּוֹשֵׁ֣ב בְּחֶבְרוֹן֒ וְשֵׁם־חֶבְר֥וֹן לְפָנִ֖ים קִרְיַ֣ת אַרְבַּ֑ע
לד מל	11 וַיַּכּ֕וּ אֶת־שֵׁשַׁ֥י וְאֶת־אֲחִימַ֖ן וְאֶת־תַּלְמָ֑י וַיֵּ֣לֶךְ מִשָּׁ֔ם אֶל־יוֹשְׁבֵ֖י
	דְבִ֑יר וְשֵׁם־דְּבִ֥יר לְפָנִ֖ים קִרְיַת־סֵֽפֶר׃ 12 וַיֹּ֣אמֶר כָּלֵ֔ב אֲשֶׁר־יַכֶּ֥ה
	אֶת־קִרְיַת־סֵ֖פֶר וּלְכָדָ֑הּ וְנָתַ֥תִּי ל֛וֹ אֶת־עַכְסָ֥ה בִתִּ֖י לְאִשָּֽׁה׃
	13 וַֽיִּלְכְּדָהּ֙ עָתְנִיאֵ֣ל בֶּן־קְנַ֔ז אֲחִ֥י כָלֵ֖ב הַקָּטֹ֣ן מִמֶּ֑נּוּ וַיִּתֶּן־ל֣וֹ אֶת־
ב מל. ב. וחסׁ״י. ל	עַכְסָ֥ה בִתּ֖וֹ לְאִשָּֽׁה׃ 14 וַיְהִ֞י בְּבוֹאָ֗הּ וַתְּסִיתֵ֙הוּ֙ לִשְׁא֤וֹל מֵֽאֵת־אָבִ֔יהָ

Masora *Magna*

Cp 1 ¹Mm 794. ²Mm 1388. ³Mm 1389. ⁴Mm 917. ⁵Mm 3870. ⁶Mm 1390. ⁷Mm 3286. ⁸Mm 1391.
⁹Mm 1392. ¹⁰Mp sub loco. ¹¹Mm 1393 contra textum.

Critical Apparatus

Cp 1,1 ᵃ frt orig מֹשֶׁה cf 2,6 ‖ 10 ᵃ prp כָּלֵב cf Jos 15,13 sq ‖ ᵇ 𝔊 καὶ ἐξῆλθεν Χεβρων ἐξ ἐναντίας ‖ ᶜ⁻ᶜ 𝔊 Καριαθαρβοκσεφερ ex א ק׳ et ᵈ סֵפֶר ק׳ cf 11ᵇ⁻ᵇ ‖ ᵈ prp וַיַּ֖ךְ ‖ 11 ᵃ 𝔊ᵃ καὶ ἀνέβησαν, l וַיַּעַל cf Jos 15,15 ‖ ᵇ⁻ᵇ 𝔊 Πόλις γραμμάτων (𝔊ᴮ ᵐⁱⁿ pr Καριασωφαρ); 𝔙 qrjt 'lk'tb ק׳ סֵפֶר cf Jos 15,15ᵃ⁻ᵃ ‖ 12 ᵃ⁻ᵃ 𝔊 τὴν Πόλιν τῶν γραμμάτων ‖ 13 ᵃ⁻ᵃ cf Jos 15,17ᵃ ‖ 14 ᵃ 𝔊(𝔙) καὶ ἐπέσεισεν αὐτήν, l וַיְסִיתָהּ; cf Jos 15,18ᵃ.

Hebrew Judges 1 in the **Biblia Hebraica Quinta (BHQ)** Judges. This page shows a facsimile of the text of the Leningrad Codex, **Masorah Parva, Masorah Magna,** and the Critical Apparatus.

Book Title

שפטים JUDGES

וַיְהִ֗י אַחֲרֵי֙ מ֣וֹת יְהוֹשֻׁ֔עַ וַֽיִּשְׁאֲלוּ֙ בְּנֵ֣י יִשְׂרָאֵ֔ל בַּיהוָ֖ה לֵאמֹ֑ר מִ֣י 1

יַעֲלֶה־לָּ֧נוּ אֶל־הַֽכְּנַעֲנִ֛י בַּתְּחִלָּ֖ה לְהִלָּ֥חֶם בּֽוֹ׃ וַיֹּ֣אמֶר יְהוָ֖ה יְהוּדָ֣ה 2

יַעֲלֶ֑ה הִנֵּ֛ה נָתַ֥תִּי אֶת־הָאָ֖רֶץ בְּיָדֽוֹ׃ וַיֹּ֣אמֶר יְהוּדָה֩ לְשִׁמְע֨וֹן אָחִ֜יו 3

עֲלֵ֧ה אִתִּ֣י בְגוֹרָלִ֗י וְנִֽלָּחֲמָה֙ בַּֽכְּנַעֲנִ֔י וְהָלַכְתִּ֧י גַם־אֲנִ֛י אִתְּךָ֖ בְּגוֹרָלֶ֑ךָ 4

וַיֵּ֥לֶךְ אִתּ֖וֹ שִׁמְעֽוֹן׃ וַיַּ֣עַל יְהוּדָ֗ה וַיִּתֵּ֧ן יְהוָ֛ה אֶת־הַכְּנַעֲנִ֥י וְהַפְּרִזִּ֖י 5

בְּיָדָ֑ם וַיַּכּ֣וּם בְּבֶ֔זֶק עֲשֶׂ֥רֶת אֲלָפִ֖ים אִֽישׁ׃ וַֽיִּמְצְא֞וּ אֶת־אֲדֹנִ֣י בֶ֗זֶק 6

בְּבֶ֙זֶק֙ וַיִּֽלָּ֣חֲמוּ ב֔וֹ וַיַּכּ֕וּ אֶת־הַֽכְּנַעֲנִ֖י וְאֶת־הַפְּרִזִּֽי׃ וַיָּ֙נָס֙ אֲדֹנִ֣י בֶ֔זֶק

וַיִּרְדְּפ֖וּ אַחֲרָ֑יו וַיֹּאחֲז֣וּ אֹת֔וֹ וַֽיְקַצְּצ֔וּ אֶת־בְּהֹנ֥וֹת יָדָ֖יו וְרַגְלָֽיו׃

וַיֹּ֣אמֶר אֲדֹֽנִי־בֶ֗זֶק שִׁבְעִ֣ים ׀ מְלָכִ֡ים בְּֽהֹנוֹת֩ יְדֵיהֶ֨ם וְרַגְלֵיהֶ֜ם 7

מְקֻצָּצִ֗ים הָי֤וּ מְלַקְּטִים֙ תַּ֣חַת שֻׁלְחָנִ֔י כַּאֲשֶׁ֣ר עָשִׂ֔יתִי כֵּ֥ן שִׁלַּם־לִ֖י

אֱלֹהִ֑ים וַיְבִיא֥וּהוּ יְרוּשָׁלַ֖͏ִם וַיָּ֥מָת שָֽׁם׃ וַיִּֽלָּחֲמ֤וּ בְנֵֽי־יְהוּדָה֙ 8

בִּיר֣וּשָׁלַ֔͏ִם וַֽיִּלְכְּד֣וּ אוֹתָ֔הּ וַיַּכּ֖וּהָ לְפִי־חָ֑רֶב וְאֶת־הָעִ֖יר שִׁלְּח֥וּ בָאֵֽשׁ׃

וְאַחַ֗ר יָֽרְדוּ֙ בְּנֵ֣י יְהוּדָ֔ה לְהִלָּחֵ֖ם בַּֽכְּנַעֲנִ֑י יוֹשֵׁ֣ב הָהָ֔ר וְהַנֶּ֖גֶב 9

וְהַשְּׁפֵלָֽה׃ וַיֵּ֣לֶךְ יְהוּדָ֗ה אֶל־הַֽכְּנַעֲנִי֙ הַיּוֹשֵׁ֣ב בְּחֶבְר֔וֹן וְשֵׁם־חֶבְר֥וֹן 10

לְפָנִ֖ים קִרְיַ֣ת אַרְבַּ֑ע וַיַּכּ֣וּ אֶת־שֵׁשַׁ֤י וְאֶת־אֲחִימַן֙ וְאֶת־תַּלְמָ֔י וַיֵּ֙לֶךְ֙ 11

Masora *Parva*

Masora *Magna*

[1:1] שא שאלה לאמר ב̇ מי יעלה לנו . האוסיף ו̇:ס . ונלחמה ד̇ וסמנהון ונלחמה [3] בכנעני . בבני עמון . ונלחמה יחד . ונלחמה במישור ס:[7] מלקטים ב̇ וסמנהון היו מלקטים תחת . הבנים מלקטים עצים ס:. רבאהו ד̇ אדני בזק . ופלשתים . בסוגר . ממדיות . ורכבהם . אחזוהו . אוריהו ס:[8] ואת העיר באש ו̇ וילחמו בני יהודה . והמה לקחו . והוספתי על ימ̇ך ד̇ מלכים . ומכף מלך אשור דישעיהו . ונתתי את הבית . ככה . ונטשתי . ואת כל נשך ס:

Critical Aparatus

1:1 יְהוֹשֻׁעַ ⁺ • 4 בְּיָדָם V S T | ἐν χειρὶ αὐτοῦ G θ' ‖ pref בְּיָדוֹ see G θ' יְהוּדָה 10 ⁺ • אֲדֹנִי בֶזֶק V S T | καὶ ἐπάταξεν αὐτούς G • 5 וַיַּכּוּם ⁺ • קִרְיַת ⁺ • בְּחֶבְרוֹן G* V S T | foll καὶ ἐξῆλθεν Χεβρων (ἐξ ἐναντίας) Gᴹˢˢ אַרְבַּע V S T | Καριαθαρβοκασεφερ G (confl) ⁺ • וַיַּכּוּ G* S T | 3 sg Gᴹˢˢ V ⁺ • תַּלְמָי V S T | foll γεννήματα τοῦ Ἐνάκ G (gloss) ⁺ • 11 וַיֵּלֶךְ Gᴹˢˢ V S T | ἀνέβησαν G* (assim-Josh 15:15) ⁺ •

Used with permissions from *Biblia Hebraica Quinta*, Fascicle 7: *Judges*, prepared by Natalio Fernández Marcos, © 2011 Deutsche Bibelgesellschaft, Stuttgart.

The Mm notes are located mostly in the top or bottom margins of the manuscripts. In *BHS*, the Mm are listed directly below the biblical text and refer to an external volume of collected lists. These entries follow the lists found in Mᴸ. They are listed in numerical order in the volumes edited by Gérard Weil.[124] For example, Judg 1:3 includes a circellus with the eighth word ונלחמה "so that we should fight" (see Judges 1 *BHS*).[125] The second Mp note of the line reads ³ד, meaning "four." The superscript 3 refers to the Mm at the bottom of the page immediately

---

[124] Gérard E. Weil, *Massorah Gedolah iuxta codicem Leningradensem B 19 a*, 4 vols. (Rome: Pontifical Biblical Institute, 1971).

[125] *BHS*, 397.

below. Following "Cp 1" (chapter one), the reference Mm 1389 points to the *Massorah Gedolah*: וְנִלְחֲמָה ד׳ וסימנהון.[126] The first word, וְנִלְחֲמָה, cites the same word from Judg 1:3. The sign ד׳ in both the Mp and the note compiled in *Massorah Gedolah* indicates that וְנִלְחֲמָה occurs four times in the Hebrew Bible. Altogether, ד׳ וסימנהון means "four times and their references (are)." The examples are listed with the chapter-verse references and the short sequences, or catchwords, from M^L in Weil's critical edition:

ונלחמה בכנעני (Judg 1:3)
בבני עמון (Judg 11:6)
ונלחמה יחד (1 Sam 17:10)
ונלחמה אותם במישור (1 Kgs 20:25)

BHQ includes the same data but does not require referencing a separate volume for the four other instances (see Judges 1 *BHQ*).[127] They are produced in the apparatus below the biblical text as catchwords only. The modern chapter-verse references are included in the textual commentary at the end of the volume.

Qere perpetuum (always read). Another type of Masoretic reading tradition relates to the divine name. It is a special kind of *qere* that has been codified in the Masoretic vocalization. When the consonants of the divine name יהוה appear in the text, the Masoretes commonly inserted the vowels for אֲדֹנָי "lord, master," yielding the amalgamation יְהוָה.[128] Sometimes the Masoretes utilized the vowels for the Aramaic word שְׁמָא "the name," which resulted in the alternative vocalization יְהוָה.[129] Other times the form is יְהוִה where the Masoretes read אֱלֹהִים "God." Robert Gordis identified this special *qere* as the initial stage of the *ketiv-qere*.[130] Another well-known example is the third-person personal pronouns:

ketiv (with vowels):	הוא
qere perpetuum:	היא

Yet another is the pronunciation of Jerusalem as יְרוּשָׁלַיִם which is read even when the form is missing the final *yod* (יְרוּשָׁלַם).

Ketiv-Qere. The interplay between oral tradition and textual transmission can be illustrated by examining the Masoretic phenomenon known as the *ketiv-qere*.[131] In the MT, *ketiv-qere* readings occur when the consonantal text does not match the Masoretic reading of that text. In such instances, the consonants of the word in question are vocalized according to how the Masoretes read it. The Masoretes would mark the *ketiv* (or, "what is written") with a superscript circle (i.e., circellus) above the word, directing the reader to the side margin (Mp) where the consonants

---

[126] Weil, *Massorah Gedolah*, 1:165.

[127] *BHQ* 7:3, 27*.

[128] Note that this is the origin of the name Jehovah.

[129] Würthwein, *Text of the Old Testament*, 22.

[130] Robert Gordis, *The Biblical Text in the Making: A Study of the Kethib-Qere*, 2nd ed. (New York: KTAV, 1971), 39.

[131] The Aramaic terms are passive participles: כְּתִיב "what is written" and קְרֵי "what is read."

of the *qere* (or "what is read") are indicated (listed above the *BHS* siglum קֿ). The *qere* originated from an earlier reading tradition that the Masoretes only later committed to writing in the right-hand margins of the consonantal text.[132] We note the following example from Isa 10:32. The MT reads:

יְנֹפֵף יָדוֹ הַר בַּית־צִיּוֹן

He shakes his hand at the mountain of **[the house/daughter?]** of Zion.

The word in question is בַּית whose vowels do not match its consonantal structure. The Mp *qere* indicates the alternative consonants as בת. When combined with the vowels in the *ketiv*, the *qere* reads בַּת, "daughter." According to the *qere*, the text is to be understood, "He shakes his hand at the mountain of the daughter of (בַּת) Zion." The *ketiv* rather indicates בֵּית, presumably, "house," yielding the alternate translation, "He shakes his hand at the mountain of the house of (בֵּית) Zion."

There are somewhere between 1,000 and 1,500 instances of *ketiv-qere* attested throughout the Masoretic text, depending upon the particular manuscript in question.[133] A large portion of these interchange *waw* and *yod*, which were easily confused in the square script since the downstroke of *waw* is slightly longer than *yod*. Note the following example from Num 25:9:

| *ketiv* | קרואי | |
| *qere* | קְרִיאֵי | "assembled ones" |

Other instances appear to reflect the preservation of an older orthography. Several *ketiv* examples attest a *he* for the 3MS personal pronoun instead of the usual *waw*, as in Exod 22:4:

| *ketiv* | בעירה | (i.e., בְּעִירֹה "in his city") |
| *qere* | בְּעִירוֹ | "in his city" |

In such cases the Masoretes appear to be reading the form in question with a *waw*. The {h} orthography for the 3MS pronominal suffix routinely occurs in Hebrew inscriptions from the first millennium BC, as in the ostracon Arad 17, line 6:

wḥtm 'th bḥtmk "seal **it** with your seal"

Orthography seems to be at issue when certain words may or may not have a final *qameṣ*. Numerous *qere* readings include spellings with the *mater* ה where final vowel is expected:

1 Sam 24:19

את (*ketiv*) vs. אַתָּה (*qere*)   "you"

2 Sam 21:9

הם (*ketiv*) vs. הֵמָּה (*qere*)   "they"

---

[132] Dotan, "Masorah," 13:609.
[133] H. M. Orlinsky, "The Origin of the Kethib-Qere System: A New Approach," in *Congress Volume Oxford 1959*, ed. G. W. Anderson et al., VTSup 7 (Leiden: Brill, 1960), 184 n. 2.; Dotan, "Masorah," 13:616.

Ps 74:6

וְעֵת (*ketiv*) vs. וְעַתָּה (*qere*)   "now"

Defective and plene spellings constitute another kind of spelling difference. In Job 1:10 a plene spelling of a *Qal* prefix verb unexpectedly occurs before the *maqqep* (אשמור־לֹו). The *maqqep* should change the accent of the previous word, resulting in a closed, unaccented final syllable. The *ketiv* with *ḥolem-waw*, according to Masoretic vocalization, is not permissible. The *qere* reads the verbal form without *waw* and vocalizes it with *qames-ḥaṭup*, אֶשְׁמָר־לֹו "I will guard for him." This example indicates that markings such as the *maqqep* were added to an already existing consonantal text that sometimes did not agree with the vocalization tradition.

In many instances, *ketiv-qere* readings register different grammatical interpretations of individual words. In Ruth 1:8 the *ketiv* indicates a long prefix conjugation form, whereas the *qere* reads a shortened (i.e., jussive) form:[134]

ketiv	יעשה יהוה עמכם חסד	"Yahweh **will deal** kindly with you"
qere	יַעַשׂ יהוה עִמָּכֶם חֶסֶד	"May Yahweh **deal** kindly with you"

The first reading takes Naomi's words as a statement of fact while the second one takes it as a prayer. A similar phenomenon occurs in 1 Kgs 1:37, only this time the *qere* reads a prefix form in place of the *ketiv* jussive:

ketiv	כן יהי עם שלמה	"thus **may** he [Yahweh] **be** with Solomon"
qere	כֵּן יִהְיֶה עִם־שְׁלֹמֹה	"thus he [Yahweh] **will be** with Solomon"

In 1 Kgs 8:48 the *qere* reads a 1CS form instead of the 2MS of the *ketiv*:

ketiv	והבית אשר־בנית	"the house which **you built**"
qere	וְהַבַּיִת אֲשֶׁר־בָּנִיתִי	"the house which **I built**"

Although the *qere* may be preferable in this context—after all, it is Solomon who physically built the temple—the *ketiv* is not entirely indefensible. The statement from Solomon may simply defer the responsibility for the temple construction ultimately to God (i.e., the house which you enabled me to build).

Grammatical difficulties involving pronouns appear in the *ketiv-qere* as well. The *qere* often reads an expected masculine pronoun where the *ketiv* has a feminine and vice versa. For instance, an independent pronoun attests the consonants הוא (3MS) for what should be a 3FS in Deut 13:16:

ketiv	ישבי העיר ההוא	"the inhabitants of **that (M)** city (F)"
qere	יֹשְׁבֵי הָעִיר הַהִיא	"the inhabitants of **that (F)** city (F)"

This same phenomenon is attested for adjectives. In 2 Sam 17:12, the feminine singular adjective אחת (*ketiv*) "one" is read as masculine אֶחָד (*qere*).

Many of the *waw/yod* examples concern the difference between singular noun pronominal suffixes and plural noun suffixes. In Ps 24:6, for example, the *qere* reads a *yod* before the final *waw* reading the noun as plural:

---

[134] For more on the prefix and suffix conjugations, see chapter 8.

ketiv	זה דור דרשו	"this is the generation of **the one seeking him**"
qere	זֶה דּוֹר דֹּרְשָׁיו	"this is the generation of **those seeking him**"

The plural reading may be influenced by the plural participle immediately following: מְבַקְשֵׁי פָנֶיךָ "those seeking your face." In Ps 105:28 the consonantal text attests two *waw*s in the pronominal suffix, which the *qere* reads as one *waw*:

ketiv	ולא מרו את דברוו	"they did not rebel against **his words** (?)"
qere	וְלֹא־מָרוּ אֶת־דְּבָרוֹ	"they did not rebel against **his word**"

The *ketiv* could have arisen from confusion of a *waw* for a *yod*, which originally might have been דְּבָרָיו "his words."

Verbal pronominal suffixes with prefix forms exhibit discrepancies in the *ketiv-qere* between the 1CP (נו) and 1CS (ני). See Ps 71:20:

ketiv	תחיינו . . . הראיתנו	"you have shown us . . . **will you preserve us?**"
qere	תְּחַיֵּינִי . . . הִרְאִיתַנִי	"you have shown me . . . **will you preserve me?**"

Another *waw/yod* confusion occurs for the 1CS and 3MS pronominal suffixes in Job 33:28:

ketiv	נפשי	"my soul"
qere	נַפְשׁוֹ	"his soul"

In 1 Sam 18:1 the *ketiv-qere* attests two spellings for the 3MS pronominal suffix attached to verbs, /ô/ compared to /ēhû/:

ketiv	ויאהבו	"he loved him"
qere	וַיֶּאֱהָבֵהוּ	"he loved him"

Other types of discrepancies in the *ketiv-qere* have to do with different words that happen to have the same pronunciation (homophones, see above). The most common example of this feature is the negative particle לֹא "not" and the *lamed* preposition with the 3MS pronominal suffix לוֹ "to/for him." Such a case comes from Ps 100:3:

ketiv	הוא עשנו ולא אנחנו	"he is our maker, and **not** we ourselves"
qere	הוּא־עָשָׂנוּ וְלוֹ אֲנַחְנוּ	"he is our maker, and we belong **to him**"

Interestingly, the Septuagint aligns with the *ketiv* in this instance: καὶ οὐχ ἡμεῖς "and not us," as does the Syriac Peshitta: ḥnn hwʾ wlʾ "and not us." Targum Psalms, on the other hand, agrees with the Masoretic *qere*: ודיליה אנחנא "we belong to him."[135]
A similar phenomenon occurs again in 1 Sam 20:2:

ketiv	הנה לו עשה אבי	"look, my father **has done to him** (?)"
qere	הִנֵּה לֹא־יַעֲשֶׂה אָבִי	"look, my father **would not do**"

---

[135] The situation here reflects the modern versions. The KJV and NASB follow the *ketiv* "not we ourselves," whereas most English versions have adopted the *qere* "we are his" (ESV, NIV, NLT, RSV, NRSV, etc.).

Clearly, the prepositional phrase makes little sense in this context. It is possible, however, that the *ketiv* is preserving the less commonly used particle לֻ used in *irrealis* clauses, meaning "O that" or "if only."[136] It is typically used with suffix conjugation verbs. The *ketiv* would mean, "Would my father do anything great or small and not tell me?"

Many *ketiv-qere* relate to commonly confused consonants. These consonants are visually similar in the square script, much like the similarity of *waw* and *yod* mentioned above.

בּ vs. כּ (Prov 21:29)

| יָכִין דרכי | "he establishes his ways" (*ketiv*) |
| יָבִין דַּרְכּוֹ | "he understands his way" (*qere*)[137] |

ה vs. ח and ר vs. ד (2 Sam 13:37)

| עמיחור | PN Ammiḥur (*ketiv*) |
| עַמִּיהוּד | PN Ammihud (*qere*) |

ך vs. ד (1 Sam 4:13)

| יד דרך | "he strikes (?) the road" |
| יַד דֶּרֶךְ | "beside the road" |

Several examples of flip-flopped consonants occur as well, as in 1 Sam 14:27:

| *ketiv* | וַתְּרֶאנָה עיניו | "his eyes saw" (√ ראה "to see") |
| *qere* | וַתָּאֹרְנָה עֵינָיו | "his eyes grew bright" (√ אור "to shine") |

A final category contains various interpretive difficulties. Many examples deal with objectionable or offensive material. For instance, in 1 Sam 5:6 the *qere* calls the reader to replace the *ketiv* with an entirely different word:[138]

| *ketiv* | ויך אתם בעפלים | "he struck them **with hemorrhoids**" |
| *qere* | וַיַּךְ אֹתָם בַּטְחֹרִים | "he struck them **with tumors**" |

Whereas the previous *ketiv-qere* examples involve the difference of one letter (often *w* vs. *y*), this type is exceptional in replacing the *ketiv* entirely.[139]

Two reigning paradigms have existed among scholars concerning the origins of the Masoretic *ketiv-qere*. The oldest view is what is sometime called "the

---

[136] BDB, 530.

[137] The second word is also a *ketiv-qere*: the *ketiv* reads the object as a plural noun with the pronominal suffix; *qere* as a singular with suffix.

[138] See also 1 Sam 5:9, 12; 6:4, 5; 14:32.

[139] See James Barr, "A New Look at Kethibh-Qere," in *Remembering All the Way: A Collection of Old Testament Studies Published on the Occasion of the Fortieth Anniversary of the Oudtestamentisch Werkgezelschap in Nederland*, ed. A. S. van der Woude, Oudtestamentisch Studiën 21 (Leiden: Brill, 1981), 25–26. Barr remarks that since *ketiv-qere* mostly differ in terms of one consonant, it is unlikely that the *qere* arose as a result of variant readings alone. Thus, apart from indecent terms as the one cited here, "a word does not find its way into the Q unless it is, in its consonantal form, graphically extremely similar to the K" (26).

correction theory," which has long assumed that the *ketiv-qere* arose from Masoretic corrections of erroneous readings in the text. Several problems have been noted for this view, one of the more significant being that in many cases the *qere* is inferior to the *ketiv*. Why would correctors propose a problematic reading for a perfectly fine text?[140] Other scholars counter that this phenomenon represents the preservation of variant readings. Orlinsky argues that the *ketiv-qere* represent readings of the best three manuscripts available to Masoretic scribes. Where the texts differed, the Masoretes selected the best reading and vocalized it as the *qere*, whereas the minority reading was left unvocalized as the *ketiv*.[141] Alternatively, Bertil Albrektson registers doubt that Jewish rabbis concerned themselves with the text-critical aim of establishing the most reliable text of the Hebrew Bible.[142] Rather, he argues that the lack of textual uniformity attested in the MT tradition would suggest quite the contrary—they were content with multiple readings at the same time, as the *ketiv-qere* indicate. This is not to say that early rabbis were not interested in preserving a reliable text, as their meticulous copying methods suggest. Albrektson thinks that the evidence of multiple readings was an asset, "or at least did not find it necessary to enforce absolute unity, to single out one possibility while discarding all others."[143]

Robert Gordis opposed the correction theory on two grounds: (1) the reverence the Masoretes had for the Hebrew text would surely have prevented them from correcting the revered text; and (2) many of the supposed corrections in the *qere* appear to be inferior readings to the *ketiv*.[144] Instead, he proposed a somewhat amalgamated version of the pronunciation and textual-correction theories. Gordis sought to show that the *ketiv-qere* initially served as "guides to the correct reading in the absence of vowels."[145] He argued that the initial development of *ketiv-qere* occurred with the Tetragrammaton, in that the reading tradition replaced the divine name יהוה with אדני "Lord" or אלהים "God" (see *Qere perpetuum* above).[146] Nonetheless, the ongoing commitment of the Masoretes to preserve the sacred text was met with the ever-growing problem of textual variation. This pressure led them to adopt a textual archetype or standard text.[147] As Gordis concludes, the written text, which includes the *ketiv*, is essentially the textual archetype, while the *qere* readings constitute a "worth-while reading from other non-archetypal manuscripts."[148]

---

[140] H. M. Orlinsky, "The Origin of the Kethib-Qere System: A New Approach," in *Congress Volume Oxford 1959*, ed. G. W. Anderson et al., VTSup 7 (Leiden: Brill, 1960), 185–86.

[141] Orlinski, "The Origin of the Kethib-Qere System," 187.

[142] Bertil Albrektson, "Reflections on the Emergence of a Standard Text of the Hebrew Bible," in *Congress Volume Göttingen 1977*, ed. J. A. Emerton, VTSup 29 (Leiden: Brill, 1978), 49–65.

[143] Albrektson, "Reflections," 61.

[144] Gordis, The Biblical Text in the Making, 24.

[145] Gordis, 35.

[146] According to Gordis, this phenomenon occurs 6,823 times in the Hebrew text, which, if included with the total number of *ketiv-qere* (1,350×), would constitute 87 percent of all examples. Gordis, 39.

[147] Gordis, 44–47.

[148] Gordis, 48.

Geoffrey Khan discusses these *ketiv-qere* questions in the wider context of the Tiberian Hebrew scribal tradition. He stresses the nature of the *qere* as distinguishing the oral reading of the Masoretes and the written marginal notes inscribing those readings. Essentially, Khan emphasizes that the *qere* did not originate "as written marginal corrections," but rather reflect "an orally transmitted reading tradition of the written text, i.e., a memorized tradition of oral recitation."[149] It was a reading system that originated before the written system of Masoretic vocalization and was handed down orally for the "oral performance" of the Hebrew text.[150] Only later were the written text and its oral recitation intertwined in a textualized form.

It may be argued, then, that the oral origins of the *ketiv-qere* deserve a more prominent place in our understanding. The fact that the Masoretes used the language of the *qere* "read" versus the *ketiv* "written" indicates they were encoding reading traditions that differed at times from their consonantal text.[151] As James Barr put it: "The K is the consonantal graphic tradition accepted for the MT, the Q is the oral reading tradition."[152] This suggestion does not ignore the varied factors that may have produced the variant readings in the text itself. In summary, the variety in the kinds of textual discrepancies attested in the *ketiv-qere* reflect a stage of oral transmission that already existed before the Masoretes recorded them in the textual tradition.

This chapter discussed the language of Biblical Hebrew, showing its place within the Northwest Semitic linguistic context. We surveyed the internal and external factors involved in its periodization and textual transmission. Our discussion concluded with a consideration of the Hebrew Bible's textual and oral transmission. In not a few places, an accurate knowledge of these complex issues contributes to better exegetical insights into the foreign world of the Hebrew Bible. We now turn our attention to detailing the ancient sources. This next chapter provides vital data to understand text criticism.

---

[149] Khan, *Tiberian Pronunciation Tradition*, 1:37, also see 38–39.

[150] Khan, 1:39. One should also note that Khan proposes that many of the linguistic differences reflected in the *ketiv-qere* may reflect dialectical differences in the language (39–40). As he observes, the orthographic variations between the consonantal form of the pronominal suffixes and their vocalizations are attested in the Qumran manuscripts. For example, the 2MS suffixes ךְ- and תְ- are vocalized with final vowels: ךָ- and תָּ-. For more examples, see Elisha Qimron, *The Hebrew of the Dead Sea Scrolls*, HSS 29 (Winona Lake, IN: Eisenbrauns, 2008), 43–44, 58–60. Note, however, that both כה- [900×] and ךְ- [160×], as well as תה- [250×] and תְ- [5×], are attested at Qumran. The orthography of the Qumran manuscripts for these suffixes likewise reflects final vowels: כה- and תה-. This reality may therefore indicate the existence of two distinct contemporaneous orthographies reflective of dialectical variation.

[151] See Emanuel Tov, "The Ketiv/Qere Variations in Light of the Manuscripts from the Judean Desert," in *The Hebrew Bible, Greek Bible, and Qumran: Collected Essays*, TSAJ 121 (Tübingen: Mohr Siebeck, 2008), 203–204.

[152] Barr, "New Look," 27.

CHAPTER 2

////////////////

RETRIEVING THE TEXT OF
THE HEBREW BIBLE

I n chapter 1, we surveyed the history of writing and scribal culture in the wider
ancient Near Eastern world and ancient Israel in particular. The history of the Hebrew Bible was recounted in broad strokes, but from this general introduction the
student can begin to grasp the complexity of the transmission of the Hebrew Bible.
In this chapter,[1] we introduce the need for Hebrew Bible textual criticism and describe in some detail the character of the ancient textual witnesses to the Hebrew
Bible so that the student can recognize them in the apparatus of *BHS* and *BHQ* and
have some knowledge of what the source behind the siglum tells us about the text.
For example, the student should not only know that the siglum α′ stands for Aquila
but also that Aquila was a Jewish reviser of the Septuagint in the early second century AD and rendered the Hebrew text into Greek with an ultra-literal translation
approach, thus allowing one to reconstruct his Hebrew parent text with greater
probability. The following in-depth descriptions will help students appreciate the
biblical sources and become acquainted with a method to solve textual problems.
In the guided example, we will walk the reader through a step-by-step method for
solving problems that arose in the textual history of the Hebrew Bible.

2.1 GOING DEEPER WITH THE TEXT OF THE HEBREW BIBLE

Students of the Bible are more aware of the necessity for biblical textual criticism
than they first realize due to the notes that signal such variants in our English
translations. Consider the note in the text of our English Bibles at the ending of

---

[1] This chapter is authored by John D. Meade.

Mark 16:8, where we have read at one time or another, "[Some of the earliest mss conclude with 16:8.]" (CSB), but then the footnote says:

> Other mss include vv. 9–20 as a longer ending. The following shorter ending is found in some mss between v. 8 and v. 9 and in one MS after v. 8 (each of which omits vv. 9– 20): *And all that had been commanded to them they quickly reported to those around Peter. After these things, Jesus himself sent out through them from east to west, the holy and imperishable proclamation of eternal salvation. Amen."* (CSB)

Not all textual problems are this notable—or notorious.

Nevertheless, there are many textual problems in the Hebrew Bible that influence the translation and meaning of passages that sometimes receive a footnote requiring the reader to look at the bottom of the page. Zechariah 5:6 (CSB) says, "And he continued, 'This is their iniquity [עֲוֺנָם] in all the land,'" while the KJV says, "He said moreover, This is their resemblance [עֵינָם lit. "eye"] through all the earth." The slight difference of one letter *waw/yod* changes the meaning of the word and even the passage, for "their eye/resemblance" probably refers to the evil desires within the community, while "their iniquity" probably refers to the result of those evil desires. Be that as it may, there is a note in most English versions indicating the variant reading. But what about the readings that our English translations do not footnote?

In 1 Sam 2:27, the CSB has, "Didn't I reveal myself to your forefather's family when they were in Egypt and belonged to Pharaoh's palace?" while the ESV has, "Did I indeed reveal myself to the house of your father when they were in Egypt *subject* [עֲבָדִים] to the house of Pharaoh?" Here, neither version leaves a footnote but, for those with eyes to see, the ESV follows the Old Greek and Dead Sea Scrolls, while the CSB follows the Masoretic Text. Which reading is the original? A budding exegete would do well to learn how to navigate textual issues like these ones in the Hebrew Bible as part of an interpretation of a passage.

Because an ancient author's wording may be modified due to later scribal activity, textual criticism retrieves the original text by comparing the remaining manuscript copies of the books and providing a critically corrected text.[2] Most scribal errors are insignificant, but many scribal errors are true variants that often impact the wording and, therefore, the meaning of a text. Thus, if the goal of exegesis is to draw out the meaning of the text according to its grammar, textual criticism is the discipline that establishes the original text for exegesis in the first place. The student, therefore, should gain facility and competency in Hebrew Bible textual criticism, learning the primary sources and the kinds of scribal modifications

---

[2] On the question of the original text and the genealogical method, which need not detain us here, see Paolo Trovato, *Everything You Always Wanted to Know about Lachmann's Method: A Non-Standard Handbook of Genealogical Textual Criticism in the Age of Post-Structuralism, Cladistics, and Copy-Text* (Padova: Libreriauniversitaria, 2014); for reconstructing the OT text(s), see Ellis R. Brotzman and Eric J. Tully, *Old Testament Textual Criticism: A Practical Introduction* (Grand Rapids: Baker, 2016), 219–26.

evident within them. Although mastering the discipline of Hebrew Bible textual criticism takes serious time and discipline, the rest of this chapter will prime the student for meaningful interaction with the practice of textual criticism to prepare the student for Hebrew exegesis.

2.2 THE PRIMARY SOURCES FOR HEBREW BIBLE TEXTUAL CRITICISM

For Hebrew Bible (OT) textual criticism, our evidence can be divided into two types: those witnesses directly preserving the Hebrew text and those witnesses indirectly preserving the Hebrew text in translation or what are called the Ancient Versions. First, we will describe the state of the Hebrew evidence according to the Masoretic Text (𝕸), the Samaritan Pentateuch (𝔪), and the Dead Sea Scrolls from Qumran (𝕼) and other sites. We will then turn to the textual critical usage of the Versions for establishing the text of the Hebrew Bible: Septuagint or Old Greek (𝕲); the pre-hexaplaric translations of Theodotion (θ′), Aquila (α′), Symmachus (σ′), Quinta (ε′), Sexta (ς′); Latin Vulgate (𝖁); Syriac Peshitta (𝕾); and Aramaic Targums (𝕿).[3]

2.3 DIRECT WITNESSES OF THE HEBREW MANUSCRIPTS

Before the discovery of the Dead Sea Scrolls in 1947, the only direct evidence for the OT text in Hebrew came from late medieval manuscripts that had been prepared and copied by the Masoretes according to two key families in Tiberius: Ben Asher and Ben Naphtali. Though sparsely attested, the Babylonian and Palestinian medieval traditions were eventually supplanted by the Tiberian.[4] After their discovery, the Dead Sea Scrolls afforded us direct knowledge of the state of the text between 250 BC and AD 135. We, therefore, can speak of four general periods of the transmission of the OT text: (1) the period before 250 BC; (2) the period between 250 BC and AD 135; (3) the period between AD 135 and 800; and (4) the period between 800 and the end of the Middle Ages.[5] Since there is evidence that the consonantal text of proto-𝕸 was relatively stable in the second period and represented the dominant text transmitted in the third and fourth periods with minor differences, scholars believe proto-𝕸 was an important textual tradition in the first, hypothetical period, the period before our evidence surfaces.[6]

---

[3] See the Bibliography of "Guided Lesson א: Textual Criticism" for the text editions of these sources.

[4] Dominique Barthélemy, *Studies in the Text of the Old Testament: An Introduction to the Hebrew Old Testament Text Project* (Winona Lake, IN: Eisenbrauns, 2012), 273–75.

[5] For a textual history of the Old Testament, see chapter 1 in the present volume; Peter J. Gentry, "The Text of the Old Testament," *JETS* 52 (2009): 19–45.

[6] Emanuel Tov, *Textual Criticism of the Hebrew Bible,* 3rd ed. (Minneapolis: Fortress, 2012), 28; see also Emanuel Tov, *Textual Criticism of the Hebrew Bible*, 4th ed. (Minneapolis: Fortress, 2022), 75.

2.3.1 Masoretic Text [תֹ]

The Masoretic Text is the medieval Hebrew text that combines the ancient consonantal text (= proto-תֹ), the graphemic representation of the vocalization of the
text, specific layouts of the text, the accent system, and other paratextual features
in and around the text.[7] How many such manuscripts are there? If we include some
24,000 fragments from the Cambridge University Library Cairo Genizah collections and some 10,800 records of manuscripts and fragments from the National
Library of Israel, there are around thirty-five thousand manuscripts and separately
catalogued fragments from the fifteenth century or earlier.[8]

As we will see below, many fragments of the Dead Sea Scrolls attest the text
of proto-תֹ. But there is a large gap in our evidence between those texts and later
תֹ manuscripts. There are, however, precious few fragments of the text from this
period that show proto-תֹ was the dominant text during this time (see Table 1).[9]

TABLE 1. HEBREW MANUSCRIPTS FROM THE THIRD THROUGH THE EIGHTH CENTURIES AD	
Torah (frag-ments from same 7th–8th century scroll)[10]	**1.** Cambridge, T-S AS 36.30: Gen 10:28–13:9 **2.** Cambridge, T-S AS 36.31 + Cambridge, T-S AS 37.26: Gen 44:23–46:20 **3.** Cambridge, T-S AS 37.1 + Cambridge, T-S AS 37.22: Gen 47:17–50:23 **4.** Cambridge, T-S AS 36.36: Exod 2:14–3:21 **5.** London, Jews' College 31: Exod 9:18–13:2 **6.** Cambridge, T-S AS 36.19 + Cambridge, T-S AS 37.8 + Durham, Duke University, Ashkar Collection 2: Exod 13:2–16:1 **7.** Cambridge, T-S NS 282.88: Exod 17:5–18:14 **8.** Cambridge, T-S AS 36.10: Num 10:16–35 **9.** Durham, Duke University, Ashkar Collection 21: Deut 2:9–3:12 **10.** Cambridge, T-S AS 37.10 + ENA 4117.13: Deut 32:50–end of the Pentateuch
Genesis	Cambridge T-S NS 3.21 and 4.3
Exodus	Oxford Bodleian Lib. Ms. Heb. D.89
Leviticus	En Gedi[11]
Numbers	Berlin, Staatsliche Museum, P 10598

---

[7] For a slightly more detailed description of תֹ, see John D. Meade, "Masoretic Text," in *Dictionary
of the Bible and Ancient Media*, ed. Chris Keith (London: Bloomsbury T&T Clark, 2016), 215–17.

[8] Drew Longacre, "The Parting of the Ways of Old and New Testament Textual Criticism:
Deconstructing a Disciplinary Division," in *Written for Our Instruction: Essays in Honor of William
Varner*, ed. Abner Chou and Christian Locatell (Dallas: Fontes, 2021), 90–91.

[9] Peter J. Gentry, "Text of the Old Testament," 22, was the first scholar to provide a list of MSS
from this period. In accordance with Armin Lange, "Ancient and Late Ancient Hebrew and Aramaic
Jewish Texts," in *THB* 1A:121–22, I have added the recently analyzed Ashkar-Gilson and Ein Gedi
MSS to the list, and the even more recent data on the 7th–8th century (fragmentary) Torah scroll.

[10] For more on the ten fragments that make up this scroll, see "Genizah Fragments," *Newsletter
of the Taylor-Schechter Genizah Research Unit* 77, April 2019, https://www.lib.cam.ac.uk/files/ge-
nizah_77.pdf.

[11] On the virtual "unwrapping" of this scroll, see VisCenter, "Virtually Unwrapping the En-
Gedi Scroll (English)," YouTube Video, 2:13, September 21, 2016, https://www.youtube.com
/watch?v=GduCExxB0vw. On the third or fourth century date of this scroll, see Drew Longacre,
"Reconsidering the Date of the En-Gedi Leviticus Scroll (EGLev): Exploring the Limitations of the
Comparative-Typological Paleographic Method," *Textus* 27 (2018): 44–84.

TABLE 1. HEBREW MANUSCRIPTS FROM THE THIRD THROUGH THE EIGHTH CENTURIES AD	
Kings	Oxford, Ashmolean Museum, Pap. 47–48
Job	Oxford, Ashmolean Museum, Ant. Pap. 49–50

As an example, Ashkar Collection 2 shows very conservative copying of the text. In the parts of the text of Exodus 13–16 it preserves, the MS contains only a couple minor differences in the use of *matres lectiones* as compared with the later 𝔐 MSS.[12] Most interesting, this text preserves the elaborate poetic layout of Moses's Song by the Sea in Exodus 15. The Talmud says that all the songs [of the Bible] are written in a poetic layout described as "a half-brick over a whole brick, and a whole brick over a half-brick."[13] We can represent four lines as follows:

Masoretic MSS from the tenth and eleventh centuries showed this elaborate structure, but the Ashkar-Gilson text shows that scribes were copying Moses's Song in this manner from at least the seventh or eighth century and most probably long before then. These fragmentary texts confirm that by this time proto-𝔐 had become the dominant text that was copied in Hebrew, and certainly the later Masoretic scribes considered this text to be the model that they copied. The most significant MSS before 1100 are listed in Table 2.

TABLE 2. SIGNIFICANT 𝔐 MSS BEFORE 1100[14]			
MS	SIGLUM	DATE	CONTENTS
Aleppo Codex	A	930	Complete Hebrew Bible (most Torah lost)
British Library Or. 4445	B	825–50 or 925	Most of Torah
Cairo Codex of the Prophets	C	895 or end of 10th cent.	Prophets
Cairo Pentateuch Codex	C^3	10th cent.	Complete Torah
Codex Leningradensis, Codex EBP I B 19a	L	1009	Complete Hebrew Bible
Codex EBP II B 10	L^{10}	900–950	Most of Torah

---

[12] For the best analysis, see Paul Sanders, "The Ashkar-Gilson Manuscript: Remnant of a Proto-Masoretic Model Scroll of the Torah" *Journal of Hebrew Scriptures* 14 (2014): 1–25.

[13] b. Meg. 16b: אריח על גבי לבינה ולבינה על גבי אריח; that is, text over non-text (or space) in the following line and vice versa.

[14] For more information on these MSS (except Ba) and a few later ones, see Lange, "Ancient and Late Ancient Hebrew," in *THB* 1A:117–20.

TABLE 2. SIGNIFICANT 𝕸 MSS BEFORE 1100			
MS	**SIGLUM**	**DATE**	**CONTENTS**
Codex EBP II B 17	L[17]	929	Most of Torah
Codex EBP II B 34	L[34]	975	Writings (incomplete)
Codex EBP II B 94	L[94]	1100	Former Prophets + Writings (incomplete)
Codex New York	N	10th/11th cent.	Latter Prophets (incomplete)
Codex Bablynicus Petropolitanus	P	916	Latter Prophets
Sassoon 1053	S[1]	10th cent.	Complete Hebrew Bible
Sassoon 507 (Damascus Pentateuch)	S[5]	1000	Most of Torah
Vatican ebr. 448	V	1100	Complete Torah
Berlin Or. qu. 680 + JTh 510[15]	Ba	9th cent.	Most of Writings
The Washington Pentateuch[16]	n/a	ca. 1000	Torah

2.3.2 Samaritan Pentateuch [𝕸]

The Samaritan Pentateuch is preserved in several medieval MSS dating from the ninth to the fourteenth centuries AD, the most important to Samaritans being the Abisha Scroll of Deuteronomy dated to the fourteenth century. The Samaritan Pentateuch was probably in circulation at or near Shechem and Mount Gerizim in the second century BC since (1) the script of its medieval MSS goes back to the Old Hebrew script of the second century BC; and (2) John Hyrcanus destroyed the Samaritan sanctuary on Mount Gerizim in 111–110 BC, causing the definitive divide between Jews and Samaritans and further causing the latter to identify their authoritative text as a distinct tradition.[17]

Before the pre-Samaritan texts were discovered at Qumran, scholars viewed 𝕸 as a secondary accretion of 𝕸.[18] That is, the text was understood as basically proto-𝕸 (with some spelling differences and minor agreements with 𝕲) with a clear Samaritan editorial layer over top. Evidence of this theory can be found in Exod 20:17a:

---

[15] On this MS, see Barthélemy, *Studies*, 241–42.

[16] The MS is on display at the Museum of the Bible, which has digitized and uploaded its images here: https://www.museumofthebible.org/collections/artifacts/34293–the-washington-pentateuch.

[17] Sidnie White Crawford, "Samaritan Pentateuch," in *THB* 1A:169. Here, Crawford also cites less clear evidence of editorial work in 4QNum[b] and 4Q365 (both texts date from the mid to late first century BC) that happened after the Samaritans departed from the Palestinian text. Perhaps, there was also a distinctive Samaritan reading tradition in place by the late second or early first centuries BC that would indicate a distinctive Samaritan text by that time.

[18] See Bruce K. Waltke, "Samaritan Pentateuch," in *ABD* 5:932–40, esp. 936–38, for a thorough portrait of 𝕸 vis-à-vis 𝕸.

𝔐	לֹא תַחְמֹד בֵּית רֵעֶךָ לֹא־תַחְמֹד אֵשֶׁת רֵעֶךָ וְעַבְדּוֹ	You shall not covet your neighbor's **house**. You shall not covet your neighbor's wife or his male servant...
𝔪	לא תחמד בית רעך ולא תחמד אשת רעך שדהו עבדו	You shall not covet your neighbor's **house**. You shall not covet your neighbor's wife, **his field**, his male servant...
𝔊	οὐκ ἐπιθυμήσεις **τὴν γυναῖκα** τοῦ πλησίον σου. οὐκ ἐπιθυμήσεις **τὴν οἰκίαν** τοῦ πλησίον σου οὔτε **τὸν ἀγρὸν αὐτοῦ** οὔτε τὸν παῖδα αὐτοῦ	You shall not covet your neighbor's **wife**. You shall not covet your neighbor's **house** or **his field** or his male servant...

As seen above, 𝔪 and 𝔊 agree on the accretion שׁדהו "his field," absent in 𝔐. But earlier in the verse, 𝔪 and 𝔐 agree against 𝔊 by preserving "neighbor's house" before "neighbor's wife." From this, we can assume that 𝔪 mainly transmits proto-𝔐 with some influence from the Hebrew source of 𝔊.

Due to inner-Pentateuchal harmonization in 𝔪, we observe some rare large-scale insertions to the basic text of proto-𝔐.[19] Exodus 20:17b is lacking from the other traditions, but 𝔪 adds a commandment on erecting the altar mostly adapted from Deut 27:1–7:

> (𝔪 Exod 20:17a) You shall not covet the house of your neighbor. You shall not covet your neighbor's wife, his field, his male servant or his female servant, his bull or his donkey or anything belonging to your neighbor (𝔪 Exod 20:17b) And it will be when Yahweh your God brings you to the land of the Canaanite where you are going to disposes it and you will set up for yourself great stones and plaster them with plaster and write on the stones all the words of this Torah (cf. Deut 11:29a; 27:1–3a). And it will be when you cross the Jordan, you will set up these stones which I am commanding you today on Mount Gerizim and you will build there an altar to Yahweh your God, an altar of stones on which you did not cut with iron.[20] With whole stones you will build the altar to Yahweh your God, and you will offer whole burnt offerings on it to Yahweh your God and you will sacrifice peace offerings, and you will eat there and rejoice before Yahweh your God (cf. Deut 27:4–7). That mountain is on the other side of the Jordan, behind the western horizon in the land of the Canaanite who dwells in the Arabah opposite Gilgal next to Alon-Moreh opposite Shechem (cf. Deut 11:30).[21]

After this long insertion, the text of Exod 20:18 in 𝔪 continues similarly as proto-𝔐. Here, as in 𝔪 Deut 27:4, 𝔪 has the altar situated on Mount Gerizim, while 𝔐 has it on Mount Ebal. This large-scale insertion, and the relative few others like it, probably arose to harmonize elements of Samaritan theology. These

---

[19] The large-scale insertions are mainly limited to places where material from Deuteronomy has been added to passages in Exodus (some 4×) and Numbers (some 11×). Genesis, Leviticus, and Deuteronomy feature different kinds of revisions, but overall 𝔪 in these books continues to harmonize passages that appear to disagree with each other.

[20] Mount Gerizim is Ebal in 𝔐 Deut 27:4.

[21] Author's translation.

texts informed the Samaritan woman's theology while she was conversing with Jesus about the different places Samaritans and Jews worship God in John 4.

Around 7 ⵀ MSS attest what is usually referred to as the pre-Samaritan text.[22] Researchers debate how close the relationship between these texts and 𝔐 is.[23] The texts of 4QpaleoExod^m, 4QNum^b, 4Q364, and 4Q365 show similar insertions as 𝔐, but 4QNum^b and 4Q365 contain additional editorial changes not found in 𝔐, and furthermore they do not agree with one another. Thus, there are three phases to its textual history:

(1) Texts like 4QpaleoExod^m contained the major insertions or editorial changes to proto-𝔐 known already from 𝔐 Exod but did not contain the "Samaritan layer" (e.g., the choice of Mount Gerizim).

(2) In the second century BC, 𝔐 scribes edited this earlier text that was similar to proto-𝔐, though now containing the large-scale additions, to include the choice of Mount Gerizim and other Samaritan ideals.

(3) Texts like 4QNum^b and 4Q365 (mid-first century BC) show a third development, but they did not harmonize the Pentateuch in the same ways.

Therefore, 𝔐 is an interesting witness to the textual history of the Hebrew Bible. Its updates and additions to proto-𝔐 indirectly attest to the antiquity of proto-𝔐. Since 𝔐 scribes edited and expanded that text in the second century BC, proto-𝔐 must be an older, more conservative text.

2.3.3 Dead Sea Scrolls [DSS]

"Dead Sea Scrolls" is the general term for the manuscripts, and fragments of manuscripts, discovered in caves on the west side of the Dead Sea near Khirbet Qumran, Wadi Murabbaʿat, Wadi Sdeir, Naḥal Ḥever, Naḥal Ṣeʾelim, and Ein Gedi as well as at the site of Masada. Of about 900 manuscripts discovered near Qumran, 210 to 212 are biblical scrolls containing 224 to 226 Hebrew/Aramaic copies of the biblical material. Some Pentateuch MSS contain passages from two books. About forty were discovered outside of the area around Qumran. Most come from Masada, but some are unprovenanced. Together these texts provide a glimpse into the state of the Hebrew and Aramaic text from about 250 BC to AD 115.[24]

---

[22] They are 4QExod-Lev^f, 4QpaleoExod^m, 4QLev^d, 4QNum^b, 4Q158, 4Q364, and perhaps 4Q365; cf. Crawford, "Samaritan Pentateuch," *THB* 1A:167.

[23] Crawford, "Samarian Pentateuch," *THB* 1A:169–71.

[24] Regarding the dates of these texts, see Tov, *Textual Criticism*, 99; see also Tov, *Textual Criticism of the Hebrew Bible*, 4th ed., 111.

HOW TO READ QUMRAN ABBREVIATIONS

1ⵕIsaᵃ:

1 indicates cave number

ⵕ indicates Qumran

Isa stands for Isaiah

Superscript "a" distinguishes this scroll from 1ⵕIsaᵇ, another Isaiah scroll

2.3.3.1 Dead Sea Scrolls Manuscripts from Qumran [ⵕ]

From the Dead Sea Scrolls found at Qumran, evidence was discovered of every book that would be recognized as part of the Hebrew canon except Esther (see Table 3). These texts often agree with the consonantal texts of proto-𝔐, the Hebrew parent text of 𝔊, or 𝔪. There is discussion over whether some of these texts are non-aligned with these previous three textual traditions.[25] Our intention here is to introduce the student to the kinds of differences found in the Scrolls to provide necessary context for making textual decisions.

TABLE 3. HEBREW/ARAMAIC BIBLICAL TEXTS FROM QUMRAN[26]	
	NUMBER OF COPIES
Genesis	23–24
Exodus	21
Leviticus	15
Numbers	9
Deuteronomy	35
Joshua	2
Judges	3
1–2 Samuel	4

---

[25] For a discussion and comparison of Tov's and Lange's analysis of this category, see Lange, "Ancient and Late Ancient Hebrew," *THB* 1A:123–27. For a response to the category of "Non-Aligned," see Chiesa, "Textual History," 1:257–72; Anthony Michael Ferguson, "A Comparison of the Non-Aligned Texts of Qumran to the Masoretic Text" (PhD diss., The Southern Baptist Theological Seminary, 2018). For a description and good interpretation of the conservative and facilitating scribal models at Qumran, see David Andrew Teeter, *Scribal Laws: Exegetical Variation in the Textual Transmission of Biblical Law in the Late Second Temple Period,* FAT 92 (Tübingen: Mohr Siebeck, 2014), 254–55, 267.

[26] Adapted from Emanuel Tov, *Revised Lists of the Texts from the Judaean Desert* (Leiden: Brill, 2010), 113–23. The numbers for the Pentateuch would be lower if the so-called Reworked Pentateuch MSS (4ⵕ158, 4ⵕ364–367) were not included.

TABLE 3. HEBREW/ARAMAIC BIBLICAL TEXTS FROM QUMRAN	
	NUMBER OF COPIES
1–2 Kings	3
Isaiah	21
Jeremiah	6
Ezekiel	6
The Twelve	8–9
Psalms	36
Job	4
Proverbs	4
Ruth	4
Song of Songs	4
Ecclesiastes	2
Lamentations	4
Daniel	8
Ezra-Nehemiah	1
1–2 Chronicles	1

2.3.3.2 Dead Sea Scroll Manuscripts from Other Sites

The roughly forty MSS from outside of Qumran exclusively attest proto-𝔐 (see Table 4). Texts from Masada are dated between 50 BC and AD 30, while texts from Wadi Murabbaʿat, Wadi Sdeir, Naḥal Ḥever, Naḥal Ḥever/Seiyal, Naḥal Ṣeʾelim, Naḥal Arugot/Ein Gedi are dated between 20 BC and AD 115.[27] Not only is the wording between these texts and 𝔐 nearly the same, but Gentry and Meade concluded for MasPsᵃ that the line divisions (or stichometries) can be traced to a common source, or that the Aleppo codex came from an intermediate copy that was derived and developed from MasPsᵃ.[28] Proto-𝔐, therefore, has strong roots in the earliest evidence of the text's history.

---

[27] Regarding the dates of these texts, see Tov, *Textual Criticism*, 99; see also Tov, *Textual Criticism of the Hebrew Bible*, 4th ed., 111.

[28] Peter J. Gentry and John D. Meade, "MasPsᵃ and the Early History of the Hebrew Psalter," in *From Scribal Error to Rewriting: How Ancient Texts Could and Could Not Be Changed*, ed. Anneli Aejmelaeus, Drew Longacre, and Natia Mirotadze (Göttingen: Vandenhoeck & Ruprecht, 2020), 140–41.

TABLE 4. HEBREW/ARAMAIC TEXTS FROM OTHER DEAD SEA SITES[29]		
LOCATION	BOOK	NUMBER OF COPIES
Masada (7)		
	Genesis	1
	Leviticus	2
	Deuteronomy	1
	Ezekiel	1
	Psalms	2
Murabbaᶜat (6)		
	Genesis	1
	Exodus	1
	Numbers	1
	Deuteronomy	1
	Isaiah	1
	The Twelve	1
Sdeir (1)		
	Genesis	1
Ḥever (2)		
	Numbers	1
	Psalms	1
Ḥever/Seiymal (2)		
	Numbers	1
	Deuteronomy	1
Ṣeʾelim (1)		
	Numbers	1
Arugot/Ein Gedi (1)		
	Leviticus	1
Unprovenanced (23)		
	Genesis	2
	Exodus	2
	Leviticus	4
	Deuteronomy	4
	Joshua	1
	Judges	4
	Isaiah	1
	Jeremiah	1
	Daniel	3
	Ezra-Nehemiah	1

---

[29] Adapted from Tov, *Revised Lists*, 126–29.

2.3.3.3 Textual Changes in the Dead Sea Scrolls

Scholarship on the DSS and what they tell us about the text history of the Hebrew Bible is still in its infancy. Some of the *editiones principes* of these texts were only published in the early 2000s, but we can summarize the kinds of variations contained in the DSS under the following categories: (1) spelling; (2) vocalization; (3) individual consonants and words; (4) longer pluses and minuses; and (5) large-scale differences.

2.3.3.3.1 Spelling. Texts change but not all changes are equally important for the text's history. Some evidence a different orthography from what we encounter in 𝔐. For example, 4QSamᵃ (4Q51) spells the name "David" as דויד with internal *yod* (2 Sam 3:1, 2, etc.), while early texts in 𝔐 (e.g., Samuel-Kings) represent it as דוד without internal *yod* (though see a rare exception in 1 Kgs 3:14). This is not a textual variant or even an error, but rather an indication of a change in orthography on the part of later scribes. Earlier biblical texts like Samuel-Kings on the whole show that David's name was spelled דוד (as preserved in 𝔐), while without exception later texts like Ezra-Nehemiah and Chronicles spell the name דויד. Later 𝔔 scribes applied this updated spelling of David in their freely copied texts. A clue that later scribes updated the text comes from the ninth-century BC Tel Dan inscription in which the short form of David is seen. Not only does this example show orthography can change across the centuries, but it also shows that much later manuscripts like 𝔐 can preserve a spelling older than a manuscript (4QSamᵃ) almost one thousand years older than it.[30] In this case, the older manuscript shows updating or a newer text, while the later manuscript shows conservatism or an older text.

2.3.3.3.2 Vocalization. But not all changes between the MSS are so simple. Other changes involved a scribe reading and interpreting the consonantal text differently. For example, in Isa 53:8, the later 𝔐 vocalized נגע as a noun נֶגַע "strike," while 1QIsaᵃ reads נוגע. In DSS, the ו likely represents the /u/ vowel, and therefore this form is probably read as a *Pual* perfect "he was stricken" (Tiberian נֻגַּע).[31]

2.3.3.3.3 Consonants and Words. Errors due to the confusion of similar letters occur in the transmission of the text.[32] For example, the graphic similarity between ד/ר causes a different reading at Isa 23:10:

> 𝔐: עִבְרִי "cross over [your land]"
> 1QIsaᵃ: עבדי "till [your land]"

At Isa 10:4, there is confusion of ו/י:

> 𝔐: אַסִּיר "[among the] prisoners"
> 1QIsaᵃ: אסור "[among the] fetters" (if אֱסוּר; read as "bound" if אָסוּר)

Even though *waw* and *yod* are more discernable in 1QIsaᵃ, the reading of 1QIsaᵃ arose due to confusion of *waw* and *yod* in the scribe's exemplar. Its text,

---

[30] Hendel and Joosten, *Hebrew Bible*, 3.

[31] Qimron, *Hebrew of the Dead Sea Scrolls*, 17.

[32] P. Kyle McCarter Jr., *Textual Criticism: Recovering the Text of the Hebrew Bible* (Philadelphia: Fortress, 1986), 43–49 has a good catalogue of these kinds of errors.

however, still reflects an early interpretation that derives from the reading of proto-𝔐.[33]

Metathesis, or the transposition of consonants, creates variants in the text. Note the example in Deut 31:1:

𝔐: וַיֵּלֶךְ מֹשֶׁה וַיְדַבֵּר "And Moses walked, and spoke"
1QDeut[b]: ויכל משה לדבר "And Moses ceased to speak"

In this example, one scribe transposed the letters כ and ל in the first word, resulting in verbs from הלך and כלה respectively. Although a decision on the original text is difficult, 𝔐 probably has the original text because 𝔔 and 𝔖 attest a text with the transposition and a secondary modification to the parallel passage in Deut 32:45: וַיְכַל מֹשֶׁה לְדַבֵּר "And Moses finished speaking." On the other hand, 𝔔 and 𝔖 could attest the original text while 𝔐 committed the error of transposition from ויכל to וילך and then altered the syntax of the next clause (לדבר → וַיְדַבֵּר).[34] But transposition and parallel passages probably explain how the reading in 1QDeut[b] arose, while 𝔐's reading is best explained if it is the original text.

2.3.3.3.4 Longer Pluses and Minuses. The DSS contain longer and shorter texts vis-à-vis 𝔐. Some of these minuses or shorter readings are probably due to a very common sight error known as parablepsis (lit. a glance to the side) or an omission known as homoioarcton or homoioteleuton that occurred while the scribe miscopied text appearing between similar letters and words as he looked from his exemplar to his copy (see §2.4.1.3.3 for more examples). Isaiah 40:7–8 is a perfect example of this phenomenon.

	1QIsa[a]	𝔐
v. 7		יָבֵשׁ חָצִיר נָבֵל צִיץ כִּי רוּחַ יְהוָה נָשְׁבָה בּוֹ אָכֵן חָצִיר הָעָם:
		The grass withers, the flower fades, when the breath of Yahweh blows on it; surely the people are grass.
v. 8	יבש חציר נבל ציץ ודבר אלוהינו יקום לעולם	יָבֵשׁ חָצִיר נָבֵל צִיץ וּדְבַר־אֱלֹהֵינוּ יָקוּם לְעוֹלָם:
	The grass withers, the flower fades, but the Word of our God will stand forever.	**The grass withers, the flower fades,** but the Word of our God will stand forever.

In this example, the eye of the scribe of 1QIsa[a] accidentally skipped from the first instance of "the grass withers, the flower fades" in verse 7 to the second instance in verse 8, thus accidentally omitting all of verse 7. Interestingly, the scribe of 1QIsa[a] or a later corrector actually caught the mistake and added the omitted text between lines and down the left margin of the scroll.

---

[33] Jan de Waard, *A Handbook on Isaiah* (Winona Lake, IN: Eisenbrauns, 1997), 47.

[34] Dominique Barthélemy et al., *The Preliminary and Interim Report on the Hebrew Old Testament Text Project* (New York: United Bible Societies, 1979), 1:299 assigned a C rating or one of "considerable doubt" to the text of 𝔐, indicating that the reconstruction is between a "high probability" A rating and "highly doubtful or relatively much lower probability" D rating.

Psalm 145:13–14 provides a good example where a scroll like 11ⵖPsᵃ contains the correct longer reading and 𝔐 has the incorrect shorter text. Furthermore, the added refrain in 11ⵖPsᵃ (lacking in all other texts) shows that an older text like 𝔐 could be updated or resignified for the liturgical needs of the community and that the same resignified text could also preserve the original text as 11ⵖPsᵃ preserves the missing verse * in the psalm.[35]

	11ⵖPSᵃ	𝔐
13	מלכותכה מלכות כול עולמים וממשלתכה בכול דור ודור ברוך יהוה וברוך שמו לעולם ועד	מַלְכוּתְךָ מַלְכוּת כָּל־עֹלָמִים וּמֶמְשֶׁלְתְּךָ בְּכָל־דּוֹר וָדוֹר:
	Your kingdom is an everlasting kingdom, and your dominion is to all generations. **Blessed be Yahweh and blessed be his name forever and ever.**	Your kingdom is an everlasting kingdom, and your dominion is to all generations.
*	נאמן אלוהים בדבריו וחסיד בכול מעשיו ברוך יהוה וברוך שמו לעולם ועד	
	Faithful is God[36] in his words and loyal in all his deeds. **Blessed be Yahweh and blessed be his name forever and ever.**	
14	סומך יהוה לכול הנופלים וזוקף לכול הכפופים ברוך יהוה וברוך שמו לעולם ועד	סוֹמֵךְ יְהוָה לְכָל־הַנֹּפְלִים וְזוֹקֵף לְכָל־הַכְּפוּפִים:
	Yahweh upholds all who are falling and raises up all who are bowed. **Blessed be Yahweh and blessed be his name forever and ever.**	Yahweh upholds all who are falling and raises up all who are bowed.

Since Psalm 145 is otherwise a complete acrostic, it is clear that 𝔐's text has been corrupted. It is missing the line that is supposed to begin with *nun*. The line is present in 11ⵖPsᵃ as well as 𝔊, 𝔖, and Kennicott MS 142. A copyist error of sight like *parablepsis* does not explain the omission in 𝔐. Thus, there was probably a mutilation at the top or bottom of a scroll.[37]

2.3.3.3.5 Large-Scale Differences. When large textual differences (i.e., differences not attributed to normal copying process) occur regularly throughout a copy of a single book, these books or sections are said to appear in variant literary editions.[38] Although many large-scale differences occur in 𝔊, the DSS show some signs of variant

---

[35] On "resignification," see Gentry, "Text of the Old Testament," 33.
[36] Benjamin Kennicott, *Vetus Testamentum Hebraicum: cum variis lectionibus* (Oxford: Clarendon, 1776–1780), 2:434 has יהו, 𝔊 reads κύριος "Lord," and 𝔖 has *mryʾ* "Lord" respectively.
[37] See Gentry, "Text of the Old Testament," 31.
[38] Julio Trebolle Barrera, "Textual Criticism: Hebrew Bible," in *The Oxford Encyclopedia of Biblical Interpretation,* ed. Steven L. McKenzie (Oxford: Oxford University Press, 2013), 2:367–68; Gentry, "Text of the Old Testament," 39–44.

editions; however, we do not know the function of these variant literary editions in their original communities, and researchers continue to pursue answers to these questions.

In 4QDeut[n], the scribe worked with a proto-𝔐-like text in which he placed Deuteronomy 8:5–10 before 5:1–6:1 as an introduction to the Decalogue, and thus he made a secondary, excerpted text with some harmonizations. Here are some of the more significant harmonizations in 5:1–6:1 with commentary.

	4QDEUT[n]	𝔐
5:5	ואנוכי עומד בין יהוה וביניכם בעת ההיא להגיד לכם את דברי יהוה **אלוהיכם** [39] כי יראתם מפני האש ולוא עליתם בהר לאמר	אָנֹכִי עֹמֵד בֵּין־יְהוָה וּבֵינֵיכֶם בָּעֵת הַהִוא לְהַגִּיד לָכֶם אֶת־דְּבַר יְהוָה כִּי יְרֵאתֶם מִפְּנֵי הָאֵשׁ וְלֹא־עֲלִיתֶם בָּהָר לֵאמֹר׃
5:14	**וביום** [40] השביעי שבת ליהוה אלוהיך לוא תעשה **בו** [41] כל מלאכה אתה ובנך בתך עבדך ואמתך שורך וחמורך ובהמתך גרך אשר בשעריך למען ינוח עבדך ואמתך כמוך	וְיוֹם הַשְּׁבִיעִי שַׁבָּת ׀ לַיהוָה אֱלֹהֶיךָ לֹא תַעֲשֶׂה כָל־מְלָאכָה אַתָּה וּבִנְךָ־וּבִתֶּךָ וְעַבְדְּךָ־וַאֲמָתֶךָ וְשׁוֹרְךָ וַחֲמֹרְךָ וְכָל־בְּהֶמְתֶּךָ וְגֵרְךָ אֲשֶׁר בִּשְׁעָרֶיךָ לְמַעַן יָנוּחַ עַבְדְּךָ וַאֲמָתְךָ כָּמוֹךָ׃
5:15	וזכרתה כי עבד היית בארץ מצרים ויציאך יהוה אלוהיך משם ביד חזקה ובזרוע נטויה על כן צוך יהוה אלוהיך **לשמור** [42] את יום השבת	וְזָכַרְתָּ כִּי־עֶבֶד הָיִיתָ ׀ בְּאֶרֶץ מִצְרַיִם וַיֹּצִאֲךָ יְהוָה אֱלֹהֶיךָ מִשָּׁם בְּיָד חֲזָקָה וּבִזְרֹעַ נְטוּיָה עַל־כֵּן צִוְּךָ יְהוָה אֱלֹהֶיךָ לַעֲשׂוֹת אֶת־יוֹם הַשַּׁבָּת׃
~ Exod 20:11	|לקדשו| כי ששת ימים עשה יהוה את השמים ואת הארץ את הים וכול אשר בם וינוח ביום השביעי על כן ברך יהוה את יום השבת |לקדשו| [43]	
5:22	את הדברים האלה דבר יהוה אל כול קהלכם בהר מתוך האש **חושך** [44] ענן וערפל קול ג[ד]ול ולוא יסף ויכותבם על שני לוחות אבנים ויתנם אלי	אֶת־הַדְּבָרִים הָאֵלֶּה דִּבֶּר יְהוָה אֶל־כָּל־קְהַלְכֶם בָּהָר מִתּוֹךְ הָאֵשׁ הֶעָנָן וְהָעֲרָפֶל קוֹל גָּדוֹל וְלֹא יָסָף וַיִּכְתְּבֵם עַל־שְׁנֵי לֻחֹת אֲבָנִים וַיִּתְּנֵם אֵלָי׃

[39] The scribe added "your God" to harmonize with the phrase, "Yahweh, your God," a common phrase in Deuteronomy (e.g. Deut 1:10).

[40] The ב is probably an assimilation to Exod 16:26, 35:2, et al.

[41] Due to the harmonization of יום to ביום, the scribe also follows texts like Exod 35:2 which include the phrase בו "in it."

[42] The scribe harmonized this word to Deut 5:12.

[43] The scribe has included the rationale for keeping the Sabbath in Exod 20:11 within the Decalogue's flow in Deuteronomy. The repetition of לקדשו "to sanctify it" brackets the added text and is called resumptive repetition, a scribal technique that shows a later scribe is aware that he is drawing from another earlier text. See William M. Schniedewind, *How the Bible Became a Book: The Textualization of Ancient Israel* (Cambridge: Cambridge University Press, 2004), 21.

[44] חשך is in Deut 4:11: "darkness, cloud, and gloom," and in 5:23: "when you heard the voice from the midst of the darkness."

Analysis of this entire scroll reveals that 4QDeut[n] is a text close to proto-𝔐 Deuteronomy with secondary harmonization to other texts like proto-𝔐 Exodus and other passages within Deuteronomy. This scroll shows the late Second Temple scribal practices of harmonization and excerption and also the antiquity of proto-𝔐, since the scribe used this text to make his new text.[45] Researchers do not know the purpose of this text or the extent of the scribe's work, since the text breaks off around 6:1.[46]

4QJosh[a] probably shows a different version than 𝔐. In this text, it appears that Josh 8:34–35 comes before 5:1–2. Researchers still debate whether this text reflects (1) an older edition than 𝔐 with a different narrative sequence (Gilgal [𝔐 4.19–24] → Torah Reading [𝔐 8:30–35] → Circumcision [𝔐 5:1 2]); (2) a text that reflects a late, secondary insertion of the Torah reading into an 𝔐-like text in order to show that the Torah was observed at the entrance into the land; or (3) the Torah reading [𝔐 8:30–35] was duplicated to harmonize a difficulty in the narrative sequence.[47]

2.3.3.3.6 Summary. The 𝔐, 𝔊, and DSS provide direct evidence of the state of the Hebrew text and even the kinds of scribal modifications that happened throughout the text's history. In these sources, we observe spelling changes; variants in vocalization, consonants, and words; pluses and minuses due to *parablepsis* or defective exemplar; and large-scale differences/variant literary editions due to harmonization, and even perhaps, earlier editions. The student would do well to be familiar with these modifications in Hebrew manuscripts before learning to "see" them in the Ancient Versions to which we now turn.

2.4 INDIRECT EVIDENCE OF THE ANCIENT VERSIONS

Before the discovery of the DSS in 1947, only the late medieval MSS of 𝔐 and 𝔊 attested the text of the Hebrew Bible. Text critics also made extensive use of what are known as the Ancient Versions in establishing the original text of the Hebrew Bible. These include several Greek, Latin, Syriac, and Aramaic translations. In particular, the fourth-century AD manuscripts of the Greek translation (e.g., Codex Vaticanus) furnished earlier material evidence for the Hebrew Bible than our earliest Hebrew manuscripts from the tenth century AD. But remember *an earlier manuscript does not necessarily preserve the more original text.*

The student of Hebrew Bible textual criticism should learn the general character of each Ancient Version and gain some competency in the use of them for textual criticism. Below, I will provide a description of the character of each Ancient Version with a couple of examples to illustrate how they operated in translating the

---

[45] Lange, "Ancient and Late Ancient Hebrew," *THB* 1A:131.

[46] Tov, "Biblical Texts," 152, classifies this text as excerpted, "probably for liturgical purposes."

[47] For a good summary of this discussion, see Karen Finsterbusch, "Other Texts," in *THB* 1B:266–67.

Hebrew text in front of them (i.e., the parent text; German *Vorlage*).[48] Knowledge of the character of these witnesses, however elementary, will help the student make decisions between textual variants.

2.4.1 Greek Versions

The history of the Hebrew Bible incorporates the testimony of several early Greek versions. The earliest and chief ones came to be called popularly "the Septuagint" (abbreviated from Lat. *Septuaginta* "the Seventy"), while others were done by the later Jewish translators or, more accurately, revisers: Theodotion, Aquila, and Symmachus. The Jews also made other early Greek translations that remained anonymous, and we learn about them from early Christian scholars like Origen of Alexandria (d. AD 254) and Eusebius of Caesarea (d. AD 339).

2.4.1.1 The Old Greek Translations [𝕲]

Although popularly and traditionally called "the Septuagint" or "the Greek Old Testament," scholars refer to the earliest Greek translations of the Hebrew Scriptures as "Old Greek" (e.g., "Old Greek Job").[49] The *Letter of Aristeas* (ca. 100 BC) only describes the work of the Seventy as translating "the Law," and therefore, "the Seventy" referred historically to a narrow corpus of translations. But by Justin Martyr's time (d. AD 165), "the Seventy" (often abbreviated LXX) had become the traditional title for the Jewish translation of all the Hebrew Scriptures into *koine* Greek. The primary translations of the Pentateuch were done around 280 BC and the latest translations like Esther are dated from around 100 BC.[50] The Prologue to Ben Sira (ca. 132 BC) assumes that most of the books that comprise "the Law, the Prophets, and the other books" had been translated by this time.

In late antiquity, early Christians rendered these Greek translations into several languages: Coptic (Akhmimic, Sahidic, Bohairic, Fayyumic, Mesokemic), Armenian, Georgian, Ethiopic, Syriac, Christian Palestinian Aramaic, Arabic, Latin (i.e., *Vetus Latina* or Old Latin), Gothic, and Old Church Slavonic. Editors of the Göttingen *Septuaginta* volumes have incorporated many but not all of these so-called daughter versions into their editions. More research into these versions of the Septuagint remains outstanding.

2.4.1.2 Old Greek as Translation

The title "Septuagint" gives the impression that this version is a monolith similar to modern translations produced by committees of translators. But the reality is, each

---

[48] The German term *Vorlage* is used in much of the literature on this subject.

[49] See Claude Cox, "Some Things Biblical Scholars Should Know about the Septuagint," *Restoration Quarterly* 56.2 (2014): 87–89, for the distinction between the narrower sense of the term "Septuagint" that refers historically only to the translation of the Pentateuch and the extension of the same term to include those translations and writings that comprise the Greek corpus that began with the translation of the Torah.

[50] For a general and accessible introduction to the Septuagint and the matter of dating certain books, see Dines, *Septuagint*, 41–46.

book or perhaps parts of books (as might be the case in Samuel-Kings) was produced by a single translator with each translator varying in approach—some more
literal and others more dynamic. The upshot is when we approach these early Greek
versions, we must ask what kind of translation it is before we use it for text-critical
purposes. For example, the translator of 𝔊 Ecclesiastes rendered his Hebrew source
with an ultra-literal approach to the point that he usually translated the Hebrew definite direct object marker אֵת (usually untranslated) with Greek σύν "with" + accusative—not the normal dative case according to normal conventions of Greek grammar:

	𝔐	𝔊
Eccl 1:14a	רָאִיתִי אֶת־כָּל־הַמַּעֲשִׂים	εἶδον σὺν πάντα τὰ ποιήματα
	I saw all the works . . .	I saw all the works . . .

A translation that renders every word of its Hebrew source will be valuable when
using that translation as a witness to the Hebrew text. But not all 𝔊 translations are
ultra-literal, so we need to be more careful in using them in textual criticism.

On the other side of the translation spectrum, 𝔊 Job exhibits a very free approach
to proto-𝔐 (not a shorter Hebrew text).[51] The translator worked as a paraphrast,
or even epitomizer, of proto-𝔐 to the extent that the Greek translation is one-sixth
shorter than the Hebrew source.[52] For example, in Job 29:13, we have:

	𝔐	𝔊
13a	בִּרְכַּת אֹבֵד עָלַי תָּבֹא	στόμα δὲ χήρας με εὐλόγησεν.
	May the blessing of the perishing come on me	And the mouth of the widow blessed me.
13b	וְלֵב אַלְמָנָה אַרְנִן׃	
	and the heart of the widow I will cause to exult.	

The original translator reduced both 29:13a and 13b of the Hebrew text into one
line using elements from both lines to convey the meaning of the whole verse. In
𝔊, verse 13 concludes a list of Job's deeds on behalf of society's marginalized
with the blessing from a widow. The translator did not simply omit 13a or 13b; he
combined them.[53] At times this paraphrastic approach omitted several lines. In Job
29:24a–30:1, the translator omitted four lines, 29:24b and 25abc, and used different forms of the root שׂחק "to laugh" (29:24a; 30:1a) as catchwords to bind lines
29:24a and 30:1a together. Thus, the translator of 𝔊 Job worked more dynamically
than other more literal translators like that of Ecclesiastes.

---

[51] For a treatment of Old Greek Job in its own polysystem, see Marieke Dhont, *Style and Context of Old Greek Job,* JSJSup 183 (Leiden: Brill, 2018).

[52] For the most up to date analysis and summary, see Claude Cox, "Septuagint," in *THB* 1C:175–81.

[53] Thus a few centuries later when Origen of Alexandria healed the difference between the Hebrew and Greek texts, he added an equivalent for Hebrew Job 29:13a from Theodotion (cf. below): εὐλογία ἀπολλυμένου ἐπ' ἐμὲ ἔλθοι "may the blessing of the perishing come upon me." Now the Greek edition has two lines, with each line having someone bless Job.

Old Greek Isaiah 53 in the **Göttingen Septuaginta Critical Edition**. This page shows the critically established text, Apparatus 1 with variants to that text, and Apparatus 2 with readings from the hexaplaric tradition.

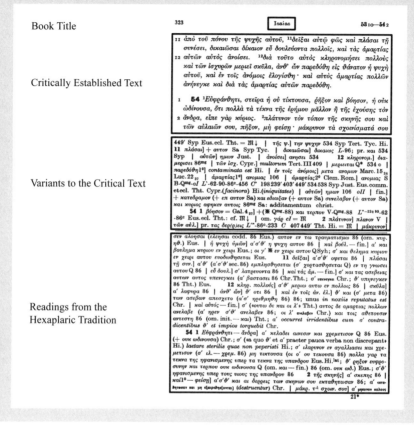

Book Title	
Critically Established Text	
Variants to the Critical Text	
Readings from the Hexaplaric Tradition	

In between these translations, there are translations like 𝕲 Isaiah, which rendered a source like proto-𝔐 with varied approaches. On the one hand, 𝕲 Isaiah transcribed שְׂרָפִים with σεραφιν in 6:2, 6, but in Isa 14:29, שָׂרָף מְעוֹפֵף "winged serpent" is translated into Greek ὄφεις πετόμενοι "flying serpents." The variation between transcription and translation shows a freer approach to the translation task. Furthermore, 𝕲 Isaiah employs exegesis of proto-𝔐 in some of its renderings like 9:9(10):

	𝔐	𝕲
v. 9	לְבֵנִים נָפָלוּ וְגָזִית נִבְנֶה שִׁקְמִים גֻּדָּעוּ וַאֲרָזִים נַחֲלִיף:	Πλίνθοι πεπτώκασιν, ἀλλὰ δεῦτε λαξεύσω-μεν λίθους καὶ ἐκκόψωμεν συκαμίνους καὶ κέδρους **καὶ οἰκοδομήσωμεν ἑαυτοῖς πύργον.**
	Bricks have fallen, but we will build with dressed stone; sycamores have been cut down, but we will replace them with cedars.	Bricks have fallen but come! Let us hew out stones and let us cut down syca-mores and cedars, **and let us build for ourselves a tower!**

The 𝔊 Isaiah text is longer than 𝔐, but probably not due to a different, longer Hebrew source. Rather, the translator appears to allude to Gen 11:3–4 due to the Hebrew word לְבֵנִים "bricks" in both contexts. That word appears infrequently in the Hebrew Bible (Gen 11:3; the Exodus narrative [Exod 1:14; 5:7, 8, 16, 18]; and 2 Sam 12:31 [in a context of tyranny]) outside of here in Isaiah. Probably, the translator remembered this word from Gen 11:3 and intended to cast Israel's prideful leadership in the shade of Babel's arrogant leadership.

While we cannot give an exhaustive catalogue of examples here, the few presented above illustrate that the Old Greek translations can be oriented on a spectrum from ultra-literal to paraphrase with less literal and exegetical translations in between. Before using an Old Greek translation for textual criticism, one must ask: What kind of translation is this? The student is encouraged to consult works like the first volume of *Textual History of the Bible* or *T&T Clark Companion to the Septuagint* to learn more about the character and description of each of the Old Greek translations before using them for textual criticism. Translations closer to the free or dynamic end of the spectrum can be used for OT textual criticism but great caution is required.

2.4.1.3 The Old Greek and the Text of the Hebrew Bible

The Old Greek translations preserve the same kinds of errors and variants that we observed in the Hebrew MSS: vocalization; consonants; words; longer additions and subtractions; and perhaps to a greater extent than the scrolls found at Qumran, large-scale differences.

2.4.1.3.1 Vocalization. In Gen 47:31, did Jacob rest upon the top of his "bed" (מִטָּה 𝔐) or his "staff" (מַטֶּה = ῥάβδος 𝔊)? The same three consonants caused both readings. Here 𝔊 was probably influenced by an earlier mention of Jacob's staff (cf. מַקֵּל in 32:11[10]) and thus rendered the consonants in 47:31 accordingly. 𝔐 probably preserves the original vocalization because it is difficult otherwise to discover how its reading arose.

Occasionally, postbiblical Hebrew or Aramaic interfered with a translator's reading of the text, creating a seemingly wild variant. 𝔊 Eccl 2:12c has βουλή "counsel" for 𝔐 מֶלֶךְ "king" from root I מלך "to reign." On the surface, this appears to be a very different text. But in Aramaic, root II מלך "to consult, ask for advice" is well attested, and this meaning influenced 𝔊 Ecclesiastes in this case.[54] Although the difference appears significant, the Greek version still attests the same Hebrew consonants as 𝔐.

2.4.1.3.2 Consonants and Words. 𝔊 attests to variant readings at the word level due to many factors including similar consonants and improper word division. In 𝔊 Eccl 5:16(17), καὶ ἐν πένθει probably reflects וּבְאֵבֶל "and in mourning," but 𝔐 has יֹאכֵל "he will eat." Here, the source of 𝔊 probably confused ו/י and כ/ב, creating a noun instead of the original verb and probably leading the scribe to add a

---

[54] Peter J. Gentry, "Propaedeutic to a Lexicon of the Three: The Priority of a New Critical Edition of Hexaplaric Fragments," *Aramaic Studies* 2.2 (2004): 164.

בְּ preposition to the noun in accordance with normal Hebrew syntax. ᚷ rendered this secondary Hebrew text.

In Jer 23:33, 𝔐 has: וְאָמַרְתָּ אֲלֵיהֶם אֶת־מַה־מַשָּׂא "and you will say to them, 'What burden?'" But this reading arose due either to misdivision of words or even theological facilitation, since ᚷ (καὶ ἐρεῖς αὐτοῖς Ὑμεῖς ἐστε τὸ λῆμμα) attests a harder reading אַתֶּם הַמַּשָּׂא "you are the burden." 𝔐 protects the honor of Israel, since they are not God's burden, and perhaps protects the impassible transcendence of God for whom nothing can be a burden.[55] A similar issue appears in Job 7:20 where ᚷ has "why am I burden to *you* [i.e., God]?," while 𝔐 has "why am I a burden to *myself?*"

2.4.1.3.3 Larger Pluses and Minuses. At times, the Hebrew source text of ᚷ attests to a longer text than 𝔐. In Gen 4:8, 𝔐 has וַיֹּאמֶר קַיִן אֶל־הֶבֶל אָחִיו וַיְהִי בִּהְיוֹתָם בַּשָּׂדֶה "And Cain spoke to Abel, his brother. And it happened when they were in the field" whereas ᚷ's Vorlage has ויאמר קין אל הבל אחיו נלכה השדה ויהי בהיותם בשדה (= καὶ εἶπεν Κάιν πρὸς Ἄβελ τὸν ἀδελφὸν αὐτοῦ Διέλθωμεν εἰς τὸ πεδίον. καὶ ἐγένετο ἐν τῷ εἶναι αὐτοὺς ἐν τῷ πεδίῳ) "And Cain said to Abel, his brother, 'Let us go out to the field.' And it happened when they were in the field." Some suggest that ᚷ and the other versions preserve the original, longer text because 𝔐's text is awkward for having no quoted speech.[56] Others see the easier reading in ᚷ as the result of a later scribe smoothing out of the difficult text of 𝔐.[57] Thus the longer text could be a secondary scribal amplification of the original, shorter text. An error of parablepsis due to the scribe's eye skipping from the alleged, first instance of שָׂדֶה to the second is not plausible, since the entire text between the two instances, including וַיְהִי בִּהְיוֹתָם, would have been omitted and the נֵלְכָה "let us go" before the first instance would have been copied. Thus, a simple scribal explanation for the original, longer text fails.

Our next example shows how a longer, original text becomes shorter in the copying process. In 1 Sam 13:15, the Hebrew source of ᚷ is longer because proto-𝔐's scribe committed a mistake of parablepsis (cf. §2.3.3.3.4) due to his eye skipping from the first instance of מן הגלגל to the second where he continued copying the rest of the verse:

---

[55] *CTAT* 2:649; Jan de Waard, *A Handbook on Jeremiah* (Winona Lake, IN: Eisenbrauns, 2003), 104.

[56] McCarter, *Textual Criticism*, 42.

[57] Barthélemy et al., *Preliminary and Interim Report*, 1:8.

𝔐	𝔊[58]
v. 15 וַיָּקָם שְׁמוּאֵל וַיַּעַל מִן־הַגִּלְגָּל גִּבְעַת בִּנְיָמִן וַיִּפְקֹד שָׁאוּל אֶת־הָעָם הַנִּמְצְאִים עִמּוֹ כְּשֵׁשׁ מֵאוֹת אִישׁ׃	ויקם שמואל ויעל מן הגלגל וילך לדרכו ויתר העם עלה אחרי שאול לקראת עם המלחמה ויבאו מן הגלגל גבעת בנימן ויפקד שאול את העם הנמצאים עמו כשש מאות איש
And Samuel rose and went up from Gilgal, Gibeah of Benjamin. And Saul numbered the people who were present with him, about six-hundred men.	And Samuel rose and went up **from Gilgal, and he went on his way. But the rest of the people went up after Saul to meet the people of the battle, and they came** from Gilgal, Gibeah of Benjamin. And Saul numbered the people who were present with him, about six-hundred men.

This mistake must have happened early in the transmission of the text since the 𝔖, 𝔙, and 𝔗 all read the shorter, miscopied text of proto-𝔐.

A similar example can be found in 2 Sam 13:21–22, but this time a fragment from 4QSam[a] shows part of the longer Hebrew text:

𝔐	𝔊[59]	4QSam[a]
v. 21 וְהַמֶּלֶךְ דָּוִד שָׁמַע אֵת כָּל־הַדְּבָרִים הָאֵלֶּה וַיִּחַר לוֹ מְאֹד׃	והמלך דוד שמע את כל הדברים האלה ויחר לו מאד **ולא עצב את רוח אמנון בנו כי אהבו כי בכרו הוא**	[והמלך דויד] שמע את [כול] [הדברים האלה ויחר לו מאד **ולוא עצב את רוח אמנון בנו כי אה**[בו כי בכור]ו הוא]
And King David heard all these words and became very angry.	And King David heard all these words and was very angry, **and he did not grieve the spirit of Amnon his son for he loved him because he was his firstborn.**	[And king David] heard [all these words and was very angry, **and he did not grieve the spirit of Amnon his son for he lov**]ed him because [he was his] firstborn.]
v. 22 וְלֹא־דִבֶּר	ולא דבר	[. . .]
And (Absalom) did not speak …	And (Absalom) did not speak …	[. . .]

---

[58] Hebrew retroversion from Barthélemy et al., *Preliminary and Interim Report*, 1:173–74. Rahlfs's Edition has: καὶ ἀνέστη Σαμουηλ καὶ ἀπῆλθεν ἐκ Γαλγαλων εἰς ὁδὸν αὐτοῦ. καὶ τὸ κατάλειμμα τοῦ λαοῦ ἀνέβη ὀπίσω Σαουλ εἰς ἀπάντησιν ὀπίσω τοῦ λαοῦ τοῦ πολεμιστοῦ. αὐτῶν παραγενομένων ἐκ Γαλγαλων εἰς Γαβαα Βενιαμιν καὶ ἐπεσκέψατο Σαουλ τὸν λαὸν τὸν εὑρεθέντα μετ' αὐτοῦ ὡς ἑξακοσίους ἄνδρας.

[59] Hebrew retroversion from *CTAT* 1:265. Rahlfs's Edition: καὶ ἤκουσεν ὁ βασιλεὺς Δαυιδ πάντας τοὺς λόγους τούτους καὶ ἐθυμώθη σφόδρα· καὶ οὐκ ἐλύπησεν τὸ πνεῦμα Αμνων τοῦ υἱοῦ αὐτοῦ, ὅτι ἠγάπα αὐτόν, ὅτι πρωτότοκος αὐτοῦ ἦν. καὶ οὐκ ἐλάλησεν.

Once again, the shorter reading probably arose from the scribe's eye skipping from the first לא‎ו to the second in verse 22, and 4QSam^a confirms that 𝕲 translated the original, longer Hebrew text.

2.4.1.3.4 Large-Scale Differences between 𝕸 and 𝕲. There are situations where real textual differences between 𝕸 and 𝕲 form a pattern so that the only explanation is that one or the other of these represents a variant edition or recension in the history of a biblical book. All scholars would agree on the following: (1) 𝕲 Jeremiah is a translation of a shorter Hebrew version than 𝕸 Jeremiah; (2) 𝕲 Ezekiel translates a shorter version than 𝕸 Ezekiel; (3) 𝕲 1 Samuel 16–18 translates a shorter version than 𝕸 1 Samuel 16–18; (4) the literary shape of several chapters of 1 Esdras is older than the 𝕸 edition of the parallel chapters in Ezra-Nehemiah and Chronicles; (5) 𝕲 Joshua and (6) 𝕲 Judges show a pattern of textual variants that attest different literary editions than proto-𝕸 for the books of Joshua and Judges.[60]

The presence of different editions in the Dead Sea Scrolls (see §2.3.3.3.5) and 𝕲 has been interpreted in various ways with two chief options. (1) Focusing on diachronic sequence, Eugene Ulrich has argued, "The principal way that the biblical text developed in the Second Temple period was through successive revised and expanded editions of each book."[61] (2) The different texts represent synchronic editions produced by conservative (focus on exact copying) and facilitating (focus on aiding understanding) scribal models within variegated Judaism and were probably intended to complement one another.[62] At times, 𝕸 appears to be the facilitating text and 𝕲 the conservative text (e.g., Jeremiah), but at other times, 𝕸 is the conservative text and 𝕲 the facilitating text (e.g., Daniel).

2.4.1.4 Later Greek Versions

Origen of Alexandria's text critical work on the Greek Scriptures influenced the textual history of 𝕲 so significantly that now researchers talk about Greek versions before his *Hexapla* (i.e., pre-hexaplaric versions) and after it (i.e., post-hexaplaric versions).

Before the Old Greek translations were finished, Jews began to revise already existing translations, focusing on translating the consonantal text of proto-𝕸 in a more literal fashion. These revisions began as early as the second and first centuries BC (4QLXXNum; Papyrus Fouad Inv. 266b-c [Deuteronomy]; 5QDeut [supralinear corrections]).[63]

---

[60] Emanuel Tov, "Septuagint," in *THB* 1A:201–4, summarizes these cases and adds more.

[61] Eugene Ulrich, *The Dead Sea Scrolls and the Developmental Composition of the Bible* (Leiden: Brill, 2015), 41.

[62] Teeter, *Scribal Laws*, 267.

[63] Armin Lange, "'Nobody Dared to Add to Them, to Take from Them, or to Make Changes,' (Jospehus, Ag. Ap. 1.42): The Textual Standardization of Jewish Scriptures in Light of the Dead Sea Scrolls," in *Flores Florentino: Dead Sea Scrolls and Other Early Jewish Studies in Honour of Florentino García Martínez*, ed. A. Hilhorst, É. Puech, and E. J. C. Tigchelaar, JSJSup 122 (Leiden: Brill, 2007), 105–26.

Dated from the latter half of the first century BC to the first half of the first century AD, a Greek Minor Prophets scroll (8HevXIIgr) shows what some researchers have sometimes called the "*kaige* recension/revision" or "*kaige*-Theodotion," since the reviser of the Book of the Twelve rendered גם/וגם with καίγε.[64] More recent analysis calls 8HevXIIgr and other texts affiliated with it the "*kaige* tradition"—a term that encompasses a nonhomogeneous tradition of new translations and revisions of proto-𝔐 characterized by increasingly formal translation approaches anticipating the subsequent extreme literalness of Aquila around AD 130.[65]

Theodotion (ca. 30 BC–AD 30) was a member of the *kaige* tradition.[66] Aquila represents the flowering of the *kaige* tradition since he refined the tradition's formal equivalence by rendering all derivatives of a single Hebrew root with derivatives from a single Greek root and by employing an etymologizing approach. Symmachus (flourished around AD 200) represents something of a response to the literalness of the *kaige* tradition and employed a more functional equivalence translation approach to the same Hebrew source though still rendering each word of the source.

Although Theodotion (θ′), Aquila (α′), and Symmachus (σ′) were the more noteworthy editions, early Christians (cf. Eusebius *Historia ecclesiastica* 6.16) mention that Origen found three other editions which he named: the Fifth (*Quinta*, ε′), the Sixth (*Sexta*, ς′), and the Seventh (*Septima*).[67] There is no trace of the *Septima* and it is debated whether it ever existed or has been lost. The *Quinta* and *Sexta* have many attested readings in Psalms and Song of Songs, which probably indicates that Origen found these revisions for only a few books of the Hebrew canon.

After having moved to Caesarea around AD 232, Origen began work on his *Hexapla* (ἑξαπλᾶ "sixfold" or "six-columned") around AD 235, inspired by his dialogues with the Jewish population there. He never called his six-columned Old Testament the *Hexapla* (his followers did that), but later sources and analysis of the fragmentary remains of the synopsis lead to the following description:

---

[64] Tov, *Textual Criticism*, 143; Brotzman and Tully, *Old Testament Textual Criticism*, 68 ; see also Tov, *Textual Criticism of the Hebrew Bible*, 4th ed., 255.

[65] Peter Gentry, "Pre-Hexaplaric Translations, Hexapla, Post-Hexaplaric Translations," in *THB* 1A:213. Leaving open the possibility that further research might show that 𝔊 Psalms represents an early stage of the *kaige* tradition, Gentry assigns the following texts to this tradition: the asterisked materials (cf. Origen below) of Job, θ′ Daniel (an exhaustive analysis is still a *desideratum*), 𝔊 Lamentations, 𝔊 Ecclesiastes, 𝔊 2 Sam 11:1–1 Kgs 2:11, and 𝔊 Song of Songs (2:22–25).

[66] The challenge to dating Theodotion to the first century is that the fourth-century father, Epiphanius dates him to the second century during the reign of Emperor Commodus (ca. AD 180). But it appears that Epiphanius has confused his sources in his attempt to give a chronology for the order of "the Three" given in the *Hexapla*: Aquila, Symmachus, and Theodotion. The chronological order is probably Theodotion, Aquila, and Symmachus, and Jerome's comment in *Epistulae* 112.19 could be read as referring to Theodotion in the first century.

[67] Eusebius's account of exactly where Origen found these editions is not clear, but slightly later Epiphanius interprets Eusebius's statements as saying that Origen found the *Quinta* edition in large jars at Jericho and the *Sexta* edition in jars in Nicopolis (in Greece) near Actium. See Epiphanius, *On Weights and Measures*, 18.

COLUMN 1	COLUMN 2	COLUMN 3	COLUMN 4	COLUMN 5	COLUMN 6
Hebrew	Greek Transcription of Hebrew	Aquila	Symmachus	Septuagint	Theodotion

Almost every detail about the history of the *Hexapla* is debated. Probably, there was one Hebrew word and the corresponding Greek equivalents in each line at about forty lines per page. Thus, the *Hexapla* would have filled almost forty codices of 400 leaves or 800 pages per codex.[68] This reconstruction probably explains why the entire *Hexapla* was never copied, and perhaps only individual books like Psalms were ever copied in the columnar form. Thus, today we only have access to the remains of the *Hexapla* and only read the editions of "the Three" (i.e., Aquila, Symmachus, and Theodotion) via remaining fragments in manuscripts, patristic commentaries, and ancient translations.

After Origen's *Hexapla*, there were probably three later scholarly editions. The Caesarean edition (or *Tetrapla*), which Origen probably began to prepare, and his followers like Pamphilus and Eusebius finalized and refined. In the Enaton monastery near Alexandria, Egypt in AD 616, bishop Paul of Tella (a town in modern-day Syria) translated the *Tetrapla* into Syriac, now called the Syro-Hexapla.[69] The second edition was the Hesychian undertaken in Egypt. Little is known about the Hesychian edition from Egypt.[70] The third Lucianic edition came from Antioch.[71] Many of the Göttingen Septuagint editions assign *O* to a group of MSS from Origen and Caesarea (i.e., the Origenic revision) and *L* to a group of MSS from Lucian and Antioch (i.e., the Lucianic revision).

Usually, the pre-hexaplaric Greek versions agree in every detail with 𝕸, but not always. For example, in Isa 7:11, 𝕸 has שְׁאָלָה, a form which may be interpreted as a *Qal* IMPV 2MS + *he* from שאל "to ask" (cf. KJV "*ask* it either in the depth") or a NP שְׁאֹלָה "to Sheol," due either to pause or assonance with the preceding לְמָעְלָה "to the height." 𝕮 and 𝕾 anticipated reading שאלה as an imperative of שאל and thus rendered it with respective imperatives, while θ′, α′, and σ′ have εἰς ᾅδην "to Hades" (cf. *inferni* 𝖁), which renders the NP "to Sheol," the reading accepted by most interpreters.[72] In favor of the first option, the analogous forms of יְרֵשָׁה "possess" (Deut 33:23), וּסְעָדָה "support" (1 Kgs 13:7), שָׁמָעָה "listen," and סָלְחָה

---

[68] Anthony Grafton and Megan Williams, *Christianity and the Transformation of the Book: Origen, Eusebius, and the Library of Caesarea* (Cambridge: Harvard University Press, 2006), 104–5.

[69] Peter J. Gentry, "The Septuagint and Origen's Hexapla," in *The T&T Clark Handbook of Septuagint Research*, ed. William A. Ross and W. Edward Glenny (London: Bloomsbury T&T Clark, 2021), 191–206.

[70] Peter Gentry's critical edition of Ecclesiastes identifies an Egyptian group of MSS; see *Ecclesiastes*, SVTG 11.2 (Göttingen: Vandenhoeck & Ruprecht, 2019), 56. The earliest MS witness (RA 998) is dated to around AD 300 and could have come from a bishop known as Hesychius.

[71] Gentry, "Pre-Hexaplaric Translations," *THB* 1A:232–35. Jerome attests to this *trifaria varietas* "threefold variation" in his *Preface to Paralipomenon*.

[72] *CTAT* 2:47; de Waard, *Handbook on Isaiah*, 32–33.

"forgive" (Dan 9:19) probably show the Masoretes intended שאלה to be read as an imperative and not as שְׁאֹלָה "to Sheol," which appears with this vocalization consistently in 𝔐.[73] But in favor of the veiled form, the Masoretes could have knowingly hid the reference to Sheol due to the theological difficulty it created.[74] On the first option, 𝔐 modified the vocalization *and the meaning* of the original text to avoid a theological difficulty, while the Three preserved the original vocalization and meaning. On the second option, 𝔐 intentionally veiled the text's original vocalization—but not its meaning—to avoid the implication that God asked Ahaz to disobey the command from Deut 18:9–14. In either case, the Three preserve the original reading of proto-𝔐 "to Sheol." 𝔐 probably modified the vocalization and the meaning resulting in the imperative "ask," but it is possible that 𝔐 only modified the vocalization and preserved the same meaning as clearly shown in the Three.

2.4.2 Latin Vulgate [𝔙]

Around AD 391, Jerome began translating the Old Testament from Hebrew into Latin and appears to have completed the project by around AD 405.[75] Although his edition became called the "Vulgate" in the sixteenth century, Jerome referred to it as *iuxta Hebraicum* "according to the Hebrew" to distinguish it from previous Latin translations of the Old Testament. Before Jerome's Vulgate, there was the *Vetus Latina* (VL) "Old Latin," which was a translation of the Greek Septuagint, and Jerome's own Latin translations of the hexaplaric editions of Psalms (called the Gallican Psalter), Job, Song of Songs, Proverbs, and 1–2 Chronicles in the late 380s.

Jerome's Vulgate generally reflects a Hebrew *Vorlage* identical with proto-𝔐. That is, it does not yield many textual variants to 𝔐. Furthermore, Jerome's more functional translation approach (i.e., "sense for sense") and inconsistent translation equivalents creates challenges for reconstructing his Hebrew parent text with certainty. But sometimes, 𝔙 does contain variants to 𝔐. At Jer 10:18, 𝔐 has לְמַעַן יִמְצָאוּ "that they might find," while 𝔙's *ut inveniantur* "that they might be discovered" probably reflects the Niphal יִמָּצְאוּ "that they might be found."

We should consider linguistic differences between Hebrew and Latin when using the Vulgate for textual criticism. At Isa 11:4, in the second instance of אֶרֶץ "land," 1QIsaᵃ has הארץ "the land" while 𝔐 has אֶרֶץ "land." 𝔙 has *terram* "land," but since Latin does not contain a definite article, one cannot use the Vulgate as a witness to the presence or absence of the Hebrew article here.

Occasionally, Jerome used Aquila and Symmachus to aid him with difficult Hebrew terms and expressions, but it is not always straightforward to discern when he relies on a reviser or is only reading the same Hebrew text. Certainly, at Ezek 1:14,

---

[73] *CTAT* 2:46. See Gen 37:35 (pause); 42:38 (pause); 44:29 (pause), 31 (pause); Num 16:30 (pause), 33 (pause); Ezek 31:15, 16, 17; Ps 9:18 (pause) for שְׁאֹ(וֹ)לָה in 𝔐, whether in pause or not.

[74] Hugh G. M. Williamson, *Isaiah 6–12: A Critical and Exegetical Commentary* (New York: Bloomsbury, 2018), 138.

[75] Michael Graves, "Vulgate," in *THB* 1A:279.

he tells the reader that he had הַבְּזָק (a *hapax* in the Hebrew Bible) in his Hebrew text and he relied on Symmachus's version (ἀκτῖνος ἀστραπῆς "flashing lightning") for his own rendering: *fulguris corscantis* "flashing lightning."[76]

2.4.3 Syriac Peshitta [𝕾]

The title "Peshitta" refers to the "common" Syriac translation of the Hebrew and probably received its name to distinguish it from the so-called Syro-Hexapla (see §2.4.1.4). The origins of 𝕾 are largely unknown. In order to account for what appears to be both Jewish and Christian elements within the translation, most scholars think that the translators were Jewish but at some time converted to Christianity in Edessa around the middle of the second century AD.[77]

𝕾 translates and attests primarily to the Hebrew text of proto-𝔐 from the middle of second century AD. Since the translators were probably more interested in exegesis of the Hebrew, one needs to be cautious when using it for textual criticism. Furthermore, 𝕾 and 𝕲 agree against 𝔐 occasionally. This agreement occurs due to several factors: (1) 𝕾 and 𝕲 had the same Hebrew text that differed from 𝔐; (2) 𝕾 and 𝕲 have the same translation coincidentally due to contextual factors (i.e., polygenesis); (3) 𝕾 and 𝕲 agree due to a common exegetical tradition or shared interpretation with other ancient versions; and (4) 𝕾 depends on 𝕲 sporadically and unsystematically.[78] For example, 𝕾's reading in Eccl 5:5(6) *wl ʾ t ʾmr qdm ʾlh ʾ* "and do not say before God" agrees with 𝕲's καὶ μὴ εἴπης πρὸ προσώπου τοῦ θεοῦ "and do not say before God" against 𝔐's וְאַל־תֹּאמַר לִפְנֵי הַמַּלְאָךְ "and do not say before the messenger/angel." The other versions agree with 𝔐 showing that 𝕾's exegesis depends on 𝕲 or other contextual factors.[79]

Sometimes 𝕾 preserves a variant to 𝔐. In Ezek 27:16, 𝕾 (ʾdwm "Edom") reads "Edom" (אֱדֹם), while 𝔐 has אֲרָם "Aram." Moreover, α′ (Ἐδώμ "Edom") supports 𝕾, while θ′ and σ′ (Συρία "Syria"), 𝔙 (*Syrus* "Syria"), and 𝕮 (אֲרָם "Aram") support 𝔐. 𝕲 (ἀνθρώπους "humans") supports the consonantal text אדם but reads it as "humanity" (Tiberian אָדָם). This is a complex case where a certain decision is not possible either way. The error arose due to the graphemic similarity of the ר and ד, and both readings have strong testimony.[80]

At times, researchers are more confident that 𝕾 preserves the more original reading than 𝔐. In Isa 1:12, 𝕾 (*lmḥzʾ* "to see [my face]") reads proto-𝔐's consonantal

---

[76] Barthélemy, *Studies*, 548–49.

[77] Ignacio Carbajosa, "Peshitta," in *THB* 1A:263–66.

[78] Michael P. Weitzman, "Peshitta, Septuagint, and Targum," in *VI Symposium Syriacum 1992: University of Cambridge, Faculty of Divinity, 30 August–2 September 1992*, ed. René Lavenant (Rome: Pontifical Biblical Institute, 1994), 51–84.

[79] John D. Meade, "The Relationship of Peshitta Qoheleth to Greek Ecclesiastes," in *Like Nails Firmly Fixed (Qoh 12:11): Essays on the Text and Language of the Hebrew and Greek Scriptures, Presented to Peter J. Gentry on the Occasion of His Retirement*, ed. Phillip S. Marshall, John D. Meade, and Jonathan Kiel, CBET 115 (Leuven: Peeters, 2023), 360.

[80] *CTAT*, 2:228 reports a split decision between the readings, with three committee members assigning a C rating to each of the readings.

text לִרְאוֹת as the Qal infinitive construct "to see" (Tiberian לִרְאוֹת), while 𝔐 and the rest of the versions read "to appear [before me]" (Tiberian לֵרָאוֹת).[81] Textual critics have concluded that 𝔖 in Isa 1:12 preserves the original vocalization of the same consonantal text, while 𝔐 and the rest of the versions have facilitated this reading to avoid the theological difficulty of a person seeing the face of God (cf. Exod 33:20), an expression which originally meant "to visit the temple (e.g., Exod 23:17)."[82]

2.4.4 Aramaic Targums [𝔗]

The term, "targum," means "translation," and in our context, it refers to a wide corpus of Aramaic translations, chiefly of the Hebrew Scriptures. Three types of texts have been categorized as Targums, or Targumim: (1) the Aramaic translations of the Hebrew Scriptures of proto-𝔐 dated from the early centuries AD to the early Middle Ages; (2) the fragmentary remains of the Aramaic translations of biblical books of Leviticus and Job found at Qumran (4QtgLev; 4QtgJob; 11QtgJob); (3) Aramaic translations of the Samaritan Pentateuch known as the Samaritan Targum.[83]

The *Sitz im Leben* of targum literature is debated with the main options being either the synagogue or the school, also known as the Bet Midrash ("house of learning"). The former option emphasizes the reading of the targumim after the reading of the Hebrew text in the synagogue, while the latter sees a written origin for the targumim in schools.[84]

2.5 THE USE OF ANCIENT VERSIONS IN TEXTUAL CRITICISM[85]

As the above has shown, one's skill in textual criticism of the Hebrew Bible depends in large measure on one's ability to engage the Ancient Versions, especially the Old Greek translations. Although we addressed the following points above in passing, we need to consider them systematically so we can use the Ancient Versions intelligently for textual criticism.

First, one must recognize the nature and limitations of the target language in contrast to those of the source language. That is, languages employ different codes of communication that do not often overlap in their surface structures, but this

---

[81] It is unusual but not unattested in Biblical Hebrew (cf. לַעֲנֹת "to bend" in Exod 10:3) for the ה of the *Niphal* INF CSTR to be syncopated. But in only three of nine cases of the *Niphal* INF CSTR of רָאָה + PREP do we observe the syncopation. In Exod 34:24 (אֶת־פְּנֵי יְהוָה אֱלֹהֶיךָ); Deut 31:11 (אֶת־ פְּנֵי יְהוָה אֱלֹהֶיךָ); and here, the face of God is the direct object. In all three cases, 𝔊 (ὀφθῆναι "to appear") already read the consonantal text as *Niphal* in an attempt to facilitate the theological difficulty of seeing the "face of God," even if that expression only originally meant "to visit the shrine."

[82] *CTAT*, 2:5; de Waard, *Handbook on Isaiah*, 5; Hendel and Joosten, *Hebrew Bible*, 49.

[83] Beate Ego, "Targumim," in *THB* 1A:239–41.

[84] For a synthesis of these views, see Ego, "Targumim," *THB* 1A:250–51.

[85] John W. Wevers, "The Use of Versions for Text Criticism: The Septuagint," in *La Septuaginta en la investigacion contemporanea (V Congreso de la IOSCS)*, ed. Natalio Fernández Marcos (Madrid: CSIC, 1985), 15–24; Gentry, "Text of the Old Testament," 26–30.

reality does not render useless the Ancient Versions in textual criticism. One needs to be acquainted with the different codes to use an Ancient Version intelligently. For example, Latin's code does not have the definite article, and therefore one cannot appeal to the absence of the article in the Latin Vulgate to make a determination of whether Jerome's Hebrew source had the article or not. Likewise, Greek nouns are inflected for gender, number, and case. Hebrew does not encode nouns grammatically in the same way as Greek, especially regarding the case of a noun. When a Greek translator came to עַל הַמִּזְבֵּחַ "on the altar," he would probably use ἐπί, but he must choose the object's case: τῷ θυσιαστηρίῳ, τοῦ θυσιαστηρίου, or τὸ θυσιαστήριον.

Second, one must use the original translation for textual criticism, not inner-transmissional corruptions or revisions of the Version. At Eccl 1:17, the Hebrew and Rahlfs's 𝕲 edition of the Greek text have:

𝔐	RAHLFS' 𝕲
וָאֶתְּנָה לִבִּי לָדַעַת חָכְמָה וְדַעַת הוֹלֵלוֹת וְשִׂכְלוּת	καὶ ἔδωκα καρδίαν μου τοῦ γνῶναι σοφίαν καὶ γνῶσιν, **παραβολὰς** καὶ ἐπιστήμην
And I set my heart to know wisdom and knowledge, **madness** and folly	And I gave my heart to know wisdom and knowledge, **parables** and understanding

𝕲 appears to have a different and interpretive rendering of its Hebrew source. However, Peter Gentry's *Ecclesiastes* reads παραφοράς "derangements."[86] Thus, παραφοράς "derangements" is the original text, and παραβολάς "parables" resulted from an early copyist mistake, which made its way into most witnesses. Thus, the textual critic will use the original version παραφοράς not the early inner-Greek corruption παραβολάς in analysis of this problem.[87]

Third, one must be acquainted with the diverse translation approaches contained in 𝕲 (see §2.4.1.2).

Fourth, sometimes Greek translators had an ancient consonantal text in front of them but supplied meanings from postbiblical Hebrew and Aramaic (see §2.4.1.3.1). Thus, the translation is based on the consonantal text of proto-𝔐 and the divergence is due to Aramaic interference or influence.

Becoming acquainted with the major witnesses to the text of the Hebrew Bible is the first step to gaining competency in Hebrew Bible textual criticism. We have observed several examples of scribal modifications (both intentional and unintentional) that appear in Hebrew manuscripts and the Ancient Versions. Only continued reading and probing of these sources will continue to grant confidence

---

[86] Gentry's apparatus has: παραφοράς 788^sup lin = Gord. 1937; περιφοραν Gra.; παραβολην *k* Sa¹ Fa1²; παραβολας rel (788* Geo = 𝔖): cf 2:12b 7:25d.

[87] John D. Meade and Peter J. Gentry, "Evaluating Evaluations: The Commentary of *BHQ* and the Problem of הוֹלֵלוֹת in Ecclesiastes 1:17," in *Sophia-Paideia: Sapienza e Educazione (Sir 1,27): Miscellanea di studi offerti in onore del prof. Don Mario Cimosa*, ed. G. Bonney and R. Vicent (Rome: Libreria Ateneo Salesiano, 2012), 197–217.

in this challenging area of the exegetical process. Furthermore, one must be aware of the challenges in using a translation for determining whether a version supports a Hebrew reading or constitutes a variant.

The interpreter of Scripture must engage the challenging exegetical task of retrieving the text. Christians have widely recognized that their Scriptures were divinely inspired, but at times later scribes miscopied them and their manuscripts contained mistakes. Thus, Christian philologists like Origen of Alexandria corrected mistakes in the copies of the Scriptures (cf. *Commentarium in evangelium Matthaei* 15.14). Although modern textual criticism is complicated, its aims are no different: to correct mistakes and later scribal interventions in order to restore the original text. The student should continue to hone the skill of textual criticism to better interpret the text of the Scriptures. Having now surveyed and described the most salient ancient sources for Hebrew Bible textual criticism, we will build on this foundation when we come to the guided example later in this book. In the "Guided Lesson א: Textual Criticism," students will learn a method for how to go about solving the various textual problems encountered in the text and will see a guided example.

//

PART B

//

PART B

///////////////

CHAPTER 3

THE VERBAL SYSTEM

The Hebrew verbal system poses several daunting challenges for beginning readers. The verb morphology can be quite complex. Even after mastering all the forms of the stems and various weak roots, one still faces the complexities of verbal semantics and syntax. In most cases a direct link exists between a verb's morphology and its semantic meanings or syntactical functions (morphosyntax). Yet, determining connotative meaning requires attention to the pragmatic details of the clause and larger discourse context. The major morphosyntactic and semantic features of the Hebrew verbal system are reviewed below. The various stems and conjugations are discussed in the following chapters.

3.1 GOING DEEPER WITH HEBREW VERBS

The casuistic law of the goring ox in Exod 21:28–30 offers an interesting array of verbal constructions illustrating grammatical voice, fientivity/stativity, causality, and more. This passage raises several significant interpretative issues involving the sanctity of human life and the gradations of culpability in situations involving manslaughter.[1]

---

[1] For more on biblical casuistic laws, see Roy E. Gane, *Old Testament Law for Christians: Original Context and Enduring Application* (Grand Rapids: Baker Academic, 2017), 89–92; William S. Morrow, *An Introduction to Biblical Law* (Grand Rapids: Eerdmans, 2017), 74; Raymond Westbrook and Bruce Wells, *Everyday Law in Biblical Israel: An Introduction* (Louisville: Westminster John Knox, 2009), 24–25.

Exod 21:28–29

וְכִי־יִגַּח שׁוֹר אֶת־אִישׁ אוֹ אֶת־אִשָּׁה וָמֵת סָקוֹל יִסָּקֵל הַשּׁוֹר וְלֹא יֵאָכֵל אֶת־בְּשָׂרוֹ
וּבַעַל הַשּׁוֹר נָקִי: וְאִם שׁוֹר נַגָּח הוּא מִתְּמֹל שִׁלְשֹׁם וְהוּעַד בִּבְעָלָיו וְלֹא יִשְׁמְרֶנּוּ
וְהֵמִית אִישׁ אוֹ אִשָּׁה הַשּׁוֹר יִסָּקֵל וְגַם־בְּעָלָיו יוּמָת:

If an ox **gores** a man or woman and [that person] **dies**, the ox **must be stoned** to death, but its flesh **should** not **be eaten**. The owner of the ox, however, is innocent. But if the ox is in the habit of goring—and its owner **is warned** and **does** not **safeguard** it—and it **kills** a man or woman, the ox **must be stoned**, and even its owner **must be put to death**.

In the opening protasis, we find two indefinite objects accompanied by the direct object marker, which typically marks definite objects.[2] Gesenius suggests that this construction could have arisen to avoid reading a construct phrase, שׁוֹר אִישׁ "ox of a man."[3] The verb יִגַּח (√נגח) is active fientive (i.e., action) with an indefinite subject and the indefinite objects, "man or woman."

The second part of the condition clause specifies the situation in which the action of the goring ox results in someone's death. The stative verb וָמֵת "he is dead" is a 3MS form and refers to either of the indefinite objects of the previous clause, regardless of the gender of the referent: "if an ox gores a man or woman and [that person] dies." Importantly, the stipulation differentiates between death of a man and a woman, but their equality is assumed in requiring the same punishment in either case.

Several passive verbal forms occur in this passage. The Hebrew passive stems (*Niphal, Pual,* and *Hophal*) should primarily be considered <u>de-agentive</u>. That is, clauses with these verb types do not stipulate the agent. Hebrew, unlike English and Greek, does not allow for a secondary presentation of the agent in an adjunct phrase (e.g., "by the community") and may or may not move the patient to the subject position. For instance, the *Niphal* verbs of verse 28 exclude the agent from the clause. Neither the agent of the stoning (סקל) nor of the eating (אכל) is expressed. The patient more typically functions as the clause subject (Exod 21:28a), but it may instead remain in the object position with a dummy subject (Exod 21:28b):

סָקוֹל יִסָּקֵל הַשּׁוֹר וְלֹא יֵאָכֵל אֶת־בְּשָׂרוֹ

(a) The ox must be stoned, (b) but its flesh should not be eaten.

The agent of the stoning is unidentified and unspecified. The passive construction serves to place both the culpability and the responsibility on the whole community effected by the loss of human life. It also leaves open the intriguing idea that the owner himself may share in the responsibility to carry out this act of justice. Yet, in this scenario, while the owner suffers the loss of the animal and even its value as food, he is considered clear of any personal guilt (נָקִי lit. "clean").

---

[2] Peter Bekins claims that only 1 percent of object marking occurs with an indefinite NP in SBH. See *Transitivity and Object Marking in Biblical Hebrew: An Investigation of the Object Preposition* ʾet, HSS 64 (Winona Lake, IN: Eisenbrauns, 2014), 93–94.

[3] GKC §116d. Gesenius lists a few other examples of אֵת followed by an indefinite object.

The second condition outlines a situation in which an ox is in the habit of goring, but its owner, fully aware of the problem, is delinquent in securing it. The
Hophal verb וְהוּעַד is a de-agentive causative followed by a prepositional phrase
(בִּבְעָלָיו).[4] The active expression utilizes the *Hiphil* stem of the verb עוּד "advise,
counsel" as a transitive verb with the preposition marking the object, הֵעִיד בְּ-
"warn (someone)."[5] The passive construction eliminates the agent. Like the *Niphal*
verb יֵאָכֵל in verse 28, the patient remains in its syntactic position as the object of
the בְּ preposition.[6]

Active	וְהוֹעַד בִּבְעָלָיו	"he warns its owner"
Passive	וְהוּעַד בִּבְעָלָיו	"its owner is warned"

Despite being warned, should the ox owner fail to keep the animal from goring
(וְלֹא־יִשְׁמְרֶנּוּ "he does not safeguard it"), he would be responsible for the death of
a man or woman. The subject of וְהֵמִית indicates the semantic role of causer (i.e.,
the ox owner). Interpretively, his negligence in restraining his animal endangers
the lives of others. Inaction portends manslaughter. This time, however, the ox
is stoned, *and* its owner is under the sentence of death. The *Hophal* renders a
de-agentive causative: בְּעָלָיו יוּמָת "its owner is made to die."

Keeping an ox in ancient Israel carried with it a certain level of risk. Large animals are "dangerous and unpredictable."[7] Though never forbidding one from having such animals, the Torah urges owners to exercise due caution in safeguarding
the life of their neighbors. Life is sacred and more valuable than possessions and
convenience. While accidental death in an unforeseen situation is certainly tragic,
an owner is not guilty of a capital crime. A habitually dangerous and unrestrained
animal is another matter entirely. Its owner risks execution on account of neglect.
This law demonstrates a commitment to protecting human life, whether male or
female. It makes allowance for tragedy, yet at the same time holds the negligent
accountable for harm done to others.

These two short verses illustrate richly the many facets of the Hebrew verbal
system. We now turn our attention to discussing both the semantic and syntactic
nuances discussed in this section.

3.2 CHAPTER OBJECTIVES

This chapter introduces the Hebrew verbal system. For most students, the morphology should be mostly review. The descriptions provide a reference for understanding

---

[4] Note that the noun בַּעַל routinely occurs with pronominal suffixes attached to the plural form
(בְּעָלָיו) in contexts where the sense is singular (i.e. בְּעָלָיו instead of בְּעָלוֹ). See BDB, 127.

[5] *DCH* 6, s.v. "עוּד," 287–88.

[6] Similarly, the direct object marker אֶת is retained in וְלֹא יֵאָכֵל אֶת־בְּשָׂרוֹ "its flesh should not be
eaten" (v. 28). Hypothetically, the non-de-agentive construction is: וְלֹא יֹאכַל אֶת־בְּשָׂרוֹ "one may not
eat its flesh."

[7] See William H. C. Propp, *Exodus 19–40*, AB 2A (New York: Doubleday, 2006), 232–33.

the main categories of verbal meaning and usage. The sections describe semantic roles and semantic situations including voice, dynamism, completion, causation, and plurality. Finally, we outline the contours of the *Qal* and *Qal* passive stems.

3.3 INTRODUCTION

The verb serves as the semantic and syntactic nerve center of the <u>clause</u>. It organizes other elements around it into units of meaning. On the most basic semantic level, a verb describes something about the <u>subject</u>. It expresses an action, event, or state. The <u>object</u> is the clause element entailed by the verb. Verbs indicate the expected semantic roles of the clause <u>constituents</u> as distinct from the relationships among other nonessential <u>adjuncts</u>, like adverbs and prepositional phrases. Further, the different verb inflections convey a large amount of semantic information about the action itself.

3.4 VERB MORPHOLOGY

The basic verb morphology includes the root, person, number, and gender. The connections between form and meaning are identified using these properties. For example, the verb כָּתַבְתִּי "I wrote" has a consonantal <u>root</u> structure כתב (see §3.4.1). The root provides basic semantic information about the verbal action, in this case "inscribing symbols to represent language." Other morphological components specify elements of the verbal semantics and syntax. The suffix -תִּי designates the <u>person</u>, <u>gender</u>, and <u>number</u> of the subject (§3.4.2). The conjugation additionally indicates the <u>tense</u>, <u>aspect</u>, and <u>modality</u> (chapters 5 and 6). The vowels ◌ְ◌ and consonant pattern designate the verb's *Aktionsart* (§3.6), including <u>voice</u> (§3.6.1), <u>stative</u> properties (§3.6.2), <u>transitivity</u> and <u>valency</u> (§3.6.3), <u>causation</u> (§3.6.4), and plurality (§3.6.5). These elements indicate that the action necessitates the other components of a <u>clause</u> (see Guided Lesson ג). Putting these properties together is further complicated by contextual and syntactical factors that may augment or even reverse the "standard" meaning of the morphological features. These categories of form and meaning combine to help the reader understand the semantics of the verb.

3.4.1 Verbal Roots

Hebrew verb morphology is principally built on the combination of (1) a root structure; (2) a framework (or pattern) of vowels and consonants (including elongation or doubling of root letters); and (3) <u>affixes</u> (namely prefixes, suffixes, and infixes). The root structure (שׁוֹרֶשׁ "root") provides the basic semantic core of the action.[8] For example, the abstracted root כתב designates a wide range of activities involving the act of "writing" or "inscribing," that is, marking characters to represent language. The vocalic and consonantal pattern and other combining elements (i.e., affixes) can change the voice (נִכְתַּב "was written"), transitivity (כָּתַב עַל "wrote on"), modality (אֶכְתְּבָה "let me write"), and causality (יַכְתִּיב "cause to write"), but the action, at its core, is still centered on the notion of "inscribing." Words other than verbs can also be construed around the root structure using different patterns and affixes: כְּתָב "document"; כְּתֹבֶת "tattoo"; and מִכְתָּב "script, text" (see chapter 7).

ROOT NOMENCLATURE

Most Semitic roots are structured on three consonants. A regular or <u>strong verb</u> is defined as having three non-weak root consonants, or radicals. A verb with three root consonants is called a <u>triradical</u> or <u>triliteral</u> root. The <u>radicals</u> are often described as R1, R2, and R3. For the root כתב, the first letter כ is R1, ת R2, and ב R3. Some notate these root letters as I-כ, II-ת, and III-ב (read: first-*kap*, second-*taw*, and third-*bet*, respectively). Based on the Semitic root פָּעַל "do," others use פ״ך, ע״ת, and ל״ב (read: *pe-kap*, *'ayin-taw*, and *lamed-bet*). The root may also be written √KTB with the "square-root" notation plus transliterated Latin letters. Notice that the Latin representation is ordered from left to right.

THIRD RADICAL	SECOND RADICAL	FIRST RADICAL	כתב (√KTB)
R3 *B*	R2 *T*	R1 *K*	Option 1 (Numbered)
III-ב	II-ת	I-כ	Option 2 (Roman Numerals)
ל״ב	ע״ת	פ״ך	Option 3 (פָּעַל Structure)

An irregular or <u>weak verb</u> consists of one or more weak consonants. Weak radicals are consonants that may be lost or unpronounced in certain situations. The most common include ו and י but may include א, ה, or נ. The so-called guttural consonants (א, ה, ח, and ע) and ר are sometimes considered weak roots. But these consonantal values are pronounced in Biblical Hebrew, except syllable closing *'alep*. Weak verbs are classified by similar forms and named for the weak root consonant. R1, or first-weak verbs consist of I-י (פ״י), I-ו (פ״ו), and sometimes I-נ (פ״נ) roots. R2, or second-weak verbs are called <u>hollow verbs</u> because the II-ו (ע״ו) and II-י (ע״י) often become vowels, leaving only the first and third root letters (e.g., קָם "he rose" from √QWM or the <u>lemma</u> קום). R3, or third-weak roots are often designated third-*he*, III-ה, or ל״ה verbs. The dictionary form of these verbs is

---

[8] There are more than 1,600 different verbal roots in Biblical Hebrew.

written with a final *he* (e.g., בנה "build"), but the ה should not be confused with a root letter.[9] It is instead a consonant to represent a vowel (i.e., *mater lectionis*). The third-weak consonant likely originated as either a *yod* or *waw*.

TYPES OF WEAK VERBS			
R3 WEAK[10]	R2 WEAK	R1 WEAK[11]	WEAK CONSONANT
רָמָה "throw"	שִׂים "put"	יָבֵשׁ "be dry"	י
רָבָה "increase"	קוּם "rise"	יָרֵשׁ "inherit"	ו

Certain roots with *nun* and doubled consonants look like the weak verbs in some conjugations. First-*nun* verbs are similar to first-weak roots in imperative and infinitive construct forms. The idiosyncratic roots הלך "walk" and לקח "take" also follow this patterning. Roots with identical R2 and R3 consonants (designated as geminate or ע״ע) may be confused with weak verbal forms. In particular, the geminate prefix conjugation uses similar patterning as either first-*nun* or hollow verbs.

Some roots are doubly weak. These combine features of more than one weak-verb type. Two relatively frequent roots are first-*nun* and final-weak roots: נטה "stretch out" (*Qal*) and נכה "strike" (*Hiphil*). Several more are attested less frequently.[12] Other verbs are composed of first and final-weak radicals, like ידה "praise."[13] Some roots include R2 and R3 weak roots, such as היה "be" and חיה "live."

One of the very few exceptions to the regular three consonant root structures is the verb תרגם "translate." It is one of the small number of roots with more than three consonants.[14] Four radical roots are called quadriliteral or quadriconsonantal.

---

[9] Unlike English or Greek dictionaries, Hebrew lexicons categorize most verbs according to the *Qal* perfect 3MS form. Middle-weak verbs are listed according to their infinitive construct forms (e.g. קוּם "rise"). Third-weak verbs follow the regular pattern בָּנָה "he built." The final letter of this form is not a consonant but a *matres lectionis*. A few verbs, however, do end with a consonantal *he*. One example is: גבה "be high." The *mappiq* (final dot) is used to designate the voiceless glottal fricative [h]. These roots pattern after other strong roots (e.g. גָּבַהְתָּ "you were high" rather than בָּנִיתָ "you built").

[10] These roots are only separable using comparative phonology with other Semitic languages.

[11] In Hebrew and other Northwest Semitic languages, the paradigm of verbs with R1-*waw* is identical to the R1-*yod* roots. These may only be separated by using comparative data.

[12] Others notably include: נאה "be pleasing"; נדה "put away, exclude"; נהה "lament"; נהה "stick to"; נוה "achieve"; נוה "adorn, beautify"; נזה "spatter"; נחה "lead, guide"; נחה "stand by"; נלה "destroy"; נסה "test."

[13] Others include: יאה "befit"; יגה "grieve"; יגה "remove"; ידה "cast"; ינה "oppress"; יעה "sweep together"; יפה "be beautiful"; ירה "throw."

[14] The rest are: חספס "be scale-like"; חצצר "blow"; טאטא "sweep"; כרבל "be wrapped"; כרסם "eat away"; פרשז "spread out"; רטפש "become fresh"; שמאל "go left."

3.4.2 Person, Gender, and Number

Verb affixes indicate subject-verb agreement. The presence or absence of prefixes and suffixes stipulate the relationship of the verb to the subject. The affixes indicate three grammatical categories of agreement—person, gender, and number.

Grammatical <u>person</u> refers to the distinction of the subject as the speaker (first person: "I"), the one being addressed (second person: "you"), or all other participants (third person: "he, she, it, they"). With prefix conjugations, the third-person prefixes are -י or -ת, second-person -ת, and first-person -א or -נ. For suffix conjugations, the third-person suffixes are ∅-, הָ֯-, or וּ-, second-person ת-, תֶּם-, or תֶּן-, and first-person are תִּי- or נוּ-.

VERB-PERSON AGREEMENT AFFIXES					
SUFFIX CONJUGATION				PREFIX CONJUGATION	
Plural	Singular	Person		Plural	Singular
וּ- "they"	∅- "he" הָ֯- "she"	3		-י "they (M)" -ת "they (F)"	-י "he" -ת "she"
תֶּם- "you (M)" תֶּן- "you (F)"	תָּ- "you (M)" תְּ- "you (F)"	2		-ת "you"	-ת "you"
נוּ- "we"	תִּי- "I"	1		-נ "we"	-א "I"

Grammatical <u>gender</u> refers to the categorization of nouns into distinct classes. Hebrew uses a binary designation of nouns as either masculine or feminine (see chapter 7). The verbal forms correspond to the gender of the subject. Typically, <u>unmarked</u> forms are used for <u>masculine</u> entities and <u>marked</u> forms for <u>feminine</u>. The morphological difference between the genders of the verb suffixes consists of the alternation of a vowel, ∅- "he" or הָ֯- "she" and תָּ- "you (MS)" or תְּ- "you (FS)," or a consonant change, תֶּם- "you (MP)" or תֶּן- "you (FP)." The prefix conjugation differentiates the masculine and feminine forms based on the prefixed consonant, -י "he" or -ת "she," the suffix, ∅- "you (MS)" or י֯- "you (FS)," and וּ- "you (MP)" or נָה- "you (FP)," or a combination of both. Some verbs have a <u>common</u> form without a formal distinction for grammatical gender. The common forms include all first-person forms and the third-person plural suffix conjugation.

QAL PREFIX AND SUFFIX CONJUGATIONS			
SUFFIX CONJUGATION		PREFIX CONJUGATION	
כָּתְבוּ "they (C) wrote"	כָּתַב "he wrote" כָּתְבָה "she wrote"	יִכְתְּבוּ "they (M) write" תִּכְתֹּבְנָה "they (F) write"	יִכְתֹּב "he writes" תִּכְתֹּב "she writes"

QAL PREFIX AND SUFFIX CONJUGATIONS			
SUFFIX CONJUGATION		PREFIX CONJUGATION	
כְּתַבְתֶּם	כָּתַ֫בְתָּ	תִּכְתְּבוּ	תִּכְתֹּב
"you (MP) wrote"	"you (MS) wrote"	"you (MP) write"	"you (MS) write"
כְּתַבְתֶּן	כָּתַבְתְּ	תִּכְתֹּ֫בְנָה	תִּכְתְּבִי
"you (FP) wrote"	"you (FS) wrote"	"you (FP) write"	"you (FS) write"
כָּתַ֫בְנוּ "we wrote"	כָּתַ֫בְתִּי "I wrote"	נִכְתֹּב "we write"	אֶכְתֹּב "I write"

Grammatical <u>number</u> distinguishes entities that are viewed as either singular (*he/she/it*) or plural (*they*). This difference generally matches the nominal morphology.[15] Where a dual noun is the subject, the Hebrew verb uses plural number agreement. In the PC, only the first-person forms differentiate between the singular -אָ "I" and plural -נ "we," using consonant prefixes. All the other forms are distinguished using dissimilar suffixes: Ø-/יִ-/הִ- (S) or ו-/נָה- (P) and תְ-/תָ- (S) or תֶם-/תֶן- (P).

When the subject is provided in a clause, the verb agrees in person, gender, and number. Unlike most English clauses, the subject is not required to be stated explicitly but may be implied. Examples of both explicit and implicit subjects are found at Gen 12:5. In the first clause, the first third-person masculine singular verb וַיִּקַּח "(he) took" indicates that Abram is the subject.[16] The following clause does not express an overt subject. Rather the third-person masculine plural verb וַיֵּצְאוּ "they left" designates the subject as Abram, Sarai (see below for the issue of gender agreement), and Lot, who were named in the previous clause. English requires the word *they*, even though the Hebrew clause does not include an independent subject pronoun.

Gen 12:5

וַיִּקַּח אַבְרָם אֶת־שָׂרַי אִשְׁתּוֹ וְאֶת־לוֹט בֶּן־אָחִיו . . . וַיֵּצְאוּ לָלֶ֫כֶת אַ֫רְצָה כְּנַ֫עַן

Abram took Sarai his wife and Lot his nephew . . . **They left** to go to the land of Canaan.

The lack of an explicit subject, at times, causes confusion regarding who (<u>subject</u>) is doing what (<u>verb</u>) to whom (<u>object</u>). Two examples from Gen 14:18–20 demonstrate potentially confusing or ambiguous situations.

---

[15] An exception to this situation occurs with nouns that are morphologically singular but refer to a plurality. These nouns are called <u>collectives</u>. An English example is the word *deer*. E.g., *the deer is trampling the garden* or *the deer are gathering in the field*. See further chapter 7.

[16] The verb לקח "take" is irregular, functioning like a I-*nun* root.

Gen 14:18–20

וּמַלְכִּי־צֶדֶק מֶלֶךְ שָׁלֵם הוֹצִיא לֶחֶם וָיָיִן וְהוּא כֹהֵן לְאֵל עֶלְיוֹן: וַיְבָרְכֵהוּ וַיֹּאמַר בָּרוּךְ אַבְרָם לְאֵל עֶלְיוֹן קֹנֵה שָׁמַיִם וָאָרֶץ: וּבָרוּךְ אֵל עֶלְיוֹן אֲשֶׁר־מִגֵּן צָרֶיךָ בְּיָדֶךָ וַיִּתֶּן־לוֹ מַעֲשֵׂר מִכֹּל:

Melchizedek, king of Salem, brought out bread and wine. (He was a priest of El Elyon.) **He blessed him** and said: "Blessed be Abram by El Elyon, Creator of heaven and earth. And blessed be El Elyon who gave your enemies into your hand." **He gave him** a tenth from everything.

In verses 18–19, a new character, Melchizedek, is introduced in the ongoing Abram saga. He gives food to Abram (v. 18a) and is called a priest (v. 18b). The following verse reads: וַיְבָרְכֵהוּ וַיֹּאמַר "he blessed him and said" (v. 19). The verb forms do not indicate who blesses whom. Both Abram and Melchizedek could be the referents of either the 3MS verb or the 3MS object suffix. As an independent clause, either option is possible: "Abram blessed Melchizedek," or "Melchizedek blessed Abram." How does one decide? Grammar and exegesis, of course! The following guideline helps provide a solution: *The actor in the preceding clause will typically continue to be the subject until another actor is designated (topic shift), or the broader context requires otherwise.* Melchizedek is the subject of the last verb in verse 18 (הוֹצִיא "he brought out"), so the expectation is that he remains the subject in verse 19. The same actor pronounces, "Blessed be Abram," in verse 19 and specifies צָרֶיךָ "your enemies" and יָדֶךָ "your hand" in verse 20. Also, it would be exceedingly odd for Abram to bless himself in the hearing of another. Further the context clarifies that Abram is the one who defeated his enemies (vv. 14–17).

In the latter part of verse 20, another clause contains a 3MS verb (נתן "give") and a 3MS pronominal suffix. Applying the same guideline to this verse, one might expect that Melchizedek gave Abram the tithe, since he was the actor in the preceding clauses. However, most translations and the book of Hebrews indicate otherwise.[17] The contextual key is to determine what is being given (object)—this indicates who the subject is. Is the text saying that Melchizedek gave Abram a tenth of the bread and wine or possibly a tenth of his kingdom? Or is the gift a tenth of the booty that Abram just acquired in verse sixteen and becomes a source of a debate with the king of Sodom in the following verses (vv. 21–24)? It seems clear that the latter situation is intended.

Some exceptions can lead to disagreements in the person, gender, and number between a verb and its subject. A single actor can serve as a representative of an entire group. In such cases, the verb may designate a primary actor even when others are included in the verbal action. In Gen 12:10, Abram and Sarai travel to Egypt (see vv. 11–13), but Abram alone is the subject of the 3MS verb (ירד "go down").

---

[17] The LXX text—καὶ ἔδωκεν αὐτῷ δεκάτην ἀπὸ πάντων—follows the Hebrew in not designating a specific subject. According to the discussion of Melchizedek in Heb 7:4, however, the author says: "Now consider how great this man was—even Abraham the patriarch gave a tenth of the plunder to him."

The narrator indicates the principal status of Abram in this action and the broader story. Abram is <u>topicalized</u>. He is the one who goes down to Egypt trusting in his own craftiness to protect himself at the expense of his wife Sarai instead of hoping in the promise of God (17:16).

Gen 12:10

וַיֵּרֶד אַבְרָם מִצְרַיְמָה לָגוּר שָׁם כִּי־כָבֵד הָרָעָב בָּאָרֶץ׃

Abram went down to Egypt to sojourn there because the famine in the land [of Canaan] was severe.

On some occasions when a primary actor is in view, the secondary actors can be identified in a subsequent phrase. One such example is in Gen 13:1. Abram is the lone subject of the 3MS verb (עלה "go up"). Those accompanying him are enumerated at the end of the clause, הוּא וְאִשְׁתּוֹ וְכָל־אֲשֶׁר־לוֹ וְלוֹט עִמּוֹ "he, his wife, all his possessions, and Lot with him." Abram is the primary actor in the sojourn from Egypt, but others who are important for the narrative are specified with the secondary structure.

Gen 13:1

וַיַּעַל אַבְרָם מִמִּצְרַיִם הוּא וְאִשְׁתּוֹ וְכָל־אֲשֶׁר־לוֹ וְלוֹט עִמּוֹ הַנֶּגְבָּה׃

Abram went up from Egypt to the Negev—**he, his wife, all their possessions, and Lot** with him.

For subjects including feminine and masculine referents, the default gender is the unmarked (masculine) plural verb form. This agreement holds regardless of the proportion of the feminine to masculine entities. In other words, even if the subject is a mixed group of women and only one man, the masculine plural verbal form is used. The second clause of Gen 12:5 provides an example. Abram, Lot, and Sarai are the subjects of the third-person masculine plural verb.

Gen 12:5

וַיִּקַּח אַבְרָם אֶת־שָׂרַי אִשְׁתּוֹ וְאֶת־לוֹט בֶּן־אָחִיו . . . וַיֵּצְאוּ לָלֶכֶת אַרְצָה כְּנַעַן

Abram took Sarai his wife and Lot his nephew . . . **They (MP) left** to go to the land of Canaan.

3.5 SEMANTIC ROLES

<u>Semantic roles</u> (or <u>thematic relations</u>) indicate the ways in which the clause participants are involved with an action or event. These semantic relations may be contrasted with the grammatical relations of the clause constituents and adjuncts, as discussed in the previous section. The following semantic roles are only the most common. The doer, initiator, or direct cause of the action or event is the <u>agent</u>. Some differentiate further animate agents from inanimate ones (e.g., <u>force</u> or <u>instrument</u>). The target, affected thing/person, or goal is the <u>patient</u>. A <u>causer</u>

brings about or prompts an action or event carried out by an agent (<u>causee</u>). The patient undergoing the effect of the action is the <u>experiencer</u> (traditionally <u>dative</u>). Several other semantic roles may additionally be designated to label the result, goal, source, manner, or purpose of an action. The section discussing grammatical voice (§3.6.1) explains how these semantic roles correspond to the constituents of a clause, such as the subject and object among others.

PRIMARY SEMANTIC ROLES		
ROLE	DEFINITION	EXAMPLE
Agent	the doer, initiator, or direct cause of the action or event	*The **officials** gave a decree.* Agent: *officials*
Patient	the target, affected thing/person, or goal of the action or event	*The officials gave a **decree**.* Patient: *decree*
Experiencer	the patient undergoing the effect of the action or event	*The officials gave a decree to the **people**.* Experiencer: *people*
Causer	the instigator who brings about an action or event	*The **queen** caused the officials to give a decree to the people.* Causer: *queen*

3.6 TYPES OF SEMANTIC SITUATIONS

The semantic categories of verbs may be further differentiated by referential events or <u>semantic situations</u>. These properties include grammatical voice, fientivity, transitivity, plurality, distributivity, causativity, and others. Several of these semantic situations are associated with what grammarians call *Aktionsart*, or situation aspect.[18] In

---

[18] Stuart Creason describes *Aktionsart* as "the properties by which situations may be distinguished from each other" ("Semantic Classes of Verbs: A Study of Aktionsart in the Hebrew Verbal System," [PhD diss., The University of Chicago, 1995], 5). See further the classic study by David Dowty, *Word Meaning and Montague Grammar: The Semantics of Verbs and Times in Generative Semantics and in Montague's PTQ*, Studies in Linguistics and Philosophy 7 (Dordrecht: Kluwer, 1979).
Students (and sometimes even scholars!) may confuse this term with aspect, which most often refers to the vantage point of action (e.g., perfective and imperfective). The German term *Aktionsart* roughly translates "kind, or manner, of action" (e.g., terminative, durative, iterative, inceptive, resultative), thus adding to the confusion. Even the scholarly literature, at times, tends to conflate these two notions. Further confusion arises for students familiar with the discussion of tense/aspect in Biblical Greek. F. Blass et al., for instance, identifies the most important "kinds of action" (*Aktsionsarten*) in Greek as (1) punctiliar (momentary); (2) durative (linear or progressive); (3) iterative; (4) perfective; and (5) "perfectivizing" by means of prepositions (BDF §318). A. T. Robertson tied *Aktionsart* to the semantics of the Greek verbal stem, identifying three "kinds of action:" punctiliar, durative, and perfected. *Grammar of the Greek New Testament in the Light of Historical Research*, 3rd ed. (London: Dorian, 1919), 823, 328. David A. Black observes that the most important element of verbal tense is the "kind of action," which "is called *aspect* or *Aktionsart*," again, assuming these terms refer to roughly the same thing; see *Linguistics for Students of New Testament Greek: A Survey of Basic Concepts and Application*, 2nd ed. (Grand Rapids: Baker, 1995), 84. In this approach, features of aspect and *Aktionsart* bleed together indistinguishably. Yet, Stanley E. Porter distinguishes *Aktionsart* and verbal aspect as two historically distinct approaches to the Greek verbal system, which, in certain ways, are mutually exclusive. See *Idioms of the Greek New Testament*, 2nd ed. (Sheffield, UK:

this grammar, we differentiate <u>viewpoint aspect</u> from <u>situation aspect</u>.[19] Carl Bache classifies the difference as follows:

> Aktionsart concerns the procedural characteristics (i.e., the "phrasal structure," "time extension" and "manner of development") ascribed to any given situation referred to by a verb phrase whereas aspect reflects the situational focus with which a situation is represented.[20]

For our purposes, viewpoint aspect, or merely <u>aspect</u>, describes the speaker's or author's portrayal of a verbal action as, for instance, perfective or imperfective (see chapter 5).[21] Situation aspect refers to a range of semantic characteristics involved in a verbal action excluding traditional notions of TAM (tense-aspect-mood).

In a similar vein, Waltke and O'Connor define *Aktionsart* in Biblical Hebrew as "the category of morphological phenomena that describe the kind of situation a verb refers to."[22] They outline five parameters of *Aktionsart*.[23] These semantic situations correspond to five grammatical categories:

1. Grammatical Voice (active, passive, reflexive, and middle voice);
2. Dynamism (fientivity and stativity);
3. Completion (transitivity, intransitivity, ditransitivity, and ambitransitivity) and Valency;
4. Causation (causative and anticausative, resultativity and factitivity);
5. Plurality (iterative, habitual, distributive, intensive, and reciprocality).

Each of these categories is outlined in the following sections. The semantic situations combine to describe the semantic-syntactic properties of the verbal action.

Sheffield Academic, 1994), 27–29; see also his detailed survey of the issue in *Verbal Aspect in the Greek of the New Testament, with Reference to Tense and Mood*, Studies in Biblical Greek (New York: Lang, 1989), 17– 65.

The broader literature on the question of verbal aspect, however, seems to focus on the relationship between the grammatical/syntactical categories associated with the terms *Aktionsart* and aspect, even if the terms themselves are altered or abandoned. See Bernard Comrie, *Aspect: An Introduction to the Study of Verbal Aspect and Related Problems*, Cambridge Textbooks in Linguistics (Cambridge: Cambridge University Press, 1976), 6–7 n. 4. For Comrie, the concept of *Aktionsart* has been renamed "inherent meaning" (41–51). Others have noted the confusion in the literature resulting from the inconsistent use of these terms; see John A. Cook, *Time and the Biblical Hebrew Verb: The Expression of Tense, Aspect, and Modality in Biblical Hebrew*, LSAWS 7 (Winona Lake, IN: Eisenbrauns, 2012), 18–19.

[19] See the overview in Hana Filip, "Aspectual Class and Aktionsart," in *Semantics: An International Handbook of Natural Language Meaning*, ed. Claudia Maienborn, Klaus von Heusinger, and Paul Portner (Berlin: de Gruyter, 2011), 1186–217.

[20] Carl Bache, "Aspect and Aktionsart: Towards a Semantic Distinction," *Journal of Linguistics* 18 (1982): 70.

[21] For a fuller treatment of verbal aspect, see §7.10.3.

[22] *IBHS* §20.2j.

[23] Waltke and O'Connor (*IBHS* §20.2o) summarize the five parameters as (1) "voice: active passive middle"; (2) "type of movement/activity: fientive stative"; (3) "contour of movement/activity: transitive intransitive"; (4) "causation: causative resultative/factitive declarative"; and (5) "double-status action: reflexive reciprocal tolerative."

And they are helpful in explaining the correlations among the different Hebrew stems (see chapter 4).

3.6.1 Grammatical Voice

Voice (or diathesis) describes the relationship of the agent and patient to the verb in a clause. It links these semantic roles with the syntactic functions of the clause constituents (i.e., subject and object).[24] Alternating the grammatical voice of a verb signals that the main clause constituents participate in the action in different ways. The principal verb alternations produce binary oppositions of active (agentive) and passive (de-agentive), reflexive and middle, and causative and anticausative.

In accusative languages, like English and Biblical Hebrew, the basic voice is the active voice. The active voice designates that the semantic role of the agent is the subject of the verbal action. The agentive subject is the doer of the action or the one who acts on others. For transitive verbs, the patient is effected by the action and is a complement (object). With the clause, *the student closes the door*, the agent (*the student*) does the action (*closes*), whereas the patient is the target constituent, receiving the verbal action (i.e., *the door*).

ACTIVE VOICE			
SEMANTIC ROLE	AGENT	ACTION	PATIENT
EXAMPLE	*The student*	*closes*	*the door*
SYNTACTIC FUNCTION	Subject	Verb	Object

The active-passive voice alternation interchanges the syntactic subject between the agent and the patient. The passive voice eliminates the agent and typically designates the patient as the syntactic role of the subject. The English passive is signaled with an auxiliary (*be*) and the past participle (*closed*). The agent may be deleted entirely from the clause or included as an adjunct (i.e., an adjunct, *by the student*). Unlike English, the passive constructions in most Semitic languages do not specify the agent of the verbal action as a clause participant.

PASSIVE VOICE			
SEMANTIC ROLE	PATIENT	ACTION	AGENT
EXAMPLE	*The door*	*is closed*	*by the student*
SYNTACTIC FUNCTION	Subject	Verb	Prepositional Phrase

---

[24] The morphosyntactic property of voice serves as a type of "mechanism" that selects a "prominent syntactic constituent . . . from the underlying semantic functions (case or thematic roles) of a clause." See Maysayoshi Shibatani, *Passive and Voice*, Typological Studies in Language 16 (Amsterdam: Benjamins, 1998), 3. Most languages have a basic voice strategy that can be augmented secondarily to change the relationship of the roles and functions of the constituents.

With the reflexive voice, the agent entails a patient similar to the active voice, but the agent and patient are identical. That is to say, the subject acts upon itself or for its own benefit. English reflexives are expressed using the reflexive pronoun: *oneself, himself, herself, themselves, yourself* (e.g., *the door closes itself*).

REFLEXIVE VOICE			
SEMANTIC ROLE	AGENT	ACTION	PATIENT
EXAMPLE	*The door*	*closes*	*Itself*
SYNTACTIC FUNCTION	Subject	Verb	Pronoun

The middle voice expresses an action in which the verb involves the agent in the verbal notion. That is to say, the subject performs an action in which it also undergoes or experiences the action in some way.[25] In English, the middle takes the same form as the reflexive but is intransitive; that is, it does not take the reflexive pronoun (see below §3.6.3). Unlike the passive, the patient cannot be expressed as an adjunct. Transitivity and constituency limitations differentiate the middle from the reflexive (e.g., *The door closes* [middle]; *The door closes itself* [reflexive]) and from the passive (e.g., **The door closes by the student* [middle]; *The door is closed by the student* [passive]). Because of the related diathetic domains, some grammarians prefer to group together both the middle and passive voices under the category mediopassive.

MIDDLE VOICE			
SEMANTIC ROLE	AGENT	ACTION	PATIENT
EXAMPLE	*The door*	*closes*	Ø
SYNTACTIC FUNCTION	Subject	Verb	N/A

The final alternation concerns causative and anticausative verbs. A causative verb indicates the causer as an agentive participant of the action. Some causative verbs require a special auxiliary (e.g., *cause, get, make*; see §3.6.4). The alternation is between the clause without a causer, *the door closes*, and one with an expressed agent, *the wind closes the door*.

CAUSATIVE			
SEMANTIC ROLE	CAUSER	ACTION	PATIENT
EXAMPLE	*The wind*	*causes ___ to close*	*the door*
SYNTACTIC FUNCTION	Subject	Verb + Infinitive	Object of Auxiliary

---

[25] See the classic study of classical Greek by John Lyons, *Introduction to Theoretical Linguistics* (Cambridge: Cambridge University Press, 1969); see also Suzanne Kemmer, *The Middle Voice*, Typological Studies in Language 23 (Amsterdam: Benjamins, 1993).

Other causative verbs are lexicalized with certain transitive verbs (e.g., *cook, break, split*). These verbs do not need a special construction or auxiliary verb, but the core of the semantic notion is causer oriented. They could alternatively be construed with the auxiliary and an intransitive or stative verb as *cause to V* ₍Intransitive₎ (e.g., *split = cause to be split*).[26]

The intransitive use of causative verbs is described as anticausative. An <u>anti-causative</u> verb does not indicate the cause of the action, even though the action assumes volitional agency (i.e., a causer). These de-agentive constructions include only one argument, and it is what undergoes the action.[27] The verb *cook* includes a causer as part of its lexical semantics (e.g., *the chef cooks the soup*). The anti-causative selects the patient as the subject and eliminates the causer from the clause. In English, some anticausative verbs do not require a different form (e.g., *the soup cooks*); others employ a passive-like construction (e.g., *the soup is cooked*).

BASIC (CAUSATIVE) VERB			
SEMANTIC ROLE	CAUSER/AGENT	ACTION	PATIENT
EXAMPLE	*The chef*	*cooks*	*the soup*
SYNTACTIC FUNCTION	Subject	Verb	Object

ANTICAUSATIVE VERB			
SEMANTIC ROLE	PATIENT	ACTION	CAUSER/AGENT
EXAMPLE 1	*The soup*	*cooks*	Ø
EXAMPLE 2	*The soup*	*is cooked*	Ø
SYNTACTIC FUNCTION	Subject	Verb	N/A

3.6.2 Dynamism

Verbs can designate the situation <u>dynamism</u> as a non-static, mutable event, or as a static, immutable event. This semantic difference may be represented by the difference between the English verbs *do* (non-static or fientivity) and *be* (static or stativity).[28] <u>Fientivity</u> refers to dynamic situations (e.g., *the woman does a puzzle*). <u>Stativity</u> expresses non-dynamic states of being, describing a characteristic (e.g., *the man is heavy*), an external circumstance (e.g., *the animal dies*), or an emotional/rational status (e.g., *the child knows*).[29] Stative and fientive verbs may inversely be

---

[26] Beth Levin, *English Verb Classes and Alternations* (Chicago: University of Chicago Press, 1993).

[27] More properly, an anticausative is a type of unaccusative verb. See Beth Levin and Malka Rappaport Hovav, *Unaccusativity: At the Syntax-Lexical Semantics Interface* (Cambridge, MA: MIT Press, 1995), 79–133.

[28] Included with the idea of state (i.e., *be*) is the related notion of process (i.e., *become*).

[29] *IBHS* §22.4; Steven W. Boyd further characterizes three stative subclasses (atelic state, point state, and transitory state) and four fientive subclasses (semelfactive, activity, accomplishment, and

conceptualized as the lack of change as opposed to the change motivated by action. Bernard Comrie distinguishes these semantic characteristics by explaining that a state exists indefinitely, whereas a dynamic situation continues only with the on-going input of new energy or action.[30] As a result, stativity would be the more basic situation.

3.6.3 Completion and Valency

The semantic notion of completion, or semantic transitivity, indicates whether the endpoint of an action is identified or unidentified.[31] Completion is indicated by the presence or absence of a verbal complement. An active voice verb is complete when its patient is expressed as a complement. For example, the verb *build* is complete in the clause, *she builds the house*. A house is the *telos* or completion of the action, *build*. Verbs are considered incomplete when the patient is not present. The clause, *the student runs*, does not have an inherent endpoint, and it is considered incomplete. Completion may vary even with similar events or actions. For instance, verbs for spoken communication may indicate a complement, *he says every word*, or not, *he talks*. The same verb may, at times, represent either an incomplete or complete event (e.g., *the student runs*, or *the student runs the marathon*; *she speaks* or *she speaks every word*; and even, *he talks the talk*).

Completion corresponds to the syntactic property of transitivity. Transitivity concerns the expectation of a verb to take objects and describes the number of objects in a verb phrase, or predicate. *Transitive* verbs have at least one object. Intransitive verbs lack objects. Ditransitive verbs (e.g., *tell, give*) require two objects. Other verbs may be termed ambitransitive because they can be fashioned as either transitive or intransitive (e.g., *speak, run*). An internal object is one that is implied and need not be expressed.

Transitivity is associated with the broader syntactic concept of valency. Valency describes the number of core constituents in a clause. Constituents include the subject and the clause complements (i.e., arguments). The number of these obligatory elements is determined by the verb semantics and voice of the verb. The clause, *Now she catches adroitly the ball with her hand*, has a valency of two, counting the constituents: *she* and *the ball*. The other nonobligatory elements are called adjuncts. They include conjunctives, *now*, prepositional phrases, *with her hand*, and adverbs, *adroitly*. Adjuncts are considered optional and not counted in valency.

The grammatical voice and dynamism of the verb determine valency. Valency can vary depending on the specific verb form and construction of the clause. An

---

achievement) using the temporal features of telicity and durativity. Boyd, "The Binyamin (Verbal Stems)," in *Where Shall Wisdom Be Found? A Grammatical Tribute to Professor Stephen A. Kaufman*, ed. Hélène M. Dallaire, Benjamin J. Noonan, and Jennifer E. Noonan (Winona Lake, IN: Eisenbrauns, 2017), 91–94

[30] Comrie, *Aspect*, 49.

[31] This distinction should not be confused with imperfective or perfective grammatical aspect (i.e., completion or duration in time).

impersonal verb (e.g., *rain*) does not require any constituents and has zero valency. The clause *it rains* is <u>avalent</u>. In this instance, *it* does not express the semantic role of agent or patient but is a dummy subject. A <u>univalent</u> verb has one constituent. In English, this element must be the subject (e.g., *the student is full*). It may either be an agent (e.g., *the student runs*) or patient (e.g., *the door is closed*). <u>Bivalent</u> verbs, such as *close*, are transitive taking two core constituents, and <u>trivalent</u> verbs, like *put*, *give*, are transitive or <u>ditransitive</u> having three (see examples in the chart below). Some verbs allow for different numbers of core constituents (e.g., *run*, *tell*).

VALENCY AND TRANSITIVITY	
AVALENT	*It rains.* (Impersonal)
UNIVALENT	*The door is closed.* (Passive) *The door closes.* (Middle) *The student is full.* (Intransitive, Stative) *The student runs.* (Active, Intransitive, Fientive)
BIVALENT	*The door closes itself.* (Reflexive) *The teacher is full of knowledge.* (Stative, Transitive) *The student closes the door.* (Transitive) *The student runs a race.* (Transitive) *The student tells a story.* (Transitive) *The storm causes the student to run away.* (Ditransitive, Causative)
TRIVALENT	*The student puts the pencil on his desk.* (Transitive) *The student gives a pencil to her.* (Transitive) *The student tells him a story.* (Ditransitive) *The student gives her a pencil.* (Ditransitive) *The storm causes the student to close the door.* (Ditransitive, Causative)

3.6.4 Causation

<u>Causation</u> denotes an event where a clause element brings about a consequent action or a resulting state. The semantic role of <u>causer</u> may serve as the grammatical subject. For example, the causative clause, *George grew vegetables*, does not suggest that the causer (George) sprouted or developed; rather he brings about the flourishing of the vegetables. The clause valency often increases by introducing an additional participant or argument as compared to the same action in a non-causative situation, as with *the vegetables grew*. Another clause participant can indicate the agent or doer of the action, that is, the <u>causee</u>. While the causer (subject) prompts or brings about an event or action, the causee accomplishes the verbal notion and may be indicated as an object. In the clause *Elizabeth walks the dog*, the causer is *Elizabeth* and the causee is *the dog*.

Causative verbs may further be described as resultative or factitive. The <u>resultative</u> indicates that the occasioned action or event is fientive (dynamic). The <u>factitive</u>

describes a stative situation (non-dynamic).[32] Factitives are commonly associated with adjectives (e.g., *The dog tires Elizabeth / Elizabeth is tired*).

CAUSATION, DYNAMISM, AND VALENCY		
NON-CAUSATIVE, FIENTIVE	*The dog walks.*	+ 1 VALENCY
RESULTATIVE	*Elizabeth* [causer] *walks the dog* [causee].	
NON-CAUSATIVE, STATIVE	*Elizabeth is tired.*	+ 1 VALENCY
FACTITIVE	*The dog* [causer] *makes Elizabeth* [causee] *tired.*	

English verbs designate causation through a range of morphosyntactic characteristics. Primary among these properties is a change of the argument structure of causative clauses. Some verbs may indicate causative situations simply by increasing the valency by including an additional core constituent. Examples include *walk, fell, rest, grow, break, trip, vanish, dry, melt, boil, march*. Other verbs indicate causation with alternative morphology. Possibly the most widespread indication of causation is the use of auxiliary verbs (*cause, get, make*). These are accompanied with an infinitive or participle indicating the consequent action. The auxiliary may or may not be followed by the preposition (e.g., *Sarah causes the students to work the problem set*; *Sarah gets the students moving to second period*; *Sarah makes the students study the lesson*). A range of affixes can also indicate causation, particularly with adjectives. With the suffix *-en, -ize, -ify*, examples include *darken, liken, electrify*, and *legalize*. Prefixes such as *en-* and *be-* are also used to create causatives, such as *belittle* and *enrage*.

A third morphological indication of causation employs apophony, specifically the alternation of internal vowels (also called ablaut or vowel gradation). Examples include:

The tree falls. / The lumberjack fells the tree.
The bottle is full. / Esther fills the bottle.
The plate sits on the table. / Mordecai sets the plate on the table.

Finally, a different verb may be paired to indicate causation. This stem change is called suppletion. For instance, *feed* is the causative of *eat*.[33]

MORPHOLOGY OF ENGLISH CAUSATION	
AUXILIARY	*cause (to), get, make*
AFFIXES	*dark/darken, electric/electrify, legal/legalize, like/liken, little/belittle, rage/enrage*

---

[32] Some further differentiate inchoative, direct causative, and indirect causative verbs. See, for instance, Leonhard Lipka, "Causatives and Inchoatives in English and their Treatment in Recent Lexicographic Practice," *Studia Anglica Posnaniensia* 14 (1982): 3–16.

[33] See, also, *kill* (i.e., make die), *teach* (i.e., cause to learn), and *show* (i.e., make see).

MORPHOLOGY OF ENGLISH CAUSATION	
APOPHONY	*bound/bind, fall/fell, full/fill, lie/lay, rise/raise, sit/set*
SUPPLETION	*eat/feed, die/kill, learn/teach, see/show*

3.6.5 Plurality

The notion of <u>verb plurality</u>, sometimes called <u>pluractionality</u>, involves the multiplicity of an event action. Like noun plurality which represents multiple entities of like kind, verb plurality indicates multiple, separate events of like kind.

Verb plurality can be expressed morphologically, syntactically, lexically, and adverbially. It can overlap with the more traditional notion of plural number.[34] A morphologically plural subject may indicate a single action (e.g., *they bathe* = a group bathes at the same time) or a multiplicity of events (e.g., *they bathe* = each one in a group bathes individually). Plural verbal action may be signaled with other plural clause participants, such as an object (e.g., *he bathes them* = he bathes a group at the same time, or *he bathes them* = he bathes each one in a group individually). Some verbs can describe a single event (e.g., *he bathes* = he takes one bath) or a multiplicity of events (e.g., *he bathes* = he bathes habitually). Other clause adjuncts can clarify verbal plurality (e.g., *he bathes each day*).

Semantically, verb plurality represents a range of event multiplicities.[35] First, the simplest event multiplication results from the same action being repeated more than once. Some lexemes imply multiplication, as with *the dog barks* and *the hen pecks her food*. Repetitive action may be signaled by verb morphology, adverbial modification, verb semantics, or a combination of these. For example, a singular event, *he watched the video last night*, can be replicated as *he watched the video again*. Various numbering, frequency, and additive adverbs indicate event repetition: *he watched the video three times*, *he watched the video often*, and *he watched the video again*. An <u>iterative</u> event includes a recurring action at different, disconnected times (e.g., *he rewatched the video again and again*) or segments (e.g., *they chitchatted back and forth*). Sometimes the difference between repeated and recurring actions is not altogether transparent. For instance, compare the action *chop* (e.g., *she chops firewood*) and *chop up* (e.g., *she chops up firewood*). A <u>habitual</u> event comprises a regular enactment of the action (e.g., *he watched the video daily*). Similarly, a <u>distributive</u> event spreads an action into different spatial locations or temporal contexts. Some examples include:

> *He watched the video on several devices* (distributive with different spatial locations)
> *He watched the video a little at a time* (distributive with different temporal contexts)

---

[34] For a discussion of number more broadly, see G. G. Corbett, *Number* (Cambridge: Cambridge University Press, 2000).

[35] W. Dressler, *Studien zur verbalen Pluralität* (Wien: Bühlau in Kommission, 1968) provides an extensive overview of the semantic notes of event plurality.

Second, some repeated events indicate continuous or ongoing actions. This kind of event continuity may be observed with *the man talked and talked* or *the young boy stuttered*. Adverbs can indicate ongoing actions, such as *he watched the video constantly*. A <u>progressive event</u> involves a durative, dynamic action that is not bounded by time (e.g., *he kept watching the video*). Event boundedness also overlaps with verbal aspect. Such progressive events may comprise an <u>intensive action</u> that is escalating in intensity. Such verbs are continuous and increasing in scope, as with *he watched the video more and more intently*.

Third, event plurality may be indicated in a clause with plural participants. The existence of multiple arguments can elicit separate events. The following examples demonstrate plural participants as the agent, patient, and recipient. In each case, the verb can indicate multiple events.

> *They watched the video* (different actors, same patient)
> *He watched the videos* (same actor, different patients)
> *She gave the video to (each of) them* (same actor, same patient, different recipient)

Finally, verb plurality can be signified by <u>reciprocality</u>. A reciprocal verb denotes a shared action (or event) between the multiple agents. For example, *they watched each other*. This notion is often confused with <u>reflexivity</u> in which the agent and patient are coreferential, as with *they watched themselves* (see above §3.6.1).

3.7 QAL STEM

The *Qal* stem forms the foundation of the Hebrew verbal system. It is referred to as the G stem from German *Grundstamm* "ground (or basic) stem."[36] The *Qal* serves as the initial morphosemantic building block (בִּנְיָן) upon which all other verbal stems (בִּנְיָנִים) are built.[37] For this reason, beginning grammars introduce students to the *Qal* stem first. Its inflectional morphology—suffixes and prefix consonants—is common among the other stems. Generally, it specifies the core semantic notion from which the other stems augment or derive various semantic situations. Students should learn the basic stem and notional meanings for each lexeme starting with the *Qal*.

The *Qal* stem verbs may be classified according to the properties of grammatical voice, dynamism, and completion. The *Qal* functions as primarily active voice. In active voice constructions, the subject of the verb performs the verbal action (agent), and where present, the object is the affected object (patient). The actor/subject may or may not be explicitly expressed. The patient can be a pronominal element (Exod 17:4) or a nominal (Exod 16:12).

---

[36] The name *Qal* comes from the Hebrew term קַל "light, simple."
[37] Gesenius calls it "the pure stem" (GKC §43a).

Exod 17:4

וּסְקָלֻנִי

They will stone me.

Exod 16:12

תֹּאכְלוּ בָשָׂר

You will eat meat.

Hebrew active verb constructions have from zero to two objects. *Qal* verbs can be described as intransitive stative (זָקֵן "be old"), transitive stative (מָלֵא "be full of"), intransitive fientive (הָלַךְ "walk"), and transitive fientive (נָתַן "give"). Transitive fientive and stative verbs take objects, whereas intransitive fientive and statives verbs do not.[38] Some *Qal* verbs can indicate the reflexive voice (רָחַץ "wash") or ditransitive completion (נָתַן "give").[39] With certain verbs (נגע "touch"), an intransitive may designate an effected constituent as a prepositional phrase (1 Kgs 19:7). Event plurality is not expressly marked with *Qal* stem verbs (§3.6.5). Lexical causatives are not uncommon (§3.6.4).

QAL SEMANTICS OF DYNAMISM AND COMPLETION			
Intransitive Stative	וְאַבְרָהָם זָקֵן	Abraham **was old**.	Gen 24:1
Transitive Stative	וְהַבַּיִת מָלֵא הָאֲנָשִׁים וְהַנָּשִׁים	The temple **was full of** men and women.	Judg 16:27
Intransitive Fientive	וַאֲבִימֶלֶךְ הָלַךְ אֵלָיו	Abimelech **went** toward him.	Gen 26:26
Transitive Fientive	נָתַתִּי אֶת־הָאָרֶץ בְּיָדוֹ	I **have given** the land into his hand.	Judg 1:2
Ditransitive	נְתַתִּיךָ אֱלֹהִים לְפַרְעֹה	I **made** you a god to Pharaoh	Exod 7:1
Reflexive	יִרְחַץ בַּמָּיִם	He **will wash himself** with water.	Deut 23:12
Intransitive	וַיִּגַּע־בּוֹ	He **touched him**.	1 Kgs 19:7

---

[38] Definite direct objects are typically preceded by the particle אֵת (as with Judg 1:2), and indefinite objects are unmarked (as with Exod 7:1). The preposition לְ may designate the complement with some verbs. In Gen 8:6, the transitive verb פתח "open" acts upon the definite object (וַיִּפְתַּח נֹחַ אֶת־חַלּוֹן הַתֵּבָה "Noah opened the ark's window"). Some confusion is possible with Exod 21:33 (וְכִי־יִפְתַּח אִישׁ בּוֹר "When someone opens a pit"). An indefinite subject and indefinite object are found with the same verb (פתח "open"). The semantics of the two indefinites and the word order help to distinguish the doer (אִישׁ "one") and receiver of the action (בּוֹר "pit"). The doer is the more animate clause element. For some transitive verbs like ילד "give birth to" as in Gen 4:1, the Hebrew verb phrase has a direct object even if the English verb designates the one birthed in a prepositional phrase (וְהָאָדָם יָדַע אֶת־חַוָּה אִשְׁתּוֹ וַתַּהַר וַתֵּלֶד אֶת־קַיִן "Now the man knew Eve his wife. She conceived and gave birth to Cain.")

[39] Joüon-Muraoka §41a.

A very small number of verbs can express different situational dynamisms. The stative verb יָרֵא does not require a complement but can include an object (e.g., "he fears [someone]," Gen 31:31; "he is afraid," 1 Sam 15:24). Another example is אָהֵב "love." In Prov 17:17, the construction does not have an expressed object. Both examples in Gen 25:28 have objects.

Intransitive/Transitive (ירא)

יָרֵ֫אתִי   I **was afraid**. (Gen 31:31)

יָרֵ֫אתִי֙ אֶת־הָעָ֔ם   I **feared** the people (1 Sam 15:24)

Intransitive/Transitive (אהב)

בְּכָל־עֵת אֹהֵב הָרֵעַ   At all times, a friend **loves**. (Prov 17:17)

וַיֶּאֱהַב יִצְחָק אֶת־עֵשָׂו...   Isaac **loved** Esau . . .

וְרִבְקָה אֹהֶ֫בֶת אֶת־יַעֲקֹב   but Rebecca **loved** Jacob (Gen 25:28)

Impersonal verbs express an action that does not have a clear agent and are considered avalent. Hebrew impersonal verbs occur with third-person verb forms without a clear subject referent. This construction is most common with the narrative frame וַיְהִי "it happened" (e.g., וַיְהִי אַחַר הַדְּבָרִים הָאֵלֶּה "After these things happened" [lit. "it was after these things"]). The impersonal verbs are found with certain environmental or astrological phenomena. For instance, the third-person suffix conjugation, אוֹר "it grows light" (1 Sam 29:10). With the environmental verb "snow," the 3FS prefix conjugation serves to designate the dummy subject at Ps 68:15. The 3FS suffix conjugation, חָשְׁכָה "it grows dark" (Mic 3:6) may have the feminine subject שֶׁמֶשׁ "sun" in view as the subject. The sun and the heavens may be assessed as the subject of verbs: נטף "falling rain" (e.g., Judg 5:4; Ps 68:9) and חמם "growing warm" (e.g., Exod 16:21). God could be designated as the agent sending the rain (מטר "rain," Gen 2:5) and causing the storms (שׁער/סער "storm," Ps 58:10; Zech 7:14).

1 Sam 29:10

וְא֥וֹר לָכֶ֖ם וָלֵֽכוּ

When it **grows light** for you, go!

Ps 68:15

תַּשְׁלֵ֥ג בְּצַלְמֽוֹן

It snows on Zalmon.

Mic 3:6

וְחָשְׁכָ֥ה לָכֶ֖ם מִקְּסֹֽם

It will grow dark for you without divination.

The preposition לְ "to, for" can serve to designate a clause argument entailed by an impersonal verb. Such adjuncts represent who benefits from an agentless verbal action. In Gen 12:13, Abram addresses his wife Sarai and claims ייטב־לי "it will be good/better for me." Sometimes the prepositional object may be best translated as the subject of the clause as in Job 3:13 (יָנוּחַ לִי "I would be at rest") and Gen 32:8 (וַיֵּצֶר לוֹ "he was troubled"). The construction, וַיִּחַר ל "it became hot" (see, e.g., Gen 31:36), may be understood similarly ("Jacob was angry") or as having the implied subject, אַף "nose" (e.g., Gen 39:19, וַיִּחַר אַפּוֹ "his nose became hot" = "he became angry").[40]

Gen 12:13

אִמְרִי־נָא אֲחֹתִי אָתְּ לְמַעַן יִיטַב־לִי בַעֲבוּרֵךְ

Please say: "You are only my sister, so that **it will be good to me** on account of you."

Job 3:13

יָשַׁנְתִּי אָז | יָנוּחַ לִי

I would be sleeping, then **it would be rest for me**.

Gen 32:8

וַיִּירָא יַעֲקֹב מְאֹד וַיֵּצֶר לוֹ

Jacob was very afraid, and **it was troubling to him**.

Gen 31:36

וַיִּחַר לְיַעֲקֹב

It became hot to Jacob.

Finally, the impersonal verb should be distinguished from an <u>indefinite subject</u>. The indefinite subject is used when the verb has a nonspecific or unknown agent. These verbal constructions are third person and commonly plural (Gen 47:14).

Gen 47:14

וַיְלַקֵּט יוֹסֵף אֶת־כָּל־הַכֶּסֶף הַנִּמְצָא בְאֶרֶץ־מִצְרַיִם וּבְאֶרֶץ כְּנַעַן בַּשֶּׁבֶר אֲשֶׁר־הֵם שֹׁבְרִים

Joseph assembled all the money found in the land of Egypt and Canaan for the grain that **they** were purchasing.

3.7.1 Qal Morphosemantics

The morphology of the *Qal* stem relates to its semantics through different vowel patterns for some roots. The morphosemantic categories are lexicalized with specific roots, that is, the vowel patterns should be considered as part of the dictionary form. The standard fientive suffix conjugation consists of two /a/ vowels: שָׁמַר "he

---

[40] The clause construction with אַף "nose" does not designate the one who is angry with ל as the impersonal verb construction does. The preposition -בְּ is used to designate the one upon whom the anger is directed (Gen 30:2; 44:18; Exod 4:14; 32:10, 11; Num 11:33; 12:9; 25:3; 32:10, 13; Deut 6:15; 7:4; 11:17; Judg 6:39; 2 Kgs 13:3; 1 Chr 13:10; 2 Chr 25:10; Job 32:2; Ps 106:40; Isa 5:25; Hos 8:51).

guarded," the first being *qameṣ* (<u>stem vowel</u>) followed by *pataḥ* (<u>theme vowel</u>). The historical vowels of the *Qal* suffix form are simply two short /a/-class vowels (Proto-Hebrew **qatal*, Tiberian קָטַל).[41] Comparative studies represent these forms with Latin letters. The form שָׁמַר "he guarded" is composed of the root ŠMR and the pattern **qatal*. Its historical, or Proto-Hebrew form can be written as **šamar*, and שָׁמַר represents its Tiberian spelling.

Other suffix conjugation patterns, **qatil* and **qatul*, are used with specific roots. A variant pattern for the *Qal* suffix conjugation substitutes the second /a/ vowel for an /i/-class theme vowel, which typically realizes as *ṣere* (**qatil*, Tiberian קָטֵל). This form serves mainly to mark verbs with stative semantics: יָרֵא "he is afraid," צָדֵק "he is righteous" (denominative of צְדָקָה "righteousness"), and כָּבֵד "he is heavy."[42] Another rare stative pattern attests an /o/ theme vowel (**qatul*, Tiberian קָטֹל), as in קָטֹן "he is small." While these verb patterns are commonly associated with fientive and stative semantics, they may be found with a variety of semantic situations. Many verbs with stative semantics, for instance, follow the more common /a/-class pattern, such as גָּדַל "he is great," or are analogous to other morphological patterns associated with weak verbs, such as כָּלָה "he is finished."

The *Qal* prefix conjugation attests three different historical patterns with unique realizations in Tiberian Hebrew. The prefix (preformative) vowels are analogous, but the vowel of the second syllable can be (1) theme vowel *holem* (historical **u*: **yaqtul* → יִקְטֹל), (2) theme vowel *pataḥ* (historical **a*: **yaqtal* → יִקְטַל), or rarely (3) theme vowel *ṣere* (historical **i*: **yaqtil* → יִקְטֵל).[43] The most frequent theme vowel is *holem* class, like יִשְׁמֹר "he guards" and יִכְתֹּב "he writes." The theme vowel reduces in forms with vocalic suffixes (יִכְתְּבוּ "they write") but is retained elsewhere (תַּעֲמֹדְנָה "they stand;" תִּרְכַּב "she rides;" יִתֶּנְךָ "he gives you").

These suffix and prefix conjugation patterns combine in a limited number of permutations. Students would do well to learn the associated pattern as part of each lexical form. The specific combination of forms is particular to the lexical root and often relate to the semantics of the lexeme. Most קָטַל-type fientive verbs correspond to the /o/ theme vowel prefix conjugation pattern of יִקְטֹל (*a ~ o*, see the chart below). Stative verbs often attest /a/ theme vowels with their prefix conjugations (**yaqtalu*) rather than /o/ (e.g., יִירָא, יִצְדַּק, יִכְבַּד, and also יִגְדַּל). Further analysis of the *Qal* vowel patterns reveal a total of six verbal alternations between

---

[41] An original final /a/ case vowel (**qatala* > **qatal*) was lost before the earliest evidence of Hebrew. Some vestiges of this vowel are evident with certain pronominal suffixes (e.g., אֲכָלַנִי "It consumed me," Gen 31:40). The /u/ case vowel of the prefix conjugation (**yaqtulu* > **yaqtul*) was also lost.

[42] For more on the Hebrew statives in the Exodus narrative's description of Pharaoh's heart, see §4.1.

[43] Certain Tiberian Hebrew forms do exhibit morphological differences between the short and long prefix conjugations (i.e. **yaqtulØ* and **yaqtulu*). For more on the historical development of the suffix and prefix verbal forms, see §§5.6.1, 5.7.1.

suffix and prefix conjugations: (1) $a \sim o$, (2) $a \sim a$, (3) $a \sim e$, (4) $e \sim a$, (5) $e \sim o$, and (6) $o \sim a$.[44]

	QAL THEME VOWEL ALTERNATIONS				
PATTERN	SUFFIX CONJ.		THEME VOWEL	PREFIX CONJ.	
1	כָּתַב	*qatal	he wrote	$a \sim o$	יִכְתֹּב	*yaqtul	he writes
2	שָׁכַב	*qatal	he reclined	$a \sim a$	יִשְׁכַּב	*yaqtal	he reclines
3	נָתַן	*qatal	he gave	$a \sim e$	יִתֵּן	*yaqtil	he gives
4	כָּבֵד	*qatil	he is heavy	$e \sim a$	יִכְבַּד	*yaqtal	he is heavy
5	נָבֵל	*qatil	he withered	$e \sim o$	יִבֹּל	*yaqtul	he withers
6	קָטֹן	*qatul	he is small	$o \sim a$	יִקְטַן	*yaqtal	he is small

Pattern 1 is the most common type and is found with most fientive verbs. Less commonly, fientive verbs follow patterns 2, 3, and 5. Patterns 4 and 6 are primarily identified with stative verbal semantics.

THE ORIGIN OF STATIVE VERBS IN SEMITIC

Stative verbs and adjectives have closely related morphosemantics and are linked historically through similar Semitic forms. For instance, the root כבד attests both the *Qal* stative verb כָּבֵד "to be heavy" and the homonymous adjective כָּבֵד "heavy," both following the *qatil* pattern. We know, however, that these represent two separate lexemes because they have different productive finite forms in Hebrew:

STATIVE VERB		ADJECTIVE	
(3CP) כָּבְדוּ	(3MS) כָּבֵד	(MP ABS) כְּבֵדִים	(MS ABS) כָּבֵד
	(3FS) כָּבְדָה	(MP CSTR) כִּבְדֵי	(MS CSTR) כְּבַד

Grammarians propose that stative verbs were originally derived from *qatil*- and *qatul*-type adjectives at a nascent phase of the language (see chapter 8).

---

[44] Michael Rand, "Fientivity, Transitivity, and Stem Vowel Variation in Byzantine *Piyyuṭ*," *JQR* 93 (2003): 471.

A few verbal roots attest two different patterns but do so in environments without a clear distinction in meaning. The root לבש attests both pattern 2 and 4. The suffix conjugations לָבֵשׁ and לָבַשׁ are fientive meaning "he puts on:"[45]

SC /a/-Class Theme Vowel

Lev 6:3

וְלָבַשׁ הַכֹּהֵן מִדּוֹ בַד

The priest **will put on** his linen garment.

SC /e/-Class Theme Vowel

Ps 93:1

יְהוָה מָלָךְ גֵּאוּת לָבֵשׁ

Yahweh reigns: he **puts on** majesty.

In rare cases, the prefix conjugation may evidence different theme vowels without clear semantic differences.[46] For example, קצר occurs with both the /o/ theme vowel and the /a/ theme vowels:[47]

PC /o/-Class Theme Vowel

Prov 10:27

וּשְׁנוֹת רְשָׁעִים תִּקְצֹרְנָה

But the years of the wicked **will be cut short**.

PC /a/-Class Theme Vowel

Job 21:4

וְאִם־מַדּוּעַ לֹא־תִקְצַר רוּחִי

Or why should my spirit not **be cut short**?

Other inconsistencies exist between the semantic expectations and the morphological patterns. Some semantically stative verbs exhibit non-stative verbal patterns. The verbs חָזַק and גָּדַל, for instance, are stative: "he is strong" and "he is great." Yet their prefixed forms, יֶחֱזַק and יִגְדַּל, follow the שׁכב *a ~ a* pattern. Conversely, a small number of fientive verbs exhibit a *e ~ a* stative-type verbal pattern, as with אֲהֵבְךָ "he loves you" at Deut 15:16 and תֶּאֱהָבוּ "you will love" at Zech

---

[45] Rand, "Stem Vowel Variation," 473. See further Stephen Coleman, *The Biblical Hebrew Transitivity Alternation in Cognitive Linguistic Perspective*, Abhandlungen für die Kunde des Morgenlandes 114 (Wiesbaden: Harrassowitz, 2018), 84–97. The second vowel may also vary with some inflectional forms of קרב "to approach." The 3FS is קָרְבָה "she approached," and 3MS קָרַב "he approached." See H. H. Hardy II, *Exegetical Gems from Biblical Hebrew* (Grand Rapids: Baker Academic, 2019): 108–10.

[46] Vestiges of the fientive-stative-type alternation are present with a small number of verbal roots, even though the semantic distinctions are no longer fully operative. For example, נשׁך attests prefix forms יִשֹּׁךְ (Eccl 10:11) and יִשָּׁךְ (Prov 23:32), both meaning "it [the snake] bites." The root חפץ yields the forms יַחְפֹּץ (Deut 25:7) and יֶחְפָּץ (Ps 68:31) meaning, "he delights in" (GKC §47i; Rand, "Stem Vowel Variation," 474).

[47] See GKC §47i; BDB, 894.

8:17. But notice elsewhere the expected fientive pattern, וְיִשְׂרָאֵל אָהַב אֶת־יוֹסֵף מִכָּל־בָּנָיו "Israel **loved** Joseph more than his sons" (Gen 37:3).

3.7.2 Qal Transitivity and Valency

Qal verbs can be complete or incomplete. Completion is signaled by a verb's transitivity as part of the mental lexicon. In other words, the argument structure is determined by the semantics of each individual lexeme. For the most part, fientive verbs are either complete and transitive (e.g., אמר "say"; אחז "hold") or incomplete and intransitive (e.g., הלך "go"; אבד "perish"). On the other hand, most stative verbs, like אמץ "be strong," are intransitive and inherently incomplete.[48] A small number of *Qal* fientive verbs can also function in ditransitive constructions:

Transitive/Ditransitive (נתן)

וּנְתַתִּיךָ לְגוֹיִם   I **will make** you into nations (Gen 12:6)

אַב־הֲמוֹן גּוֹיִם נְתַתִּיךָ   I **will make** you a father of a multitude of nations (Gen 12:5)

For <u>ditransitive verbs</u> with two marked objects in Hebrew, English translations often designate the secondary object in a prepositional phrase. In contrast with a <u>direct object (DO)</u>, secondary objects are either an <u>object complement</u> (OC) or an <u>indirect object (IO)</u>. For example, the verb נתן "give" in Gen 17:5 has two objects: the 2MS pronominal suffix ךָ- "you" and אב המון גוים "a father of a multitude of nations." The relationship is one of object and OC—they may be equated or renamed with the copula, as in Object₁ is Object₂ ("you [are] a father of a multitude of nations," Gen 17:5).

Gen 17:5

כִּי אַב־הֲמוֹן גּוֹיִם נְתַתִּיךָ

For I made you a father of a multitude of nations.

An indirect object (IO) is more commonly indicated with a prepositional phrase. The phrases לָכֶם "to you" (Gen 9:3) and אֵלַי "to me" (Deut 10:4) designate the goal or benefit of the verbal action. A clause may even contain both constructions, combining a ditransitive verb and an indirect object as with 1 Kgs 9:16.

Gen 9:3

נָתַתִּי לָכֶם אֶת־כֹּל

I gave you (IO) everything (DO).

---

[48] Some primarily intransitive stative verbs exhibit a small number of cases with transitive structures. The stative verb חָזַק "be strong" is generally intransitive; however, a few instances evidence an object designating a goal: חֲזַקְתַּנִי וַתּוּכָל "you seized me, and you prevailed" (Jer 20:7), וְלֹא חֲזָקוֹ "he did not strengthen him" (2 Chr 28:20), וַיֶּחֱזַק הָעָם אֲשֶׁר אַחֲרֵי עָמְרִי אֶת־הָעָם אֲשֶׁר אַחֲרֵי תִבְנִי בֶן־גִּינַת "the people following Omri took hold of the people following Tibni ben-Ginath" (1 Kgs 16:22).

Deut 10:4

וַיִּתְּנֵם יְהוָה אֵלַי

Yahweh gave them (DO) to me (IO).

1 Kgs 9:16

וַיִּתְּנָהּ שִׁלֻּחִים לְבִתּוֹ אֵשֶׁת שְׁלֹמֹה

He gave it (DO) as a dowry (OC) to his daughter (IO), the wife of Solomon.

Two more examples of common ditransitive roots are שִׂים "make (someone) (something)" and קרא "call (someone) (something)." In 1 Sam 8:1, the prophet Samuel is said to be old and hands over his responsibilities. The verb, שִׂים "put, make," designates the first object בָּנָיו "his sons" with the definite direct object marker, and the object complement is the indefinite noun, שֹׁפְטִים "judges." The verb, קרא "call," can express the idea of naming something or someone as in Gen 3:20. The objects are the phrase, שֵׁם אִשְׁתּוֹ "his wife's name," and the proper noun, חַוָּה "Eve."

1 Sam 8:1

וַיָּשֶׂם אֶת־בָּנָיו שֹׁפְטִים לְיִשְׂרָאֵל

He made his sons (DO) judges (OC) for Israel.

Gen 3:20

וַיִּקְרָא הָאָדָם שֵׁם אִשְׁתּוֹ חַוָּה

The man called his wife's name (DO) Eve (OC).

A small number of verbs are <u>ambitransitive</u>. The verb argument structure (valency, §3.6.3) can vary among the previously discussed patterns. The root גמל "repay; ripen" provides examples of taking zero (Ps 13:6), one (Isa 3:9), or two objects (1 Sam 24:18). Similarly, קרא is used without an object (1 Sam 3:5), as intransitive with the preposition אֶל (1 Sam 3:4), as transitive (1 Sam 3:6), or as ditransitive (1 Sam 1:20).

AMBITRANSITIVE VERBS		
VALENCY	גמל	קרא
1	כִּי גָמַל עָלָי For **he will repay** on me. (Ps 13:6)	וַיֹּאמֶר לֹא־קָרָאתִי שׁוּב שְׁכָב But he responded: "**I did not call.** Go back to sleep!" (1 Sam 3:5)
		וַיִּקְרָא יְהוָה אֶל־שְׁמוּאֵל וַיֹּאמֶר הִנֵּנִי: Yahweh **called to** Samuel. And he replied: "I am here!" (1 Sam 3:4)

AMBITRANSITIVE VERBS		
VALENCY	גמל	קרא
2	גָּמְלוּ לָהֶם רָעָה **They repaid** evil to them. (Isa 3:9)	וַיֹּסֶף יְהֹוָה קְרֹא עוֹד שְׁמוּאֵל Yahweh again **called** Samuel once more. (1 Sam 3:6)
3	אַתָּה גְּמַלְתַּנִי הַטּוֹבָה As for you, **you repaid** me [with] good. (1 Sam 24:18)	וַתִּקְרָא אֶת־שְׁמוֹ שְׁמוּאֵל She **called** his name Samuel. (1 Sam 1:20)

Some ambitransitive verbs may alternate between the transitive and the reflexive or middle voice with <u>internal objects</u> that are implied even when not stated. For instance, רחץ "bathe" can designate a direct object: "face" (Gen 43:31, וַיִּרְחַץ פָּנָיו "he washed his face"), "hands" (Deut 21:6, יִרְחֲצוּ אֶת־יְדֵיהֶם "they should wash their hands"), "feet" (Gen 18:4, רַחֲצוּ רַגְלֵיכֶם "wash your feet"), or "persons" (Exod 40:12, וְרָחַצְתָּ אֹתָם בַּמָּיִם "You shall bathe them in water"). Notice, however, the interchange of similar clauses designating the object washed (Lev 14:9) and not designating an object (Lev 14:8).

Lev 14:9
וְרָחַץ אֶת־בְּשָׂרוֹ בַּמָּיִם
He **shall bathe** his body with water.

Lev 14:8
וְרָחַץ בַּמַּיִם
He **shall bathe** [himself] with water.

Similarly, גלח "shave" may take a complement, such as רֹאשׁ "head" (e.g., Num 6:18) or שֵׂעָר "hair" (e.g., Lev 14:8–9), but at times it has no object (see Gen 41:14).

Gen 41:14
וַיְרִיצֻהוּ מִן־הַבּוֹר **וַיְגַלַּח** וַיְחַלֵּף שִׂמְלֹתָיו
They fetched him from the pit. **He shaved** and changed his clothes.

3.7.3 Qal Denominative

Some *Qal* stem verbs originate from primary nouns. These verbs are labeled <u>denominative</u>—that is, deriving from nouns. In English, numerous verbs are in this class: *to mother, to google, to muscle, to friend, to message.* They are most commonly incorporated into the standard morphosyntactic system. The result is familiar paradigmatic usage: *he googles, she googled, they are googling, we have googled.*

The following list of Hebrew lexemes includes examples of denominative *Qal* stem verbs. The nominal idea may be transformed into a dynamic action (e.g., אָבַר

"to fly"), identify a characteristic (e.g., בָּעַר "to be foolish"), or enact a transformed reality (e.g., גָּבַל "to form a boundary"). Most denominatives take the verbal pattern, קָטַל and יְקְטֹל/יְקְטַל (Pattern 1 or 2, see §3.7.1).[49] Some biconsonantal nouns repattern based on etymological roots different from their assumed origin. For instance, the verb דִּיג "to fish" is middle weak, but the related noun is likely derived from the third-weak root דָּגָה "to increase."

QAL STEM DENOMINATIVE VERBS	
NOUN	**VERB**
אֵבֶר "wing"	אבר (יְאַבֵּר)* "to fly" ("to glide on wings")
אֹהֶל "tent"	אהל (יְאֱהַל)* "to pitch a tent"
אֵפוֹד "ephod"	אָפַד (יְאֹפֵד) "to gird" ("to wear an ephod")
אֵצֶל "side"	אָצַל "to withhold" ("to lay aside")
בֶּדֶק "repair"	בדק* "to repair"[50]
בַּעַר "fool"	בער (יִבְעֲרוּ)* "to be foolish"
בָּרָד "hail"	בָּרַד "to hail"
גְּבוּל "boundary"	גָּבַל (יִגְבּוֹל) "to form a boundary"
דָּג "fish"	דִּיג "to fish"
דֶּגֶל "banner"	דגל (נִדְגֹּל)* "to raise a banner"
הֶבֶל "vanity"	הבל (תֶּהְבָּלוּ)* "to be vain"
חִידָה "riddle"	חוד (אָחוּדָה) "to riddle"
חֹמֶר "mortar"	חמר (תַּחְמְרָה)* "to mortar"
חֹרֶף "winter"	חרף (תֶּחֱרַף)* "to spend the winter"
כֹּפֶר "pitch"	כָּפַר "to cover with pitch"
לְבֵנָה "brick"	לבן (נִלְבְּנָה)* "to make brick"
מֹהַר "dowry; bride price"	מָהַר "to pay a dowry"
מֶלַח "salt"	מלח (תִּמְלָח)* "to salt"
מָשָׁל "proverb"	משׁל (יִמְשֹׁל)* "to tell a proverb"
נְאֻם "utterance"	נאם (יִנְאֲמוּ)* "to utter"
נַחֲלָה "possession"	נָחַל (יִנְחַל) "to possess"

---

[49] The root צדק "to be righteous" takes the stative pattern יִצְדַּק for the prefixed conjugation.
[50] Only the infinitive construct לִבְדֹק is evidenced.

QAL STEM DENOMINATIVE VERBS	
NOUN	**VERB**
נַעַל "shoe, sandal"	נעל* (אֶנְעָלֵךְ) "to shoe"
נֶשֶׁךְ "usury, interest"	נשׁך* (יִשָּׁךְ) "to earn interest"
עֲבוֹט "pledge"	עבט (תַּעֲבֹט)* "to pledge"
עֻגָה "cake, bread"	עוג* (תְּעֻגֶנָה) "to bake"
עֲנָק "necklace"	עָנַק "to be a necklace"
עֹנֶשׁ "fine, punishment"	עָנַשׁ (יַעֲנֹשׁ) "to fine"
עֹרֶף "neck"	עָרַף (יַעֲרֹף) "to break a neck"
עֶשֶׂר "ten"	עשׂר (יְעַשֵּׂר)* "to take a tenth"
עָשָׁן "smoke"	עָשַׁן (יֶעְשְׁנוּ) "to smoke"
פֶּתִי "simple"	פתה (יִפְתֶּה)* "to be simple"
צְדָקָה "righteousness"	צָדַק (יִצְדַּק) "to be righteous"
קֹדֶשׁ "holy"	קָדַשׁ (יִקְדַּשׁ) "to consecrate"
קֶסֶם "divination"	קסם* (יִקְסֹמוּ) "to divinate"
רֹבַע "four sides"	רבע* "to be square"[51]
רַעַם "thunder"	רעם* (יִרְעַם) "to thunder"
רַע "evil"	רַע (יֵרַע) "to do evil"
רֶשַׁע "wickedness"	רָשַׁע (תִּרְשַׁע) "to be wicked"
שָׂטָן "adversary"	שׂטן (יִשְׂטְנוּנִי)* "to be an adversary"
שִׂיחַ "musing"	שִׂיחַ "to muse"
שֵׂעָר "hair"	שָׂעַר (יִשְׂעֲרוּ) "to have your hair stand up"
שַׂר "prince"	שׂרר* (וַיִּשַׂר) "to rule"
שֶׁבֶר "grain"	שׁבר* (תִּשְׁבְּרוּ) "to buy grain"
שַׁבָּת "Sabbath"	שָׁבַת (יִשְׁבֹּת) "to sabbath" (i.e., cease)

---

[51] Only the passive participle רָבוּעַ is evidenced.

3.8 QAL PASSIVE

The Hebrew "passive" stems include *Qal* passive, *Niphal*, *Pual*, and *Hophal*. They should primarily be considered a <u>de-agentive</u> verb construction. That is, clauses with these verb types do not stipulate an agent. Hebrew, unlike English and Greek, rarely allows for a secondary presentation of the agent in an adjunct phrase, and it may or may not "promote" the patient to the subject position.

The internal Hebrew evidence and the Semitic G-passive stem make the reconstruction of a *Qal* passive stem in BH highly plausible. Scholars have long suggested that Biblical Hebrew has a *Qal* passive form (**qutal*) akin to the Arabic internal passive stem *qutila*.[52] It is argued that certain verbs, vocalized in Tiberian Hebrew with the *Pual* suffix conjugation (**quttal*, Tiberian קֻטַּל), should instead be analyzed as *Qal* passives.[53] At some late stage of the reading tradition, the archaic **qutal* form was likely confused with **quttal* and understood as *Pual*. This understanding of the *Qal* passive poses several morphological challenges. One difficulty is how to account for the doubling of the middle root consonant. The doubling may have resulted from the Masoretes' desire to preserve the distinctive short /u/ as the morphological demarcation of the internal passive, which would have reduced otherwise.[54] This practice may have led them to be misunderstood as *Pual* stems.

Grammarians note several features to identify potential *Qal* passive verbs. These relate to the distribution of its forms in Biblical Hebrew.[55] First, some *Pual* forms of a given root do not attest a corresponding *Piel*, which is especially unusual for widely attested roots such as אכל. Second, other roots have *Piel* forms that do not correspond to the meaning of the *Pual*. For example, the *Piel* designates specifically "to serve as a midwife (i.e., to help someone in the state of giving birth)" (e.g., Exod 1:16) whereas the *Pual* of ילד means "to be born" (e.g., Gen 6:1). Third, certain

---

[52] See Frank R. Blake, "The Internal Passive in Semitic," *JAOS* 22 (1901): 54. As Blake observed, the Hebrew development of the /a/ of the old *Qal* internal passive **qutal* may have been analogous to the /a/ theme vowel of the suffix conjugation **qatal*, in distinction from Arabic *qutila*.

[53] Gesenius listed the following roots for which the *Pual* suffix forms are potentially *Qal* passives: קרא, עשׂה, עֻזב, עבד, נפח, מרט, כרת, לקח, יצר, ילד, טרף, חצב, חפשׂ, זרק, זרע, הרג, הרה, זנה, בזו, אסר, ראה, שׂרף, שׂגל, שׁטף, שׁפך (GKC §52e).

[54] See BL §42q; Blake, "Internal Passive," 54; GKC §52e; and most recently, Khan, *Tiberian Pronunciation*, 351 (§I.3.1.5.1).

[55] See GKC §52e, following the work of Mayer Lambert, "L'Emploi du nifal en Hébreu," *Revue des études Juives* 41 (1900): 196–214 and Jacob Barth, "Das passive Qal und seine Participien," in *Jubelschrift zum siebzigsten Geburtstag des Dr. Israel Hildesheimer* (Berlin: Engel, 1890), 145–53. See also the earlier work of Friedrich Böttcher, *Ausführliches Lehrbuch der hebräischen Sprache* (Leipzig: Barth, 1866), §§109–906. For more recent assessments of the *Qal* passive, see Ronald J. Williams, "The Passive Qal Theme in Hebrew," in *Essays on the Ancient Semitic World*, ed. J. W. Wevers and D. B. Redford (Toronto: University of Toronto Press, 1970), 43–50; Daniel Sivan, "The Internal Passive of G-Stems in Northwest Semitic Languages," (Hebrew) in *Mas'at Aharon: Linguistic Studies Presented to Aaron Dotan*, ed. M. Bar-Asher and C. E. Cohen (Jerusalem: Bialik, 2009), 47–56; Eric D. Reymond, "The Passive Qal in the Hebrew of the Second Temple Period, Especially as Found in the Wisdom of Ben Sira," in *Sibyls, Scriptures, and Scrolls: John Collins at Seventy*, ed. Joel Baden et al., Supplements to the Journal for the Study of Judaism 175 (Leiden: Brill, 2017), 1110–27.

strong roots exclusively attest the *Pual* in the suffix conjugation and the *Niphal* in the prefix conjugation (e.g., טרף: SC טֹרַף, PC יְטֹרַף; חצב: SC חֻצַּבְתֶּם, PC יֵחָצְבוּן). Since the consonantal forms of the *Niphal* and *Pual* are identical in the prefix conjugation (יקטל), they could be vocalized as either stem (e.g., *Niphal* יְטֹרַף ~ *Pual* יְטֹרַף*). Scholars argue that these *Niphal* forms may represent old PC *Qal* passives that were reanalyzed as *Niphal* stems once the *Qal* passive fell out of use.

These factors have led scholars to reconstruct a *Qal* passive that functioned as the passive suffix conjugation form in opposition to the *Niphal* prefix conjugation, as outlined with the following examples:

	ACTIVE SC	ACTIVE PC	PASSIVE SC		PASSIVE PC	
	Qal		Niphal	Pual	Niphal	Pual
טרף	טָרַף "he tore" (Job 16:9)	אֶטְרֹף "I tear" (Hos 5:14)	Ø	טֹרַף "he has been torn" (Gen 37:33)	יִטָּרֵף "he is torn" (Exod 22:12)	Ø
עבד	עָבְדוּ "they served" (Deut 7:4)	יַעֲבֹד "they serve" (Gen 25:23)	נֶעֶבְדְתֶּם "you are worked" (Ezek 36:9)	לֹא־עֻבַּד "was not worked" (Deut 21:3)	לֹא־יֵעָבֵד "it will not be worked" (Deut 21:4)	Ø
שטף	שָׁטַף "it overflowed" (Isa 8:8)	Ø	Ø	וְשֻׁטַּף "it will be rinsed" (Lev 6:21)	יִשָּׁטֵף "it will be rinsed" (Lev 15:12)	Ø

A few roots attest both *Niphal* and *Pual* suffix forms (e.g., עבד), but all roots in this category except one have no corresponding *Pual* prefix form.[56] Yet, the identification of *Qal* passive verbs is not without difficulty. One problem is that many are so meagerly attested in the Hebrew Bible. More widely attested roots like עבד show both a *Niphal* and *Pual* suffix form but not a *Pual* prefix form. As Eric Reymond aptly cautions, the absence of *Pual* prefix forms or *Niphal* suffix forms may simply be coincidental.[57]

In conclusion, this chapter presents an overview of the Biblical Hebrew verbs. It describes semantic roles, semantic situations, and the foundational stem of the verbal system. This discussion covers the basic *Qal* stem as well as the purported *Qal* passive stem. In the following chapter, we consider the derived stems including the *Niphal*, *Piel*, *Pual*, *Hitpael*, *Hiphil*, *Hophal*, and other reduplicated stems.

---

[56] See תֵּאָכֵלוּ "will be devoured" in Isa 1:20.

[57] Reymond, "Passive Qal," 1115. Reymond goes on to hypothesize that the *Qal* passive likely disappeared from the literary from of the language by the late Second Temple period.

3.9 EXERCISES

Translate the following Hebrew sentences into English. Describe the verbal semantics of all the bold finite verbs in the following passage and comment on their interpretive significance.

1. וַיְהִ֗י אַחֲרֵ֛י מ֥וֹת מֹשֶׁ֖ה עֶ֣בֶד יְהוָ֑ה **וַיֹּ֤אמֶר** יְהוָה֙ אֶל־יְהוֹשֻׁ֣עַ בִּן־נ֔וּן מְשָׁרֵ֥ת מֹשֶׁ֖ה
   לֵאמֹֽר׃ (Josh 1:1)

2. מֹשֶׁ֥ה עַבְדִּ֖י מֵ֑ת וְעַתָּה֩ **ק֨וּם** עֲבֹ֜ר אֶת־הַיַּרְדֵּ֣ן הַזֶּ֗ה אַתָּה֙ וְכָל־הָעָ֣ם הַזֶּ֔ה אֶל־הָאָ֕רֶץ
   אֲשֶׁ֧ר אָנֹכִ֛י נֹתֵ֥ן לָהֶ֖ם לִבְנֵ֥י יִשְׂרָאֵֽל׃ (Josh 1:2)

3. כָּל־מָק֗וֹם אֲשֶׁ֨ר **תִּדְרֹ֧ךְ** כַּף־רַגְלְכֶ֛ם בּ֖וֹ לָכֶ֣ם **נְתַתִּ֑יו** כַּאֲשֶׁ֥ר **דִּבַּ֖רְתִּי** אֶל־מֹשֶֽׁה׃
   (Josh 1:3)

4. מֵהַמִּדְבָּר֩ וְהַלְּבָנ֨וֹן הַזֶּ֜ה וְעַד־הַנָּהָ֤ר הַגָּדוֹל֙ נְהַר־פְּרָ֔ת כֹּ֖ל אֶ֣רֶץ הַֽחִתִּ֑ים וְעַד־הַיָּ֧ם
   הַגָּד֛וֹל מְב֥וֹא הַשָּׁ֖מֶשׁ **יִהְיֶ֥ה** גְּבוּלְכֶֽם׃ (Josh 1:4)

5. לֹֽא־**יִתְיַצֵּ֥ב** אִישׁ֙ לְפָנֶ֔יךָ כֹּ֖ל יְמֵ֣י חַיֶּ֑יךָ כַּאֲשֶׁ֨ר הָיִ֤יתִי עִם־מֹשֶׁה֙ **אֶהְיֶ֣ה** עִמָּ֔ךְ לֹ֥א
   אַרְפְּךָ֖ וְלֹ֥א **אֶעֶזְבֶֽךָ**׃ (Josh 1:5)

Translate the following sentences and identify each finite verb in the following passage as either fientive or stative.

6. **וַיֶּחֱזַק֙** לֵ֣ב פַּרְעֹ֔ה וְלֹ֥א **שָׁמַ֖ע** אֲלֵהֶ֑ם כַּאֲשֶׁ֖ר **דִּבֶּ֥ר** יְהוָֽה׃ **וַיֹּ֤אמֶר** יְהוָה֙ אֶל־מֹשֶׁ֔ה
   כָּבֵ֖ד לֵ֣ב פַּרְעֹ֑ה מֵאֵ֖ן לְשַׁלַּ֥ח הָעָֽם׃ (Exod 7:13–14)

7. וְכֹל אֲשֶׁר־**יִפֹּל**־עָלָיו מֵהֶם | בְּמֹתָם **יִטְמָא** מִכָּל־כְּלִי־עֵץ אוֹ בֶגֶד אוֹ־עוֹר אוֹ שָׂק כָּל־כְּלִי אֲשֶׁר־**יֵעָשֶׂה** מְלָאכָה בָּהֶם בַּמַּיִם **יוּבָא** **וְטָמֵא** עַד־הָעֶרֶב **וְטָהֵר**: (Lev 11:32)

Translate the following sentences and determine the agent, patient, and valency for each verb phrase.

8. **וַיֹּאמֶר** לוֹ יְהוָה לָכֵן כָּל־הֹרֵג קַיִן שִׁבְעָתַיִם **יֻקָּם** **וַיָּשֶׂם** יְהוָה לְקַיִן אוֹת לְבִלְתִּי **הַכּוֹת**־אֹתוֹ כָּל־מֹצְאוֹ: (Gen 4:15)

9. **וַיְעַזְּקֵהוּ** **וַיְסַקְּלֵהוּ** **וַיִּטָּעֵהוּ** שֹׂרֵק **וַיִּבֶן** מִגְדָּל בְּתוֹכוֹ וְגַם־יֶקֶב **חָצֵב** בּוֹ **וַיְקַו** לַעֲשׂוֹת עֲנָבִים **וַיַּעַשׂ** בְּאֻשִׁים: (Isa 5:2)

10. יַעַן אֲשֶׁר **הֲרִימֹתִיךָ** מִן־הֶעָפָר **וָאֶתֶּנְךָ** נָגִיד עַל עַמִּי יִשְׂרָאֵל **וַתֵּלֶךְ** | בְּדֶרֶךְ יָרָבְעָם **וַתַּחֲטִא** אֶת־עַמִּי יִשְׂרָאֵל לְהַכְעִיסֵנִי בְּחַטֹּאתָם: הִנְנִי **מַבְעִיר** אַחֲרֵי בַעְשָׁא וְאַחֲרֵי בֵיתוֹ **וְנָתַתִּי** אֶת־בֵּיתְךָ כְּבֵית יָרָבְעָם בֶּן־נְבָט: (1 Kgs 16:2–3)

Translate from English to Hebrew.

11. The King of Egypt rose, attacked Israel, and became strong before them.

12. Saul killed the cow, and then it was slaughtered, and its blood filled the vessels of the temple.

13. Ruth became angry because they did not believe her.

14.   You will no longer be called Hoshea. I will call your name Joshua.

15.   I am bringing you out of Egypt with a strong hand.

Guided Reading: 1 Kgs 1:1–10

1 וְהַמֶּ֙לֶךְ֙ דָּוִד֙ זָקֵ֔ן בָּ֖א בַּיָּמִ֑ים וַיְכַסֻּ֙הוּ֙ בַּבְּגָדִ֔ים וְלֹ֥א יִחַ֖ם לֽוֹ׃ 2 וַיֹּ֧אמְרוּ ל֣וֹ עֲבָדָ֗יו יְבַקְשׁ֞וּ לַאדֹנִ֤י הַמֶּ֙לֶךְ֙ נַעֲרָ֣ה בְתוּלָ֔ה וְעָֽמְדָ֖ה לִפְנֵ֣י הַמֶּ֑לֶךְ וּתְהִי־ל֣וֹ סֹכֶ֔נֶת וְשָֽׁכְבָ֣ה בְחֵיקֶ֔ךָ וְחַ֖ם לַֽאדֹנִ֥י הַמֶּֽלֶךְ׃ 3 וַיְבַקְשׁוּ֙ נַעֲרָ֣ה יָפָ֔ה בְּכֹ֖ל גְּב֣וּל יִשְׂרָאֵ֑ל וַֽיִּמְצְא֗וּ אֶת־אֲבִישַׁג֙ הַשּׁ֣וּנַמִּ֔ית וַיָּבִ֥אוּ אֹתָ֖הּ לַמֶּֽלֶךְ׃ 4 וְהַֽנַּעֲרָ֖ה יָפָ֣ה עַד־מְאֹ֑ד וַתְּהִ֨י לַמֶּ֤לֶךְ סֹכֶ֙נֶת֙ וַתְּשָׁ֣רְתֵ֔הוּ וְהַמֶּ֖לֶךְ לֹ֥א יְדָעָֽהּ׃ 5 וַאֲדֹנִיָּ֧ה בֶן־חַגִּ֛ית מִתְנַשֵּׂ֥א לֵאמֹ֖ר אֲנִ֣י אֶמְלֹ֑ךְ וַיַּ֣עַשׂ ל֗וֹ רֶ֚כֶב וּפָ֣רָשִׁ֔ים וַחֲמִשִּׁ֥ים אִ֖ישׁ רָצִ֥ים לְפָנָֽיו׃ 6 וְלֹֽא־עֲצָב֨וֹ אָבִ֤יו מִיָּמָיו֙ לֵאמֹ֔ר מַדּ֖וּעַ כָּ֣כָה עָשִׂ֑יתָ וְגַם־ה֤וּא טֽוֹב־תֹּ֙אַר֙ מְאֹ֔ד וְאֹת֥וֹ יָלְדָ֖ה אַחֲרֵ֥י אַבְשָׁלֽוֹם׃ 7 וַיִּהְי֣וּ דְבָרָ֔יו עִ֚ם יוֹאָ֣ב בֶּן־צְרוּיָ֔ה וְעִ֖ם אֶבְיָתָ֣ר הַכֹּהֵ֑ן וַֽיַּעְזְר֔וּ אַחֲרֵ֖י אֲדֹנִיָּֽה׃ 8 וְצָד֣וֹק הַ֠כֹּהֵן וּבְנָיָ֨הוּ בֶן־יְהוֹיָדָ֜ע וְנָתָ֣ן הַנָּבִ֗יא וְשִׁמְעִי֙ וְרֵעִ֔י וְהַגִּבּוֹרִ֖ים אֲשֶׁ֣ר לְדָוִ֑ד לֹ֥א הָי֖וּ עִם־אֲדֹנִיָּֽהוּ׃ 9 וַיִּזְבַּ֣ח אֲדֹנִיָּ֗הוּ צֹ֤אן וּבָקָר֙ וּמְרִ֔יא עִ֚ם אֶ֣בֶן הַזֹּחֶ֔לֶת אֲשֶׁר־אֵ֖צֶל עֵ֣ין רֹגֵ֑ל וַיִּקְרָ֗א אֶת־כָּל־אֶחָיו֙ בְּנֵ֣י הַמֶּ֔לֶךְ וּלְכָל־אַנְשֵׁ֥י יְהוּדָ֖ה עַבְדֵ֥י הַמֶּֽלֶךְ׃ 10 וְֽאֶת־נָתָן֩ הַנָּבִ֨יא וּבְנָיָ֜הוּ וְאֶת־הַגִּבּוֹרִ֧ים וְאֶת־שְׁלֹמֹ֛ה אָחִ֖יו לֹ֥א קָרָֽא׃

VOCABULARY AND NOTES

Verse 1

זָקֵן	*Qal*			"be old; grow old"
וַיְכַסֻּהוּ	*Piel*	CP 3MP + 3MS SF	כסה	"to cover"
יִחַם	*Qal*			"be(come) warm"

Verse 2

יְבַקְשׁוּ	*Piel*	PC/JUSS 3MP	בקשׁ	"seek; require; consult"
נַעֲרָה		N.FS		"young girl; maidservant"
בְתוּלָה		N.FS		"virgin"
וְעָמְדָה	*Qal waqātal*	3FS	עמד	

וַתְּהִי	Qal	JUSS 3FS	היה	
סֹכֶנֶת	Qal	PTCL FS	סכן	"official; administrator"
וְשָׁכְבָה	Qal wəqātal	3FS	שכב	
חֵיקֶךָ		N.MS		"bosom, lap"

Verse 3

וַיְבַקְשׁוּ	Piel	CP 3MP	בקש	
יָפָה		ADJ.FS		"beautiful; fair"
אֲבִישַׁג		PN		"Abishag"
שׁוּנַמִּית		ADJ.FS		"Shunammite"
וַיָּבִאוּ	Hiphil	CP 3MP	בוא	

Verse 4

וַתְּהִי	Qal	CP 3FS	היה	
וַתְּשָׁרְתֵהוּ	Piel	CP 3FS + 3MS SF	שרת	"serve"
יְדָעָהּ	Qal	SC 3FS	ידע	

Verse 5

אֲדֹנִיָּה		PN		
חַגִּית		PN		
מִתְנַשֵּׂא	Hitpael	PTCL MS	נשא	
אֶמְלֹךְ	Qal	PC 1CS	מלך	
רֶכֶב		N.MS		"chariot"
פָּרָשִׁים		N.MP		"horse, steed"
חֲמִשִּׁים		N.M		"fifty"
רָצִים	Qal			"run"

Verse 6

עֲצָבוֹ	Qal	|SC 3MS + 3MS SF|	עצב	"hurt; grieve"
מַדּוּעַ		INTR		"why?"
כָּכָה		ADV		"thus"
עָשִׂיתָ	Qal	|SC 2MS|	עשה	
תֹּאַר		N.MS		"form"

יָלְדָה	Qal	|SC 3FS|	יָלַד	
אַבְשָׁלוֹם		PN		"Absalom"

Verse 7

יוֹאָב		PN		"Joab"
צְרוּיָה		PN		"Zeruiah"
אֶבְיָתָר		PN		"Abiathar"
וַיַּעְזְרוּ	Qal			"help"

Verse 8

צָדוֹק		P		"Zadok"
בְּנָיָהוּ		PN		"Benaiah"
יְהוֹיָדָע		PN		"Jehoiada"
נָתָן		PN		"Nathan"
שִׁמְעִי		PN		"Shimei"
רֵעִי		PN		"Rei"
גִבּוֹרִים		N.MP		"strong, mighty; hero"

Verse 9

וַיִּזְבַּח	Qal			"slaughter; sacrificial slaughter"
בָּקָר		N.MS		"cattle, herd, ox"
מְרִיא		N.MS		"fatling, fatted steer"
אֶבֶן הַזֹּחֶ־לֶת		PN		"Eben-zoheleth"
אֵצֶל		PREP		"beside"
עֵין רֹגֵל		PN		"En-rogel"

Verse 10

נָתָן		PN		"Nathan"

///////////////

CHAPTER 4

VERBAL STEMS

The Hebrew verbal stems provide a special challenge to English speakers. This language structure does not easily map one for one to English verb phrases. The semantic notions of each stem resist all-encompassing explanations, broad definitions, and translation equivalences. Moreover, the differences are not always readily apparent. Sometimes the same root with different stems is rendered in similar ways. This chapter discusses how the stems work to create meaning in Hebrew and the various approaches to understanding their variety.

4.1 GOING DEEPER WITH VERB STEMS

The showdown between Moses and Pharaoh in the opening scenes of the book of Exodus represents an apologetic for Yahweh's superiority over Egypt and her gods, of which Pharaoh is the human representative. The theological importance of this episode in the Hebrew Bible cannot be overstated. One of the dominant motifs in this episode is the heart of Pharaoh and its submission to the divine will. Theologians often ask questions about the nature of God's influence on Pharaoh's volition, particularly, the extent of his involvement in the activity of hardening Pharaoh's heart. This primary question is not merely a theological one, but it requires a thorough grammatical investigation.[1] In order to grapple with the theological issues arising in these texts, we first must wrestle with the grammar and syntax of the verbal forms that describe what was taking place in Pharaoh's heart. The Hebrew stems are front and center in this inquiry.

---

[1] The following discussion is informed by Matthew McAffee, "The Heart of Pharaoh in Exodus 4–15," *BBR* 20 (2010): 10–16.

Exodus 4–11 attests an assortment of verbs describing Pharaoh's heart. Despite the uniformity of English translations, the descriptions employ three distinct roots: (1) קשה "to be hard"; (2) כבד "to be heavy"; and (3) חזק "to be strong." Beyond the lexical distinctions, the narrative distinguishes this "hardening" activity with the employment of *Qal*, *Piel*, and *Hiphil* stems. Understanding this variation provides the interpreter useful information about Pharaoh's mental and emotional status. All three basic roots are stative, meaning that they refer to a status or condition of the heart rather than a dynamic activity. The *Qal* stem expresses that the heart of Pharaoh is hard/heavy/strong. In the *Piel*, the intransitive stative is transformed into a factitive transitive (i.e., he makes the heart hard/heavy/strong). As we will explain later in this chapter, factitive verbs can denote actions that produce a state. The *Hiphil* stem indicates causation in the sense that the subject causes an act of hardening, weighing down, or strengthening or causes another actor to harden, weigh down, or strengthen something. The following chart maps the interplay between narrative description and dynamic events as it relates to Pharaoh's heart throughout Exodus 4–15:

INTRANSITIVE	TRANSITIVE (HEART = OBJECT)	ROOT	STEM
	4:21: SUBJ Yahweh (discourse prediction)	חזק	*Piel*
	7:3: SUBJ Yahweh (discourse prediction)	קשה	*Hiphil*
7:13: SUBJ heart (narrative description)		חזק	*Qal*
7:14: SUBJ heart (narrative description)		כבד	*Qal*
7:22: SUBJ heart (narrative description)		חזק	*Qal*
	8:15[11]: SUBJ Pharaoh (narrative event)	כבד	*Hiphil*
8:19[15]: SUBJ heart (narrative description)		חזק	*Qal*
	8:32[28]: SUBJ Pharaoh (narrative event)	כבד	*Hiphil*
9:7: SUBJ heart (narrative description)		כבד	*Qal*
	9:12: SUBJ Yahweh (narrative event)	חזק	*Piel*
	9:34: SUBJ Pharaoh (narrative event)	כבד	*Hiphil*
9:35: SUBJ heart (narrative description)		חזק	*Qal*
	10:1: SUBJ Yahweh (discourse acknowledgment)	כבד	*Hiphil*

INTRANSITIVE	TRANSITIVE (HEART = OBJECT)	ROOT	STEM
	10:20: SUBJ Yahweh (narrative event)	חזק	*Piel*
	10:27: SUBJ Yahweh (narrative event)	חזק	*Piel*
	11:10: SUBJ Yahweh (narrative event)	חזק	*Piel*
	14:4: SUBJ Yahweh (discourse prediction)	חזק	*Piel*
	14:8: SUBJ Yahweh (narrative event)	חזק	*Piel*
	14:17: SUBJ Yahweh (discourse acknowledgment)	חזק	*Piel*

The English translations are not always clear in maintaining these morphosemantic distinctions. Exodus 7:13 is an example: וַיֶּחֱזַק לֵב פַּרְעֹה "The heart of Pharaoh was strong." The versions, however, render the stative verb in a variety of ways, with only the NLT and the CSB maintaining its descriptive quality:

NLT	Pharaoh's heart, however, remained hard.	*Descriptive*
CSB	However, Pharaoh's heart was hard.	*Descriptive*
NIV, NKJV	Yet Pharaoh's heart became/grew hard.	*Ingressive*
KJV	And he hardened Pharaoh's heart.	*Active*
RSV, NRSV NASB, ESV	Yet/still Pharaoh was hardened.	*Passive*

Several versions translate the Hebrew stative as a passive with Pharaoh as subject. However, the Hebrew text describes the status of Pharaoh's heart in the face of Yahweh's action (i.e., his heart was strong). This rendering gives the impression that he is being acted upon by an external agent, eliminating the readers option to understand that Pharaoh could be the one responsible for his own heart's state. Brevard Childs concludes: "The hardening is not a definite reaction to the plagues, but the description of a state."[2] These versions confuse the matter.

The *Piel* and *Hiphil* stems relate the actions of Pharaoh and Yahweh as they further harden/strengthen/weigh down the heart. These notices often come after the narrative descriptions of Pharaoh's disposition toward the divine will. For instance, Exod 8:11(15) reads וְהַכְבֵּד אֶת־לִבּוֹ "[Pharaoh] would weigh down his heart." The *Hiphil* of the stative root כבד "to be heavy" indicates an act of stubbornness on the part of Pharaoh, that is, he weighs down his obstinate position. With the *Piel* of the stative root חזק "to be strong" in Exod 9:12, Yahweh intensifies Pharaoh's strong

---

2 Brevard S. Childs, *The Book of Exodus*, OTL (Louisville: Westminster, 1974), 173–74.

resistance: וַיְחַזֵּק יהוה אֶת־לֵב פַּרְעֹה "Yahweh made the heart of Pharaoh strong."[3] In this case, Yahweh makes Pharaoh's heart even stronger (cf. Exodus 8:15[19]).

The different Hebrew stems (and roots) present the fascinating interplay between human action and the divine will. As the contest between Yahweh and Pharaoh begins, the narrative utilizes a series of *Qal* statives to describe the unresponsiveness of Pharaoh to Yahweh's command to release the Israelites from Egypt. In Exod 8:11(15), the *Hiphil* demonstrates Pharaoh's active resistance to Yahweh's will, after which the *Piel* reveals Yahweh's intensification of Pharaoh's obstinance. As the narrative progresses the focus shifts to Yahweh's relentless hardening of Pharaoh's heart, resulting in his leading the Egyptian army to their defeat at the sea.

This infamous episode provides a useful introduction to the semantics of Hebrew stems. We discuss how the alternation of stems can induce certain kinds of changes to meaning and syntax separate from the core lexical meaning of the root. This chapter details the ways in which different verbal forms combine these morphosyntactic properties to create meaning.

4.2 CHAPTER OBJECTIVES

The following sections clarify the terminology of verbal stems, roots, and conjugations. It outlines briefly the broader Semitic understanding of verb stems and describes the syntactic and semantic characteristics of verbs and verb phrases. Finally, each stem is explained in light of its various features.

4.3 INTRODUCTION

The terms used to describe or parse Hebrew verbs can be especially confusing because various authors use similar terminology with different referents. The following explanation attempts to follow the most widely accepted descriptions. The overlapping senses and terms are noted. We recommend familiarizing yourself with the different terminologies to be able to interact with a wide range of resources in Hebrew studies.

The nomenclature of stem is commonly distinguished from the terms *root* and *conjugation*. Root refers to the abstract consonantal structure made up of between two and four consonants. Stereotypically, three root letters (e.g., √כתב) demarcate the related semantics of a group of associated words (e.g., יִכְתֹּב "he writes"; כֹּתֵב "writing"; יִכָּתֵב "it is written"; כְּתָב "written record"; מִכְתָּב "inscription"). A root is different than the base lexeme or so-called dictionary form. Verbs are generally listed according to the SC 3MS (e.g., כָּתַב "he wrote").[4]

---

[3] For a full list of hardening statements, see McAffee, "Pharaoh in Exodus 4–15," 17.

[4] Note, however, that middle-weak verbs are organized in most lexicons by their infinitive construct forms, e.g., קוּם "arise" not קָם "he arose" (SC 3MS) and שִׂים "put, place" not שָׂם "he placed" (SC 3MS).

Conjugation describes the morphological patterns comprising prefixes and suffixes that together with a root create either a finite or nonfinite verb. The two main Hebrew finite verbs are the prefix and suffix forms (i.e., *yiqtol* and *qātal*, or the imperfect[ive] and perfect[ive]), as well as the two corresponding *waw* conjugations: the consecutive preterite (i.e., the *wayyiqtol* or *waw*-consecutive imperfect) and the converted perfect (i.e., *wəqātal*).[5] The nonfinite forms include the infinitives (absolute and construct) and the participles.

Finally, stem designates the distinct consonant and vowel patterning of the root that structure the basic verbal building blocks of syntax and semantics. Jewish grammarians identify the stems as *binyanim* (בִּנְיָנִים), the Hebrew word meaning "buildings."[6] Confusingly, a few grammarians enlist the term "conjugation" to refer to the Hebrew stems.[7] The association of this term with *binyanim* apparently goes back to Johann Reuchlin (AD 1455–1522) who rendered Qimḥi's Hebrew term *binyanim* as Latin *conjugatio*.[8] This correspondence is not typical in most English grammars and has received increasing scrutiny since conjugations in Latin are not the same as Hebrew *binyanim*. For this reason, we prefer the term stem or *binyanim* to describe these verbal patterns.

A division is made among the different stems. The medieval Jewish grammarians distinguished the *Qal* stem, which they called קַל meaning "light, simple," from the other stems, which they called כָּבֵד "heavy."[9] These two groupings are generally termed the basic and derived stems. The basic stem is the *Qal*. The derived stems are the *Niphal, Piel, Pual, Hitpael, Hiphil,* and *Hophal*.[10]

VERB STEM AND PATTERN TERMINOLOGY

The stem names derive from an approximation of the suffix conjugation third-person masculine singular form of the root פָּעַל "to do." The six primary derived stems are: נִפְעַל (Niphal), פִּעֵל (Piel), פֻּעַל (Pual), הִתְפַּעֵל (Hitpael), הִפְעִיל (Hiphil), and הָפְעַל (Hophal).

The inflectional patterns are abstracted using the root קְטֹל (or transcribed simply as qtl). For example, the verb כָּתַב "he wrote" is described as a קָטַל pattern (qātal), the prefix form יְכְתֹּב "he writes" is יִקְטֹל (yiqtol), the verb דִּבֶּר "he spoke" is קִטֵּל (qittel), and the verb הִמְלִיךְ is הִקְטִיל (hiqtîl).

---

[5] See chapter 5.

[6] See Arian J. C. Verheij, *Bits, Bytes, and Binyanim: A Quantitative Study of Verbal Lexeme Formations in the Hebrew Bible*, OLA 93 (Leuven: Peeters, 2000), 1.

[7] E.g., Joüon-Muraoka §40a.

[8] M. H. Goshen-Gottstein, "The System of Verbal Stems in the Classical Semitic Languages," in *Proceedings of the International Conference on Semitic Studies Held in Jerusalem, 19–23 July 1965* (Jerusalem: The Israel Academy of Sciences and Humanities, 1969), 70 n. 1.

[9] Joüon-Muraoka §40a n. 4.

[10] *IBHS* §21a; Goshen-Gottstein, "System of Verbal Stems," 70 n. 1. Note that Gesenius argued against the use of such terminology, preferring to reserve "stem" for the root consonants (GKC §30d).

4.4 SEMITIC CONTEXT

More recent comparative Semitic grammar discussions have tended to utilize a more generalized morphosemantic approach to naming the stems. These verbal stem names can be readily applied to most of the ancient Semitic languages. For example, they refer to the most basic stem of the languages as the G stem, based on the German word *Grund* meaning "ground, basic." Other designations point to either shared morphological or semantic characteristics of the verbal forms themselves. The N stem, for instance, identifies the *Niphal* in light of its prefixed *nun* in Hebrew (נִכְבַּד "he was heavy"). The D stem is so named for the doubling of the middle root consonant (i.e., דִּבֶּר "he spoke"). Grammatical variations of the D stem may further be identified semantically. The Dp stem refers to the internal passive (i.e., the *Pual*, דֻּבַּר "it was spoken"). The tD stem refers to the D stem with a prefixed consonantal morpheme -*t*- (i.e., *Hitpael*), designating reflexivity (i.e., הִתְכַּבֵּד "he weighed himself down"). Other Semitic languages attest to the Dt stem, with an infixed -*t*- (e.g., Akkadian *šutallumum* "he is made whole," √*ŠLM*), and even include additional *t* forms with other stems, such as the Gt stem (e.g., Targumic Aramaic אשתמעת "I was heard" [Cairo Genizah E Gen 30:8]). The C stem *(i.e., Hiphil)* is so named for its semantic characteristic of causativity. The morphology of the C stem is variously marked in the Semitic languages. Hebrew designates causation in the suffix conjugation with a prefixed *h*- and with a *ḥireq-yod* theme vowel (e.g., הִשְׁבִּית "he made cease"), whereas Akkadian and Ugaritic attest to the related prefixed *š*- (e.g., *ušapris* in Akkadian; *šaqtila* in Ugaritic). The Cp stem is the passive of the causative (e.g., יָעֳמַד "he is made to stand"). The designation in Hebrew grammar is commonly *Hophal.*

BIBLICAL HEBREW STEMS*			
ENGLISH NAME	HEBREW NAME	SEMITIC DESIGNATION	COMPARATIVE DESCRIPTION
Qal	קַל	G stem	Ground/Basic stem
Niphal	נִפְעַל	N stem	*Nun* stem
Piel	פִּעֵל	D stem	Doubled stem
Pual	פֻּעַל	Dp stem	Doubled-passive stem
Hitpael	הִתְפַּעֵל	tD stem	Doubled t-stem
Hiphil	הִפְעִיל	C stem	Causative stem
Hophal	הָפְעַל	Cp stem	Causative-passive stem

*The presence of ע in the R2 position (i.e., פעל) prevents the expected doubling in the *Piel, Pual,* and *Hitpael* stems.

4.5 SYNTACTIC-SEMANTIC FEATURES OF VERBS

Verbs encode a complex network of syntactic and semantic information. Based on the action (root) and the semantic situation (stem), a verb indicates the number of clause participants and their syntactic functions. The two primary clause constituents are the <u>subject</u> and the <u>object</u>. These syntactical units are designated in a variety of ways. Unlike English verbs which require explicit subjects, Hebrew verbs stipulate basic information about the <u>person</u>, <u>gender</u>, and <u>number</u> of their subjects through inflectional prefixes and suffixes. Overt subjects must agree with their corresponding finite verbs in person and gender.[11] Objects stereotypically follow the verb and may be a pronominal suffix or overtly expressed. Generally, the particle אֶת precedes a definite direct object (§7.9.1). Object pronouns may be attached directly to the verb or to an object marker.

While the verbal root conveys the basic action, Hebrew stems specify the number of clause constituents, the kinds of grammatical relations, the role of the clause participants, and the type of the referential event. These syntactic and semantic properties frame the relationship, for example, between the *Qal* and *Piel* verbs of the shared root למד.

> Deut 4:10
>
> הַקְהֶל־לִי אֶת־הָעָם וְאַשְׁמִעֵם אֶת־דְּבָרָי אֲשֶׁר יִלְמְדוּן לְיִרְאָה אֹתִי כָּל־הַיָּמִים אֲשֶׁר הֵם חַיִּים עַל־הָאֲדָמָה וְאֶת־בְּנֵיהֶם יְלַמֵּדוּן:
>
> Assemble the people to me in order that I may tell them my words so that **they will learn** to fear me all the days of their lives on the earth, and **they will teach** their children.

Notice the syntactic differences in the *Qal* and *Piel* stem of the same verbal root. As a *Qal*, the verb יִלְמְדוּן "they will learn" anticipates a subject as the conscious doer of the action, and no object is expected. The *Piel* יְלַמֵּדוּן "they will teach" likewise specifies an actor as the subject, but it also indicates the receiver of the verbal action as an object, אֶת־בְּנֵיהֶם "their children." Another way of thinking about the relationship of the *Qal* and *Piel* is by relating the differences in the semantics of the referential events. The *Piel* "to teach" (i.e., "to make learn") introduces a situation in which a causer brings about the primary verbal action of the *Qal* "to learn." The causer is the people, and they produce the event for the children. That is to say, the people make their children learn the fear of Yahweh. Variation in these syntactic and semantic features illustrate the nature of the Hebrew verb stems.

Further elaborating on the verb למד, the following chart represents the grammatical relationships of the verb to its clause <u>constituents</u>. For example, the *Qal* verb requires a subject which may be implicit (יִלְמְדוּ "they learn") or explicit (יִלְמַד הָעָם

---

[11] Number agreement may, at times, diverge between the verb and the subject based on sense over form, as with collective nouns (see §7.5.4).

"the people learn").[12] An optional object may be employed to designate what is learned (יִלְמְדוּ הָעָם אֶת־הַתּוֹרָה "the people learn the law"). The *Piel* verb expects at least one grammatical object. This constituent must be expressed overtly with a pronominal suffix (יְלַמְּדוּהָ "they teach it") or a noun phrase (יְלַמְּדוּ אֶת־הַתּוֹרָה "they teach the law"). Of course, the subject may also be expressed (יְלַמְּדוּ הָעָם אֶת־הַתּוֹרָה "the people teach the law"). A second object indicates the one being taught.[13]

OBJECT₂	OBJECT₁	SUBJECT	VERB	TRANSLATION
∅	∅	∅	יִלְמְדוּ	They learn (*Qal*).
∅	∅	הָעָם	יִלְמְדוּ	The people learn (*Qal*).
∅	אֶת־הַתּוֹרָה	הָעָם	יִלְמְדוּ	The people learn (*Qal*) the law.
∅	(אֹתָהּ)	∅	יְלַמְּדוּהָ	They teach (*Piel*) it.
∅	אֶת־הַתּוֹרָה	∅	יְלַמְּדוּ	They teach (*Piel*) the law.
∅	אֶת־הַתּוֹרָה	הָעָם	יְלַמְּדוּ	The people teach (*Piel*) the law.
אֶת־בְּנֵיהֶם	∅	הָעָם	יְלַמְּדוּ	The people teach (*Piel*) their children.
אֶת־בְּנֵיהֶם	אֶת־הַתּוֹרָה	הָעָם	יְלַמְּדוּ	The people teach (*Piel*) their children the law.

As in English, a second complement (traditionally called an <u>indirect object</u>) may be construed using a prepositional phrase rather than as an object. Most commonly, the preposition לְ- "to" is used as in Job 21:22.

Job 21:22
הַלְאֵל יְלַמֶּד־דָּעַת
Can one teach God knowledge?

The object is the content of what is taught (דַּעַת "knowledge"). And the one being taught is indicated with the prepositional phrase לְאֵל "to God."

4.6 DERIVED STEMS

Derived stems generally derive their semantic and syntactic properties from their base (*Qal*) form. These stems are formed by making morphological adjustments to the *Qal* by altering the vocalization patterns along with (1) consonantal augmentation (e.g., *Piel*, *Pual*); (2) the addition of prefixes (*Niphal*, *Hiphil/Hophal*); or (3)

---

[12] Number disagreement between the plural verb (יִלְמְדוּ) and the singular subject (הָעָם) may be motivated by the collective sense of the noun (i.e. "people" = "persons").

[13] An example of a double object is found at Deut 4:5 (לִמַּדְתִּי אֶתְכֶם חֻקִּים וּמִשְׁפָּטִים "I taught you statutes and ordinances").

both (*Hitpael*). These derived stems combine with the same inflectional suffixes and prefixes of the *Qal* to form the inflectional paradigms.

SUFFIX CONJUGATION INFLECTIONAL FORMS			
PLURAL		**SINGULAR**	
וֹOOO	3C	OOO	3M
		הָOOO	3F
מְתֶּOOO	2M	תָּOOO	2M
תֶּןOOO	2F	תְּOOO	2F
נוּOOO	1C	תִּיOOO	1C

PREFIX CONJUGATION INFLECTIONAL FORMS			
PLURAL		**SINGULAR**	
יOOOוֹ	3M	יOOO	3M
תOOOנָה	3F	תOOO	3F
תOOOוֹ	2M	תOOO	2M
תOOOנָה	2F	תOOOי	2F
נOOO	1C	אOOO	1C

PARTICIPLE INFLECTIONAL FORMS			
PLURAL		**SINGULAR**	
OOOים	M	OOO	M
OOOוֹת	F	OOOהָ / OOOת	F

4.6.1 Verb Stems in the Semitic Context

Many characteristics of the derived stems in Biblical Hebrew are similar to analogous stems in other Semitic languages. The *Piel* stem parallels other stems that duplicate the middle root consonant. While the vowels of the D stem SC are varied, the PC form is quite similar, following the pattern **yuqattil*. The *Hiphil* (C stem) correlates to other prefixed stems that use either an ʾ- or š-preformative. The syllable structure is similar with the SC and PC forms of the C stems. But the vowels are somewhat varied in both conjugations. The internal passive stems— Gp, Dp, and Cp—are Central Semitic innovations, and as such they do not exist in Akkadian or Ethiopic. The primary characteristic is the *u*-type vowel with the first syllable. The reflexive stem is largely limited to the doubled stem (tD) in Biblical Hebrew. Yet, a few unique lexemes may relate to the base reflexive (tG) stem (הִתְפָּקְדוּ "they mobilized themselves"; הִתְרָחַצְתִּי "I washed myself") and causative reflexive (Št) stem (חוה "bow down"). Other rare combinations of these stems do occur in BH (e.g., tGp הָתְפָּקְדוּ "they were counted"; tND נִשְׁתַּוָּה "be alike," which later in Mishnaic Hebrew is a productive stem נִתְפַּקֵּד "he was counted"). Finally, N stems are known in Arabic and Akkadian.

COMPARATIVE STEM MORPHOLOGY			
	BASE-STEM SC (PC)	**DOUBLED-STEM SC (PC)**	**Š/H/ʾ-STEM SC (PC)**
Active	BH קָטַל (יְקְטֹל) PBH *qatal (*yiqtul) Akk. qatili (iqtul)[ii] Arab. qatala (yaqtulu) Aram. qətal (yiqtob) Eth. qatala (yəqtəl)	BH קִטֵּל (יְקַטֵּל) PBH *qittil (*yuqattil) Akk. quttul[i] (uqattal) Arab. qattala (yuqattilu) Aram. qattel (yəqattel) Eth. qattala (yəqattəl)	BH הִקְטִיל (יַקְטִיל) PBH *hiqtīl (*yaqtīl) Akk. šuqtul (ušaqtal) Arab. ʾaqtala (yuqtilu) Aram. ʾaqtel (yaqtel) Eth. ʾaqtala (yāqtəl)
Passive	BH קֻטַל (יְקְטַל) PBH *qutal (*yuqtal) Arab. qutila (yuqtalu) (Aram.)[iii] qətīl	BH קֻטַל (יְקַטַּל) PBH *quttal (*yuquttal) Arab. quttila (yuqattalu) Aram. quttal	BH הֻקְטַל (יְקְטַל) PBH *huqtal (*yuqtal) Arab. ʾuqtila (yuqtalu) Aram. huqtal
Reflexive (t stem)	BH הִתְפָּקֵד (יִתְפָּקֵד) PBH *hitqatil (*yitqatil) Akk. qittuli (iqtatal) Arab. iqtatala (yaqtatilu) Aram. ʾitqətel (yitqətel) Eth. taqatla (yətqatal)	BH הִתְקַטֵּל (יִתְקַטֵּל) PBH *hitqattil (*yitqattil) Akk. ——— (uqtattal) Arab. taqattala (yataqattalu) Aram. ʾitqattal (yitqabbal) Eth. taqattala (yətqattal)	BH הִשְׁתַּחֲוָה (יִשְׁתַּחֲוֶה) PBH *hištaqtal (*yištaqtal) Akk. šutaqtuli (uštaqtal) Arab. istaqtala (yastaqtilu) Aram. ʾittaqtal (yittaqtal) Eth. ʾastaqtala (yāstaqtəl)
N stem	BH נִקְטַל (יְקְטַל) PBH *niqtal (*yinqatil) Arab. inqatala (yanqatilu) Akk. naqtuli (iqqattal)		

Arab. = Arabic; Aram. = (Targumic) Aramaic; Eth. = Ethiopic; PBH = proto-Biblical Hebrew
[i] Akk. stative
[ii] Akk. G preterite
[iii] Biblical Aramaic only

4.6.2 Hebrew Stem Distribution

The seven main Hebrew stems make up more than 99 percent of all BH verbs. The distribution of the seven stems is heavily weighted to the *Qal*, *Hiphil*, and *Piel*. These three main stems comprise nearly 91 percent of verb forms. More than two-thirds of Hebrew verbs are *Qal* (69 percent). The *Hiphil*, *Piel*, and *Niphal* are the next most frequent at 13 percent, 9 percent, and 5.7 percent respectively. The derived-stem passives and reflexives amount to a mere 2.3 percent of occurrences. None of the reduplicated and lengthened stems—such as the *Polel*, *Hitpolel*, *Poel*, and *Pilpel*—or the *Hištaphel* stem of the unique root חוה "bow down," occur more than two-tenths of one percent of the time.

HEBREW STEM DISTRIBUTION		
Qal 69%	Piel 9%	Hiphil 13%
Niphal 5.7%	Pual 0.6%	Hophal 0.5%
	Hitpael 1.2%	Seven Stem Total: 99.05% Other Stems: 0.95%

Biblical Hebrew includes more than 1,600 unique verb roots. Over half of these roots (859) occur a minimum of five times. Most of those roots appear at least once as *Qal* (82 percent). About 22 percent of roots occur with one stem to the exclusion of the other six main stems (see chart below). Of these roots, the largest number are exclusive to the *Qal* and make up about 16 percent of the lexemes with five or more occurrences. Only five roots occur in all seven main stems.[14]

NUMBER OF FREQUENT ROOTS EXCLUSIVE TO ONE STEM		
G/N stems	D stems	C stems
Qal 140 (16.3%)	Piel 19 (2.2%)	Hiphil 16 (1.9%)
Niphal[15] 4 (0.5%)	Pual 0 (0%)	Hophal 1 (0.1%)
	Hitpael 8 (0.9%)	

The G/N stems, D stems, and C stems make up the three main morphosemantic categories. About 37 percent of roots occurring five times or more are found exclusively in one of these stem categories. Most roots occur with forms evidenced in two stem categories (45.4 percent). One hundred fifty-five roots (18 percent) are found in the three main stem categories.

NUMBER OF FREQUENT ROOTS LIMITED TO ONE STEM CATEGORY		
G/Gp/N 236 (27.5%)	D/Dp/tD 50 (5.8%)	C/Cp 29 (3.4%)
NUMBER OF FREQUENT ROOTS LIMITED TO TWO STEM CATEGORIES		
G/N & D stems 173 (20.1%)	G/N & C stems 208 (24.2%)	D & C stems 9 (1.0%)
NUMBER OF FREQUENT ROOTS IN ALL THREE MAIN STEM CATEGORIES		
G/N, D, & C stems 155 (18.0%)		

---

[14] The five roots are: עקב, ידע, חלה, פקד, and גלה.
[15] Three roots occur once each as *Qal* passives: זרר, ישם, and רטפש.

4.6.3 Syntactic and Semantic Characteristics of the Derived Stems

The derived stems carry several generally predictable syntactic and semantic characteristics. It is best to understand these syntactic and semantic properties in relation to the base form (*Qal*) of each distinct lexeme.

The correspondences between the stems may be summarized particularly with reference to voice (§3.6.1) and valency (§3.6.3). Valency changes as one compares the stem categories, that is, moving horizontally across the columns from left to right on the chart that follows. The same lexeme generally will increase its transitivity from *Qal* stem to *Piel* or *Hiphil* stem.[16] In like manner, the number of clause arguments increases within each column of the chart as one moves from top to bottom. For example, the passive *Pual* stem of a lexeme generally has fewer arguments than the active *Piel* and reflexive *Hitpael*.

VOICE AND VALENCY OF DERIVED STEMS				
	Valency:			
		Avalent	Univalent	Bivalent	Trivalent
	Passive	*Niphal*[17] נִקְטַל	*Pual* קֻטַל	*Hophal* הֻקְטַל
Voice: Number of Arguments — fewer → greater	**Active**	*Qal* קָטַל	*Piel* קִטֵּל	*Hiphil* הִקְטִיל
	Reflexive Middle	*Niphal* נִקְטַל	*Hitpael* הִתְקַטֵּל	*Hitpael* הִתְקַטֵּל

Additional longitudinal comparisons consider the place of <u>dynamism</u> in assessing the different semantic characteristics of the derived stems (§3.6.2). While many of these generalizations hold across lexemes, the best way to understand the stem differences is to compare how the meanings of individual roots relate one to another in distinct stems. By evaluating similar roots, the primary characteristics may be differentiated for each stem.

In the following charts, four stative roots (כבד, קדש, ראה, ידע) and four fientive roots (קטר, כרת, שפך, בקע) allow for the identification of the semantic relationships between stems. Many roots are limited to pairings of the G and D stems (e.g., שפך, טמא), G and C stems (e.g., כרת, ראה), or infrequently D and C stems (e.g., קטר). Only occasionally is a root found with all three columns (e.g., בקע, ידע, כבד). In these cases, the D and C stem semantics are more difficult to differentiate. The *Hitpael* stem may serve as the productive reflexive for the C stem or D stem.[18]

---

[16] Holger Gzella, "Voice in Classical Hebrew against Its Semitic Background," *Or* 78 (2009): 292–325.

[17] The *Qal* passive (קֻטַל) was originally the basic middle/passive stem, but it was replaced by the *Niphal* for most lexemes in Biblical Hebrew. Some relics of the *Qal* passive form are still found (§3.8).

[18] Nineteen roots with five or more examples are found with the *Hitpael* and *Hiphil/Hophal* stems but not the *Piel/Pual* stems: קצף, באש, קדר, עשר, תמם, הפך, רגז, נפל, ראה, חרה, עלם, עטף, ידה, אבל, חרש, יכח, נגש, עלה, and לבן.

Some alternation between the *Niphal* and *Hitpael* stems (e.g., נִטְמָא/יִטַּמָּא "defile oneself") and the *Qal* passive and *Niphal* (e.g., נִכְרַת/כֻּרַּת "be cut off") is evident.[19]

STEM COMPARISON OF STATIVE VERBS		
	BASE	**FACTITIVE/PLURALITY**	**CAUSATIVE**

	BASE	**FACTITIVE/PLURALITY**	**CAUSATIVE**
Passive	*Qal* passive [Gp]/*Niphal* [N] נוֹדַע "become known" ——— רְאָה "be seen" (?) נִכְבַּד "become honored"	*Pual* [Dp] יֻדַּע "be known" מְטַמָּאָה "be defiled" ——— מְכֻבָּד "be honored"	*Hophal* [Cp] הוֹדַע "be made known" הָרְאָה "be shown"
Active	*Qal* [G] יָדַע "know; recognize" טָמֵא "be unclean" רָאָה "see" כָּבֵד "be heavy, honored"	*Piel* [D] יִדַּע "make known" טִמֵּא "defile" ——— כִּבֵּד "honor"	*Hiphil* [C] הוֹדִיעַ "cause to know" ——— הֶרְאָה "show" הִכְבִּיד "make heavy"
Middle/ Reflexive	*Niphal* [N] נוֹדַע "make (oneself) known" נִטְמָא "become unclean" נִרְאָה "appear"/"present oneself" נִכְבַּד "reveal (one")s honor"	*Hitpael* [tD] הִתְוַדַּע "make oneself known" יִטַּמָּא "defile oneself" הִתְרָאָה "look at oneself" הִתְכַּבֵּד "honor oneself"	

STEM COMPARISON OF FIENTIVE VERBS		

	BASE	**FACTITIVE/PLURALITY**	**CAUSATIVE**
Passive	*Qal* passive [Gp]/*Niphal* [N] נִבְקַע "be split; be broken" שֻׁפַּךְ/נִשְׁפַּךְ "be poured out" כֻּרַּת/נִכְרַת "be cut (off)" ———	*Pual* [Dp] יְבֻקְּעוּ "be ripped open" ——— מְקֻטֶּרֶת "be burned up"	*Hophal* [Cp] הָבְקְעָה "be broken into" הָכְרַת "be cut off, be destroyed" מָקְמָר "be offered in smoke"
Active	*Qal* [G] בָּקַע "split; break into" שָׁפַךְ "pour (out)" כָּרַת "cut, sever" ———	*Piel* [D] בִּקַּע "split; break apart" ——— קִטְּרוּ "burn up"	*Hiphil* [C] וַנִּבְקָעֶנָּה "break into" ——— הִכְרִית "cut off, destroy" הִקְטִיר "offer up in smoke"

---

[19] Seventy-four roots with more than five occurrences are found in both the *Niphal* and *Hitpael* stems. Of these roots, thirty-seven are not evidenced with the C stem. At least seventeen roots have both Gp and N stem usages (טרף, הרג, עבד, עזב, שפד, נקם, שרף, לקח, אכל, ילד, כרת, נתן, עשה, ראה, נתץ, שדד, and ארר). See further Reymond, "Passive Qal," 1110–27.

STEM COMPARISON OF FIENTIVE VERBS			
	BASE	FACTITIVE/PLURALITY	CAUSATIVE
Middle/ Reflex- ive	*Niphal* [N] נִבְקַע "break (oneself) out" ——— נִכְרַת "cut (oneself) off" ———	*Hitpael* [tD] הִתְבַּקֵּעוּ "burst (oneself) open" תִּשְׁתַּפֵּךְ "pour oneself out" ———	

Other details regarding verb situations and thematic roles are discussed as part of each verb stem description below.

4.7 NIPHAL STEM

4.7.1 Morphology of the *Niphal*

The *Niphal* is characterized morphologically by a prefixed *nun*. The *nun* is directly adjacent to the beginning of the root, and any inflectional prefixes are attached secondarily. This preformative is overt as -נִ in the strong root forms of the suffix conjugation (נִקְטַל), participle (נִקְטָל), and infinitive absolute (נִקְטֹל).[20] For the forms with inflectional prefixes, the stem preformative *nun* closes the initial syllable and assimilates to the first consonant of the root. These forms include the prefix conjugation (יִקָּטֵל), the imperative (הִקָּטֵל), the infinitive construct (הִקָּטֵל), and an alternate infinitive absolute (הִקָּטֹל). Characteristically, the assimilated *nun* forms have an *hireq* vowel with the prefix syllable and an irreducible *qameṣ* with first root letter.[21] The three-syllable structure (*CVn-R_1V-R_2VR_3) is preserved with -הִ for the imperative and the infinitives. Unlike the other derived stems, the participle does not have a *mem* preformative.

PREFORMATIVE MORPHOLOGY OF THE *NIPHAL* STEM		
	UNASSIMILATED *NUN*	ASSIMILATED *NUN*
Suffix Conjugation	נִקְטַל	———
Prefix Conjugation	———	יִקָּטֵל
Participle	נִקְטָל	———

---

[20] First-weak (e.g. ידע), middle-weak (e.g. מוג), geminate (e.g. קלל) and some first guttural roots (e.g. עשׂה) evidence a historical /a/ vowel with the preformative syllable: נוֹדַע (<*nawdaʕ); נָמוֹג, and נֶעֱשָׂה, and נָקַל.

[21] With first-guttural and first-*reš* roots, the initial vowel is *ṣere*: תֵּרָאֶה, יֵאָכֵל, etc. First-weak verbs pattern like first-*waw* roots regardless of their original root (cf. תִּוָּדַע and יִוָּשַׁע). Other first guttural roots pattern with *segol* without (נֶעְדָּר) or with secondary opening (נֶאֱסַף).

PREFORMATIVE MORPHOLOGY OF THE *NIPHAL* STEM		
	UNASSIMILATED *NUN*	ASSIMILATED *NUN*
Imperative	——	הִקָּטֵל
Infinitive Construct	——	הִקָּטֵל
Infinitive Absolute[22]	נִקְטֹל	הִקָּטֹל

4.7.2 Semantics of the *Niphal*

The *Niphal* conveys a range of mostly non-active meanings. It serves as the principal grammatically marked form for voice alternation with the *Qal*. Generally, the *Niphal* is used in situations where the actor is not overtly expressed. In cases where the semantics of the verbal root anticipate an actor or causer to be the source of the action, the *Niphal* serves to <u>de-agentify</u> or remove the semantic role of causer, doer, or instigator (i.e., agent) from a clause. The subject typically becomes the entity which undergoes, receives, or experiences the effect of the action.

COMPARATIVE SEMITICS OF THE N STEM

The semantics of the *Niphal* stem overlap with that of the N stems found in several Semitic languages. The Ugaritic N stem and Stem VII in Arabic (*infaʿala*) are de-agentified, intransitive, and anticausative stems.[23] The *Niphal* likely originated as primarily an anticausative stem. The Old Assyrian N stem denotes the mediopassive, reciprocal, and ingressive notions.[24] Notably, Semitic N stem verbs with very few exceptions do not indicate their agents as adjuncts. Unlike many European languages which can demote the agent using a nonobligatory structure (e.g., English *by*, Greek ὑπὸ, or the Latin ablative), Semitic languages do not allow for the expression of a non-subject agent.

The *Niphal* stem is best understood in relation to the semantics of the *Qal*. The overwhelming majority of roots occurring as the *Niphal* stem correspond to their *Qal* meanings.[25] The *Niphal* exhibits two negative semantic-syntactic traits as compared with the *Qal*. First, the *Niphal* obscures the semantic role of the agent. An

---

[22] Each root selects one of these forms. Half of the thirty different roots take one form and half the other.

[23] See Pierre Bordreuil and Dennis G. Pardee, *A Manuel of Ugaritic*, LSAWS 3 (Winona Lake, IN: Eisenbrauns, 2009), 47; Peter John Glanville, *The Lexical Semantics of the Arabic Verb* (Oxford: Oxford University Press, 2018), 51, 60–61, 111.

[24] N. J. C. Kouwenberg, *Introduction to Old Assyrian* (Munster: Zaphon, 2019), 98–99.

[25] For a detailed numerical analysis and discussion of the relationship to other non-*Qal* stems, see P. A. Siebesma, *The Function of the Niphʾal in Biblical Hebrew: In Relationship to Other Passive-Reflexive Verbal Stems and to the Puʾal and Hophʾal in Particular*, SSN 28 (Assen, NL: Van Gorcum, 1991).

affected entity (patient) is typically construed as the subject. Second, the *Niphal* reduces the transitivity. The result is a derivational intransitive verb form.

Traditionally the *Niphal* is described using passive, middle, reciprocal, or reflex-ive notions.[26] Others prefer the term <u>mediopassive</u> or several other designations.[27] The following sections outline the main uses of the *Niphal* as anticausative, mid-dle, passive, ingressive, reciprocal, and reflexive. These non-active *Niphal* notions are discussed as semantic and syntactic derivatives—or possibly more accurately, alternations—of a base stem, most typically the active *Qal*. A small number of *Niphal* verbs do not display obvious dissimilarity with their *Qal* usage and will be discussed at the end of this section. Finally, several *Niphal* verbs are not isolated to one of these classifications. They may be used with multiple meanings, which are only differentiated by context.

4.7.2.1 Anticausative

The causative-anticausative alternation describes the presence or absence of the se-mantic role of causer (§3.6.4). Depending on a verb's lexical semantics, the causer may be equivalent to the subject of the basic verb or require added elements. As such, a basic verb construction may include lexicalized causative semantics (e.g., *the mother wakes up the child*), or, sometimes, a special morphological form is needed to designate the presence of a specified cause (e.g., *the mother makes the child wake up*). In contrast, <u>anticausative</u> verbs eliminate the causer as a clause constituent and include only one core constituent, which is entailed by the action or event, without reference to the causer of that action or event (e.g., *the child wakes up*).

BASIC, CAUSATIVE, AND ANTICAUSATIVE ALTERNATION					
SEMANTIC ROLE:	CAUSER	AUXILIARY	AGENT	ACTION	PATIENT
Basic	*the mother*	Ø	Ø	*wakes up*	*the child*
Causative	*the mother*	*makes*	*the child*	*wake up*	Ø
Anticausative	Ø	Ø	*the child*	*wakes up*	Ø

In Hebrew, the causative semantics may be encoded with the *Qal* stem. To add the role of causer, a verb is designated morphosemantically by either the *Hiphil* or *Piel* stems. As an anticausative, the *Niphal* stem serves to remove the causer and typically expresses the remaining semantic role as the agent/subject.

The *Niphal* commonly designates the anticausative in relation to a *Qal* verb with fientive and causative semantics. For example, the *Qal* verb בקע "split, break open" designates both the causer and the patient. Psalm 74:15 demonstrates the basic

---

[26] GKC §51; Joüon-Muraoka §51c; *BHRG* §16.3.2; Blau, 227–28.

[27] Boyd, "Binyanim," 97–100. Additional descriptions include <u>tolerative</u>, <u>resultative</u>, and <u>bene-factive</u> (*IBHS* §23.4).

notion with the subject (Yahweh) as the causer of the verb. The waterways are the object/patient. The *Niphal* stem, alternatively, is anticausative. Genesis 7:11 does not indicate the causer but instead designates the waterways as the agent/subject.

בקע *Qal / Niphal*

> Ps 74:15
>
> אַתָּה בָקַעְתָּ מַעְיָן וָנָחַל
>
> You **split open** (*Qal*) the springs and wadis.

> Gen 7:11
>
> נִבְקְעוּ כָּל־מַעְיְנֹת תְּהוֹם רַבָּה
>
> All of the springs of the great deep **split open** (*Niphal*).

A similar anticausative notion is found with some usages of the *Niphal* of כרת "to cut." Joshua 3:13 describes what happened when the feet of the priests carrying the ark reached the Jordan River. The subject of the anticausative *Niphal* verb, נִכְרַת "stop, cease," is the affected entity. The causer, presumably God, is unexpressed.

> Josh 3:13
>
> מֵי הַיַּרְדֵּן יִכָּרֵתוּן הַמַּיִם הַיֹּרְדִים מִלְמָעְלָה וְיַעַמְדוּ נֵד אֶחָד׃
>
> The waters of the Jordan **stopped** (*Niphal*) the waters flowing from upriver. They stood as one heap.

Other causative-anticausative alternations are found when comparing the *Hiphil* with the *Niphal* stems of certain verbs, particularly those without *Qal* forms. For example, שאר expresses a causer with the *Hiphil* causative stem ("leave" or "allow to remain;" e.g., 1 Sam 14:36) and without a causer with the *Niphal* anticausative stem ("be left" or "remain;" e.g., 2 Kgs 10:21).

שאר *Hiphil / Niphal*

> 1 Sam 14:36
>
> וְלֹא־נַשְׁאֵר בָּהֶם אִישׁ
>
> We will not **allow** a man **to remain** (*Hiphil*) among them.

> 2 Kgs 10:21
>
> וְלֹא־נִשְׁאַר אִישׁ
>
> A man **did** not **remain** (*Niphal*).

4.7.2.2 Middle

The middle voice indicates that the subject of the verb undergoes or experiences the verbal action to some degree or way. In English, middle verbs have the same form as an active verb (e.g., *she opens the door* [active] ~ *the door opens* [middle]) as opposed to the passive verb (e.g., *the door is opened* [passive]). In Hebrew, the alternation is often signaled with the *Qal* and *Niphal*.

פתח *Qal / Niphal*

Ezek 46:12

וּפָתַח לוֹ אֶת־הַשַּׁעַר הַפֹּנֶה קָדִים

He will open (*Qal*) for him the eastern facing gate.

Nah 2:7

שַׁעֲרֵי הַנְּהָרוֹת נִפְתָּחוּ

The river gates **open** (*Niphal*).

This active-middle alternation may be observed in Num 22:25 with two forms of the verb לחץ "press, push." The first form is the *Niphal* and the second *Qal*. The *Qal* form is fientive and transitive: וַתִּלְחַץ אֶת־רֶגֶל בִּלְעָם אֶל־הַקִּיר "[the female don-key] pressed Balaam's foot against the cliff-wall." The *Niphal* form, in contrast, is middle, and the subject experiences the verbal action. The donkey both undertakes and undergoes the action: וַתִּלָּחֵץ אֶל־הַקִּיר "[the female donkey] pressed up against the cliff-wall."

Num 22:25

וַתֵּרֶא הָאָתוֹן אֶת־מַלְאַךְ יְהוָה וַתִּלָּחֵץ אֶל־הַקִּיר וַתִּלְחַץ אֶת־רֶגֶל בִּלְעָם אֶל־הַקִּיר וַיֹּסֶף לְהַכֹּתָהּ:

When the female donkey saw the angel of Yahweh, **she pressed** (*Niphal*) up against the cliff-wall and **pressed** (*Qal*) Balaam's foot against the wall. Then he struck her again.

The middle notion illuminates the action of seeing God in the Jacob narrative. The *Qal* verb ראה "see," indicates the basic notion of vision. Jacob describes his famous wrestling match at Peniel as seeing God (Gen 32:31). Later in the story, the narrator describes a second theophany and relates this manifestation with the first one. But this time, the *Niphal* of ראה is used to indicate that God undertakes or undergoes the action.[28] God "appeared" to Jacob (Gen 35:9), and he again calls his name Israel ("wrestler," cf. 32:28; 35:10).

ראה *Qal / Niphal*

Gen 32:31

רָאִיתִי אֱלֹהִים פָּנִים אֶל־פָּנִים

I saw (*Qal*) God face to face.

Gen 35:9

וַיֵּרָא אֱלֹהִים אֶל־יַעֲקֹב עוֹד

God **appeared** (*Niphal*) to Jacob again.

---

[28] Less likely is the analysis of this usage as a reflexive "make himself to be seen." See Boyd, "Binyamin," 98.

A few middle verbs express their primary meaning in the *Niphal*. Examples include transitive verbs, like נבא "to prophesy" (see below §4.8.4), and intransitive verbs, such as רדם "to sleep deeply" and מלט "to escape."

נבא *Niphal*

Jer 25:30

וְאַתָּה תִּנָּבֵא אֲלֵיהֶם אֵת כָּל־הַדְּבָרִים הָאֵלֶּה

You **must prophesy** (*Niphal*) to them all these matters.

רדם *Niphal*

Jonah 1:5

וַיִּשְׁכַּב וַיֵּרָדַם

He laid down and **slept** (*Niphal*).

מלט *Niphal*

1 Sam 19:10

וְדָוִד נָס וַיִּמָּלֵט בַּלַּיְלָה הוּא

But David ran away, and he **escaped** (*Niphal*) at night.

4.7.2.3 Passive

The <u>passive</u> notion of the *Niphal* situates the patient as the subject which undergoes an action or is acted upon. The agent of the fientive verb is not expressed but may be assumed.[29] In this way, the alternation of the basic and passive semantics is similar to the basic and anticausative (§4.7.2.1). Unlike an English passive, the agent is not expressed elsewhere in the clause. As such, it may be better to understand this usage as primarily removing the agent, that is, <u>de-agentifying</u>.

The interchange of the *Qal* and *Niphal* stems of כרת "cut" follows the active-passive alternation. The agent and patient is expressed with the *Qal* as in 2 Chr 2:15. The agent, however, is not expressed with the *Niphal* verb form as with אִם־יִכָּרֵת "If a tree should be cut down" (Job 14:7). The subject in this case is עֵץ "a tree" from the first part of the sentence.

כרת *Qal / Niphal*

2 Chr 2:15

וַאֲנַחְנוּ נִכְרֹת עֵצִים מִן־הַלְּבָנוֹן

We **will cut timber** from Lebanon (*Qal*).

---

[29] See, further, Ellen van Wolde, "The Niphal as Middle Voice and Its Consequence for Meaning," *JSOT* 43 (2019): 453–78. We do not agree with van Wolde's analysis that the *Niphal* "predominantly marks the middle voice"; rather, it expresses "various meanings—the middle and passive being only two examples" as stated by Ethan C. Jones, "Hearing the 'Voice' of the Niphal: A Response to Ellen van Wolde," *JSOT* 45 (2021): 294.

Job 14:7

כִּי יֵשׁ לָעֵץ תִּקְוָה אִם־יִכָּרֵת

For even a tree has hope if **it is cut down** (*Niphal*).

The verb שׁפך "pour out" denotes primarily the fientive action of removing a sub-stance from its usual container. These substances and containers include blood in persons/animals (Ps 106:38; Lev 4:7), water in rivers/seas/vessels (Exod 4:9; Amos 9:6; 1 Sam 17:6), drink-offering in a vessel (Isa 57:6), bile in kidneys (Job 16:13), innards in a person (2 Sam 20:10), broth in a pot (Judg 6:20), dust in a house (Lev 14:41), ashes on an altar (1 Kgs 13:3), and a number of metaphori-cal extensions. The *Qal* includes the subject/agent and the object being removed. In Deut 12:23–24, the Israelites are instructed not to consume the blood of their sacrifices, but they are to "pour out" the blood on the ground. The originating con-tainer may be implied, especially if the substance is uniquely found in only one kind of container, as with blood in living beings. The *Qal* passive and *Niphal* have equivalent de-agentifying semantics.[30] In both cases below, the patient is typically construed as the subject of the intransitive verb.

שׁפך *Qal* / *Qal* passive / *Niphal*

Deut 12:24

עַל־הָאָרֶץ תִּשְׁפְּכֶנּוּ כַּמָּיִם

Upon the ground, you **shall pour out** (*Qal*) it (i.e., the blood) like water.

Zeph 1:17

וְשֻׁפַּךְ דָּמָם כֶּעָפָר

Their blood **will be shed** (*Qal* passive[31]) like dust.

Deut 12:27

וְדַם־זְבָחֶיךָ יִשָּׁפֵךְ עַל־מִזְבַּח יהוה אֱלֹהֶיךָ

The blood of your sacrifices **shall be poured out** (*Niphal*) upon the altar of Yahweh your God.

4.7.2.4 Ingressive (Inchoative)

The *Niphal* stem of stative verbs does not function like the three previous groups. In their basic (*Qal*) form, stative verbs are intransitive. As a result, it would not seem possible to remove the subject, and no patient is available to assume the place of the subject. The *Niphal* stem of stative verbs is used principally to indicate in-gressive (or <u>inchoative</u>) notions. An <u>ingressive</u> denotes the initiation or beginning

---

[30] It is widely understood that the *Niphal* assumes the semantic space vacated by the loss of the *Qal* passive before Tiberian Hebrew. Crosslinguistically, anticausative verbs are known to take on pas-sive notions; see Bernd Heine and Tania Kuteva, *World Lexicon of Grammaticalization* (Cambridge: Cambridge University Press, 2002), 44.

[31] See *Qal* passive (§3.8) for more details on this form in Tiberian Hebrew.

of an action or state. A related description specifies "the nuance of potentiality" for the *Niphal* of stative verbs.[32]

The stative-ingressive alternation is observable with the root כבד "be honored." The *Qal* stative verb כָּבֵד "be honored" in Job 14:21 describes a son whose father is dead and knows not of his future honor. Alternatively, using the ingressive *Niphal* נִכְבַּד "become honored," Saul's daughter Michal, in 2 Sam 6:20, despises David and complains about his exuberant reaction at the return of the ark of Yahweh: "How could the king hope to begin to be honored?" Her accusation is concerned with the shame that the king brought on Israel (and her father's house) through his unseemly behavior rather than his honoring of himself (reflexive) as most modern English translations suggest (CSB, ESV, NASB, NIV).[33]

כבד *Qal / Niphal*

Job 14:21

יִכְבְּדוּ בָנָיו וְלֹא יֵדַע

[If] his sons **are honored** (*Qal*), he does not know.

2 Sam 6:20

מַה־נִּכְבַּד הַיּוֹם מֶלֶךְ יִשְׂרָאֵל אֲשֶׁר נִגְלָה הַיּוֹם לְעֵינֵי אַמְהוֹת עֲבָדָיו

How can the king of Israel **begin to be honored** (*Niphal*) today as he has been exposed today in the eyes of his servants' maidens?

4.7.2.5 Reciprocal

The reciprocal conveys a shared action (or event) between the multiple agents. It is similar to the middle but often is made up of multiple discrete actions. Frequently, this notion is expressed with a plural verb. In these cases, the plural subject consists of both the doers and the receivers of the verbal notion. In English, these expressions require reciprocal pronouns (e.g., *each other*) or noun phrases (e.g., *one to another*). Hebrew also conveys a similar notion with other constructions, like אִישׁ לְרֵעֵהוּ "each to his neighbor."

The active-reciprocal alternation is exemplified by the *Qal* and *Niphal* forms of אסף "to gather." In Gen 29:22, the *Qal* verb is used to indicate a transitive fientive action. The subject, Laban, causes the action of gathering the locals. Alternatively, the *Niphal* verb is used for multiple discrete and reciprocal actions. In Judg 9:6,

---

[32] Lambdin, §140. Lambdin includes this notion within the category of the resultative meaning of the *Niphal* of stative verbs. The resultative "describes the state of its subject which has been produced by the verbal action named by the root," and he exemplifies the active-passive-resultative as פָּתַח "to open," נִפְתַּח "to be opened," and נִפְתָּח "to be open" (§140 [177]).

[33] Another interpretation would understand some *Niphal* verb usages—particularly those with divine subjects—as נִכְבַּד "reveal (one's) honor," that is, as a tolerative: "Tolerative constructions (usually singular) involve an agent (usually human) allowing itself to undergo an action (cf. 'He let himself be chosen')." See *IBHS* §20.2n, also §23.1h; following Ernst Jenni, *Lehrbuch der hebräischen Sprache des Alten Testaments* (Basel: Helbing and Lichtenhahn, 1981).

it indicates that each of the inhabitants of Shechem and Beth-Millo gathered with one another.

אסף *Qal / Niphal*

Gen 29:22

וַיֶּאֱסֹף לָבָן אֶת־כָּל־אַנְשֵׁי הַמָּקוֹם

Laban **assembled** (*Qal*) all the men of the place.

Judg 9:6

וַיֵּאָסְפוּ כָּל־בַּעֲלֵי שְׁכֶם וְכָל־בֵּית מִלּוֹא וַיֵּלְכוּ וַיַּמְלִיכוּ אֶת־אֲבִימֶלֶךְ לְמֶלֶךְ

All the citizens of Shechem and Beth-Millo **assembled together** (*Niphal*). They went and appointed Abimelech king.

The verb לחם "to fight" is used almost exclusively in the *Niphal* stem and expresses reciprocal semantics. That is to say, the verb implies that the action includes multiple discrete actions with multiple agents. Most typically, the verb indicates multiple agents with reference to a grammatical or conceptually plural subject.[34] In 1 Sam 28:15, Saul tells the conjured prophet that the Philistines were fighting against him. The implication is that the plural subject, the Philistines, engaged Saul on multiple occasions. Rarely, the verb implies the reciprocal notion. An example is 1 Sam 8:20. The king is said to fight on behalf of the people.[35] The great irony here is Samuel had warned the people (vv. 11–12) that the king would himself conscript their sons as agents of war—it would not just be the king fighting!

לחם *Niphal / Niphal*

1 Sam 28:15

וּפְלִשְׁתִּים | נִלְחָמִים בִּי וֵאלֹהִים סָר מֵעָלַי

The Philistines **are fighting** (*Niphal*) against me, but God has abandoned me!

1 Sam 8:20

וּשְׁפָטָנוּ מַלְכֵּנוּ וְיָצָא לְפָנֵינוּ וְנִלְחַם אֶת־מִלְחֲמֹתֵנוּ

Our king will judge us, he will go out before us, and he **will fight** (*Niphal*) our battles.

4.7.2.6 Reflexive

Dissimilar from the reciprocal, the <u>reflexive</u> notion conveys an action in which the agent and patient are coreferential. In English, a reflexive is expressed using a reflexive pronoun: *oneself, himself, herself, themselves, yourself*. Hebrew typically does not indicate the reflexive with the *Niphal* but favors either the *Hitpael* stem (see §4.8.4) or a self-referential construction (e.g., נַפְשׁוֹ "himself"). In Lev 11:43,

---

[34] Camil Staps, "A Case Study of Reciprocal Middles in Biblical Hebrew: The Niphal of לחם," *Or* 87 (2018) 159–83.

[35] Notice the contrast with Exod 14:14: יהוה יִלָּחֵם לָכֶם "Yahweh will fight for you."

these three constructions are contiguous. The first clause employs a *Piel* verb with the reflexive pronoun (נַפְשֹׁתֵיכֶם "yourselves"). The second clause consists of a reflexive *Hitpael* stem of the stative verb טמא "be unclean." The third clause indicates the ingressive notion with the *Niphal* of the same root, וְנִטְמֵתֶם "you shall become unclean," rather than the reflexive sense, *you shall be unclean yourselves*.

Lev 11:43

אַל־תְּשַׁקְּצוּ אֶת־נַפְשֹׁתֵיכֶם בְּכָל־הַשֶּׁרֶץ הַשֹּׁרֵץ וְלֹא תִטַּמְּאוּ בָּהֶם וְנִטְמֵתֶם בָּם׃

Do not **make yourselves detestable** (*Piel*) with any swarming thing. You shall not **make yourselves unclean** (*Hitpael*) with them, and you shall **become unclean** (*Niphal*) with them.

4.7.2.7 Equivalent to the Qal

A very small number of roots function with indistinguishable semantics between their *Qal* and *Niphal* verbs. One example is the root כשל "stumble."[36] The verb נגשׁ "approach" is another possible example; however, the form distribution between *Niphal* suffix conjugations and *Qal* prefix conjugations may be better understood as a case of suppletion.[37]

כשל *Qal / Niphal*

Jer 6:21

הִנְנִי נֹתֵן אֶל־הָעָם הַזֶּה מִכְשֹׁלִים וְכָשְׁלוּ בָם

Beware, I am placing stumbling-blocks before this people, they **will stumble** (*Qal*) on them.

Jer 6:15

לָכֵן יִפְּלוּ בַנֹּפְלִים בְּעֵת־פְּקַדְתִּים יִכָּשְׁלוּ

Therefore, they will fall with the fallen ones; when I punish them, they **will stumble** (*Niphal*).

4.8 PIEL/PUAL/HITPAEL STEMS

4.8.1 Morphology of the *Piel*

The distinguishing morphological feature of the *Piel* is its characteristic doubling of the middle root consonant. It is sometimes called the D stem for this reason (i.e., doubling stem).

---

[36] An intriguing result of this semantic similarity is found with Isa 40:30 (וְיָעֵפוּ נְעָרִים וְיִגָעוּ וּבַחוּרִים כָּשׁוֹל יִכָּשֵׁלוּ "Lads will grow weary and exhausted, and youth will certainly stumble"). The final construction includes the *Qal* infinitive absolute paired with the finite *Niphal* verb. The more common formation pairs similar roots and stems together.

[37] *IBHS* §23.6.1c.

The SC vowel patterns are varied. The 3MS suffix conjugation features *ḥireq* with the first root radical (e.g., סִפֵּר, חִזֵּק, דִּבֵּר), while the doubled radical attests *segol*, *ṣere*, and *pataḥ*. In all subsequent forms of the SC paradigm, the non-reduced vowel with the doubled radical is always *pataḥ*. The doubling of the second radical in the בקשׁ example disappears when the vowel reduces to *shewa*, according to the *Skin 'em alive* or *Skin 'em Levi* rule.[38]

	PIEL I/E SUFFIX CONJUGATION	
P	**S**	
דִּבְּרוּ	דִּבֶּר/דִּבֵּר	3M
——	דִּבְּרָה	3F
דִּבַּרְתֶּם	דִּבַּרְתָּ	2M
דִּבַּרְתֶּן	דִּבַּרְתְּ	2F
דִּבַּרְנוּ	דִּבַּרְתִּי	1C

	PIEL I/Ē SUFFIX CONJUGATION	
P	**S**	
בִּקְשׁוּ	בִּקֵּשׁ	3M
——	בִּקְשָׁה	3F
בִּקַּשְׁתֶּם	בִּקַּשְׁתָּ	2M
בִּקַּשְׁתֶּן	בִּקַּשְׁתְּ	2F
בִּקַּשְׁנוּ	בִּקַּשְׁתִּי	1C

	PIEL I/A SUFFIX CONJUGATION	
P	**S**	
לִמְּדוּ	לִמַּד	3M
——	לִמְּדָה	3F
לִמַּדְתֶּם	לִמַּדְתָּ	2M
לִמַּדְתֶּן	לִמַּדְתְּ	2F
לִמַּדְנוּ	לִמַּדְתִּי	1C

---

[38] When the doubled consonants שׂ/ס, ק, נ, מ, ל, ו, or י (thus, *Skin 'em Levi*) are followed by a *shewa*, the doubling typically disappears. The most cited example is וַיְהִי, for which one would expect *וַיְּהִי. Note, however, that the doubling is preserved in the root למד (e.g., לִמְּדוּ).

As already mentioned, the Masoretic tradition shows vowel variation between *segol* and *ṣere* with the doubled radical, even within a single root (דִּבֶּר vs. דִּבֵּר). II-guttural roots show compensatory lengthening of the first radical *ḥireq* to *ṣere*, as in בֵּרֵךְ. As with the variation of *segol* and *ṣere*, the second vowel with the doubled radical sometimes alternates with *pataḥ* (e.g., גִּדֵּל/גִּדַּל; בֵּרֵךְ/בֵּרַךְ).

PIEL SC HISTORICAL DEVELOPMENT

The underlying form behind the *Piel* SC is most likely **qattal*. The historical development would be **qattal* > **qittal* > **qittil* > *qittēl*. Comparative evidence furnishes external justification for positing an historical base **qattal*. Arabic's form II (equivalent of Semitic D stem) attests *qattala* (also in Ethiopic) in the suffix conjugation (e.g., *kabbara*), which scholars cite in support of this historical reconstruction.[39] New Kingdom Egyptian inscriptions possibly offer evidence for the second stage of development, attesting D stem *qittala*.[40] Hebrew first and second-person forms may likewise preserve this earlier stage (e.g., כִּבַּדְתַּנִי, סִפַּרְתִּי, כִּפַּרְתֶּם), which becomes *qittil* in the 3MS. The final **qittil* is also found in Phoenician proper names.[41] A different development apparently occurred in Aramaic, where one finds *qattil* (e.g., כַּתֵּב and sometimes כַּתֵּב).[42]

John Huehnergard proposes that the original D stem suffix form was **qattil* rather than **qattal*. He cites the Ugaritic syllabic form *ša-li-ma*, which he analyzes as a suffix conjugation D stem form /šallima/, from text RS 20.012 as evidence in favor of this reconstruction.[43] He argues that **qattil* eventually changed to **qittil* by way of regressive assimilation.[44] Huehnergard nonetheless admits that his reconstruction does not easily account for Arabic and Ethiopic *qattala*, which he designates as "parallel innovations."[45] Recent evidence from Ugaritic, however, has brought this analysis of the Ugaritic D stem into question. Pierre Bordrueil and Dennis Pardee cite the form *ihb* from the recent text

---

[39] See W. M. Thackston, *An Introduction to Koranic and Classical Arabic* (Bethesda, MD: IBEX, 1994), 162–64.

[40] See Anson F. Rainey, *Canaanite in the Amarna Tablets: A Linguistic Analysis of the Mixed Dialect Used by Scribes from Canaan*, vol. 2, *Morphosyntactic Analysis of the Verbal System* (Leiden: Brill, 1996), 311.

[41] The proper name *b ʾlšlk* "Baʾal has saved" is transliterated with Greek characters as βαλσιλληχ and with Latin characters as Balsillec. See Stanislav Segert, *A Grammar of Phoenician and Punic* (Munich: Beck, 1976), 140; J. Friedrich and W. Röllig, *Phönizisch-Punische Grammatik*, 3rd ed., ed. M. G. Amadasi Guzzo, AnOr 55 (Rome: Pontifical Biblical Institute, 1999), §143.

[42] Franz Rosenthal, *A Grammar of Biblical Aramaic*, 7th ed., Porta Linguarum Orientalium 5 (Wiesbaden: Harrassowitz, 2006), 64.

[43] John Huehnergard, *Ugaritic Vocabulary in Syllabic Transcription*, Rev. ed., HSS 32 (Winona Lake, IN: Eisenbrauns, 2008), 182, 321; Huehnergard, "Historical Phonology and the Hebrew Piel," in *Linguistics and Biblical Hebrew*, ed. W. R. Bodine (Winona Lake, IN: Eisenbrauns, 1992), 209–29. The form *ša-li-ma* appears in the Ugaritic syllabic text RS 20.012; see J. Nougayrol, "Textes suméro-accadiens des archives et bibliothèques privées d'Ugarit," in *Ugaritica V*, ed. Charles Virolleaud et al., Bibliothèque Archéologique et Historique 80, Mission de Ras Shamra 16 (Paris: Imprimerie Nationale, 1968), text 96. There is some dispute as to the reading of the first sign of this word. Huehnergard argues the signs should be read *šal-li-ma*, with doubled *lamed*, requiring the form to be interpreted as a D stem (*Ugaritic Vocabulary*, 182). Nougayrol, however, read *ša-li-ma* and interpreted it as a G stem stative *šalima* "he is well."

[44] Huehnergard, "Hebrew Piel," 219, 228–29.

[45] Huehnergard, 227.

RS 94.2168, which attests to *'alep-i* as the first root radical.[46] This spelling suggests the vocalization, *'ihhaba* "he loved."[47] This form accords with the evidence from Amarna Canaanite, as well as the Masoretic vocalization *qittal-* (as cited above), again pointing to an intermediary development between proto-Hebrew **qattal* and *qittēl*.

The *Piel* prefix conjugation vowel pattern is יְכַבֵּד "he makes heavy." The 3MS form consistently attests *ṣere* with the doubled radical. The prefix vowel is always reduced to *shewa* (< **yVqattil*).

PIEL PREFIX CONJUGATION		
P	S	
יְכַבְּדוּ	יְכַבֵּד	3M
תְּכַבֵּדְנָה	תְּכַבֵּד	3F
תְּכַבְּדוּ	תְּכַבְּדִי	2M
תְּכַבֵּדְנָה	תְּכַבֵּד	2F
נְכַבֵּד	אֲכַבֵּד	1C

PIEL PC HISTORICAL DEVELOPMENT

Scholars appeal to comparative evidence to reconstruct the first vowel of the *Piel* PC (i.e., **yVqattilu*). Bordreuil and Pardee cite Ugaritic 1CS forms and their consistent use of *'alep-a* for the 1CS prefix, which indicates a prefixed /a/ vowel.[48] For example, in *KTU* 1.18 I:29 we find *âlmdk* (/'alammiduka/) "I will teach you."[49] They follow other scholars in assuming that the /a/ vowel must have appeared in the second and third persons as well.[50] Against this view, Josef Tropper argues that the /a/ vowel apparent in the 1CS forms must have been a secondary development. The historical prefix vowel was originally /u/, and the /a/ of the 1CS forms arose by influence of the *'alep*.[51] His basis for positing the prefixed /u/ is largely comparative, in that Akkadian (D-stem preterite *uparris*)

---

[46] Ugaritic utilized a series of three *'aleps* (*ȧ*, *ȧ*, and *u̇*) that are thought to have indicated three vowel qualities (*a*, *i*, and *u* respectively). For more on the Ugaritic alphabet, see §1.4.2.

[47] Bordreuil and Pardee, *Manual of Ugaritic*, 259. For the *editio princeps* of RS 94.2168, see Pierre Bordreuil and Dennis Pardee with Robert Hawley, *Une bibliothèque au sud de la ville. Textes 1994–2002 en cunéiforme alphabétique de la maison d'Ourtenou*, Ras Shamra-Ougarit 18 (Paris: Maison de l'Orient et de la Méditerranée, 2012), 135–41.

[48] Bordreuil and Pardee, *Manual of Ugaritic*, 52. They cite *ȧnṣq*, vocalized /'anaššiq/ "I will assault" (RS 3.367 IV:4′).

[49] For more examples, see Tropper, *Ugaritische Grammatik*, 550–52.

[50] See also Cyrus H. Gordon, *Ugaritic Textbook: Grammar, Texts in Transliteration, Cuneiform Selections, Glossary, Indices*, rev. ed., AnOr 38 (Rome: Pontifical Biblical Institute, 1998), §9.35; Stanislav Segert, *A Basic Grammar of the Ugaritic Language* (Berkeley: University of California Press, 1984), §54.41.

[51] Tropper, *Ugaritische Grammatik*, 545.

and Arabic (form II prefix *yufaʿil-*) attest to /u/-vowel prefixes in the D stem.[52] Huehnergard likewise agrees that the /a/ vowel of the 1CS may have arisen secondarily, perhaps by way of vowel harmony.[53] He further entertains the possibility that the prefix vowel could have been /i/ based upon another syllabic spelling: ti-tar-ri(?)-za (/titarriza/ "may she hasten"), but does so "with much reservation."[54] Although the evidence from Ugaritic supports an /a/ vowel prefix in the D stem, the comparative picture leaves things much murkier. The fact that the Hebrew Masoretic tradition always reduces this vowel to *shewa* only lessens the certainty of any one proposal.

4.8.2 Semantics of the *Piel*

The function of the Hebrew *Piel* stem (Semitic D stem) has posed great difficulty for grammarians. Scholars have struggled to find a satisfactory means of explaining its semantic variability throughout the language. Front and center in these discussions is the nature of the morphological doubling of the second radical. Scholars have attempted to find a satisfactory way of tying the meaning of the *Piel* to its morphological doubling in one way or another.

4.8.2.1 Intensive Framework of the *Piel*

Many grammarians have proposed that the doubling quality is somehow related to its intensive meaning.[55] Gesenius's comments are representative of this approach:

> The fundamental idea of *Piʿēl*, to which all various shades of meaning in this conjugation may be referred, is to busy oneself eagerly with the action indicated by the stem. This intensifying of the idea of the stem, which is outwardly expressed by the strengthening of the second radical, appears in individual cases as—(a) a *strengthening* and *repetition* of the action . . . [and] (b) a *causative* sense (like *Hiphʿîl*).[56]

Gesenius also comments on the denominative use of the *Piel*, whereby the *Piel* stem is used for certain verbs derived from nouns, but he does not explain this usage as having any connection to the fundamental idea of intensity ascribed to this stem.[57]

4.8.2.2 Factitive Framework of the *Piel*

Recent grammarians have made several attempts at finding a synchronic explanation for the diverse uses of the *Piel*. Various treatments have focused on the

---

[52] Wolfram von Soden with Werner R. Mayer, *Grundriss der akkadischen Grammatik*, 3rd ed., AnOr 33 (Rome: Pontifical Biblical Institute, 1995), §88; Thackston, *Koranic and Classical Arabic*, 163.

[53] Huehnergard, *An Introduction to Ugaritic* (Peabody, MA: Hendrickson, 2012), 64.

[54] Huehnergard, *Introduction to Ugaritic*, 64; Huehnergard, *Ugaritic Vocabulary*, 403.

[55] This idea goes back to early Arab grammarians, which in turn influenced early Jewish scholars. See Albrecht Goetze, "The So-Called Intensive of the Semitic Languages," *JAOS* 62 (1942): 1.

[56] GKC §52.f–g.

[57] GKC §52.h. Gesenius defines this use as generally expressing "a being occupied with the object expressed by the noun, either to form or to make use of it."

semantic connection between the so-called intensive and the causative. The following two examples illustrate this semantic variation.

Intensive

Exod 32:19

וַיְשַׁבֵּר אֹתָם

[Moses] **smashed** [the tablets] **in pieces**.

Causative

Exod 9:12

וַיְחַזֵּק יְהוָה אֶת־לֵב פַּרְעֹה

Yahweh **made** the heart of Pharaoh **strong**.

In an influential article on the Semitic "intensives," Albrecht Goetze challenged the long-held idea that the doubled middle radical was in any way related to the semantics of the D stem. This notion must be discarded, he urged. Its meaning must be determined by a broad survey of actual uses and their accompanying contexts.[58] His analysis focuses on the Akkadian D stem and its relationship to the G stem stative with regard to transitivity. By nature, stative verbs are <u>denominal</u> (or perhaps more accurately, "de-adjectival," or derived from adjectives), and are thus intransitive.[59] D stem verbs are by nature transitive but are related to stative verbs semantically. In fact, Goetze concluded that "in Akkadian all D stems . . . are in parallelism with statives" and are in actuality derived from them. He outlines the correlation between D stem types and three categories of statives:[60]

1. *The durative stative*: "an inherent quality of a person or thing" (e.g., *ṭāb* "is good," *šalim* "is well," *ḫaliq* "is lost")
2. *The perfective stative*: "a condition which results from the subject's own action with reference to a person or thing" (e.g., *aḫiz* "holds," *maḫer* "has received," *lamid* "has learnt")
3. *The passive stative*: "a state of affairs which results from another person's action; but the agent remains unspecified" (e.g., *aḫiz* "(is) held," *maḫer* "(is) received," *lamid* "(is) learnt").

The class of D stem denominatives, for which classification has eluded grammarians, essentially represents the fundamental notion of this stem, since it is derived from the stative, whose origin is found in the adjective.[61] The result of this formulation is that the fundamental notion of the D stem is to transitivize the stative, so that the action of the D stem produces a resulting state. In other words, the D stem is essentially factitive. The exception to Goetze's assertion, however, is a small

---

[58] Goetze, "So-Called Intensive," 2.
[59] See our discussion of verb completion and valency, §3.6.3.
[60] Goetze, "So-Called Intensive," 5.
[61] Goetze, 6.

subclass of Akkadian D stem verbs that do not fit his thesis.[62] These verbs describe a state of continuous action and thus cannot easily be derived from the stative.

Other scholars since Goetze have adapted his factitive interpretation of the Akkadian D stem to the Hebrew *Piel*. Ernst Jenni goes further than Goetze in arguing that all *Piel* verbs can be explained according to the factitive thesis.[63] Stuart A. Ryder advances Goetze's view that the D stem denominatives are derived from G stem statives a step further by suggesting that the D stem arose rather independently of the verbal stems. All D stem verbs are denominal in that they arose in opposition to nominal. He posits that the morphological doubling of the second radical may have been an attempt to imitate quadriliterals (four root-letter verbs), which were exclusively denominal verbs in the Semitic languages. This newly created "quadriliteral" (by virtue of the doubled second radical) was then incorporated into the verbal system as the D stem.[64]

Ryder divides the Hebrew *Piel* into two broad categories with further subdivisions:

D Stems Transformative
Associated with G stems durative stative (e.g., שָׁלֵם "be whole"/שִׁלֵּם "make whole")
Associated with G stems perfect stative (e.g., לָמַד "learn"/לִמֵּד "teach")
Associated with G stems transitive (e.g., קָבַר "bury"/קִבֵּר "bury")

D Stems Non-Transformative
Associated with nominal forms (e.g., דָּבָר "word"/דִּבֵּר "speak")
Associated with G stems intransitive (e.g., הָלַךְ "walk"/הִלֵּךְ "walk")[65]

Much like Goetze, Ryder is not compelled to insist that all uses of the *Piel* fall within the category of factitive.[66] One would expect outliers given that the stem was originally derived from nominals with diverse lexical content.

Bruce Waltke and Michael O'Connor follow Jenni in proposing that all *Piel* verbs can be explained in terms of a factitive framework. The *Piel* is primarily

---

[62] Goetze, 6–7 lists the following examples: *uḫḫurum* "to lag behind," *lupputum* "to loiter," *nubbūm* "to bawl," *qubbûm* "to shout," *ruppudum* "to roam," *ruqqudum* "to dance," *dullupum* "to run relentlessly to and fro," *lussumum* "to sprint," *nummušum* "to roam."

[63] Ernst Jenni, *Das hebräische Pi'el: Syntaktisch-semasiologische Untersuchung einer Verbalform im Alten Testament* (Zurich: EVZ Verlag, 1968), 264–74.

[64] Stuart A. Ryder, *The D-Stem in Western Semitic* (The Hague: Mouton, 1974), 43. Ryder explains further: "The gemination of the D-stem seems to be a similar extension of the triliteral root in order to confirm to a quadriliteral pattern originally associated with denominative (or nominal) verbs. These denominatives in turn seem to have come into existence as a result of an impulse external to the verbal system proper, whereby the prefixal and suffixal morphemes of the verbal system were combined with the nominal stems to create new verbal forms" (164).

[65] For a full list of Hebrew roots for each category, see Ryder, *D-Stem*, 97–105, 108–18, 123–28, and 130–34.

[66] Ryder, *D-Stem*, 46, qualifies that the denominal origin of the D stem does not mean that every usage can be traced back to a denominative meaning. Of the denominative usage, he states that it "would have given this stem predominance in the area of denominative verbs, tending to usurp this function when it arose in the simple triliteral stem and only later yielding ground to the *hiph'il* forms."

"associated with causation: the *Piel* causes a state rather than an action (as the *Hiphil*), for which we reserve the term causative." They continue, "Since the object of causation is in a state of suffering the effects of an action, it is inherently passive in part." Waltke and O'Connor argue that this formulation accords with Jenni's desire to find "the 'living' unity of the stem system."[67] This system divides the uses of the *Piel* into the following categories:[68]

1. *Factitive* (*Qal* intransitive > *Piel* factitive > *Hiphil* causative). The *Piel* puts its object into the state described by the corresponding *Qal*. The *Hiphil* indicates the cause of the action.

צדק *Qal* / *Piel* / *Hiphil*

Job 35:7

אִם־צָדַקְתָּ מַה־תִּתֶּן־לֹו
If **you are righteous** (*Qal*), what will you give him?

Job 32:2

חָרָה אַפּוֹ עַל־צַדְּקוֹ נַפְשׁוֹ מֵאֱלֹהִים
His anger burned because **he justified** (*Piel*) himself more than God.

Job 27:5

חָלִילָה לִּי אִם־אַצְדִּיק אֶתְכֶם עַד־אֶגְוָע
May I not **declare** you **to be right** (*Hiphil*) until I perish.

כבד *Qal* / *Piel* / *Hiphil*

Isa 66:5

יִכְבַּד יְהוָֹה וְנִרְאֶה בְשִׂמְחַתְכֶם
Let Yahweh **be honored** (*Qal*), that we may see your gladness.

Mal 1:6

בֵּן יְכַבֵּד אָב וְעֶבֶד אֲדֹנָיו
A son **honors** (*Piel*) a father, and a servant his master.

Exod 8:11(15)

וְהַכְבֵּד אֶת־לִבּוֹ
[Pharaoh] **would weigh down** (*Hiphil*) his heart."

2. *Resultative* (*Qal* transitive > *Piel* resultative > *Hiphil* causative). The *Qal* focuses on the execution of the act, whereas the *Piel* emphasizes the achieved result of the action and the *Hiphil* focuses on the cause of the action.

---

[67] *IBHS* §24.1i.

[68] The following major categories are adapted from *IBHS* §24.2–5, which relies heavily on Jenni (*Das hebräische Pi'el*) throughout the discussion.

אבד *Qal / Piel / Hiphil*

Deut 11:17

וַאֲבַדְתֶּם מְהֵרָה מֵעַל הָאָרֶץ הַטֹּבָה אֲשֶׁר יְהוָה נֹתֵן לָכֶם

You will perish (*Qal*) quickly from upon the good land Yahweh is giving you.

2 Kgs 11:1

וַתְּאַבֵּד אֵת כָּל־זֶרַע הַמַּמְלָכָה

She **made** all the royal seed **perish** (*Piel*).

Lev 23:30

וְהַאֲבַדְתִּי אֶת־הַנֶּפֶשׁ הַהִוא מִקֶּרֶב עַמָּהּ

I will **cause** that soul **to perish** (*Hiphil*) from the midst of its people.

3. *Denominative* (*Piel* verbs derived from nominals).

דבר Noun / *Piel*

2 Sam 3:17

וּדְבַר־אַבְנֵר הָיָה עִם־זִקְנֵי יִשְׂרָאֵל

The **word** (noun) of Abner was with the elders of Israel.

Gen 12:4

וַיֵּלֶךְ אַבְרָם כַּאֲשֶׁר דִּבֶּר אֵלָיו יְהוָה

Abram went as Yahweh **had spoken** (i.e., spoke a word, *Piel*) to him.

כהן Noun / *Piel*

Gen 14:18

וְהוּא כֹהֵן לְאֵל עֶלְיוֹן

Now he [Melchizedek] was **priest** (noun) to El Elyon.

Num 3:4

וַיְכַהֵן אֶלְעָזָר וְאִיתָמָר עַל־פְּנֵי אַהֲרֹן אֲבִיהֶם

Eleazar and Ithamar **served as priest** (*Piel*) before Aaron their father.

4. *Frequentative* (*Qal* intransitives denoting physical movement or effort > *Piel* frequentative aspect[69]).

---

[69] Cf. this function of the *Piel* with the iterative/frequentative (also called habitual or customary) use of the prefix/*wəqātal* conjugations, as in 1 Sam 7:16:

וְהָלַךְ מִדֵּי שָׁנָה בְּשָׁנָה וְסָבַב בֵּית־אֵל וְהַגִּלְגָּל וְהַמִּצְפָּה וְשָׁפַט אֶת־יִשְׂרָאֵל אֵת כָּל־הַמְּקוֹמוֹת הָאֵלֶּה׃

Now Samuel would go around yearly to Bethel, Gilgal, and Mizpah and would judge Israel at all these places.

For more on this use of the prefix conjugation, see §5.7.2.1.

הלך *Qal / Piel*

Gen 18:33

וַיֵּלֶךְ יְהוָֹה כַּאֲשֶׁר כִּלָּה לְדַבֵּר אֶל־אַבְרָהָם

Yahweh **departed** (*Qal*) when he had finished speaking to Abraham.

Ps 55:15

אֲשֶׁר יַחְדָּו נַמְתִּיק סוֹד בְּבֵית אֱלֹהִים נְהַלֵּךְ בְּרָגֶשׁ:

We, who together made sweet counsel, in the house of God, **would frequently walk** (*Piel*) in procession.

קוה *Qal / Piel*

Ps 69:7

אַל־יֵבֹשׁוּ בִי| קֹוֶיךָ אֲדֹנָי יְהוִה צְבָאוֹת

Let **those waiting** (*Qal*) on you not be ashamed on account of me, Lord Yahweh of armies.

Gen 49:18

לִישׁוּעָתְךָ קִוִּיתִי יְהוָה:

For your salvation **I wait and wait** (*Piel*), Yahweh.

4.8.2.3 Transitivity and Verbal Plurality Framework of the Piel

Waltke and O'Connor specify a fifth category they call "other," under which they discuss Jenni's proposed verbal plurality use—distinguishing between *Qal* verbs that transmit action to a single object versus *Piel* verbs that transmit action to multiple objects.[70] They surmise, however, that such examples may reflect "an analogical extension of the frequentative from (a relatively few) intransitive verbs to transitive verbs."[71] This disagreement raises broader questions related to the role of transitivity and verbal plurality (§3.6.5) in the semantics of the *Piel*.

Other grammarians have appealed to the linguistic concept of semantic transitivity, or what we have called completion (§3.6.3), as one means of explaining the D stem synchronically. John Beckman defines semantic transitivity as "the extent to which the subject of the clause affects the direct object."[72] Unlike syntactical transitivity, which indicates whether the verb has or does not have a direct object, semantic transitivity can have a high level of transitivity (the verb significantly entails its object) or low transitivity (the verb has a limited or no effect on the object). For example, G stem stative verbs are low in semantic transitivity because the subject of the verb is a patient of the state. In other words, the patient status of the subject is reflected because it is being described by the verb. Grammatically

---

[70] *IBHS* §24.3.3, citing Jenni, *Das hebräische Pi'el*, 143.

[71] *IBHS* §24.3.3.

[72] John C. Beckman, "Toward the Meaning of the Biblical Hebrew Piel Stem" (PhD diss., Harvard University, 2015), 22.

speaking, stative verbs describe the state or condition of the subject rather than its activity (e.g., *he is great*), and therefore cannot take a direct object. This situation represents low semantic transitivity. Stative verbs raise their transitivity in the D stem, in that they add a verbal agent (the subject), which now entails its patient (e.g., *he makes X great*).[73] In this scenario, the patient of the G stem has been transformed into the agent of the newly introduced patient (i.e., it has changed its valency).

N. J. C. Kouwenberg helpfully outlines the following transitive/intransitive categories for the Akkadian G and D stems:[74]

Type I: verbs that are transitive in both the G and D stems
Type II: verbs that are intransitive in both the G and D stems
Type III: verbs that are intransitive in the G stem, but transitive in the D stem
Type IV: verbs that are transitive in the G stem, but doubly transitive in the D stem

He summarizes the uses of the D stem in light of these types as follows:

1. D stems of intransitive process verbs (what he calls "adjectival" or stative verbs) are factitive, their essential feature being that they change the nature of the subject from non-agentive to agentive ("the agentive counterpart of the G-stem;" e.g., *qatû* G "to come to an end," D "to end, finish").[75]

2. D stems of intransitive action verbs are also intransitive consisting of a small number of <u>atelic</u> action verbs with narrow ranges of meanings including sounds (*nabāḫu* G and D "to bark"), bodily functions *saʾalu* G and D "to cough"), and mental activities (*kapādu* G and D "to think, plan").[76]

3. D stems of transitive process verbs, which are small in number, work the same way as intransitive process verbs, and are therefore factitive (*labāšu* G "to wear, put on," D "to dress someone"; *lamādu* G "to know, learn," D "to inform")[77]

4. D stems of transitive action verbs produce specialized meanings. Many examples underscore the plurality of events and/or participants. Kouwenberg clarifies: "The greater the effect of an action on the patient, the stronger the tendency to use the D-stem if the direct object is plural."[78] Some verbs indicate intensive actions, as in prolonged or forceful action. Still others take on idiomatic meanings.

---

[73] Beckman, 213.
[74] N. J. C. Kouwenberg, *Gemination in the Akkadian Verb* (Assen: Van Gorcum, 1997), 91.
[75] Kouwenberg, *The Akkadian Verb and Its Semitic Background* (Winona Lake, IN: Eisenbrauns, 2010), 272.
[76] Kouwenberg, 274.
[77] Kouwenberg, 274.
[78] Kouwenberg, 274–75.

The fundamental relationship between the G and D stems, according to Kouwen-berg, involves a raise in transitivity, most clearly demonstrated by G intransitive verbs in opposition to their D transitive counterparts. Kouwenberg explains:

> If the G-stem itself is intransitive, there is a sharp contrast in transitivity between G and D; they occupy opposite positions on either end of the transitivity scale; if it is transitive, the difference in transitivity is small, and their positions on the transitivity scale are more or less contiguous. This explains why the relationship between the G- and D-stems of transitive is quite different from that of intransitive verbs.[79]

Another important consideration for articulating the meaning of the D stem—and one that factors into Kouwenberg's approach—is verbal plurality. As mentioned earlier in this chapter, verbal plurality concerns the multiplicity of an event.[80] Scholars have applied this crosslinguistic formulation of verbal plurality to the meanings proposed for the D stem in the Semitic languages. As Beckman notes, it unifies Gesenius's intensive and iterative meanings, but not his causative (i.e., factitive), declarative, or denominative.[81] Nonetheless, Abdelkader Fehri appeals directly to verbal plurality as a means of demonstrating the link between intensive and factitive uses of the *Piel*.[82] He argues that the doubled middle root consonant expresses verbal plurality, which can represent repeated action or multiple subjects acting on multiple objects for transitive verbs on the one hand. It can convert syntactically intransitive verbs to transitive verbs with the addition of an object on the other.

Other scholars have argued that the factitive meaning cannot be subsumed under verbal plurality, however.[83] For example, Kouwenberg proposes the factitive developed historically from adjectives marked for intensity (much like Ryder's development from adjectives > denominatives > the D stem).[84] Beckman rather notes that the move from iterative to factitive may actually involve a change in

---

[79] Kouwenberg, *Gemination*, 105.

[80] Wolfgang Dressler divides verbal plurality into four categories: (1) iterative (repeated action); (2) distributive (action affecting multiple subjects or objects or a state affecting multiple subjects); (3) continuous (habitual or customary action); and (4) intensive (action with a heightened degree of certainty). See *Studien zur verbalen Pluralität: Iterativum, Distributivum, Durativum, Intensivum in der allgemeinen Grammatik, im Lateinischen und Hethitischen* (Vienna: Böhlau im Kommission, 1968), cited in Beckman, "Piel Stem," 56.

[81] Beckman, "Piel Stem," 59–60, referencing GKC §52f–h.

[82] Abdelkader Fassi Fehri, "Verbal Plurality, Transitivity, and Causativity," in *Research in Afroasiatic Grammar 2: Selected Papers from the Fifth Conference on Afroasiatic Languages, Paris, 2000*, ed. Jacqueline Lecarme (Philadelphia: Benjamins, 2003), 151–85.

[83] E.g., Kouwenberg, *Gemination*, 117–75; Stephen A. Kaufman, "Semitics: Directions and Re-Directions," in *The Study of the Ancient Near East in the Twenty-First Century: The William Foxwell Albright Centennial Conference*, ed. Jerrold S. Cooper and Glenn M. Schwartz (Winona Lake, IN: Eisenbrauns, 1996), 280–82; Joseph Greenberg, "The Last Stages of Grammatical Elements: Contractive and Expansive Desemanticization," in *Approaches to Grammaticalization*, ed. E. Traugott and B. Heine (Amsterdam: Benjamins, 1991), 301–14.

[84] Kouwenberg, *Gemination*, 435–37.

semantic transitivity and is thus an extension of Dressler's plurality of intensity (category 4). High semantic transitivity indicates the subject greatly impacts the object, whereas low semantic transitivity suggests little to no effect on the object.[85] In terms of plurality, "intensive verbal plurality increases semantic transitivity by increasing the affectedness of the object," while "iterative and continuous verbal plurality decrease semantic transitivity because they are intrinsically imperfective and atelic."[86] The verb's intensification effect on the object results in a productive function of the D stem.

Waltke and O'Connor's adaptation of Jenni presents a comprehensive system that is able to account for the majority of the uses of the Hebrew *Piel*. There are, however, a few alleged shortcomings. Beckman points out that their distinction between the *Piel* as producing a state and the *Hiphil* as causing an action does not always hold true. Three verbal roots attest to *Piel* uses in which the subject causes an action: I-אשׁר "to walk (as lifestyle)" in the *Piel* can mean "to cause someone to carry out the process of walking" (Prov 23:19); ילד "to give birth" in the *Piel* can indicate "to help someone do the process of giving birth" (Exod 1:16); and צחק "to laugh" in the *Piel* means "to cause someone to laugh" (Judg 16:25).[87] On the surface, these examples appear to violate Waltke and O'Connor's restriction of the *Piel* exclusively to factitive meanings, but further analysis brings this criticism into question. In the first example from Prov 23:19, the root-I אשׁר does not simply mean "to walk as a lifestyle," as Beckman defines it, but "to walk in a straight or morally upright manner." We might translate the text in this way: וְאַשֵּׁר בַּדֶּרֶךְ לִבֶּךָ "Make your heart walk uprightly in the way." This usage could just as well be explained as a factitive: to produce a state of upright behavior. Exodus 1:16 reads: בְּיַלֶּדְכֶן אֶת־הָעִבְרִיּוֹת "when you assist the Hebrew women in giving birth." A strictly causative interpretation will not work, since the midwives were not causing them to enter into the process of giving birth. Rather, they were assisting those who were in the state of childbirth. Here, the factitive meaning is plausible, while a causative meaning is unworkable. Besides, the causative *Hiphil* of this root is reserved for the act of conception itself.[88] Finally, we have been unable to find a causative use for the *Piel* of צחק. The closest one finds is Judg 16:25: קִרְאוּ לְשִׁמְשׁוֹן וִישַׂחֶק־לָנוּ "Call in Samson that he might make us laugh." The *lāmed* preposition, however, would suggest the meaning "make sport for us," which again seems to indicate a state of amusement.[89]

The above survey highlights the difficulty scholars have had in assessing the function of the D stem. The conversation, however, demonstrates significant progress toward agreement. The Jenni/Waltke and O'Connor approach is extremely

---

[85] See Beckman, "Piel Stem," 21–22.
[86] Beckman, 61.
[87] Beckman, 218.
[88] See BDB, 409.
[89] Beckman entertains this possibility, but finds it unconvincing ("Piel Stem," 218 n. 127).

appealing considering its elegance as a systematic explanation, and the criticisms leveled against it are not devastating but may only require further refinement.

In summary, Beckman demonstrates the usefulness of semantic transitivity and verbal plurality in explaining most uses of the Hebrew *Piel* (D stem). Beckman compares the framework of Waltke and O'Connor and that of Kouwenberg. By placing these two theoretical approaches together, he provides unique solutions for the difficulties inherent in previous scholarship. We would agree that both frameworks are valuable for better understanding the semantic character of this debated verb morphology, even though the two approaches come from different theoretical starting points. For students of Biblical Hebrew, Kouwenberg's proposal is perhaps less familiar, but Beckman's appropriation of it is an important step forward in our understanding of this stem.

4.8.3 Pual: Morphology and Semantics

Morphology. The theme vowel of the *Pual* is /u/ throughout the verbal conjugations. The historical form of the suffix conjugation was presumably *quttal. The prefix conjugation was likely *yaquttal with prefix /ya-/, that is, if we adopt the reconstructed prefix vowel for the *Piel* as outlined above. The *Pual* is meagerly attested in Biblical Hebrew, so full verbal paradigms are not possible. The following forms illustrate the general morphology of the stem.

SC:	לֻמַּד	"he is taught" (Jer 31:18)
PC:	יְבֻקַּשׁ	"he is sought after" (Jer 50:20)
PTCL:	מְגֻדָּלִים	"be brought up" (Ps 144:12)
INF ABS:	גֻּנֹּב	"stolen" (Gen 40:15)
INF CSTR:	עֻנּוֹתוֹ	"his infliction" (Ps 132:1)

When the middle root consonant is a guttural א, ע, ר, the preceding short /u/ (Tiberian: *qibbuṣ*) undergoes compensatory lengthening to *holem*, as in the root ברך: יְבֹרַךְ "he is blessed" (2 Sam 7:29); מְבֹרָךְ "one who is blessed" (Num 22:6).

Function. The *Pual* functions as the passive voice of the *Piel*. The factitive meaning of the *Piel* involves the subject transforming the syntactical object into the state resulting from the action of the verb (§4.8.2.2). The *Pual* is an alternation of the *Piel*. The object affected by the resulting state produced by the *Piel* changes into the passive subject of the verb. No agent is expressed.

	S	V	O
Piel	Samuel angered the man (i.e., Samuel made the man angry).		
	S	V	
Pual	The man was angered (i.e., the man was made angry).		

This *Piel* ~ *Pual* alternation is exemplified with the intransitive and transitive verbs: גדל "be large," למד "learn," and חלק "divide, share."

גדל *Intransitive* Qal
    Qal "to be large"
    Piel "to make large, great"
    Pual "to be made large, great"

PIEL		PUAL	
בַּיּוֹם הַהוּא **גִּדַּל** יְהוָה אֶת־יְהוֹשֻׁעַ בְּעֵינֵי כָּל־יִשְׂרָאֵל	In that day, Yahweh **made** Joshua **great** in the eyes of all Israel (Josh 4:14).	אֲשֶׁר בָּנֵינוּ׀ כִּנְטִעִים֙ **מְגֻדָּלִים**	In that our sons are like **raised** plants (Ps 144:12).

למד *Intransitive* Qal
    Qal "to learn"
    Piel "to teach"
    Pual "to be taught"

PIEL		PUAL	
וְיֹתֵר שֶׁהָיָה קֹהֶלֶת חָכָם עוֹד **לִמַּד־דַּעַת** אֶת־הָעָם	In addition to the fact that he was wise, Qoheleth also **taught** the people knowledge (Eccl 12:9).	וַתְּהִי יִרְאָתָם֙ אֹתִי מִצְוַת אֲנָשִׁים **מְלֻמָּדָה**׃	Their fear of me was a commandment **learned** from men (Isa 29:13).

חלק *Transitive* Qal
    Qal "to divide, share"
    Piel "to apportion"
    Pual "to be apportioned"

PIEL		PUAL	
וְיָדוֹ **חִלְּקַתָּה** לָהֶם בַּקָּו	His hand **has apportioned** it to them by line (Isa 34:17).	וְאַדְמָתְךָ בַּחֶבֶל **תְּחֻלָּק**	Your land **will be apportioned** by the sword (Amos 7:17).

4.8.4 Hitpael: Morphosemantics

Morphology. The *Hitpael* or tD stem is formed by prefixing {t} to the *Piel* or D stem. We propose that the prefix conjugation yields a historical base *yatqattal (> *yitqattēl*). Scholars have proposed that the vowel under the second root consonant was historically short /a/ in the prefix and suffix conjugations based on comparative evidence. Ugaritic III-ʾalep verbs, for instance, attest {å} in the prefix conjugation, which likely indicates an /a/ vowel: *yštål* (*yišta"al*) in *KTU* 2.42:23.[90] Arabic likewise attests prefix form *tafaᶜala* and suffix form *yatafaᶜalu*.[91] The corresponding Aramaic forms are similar: prefix form *yitqattal*; suffix forms *hitqattal/ 'itqattal*.[92] The /a/ vowel proposal finds support within Hebrew itself, however, in that forms whose third root consonant begins a stressed syllable attest *pataḥ* (יִתְהַלֵּךְ vs. וַיִּתְהַלְּכְנָה). Although this morphological aspect is not unique to the *Hitpael*,[93] it does contrast with the *Piel*, where the same stressed syllable yields *ṣere* instead (e.g., וַתְּדַבֵּרְנָה in 1 Sam 4:20). In addition to the prefixed {t}, the suffix conjugation adds a prefixed {h} with short /i/ *ḥireq*: *hatqattal (> *hitqattēl*). The historical basis of the prefixed {h} is difficult to account for and may have arisen on analogy to the prefixed {h} of the *Hiphil*.[94] Evidence for this analogy may reside in the fact that Aramaic attests the variations *hit-* and *'it-* for the tD stem, which is analogous to the C stem variations *ha-* (*Haphel*) and *'a-* (*'Aphel*). At one time, Hebrew likely had a Gt stem, which eventually fell out of use and collapsed with the other reflexive stems. Sometimes the *Hitpael* of certain roots seems to express reciprocal action of the *Qal* semantics rather than the *Piel*. This phenomenon may also point to an original Gt stem.[95]

The following examples of the widely attested root הלך "to walk" (*Hitpael*: "to walk around, about") illustrate the main forms of the various paradigms:

SC:	הִתְהַלֵּךְ	"he walked around" (Gen 6:9)
PC:	יִתְהַלֵּךְ	"it goes around" (Prov 23:31)
CP:	וַיִּתְהַלְּכוּ	"they went about" (Judg 21:24)
IMPV:	הִתְהַלֵּךְ	"walk about" (Gen 13:17)
PTCL:	מִתְהַלֵּךְ	"walking around" (Gen 3:8)
INF CSTR:	לְהִתְהַלֵּךְ	"to walk about" (Ps 56:14)

The first root consonant will augment this infixed {t} in two ways. First, if the initial consonant is a dental (i.e., unvoiced ת, voiced ד, or emphatic ט), the infixed {t} assimilates to the following consonant. Second, if the first root consonant is a sibilant (i.e., ז, ס, שׂ, שׁ, or emphatic צ), the form undergoes metathesis, whereby the infixed {t} and the first root consonant switch places. Furthermore, in the case of the emphatic sibilant צ, the infixed {t} transforms to the corresponding emphatic dental ט.

---

[90] See Tropper, *Ugaritische Grammatik*, 571; Bordreuil and Pardee, *Manual of Ugaritic*, 53.

[91] Thackston, *Koranic and Classical Arabic*, 174.

[92] See Rosenthal, *Biblical Aramaic*, 48, 66–67; Steven E. Fassberg, *A Grammar of Palestinian Targum Fragments from the Cairo Genizah*, HSS 38 (Atlanta: Scholars Press, 1990), 178.

[93] It also occurs for the *Niphal* (יִשָּׁמֵר vs. יִשָּׁמַרְנָה).

[94] Blau, 233.

[95] Blau, 232, cites תִּתְרָאוּ meaning "you look on each other" in Gen 42:1. Note that Huehnergard reconstructs theme vowel /i/ for the Gt in Ugaritic: *'iqatila* (SC) and *yiqtatilu* (PC). See "A Dt in Stem in Ugaritic?," *UF* 17 (1986): 402; followed by Bordreuil and Pardee, *Manual of Ugaritic*, 53. This accords with the Aramaic reflexive stem, written with *ṣere*, e.g. אתקטל in Cairo Genizah Targum Fragment Gen 37:33; see Fassberg, *Palestinian Targum Fragments*, 177.

Reflexive. The primary function of the *Hitpael* in Hebrew is to express the reflexive of the *Piel*. Reflexivity means that the agent and patient of the verbal action are the same, or in syntactical terms, the verbal action affects the subject of that action (§3.6.1). Since the factitive meaning of the *Piel* indicates action resulting in a state, the *Hitpael* thus produces a state in the one doing the action.

צדק

> *Qal* "to be just, righteous"
> *Piel* "to make someone just, righteous"
> *Hitpael* "to justify oneself"

Gen 44:16

וּמַה־**נִּצְטַדָּק**

How **can we justify ourselves**?

קדשׁ

> *Qal* "to be holy"
> *Piel* "to consecrate someone/something"
> *Hitpael* "to consecrate oneself"

Josh 3:5

הִתְקַדָּשׁוּ כִּי מָחָר יַעֲשֶׂה יְהוָה בְּקִרְבְּכֶם נִפְלָאֹות:

Consecrate yourselves for tomorrow Yahweh will perform wonders in your midst.

Indirect Reflexive. Some *Hitpael* verbs denote actions that influences the grammatical subject indirectly rather than directly. In the following example (Exod 33:6), the action done to the object indirectly affects the subject

Exod 33:6

וַיִּתְנַצְּלוּ בְנֵי־יִשְׂרָאֵל אֶת־עֶדְיָם

The sons of Israel **stripped themselves** of their ornaments.

Sometimes the indirect action is done for the advantage of the subject, as in the use פלל "to pray to a deity on behalf of oneself" (Isa 44:17).

Isa 44:17

וְיִתְפַּלֵּל אֵלָיו וְיֹאמַר הַצִּילֵנִי כִּי אֵלִי אָתָּה:

He prays to it **for himself** and says, "Deliver me, for you are my god."

Reciprocal. Reciprocal action involves multiple entities being affected by the verbal action. Reciprocity falls under the category of verbal plurality (§3.6.5). A commonly cited example is found in Genesis 42:1.

Gen 42:1

וַיֹּאמֶר יַעֲקֹב לְבָנָיו לָמָּה **תִּתְרָאוּ**:

Jacob said to his sons, "Why are you **looking at one another**?"

Denominative. Several *Hitpael* denominatives indicate the notion of pretension. One prominent example discussed in the literature is הִתְנַבֵּא "to prophesy," from the noun נָבִיא "prophet." Simon B. Parker once argued that the *Hitpael* (and *Niphal*) form represented the remnants of an earlier Canaanite form of prophecy characterized by ecstatic utterance distinct from the usual activity of the נָבִיא elsewhere in the HB. He defined this meaning, "to be in, or to fall into, a possession trance."[96] As he argued, the Israelites adopted this system of prophecy—distinct from mediatory prophetic activity—from Phoenicia for the purposes of confirming Yahweh's endorsement of an individual for a new office through trance-like activity, as in the case of the newly appointed King Saul among the prophets (1 Sam 18:10).[97]

Recently, Klaus-Peter Adam has challenged this view concerning the *Hitpael* of נבא.[98] He instead argues that the *Hitpael* stem conveys pretention, specifically, pretending to be in the social status indicated by the corresponding verbal root.[99] In this case, הִתְנַבֵּא means to pretend to be in the class of prophet, and therefore, instead of emphasizing verbal action, the focus is on the resultant status the verbal action produces.[100] The example of Saul's behavior among the prophets in 1 Sam 10:13 thus indicated that he was acting like a prophet, perhaps signaling in the broader narrative a social status subservient to Samuel. After Saul's disobedience and the divine rejection of his kingship this role is portrayed negatively: he acts like a prophet when he tries to kill David in 1 Sam 18:10.[101]

Passive. Scholars have noted several cases in Biblical Hebrew in which the *Hitpael* seems to function passively.[102] Joel S. Baden has queried the stability of this semantic category for the *Hitpael*, noting that many proposed *Hitpael* passives can also be understood reflexively.[103] For example, Waltke and O'Connor cite הִיא הִתְהַלָּל "she is praised" in Prov 31:30, which Baden argues could plausibly mean "she

---

[96] Simon B. Parker, "Possession Trance and Prophecy in Pre-Exilic Israel, *VT* 28 (1978): 274.

[97] Parker, "Possession Trance," 275–79.

[98] Klaus-Peter Adam, "'And He Behaved Like a Prophet among Them.' (1 Sam 10:11b): The Depreciative Use of נבא *Hitpael* and the Comparative Evidence of Ecstatic Prophecy," *Die Welt des Orients* 39 (2009): 3–57.

[99] Adam, "Ecstatic Prophecy," 8–11. He argues that the *Hitpael* also indicates pretention in the following roots: שנה "to disguise oneself" (1 Kgs 14:2); אבל "to pretend to be a mourner" (2 Sam 14:2); חפש "to make oneself unrecognizable" (1 Kgs 22:30 ‖ 2 Chr 18:29); חלה "to pretend to be sick" (2 Sam 13:2, 5, 6); שכר "to pretend (?) to be intoxicated" (1 Sam 1:14); בשר "to pretend to receive good news" (2 Sam 18:31); שגה "to pretend madness" (1 Sam 21:15); נשא "to raise oneself to a certain social position" (1 Kgs 1:5); ציד "to pretend to take provisions" (Josh 9:12); בקע "to pretend to make torn" (Josh 9:13); שרר "to pretend to be a ruler" (Num 16:13); יפח "to show oneself breathing heavily" (Jer 4:31); עשר "to pretend to be rich" (Prov 13:7); עלף "to pretend to be a prostitute" (Gen 38:14); יהד "to pretend to be Jewish" (Esth 8:17).

[100] Adam, "Ecstatic Prophecy," 22, 24. Cf. Waltke and O'Connor's description of this usage as "estimative-declarative" (*IBHS* §26.4a).

[101] See Adam, "Ecstatic Prophecy," 12–15.

[102] GKC §54g–h; Joüon-Muraoka §53g–h; *IBHS* §26.3a–b.

[103] Joel S. Baden, "Hithpael and Niphal in Biblical Hebrew: Semantic and Morphological Overlap," *VT* 60 (2010): 34–35.

gains praise for herself," or "she is praiseworthy."[104] Baden identifies only three clear examples of the passive *Hitpael* in Biblical Hebrew, which he believes are "statistically insignificant."[105] Instead, the so-called *Hitpael* passive may have developed as a result of the semantic and morphological overlap between the *Hitpael* and the *Niphal*. The shared semantics of reflexivity are well attested, though it is one-sided. The *Niphal* routinely shares the reflexive meaning of the *Hitpael*, whereas the *Hitpael* rarely ever takes on passive meanings associated with the *Niphal*. The morphological overlap further suggests that *Niphal verb*s of certain root types could have been reanalyzed as *Hitpael verb*s in the consonantal text. For example, in the case of I-dentals, the prefixed {t} of the *Hitpael* assimilates to the following consonant, making the prefix conjugation form identical with the *Niphal* in unvocalized texts (e.g., אדמה in Isa 14:14; והטהרו in Gen 35:2; והתמהו in Hab 1:5).[106] Baden further illustrates this feature with the root טמא, which means "to purify oneself" in both the *Niphal* and *Hitpael* stems. All instances of the *Niphal* (18×) are found in the suffix conjugation, where the prefixed *nun* distinguishes the form as a *Niphal*. All occurrences of the *Hitpael* (15×) for this root, however, are in the prefix conjugation, a form that is indistinguishable from the *Niphal* in an unvocalized text:[107]

		יִטַּמֵא (*Hitpael*)
יטמא	=	or
		יִטָּמֵא (*Niphal*)

Both forms would have been pronounced the same, furthering the confusion between graphic representation and vocalization.

4.9 HIPHIL/HOPHAL STEMS

4.9.1 Morphology of the *Hiphil*

The internal vowel pattern of the *Hiphil* suffix conjugation alternates between a theme vowel /a/ and long /i/ vowel (*ḥireq-yod*). The 3MS (Ø suffix), 3FS (vocalic suffix *â*), and 3CP (vocalic suffix *û*) forms attest theme vowel *ḥireq-yod*. All other suffixal forms attest theme vowel short /a/, which is in a closed, accented syllable with the addition of CV (2MS, 2FS, 1CS, 1CP) and CVC (2MP, 2FP) pronominal suffixes. The suffix conjugation also attaches a {h} prefix with an accompanying short /i/ vowel (*ḥireq*).

---

[104] *IBHS* §26.3a.

[105] אָם־יְתְכַּפֵּר עֲוֹן בֵּית־עֵלִי "the iniquity of the house of Eli will not be atoned for" (1 Sam 3:14); וְיִשְׁתַּכְּחוּ "they are forgotten" (Eccl 8:10); תִּשְׁתַּפֵּכְנָה אַבְנֵי־קֹדֶשׁ "the sacred stones are poured out" (Lam 4:1).

[106] Baden, "Hithpael and Niphal," 35–38.

[107] Baden, 38–39.

HIPHIL SUFFIX CONJUGATION		
P	**S**	
הִשְׁמִירוּ	הִשְׁמִיר	3M
———	הִשְׁמִירָה	3F
הִשְׁמַרְתֶּם	הִשְׁמַרְתָּ	2M
הִשְׁמַרְתֶּן	הִשְׁמַרְתְּ	2F
הִשְׁמַרְנוּ	הִשְׁמַרְתִּי	1C

The prefix conjugation undergoes the apocopation of the prefixed {h} with the addition of the pronominal prefixes, which take the short /a/ vowel (*pataḥ*) instead of the short /i/ (*ḥireq*) of the *Qal*. The prefix conjugation theme vowel is the long /i/ *ḥireq-yod*, except for 3FP and 2FP where the addition of the CV pronominal suffixes causes the theme vowel to contract to *ṣere* in closed, accented syllable. We note that this *ṣere* vowel stands in contrast with the short /a/ attested in the closed, accented syllables of the suffixal paradigm listed above.

HIPHIL PREFIX CONJUGATION		
P	**S**	
יַכְתִּיבוּ	יַכְתִּיב	3M
תַּכְתֵּבְנָה	תַּכְתִּיב	3F
תַּכְתִּיבוּ	תַּכְתִּיב	2M
תַּכְתֵּבְנָה	תַּכְתִּיבִי	2F
נַכְתִּיב	אַכְתִּיב	1C

HIPHIL SC HISTORICAL DEVELOPMENT

The historical origin of the *ḥireq-yod* theme vowel for the Hebrew Hiphil has posed difficulties for grammarians. The suffix conjugation may have taken the following developmental path historically (*haqtal > *hiqtal > *hiqtil > hiqtîl*). Gesenius proposed a proto-form *haqtal on the basis of Arabic form IV suffix conjugation ʾaqtala, with the prefix /i/ arising by way of attenuation in a closed syllable (*haq- > hiq-*).[108] The prefix of the causative stem is sometimes {š} in other languages (i.e., Š stem), such as Akkadian preterite ušapris and Ugaritic suffixal form šaqtila.[109] Many scholars have proposed that the {š} of the commonly attested Hebrew verb הִשְׁתַּחֲוָה "to bow down, prostrate oneself,"

---

108 GKC §53.a; Blau, 235.
109 Note the uncertainty of the second vowel; see Bordreuil and Pardee, *Manuel of Ugaritic*, 53.

offers vestigial evidence of an old Št stem in the Hebrew language.[110] Aramaic attests both prefixes {h} and {ʾ} (i.e., *Haphel*/ʾ*Aphel*) for this stem—the latter being the "phonetic alternative" to {h}.[111] Phoenician's prefixed {y} (i.e., *Yiphil*) may reflect a phonetic development unique to the language.[112] The theme vowel *ḥireq-yod* throughout the suffix conjugation is difficult to derive from the historical /a/ vowel (**haqtala*), and may have developed on analogy to the prefix conjugation.[113]

The prefix conjugation's *ḥireq-yod* likely goes back to an historical short /i/ in a closed unaccented syllable: **yahaqtil*. Short /i/ appears in forms with pronominal suffix (e.g., יְמַצְאֶנּוּ, Job 34:11).[114] The intervocalic {h} apparently apocopated, resulting in the form **yaqtil*. The loss of final vowels (i.e., /u/ indicative; /a/ volitive) in all prefix forms meant that the final stress thus fell on the /i/ vowel, which lengthened to *ḥireq-yod* under stress. This lengthening could have taken place on analogy with Hiphil middle-weak forms like יָקִים.[115]

The consecutive preterite, jussive, and imperative forms are all distinguished from the prefix conjugation by *ṣere*:

PC:	יַזְכִּיר	"he brings to mind"
CP:	*וַיַּזְכֵּר	"he brought to mind"
JUSS:	יַזְכֵּר	"let him bring to mind"
IMPV:	הַזְכֵּר	"bring to mind"[116]

The *ṣere* in these forms represent a contraction or shortening of the *ḥireq-yod* and allows the *Hiphil* morphologically to mark distinct syntactical functions where no such distinction exists for the *Qal*.

---

[110] For references, see *HALOT*, s.v. "הוח II." Scholars cite the Ugaritic form *tšthwy* (√*ḤWY* "to live") in support of this proposal. See also Gregorio del Olmo Lete and Joaquín Sanmartín, *A Dictionary of the Ugaritic Language in the Alphabetic Tradition*, 3rd rev. ed., trans. Wilfred G. E. Watson, Handbook of Oriental Studies, Section 1: The Near and Middle East 112 (Leiden: Brill, 2015), 375–76. The traditional understanding of this form has been to analyze it as a Hitpael of the root ŠḤH. For a defense of the traditional, non-Š stem view of this verb, see J. A. Emerton, "The Etymology of *hištaḥawāh*," *Oudtestamentische Studiën* 20 (1977): 41–55, reprinted in *Studies on the Language and Literature of the Bible: Selected Works of J. A. Emerton*, ed. Graham Davies and Robert Gordon, VTSup 165 (Leiden: Brill, 2015), 83–96.

[111] Blau, 234. The *Haphel* appears in the earliest dialects of Aramaic and has all but disappeared by the Middle Aramaic period; see Stuart Creason, "Aramaic," in *The Cambridge Encyclopedia of the World's Ancient Languages*, ed. Roger D. Woodard (Cambridge: Cambridge University Press, 2004), 409.

[112] Creason, "Aramaic," 409. He explains it as a secondary development that may have arisen as a glide following the negative אי. On the Phoenician *yiphil*, see Friedrich and Röllig, *Phönizisch-Punische Grammatik*, §§146–48; Segert, *Grammar of Phoenician and Punic*, 142–43.

[113] See GKC §53.a n. 1.

[114] Note also the FP forms: *segol* in וַתֵּצֶאןָ (Exod 15:20); *patah* under the influence of a guttural in תִּבְּעֶנָה (Ps 119:171).

[115] Joüon-Muraoka §54a. Blau strongly asserts that this is the only means of explaining the origin of the *ḥireq-yod* in the *Hiphil* morphology (235).

[116] Note that the infinitive absolute also attests *ṣere*, as in הַכְבֵּד (Exod 8:11).

HIPHIL PC HISTORICAL DEVELOPMENT

The prefix vowel of the *Hiphil* is *pataḥ* (e.g., יַצִּיב "he stations;" יַקְרִיב "he brings near") and likely goes back to historical /a/ as well (*yahaqtil*), despite recent arguments to the contrary. For example, Blau, much like his argument for the *Piel*, believes the historical prefix vowel was /u/, as in *yuhaqtil* on the basis of Akkadian C stem (*ušapris/ušapras*) and Arabic form IV (*yuqtilu*).[117] Aramaic attests prefix /a/ vowel, as in Targum Cairo Genizah יַדְבֵּק (Deut 28:21).[118] The evidence from Ugaritic regarding the Š stem prefix is similar to that of the D stem—1CS forms occur with *ʾalep-a*, again suggesting an /a/ prefix vowel (e.g., *ašhlk* /ʾašahliku/ "I make X walk," *KTU* 1.3 V:24; 1.18 I:11).[119]

4.9.2 The Semantics of the *Hiphil*

The *Hiphil* stem denotes causative action of the *Qal*. As noted above, causation often involves the addition of an agent of the verbal action (§3.6.4). The subject of the verb causes another agent to bring about the action of the verb. Syntactically, the *Hiphil* of *Qal* intransitive verbs results in single accusative. We can illustrate this usage with the English verb walk:

Bill caused Jim₁ to walk.

The *Hiphil* of *Qal* transitive verbs potentially yields a double accusative:

Bill caused <u>Jim₁</u> to kick <u>the ball₂</u>.

The following examples from Hebrew illustrate this usage further:

		QAL	*HIPHIL*	*EXAMPLE*	
Intransitive	מלך	"reign, act as king"	"make someone king"	וַתַּמְלִיכוּ אֶת־אֲבִימֶלֶךְ	**You made** Abimelech **king** (Judg 9:16)
Transitive	נשא	"carry, bear"	"make someone bear something"	וְהִשִּׂיאוּ אוֹתָם עֲוֹן אַשְׁמָה	So that **they make** them **bear** the iniquity of guilt (Lev 22:16)

The verb פשט "to strip, take off," paired with לבש "to clothe, put on" in Num 20:28 demonstrates how *Qal* transitives can convert to *Hiphil* double accusatives.

---

[117] Blau, 236. Tropper (*Ugaritische Grammatik*, 587–88) believes that although the 1CS prefix had an /a/ vowel, all other persons had /u/, which is a rather complicated reading of the data.

[118] See Fassberg, *Grammar of Palestinian Targum Fragments*, 177. Note that the {h} does not apocopate in Biblical Aramaic prefix forms, yielding a reduced vowel in the prefix: e.g., תְּהַשְׁכַּח (Ezr 4:15; 7:16).

[119] See Bordreuil and Pardee, *Manual of Ugaritic*, 53

Num 20:28

וַיַּפְשֵׁט מֹשֶׁה אֶת־אַהֲרֹן אֶת־בְּגָדָיו וַיַּלְבֵּשׁ אֹתָם אֶת־אֶלְעָזָר בְּנוֹ

Moses **made** <u>Aaron</u> **remove** <u>his garments</u> and he **made** <u>them</u> **to be put on** <u>Eleazar</u> his son.

The meaning of the *Hiphil* in distinction from the *Piel* is often difficult to discern. Some grammarians have defined the *Hiphil* and *Piel* as both expressing causativity.[120] As discussed above, however, the basic notion of the *Piel* is to bring about a state, whereas the *Hiphil* seems to focus on the causation of actions. Waltke and O'Connor identify causation of actions or events as the defining feature of the *Hiphil* in opposition to the *Piel*. Even though "both stems involve causation, the factitive-resultative *Piel* generally has to do with the bringing about of a state or condition, and the causative *Hiphil* with the causing of an event."[121] They further note that the relationship between the subject and object of each stem is somewhat different, even though they are both syntactically transitive. In the *Piel* the object is passively brought into the resulting state or condition, whereas objects of *Hiphil* verbs are actively involved in the caused action.[122] Kouwenberg similarly distinguishes the functions of the Akkadian D and Š stems in terms of action verbs (causatives) versus process verbs (factitives) and whether they are able to take what he calls an "agentive subject" or not. He explains:

> For action verbs, the addition of an extra agent on top of one that is inherently present results in a prototypical causative event in which not only the original event and the external agent are clearly distinguishable but often also the original agent, the "causee," who may keep a certain control over the action. . . . Process verbs, on the other hand, do not have an inherent agent, and the addition of an agent to instigate the process in question usually results in a two-participant clause that is not significantly different from that of an ordinary transitive clause. . . . A factitive D-stem, then, does not indicate the presence of an additional agent but a change in the subject from non-agentive to agentive.[123]

The D stem factitive denotes <u>qualitative valency</u> (i.e., changing the subject from non-agentive to agentive), whereas the Š-stem causative denotes <u>quantitative valency</u> (i.e., the addition of an agent).[124]

Hiphil of Qal Intransitive. The first group of *Hiphil* verbs to describe are those whose *Qal* is intransitive. These come in two types: fientive or event verbs and stative verbs.

---

[120] See GKC §§52.g, 53.c.
[121] *IBHS* §27.1d, following Jenni, *Das hebräische Pi'el*, 25–33.
[122] *IBHS* §27.1d.
[123] Kouwenberg, *Akkadian Verb*, 257.
[124] Kouwenberg, 257.

1) Fientive Verbs

בוא
Qal "to come, go"
Hiphil "to make X go"

Mal 3:10
הָבִ֣יאוּ אֶת־כָּל־הַֽמַּעֲשֵׂר֮ אֶל־בֵּ֣ית הָאוֹצָר֒
Bring all the tithes into the storehouse.

הלך
Qal "to walk"
Hiphil "to make walk"

2 Sam 13:13
וַאֲנִ֗י אָ֤נָה אוֹלִיךְ֙ אֶת־חֶרְפָּתִ֔י
As for me, where could **I take** my reproach (lit., make my reproach go)?

עבר
Qal "to pass over"
Hiphil "to make pass over"

Gen 8:1
וַיַּעֲבֵ֨ר אֱלֹהִ֥ים ר֙וּחַ֙ עַל־הָאָ֔רֶץ וַיָּשֹׁ֖כּוּ הַמָּֽיִם׃
God **made** a wind **pass** over the earth and the waters receded.

ילד
Qal "to give birth"
Hiphil "to father a child" (lit. "to make someone conceive")

Gen 5:4
וַיִּֽהְי֣וּ יְמֵי־אָדָ֗ם אַֽחֲרֵי֙ הוֹלִיד֣וֹ אֶת־שֵׁ֔ת שְׁמֹנֶ֥ה מֵאֹ֖ת שָׁנָ֑ה וַיּ֥וֹלֶד בָּנִ֖ים וּבָנֽוֹת׃
The days of Adam after **he fathered** Seth were 800 years, and **he fathered** sons and daughters.

קום
Qal "to arise"
Hiphil "to raise something" Exod 6:4)

Exod 6:4
וְגַ֨ם הֲקִמֹ֤תִי אֶת־בְּרִיתִי֙ אִתָּ֔ם
I also **raised** (i.e., upheld) my covenant with them.

2) Stative Verbs

אבד

Qal "to perish" (i.e., "come to ruin")
Piel "to make perish" (i.e., "bring to ruin")
Hiphil "to cause an act of destruction" (i.e., "to put to death")

2 Kgs 10:19

וְיֵהוּא עָשָׂה בְעָקְבָּה לְמַעַן **הַאֲבִיד** אֶת־עֹבְדֵי הַבָּעַל:

But Jehu acted cunningly so that **he might put** the prophets of Baal **to death**.

בוש

Qal "to be ashamed"
Hiphil "to put to shame"

Ps 119:31

דָּבַקְתִּי בְעֵדְוֹתֶיךָ יְהוָה **אַל־תְּבִישֵׁנִי**:

I cling to your testimonies; O Yahweh, **do not put me to shame**.

גדל

Qal "to be large, grow up"
Piel "to make grow" (i.e., "to bring into a state of growth")
Hiphil "to magnify (i.e., "to cause something/someone to be great")

Eccl 2:4

הִגְדַּלְתִּי מַעֲשָׂי בָּנִיתִי לִי בָּתִּים נָטַעְתִּי לִי כְּרָמִים:

I have made my works **great**: I have built my own houses and planted my own vineyards.

Hiphil of Qal Transitive. A second group of *Hiphil* verbs are syntactically transitive in the *Qal*, meaning that they can take an object. A few verbs are both transitive and intransitive, such as בער, which can mean either "to be kindled" or "to burn, consume something."

Qal Intransitive בער

Ps 39:4

חַם־לִבִּי ׀ בְּקִרְבִּי בַּהֲגִיגִי **תִבְעַר־אֵשׁ**

My heart grew hot within me,
In my musing a fire **was kindled**.

Qal Transitive בער

Ps 83:15

כְּאֵשׁ תִּבְעַר־יָעַר וּכְלֶהָבָ֫ה תְּלַהֵט הָרִים:

As a flame **burns** a forest,
And a flame ignites mountains.

Hiphil Causative בער

2 Chr 28:3

וַיַּבְעֵר אֶת־בָּנָיו בָּאֵשׁ כְּתֹעֲבוֹת הַגּוֹיִם אֲשֶׁר הֹרִישׁ יְהוָה מִפְּנֵי בְּנֵי יִשְׂרָאֵל:

He **caused** his sons **to be consumed** by fire according to the abominations
of the nations whom Yahweh dispossessed from before the sons of Israel.

Many *Qal* transitive verbs helpfully illustrate the meaning of the *Hiphil* in relation to the meaning of other stems.

זכר
Qal "to remember" (Gen 40:14)
Niphal "to be remembered" (Isa 65:17)
Hiphil "to bring to remembrance" (lit., "to cause to remember")

2 Sam 18:18

אֵין־לִ֫י בֵּן בַּעֲבוּר הַזְכִּיר שְׁמִי

I have no son to **bring** my name **to remembrance.**

ידע
Qal "to know" (1 Kgs 2:15)
Niphal "to be known" (Exod 2:14)
Hiphil "to make someone know"

Gen 41:39

אַחֲרֵי הוֹדִיעַ אֱלֹהִים אוֹתְךָ אֶת־כָּל־זֹאת אֵין־נָבוֹן וְחָכָם כָּמ֫וֹךָ:

Since God has **made** you **know** all this, there is no one as understanding and wise as you.

אמן
Qal "to support" (Esth 2:7)
Niphal "to be confirmed, made firm, reliable" (2 Sam 7:16; 1 Sam 2:35)
Hiphil "to make firm, treat someone as firm" (i.e., trust, believe)

Exod 4:31

וַיַּאֲמֵן הָעָם

The people **believed.**

שׁלח
Qal "to send" (Gen 42:4)
Niphal "to be sent" (Esth 3:13)
Piel "to send off, dismiss, release" (1 Kgs 9:7; Lev 16:22)
Hiphil "to cause to come, enter" (Exod 8:17; Amos 8:11)

Amos 8:11
הִנֵּ֣ה | יָמִ֣ים בָּאִ֗ים נְאֻם֙ אֲדֹנָ֣י יְהוִ֔ה וְהִשְׁלַחְתִּ֥י רָעָ֖ב בָּאָ֑רֶץ
Look, days are coming, declares Yahweh, when **I will cause** famine **to enter** the land.

Some verbal roots attest to the *Hiphil* stem with no accompanying *Qal* stem. The following examples may warrant reconstructing a *Qal* intransitive

נכה "to strike"
*Qal "to be defeated"?
Hiphil "to cause an injury"?

Num 22:23
וַיַּ֥ךְ בִּלְעָם֙ אֶת־הָאָת֔וֹן
Balaam **struck** the donkey.

שׁלך "to cast"
*Qal "to travel a road"?
Hiphil "to cast, throw" (< "to cause to travel"?)

Exod 15:25
וַיּוֹרֵ֣הוּ יְהוָ֗ה עֵ֚ץ וַיַּשְׁלֵךְ֙ אֶל־הַמַּ֔יִם וַֽיִּמְתְּק֖וּ הַמָּ֑יִם
Yahweh showed him a tree and **he cast** [it] into the waters and the waters became sweet.

Denominatives. Several denominatives are attested in the *Hiphil*. As with all denominatives, these *Hiphil* verbs are derived from nouns. One prominent example is the verb שׁכם meaning "to rise early" (Gen 22:3). This verb appears to be derived from the noun שְׁכֶם "shoulder," but the semantic development from "shoulder" to "rise early" has puzzled scholars.[125] Marvin Pope explained that it may relate to the fact that rising early involved breaking up camp, which would have required the shoulders of man and beast.[126] This explanation is plausible, yet somewhat speculative.

---

[125] See Victor P. Hamilton, "שָׁכַם," *TWOT* 2:924. Hamilton notes that the meaning "rise early *in the morning*" is only possible with the adverbial בַּבֹּקֶר. Other contexts suggest the basic notion of the root is to do something eagerly or intently (e.g., Jer 7:13). The expression "rise early in the morning" would therefore indicate an eagerness to start the day.
[126] Marvin H. Pope, *Job*, AB 15 (New York: Doubleday, 1965), 8.

שׁכם
Noun שְׁכֶם "shoulder"
Hiphil "to rise early"

Gen 22:3

וַיַּשְׁכֵּם אַבְרָהָם בַּבֹּקֶר וַיַּחֲבֹשׁ אֶת־חֲמֹרוֹ וַיִּקַּח אֶת־שְׁנֵי נְעָרָיו אִתּוֹ וְאֵת יִצְחָק בְּנוֹ
Abraham **rose early** in the morning and saddled his donkey and took two
of his young men with him and Isaac, his son.

4.9.3 The Morphology of the *Hophal*

The distinctive morphological feature of the *Hophal* is the vowel in the first syllable. It can be an /o/ or /u/ vowel with a *pataḥ* theme vowel. The prefix vowel was
historically **u*, which is realized as *qames-ḥaṭup* and *qibbuṣ* (הָפְקַד/הֻפְקַד). *Qib-*
buṣ commonly occurs with *Hophal* participles and I-*nun* roots.[127] Like the *Hiphil*,
the suffix conjugation contains the {h} prefix, which then <u>apocopates</u> in the prefix
conjugation (**yahuqtal* > ** yəhuqtal* > יָקְטַל).[128] Due to the *Hophal*'s sparsity, we
only include a partial paradigm.

HOPHAL CONJUGATIONS		
	WITH /O/	WITH /U/
SC	הָשְׁלַכְתָּ	הֻשְׁלַךְ
PC	יָשְׁלַךְ	יֻשְׁלְכוּ
CP	—	וַיֻּתַּן
IMPV[129]	הָשְׁכְּבָה	—
PTCL	מָשְׁחַת	מֻשְׁלָךְ
INF ABS	הָחְתֵּל	—

4.9.4 The Semantics of the *Hophal*

The *Hophal* functions as the passive stem of the *Hiphil*. In the *Hiphil* the syntactical subject causes an action or event to occur, while in the *Hophal* the subject
experiences an action caused by an external agent.

Hophal of Qal Transitives. The *Hiphil* of *Qal* transitive verbs produces causative
verbs with the potential of a double accusative: Someone causes someone else to
do something. The *Hophal* of such verbs converts the secondary agent (i.e., the one

---

[127] GKC §53s.
[128] However, note the non-apocopated form מְהֻקְצָעוֹת in Ezek 46:22.
[129] Occurs only twice in BH (Jer 49:8; Ezek 32:19).

caused to do something) into a passive subject who is made to produce the action: Someone is caused to do something.

יָדַע

Qal "to know"
Hiphil "to make someone know something"
Hophal "someone is made to know something"

HIPHIL		HOPHAL	
תּוֹדִיעֵ֫נִי אֹ֣רַח חַיִּ֑ים	**Make me know** the path of life (Ps 16:11).	אוֹ־הוֹדַ֤ע אֵלָיו֙ חַטָּאתוֹ֙ אֲשֶׁ֣ר חָטָ֔א בָּ֑הּ	If the sin which he has committed **is made known** to him (Lev 4:23).

Hophal of Qal Intransitives. In *Hiphil* verbs derived from *Qal* intransitive fientive verbs the syntactical subject causes the object to do an action or bring about an event.[130] The *Hophal* transforms the syntactical object of causation into a passive subject, and thus has no syntactical object.

יָצָא

Qal "to go out"
Hiphil "to make someone/something go out"
Hophal "to be made to go out"

HIPHIL		HOPHAL	
אֲשֶׁ֤ר הוֹצֵ֨אתָ֙ מֵאֶ֣רֶץ מִצְרָ֑יִם	Whom **you brought out** of the land of Egypt (Exod 22:11).	וְהִיא֙ מֵעַמִּ֔ים הוּצָ֫אָה	[Israel] **was brought out** from the peoples (Ezek 38:8).

עָמַד

Qal "to stand"
Hiphil "to make someone/something stand"
Hophal "to be made to stand"

HIPHIL		HOPHAL	
וַיַּעֲמִ֤ידוּ אוֹתוֹ֙ בֵּ֣ין הָֽעַמּוּדִ֑ים	**They stationed** him [Samson] between the pillars (Judg 16:25).	וְהַמֶּ֨לֶךְ֙ הָיָ֣ה מָעֳמָ֔ד בַּמֶּרְכָּבָ֖ה נֹ֣כַח אֲרָ֑ם	The king **was propped up** in the chariot in front of the Arameans (2 Kgs 22:35).

---

[130] As Waltke and O'Connor (*IBHS* §28.2c) note, passive causatives of *Qal* intransitive stative verbs are extremely rare.

4.10 OTHER STEMS: *PILPEL, POEL, POLEL,* AND SO ON

Several other stems are found with various Hebrew roots. The Westminster Hebrew Morphology database identifies fifteen minor stems.[131] Their total number account for less than three-quarters of one percent of verbs in the Hebrew Bible. These rare stems are enumerated as follows:

MINOR VERB STEMS		
STEM	OCCURRENCES	PERCENTAGE
Pulel	7	0.010%
Pealal	6	0.008%
Pilel	3	0.004%
Pilpel	50	0.069%
Polel	180	0.249%
Polal	11	0.015%
Polpal	2	0.003%
Pulal	15	0.021%
Poel	83	0.115%
Poal	8	0.011%
Tiphil	1	0.001%
Hotpaal	8	0.011%
Hitpolel	114	0.157%
Hitpalpel	21	0.029%
Nitpael	3	0.004%
TOTAL	512 / 72,404	0.707%

4.10.1 Morphology

The morphology of the rare stems can be described as either root reduplicating (R stem), vowel lengthening (L stem), or both (RL stem). Nearly all of these verbs are weak, namely geminate or middle-weak roots. R stems are akin to verb forms found in Arabic (form IX) and Akkadian. In BH, the root reduplication may include only the final consonant (*Palel*) or more commonly two consonants (*Pilpel, Polpal, Hitpalpel*). Typically, these stems correlate with geminate roots. Arabic (form III), Ethiopian, and the Modern South Arabian languages evidence L stems in which the vowel following the first root radical is a long $\bar{a}$ (BH *o*).[132] This stem

---

[131] Compare "a dozen or so" (*IBHS* §21.2.3). To this number could be added the *Hištaph'el* stem; see Graham I. Davies, "A Note on the Etymology of *hištaḥawāh*," *VT* 29 (1979): 493–95.

[132] See John Huehnergard, "Proto-Semitic," in *The Semitic Languages*, 2nd ed., ed. John Huehnergard and Na'ama Pat-El (London: Routledge, 2019), 65.

morphology corresponds to BH *Poel, Poal,* and *Hitpolel* and geminate roots. Finally, some stems incorporate both the reduplication and lengthen to form RL stems: *Polel, Polal, Hitpolel*. These stems occur with middle-weak root verbs.

4.10.2 Semantics

The R, L, and RL stems are constructed as variations of the D stem with particular weak roots. Each of the minor stems may be understood as "morphemic variants of the major [stems]."[133] Semantically, most of these stems may be aligned with the active (*Piel*), passive (*Pual*), and reflexive notions (*Hitpael*) of the D stem.[134] The roots occurring more than five times or more in these minor stems include:

R STEMS			
PILPEL/POLPAL/HITPALPEL			
	Pilpel (active)	*Polpal* (passive)	*Hitpalpel* (reflexive)
כול	"contain; sustain"	"be sustained"	———
מהה	———	———	"delay, tarry"
שעע	"delight in"	"be played with"	"take pleasure in"
גלל	"roll"	"rolled"	"roll over"[135]

Palel

שאן   "be at ease, be secure"

Pulal

אמל   "languish; dwindle"

L STEMS			
POEL/POAL/HITPOLEL			
	Poel (active)	*Poal* (passive)	*Hitpolel* (reflexive)
סבב	"encompass; surround"	———	———
ענן	"interpret signs; practice witchcraft"	———	———
חקק	"inscribe; enact"	———	———
גדד			"cut"
עלל	"glean; deal severely"	"be inflicted (with pain)"	"act deceitfully"
קשש	"gather stubble"	———	"gather oneself"

---

[133] *IBHS* §21.2.3a.
[134] Joüon-Muraoka §59.
[135] The *Hitpolel* stem possibly differentiates a reciprocal nuance: "wallow."

L STEMS		
POEL/POAL/HITPOLEL		
	Poel (active)	*Poal* (passive)	*Hitpolel* (reflexive)
שׁמם	"cause horror"	———	"be appalled; cause oneself ruin"
הלל	"make a mockery of"	"be foolish"	"act crazy"

RL STEMS		
Polel/Polal/Hitpolel		
	Polel (active)	*Polal* (passive)	*Hitpolel* (reflexive)
שׁיר	"sing"	———	———
שׁוב	"bring back; restore"	———	———
מות	"kill"	———	———
קין	"sing a dirge"	———	———
בין	"take care of"	———	"get understanding"
עור	"awaken; disturb"	———	"arise; stir oneself up"
עוף	"fly"	———	"fly about"
שׁוט	"roam about"	———	"turn back and forth"
קום	"raise up"	———	"rise up"
מוג	"dissolve; soften"	———	"melt"
כון	"establish"	"be established"	"established oneself"
רום	"raise; exalt"	"be raised; be exalted"	"exalt oneself"
חיל	"bring on labor pains"	"be birthed"	"writhe about"

The derived stems often overwhelm beginning students learning Biblical Hebrew. Even once their morphological distinctions are mastered, the corresponding semantics are not easily described or qualified with clearly defined categories or characteristics. Students would do well to begin thinking about this semantic variability as a product of the relationship between the *Qal* and the derived stems with the same verbal roots (and even between various derived stems themselves). The meaning of the stems is best understood in their opposition to one another. The above material surveys many of the semantic alternatives latent within each derived stem. In the next chapter, we outline the meaning and use of the finite conjugations.

4.11 EXERCISES

Translate the following Hebrew sentences into English. Parse the bold verbs by giving the stem, conjugation, person, gender, number, and three letter Hebrew root. Provide the basic meaning and theme vowel alternations of the verb using a lexicon.

1. וַיְהִי֩ כִשְׁמֹ֨עַ אַחְאָ֜ב אֶת־הַדְּבָרִ֣ים הָאֵ֗לֶּה וַיִּקְרַ֣ע בְּגָדָ֔יו **וַיָּ֥שֶׂם**־שַׂ֖ק עַל־בְּשָׂר֑וֹ **וַיָּצ֥וֹם** וַיִּשְׁכַּ֣ב בַּשָּׂ֔ק **וַיְהַלֵּ֖ךְ** אַֽט׃ (1 Kgs 21:27)

2. **תִּכְבַּ֧ד** הָעֲבֹדָ֛ה עַל־הָאֲנָשִׁ֖ים **וְיַעֲשׂוּ**־בָ֑הּ **וְאַל־יִשְׁע֖וּ** בְּדִבְרֵי־שָֽׁקֶר׃ (Exod 5:9)

3. וְֽהָיָ֗ה כְּעֵץ֮ שָׁת֪וּל עַֽל־פַּלְגֵ֫י מָ֥יִם אֲשֶׁ֤ר פִּרְי֨וֹ ׀ **יִתֵּ֬ן** בְּעִתּ֗וֹ וְעָלֵ֥הוּ לֹֽא־**יִבּ֑וֹל** וְכֹ֖ל אֲשֶׁר־יַעֲשֶׂ֣ה **יַצְלִֽיחַ**׃ (Ps 1:3)

Translate the following sentences. Parse the bold verbs and describe whether they are fientive or stative in this context, and if they are transitive, ditransitive, or intransitive.

4. **וַיִּקַּ֨ח** תֶּ֜רַח אֶת־אַבְרָ֣ם בְּנ֗וֹ וְאֶת־ל֤וֹט בֶּן־הָרָן֙ בֶּן־בְּנ֔וֹ וְאֵת֙ שָׂרַ֣י כַּלָּת֔וֹ אֵ֖שֶׁת אַבְרָ֣ם בְּנ֑וֹ **וַיֵּצְא֣וּ** אִתָּ֡ם מֵא֣וּר כַּשְׂדִּים֩ לָלֶ֨כֶת אַ֜רְצָה כְּנַ֗עַן **וַיָּבֹ֤אוּ** עַד־חָרָן֙ וַיֵּ֥שְׁבוּ שָֽׁם׃ (Gen 11:31)

5. וַיַּ֨עַן יִצְחָ֜ק וַיֹּ֣אמֶר לְעֵשָׂ֗ו הֵ֣ן גְּבִ֞יר **שַׂמְתִּ֥יו** לָךְ֙ וְאֶת־כָּל־אֶחָ֗יו **נָתַ֤תִּי** ל֙וֹ לַעֲבָדִ֔ים וְדָגָ֥ן וְתִירֹ֖שׁ **סְמַכְתִּ֑יו** וּלְכָ֣ה אֵפ֔וֹא מָ֥ה **אֶֽעֱשֶׂ֖ה** בְּנִֽי׃ (Gen 27:37)

6. וְגַ֣ם אָנֹכִ֡י **מָנַ֣עְתִּי** מִכֶּם֩ אֶת־הַגֶּ֨שֶׁם בְּע֜וֹד שְׁלֹשָׁ֤ה חֳדָשִׁים֙ לַקָּצִ֔יר וְהִמְטַרְתִּי֙ עַל־עִ֣יר אֶחָ֔ת וְעַל־עִ֥יר אַחַ֖ת לֹ֣א **אַמְטִ֑יר** חֶלְקָ֤ה אַחַת֙ **תִּמָּטֵ֔ר** וְחֶלְקָ֛ה אֲשֶׁר־לֹֽא־**תַמְטִ֥יר** עָלֶ֖יהָ **תִּיבָֽשׁ**׃ (Amos 4:7)

Translate the following sentences. Parse and designate the voice of the bold verbs as active, passive, reflexive, or middle. Give the syntactic subject and object(s) and the semantic role (agent, patient, experiencer, causer) of each subject and object(s).

7.　　　　　(Exod 19:10) :לֵךְ אֶל־הָעָם וְ**קִדַּשְׁתָּם** הַיּוֹם וּמָחָר וְ**כִבְּסוּ** שִׂמְלֹתָם

8.　וְ**הֱבִיאֲךָ** יְהוָה אֱלֹהֶיךָ אֶל־הָאָרֶץ אֲשֶׁר־יָרְשׁוּ אֲבֹתֶיךָ וִירִשְׁתָּהּ וְהֵיטִבְךָ וְהִרְבְּךָ
　מֵאֲבֹתֶיךָ: (Deut 30:5)

9.　**וַיִּקְחוּ** אֶת־בְּנוֹתֵיהֶם לָהֶם לְנָשִׁים וְאֶת־בְּנוֹתֵיהֶם נָתְנוּ לִבְנֵיהֶם **וַיַּעַבְדוּ** אֶת־
　אֱלֹהֵיהֶם: (Judg 3:6)

10.　לֹא לָכֶם לְהִלָּחֵם בָּזֹאת הִ**תְיַצְּבוּ** עִמְדוּ וּ**רְאוּ** אֶת־יְשׁוּעַת יְהוָה עִמָּכֶם
　יְהוּדָה וִירוּשָׁלַםִ אַל־**תִּירְאוּ** וְאַל־**תֵּחַתּוּ** מָחָר צְאוּ לִפְנֵיהֶם וַיהוָה עִמָּכֶם:
　(2 Chr 20:17)

Translate from English to Hebrew.

11.　She will teach her mother's wise instructions to her sons.

12.　The Spirit of God covered the house and filled the city with a dark cloud.

13.　Samuel went to Saul and commanded: "You have defiled yourself and must wash with pure water."

14. God appeared to him and said: "I will make you the father of all peoples. You will fear me with all your heart."

15. Noah and his sons covered the boat with pitch. They were righteous among all the nations of the earth.

Guided Reading: Psalm 29

¹ מִזְמֹ֗ור לְדָ֫וִ֥ד הָב֣וּ לַֽ֭יהוָה בְּנֵ֣י אֵלִ֑ים הָב֥וּ לַ֝יהוָ֗ה כָּב֥וֹד וָעֹֽז: ² הָב֣וּ לַֽ֭יהוָה כְּב֣וֹד שְׁמ֑וֹ הִשְׁתַּחֲו֥וּ לַ֝יהוָ֗ה בְּהַדְרַת־קֹֽדֶשׁ: ³ ק֥וֹל יְהוָ֗ה עַל־הַ֫מָּ֥יִם אֵֽל־הַכָּב֥וֹד הִרְעִ֑ים יְ֝הוָ֗ה עַל־מַ֥יִם רַבִּֽים: ⁴ קוֹל־יְהוָ֥ה בַּכֹּ֑חַ ק֥וֹל יְ֝הוָ֗ה בֶּהָדָֽר: ⁵ ק֣וֹל יְ֭הוָה שֹׁבֵ֣ר אֲרָזִ֑ים וַיְשַׁבֵּ֥ר יְ֝הוָ֗ה אֶת־אַרְזֵ֥י הַלְּבָנֽוֹן: ⁶ וַיַּרְקִידֵ֥ם כְּמוֹ־עֵ֑גֶל לְבָנ֥וֹן וְ֝שִׂרְיֹ֗ן כְּמ֣וֹ בֶן־רְאֵמִֽים: ⁷ קוֹל־יְהוָ֥ה חֹצֵ֗ב לַהֲב֥וֹת אֵֽשׁ: ⁸ ק֣וֹל יְ֭הוָה יָחִ֣יל מִדְבָּ֑ר יָחִ֥יל יְ֝הוָ֗ה מִדְבַּ֥ר קָדֵֽשׁ: ⁹ ק֤וֹל יְהוָ֨ה ׀ יְחוֹלֵ֣ל אַיָּלוֹת֮ וַֽיֶּחֱשֹׂ֪ף יְעָ֫ר֥וֹת וּבְהֵיכָל֑וֹ כֻּ֝לּ֗וֹ אֹמֵ֥ר כָּבֽוֹד: ¹⁰ יְ֭הוָה לַמַּבּ֣וּל יָשָׁ֑ב וַיֵּ֥שֶׁב יְ֝הוָ֗ה מֶ֣לֶךְ לְעוֹלָֽם: ¹¹ יְֽהוָ֗ה עֹ֭ז לְעַמּ֣וֹ יִתֵּ֑ן יְהוָ֓ה ׀ יְבָרֵ֖ךְ אֶת־עַמּ֣וֹ בַשָּׁלֽוֹם:

VOCABULARY AND NOTES

Verse 1

מִזְמֹור		N.MS		"psalm; melody"
הָבוּ	Qal	IMPV MP	יהב	"give"
עֹז		N.MS		"strength, might"

Verse 2

הִשְׁתַּחֲווּ	Hištaphel	IMPV MP	חוה	"worship"
הַדְרַת		N		"ornament; majesty"

Verse 3

הִרְעִים	Hiphil	SC 3MS	רעם	"cause to thunder"

Verse 4

כֹּחַ		N.MS		"power, strength"
הָדָר		N.MS		"splendor; honor"

Verse 5

שֹׁבֵר	*Qal*			"break"
אֲרָזִים		N.MP		"cedar"
וַיְשַׁבֵּר	*Piel*	CP 3MS	שבר	"shatter; break apart"
לְבָנוֹן		PN		" Lebanon "

Verse 6

וַיַּרְקִידֵם	*Hiphil*	CP 3MS	רקד	"make to leap"
כְּמוֹ		PREP		"like; as"
עֵגֶל		N.MS		"calf"
שִׂרְיֹן		PN		"Sirion" (Syria)
רְאֵמִים		N.MP		"ox"

Verse 7

חֹצֵב	*Qal*			"rake"
לַהֲבוֹת		N.FP		"flame"

Verse 8

יָחִיל	*Hiphil*	PC 3MS	חיל	"cause to tremble"
קָדֵשׁ		PN		"Kadesh"

Verse 9

יְחוֹלֵל	*Polel*	PC 3MS	חיל	"bring on labor pains"
אַיָּלוֹת		N.FP		"hind; doe"
וַיֶּחֱשֹׂף	*Qal*	CP 3MS	חשׂף	"birth prematurely"
יְעָרוֹת		N.FP		"wood, forest"
הֵיכָלוֹ		N.MS + 3MS SF		"temple"

Verse 10

מַבּוּל		N.MS		"flood"

Verse 11

עֹז		N.MS		"refuge"
יְבָרֵךְ	*Piel*	PC 3MS	ברך	

CHAPTER 5

////////////////

PREFIX AND SUFFIX CONJUGATIONS

The verbal conjugations continue to be one of the most discussed components of Biblical Hebrew grammar. Morphologically speaking, little of the debate concerns the differences in forms. Semantically, the system is complex and debated. Questions include: Do different verbal forms mark time or aspect? Do similar forms always have the same meaning? Is context the primary factor in determining meaning? What is the best translation value for each?

Part of the complexity is that Semitic languages typically have a small number of forms designating verb tense, aspect, and modality (TAM). Hebrew has only four distinct, productive forms marking tense and aspect, while English and Greek designate tense-aspect with a proliferation of different forms (e.g., the future perfect continuous: *I will have been writing*). As compared to the many forms of Greek verbs, Hebrew morphology appears underdetermined. Unlike English, Hebrew does not use auxiliaries (*will, do, have, shall*) to designate various semantic meanings.

To complicate matters further, the principal Hebrew conjugations function with seemingly opposite senses. And the semantic categories are not easily mapped one-to-one onto the morphology. The English verbal system provides similar issues of polysemy (e.g., *I write* can be present, past, or future depending on context) and synonymity—semantic equivalence with different verbs (e.g., *I will write; I am going to write*). Meaning is understood with a combination of several factors, some morphological while others syntactic and contextual. Another important error to be avoided is the common confusion of translation value as compared with what the forms indicated to the ancient Hebrews. While beginning grammar texts provide helpful, broad-ranging groupings for the various conjugations, the actual senses of these forms are far more nuanced than these presentations convey.

173

5.1 GOING DEEPER WITH VERB CONJUGATIONS

The sons of the gods and the daughters of man in Genesis 6 have puzzled commentators for centuries. No simple solution exists for understanding the meaning of these enigmatic references. It is particularly difficult to determine both the nature of the strange union between the divine sons and the human daughters as well as the story's function in the narrative of the larger flood narrative. Careful attention to the verb usage provides helpful clues concerning how to understand these verses better and the interconnections among the sons of God, the daughters of man, their offspring, and the perplexing Nephilim.

The narrative begins with a temporal clause setting the scene in the antediluvian world. The number of human beings on the earth was increasing significantly. Verse one reads:

Gen 6:1

וַיְהִי כִּי־הֵחֵל הָאָדָם לָרֹב עַל־פְּנֵי הָאֲדָמָה וּבָנוֹת יֻלְּדוּ לָהֶם:

When humanity **began** to increase upon the face of the ground and daughters **were born** to them.

The clause beginning with היה followed by כי is one of the ways Hebrew marks dependent temporal clauses and can be translated as "when" or "whenever."[1] Some morpheme-for-morpheme translations render וַיְהִי כִּי as "Now it came about" (NASB) or "And it came to pass" (KJV). Most English speakers find these frames dated, and they do not fit the translation theory of most modern versions. The semantics of the *Hiphil* verb חלל designates the beginning of a state or event (<u>inchoative</u> action). The description of the setting continues with the following clause. The verb (יֻלְּדוּ) is a passive suffix conjugation and is the second element of the clause (X + *qātal*). This usage indicates <u>perfective</u> aspect.

Main narrative events are generally sequenced using prefix conjugation verbs with a prefixed *waw* consecutive (i.e., *wayyiqtol*, or CP). The *wayyiqtol* verb marks the verbal aspect as <u>perfective</u>, presenting the event as completed action in narrative. In verse 2, two sequential clauses begin with וַיִּרְאוּ "they saw" and then וַיִּקְחוּ "they took":

Gen 6:2

וַיִּרְאוּ בְנֵי־הָאֱלֹהִים אֶת־בְּנוֹת הָאָדָם כִּי טֹבֹת הֵנָּה וַיִּקְחוּ לָהֶם נָשִׁים מִכֹּל אֲשֶׁר בָּחָרוּ:

The sons of the gods **saw** that the daughters of humanity were beautiful and **took** them for themselves as wives from any they chose.

Verse three continues the narrative with an evaluation in the form of a quotation:

---

[1] Other ways Hebrew marks temporal dependent clauses are: (1) perfective aspect: וַיְהִי בְּ "in/during"; וַיְהִי אַחֲרֵי "after"; וַיְהִי כַּאֲשֶׁר "when"; (2) imperfective aspect: וְהָיָה בְּ "in/during"; וְהָיָה כִּי "when." See Lambdin, §110.

Gen 6:3

וַיֹּאמֶר יְהֹוָה לֹא־יָדוֹן רוּחִי בָאָדָם לְעֹלָם בְּשַׁגַּם הוּא בָשָׂר וְהָיוּ יָמָיו מֵאָה וְעֶשְׂרִים שָׁנָה:

Yahweh said, "My spirit will not remain with humanity forever because they are flesh, and their days will be [limited to] 120 years."

As part of the divine direct speech, the *yiqtol* and *wəqātal* verbs indicate an ongoing event (<u>continuous</u> aspect) and an <u>imperfective</u> state.

We find more evidence of the severity of the situation in verse four. The <u>fronted</u> topic is the Nephilim with the SC verb (X + *qātal*): הַנְּפִלִים הָיוּ בָאָרֶץ "The Nephilim were in the land." Standing outside of the previous narrative sequence, this perfective verb presents a complete, realized state. The following temporal phrases clarify that the presence of the Nephilim in the land preceded the circumstances being described (בַּיָּמִים הָהֵם "in those days") and followed after them as well (וְגַם אַחֲרֵי־כֵן "and even afterwards"). The latter situation is further described using a relative with two imperfective aspect clauses: וְגַם אַחֲרֵי־כֵן אֲשֶׁר יָבֹאוּ בְּנֵי הָאֱלֹהִים אֶל־בְּנוֹת הָאָדָם וְיָלְדוּ לָהֶם "And even afterwards, when the sons of the gods were going in (*yiqtol*) to the daughters of man, and they were bearing (*wəqātal*) them children." The Nephilim could not be the offspring of the illicit relationship described. Rather they coexisted at the same place and time as the coupling of the sons of the gods and the daughters of man. And they were recognized as "the valiant, renowned warriors from ancient times" (הֵמָּה הַגִּבֹּרִים אֲשֶׁר מֵעוֹלָם אַנְשֵׁי הַשֵּׁם).

The narrative employs the Hebrew verbal forms in several different ways to add depth and texture to the story. We can summarize their usage in verses 1 through 4 as follows:

- וַיְהִי (v. 1): *wayyiqtol* expressing perfective aspect (event as a whole), marking the setting of the new story about the sons of the gods, and connecting this narrative with the genealogical material (ending with Noah) in the previous chapter.
- כִּי־הֵחֵל הָאָדָם לָרֹב (v. 1): temporal כִּי + *qātal* (suffix conjugation) expressing perfective aspect (event as a whole), bringing the setting of the story to the beginning of humanity's increase upon the face of the earth.
- וּבָנוֹת יֻלְּדוּ לָהֶם (v. 1): the fronted subject places the narrative focus on the daughters being born to human beings. The X + *qātal* (Qal passive SC) expresses the perfective aspect, viewing the event as a whole as part of the temporal setting.
- וַיִּרְאוּ . . . וַיִּקְחוּ . . . וַיֹּאמֶר (vv. 2–3): *wayyiqtol* expressing the consecutive narrative actions. The population increase—particularly the beauty of the daughters—brought the notice of the sons of god, who took them as mates. Finally, human mortality is affirmed in the divine discourse.

הַנְּפִלִים הָיוּ בָאָרֶץ (v. 4): the fronted subject focuses the narrative on a new topic, the Nephilim. The X + *qātal* expresses the perfective aspect—the Nephilim lived in the land at that time. The specific timeframe is designated by the prepositional phrase.

בַּיָּמִים הָהֵם וְגַם אַחֲרֵי־כֵן (v. 4): the conjunction and temporal marker indicating what was happening during the time of the Nephilim and afterwards.

אֲשֶׁר יָבֹאוּ ... וְיָלְדוּ (v. 4): a compound dependent relative clause connecting to the temporal situation expressed in verse two. The sons of the gods were "going in" to the daughters of men and having children.[2] The *yiqtol* (PC) and *wəqātal* express imperfective actions—the activity is portrayed as continuous, "they [the daughters of man?] were bearing children" or even habitual, "they kept bearing them children."

The key to interpreting this passage is the meaning of the phrase, בְּנֵי־הָאֱלֹהִים "the sons of the gods." Interpreters have proposed three main views. The oldest view states that the sons of the gods were divine (or angelic) beings who were having sexual relations with human daughters.[3] This view makes use of the typical sense of the phrase, which almost always refers to divine beings in the Old Testament. And such an interpretation appears to inform the arguments of New Testament authors Peter and Jude regarding divine judgment (see 1 Pet 3:19–20; 2 Pet 2:4; Jude 6–7). Nonetheless, sexual relations between humans and angels appear to be problematic according to the theology of the New Testament (see Matt 22:30; Mark 12:25). Another view argues that the sin in this text involves the godly line of Seth (i.e., "divine sons") intermarrying with the ungodly line of Cain (i.e., "human daughters").[4] Though it avoids some of the problems of the first view, its interpretation of בְּנֵי־הָאֱלֹהִים is less convincing as nowhere else is Seth's patriline referred to in this manner. A more recent view appeals to the well-attested notion of divine kingship in the ancient world. It suggests that "the sons of the gods" were tyrannical kings descended from Cain who claimed to be divine and who indiscriminately took many wives for themselves in defiance of God's rule.[5] This proposal is rather promising from a purely Old Testament point of view, but it is difficult to reconcile with allusions to this event in Peter and Jude cited above. For this reason, Bruce K. Waltke suggests a combination of the angelic and divine kingship views, concluding, "The tyrants were demon possessed."[6] In sum, a conclusive interpretation

---

[2] The expression "go into" (בא + אל/על) commonly indicates sexual intercourse, usually with the focus on the male's role in the activity (see BDB, 98). Similar phraseology occurs in Gen 16:2 when Sarah instructs Abraham concerning Hagar: בֹּא־נָא אֶל־שִׁפְחָתִי "Please, go in to my maidservant."

[3] Amar Annus, "On the Origin of Watchers: A Comparative Study of the Antediluvian Wisdom in Mesopotamian and Jewish Traditions," *Journal for the Study of the Pseudepigrapha* 19 (2010): 277–320, provides an up-to-date analysis of this interpretation in light of the comparative ancient Near Eastern and Jewish evidence.

[4] For a defense of this view, see Kenneth A. Mathews, *Genesis 1–11:26*, NAC 1A (Nashville: Broadman & Holman, 1996), 329–32.

[5] See Meredith G. Kline, "Divine Kingship and Sons of God in Genesis 6:1–4," *Westminster Theological Journal* 24 (1962): 187–204.

[6] Bruce K. Waltke, *Genesis: A Commentary* (Grand Rapids: Zondervan, 2001), 117.

remains tentative, acknowledging the multiple difficulties and multilayered traditions of such an elusive text.

Recognizing the difficulty of this passage, however, does not mean we are unable to understand its thrust in the overall narrative. The main point of the passage is that as humanity increased upon the earth, so did sin. God's intent involved human flourishing (Gen 1:28), but instead "human wickedness" had increased and "every inclination of the human mind was nothing but evil all the time" (Gen 6:5). The narrative progression emphasizes this development, even if the specific nature of the sin remains mysterious in 6:1–4. Furthermore, the force of God's displeasure and the responsibility for this sin falls squarely upon humankind (not divine beings) for its participation in these sexual unions.

This exposition of Genesis 6 demonstrates a particularly diverse assortment of verb forms and other pragmatic markers in a narrative. This chapter will focus on the meanings of the finite verb conjugations. We seek to develop a broader understanding of the sequencing of these forms to form connections and disjunctions in contexts larger than a sentence.

5.2 CHAPTER OBJECTIVE

This chapter introduces the prefix and suffix conjugations and their functions within the Hebrew verbal system. This discussion begins with a discussion of the semantics of tense and aspect. The finite forms describe the suffix conjugation, the prefix conjugation, and the *waw* conjugations.

5.3 INTRODUCTION

Hebrew verbs can be divided into two groups of finiteness: finite and nonfinite conjugations. Finite verbs are forms inflected for person (3, 2, or 1), gender (M or F), and number (S or P). They are used in independent clauses and are marked for tense, aspect, and modality (TAM). Hebrew finite verbs include the prefix (*yiqtol*) and suffix (*qātal*) conjugations, the *waw* consecutive imperfect (*wayyiqtol*, or CP), and the *waw* consecutive perfect (*wəqātal*, sometimes called the converted perfect), as well as the Hebrew volitive forms (jussives, imperatives, and cohortatives). Conversely, nonfinite verbs are not inflected for person or TAM. Nonfinite verbal forms are rarely used in independent clauses, and their syntactical function resembles that of nouns rather than verbs. Nonfinite verbs include the infinitive construct, the infinitive absolute, and the active and passive participles.

The prefix and suffix conjugations constitute a binary pair of opposing meanings (*qātal* ~ *yiqtol*). The simplicity of this binary opposition is often lost to students once they discover the array of uses each conjugation employs. Nonetheless, this traditional formulation of the Hebrew conjugations provides a helpful and eloquent accounting. The consecutive forms (*wayyiqtol* ~ *wəqātal*) create a similar pairing. Scholars have proposed theories for explaining the semantics of these binary oppositions.

5.4 TENSE-ASPECT AND HEBREW CONJUGATIONS

5.4.1 Definition of Tense and Aspect

Hebrew grammarians are divided over the nature of the Hebrew verbal system, and they can be put into two groups. On one side are those who believe the Hebrew verbal system is primarily a tense-based system.[7] The term *tense* most often connotes the idea of time or temporality. In tense-based languages the verb is morphologically marked (inflected) in reference to a temporal reference point. For instance, it can designate the past, present, or future. These tenses are familiar to speakers of English, which is a tense language, along with a number of other Indo-European languages still spoken today.

On the other side are those who argue that Hebrew verbs are based primarily upon aspect differences.[8] Aspect focuses on the extent and duration of action indicated by the verb rather than the time frame of the action.[9] It provides different ways of viewing the completeness of an action from within the situation, from the point of view of the writer or speaker.[10] In this way a given verbal action may be described as perfective or imperfective. Hebrew students are often confused by this terminology because it resembles the traditional designations of the suffix and prefix conjugations as perfect and imperfect, respectively. Perfective and imperfective *aspect*, however, refer to the way in which the verbal action is portrayed

---

[7] E.g., Robert Hetzron, "Hebrew," in *The Major Languages of South Asia, the Middle East, and Africa*, ed. Bernard Comrie (London: Routledge, 1987), 192–210; E. John Revell, "The System of the Verb in Standard Biblical Prose," *HUCA* 60 (1989): 1–37; Alverio Niccacci, *The Syntax of the Verb in Classical Hebrew Prose*, JSOTSup 86 (Sheffield: JSOT Press, 1990); Vincent J. J. DeCean, "Ewald and Driver on Biblical Hebrew 'Aspect': Anteriority and the Orientalist Framework," *ZAH* 9 (1996): 126–51; Tal Goldfajn, *Word Order and Time in Biblical Hebrew Narrative*, Oxford Theological Monographs (Oxford: Clarendon, 1998); Ziony Zevit, *The Anterior Construction in Classical Hebrew*, SBLMS 50 (Atlanta: Scholars Press, 1998); Jan Joosten, "Do the Finite Verbal Forms in Biblical Hebrew Express Aspect?" *JANES* 29 (2002): 49–70; Blau, 187–93.

[8] E.g., *IBHS* §20.2g–i; Douglas M. Gropp, "The Function of the Finite Verb in Classical Biblical Hebrew," *Hebrew Annual Review* 13 (1991): 45–62; Peter J. Gentry, "The System of the Finite Verb in Classical Biblical Hebrew," *HS* 39 (1998): 7–39; F. W. Dobbs-Allsopp, "Biblical Hebrew Statives and Situation Aspect," *JSS* 45 (2000): 21–53; Galia Hatav, "Anchoring World and Time in Biblical Hebrew," *Journal of Linguistics* 40 (2004): 491–526; Cook, *Time and the Biblical Hebrew Verb*, 77–175; Dennis G. Pardee, "The Biblical Hebrew Verbal System in a Nutshell," in *Language and Nature: Papers Presented to John Huehnergard on the Occasion of His 60th Birthday*, ed. Rebecca Hasselbach and Naʿama Pat-El, SAOC 67 (Chicago: The Oriental Institute, 2012), 285–317.

[9] Some grammarians equate aspect and *Aktionsart* (a German word meaning "type of action") (e.g., *IBHS* §20.2j). Others maintain, however, that they are distinct: aspect is marked by the verbal form, while *Aktionsart* is conditioned upon the lexical meaning of a given verb (see Creason, "Semantic Classes of Hebrew Verbs," 6–7). See further below.

[10] See Comrie, *Aspect*, 3.

and are not necessarily aligned directly with the Hebrew conjugations, traditionally called the perfect and imperfect. Perfective aspect presents the verbal action
as completed, regardless of its place in the present or the past time (e.g., *I learned
Hebrew in the fall semester*). It depicts the action from outside the situation in
which it occurs, describing the action as whole or complete. Conversely, imperfective aspect shows the action in progress, depicting it from within the situation
as the event is in the process of happening (e.g., *I was learning Hebrew*). The notions of <u>iterativity</u> (or <u>frequentativity</u>, e.g., *Sam reexamined his vocabulary words*)
and <u>distributive</u> (e.g., *Sam examined each word*) concern the repetition of a given
action and are related to aspect.[11] Another category is <u>habitual</u> aspect, which is a
repeated action that is customary in nature, as in the examples, *I used to drink too
much coffee* or *Sam used to practice regularly*.[12]

5.4.2 Tense-Based Approach

The earliest understanding of the verbal system in the modern study of Hebrew
grammar was based upon tense. Leslie McFall summarizes the period of grammatical study before 1827 by noting that European grammarians apparently assumed
"that every language in the world had a tense system; therefore it was natural for
them to look for the Indo-European tense system in BH."[13] Blau argues that tense
generally appears to be indicated consistently.[14] Biblical Hebrew "marks the same
tenses as do many modern Indo-European languages, including English, viz., past,
present, and future." E. J. Revell concedes that the utility of basing Hebrew verbs
on tense may stem from our familiarity with English, but at the same time he sees
no reason to doubt this formulation.[15]

Other scholars believe the Hebrew verbal system allows for both tense and aspect, but that its fundamental operation is still prominently tense. Alverio Niccacci, for instance, thinks the *wayyiqtol* form functions as the "narrative tense."
Aspect, on the other hand, is indicated by nonverbal elements of the sentence including nonverb initial clause types.[16] The verbal forms in direct speech follow the

---

[11] *IBHS* §20.2i.

[12] Note that Comrie distinguishes between iterative and habitual action, clarifying that "the repetition of a situation is not sufficient for that situation to be referred to by a specifically habitual (or,
indeed, imperfective) form." He thus defines habitual action as "a situation which is characteristic of
an extended period of time, so extended that the situation referred to is viewed not as an incidental
property of the moment but, precisely, as a characteristic feature of a whole period" (*Aspect*, 27–28).

[13] Leslie McFall, *The Enigma of the Hebrew Verbal System: Solutions from Ewald to the Present
Day* (Sheffield, UK: Almond, 1982), 16.

[14] Blau, 189–90.

[15] Revell, "System of the Verb," 3.

[16] Alverio Niccacci, "Basic Facts and Theory of the Biblical Hebrew Verb System in Prose,"
in *Narrative Syntax and the Hebrew Bible: Papers of the Tilburg Conference 1996*, ed. Ellen van
Wolde (Leiden: Brill, 1997), 15, 31–32. Note, however, that in subsequent publications Niccacci
has developed his theory of the verbal system in light of the text-linguistic approach of Harald
Weinrich, *Tempus: Besprochene und erzählte Welt*, 4th ed. (Stuttgart: Beck, 1985). See Niccacci, "An
Integrated Verb System for Biblical Hebrew Prose and Poetry," in *Congress Volume Ljubljana 2007*,
ed. A. Lemaire, VTSup 133 (Leiden: Brill, 2010), 99. His view is not simply characterized as "time"

threefold tense understanding. For example, in 1 Sam 26:3 the *wayyiqtol* of the first clause is said to indicate the narrated event in past time, and the participle of the second clause (a nonverbal clause according to Niccacci's terminology) lends important antecedent information leading up to the narrated event:

1 Sam 26:3

וַיִּחַן שָׁאוּל בְּגִבְעַת הַחֲכִילָה . . . וְדָוִד יֹשֵׁב בַּמִּדְבָּר

Saul **encamped** on the hill of Hachilah . . . while David **was dwelling** in the desert.[17]

Mainline finite verbal forms mark time. Second-line sentence constituents and nonverb initial clauses (i.e., X+*qātal*) indicate aspect or other types of information. Stated differently, tense is seen as the primary feature of finite verbal forms while aspect is a primary feature of nonfinite verbal forms.[18]

The tense understanding typically assumes three tenses for Hebrew:

FORM	TENSE
קָטַל (*qātal* or SC)	Past
קֹטֵל (PTCL)	Present[19]
יִקְטֹל (*yiqtol* or PC)	Future

For this theory Gen 1:1 would illustrate the *qātal* functioning as past time:

Gen 1:1

בְּרֵאשִׁית בָּרָא אֱלֹהִים אֵת הַשָּׁמַיִם וְאֵת הָאָרֶץ׃

In the beginning God **created** the heavens and the earth.

The participle functions as the present tense in the next verse:

---

based but rather looks to the textual environment of each verbal form in terms of its marking narrative foreground or background. Note the following summary statement: "For me, each form refers to its own temporal axis—Qatal and Wayyiqtol to the past, Yiqtol and Weqatal to the future—and express a main-level information (§ 1). However, Yiqtol and Weqatal can also refer to the past (§ 2), as Qatal and Wayyiqtol can also refer to the future (§ 3). In both cases, the verb forms referring to a temporal axis different from their own convey an information that is of secondary level of communication." See "Problematic Points that Seem to Contradict a Coherent System of Biblical Hebrew Syntax in Poetry," *KUSATU* 15 (2013): 93–94. This approach still assumes a verbal system based in time categories, even if it is relative time.

[17] Niccacci, "Biblical Hebrew Verb System in Prose," 14.

[18] John Huehnergard nuances his description of tense and aspect. He also admits that the situation is more complicated than simply affirming that the Hebrew verbal system marks either tense or aspect. Rather, some forms primarily mark tense, while others primarily mark aspect. See "The Early Hebrew Prefix-Conjugations," *HS* 29 (1988): 20–21.

[19] Some argue the infinitive + pronominal suffix marks the present, e.g., Saadin Gaon (see Goldfajn, *Word Order*, 39).

Gen 1:2

וְרוּחַ אֱלֹהִים מְרַחֶפֶת עַל־פְּנֵי הַמָּיִם:

Now the Spirit of God **is hovering** upon the face of the waters.

The *yiqtol* PC for future time is found in the divine command:[20]

Gen 1:29

לָכֶם יִהְיֶה לְאָכְלָה

It **will be** food for you.

An earlier theory among some Jewish scholars was called the <u>conversive theory</u>, which stated that past and future forms could be "converted" into the opposite tense by attaching a *waw* (i.e., converted forms).[21] In other words, the past tense *waw* + *qātal* "converts" the *qātal* into a future, as in Exod 3:20.

Exod 3:20

וְשָׁלַחְתִּי אֶת־יָדִי וְהִכֵּיתִי אֶת־מִצְרַיִם בְּכֹל נִפְלְאֹתַי אֲשֶׁר אֶעֱשֶׂה בְּקִרְבּוֹ

I will send forth my hand and **will strike** Egypt with all my wonders which I will perform in its midst.

The *wayyiqtol* form would be another converted form, only in this case a *waw* + *pataḥ* + doubling precedes the PC (*yiqtol*) instead of the simple וֹ. For example, the first clause of Gen 1:4 continues the past tense from the previous verse.

Gen 1:5

וַיִּקְרָא אֱלֹהִים ׀ לָאוֹר יוֹם וְלַחֹשֶׁךְ קָרָא לָיְלָה

God **called** the light day, but the darkness he called night.

Ziony Zevit prefers to speak of only two Hebrew tenses, indicated by the four forms outlined above: the past marked by either the *qātal* suffix form or the *wayyiqtol* consecutive form, and the present-future marked by either the *yiqtol* prefix form or the *wəqātal* "converted" form.[22] How might we explain the fact that a prefixed form typically used for the present-future can also be appropriated for past narration? This question has posed a major problem for many scholars who have come to reject the tense-based theory for the Hebrew verbal system and accept an aspectual approach.

5.4.3 Aspect-Based Approach

The first scholar to articulate a full view of the Hebrew verbal system based on aspect rather than tense was G. H. A. von Ewald.[23] He distinguished between perfect (*qātal*) and imperfect (*yiqtol*) verbal forms marking complete and incomplete

---

[20] According to Niccacci ("Biblical Hebrew Verb System in Prose," 32), the indicative future tense is indicated by "initial x-yiqtol together with its continuation form weqatal" in direct speech.

[21] Goldfajn, *Word Order*, 17.

[22] Zevit, *Anterior Construction*, 48.

[23] First expressed in his Arabic grammar, G. H. A. von Ewald, *Grammatica critica linguae Arabicae*, 2 vols. (Leipzig: Hahn, 1831–1833), 1:112–13.

actions respectively.[24] The study of Hebrew grammar inherited the nomenclature "perfect" for the SC and "imperfect" for the PC largely from Ewald's contribution. The subsequent work of S. R. Driver on the Hebrew verbal system drew similar conclusions regarding its aspectual nature, with minor points of variation.[25] For instance, instead of referring to imperfect or incomplete action, Driver described the *yiqtol* form as "nascent" or initiatory action in opposition to the completed action of *qātal* forms.[26] Since Ewald and Driver, aspect has become the reigning paradigm for analyzing the Hebrew verbal system.[27]

The aspectual approach does not deny that Hebrew verbs express time reference, but rather assumes it is secondary to aspect. Completed actions are typically presented as having occurred in the past, while incomplete actions typically persist or continue into the present time of the speaker. The temporal point of reference is therefore that of the narrator or the speaker within the narrative. In this way aspect and tense refer to relative rather than the absolute time of a given action or event.[28] However, not all completed actions are necessarily presented in the past, nor are all incomplete actions portrayed in the present.

Aspect generally identifies two opposing verbal perspectives: perfective/complete action versus imperfective/incomplete action. In Hebrew, for instance, viewpoint aspect is marked by verbal morphology: the *yiqtol/wəqātal* denoting imperfective action, and *qātal/wayyiqtol* perfective action.[29]

ASPECT-BASED APPROACH	
FORM	ASPECT
יִקְטֹל (*yiqtol* or PC)	Imperfective
וְקָטַל (*wəqātal*)	
קָטַל (*qātal* or SC)	Perfective
וַיִּקְטֹל (*wayyiqtol* or CP)	

---

[24] See McFall, *Enigma*, 44–47.

[25] S. R. Driver, *A Treatise on the Use of the Tenses in Hebrew*, 3rd ed. (Oxford: Clarendon, 1892).

[26] For an overview, see McFall, *Enigma*, 61–69.

[27] McFall, *Enigma*, 27; Zevit, *Anterior Construction*, 46; Cook, *Time and the Biblical Hebrew Verb*, 83. Pardee refers to the "century-old tide of explaining the Biblical Hebrew verbal system as aspectual, rather than tensed." See Pardee, review of *The Anterior Construction in Classical Hebrew*, by Ziony Zevit, *JANES* 60 (2001): 308; also noted in Joosten, "Finite Verbal Forms," 50 n. 7.

[28] Earlier tense-based approaches also allowed for relative time (to be distinguished from absolute time) in the Hebrew verbal system. See the discussion of N. W. Schroeder's relative tense theory in McFall, *Enigma*, 21–24.

[29] Pardee, "Biblical Hebrew Verbal System," 287; Cook, *Time and the Biblical Hebrew Verb*, 199–201.

The position of the verb in the clause determines the choice of the verbal form.[30] For instance, the clause-initial verb expressing perfective aspect (or completed action) is *wayyiqtol*. In 1 Sam 1:1, וַיְהִי marks the beginning of the narrative:

1 Sam 1:1

וַיְהִי֩ אִ֨ישׁ אֶחָ֜ד מִן־הָרָמָתַ֛יִם

There was a man from Haramathaim

The *qātal* SC, on the other hand, indicates completed action in the non-clause-initial position when a word other than the verb is fronted in the sentence. We see this in Gen 4:1:

Gen 4:1

וְהָ֣אָדָ֔ם יָדַ֖ע אֶת־חַוָּ֣ה אִשְׁתּ֑וֹ וַתַּ֙הַר֙ וַתֵּ֣לֶד אֶת־קַ֔יִן

But the man **knew** Eve, his wife, and she conceived and bore Cain.

This example also illustrates the correlation between the *qātal* and *wayyiqtol* forms. One form is used for clause-internal position and the other for clause-initial position, but both mark perfective action. The aspectual opposite of the perfective SC (*qātal*) is the imperfective PC (*yiqtol*). Note the imperfective aspect of the *yiqtol* form in Josh 9:8:

Josh 9:8

וַיֹּ֨אמֶר אֲלֵהֶ֤ם יְהוֹשֻׁ֙עַ֙ מִ֣י אַתֶּ֔ם וּמֵאַ֖יִן **תָּבֹֽאוּ**

Joshua said to them, "Who are you and from where **are you coming**?"

Even though imperfective action often corresponds to present time, such is not always the case. From within the confines of Hebrew narrative *yiqtol* forms regularly report past events as in the following example.

Gen 6:4

הַנְּפִלִ֞ים הָי֣וּ בָאָרֶץ֮ בַּיָּמִ֣ים הָהֵם֒ וְגַ֣ם אַֽחֲרֵי־כֵ֗ן אֲשֶׁ֨ר **יָבֹ֜אוּ** בְּנֵ֤י הָֽאֱלֹהִים֙ אֶל־בְּנ֣וֹת הָֽאָדָ֔ם

The Nephilim were in the land in those days, and even afterwards, when the sons of the gods **were going** into the daughters of humankind.

In aspectual terms, the opposition signifies perfectivity for the suffix conjugation (*qātal*) and imperfectivity for the prefix conjugation (*yiqtol*). The corresponding *waw*-sequential forms likewise function as an opposing pair of perfectives (*wayyiqtol*) and imperfectives (*wəqātal*) in clause-initial position.[31]

---

[30] Gentry, "System of the Finite Verb," 13; Pardee, "Biblical Hebrew Verbal System," 290.

[31] See the helpful discussion in Cook, *Time and the Biblical Hebrew Verb*, 199–201 and McFall, *Enigma*. Cook singles out Jan Joosten's proposed opposition between indicative and non-indicative modality, noting its inability to be distinguished adequately in the Hebrew verbal system. See Jan Joosten, "The Long Form of the Prefixed Conjugation Referring to the Past in Biblical Hebrew Prose," *HS* 40 (1999): 15–26, and Cook's interaction with this view (141–43).

5.4.4 Assessment

Providing a complete assessment of all the views on tense and aspect is beyond the scope of the present chapter. Numerous articles and monographs have been written for just that purpose and present the various viewpoints.[32] For that reason, we will simply indicate which approach seems more plausible and why.

In this book we adopt an aspect-prominence approach to the Hebrew verbal system.[33] One of the problems with the tense-based system is its inability to account satisfactorily for significant exceptions to the tensed interpretations of certain forms.[34] This theory explains the use of *qātal* and *wayyiqtol* forms to refer to future events in prophetic texts, as in Isa 9:5.

Isa 9:5

כִּי־יֶ֣לֶד יֻלַּד־לָ֗נוּ
בֵּ֚ן נִתַּן־לָ֔נוּ
וַתְּהִ֥י הַמִּשְׂרָ֖ה עַל־שִׁכְמ֑וֹ
וַיִּקְרָ֨א שְׁמ֜וֹ פֶּ֣לֶא יוֹעֵץ֒ . . .

For a child **will be born** to us,
A son **will be given**.
Then the government **will be** upon his shoulder,
And his name **will be called** Wonderful Counselor . . .

The same problem occurs for *yiqtol* verbs in what look like past contexts and *qātal* verbs in what look like future contexts:

Judg 2:1

וַיֹּ֖אמֶר **אַעֲלֶ֤ה** אֶתְכֶם֙ מִמִּצְרַ֔יִם
He said, "**I brought** you up from Egypt."

Gen 17:16

וּבֵרַכְתִּ֣י אֹתָ֔הּ וְגַ֨ם **נָתַ֧תִּי** מִמֶּ֛נָּה לְךָ֖ בֵּ֑ן
I will bless her, and also **I will give** you a son from her.

To deal with such cases, tense-based advocates appeal to the notion of relative tense. They assert the time is not actual, absolute time of a given event but is time as it is intentionally portrayed by the speaker or narrator.[35] This explanation, however,

---

[32] E.g., Cook, *Time and the Biblical Hebrew Verb*.

[33] We have adopted this language from Aaron D. Hornkohl, "Biblical Hebrew Tense-Aspect-Mood, Word Order and Pragmatics: Some Observations on Recent Approaches," in *Studies in Semitic Linguistics and Manuscripts: A Liber Discipulorum in Honour of Professor Geoffrey Khan*, ed. Nadia Vidro et al. (Uppsala: University of Uppsala Press, 2018), 30. Hornkohl distinguishes between tense-prominent and aspect-prominent approaches to the Hebrew verbal system. Note, however, that he prefers a tense-prominent approach over an aspect-prominent approach.

[34] This criticism relies heavily on the analysis of McFall, *Enigma*, 18–21, 176–77.

[35] For instance, Galia Hatav suggests that application of the past tense *wayyiqtol* to future circumstances in the prophets is permissible because "prophets may be able to see in the future." She explains that in cases where God chooses to reveal certain events to someone, "that person would be

is unnecessary if one adopts the view that these Hebrew verbal forms are instead marking two kinds of aspects—perfective/complete action (*qātal* and *wayyiqtol*) and imperfective/incomplete action (*yiqtol* and *wəqātal*). The time of these verbal forms is relative to the situation as described in the narrative and is therefore not marked by the verbal conjugations. In our view, this formulation is the best means of accounting for most cases of verbal usage in the Biblical Hebrew.

5.5 MODALITY

Modality or mood refers to how a verbal action is portrayed in relation to reality. Some discussions distinguish mood simply as declarative and nondeclarative statements, one being factual and the other not factual. Recent approaches instead speak of realis versus irrealis verbal statements. Realis statements portray situations that have been actualized or perceived as real life circumstances. Irrealis statements on the other hand portray situations that are not actualized but that the speaker considers may potentially occur.[36] In many of the Indo-European languages mood is distinguished by two opposing forms: (1) indicative for realis and (2) subjunctive for irrealis.[37] Irrealis in these languages includes the imperative to assert the will of the speaker.

For this reason, we need to stress that mood constitutes the speaker's portrayal of realis or irrealis verbal action, since in many cases the modal statement expresses what the speaker wills to become reality and not necessarily what is reality. Linguists call this deontic modality (or *event modality*) because it deals with events or situations that are not yet realized but exist as mere potential in the mind of the speaker.[38] These statements specifically have to do with the assertion of the speaker's will for a situation or event to happen in reality. In contrast, epistemic modality (or *propositional modality*) refers to the speaker's attitude toward or knowledge about the truth or factuality of the proposition being asserted.[39] Such statements can express belief, doubts, or expectations held by the speaker.[40]

The most common mood in Biblical Hebrew is the indicative, the mood of declaration or portrayal of realis.[41] The Hebrew language formally marks mood only in the volitive forms—certain forms of the jussive (e.g., hollow and III-weak roots, as well as the *Hiphil*), imperative, and cohortative.[42] Volitive semantics mainly

---

able to pick out the actual world in which those events are to take place and use *wayyiqtol* clauses to report them." See "Past and Future Interpretation of Wayyiqtol," *JSS* 56 [2011]: 105.

[36] F. R. Palmer, *Mood and Modality*, 2nd ed., Cambridge Textbooks in Linguistics (Cambridge: Cambridge University Press, 2001), 1.

[37] Greek verbs are morphologically different when indicative and subjective.

[38] Palmer, *Mood and Modality*, 8.

[39] Palmer, 8. See also Ronald S. Hendel, "In the Margins of the Hebrew Verbal System," *ZAH* 9 (1996): 169.

[40] Palmer, *Mood and Modality*, 8.

[41] *IBHS* §20.2f.

[42] Hendel, "In the Margins," 169.

concerns deontic or event modality in that they express the speaker's desire that a given situation or event take place in reality. The types of assertions available range from strong commands to polite requests, the former being potentially more likely to become realized than the latter.

Vestiges of energic forms in Biblical Hebrew suggest another possible "mood" having existed at an earlier stage of the language. The energic form often is found with a suffixed -*n* preserved between a prefix conjugation and its pronominal suffix. The energics can occur with an unassimilated *nun* (e.g., יְסֹבְבֶנְהוּ in Deut 32:10) or an assimilated *nun* (e.g., יִשְׁמְרֶנּוּ in Exod 21:29).[43] Their function in the language remains unknown.

Other irrealis moods are expressed in Hebrew, but these are marked by syntax rather than morphology. The *wǝyiqtol* forms can express purpose, goal, and result.[44] This same irrealis mood can also be expressed when *wǝyiqtol* is sequenced after non-volitive verbal forms, though it is less common than in those cases following volitives.[45] We will cover this issue more fully in our treatment of volitive verbs in chapter 6. Other modal uses of the prefix conjugation (*yiqtol*) denote irrealis notions such as capability, permission, possibility, deliberation, obligation, and desire.[46] These uses must be determined from context.

5.6 SUFFIX CONJUGATION

The distinctive morphological feature of the Hebrew suffix conjugation or *qātal* is the attachment of pronominal suffixes (except for the 3MS) throughout the paradigm. These suffixes are historically related to the independent pronouns, as the following comparisons illustrate:

PLURAL		SINGULAR		
SC	PRONOUN	SC	PRONOUN	
כָּתְבוּ	הֵם	כָּתַב	הוּא	3M
	הֵנָּה	כָּתְבָה	הִיא	3F
כְּתַבְתֶּם	אַתֶּם	כָּתַבְתָּ	(אַתָּ(ה	2M
כְּתַבְתֶּן	אַתֵּנָה	כָּתַבְתְּ	אַתְּ	2F
כְּתַבְנוּ	אֲנַחְנוּ	כָּתַבְתִּי	אֲנִי/אָנֹכִי	1C

---

[43] For more examples, see *IBHS* §31.7.2a–b.

[44] Lambdin §107c (119).

[45] Pardee, "Biblical Hebrew Verbal System," 293.

[46] *IBHS* §31.4. Waltke and O'Connor note certain contexts in which the suffix conjugation denotes an irrealis situation: (1) certain conditional clauses where the suffix conjugation expresses hypothetical circumstances, and (2) the so-called "precative perfective" or "perfective of prayer" (493–94).

This form has been more commonly called the perfect, going back to the aspectual designations of G. H. A. von Ewald who labeled the <u>perfective</u> form the "perfect" and the <u>imperfective</u> form the "imperfect."[47] The aspectual meaning of the suffix conjugation is completed action or action viewed from the perspective of the whole in contrast with the imperfective aspect of the prefix conjugation, which typically portrays the action in progress.

5.6.1 Historical Development

The historical development of the suffix conjugation necessitates we revisit the Hebrew statives. In chapter 3, we noted that Hebrew verbs distinguish between <u>fientive</u> (expressing actions) and <u>stative</u> verbs (expressing a state of being). In certain forms of the prefix conjugation the fientive and stative verbs are identified by different theme vowels. For example, the stative root כבד "to be heavy" in the 3MS of the Qal PC is כָּבֵד (*i*-type theme vowel), whereas the fientive root כתב "to write" is כָּתַב (*a*-type theme vowel).

The historical origin of the stative is an adjective form. A whole class of adjectives are formed with the vowel pattern *a-i* (i.e., *qatil). Examples include זָקֵן "old," חָנֵף "profane," כָּבֵד "heavy." The result of this development is that it is often difficult to determine whether the form כָּבֵד should be analyzed as the 3MS *Qal* stative "he is heavy" or the MS adjective "heavy."[48]

COMPARATIVE SEMITICS AND THE STATIVE VERB

The East Semitic language of Akkadian attested a form grammarians call the verbal adjective or stative, which is related to the Hebrew *qatil adjective. The dominant theme vowel of the Akkadian verbal adjective was *i*, but it also attested theme vowels *a* and *u*.[49] Analogically, Hebrew attests these same vowel patterns in the Qal stem with different semantic values: *qatal for the Qal active, *qatil for the Qal stative, and in rare cases *qatul for the Qal stative (קָטֹנְתִּי "I am small"; יָכֹל "he is able").

5.6.2 Meaning and Function

The perfective semantics of the suffix conjugation naturally developed from its origin as a descriptor. Adjectives describe certain qualities of the entities they modify. A handy illustration of this point is the Hebrew stative adjectives that describe qualities with no reference to time: זָקֵן "He is old" rather than "He was old," and

---

[47] McFall, *Enigma*, 44.

[48] For more examples, see Joüon-Muroaka §41f.

[49] Huehnergard, *Grammar of Akkadian*, 25–26. For example, Akkadian attests the verbal adjectives *damqum* (< *damiq-*) "good," *rapšum* (< *rapaš-*) "wide," and *zaprum* (< *zapur-*) "malicious." The theme vowel only occurs in the feminine singular forms because when case vowels are attached, vowel syncope occurs: *damqum* (MS) vs. *damiqtum* (FS).

קָטֹן "He is small" rather than "He was small." In this regard, the suffix conjugation is more highly marked than the prefix conjugation. Fientive verbs describe the subject as carrying out an action. Typically, such events are understood as taking place in the past though not always. Compare the following two examples:

Job 1:22

בְּכָל־זֹאת לֹא־חָטָא אִיּוֹב

In all this, Job **did not sin**.

Ps 1:1

אַשְׁרֵי־הָאִישׁ אֲשֶׁר ׀ לֹא הָלַךְ בַּעֲצַת רְשָׁעִים

Blessed in the man who **does not walk** in the counsel of the wicked.

As we concluded in the previous sections, the suffix forms are not tied to a specific referent, but may describe actions in the past, present, and even future.

What role does time play for this form, if any? The tense model of the Hebrew verbal system designates the suffix conjugation as the default past tense. The close association of this conjugation with past time is not without merit, however, even if one adopts a more aspectual model. It is reasonable to conclude that perfective verbs are most often associated with past time, since the portrayal of completed actions is commonly done so after the fact. Cook helpfully qualifies in this regard that perfective aspect is "the defining property" of the suffix forms, while their association with past tense is "an accidental property that can be explained in terms of implication."[50] In other words, the contexts of certain suffixal forms imply that the verbal action takes place in the past. This feature is important to keep in mind, but it is one that can also be superseded in certain contexts by pragmatic factors. The suffix conjugation sometimes portrays a completed action before it happens, thus giving it a future referent. The same can be said of those cases wherein the suffix conjugation describes something as it currently stands, giving the impression of a present time referent.

We have chosen to categorize the suffix conjugation syntax along the lines of narrative uses versus direct discourse uses. Narrative use refers to those instances of the suffix forms in narrative prose, which constitutes a large portion of the attested forms. Discourse use is more difficult to define but is nonetheless a useful categorization. This includes reported speech embedded within narrative prose, but it also includes other types of direct speech such as that recorded in Ecclesiastes, the Ezra-Nehemiah memoirs, the Psalter, or the poetic speech of the Hebrew prophets.

5.6.2.1 Narrative Uses

Past. The suffix conjugation provides the default verbal form for reporting completed action. Most of these contexts involve actions reported as a whole after-the-fact, and thus with a past time referent. The aspect of this form is the same as the

---

[50] Cook, *Time and the Biblical Hebrew Verb*, 180–81.

narrative *wayyiqtol* (also called the *waw* consecutive), which we will discuss more fully below.

Judg 2:15

בְּכֹל ׀ אֲשֶׁר **יָצְאוּ** יַד־יְהוָה **הָיְתָה**־בָּם לְרָעָה כַּאֲשֶׁר דִּבֶּר יְהוָה וְכַאֲשֶׁר נִשְׁבַּע יְהוָה לָהֶם

Every time **they went out** the hand of Yahweh **was** against them for evil as Yahweh had spoken and as Yahweh had sworn to them.

1 Sam 5:1

וּפְלִשְׁתִּים **לָקְחוּ** אֵת אֲרוֹן הָאֱלֹהִים וַיְבִאֻהוּ מֵאֶבֶן הָעֵזֶר אַשְׁדּוֹדָה:

The Philistines **took** the ark of God and brought it from Ebenezer to Ashdod.

Isa 7:1

וַיְהִי בִּימֵי אָחָז בֶּן־יוֹתָם בֶּן־עֻזִּיָּהוּ מֶלֶךְ יְהוּדָה **עָלָה** רְצִין מֶלֶךְ־אֲרָם וּפֶקַח בֶּן־רְמַלְיָהוּ מֶלֶךְ־יִשְׂרָאֵל יְרוּשָׁלַם לַמִּלְחָמָה עָלֶיהָ **וְלֹא יָכֹל** לְהִלָּחֵם עָלֶיהָ:

In the days of Ahaz, son of Jotham, son of Uzziah, king of Judah, Rezin, king of Aram, and Pekah, son of Remaliah, king of Israel, **went up** to Jerusalem to wage battle against it, but **was not able** to prevail against it.

Perfect. The perfect use of the suffix conjugation portrays completeness or the entrance into a state of being. Narrative perfects are best translated in English as past perfects (i.e., "X had occurred") and are much like the Greek pluperfect (e.g., συνετέθειντο "they had agreed" John 9:22).[51] The following example reports onset of Eli's impaired vision that had already begun to inflict him before the events being narrated:

1 Sam 3:2

וְעֵינָו **הֵחֵלּוּ** כֵהוֹת לֹא יוּכַל לִרְאוֹת:

Now his eyes[52] **had begun** growing dim. He could not see.

Judg 2:15

בְּכֹל ׀ אֲשֶׁר **יָצְאוּ** יַד־יְהוָה **הָיְתָה**־בָּם לְרָעָה כַּאֲשֶׁר **דִּבֶּר** יְהוָה וְכַאֲשֶׁר **נִשְׁבַּע** יְהוָה לָהֶם

Every time they went out the hand of Yahweh was against them for evil as Yahweh **had spoken** and as Yahweh **had sworn** to them.

The second example describes what the Philistines had come to understand once they heard the cry from the camp of the Israelites:

---

[51] On the Greek pluperfect, see BDF §347.
[52] Reading with the *qere*: ועיניו "his eyes."

1 Sam 4:6

וַיֵּדְעוּ כִּי אֲרוֹן יְהוָה **בָּא** אֶל־הַמַּחֲנֶה׃

They knew that the ark of Yahweh **had entered** the camp.

5.6.2.2 Discourse Uses

Past. Reported speech also utilizes the suffixal forms to depict completed action or action as a whole. Sometimes the speaker refers to actions or events that have already occurred in the past, much like a narrator recounts past events. For example, messengers approach Job and report to him the tragic deaths of his children:

Job 1:19

וְהִנֵּה רוּחַ גְּדוֹלָה **בָּאָה** ׀ מֵעֵבֶר הַמִּדְבָּר וַיִּגַּע בְּאַרְבַּע פִּנּוֹת הַבַּיִת וַיִּפֹּל עַל־הַנְּעָרִים

וַיָּמוּתוּ

Behold, a great wind **came** from across the wilderness and struck the four corners of the house and it fell upon the youths and they died.

The psalmist describes that he rested in the midst of the trouble because Yahweh protected him:

Ps 3:6

אֲנִי **שָׁכַבְתִּי** וָאִישָׁנָה **הֱקִיצוֹתִי** כִּי יְהוָה יִסְמְכֵנִי׃

As for me, **I lay down** and then slept. **I awoke**, for Yahweh supports me.

Elsewhere the psalmist describes his confession of sin:

Ps 51:6

הֵן־בְּעָווֹן **חוֹלָלְתִּי** וּבְחֵטְא **יֶחֱמַתְנִי** אִמִּי׃

Behold, in iniquity **I was brought forth**; in sin my mother **conceived** me.

Present. More commonly in direct speech the suffix conjugation describes present realities (also called the gnomic perfect or proverbial perfect).[53] The aspect of this verbal form enables the speaker to describe the action, event, or circumstances as a whole. In Ps 6:4, the psalmist laments his present distressed soul before Yahweh.

Ps 6:4(3)

וְנַפְשִׁי **נִבְהֲלָה** מְאֹד וְאַתָּ יְהוָה עַד־מָתָי׃

My soul **is** exceedingly **distressed**; but you, O Yahweh, how long?

The prologue of Proverbs describes the tendencies of fools with a suffixal form preceded by a contrastive verbless clause describing the beginning of wisdom:

---

[53] *IBHS* §30.5.1c.

Prov 1:7

יִרְאַת יְהוָה רֵאשִׁית דָּעַת חָכְמָה וּמוּסָר אֱוִילִים בָּזוּ׃

The fear of Yahweh is the beginning of knowledge; fools **despise** discipline.

In the opening speech of Lady Wisdom, we find a suffixal form sandwiched between two prefix forms. Regarding the naïve, the prefix forms emphasize the habitual love for simplicity and hatred of knowledge, whereas the suffixal form describes their characteristic delight in scoffing:

Prov 1:22

עַד־מָתַי | פְּתָיִם תְּאֵהֲבוּ פֶתִי וְלֵצִים לָצוֹן חָמְדוּ לָהֶם וּכְסִילִים יִשְׂנְאוּ־דָעַת׃

How long will you go on loving simple things, O simple ones? Scoffers **delight in** their scorning, and fools hate knowledge.

Perfect. Speakers can utilize the suffix conjugation to refer to states that have come into effect before the moment of speaking. In direct speech, this state is more immediately relevant to the context than is the case for narrative, which describes the state as somewhat remote from the context of the reader (e.g., 1 Sam 8:5). This use of the suffix conjugation is much like the Greek perfect and is best translated in English as "X has/have occurred" (e.g., Ps 2:7; Jer 1:18).

1 Sam 8:5

הִנֵּה אַתָּה זָקַנְתָּ וּבָנֶיךָ לֹא הָלְכוּ בִּדְרָכֶיךָ

Behold, **you have grown old**, and your sons **have** not **walked** in your ways.

Ps 2:7

אֲסַפְּרָה אֶל חֹק יְהוָה אָמַר אֵלַי בְּנִי אַתָּה אֲנִי הַיּוֹם יְלִדְתִּיךָ׃

Let me declare the statute of Yahweh. He said to me: "You are my son; today **I have begotten you**."

Jer 1:18

וַאֲנִי הִנֵּה נְתַתִּיךָ הַיּוֹם לְעִיר מִבְצָר וּלְעַמּוּד בַּרְזֶל וּלְחֹמוֹת נְחֹשֶׁת עַל־כָּל־הָאָרֶץ לְמַלְכֵי יְהוּדָה לְשָׂרֶיהָ לְכֹהֲנֶיהָ וּלְעַם הָאָרֶץ׃

Behold, **I have set you** today as a fortified city and as a pillar of iron and as a wall of bronze against all the land, against the kings of Judah, against its princes, against its priests, and against the people of the land.

5.6.2.3 Prophetic Future

The prophetic perfect refers to an action or event that will take place in the future (also called the rhetorical future, accidental perfective, perfect of confidence, or persistent future perfective).[54] The action is presented as though it has already been completed, thus emphasizing the surety that it is as good as done. The prophet Isaiah portrays future acts of divine judgment as though they have already occurred:

Isa 2:11

עֵינֵי גַבְהוּת אָדָם **שָׁפֵל** וְשַׁח רוּם אֲנָשִׁים וְנִשְׂגַּב יְהוָה לְבַדּוֹ בַּיּוֹם הַהוּא:

The man with lofty eyes **will be abased**, the haughtiness of men will be brought low, and Yahweh alone will be exalted in that day.

He likewise portrays the righteous reign of the branch as though it had already come into effect in Isa 11:9.

Isa 11:9

לֹא־יָרֵעוּ וְלֹא־יַשְׁחִיתוּ בְּכָל־הַר קָדְשִׁי כִּי־**מָלְאָה** הָאָרֶץ דֵּעָה אֶת־יְהוָה כַּמַּיִם לַיָּם מְכַסִּים:

They will not fear, and they will not be dismayed in my holy mountain, for the land **will be full** of the knowledge of Yahweh as the waters cover the sea.

This use is common to the Hebrew prophets but is not limited to them. In the following two instances (one from Psalms, the second from Proverbs), the construction כִּי + suffixal form follows two imperatives, indicating that the suffix conjugation is describing what will occur if the imperatives are acted upon.

Ps 3:8

קוּמָה יְהוָה | הוֹשִׁיעֵנִי אֱלֹהַי כִּי־**הִכִּיתָ** אֶת־כָּל־אֹיְבַי לֶחִי שִׁנֵּי רְשָׁעִים **שִׁבַּרְתָּ**:

Arise, O Yahweh. Deliver me, O my God, for **you will strike** all my enemies on the cheek; **you will shatter** the teeth of the wicked.[55]

Prov 4:1–2

שִׁמְעוּ בָנִים מוּסַר אָב וְהַקְשִׁיבוּ לָדַעַת בִּינָה: כִּי לֶקַח טוֹב **נָתַתִּי** לָכֶם

Hear, my sons, the instruction of a father, and give attention to the knowledge of understanding, for **I will give** you sound teaching.

5.6.2.4 Irrealis Uses

Conditional Constructions. It is fairly common to find the suffix conjugation in conditional constructions, either stating the protasis or the apodosis.

---

[54] *IBHS* §30.5.1e; Williams §165. Gesenius called this use *perfectum confidentiae*, which expresses "facts which are undoubtedly imminent, and, therefore, in the imagination of the speaker, already accomplished," also noting that it is most frequent in prophetic language (*perfectum propheticum*; GKC §106m–n).

[55] The effect of this prayer from the psalmist is one of confident trust in Yahweh's ability to defeat his enemies. In fact, we could translate these suffix forms as perfects, which again portrays the rescuing acts of Yahweh as though they have already occurred: "for you have struck all my enemies on the cheek; you have shattered the teeth of the wicked."

As a protasis:

Ps 44:21–22

אִם־שָׁכַחְנוּ שֵׁם אֱלֹהֵינוּ וַנִּפְרֹשׂ כַּפֵּינוּ לְאֵל זָר: הֲלֹא אֱלֹהִים יַחֲקָר־זֹאת

If **we denied** the name of our God and then extended our hand to another God, would he not find it out?

As an apodosis:

1 Sam 6:9

אִם־דֶּרֶךְ גְּבוּלוֹ יַעֲלֶה בֵּית שֶׁמֶשׁ הוּא **עָשָׂה** לָנוּ אֶת־הָרָעָה הַגְּדוֹלָה הַזֹּאת

If [the ark] would go up by the way of its territory to Beth-Shemesh, then certainly he **has done** to us this great evil.

Ps 11:3 (with כִּי)

כִּי הַשָּׁתוֹת יֵהָרֵסוּן צַדִּיק מַה־**פָּעָל**:

If the foundations are demolished, what can the righteous **do**?

Other Irrealis Uses. The suffix form can follow כִּי expressing the resulting content of the preceding verbal action. Here, it provides what is known (ידע):

1 Sam 6:9

וְיָדַעְנוּ כִּי לֹא יָדוֹ **נָגְעָה** בָּנוּ

We will know that his hand did not **strike** us.

Sometimes the suffix conjugation can function as a modal. For example, Job declares a *potential* act of denying God.

Job 31:28

גַּם־הוּא עָוֹן פְּלִילִי כִּי־**כִחַשְׁתִּי** לָאֵל מִמָּעַל:

That too would be an iniquity deserving judgment, for **I would have denied** the God above.

5.6.2.5 Special Uses

Introductory Formula with אמר. The standard formula for introducing divine speech in the prophets utilizes the 3MS *Qal* suffix conjugation of the root אמר "to say." Analysis of the situation aspect of the suffix conjugation in this formula indicates that it presents the divine speech as a whole unit. The common translation value for כֹּה אָמַר אֲדֹנָי "thus says the Lord," could alternatively be rendered, "The Lord has spoken the following."

Performative. The category performative borrows relatively recent terminology, even though the basic concept of a performative utterance has been identified in Hebrew grammars for quite some time. GKC lists two categories of the suffix conjugation relate to utterances that accomplish actions once they are spoken.[56] More recently, Waltke and O'Connor identify the "instantaneous perfective,"

---

[56] GKC §§106*i* and *m*.

which "represents a situation occurring at the very instant the expression is being uttered." They associate this particular usage of the suffix conjugation with verbs of speech such as swearing, declaring, advising, and the like.[57] The first English edition of Joüon and Muraoka's grammar offers a similar explanation and identifies this usage as performative.[58] The earliest sustained treatment of the performative in Biblical Hebrew occurs in an article by Delbert R. Hillers, who borrows the concept from the theoretical work of philosopher J. L. Austin and applies it to the suffix conjugation.[59] This concept as a modern grammatical category apparently originates with Erwin Koschmieder, who coined the German term *Koinzindenzfall* in describing the usage of a Greek aorist verb.[60] Drawing upon Koschmieder's formulation, Dennis Pardee and Robert Whiting define a performative as "an utterance which actually performs, effects," or "brings about the event." Seth L. Sanders similarly qualifies that they "simultaneously say something and do something by talking about saying and talking about doing."[61]

The performative is limited to certain verbs in direct discourse. In specific environments, the utterance is the action bringing about what is stated. In Northwest Semitic languages, the suffix conjugation is the verb of choice in these contexts, likely because it is the least marked verbal form, having derived historically from the verbal adjective/stative. It is descriptive in nature and in that sense less tied to a particular time referent. According to Sanders, this form "by itself does not specify a relation to the moment of speaking." Rather, when it is spoken by an authorized person in the right circumstances, "the performative actually brings about the relationship between the first-person referent and the second-person referent denoted by the performative verb in the utterance."[62] In other words, the descriptive nature of the suffixal form enables the speaker to unite himself and the hearer with the

---

[57] *IBHS* §30.5.1d.

[58] They state: "The qatal is used for an instantaneous action which, being performed at the very moment of the utterance, is assumed to belong to the past. Hence this use of the perfect is sometimes called 'performative'" (Joüon-Muroaka §112f). The second English edition in the same paragraph adds the following explanation at the end of the first sentence: "whereby the actor is, as it were, acting out his utterance," citing an article by I. Zatelli, "I prodromi della definizione di verbo performativo nelle grammatiche tradizionali dell'ebraico biblico," in *Semitic and Assyriological Studies Presented to Pelio Fronzaroli by Pupils and Colleagues*, ed. Paolo Marrassini (Wiesbaden: Harrassowitz, 2003), 690–97. In the revised and expanded edition of Ronald J. Williams's *Hebrew Syntax*, John C. Beckman identifies Williams's "instantaneous" perfect with the "performative perfect," which "indicates a speech act, meaning that the action denoted by the verb occurs by means of speaking the sentence (or other linguistic unit) in which the verb occurs" (Williams §164).

[59] Delbert R. Hillers, "Some Performative Utterances in the Bible," in *Pomegranates and Golden Bells: Studies in Biblical, Jewish, and Near Eastern Ritual, Law, and Literature in Honor of Jacob Milgrom*, ed. David P. Wright, David Noel Freedman, and Avi Hurvitz (Winona Lake, IN: Eisenbrauns, 1995), 757–66; J. L. Austin, *How to Do Things with Words*, 2nd ed., ed. J. O. Urmson and Marin Sbisa (Cambridge: Harvard University Press, 1962).

[60] Erwin Koschmieder, "Zu den Grundfragen der Aspekttheorie," *IF* 53 (1935): 280–300, as identified in Dennis Pardee and Robert M. Whiting, "Aspects of Epistolary Verbal Usage in Ugaritic and Akkadian," *BSOAS* 50 (1987): 23.

[61] Seth L. Sanders, "Performatives Utterances and Divine Language in Ugaritic," *JNES* 63 (2004): 167.

[62] Sanders, "Performatives Utterances," 169.

utterance instantaneously. Moreover, the performative is lexically, contextually, and culturally defined by performative utterance contexts. Examples include:

Gen 15:18

לְזַרְעֲךָ֗ **נָתַ֙תִּי֙** אֶת־הָאָ֣רֶץ הַזֹּ֔את מִנְּהַ֣ר מִצְרַ֔יִם עַד־הַנָּהָ֥ר הַגָּדֹ֖ל נְהַר־פְּרָֽת׃

To your seed **I give** this land, from the river of Egypt to the great river Euphrates.

Gen 23:11

לֹֽא־אֲדֹנִ֣י שְׁמָעֵ֔נִי הַשָּׂדֶה֙ **נָתַ֣תִּי** לָ֔ךְ וְהַמְּעָרָ֥ה אֲשֶׁר־בּ֖וֹ לְךָ֣ **נְתַתִּ֑יהָ** לְעֵינֵ֧י בְנֵי־עַמִּ֛י **נְתַתִּ֥יהָ** לָּ֖ךְ קְבֹ֥ר מֵתֶֽךָ׃

No, my lord. Listen to me. **I give** the field to you, and the cave which is in it **I give** to you. Before the eyes of the sons of my people, **I give** it to you; bury your dead.

Deut 4:26

הַעִידֹ֩תִי֩ בָכֶ֨ם הַיּ֜וֹם אֶת־הַשָּׁמַ֣יִם וְאֶת־הָאָ֗רֶץ כִּֽי־אָבֹ֣ד תֹּאבֵדוּן֮ מַהֵר֒ מֵעַ֣ל הָאָ֔רֶץ אֲשֶׁ֨ר אַתֶּ֜ם עֹבְרִ֧ים אֶת־הַיַּרְדֵּ֛ן שָׁ֖מָּה לְרִשְׁתָּ֑הּ

I call heaven and earth **as witnesses** against you this day, that you will surely perish quickly from upon the land which you are crossing over the Jordan to possess.

Judg 17:3

הַקְדֵּ֣שׁ **הִקְדַּ֣שְׁתִּי** אֶת־הַכֶּ֧סֶף לַיהוָ֛ה מִיָּדִ֖י לִבְנִ֑י לַעֲשׂוֹת֙ פֶּ֣סֶל וּמַסֵּכָ֔ה

I wholly **dedicate** the silver from my hand to Yahweh for my son to build an idol and molten image.

Epistolary Perfect. Dennis Pardee's work on the epistolary perfect in Hebrew letters and his joint publication with Robert M. Whiting on the epistolary perfect in the Ugaritic and Akkadian lay the groundwork for subsequent discussions of this category in the Semitic languages.[63] Pardee borrowed the verbal category <u>epistolary</u> from Classical Greek and applied it to various suffixal verbal forms in the corpus of Hebrew letters.[64] The epistolary usage occurs when the writer "puts himself in the situation of the reader or beholder who views the action as past."[65] There appears to be some confusion as to whether the epistolary perfect is a type of performative. Pardee and Whiting distinguish the epistolary perfect from the performative, arguing that the epistolary perfect is not a performative because it

---

[63] Dennis Pardee, "The 'Epistolary Perfect' in Hebrew Letters," *BN* 22 (1983): 34–40; Pardee and Whiting, "Verbal Usage," 1–31.

[64] Pardee, "Epistolary Perfect," 34. For more on the Hebrew letters, see Pardee, *Handbook of Hebrew Letters*, SBL Sources for Biblical Study 15 (Chico, CA: Scholars Press, 1982); F. W. Dobbs-Allsopp et al., *Hebrew Inscriptions: Texts from the Monarchy with Concordance* (New Haven: Yale University Press, 2005).

[65] Herbert Weir Smyth, *Greek Grammar*, rev. ed., ed. Gordon Messing (Cambridge: Harvard University Press, 1956), §1942.

only reports an act and is not an action itself.[66] Only two occurrences are found in BH (2 Kgs 5:6; 2 Chr 2:12), but the extrabiblical letters justify their categorization.

2 Kgs 5:6

וְעַתָּ֗ה כְּב֞וֹא הַסֵּ֤פֶר הַזֶּה֙ אֵלֶ֔יךָ הִנֵּ֨ה שָׁלַ֤חְתִּי אֵלֶ֨יךָ֙ אֶת־נַעֲמָ֣ן עַבְדִּ֔י וַאֲסַפְתֹּ֖ו מִצָּֽרַעְתֹּֽו׃

Now, when this letter comes to you, behold, **I have sent** to you Naaman, my servant, that you might heal him of his leprosy.

2 Chr 2:12

וְעַתָּ֗ה שָׁלַ֤חְתִּי אִישׁ־חָכָ֛ם יוֹדֵ֥עַ בִּינָ֖ה לְחוּרָ֥ם אָבִֽי׃

Now, **I have sent** Huram-abi, a man of wisdom, knowing understanding.

5.7 PREFIX CONJUGATION

The prefix conjugation (more commonly called the imperfect[67]) is the main non-perfective verb for BH. The prefix of the prefix conjugation form derives from pronouns attached to the verbal root. The traditional nomenclature of "imperfect" often leads students to identify the imperfect conjugation exclusively with imperfective aspect. This term lends itself to the confusion of form and function. We have therefore adopted the descriptive morphological designation "prefix conjugation" (PC or *yiqtol*) in this grammar. The tense-based grammarians interpret the PC as a future tense, but as we have argued above (§5.4.2) this approach is unable to account for the numerous examples to the contrary. Rather, the PC appears to mark non-perfective action or action that is not portrayed as a whole, that is, incomplete.

5.7.1 Historical Development

The historical development of the prefix conjugation yields a number of important observations. This discussion takes us to the El Amarna letters which preserved Canaanite language(s) from the early fourteenth century BC. William L. Moran identifies in these texts three distinct prefixed verbal forms: *yaqtulu*, *yaqtul*, and *yaqtula*. The distinguishing feature of the series is the final vowel. Moran understood the final-*u* as marking an indicative, -Ø (null ending) as marking the so-called preterite, and -*a* as marking the jussive.[68] Anson R. Rainey argues that Amarna Canaanite evidences a fully productive system of tense and modality, which he believes should inform our interpretation of the Hebrew verbal system.[69] John Huehnergard states that "Rainey overstates the matter in insisting that the forms he calls 'indicative' constitute a system of tenses rather than aspect—remarks intended to

---

[66] Pardee and Whiting, "Verbal Usage," 26.
[67] Going back to G. H. A. von Ewald (see McFall, *Enigma*, 44).
[68] William L. Moran, "Early Canaanite *yaqtula*," *Or* 29 (1960): 7–8.
[69] Anson F. Rainey, "The Ancient Hebrew Prefix Conjugation in the Light of Amarna Canaanite," *HS* 27 (1986): 4–5.

counter the now very outdated implication that the ancient Semites never know what time it was and must have had a lot of trouble arranging panel discussions."[70] Whether or not we adopt the tense interpretation does not lessen the importance of the Amarna evidence for explaining the development of the prefix forms. Ugaritic appears to have preserved vestiges of a similar distinction between indicative and non-indicative forms. Altogether, this evidence allows us to reconstruct the following system of verbal forms in early Northwest Semitic as the precursor to BH:[71]

INDICATIVE		VOLITIVE	
Perfective	*qatala	Imperative	*qutul
Imperfective	*yaqtulu	Jussive	*yaqtul
		Cohortative	*yaqtula

For BH, the distinction between the short and long PC forms, *yaqtulu indicative and jussive *yaqtul, are mostly but not entirely lost. At some point in the historical development of the language, Hebrew verbs lost their final short vowels. For most strong verbs, this change meant the indicative and volitive forms were no longer distinguishable.[72] Only context can tell us whether יִכְתֹּב is the indicative "he writes" or the jussive "may he write." Biblical Hebrew cohortatives largely preserve the volitive final-a ending, but this is limited to the first-person forms of strong verbs (e.g., אֶשְׁמְעָה "let me hear").

III-weak roots, middle-weak roots, and *Hiphil* stem verbs mostly preserve the distinction and provide evidence that Hebrew at one time marked indicative and volitive forms much like the situation attested in earlier Northwest Semitic. For the indicative, III-weak roots distinguished two forms by the presence or absence of a final-u vowel. Biblical Hebrew III-weak roots attest so-called long and short prefix forms and may reflect vestiges of indicative and non-indicative forms. For example, the root בנה attests both the indicative יִבְנֶה "he builds" and jussive יִבֶן "let him build." The same distinction shows up in the doubly-weak verbs היה "to be" and חיה "to live," יִהְיֶה "he is" and יְהִי "let him be," and יִחְיֶה "he lives" and יְחִי "let him live."

SHORT AND LONG PC VERBS WITH III-WEAK ROOTS			
INDICATIVE		VOLITIVE	
Perfective	בָּנָה	Imperative	בְּנֵה
Imperfective	יִבְנֶה	Jussive	יִבֶן
		Cohortative	אֶשְׁמְעָה[73]

---

[70] See Huehnergard, "Early Hebrew Prefix-Conjugation," 20.

[71] As adapted from Dennis G. Pardee, review of *Canaanite in the Amarna Tablets,* by Anson F. Rainey, *JNES* 58 (1999): 314.

[72] See a review of the different views of this process in Benjamin D. Suchard, *The Development of the Biblical Hebrew Vowels,* SSLL 99 (Leiden: Brill, 2020), 190–220.

[73] The final -a of the cohortative is not preserved in III-weak verbs (Joüon-Muraoka §79o).

HISTORICAL DEVELOPMENT OF PC SHORT AND LONG FORMS

How do we explain the development of the PC short and long forms? The historical argument suggests that the Hebrew long forms demonstrate what once was a *yaqtulu* for prefix forms with theme vowel /u/ (e.g., יִכְתֹּב), *yiqtalu* for theme vowel /a/ verbs (e.g., יִכְבַּד), and *yaqtilu* for theme vowel /i/ verbs (e.g., יֵשֵׁב).[74] For BH בנה (*yiqtal* pattern), we may reconstruct the following development: *yibnayu > yibneh*. The short form would have likely developed along the following lines: *yibnayØ > *yibn > yíben*.

Middle-weak roots preserve the difference in the PC morphology. The long form is יָקוּם "he will arise," and the short form is יָקֻם "may he arise" (once וַיָּקָם occurs at Job 22:28). The imperative forms are קוּם (MS), קוּמִי (FS), and קוּמוּ (MP) but קֹמְנָה (FP). The cohortative is also the long form.

SHORT AND LONG PC VERBS WITH MIDDLE-WEAK ROOTS			
INDICATIVE		VOLITIVE	
Perfective	קָם	**Imperative**	קֹמְנָה/קוּם
Imperfective	יָקוּם	**Jussive**	(וַיָּקָם) יָקֻם
Wayyiqtol	וַיָּקָם	**Cohortative**	נָקוּמָה

The *Hiphil* stem attests a series of short and long prefix verbs demarcating volitives and indicatives. The prefix indicative forms are written with the theme vowel *ḥireq-yod*, while the volitive forms contract it to *ṣere*. The *Hiphil* prefix form of the root כרת is יַכְרִית "he cuts off" (Deut 12:29), but the jussive is יַכְרֵת "may he cut off" (Ps 12:4). The same distinction occurs for the imperative, as illustrated by the root שכם "to rise early:" תַּשְׁכִּים "you rise early" (Judg 9:33) and הַשְׁכֵּם "may he rise early" (Exod 8:16). When endings are attached which create an open second syllable, however, *ḥireq-yod* reappears, thereby removing any distinction. We can observe this morphological characteristic in the masculine plural imperative, as with הַזְכִּירוּ (Isa 12:4).

SHORT AND LONG PC VERBS WITH THE *HIPHIL* STEM			
INDICATIVE		VOLITIVE	
Perfective	הִשְׁכִּים	**Imperative**	הַזְכִּירוּ/הַשְׁכֵּם
Imperfective	יַשְׁכִּים	**Jussive**	יַשְׁכֵּם
		Cohortative	אַשְׁכִּימָה

---

[74] For more on the historical development of III-weak verbs, see BL §57; Blau, 248–52.

5.7.2 Meaning and Function

The diverse uses of the prefix conjugation is often confusing to students. It is helpful to remember, however, that the basic notion of the verbal form is the imperfective aspect, which is used in opposition to its perfective counterpart **qatala*. The PC is primarily undefined and incomplete action viewed from within the situation being described. Waltke and O'Connor prefer to call this form the non-perfective conjugation and identify two values: (1) to mark an imperfective situation in past or present time, and (2) to mark a dependent situation.[75] We suggest it may be more correct to remove the time element from Waltke and O'Connor's definition and simply say that it marks imperfective and dependent situations. Cook categorizes the prefix conjugation as both imperfective *yiqtol* and irrealis *yiqtol*.[76] The irrealis mood corresponds to Waltke and O'Connor's dependent situations, which entails actions or situations that are not actualized but that exist in the mind of the speaker as potential.

The standard grammars identify several functions of the prefix forms. Their semantics primarily include imperfective and modal uses.

5.7.2.1 Imperfective Uses

Progressive. The default meaning of the prefix conjugation is <u>progression</u>. The context can portray the progressive action as either occurring in the past or non-past. These prefix uses the take the reader inside the action as though it were in progress and therefore incomplete.

Exod 15:5 (past)

תְּהֹמֹת יְכַסְיֻמוּ יָרְדוּ בִמְצוֹלֹת כְּמוֹ־אָבֶן׃

The deeps **covered them**; **they went down** into the depths like a stone.

Gen 24:31 (non-past)

וַיֹּאמֶר בּוֹא בְּרוּךְ יְהוָה לָמָּה תַעֲמֹד בַּחוּץ וְאָנֹכִי פִּנִּיתִי הַבַּיִת וּמָקוֹם לַגְּמַלִּים׃

And he said, "Come, blessed of Yahweh. Why **are you standing** outside? I have prepared the house and a place for the camels."

Exod 14:14 (non-past)

יְהוָה יִלָּחֵם לָכֶם וְאַתֶּם תַּחֲרִישׁוּן׃

Yahweh **is fighting** for you, but you must remain silent.

Iterative/Frequentative. Sometimes the prefix conjugation denotes action that occurs at various intervals over time. Grammarians often label this category <u>customary</u> or <u>habitual</u>, but this categorization may be too narrow. More than simply habitual or customary behavior, this usage depicts a single action that takes place multiple times or is repeated over time under certain conditions. The time of the

---

[75] *IBHS* §31.2.
[76] Cook, *Time and the Biblical Hebrew Verb*, 222.

frequentative action can either be past or present, depending on the temporal indicators of the context.

Num 9:18 (past)

עַל־פִּי יְהוָה יִסְעוּ בְּנֵי יִשְׂרָאֵל וְעַל־פִּי יְהוָה יַחֲנוּ כָּל־יְמֵי אֲשֶׁר יִשְׁכֹּן הֶעָנָן עַל־הַמִּשְׁכָּן יַחֲנוּ:

At the command the Yahweh the sons of Israel **would set out**, and at the command of Yahweh **they would set up camp**. As long as the cloud remained over the camp, **they would remain encamped**.

Judg 2:19 (past)

וְהָיָה | בְּמוֹת הַשּׁוֹפֵט יָשֻׁבוּ וְהִשְׁחִיתוּ מֵאֲבוֹתָם לָלֶכֶת אַחֲרֵי אֱלֹהִים אֲחֵרִים

Whenever the judge would die, **they would turn back** and then become more corrupt than their fathers following other gods.

Prov 1:18 (non-past)

וְהֵם לְדָמָם יֶאֱרֹבוּ יִצְפְּנוּ לְנַפְשֹׁתָם:

They would regularly **lie in wait** for their own blood; **they ambush** their own souls.

Incipient/Ingressive/Inchoate. This conjugation is also able to focus on the initiation of an incomplete action, shining the spotlight upon the circumstances inaugurating the activity.

Gen 29:32 (non-past)

וַתַּהַר לֵאָה וַתֵּלֶד בֵּן וַתִּקְרָא שְׁמוֹ רְאוּבֵן כִּי אָמְרָה כִּי־רָאָה יְהוָה בְּעָנְיִי כִּי עַתָּה יֶאֱהָבַנִי אִישִׁי:

Leah conceived and bore a son, and she called his name Reuben, for she said, "Yahweh has seen my affliction. Surely now my husband **will start loving me**."

Exod 15:1 (past)

אָז יָשִׁיר־מֹשֶׁה וּבְנֵי יִשְׂרָאֵל אֶת־הַשִּׁירָה הַזֹּאת לַיהוָה

Then Moses and the sons of Israel **began singing** this song to Yahweh.

Resultative/Culminative. Likewise, the prefix conjugation can emphasize the culminating effects of a given action, drawing attention to the final moments of the event.

Gen 29:8 (non-past)

וְאָנֹכִי לֹא אוּכַל לְהִמָּלֵט הָהָרָה פֶּן־תִּדְבָּקַנִי הָרָעָה וָמַתִּי:

I am unable to flee to the mountain lest calamity **overtake me**, and I die.

Gen 38:11 (non-past)

וַיֹּאמֶר יְהוּדָה לְתָמָר כַּלָּתוֹ שְׁבִי אַלְמָנָה בֵית־אָבִיךְ עַד־יִגְדַּל שֵׁלָה בְנִי

Judah said to Tamar, his daughter-in-law, "Remain a widow in the house of your father until Shela, my son, **grows up**."

5.7.2.2 Modal Uses

The modal uses occur in clauses that express a number of irrealis or potential actions, should the right conditions come into effect.

Capability. This category of usage occurs when the potential action in view signifies what the subject is capable of doing. In other words, the subject has the ability to carry out the action given the right circumstances.

Gen 44:15 (non-past)

מַה־הַמַּעֲשֶׂה הַזֶּה אֲשֶׁר עֲשִׂיתֶם הֲלוֹא יְדַעְתֶּם כִּי־נַחֵשׁ יְנַחֵשׁ אִישׁ אֲשֶׁר כָּמֹנִי:

What is this deed that you have done? Do you not know that a man such as I **can** indeed **practice** divination?

In certain contexts, the prefix form indicates what the subject is incapable of doing.

Gen 39:9 (non-past)

וְאֵיךְ אֶעֱשֶׂה הָרָעָה הַגְּדֹלָה הַזֹּאת וְחָטָאתִי לֵאלֹהִים:

How **could I do** this great evil and sin against God?

Permission. In this use the subject of the verb is permitted to carry out the action.

1 Sam 21:16 (non-past)

חֲסַר מְשֻׁגָּעִים אָנִי כִּי־הֲבֵאתֶם אֶת־זֶה לְהִשְׁתַּגֵּעַ עָלָי הֲזֶה יָבוֹא אֶל־בֵּיתִי:

Am I lacking madmen that you have brought this one to act madly before me? **Should** this one **enter** my house?

1 Sam 23:2 (non-past)

וַיִּשְׁאַל דָּוִד בַּיהוָה לֵאמֹר הַאֵלֵךְ וְהִכֵּיתִי בַּפְּלִשְׁתִּים הָאֵלֶּה

And David asked Yahweh saying, "**May I go** and strike these Philistines?"

When a negative particle accompanies the prefix form it denotes actions that are not permissible.

Gen 20:9 (non-past)

וּמֶה־חָטָאתִי לָךְ כִּי־הֵבֵאתָ עָלַי וְעַל־מַמְלַכְתִּי חֲטָאָה גְדֹלָה מַעֲשִׂים אֲשֶׁר לֹא־יֵעָשׂוּ עָשִׂיתָ עִמָּדִי:

How have I sinned against you that you would bring this great sin upon me and my kingdom? [Why] have you done to me the things that **ought not to be done**?

1 Sam 27:9 (non-past)

וְהִכָּה דָוִד אֶת־הָאָרֶץ **וְלֹא יְחַיֶּה** אִישׁ וְאִשָּׁה

David struck the land and **did not allow** a man or woman **to live**.

Possibility. Sometimes the prefix form can indicate potential actions that have a high likelihood happening.

Gen 44:34 (non-past)

כִּי־אֵיךְ אֶעֱלֶה אֶל־אָבִי וְהַנַּעַר אֵינֶנּוּ אִתִּי פֶּן אֶרְאֶה בָרָע אֲשֶׁר **יִמְצָא** אֶת־אָבִי׃

For how shall I go up to my father and the youth not be with me, lest I see the evil that **would find** my father?

Deliberation. In other instances, the verbal phrase indicates a deliberation of outcomes in a given situation. This usage is similar to possibility in that it deals with what may or may not occur.

Gen 50:15 (non-past)

וַיֹּאמְרוּ לוּ **יִשְׂטְמֵנוּ** יוֹסֵף וְהָשֵׁב יָשִׁיב לָנוּ אֵת כָּל־הָרָעָה אֲשֶׁר גָּמַלְנוּ אֹתוֹ׃

They said, "Perhaps Joseph **will begrudge us** and indeed return against us all the evil that we did to him."

Exod 16:4 (non-past)

וְיָצָא הָעָם וְלָקְטוּ דְּבַר־יוֹם בְּיוֹמוֹ לְמַעַן אֲנַסֶּנּוּ **הֲיֵלֵךְ** בְּתוֹרָתִי אִם־לֹא׃

The people will go out and gather a day's portion so that I may test them, **whether they will walk** in my instruction or not.

Obligation. The prefix conjugation can also express an obligation the subject is expected to fulfill.

Exod 5:2 (non-past)

וַיֹּאמֶר פַּרְעֹה מִי יְהוָה אֲשֶׁר **אֶשְׁמַע** בְּקֹלוֹ לְשַׁלַּח אֶת־יִשְׂרָאֵל

Pharaoh said, "Who is Yahweh that **I should listen** to his voice to let Israel go?"

Mal 2:7 (non-past)

כִּי־שִׂפְתֵי כֹהֵן **יִשְׁמְרוּ**־דַעַת וְתוֹרָה **יְבַקְשׁוּ** מִפִּיהוּ

For the lips of the priests **must guard** knowledge, and instruction **they must seek** from his mouth.

Desire. The subject's desire for a given action to occur is another common use of the prefix form.

Gen 42:36 (non-past)

אֹתִי שִׁכַּלְתֶּם יוֹסֵף אֵינֶנּוּ וְשִׁמְעוֹן אֵינֶנּוּ וְאֶת־בִּנְיָמִן **תִּקָּחוּ**

You have bereft me of children. Joseph is no more and Simeon is no more, and now **you want to take** Benjamin?

5.7.2.3 Other Uses

Conditional Constructions. The prefix conjugation functions in a number of conditional constructions. Again, its imperfective aspect presents the action as though it is in progress or, to put it another way, portrays the event from within the action rather than as a whole.

As the protasis:

Jer 12:17 (non-past)

וְאִם לֹא **יִשְׁמָעוּ** וְנָתַשְׁתִּי אֶת־הַגּוֹי הַהוּא נָתוֹשׁ וְאַבֵּד נְאֻם־יְהוָה׃

If **they** do not **listen**, then I will surely uproot that nation and destroy it, declares Yahweh.

As the protasis and apodosis:

Exod 15:26 (non-past)

אִם־שָׁמוֹעַ **תִּשְׁמַע** לְקוֹל ׀ יְהוָה אֱלֹהֶיךָ וְהַיָּשָׁר בְּעֵינָיו **תַּעֲשֶׂה** וְהַאֲזַנְתָּ לְמִצְוֹתָיו וְשָׁמַרְתָּ כָּל־חֻקָּיו כָּל־הַמַּחֲלָה אֲשֶׁר־שַׂמְתִּי בְמִצְרַיִם לֹא־**אָשִׂים** עָלֶיךָ כִּי אֲנִי יְהוָה רֹפְאֶךָ׃

If **you** indeed **listen** to the voice of Yahweh your God (and) **do** what is upright in his eyes to give ear to his commandments and guard all his statutes, (then) **I will** not **set** upon you every malady I put on Egypt, for I am Yahweh, your healer.

Positive Commands. Sometimes second-person forms of the prefix conjugation can take on imperatival force as a strong command. This use of the prefix conjugation is common in apodictic laws scattered throughout various law collections in the Pentateuch.[77] The following example comes from the Covenant Code in Exod 20:22–23:33:

Exod 20:24 (non-past)

מִזְבַּח אֲדָמָה **תַּעֲשֶׂה**־לִּי וְזָבַחְתָּ עָלָיו אֶת־עֹלֹתֶיךָ וְאֶת־שְׁלָמֶיךָ אֶת־צֹאנְךָ וְאֶת־בְּקָרֶךָ

You shall make an earthen altar for me to sacrifice upon it your burnt offerings and your well-being offerings, your sheep and your cattle.

Exod 23:10 (non-past)

וְשֵׁשׁ שָׁנִים **תִּזְרַע** אֶת־אַרְצֶךָ וְאָסַפְתָּ אֶת־תְּבוּאָתָהּ׃

Six years **you shall sow** your land and then gather its yield.

Negative Commands. Finally, when accompanied by the negative particle לֹא, the prefix conjugation can function as a negative imperative. This prohibition is

---

[77] Apodictic laws are typically stated in second person (e.g., "You shall do X," or "You shall not do X") and are to be distinguished from casuistic laws, which take the form of conditional statements (e.g., "If X occurs, then do Y"). For more on these two kinds of Old Testament laws, see Gane, *Old Testament Law*, 85–93, and more briefly Morrow, *Introduction to Biblical Law*, 74–75.

understood as stronger in force than אַל + the jussive.[78] The negative commands are well-known from the Decalogue (Exod 20:1–21; Deut 5:6–21). They appear in the apodictic laws of the Pentateuch as well.

Exod 20:16

לֹא־תַעֲנֶה בְרֵעֲךָ עֵד שָׁקֶר׃

You shall not ever answer with a false witness against your neighbor.

Exod 23:1

לֹא תִשָּׂא שֵׁמַע שָׁוְא אַל־תָּשֶׁת יָדְךָ עִם־רָשָׁע לִהְיֹת עֵד חָמָס׃

You shall not ever bear an empty report. Do not set your hand with a wicked person to be a malicious witness.

5.8 WAW CONJUGATIONS

The *waw* conjugations of the Hebrew verbal system have been variously explained. The two verbal forms—*wayyiqtol* and *wəqātal*—consist of the attachment of *waw* to what resembles the prefix conjugation and the suffix conjugation, respectively. This morphological observation, however, does not explain the meaning and function of these two forms. We will discuss morphological features of each of these two forms in view of their historical development. This discussion is followed by an assessment of their use in Hebrew narrative.

5.8.1 *Waw* + Prefix Conjugation

The *wayyiqtol* is commonly identified in the grammars as the *waw* or *vav* consecutive imperfect.[79] It has been called by several other names: *waw* conversive,[80] imperfect consecutive,[81] converted imperfect,[82] inverted future,[83] *waw* relative,[84] consecutive preterite,[85] and no doubt several others. The variety and multiplicity of nomenclatures for this form represent some of the disagreement among scholars regarding its meaning and function.

---

[78] *GKC* §107o; Joüon-Muroaka §113m. Jo Ann Hackett describes this construction as a "universal prohibition" in *A Basic Introduction to Biblical Hebrew* (Peabody, MA: Hendrickson, 2010), 84.

[79] Page H. Kelley, *Biblical Hebrew: An Introductory Grammar* (Grand Rapids: Eerdmans, 1992), §43; Gary D. Pratico and Miles V. Van Pelt, *Basics of Biblical Hebrew Grammar* (Grand Rapids: Zondervan, 2001), §17; Allen P. Ross, *Introducing Biblical Hebrew* (Grand Rapids: Baker Academic, 2001), §18; Williams §77a.

[80] Lambdin §98 (108).

[81] GKC §111a; J. Wash Watts, *A Survey of Syntax in the Hebrew Old Testament* (Grand Rapids: Eerdmans, 1964), 61.

[82] Williams §77a.

[83] Joüon-Muroaka §118.

[84] *IBHS* §33.

[85] Hackett, *Biblical Hebrew*, 89–90

The converted imperfect (or inverted future) theory attempts to explain that the prefixed *waw* converts the imperfect form from future to past tense. The same would be true for *wǝqātal*, which converts the suffix form *qātal* from past tense to future tense. This understanding of the *waw* verbal forms comes from medieval Jewish grammarians and has been articulated in great detail by Granville Sharp.[86] Scholars have noted problems with this explanation, one of them being the fact that sometimes *yiqtol* forms refer to past actions while certain *wayyiqtol* forms refer to future actions.[87] Moreover, this viewpoint assumes that the Hebrew conjugations primarily mark time rather than aspect. Robert S. Kawashima concludes regarding *wayyiqtol* and *wǝqātal* that regardless of one's understanding of the diachronic development of these forms, they undeniably "converted tenses" in the eyes of native speakers of Classical Hebrew.[88] This temporal interpretation, however, is not universally assumed by all grammarians.

Other scholars point out the sequential nature of the *wayyiqtol*. It distinguishes action having taken place subsequent to a preceding verb. Thomas O. Lambdin explains that *wayyiqtol* primarily marks a sequence wherein "each verb is temporally or logically consequent upon the preceding verb."[89] Traditionally, beginning students often learn to translate *wayyiqtol* forms with some variation of "*and then* X occurred" indicating consecutive action. This formulation goes back to Ewald, who proposed that the prefixed *wa-* did not simply mean "and," but rather "then" or even "so." As he explained, when the suffixal form *qātal* is followed by *wayyiqtol* in a narrative, the combined *wayyiqtol* indicates "successive consequence." It yields an entirely new form independent of the prefix form *yiqtol*.[90]

Advocates of the discourse analysis perspective maintain that sequential verbs delineate the foreground of the narrative and that nonsequential verbs represent a break in the narrative signaling background information.[91] Robert E. Longacre advances this foreground and background framework within his influential

---

[86] McFall, *Enigma*, 17, 219–20 n. 17–1; Granville Sharp, *A Letter to a Learned Friend Respecting Some Particularities of the Hebrew Syntax* (London: Vernor and Hood, 1803), 13–17; recently reprinted by Brian Tice, ed., *A Letter Respecting Some Particularities of the Hebrew Syntax* (Grand Rapids: MJR Press, 2017).

[87] McFall lists several examples: *wayyiqtol* as future (Isa 9:6[5] [2×]; 51:3; Pss 55:17[18]; 64:9; 94:23), *yiqtol* as past (Judg 2:1; 1 Sam 9:9; Deut 11:10). See *Enigma*, 18–19.

[88] Robert S. Kawashima, "'Orphaned' Converted Tense Forms in Classical Biblical Hebrew Prose," *JSS* 55 (2010): 16.

[89] Lambdin §98.

[90] G. H. A. von Ewald, *A Grammar of the Hebrew Language of the Old Testament*, trans. John Nicholson (London: Whittaker, 1836), §296. See also McFall, *Enigma*, 47–50.

[91] As described by Gentry, "System of the Finite Verb," 13. The earliest advocates of narrative "grounding" referred to the notions of "topic" and "comment," which, according to the Prague school of the 1930s, distinguished between the things talked about and what is said about the things talked about. See Ellen van Wolde, "The Verbless Clause and its Textual Function," in *The Verbless Clause in Biblical Hebrew: Linguistic Approaches*, ed. Cynthia L. Miller; LSAWS 1 (Winona Lake, IN: Eisenbrauns, 1999), 223–25. Later studies have developed this concept further by emphasizing "given" versus "new" information; see Weinrich, *Tempus*; William Labov, "The Transformation of Experience in Narrative Syntax," in *Language in the Inner City*, ed., William Labov (Philadelphia: University of Pennsylvania Press, 1972), 354–96; Paul Hopper, "Aspect and Foregrounding in

discourse analysis of the Joseph story in Genesis.[92] Sequential forms thus do more than simply narrate consecutive events; they represent the baseline of the narrative with nonsequential verbs representing circumstantial information. Alviero Niccacci explains the functional difference between *wayyiqtol* and *qātal* as follows:

> *Wayyiqtol* is the narrative verb form par excellence because it is the only one indicating the main line of communication. *Qatal*, on the contrary, indicates a secondary line of communication in historical narrative, i.e., background (circumstance, or contrast) to a preceding *wayyiqtol* . . . or antecedent information to a following *wayyiqtol*.[93]

Unfortunately, this distinction between background and foreground is not always clear. Jean-Marc Heimerdinger gives two convincing reasons.[94] For one, this theory assumes that the *wayyiqtol* fundamentally represents a chronological sequence in which the verbal actions move the narrative forward in time, but this is not so. Sometimes this form can occur in the future, as seen in Isa 9:5 (see also §5.4.4).

Isa 9:5

כִּי־יֶ֣לֶד יֻלַּד־לָ֗נוּ
בֵּ֚ן נִתַּן־לָ֔נוּ
וַתְּהִ֥י הַמִּשְׂרָ֖ה עַל־שִׁכְמ֑וֹ
וַיִּקְרָ֨א שְׁמ֜וֹ פֶּ֣לֶא יוֹעֵ֗ץ

For a child will be born to us,
A son will be given.
Then the government **will be** upon his shoulder,
And then his name **will be called** Wonderful Counselor.

Nonsequential forms can also depict obligatory (or "foregrounded") elements of the narrative. Heimerdinger notes the following example where noninitial *qātal* marks foregrounded elements of the narrative:[95]

Jonah 1:4

וַיהוָ֗ה הֵטִ֤יל רֽוּחַ־גְּדוֹלָה֙ אֶל־הַיָּ֔ם
וַיְהִ֥י סַֽעַר־גָּד֖וֹל בַּיָּֽם

Discourse," in *Discourse Syntax*, ed. T. Givón, Syntax and Semantics 12 (New York: Academic Press, 1979), 231–41.

[92] Robert E. Longacre, *Joseph: A Story of Divine Providence: A Text Theoretical and Textlinguistic Analsysi of Genesis 37 and 39–40* (Winona Lake, IN: Eisenbrauns, 1989). Note also Francis I. Andersen, *The Sentence in Biblical Hebrew* (The Hague: Mouton, 1974); Niccacci, *Syntax of the Verb*.

[93] Niccacci, "Biblical Hebrew Verb System," 10.

[94] Jean-Marc Heimerdinger, *Topic, Focus and Foreground in Ancient Hebrew Narratives*, JSOTSup 295 (Sheffield: Sheffield Academic, 1999), 261–62. This work is also referenced in Pardee, "Nutshell," 291.

[95] Heimerdinger, *Topic*, 236.

וַיְהוָה הֵטִיל רוּחַ־גְּדוֹלָה אֶל־הַיָּם

Yahweh **hurled** a great wind to the sea,
And there was a great tempest on the sea;
The ship **was about** to break in pieces.

While it is plausible to understand these as background events, the verbs indicate completed aspect in both cases.

The comparative-historical approach explains the origin and development of *wayyiqtol* in light of comparative data drawn from the Semitic languages. We have already introduced the **yaqtulu/*yaqtul* distinction when we discussed the prefix conjugation above. The historical forms of *wayyiqtol* are relevant to this discussion.

Scholars generally agree that at an earlier stage of the language Hebrew attested both an imperfective **yaqtulu* with final -*u* and perfective **yaqtul* with Ø final vowel. The latter form underlies the jussive, as noted above (§5.7.1), but it likewise underlies *wayyiqtol*. We can demonstrate this once again from the III-weak and middle-weak roots where shortened forms are used for *wayyiqtol* (וַיִּבֶן "he built"; וַיָּקָם "he arose") as compared with long forms (יִבְנֶה "he builds"; יָקוּם "he arises"). But does the **yaqtul* perfective ever occur independently of the prefixed *wa-* of *wayyiqtol*? The answer to this question is disputed.

For quite some time now a number of scholars have posited that some Ugaritic and Hebrew prefix conjugation forms should be reanalyzed as **yaqtul* perfectives or preterites.[96] Identification of the shorter form is extremely problematic, since strong roots of both languages no longer distinguish between **yaqtul-Ø* and

---

[96] Gordon, *Ugaritic Textbook*, §9.2; Tropper, *Ugaritische Grammatik*, 431; Huehnergard, "Early Hebrew Prefix-Conjugations," 19–23; Jo Ann Hackett, "Yaqtul and a Ugaritic Incantation Text," in *Language and Nature: Papers Presented to John Huehnergard on the Occasion of His 60th Birthday*, ed. Rebecca Hasselbach and Naʿama Pat-El, SAOC 67 (Chicago: Oriental Institute, 2012), 111–17; Tania Notarius, "Narrative Tenses in Archaic Hebrew in the North-West Semitic Linguistic Context," in *Neue Beiträge zur Semitistik*, ed. Viktor Golinets et al. (Münster: Ugarit Verlag, 2015), 237–59; Krzystof J. Baranowski, "The Biblical Hebrew *wayyiqtol* and the Evidence of the Amarna Letters from Canaan," *JHS* 16 (2016): 1–18; Alexand Andrason and Juan-Pablo Vita, "The YQTL-Ø 'Preterite' in Ugaritic Epic Poetry," *ArOr* 85 (2017): 345–87.

Edward L. Greenstein's work on the prefix forms in Ugaritic marks an important contribution to this discussion ("Forms and Functions of the Finite Verb in Ugaritic Narrative Verse," in *Biblical Hebrew in Its Northwest Semitic Setting: Typology and Historical Perspectives*, ed. Steven E. Fassberg and Avi Hurwitz [Winona Lake, IN: Eisenbrauns, 2006], 75–102.). He analyzes the III-weak verbs attested in Ugaritic narrative poetry to see if short forms correspond to perfective meaning and long forms to imperfective meaning. For example, does *ybk* (= /yabkī/ or /yabki/) represent the perfective "he wept" and *ybky* (= /yabkiyu/) the imperfective "he weeps"? The distribution of forms like these indicates either a phonological, lexical, or even stylistic phenomenon, but most likely not a morphosemantic one. For instance, the poet of Aqhat prefers the long form of *ybky* "he weeps" (7×) over the short form *ybk* "he weeps" (2×). The Long form is *ybky* (*KTU* 1.14 I:26–27, 38–41; 1.16 I:6, 12, 55; 1.16 II:35, 44–45) and the short form *ybk* (*KTU* 1.15 V:12, 14; 1.15 VI:6). Greenstein, "Finite Verb," 85. The lexical feature is demonstrated by the fact that prefix forms of one root such as *bky* generally attest long forms (see previous examples), whereas *ḥdy* favors short (e.g., *yḥd* "he sees;" see *KTU* 1.19 III:3–4, 15, 19, 24, 29, 33) (85). This evidence from Ugaritic does not support the view that the language possessed a fully productive **yaqtul* perfective. Even Hackett's attempt to justify this position from Ugaritic III-ʾalep verbs only turns up three examples that are not *yaqtulu*. In addition to the short and long forms of the weak roots, scholars also note prefix forms with or without the suffix *n* when accompanied by a pronominal suffix (e.g., יְמִיתֵהוּ vs. יְמִתֶנּוּ). It is often argued that forms with the *n* suffix preserve the *yaqtulu(n)* imperfective and those without it represent the *yaqtul* perfective. Jo Ann Hackett adds that 1CS III-ʾ*alep* verbs ending in *i*, demonstrating long /ī/ after the ʾ*alep*, may also reflect *yaqtul* perfectives.[97] Another morphological distinction occurs for the *Hiphil* stem, generally showing *plene* spelling for the prefix conjugation (e.g., יַכְרִית "he cuts off") and defective spelling for *wayyiqtol* (e.g., וַיַּכְבֵּד "he made heavy") and the jussive (e.g., יַכְרֵת "let him cut off").

Tania Notarius likewise argues that *yaqtul* perfectives have been preserved in archaic Hebrew poems of the Old Testament. She analyzes a number of prefix forms throughout these poems that occur in contexts suggestive of a preterite or past meaning. She cites several examples from Deut 32:8–20 and 2 Sam 22:5–20.[98] Note the prefix form in the following example, which she interprets perfectively:

Deut 32:8

בְּהַנְחֵל עֶלְיוֹן גּוֹיִם בְּהַפְרִידוֹ בְּנֵי אָדָם **יַצֵּב** גְּבֻלֹת עַמִּים
When the Most High apportioned the nations, when he divided humankind, **he fixed** the boundaries of the peoples[99]

The basis for this interpretation is largely contextual as informed by noninitial position and circumstantial clauses. Waltke and O'Connor similarly identify cases where prefix verbs should be interpreted as perfective, citing the following example:[100]

Judg 2:1

אַעֲלֶה אֶתְכֶם מִמִּצְרַיִם וָאָבִיא אֶתְכֶם אֶל־הָאָרֶץ אֲשֶׁר נִשְׁבַּעְתִּי לַאֲבֹתֵיכֶם
I brought you **up** from Egypt and I brought you into the land that I swore to your fathers.

The problem with this example, however, is that it is a long prefix form of a III-weak root, which is difficult to derive from a short *yaqtul* perfective. It is not impossible to render this form as an imperfective, perhaps as an ingressive focusing on the initiation of Israel's rescue from Egypt.[101]

Notarius identifies two prefix forms in Deuteronomy 32 having pronominal suffixes without affix -*n*, which is likewise thought to mark the *yaqtul* perfective (e.g., יִמְצָאֵהוּ "he found him," v. 10; יִקָּחֵהוּ "he took him," v. 11). Anson F. Rainey

---

conclusive ("Ugaritic Incantation Text," 112–14). The best we can glean from the linguistic data are vestigial forms reflective of an earlier stage of the language.

[97] Hackett, "Ugaritic Incantation Text," 112.
[98] Notarius, "Narrative Tenses," 239–41.
[99] As translated by Notarius, "Narrative Tenses," 239.
[100] *IBHS* §31.1.1d.
[101] As suggested by Dennis Pardee (personal communication).

has articulated extensively the merits of this proposal.[102] This morphological distinction is not consistently maintained in Biblical Hebrew, however, as the oft cited example demonstrates:

Exod 15:2

זֶה אֵלִי וְאַנְוֵהוּ

אֱלֹהֵי אָבִי וַאֲרֹמְמֶנְהוּ׃

This is my God, and **I will praise him**.

The God of my father, and **I will exalt him**.

Both forms are markedly imperfective, but the first is with -*n* and the latter is without -*n*.

Nonetheless, the central question here is: *how* has the *yaqtul perfective been preserved in Hebrew—not *if* it has been preserved? Hebrew evidence for this form is found with the *wayyiqtol*, but it appears to be preserved only here as a productive form, and not in self-standing forms without the prefixed *wa*-. That is not to say that vestiges of an earlier *yaqtul perfective outside the *wayyiqtol* have not survived in Hebrew or Ugaritic. Certain contexts in Ugaritic seem to preserve a *yaqtul perfective and *yaqtulu imperfective distinction for III-weak roots.[103] Pierre Bordreuil and Dennis Pardee rightly qualify the Ugaritic cases as "archaisms."[104] Examples may be culled from Hebrew as well. For example, a potential self-standing short form תֶּשִׁי appears in the MT Deuteronomy, which Notarius renders:

Deut 32:18

צוּר יְלָדְךָ תֶּשִׁי

You were unmindful of the Rock that bore you.[105]

This form is textually problematic, however.[106] Clearer cases for self-standing prefixed perfectives are those following the adverbials אָז, טֶרֶם, and בְּטֶרֶם, but these are contextually conditioned. For instance, a survey of אָז + prefix conjugation yields mixed results. A number of contexts do suggest a past time referent seemingly reflective of perfective action.

---

[102] See Anson F. Rainey, "The Prefix Conjugation Patterns of Early Northwest Semitic," in *Lingering over Words: Studies in Ancient Near Eastern Literature in Honor of William F. Moran*, ed. Tzvi Abusch et al.; HSS 37 (Atlanta: Scholars Press, 1990), 407–20.

[103] The epic of Aqhat provides examples:

KTU 1.17 VI:30	k bʿl **kyḥwy**	"like Baʿlu **when he was revived**"
KTU 1.17 VI:32	ȧp ȧnk **ȧḥwy** ȧqht [ġ]zr	"Even I myself **will make** the hero ʾAqhatu **live**"
KTU 1.18 IV:27	ȧp mprh ȧnk **lȧḥwy**	"Even I myself **will not let** the soldier **live**"
KTU 1.19 I:16	ʿl qsʿth hwt **lȧḥw**	"On account of his arrows **I did not let** that one **live**"

[104] Bordreuil and Pardee, *Manual of Ugaritic*, 49.

[105] Notarius, "Narrative Tenses," 240.

[106] *HALOT*, s.v. "שׁיה."

Josh 10:12

אָז יְדַבֵּר יְהוֹשֻׁעַ לַיהוָה בְּיוֹם תֵּת יְהוָה אֶת־הָאֱמֹרִי לִפְנֵי בְּנֵי יִשְׂרָאֵל

Then Joshua **said** to Yahweh on the day Yahweh gave up the Amorites
before the sons of Israel.

1 Kgs 3:16

אָז יַקְהֵל שְׁלֹמֹה אֶת־זִקְנֵי יִשְׂרָאֵל

Then Solomon **assembled** the elders of Israel.

This second example utilizes the defective spelling of the *Hiphil*, which constitutes a shortened form. What we do not find are examples of shortened III-weak
verbs following אָז, but, rather surprisingly, several of these contexts yield long
III-weak forms:

Exod 15:1

אָז יָשִׁיר־מֹשֶׁה וּבְנֵי יִשְׂרָאֵל אֶת־הַשִּׁירָה הַזֹּאת לַיהוָה

Then Moses **sang** this song to Yahweh with the children of Israel.

Josh 1:8

אָז יִבְנֶה יְהוֹשֻׁעַ מִזְבֵּחַ לַיהוָה אֱלֹהֵי יִשְׂרָאֵל בְּהַר עֵיבָל:

Then Joshua **built** an altar to Yahweh, God of Israel, on Mount Ebal.

2 Kgs 12:18

אָז יַעֲלֶה חֲזָאֵל מֶלֶךְ אֲרָם וַיִּלָּחֶם עַל־גַּת וַיִּלְכְּדָהּ

Then Hazael, king of Aram, **went up** and fought against Gath and captured it.

The plene spelling of the *Hiphil* occurs in the following as well:

Deut 4:41[107]

אָז יַבְדִּיל מֹשֶׁה שָׁלֹשׁ עָרִים

Then Moses **designated** three cities.

These examples reflect the mixed situation reflected for *wayyiqtol*. Even though
the *wayyiqtol* prefers apocopated forms for III-weak roots, this is not always the
case. For example, Gen 21:16 attests the expected וַתֵּבְךְ "she wept," but in 1 Sam
1:7 we find וַתִּבְכֶּה "she wept." Likewise in Isa 5:2 the *wayyiqtol* of the root עשׂה
is וַיַּעַשׂ "he made," whereas in 1 Kgs 16:25 it is וַיַּעֲשֶׂה "he made."

In conclusion, the linguistic evidence as it has been preserved in Biblical Hebrew represents a mixed situation and does not suggest a fully productive paradigm whereby **yaqtul* perfective and **yaqtulu* imperfective are consistently distinguished.[108] It reflects a circumstance similar to what Mark S. Smith refers to

---

[107] Also noted in Edward L. Greenstein, "On the Prefixed Preterite in Biblical Hebrew," *HS* 29
(1988): 8.
[108] Similarly concluded by *IBHS* §31.1.1g–h.

as "obsolescence."[109] The suffix form *qātal* has apparently replaced the earlier **yaqtul* as the default perfective in narrative prose in BH.

5.8.2 Waw + Suffix Conjugation

The second *waw* form in Hebrew is the *wəqātal*, also called the consecutive perfect or converted perfect. This terminology comes from the fact that the *wəqātal* likely arose as a counterpart to *wayyiqtol*.[110] In other words, before the period of Biblical Hebrew, a fully developed system of opposite forms emerged: one pair of imperfectives consisting of a clause-initial form and non-clause-initial counterpart, and an opposing pair of perfectives, likewise consisting of a clause-initial and non-clause-initial counterpart. We may summarize these opposing pairs in the following chart:

	PERFECTIVE	IMPERFECTIVE
Clause initial	*wayyiqtol*	*wəqātal*
Non-clause initial	X + *qātal*	X + *yiqtol*

Scholars have looked to the suffix conjugation as a means of explaining the historical development of *wəqātal*. H. L. Ginsberg proposed that its use in irrealis contexts as an optative or precative eventually led to the formation of *wəqātal*.[111] Others point to the appearance of the suffix conjugation in conditional statements as the impetus for this form. As noted earlier in this chapter (§5.6.2.4), the suffix conjugation can serve as the verb of both protasis (i.e., "if") and apodosis (i.e., "then") clauses, which constitute an irrealis application. Note the following two examples:

Ps 44:21–22

אִם־שָׁכַחְנוּ שֵׁם אֱלֹהֵינוּ וַנִּפְרֹשׂ כַּפֵּינוּ לְאֵל זָר׃ הֲלֹא אֱלֹהִים יַחֲקָר־זֹאת

If **we denied** the name of our God and then extended our hand to another God, would he not find it out?

---

[109] Mark S. Smith, *The Origins and Development of the* Waw-*Consecutive: Northwest Semitic Evidence from Ugarit to Qumran*, HSS 39 (Atlanta: Scholars Press, 1991), 12.

[110] As articulated in Gotthelf Bergsträsser, *Hebräische Grammatik: Mit Benutzung der von E. Kautzsch bearbeiteten 28, Auflage von Wilhelm Gesenius' hebräischer Grammatik*, vol. 2 (Leipzig: Vogel, 1918), §3g, also referenced in Smith, Waw-*Consecutive*, 6. See also *GKC* §112b n. 2. See the recent exhaustive treatment of this form by W. R. Garr, "The Coordinated Perfect," in *"Like 'Ilu Are You Wise": Studies in Northwest Semitic Languages and Literatures in Honor of Dennis G. Pardee*, ed. H. H. Hardy II, Joseph Lam, and Eric Reymond, SAOC 73 (Chicago: The Oriental Institute, 2022), 493–521.

[111] H. L. Ginsberg notes that the "perfect consecutive was not purely a polar consequence of the development of the imperfect consecutive, but was favoured by the fact that one of the original functions of the perfect was that of an optative and precative." See "The Rebellion and Death of Ba'lu," *Or* 5 (1936): 177.

1 Sam 6:9

אִם־דֶּרֶךְ גְּבוּלוֹ יַעֲלֶה בֵּית שֶׁמֶשׁ הוּא עָשָׂה לָנוּ אֶת־הָרָעָה הַגְּדוֹלָה הַזֹּאת

If [the ark] would go up by the way of its territory to Beth-shemesh, **then surely he has done** to us this great evil.

Moran argues that the Amarna letters provide explicit evidence for this historical development. These texts attest some thirty-three instances of the suffix conjugation appearing in contexts referring to future actions or events.[112] Twenty-four of these are accompanied by the conjunction *u* "and," much like Hebrew *wəqātal*, and eight of the twenty-four occur in the apodosis of a conditional clause. Scholars have noted a similar verbal construction in Ugaritic as well.[113] These examples of conjunction + suffix conjugation in dependent syntactical environments offer important antecedents to Hebrew *wəqātal* in Amarna Canaanite and Ugaritic, but no precedent for its independent use is thus far known.

Clause-initial *wəqātal* commonly functions as the default consecutive imperfective in much the same way that *wayyiqtol* functions as the consecutive perfective in narrative prose. This form has the potential to perform any of the uses identified for the prefix conjugation outlined above. When it occurs sequentially following a prefix form, the use of the previous form usually carries through to the *wəqātal*.[114] For example, *wəqātal* may follow the prefix conjugation and continue the portrayal of frequentative action from a past time referent:

Gen 2:6

וְאֵד יַעֲלֶה מִן־הָאָרֶץ וְהִשְׁקָה אֶת־כָּל־פְּנֵי־הָאֲדָמָה׃

A mist would go up (PC) from the earth **and would water** (*wəqātal*) all the face of the ground.

Nonetheless, *wəqātal* can occur in nonconsecutive contexts as well, functioning independently from the immediately preceding verb.[115] In this way, *wəqātal* serves as the true clause-initial counterpart to *yiqtol*. One finds an explicit break in X + *qātal* forms:

---

[112] William L. Moran, "The Hebrew Language in Its Northwest Semitic Background," in *The Bible and the Ancient Near East: Essays in Honor of William Foxwell Albright*, ed. G. Ernest Wright (Garden City, NY: Doubleday, 1961), 64–65, cites the following example:

| *allu paṭārima awīlūt ḫupši* **u ṣabtū** *Ḫapirū āla* | Behold! if the serfs desert, **then** the Hapiru **will seize** the city. |

[113] Smith (Waw-*Consecutive*, 13) cites two, one from the letter *KTU* 2.30:16–20, and another from the prayer *KTU* 1.119:34–36. The second example is more problematic, but *KTU* 2.30 seems plausible:

whm ḫt 'l	If the Hittite (forces) goes up,
wlikt *'mk*	**Then I will send** you a message;
whm l'l	And if they do not go up,
wlåkm *ilåk*	**Then I will** surely **send a message**.

[114] Lambdin §98b.

[115] Pardee, "Nutshell," 290; Pardee, review of *An Introduction to Biblical Hebrew Syntax*, by Bruce Waltke and Michael Patrick O'Connor, *JNES* 53 (1994): 152 n. 3.

Gen 34:5

וְיַעֲקֹב שָׁמַע כִּי טִמֵּא אֶת־דִּינָה בִתּוֹ וּבָנָיו הָיוּ אֶת־מִקְנֵהוּ בַּשָּׂדֶה **וְהֶחֱרִשׁ יַעֲקֹב**
עַד־בֹּאָם:

Jacob heard (X + *qātal*) that he had defiled Dinah, his daughter, but his
sons were (X + *qātal*) with his cattle in the field, **so Jacob kept silent**
(*wəqātal*) until they came (back).

Here, *wəqātal* interrupts the narrative events, focusing instead on the durative aspect of Jacob's silence. This example poses problems for those who view *wəqātal*
as a converted future, since its timeframe in this case is past. It also makes the consecutive explanation less likely since the aspect of *wəqātal* is not simply carried
through from the preceding verbal form.

The independent quality of *wəqātal* is also evident when it is followed by
wayyiqtol:

Gen 15:6

וְהֶאֱמִן בַּיהוָה וַיַּחְשְׁבֶהָ לּוֹ צְדָקָה:

[Abram] **continued trusting** in Yahweh, and he accounted it to him as
righteousness.

In this example, the imperfective force of *wəqātal* highlights Abraham's continued
trust in Yahweh. Other independent uses occur in direct discourse. In Exod 3:20,
wəqātal portrays the action of the verb as a future progressive, following a suffixal
form:

Exod 3:19–20

וַאֲנִי יָדַעְתִּי כִּי לֹא־יִתֵּן אֶתְכֶם מֶלֶךְ מִצְרַיִם לַהֲלֹךְ וְלֹא בְּיָד חֲזָקָה: **וְשָׁלַחְתִּי אֶת־יָדִי**
וְהִכֵּיתִי אֶת־מִצְרַיִם בְּכֹל נִפְלְאֹתַי אֲשֶׁר אֶעֱשֶׂה בְּקִרְבּוֹ

I know that the king of Egypt will not allow you to go except with a
strong hand. **I am about to stretch** out my hand **and strike** Egypt with all
my wonders that I am about to perform in its midst.

It can also take on imperatival force on its own, as in the following example:

Exod 4:15

וְדִבַּרְתָּ אֵלָיו וְשַׂמְתָּ אֶת־הַדְּבָרִים בְּפִיו

You shall speak to him and put the words in his mouth.[116]

These examples demonstrate that even though *wəqātal* often continues the
verbal action immediately preceding imperfectives, it can just as well function
imperfectively on its own, even following a perfective form. The terminology

---

[116] The *wəqātal* in this instance follows two other *wəqātal* forms in v. 14, which are not, techni-
cally speaking, imperatival: יָדַעְתִּי כִּי־דַבֵּר יְדַבֵּר הוּא וְגַם הִנֵּה־הוּא יֹצֵא לִקְרָאתֶךָ וְרָאֲךָ וְשָׂמַח בְּלִבּוֹ "I know
that he [Aaron] can speak well. He is already coming out to meet you. He shall see you and rejoice
in his heart." The subsequent *wəqātal* וְדִבַּרְתָּ "you shall speak," indicates a change in topic, signaled
by the switch from third to second person. It represents a situation "relative" to or subordinate to the
main verb.

"*waw*-conversive" does not adequately represent the function of this form. Waltke and O'Connor prefer the term "*waw*-relative" in light of the fact that *wəqātal* "has the values of the prefix conjugation and represents a situation relative (that is subordinate) to the leading verb (or equivalent)."[117] Pardee criticizes this terminology in light of its possible confusion with relative clauses and for the simple fact that not all *wəqātal* are relative to a preceding verb, which is demonstrated by their independent uses.[118] Instead, he proposes calling both *wayyiqtol* and *wəqātal* "*waw*-retentive" forms as a means of expressing their diachronic reality. As he explains, the binary (*qātal* :: *wayyiqtol* and *yiqtol* :: *wəqātal*) provides two forms that came to express perfective and imperfective aspect respectively, *qātal* and *yiqtol* in non-clause-initial position and *wayyiqtol* and *wəqātal* in initial position. The two-clause-initial *waw* forms constitute "frozen usages retained from a previous stage of the language when the perfective or preterit was expressed by *yaqtul while *qatala (and its variants) expressed stativity."[119] This formulation accounts for the earlier existence of perfective *yaqtul and the original stative, adjectival quality of *qatala/*qatila/*qatula (e.g., *kabida > כָּבֵד "he is heavy").

5.8.3 Verbal Sequences Involving *wayyiqtol*, *wəqātal*, and *wəyiqtol*

Hebrew utilizes the *wayyiqtol* and *wəqātal* forms of the verbal root הָיָה in a variety of temporal clauses and phrases which provide background information to the main line of the narrative. The *wayyiqtol* form וַיְהִי introduces background information to the narrative perfectively, while *wəqātal* וְהָיָה provides its imperfective counterpart. The following examples illustrate these constructions:

PERFECTIVE וַיְהִי		
Gen 4:3	וַיְהִי מִקֵּץ יָמִים וַיָּבֵא קַיִן מִפְּרִי הָאֲדָמָה מִנְחָה לַיהוָה	**At the end of the days** Cain brought from the fruit of the ground an offering to Yahweh.
Gen 12:11	וַיְהִי כַּאֲשֶׁר הִקְרִיב לָבוֹא מִצְרָיְמָה וַיֹּאמֶר אֶל־שָׂרַי אִשְׁתּוֹ	**As he drew near to entering Egypt**, he said to Sarai, his wife.
Gen 21:22	וַיְהִי בָּעֵת הַהִוא וַיֹּאמֶר אֲבִימֶלֶךְ וּפִיכֹל	**At that time**, Abimelech and Phicol said
Gen 22:1	וַיְהִי אַחַר הַדְּבָרִים הָאֵלֶּה וְהָאֱלֹהִים נִסָּה אֶת־אַבְרָהָם	**After these things**, God tested Abraham
Exod 13:15	וַיְהִי כִּי־הִקְשָׁה פַרְעֹה לְשַׁלְּחֵנוּ וַיַּהֲרֹג יְהוָה כָּל־בְּכוֹר בְּאֶרֶץ מִצְרָיִם	**When Pharaoh became opposed to sending us**, Yahweh slew every firstborn in the land of Egypt.

---

[117] *IBHS* §32.2a.
[118] Pardee, review of *An Introduction to Biblical Hebrew*, 152 n. 3.
[119] Pardee, "Nutshell," 287 n. 10.

IMPERFECTIVE וְהָיָה		
Gen 4:14	וְהָיָה כָל־מֹצְאִי יַהַרְגֵנִי	**Anyone who finds me** will kill me.
Gen 27:40	וְהָיָה כַּאֲשֶׁר תָּרִיד וּפָרַקְתָּ עֻלּוֹ מֵעַל צַוָּארֶךָ	**When you become restless**, you will break his yoke from upon your neck
Exod 12:25	וְהָיָה כִּי־תָבֹאוּ אֶל־הָאָרֶץ אֲשֶׁר יִתֵּן יְהוָה לָכֶם כַּאֲשֶׁר דִּבֵּר וּשְׁמַרְתֶּם אֶת־הָעֲבֹדָה הַזֹּאת	**When you enter the land which Yahweh is giving to you**, as he has spoken, you shall keep this service.
Exod 17:11	וְהָיָה כַּאֲשֶׁר יָרִים מֹשֶׁה יָדוֹ וְגָבַר יִשְׂרָאֵל	**As Moses would raise his hand**, Israel would prevail.
Exod 33:22	וְהָיָה בַּעֲבֹר כְּבֹדִי וְשַׂמְתִּיךָ בְּנִקְרַת הַצּוּר	**As my glory passes by**, I will set you in the crevice of the rock
Deut 27:4	וְהָיָה בְּעָבְרְכֶם אֶת־הַיַּרְדֵּן תָּקִימוּ אֶת־הָאֲבָנִים הָאֵלֶּה	**When you cross over the Jordan**, you shall set up these stones

The Guided Lesson ג: Syntactic Analysis further discusses these forms in an extended sequence. The following chart summarizes the function of verbal forms in narrative sequence, focusing particularly on the clausal position of the verb:[120]

BEGINNING OF THE NARRATIVE = ANTECEDENT (SECONDARY LEVEL)	→ BEGINNING OF THE MAIN LINE = FOREGROUND (MAIN LEVEL, NARRATIVE CHAIN)	→ OFF LINE = BACKGROUND (SECONDARY LEVEL)
X + qātal or: nonverbal sentence (waw) X + yiqtol wəqātal	→ wayyiqtol in a chain of coordinate verb forms (↔)	→ (waw) X + qātal → nonverbal sentence → (waw) X + yiqtol → wəqātal

Another verbal sequence involves the dependent use of *wəqātal* following a volitive. Lambdin outlines three volitive sequences:[121]

a. Imperative + Imperative
b. Imperative + Perfect
c. Imperative, Jussive, or Cohortative + Imperfect or Cohortative

We will discuss volitives more fully in the next chapter. For now, it is important to observe the second and third type. The second consists of a volitive followed by *wəqātal*, which Lambdin identifies as expressing "explicit consecution," which

---

[120] Adapted from Niccacci, "Integrated Verb System," 103. Niccacci uses the symbol → to indicate "a transition to a verb form or construction of a different syntactic level" and the symbol ↔ for "a transition to a verb form of the same syntactic level."
[121] Lambdin §107.

means that the *wəqātal* expresses a volitive action consequent upon the previous volitive. For example, we read:

Exod 45:9

מַהֲרוּ֮ וַעֲל֣וּ אֶל־אָבִי֒ וַאֲמַרְתֶּ֣ם אֵלָ֔יו

Quickly, **go up** to your father **and say** to him.

In this context, Joseph's brothers cannot speak to their father until after they have returned to Canaan.

The third type introduces a form we have yet to encounter in this chapter: *wəyiqtol*. This form seems to mirror the formation of *wəqātal* as an imperfective *waw* conjugation, distinguished morphologically from *wayyiqtol* by the simple *waw* prefixed with a reduced vowel. The historical development of this form is difficult to reconstruct. It is possible that at an earlier stage of the language a perfective *wa-qatal existed alongside an imperfective *wa-yaqtul. There are a few rare instances where *wəqātal* seems to be used as a perfective. Pardee surmises that perfective *wa-qatal was abandoned because of the language's proclivity for perfective *wayyiqtol*. On the other hand, imperfective *wa-yaqtul survived as *wəyiqtol* "by taking on a particular function" in such a way that was not confused with other forms of the verbal system.[122]

The function of *wəyiqtol* appears to be confined to this volitive sequence and its meaning tends to be more precise than volitive + *wəqātal*. Lambdin suggests that it expresses purpose or result.[123] Note the following examples:

Num 5:2

צַ֚ו אֶת־בְּנֵ֣י יִשְׂרָאֵ֔ל **וִֽישַׁלְּחוּ֙** מִן־הַֽמַּחֲנֶ֔ה כָּל־צָר֖וּעַ

Command the sons of Israel **that they might send away** from the camp every leprous person.

Num 13:2

שְׁלַח־לְךָ֣ אֲנָשִׁ֗ים **וְיָתֻ֨רוּ֙** אֶת־אֶ֣רֶץ כְּנַ֔עַן

Send out men **that they might explore** the land of Canaan.

It is also common to see the simple *waw* attached to the cohortative, also expressing purpose or result:

Gen 17:1b–2

וֶהְיֵ֥ה תָמִֽים: **וְאֶתְּנָ֥ה** בְרִיתִ֖י בֵּינִ֣י וּבֵינֶ֑ךָ **וְאַרְבֶּ֥ה** אוֹתְךָ֖ בִּמְאֹ֥ד מְאֹֽד:

Be blameless, **that I may establish** my covenant between me and between you **and that I may multiply** you exceedingly.

---

[122] Pardee, "Nutshell," 294–95.
[123] Pardee, 294–95. See also Pardee, review of *An Introduction to Biblical Hebrew Syntax* (Waltke and O'Connor), 152–53; Niccacci, "Integrated Verb System," 113.

Pardee has also identified *wəyiqtol* marking purpose or result in non-volitive sequence.[124] He cites the following example from 2 Sam 9:1:

2 Sam 9:1

הֲכִי יֶשׁ־עוֹד אֲשֶׁר נוֹתַר לְבֵית שָׁאוּל וְאֶעֱשֶׂה עִמּוֹ חֶסֶד

Is there anyone left of the house of Saul, **that I may show** him kindness?

In conclusion, we organize three volitive sequences. Each is initiated with a volitive form. The following clause can build on this form to create a sequence. To accomplish this structure, a subsequent clause begins with one of the three forms: (a) volitive, (b) *wəqātal*, or (c) *wəyiqtol* or cohortative. The semantics of the sequence can denote consecution or purpose/result.

VOLITIVE SEQUENCES					
	INITIAL CLAUSE		SUBSEQUENT CLAUSE		SEMANTICS OF SEQUENCE
(a)	Volitive	+	Volitive	=	Potential Consecution
(b)	Volitive	+	*wəqātal*	=	Explicit Consecution
(c)	Volitive	+	*wəyiqtol* or cohortative	=	Purpose or Result

According to Niccacci, the usage of sequential verbs in direct speech parallels that of narrative prose. Their clausal position similarly marks foreground and background information, as the following chart outlines:[125]

	MAIN LEVEL (FOREGROUND)	→ SECONDARY LEVEL (BACKGROUND)
a. Perfective Indicative	(X +) *qātal* ↔ continuation *wayyiqtol* (coordinate, main level)	→ X + *qātal*, nonverbal sentence X + *yiqtol*, *wəqātal*
b. Imperfective Indicative	Nonverbal sentence (especially with PTCP ↔ continuation *wəqātal* or: Initial X + *yiqtol* ↔ continuation *wəqātal* (in a chain)	→ X + *yiqtol*
c. Volitive	Imperative ↔ *wəyiqtol* or: (X +) *yiqtol* cohortative/jussive ↔ *wəyiqtol*	→ X + imperative → X + *yiqtol*

---

[124] Pardee, "Nutshell," 293.

[125] Adapted from Niccacci, "Integrated Verb System," 110. Niccacci uses the symbol → to indicate "a transition to a verb form or construction of a different syntactic level" and the symbol ↔ for "a transition to a verb form of the same syntactic level."

Generally, beginning grammars provide a basic model for verb conjugation meaning. As students read, these early summaries are too simplistic to explain the semantic variety of BH texts. An elaborate system of alternating forms and syntax displays the beautiful elegance of the verb system. This chapter outlines many of the ways that finite conjugations produce meaning. The following chapter builds upon these notions by focusing on the modality of the volitive forms.

5.9 EXERCISES

Translate the following Hebrew sentences into English. Parse all verbs in the following verses (stem, conjugation, person, gender, number, and root). Analyze the function of PC and SC forms in light of the functional categories discussed in this chapter. Take special note of shifts between PC and SC and their interpretive significance. Also, identify any narrative sequences as they occur.

1. וַיֹּ֣אמֶר ׀ יְהוָ֣ה אֱלֹהִ֗ים הֵ֤ן הָֽאָדָם֙ הָיָה֙ כְּאַחַ֣ד מִמֶּ֔נּוּ לָדַ֖עַת ט֣וֹב וָרָ֑ע וְעַתָּ֣ה ׀ פֶּן־
יִשְׁלַ֣ח יָד֗וֹ וְלָקַח֙ גַּ֚ם מֵעֵ֣ץ הַֽחַיִּ֔ים וְאָכַ֖ל וָחַ֥י לְעֹלָֽם׃ (Gen 3:22)

2. וְיִשְׂרָאֵ֗ל אָהַ֤ב אֶת־יוֹסֵף֙ מִכָּל־בָּנָ֔יו כִּֽי־בֶן־זְקֻנִ֥ים ה֖וּא ל֑וֹ וְעָ֥שָׂה ל֖וֹ כְּתֹ֥נֶת פַּסִּֽים׃
וַיִּרְא֣וּ אֶחָ֗יו כִּֽי־אֹת֞וֹ אָהַ֤ב אֲבִיהֶם֙ מִכָּל־אֶחָ֔יו וַֽיִּשְׂנְא֖וּ אֹת֑וֹ וְלֹ֥א יָכְל֖וּ דַּבְּר֥וֹ
לְשָׁלֹֽם׃ (Gen 37:3–4)

3. וְהָיָ֡ה אִם־לֹ֣א יַאֲמִ֡ינוּ גַּם֩ לִשְׁנֵ֨י הָאֹת֜וֹת הָאֵ֗לֶּה וְלֹ֤א יִשְׁמְעוּן֙ לְקֹלֶ֔ךָ וְלָקַחְתָּ֙ מִמֵּימֵ֣י
הַיְאֹ֔ר וְשָׁפַכְתָּ֖ הַיַּבָּשָׁ֑ה וְהָי֤וּ הַמַּ֙יִם֙ אֲשֶׁ֣ר תִּקַּ֣ח מִן־הַיְאֹ֔ר וְהָי֥וּ לְדָ֖ם בַּיַּבָּֽשֶׁת׃
(Exod 4:9)

4. וַיְהִ֡י בְּיוֹם֩ כַּלּ֨וֹת מֹשֶׁ֜ה לְהָקִ֣ים אֶת־הַמִּשְׁכָּ֗ן וַיִּמְשַׁ֨ח אֹת֜וֹ וַיְקַדֵּ֤שׁ אֹתוֹ֙ וְאֶת־כָּל־
כֵּלָ֔יו וְאֶת־הַמִּזְבֵּ֖חַ וְאֶת־כָּל־כֵּלָ֑יו וַיִּמְשָׁחֵ֖ם וַיְקַדֵּ֥שׁ אֹתָֽם׃ (Num 7:1)

5. וְעָלָה הָאִישׁ הַהוּא מֵעִירוֹ מִיָּמִים | יָמִימָה לְהִשְׁתַּחֲוֹת וְלִזְבֹּחַ לַיהוָה צְבָאוֹת
בְּשִׁלֹה וְשָׁם שְׁנֵי בְנֵי־עֵלִי חָפְנִי וּפִנְחָס כֹּהֲנִים לַיהוָה: וַיְהִי הַיּוֹם וַיִּזְבַּח אֶלְקָנָה
וְנָתַן לִפְנִנָּה אִשְׁתּוֹ וּלְכָל־בָּנֶיהָ וּבְנוֹתֶיהָ מָנוֹת: (1 Sam 1:3–4)

6. בְּהֵעָצֵר שָׁמַיִם וְלֹא־יִהְיֶה מָטָר כִּי יֶחֶטְאוּ־לָךְ וְהִתְפַּלְלוּ אֶל־הַמָּקוֹם הַזֶּה וְהוֹדוּ
אֶת־שְׁמֶךָ וּמֵחַטָּאתָם יְשׁוּבוּן כִּי תַעֲנֵם: (1 Kgs 8:35)

7. הָאֹמְרִים יְמַהֵר | יָחִישָׁה מַעֲשֵׂהוּ לְמַעַן נִרְאֶה וְתִקְרַב וְתָבוֹאָה עֲצַת קְדוֹשׁ
יִשְׂרָאֵל וְנֵדָעָה: (Isa 5:19)

8. עָלָיו יִשְׁאֲגוּ כְפִרִים נָתְנוּ קוֹלָם וַיָּשִׁיתוּ אַרְצוֹ לְשַׁמָּה עָרָיו נִצְּתָה מִבְּלִי יֹשֵׁב:
(Jer 2:15)

9. וּבְשׁוּב צַדִּיק מִצִּדְקוֹ וְעָשָׂה עָוֶל וְנָתַתִּי מִכְשׁוֹל לְפָנָיו הוּא יָמוּת כִּי לֹא
הִזְהַרְתּוֹ בְּחַטָּאתוֹ יָמוּת וְלֹא תִזָּכַרְןָ צִדְקֹתָו אֲשֶׁר עָשָׂה וְדָמוֹ מִיָּדְךָ אֲבַקֵּשׁ:
(Ezek 3:20)

10. אֵלֶּה אֶזְכְּרָה | וְאֶשְׁפְּכָה עָלַי | נַפְשִׁי כִּי אֶעֱבֹר | בַּסָּךְ אֶדַּדֵּם עַד־בֵּית אֱלֹהִים בְּקוֹל־
רִנָּה וְתוֹדָה הָמוֹן חוֹגֵג: מַה־תִּשְׁתּוֹחֲחִי | נַפְשִׁי וַתֶּהֱמִי עָלָי הוֹחִילִי לֵאלֹהִים
כִּי־עוֹד אוֹדֶנּוּ יְשׁוּעוֹת פָּנָיו: (Ps 42:5–6)

Translate from English to Hebrew.

11. The tribe of Benjamin went out of the city and took the gold to the temple.

12. You lay down each day and rise up again.

13. Ahab did not walk according to the ways of his father David, and he did evil in the eyes of the people in all the land.

14. The prophet said: "The land will overflow with milk and honey because God's word will cover all nations."

15. If I listen to his instruction and do what is right in his eyes, Yahweh will certainly give me favor before my enemies and then he will save me from those hating me.

Guided Reading: Job 1:1–8

1 אִישׁ הָיָה בְאֶרֶץ־עוּץ אִיּוֹב שְׁמוֹ וְהָיָה | הָאִישׁ הַהוּא תָּם וְיָשָׁר וִירֵא אֱלֹהִים וְסָר מֵרָע:
2 וַיִּוָּלְדוּ לוֹ שִׁבְעָה בָנִים וְשָׁלוֹשׁ בָּנוֹת: 3 וַיְהִי מִקְנֵהוּ שִׁבְעַת אַלְפֵי־צֹאן וּשְׁלֹשֶׁת אַלְפֵי
גְמַלִּים וַחֲמֵשׁ מֵאוֹת צֶמֶד־בָּקָר וַחֲמֵשׁ מֵאוֹת אֲתוֹנוֹת וַעֲבֻדָּה רַבָּה מְאֹד וַיְהִי הָאִישׁ הַהוּא
גָּדוֹל מִכָּל־בְּנֵי־קֶדֶם: 4 וְהָלְכוּ בָנָיו וְעָשׂוּ מִשְׁתֶּה בֵּית אִישׁ יוֹמוֹ וְשָׁלְחוּ וְקָרְאוּ לִשְׁלֹשֶׁת
אַחְיֹתֵיהֶם לֶאֱכֹל וְלִשְׁתּוֹת עִמָּהֶם: 5 וַיְהִי כִּי הִקִּיפוּ יְמֵי הַמִּשְׁתֶּה וַיִּשְׁלַח אִיּוֹב וַיְקַדְּשֵׁם
וְהִשְׁכִּים בַּבֹּקֶר וְהֶעֱלָה עֹלוֹת מִסְפַּר כֻּלָּם כִּי אָמַר אִיּוֹב אוּלַי חָטְאוּ בָנַי וּבֵרְכוּ אֱלֹהִים
בִּלְבָבָם כָּכָה יַעֲשֶׂה אִיּוֹב כָּל־הַיָּמִים: 6 וַיְהִי הַיּוֹם וַיָּבֹאוּ בְּנֵי הָאֱלֹהִים לְהִתְיַצֵּב עַל־יְהוָה
וַיָּבוֹא גַם־הַשָּׂטָן בְּתוֹכָם: 7 וַיֹּאמֶר יְהוָה אֶל־הַשָּׂטָן מֵאַיִן תָּבֹא וַיַּעַן הַשָּׂטָן אֶת־יְהוָה וַיֹּאמַר
מִשּׁוּט בָּאָרֶץ וּמֵהִתְהַלֵּךְ בָּהּ: 8 וַיֹּאמֶר יְהוָה אֶל־הַשָּׂטָן הֲשַׂמְתָּ לִבְּךָ עַל־עַבְדִּי אִיּוֹב כִּי אֵין
כָּמֹהוּ בָּאָרֶץ אִישׁ תָּם וְיָשָׁר יְרֵא אֱלֹהִים וְסָר מֵרָע:

VOCABULARY AND NOTES

Verse 1

Hebrew		Parse	Root	Gloss
עוּץ		PN		"Uz"
אִיּוֹב		PN		"Job"
תָּם		ADJ.MS		"whole"
יָשָׁר		ADJ.MS		"upright"
יְרֵא		ADJ.MS CSTR		"fearing"

Verse 2

Hebrew		Parse	Root	Gloss
וַיִּוָּלְדוּ	*Niphal*	CP 3MP	ילד	"be born"

Verse 3

Hebrew		Parse	Root	Gloss
מִקְנֵהוּ		N.MS + 3MS SF		"possession"
גְמַלִּים		N.MP		"camel"
צֶמֶד		N.MS CSTR		"pair"
בָּקָר		N.MS		"cattle"
אֲתוֹנוֹת		N.FP		"female donkey"
עֲבֻדָּה		N.FS		"livestock"
קֶדֶם		N.MS		"east"

Verse 4

Hebrew		Parse	Root	Gloss
מִשְׁתֶּה		N.MS		"feast"
אַחְיֹתֵיהֶם		N.FP + 3MP SF	אָחוֹת	"sister"

Verse 5

Hebrew		Parse	Root	Gloss
הִקִּיפוּ	*Hiphil*	SC 3MP	נקף	"come to an end"
וַיְקַדֵּשׁ	*Piel*	CP 3MS + 3MP SF	קדשׁ	"consecrate"
וְהִשְׁכִּים	*Hiphil* wəqāṭal	3MS	שׁכם	"arise early"
וְהֶעֱלָה	*Hiphil* wəqāṭal	3MS	עלה	"offer up"
מִסְפַּר		N.MS CSTR		"number"
כֻּלָּם		N.MS + 3MP SF		"all of them"
אוּלַי		ADV		"perhaps"
וּבֵרְכוּ	*Piel*	SC 3MP	ברך	
לְבָבָם		N.MS + 3MP SF		
כָּכָה		ADV		"thus"

Verse 6

Hebrew		Parse	Root	Gloss
הִתְיַצֵּב	*Hitpael*	INF CSTR	יצב	"stand"

| שָׂטָן | | N.MS | | "adversary" |

Verse 7

מֵאַיִן		INTR		"from where?"
שׁוּט	Qal			"roam; row"
הִתְהַלֵּךְ	Hitpael	INF CSTR	הלך	"walk about"

Verse 8

| כָּמֹהוּ | | PREP + 3MS | | "like him" |

CHAPTER 6

//////////////

VOLITIVES

The Hebrew volitives are a central component of direct discourse embedded in the narratives of the Hebrew Bible. This chapter outlines the three morphological categories of volition: jussive, imperative, and cohortative. It also demonstrates how ancient speakers used them in a variety of social situations to influence others, ranging from indirect requests to assertive commands.

6.1 GOING DEEPER WITH VOLITIVES

The deliberation of Joseph's brothers in Genesis 37 offers a fascinating exchange of volitive forms. As they argue among themselves about the fate of their younger brother Joseph, a struggle for dominance begins to emerge. This sibling rivalry is especially evident in their exchange of volitive forms. Their choice of volitive forms demonstrates the sibling rivalries of Jacob's twelve sons.

Initially, the text does not name a spokesman but instead portrays the brothers as a group deliberating their course of action. The plural cohortative provides an anonymous introduction to the brothers as they decide to move on to Dothan: נֵלְכָה דֹתָיְנָה "Let us go to Dothan" (Gen 37:17). As Joseph approaches them to find out their welfare for his father, the narrative tells the reader that the brothers proceed to conspire about how they might rid themselves of their annoying little brother: וַיֹּאמְרוּ אִישׁ אֶל־אָחִיו "They said to one another" (Gen 37:19). This phrase signals to the reader that a superior to inferior relationship is not meant by the plural imperative that follows: לְכוּ "Come on!" (Gen 37:20). Instead, the imperative is to be interpreted in the context of a unified group making a decision to act. They are united in their desire to teach Joseph a lesson.

But suddenly, the focus shifts from the group to an individual, Reuben, the firstborn, tries to assert himself over the group. His speech begins with a negative statement (לֹא + prefix conjugation), followed by a second-person negative jussive and a marked imperative: לֹא נַכֶּנּוּ נָפֶשׁ . . . אַל־תִּשְׁפְּכוּ־דָם הַשְׁלִיכוּ אֹתוֹ אֶל־הַבּוֹר הַזֶּה "We should not strike him . . . Do not shed blood. Throw him into this pit" (Gen 37:21b, 22).

Yet a second shift in focus takes place in the story as Judah, the fourth son of Jacob, also attempts to assert influence over the group. He does so more discretely by using less direct volitive forms—a plural cohortative and a third-person negative jussive: לְכוּ וְנִמְכְּרֶנּוּ לַיִּשְׁמְעֵאלִים וְיָדֵנוּ אַל־תְּהִי־בוֹ כִּי־אָחִינוּ בְשָׂרֵנוּ הוּא "Come, let us sell him to the Ishmaelites, but let not our hand be against him, for he is our brother, our own flesh" (Gen 37:27). The first two volitional statements in Judah's speech parallel those of the group, while Reuben's do not:

The Group: Imperative (לְכוּ)
             Cohortative

Reuben: Negative Imperative (לֹא + PC)
             Second-Person Negative Jussive
             Imperative

Judah: Imperative (לְכוּ)
             Cohortative
             Third-Person Negative Jussive

Judah ends up winning over the will of the group with his softer tone. Reuben, however, falls out of favor with them, despite his more direct and forceful commands. The passage shows a desperate older brother who fails to convince his younger siblings to follow his lead. The narrative interest in Judah becomes more pronounced as the reader moves forward in the Joseph story.[1]

The narrator of the Joseph story skillfully weaves together narrative description and corresponding direct discourse. Volitive forms drive the plot line to its climax and subsequent aftermath. We now turn our attention to describe the morphosemantics of the Hebrew volitive.

6.2 CHAPTER OBJECTIVES

This chapter aims to introduce the reader to the Hebrew volitive forms. These forms include the imperative, jussive, and cohortative. The following discussion will introduce their morphology and offer an overview of usage throughout the Hebrew Bible. This chapter will also give some attention to the social status of both speaker and addressee.

---

[1] The Judah and Tamar episode (Gen 38); Judah the spokesman of the brothers (Gen 43:8; 44:16–34); Judah the heir of the scepter (Gen 49:8–12).

6.3 INTRODUCTION

The volitive mood is to be distinguished from the indicative mood in its assertion of the will or "volition" of the speaker onto the recipient. The role of the indicative mood is to convey verbal actions or states of being, and the indicative accounts for the bulk of verbal expression throughout the Hebrew Bible. Volitional utterances are unique from other aspects of the Hebrew verbal system because they are the product of direct discourse and rarely occur outside of direct speech. The volitive mood deals with irrealis, which refers to actions or situations that are not yet realized, but that exist as potential in the mind of the speaker. The volitive mood expresses the wish or desire that the speaker wants to become reality. As we will observe below, these expressions of volition vary from strong or direct assertions to soft or indirect requests. On account of these usages, some classify volitionals as a form of indirect commands.

6.4 VOLITIVES AND SOCIAL STATUS

The social status of the speakers who utilize Hebrew volitive forms is an important component of their interpretation. This aspect is important for two reasons. The first problem to overcome is our distance from the ancient setting of Classical Biblical Hebrew. Since it is a dead language, we do not have access to the native speakers of the language, thus further removing us from the social context in which these volitives were originally uttered. The second factor to remember is that each volitive utterance is embedded in carefully crafted narratives with overarching literary purposes. This acknowledgment does not necessarily shut us off from genuinely reported speech from the ancient world, but rather alerts us to its complex literary setting in the Hebrew Bible.

Volitive forms occurring in speeches reported by the narrator require us to pay close attention to their social contexts. The perceived social status of the speaker is a major factor in the form chosen to express his or her wish. Scholars refer to this perceived status as the "relative status," meaning that every speaker makes volitive utterances according to accepted social norms that vary depending on the nature of the exchange. Ahouva Shulman explains her criteria for determining relative status: "In each speech situation examined . . . the relative status of the participants is determined according to the participants' recognition and perception of their status in relation to the addressee, or to the speaker, at the time of the utterance."[2]

The main indicator of this recognition and perception of status comes from the speech itself. As Cynthia Miller has noted, a given speech will often "index the social relation" of the speaker to the addressee by using terms that demarcate "social distance (the speaker indexes him/herself in an inferior relation to the addressee) or

---

[2] Ahouva Shulman, "The Use of Modal Verb Forms in Biblical Hebrew Prose" (PhD diss., University of Toronto, 1996), 24–25.

social intimacy."[3] Terms like "father," "lord/master," and "king" all designate deferential language whereby an inferior addresses a superior. Esau asks his father to arise and eat from the game he had prepared, deferentially addressing him as "my father:"

Gen 27:31

יָקֻם אָבִי וְיֹאכַל מִצֵּיד בְּנוֹ

Let **my father** arise and eat from the game of his son.

Similarly, expressions such as "your servant" or "your maidservant" allow an inferior to reference himself or herself when speaking to a superior. Bathsheba appeals to King David in this manner:

1 Kgs 1:17

אֲדֹנִי אַתָּה נִשְׁבַּעְתָּ בַּיהוָה אֱלֹהֶיךָ לַאֲמָתֶךָ

My lord, you swore **to your maidservant** by Yahweh your God.

Interestingly, Miller notes that no terms of address are used when a superior speaks to an inferior.[4] There is a relative terseness about a superior's address to an inferior, which contrasts the rather lengthy and roundabout ways an inferior makes a request to a superior. Joseph's command to his household servant to pursue his brothers, for instance, is rather terse:

Gen 44:4

קוּם רְדֹף אַחֲרֵי הָאֲנָשִׁים

Get up. Pursue the men.

The notion of polite versus impolite speech is an important aspect of direct discourse. Richard J. Watts has defined polite speech in a way that emphasizes the behavioral aspect of the exchange. Whether verbal or nonverbal, polite speech concerns what is appropriate for "ongoing social interaction."[5] Watts outlines two means of marking polite speech. The first is what he calls "formulaic utterances." They contain explicit markers of politeness such as terms of deference like "lord" or "king" as identified in the above examples. The second way to signify polite speech is "semi-formulaic utterances," which he characterizes as indirect linguistic expressions.[6] The indirect volitional utterance of an inferior to a superior in Biblical Hebrew is representative of this kind of polite speech.

Another way of describing social distance versus social intimacy is in terms of social equality or inequality. On the polar ends of the spectrum speakers register social superiority versus inferiority. Somewhere in the middle one finds varying degrees of social equality. Admittedly, the advantage of distance and intimacy as a means of identifying social status is that a speech could conceivably occur between

---

[3] Cynthia Miller, "Reported Speech" (PhD diss., University of Chicago, 1993), 215.

[4] Miller, 215.

[5] Richard J. Watts, *Politeness*, Key Topics in Sociolinguistics (Cambridge: Cambridge University Press, 2003), 20.

[6] Watts, 168–69.

a superior and inferior, and yet take place in an intimate social setting. However, in the ancient world of the Hebrew Bible, deferential speech occurred in both distant and intimate settings, making it all the more useful to identify social equals. For example, a conversation among brothers exhibits varying degrees of social equality, notwithstanding the pecking order of older and younger siblings and the rivalries it produces. For instance, the Joseph story records the discussion among Joseph's brothers as Joseph approached them in the field. The conversation takes place in an intimate setting, yet Reuben is seeking to assert himself as the eldest brother and therefore utilizes several direct volitive statements:

Gen 37:21b–22a

לֹא נַכֶּנּוּ נָפֶשׁ: אַל־תִּשְׁפְּכוּ־דָם֩ הַשְׁלִיכוּ אֹתוֹ אֶל־הַבּוֹר הַזֶּה אֲשֶׁר בַּמִּדְבָּר וְיָד אַל־תִּשְׁלְחוּ־בוֹ

We shall not strike (his) soul.
Do not shed blood. **Throw** him into this pit which is in the wilderness, but **do not lay** a hand against him.

The other means of identifying the perceived status of an individual speaker is to examine the surrounding context of the narrative in which the utterance is recorded. Once again, we must remember that each speech serves the literary agenda of the narrative. Furthermore, the final control in determining meaning in these contexts is the narrative itself. The introductory example from the Joseph story demonstrates this point. The narrative introduces characters in identifiable ways. In most cases the social setting is already set in place before the character of the story speaks. Similar terms of identification like "king," "servant," "brother," or "father" alert the reader to the social situation in view. In some settings, however, a given utterance may surprise the reader with an inversion or subversion of expected social norms. Even though the narrative context may indicate an inferior to superior address, the terms of address do not. These examples often occur for rhetorical effect to highlight flaws of character or to stress the dire nature of the circumstances. For instance, Nabal, a social inferior, responds to the messengers of David (who are speaking in David's name) with a rhetorical question as a means of challenging David's authority:

1 Sam 25:10

מִי דָוִד וּמִי בֶן־יִשָׁי

Who is David and who is the son of Jesse?

A group of young boys show disrespect to the prophet Elisha on his way to Bethel, shouting at him:

2 Kgs 2:23

עֲלֵה קֵרֵחַ עֲלֵה קֵרֵחַ:

Go up, baldy! **Go up**, baldy!

God addresses the problem of offering blemished sacrifices on the temple altar, asking sarcastically:

Mal 1:8

הַקְרִיבֵ֨הוּ נָ֜א לְפֶחָתֶ֗ךָ הֲיִרְצְךָ֙ א֣וֹ הֲיִשָּׂ֣א פָנֶ֔יךָ

Please, offer it to your governor. Would he be pleased with you? Or would he show you favor?

Since we are dealing with volitional statements, it is not always immediately apparent whether the speaker's perception is reflective of reality. Beyond the fact that the speaker asserts what he or she wants to become reality (i.e., irrealis), one also must evaluate how the speaker perceives his or her social status in the exchange, as the above examples illustrate. It is useful to consider the following three possibilities in making such an assessment:

1. The actual social status of the speaker.
2. The perceived social status of the speaker.
3. The desired social status of the speaker.

To identify one of these possibilities, the interpreter has to rely upon the cues of the narrative. Furthermore, the social status of an individual is not a static classification, since one person can fill different roles in various circumstances (e.g., husband, father, servant, younger son). A person can also experience a dramatic change of status through some significant event or experience, a gradual process stemming from the natural developments of life, or even a self-conscious effort to assert oneself in a particular manner. Once again, Joseph's change of status from annoying, younger brother to governor of Egypt well demonstrates this kind of situation. Judah deferentially pleads to speak in the hearing of the Egyptian overlord, not knowing it is his younger brother, Joseph:

Gen 44:18

בִּ֣י אֲדֹנִ֗י יְדַבֶּר־נָ֨א עַבְדְּךָ֤ דָבָר֙ בְּאָזְנֵ֣י אֲדֹנִ֔י וְאַל־יִ֥חַר אַפְּךָ֖ בְּעַבְדֶּ֑ךָ

My lord, **please let** your servant **speak** a word in the ears of my lord. Do not let your anger kindle against your servant.

The social contexts of narrative-imbedded speeches are thus complex and multilayered, requiring careful consideration. For this reason, our interpretation of the volitive forms needs to be accompanied by a close reading of the social settings in which they occur. In the course of this chapter on Hebrew volitives (e.g., imperatives, jussives, and cohortatives) we will comment on the ways in which they relate to the social status of those who utter them in direct discourse.

6.5 THE IMPERATIVE

6.5.1 Morphology and Historical Development

The Hebrew imperative is the second-person volitional form of the verbal system. The historical development of the imperative form has been understood in different ways. Earlier scholars argued that the imperative was formed by removing the personal pronoun prefixes from the prefix conjugation. G. H. A. von Ewald, for instance, argued that the *Qal* imperative is derived from the jussive, thus making the imperative "short and emphatic."[7] The following chart illustrates this derivation:

QAL PC	QAL IMPV	
תִּשְׁמֹר	שְׁמֹר	2MS
תִּשְׁמְרִי	שִׁמְרִי	2FS
תִּשְׁמְרוּ	שִׁמְרוּ	2MP
תִּשְׁמֹרְנָה	שְׁמֹרְנָה	2FP

Most beginning grammars use this heuristic explanation to describe the surface forms because it is easy to memorize. Despite the surface-level correspondence, however, closer examination reveals several difficulties.

First, the formation of the imperative in the derived stems complicates matters. Three of the derived stems have a prefixed syllable. The *Hiphil*, for instance, has a prefixed ה- + a *ḥireq* vowel in the suffix conjugation and a theme vowel -ִי. The prefixed ה- apocopates when the pronominal prefixes of the prefix conjugation are attached and the prefixed *ḥireq* changes to *pataḥ*: הִכְתִּיב (SC) versus תַּכְתִּיב (PC). The *Hiphil* imperative maintains the /a/ vowel of the prefixed ה- and shortens the *ḥireq-yod* theme vowel to *ṣere*: הַכְתֵּב. Shortening the *ḥireq-yod* to *ṣere* does parallel what happens in the jussive: PC יַכְתִּיב, JUSS יַכְתֵּב. Grammarians have suggested that the imperative is taking the vowel of the jussive since they are both volitive moods.[8] The prefixed ה of the *Hitpael* behaves similarly to that of the *Hiphil*, but it occurs with a *ḥireq* in both the suffix conjugation and the imperative (see chart below). The *Hitpael* imperative is distinguished from the other forms with a *pataḥ* in the third syllable, but it is only visible in the masculine singular (הִתְהַלֵּךְ vs. הִתְהַלֵּךְ). The *Niphal* poses similar challenges. Its PC form is יִכָּתֵב, but the imperative is הִכָּתֵב, again with prefixed ה analogical to the *Hiphil* imperative. Removing the pronominal prefix from the *Hiphil* or *Niphal* PC does not yield the imperative form. Strictly speaking, these imperatives are not derived from the PC.

---

[7] Ewald, *Grammar*, §291. More recently, see M. M. Bravmann, "Notes on the Forms of the Imperative in Hebrew and Arabic," *JQR* 42 (1951): 56. He similarly argues that the *Qal* imperative is derived from the prefix conjugation, reasoning that the intensity associated with the utterance of commands produces shortened forms. The association of shortness with direct commands works for the *Qal* imperative, but it is not true of the shortened jussive. Though the jussive is characteristically a "short" volitive form, it is at the same time a less direct volitional statement.

[8] Joüon-Muraoka §48a.

	SC	PC	IMPV	JUSS
Hiphil	הִקְטִיל	תַּקְטִיל	הַקְטֵל	תַּקְטֵל
Niphal	נִקְטַל	תִּקָּטֵל	הִקָּטֵל	תִּקָּטֵל
Hitpael	הִתְהַלֵּךְ	תִּתְהַלֵּךְ	הִתְהַלֵּךְ	תִּתְהַלֵּךְ

We now return our attention to the *Qal* imperative. Despite the visual similarity between the 2MS forms of the imperative and the PC (see chart below), the *shewa* of the PC is not pronounced (i.e., *tišmor*) while in the imperative it is vocal (i.e., *šəmor*). The initial form of the imperative would have contained an initial consonant cluster (e.g., **šmor*), something that cannot occur in Biblical Hebrew. The vocal *shewa* would have developed secondarily as a means of mitigating the consonant cluster. Second, when the final vowel is added to the 2FS (◌ִ-) and 2MP (וּ-) *Qal* prefix forms, it creates another problem. Once the pronominal prefixes are removed, the expected reduction pattern produces two consecutive *shewas* at the beginning of the word. This phonological situation requires one to apply the rule of *shewa*—when two *shewas* occur at the beginning of the word, the first one changes to *hireq* (שִׁמְרוּ < שְׁמְרוּ*).

The *Qal* stem furthermore exhibits three different theme vowels in the prefix forms: *a*, *o* (historically *u*), and *i*. In most cases the theme vowel of the prefix form matches that of the imperative, again allowing one to remove the pronominal prefixes to form the imperative, as demonstrated in the following chart:

VOWEL CLASS	QAL PC	QAL IMPV
o-class	תִּשְׁמֹר	שְׁמֹר
	תַּעֲבֹר	עֲבֹר
a-class	תִּשְׁלַח	שְׁלַח
	תִּלְבַּשׁ	לְבַשׁ
i-class	תִּתֵּן	תֵּן
	תֵּצֵא	צֵא

A significant number of forms do not suggest a correspondence between the *Qal* PC and imperative, however. For example, the root כרת suggests that their underlying historical bases are different. When the imperative is bound to the following word by a *maqqep*, the theme vowel is short /o/ (*qameṣ-ḥaṭup*) with a reduced vowel in the first syllable: כְּרָת־לָנוּ (1 Sam 11:1). When the imperative takes suffixes (e.g., 2FS, 2MP, 2FP, pronominal suffixes) the vowel of the first syllable is also short /o/ (*qameṣ-ḥaṭup*): כָּרְתָה (2 Sam 3:12). The same forms occur for the root מלך as well: מְלָךְ־עָלֵינוּ (Judg 9:14); מָלְכָה (Judg 9:8). The evidence for some roots is mixed, as in the root כתב: כָּתְבוּ (Deut 31:19); כָּתְבָה (Isa 30:8). Similarly, the root משׁך attests both מָשְׁכוּ (Exod 12:21) and מָשְׁכֵנִי (Song 1:4).[9]

These morphological developments complicate the idea that the *Qal* imperative is formed from the PC by the removal of pronominal prefixes. The consensus among grammarians is to propose the historical bases *qutul*, *qatal*, and *qitil* for the *Qal* imperative, independent of the PC, whose base was most likely *yaqtulu* (see §6.5.1).[10] The *qutul* and *qatal* bases have produced the /o/ and /a/ theme vowel imperatives respectively: שְׁמֹר (< *šumur*); מָלְכָה (< *mulukat*); שְׁלַח (< *šalah*). The proposed *qitil* base is no longer detectible from the morphological evidence. Once the *Qal* imperative reduced the initial vowel, the *i*-class roots may have collapsed with the *a*-class roots (perhaps *qitil* > *qatal*), since no strong root shows a *qatil* pattern.[11] The presence of an /i/ vowel in forms like the I-weak צֵא "go out" (note the pausal form צֵאוּ [Isa 49:9] vs. non-pausal צְאוּ [Gen 19:14]) and I-*nun* תֵּן "give" may preserve vestigial *qitil* imperatives. The presence of the /i/ vowel in suffixal forms like כִּתְבוּ (*u*-class) "write" or שִׁכְבָה (*a*-class) "lie down" apparently show a secondary application of the rule of *shewa* and not the preservation of an historical /i/ of a *qitil* imperative.

HISTORICAL BASE	SAMPLE FORMS
qutul	מָלְכָה, אֱמֹר, שְׁמֹר, עֲמֹר
qatal	שָׂא, גַּשׁ, מְנַע, שְׁלַח
qitil	רֵד, צֵא, תֵּן

The morphological data surveyed in this section suggest that deriving the *Qal* imperative from the PC, though convenient for memorization purposes, at best misrepresents the evidence. It is not entirely inaccurate, however, since it becomes the means of forming the imperative in Mishnaic Hebrew. Blau argues that already in Biblical Hebrew the formation of the imperative is being restructured according to the prefix conjugation, in spite of their distinct historical developments.[12] Itsik Pariente has reached a similar conclusion in his study of spirantization in imperative forms.[13] He points out that spirantization of the *bgdkpt* letters (i.e., without *dageš lene*) generally takes place when they follow a vowel, while their non-spirantized (i.e., with *dageš lene*) forms occur everywhere else.[14] For example,

---

[9] For more examples, see GKC §46d.

[10] See Carl Brockelmann, *Grundriss der vergleichenden Grammatik der semitischen Sprachen* (Berlin: Reuther & Reichard, 1908–1913; repr. Hildesheim: Olms, 1961), 1:544–54; BL §42; GKC §46a. Joshua Blau even suggests that the prefix forms may have been derived from the imperatives (Blau, 224).

[11] As noted in BL §42f.

[12] Blau, 224.

[13] Itsik Pariente, "On the Formation of the Tiberian Hebrew Imperatives: Evidence from Spirantization," *HS* 45 (2004): 71–77.

[14] Sometimes the spirantized *bgdkpt* letters are transliterated as follows: *v, γ, δ, x, f*, and *θ*.

the ת is spirantized in כָּתַב "he wrote," but not in יִכְתֹּב "he writes." This observation is relevant to the imperative because the *bgdkpt* letters do not adhere to the expected spirantization patterns in certain forms. Pariente cites the feminine singular of the root שׁכב. The 2FS of the prefix form is תִּשְׁכְּבִי "you will lie down," whereas the FS imperative is שִׁכְבִי "lie down." Were the imperative derived from the prefix form, one might expect שִׁכְבִי mirroring the post-vocalic stop in תִּשְׁכְּבִי. Also, in שִׁכְבִי the ב is spirantized following a consonant, again violating the general pattern, and perhaps indicating that the imperative form with the FS suffix is mirroring the masculine singular imperative where the ב is spirantized: שְׁכַב.[15] In summary, the evidence shows that *bgdkpt* letters break the regular spirantization tendencies to align with the masculine singular imperative, not the prefix form.

Some I-*nun* verbs provide similar evidence for alignment with the imperative rather than the PC. Two examples will suffice. A few I-*nun* imperatives appear to be derived from the PC, like גַּשׁ (root נגשׁ "to draw near), which is analogous to the prefix form תִּגַּשׁ. However, for the root נקם the initial *nun* reappears in the imperative: נְקֹם (Num 31:2), not קֹם as expected.[16] The evidence for the root נשׂא attests both types: שָׂא (Gen 13:14) and נְשָׂא (Ps 10:12). These forms seem to confirm the conclusion that Biblical Hebrew witnesses a change in the way the *Qal* imperatives are being formed. They began to move away from their historical origin and shifted morphologically toward a greater conformity to PC patterns.[17]

6.5.2 Use of the Imperative

The imperative appears to be the preferred mode of volition for one to address an individual of inferior social status. Depending on whether the speaker addresses a group or individual, the superior will use the singular or plural. The semantics of the imperative form communicate terse commands in a variety of social contexts that for the most part are perceived by inferiors as binding requests. The imperative is both strong and direct. Not every "short" volitional form indicates terseness or directness, however. The jussive is a "shortened" form of the prefix conjugation but is viewed as less direct than the imperative. The directness of the imperative is less tied to the shortness of its morphology and is probably more related to it being in the second person—"You, do X!" One can mitigate the directness of the command by stating it in the plural or by means of other suffixes or volitional particles (e.g., the הָ- suffix, precative לְ, or particle נָא).

General Command. Most times the imperative relates specific commands to a superior's subordinate(s) in both socially distant and intimate contexts. The following examples come from the Joseph story.

---

[15] For the details of this argument, see Pariente, "Tiberian Hebrew Imperatives," 75–76.
[16] This example is cited in Pariente, 77.
[17] With Blau, 224, and Pariente, "Tiberian Hebrew Imperatives," 77.

Gen 43:16 (Joseph to his household servants)

הָבֵא אֶת־הָאֲנָשִׁים הַבָּיְתָה וּטְבֹחַ טֶבַח וְהָכֵן כִּי אִתִּי יֹאכְלוּ הָאֲנָשִׁים בַּצָּהֳרָיִם:

Take the men to the house and **slaughter** a slaughter and **prepare** (it), for the men are going to eat with me at noon.

Gen 45:17 (Pharaoh to Joseph)

אֱמֹר אֶל־אַחֶיךָ זֹאת עֲשׂוּ טַעֲנוּ אֶת־בְּעִירְכֶם וּלְכוּ־בֹאוּ אַרְצָה כְּנָעַן:

Say to your brothers: "**Do** this: load your beasts and **go**[18] to the land of Canaan.'"

Gen 43:11 (Jacob to his sons)

אִם־כֵּן | אֵפוֹא זֹאת עֲשׂוּ קְחוּ מִזִּמְרַת הָאָרֶץ בִּכְלֵיכֶם וְהוֹרִידוּ לָאִישׁ מִנְחָה מְעַט צֳרִי וּמְעַט דְּבַשׁ נְכֹאת וָלֹט בָּטְנִים וּשְׁקֵדִים:

If this is so, then this is what **you must do**: **Take** from the best products of the land in your sacks and **carry** (them) **down** to the man as a gift (offering), a little balm and a little honey, *ladanum*-spice and myrrh, pistachio nuts, and almonds.

Similarly, the prologue to the book of Proverbs couches the reception of wisdom's teaching as that of a father instructing his son. The imperative is commonly attested in this material, as in:

Prov 1:8

שְׁמַע בְּנִי מוּסַר אָבִיךָ

Hear, my son, the instruction of your father.

Prov 25:16

דְּבַשׁ מָצָאתָ אֱכֹל דַּיֶּךָ פֶּן־תִּשְׂבָּעֶנּוּ וַהֲקֵאתוֹ:

(If) you have found honey, **eat** what is sufficient for you, lest you have too much and vomit it.

The imperative is broadly applied to instruction in general, including the psalms where the psalmist instructs Israel corporately:

Ps 34:10, 14–15

יְראוּ אֶת־יְהוָה קְדֹשָׁיו . . . נְצֹר לְשׁוֹנְךָ מֵרָע וּשְׂפָתֶיךָ מִדַּבֵּר מִרְמָה: סוּר מֵרָע וַעֲשֵׂה־טוֹב בַּקֵּשׁ שָׁלוֹם וְרָדְפֵהוּ:

Fear Yahweh, O you his saints. . . . **Guard** your tongue from evil, and your lips from speaking deceit. **Turn** from evil and **do** good. **Seek** peace and **pursue** it.

Commands are not always obeyed, however. This outcome tends to occur within a familiar or familial social context. For instance, Jacob tells his sons to return to Egypt to buy provisions, but they refuse:

---

18 Note that there are two imperatives here: וּלְכוּ "Come!" and בֹאוּ "Go."

Gen 43:2

שֻׁבוּ שִׁבְרוּ־לָנוּ מְעַט־אֹכֶל

Go back, **buy** for us a little food.

Someone may use the imperative to portray himself in a particular way. Reuben
tries to assert his elder position over his younger brothers by commanding them
not to take the life of Joseph.

Gen 37:22

וַיֹּאמֶר אֲלֵהֶם| רְאוּבֵן אַל־תִּשְׁפְּכוּ־דָם **הַשְׁלִיכוּ** אֹתוֹ אֶל־הַבּוֹר הַזֶּה אֲשֶׁר בַּמִּדְבָּר
וְיָד אַל־תִּשְׁלְחוּ־בוֹ לְמַעַן הַצִּיל אֹתוֹ מִיָּדָם לַהֲשִׁיבוֹ אֶל־אָבִיו:

Reuben said to them: "Do not shed blood. **Throw** him into this pit in the
wilderness, but do not lay a hand upon him!" that he might rescue him
from their hands to return him to his father.

This use of the imperative attempts to persuade others with one's wishes and does
not have the same force as a recognized superior's command to an inferior. The act
of persuasion can occur among peers as well. The wise father warns his son about
the pressure to join in the violence of his peers:

Prov 1:11

אִם־יֹאמְרוּ לְכָה אִתָּנוּ

If they say: "**Come** with us!"

Divine Command. The imperative is often associated with divine commands
expressed in covenantal contexts. A most familiar example comes from the
Decalogue:

Exod 20:12

כַּבֵּד אֶת־אָבִיךָ וְאֶת־אִמֶּךָ

Honor your father and mother.

Divine commands instruct the people of Israel in their ritual obligations, as in:

Lev 9:2

וַיֹּאמֶר אֶל־אַהֲרֹן **קַח־לְךָ** עֵגֶל בֶּן־בָּקָר לְחַטָּאת וְאַיִל לְעֹלָה תְּמִימִם

[Moses] said to Aaron: "**Take** a bull calf for a sin offering and a ram for a
whole burnt offering, both unblemished."

Moses speaks the command of Yahweh to Pharaoh in Exod 5:1, which is rather
jarring considering Pharaoh's divine status as king of Egypt:

Exod 5:1

כֹּה־אָמַר יְהוָֹה אֱלֹהֵי יִשְׂרָאֵל **שַׁלַּח** אֶת־עַמִּי וְיָחֹגּוּ לִי בַּמִּדְבָּר:

Thus says Yahweh, the God of Israel: "**Send away** my people that they
may celebrate a festival to me in the wilderness."

Divine commands are common throughout the Hebrew prophets. Yahweh commands the prophet Isaiah:

Isa 7:3

וַיֹּאמֶר לֵךְ וְאָמַרְתָּ לָעָם הַזֶּה

And he said: "**Go** and speak to this people."

The prophet as the spokesman of Yahweh regularly commands the covenant people to hear the word of Yahweh.

Jer 44:24

שִׁמְעוּ דְבַר־יְהוָה כָּל־יְהוּדָה אֲשֶׁר בְּאֶרֶץ מִצְרָיִם׃

Hear the word of Yahweh, all Judah who are in the land of Egypt.

Other Types of Commands. Several other uses of the imperative as a command do not fit the contexts of the examples discussed above. The lament psalms are replete with words directed against oppressors. Sometimes the psalmist commands his oppressor *in absentia*, which rhetorically elevates the status of the oppressed over his oppressor.

Ps 6:9

סוּרוּ מִמֶּנִּי כָּל־פֹּעֲלֵי אָוֶן כִּי־שָׁמַע יְהוָה קוֹל בִּכְיִי׃

Depart from me, all you workers of iniquity,
For Yahweh has heard the voice of my weeping.

The psalmist commonly exhorts himself with commands, often addressed to the soul or *nepeš*. After asking his soul why it is downcast in Ps 42:6, the psalmist exhorts himself:

Ps 42:6

הוֹחִילִי לֵאלֹהִים כִּי־עוֹד אוֹדֶנּוּ יְשׁוּעוֹת פָּנָיו׃

Wait for God, for I will yet give him praise for the deliverances of his presence.

The well-known *inclusio* of Ps 103:2, 22 instructs the soul:

Ps 103:2, 22

בָּרְכִי נַפְשִׁי אֶת־יְהוָה . . . בָּרְכִי נַפְשִׁי אֶת־יְהוָה׃

Bless Yahweh, O my soul. . . .
Bless Yahweh, O my soul.

Corporate Injunction. Sometimes the imperative expresses corporate injunctions, which are more hortatory in nature, even though they are couched as a command. This usage occurs in contexts where an individual addresses a group urging them to act in a particular manner. The Shema offers a prominent example:

Deut 6:4

שְׁמַע יִשְׂרָאֵל יְהוָה אֱלֹהֵינוּ יְהוָה ׀ אֶחָד׃

Hear, O Israel, Yahweh is our God, Yahweh alone.

The corporate injunction is common in the psalms as well:

Ps 29:2

הָבוּ לַיהוָה כְּבוֹד שְׁמוֹ הִשְׁתַּחֲווּ לַיהוָה בְּהַדְרַת־קֹדֶשׁ׃

Ascribe to Yahweh the glory of his name;
Bow down to Yahweh in the splendor of holiness.

Ps 95:6

בֹּאוּ נִשְׁתַּחֲוֶה וְנִכְרָעָה נִבְרְכָה לִפְנֵי־יְהוָה עֹשֵׂנוּ׃

Come, let us prostrate and bow down;
Let us kneel before Yahweh our maker.

Entreaty. The dominant use of the imperative is to give commands, typically from a social superior to an inferior. However, the psalms indicate that the imperative can also be used by the psalmist to express prayers of entreaty to God. These utterances are expressed in times of distress as the petitioner urges God to act swiftly on his behalf. When the imperative is used in this way it indicates a strong and urgent request. Deferential titles accompany these requests, thus softening the intensity of the imperative's directness. The following examples illustrate this usage:

Ps 5:11

הַאֲשִׁימֵם ׀ אֱלֹהִים יִפְּלוּ מִמֹּעֲצוֹתֵיהֶם בְּרֹב פִּשְׁעֵיהֶם הַדִּיחֵמוֹ כִּי־מָרוּ בָךְ׃

Make them **bear** their **guilt**, O God,
May they fall by their own plans.
Because of the increase of their transgressions **drive them out**,
For they have rebelled against you.

Ps 6:3

חָנֵּנִי יְהוָה כִּי אֻמְלַל אָנִי רְפָאֵנִי יְהוָה כִּי נִבְהֲלוּ עֲצָמָי׃

Be gracious to me, O Yahweh, for I am feeble,
Heal me, O Yahweh, for my bones are dismayed.

Ps 17:6

אֲנִי־קְרָאתִיךָ כִי־תַעֲנֵנִי אֵל הַט־אָזְנְךָ לִי שְׁמַע אִמְרָתִי׃

I have called you, for you will answer me, O God;
Stretch out your ear to me, **hear** my speech.

Ps 25:6

זְכֹר־רַחֲמֶיךָ יְהוָה וַחֲסָדֶיךָ כִּי מֵעוֹלָם הֵמָּה׃

Remember, O Yahweh, your compassions and lovingkindness,
For they have been from of old.

Permission. Grammarians have identified a few occasions in the Old Testament where the imperative is used in the context of granting permission. One commonly cited passage for this purported usage is 2 Sam 18:23.[19] The setting is Absalom's death at the hands of Joab. Joab sends the Cushite to relay the message to King David that his son is dead and that the coup is over. Ahimaaz, son of Zadok had originally requested to relay the message (אָרוּצָה נָּא "Please, let me run!" in v. 19), but Joab sent the Cushite instead. After the Cushite leaves, Ahimaaz asks permission to run after him:

2 Sam 18:22b–23

וִיהִי מָה אָרֻצָה־נָּא גַם־אָנִי אַחֲרֵי הַכּוּשִׁי וַיֹּאמֶר יוֹאָב לָמָּה־זֶּה אַתָּה רָץ בְּנִי וּלְכָה אֵין־בְּשׂוֹרָה מֹצֵאת: וִיהִי־מָה אָרוּץ וַיֹּאמֶר לֹו רֻץ

"Whatever occurs, please let me also run after the Cushite." And Joab said to him, "Why would you run, my son, and no reward come to you?" [Ahimaaz responded,] "Whatever occurs, I will run." And he said to him, "**Run.**"

Clearly, this dialogue records a negotiation between Ahimaaz and Joab, with Ahimaaz attempting to convince Joab to let him follow after the Cushite messenger. In the end, Joab concedes and allows Ahimaaz to go. But the force of the imperative in this case is not necessarily permission. The context of the imperative may indicate permission, but the imperative itself simply expresses a command from a superior to an inferior, even if the command was uttered as a result of coercion. Waltke and O'Connor provide another example for this usage that likewise expresses a command from a superior in response to the request of an inferior:

Gen 50:6

וַיֹּאמֶר פַּרְעֹה עֲלֵה וּקְבֹר אֶת־אָבִיךָ כַּאֲשֶׁר הִשְׁבִּיעֶךָ:

Pharaoh said, "**Go up** and **bury** your father, as he made you swear."

Infinitive Absolute as a Command. The infinitive absolute is used sometimes for a command much like the imperative. The two versions of the fourth word of the Decalogue in Exodus 20 and Deuteronomy 5 illustrate this usage:

Exod 20:8

זָכוֹר אֶת־יֹום הַשַּׁבָּת לְקַדְּשֹׁו:

Remember the Sabbath day by sanctifying it.

Deut 5:12

שָׁמוֹר אֶת־יֹום הַשַּׁבָּת לְקַדְּשֹׁו כַּאֲשֶׁר צִוְּךָ| יְהֹוָה אֱלֹהֶיךָ:

Keep the Sabbath day by sanctifying it, as Yahweh your God commanded you.

---

[19] See GKC §110b; *IBHS* §34.4b.

6.5.3 The Long Imperative

The morphological characteristic of the long imperative is the הָ◌- suffix. The examples highlighted in Ps 39:13 illustrate the form:

Ps 39:13

שִׁמְעָה־תְפִלָּתִי ׀ יְהוָה וְשַׁוְעָתִי ׀ הַאֲזִינָה

Hear my prayer, Yahweh,
Give ear to my cry.

The long imperative most commonly occurs in the *Qal* stem and is attested for all vowel types: מְלֹכָה "Rule" (*o*-type; Judg 9:8), שִׁכְבָה "Lie down" (*a*-type; Gen 39:7), and וָצְאָה "And come out" (*i*-type; Judg 9:29). It is also attested in the derived stems, as in the *Niphal* הִשָּׁבְעָה "Swear" (Gen 21:23),[20] the *Hiphil* הַקְשִׁיבָה "Give attention" (Ps 5:3[2]), or the *Piel* סַפְּרָה־נָא "Please, tell" (2 Kgs 8:4). The long imperative is phonologically restricted to the masculine singular, since the feminine singular, feminine plural, and masculine plural suffixes prevent the הָ◌- from occurring. Also, III-weak verbs with their characteristic final ה in the masculine singular form eliminate any distinction between short and long imperative forms.

For a long time, scholars have struggled to understand the syntactical function of this morpheme. Steven E. Fassberg surveys the history of its interpretation from medieval grammarians up into the modern era.[21] He notes that the earliest grammarians by and large did not comment on its function but instead focused on its morphology. He takes this silence as an indication that they did not believe there to be any difference in function between the short and long imperatives.[22] The earliest view on a distinction in function was that the lengthened form demarcated emphasis. This idea was largely based upon the emphatic imperative in Arabic, which also attests a final long /a/ vowel in pausal forms.[23] Ugaritic attests a productive long imperative with final /a/ (i.e., *qutula*), while Amorite preserves one in a proper name.[24] The Arabic, Ugaritic, and Amorite forms are all likely related to the energic patterns of the prefix conjugation, which contained an afformative *-an(na)*. In some phonological environments (like pause in the case of Arabic), only the *-a* remained.

---

[20] Gesenius points out that the masculine singular imperative of this root always attests the long form (GKC §51o).

[21] Steven E. Fassberg, "The Lengthened Imperative קָטְלָה in Biblical Hebrew," *HS* 40 (1999): 7–9.

[22] Fassberg, 8.

[23] See W. Wright, *Arabic Grammar* (Mineola, NY: Dover, 2005), §99d, cf. §97d; also noted in GKC §48i.

[24] In Ugaritic, Josef Tropper cites the form *šā* (*KTU* 1.5 V:13; 1.14 II:22; 6.48:3), vocalized as /šaʾa/ or /šaʾā/ meaning "Lift up!" (*Ugaritische Grammatik*, 429). See also John Huehnergard, *An Introduction to Ugaritic* (Peabody, MA: Hendrickson, 2012), 50. In his review of Tropper's *Ugaritische Grammatik*, Michael P. Streck also cites an Amorite personal name containing the long imperative: *Šūba-ḫālī*, which he translates "Turn to me, my mother's brother" (*Wende dich zu, mein Mutterbruder*). See review of *Ugaritische Grammatik*, by J. Tropper, *ZDMG* 152 (2002): 189. Streck's observation is also noted in Joüon-Muraoka §48d n. 4.

G. H. A. von Ewald argued that the long imperative indicates a more urgent command.[25] Gesenius suggested that it is more frequently emphatic, but also admitted that its distinct function is not always perceptible.[26] Others have maintained that while an emphatic meaning may have been functional at an earlier stage of the language, it is no longer detected in Biblical Hebrew.[27] The following comment from Matitiahu Tsevat is indicative of this approach: "These two imperatives can rightly be juxtaposed for comparison, since no differences in meaning between them can be detected."[28] Another way of describing this approach is to say that the long imperative is stylistic, with no distinction in meaning.[29] Waltke and O'Connor believe the long imperative is lexically conditioned, since some roots exclusively attest the lengthened form (as in הַקְשִׁיבָה cited above).[30]

Other scholars have emphasized the volitional function of the long imperative. Mayer Lambert accepted its historical derivation from the energic afformative attested in Arabic with earlier grammarians, but he did not believe it denotes emphasis.[31] Rather, he understood it to be a special volitional form marking respect.[32] He argued that Hebrew has retained the old energic afformative *-anna in the volitional particle נָא (< *-na < *-anna), traditionally rendered "please." Furthermore, the נָא particle is historically related to the final הָ֯- of the cohortative, the first-person Hebrew volitive. He proposed that the cohortative is akin to Arabic subjunctives which also attest a final /a/ vowel.[33] Lambert was trying to reconstruct a workable solution for explaining these Hebrew volitive morphemes. Stephen Kaufman's article on the נָא particle advances this proposal considerably.[34] For him, the historical development and function of the long imperative cannot be

---

[25] Ewald, *Grammar*, §293. Fassberg ("Lengthened Imperative," 8) also mentions Rudolf Meyer as sharing this view in his *Hebräische Grammatik*, 3rd ed., (Berlin: de Gruyter, 1972), §63.5b.

[26] GKC §48k.

[27] Joüon-Muraoka §48d.

[28] Matitiahu Tsevat, *A Study of the Language of the Biblical Psalms*, JBL Monograph Series 9 (Philadelphia: SBL, 1955), 111 n. 254.

[29] Tsevat (*Biblical Psalms*, 25) claims that the long imperative is the normal imperative of the psalms, stating that it is eight times as frequent as the regular imperative. Hélène Dallaire has challenged this claim, however, contending that the frequency of the long imperative to the regular imperative in Psalms is 1:1. See Dallaire, "The Syntax of Volitives in Northwest Semitic Prose" (PhD diss., Hebrew Union College, 2002), 70. (Note that this assertion does not appear in the 2014 published version of this work). Neither of these assessments are accurate. In the Psalter, the imperative occurs a total of 701 times. Of those 701 instances, the masculine singular (the only form that can be lengthened) is found 451 times. Only 111 of those forms are lengthened, which means that for the MS imperative the long form occurs 25 percent of the time in Psalms.

[30] *IBHS* §34.4a; Dallaire categorizes the view of Waltke and O'Connor and Tsevat as "stylistic variation." See *The Syntax of Volitives in Biblical Hebrew and Amarna Canaanite Prose*, LSAWS 9 (Winona Lake, IN: Eisenbrauns, 2014), 69.

[31] Mayer Lambert, *Traité de grammaire hébraïque* (Paris: Presses universitaires de France, 1946), 257 n. 2. This grammar is referenced in Dallaire, *Syntax of Volitives*, 68 n. 135, but without interaction.

[32] Lambert, *Traité de grammaire hébraïque*, 256 n. 1, notes the following contexts in which honorific requests are made: of God (Ps 5:2); of a father (Gen 27:19); of a prophet (Num 22:6); and of a priest (1 Sam 14:18).

[33] Lambert, 257 n. 2.

[34] Stephen A. Kaufman, "An Emphatic Plea for Please," *Maarav* 7 (1991):196–97.

separated from the particle נָא. For example, a first-person energic verb such as
'aktubanna was eventually realized in Hebrew as אֶכְתְּבָה־נָּא.[35] In other words,
the נָא particle developed as a result of separating the last syllable from energic
verbs. Dividing affixes from verbs is not unheard of among Northwest Semitic
languages, as Kaufman rightly notes. In Ugaritic pronominal suffixes can be separated from the verb by a word divider, as in the following example from *KTU* 1.16
VI:10:

trḥṣ . nn	She washes **him**

Also relevant to this discussion are pronominal suffixes attached to first-person
prefix verbs. It is argued that the ־ָה affix of the cohortative and the long imperative are historically related. John Huehnergard, for instance, notes that when
prefixed verbs with pronominal suffixes appear in contexts that suggest a cohortative function, the *nun* formation occurs (e.g.,אֲגָרְשֶׁנּוּ "Let me drive him out,"
Exod 23:29). Conversely, first-person consecutive preterites take pronominal suffixes without *nun* (e.g., וָאַכְרִחֵהוּ "I let him flee," Neh 13:28).[36] This observation
has to be qualified as typical, however, since exceptions do exist. For example, a
first-person consecutive preterite occurs with a *nun* suffix in Judg 15:2: וָאֶתְּנֶנָּה instead of the expected וָאֶתְּנֶהוּ*.[37] Furthermore, we need to distinguish cases where
the cohortative occurs as a stand-alone volitive form from first-person prefix forms
in volitive sequence (i.e., the *wəyiqtol*). The following example in 1 Sam 18:21
represents a stand-alone cohortative with a *nun* suffix:

1 Sam 18:21

וַיֹּאמֶר שָׁאוּל אֶתְּנֶנָּה לּוֹ וּתְהִי־לוֹ לְמוֹקֵשׁ

Saul said, "**Let me give her** to him that she might become a snare to
him."

In cases like this one, it might be better to say that the *nun* suffixal formation
is a morphological indicator of the cohortative. We will address this again in our
discussion of the cohortative below. At this point we simply observe that scholars
have long argued for a historical relationship between energic and volitive verbs.
The initial separation of the energic affix yielded the long imperative + נָא. By the
time of Biblical Hebrew, the long imperative could occur with or without נָא.

Several scholars have voiced opposition to the long imperative's volitional function. Fassberg has proposed that the long imperative indicates commands directed

---

[35] As argued by Thomas O. Lambdin, "The Junctural Origin of the West Semitic Definite Article,"
in *Near Eastern Studies in Honor of William Foxwell Albright*, ed., H. Goedicke (Baltimore:
Johns Hopkins University Press, 1971), 326 and noted by Huehnergard, "Early Hebrew Prefix-
Conjugations," 23.

[36] Huehnergard, "Early Hebrew Prefix-Conjugations," 23. See the similar observation by E. J.
Revell, "System of the Verb," 15–16.

[37] We could only find one example of this formation.

toward the speaker, as opposed to the regular imperatives, which expresses commands directed elsewhere. Sometimes the long imperative exhibits a more general relationship to the speaker, such as action benefiting the speaker or being performed with or in the presence of the speaker.[38] Direction is marked contextually, most usually by the לְ preposition with first-person pronouns. The following two examples illustrate the long imperatives investment in the speaker's interests: הִשָּׁבְעָה לִּי "Swear to me" (directed toward the speaker) versus הִשָּׁמֶר לְךָ "Watch yourself" (directed away from the speaker).[39] Shulman reaches a similar conclusion in her analysis of the Pentateuch and Former Prophets. Of the 116 instances of the long imperative, 61 of them are followed by a preposition with a first-person pronominal suffix. Another 51 of the 116 imply a preposition and pronoun, meaning that in "112 cases (97%) the speaker is requesting that an action be done for him, to him, with him, or towards him." The contexts of the remaining four occurrences, she argues, imply action that personally benefits the speaker.[40] The directional theory has been supported by Jan Joosten, who analyzes second-masculine imperatives with *nun*-pronominal suffixes of the third person as further evidence for this view.[41]

One immediate problem with this theory is that the imperative by itself already indicates the volitional desire of the speaker, which would seem to express a command that has some level of self-interest.[42] Secondly, the directional model does not adequately account for the exceptions where direction toward the speaker is not detected. Even if we were to grant that direction is the main function of the הָ-suffix of the long imperative, it apparently lost its semantic force in Biblical Hebrew, since both the preposition and pronominal suffixes were needed. It is also true that Hebrew has a fully functioning directional הָ. Its analogy to the long imperative, however, is not without difficulty. The directional הָ never takes the accent. The accent falls on the previous syllable of the word to which it is attached, unlike the long imperative whose stress falls on the final syllable.

DIRECTIONAL הָ	IMPERATIVE הָ
יָמָּה "toward the sea" (Gen 28:14)	תְּנָה אֹתוֹ "Give him up" (Gen 42:37)

The analogy with the cohortative הָ and its connection to the energic verbs as discussed above provides a more suitable option historically. Lambert's suggestion that it marks elevated requests provides a satisfactory means of explaining the long imperative's historical development and resulting function. The so-called energics were modal forms and did not necessarily indicate emphasis, which leads

---

[38] Fassberg, "Lengthened Imperative," 10.
[39] Fassberg, 10.
[40] Shulman, "Modal Verb Forms," 66.
[41] Jan Joosten, "The Lengthened Imperative with Accusative Suffix in Biblical Hebrew," *ZAW* 111 (1999): 423–26.
[42] Similarly, it is noted in Joüon-Muraoka §48d n. 1: "Of course, the imperative, by definition, is an expression of the speaker's interest."

Kaufman to suggest that the long imperative represents "a softening rather than a strengthening!"[43]

In Hebrew narrative prose, the long imperative is used by both superiors and inferiors to mark requests. In the Joseph story, for instance, inferiors and superiors use this form in familiar and unfamiliar social exchanges, in urgent and socially awkward circumstances. Twice Potiphar's wife softly requests that he lie with her:

> Gen 39:7, also v. 12
>
> שִׁכְבָה עִמִּי
>
> **Won't you lie** with me!

The longer form of the imperative has the effect of muting the abruptness of the command, turning it into a softer appeal. It is a rather shocking proposal. Similarly, Reuben pledges the lives of his two sons as collateral if Benjamin does not safely return home from their trip to Egypt to request food from Pharaoh. This appeal is expressed using the long imperative form:

> Gen 42:37
>
> אֶת־שְׁנֵי בָנַי תָּמִית אִם־לֹא אֲבִיאֶנּוּ אֵלֶיךָ תְּנָה אֹתוֹ עַל־יָדִי וַאֲנִי אֲשִׁיבֶנּוּ אֵלֶיךָ׃
>
> My two sons you may put to death if I do not bring him back to you.
> **Won't you give** him over to my hand and I will bring him back to you!

The contexts in which the long imperative occurs suggests the directness of the command has been transformed into a persuasive request. Ernst Jenni helpfully emphasizes the will of the addressee in such exchanges. He maintains that the long imperative indicates politeness in making requests but adds that the choice of the short or long form depends upon how likely it is that the addressee will act on the request. For example, short imperatives are appropriate for situations in which the fulfillment of the request is relatively certain. Long imperatives, on the other hand, do not presume the hearer will act upon a given request but rather assume it requires special consideration.[44] In the above examples, the addressee's willingness to grant what is being requested is uncertain. In the case of Potiphar's wife, she had been unsuccessful in convincing Joseph to lie with her. Jenni's insight offers a way of explaining why the long imperative is used in extenuating circumstances.

These same features are evident for long imperatives in poetic environments. The long imperative routinely appears in the psalms. In Psalm 3 the psalmist laments the affliction of the wicked, pleading with Yahweh to come to his defense. We see a similar usage in Psalm 5.

> Ps 3:8
>
> קוּמָה יְהוָה | הוֹשִׁיעֵנִי אֱלֹהַי
>
> **Arise**, Yahweh; Save me, my God.

---

[43] Kaufman, "Emphatic Plea," 197.

[44] Ernst Jenni, "Höfliche Bitte im Alten Testament," in *Congress Volume: Basel, 2001*, ed. A. Lemaire, VTSup 92 (Leiden: Brill, 2002), 10.

Ps 5:2

אֲמָרַי הַאֲזִינָה | יְהֹוָה בִּינָה הֲגִיגִי:

Give ear to my words, Yahweh,
Understand my groaning.

As Jenni explains, short imperatives do not necessarily constitute an inferior commanding God. Rather, they often appear when the psalmist is asking God to defend his people from their enemies and to remember his covenantal faithfulness. They are made in light of God's record of activity in the past.[45] When the psalmist makes entreaties like these in the above examples, he is less certain about the way in which God will respond. The long imperative therefore expresses the psalmist's plea for divine intervention on his behalf.

6.6 THE JUSSIVE

6.6.1 Morphology and Historical Development

The Hebrew jussive functions as a third, second, or first-person volitive form and can be organized into two morphological categories: primarily and secondarily marked jussives. The reason for this twofold categorization is that Hebrew marks the jussive in one of two ways. The primary marking feature is to use a morphologically shortened/apocopated form wherever possible. Third and middle-weak roots of *Qal* verbs provide the most common shortening possibility. Third-weak roots are characterized historically as having a {y} or {w} in the third root position. In Hebrew, the final {y} or {w} has been replaced by a vowel with a final *mater* {h}. As we mentioned in chapter 4, the prefix conjugation historically ended in final /u/: *yaqtulu*. The jussive form had no final vowel, which is no longer traceable in strong roots. Third-weak roots attest shortened forms in the jussive, having developed from the absence of final /u/. Hollow (or second-weak) roots likewise exhibit shortened forms in the jussive, also because it ends with Ø vowel. The long vowel of the middle root position in prefix forms is shortened in the jussive. The following chart outlines these developments:

	PREFIX CONJUGATION		JUSSIVE	
	HEBREW	**HISTORICAL DEVELOPMENT**	**HEBREW**	**HISTORICAL DEVELOPMENT**
III-weak	יִבְנֶה	*yibnayu* > *yibnay* > yibnê	יִבֶן	*yibnayØ* > *yibna* > *yibn* > yiben
Hollow	יָקוּם	*yaqūmu* > yāqūm	יָקָם	*yaqūmØ* > yāqum

---

[45] Jenni, "Höfliche Bitte," 11.

A third primarily marked jussive occurs in the *Hiphil* stem. The *hireq-yod* of the prefix conjugation is shortened to *sere* in the jussive (PC יַשְׁכִין* "he settles" vs. JUSS יַשְׁכֵן "let him settle"). This pattern is also applied to the middle-weak verbs (PC יָקִים "he makes rise" vs. JUSS יָקֵם "let him make rise"). Again, the historical absence of final /u/ in the jussive contributes to these vocalic changes.

	PREFIX CONJUGATION		JUSSIVE	
	HEBREW	**HISTORICAL DEVELOPMENT**	**HEBREW**	**HISTORICAL DEVELOPMENT**
אמן	יַאֲמִין	**yaha'minu > *ya'min > ya'mîn*	יַאֲמֵן	**yaha'minØ > *ya'min > ya'mēn*
יצא	יוֹצִיא	**yahawṣi'u > *yôṣi' > yôṣî'*	תוֹצֵא	**yahawṣi'Ø > *yôṣi' > yôṣē'*

Secondarily marked jussives occur when separate volitional particles are connected to the jussive. The reason we identify these forms as secondarily marked is because the forms themselves are indistinguishable morphologically from prefix forms. Secondary indicators offer an external means of disambiguating otherwise indistinguishable forms (e.g., strong roots). At an earlier stage of the language the external volitive markers must have correlated with the shortened forms:

NEGATIVE PREFIX CONJUGATION	NEGATIVE JUSSIVE
*lā' yaqtulu[46]	**'al yaqtulØ*

In Biblical Hebrew, negative jussives are marked with the volitive negative particle אַל in both third and second-person forms.

	PREFIX CONJUGATION	NEGATIVE JUSSIVE
3MS	יִכְתֹּב "he will write" or "let him write"	אַל־יִכְתֹּב "let him not write"
2MP	תִּירְאוּ "you will fear" or "you shall fear"	אַל־תִּירְאוּ "do not fear"

Even though the above verbal forms are identical morphologically, the negative particle secondarily marks them as jussives. Without the negative, only context can determine whether they should be read as prefix or jussive forms. The volitive particle נָא can also secondarily mark jussives, with or without negative אַל (see examples below).

The correlation between primary morphological demarcation (i.e., morphological shortening) and the volitive negative particle throughout Classical Hebrew prose is rather instructive.[47] Second-person negative jussives are the most common,

---

[46] Note that the Hebrew long /o/ in לֹא was historically long **ā*.

[47] For the purposes of this analysis, we are limiting Classical Hebrew prose to the prose sections of Genesis through 2 Kings.

occurring 142 times, while third-person negative jussives occur 55 times.[48] The morphology of these second-person jussives is distinct from third-person forms when the volitive negative accompanies them. Of the twenty-nine third-person jussives that permit morphological shortening (i.e., *Qal* hollow and III-weak forms, *Hiphil* forms of all roots), only two do not.[49] This observation contrasts the situation of the second-person jussives in which thirteen of the thirty-four morphological candidates do not exemplify the shortened jussive form.[50] The greater tendency not to shorten the second-person jussive may stem from the fact that its function is likewise distinguished from the third-person jussive. The shortened form of the third person may correspond to its function as an indirect volitional form, which contrasts the forceful nature of the second-person negativized jussive.

6.6.2 Non-Volitive Shortened Forms

Biblical Hebrew attests a few first-person prefix verbs exhibiting the morphological shortening characteristic of the jussive. Hélène Dallaire lists thirteen such examples, mostly attested in poetic texts.[51] To her list we add Isa 42:6, which attests the form וָאֹחֵז "and I seize," an apocopation of the *Hiphil* אַחְזִיק. One of the clearer examples of a first-person jussive with volitional force is וְנִרְא. It is found in the consonantal text of MT Isaiah:

Isa 41:23

הַגִּ֤ידוּ הָאֹתִיּוֹת֙ לְאָח֔וֹר וְנֵ֣דְעָ֔ה כִּ֥י אֱלֹהִ֖ים אַתֶּ֑ם אַף־תֵּיטִ֣יבוּ וְתָרֵ֔עוּ וְנִשְׁתָּעָ֖ה וְנִרְא֥

יַחְדָּֽו׃

Declare the things coming afterwards, that we may know that you are gods. Also, do good or evil, that we **may look and see** together.

The form in question follows a clearly marked cohortative (וְנִשְׁתָּעָה), which is sequential to two prefix conjugations functioning as imperatives. The Masoretes likely perceived the form as problematic, indicating that the written (*ketiv*) form

---

[48] Second-person negatives with אַל: Gen 15:1; 19:8, 17 (2×); 21:17; 22:12 (2×); 24:56; 26:2, 24; 35:17; 37:22 (2×); 42:22; 43:23; 45:5, 9, 24; 46:3; 49:4; 50:19, 21; Exod 3:5; 10:28; 12:9; 14:13; 19:15; 20:20; 23:1, 7, 21; 33:15; Lev 10:9; 11:43; 18:24; 19:4, 29, 31 (2×); 25:36; Num 4:18; 14:9 (3×), 42; 16:15, 26; 21:34; 32:5; Deut 1:21 (2×); 2:5, 9, 19 (2×); 3:2, 26; 9:4, 7, 26, 27; 20:3 (3×); 21:8; 31:6 (2×); Josh 1:7, 9 (2×); 3:4; 7:3, 19; 8:1, 4; 10:6, 8, 19 (2×), 25 (2×); 11:6; 22:19, 22; Judg 4:18; 6:18, 23; 13:4, 7; 18:9, 25; 19:20, 23 (2×); Ruth 1:20; 3:3, 11, 17; 1 Sam 1:16; 2:3; 3:17; 4:20; 6:3; 7:8; 9:20; 12:20; 16:7; 20:38; 22:23; 23:17; 26:9; 28:13; 2 Sam 1:20 (2×); 9:7; 13:12 (2×), 20, 28; 14:2, 18; 17:16; 19:20; 1 Kgs 2:9, 16; 3:26; 17:13; 20:8; 2 Kgs 1:15; 2:18; 4:3, 16, 24; 6:16; 12:8; 18:26, 31, 32; 19:6; 25:24. Third-person negatives with אַל: Gen 18:30, 32; 21:12; 31:35; 37:27; 44:18; 45:5, 20; 49:6 (2×); Exod 8:25; 16:19, 29; 19:24; 20:19; 32:22; 34:3 (2×); 36:6; Lev 16:2; Num 12:12; Deut 20:3; Josh 7:3; Judg 6:39; 13:14 (2×); Ruth 3:14; 1 Sam 17:32; 18:17; 19:4; 20:3; 21:3; 22:15; 25:25; 26:20; 2 Sam 3:29; 11:25; 13:26, 33; 19:20; 1 Kgs 2:20; 8:57 (2×); 18:40; 20:11; 22:8; 2 Kgs 6:27; 9:15; 10:19, 25; 11:15; 18:29, 30; 19:10; 23:18.

[49] 1 Sam 25:25; 2 Kgs 18:29.

[50] Gen 19:17; Num 4:18; Josh 1:7; 8:4; 22:22; Ruth 3:17; 1 Sam 12:20; 26:9; 2 Sam 13:12, 20; 14:2; 1 Kgs 3:26; 2 Kgs 4:3. See also *IBHS* §34.2.1.

[51] Deut 18:16; 1 Sam 14:36; Isa 41:23; Ezek 5:16; Hos 9:15; 11:4; Job 23:9, 11; Zeph 1:2, 3 (2×); Neh 1:4 (Dallaire, *Syntax of Volitives*, 92 n. 172).

וַנֵּרָא was to be read (*qere*) as וְנִרְאֶה (i.e., the non-apocopated form). Given that it is a III-weak root, the cohortative morpheme is no longer discernible. The apocopated form is without question problematic in this syntactical environment.

Other candidates for the first-person jussives occur in contexts not suggestive of volitional force:

> Isa 41:28
>
> וְאֵרֶא וְאֵין אִישׁ
>
> **I look**, and there is no one.

> Ezek 5:16
>
> וְרָעָב אֹסֵף עֲלֵיכֶם
>
> Famine **I will increase** (*Hiphil*) against you.

> Hos 11:4
>
> וְאַט אֵלָיו אוֹכִיל
>
> **I incline** to him (and) feed (him).

Several purported first-person jussives in the above list occur with the negative particle לֹא (Deut 18:16; 1 Sam 14:36; Hos 9:15; Job 23:9, 11). The use of לֹא suggests that the apocopated forms are not being analyzed as volitives, which are negated with אַל. It is possible that some of these shortened prefix forms represent vestiges of the old perfective preterite.[52] The following example from Job 23:11 illustrates this possibility:

> Job 23:11
>
> בַּאֲשֻׁרוֹ אָחֲזָה רַגְלִי דַּרְכּוֹ שָׁמַרְתִּי וְלֹא־אָט׃
>
> His pathway my foot grasped; his way I have kept **and not turned aside.**

The apocopated form follows a series of suffix conjugation forms indicating perfective action. Were this verb a regular prefix conjugation one would expect אַטֶּה as attested elsewhere.[53]

Several second and third-person jussives pose similar inconstancy in the use of apocopated and non-apocopated forms. Sometimes the second-person shortened form is used in a context suggesting perfective action, again possibly reflecting an archaic preterite.

---

[52] See §6.6.1. Similarly noted in *IBHS* §34.2.1c. Waltke and O'Connor also point out that wherever לֹא occurs with the jussive it indicates these verbal forms are "confounded in the Masoretic tradition" (*IBHS* §34.2.1d). Gesenius's grammar similarly suggests that these jussives may represent a misunderstanding of defective writings, but alternatively proposes that some cases (e.g., Gen 24:8) are the result of "rhythmical shortening due to the strong influence of the tone" (GKC §109d, k).

[53] See Jer 6:12; Ps 49:5.

Deut 32:18

צוּר יְלָדְךָ תֶּשִׁי

You were unmindful of the Rock that bore you[54]

Some seventy-one instances of the shortened/apocopated third-person form do not function volitionally.[55] Like the first-person forms cited above, its use with the negative particle לֹא indicates a non-volitional usage.

Gen 4:12

כִּי תַעֲבֹד אֶת־הָאֲדָמָה לֹא־תֹסֵף תֵּת־כֹּחָהּ לָךְ

When you cultivate the ground, **it will no longer** give its yield to you.

In many cases, the apocopated form occurs in contexts suggesting perfective action. In Deut 32:8, the shortened *Hiphil* refers to the point in time when God fixed the boundaries of the nations:

Deut 32:8

בְּהַנְחֵל עֶלְיוֹן גּוֹיִם בְּהַפְרִידוֹ בְּנֵי אָדָם יַצֵּב גְּבֻלֹת עַמִּים לְמִסְפַּר בְּנֵי יִשְׂרָאֵל׃

When the Most High made the nations inherit, when he divided the sons of man, **he established** the boundaries of the people, according to the number of the sons of Israel.

It may follow the adverb אָז "then:"

1 Kgs 8:1

אָז יַקְהֵל שְׁלֹמֹה אֶת־זִקְנֵי יִשְׂרָאֵל

Then Solomon **assembled** the elders of Israel.

Both of these examples could be explained as vestiges of an old preterite, as we have done for the first and second-person forms. Most of the other examples occur primarily in poetic texts.

Needless to say, we cannot reconstruct a consistent distribution of functioning preterites in Biblical Hebrew. What we have instead is a mixture of forms with inconsistent usage. This reality is evident even within the first person shortened prefix verbs. For example, its occurrence in Hos 9:15 follows another imperfective form:

Hos 9:15

עַל רֹעַ מַעַלְלֵיהֶם מִבֵּיתִי אֲגָרְשֵׁם לֹא אוֹסֵף אַהֲבָתָם

Because of their deeds, I will drive them from my house; **I will no longer** love them.

---

[54] Also referenced in §6.6.1.

[55] Exod 22:4; Num 22:19; 24:19; Deut 28:8, 21, 36; 32:8; 1 Sam 2:10; 10:5; 1 Kgs 8:1; Isa 12:1; 27:6; 41:2; 50:2; 63:3; Ezek 14:7; 16:15; 48:14; Hos 6:1; Joel 2:2, 20; Mic 3:4; 7:10; Nah 3:11; Hab 2:3; Zech 9:5; Pss 18:12; 25:9; 47:4; 58:5; 78:26; 85:14; 91:4; 107:29, 33, 35; 147:18; Job 15:33; 18:9, 12; 20:23, 26, 28; 24:14, 25; 27:8, 22; 33:11, 21, 27; 34:37; 36:14, 15; 37:4, 5; 38:24; 39:26; Prov 12:26; 15:25; Eccl 12:7; Lam 3:50; Dan 8:12; 11:4, 10, 16, 17, 18, 19, 25, 28, 30.

The context does not favor interpreting אֹסֵף perfectively. This class of shortened forms represent vestigial forms whose development were likely distinct from the jussive, even though they are no longer morphologically distinguishable in Biblical Hebrew due to the loss of final short vowels.

6.6.3 Use of the Second-Person Jussive

Negative Command. The second-person jussive mostly appears with the volitive negative אַל and functions as the negative imperative. It serves as the negative counterpart to the regular imperative—the imperative is never negated in Hebrew. The negative command routinely comes from the mouth of a social superior to an inferior. For instance, God commands Jacob not to be afraid of going down to Egypt where he will become a great nation:

Gen 46:3

אַל־תִּירָא מֵרְדָה מִצְרַיְמָה כִּי־לְגוֹי גָּדוֹל אֲשִׂימְךָ שָׁם:

Do not be afraid of going down to Egypt, for I will make you a great nation there.

In Gen 49:4, Jacob rebukes Reuben for his sin against him:

Gen 49:4

אַל־תּוֹתַר כִּי עָלִיתָ מִשְׁכְּבֵי אָבִיךָ

You shall not have preeminence, because you defiled the bed of your father.

The negative imperative is sometimes found in mixed social situations, where two relationships are in view. Returning to the Joseph story, the situation with the family of Jacob brings Reuben's firstborn status into question. He appears to be losing influence on his younger brother, Judah. Therefore, although Reuben is undeniably the firstborn of the family, he is seemingly portrayed as one among equals (i.e., equal to equal vs. superior to inferior).[56] In the deliberation of Jacob's sons concerning the fate of Joseph, one finds two second-person negative commands before and after an imperative as Reuben attempts to assert his firstborn

---

[56] The subtle interplay of these volitive forms in this episode is lost on those who wish to divide Genesis 37 into two independent narratives on source-critical grounds. Source critics typically divide the story into J and E along the lines of Judah and the Ishmaelites (assigned to J) versus Reuben and the Midianites (assigned to E); e.g., Baruch J. Schwartz, "How the Compiler of the Pentateuch Worked: the Composition of Genesis 37," in *The Book of Genesis: Composition, Reception, and Interpretation*, ed. Craig A. Evans et al.; VTSup 152 (Leiden: Brill, 2012), 265–67; Joel S. Baden, *The Composition of the Pentateuch: Renewing the Documentary Hypothesis* (New Haven: Yale University Press, 2012), 37; Jeffery Stackert, "Pentateuchal Coherence and the Science of Reading," in *The Formation of the Pentateuch: Bridging the Academic Cultures of Europe, Israel, and North America*, ed. Jan C. Gertz et al. FAT 111 (Tübingen: Mohr Siebeck, 2016), 260–61. One argument against this approach and in favor of narrative unity is the sustained emphasis throughout the Joseph story on the struggle between Reuben and Judah, with Judah gaining the upper hand. A study of the narrative's careful choice of volitive forms for the verbal exchanges among Jacob's brothers further supports this interest.

authority over his brothers.[57] This example demonstrates the imperatival thrust of the second-person jussive:

Gen 37:22

אַל־תִּשְׁפְּכוּ־דָם֩ הַשְׁלִ֨יכוּ אֹת֜וֹ אֶל־הַבּ֣וֹר הַזֶּ֗ה אֲשֶׁ֤ר בַּמִּדְבָּר֙ וְיָ֖ד אַל־תִּשְׁלְחוּ־ב֑וֹ

Do not shed blood. Throw him into this pit which is in the wilderness, but **do not lay** a hand on him.

Like the imperative, the negative imperative is not limited to superior-inferior relationships but can also be expressed by an inferior to a superior. This usage often takes place in human entreaties to God, as when Moses petitions God not to accept the offering of the sons of Korah:

Num 16:15

אַל־תֵּ֖פֶן אֶל־מִנְחָתָ֑ם

Do not regard their offering!

The people of Israel cried out to the prophet Samuel, urging him not to cease praying to Yahweh on their behalf:

1 Sam 7:8

אַל־תַּחֲרֵ֣שׁ מִמֶּ֔נּוּ מִזְּעֹ֖ק אֶל־יְהוָ֣ה אֱלֹהֵ֑ינוּ וְיֹשִׁעֵ֖נוּ מִיַּ֥ד פְּלִשְׁתִּֽים׃

Do not cease crying out for us to Yahweh our God, that he might save us from the hand of the Philistines.

Positive Command. In a few cases, the second-person jussive communicates a positive command. In 1 Sam 10:8, the prophet Samuel instructs King Saul to wait for him at Gilgal where he will offer sacrifices to Yahweh before the battle against the Philistines:

1 Sam 10:8

שִׁבְעַ֣ת יָמִ֣ים תּוֹחֵ֗ל עַד־בּוֹאִ֣י אֵלֶ֔יךָ וְהוֹדַעְתִּ֣י לְךָ֔ אֵ֖ת אֲשֶׁ֥ר תַּעֲשֶֽׂה׃

Seven days **you shall wait** until I come to you and inform you what you must do.

The shortened form of the *Hiphil* marks the form as a jussive and not the prefix conjugation (i.e., תּוֹחֵל not תּוֹחִיל). Similarly, God commands Ezekiel to feed his stomach.

Ezek 3:3

בֶּן־אָדָ֗ם בִּטְנְךָ֤ תַֽאֲכֵל֙ וּמֵעֶ֣יךָ תְמַלֵּ֔א אֵ֚ת הַמְּגִלָּ֣ה הַזֹּ֔את אֲשֶׁ֥ר אֲנִ֖י נֹתֵ֣ן אֵלֶ֑יךָ

Son of man, **feed** your stomach and fill your innards with this scroll I am giving to you.

---

[57] This point is important in understanding the social status of the speaker because he is simply an equal trying to assert himself as a superior. See Judith Irvine, "Strategies of Status Manipulation in the Wolof Greeting" in *Explorations in the Ethnography of Speaking*, ed. Richard Bauman and Joel Sherzer (Cambridge: Cambridge University Press, 1974), 167.

Once again, the shortened *Hiphil* formally marks the verb as a jussive (i.e., תֹּאכֵל, not תַּאֲכִיל).

This usage is more difficult to detect in Biblical Hebrew insofar as the distinction in most verbal roots between the prefix and jussive forms is no longer evident. Furthermore, for those verbs that permit the morphological shortening characteristic of the jussive, the shortened form is not always used. Part of the problem may stem from the prefix conjugation's ability to function as a positive command (see chapter 5). Admittedly, some of these prefix forms may have been jussives before the loss of final vowels in Hebrew. Nonetheless, a few non-shortened forms appear to function as positive commands, as in the following example:

Exod 24:24

מִזְבַּח אֲדָמָה֙ תַּעֲשֶׂה־לִּי֒ וְזָבַחְתָּ עָלָיו אֶת־עֹלֹתֶ֙יךָ֙ וְאֶת־שְׁלָמֶ֔יךָ אֶת־צֹאנְךָ֖ וְאֶת־בְּקָרֶ֑ךָ

An earthen altar **you shall make** for me and you shall sacrifice upon it your burnt offerings, your well-being offerings, your sheep, and your cattle.

The jussive form for this III-weak root would have been תַּֽעַשׂ, but the long form occurs instead.

Conversely, in situations where we might expect a prefix form, we sometimes find a shortened jussive. In Job 40:9 the shortened form follows a series of prefix verbs expressing God's questions to Job.

Job 40:8–9

הַאַף תָּפֵר מִשְׁפָּטִ֑י תַּ֝רְשִׁיעֵ֗נִי לְמַ֣עַן תִּצְדָּֽק׃ וְאִם־זְר֖וֹעַ כָּאֵ֥ל ׀ לָ֑ךְ וּ֝בְק֗וֹל כָּמֹ֥הוּ תַרְעֵֽם׃

Will you also frustrate my justice? Will you condemn me so that you are just? Or do you have an arm like God? With a voice like his **can you thunder**?

In this context, the shortened form most likely does not indicate a jussive function.

Overall, this category is relatively small in Biblical Hebrew, yielding only eleven potential examples of a morphologically marked second-person jussive.[58] The default positive command in Biblical Hebrew is the imperative, with the second-person prefix conjugation providing a secondary means of expressing commands. In short, the second-person jussive as a positive command is largely redundant and unnecessary, which explains its paucity of usage in the Hebrew Bible. So, the second-person jussive is mainly reserved for expressing negative commands.

---

[58] Deut 32:18; 1 Sam 10:8; 2 Kgs 10:25; Isa 58:10; Ezek 3:3; Pss 71:21; 104:20; Job 10:17; 13:27; 40:9; Dan 9:25.

6.6.4 Use of the Third-Person Jussive

Indirect Request. The third-person jussive offers a means of expressing concern or desire in an indirect manner.[59] It avoids the forcefulness of the imperative and the negated second-person jussive. The third-person jussive is used to express an indirect request in one of three ways:

1. An indirect request that concerns the action of the addressee.
2. An indirect request that concerns the action of the speaker.
3. An indirect request that concerns the action of a third party.

Genesis 37:27 illustrates a request involving the action of the addressees.

Gen 37:27

לְכוּ וְנִמְכְּרֶנּוּ לַיִּשְׁמְעֵאלִים וְיָדֵנוּ **אַל־תְּהִי־בֹו** כִּי־אָחִינוּ בְשָׂרֵנוּ הוּא

Come on, let us sell him to the Ishmaelites; **let** our hand **not be** against him for he is our brother, our flesh.

Here, Judah successfully convinces his brothers to spare the life of Joseph, even though he is not the elder brother. The third-person jussive imbeds a volitive sequence: imperative + consecutive preterite + jussive. Judah begins with a forceful command that is, nevertheless, a virtual interjection or call to action, followed by an indirect reminder that Joseph is still their brother. The social situation is complex and may reflect two siblings, Reuben and Judah, each attempting to assert himself as the legitimate family leader.

In 2 Sam 13:33, Joab asks David not to take Absalom's death to heart in thinking that all his sons are dead. The request comes from an inferior to a superior and concerns the action of the addressee:

2 Sam 13:33

וְעַתָּה **אַל־יָשֵׂם** אֲדֹנִי הַמֶּלֶךְ אֶל־לִבּוֹ דָּבָר לֵאמֹר כָּל־בְּנֵי הַמֶּלֶךְ מֵתוּ

Now, **let not** my lord the king **take** the matter to heart, saying all the sons of the king have died.

The following two examples illustrate indirect requests that relate to the action of the speaker:

Num 23:10

תָּמֹת נַפְשִׁי מוֹת יְשָׁרִים

Let my soul **die** the death of the upright.

---

[59] This use of terminology is not the same as Douglas M. Gropp, who attempts to establish categories "direct" and "indirect" volitives on the following basis: "The negative counterpart of a coordinated direct volitive is wə'al- + jussive/cohortative, while the negative counterpart for an indirect volitive is wəlō' + imperfect." See "Function of the Finite Verb," 51.

1 Kgs 20:32

תְּחִי־נָא נַפְשִׁי

Please, **let** my soul **live**.

At other times, the request concerns the action of a third party:

Gen 44:33

וְהַנַּעַר יַעַל עִם־אֶחָיו

Let the lad **go up** with his brothers.

Exod 16:19

אִישׁ אַל־יוֹתֵר מִמֶּנּוּ עַד־בֹּקֶר

Let no one **leave** any of it until morning.

Allowance. In several contexts social superiors use the third-person jussive to express allowance. These statements grant permission for the addressee to act in his or her own favor. For example, the military commanders are to give permission to a man to return home to dedicate his new dwelling.

Deut 20:5

מִי־הָאִישׁ אֲשֶׁר בָּנָה בַיִת־חָדָשׁ וְלֹא חֲנָכוֹ יֵלֵךְ וְיָשֹׁב לְבֵיתוֹ פֶּן־יָמוּת בַּמִּלְחָמָה
וְאִישׁ אַחֵר יַחְנְכֶנּוּ׃

Who is the man who has built a new house but has not dedicated it? **Let him go** and **return** to his house lest he die in battle and other man dedicate it.

Similarly, those afraid of the horrors of battle are relinquished of their military obligations:

Judges 7:3

מִי־יָרֵא וְחָרֵד יָשֹׁב וְיִצְפֹּר[60] מֵהַר הַגִּלְעָד

Whoever is afraid and trembling, **let him turn back** and depart from Mount Gilead.

Indirect Command. The third-person jussive can also relate indirect commands. Several examples of this usage are found in the ritual material from the Pentateuch, though it is not limited to that genre. For instance, the jussive offers instruction concerning the restitution of a person who has sinned:

Lev 5:16

וְאֶת־חֲמִישִׁתוֹ יוֹסֵף עָלָיו וְנָתַן אֹתוֹ לַכֹּהֵן

Let him add a fifth to it and give it to the priest.

In Judg 13:14, the angel of Yahweh instructs Manoah regarding his wife's obligations during her pregnancy with Samson:

---

[60] Note that this verb is not primarily or secondarily marked as a jussive. However, the context indicates it should be interpreted as a jussive in sequence with יָשֹׁב.

Judg 13:14

מִכֹּל אֲשֶׁר־יֵצֵא מִגֶּפֶן הַיַּיִן לֹא תֹאכַל וְיַיִן וְשֵׁכָר **אַל־תֵּשְׁתְּ** וְכָל־טֻמְאָה אַל־תֹּאכַל

From anything that comes from the vine she shall not eat. Wine or strong drink **let her not drink**, nor let her eat any unclean thing.

Prayer. This third-person jussive occurs in prayers to God. Its indirectness in such contexts communicates humble entreaty. Eli asks for Yahweh to bless El-kanah and Hannah with many more children in the place of Samuel.

1 Sam 2:20

יָשֵׂם יְהוָה לְךָ זֶרַע מִן־הָאִשָּׁה הַזֹּאת תַּחַת הַשְּׁאֵלָה אֲשֶׁר שָׁאַל לַיהוָה

May Yahweh **establish** seed for you from this woman in place of the request that he made to Yahweh.

Following Solomon's dedication of the temple, he prays the following benediction.

1 Kgs 8:57

יְהִי יְהוָה אֱלֹהֵינוּ עִמָּנוּ כַּאֲשֶׁר הָיָה עִם־אֲבֹתֵינוּ אַל־יַעַזְבֵנוּ וְאַל־יִטְּשֵׁנוּ׃

May Yahweh our God **be** with us as he was with our fathers. May he not leave us or forsake us.

Special Declaration. A final category of usage involves special declarations. These declarations are statements that are to be understood as actions, or what are sometimes called "speech acts" or "performatives." In chapter 5 (§5.6.2.5) we discussed the performative use of the suffix conjugation, in which the utterance is simultaneously the action that brings about what is stated in the utterance. The clearest examples of the jussive used in this way are found in the creation account of Genesis 1. The initial declaration of creation indicates that the spoken word of God simultaneously brought the created thing into existence.

Gen 1:3

וַיֹּאמֶר אֱלֹהִים יְהִי אוֹר וַיְהִי־אוֹר׃

God said, "**Let there be** light," and there was light.[61]

The consecutive preterite following the jussive reinforces its performativity by stating perfectively that the result of the declaration is that light now exists.

A similar usage occurs in the formulaic "Long live the king" statements throughout the Hebrew Bible. For example, Hushai declares his support of Absalom's rise to power:

---

[61] See also Gen 1:6, 9 (unmarked jussive), 11, 14, 20 (unmarked jussive), 22, 24. Note the shift in person for the creation of humanity in verse 26: נַעֲשֶׂה אָדָם "Let us make man" (unmarked cohortative). Rather than the function of a performative jussive, the cohortative states the action that God is going to do. The act of creation is expressed in verse 27: וַיִּבְרָא אֱלֹהִים אֶת־הָאָדָם "God created man." The use of the first-person verbal form contrasts with the indirect nature of the jussive, instead emphasizing God's personal investment in the creation of humanity.

2 Sam 16:16

יְחִי הַמֶּלֶךְ יְחִי הַמֶּלֶךְ:

Let the king **live**! **Let** the king **live**!

Tryggve N. D. Mettinger describes this formula as an "elliptic oath" signifying the declaration of a royal covenant.[62] He notes that swearing this oath not only recognizes the authority of the king, but also indicates one's acceptance of and submission to that authority.[63] The oath therefore functions performatively as an act of verbal allegiance.

6.7 THE COHORTATIVE

6.7.1 Morphology and Historical Development

The cohortative volitional form as it appears in MT looks like a first-person prefix conjugation with an unaccented הֲ- suffix. The cohortative is exclusive to the first person and can be either singular or plural.

	PREFIX CONJUGATION	COHORTATIVE
1CS	אֲדַבֵּר "I will speak"	אֲדַבְּרָה "Let me speak"
1CP	נִכְרֹת "We will cut"	נִכְרְתָה "Let us cut"

III-weak verbs prohibit this morphological distinction because the third-weak consonant has been replaced with a final vowel: נַעֲשֶׂה "We will make" or "Let us make." In such cases only context can determine whether it is a cohortative or not. Also, once pronominal suffixes are attached the final /a/ is no longer present. However, scholars have noted that *n* suffixes may in some cases preserve the cohortative ending (see §6.5.3 above).

As with the jussive, scholars have appealed to the comparative linguistic data in explaining the morphological development of the Hebrew cohortative. William L. Moran's influential study cites El Amarna **yaqtula* as the predecessor of Hebrew cohortatives.[64] Its corresponding forms are as follows:

INDICATIVE		VOLITIVE	
Imperfective	**yaqtulu*	Jussive	**yaqtulØ*
		Cohortative	**yaqtula*

---

[62] Tryggve N. D. Mettinger, *King and Messiah: The Civil and Sacral Legitimation of the Israelite Kings*, Coniectanea Biblica: Old Testament Series 8 (Lund: CWK Gleerup, 1976), 131–36.

[63] Mettinger, 134.

[64] Moran, "Early Canaanite *yaqtula*," 1–19.

Other scholars, however, have questioned this reconstruction. Steven E. Fassberg connects the final /a/ of the cohortative and the long imperative to the Akkadian ventive morpheme -a(m).[65] The Akkadian ventive is attached to verbs of motion marking the action as being directed toward the speaker or writer. For example, *ana bītim īrub* means "he went into the house," whereas *ana bītim īrub**am*** means "he came into the house," indicating that the motion is toward the speaker/writer.[66] Fassberg and others have thus argued that the cohortative הָ◌- marks action directed toward the speaker, not volition.[67] We have already treated this argument for the long imperative above and found it lacking. Similar objections apply to the cohortative as well. Beyond matters of function, however, the morphological correspondence between these morphemes poses other problems. The Akkadian ventive alters its form according to the following situations: -a(m) on verbs without endings, -m after -ī of the 2FS, and -nim after -ū and -ā of the 2P and 3P.[68] In other words, the -m functions as the primary morpheme of the ventive, not the -a. Furthermore, this same morpheme can also mark the 1CS dative suffix, "to me," and is often not clearly distinguishable from its ventive usage.[69] Although the directional meaning of the Akkadian ventive is largely accepted, its morphological and functional correspondence to the Hebrew cohortative הָ◌- poses serious problems.

As Moran noted, the vast majority of *yaqtula* forms attested in the Amarna Canaanite texts cannot be explained as ventives. Instead, they occur in speech contexts that indicate volitive usage. It is more likely that this form represented a West Semitic volitive—preserved in the Hebrew cohortative—and not the Akkadian ventive. Moran identified two categories of volitional usage for *yaqtula*: (1) to express a wish, request, or command, and (2) to express purpose or result in dependent clauses.[70]

6.7.2 Use of the Cohortative

The Hebrew cohortative represents the functional equivalent of the third-person jussive. It provides a means of expressing the wish or desire of the speaker in the first person. By using this form to address circumstances that concern himself or his associates, the speaker can make his will known without coming across forcefully. The singular form refers exclusively to actions related the speaker (i.e., "Let me X"), while the plural form involves the speaker and one or more associate(s) (i.e., "Let us X"). The major concern of the speaker is to impress his own desire

---

[65] See Stephen E. Fassberg, *Studies in the Syntax of Biblical Hebrew* (Hebrew) (Jerusalem: Magnes, 1994), 34–35 n. 100; Fassberg, "Lengthened Imperative," 13.

[66] Huehnergard, *Grammar of Akkadian*, 133–34. See also von Soden and Mayer, *Grundriss der akkadischen Grammatik*, §82.

[67] See also Gentry, "System of the Finite Verb," 29.

[68] Huehnergard, *Grammar of Akkadian*, 133.

[69] Huehnergard, 135; Richard Caplice with Daniel Snell, *Introduction to Akkadian*, 4th ed. (Rome: Pontifical Biblical Institute, 2002), §36.

[70] Moran, "Early Canaanite *yaqtula*," 2–6. For more on dependent clauses in verbal sequence, see §5.8.3

upon the addressee politely so that that person might accommodate the will of the speaker.

Request. The cohortative commonly indicates the request of an individual, either to a superior or inferior, or to an individual or group. Both singular and plural forms of the cohortative can make requests. Singular forms represent the request of an individual, whereas plural forms express the collective request of a group.

Individual to a Superior

1 Sam 9:6

עַתָּה֙ **נֵֽלֲכָה** שָּׁ֔ם אוּלַ֗י יַגִּ֤יד לָ֨נוּ֙ אֶת־דַּרְכֵּ֔נוּ אֲשֶׁר־הָלַ֖כְנוּ עָלֶֽיהָ׃

Now **let us go** there. Perhaps he will relate to us the journey on which we are going.

Individual to an Inferior

1 Sam 9:10

לְכָ֣ה ׀ **וְנֵלֵ֑כָה**

Come, **let us go**.

Individual to a Group

Judg 8:24

אֶשְׁאֲלָ֤ה מִכֶּם֙ שְׁאֵלָ֔ה וּתְנוּ־לִ֕י אִ֖ישׁ נֶ֥זֶם שְׁלָלֹ֑ו

Let me make a request of you that each of you give to me a ring of his spoil.

Group to a Superior

Exod 5:3

נֵ֣לֲכָה נָּ֞א דֶּ֣רֶךְ֙ שְׁלֹ֣שֶׁת יָמִ֣ים בַּמִּדְבָּ֔ר

Please, **let us go** a three-day journey into the wilderness.

Suggestion. This category of usage arises because a number of examples defy being categorized as requests, but instead reflect suggestions. These suggestions occur with either singular or plural cohortatives and can address individuals or groups.

Gen 19:8

אֹוצִֽיאָה־נָּ֤א אֶתְהֶן֙ אֲלֵיכֶ֔ם וַעֲשׂ֣וּ לָהֶ֔ן כַּטֹּ֖וב בְּעֵינֵיכֶ֑ם

Please, **let me bring** them to you. Do to them what is good in your eyes.

Deut 13:3

נֵֽלְכָ֞ה אַחֲרֵ֨י אֱלֹהִ֤ים אֲחֵרִים֙ אֲשֶׁ֣ר לֹֽא־יְדַעְתָּ֔ם וְנָֽעָבְדֵֽם׃

Let us go after other gods whom we do not know that we might serve them.

Deliberation. The cohortative can also indicate deliberation. As a deliberative statement, the singular cohortative expresses the personal deliberation of an individual, while the plural reflects the deliberation of a group. This category overlaps with the category "suggestion" listed above. However, the example of personal deliberation seems to fall outside the lines of "suggestion," and warrants a separate category.

Personal Deliberation

Exod 3:3

אָסֻרָה־נָּא וְאֶרְאֶה אֶת־הַמַּרְאֶה הַגָּדֹל הַזֶּה מַדּוּעַ לֹא־יִבְעַר הַסְּנֶה׃

Please, **let me turn aside** and see this great sight, why the bush is not burned up.

Group Deliberation

Gen 37:17

נֵלְכָה דֹּתָיְנָה

Let us go to Dothan.

Statement of Desire. The cohortative can declare the will or desire of the speaker, but in such a way that does not reflect a request, suggestion, or deliberation. This usage denotes the unrealized will of the speaker, which is in keeping with the irrealis nature of volitive forms in general.

Exod 15:1

אָשִׁירָה לַיהוָה כִּי־גָאֹה גָּאָה

I will sing to Yahweh, for he is highly exalted.

Judg 15:1

אָבֹאָה אֶל־אִשְׁתִּי הֶחָדְרָה

I will go to my wife in her room.

In Other Irrealis Utterances. The cohortative often occurs in conditional clauses, functioning as either the protasis or apodosis statement.

Protasis

Job 16:6

אִם־אֲדַבְּרָה לֹא־יֵחָשֵׂךְ כְּאֵבִי

If **I speak**, my pain is not relieved.

Apodosis

1 Kgs 21:2

אִם טוֹב בְּעֵינֶיךָ אֶתְּנָה־לְךָ כֶּסֶף מְחִיר זֶה׃

If it is good in your eyes, **I will give** you silver at this price.

Long Consecutives. Finally, the cohortative attests several lengthened forms that also exhibit the consecutive prefix—i.e., *wa-* + doubled prefix consonant. These forms may represent a shift in the cohortative's usage, which may signify that the original volitional meaning was losing its force. Some scholars have noted that this usage tends to frequent later Biblical Hebrew texts.[71] It is a dominant feature of Qumran Hebrew as well.[72] These observations are tempered by the existence of an indicative *yaqtula* in the Amarna corpus as well.[73] As Moran explains, the use of the cohortative in sequential result clauses could have yielded a shift from the expression of willed result to that of actual result.[74]

Num 8:19

וָאֶתְּנָה אֶת־הַלְוִיִּם נְתֻנִים | לְאַהֲרֹן

I have given the Levites as a gift to Aaron.

2 Sam 7:9

וָאַכְרִתָה אֶת־כָּל־אֹיְבֶיךָ מִפָּנֶיךָ

I have cut off all your enemies from before you.

6.8 THE PARTICLE נָא

The נָא particle is traditionally identified as the particle of entreaty. Gesenius translated this particle as "pray!" and explained it as an emphatic interjection used to emphasize a demand, warning, or entreaty.[75] Joüon and Muraoka call it an "entreating interjection" used to add a "usually weak entreating nuance equivalent to a stressed and lengthened *please* in English."[76] Most of the time it is attached to one of the volitive forms, usually with a *maqqep*, as the following examples illustrate:

Imperative (Short)	Gen 45:4	גְּשׁוּ־נָא אֵלַי	**Please**, come closer to me.
Imperative (Long)	Judg 16:10	עַתָּה הַגִּידָה־נָּא לִי בַּמֶּה תֵּאָסֵר	Now **please**, tell me how you might be bound.
Jussive	Gen 47:4	יֵשְׁבוּ־נָא עֲבָדֶיךָ בְּאֶרֶץ גֹּשֶׁן	**Please**, let your servants dwell in the land of Goshen.
Cohortative	Exod 5:3	נֵלֲכָה נָּא דֶּרֶךְ שְׁלֹשֶׁת יָמִים בַּמִּדְבָּר	**Please**, let us go a three-days journey into the wilderness.

---

[71] E.g., Gentry, "System of the Finite Verb," 24.

[72] See Elisha Qimron, *The Hebrew of the Dead Sea Scrolls*, HSS 29 (Winona Lake, IN: Eisenbrauns, 1986), 44.

[73] Moran, "Early Canaanite *yaqtula*," 16, 17–18.

[74] Moran, 18.

[75] GKC §105b.

[76] Joüon-Muraoka §105c.

Gesenius also claimed that the נָא particle occurs once in the Hebrew Old Testament with a suffix conjugation verb.[77] He references:

Gen 40:14

וְעָשִׂיתָ־נָּא עִמָּדִי חֶסֶד

Please, show me kindness.

The presence of נָא with *wəqātal* in this example indicates it is more likely analyzed as a second-person unmarked volitive. It stands as the first of a three-member volitive sequence expressing explicit consecution:[78]

וְעָשִׂיתָ־נָּא	Please, show . . .
וְהִזְכַּרְתַּנִי	and mention me . . .
וְהוֹצֵאתַנִי	and bring me out . . .

In addition to verbal forms, נָא can be attached to the presentative particle הִנֵּה "look, behold." This usage takes place when something is being presented in the context of a request or entreaty.[79] When Abram and Sarai sojourned in Egypt, Abram asked Sarai to pretend she was his sister because of her physical beauty:

Gen 12:11

הִנֵּה־נָא יָדַעְתִּי כִּי אִשָּׁה יְפַת־מַרְאֶה אָתְּ

Look, please! I know that you are woman beautiful in appearance.

The combination הִנֵּה־נָא signals that the speaker is making a request, here in an extenuating circumstance. The actual request comes later in verse 13 in the form of an imperative + נָא:

Gen 12:13

אִמְרִי־נָא אֲחֹתִי אָתְּ לְמַעַן יִיטַב־לִי בַעֲבוּרֵךְ

Please, say you are my sister, so that it will go well for me on your account.

Similarly, in 1 Kgs 20:31 הִנֵּה־נָא anticipates a request, this time with cohortative + נָא:

---

[77] Joüon-Muraoka §105b (308 n. 1).

[78] See §5.8.3

[79] BDB, 244.

1 Kgs 20:31

הִנֵּה־נָא שָׁמַעְנוּ כִּי מַלְכֵי בֵּית יִשְׂרָאֵל כִּי־מַלְכֵי חֶסֶד הֵם נָשִׂימָה נָּא שַׂקִּים בְּמָתְנֵינוּ וַחֲבָלִים בְּרֹאשֵׁנוּ

See here! We have heard that the kings of the house of Israel are indeed merciful kings. **Please, let us put** sackcloth on our loins and cords on our heads.

The same sense of entreaty is observable when נָא accompanies the conditional particle אִם. In such examples נָא stands with אִם at the head of the protasis, and then is repeated in the stated request, which occurs in the apodosis.

Gen 18:3

אִם־נָא מָצָאתִי חֵן בְּעֵינֶיךָ אַל־נָא תַעֲבֹר מֵעַל עַבְדֶּךָ

Please, if I have found favor in your eyes, **please do not pass by** your servant.

This expression is structurally the same as הִנֵּה־נָא. Also, this example illustrates נָא with אַל, the marker of negative volitives. As a volitive particle, whenever נָא appears with a volitive statement, it will come after the negative particle אַל. This condition only applies to jussives (second or third-person) and cohortatives, however, since Hebrew never negates the imperative form itself. Instead, Hebrew negates second-person commands by attaching אַל to the second-person jussive (see above). Speakers can also use the stronger negative command consisting of the prefix conjugation + לֹא, traditionally rendered in English, "You shall not X."[80] The forceful nature of the latter negative command does not allow for a combination with נָא, which typically occurs in the context of entreaty.

A different interpretation of נָא has challenged its status as a volitional particle. Thomas O. Lambdin has argued the entreaty interpretation is unfounded, instead proposing it is a logical particle marking consequence. He explains, "The particle seems rather to denote that the command in question is a logical consequence, either of an immediately preceding statement or the general situation in which it is uttered."[81] Lambdin points to its appearance with הִנֵּה as exemplary, since a הִנֵּה clause often results in an imperatival statement. He cites the following example from Judg 19:9, interpreting the נָא attached to the imperative as marking the consequence of the preceding הִנֵּה clause:

Judg 19:9

הִנֵּה נָא רָפָה הַיּוֹם לַעֲרֹב לִינוּ־נָא

Since the day has drawn to a close, spend the night here (trans. Lambdin).

Waltke and O'Connor and Fassberg all follow Lambdin's analysis of נָא.[82]

---

[80] See §5.7.2.

[81] Lambdin §136.

[82] *IBHS* §34.7a; Fassberg, *Syntax of Biblical Hebrew*, 70–73. Both Kaufman ("Emphatic Plea," 196) and Shulman ("Particle נָא," 58) criticize Waltke and O'Connor for their inconsistency in

Other scholars have been critical of this recent interpretation. Timothy Wilt outlines several objections:[83]

1. Why does נָא occur in some utterances showing a logical link with prior statements or situations but not others?
2. Why is נָא attached to volitives initiating an utterance no more closely linked with the context than others without נָא?
3. How would one explain the difference between נָא and וְעַתָּה, the latter of which does function as a logical connector?
4. What would נָא functionally add to the grammatical structure of requests (e.g., circumstantial sentence + volitional sentence + desired result)?
5. Why does נָא appear in narrative records of conversation but never in Leviticus and only twice in Deuteronomy, although they are filled with volitive expressions?

For these reasons, Wilt believes earlier explanations of נָא as marking politeness were more acceptable. He appeals to the sociolinguistic contexts of volitional statements, particularly as it relates to politeness. When נָא is attached to volitional forms, it represents "redressive action," that is, indirect requests in which the speaker has regard for the face of the hearer. To put it another way, "volitionals without *nā'* are *relatively* balder than those with *nā'*."[84]

Shulman has also challenged the Lambdin hypothesis in her diachronic study of נָא.[85] She limits her corpus to the narrative prose material found in the Pentateuch and Former Prophets, analyzing every instance of נָא. Shulman concludes that this particle has a single function—to designate a given utterance as a "polite and personal request."[86] More specifically, when נָא follows a jussive it marks an explicit request; without it the jussive makes a request or expresses a wish in third person. With an imperative it turns a typically forceful command into a polite and personal request. When נָא is used with the cohortative, it seeks permission or approval to act; with נָא the cohortative expresses the speaker's intention to act. It occurs with הִנֵּה and אִם in contexts where a request is being made.[87]

Shulman's study offers a compelling interpretive framework for the function of נָא. Nonetheless, Brent Christiansen has isolated a set of Shulman's examples that resist being designated a polite request.[88] These are cohortatives with נָא in soliloquy, which would involve the speaker making a polite request of himself.

---

identifying it as the "precative particle" or "particle of entreaty" (*IBHS* 31.7.2.a [517 n. 63] and 32.2.3.d [533 n. 32], respectively).

[83] Timothy Wilt, "A Sociolinguistic Analysis of *nā'*," *VT* 46 (1996): 237–39.
[84] Wilt, "Analysis of *nā'*," 242.
[85] Shulman, "The Particle נָא in Biblical Hebrew Prose," *HS* 40 (1999): 57–82.
[86] Shulman, 81.
[87] Shulman, 81–82.
[88] Brent Christiansen, "A Linguistic Analysis of the Biblical Particle *nā'*: A Test Case," *VT* 59 (2009): 379–93.

Christiansen points out four examples that make less sense when נָא is translated as "Please."[89]

Gen 18:21	אֵרֲדָה־נָּא וְאֶרְאֶה	**"Please**, let me go down and see" (God speaking to himself)
Exod 3:3	אָסֻרָה־נָּא וְאֶרְאֶה אֶת־הַמַּרְאֶה הַגָּדֹל הַזֶּה	**"Please**, let me turn aside and see this great sight" (Moses speaking to himself)
2 Sam 14:15	אֲדַבְּרָה־נָּא אֶל־הַמֶּלֶךְ	**"Please**, let me speak to the king" (woman of Tekoa speaking to herself)
Ps 122:8	אֲדַבְּרָה־נָּא שָׁלוֹם בָּךְ	**"Please**, let me say: Peace to you" (David speaking to himself)

Christiansen proposes that נָא marks a propositive clause—that is, a clause introducing a proposal or suggestions.[90] This meaning includes the notion of entreaty advanced in Shulman's study, but also broadens it, since a proposal "has a softening effect on the speech segment conveyed to the addressee, suggesting that his response or compliance to the proposal is elective."[91] Christiansen's approach reintroduces the connection between נָא and the long imperative, as discussed above. If the modal energics provide the historical origins of these two volitional features in the Hebrew language, it is reasonable to explain how this propositive meaning could have developed. As an irrealis mood conveying actions the speaker wishes to be realized, these energic morphological elements were then adapted to mark polite ways of making requests and offering suggestions.[92] The *-anna* affix was initially applied to the imperative, but once *-(n)na* became a separate morpheme it could be used with any volitional verb.

Finally, Peter Juhás has offered an entire monograph on the particle נָא. Juhás examines the way in which the ancient versions (LXX, Peshitta, and Vulgate) translated this particle as a means of understanding its meaning and function in Hebrew. He believes the evidence from its distributive usage throughout the Old Testament and the Ancient Versions defies a single categorization like politeness. Instead, its meaning depends on whether it occurs in one of two levels of discourse—the interaction level versus the representational level. The interaction level discourse refers to interpersonal dialogue, whereas the representational level refers to interjections or assertions. At the representational level, the main function of the particle נָא is to mark assertion, or even sometimes emotionality. In such cases the particle draws the attention of the hearer to the focal point of the utterance. The interaction level is a secondary function, what Juhás calls a "side effect" (*Nebeneffekt*) of assertion. The notion of politeness shows up in interpersonal dialogue where the will of the speaker is being impressed upon the listener. The communicative effect can be

---

89 Christiansen, "Biblical Particle *nā*'," 385.
90 Christiansen, 387, 92.
91 Christiansen, 392.
92 Kaufman, "Emphatic Plea," 197.

both positive (polite entreaty) or negative, however, since nonpolite expressions containing נָא can occur.[93] For example, God states rather sarcastically to postexilic Israel through Malachi, "Please, offer it to your governor!" (Mal 1:8).

Juhás's study advances our understanding of נָא considerably. For one, it demonstrates the difficulty ancient translators had in knowing how to render this particle, with less than consistent results. His emphasis on its representational nature is helpful, although it may not upend previous proposals to interpret נָא as a form of polite speech. If it were truly a representational/presentative particle by definition, it is difficult to explain why the addition of הִנֵּה would have been necessary in certain environments. Even though Christiansen's treatment is much briefer, his model has more explanatory power in accounting for its breadth of usage.

In this chapter we have discussed the morphosyntax of Hebrew volitives. We have also considered the social status of speaker and addressee, as well as how these roles impact our interpretation of volitional exchange.

6.9 EXERCISES

Translate the following Hebrew sentences into English. Parse all volitive forms (stem, conjugation, person, gender, number, and root) and analyze their function. Identify any volitive sequences as they occur. Also, consider how the social status of the speaker and addressee impact interpretation.

1. וַיֹּאמֶר אֱלֹהִים יְהִי מְאֹרֹת בִּרְקִיעַ הַשָּׁמַיִם לְהַבְדִּיל בֵּין הַיּוֹם וּבֵין הַלָּיְלָה וְהָיוּ לְאֹתֹת וּלְמוֹעֲדִים וּלְיָמִים וְשָׁנִים: (Gen 1:14)

2. וְסָמַךְ יָדוֹ עַל רֹאשׁ הָעֹלָה וְנִרְצָה לוֹ לְכַפֵּר עָלָיו: וְשָׁחַט אֶת־בֶּן הַבָּקָר לִפְנֵי יְהוָה וְהִקְרִיבוּ בְּנֵי אַהֲרֹן הַכֹּהֲנִים אֶת־הַדָּם וְזָרְקוּ אֶת־הַדָּם עַל־הַמִּזְבֵּחַ סָבִיב אֲשֶׁר־פֶּתַח אֹהֶל מוֹעֵד: (Lev 1:4–5)

3. וַיֹּאמֶר יְהוֹשֻׁעַ אֶל־עָכָן בְּנִי שִׂים־נָא כָבוֹד לַיהוָה אֱלֹהֵי יִשְׂרָאֵל וְתֶן־לוֹ תוֹדָה וְהַגֶּד־נָא לִי מֶה עָשִׂיתָ אַל־תְּכַחֵד מִמֶּנִּי: (Josh 7:19)

[93] Peter Juhás, *Die biblisch-hebräische Partikel* נָא *im Lichte der antiken Bibelübersetzungen: unter besonderer Berücksichtigung ihrer vermuteten Höflichkeitsfunktion*, SSN 67 (Leiden: Brill, 2017), 201, 203.

4. וַיֹּאמֶר שְׁמוּאֵל אֶל־הָעָם אַל־תִּירָאוּ אַתֶּם עֲשִׂיתֶם אֵת כָּל־הָרָעָה הַזֹּאת אַךְ
אַל־תָּסוּרוּ מֵאַחֲרֵי יְהוָה וַעֲבַדְתֶּם אֶת־יְהוָה בְּכָל־לְבַבְכֶם: (1 Sam 12:20)

5. שְׁאַל אֶת־נְעָרֶיךָ וְיַגִּידוּ לָךְ וְיִמְצְאוּ הַנְּעָרִים חֵן בְּעֵינֶיךָ כִּי־עַל־יוֹם טוֹב בָּנוּ תְּנָה־
נָּא אֵת אֲשֶׁר תִּמְצָא יָדְךָ לַעֲבָדֶיךָ וּלְבִנְךָ לְדָוִד: (1 Sam 25:8)

6. יְהִי יְהוָה אֱלֹהֵינוּ עִמָּנוּ כַּאֲשֶׁר הָיָה עִם־אֲבֹתֵינוּ אַל־יַעַזְבֵנוּ וְאַל־יִטְּשֵׁנוּ:
(1 Kgs 8:57)

7. לְכוּ־נָא וְנִוָּכְחָה יֹאמַר יְהוָה אִם־יִהְיוּ חֲטָאֵיכֶם כַּשָּׁנִים כַּשֶּׁלֶג יַלְבִּינוּ אִם־יַאְדִּימוּ
כַתּוֹלָע כַּצֶּמֶר יִהְיוּ: (Isa 1:18)

8. נִשְׁכְּבָה בְּבָשְׁתֵּנוּ וּתְכַסֵּנוּ כְּלִמָּתֵנוּ כִּי לַיהוָה אֱלֹהֵינוּ חָטָאנוּ אֲנַחְנוּ וַאֲבוֹתֵינוּ
מִנְּעוּרֵינוּ וְעַד־הַיּוֹם הַזֶּה וְלֹא שָׁמַעְנוּ בְּקוֹל יְהוָה אֱלֹהֵינוּ: (Jer 3:25)

9. וְכִי־יִשְׁמְעוּ הַשָּׂרִים כִּי־דִבַּרְתִּי אִתָּךְ וּבָאוּ אֵלֶיךָ וְאָמְרוּ אֵלֶיךָ הַגִּידָה־נָּא לָנוּ
מַה־דִּבַּרְתָּ אֶל־הַמֶּלֶךְ אַל־תְּכַחֵד מִמֶּנּוּ וְלֹא נְמִיתֶךָ וּמַה־דִּבֶּר אֵלֶיךָ הַמֶּלֶךְ:
(Jer 38:25)

10. קוּמָה אֱלֹהִים שָׁפְטָה הָאָרֶץ כִּי־אַתָּה תִנְחַל בְּכָל־הַגּוֹיִם: (Ps 82:8)

Translate from English to Hebrew.

11.   God said: "Let there be living beings on the face of the earth."

12.   May my servant David arise, pursue after his enemies, and then strike them in the wilderness.

13.   Please let your maidservant dwell among her people. Give her food and let her soul live so that she shall not die.

14.   Hear the words of Yahweh. Let us serve our God with all our heart and all our souls.

15.   Enter the city, slaughter the inhabitants, and take the silver. Capture the king, carry him away, and kill him.

Guided Reading: Num 19:1–10

וַיְדַבֵּ֣ר יְהוָ֔ה אֶל־מֹשֶׁ֥ה וְאֶֽל־אַהֲרֹ֖ן לֵאמֹֽר: 2 זֹ֚את חֻקַּ֣ת הַתּוֹרָ֔ה אֲשֶׁר־צִוָּ֥ה יְהוָ֖ה לֵאמֹ֑ר
דַּבֵּ֣ר | אֶל־בְּנֵ֣י יִשְׂרָאֵ֗ל וְיִקְח֣וּ אֵלֶיךָ֩ פָרָ֨ה אֲדֻמָּ֜ה תְּמִימָ֗ה אֲשֶׁ֤ר אֵֽין־בָּהּ֙ מ֔וּם אֲשֶׁ֛ר לֹא־עָלָ֥ה
עָלֶ֖יהָ עֹֽל: 3 וּנְתַתֶּ֣ם אֹתָ֔הּ אֶל־אֶלְעָזָ֖ר הַכֹּהֵ֑ן וְהוֹצִ֤יא אֹתָהּ֙ אֶל־מִח֣וּץ לַֽמַּחֲנֶ֔ה וְשָׁחַ֥ט אֹתָ֖הּ
לְפָנָֽיו: 4 וְלָקַ֞ח אֶלְעָזָ֧ר הַכֹּהֵ֛ן מִדָּמָ֖הּ בְּאֶצְבָּע֑וֹ וְהִזָּ֞ה אֶל־נֹ֨כַח פְּנֵ֧י אֹֽהֶל־מוֹעֵ֛ד מִדָּמָ֖הּ שֶׁ֥בַע
פְּעָמִֽים: 5 וְשָׂרַ֥ף אֶת־הַפָּרָ֖ה לְעֵינָ֑יו אֶת־עֹרָ֤הּ וְאֶת־בְּשָׂרָהּ֙ וְאֶת־דָּמָ֔הּ עַל־פִּרְשָׁ֖הּ יִשְׂרֹֽף: 6
וְלָקַ֣ח הַכֹּהֵ֗ן עֵ֥ץ אֶ֛רֶז וְאֵז֖וֹב וּשְׁנִ֣י תוֹלָ֑עַת וְהִשְׁלִ֕יךְ אֶל־תּ֖וֹךְ שְׂרֵפַ֥ת הַפָּרָֽה: 7 וְכִבֶּ֨ס בְּגָדָ֜יו
הַכֹּהֵ֗ן וְרָחַ֤ץ בְּשָׂרוֹ֙ בַּמַּ֔יִם וְאַחַ֖ר יָבֹ֣א אֶל־הַֽמַּחֲנֶ֑ה וְטָמֵ֥א הַכֹּהֵ֖ן עַד־הָעָֽרֶב: 8 וְהַשֹּׂרֵ֣ף אֹתָ֗הּ
יְכַבֵּ֤ס בְּגָדָיו֙ בַּמַּ֔יִם וְרָחַ֥ץ בְּשָׂר֖וֹ בַּמָּ֑יִם וְטָמֵ֖א עַד־הָעָֽרֶב: 9 וְאָסַ֣ף | אִ֣ישׁ טָה֗וֹר אֵ֚ת אֵ֣פֶר
הַפָּרָ֔ה וְהִנִּ֛יחַ מִח֥וּץ לַֽמַּחֲנֶ֖ה בְּמָק֣וֹם טָה֑וֹר וְֽהָיְתָ֞ה לַעֲדַ֣ת בְּנֵֽי־יִשְׂרָאֵ֗ל לְמִשְׁמֶ֛רֶת לְמֵ֥י נִדָּ֖ה

חַטָּאת הָוא: 10 וְכִבֶּס הָאֹסֵף אֶת־אֵפֶר הַפָּרָה אֶת־בְּגָדָיו וְטָמֵא עַד־הָעֶרֶב וְהָיְתָה לִבְנֵי
יִשְׂרָאֵל וְלַגֵּר הַגָּר בְּתוֹכָם לְחֻקַּת עוֹלָם:

VOCABULARY AND NOTES

Verse 2

חֻקַּת		N.FS CSTR		"statute"
צִוָּה	*Piel*	SC 3MS	צוה	"command"
דַּבֵּר	*Piel*	IMPV MS	דבר	
וְיִקְחוּ	*Qal*	PC 3MP	לקח	
פָּרָה		N.FS		"cow"
אֲדֻמָּה		ADJ.FS		"red"
תְּמִימָה		ADJ.FS		"perfect"
מוּם		N.MS		"blemish"
עֹל		N.MS		"yoke"

Verse 3

וּנְתַתֶּם	*Qal wəqāṭal*	2MP	נתן	
אֶלְעָזָר		PN		"Eleazar"
וְהוֹצִיא	*Hiphil wəqāṭal*	3MS	יצא	"lead out"
חוּץ		N.MS		"outside"
שָׁחַט	*Qal*			"slaughter"

Verse 4

דָּמָהּ		N.MS + 3FS SF		
אֶצְבָּעוֹ		N.FS + 3MS SF		"finger"
וְהִזָּה	*Hiphil wəqāṭal*	3MS	נזה	"sprinkle"
נֹכַח		N.MS		"front; opposite"
פְּעָמִים		N.MP		"times"

Verse 5

וְשָׂרַף	*Qal wəqāṭal*	3MS	שׂרף	"burn"
עֹרָהּ		N.MS + 3FS SF		"skin"
בְּשָׂרָהּ		N.MS + 3FS SF		"meat"
פִּרְשָׁהּ		N.MS + 3FS SF		"intestines"
יִשְׂרֹף	*Qal*	PC 3MS	שׂרף	

Verse 6

אֶרֶז		N.MS		"cedar"
אֵזוֹב		N.MS		"hyssop"

שְׁנִי תוֹלַ֫עַת		N.M		"scarlet yarn"
וְהִשְׁלִיךְ	Hiphil wəqātal	3MS	שלך	"throw"
שְׂרֵפַת		N.FS CSTR		"burning"

Verse 7

וְכִבֶּס	Piel wəqātal	3MS	כבס	"wash"
וְרָחַץ	Qal wəqātal	3MS	רחץ	"bathe"
וְטָמֵא	Qal wəqātal	3MS	טמא	"be unclean"
עָ֫רֶב		N.MS		"evening"

Verse 8

שֹׂרֵף	Qal	ACT PTCL MS	שרף	
יְכַבֵּס	Piel	PC 3MS	כבס	

Verse 9

טָהוֹר		ADJ		"clean"
אֵ֫פֶר		N.MS		"ash"
וְהִנִּיחַ	Hiphil wəqātal	3MS	נוח	"put, leave"
חוּץ		N.MS		"outside; street"
עֲדַת		N.FS CSTR		"assembly"
מִשְׁמֶ֫רֶת		N.FS		"observance"
נִדָּה		N.FS		"impurity"

Verse 10

גֵּר		N.MS		"immigrant, refugee"
גֵּר	Qal	ACT PTC MS	גור	"reside"
חֻקַּת		N.FS CSTR		"statute"

//

PART C

//

///////////////

CHAPTER 7

NOUNS AND NOUN PHRASES

Nouns describe the realities that we observe daily around us. Some of those realities are physical and concrete while others are immaterial and intangible or somewhere in between. These entities serve as the primary actors, participants, and concepts in the communication of events and ideas. Special attention is given in this chapter to the way in which the Hebrew language encodes various noun characteristics. These properties and strategies are collectively called the grammar of the Hebrew noun (N) and noun phrase (NP).

7.1 GOING DEEPER WITH NOUNS

The creation account in the first chapter of the book of Genesis is arguably one of the most marvelous, densely theological and anthropological texts in the entire Bible. Beginning in ancient times until today, readers have been fascinated by the beauty of the story and beguiled by its description of God's creative work.[1] The three-by-three matrix of days corresponds ingeniously to the forming and filling of creation with habitants.[2] The first verses of chapter 2 complete the work week—embodying cessation and sanctity as the culmination of divine labor.

Within this inventive portrayal, the penultimate day contains two fecund speeches (vv. 24, 26) and two creative actions (vv. 25, 27). Corresponding to the twofold speech-acts of day three (vv. 9, 11), the ensuing performance (וַתּוֹצֵא הָאָרֶץ "the earth brought forth . . ." v. 12) serves as the starting point of day six's drama (וַיֹּאמֶר אֱלֹהִים תּוֹצֵא הָאָרֶץ "God said: Let the earth bring forth . . ." v. 24) and the encore

---

[1] Kyle Greenwood, ed. *Since the Beginning: Interpreting Genesis 1 and 2 through the Ages* (Grand Rapids: Baker Academic, 2018).
[2] Mathews, *Genesis 1–11:26*, 144.

of its food provision (עֵשֶׂב "herbs," זֶרַע "seed," עֵץ "trees;" vv. 11–12, 29–30). Yet, the second divine word of day six—which enacts the final creative work of the entire account—imprints God's very image on his domain. Humans become both residents and surrogate sovereigns over his bourgeoning, goodly realm.

While the concepts signified by "image" and "likeness" continue to enliven spirited speculation, the first occurrence of the noun אָדָם stimulates a range of intriguing grammatical questions. For readers relying on English translations, one oddity is clear: *they* and *him* point to changing references and agreement number between the pronouns and their antecedent *man*. See, for instance, the CSB.

Gen 1:26–28	CSB Translation
וַיֹּאמֶר אֱלֹהִים	Then God said,
נַעֲשֶׂה **אָדָם** בְּצַלְמֵנוּ כִּדְמוּתֵנוּ	"Let us make **man** in our image, according to our likeness
וְיִרְדּוּ בִדְגַת הַיָּם וּבְעוֹף הַשָּׁמַיִם	**They will rule** the fish of the sea, the birds of the sky,
וּבַבְּהֵמָה וּבְכָל־הָאָרֶץ	the livestock, the whole earth,
וּבְכָל־הָרֶמֶשׂ הָרֹמֵשׂ עַל־הָאָרֶץ:	and the creatures that crawl on the earth."
וַיִּבְרָא אֱלֹהִים ׀ אֶת־הָאָדָם בְּצַלְמוֹ	So God created **man** in his own image;
בְּצֶלֶם אֱלֹהִים בָּרָא אֹתוֹ	he created **him** in the image of God;
זָכָר וּנְקֵבָה בָּרָא אֹתָם:	he created **them** male and female.
וַיְבָרֶךְ **אֹתָם** אֱלֹהִים	God blessed **them**,
וַיֹּאמֶר לָהֶם אֱלֹהִים	and God said to **them**,
פְּרוּ וּרְבוּ וּמִלְאוּ אֶת־הָאָרֶץ וְכִבְשֻׁהָ	"**Be fruitful**, **multiply**, **fill** the earth, and **subdue** it.
וּרְדוּ בִּדְגַת הַיָּם וּבְעוֹף הַשָּׁמַיִם	**Rule** the fish of the sea, the birds of the sky,
וּבְכָל־חַיָּה הָרֹמֶשֶׂת עַל־הָאָרֶץ:	and every creature that crawls on the earth."

For the student of Hebrew, this translation follows a straightforward substitutionary approach. The usual English gloss of אָדָם is "man." The direct object pronouns in verses 27–28 are אֹתוֹ "him" (3MS), and אֹתָם "them" (3MP). And the related verb forms are all plural: וְיִרְדּוּ "they will rule," פְּרוּ "[You (P)] be fruitful," רְבוּ "[You (P)] multiply," מִלְאוּ "[You (P)] fill," כִּבְשֻׁהָ "[You (P)] subdue it," and רְדוּ "[You (P)] rule" (vv. 26, 28).

The problem surfaces with the English word *man*. What exactly is referenced by this term? And what pronouns should be used? Present-day English speakers normally use this word to speak of an individual male human, and the corresponding pronoun would be "he." Few today use the archaic meaning describing a generic human being without reference to sex, except in certain idioms (e.g., *c'mon man!*). Even more antiquarian is its allusion to a group of people (i.e., the human species, humanity). In these verses, many contemporary English versions preserve almost word-for-word the translation tradition originating half a millennium ago with Tyndale and Coverdale. For instance, the King James Version of verse 27 only differs from the CSB in word order:

> So God created man in his own image,
> in the image of God created he him;
> male and female created he them.

In situations like this passage, many modern readers are left engaging the ancient Hebrew text through an outmoded English translation. They find themselves several steps removed. They need to translate their translation. And two translation principles create a paradox. The first is the convention of maintaining the wording of previous English Bible renditions, and the second is the assumption that a contemporary version would employ the best common idiom.[3] Inevitably, this linguistic distance leads to bewilderment or worse misunderstanding.

While acknowledging the changing nature of English, another aspect is the need to go deeper in understanding the meaning and grammar of Hebrew אָדָם. An examination of a Hebrew lexicon, like the *Dictionary of Classical Hebrew*, provides a helpful appraisal of the potential range of usage of the term beyond a simple comparable English gloss. There, two basic definitions are provided:

1. collective, **humanity**, **people** (as distinct from God or animals), persons in general (usually without regard to sex, e.g., Gn 5:2), human race as a whole, also with reference to smaller groups, e.g., inhabitants of a city; of persons in general.[4]

2a.**individual**, whether a particular person or a typical human [. . .]

2b.with article, **the man**, i.e., Adam, in Gn 2–3.[5]

Further, an added note explains that the distinction between the collective and the individual usage is not always clear and that אָדָם may rarely take the plural verb. Said another way, אָדָם references entities similar to the English terms: *humans, humanity* (i.e., a group of persons or humankind in general) or *man, person* (i.e., a lone male human, a generic human without reference to sex). The former reference is to a collective group, and the latter is to an individual.[6] The English gloss should be updated to *human race, humanity*; *man, person*. Morphologically,

---

[3] Several recent translations update this passage (see CEB, ISV, NIV, NLT, and NRSV).

[4] *DCH 1*, s.v. "אדם," 123–24.

[5] *DCH 1*, s.v. "אדם," 126–27.

[6] The male individual referenced in Genesis 2–3 is found with the article, הָאָדָם "the man," but subsequently אָדָם serves as a proper noun, *Adam*. See Richard Hess, "Splitting the Adam: The Usage of 'ādām in Genesis i–v," in *Studies in the Pentateuch*, ed. J. Emerton, VTSup 41, (Leiden: Brill, 1990), 1–15.

Hebrew אָדָם is never plural, but semantically the noun can represent multiple (or even all) humans. As such, the number agreement can be singular or plural with pronouns and verbs. Finally, the common noun—unlike proper name *Adam*—takes the definite article.

This grammar of אָדָם provides a basis to read Gen 1:26–28 as voicing the origin and distinctiveness of all humanity. The first verse indicates that God plans to construct אָדָם in a unique way. It might be tempting to understand the noun with reference only to Adam, but the following plural agreement with the verb וְיִרְדּוּ requires the collective reference to humanity as a group. Consequently, God endows collective humankind (הָאָדָם)—the aforementioned group he just created and not just a lone individual (Adam)—with the image of God. And humans are entrusted with dominion over the other earthly inhabitants. This notion is repeated twice more in the threefold parallelistic structure of the following verse.

Gen 1:27

וַיִּבְרָא אֱלֹהִים ׀ אֶת־הָאָדָם בְּצַלְמוֹ	God created	הָאָדָם	in his image
בְּצֶלֶם אֱלֹהִים בָּרָא	created	אֹתוֹ	in God's image;
זָכָר וּנְקֵבָה בָּרָא אֹתָם:	created	אֹתָם	male and female.

Each line identifies an identical subject, verb, and object, while each element differs slightly. אֱלֹהִים "God" is explicitly mentioned only in the first line, tacitly continuing as the primary actor thereafter. The verb ברא "create" alternates from a sequential narrative preterite (*wayyiqtol*) to a noninitial suffix conjugation (*qātal*) in the second and third clauses. The object is the previously specified אָדָם "humanity" from verse 26.[7] A definite article indicates the connection with this known entity. The second line specifies the collective referent (e.g., humanity) agreeing with the singular morphology of the noun. The third object, then, changes to a plural pronoun. The shift appears to be motivated by the focus on the plural notion of אָדָם "humanity" as זָכָר וּנְקֵבָה "male and female" in place of the singular. Finally, the adverbial modification crescendos with each subsequent refrain. The culminating lyric of verse 27 sings the intention of human creation. This lyric connects the pronouncement of humanity's purpose in verse 26 and the divine command of verse 28.

With these issues in mind, a suggested modernized English rendering of this passage is as follows:

God said,

> "Let us make human beings in our image, according to our likeness, so that they might rule over the fish of the sea, the birds of the heavens, and

---

[7] The other group references employ singulars as well: וְיִרְדּוּ בִדְגַת הַיָּם וּבְעוֹף הַשָּׁמַיִם וּבַבְּהֵמָה וּבְכָל־ הָאָרֶץ וּבְכָל־הָרֶמֶשׂ הָרֹמֵשׂ עַל־הָאָרֶץ: "So that [humans] might rule over the sea-**fish**, the heaven-**bird**(s), the **livestock** as well as everything on the earth, and every **critter** crawling on the land" (v. 26).

the animals along with everything on the earth, and all the critters crawling on the land."

God created the human beings in his image.
In the image of God, he created humankind.
He created them male and female.

God blessed them and said to them:
"Be fruitful and increase, fill the earth and subdue it, and rule over the fish of the sea, the birds of the heavens, and all living beings crawling on the land."

To sort out these nuances, we turn our attention in this chapter to describing the grammar of nouns and noun phrases. While it is tempting to assume continuity between these categories in English and Hebrew, the differences can be significant. As seen in this brief example, translations can provide a false sense of correspondence with similar language structures. Our task is to notice the ways the words mean and the ways they are used in BH. At times, these resemble English constructions, but critically they sometimes do not.

7.2 CHAPTER OBJECTIVES

This chapter describes the grammar of Hebrew nouns and noun phrases. The following section provides basic grammatical and notional definitions of nouns in relation to other parts of speech (§7.3). The subsequent sections survey the various types and functions of noun phrases (§7.4), the grammatical and semantic classification of nouns (§7.5), and the morphosyntax of noun phrases along with numerals (§7.6–9).

7.3 INTRODUCTION

According to traditional grammatical descriptions, words are grouped into a discrete number of lexical categories—called <u>word classes</u> or <u>parts of speech</u>. These categories are not the same for all languages.[8] English parts of speech traditionally include nouns, pronouns, adjectives, numerals, verbs, adverbs, prepositions, conjunctions, interjections, and articles. The earliest Indo-European grammarians describe four categories of word classes.[9] And Semitic grammarians often

---

[8] For the various difficulties in applying a crosslinguistic framework, see Martin Haspelmath, "Word Classes and Parts of Speech," in *International Encyclopedia of the Social & Behavioral Sciences*, ed. P. B. Baltes and N. J. Smelser (Amsterdam: Pergamon, 2001), 16538–45.

[9] These are commonly labeled, *nāman* "noun," *ākhyāta* "verb," *upasarga* "preverb," and *nipāta* "particle," in Sanskrit and ὄνομα "noun," ῥῆμα "verb," σύνδεσμος "link" (i.e., particle), ἄρθρον "joint" (i.e., article) in Greek. See Emilie Aussant. "To Classify Words: Western and Indian Grammatical

circumscribe three categories: noun, verb, and particles.[10] While the number of word classes varies, the broad grouping of at least nouns and verbs is almost universally recognized across nearly all the world's languages. However, the characteristics of each word class must be described for each individual language.

In chapters 3 through 6, the various morphosyntactic nuances of Hebrew verbs were introduced. The present chapter describes Hebrew nouns. The following sections elaborate on noun semantics, morphology, and usage.

Semantically, nouns designate words that refer to concrete objects (e.g., persons, places, things) or abstract entities.[11] Cognitive grammar approaches provide a more sophisticated notional understanding of nouns as the prototype *thing*, or "a reified group of interconnected entities," which are distinguished from verbs as *process*, expressing development through time.[12] Others define word classes with the focus on the degree of *time-stability*. In this understanding, temporality provides the semantic criterion to identify nouns, adjectives, and verbs, along a progression ranging from permanent states with stable time to changing processes indicating rapid change (see Figure A).[13]

Figure A: Time-Stability of Word Classes[14]

More Stable - Less Stable

Nouns	Adjectives		Verbs	
(*rock, person*)	(*green*)	(*sad*)	(*know*)	(*walk, shoot*)

Some words describe the states (e.g., *green*) or emotions (e.g., *sad*) of other entities. These are more time-stable than verbs but less so than nouns. In certain word class systems, these descriptors are placed in their own category, often called adjectives, while other grammatical organizations include adjectives together with nouns as substantives.[15]

Approaches," in *Sanskrit Syntax: Selected Papers Presented at the Seminar on Sanskrit Syntax and Discourse Structures, 13–15 June 2013, Université Paris Diderot, with an Updated and Revised Bibliography by Hans Henrich Hock*, ed. Peter M. Scharf (Providence, RI: The Sanskrit Library, 2015), 213–35.

[10] The Arabic grammatical tradition designates three word classes (*ism* "name," *fi'l* "verb," and *harf* "particle").

[11] Latin *nomen*, Greek ὄνομα, and English *noun*—each mean "name."

[12] Ronald W. Langacker, *Cognitive Grammar: A Basic Introduction* (Oxford: Oxford University Press, 2008), 103–12. See further Mark Baker and William Croft, "Lexical Categories: Legacy, Lacuna, and Opportunity for Functionalists and Formalists," *Annual Review of Linguistics* 3 (2017): 179–197.

[13] Talmy Givón, *Syntax: An Introduction* (Amsterdam: Benjamins, 2001), 1:50–54. See the criticism of, among others, John R. Taylor, *Cognitive Grammar* (Oxford: Oxford University Press, 2002), 177.

[14] Adapted from Talmy Givón, *On Understanding Grammar*, rev. ed. (Amsterdam: Benjamins, 2018), 253.

[15] Sometimes the term substantive is used as a more specific term for more time-stable words, whereas *noun* covers the boarder category, inclusive of substantives and adjectives. In the Arabic

Other words share characteristics of nouns, including functioning in sentences like nouns, yet are primarily categorized as another part of speech. In linguistic terminology, a <u>nominal</u> is a functional descriptor that is inclusive of noun-like words. This category includes any word or phrase, not just nouns, that functions in noun-like ways in a sentence. Adjectives (*rich*) and even verbs (*walk*) can be considered nominals based on their usage (e.g., *the rich are miserly*; *he went on a walk*).

Morphologically, nouns are grouped as having similar inflections. <u>Inflection</u> refers to the various forms of a word that do not change its part of speech or basic meaning. This variation commonly includes an <u>affix</u> change and expresses different grammatical categories (e.g., gender, number, case). In English, for example, the inflectional suffix *-s* designates plural nouns (e.g., *word ~ words*), and several different affixes are used for feminine gender nouns: *she-* (*she-wolf*), *-ine* (*heroine*), *-ette* (*bachelorette*), *-ess* (*lioness*), and *-trix* (*aviatrix*).[16] Case inflections—like what is seen in the Greek nominal system—indicate syntactically similar entities. That is, different inflectional forms designate the doer of an action, or <u>subject</u> (e.g., with -ς, i.e., the nominative form: λογος, πόλις) or the one that is entailed by an action, or <u>object</u> (e.g., with -ν, i.e., the accusative form: λογον, πόλιν).

Some more recent linguistic approaches attempt to define <u>phrasal units</u> instead of individual words by usage categories. As distinct from lexical categories, syntactic categorization defines combinations of words as <u>noun phrases</u>, <u>verb phrases</u>, and <u>clauses</u>. These phrases then serve syntactic structures. They are described based on their phrasal head and function in a clause. For instance, a noun phrase (*the Hebrew student*) can be a subject (*the Hebrew student passed*), a prepositional complement (*vocabulary is difficult for the Hebrew student*), or an object of a verb (*she helps the Hebrew student*). A verb phrase (*was diligent*) can be used in an independent (*the Hebrew student was diligent*), dependent (*because the Hebrew student was diligent, she learned to read*), or a relative clause (*the one who was diligent learned to read*) as a predicate.

7.4 NOUN PHRASES

A noun phrase is a group of words that includes at least one nominal element and functions syntactically like a noun. Along with the primary nominal constituent, a NP may include other components. These commonly include articles, demonstratives, quantifiers, numerals, measure words, relatives, and additional nouns.

---

grammatical tradition, *ism* "name" describes the word class including nouns, adjectives, participles, pronouns, numerals, names, and certain adverbs.

[16] The suffix *-s* alternately can designate present tense verbs (e.g. *walk ~ walks*), but only verbs can have a form with *-ed* (e.g. *walked*).

7.4.1 Types of Noun Phrases

Varying degrees of complexity are evidenced with Hebrew NPs. These include a single noun (1a), multiple nouns (1b), a noun with a pronominal element (1c), a noun with an article (1d), a noun with a demonstrative (1e), a noun with a quantifier (1f), a noun with a numeral (1g), a noun with an adjective (1h), a noun with a relative clause (1i), or a combination of these (1j).

(1a)	דָּבָר	a word; discourse; matter
(1b)	דְּבַר־הַמֶּלֶךְ	the king's word
(1c)	דְּבָרוֹ	his word
(1d)	הַדָּבָר	the word
(1e)	הַדָּבָר הַזֶּה	this word
(1f)	כֹּל דָּבָר	every word
(1g)	דָּבָר אֶחָד	one word
(1h)	דְּבַר טוֹב	a favorable word
(1i)	הַדָּבָר אֲשֶׁר לֹא־דִבְּרוֹ יהוה	the word which Yahweh did not speak (Deut 18:22)
(1j)	כֹּל דְּבָרוֹ הַטּוֹב אֲשֶׁר דִּבֶּר בְּיַד מֹשֶׁה עַבְדּוֹ	his every good word which he spoke through Moses his servant (1 Kgs 8:56)

7.4.2 Functions of Noun Phrases

Each NP type may function syntactically as a noun in a clause. In BH, the syntactic function of NPs is not marked by a case system as found in many other languages (e.g., Arabic, Greek, Korean, German, Turkish, Latin, Tamil, Hungarian, Hindi).[17] Grammatical case is not formally distinguished by morphology—that is, nominal inflection.[18] Certain BH grammars, however, refer to traditional case distinctions to describe nouns (e.g., nominative, accusative).[19] Some vestigial evidence exists for a mixed diptotic and triptotic case system in proto-Hebrew, which resembles that of several genetically related Semitic languages.[20] The following discussion takes a functional approach to describing NPs (e.g., subject, object).

Hebrew NPs may function in a clause as the subject: הַמֶּלֶךְ "the king" (1 Sam 21:3), object: נָשִׁים נָכְרִיּוֹת רַבּוֹת "many foreign women" (1 Kgs 11:1), adverb:

---

[17] Michèle Fruyt, Michel Mazoyer, and Dennis Pardee, eds., *Grammatical Case in the Languages of the Middle East and Europe Acts of the International Colloquium Variations, Concurrence et Évolution des cas dans divers domaines linguistiques, Paris, 2–4 April 2007*, SAOC 64 (Chicago: The Oriental Institute, 2011).

[18] *IBHS* §8.1; *BHRG* §25.1.1; Joüon-Muraoka §124t.

[19] GKC §90.

[20] Dennis G. Pardee, "Vestiges du système casuel entre le nom et le pronom suffixe en hébreu biblique," in *Grammatical Case in the Languages of the Middle East and Europe: Acts of the International Colloquium "Variations, Concurrence et Evolution des cas dans divers domaines linguistiques," Paris, 2–4 April 2007*, ed. Michèle Fruyt, Michel Mazoyer, and Dennis Pardee, SAOC 64 (Chicago: University of Chicago, 2011), 113–21.

שְׁלֹשִׁים יוֹם "thirty days" (Num 20:29), object of a preposition: לְבִּי "my heart" (Jer 3:15), nominal modifier: יִשְׂרָאֵל "Israel" (Num 20:29), indirect object: הָאַרְיֵה "the lion" (1 Kgs 13:26), object complement: חַוָּה "Eve" (Gen 3:20), subject complement: הָאֱלֹהִים "God" (1 Kgs 18:21), or apposition to another element: דָּוִד "David" (2 Sam 5:3). Sometimes a NP can stand outside of the clause structure as a vocative (Isa 42:18).[21] The NP participant may also be compounded as adverbs דֵּעָה וְהַשְׂכֵּיל "knowledgeably and skillfully" (Jer 3:15).

1 Sam 21:3
הַמֶּלֶךְ צִוַּנִי דָבָר
The king issued me a command.

1 Kgs 11:1
וְהַמֶּלֶךְ שְׁלֹמֹה אָהַב נָשִׁים נָכְרִיּוֹת רַבּוֹת
King Solomon loved **many foreign women**.

Num 20:29
וַיִּבְכּוּ אֶת־אַהֲרֹן שְׁלֹשִׁים יוֹם כֹּל בֵּית יִשְׂרָאֵל
The entire house of Israel mourned Aaron **thirty days**.

Jer 3:15
וְנָתַתִּי לָכֶם רֹעִים כְּלִבִּי
I will give you shepherds **according to my heart**.

Num 20:29
וַיִּבְכּוּ אֶת־אַהֲרֹן שְׁלֹשִׁים יוֹם כֹּל בֵּית יִשְׂרָאֵל
The entire house of **Israel** mourned Aaron thirty days.

1 Kgs 13:26
וַיִּתְּנֵהוּ יְהֹוָה לָאַרְיֵה
Yahweh gave him **to the lion**.

Gen 3:20
וַיִּקְרָא הָאָדָם שֵׁם אִשְׁתּוֹ חַוָּה כִּי הִוא הָיְתָה אֵם כָּל־חָי
The man called his wife's name **Eve** because she was the mother of all living.

1 Kgs 18:21
אִם־יְהֹוָה הָאֱלֹהִים לְכוּ אַחֲרָיו
If Yahweh is **God**, follow him.

---

[21] Interjections also stand outside of the typical clause structure. BH interjections mostly include particles and verbal elements (see chapter 10).

2 Sam 5:3

וַיִּכְרֹת לָהֶם֩ הַמֶּ֨לֶךְ דָּוִ֥ד בְּרִ֛ית בְּחֶבְר֖וֹן לִפְנֵ֣י יְהוָ֑ה

King David cut a covenant with them at Hebron in Yahweh's presence.

Isa 42:18

הַחֵרְשִׁ֖ים שְׁמָ֑עוּ וְהַעִוְרִ֖ים הַבִּ֥יטוּ לִרְאֽוֹת

Listen, **O deaf ones**! Try to see, **O blind ones**!

Jer 3:15

וְרָע֥וּ אֶתְכֶ֖ם דֵּעָ֥ה וְהַשְׂכֵּֽיל

[Shepherds] will guide you **knowledgeably and skillfully**.

Noun phrase functions are indicated by a network of morphosyntactic characteristics. English NPs are indicated by syntactic position rather than grammatical
words or cases. In BH, subjective NPs are designated as such by being <u>animate</u>
and identified entities that are ordinarily in near proximity to the verb and the head
noun and the finite verb agree in gender and number. In 1 Sam 21:3 (see above),
the subject, הַמֶּלֶךְ "the king," is both animate and definite. The subject NP immediately precedes the verb in 1 Sam 21:3 and 1 Kgs 11:1 and follows in 1 Kgs 13:26
and Gen 3:20. The adjacency of the subject and verb can be interrupted by a prepositional phrase, such as 2 Sam 5:3. For other pragmatic reasons, the subject may
come at the end of a clause, such as Num 20:29. Subject-verb agreement is found
with all clauses with an expressed verb.

A subject complement provides a description of the subject as a predicate of a
<u>copula</u> type clause. Generally, the predicate may comprise an adjective, prepo-
sitional phrase, participle, or noun phrase. First Kings 18:21 includes the definite
subject complement הָאֱלֹהִים "God" (see further below §7.9.1).

Objective NPs occur with more variation but are typically found after the verb.
As seen in the examples above, an object may be an unspecified, indefinite constituent: דָּבָר "a word, command" (1 Sam 21:3), נָשִׁים נָכְרִיּוֹת רַבּוֹת "many foreign
women" (1 Kgs 11:1), רֹעִים "shepherds" (Num 20:29), and בְּרִית "a covenant"
(1 Kgs 18:21). Or the NP can be specified: אַהֲרֹן "Aaron" (Num 20:29) and שֵׁם
אִשְׁתּוֹ "his wife's name" (Gen 3:20). A known object is often indicated with the
definite direct object marker אֶת־אַהֲרֹן "Aaron" (Num 20:29), but the particle is not
required in every instance (Gen 3:20).

Secondary verbal objects may be designated as an <u>object complement</u>, as with
חַוָּה "Eve" (Gen 3:20), or as an <u>indirect object</u>, sometimes marked with the ל
preposition as with לָאַרְיֵה "to the lion" (1 Kgs 13:26). NP prepositional objects are
contiguous with a preposition: לִבִּי "my heart" (Jer 3:15), בְּחֶבְרוֹן "in Hebron," and
לִפְנֵי יהוה "before Yahweh" (2 Sam 5:3). Adverbial NPs, like שְׁלֹשִׁים יוֹם "for thirty

days" (Num 20:29), are in many ways indistinguishable from objective NPs.[22] And they are ultimately assessed by their semantics.

Two or more NPs may conjoin to serve a single function. For instance, Jer 3:15 includes the adverbial compound NP דֵעָה וְהַשְׂכֵּיל "knowledgeably and skillfully." Two or more nouns may be combined in construct relationship, as with בֵּית יִשְׂרָאֵל "House of Israel" (Num 20:29), שֵׁם אִשְׁתּוֹ "his wife's name," and אֵם כָּל־חָי "mother of all living" (Gen 3:20). Alternatively, two NPs may serve appositionally in the same syntactic function, like הַמֶּלֶךְ שְׁלֹמֹה "King Solomon" (1 Kgs 11:1), שְׁלֹשִׁים יוֹם "thirty days" (Num 20:29), and אֲדֹנָי יְהוִה "Lord Yahweh" (Ezek 18:3).

Finally, almost any NP may be replaced by a pronoun of <u>anaphoric</u> reference. Examples include the subject: הוּא "she" (Gen 3:20), direct object: אֶתְכֶם "you" (Jer 3:15), indirect objects: צַוֵּנִי "command **me**" (1 Sam 21:3) and לָכֶם "to you" (Jer 3:15), possessive: אִשְׁתּוֹ "**his** wife" (Gen 3:20), and preposition object: אַחֲרָיו "after **him**" (1 Kgs 18:21).

7.5 NOUN CLASSES

A <u>noun class</u> organizes nouns with similar semantic and grammatical characteristics. Some are distinct groups (e.g., count and noncount nouns), while others should be understood as overlapping (e.g., common and proper nouns). Grammatical gender is a familiar noun class. It separates Hebrew nouns into masculine and feminine subclasses. These subclasses are based on related agreement structures and lexical semantics (see more below §7.6.2). Other noun classes include common and proper, concrete and abstract, count and noncount, and individuative and collective nouns. For the most part, these BH categorizations comprise binary groupings. In other words, the elements of each paired subclass are distinct and closed (masculine ~ feminine, concrete ~ abstract, common ~ proper). A lexeme is seldom found in both groups (e.g., proper *and* common nouns) and rarely changes subclass (e.g., proper noun → common noun).[23] While each subclass represents distinct elements and is closed, a noun is characterized by more than one noun class. For instance, צְדָקָה "righteousness" is characterized as feminine, abstract, common, and individuative.

---

[22] A helpful data-driven approach to distinguishing NPs as temporal adverbs is found in Cody Kingham, "Parts of Speech in Biblical Hebrew Time Phrases: A Cognitive-Statistical Analysis," in *New Perspectives in Biblical and Rabbinic Hebrew*, ed. Aaron Hornkohl and Geoffrey Khan, Cambridge Semitic Languages and Cultures 7 (Cambridge: Open Book, 2021), 497–545.

[23] In the few occasions where a noun may be grouped into more than one subclass, semantic variation typifies the relationship. Examples include the feminine עַיִן "eye," as compared with the masculine עַיִן "facet," and the feminine שֵׁן "tooth," as compared to the masculine שֵׁן "tine, prong," etc. (*IBHS* §6.4.1d).

7.5.1 Proper and Common Nouns

The subclasses of common and proper nouns differentiate between nonspecific and specific entities. <u>Common nouns</u> specify nonspecific entities with lexical meaning (e.g., עִיר "city," אִשָּׁה "woman," עַם "people," and נָהָר "river"). On a grammatical level, they are fully inflected, take nominal modifiers, and require a definite modifier to indicate specific referentiality.

<u>Proper nouns</u> (i.e., <u>names</u>) refer to specific entities. They are similar to pronouns in that they have fixed denotation, that is, they refer to unique entities. Examples include: יְרוּשָׁלַם "Jerusalem," חַוָּה "Eve," מִצְרַיִם "Egypt," and חִדֶּקֶל "the Tigris (River)." Proper nouns do not have lexical meaning—they cannot be defined.[24] Rather proper nouns include at least one basic category sense, which normally has a related common noun. Syntactic agreement is based on congruence with these related concepts: יְרוּשָׁלַם "Jerusalem" and חַוָּה "Eve" are feminine like עִיר "city" and אִשָּׁה "woman," while מִצְרַיִם "Egypt" and חִדֶּקֶל "Tigris" are masculine corresponding to עַם "people" and נָהָר "river."[25] Pronoun substitution demonstrates this grammatical congruence: הִיא replaces יְרוּשָׁלַם "Jerusalem" and חַוָּה "Eve," while הוּא may be exchanged for מִצְרַיִם "Egypt" or חִדֶּקֶל "Tigris."

On a grammatical level, proper nouns are not characteristically inflected for number or state.[26] As a function of their specific referentiality, proper nouns are intrinsically definite. They do not take typical nominal modifiers (e.g., pronominal suffixes, adjectives, determiners, quantifiers, demonstratives, definite articles).[27] The only productive exception is the unaccented directive suffix on place names

---

[24] These pragmatic-semantic properties explain why most names are transferred from one language to another through simple phonological adaptation (<u>rendering</u>) rather than translation. Like common nouns, proper nouns may have associated connotative meanings. See, further, Willy Van Langendonck and Mark Van de Velde, "Names and Grammar," in *The Oxford Handbook of Names and Naming*, ed. Carole Hough (Oxford: Oxford University Press, 2016), 20–33.

[25] Some proper nouns (e.g., אֱדוֹם "Edom") specify multiple basic category senses (אִישׁ "man," עַם "people," and אֶרֶץ "land"). The congruency follows the gender of the usage. Typically, the noun is masculine in reference to the person (Gen 36:8) and the people (Num 20:18–21) but feminine in reference to the place (Num 24:18).

[26] Most Hebrew names are derived from common nouns. Through time, they developed variable and then independent status from their originating lexemes. This independent status created the fixity of their form and the disassociation of the name from its etymological origin. That is to say, distinct morphemes are no longer considered grammatical but are part of the phonology of the word. For instance, proper nouns, such as קִרְיָתַיִם "Kiriathaim," אֶלְיָקִים "Eliakim," and עֲנָתוֹת "Anathoth," have etymologically transparent number morphemes, but these suffixes are considered part of the proper noun and do not take plural referents.

[27] Some names include analyzable modifiers, for example the definite article with הַבָּשָׁן "the Bashan," הַגִּלְגָּל "the Gilgal," הַגָּלִיל "the Galilee," הַגִּלְעָד "the Gilead," הַיַּרְדֵּן "the Jordan (River)," הַלְּבָנוֹן "the Lebanon," הַלּוֹחֵשׁ "the Hallohesh," הַכַּרְמֶל "the (Mount) Carmel," הַמִּדָתָא "the Hammedatha," הַמַּכְפֵּלָה "the Machpelah," הַמֹּלֶךְ "the Molech," הַמּוֹרִיָּה "the Moriah," הַמִּצְפָּה "the Mizpah," הָעַי "the Ai," הָעֹפֶל "the Ophel," הַפִּסְגָּה "the Pisgah," הַקּוֹץ "the Hakkoz," הָרָמָה "the Ramah," הַשִּׂדִּים "the Siddim," הַשָּׁרוֹן "the Sharon," and הַתֹּפֶת "the Topheth." These examples are etymological and not productive elements. One exception is יְאֹר "Nile," which lexicalizes as a general word for river (Dan 12:5–7) and the multiple tributaries of the Nile delta (יְאֹרֵי מִצְרַיִם, Isa 7:18).

(e.g., מִצְרַיְמָה "toward Egypt").[28] Proper nouns ending in ◌ָה- evidence the original feminine ending *t with the directive *he* (e.g., the form עָפְרָה "Oprah" becomes עָפְרָתָה "toward Oprah;" גִּבְעָה "Gibeah" becomes גִּבְעָתָה "toward Gibeah").[29] The chart below indicates the normal inflectional variation between proper (I) and common nouns (III).

	PROPER AND COMMON NOUN INFLECTIONS		
	PROPER NOUNS – – – – – – – – – – – – COMMON NOUNS		
	I	II	III
Absolute	חַוָּה "Eve"	גִּבְעָה "Gibeah/hill"	עֵצָה "counsel"
Construct	חַוַּת** "Eve of"	גִּבְעַת "Gibeah/hill of"	עֲצַת "counsel of"
Pronominal	חַוָּתִי** "my Eve"	יְאֹרִי "my Nile/watercourse"	עֲצָתִי "my counsel"
Plural	חַוּוֹת** "Eves"	גְּבָעוֹת** "Gibeahs"	עֵצוֹת "counsels"
Definite	הַחַוָּה** "the Eve"	הַגִּבְעָה "the Gibeah/hill"	הָעֵצָה "the counsel"
Quantifier	כָּל־חַוָּה** "every Eve"	כָּל־גִּבְעָה** "every Gibeah"	כָּל־עֲצַת "every counsel of"
Adjective	טוֹבָה חַוָּה** "good Eve"	טוֹבָה גִּבְעָה** "good Gibeah"	טוֹבָה עֲצַת "good counsel of"

Some overlap of these characteristics is evidenced for homonyms with etymologically similar proper and common nouns (cf. גִּבְעָה "Gibeah" and גִּבְעָה "hill" in column II). In these cases, the construct state may be used to differentiate between two similarly named entities, such as גִּבְעַת בִּנְיָמִין "Gibeah of Benjamin" and גִּבְעַת שָׁאוּל "Gibeah of Saul," or רָמַת לֶחִי "Ramath-lehi" and רָמַת הַמִּצְפֶּה "Ramath-mizpeh."[30] The use of pronominal suffixes is limited to names closely associated with common nouns: יְאֹרִי "my Nile/watercourse."[31]

---

[28] For multiword names, the suffix may be attached to the first element, similar to other construct phrases (בֵּיתָה פַרְעֹה "into the house of Pharaoh," Gen 47:14). Examples include: פַּדֶּנָה אֲרָם "toward Paddan-Aram" (Gen 28:2), בְּאֵרָה שֶׁבַע "toward Beer-Sheba" (Gen 46:1), and בְּאָבֵלָה בֵּית הַמַּעֲכָה "in Abel beth-ha-Maacah" (2 Sam 20:15). Sometimes the name forms an indivisible unit, and the suffix is instead added at the end of the sequence, as found with בְּעַלְמֹן דִּבְלָתָיְמָה "toward Almon-diblathaim" (Num 33:46, also cf. v. 47) and יִזְרְעֶאלָה "toward Jezreel" (2 Kgs 9:16).

[29] The etymological plural forms include the suffix with the absolute ending: כַּשְׂדִּימָה "toward Chaldea."

[30] Another way to differentiate between two similarly named places is to provide further specified information with a relative clause. Examples include: הַגִּבְעָתָה אֲשֶׁר לְבִנְיָמִן "to the Gibeah, which belongs to Benjamin" (Judg 20:4), and וּמִשָּׁם בְּאֵרָה הוּא הַבְּאֵר אֲשֶׁר אָמַר יְהֹוָה לְמֹשֶׁה "from there, [they went] into Beer, that is the Beer which Yahweh told to Moses . . ." (Num 21:16).

[31] The noun יְאֹר "Nile" appears to have been borrowed into Hebrew from Egyptian (*itrw* "Nile") as a transcribed proper noun. It either was relexicalized or borrowed separately as a common noun for a general "watercourse": יְאֹרִי/יְאֹרוֹ "my/his Nile" (Ezek 29:3), יְאֹרֶיךָ/יְאֹרֵיהֶם "Your/Their Niles"

7.5.2 Concrete and Abstract Nouns

In BH, concrete and abstract nouns are mainly differentiated based on semantics. <u>Concrete nouns</u> signify physical objects, such as עִיר "city," דּוֹד "uncle," and בְּתוּלָה "virgin." <u>Abstract nouns</u> have nonphysical referents (e.g., אַהֲבָה "love").

Some morphological identifiers are recognizable within the abstract noun sub-class. The suffix -וּת indicates an abstract concept (e.g., זְנוּת "fornication").[32] Plurality and feminine gender may also suggest abstracts, especially where parallel non-plural or masculine forms exist. Examples include the concrete singular nouns, דּוֹד "uncle"/דֹּדָה "aunt" and בְּתוּלָה "virgin" as compared with their respective plural forms as abstract nouns, דֹּדִים "love" and בְּתוּלִים "virginity." Feminine abstract nouns (e.g., טוֹבָה "welfare," דַּלָּה "the poor") may be formed from masculine adjectives (טוֹב "prosperity," דַּל "poor [person]"). The definite article also, at times, indicates abstract concepts (e.g., בִּלַּע הַמָּוֶת לָנֶצַח "he will devour [the] death for all time" Isa 25:8).

EXAMPLES OF CONCRETE AND ABSTRACT NOUNS			
CONCRETE		**ABSTRACT**	
Masculine	Feminine	Masculine	Feminine
————	————	זְנוּנִים "fornication(s)"	זְנוּת "fornication"
דּוֹד "uncle"	דֹּדָה "aunt"	דֹּדִים "love"	אַהֲבָה "love"
————	בְּתוּלָה "virgin"	————	בְּתוּלִים "virginity"
טוֹב "good"	————	טוֹב "prosperity"	טוֹבָה "welfare"
דַּל "poor (person)"	————	————	דַּלָּה "the poor"

7.5.3 Count and Noncount Nouns

Common nouns may be further described as either count nouns or noncount nouns (i.e., mass nouns). This division is based on the difference between counting and measuring. The former describes referents using a number amount or quantity (i.e., how many), while the latter is numbered using measurement, degree, or quality (i.e., how much).

<u>Count nouns</u> can typically be construed as both singular and plural forms (e.g., אִשָּׁה "woman; wife" ~ נָשִׁים "women; wives," פַּר "bull" ~ פָּרִים "bulls," and שָׁנָה

(Exod 7:19; Ezek 29:4), and יְאֹרֵי מִצְרַיִם/הַיְאֹרִים "Niles/Niles of Egypt" (Exod 8:1; Isa 7:18). Note also the well-known Kuntillet ʿAjrud graffiti "Yahweh and his Asherah (ʾšrth)." See Jeremy Smoak and William Schniedewind, "Religion at Kuntillet ʿAjrud," *Religions* 10.3.211 (2019): 1–18.

[32] Only four of the sixty-three instances of nouns with this suffix are *not* abstract: הַלְמוּת "hammer, mallet," כְּסוּת "clothing," חַלָּמוּת "type of plant product; alkanet," and רְעוּת "female companion, friend."

"year" ~ שָׁנִים "years"). They can also be quantified by a cardinal number (e.g., שְׁתַּיִם נָשִׁים "two women," פָּרִים עֲשָׂרָה "ten bulls," and מְאַת שָׁנָה "one hundred years"). Most common nouns are countable.[33] Syntactic agreement follows the morphological forms.

<u>Noncount nouns</u> do not take plural morphemes and cannot be quantified with a cardinal number except with a <u>measure word</u>. Grammatical concord is characteristically singular in line with the morphology. Generally, abstract nouns are noncount nouns. Examples include טוֹבָה "bounty" and טוֹב "good." Some abstract nouns behave more like count nouns, including צְדָקוֹת ~ צְדָקָה "righteousness" (but not צֶדֶק "righteousness").[34] Most concrete noncount nouns designate various kinds of materials, such as זָהָב "gold," עָפָר "dust," מֹר "myrrh," and סֹלֶת "fine flour." These may be grouped according to similar semantic types (e.g., metals, particles, amorphous materials, conflagrant elements, meteorological substances, foodstuffs, fluids, clothing materials, and intervals).

TYPE OF MATERIAL	EXAMPLES	UNITS OF MEASUREMENT
Metals	זָהָב "gold," בַּרְזֶל "iron," נְחוּשָׁה "copper, bronze," כֶּתֶם "gold," פַּז "refined gold," סָגוּר "gold," בְּדִיל "tin; plummet, lead weight," עֹפֶרֶת "lead"	שֶׁקֶל "shekel," כִּכָּר "talent," בֶּקַע "half-shekel," גֵּרָה "gerah," מָנֶה "mina"
Particles	תֶּבֶן "straw," מֹץ "chaff," קַשׁ "chaff," אֵפֶר "dust; ash," חוֹל "sand," עָפָר "dust"	מִקְוֶה "particle, grain," מָעָה "group," שְׁעָלִים "handfuls"
Amorphous	חֹמֶר "cement, mortar; clay," סַפִּיר "lapis-lazuli," טִיט "mud; clay," רֶפֶשׁ "mud," לְבוֹנָה "frankincense," כַּרְכֹּם "saffron," קִנָּמוֹן "cinnamon," נֵרְדְּ "nard," מֹר "myrrh," גַּד "coriander"	שֶׁקֶל "shekel," לְבֵנָה "brick," מְרְקָחָה "pot," זֶרַע "seed"
Conflagrant	אֵשׁ "fire," קְטֹרֶת "smoke; incense," עָשָׁן "smoke," עֲרָפֶל "heavy darkness; thick cloud," רֵיחַ "odor, scent"	עַמּוּד "pillars"
Meteorological	בָּרָד "hail," שֶׁלֶג "snow," קֶרַח "frost, ice," כְּפוֹר "frost"	אֶבֶן "stone"

---

[33] Langacker, *Cognitive Grammar*, 129–31.
[34] The plural may alternatively refer to discrete "righteous deeds" (*DCH* 7, s.v. "צדק," 85). See also M. Bar-Asher, "The Gender of Nouns in Biblical Hebrew," *Semitics* 6 (1978): 1–14.

TYPE OF MATERIAL	EXAMPLES	UNITS OF MEASUREMENT
Agronomy and Foodstuffs	לֶחֶם "food; bread," דְּבַשׁ "honey," סֹלֶת "fine flour," מֶלַח "salt," קֶמַח "flour," מָן "manna," נֹפֶת "honey," מַאֲכָל "food," בַּר "grain; produce," דֶּשֶׁא "grass," יְבוּל "produce," אָבִיב "grain," פְּרִי "ears (of grain)," דָּגָן "grain," חָצִיר "fruit, produce; offspring," אֹכֶל "food," אָבִיב "grass," חריונים/דביונים "barley ears," "dung"	קֹמֶץ "handful," סַל "basket," פַּת "cake," כִּכָּר "loaf," בַּקְבֻּק "piece," עֲרֵמָה "bottle, jar," סְאָה "heap," אֵיפָה "seah-measure," חֹמֶר "ephah-measure," לֶתֶךְ "homer-measure," עֹמֶר "cor-measure," שְׁעָלִים "le-thech-measure," "sheaf," "handfuls"
Fluids	יַיִן "wine," חָלָב "milk," תִּירוֹשׁ "new wine," יִצְהָר "oil," שֵׁכָר "alcoholic beverage, beer," עָסִיס "sweet wine," שֶׁמֶן "oil"	בַּת "bath-measure," הִין "hin-measure," חֹק "portion," כֹּר "cor-measure," לֹג "log-measure"
Clothing	אַרְגָּמָן "red-purple wool," שֵׁשׁ "linen," צֶמֶר "wool," בּוּץ "linen," תְּכֵלֶת "blue/violet thread," כַּרְמִיל "crimson," מַטְוֶה "yarn"	בֶּגֶד "garment," לְבוּשׁ "clothing," אַיִל "ram (pelts)," עוֹר "skin"
Intervals	אֹרֶךְ "length," רֹחַב "width," קוֹמָה "height," גֹּבַהּ "height, עֲבִי "thickness"	אַמָּה "cubit," קָנֶה "rod, reed," זֶרֶת "span," טֶפַח "handbreadth (four fingers or palm length)," אֶצְבַּע "finger"

Noncount nouns can be numbered but entail the inclusion of a unit of measure or a noun classifier. (Sometimes the measure word is implicit, see §7.9.6.) In Josh 7:21, the first item is a count noun (אַדֶּרֶת "garment"), and the other two items are noncount nouns (כֶּסֶף "silver," זָהָב "gold"). Metals require a unit to be counted (לָשׁוֹן "tongue-shaped brick") or an amount to be measured (שֶׁקֶל "shekel weight," מִשְׁקָל "weight").

Josh 7:21

וָאֵרְאֶה בַשָּׁלָל אַדֶּרֶת שִׁנְעָר אַחַת טוֹבָה וּמָאתַיִם שְׁקָלִים כֶּסֶף וּלְשׁוֹן זָהָב אֶחָד חֲמִשִּׁים שְׁקָלִים מִשְׁקָלוֹ

I saw in the spoil a nice Babylonian **garment**, two hundred shekels of **silver**, and an ingot of **gold** weighing fifty shekels.

Some common nouns do not have a singular form. The most common of these may be designated plural-only nouns (Latin: *plural tantum*). They include common nouns, such as פָּנִים "face; front," שָׁמַיִם "heavens; sky," מַיִם "water," גִּלֻּלִים "idols," מַעֲלָלִים "deeds; practice," בַּדִּים "polls; shoots," תּוֹלְדוֹת "generations,"

מֵעִים "internal parts, entrails, belly," and כְּלָיוֹת "kidneys."[35] Abstract concepts may be construed as plural-only nouns (§7.5.2). Examples are נְעוּרִים "youth; early life," רַחֲמִים "compassion," תַּהְפֻּכוֹת "perversion," and בְּתוּלִים "virginity." With only rare exceptions, these nouns have plural agreement. The nouns אֱלֹהִים "god, deity" and אֲדֹנָי "Lord" should probably be put into a separate category, often called *pluralis maiestatis* "plural of majesty (or rank)."[36] These words used with unique reference to God function like proper nouns, and they typically employ singular agreement.

Other nouns occur exclusively as duals. In these cases, the twofold referent is, in a sense, indivisible.[37] These include paired body parts (מָתְנַיִם "loins," חֲלָצַיִם "loins," עַפְעַפַּיִם "eyes; eyelids," חָפְנַיִם "hollows of hand," דַּדַּיִם "breasts; nipples"), bifurcated implements (מֹאזְנַיִם "balance," מֶלְקָחַיִם "tongs, snuffer," רֵחַיִם "hand-mill," אָבְנָיִם "potter's wheel; birth stool"), and other bifurcated items (מִכְנָסַיִם "pants, undergarments," מִשְׁפְּתַיִם "saddlebags").

7.5.4 Individuative and Collective Nouns

Count nouns can be subdivided further based on their semantic and grammatical properties relating to plurality. Semantically, an <u>individuative noun</u> designates a distinct referent. Most of these nouns may be pluralized to indicate more than one entity. This category comprises the majority of count nouns (e.g., אִשָּׁה "woman; wife" ~ נָשִׁים "women; wives;" בַּיִת "house" ~ בָּתִּים "houses"). Predictably, number congruence follows the noun morphology (e.g., וַיָּבֹאוּ נָשִׁים "women entered;" נָשִׁים רַבּוֹת "many women;" הָאִשָּׁה וִילָדֶיהָ "the woman and her children").

A <u>collective noun</u> is morphologically singular but refers to an assemblage of entities. English examples include *flock*, *clergy*, and *family*.[38] Such nouns usually show variation in number agreement, particularly with verbs.[39] Collectives may be considered a unit and agree with the morphological marking as singular. Plural concord is used when separable members are in view, following the notional plural

---

[35] Others are רְבִיבִים "raindrops," תּוֹצָאוֹת "exit, extremities; origin," פִּקּוּדִים "precepts," פְּסִילִים "images," מְתִים "people," בִּכּוּרִים "first fruits," גֶּחָלִים "embers," סַמִּים "spices; perfume," מִלֻּאִים "or-dination; setting," לֻלָאֹת "loops," מְרַאֲשׁוֹת "head position," מַעֲמַקִּים "depths," and קְלָעִים "curtains." (The related terms מָסָךְ "curtain; covering" and פָּרֹכֶת "curtain" are always singular.) For several plant terms, the plural form corresponds to the agricultural by-product of a singular entity: עֵצִים "wood, timber," שְׂעֹרִים "measured barley grain," חִטִּים "wheat kernels," and שִׁבֳּלִים "heads of grain." The corresponding plurals occur with numbers, for instance: רְכֵב "[Joshua] hung [the five kings] on five wood (stakes)" (Josh 10:26); וַיָּמָד שֵׁשׁ־שְׂעֹרִים "[Boaz] measured six [measures of] barley grain" (Ruth 3:15); but וּשְׁלֹמֹה נָתַן לְחִירָם עֶשְׂרִים אֶלֶף כֹּר חִטִּים מַכֹּלֶת לְבֵיתוֹ "Solomon gave Hiram 20,000 *kor*-measures of wheat" (1 Kgs 5:25).

[36] See Blau, 272. The singular noun אֱלֹהַּ may represent a backformation of the plural אֱלֹהִים.

[37] Interestingly, תְּאוֹמִים "twins" is not a dual but a plural-only noun.

[38] Some grammars categorize noncount nouns (§7.5.3) together with collective nouns; see Heinrich von Siebenthal, "'Collectives' in Ancient Hebrew: A Closer Look at the Semantics of an Intriguing Noun Category," *KUSATU* 10 (2009): 67–81.

[39] Some proper names, like יִשְׂרָאֵל "Israel," also share congruence properties with collective nouns.

(i.e., the semantic sense, Latin: *constructio ad sensum*).[40] With נְבֵלָה "corpse(s)," for example, the subject-verb number congruence can match the singular morphology of the noun (Jer 7:33) or the plural semantics of the noun (Isa 26:19).

Jer 7:33

וְהָיְתָה **נִבְלַת** הָעָם הַזֶּה לְמַאֲכָל

The corpse of this people will become (S) food.

Isa 26:19

יִחְיוּ מֵתֶיךָ **נְבֵלָתִי** יְקוּמוּן

Your dead ones will live; **my corpse(s)** will arise (P)!

The same noun, at times, may be used in both ways with little to no obvious notional differences (Josh 6:5, 20) and may even change within the same context (Exod 16:4).

Josh 6:5

וְעָלוּ הָעָם אִישׁ נֶגְדּוֹ

The people **are to go up** (P) each straight ahead.

Josh 6:20

וַיַּעַל הָעָם הָעִירָה אִישׁ נֶגְדּוֹ

The people **went up** (S) into the city each straight ahead.

Exod 16:4

וְיָצָא הָעָם וְלָקְטוּ דְּבַר יוֹם בְּיוֹמוֹ

The nation **is to go out** (S) [of the camp], and **they are** (P) **to gather** a ration for each day.

Analogous to standard count nouns, some <u>collective nouns</u> can specify multiple groups with singular or plural forms and can be enumerated with cardinal numbers.[41] Examples include מִשְׁפָּחָה "clan; family," מַטֶּה "tribe," שֵׁבֶט "tribe," רֹב "multitude," and לְאֹם "people." Further subsets should be separated with גּוֹי "people; nation" and עַם "people; nation." The former uses singular adjectives, and the plural form expresses multiple groups of entities (e.g., גּוֹיֵי הָאָרֶץ "peoples of the land") or a specified number (e.g., שִׁבְעָה גוֹיִם "seven nations," Deut 7:1).[42]

---

[40] E. J. Revell, "Logic of Concord with Collectives in Biblical Narrative," *Maarav* 9 (2002): 61–91.

[41] Multiple groups of collectives can require a plural venery word (e.g., שְׁלֹשָׁה עֶדְרֵי צֹאן "three flocks of sheep"). Some label these *of*-collectives because they can characteristically be construed in NPs as a collection of something (e.g. *family of Smiths, congregation of people, army of men, flock of sheep*). Additional examples include: עֵדָה "assembly," קָהָל "assembly, congregation," יֶתֶר "rest; remainder," and שְׁבִי "captivity; captives."

[42] See further Dougald McLaren III, "Defining Collective Nouns: How Cognitive Linguistics Helps Biblical Hebrew Grammarians," *Journal for Semitics* 30, no. 2 (2021): 1–15.

The noun עַם "people; nation" is more mixed as it is used with singular and plural verbs and adjectives.

Some nouns appear to be a mixture of both individuative and collective nouns.[43] These nouns can designate a group of entities but may elsewhere reference a countable member of that same group. We have already encountered one such noun נְבֵלָה "corpse, corpses." Some of these examples do not have plural forms. Unlike noncount nouns, these no plural nouns may be enumerated without a mediating quantifier, as with אַרְבֶּה אֶחָד "one locust" (Exod 10:19). These are similar to English no plural count nouns. Examples include words like *sheep, fish, deer,* or *buffalo*. These nouns do not have a plural form, but the bare form is combined with cardinal numbers or other quantifiers (e.g. *two sheep, ten fish, few deer, many buffalo*). Another Hebrew no plural count noun is עוֹף "bird(s)." First Kings 14:11 demonstrates that the singular may be conceptualized as a plurality, as seen with the plural verbal agreement (יֹאכְלוּ).

> 1 Kgs 14:11
>
> וְהַמֵּת בַּשָּׂדֶה יֹאכְלוּ **עוֹף** הַשָּׁמָיִם
> The **bird(s)** of heaven will eat (P) the dead in the field.

Other examples include: רֶכֶב "chariot" (עֲשָׂרָה רֶכֶב "ten chariots"), בָּקָר "cattle, herd; ox" (חֲמִשָּׁה בָקָר "five cattle" but עֶדְרֵי בָקָר "herds of cattle"), צֹאן "small cattle; flock" (מֵאָה צֹאן "one hundred sheep"), and perhaps אָדָם "man, person; humans, humanity." For this last case, אָדָם can refer to a single individual, as in Josh 14:15, or to a group of people (Jer 47:2 and Eccl 7:29).

> Josh 14:15
>
> וְשֵׁם חֶבְרוֹן לְפָנִים קִרְיַת אַרְבַּע **הָאָדָם** הַגָּדוֹל בָּעֲנָקִים הוּא
> The name of Hebron used to be the city of Arba, who was a great **man** among the Anakim.

> Jer 47:2
>
> וְזָעֲקוּ **הָאָדָם** וְהֵילִל כֹּל יוֹשֵׁב הָאָרֶץ
> **The people** will cry out (P), and every inhabitant of the land will howl.

> Eccl 7:29
>
> מָצָאתִי אֲשֶׁר עָשָׂה הָאֱלֹהִים אֶת־**הָאָדָם** יָשָׁר וְהֵמָּה בִקְשׁוּ חִשְּׁבֹנוֹת רַבִּים
> I have found that God made **people** upright, but **they** have pursued (P) many schemes.

---

[43] A few nouns appear to fall into multiple categories with different semantics. For instance, בַּיִת "house" can represent either an individuated entity "house (i.e., structure)" or a collective "household; family, dynasty." The individual member of a בַּיִת "household," however, would be אָב "father," אָח "brother," אֵם "mother," or בֵּן "son," not a בַּיִת "house."

Unlike no plural nouns, however, אָדָם usually takes a classifier—such as נֶפֶשׁ "soul" (Num 31:46)—to be counted.[44]

Num 31:46

וְנֶפֶשׁ אָדָם שִׁשָּׁה עָשָׂר אָלֶף
16,000 **people**

The feminine suffix with certain nouns can also be used to indicate a single entity (Latin: *nomina unitatis*). Examples include: אֳנִי "fleet" with the discrete unit אֳנִיָּה "a ship" (but also, אֳנִיּוֹת "ships"), אֵבֶר "wings" but singular אֶבְרָה "a wing," שֵׂעָר "hair" but the singular שַׂעֲרָה "a hair" (also, שַׂעֲרוֹת רֹאשִׁי "the hairs of my head"), and עָנָן "cloud mass" but a singular עֲנָנָה "cloud." This pattern, however, is not a productive pattern for Hebrew collectives as it is in other Semitic languages.[45] In fact, some collectives, like דָּגָה "fish," appear to show the inverse relationship with the corresponding individuative דָּג "a fish."

7.6 NOUN MORPHOLOGY

Hebrew noun morphology may be separated into the categories of derivation and inflection. Derivation describes the formative elements of a word, namely, its root, pattern, and affixes. Inflection designates the different forms of the same lexeme which are grammatically conditioned. As a general rule, each lexeme is distinguished from similar lexemes based on derivation (e.g., various affixes differentiate the words *center*, *central*, *centralize*, and *centrality*). The variation of forms of the same lexeme comprises its inflection (e.g., *center*, *centers*, *centered*). Some category fluidity is feasible because affixes could be derivative, inflectional, or sometimes both. The regularity, or productivity, of certain formative elements can also lead to hazy categorical distinctions. In English, derivational morphemes, like *-ity*, *-ness*, and *-er*, create new lexemes, such as *modernity*, *tardiness*, and *helper*. Inflectional endings (e.g., *-s* and *-ed*) designate variant forms of the same lexeme (e.g., *help*, *helps*, *helped*), but some formative patterns are inflectional (e.g., vowel gradation, or ablaut: *man ~ men*; *sing ~ sang ~ sung*).

7.6.1 Noun Derivation

Hebrew word formation may be considered as building from either an originating lexeme or a notional consonantal root. This derivational source is generally represented by a verb (usually the *Qal* SC 3MS, e.g., זָבַח "slaughter") or the corresponding abstracted root (זבח). From this source, noun formation occurs through varying the morphological pattern (e.g., זֶבַח "sacrifice"), adding affixes (מִזְבֵּחַ "altar"), or using inflectional endings (זִבְחוֹ "his sacrifice;" זְבָחִים "sacrifices;" מִזְבְּחֹתָיו "his altars").

---

[44] Exceptions include one instance at the end of the book of Jonah (הַרְבֵּה מִשְׁתֵּים עֶשְׂרֵה רִבּוֹ אָדָם "more than 120,000 people," Jonah 4:11) and constructions with the number אֶחָד "one."

[45] *BHRG* §24.2.2.2.

7.6.1.1 Noun Patterns

Nouns are formed using a derivational source combined with certain patterning structures. These patterns include combinations of vowels and consonantal lengthening. The consonantal-vowel pattern is sometimes called a <u>base</u>.[46] For instance, זֶבַח "sacrifice" may be described as combining the abstracted root זבח ($\sqrt{ZBH}$) with the vowels ◌ֶ◌ֿ ($C_1\acute{e}C_2aC_3$). The morphological patterns are commonly generalized to the root QTL. As such, זֶבַח is a *qétal* form.

NOUN FORMATION	QÉTAL (*QATL)	
Pattern	◌ֶ◌ֿ	$C_1\acute{e}C_2aC_3$
Root	זבח	ZBḤ
Base Form	—	*zabḥ
Lexeme	זֶבַח	zébaḥ

This pattern is further categorized as one of the segholate-type noun patterns. <u>Segholate nouns</u> originate from the structure, *CVCC*, where *V* is an original short *a*, *i*, or *u*-class vowel. The absolute form is characterized by stress on the initial syllable and typically an eponymous *segol* forming the second syllable. These patterns are sometimes referred to as *qatl*, *qitl*, and *qutl* based on the three vowel classes.[47] The chart below exemplifies the typical dictionary forms with מֶלֶךְ "king," סֵפֶר "book," and אֹזֶן "ear." Other cases, such as בַּעַל "lord" and קֶבֶר "grave," are secondary patterns for the *qatl* and *qitl* nouns. The originating form is evident with the vocalic pronominal suffixes.

SEGHOLATE NOUNS							
	*A-CLASS (*QATL)		*I-CLASS (*QITL)				*U-CLASS (*QUTL)
Pattern	◌ֶ◌ֿ	CéCeC	◌ֶ◌ֿ	CéCeC	◌ֶ◌ֿ	CéCeC	◌ֹ◌ֿ CóCeC
Root	מלך	MLK	קבר	QBR	ספר	SPR	אזן ʾZN
Base Form	—	*malk	—	*qibr	—	*sipr	— *ʾuzn
Lexeme	מֶלֶךְ	mélek	קֶבֶר	qéber	סֵפֶר	séper	אֹזֶן ʾózen
Suffixed	מַלְכִּי	malkî	קִבְרִי	qibrî	סִפְרִי	siprî	אָזְנִי ʾoznî

---

[46] John Huehnergard, "Biblical Hebrew Nominal Patterns," in *Epigraphy, Philology, and the Hebrew Bible: Methodological Perspectives on Philological and Comparative Study of the Hebrew Bible in Honor of Jo Ann Hackett*, ed. Jeremy M. Hutton and Aaron D. Rubin, ANEM 12 (Atlanta: Society of Biblical Literature, 2015), 25–64.
[47] The asterisk is used to indicate a reconstructed earlier form.

The vowels *pataḥ* or *ḥireq* can occur in the second syllable in the context of a guttural consonant or certain glides, as with זֶבַח "sacrifice" and יַיִן "wine."

OTHER SEGHOLATE NOUN PATTERNS					
	*A-CLASS (*QATL*)		***I-CLASS** (*QITL*)		***U-CLASS** (*QUTL*)	
III-guttural	◌ֶ◌ַ◌	$C_1éC_2aC_3$	◌ֶ◌ַ◌	$C_1éC_2aC_3$	◌ֹ◌ַ◌	$C_1óC_2aC_3$
Root	זרע	ZRʿ	זבח	ZBḤ	ארח	ʾRḤ
Base Form	—	*zarʿ	—	*zabḥ		órah
Lexeme	זֶרַע	zéraʿ	זֶבַח	zébaḥ	אֹרַח	órah
Suffixed	זַרְעִי	zarʿî	זִבְחִי	zibḥî	אָרְחִי	órah
II-guttural	◌ַ◌ֹ	CáCaC				
Root	בעל	BʿL				
Base Form	—	*baʿl				
Lexeme	בַּעַל	báʿal				
Suffixed	בַּעְלִי	baʿlî				
II-/III-yod	◌ַיִ◌	CáYiC	◌ִ◌	CăCî	◌ֳ◌	CŏCî
Root	עין	ʿYN	בכי	BKY	עני	ʿNY
Base Form	—	*ʿayn	—	*biky	—	*ʿuny
Lexeme	עַיִן	ʿáyin	בְּכִי	bəkî	עֳנִי	ŏnî
Suffixed	עֵינִי	ʿêni	בְּכִיֵ	bikyî	עָנְיֵ	ʿonyî

Some noun patterns can be correlated with specific semantics. Examples include: (1) the *qōtēl* pattern as the doer of an action (e.g., כֹּהֵן "priest," שֹׁפֵט "judge"), (2) the *qattāl* pattern denoting a habitual activity, profession, or occupation (Latin: *nomen professionis*; e.g., חַטָּא "sinner," דַּיָּן "judge," מַכָּר "merchant"), and (3) the *qittēl* pattern used for bodily defects (e.g., אִסֵּר "disabled, bound," אִלֵּם "silent, mute," גִּבֵּח "balding," גִּבֵּן "hunchbacked," עִוֵּר "blind," פִּסֵּחַ "lame"). The *qōtēl* pattern is conspicuously indistinguishable from the *Qal* active participle, but dyads like מֹלֵךְ "reigning"/מֶלֶךְ "king" and סֹפֵר "enumerating"/סֵפֶר "scribe" evidence syntactic and semantic differences between the productive verbal adjective and the identical noun patterns.

NOUN FORMATION	QŌTĒL (*QĀTIL)		QATTĀL (*QATTAL)		QITTĒL (*QITTIL)	
Root	שׁפט	ŠPṬ	חטא	ḤṬʾ	עור	ʿWR
Pattern	◌ְ◌ֹ◌	$C_1\bar{o}C_2\bar{e}C_3$	◌ָ◌ַ◌	$C_1aC_2C_2\bar{a}C_3$	◌ֵ◌ִ◌	$C_1iC_2C_2\bar{e}C_3$
Lexeme	שֹׁפֵט	šōpēṭ	חַטָּא	ḥaṭṭāʾ	עִוֵּר	ʿiwwēr

7.6.1.2 Noun Affixes

Nouns may be comprised of one or more derivational affixes. The most common of these include the prefix element, -מְ (e.g., מָגוּר "sojourning, dwelling place"), the suffix, -ָה (e.g., מַלְכָּה "queen"), or both (e.g., מַמְלָכָה "kingdom;" מְנוֹרָה "lamp stand"). Other nominal affixes include: ʾalep prefixes -א, he prefixes -ה, yod prefixes -י, nun prefixes -נ, šin prefixes -שׁ, and taw prefixes -ת. Common suffixes are -ן, -ִי, -ִית, -וּת, -ם, and -ת.

NOUN AFFIXES	
SUFFIX	**EXAMPLES**
-ָה	מַלְכָּה "queen"
-ן	שֻׁלְחָן "table," אֶבְיוֹן "poor, needy"
-ִי	מִשְׁעִי "cleansing"
-ִית	אַחֲרִית "end; future; descendants"
-וּת	הֲרִיסוּת "destruction; ruin"
-ם	יוֹמָם "daytime; by day," חַרְטֹם "engraver; diviner"
-ת	אַדֶּרֶת "splendor, glory; robe, mantle"
-ָם	אָמְנָם "surely; truly," אוּלָם "alternatively," חִנָּם "undeservedly," יוֹמָם "by day," רֵיקָם "emptily, vainly"
-ִית	אַחֲרִית "end; future; descendants," חָפְשִׁית "freedom," רֵאשִׁית "beginning; chief," שְׁאֵרִית "rest, remainder; remnant," תָּבְנִית "measurement"
-וּת	גַּבְהוּת "haughtiness, pride," הוֹלֵלוּת "foolishness," יְדִדוּת "love, beloved (one)," יַלְדוּת "childhood; youth," כְּבֵדֻת "heaviness, difficulty," כְּלִמּוּת "disgrace," כְּסִילוּת "stupidity," מַלְכוּת "royalty; dominion; reign; kingdom"
-ִי (M) or -ִית (F)	נָכְרִי "foreign," אֲרַמִּי "Aramean," מִצְרִית "Egyptian woman," מוֹאֲבִיָּה "Moabite woman"

NOUN AFFIXES	
PREFIX	**EXAMPLES**
-מְ	מִזְבֵּחַ "altar," מָגוֹר "sojourning, dwelling place"
-א	אֶשְׁכָּר "tribute; payment," אַבְרֵךְ "bow, kneel down," אַזְכָּרָה "memorial," אַשְׁמוּרָה "(night) watch"
-ה	הֵידָד "shout; cheer," הַצָּלָה "deliverance," הַרְאֵל "altar; hearth," הַרְבֵּה "much, many"
-י	יְדִידוֹת "love," יְקוּם "substance, existence"
-נ	נְסִבָּה "turn of events," נָזִיד "cooked food"
-שַׁ	שַׁלְהֶבְתְיָה "flame," שַׁלְהֶבֶת "sparks"
-תִ	תְּפִלָּה "prayer," תַּלְמִיד "scholar," תּוֹדָה "thanksgiving"

Some affixes provide semantic information. For instance, the suffix -הֹ֫ indicates a marked or feminine entity. The prefix -מְ often designates a concrete object. Semantically, -םֹ֫ typically designates an adverb; - יתֹ֫ and -וּת can indicate various abstract notions; and -יֹ֫ and -יתֹ֫ are used as the *nisbe* or gentilic suffix.

Noun patterns can work together with affixes to produce various word types. One example is found with the ordinal numbers. The pattern קְטִילִי is used with the numbers "three" through "ten" to create the ordinals: שְׁלִישִׁי "third," רְבִיעִי "fourth," חֲמִישִׁי "fifth," שִׁשִּׁי "sixth," etc.[48]

7.6.2 Noun Inflection

Derivational pattern morphology indicates the distinction between the noun דָּבָר "word" and the verb דִּבֶּר "speak." Noun inflection refers to the various forms of the same lexeme. The noun דָּבָר includes the semantic plural, דְּבָרִים "words," and the forms used as the head of a noun phrase, דְּבַר "word of" and דִּבְרֵי "words of." Inflectional forms are obligatory and grammatically conditioned. Hebrew nouns are inflected primarily by adding suffixes to their base form. In some cases, the noun pattern varies, and even more rarely the root changes. These morphological characteristics are described under the semantic categories of gender, number, and state.

7.6.2.1 Gender

Gender describes a lexical and grammatical property of nouns. Similar to French or Spanish, Hebrew nouns are categorized into either masculine or feminine subclasses (e.g., אָב "father [M]" ~ אֵם "mother [F]"). Nouns are gendered as masculine

---

[48] The sixth ordinal demonstrates a variation on this pattern because of the assimilation of the original R2 stop to the final consonant. Instead of שְׁדִישִׁי* the form is שִׁשִּׁי "sixth."

and feminine in about a 2:1 ratio. In many, if not most, of these cases, the noun morphology signals grammatical gender.[49] The suffixes are the same as those with adjectives and participles: masculine singular (Ø-), masculine plural (ים-ִ◌), feminine singular (ה-ָ◌), and feminine plural (וֹת-).[50] Foundationally, though, gender is ascribed at the lexeme level and is only secondarily signaled with morphology. Grammatical gender must be learned with each individual lexeme. For instance, אֵם "mother" is feminine even though it does not have the feminine suffix.[51] The nouns אִמּוֹת "mothers" and אָבוֹת "fathers" take the morphological plural וֹת- suffix, yet the former noun is feminine, and the latter is masculine.

While the assignment of gender appears arbitrary on a semantic level for most nouns (e.g., עֹשֶׁר "wealth [M]" and יִתְרָה "wealth [F]"), some groupings are predictable. For referents with distinct biological sex, masculine and feminine gender typically correspond to male and female entities (e.g., פַּר "bull [M]" ~ פָּרָה "cow [F];" אִישׁ "man [M]" ~ אִשָּׁה "woman [F]"). A number of <u>epicene</u> nouns, however, comprise referents of both biological sexes without a dyad of <u>isomorphic</u> forms. Examples include: גָּמָל "camel," דֹּב "bear," פֶּרֶא "wild donkey," צִפּוֹר "bird," תּוֹלֵעָה "worm," תַּן "jackal," and תּוֹר "dove."[52] Other semantic groups—some body parts (particularly the paired ones), certain places, abstracts, natural forces/elements, tools/utensils, and clothing—contain a disproportionately high number of feminine nouns.

---

[49] It is widely thought that the feminine suffixes in Semitic initially indicated unmarked and marked nouns rather than gender marking.

[50] Additional feminine singular endings are found with final ת (GKC §80).

[51] Other common unmarked feminine nouns include: אֶבֶן "stone; rock," אֶזְרוֹעַ "arm," אֶצְבַּע "finger," אֶרֶץ "earth, land, ground," אָתוֹן "female donkey," אֹזֶן "ear," אֹשֶׁר "happiness," בְּאֵר "well, pit," בְּרִית "covenant; contract," בֶּטֶן "stomach; womb," בֶּרֶךְ "knee," גֹּרֶן "threshing floor," דְּיוֹ "ink," דָּת "law, decree," זְרוֹעַ "arm; forearm; shoulder; strength, force," חֲנִית "spear," חֶרֶב "sword," יָד "hand," יָמִין "right hand," יָרֵךְ "thigh; side; base," יָתֵד "peg, pin," כְּרָע "lower leg," כִּכָּר "talent, weight measurement; round district; loaf," כַּף "palm; sole; bowl," כָּבֵד "liver," כָּנָף "wing; extremity, edge," כָּרֵשׂ "stomach," כָּתֵף "shoulder; side," כּוֹס "cup," לְחִי "jaw, jawbone; cheek," מְצָד "stronghold; fortress," מִגְרָע "recess, niche," מַהֲמֹר "deep pit," מַקְהֵל "assembly," מֵעֶי "grain," נַעַל "sandal, shoe," סוּת "vestment," עִיר "city; district," עֵז "goat," עֶצֶם "bone; skeleton," עֶרֶשׂ "couch, bed," עַיִשׁ "constellation; Pleiades," עָרוּץ "dreadful," פִּלֶגֶשׁ "concubine," פַּעַם "foot; pace, footstep," צְפַרְדֵּעַ "frog," צֵלָע "rib, side," צָנֻם "hard," צָפוֹן "north," צֹהַר "roof," קִפּוֹז "tree snake," קֶרֶן "horn," קַרְסֹל "ankle," קָצוּר "small," קֹטֶן "little finger," רֶגֶל "foot," רֶצֶף "burning coal," רָחֵל "ewe," רוּחַ "spirit; breath; wind," שְׂלָו "quail," שָׂרִיק "combed," שׂוֹךְ "branch," שֵׁגָל "queen; female noble," שׁוֹק "leg; thigh, fibula," תֵּבֵל "world; earth," תֵּימָן "south country," and תּוֹר "turtledove."

[52] A small number of instances of אַיָל "deer" and חֲמוֹר "donkey" appear to be feminine even though dyad exists, אַיָּלָה "hind" and אָתוֹן "she-ass."

SEMANTIC GROUPS	FEMININE NOUNS	MASCULINE NOUNS
Body Parts	אֹזֶן "ear," אַמָּה "cubit; forearm," אֶצְבַּע "finger," בָּבָה "eye, pupil," בֶּטֶן "stomach, womb," בֶּרֶךְ "knee," זְרוֹעַ "arm; forearm; shoulder," זֶרֶת "hand-span," חֲלָצַיִם "loins," יָד "hand," יָמִין "right hand," יָרֵךְ "thigh; side," כָּנָף "wing," כַּף "palm; sole," כָּתֵף "shoulder; side," לְחִי "jaw," לָשׁוֹן "tongue," מַפְרֶקֶת "neck," עֶצֶם "bone, skeleton," עַיִן "eye," צֵלָע "rib, side," קֶרֶן "horn," שְׁמֻרָה "eyelid," רֶגֶל "foot," שֵׁן "tooth," שָׂפָה "lip," שָׁפְכָה "penis"	אַף "nose; anger," גָּרוֹן "neck; throat," מֵצַח "forehead, brow," מָתְנַיִם "loins," עָקֵב "footprint; heel," עֹרֶף "neck," פֶּה "mouth," צַוָּאר "neck; back of the head," רֶחֶם "womb," שַׁד "(female) breast," שְׁכֶם "shoulder"
Places	אֶרֶץ "land," גְּבוּלָה "border; territory," חֶלְקָה "portion, allotment," טִירָה "encampment; battlement," מַמְלָכָה "kingdom, dominion; sovereignty; reign," מִקְנָה "purchase; possession," סְבָכָה "thicket," עִיר "city," רְחוֹב "open plaza," שְׁאוֹל "underworld, afterlife; Sheol," שִׁבֹּלֶת "stream, wadi," תֵּבֵל "world; earth," תְּהוֹם "abyss; deep (waters)"	שָׂדֶה "field," גְּבוּל "border, boundary; territory; mountain," גַּיְא "valley," גַּן "garden," דֶּרֶךְ "way, road," הַר "mountain," כֶּרֶם "vineyard," מִדְבָּר "pasture; wilderness," נַחַל "wadi, stream, trench," נָהָר "stream, river"
Natural Forces/ Elements	אֶבֶן "stone; rock," אוֹר "light," אֵשׁ "fire," רוּחַ "wind," שֶׁמֶשׁ "sun"	טַל "dew," בָּרָק "lightning," בָּרָד "hail," עָב "cloud," מָטָר "rain," עֲרָפֶל "heavy cloud"
Tools/ Utensils	מַאֲכֶלֶת "knife," כּוֹס "cup," חֶרֶב "sword,"	
Clothing	אַדֶּרֶת "cloak," אֲפֻדָּה "ephod," אֵזוֹר "belt; loincloth," כְּסוּת "covering," כֻּתֹנֶת "tunic," מִגְבָּעָה "headdress," מַסֵּכָה "cloak," מִטְפַּחַת "covering," מִסְפָּחָה "covering," מַסְוֶה "veil," מַעֲטֶפֶת "cloak," מִצְנֶפֶת "turban," נַעַל "sandal," סְחָבָה "ragged cloths," שַׂלְמָה "veil," רְעָלָה "veil," תִּלְבֹּשֶׁת "cloak; clothing," "clothing"	אֵפֹד "ephod," בֶּגֶד "garment; covering," לְבוּשׁ "clothing; garment," מִכְנָסַיִם "undergarments," מְעִיל "cloak; outer garment," פְּאֵר "turban, headdress"

A very small group of nouns are found with variable gender. For most of these examples, one gender is dominant while the other is rare.[53] Some characteristically feminine nouns are masculine in a small number of instances. Conversely, certain masculine nouns are sometimes feminine.

Feminine (rarely M)	אוֹר "light," אֶרֶץ "land," אֵשׁ "fire," גֶּפֶן "vine," דַּעַת "knowledge," זְרוֹעַ "arm," יָד "hand," יְסוֹד "foundation," כָּנָף "wing," לָשׁוֹן "tongue," עִיר "city," עֵת "time," צֵלָע "rib," שְׁאוֹל "underworld, afterlife; Sheol," שַׁבָּת "Sabbath," שֶׁמֶשׁ "sun," שֵׁן "tooth; ivory; fork prong," תֵּבֵל "world; earth," תְּהוֹם "abyss; deep (waters)"
Masculine (rarely F)	אֱדוֹם "Edom," אוֹר "light," אוֹת "sign," אִי "island," אֹרַח "way, path; behavior," אֲרוֹן "ark; chest," גַּיְא "valley," גַּן "garden," דֶּרֶךְ "way, road," זָקָן "beard," חֹדֶשׁ "month; new moon," חַלּוֹן "window," חָצֵר "court; enclosure," כֶּרֶם "vineyard," מַאֲכָל "food," מָגֵן "shield," מַחֲנֶה "encampment," מַטֶּה "staff; tribe," מוֹאָב "Moab," מָקוֹם "place," מַקֵּל "staff; rod," נְחֹשֶׁת "copper, bronze," סִיר "pot," עָב "cloud," עֲבֹת "cord, rope," רֶחֶם "womb," שֵׁבֶט "rod, staff, scepter; tribe," שׁוּשַׁן "lotus, lily," שַׁעַר "gate," תַּעַר "razor; sheath"

Grammatical gender is critical to syntax. Syntactic agreement, or congruence, indicates the relationships between words and the gender of the lexeme. These relations are signaled by matching the gender of nouns with predicates (Num 13:28), adjectives (Amos 8:13), and pronominal referents (Gen 3:6).

וְהֶעָרִים בְּצֻרוֹת גְּדֹלֹת מְאֹד	The cities (F) were inaccessible [and] very large (F) (Num 13:28)
הַבְּתוּלֹת הַיָּפוֹת	The beautiful (F) virgins (F) (Amos 8:13)
תַאֲוָה־הוּא לָעֵינַיִם	It (M = הָעֵץ) was pleasing to the eyes (Gen 3:6)

The inflectional forms are described in the next two sections.

7.6.2.2 Number
Nouns inflect for <u>number</u> generally related to their countability. In Hebrew, noun inflection can differentiate one, two, and more than two entities corresponding to the singular, dual, and plural forms. Three morphological forms use distinct suffixes for masculine and feminine nouns. Most nouns only inflect as singular or plural.

P	D	S	
־ִים	־ַיִם	∅-	M
־וֹת	־ָתַיִם	־ָה	F

---

53 Joüon-Muraoka §134m.

The majority inflect by adding a suffix to their singular form. If the singular noun has no suffix, it will inflect with masculine suffixes regardless of its grammatical gender: יוֹם "day (M)," רֶ֫גֶל "foot (F)," יוֹמַ֫יִם "two days," רַגְלַ֫יִם "two feet (F)," and יָמִים "days," רְגָלִים "feet (F)." If the lexeme ends with הָ֯-, it typically inflects using feminine suffixes, such as שָׁנָה "year," שְׁנָתַ֫יִם "two years," and שָׁנוֹת "years." A small number of nouns, however, mix these forms, such as יוֹם "day (M)" ~ יָמוֹת "days (M);" שָׁנָה "year (F)" ~ שָׁנִים "years (F);" אָב "father" ~ אָבוֹת "fathers."

Certain lexemes use distinct noun patterns with their plural form. Segholate nouns have one pattern with the singular/dual and another with the plural (see chart below). The segholate noun plurals—רְגָלִים "feet," סְפָרִים "documents," and בְּקָרִים "mornings"—are formed similarly to the common plural form (e.g., דָּבָר "word" ~ דְּבָרִים "words").

SEGHOLATE NOUNS					
	A-CLASS (*QATL*)		I-CLASS (*QITL*)		U-CLASS (*QUTL*)
S/D	oǪ֫Ǫ	oǪ֫Ǫִים	oǪ֫Ǫ	——	oǪ֫Ǫ	——
	רֶ֫גֶל	רַגְלַ֫יִם	סֵ֫פֶר	——	בֹּ֫קֶר	——
P	ǪǪֹ֯יִם		ǪǪֹ֯יִם		ǪǪֹ֯יִם	
	רְגָלִים		סְפָרִים		בְּקָרִים[54]	

Other common nouns have irregular plural forms.

IRREGULAR PLURAL NOUNS	
P	**S**
יָמִים "days"	יוֹם "day"
עָרִים "cities"	עִיר "city"
בָּנִים "sons"	בֵּן "son"
רָאשִׁים "heads"	רֹאשׁ "head"
אַחִים "brothers"	אָח "brother"
בָּנוֹת "daughters"	בַּת "daughter"
בָּתִּים "houses"	בַּ֫יִת "house"
כֵּלִים "vessels"	כְּלִי "vessel; utensil"
אֲנָשִׁים "men"	אִישׁ "man"

---

[54] Another plural pattern of *qutl* type nouns is אֹהָלִים or אֳהָלִים "tents."

IRREGULAR PLURAL NOUNS	
P	**S**
נָשִׁים "women"	אִשָּׁה "woman"
פִּיּוֹת/פִּיפִיּוֹת "mouths"	פֶּה "mouth"

Most nouns employ two of the three number forms. For instance, דָּבָר "word" is restricted to the singular and the plural, דְּבָרִים "words." The dual is not productive in BH. When it does occur, the dual form generally corresponds to the singular: עַיִן "eye" and עֵינַיִם "two eyes." The dual number is limited to certain semantic groups (i.e., paired entities, body parts, and measuring units).[55]

DUAL NOUN SEMANTIC GROUPS		
	MASCULINE NOUNS	**FEMININE NOUNS**
Paired	אָבְנַיִם "potter wheel," דְּרָכַיִם "two ways," לֻחֹתַיִם "two tablets," מֹאזְנַיִם "balances, scales," נְחֻשְׁתַּיִם "shackles," נַעֲלַיִם "sandals," עַרְבַּיִם "twilight,"[56] רֵחַיִם "hand-mill," רַחֲמָתַיִם "two wombs"	חוֹמֹתַיִם "two doors," דְּלָתַיִם "double walls," מְצִלְתַּיִם "cymbals," רִקְמָתַיִם "sheep pens," מִשְׁפְּתַיִם "two garments"
Body Parts	אַפַּיִם "nostrils," אַפְסָיִם "two extremities," חָפְנַיִם "handfuls," מָתְנַיִם "loins," שָׁדַיִם "breasts"	אָזְנַיִם "ears," בִּרְכַּיִם "knees," חֲלָצַיִם "loins," יָדַיִם "two hands," יְרֵכַיִם ~ יַרְכְתַיִם "sides," כְּנָפַיִם "two wings," כַּפַּיִם "two hands," כְּרָעַיִם "legs," קַרְנַיִם "jaws," עֵינַיִם "eyes," לְחָיַיִם "two horns," רַגְלַיִם "two feet," שִׁנַּיִם "teeth," שֹׁקַיִם "legs," שְׂפָתַיִם "two lips"
Measuring Units	אַלְפַּיִם "two thousand," יוֹמַיִם "two days," כִּלְאַיִם "two kinds," כִּפְלַיִם "double," שְׁבֻעַיִם "two weeks," שְׁנַיִם "two"	אַרְבַּעְתַּיִם "two cubits," אַמָּתַיִם "four times," כִּכְּרַיִם "double weight," מָאתַיִם "two hundred," סָאתַיִם "two measures," פַּעֲמַיִם "two times," רִבֹּתַיִם "twenty thousand," שִׁבְעָתַיִם "seven times," שְׁנָתַיִם "two years," שְׁתַּיִם "two"

---

[55] The nouns שָׁמַיִם "heavens; sky" and מַיִם "water" appear to be morphologically dual, but they are best understood as plural-only nouns. Similarly, יְרוּשָׁלַם "Jerusalem" and מִצְרַיִם "Egypt" have frozen dual-like forms.

[56] The form צָהֳרַיִם "noon; midday" may be formed from an analogy on this word.

Semantically, the Hebrew number, or count distinctions, relate to the actual number or countability of the real-world referent. Some plural nouns, however, indicate various kinds of abstraction.[57] A few nouns have different but related meanings for the singular as opposed to the plural form. These include various kinds of vegetation, trees, and blood.

P	S
שְׂעֹרִים "barley (product)"	שְׂעֹרָה "barley (plant)"
חִטִּים "wheat (product)"	חִטָּה "wheat (plant)"
תַּפּוּחִים "apples"	תַּפּוּחַ "apple tree"
עֵצִים "timber, lumber"	עֵץ "tree; wood" (or collectively "trees")
דָּמִים "shed blood; bloodguilt"	דָּם "blood"

On a grammatical level, syntactical concord is limited to a binary count distinction of one as compared with more than one. That is to say, a noun referring to a single referent has singular concord (Ps 36:12), and nouns with number higher than one typically use plural concord (Gen 6:4). Dual nouns express concord with the plural (Prov 6:18).

אַל־תְּבוֹאֵנִי רֶגֶל גַּאֲוָה   Do not let the foot (S) of the proud come (S) near me. (Ps 36:12)

בַּיָּמִים הָהֵם   in those (P) days (P) . . . (Gen 6:4)

רַגְלַיִם מְמַהֲרוֹת לָרוּץ לָרָעָה   Feet (P) hastening (P) to run to evil. (Prov 6:18)

7.6.2.3 State

Hebrew does not use grammatical case (i.e., declension) to indicate the syntactic roles of nouns within a clause. Rather, nouns inflect for <u>grammatical state</u> (Lat. *status*), linking the elements within a noun phrase. With the example וַיָּבֹא מֶלֶךְ הָאָרֶץ ("The king of the land entered"), מֶלֶךְ "king" is the central semantic concept, or <u>head</u>, of the noun phrase, and הָאָרֶץ "the land" is the <u>dependent</u>. The head noun could stand on its own and perform the syntactic function of the entire phrase, that is, the subject, as in וַיָּבֹא הַמֶּלֶךְ ("The king entered").

A NP can include several dependents but only one head. Regardless of the total number of elements in the phrase, the first word is always the phrase head. All following elements are dependents specifying the head. English *of*-constructions are structured in a similar way.[58] The NP אֵם הַמֶּלֶךְ can be understood as "the mother of the king," taking the elements in order, or "the king's mother," reversing the order with the English genitive. With NPs longer than two elements, translations using the *of*-construction are generally preferable to the genitive (e.g., אֵם מֶלֶךְ הָאָרֶץ

---

[57] See Nicholas Lunn, "Differentiating Intensive and Abstract Plural Nouns in Biblical Hebrew," *JNSL* 42, no. 1 (2016): 81–99.

[58] Certain noun-adjective phrases in English (e.g. *attorney general*, *president-elect*, *mother-in-law*, *campus-wide*) are also comparable.

"the mother of the king of the land" versus "the land's king's mother"). These noun phrases are called <u>construct phrases</u>.

HEBREW			ENGLISH		
הָאָרֶץ	מֶלֶךְ	אֵם	The mother	of the king	of the land
Dependent	Dependent	Head	Head	Dependent	Dependent

Nouns are inflected for three grammatical states. The <u>absolute state</u> is the lexical or dictionary form. It is used as the final element of a construct phrase or by itself. Definiteness (§7.7) of the entire phrase is indicated with the absolute state noun.

	ABS	CSTR	
Definite	הַמֶּלֶךְ	אֵם	"the king's mother"
Indefinite	מֶלֶךְ	אֵם	"a king's mother"

Alternatively, the final element could include a pronominal suffix. In these cases, the noun with the suffix uses the <u>pronominal state</u> (e.g., מֶלֶךְ אַרְצִי "the king of my land," or "my land's king"). The forms of the pronominal state are often variations on the absolute or the construct state. Nouns with suffixes are definite even though they do not have the definite article. All non-final elements lose their primary accent and inflect with the <u>construct state</u>. Some nouns have identical absolute and construct forms (e.g., אֵם "mother," מֶלֶךְ "king"), while other nouns are variable (e.g., דָּבָר "word [ABS]" and דְּבַר "word of [CSTR]"). Most elementary grammars outline the basic synchronic guidelines for the phonological changes. The semantics of construct phrases is addressed below (§7.7).

INVARIABLE NOUNS						
FP	FD	FS		MP	MD	MS
סוּסוֹת	סוּסָתַיִם	סוּסָה	ABS	סוּסִים	סוּסַיִם	סוּס
סוּסוֹת	סוּסָתֵי	סוּסַת	CSTR	סוּסֵי	סוּסֵי	סוּס
סוּסוֹתֶיךָ	סוּסָתֶיךָ	סוּסָתִי	PRO (vocalic)	סוּסֶיךָ	סוּסֶיךָ	סוּסִי
סוּסוֹתֵיכֶם	סוּסָתֵיכֶם	סוּסַתְכֶם	PRO (heavy)	סוּסֵיכֶם	סוּסֵיכֶם	סוּסְכֶם

VARIABLE NOUNS				
FP	FS		MP	MS
צְדָקוֹת	צְדָקָה	ABS	דְּבָרִים	דָּבָר
צְדָקוֹת	צִדְקַת	CSTR	דִּבְרֵי	דְּבַר

VARIABLE NOUNS				
FP	FS		MP	MS
צִדְקֹתַיִךְ	צִדְקָתִי	PRO (vocalic)	דְּבָרֶיךָ	דְּבָרִי
צִדְקֹתֵיכֶם*	צִדְקַתְכֶם*	PRO (heavy)	דִּבְרֵיכֶם	דְּבַרְכֶם*

The construct phrase is different than the morphosyntax of the NP in case-based languages like Greek. In these systems, the head inflects with the lexical form and uses the declension required by its syntactic function in the broader clause. The dependents are variable and typically use the genitive case. Each element in the clause is definite or indefinite independent of the entire clause (e.g., ὁ λόγος τοῦ βασιλέως τῆς γῆς).

	HEBREW			GREEK		
	הָאָרֶץ	מֶלֶךְ	דְּבַר	ὁ λόγος	τοῦ βασιλέως	τῆς γῆς
Relationship	Dependent	Dependent	Head	Head	Dependent	Dependent
State/Case	Absolute	Construct	Construct	Nominative	Genitive	Genitive

In Hebrew דְּבַר מֶלֶךְ הָאָרֶץ "the word of the king of the land," only the final dependent noun uses the absolute state, and it determines the definiteness of the entire phrase. Each non-final element is in the construct state, including the invariable form מֶלֶךְ "king" and the head noun, דְּבַר "word."

7.7 CONSTRUCT PHRASE

Construct phrases are based on an initial central concept (i.e., head = H) and following modifying elements (i.e., dependents = D). The head functions as the constituent role in the clause. Dependents describe the head noun through designating various semantic roles, including: (i) agents, (ii) patients, (iii) attributes, (iv) possessors, (v) content, (vi) location, (vii) material, (viii) superlative, (ix) specification, (x) measure, or (xi) class. Each of these semantic relationships is illustrated below:

I. AGENT (OR SUBJECTIVE)	*H is done by D*
	דְּבַר יהוה "the word (H) of Yahweh (D)" (i.e., "the word which Yahweh spoke")
	עֲוֹן הָאֱמֹרִי "the sin (H) of the Amorites (D)" (i.e., "the sin which the Amorites did")

II. PATIENT (OR OBJECTIVE)	*H is done to or directed toward D*
	רֹעֵה צֹאן "a shepherd (H) of sheep (D)" (i.e., "a shepherd who directs sheep")
	יִרְאַת אֱלֹהִים "the fear (H) of God (D)" (i.e., "fear which is focused on God")
III. ATTRIBUTE	*H is characterized by D*
	נֶפֶשׁ חַיָּה "the breath (H) of life (D)" (i.e., "the breath which represents life" or "living breath")
	רוּחַ הַיּוֹם "the wind (H) of the day (D)" (i.e., "the wind characterized by the daytime" or "daily wind")
IV. POSSESSION	*H belongs to D (or H related to D)*
	בֵּית אִמָּהּ "her mother's (D) house (H)" (i.e., "a house belonging to her mother")
	בַּת מֶלֶךְ "a king's (D) daughter (H)" (i.e., "daughter related to a king")
V. CONTENT	*H contains D*
	נֵבֶל יַיִן "jar (H) of wine (D)" (i.e., "a jar contains wine")
	אֲרוֹן הָעֵדוּת "the ark (H) of the covenant (D)" (i.e., "the ark containing the covenant [document]")
VI. LOCATION	*H located within D*
	דְּגַת הַיָּם "the fish (H) of the sea (D)" (i.e., "the fish located in the sea")
	דֶּרֶךְ בֵּיתָהּ "the road (H) of her house (D)" (i.e., "the road to her house")
VII. MATERIAL	*H is made of D*
	כְּלֵי זָהָב "implements (H) of gold (D)" (i.e., "implements made of gold")
	חַלַּת לֶחֶם "loaf (H) of bread (D)" (i.e., "a loaf made of bread")
VIII. SUPERLATIVE	*The most H (in the realm) of D*
	קֹדֶשׁ קָדָשִׁים "most holy place" (i.e., "most holy [H] of holy things [D]")
	קְטֹן בָּנָיו "his youngest son" (i.e., "most small [H] of his sons [D]")
IX. SPECIFICATION	*H with regard to D*
	אִישׁ תֹּאַר "a handsome man" (i.e., "a man [H] with a goodly form [D]")
	טְמֵא שְׂפָתַיִם "unclean lips" (i.e., "unclean [H] with regard to lips [D]")
X. MEASURE	*H quantifies D*
	שְׁתֵּי פָרוֹת "two cows" (i.e., "two [H] of cows [D]")
	רֹב גְּאוֹנְךָ "your numerous splendors" (i.e., "the many [H] number of your splendors [D]")

XI. CLASS[59]	*H is exemplified by D*
	הַר צִיּוֹן "Mount Zion" (i.e., "the mountain [H] exemplified by Zion [D]")
	נְהַר־כְּבָר "The Khabur River" (i.e., "the river [H] named Khabur [D]")

Within the clause, construct phrases function as obligatory and nonobligatory elements. Required clause constituents can include subjects (2 Kgs 21:24), and some objects (Exod 29:44). Optional constituent units (adjuncts) include adverb NPs (Jer 11:23) and prepositional phrases functioning adverbially (Prov 25:6).

2 Kgs 21:24

וַיַּמְלִיכוּ עַם־הָאָרֶץ אֶת־יֹאשִׁיָּהוּ בְנוֹ תַּחְתָּיו

The people of the land enthroned Josiah, his son, in his place.

Exod 29:44

וְקִדַּשְׁתִּי אֶת־אֹהֶל מוֹעֵד וְאֶת־הַמִּזְבֵּחַ

I will consecrate **the tent of meeting** and the altar."

Jer 11:23

וּשְׁאֵרִית לֹא תִהְיֶה לָהֶם כִּי־אָבִיא רָעָה אֶל־אַנְשֵׁי עֲנָתוֹת שְׁנַת פְּקֻדָּתָם

They will not have a remnant because I will bring calamity to the people of Anathoth (in) **the year of their punishment**.

Prov 25:6

וּבִמְקוֹם גְּדֹלִים אַל־תַּעֲמֹד

Do not stand **in the place of the great**.

7.8 APPOSITION

Apposition describes two or more elements with the same constituent function and referent. The elements are typically contiguous. Syntactically, apposition can occur with any constituent function. Common examples include subjects (Gen 3:9), objects (2 Sam 6:16), and adverbs (Exod 9:18).

Gen 3:9

וַיִּקְרָא יְהוָה אֱלֹהִים אֶל־הָאָדָם

Yahweh God called to the man.

---

[59] Other similar descriptions include "genitive of association" (*IBHS* §9.5.3h) and "appositional genitive." Williams §42a.

2 Sam 6:16

וַתֵּ֡רֶא אֶת־הַמֶּ֣לֶךְ דָּוִד֩ מְפַזֵּ֨ז וּמְכַרְכֵּר֙ לִפְנֵ֣י יְהוָ֔ה

She saw **King David** leaping and dancing before Yahweh.

Exod 9:18[60]

הִנְנִ֤י מַמְטִיר֙ כָּעֵ֣ת מָחָ֔ר בָּרָ֖ד כָּבֵ֣ד מְאֹ֑ד

Beware, I am about to rain down exceptionally heavy hail **at this time tomorrow**.

The morphosyntax of nouns in apposition differs from a construct phrase. All appositive elements are in the absolute state, and nonfinal elements may take the definite article.

7.8.1 Semantics of Apposition

Apposition expresses distinct semantic notions about an equivalent referent. This description is not unlike other types of multiword NPs describing a head noun. Generally, the second appositive element specifies the meaning of the referent with regard to (i) class, (ii) material, (iii) quantity, or (iv) explication. The order may vary, but both nouns, where possible, match in definiteness. With identical elements, apposition indicates (v) a distributive connotation.

I. CLASS	דָּוִיד הַמֶּלֶךְ "King David" (1 Chr 29:9)[61]
	נַעֲרָה בְתוּלָה "a young woman, a virgin" (1 Kgs 1:2)
	דְּבוֹרָה אִשָּׁה נְבִיאָה "Deborah, the woman, the prophetess" (Judg 4:4)
II. MATERIAL	הָאֶבֶן הַבְּדִיל "the tin stone" (Zech 4:10)
	הָעֲבֹתֹת הַזָּהָב "the gold cords" (Exod 39:17)
	אֵילִים צֶמֶר "rams wool" (2 Kgs 3:4)
III. QUANTITY	עָרִים שָׁלֹשׁ "three cities" (Josh 21:32)
	שָׁלֹשׁ עָרִים "three cities" (Deut 19:7)
	הָעָם כֻּלּוֹ "the nation all of it" (Isa 9:8)

---

[60] In this example, the referent is the future time frame. This means the adverbial constituents are in apposition and not the two nouns. The prepositional phrase כָּעֵת "at the (same) time" serves the same constituent function as the noun מָחָר "tomorrow, future time" functioning as a temporal adverb. The opposite order is also evidenced מָחָר כָּעֵת הַזֹּאת "tomorrow at this time" (Josh 11:6).

[61] The more common reverse order, הַמֶּלֶךְ דָּוִיד "King David" (2 Sam 3:31; 5:3; 6:12, 16; 7:18; 8:8, 10, 11; 9:5; 13:21; 16:5, 6; 17:17, 21; 19:12, 17; 1 Kgs 1:1, 13, 28, 31, 32, 37, 38, 43, 47; 2 Kgs 11:10; 1 Chr 15:29; 17:16; 18:10, 11; 21:24; 27:24, 31; 29:24) may be understood instead as a title. The order is always PN + common noun with יהוה הָאֱלֹהִים "Yahweh God."

IV. EXPLICATION	הַבֵּן הַבְּכוֹר "the son, the firstborn" (Deut 21:15)
	דְּבָרִים נִחֻמִים "words, consolations" (Zech 1:13)
V. DISTRIBUTION	אִישׁ אִישׁ "one by one" or "anyone" (Exod 36:4)
	יוֹם יוֹם "day after day" (Gen 39:10)
	שָׁנָה שָׁנָה "each year" (Deut 14:22)
	הֲמוֹנִים הֲמוֹנִים "crowds upon crowds" (Joel 4:14)

7.8.2 Restrictive and Nonrestrictive Relatives

A restrictive relative clause defines the meaning of a NP with necessary information about its referent. A nonrestrictive relative clause provides an optional description. In English, a restrictive relative clause ordinarily begins with *that*, or a *wh*-word may be used without surrounding commas (e.g., *I see the car that is on the sidewalk*; *I see the car which is on the sidewalk*). A nonrestrictive relative is offset by commas and begins with a *wh*-word (e.g., *I see the Volkswagen, which is on the sidewalk*). Biblical Hebrew restrictive and nonrestrictive relative clauses may be marked with אֲשֶׁר, -שֶׁ, or מָה.[62] Several semantic, syntactic, and intonational features can differentiate between these two types of relative clauses.[63] Yet these criteria are ultimately assessed based on contextual evidence rather than morphological or orthographic differences.

On a syntactical level, BH relatives operate akin to apposition. The relative marker signals that a subordinate clause modifies a head noun. Generally, the relative marker follows the nominal head in the main clause like an appositive element and is in construct with the following clause. The resulting embedded clause either deletes the referent (Gen 2:2; 3:3) or replaces the referent with a resumptive pronominal element (Exod 3:5). The main-clause nominal head is not repeated in the embedded clause. Infrequently, the relative marker may be absent (Exod 18:20).

Gen 3:3

וּמִפְּרִי הָעֵץ אֲשֶׁר בְּתוֹךְ־הַגָּן אָמַר אֱלֹהִים לֹא תֹאכְלוּ מִמֶּנּוּ

From the fruit of **the tree** that [**it**] is in the middle of the garden, God said: "Never eat of it."

---

[62] See Robert D. Holmstedt, *The Relative Clause in Biblical Hebrew*, LSAWS 10 (Winona Lake, IN: Eisenbrauns, 2016). He additionally identifies the definite article and the demonstrative זֶה as relative markers.

[63] H. Van Dyke Parunak, "Discourse Implications of Resumption in Hebrew אֲשֶׁר Clauses: A Pre-liminary Assessment from Genesis," in *Literary Structure and Rhetorical Strategies in the Hebrew Bible*, ed. L. J. de Regt, J. de Waard, and J. P. Fokkelman (Winona Lake, IN: Eisenbrauns, 1996), 101–16. See also, the interaction by Holmstedt (*Relative Clause*, 168–69) as well as his discussion of nonrestrictive relative clauses (195–214, particularly 209).

Gen 2:2

וַיְכַל אֱלֹהִים בַּיּוֹם הַשְּׁבִיעִי **מְלַאכְתּוֹ** אֲשֶׁר עָשָׂה

On the seventh day, God completed **his work**, which he had done [it].

Exod 3:5

כִּי **הַמָּקוֹם** אֲשֶׁר אַתָּה עוֹמֵד **עָלָיו** אַדְמַת־קֹדֶשׁ הוּא

For **the place** that you are standing **on [it]** is sacred ground.

Exod 18:20

וְהוֹדַעְתָּ לָהֶם אֶת־הַדֶּרֶךְ [_____] יֵלְכוּ בָהּ וְאֶת־הַמַּעֲשֶׂה **אֲשֶׁר** יַעֲשׂוּן

You shall make them know the way [that] they shall walk in [it] and the labor **that** they shall do.

7.9 DETERMINERS

<u>Determiners</u> are words or morphemes that combine in noun phrases to specify the contextual reference, the deictic orientation, and the quantity of another constituent. These grammatical words refer to known or unknown entities (definiteness), the proximity or immediacy of an entity (demonstratives), or various amounts of an entity (quantifiers, numerals, and measure words). Some determiners are multifunctional—they can serve different functions as adjectives, pronouns, nouns, and even other function words.

7.9.1 Definiteness

The semantic property of <u>definiteness</u> describes the degree to which a referent is identifiable or distinguishable. Unknown, unspecified, and generic NP referents are typically indicated by common nouns (e.g., בַּיִת "[a] house," אִישׁ "[a] man; one"). If succeeding reference is made, the definite article may be used, indicated by the prefix ־הַ (*he-pataḥ* and, where possible, doubling of the first consonant, e.g., הַבַּיִת "the house," הָאִישׁ "the man"). The apocopated *he* of the definite article elides when combined with an inseparable preposition (־בְּ, ־לְ, ־כְּ; e.g., בְּהַבַּיִת* becomes בַּבַּיִת). The terms <u>anarthrous</u> and <u>arthrous</u> are sometimes used to specify the absence and presence of an article, respectively. In Gen 37:15, an unknown, unidentified man (אִישׁ) encounters Joseph in his search for his brothers near Shechem. The same man is subsequently specified by the shift in definiteness (הָאִישׁ) in the second part of the verse.

Gen 37:15

וַיִּמְצָאֵהוּ **אִישׁ** וְהִנֵּה תֹעֶה בַּשָּׂדֶה וַיִּשְׁאָלֵהוּ **הָאִישׁ** לֵאמֹר מַה־תְּבַקֵּשׁ

A man found him (i.e., Joseph), while he was wandering in the field, and **the man** asked him, "What are you looking for?

A definite article can also indicate uniqueness (Gen 1:1) or a generic reference to a class, species, or kind (Gen 6:7).[64] The definite direct object marker אֵת often accompanies a definite object.[65]

Gen 1:1

בְּרֵאשִׁית בָּרָא אֱלֹהִים אֵת הַשָּׁמַיִם וְאֵת הָאָרֶץ

In the beginning, God created **the heavens and the earth**.

Gen 6:7

אֶמְחֶה אֶת־הָאָדָם אֲשֶׁר־בָּרָאתִי מֵעַל פְּנֵי הָאֲדָמָה מֵאָדָם עַד־בְּהֵמָה עַד־רֶמֶשׂ
וְעַד־עוֹף הַשָּׁמָיִם

I will blot out **the humankind**, which I created, from the surface of the earth from human to animals, creeping things, and birds of the sky.

The numeral אֶחָד "one" (F אַחַת) may be used to indicate a specific but unknown referent. In 1 Sam 7:12, a particular stone is described and then subsequently named. A similar notion is conveyed by using English *a certain*.[66] Judges 9:53 presents אִשָּׁה אַחַת "a certain woman" who is the famed but unnamed avenger of the bloodguilt of Abimelech's brothers.

1 Sam 7:12

וַיִּקַּח שְׁמוּאֵל אֶבֶן אַחַת וַיָּשֶׂם בֵּין־הַמִּצְפָּה וּבֵין הַשֵּׁן וַיִּקְרָא אֶת־שְׁמָהּ אֶבֶן הָעָזֶר
וַיֹּאמַר עַד־הֵנָּה עֲזָרָנוּ יְהוָה

Samuel took and set up **a stone** between Mizpah and Shen. He named it Ebenezer, explaining, "Yahweh has helped us up to this point."

Judg 9:53

וַתַּשְׁלֵךְ אִשָּׁה אַחַת פֶּלַח רֶכֶב עַל־רֹאשׁ אֲבִימֶלֶךְ

A certain woman threw an upper millstone on the head of Abimelech.

Three other NP strategies are used to reference entities that are identified or known. These have been discussed previously with proper nouns (§7.5.1), the pronominal state, and definite construct phrases (§7.6.2.3).

Definiteness can help to indicate clause syntax. If two nouns could potentially be the grammatical subject, as in Gen 1:24, the subject is typically definite (הָאָרֶץ "the land"), and the object is not (נֶפֶשׁ חַיָּה "a living being").

Gen 1:24

תּוֹצֵא הָאָרֶץ נֶפֶשׁ חַיָּה לְמִינָהּ

The land will yield **animate life** according to its kind.

---

[64] Peter Bekins, "Definiteness and the Definite Article," in *Where Shall Wisdom Be Found? A Grammatical Tributer to Professor Stephen A. Kaufman*, ed. Hélène Dallaire, Benjamin J. Noonan, and Jennifer E. Noonan (Winona Lake, IN: Eisenbrauns, 2017), 28–33.

[65] Bekins, *Transitivity and Object Marking*.

[66] Other indefinite usages of אֶחָד have also been suggested (*IBHS* §13.8; Joüon-Muraoka §137u–v).

Definite objects are generally indicated by the definite direct object marker, אֵת. In clauses with more than one object, animacy distinguishes between direct objects and indirect objects (1 Kgs 2:30), and definiteness designates direct objects and object complements (Exod 37:17).

1 Kgs 2:30

וַיָּשֶׁב בְּנָיָהוּ אֶת־הַמֶּלֶךְ דָּבָר

Benaiah took **the king** [IO] a communication [DO].

Exod 37:17

וַיַּעַשׂ אֶת־הַמְּנֹרָה זָהָב טָהוֹר

He made **the lampstand** [DO] (out of) pure gold [OC].

Definiteness serves to mark agreement between a noun and an attributive. An attributive constituent, such as a demonstrative, adjective, or participle, must agree with the noun it modifies in gender, number, and definiteness. A predicative element only agrees in gender and number.

Attributive Constituent

הַמֶּלֶךְ הַזָּקֵן "the wise-old [MS] king"

הַמַּלְכוֹת הַזְּקֵנוֹת "the wise-old [FP] queens"

Predicative Element

הַמֶּלֶךְ זָקֵן "The king is wise-old [MS]."

הַמַּלְכוֹת זְקֵנוֹת "The queens are wise-old [FP]."

For verbless clauses, variation in definiteness helps to distinguish the subject as the given or known entity from the subject complement (i.e., predicate) as the new or unknown entity. With two noun clauses, such as with Gen 6:9, the subject is definite (נֹחַ "Noah"), and the subject complement is indefinite (אִישׁ צַדִּיק "a righteous man").

Gen 6:9

נֹחַ אִישׁ צַדִּיק

Noah was a righteous man.

Clauses with two definite nouns, however, are more difficult to assess.[67] In Gen 27:22, Isaac's response הַקֹּל קוֹל יַעֲקֹב be understood as "the voice is Jacob's voice" or "Jacob's voice is the voice." In such cases, Ellen van Wolde suggests that the subject-predicate arrangement is determined by a range of information, including the context, the expected word order, and the degree of definiteness.[68] The degree of definiteness is a gradient from less to more (see the full definiteness

---

[67] Francis I. Andersen, *The Hebrew Verbless Clause in the Pentateuch*, JBLMS 14 (Nashville: Abingdon, 1970) suggests that predicates composed of definite NPs either identify or classify the subject. For a summary, see *IBHS* §8.4.

[68] Van Wolde, "Verbless Clause," 321–36.

continuum at §8.6.3).[69] Higher levels of definiteness indicate that the new information is the predicate. Lower levels of definiteness signal the subject.[70] With this in mind, the higher degree of definiteness is the NP with the proper name; therefore, קוֹל יַעֲקֹב "Jacob's voice" would serve as the subject complement.

7.9.2 Demonstratives

Demonstratives point to the relative setting of a known referent. The reference point is determined from the perspective of the speaker (personal deixis) or the context of the situation (discourse deixis). If an author refers to *this place*, it does not refer to a location near the reader, and *this time* does not correspond to the moment you are reading. Such settings indicate the proximity (place deixis) or immediacy of an entity (time deixis) to the speaker/author. Determiners must be understood with regard to who is speaking, the time of speaking, the place of speaking, the speaker's (extralinguistic) gestures, and the discourse situation.

7.9.2.1 Demonstrative Personal Deixis

Biblical Hebrew demonstratives function like pronouns, adjectives, and adverbs. Proximity or immediacy may be expressed with either near or far deixis. These contrasting demonstratives correspond with their referent in grammatical gender and number.

NEAR DEMONSTRATIVES ("THIS," "THESE")		
P	S	
אֵלֶּה	זֶה	M
	זֹאת	F

FAR DEMONSTRATIVES ("THAT," "THOSE")		
P	S	
הֵמָּה/הֵם	הוּא	M
הֵנָּה	הִיא	F

Demonstratives function independently like pronouns. As subjects, they occur without an article and typically precede their predicates (Lam 2:15), but they may at times follow them (2 Sam 18:27).

Lam 2:15

הֲזֹאת הָעִיר שֶׁיֹּאמְרוּ כְּלִילַת יֹפִי מָשׂוֹשׂ לְכָל־הָאָרֶץ

Is **this** the city which they call perfect beauty, the joy of the entire earth?

---

[69] Van Wolde, 333.

[70] See also the discussion of verbless participial clauses in §§8.4.2, 8.6.3.

2 Sam 18:27

אִישׁ־טֹוב זֶ֑ה

this is a good man.

As verb complements, they can be designated with the direct object marker (Num 15:13) or without it (Isa 29:11).

Num 15:13

כָּל־הָאֶזְרָ֥ח יַעֲשֶׂה־כָּ֖כָה אֶת־אֵֽלֶּה

Every native inhabitant should prepare **these** accordingly.

Isa 29:11

קְרָ֣א נָא־זֶ֑ה וְאָמַר֙ לֹ֣א אוּכַ֔ל כִּ֥י חָת֖וּם הֽוּא

Read **this**, and he will respond: "I am not able because it is sealed."

As adverbs, a demonstrative indicates manner or repetition (Num 14:22):

Num 14:22[71]

וַיְנַסּ֣וּ אֹתִ֔י זֶ֖ה עֶ֥שֶׂר פְּעָמִ֑ים

They tested me (**this**) ten times.

Demonstratives function like adjectives in NPs. They follow their referent and agree in grammatical gender, number, and definiteness.

NEAR DEMONSTRATIVES ("THIS," "THESE")		
P	S	
הָאֲבָנִ֖ים הָאֵֽלֶּה "these stones" (Josh 4:6)	הַיֹּ֣ום הַזֶּ֑ה "this day" (Josh 5:11)	**M**
	הָעִ֥יר הַזֹּֽאת "this city" (Josh 6:26)	**F**

FAR DEMONSTRATIVES ("THAT," "THOSE")		
P	S	
הַיָּמִ֣ים הָהֵ֔ם "those days" (Jer 31:33)	הַמָּק֖וֹם הַה֑וּא "that place" (Deut 12:3)	**M**
מְעַ֛ט הַצֹּ֥אן הָהֵ֖נָּה "those few sheep" (1 Sam 17:28)	הָאָ֥רֶץ הַהִֽיא "that land" (Judg 11:21)	**F**

With construct phrases, the demonstrative follows the phrase regardless of which element it modifies (Deut 32:49, 2 Sam 12:11, Josh 20:4).

---

[71] See, also, Num 22:28: מֶֽה־עָשִׂ֣יתִי לְךָ֔ כִּ֣י הִכִּיתַ֔נִי זֶ֖ה שָׁלֹ֥שׁ רְגָלִֽים "What have I done to you that you have struck me **this three times**?"

Deut 32:49

עֲלֵה אֶל־הַר֩ הָעֲבָרִ֨ים הַזֶּ֜ה

Ascend toward **this mountain** of Abarim.

2 Sam 12:11

עֵינֵ֖י הַשֶּׁ֥מֶשׁ הַזֹּֽאת

the eyes of **this sun**

Josh 20:4

וְדִבֶּ֞ר בְּאָזְנֵ֨י זִקְנֵ֤י הָעִיר־הַהִ֨יא

He will speak in the ears of the elders of **that city**.

With a noun phrase consisting of a referent and adjective (Jer 13:10, Num 14:35, Deut 1:19), the demonstrative may come before or after the adjective. In the rare situation with two adjectives, the demonstrative follows.

Jer 13:10

הָעָם֙ הַזֶּ֣ה הָרָ֔ע

this evil nation

Num 14:35

הָעֵדָ֤ה הָרָעָה֙ הַזֹּ֔את

this evil congregation

Deut 1:19

וַנֵּ֡לֶךְ אֵ֣ת כָּל־הַמִּדְבָּ֣ר הַגָּדוֹל֩ וְהַנּוֹרָ֨א הַה֜וּא

We traversed **that** every great and formidable place.

Demonstratives, adjectives, and construct phrases combine various orders (Esth 9:29).

Esth 9:29

אִגֶּ֧רֶת הַפּוּרִ֛ים הַזֹּ֖את הַשֵּׁנִֽית

This second Purim letter

7.9.2.2 Demonstrative Discourse Deixis

Demonstratives can indicate situational references within a discourse. A <u>discourse situation</u> includes information about the speaker, addressee, and their locations in relation to each other as portrayed in an account using spatiotemporal deixis. In Josh 5:9, for instance, the description of the circumcision of the Israelite army ends with the identification of the location and the claim to the longevity of the name.

Josh 5:9

וַיִּקְרָ֞א שֵׁ֣ם הַמָּק֤וֹם הַהוּא֙ גִּלְגָּ֔ל עַ֖ד הַיּ֥וֹם הַזֶּֽה

The name of **that place** is still called Gilgal until **this day**.

Both the place and the timeframe are dependent on the situational context of the naming events. The discourse setting הַמָּקוֹם הַהוּא "that place" refers anaphorically to the geographic site previously discussed, and הַיּוֹם הַזֶּה "this day" indicates the setting of the writing of the book itself—that is to say, the author's own temporal location as distinct from the timeframe of the narrative or the reader's situation.

Demonstratives can also be used to indicate sequential references in discourses. In Exod 9:13–14, the sequential reference, פַּעַם הַזֹּאת "this time," may only be understood in light of the discourse situation of the narrative.

> Exod 9:13–14
>
> וַיֹּאמֶר יְהוָה אֶל־מֹשֶׁה הַשְׁכֵּם בַּבֹּקֶר וְהִתְיַצֵּב לִפְנֵי פַרְעֹה וְאָמַרְתָּ אֵלָיו כֹּה־אָמַר יְהוָה
> אֱלֹהֵי הָעִבְרִים שַׁלַּח אֶת־עַמִּי וְיַעַבְדֻנִי: כִּי| בַּפַּעַם הַזֹּאת אֲנִי שֹׁלֵחַ אֶת־כָּל־מַגֵּפֹתַי
> אֶל־לִבְּךָ וּבַעֲבָדֶיךָ וּבְעַמֶּךָ בַּעֲבוּר תֵּדַע כִּי אֵין כָּמֹנִי בְּכָל־הָאָרֶץ:
>
> Yahweh said to Moses: "Arise early in the morning, stand before Pharaoh, and say to him, 'Thus says Yahweh the God of the Hebrews: Let my people go and serve me! For **this time**, I am sending all my plagues on your heart, your servants, and your people so that you might know that there is none like me in all the earth.'"

The divine instruction is spoken by Moses and addressed to Pharaoh. The same command to release the Hebrews from captivity is relayed eight times in Exodus 4–10.[72] This instance, however, is different from previous encounters because the impending plagues would result in the Egyptian's recognition of Yahweh's uniqueness (v. 14) and righteousness (v. 27). If this sequential reference in Exod 9:14 had occurred in the first encounter, the relation language would not make sense.

7.9.2.3 Locative Adverbs

The discourse situations of proximity and immediacy are similarly designated using various locative and temporal adverbs. These adverbs mostly express place and time deixis using an analogous framework as the near (Gen 19:12–13) and far demonstratives (2 Kgs 6:9).

> Gen 19:12–13
>
> עֹד מִי־לְךָ **פֹה** חָתָן וּבָנֶיךָ וּבְנֹתֶיךָ וְכֹל אֲשֶׁר־לְךָ בָּעִיר הוֹצֵא מִן־הַמָּקוֹם כִּי־מַשְׁחִתִים
> אֲנַחְנוּ אֶת־הַמָּקוֹם הַזֶּה
>
> Whoever is related to you **here**—in-law, sons, daughters, or any relative in the city—take out from the place for we are about to destroy **this** place.

> 2 Kgs 6:9
>
> הִשָּׁמֶר מֵעֲבֹר הַמָּקוֹם הַזֶּה כִּי־שָׁם אֲרָם נְחִתִּים
>
> Be vigilant when passing through **this** [aforementioned] place because the Arameans are heading **there**.

---

72 These examples include Exod 4:23; 5:1; 7:16, 26; 8:16(20); 9:1, 14, and 10:3. Twice more, the command is indirectly mentioned by Yahweh (6:11) or spoken to Pharaoh by other Egyptians (10:7).

Near locative adverbs include הֲכֵן, הֵנָּה, כֹּה, and פֹּה as "here,"[73] and the far locative adverbs are שָׁם "there" and הָלְאָה "there, yonder."[74]

| LOCATIVE ADVERBS ||
FAR	NEAR
שָׁם "there" הָלְאָה "there, yonder"	הֲכֵן "here" הֵנָּה "here" כֹּה "here" (פֹּא, פֹּו) פֹּה "here"

Several locative adverbs combine the proximity notion with directionality.

| DIRECTIONAL LOCATIVE ADVERBS |||
FAR ("THERE")	NEAR ("HERE")	
שָׁמָּה "thither, toward there"	הֲלֹם "hither, toward this place" עַד־הֵנָּה "hither, to here"	GOAL (TOWARD)
מִשָּׁם "thence, from there" מֵהָלְאָה "thence, from yonder"	מִזֶּה "hence, from here"	SOURCE (FROM)

7.9.2.4 Temporal Adverbs

The logic of near and far temporality may also be mapped to what are traditionally
labeled temporal adverbs. The immediacy of a verbal action or clause is indicated
as proximal ("now") or distal ("then") to the discourse setting.

| TEMPORAL ADVERBS ||
FAR	NEAR
אָז "then"	עַתָּה "now"

These notions further convey sequence from the perspective of the implied narrative present (Josh 14:11).

---

[73] The repetition of more than one of the same adverbs can indicate differentiated locations: הֵנָּה
וְהֵנָּה "here and there" (1 Kgs 20:40), כֹּה . . . כֹּה "here . . . there" (Exod 2:12; Num 11:31; 23:15),
שָׁם . . . שָׁם "here . . . there." See also several contexts in Ezek. 40–41 indicating opposite sides, e.g.,
מִפֹּה וּמִפֹּו "from here and from there" (Ezek 40:10).

[74] The combination of מִשָּׁם וְהָלְאָה "from there and farther" (1 Sam 10:3) and מִן־הוּא וְהָלְאָה "from
that and farther" (Isa 18:2, 7) may indicate a third realm of proximity: beyond the far location.

Josh 14:11

עוֹדֶ֨נִּי הַיּ֜וֹם חָזָ֗ק כַּאֲשֶׁר֙ בְּי֨וֹם שְׁלֹ֤חַ אוֹתִי֙ מֹשֶׁ֔ה כְּכֹ֥חִֽי אָ֖ז וּכְכֹ֣חִי עָתָּ֑ה לַמִּלְחָמָ֖ה
וְלָצֵ֥את וְלָבֽוֹא

Still today, I am as strong as the day Moses sent me out—as was my
strength **then**, so too is my strength **now**—for battle as well as coming
and going.

Other temporal adverbs reckon time on, before, or after a given day. The expression הַיּוֹם "today" marks the narrative present, as with Exod 14:13.

Exod 14:13

אַל־תִּ֣ירָאוּ֮ הִֽתְיַצְּבוּ֒ וּרְאוּ֙ אֶת־יְשׁוּעַ֣ת יְהוָ֔ה אֲשֶׁר־יַעֲשֶׂ֥ה לָכֶ֖ם הַיּ֑וֹם כִּ֗י אֲשֶׁ֨ר רְאִיתֶ֤ם
אֶת־מִצְרַ֙יִם֙ הַיּ֔וֹם לֹ֥א תֹסִ֛פוּ לִרְאֹתָ֥ם ע֖וֹד עַד־עוֹלָֽם׃

Do not fear! Stand and watch Yahweh's salvation that he will accomplish
for you **today** because the Egyptians you see **today** you never again see
them forever.

A day in the relative future is designated as מָחָר or מָחֳרָת "tomorrow" (Num 11:32)
or elsewhere הַיּוֹם הָאַחֵר "the next day" (2 Kgs 6:28b–29).[75]

Num 11:32

וַיָּ֣קָם הָעָ֡ם כָּל־הַיּוֹם֩ הַה֨וּא וְכָל־הַלַּ֜יְלָה וְכֹ֣ל ׀ י֣וֹם הַֽמָּחֳרָ֗ת וַיַּֽאַסְפוּ֙ אֶת־הַשְּׂלָ֔ו
The people arose all that day and night and the entire **next day**, and they
gathered quail.

2 Kgs 6:28b–29

וַתֹּ֧אמֶר הָאִשָּׁ֣ה הַזֹּ֗את אָמְרָ֤ה אֵלַי֙ תְּנִ֣י אֶת־בְּנֵ֗ךְ וְנֹאכְלֶ֙נּוּ֙ הַיּ֔וֹם וְאֶת־בְּנִ֖י נֹאכַ֥ל מָחָֽר׃
וַנְּבַשֵּׁ֥ל אֶת־בְּנִ֖י וַנֹּֽאכְלֵ֑הוּ וָאֹמַ֨ר אֵלֶ֜יהָ בַּיּ֣וֹם הָאַחֵ֗ר תְּנִ֤י אֶת־בְּנֵךְ֙ וְנֹ֣אכְלֶ֔נּוּ וַתַּחְבִּ֖א
אֶת־בְּנָֽהּ׃

This woman responded: "She said to me: 'Give me your son so that we
can eat him **today**, and **tomorrow** we will eat my son.' So, we boiled my
son and ate him. Then I said to her **on the next day**: 'Give me your son so
that we can eat him.' But she had hidden her son."

The relatively near past is indicated as אֶתְמוֹל or תְּמוֹל "yesterday" and שִׁלְשׁוֹם
"three days ago" (Exod 5:14) or more generically "previously" (2 Sam 3:17).

Exod 5:14

מַדּ֡וּעַ לֹא֩ כִלִּיתֶ֨ם חָקְכֶ֤ם לִלְבֹּן֙ כִּתְמ֣וֹל שִׁלְשֹׁ֔ם גַּם־תְּמ֖וֹל גַּם־הַיּֽוֹם׃
Why have you not finished making your instructed number of bricks
either **yesterday** or **today** as [you did] **before yesterday**?

---

[75] The string, כָּעֵת מָחָר "the (same) time tomorrow," expresses the mapping of a present moment
onto the subsequent day (Exod 9:18; 1 Sam 9:16; 1 Kgs 19:2; 20:6; 2 Kgs 7:1, 18; 10:6).

2 Sam 3:17

גַּם־תְּמוֹל גַּם־שִׁלְשֹׁם הֱיִיתֶם מְבַקְשִׁים אֶת־דָּוִד לְמֶלֶךְ עֲלֵיכֶם

Both **yesterday** and **previously** you've sought David to be king over you.

7.9.3 Quantifiers

A quantifier designates a nonspecific number of entities. These determiners generalize the scope of the set by indicating "how many entities or how much substance
is being referred to."[76] English quantifiers include *all, whole, entire, every, no,
some, many,* and *few.* Quantifiers may modify a noun phrase or serve as an independent noun. In contrast, specific amounts are considered numerals (§7.9.4).

The most frequent BH quantifier is כֹּל "all, every." Syntactically, כֹּל is a type
of predeterminer, situated in position before a noun phrase.[77] This construction is
different from a typical construct phrase where the initial element serves as the
head noun. The bound form כָּל־ (1 Sam 4:13, Gen 9:29, Dan 12:7) and pronominal suffix forms with כָּל־ (<*kull*; Isa 22:1) assume the number and gender of the
quantified head noun or suffix.[78]

1 Sam 4:13

וַתִּזְעַק כָּל־הָעִיר

All the city (F) **cried out** (F).

Gen 9:29

וַיִּהְיוּ כָּל־יְמֵי־נֹחַ תְּשַׁע מֵאוֹת שָׁנָה וַחֲמִשִּׁים שָׁנָה

All the days (P) of Noah **were** (P) 950 years.

Dan 12:7

תִּכְלֶינָה כָל־אֵלֶּה

All these (CP) **will come to pass** (FP).

Isa 22:1

מַה־לָּךְ אֵפוֹא כִּי־עָלִית כֻּלָּךְ לַגַּגּוֹת:

What is it to you then that all you (FS) **have ascended** (FS) to your
rooftops?

Alternatively, כֹּל may serve as an independent noun with singular (Josh 21:45) or
plural agreement (Josh 23:14) or as an appositional element (Isa 9:8).[79]

---

[76] John Lyons, *Semantics* (Cambridge: Cambridge University Press, 1977), 2:455. *BHRG* §37.1,
however, defines numerals within the category of quantifiers.

[77] Randolph Quirk et al. *A Comprehensive Grammar of the English Language* (London: Longman,
1985), 253, 257–61.

[78] Yael Netzer, "Quantifier," in *EHLL* 3:311–15.

[79] Jacobus Naudé refers to this appositional function as "a floating quantifier phrase." See
"Syntactic Patterns of Quantifier Float in Biblical Hebrew," *HS* 52 (2011): 121–36.

Josh 21:45

הַכֹּל֙ בָּ֔א

All (S) **have come to pass** (S).

Josh 23:14

הַכֹּל֙ בָּ֣אוּ לָכֶ֔ם

All (P) **have come to pass** (P) for you.

Isa 9:8

וְיָדְעוּ֙ הָעָ֣ם כֻּלּ֔וֹ אֶפְרַ֖יִם וְיוֹשֵׁ֣ב שֹׁמְר֑וֹן

The people—**all of them**, Ephraim and the inhabitants of Samaria—**will know** (P).

As the initial element of a noun phrase, כֹּל can express the semantic notion of a collective quantifier (*all [of]*, *whole*, *the totality of the entity*) or a distributive quantifier (*all*, *each*).[80] For definite nouns, the quantifier designates totality or universal reference. The expression is best translated "all of the NP" or "the entire NP" (1 Sam 28:20). For indefinite nouns, the quantifier indicates inclusivity or a generic distributive reference, "every, each" (Ps 140:3).

1 Sam 28:20

גַּם־כֹּ֨חַ לֹא־הָ֤יָה בוֹ֙ כִּ֣י לֹ֤א אָכַל֙ לֶ֔חֶם כָּל־הַיּ֖וֹם וְכָל־הַלָּֽיְלָה

He did not have any strength left in him because he had not eaten food the **entire** day or night.

Ps 140:3

כָּל־י֭וֹם יָג֣וּרוּ מִלְחָמֽוֹת

Each day they keep fighting battles.

The negatives, לֹא and אֵין, may serve as a type of pre-quantifier when conjoined with another constituent.[81] In English, the negative attaches to only certain nouns: *nobody*, *no one*, *nothing*. The resulting forms may be contrasted with the distributive forms: *everybody*, *everyone*, *everything*. Hebrew negative quantifiers are less restricted. They typically quantify indefinite nouns to form a universal negative (Num 23:19, Isa 6:11, Num 16:15) or contrastive quality (Gen 27:12).

Num 23:19

לֹ֣א אִ֤ישׁ אֵל֙ וִֽיכַזֵּ֔ב

God is **no man** that he should lie.

---

[80] Jacobus A Naudé, "The Interpretation and Translation of the Biblical Hebrew Quantifier *kol*," *Journal for Semitics* 20, no. 2 (2011): 408–21.

[81] See *BHRG* §41.9.2; Cynthia Miller-Naudé and Jacobus Naudé, "The Participle and Negation in Biblical Hebrew," *KUSATU* 19 (2015): 165–99.

Isa 6:11

עַד אֲשֶׁר אִם־שָׁאוּ עָרִים מֵאֵין יוֹשֵׁב וּבָתִּים מֵאֵין אָדָם

Until cities are uninhabited with **no occupant**, and houses with **no one**.

Num 16:15

לֹא חֲמוֹר אֶחָד מֵהֶם נָשָׂאתִי

I have taken from them **not one donkey**.

Gen 27:12

וְהֵבֵאתִי עָלַי קְלָלָה וְלֹא בְרָכָה

I will bring upon myself a curse and **not a blessing**.

Elsewhere, the negative quantifier may combine with another quantifier (1 Kgs 11:39) or a construct phrase (Exod 4:10).

1 Kgs 11:39

וַאעַנֶּה אֶת־זֶרַע דָּוִד לְמַעַן זֹאת אַךְ לֹא כָל־הַיָּמִים

I will humble[82] David's offspring on account of this only **not all days**.

Exod 4:10

לֹא אִישׁ דְּבָרִים אָנֹכִי

I am **no man of words**.

Several other quantifiers relate different sets of entities to a known or assumed quantity of the full set. The pairings of מְעַט "few, some" with the adjective רַב "much, many" (Num 13:18) as well as with the infinitive absolute הַרְבֵּה "many, much" (Hag 1:6) indicate a nascent quantifier function for these opposites. מְעַט is also used as a pre-quantifier with indefinite nouns, such as water (Judg 4:19) and food (Gen 43:2). Like כֹּל "all," the construct form does not operate as the head of noun phrase (1 Sam 17:28).

Num 13:18

הַמְעַט הוּא אִם־רָב

Are [the inhabitants] **few** or **many**?

Hag 1:6

זְרַעְתֶּם הַרְבֵּה וְהָבֵא מְעָט

You planted **much** and harvested **little**.

Judg 4:19

הַשְׁקִינִי־נָא מְעַט־מַיִם כִּי צָמֵאתִי

Would you give me **some water** because I am thirsty?

---

[82] Some MT manuscripts read: וְעִנָּה.

Gen 43:2

שֻׁבוּ שִׁבְרוּ־לָנוּ מְעַט־אֹכֶל

Return, purchase for us **some food**.

1 Sam 17:28

וְעַל־מִי נָטַשְׁתָּ מְעַט הַצֹּאן הָהֵנָּה בַּמִּדְבָּר

With whom did you leave **these several sheep** in the wilderness?

The form הַרְבֵּה "many, much" may elsewhere be understood as a post-quantifier (Isa 30:33; Eccl 2:7; 5:6, 16; 6:11; 7:16; 9:18; 12:9; 12:12; Neh 4:4, 13; 2 Chr 14:12; 32:27).

Additional examples of qualifiers include מִזְעָר "few" (Isa 24:6), זְעֵיר "little" (Isa 28:10, 13; Job 36:2), יֶתֶר "rest" (2 Kgs 14:18), הָמוֹן "many" (Jer 10:13), דַּי "enough" (Prov 27:27) and עוֹד "more" (Gen 29:27). The compound, כַּמָּה "like what, how many," may also indicate a subset "few" in the phrase זֶה כַּמֶּה שָׁנִים "these several years" (Zech 7:3) as compared with זֶה עֶשְׂרִים שָׁנָה "these twenty years" (Gen 31:38, 41), זֶה אַרְבָּעִים שָׁנָה "these forty years" (Deut 2:7), and זֶה יָמִים רַבִּים "these many years" (Josh 22:3).

The final way to designate a quantity is with a מִן construction. Collocations with the preposition מִן can represent comparative and partitive notions. As a comparative, a quality, for instance טוֹב "good," גָּדוֹל "great," or יוֹתֵר "remainder," is combined with a prepositional phrase to indicate a comparative quantifier (2 Sam 17:14, Exod 18:11, Esth 6:6). This construction contrasts with the English comparative and superlative sequences (e.g., *few/fewer/fewest, little/less/least, small/smaller/smallest, large/larger/largest, many/more/most*).

2 Sam 17:14

טוֹבָה עֲצַת חוּשַׁי הָאַרְכִּי מֵעֲצַת אֲחִיתֹפֶל

The advice of Hushai the Arkite is **better than the advice** of Ahitophel.

Exod 18:11

עַתָּה יָדַעְתִּי כִּי־גָדוֹל יְהוָה מִכָּל־הָאֱלֹהִים

Now I know that Yahweh is **greater than all** the gods.

Esth 6:6

לְמִי יַחְפֹּץ הַמֶּלֶךְ לַעֲשׂוֹת יְקָר יוֹתֵר מִמֶּנִּי

Who else would the king desire to give honor **more than** me?

The partitive construction, on the other hand, designates a subset. This subset is understood relative to the complete set of entities. A few partitive quantifiers are used as predeterminers, but mostly the partitive construction is indicated with the preposition מִן "from among." A quantifier is often absent, and the generic *some* may be supplied in English translations (e.g., Gen 4:3). At times, a nonspecific quantity is found with partitive (2 Sam 16:1) and comparative collocations (Deut 7:7).

Elsewhere, numerals may designate a specific amount with the partitive מִן construction. Contrasting constructions without and with a numeral may be seen in Lev 7:14.

Gen 4:3

וַיָּבֵא קַיִן מִפְּרִי הָאֲדָמָה מִנְחָה לַיהוָה

Cain brought **some from among the fruit of the land** as an offering for Yahweh.

2 Sam 16:1

וְדָוִד עָבַר מְעַט מֵהָרֹאשׁ

David crossed over **a little distance from the summit**.

Deut 7:7

לֹא מֵרֻבְּכֶם מִכָּל־הָעַמִּים חָשַׁק יְהוָה בָּכֶם וַיִּבְחַר בָּכֶם כִּי־אַתֶּם הַמְעַט מִכָּל־הָעַמִּים׃

Not because **you are greater than** all the nations has Yahweh desired you and chose you, (rather) because you are **smaller than all** the nations.

Lev 7:14

וְהִקְרִיב מִמֶּנּוּ אֶחָד מִכָּל־קָרְבָּן תְּרוּמָה לַיהוָה

He shall offer **from among it** [i.e., his offering of unleavened cakes] **one (cake) from every offering** as a contribution for Yahweh.

7.9.4 Numerals

Distinct from quantifiers, numerals designate specific amounts of an entity. Numerals include cardinal numbers, ordinal numbers, fractions, multipliers, and classifiers.[83] In contrast to number words, the numerical quantities *one* and *two* may be specified using singular and dual morphology of the noun in place of a numeral (see above §7.6.2.2).

7.9.4.1 Cardinal Numbers

A <u>cardinal number</u> designates a numerical sum of a countable entity. A noncount noun (§7.5.3), on the other hand, is quantified using a <u>measure word</u> (§7.9.6). The cardinal numbers are the set of simple counting numerals. They designate a semantic property that enumerates a collection of things.[84] For example, the cardinals אֶחָד "one," חֲמִשָּׁה "five," עֲשָׂרָה "ten," and עֶשְׂרִים "twenty" together number the days of judgment in Num 11:4–6. God promised to nauseate the people by the unrelenting onslaught of meat (Num 11:19–20), responding to Israel's complaints

---

[83] Others categorize numerals within a larger class of quantifiers. John Screnock ("Some Oddities of Ancient Hebrew Numeral Syntax," *HS* 61 [2020]: 23–44) describes numerals as "numerically specific" quantifiers designating an exact number, following Ferdinand von Mengden, *Cardinal Numerals: Old English from a Cross-Linguistic Perspective*, Topics in English Linguistics (Berlin: de Gruyter, 2010).

[84] Screnock, "Some Oddities," 25–29.

in the desert about their lack of meat and their reminiscing about the food of Egypt. In contrast, the dual form is used for יוֹמַ֫יִם "two days," and the noun חֹ֫דֶשׁ "month; new moon" is used to indicate the full course of days of the lunar cycle.

Num 11:19–20

לֹא י֤וֹם אֶחָד֙ תֹּאכְל֔וּן וְלֹ֖א יוֹמָ֑יִם וְלֹ֣א ׀ חֲמִשָּׁ֣ה יָמִ֗ים וְלֹא֙ עֲשָׂרָ֣ה יָמִ֔ים וְלֹ֖א עֶשְׂרִ֥ים יֽוֹם׃
עַ֣ד ׀ חֹ֣דֶשׁ יָמִ֗ים עַ֤ד אֲשֶׁר־יֵצֵא֙ מֵֽאַפְּכֶ֔ם וְהָיָ֥ה לָכֶ֖ם לְזָרָ֑א יַ֗עַן כִּֽי־מְאַסְתֶּ֤ם אֶת־יְהוָה֙
אֲשֶׁ֣ר בְּקִרְבְּכֶ֔ם וַתִּבְכּ֤וּ לְפָנָיו֙ לֵאמֹ֔ר לָ֥מָּה זֶּ֖ה יָצָ֥אנוּ מִמִּצְרָֽיִם׃

You shall eat [meat] not **one day**, not **two days**, not **five days**, not **ten days**, not **twenty days**, but **an entire month of days** until it comes out of your nose, and it nauseates you because you have rejected Yahweh who is in your midst and wept before him, saying: "Why is it we left Egypt?"

The morphosyntax of the cardinal numbers is quite complicated. The gender of the number form depends on the gender of the counted entity. The state of the cardinal number varies depending on its position relative to the counted entity. And the morphological number of the counted entity, singular or plural, is based on the magnitude of the cardinal number.

The single word counting numbers (cardinals) are:

CARDINALS: 1-10				
	M		F	
	ABS	CSTR	ABS	CSTR
1. "one"	אֶחָד	אַחַד	אַחַת	אַחַת
2. "two"	שְׁנַ֫יִם	שְׁנֵי	שְׁתַּ֫יִם	שְׁתֵּי
3. "three"	שְׁלֹשָׁה	שְׁלֹ֫שֶׁת	שָׁלֹשׁ	שְׁלֹשׁ
4. "four"	אַרְבָּעָה	אַרְבַּ֫עַת	אַרְבַּע	אַרְבַּע
5. "five"	חֲמִשָּׁה	חֲמֵ֫שֶׁת	חָמֵשׁ	חֲמֵשׁ
6. "six"	שִׁשָּׁה	שֵׁ֫שֶׁת	שֵׁשׁ	שֵׁשׁ
7. "seven"	שִׁבְעָה	שִׁבְעַת	שֶׁ֫בַע	*שְׁבַע
8. "eight"	שְׁמֹנָה	שְׁמֹנַת	שְׁמֹנֶה	שְׁמֹנֶה
9. "nine"	תִּשְׁעָה	תִּשְׁעַת	תֵּ֫שַׁע	*תְּשַׁע
10. "ten"	עֲשָׂרָה	עֲשֶׂ֫רֶת	עֶ֫שֶׂר	עֶ֫שֶׂר

The word class of the cardinal numbers is not straightforward. They have morphosyntactic characteristics similar to adjectives and nouns. Lower numbers display more adjectival features, and higher numbers are more noun-like.[85] The general characteristics are outlined below for the numbers 1, 2, 3–10, 11–12, 13–19, base-ten digits ($n \times 10^1$, $n \times 10^2$, $n \times 10^3$, $n \times 10^4$), 21–99, 101–999, and higher than 1,000.

7.9.4.1.1 One. The number אֶחָד "one" is most similar to an adjective. It takes masculine, feminine, and plural forms, agreeing with the noun it modifies in definiteness (e.g., בְּנֵי אָבִינוּ הָאֶחָד "sons of our one father"; הַצִּפּוֹר הָאֶחָת "the one bird"; יָמִים אֲחָדִים "one days" [i.e., "a few days"]). The construct forms, אַחַד (M) and אַחַת (F) "one of," function with a plural entity to indicate a single item of a class (אַחַד הָעָם "one of the people"; אַחַד הֶהָרִים "one of the mountains"; אַחַת מִכָּל־מִצְוֺת "one of all the commandments"). This meaning is like the sequence of אֶחָד with a partitive מִן construction (אֶחָד מֵאֶחָיו "one among his brothers"; אַחַת מִצַּלְעֹתָיו "one from among his ribs"). The numeral gender is based on the entity enumerated even when it is not stated (e.g., אֵשֶׁת הָאֶחָד "the wife of the one [man]," Deut 25:11; שֵׁם הָאַחַת שִׁפְרָה "the name of the one [midwife] was Shiphrah," Exod 1:15). It may also be used to enumerate the first entity of an ordered sequence (see below §7.9.4.2).

7.9.4.1.2 Two. The higher cardinals follow more closely the morphosyntax of nouns. The number "two" exhibits dual-suffix morphology with both the masculine (שְׁנַיִם) and feminine form (שְׁתַּיִם). The gender of the enumerated entity determines the gender of the numeral. The counted entity is plural in number (e.g., שְׁתֵּי בְנֹתָי "your two daughters," Gen 31:41).[86] The construct form of the number precedes the noun being counted. The absolute form of the cardinal may be placed before or after a noun. A pronominal suffix with the numeral may replace a following noun (e.g., שְׁנֵינוּ "two of us"; שְׁנֵיכֶם "two of you"; שְׁנֵיהֶם and שְׁתֵּיהֶן "two of them"). The absolute form of the numeral can be followed by the preposition מִן to designate the partitive construction (e.g., שְׁנַיִם שְׁנַיִם מִכָּל־הַבָּשָׂר "two by two from among every creature," Gen 7:15).

MORPHOSYNTAX OF THE CARDINAL NUMERAL שְׁנַיִם "TWO"			
POSITION:	AFTER NOUN	BEFORE NOUN	
STATE	ABSOLUTE FORM		CONSTRUCT FORM
M	הָעַמּוּדִים שְׁנַיִם "the two pillars"	שְׁנַיִם כְּרֻבִים זָהָב "two gold cherubs"	שְׁנֵי בְּנֵי יוֹנָה "two doves"
F	עָרִים שְׁתַּיִם "two cities"	שְׁתַּיִם מַעֲרָכוֹת "two rows"	שְׁתֵּי הַמְּזוּזוֹת "the two doorposts"

7.9.4.1.3 Three through Ten. The morphosyntax of the numbers three through ten is most akin to nouns. Yet, a few oddities should be noted. First, these numbers are

---

[85] Screnock, 25–29.

[86] A noun with dual morphology is found once with the numeral "two" (שְׁתֵּי כְרָעַיִם "two lower legs"). In this case, the dual noun may refer to the double lower leg bones (i.e., tibia and fibula).

gendered with "chiastic concord."[87] The form of the feminine numbers aligns with masculine noun morphology, and the form of the masculine numbers is akin to feminine noun morphology, *-*(a)t* (i.e., ־ָה- or ־ת). Second, the numeral may precede the counted noun as a construct or absolute form. Only the absolute form follows the noun. The absolute form of the number is used with an indefinite counted entity (e.g., שָׁלֹשׁ שָׁנִים "[every] three years," see Lev 19:23; Deut 14:28), and the construct form of the number is usually found with a definite noun (e.g., לִשְׁלֹשׁ הַשָּׁנִים "for the [next] three years," Lev 25:21).[88] Third, a few plural pronominal forms exist with the cardinals (e.g., שְׁלָשְׁתְּכֶם "three of you" and שְׁלָשְׁתָּם "three of them," Num 12:4; אַרְבַּעְתָּם "four of them," Ezra 1:8; שִׁבְעָתָם "seven of them," 2 Sam 21:9). Fourth, the counted nouns between three and ten are always plural in number. The counted entity may be a demonstrative (e.g., שְׁלָשׁ־אֵלֶּה "three of these," Exod 21:11). Fifth, the number may be used with determiners, such as the demonstrative and definite article (e.g., הַשָּׁלֹשׁ הָאֵלֶּה "these three [cities]," Deut 19:9) or to form a kind of proper name (e.g., הַשְּׁלֹשָׁה "the Three," 2 Sam 23:18–19), but never with a counted noun. Sixth, the absolute state of the numeral can be used with the partitive מִן and noun (e.g., שִׁשָּׁה מִשְּׁמֹתָם "six of their names," Exod 28:10). Seventh, no plural morphology is used with the numerals three through ten (see the plural forms with base-ten digits, §7.9.4.1.6).

MORPHOSYNTAX OF THE CARDINAL NUMERALS			
POSITION:	AFTER NOUN	BEFORE NOUN	
STATE	ABSOLUTE FORM		CONSTRUCT FORM
M	שְׁעָרִים שְׁלוֹשָׁה "three gates"	שְׁלֹשָׁה בָנִים "three sons"	שְׁלֹשֶׁת יָמִים "three days"
F	עָרִים שָׁלֹשׁ "three cities"	שָׁלֹשׁ שָׁנִים "three years"	שְׁלֹשׁ הַשָּׁנִים "the three years" שְׁלֹשׁ הֶעָרִים "the three cities"

7.9.4.1.4 Eleven and Twelve. The cardinals "eleven" and "twelve" are multiword (or complex) <u>additive numbers</u>. An additive number is construed as the sum of more than one amount.[89] Hebrew uses a place value system where each numeral represents a digit of a base-ten system. The numbers "eleven" and "twelve" are formulated with the ones digit first followed by the numeral ten. Each has four

---

[87] For a modern comparative approach, see Rebecca Hasselbach, "Agreement and the Development of Gender in Semitic," *ZDMG* 164 (2014): 33–64, 319–44.

[88] Indefinite counted nouns tend to denote an abstract expression of measure, duration, or nonspecific entities. See Adina Moshavi, "Indefinite Numerical Construct Phrases in Biblical Hebrew," *JSS* 63 (2018): 99–123.

[89] Others call these "(complex) adding numerals." See, e.g., John Screnock, "The Syntax of Cardinal Numerals in Judges, Amos, Esther, and 1QM," *JSS* 63 (2018): 129–31.

possible forms—two are masculine and two are feminine. The ones digit for "eleven" may be analogous to the gendered construct form of אֶחָד "one" (אַחַד M, אַחַת F) or the older nongendered form עַשְׁתֵּי (< * ʿast).[90] The ones digit for "twelve" is the construct form either with or without <u>memation</u>. No usage difference is evident between the two masculine forms or the two feminine forms.

CARDINALS: 11 AND 12				
	M		F	
	FORM 1	FORM 2	FORM 1	FORM 2
11. "eleven"	עַשְׁתֵּי עָשָׂר	אַחַד עָשָׂר	עַשְׁתֵּי עֶשְׂרֵה	אַחַת עֶשְׂרֵה
12. "twelve"	שְׁנֵים עָשָׂר	שְׁנֵי עָשָׂר	שְׁתֵּים עֶשְׂרֵה	שְׁתֵּי עֶשְׂרֵה

The ones digit matches the gender of the counted noun (excepting עַשְׁתֵּי), and it takes the construct form. The digit "ten" is gendered with עָשָׂר as masculine and עֶשְׂרֵה as feminine. This additive ten is the same for all numerals eleven through nineteen. Most counted entities are plural and follow the numeral (e.g., אַחַד עָשָׂר יְלָדָיו "his eleven children"), but some may come before (e.g., עָרִים אַחַת־עֶשְׂרֵה "eleven cities"). Certain common quantified entities are singular (e.g., יוֹם "day," שָׁנָה "year," חֹדֶשׁ "month," אַמָּה "cubit") and come after the numeral. Such constructions can take on the role of ordinal numbers (e.g., לְעַשְׁתֵּי־עָשָׂר חֹדֶשׁ "eleventh month," Zech 1:7; עַשְׁתֵּי עֶשְׂרֵה שָׁנָה "eleventh year," Jer 1:3). At times, the counted noun is duplicated (e.g., בִּשְׁנַת שְׁתֵּים־עֶשְׂרֵה שָׁנָה "twelfth year," 2 Kgs 8:25).

7.9.4.1.5 Teens: Thirteen through Nineteen. Thirteen through nineteen are additive numbers. The ones digit is first and consists of the absolute form of the numerals three through nine with vowel reduction. The tens digit is represented by the same forms of "ten" found with "eleven" and "twelve." The first numeral is gendered according to the counted entity with chiastic concord, and the second with עָשָׂר as masculine and עֶשְׂרֵה as feminine.

CARDINALS: 13–19		
	M	F
13. "thirteen"	שְׁלֹשָׁה עָשָׂר	שְׁלֹשׁ עֶשְׂרֵה
14. "fourteen"	אַרְבָּעָה עָשָׂר	אַרְבַּע עֶשְׂרֵה
15. "fifteen"	חֲמִשָּׁה עָשָׂר	חֲמֵשׁ עֶשְׂרֵה
16. "sixteen"	שִׁשָּׁה עָשָׂר	שֵׁשׁ עֶשְׂרֵה
17. "seventeen"	שִׁבְעָה עָשָׂר	שְׁבַע עֶשְׂרֵה

---

[90] See Aren Wilson-Wright, "The Word for 'One' in Proto-Semitic," *JSS* 59 (2014): 1–13.

CARDINALS: 13–19		
	M	F
18. "eighteen"	שְׁמֹנָה עָשָׂר	שְׁמֹנֶה עֶשְׂרֵה
19. "nineteen"	תִּשְׁעָה עָשָׂר	תְּשַׁע עֶשְׂרֵה

The counted entity may come before (Josh 21:6) but more commonly after the number (Josh 21:19). And the counted nouns may be singular (Josh 21:33). Some frequently quantified entities over ten may use the singular noun form (1 Kgs 8:65).[91]

Josh 21:6

עָרִים שְׁלֹשׁ עֶשְׂרֵה

thirteen cities

Josh 21:19

שְׁלֹשׁ־עֶשְׂרֵה עָרִים וּמִגְרְשֵׁיהֶן

thirteen cities and their pasturelands

Josh 21:33

שְׁלֹשׁ־עֶשְׂרֵה עִיר וּמִגְרְשֵׁיהֶן

thirteen cities and their pasturelands

1 Kgs 8:65

וַיַּעַשׂ שְׁלֹמֹה בָעֵת־הַהִיא| אֶת־הֶחָג וְכָל־יִשְׂרָאֵל עִמּוֹ קָהָל גָּדוֹל מִלְּבוֹא חֲמָת|
עַד־נַחַל מִצְרַיִם לִפְנֵי יְהוָה אֱלֹהֵינוּ שִׁבְעַת יָמִים וְשִׁבְעַת יָמִים **אַרְבָּעָה עָשָׂר יוֹם**:

At that time, Solomon observed the festival, and all of Israel was with him. A great assembly stretched out from Lebo-Hamath to the wadi of Egypt in the presence of Yahweh our God for seven days and seven more days—**fourteen days** total.

7.9.4.1.6 Base-Ten Digits. A combination of plural and dual morphology, multiplicative numbers, and distinct lexemes indicate the base-ten digits. The various forms of "ten" are outlined above as a lone numeral (עֲשָׂרָה M ABS, עֲשֶׂרֶת M CSTR, עֶשֶׂר F) and an additive number (עָשָׂר M, עֶשְׂרֵה F). The plural form of "ten" functions as the indeclinable cardinal עֶשְׂרִים "twenty."[92] The counted entity typically follows the number and is plural (עֶשְׂרִים אֲנָשִׁים "twenty men," 2 Sam

---

[91] See further John Screnock, "The Syntax of Complex Adding Numerals and Hebrew Diachrony," *JBL* 137 (2018): 795–97.

[92] The feminine plural form עֲשָׂרֹת designates "a group of ten." For example, Moses's father-in-law advises him to set judges over the people in concentric groups: וְשַׂמְתָּ עֲלֵהֶם שָׂרֵי אֲלָפִים שָׂרֵי מֵאוֹת שָׂרֵי חֲמִשִּׁים וְשָׂרֵי **עֲשָׂרֹת** "You should put over them rulers of thousands, rulers of hundreds, rulers of fifties, and rulers of **tens**" (Exod 18:21).

3:20). Some common counted nouns are singular (עֶשְׂרִים אִישׁ "twenty men," 1 Sam 14:14; זֶה עֶשְׂרִים שָׁנָה "this twenty years," Gen 31:38).

The tens cardinals (30, 40, 50, etc.) are formed using the masculine plural suffix with the numerals 3 through 9. These numbers are indeclinable (or invariable) and typically precede the counted noun.

TENS CARDINALS: 20–90	
	COMMON GENDER
20. "twenty"	עֶשְׂרִים
30. "thirty"	שְׁלֹשִׁים
40. "forty"	אַרְבָּעִים
50. "fifty"	חֲמִשִּׁים
60. "sixty"	שִׁשִּׁים
70. "seventy"	שִׁבְעִים
80. "eighty"	שְׁמֹנִים
90. "ninety"	תִּשְׁעִים

The base forms of the larger digit numbers are מֵאָה "one hundred," אֶלֶף "one thousand," and רִבּוֹ "ten thousand." The forms found in construct with the counted noun are מְאַת "one hundred" and אֶלֶף "one thousand." These digits are indeclinable (or invariable) with regard to grammatical gender.

THREE-, FOUR-, AND FIVE-DIGIT BASE-TEN "ONES:" 100, 1,000, AND 10,000		
	ABS	CSTR
100. "one hundred"	מֵאָה	מְאַת
1,000. "one thousand"	אֶלֶף	אֶלֶף
10,000. "ten thousand"[93]	רְבָבָה (רִבּוֹא) or[94] רִבּוֹ	רִבְבוֹת (רִבְאוֹת) or רִבּוֹת

The counted entity typically follows absolute forms (Isa 65:20), and it must follow the construct forms (Gen 21:5, Deut 33:17).

---

[93] The number 10,000 may alternatively be represented as the multiplicative number עֲשֶׂרֶת אֲלָפִים.

[94] The noun רְבָבָה frequently conveys a large uncountable amount, particularly as a plural רִבְבוֹת "myriads" or with a suffix בְּרִבְבֹתָיו "his myriads."

Isa 65:20

כִּי הַנַּעַר בֶּן־מֵאָה שָׁנָה יָמוּת

For a lad will die at the age of **one hundred years**.

Gen 21:5

וְאַבְרָהָם בֶּן־מְאַת שָׁנָה

Abraham was **one hundred years old**.

Deut 33:17

וְהֵם רִבְבוֹת אֶפְרַיִם וְהֵם אַלְפֵי מְנַשֶּׁה

Ephraim is **ten thousands** [strong], and Manasseh is **thousands** [strong].

The dual suffix is used to form the numbers מָאתַיִם "two hundred," אַלְפַּיִם "two thousand," and רִבּוֹתַיִם "twenty thousand." The numeral typically is before a singular (מָאתַיִם אִישׁ "two hundred men") or plural noun (מָאתַיִם הָאֲנָשִׁים "two hundred men"), but it may follow the counted entity (עִזִּים מָאתַיִם "two hundred goats").

THREE-, FOUR-, AND FIVE-DIGIT BASE-TEN "TWOS:" 200, 2,000, AND 20,000	
	COMMON GENDER
200. "two hundred"	מָאתַיִם
2,000. "two thousand"	אַלְפַּיִם
20,000. "twenty thousand"[95]	רִבּוֹתַיִם

The higher hundreds and thousands digits are multiplicative numbers. A <u>multiplicative number</u> includes a lower numeral followed by a multiplying numeral.[96] When the lower numeral is 3–10, the multiplying unit follows the lower numeral and takes the plural absolute form (i.e., מֵאוֹת "hundreds," אֲלָפִים "thousands," or רִבּוֹת "ten thousands" [or רְבוֹאת]) analogous to a counted entity with these numbers. Multipliers above ten are construed with the singular multiplier (i.e., אֶלֶף "thousand," and רְבָבָה "ten thousand"). For example, שְׁלשׁ מֵאוֹת "three hundreds" represents 300 (3 × 100), אַרְבַּעַת אֲלָפִים "four thousands" 4,000 (4 × 1,000s), שְׁנֵים־עָשָׂר אֶלֶף "twelve thousand" 12,000 (12 × 1,000), עֶשְׂרִים אֶלֶף "twenty thousand" (20 × 1,000) or שְׁתֵּי רִבּוֹת "two ten-thousands" (2 × 10,000), מֵאָה אֶלֶף "one hundred thousand" 100,000 (100 × 1,000), and שְׁמֹנֶה מֵאוֹת אֶלֶף "eight hundreds thousand" 800,000 (8 × 100s × 1,000). The single-digit lower numeral takes the form of the feminine teens combining number with the hundreds digit (i.e., שְׁלשׁ, חֲמֵשׁ, אַרְבַּע) and the form of the masculine construct with the thousands digit (i.e.,

---

[95] The number 20,000 may also be construed as the multiplicative שְׁתֵּי רְבוֹא or שְׁתֵּי רִבּוֹת "two ten-thousand(s)."

[96] Screnock ("Cardinal Numbers," 129–31) labels these "(complex) multiplying numerals."

שְׁלֹשֶׁת, אַרְבַּעַת, חֲמֵשֶׁת).[97] An additive number can precede the multiplying digit, as with מֵאָה וְעֶשְׂרִים אֶלֶף "one hundred and twenty thousand" ([100 + 20] × 1,000 = 120,000).

The number may precede or follow the counted entity. These numbers may also be in construct with a subsequent counted noun: מֵאוֹת "hundreds of" or אַלְפֵי "thousands of" or רִבְבוֹת "ten thousands of" (Mic 6:7).

Mic 6:7

הֲיִרְצֶה יְהוָה בְּאַלְפֵי אֵילִים בְּרִבְבוֹת נַחֲלֵי־שָׁמֶן

Is Yahweh pleased **with thousands** of rams, **with ten thousands** of torrents of oil?

HUNDREDS ABOVE TWO HUNDRED: 300–900		
	ABS	CSTR
300. "three hundred"	שְׁלֹשׁ מֵאוֹת אַמָּה	———
400. "four hundred"	נְבִיאֵי הָאֲשֵׁרָה אַרְבַּע מֵאוֹת	אַרְבַּע מֵאת שֶׁקֶל־כֶּסֶף
500. "five hundred"	אֲנָשִׁים חֲמֵשׁ מֵאוֹת	———
600. "six hundred"	שֵׁשׁ־מֵאוֹת אִישׁ	———
700. "seven hundred"	בָּקָר שְׁבַע מֵאוֹת	———
800. "eight hundred"	שְׁמֹנֶה מֵאוֹת חָלָל	———
900. "nine hundred"	תְּשַׁע מֵאוֹת רֶכֶב	———

THOUSANDS ABOVE TWO THOUSAND: 3,000 AND UP		
	ABS	CSTR
3,000. "three thousand"	שְׁלֹשֶׁת אֲלָפִים אִישׁ	שְׁלֹשֶׁת אַלְפֵי אִישׁ
4,000. "four thousand"	אַרְבַּעַת אֲלָפִים שְׂעֹרִים	———
5,000. "five thousand"	חֲמֵשֶׁת אֲלָפִים אִישׁ	———
6,000. "six thousand"	שֵׁשֶׁת אֲלָפִים גְּמַלִּים	———
7,000. "seven thousand"	צֹאן שִׁבְעַת אֲלָפִים	שִׁבְעַת אַלְפֵי־צֹאן
8,000. "eight thousand"	כִּכָּרִים עֲשֶׂרֶת אֲלָפִים	———
10,000. "ten thousand"	עֲשֶׂרֶת אֲלָפִים אִישׁ	עֲשֶׂרֶת אַלְפֵי אִישׁ

---

[97] For the formation of ten thousand, the typical form of the lower digit is the masculine construct (עֲשֶׂרֶת אֲלָפִים), but the masculine absolute occasionally is found (עֲשָׂרָה אֲלָפִים 2 Sam 18:3). This difference is evident at 2 Kgs 24:14 with the vocalization following the former pattern (*qere*) and the written text (*ketiv*) the latter (עֲשָׂרָה אֲלָפִים).

THOUSANDS ABOVE TWO THOUSAND: 3,000 AND UP		
	ABS	CSTR
12,000. "twelve thousand"	שְׁנֵים־עָשָׂר אֶלֶף פָּרָשִׁים	
20,000. "twenty thousand"	כֹּרִים עֶשְׂרִים אֶלֶף דַּרְכְּמוֹנִים שְׁתֵּי רִבּוֹת	עֶשְׂרִים אֶלֶף אִישׁ רַגְלִי
40,000. "forty thousand"	אַרְבָּעִים אָלֶף	———
50,000. "fifty thousand"	חֲמִשִּׁים אָלֶף	———
60,000. "sixty thousand"	שִׁשִּׁים אֶלֶף פָּרָשִׁים	———
70,000. "seventy thousand"	שִׁבְעִים אֶלֶף אִישׁ סַבָּל	———
80,000. "eighty thousand"	שְׁמֹנִים אֶלֶף אִישׁ חֹצֵב	———
100,000. "one hundred thousand"	נֶפֶשׁ אָדָם מֵאָה אָלֶף	מֵאָה־אֶלֶף כָּרִים
120,000. "one hundred and twenty thousand"	מֵאָה וְעֶשְׂרִים אָלֶף	———
500,000. "five hundreds thousand"	חֲמֵשׁ־מֵאוֹת אֶלֶף אִישׁ	———
600,000. "six hundreds thousand"	שֵׁשׁ־מֵאוֹת אֶלֶף רַגְלִי הַגְּבָרִים	———
800,000. "eight hundreds thousand"	שְׁמֹנֶה מֵאוֹת אֶלֶף אִישׁ	———
1,000,000. "one thousand thousands"	אֶלֶף אֲלָפִים כִּכָּרִים	———
10,000,000. "ten million"[98]	———	אַלְפֵי רְבָבָה

7.9.4.1.7 Twenty-One through Ninety-Nine. The cardinal numbers between the decades (tens) consist of two-word compounds. These two-digit numerals are additive numbers combining a tens digit and a ones digit with *waw* (עֶשְׂרִים וְשָׁלֹשׁ שָׁנָה "twenty-three years," 2 Kgs 23:31). The reverse number order is also evidenced—ones digit followed by tens digit (שָׁלֹשׁ וְעֶשְׂרִים שָׁנָה "twenty-three years," Jer 25:3). The counted noun may come before (עָרִים עֶשְׂרִים וּשְׁתַּיִם "twenty-two cities," Josh 19:30) or after (עֶשְׂרִים וְשָׁלוֹשׁ עָרִים "twenty-three cities," 1 Chr 2:22) the number compound. The gender of the ones digit is determined by the grammatical gender of the counted entity (e.g., שְׁלֹשִׁים־וּשְׁנַיִם מֶלֶךְ "thirty-two kings (M)," 1 Kgs 20:16) even if the noun is not present (e.g., וּבִירוּשָׁלַם מָלַךְ שְׁלֹשִׁים וְשָׁלוֹשׁ "[David] ruled

---

[98] The number, רִבְבוֹת אַלְפֵי יִשְׂרָאֵל "ten-thousands thousands of Israel" (Num 10:36), may be best understood as a distributive.

in Jerusalem thirty-three [years (F)]," 1 Chr 29:27). Commonly counted nouns are often singular (שְׁמֹנִים וַחֲמִשָּׁה אִישׁ "eighty-five men," 1 Sam 22:18), but other entities are plural (Ezra 8:35).

Ezra 8:35

הַבָּאִים מֵהַשְּׁבִי בְנֵי־הַגּוֹלָה הִקְרִיבוּ עֹלוֹת ׀ לֵאלֹהֵי יִשְׂרָאֵל פָּרִים שְׁנֵים־עָשָׂר
עַל־כָּל־יִשְׂרָאֵל אֵילִים ׀ תִּשְׁעִים וְשִׁשָּׁה כְּבָשִׂים שִׁבְעִים וְשִׁבְעָה צְפִירֵי חַטָּאת
שְׁנֵים עָשָׂר

Those returning from the captives of the exiles offered whole burnt sacrifices to the God of Israel: twelve bulls for all of Israel, **ninety-six rams, seventy-seven ewes**, and twelve male-goats as a burnt sacrifice.

7.9.4.1.8 One Hundred One through Nine Hundred Ninety-Nine. The cardinal numbers between the hundreds are composed of multiword compounds. These three-digit numerals are additive numbers combining a hundreds digit with a ones digit (בְּאַחַת וְשֵׁשׁ־מֵאוֹת שָׁנָה "in the one and six hundreds [601st] year [of Noah's life]," Gen 8:13) or a tens digit (שְׁלֹשׁ־מֵאוֹת וְשִׁשִּׁים אִישׁ "three hundreds and sixty [360] men," 2 Sam 2:31) or both (שֶׁבַע וְעֶשְׂרִים וּמֵאָה מְדִינָה "seven and twenty and one hundred [127] provinces," Esth 1:1). The order of the digits is variable. Four permutations—ones-tens-hundreds, tens-ones-hundreds, hundreds-ones-tens, and hundreds-tens-ones—are used. The first and last are the most common. The hundreds digit is never listed between the tens and ones. Typically, a *waw* separates each compounded digit; however, it may be omitted after the hundreds (שֵׁשׁ מֵאוֹת שִׁשִּׁים וָשֵׁשׁ כִּכַּר זָהָב "six hundreds, sixty, and six [666] talents of gold," 1 Kgs 10:14). This omission of *waw* is often, but not consistently, found in lists in the books of Ezra (2:4–5) and Neh (7:31–32).

Ezra 2:4–5

בְּנֵי שְׁפַטְיָה שְׁלֹשׁ מֵאוֹת שִׁבְעִים וּשְׁנָיִם׃
בְּנֵי אָרַח שְׁבַע מֵאוֹת חֲמִשָּׁה וְשִׁבְעִים׃

The children of Shephatiah: **three hundreds, seventy, and two** [372].
The children of Arah: **seven hundreds, five, and seventy** [775].

Neh 7:31–32

אַנְשֵׁי מִכְמָס מֵאָה וְעֶשְׂרִים וּשְׁנָיִם׃
אַנְשֵׁי בֵית־אֵל וְהָעָי מֵאָה עֶשְׂרִים וּשְׁלֹשָׁה׃

The men of Michmas: **one hundred and twenty and two** [122].
The men of Bethel and Ai: **one hundred twenty and three** [123].

The digits one through ten consist of the absolute form of the cardinal number (e.g., שֶׁבַע וּשְׁלֹשִׁים וּמְאַת שָׁנָה "seven (F ABS) and thirty and one hundred [137] years," Exod 6:16) and matches the gender of the counted entity (e.g., מֵאָה וְעֶשֶׂר שָׁנִים "one hundred and ten (F) [110] years," Gen 50:22). If the numeral compound ends with מֵאָה "one hundred," it is often the construct form (e.g., חֲמִשִּׁים וּמְאַת יוֹם

"fifty and one hundred [150] days," Gen 7:24; שָׁלֹשׁ וּשְׁלֹשִׁים וּמְאַת שָׁנָה "three and thirty and one hundred [333] years," Exod 6:18).

When referring to a known numbered entity, each digit must be definite. Such is the case with the unredeemed males in Numbers 3. They are referred to as הַשְּׁלֹשָׁה וְהַשִּׁבְעִים וְהַמָּאתָיִם "the three and the seventy and the two hundred [273]" (Num 3:46). These individuals represent the difference between the 22,000 redeeming Levites (v. 39) and the 22,273 redeemed firstborn Israelite males (v. 43). They are further described attributively as הָעֹדְפִים עַל־הַלְוִיִּם מִבְּכוֹר בְּנֵי יִשְׂרָאֵל "those remaining above the Levitical firstborn of Israel." The price of redemption is set as חֲמֵשֶׁת חֲמֵשֶׁת שְׁקָלִים "five shekels apiece" (v. 47) for a total of חֲמִשָּׁה וְשִׁשִּׁים וּשְׁלֹשׁ מֵאוֹת וָאֶלֶף בְּשֶׁקֶל הַקֹּדֶשׁ "five and sixty and three hundreds and one thousand [1,365] according to the sanctuary shekel" (v. 50).

> Num 3:46
>
> וְאֵת פְּדוּיֵי הַשְּׁלֹשָׁה וְהַשִּׁבְעִים וְהַמָּאתָיִם הָעֹדְפִים עַל־הַלְוִיִּם מִבְּכוֹר בְּנֵי יִשְׂרָאֵל:
>
> As for the redemption price of the **273** remaining above the Levitical firstborn of Israel.

In this example, the counted entity is absent from the NP. When present, the noun usually comes after the numeral, but it may come before (e.g., נְבִיאֵי הַבַּעַל אַרְבַּע מֵאוֹת וַחֲמִשִּׁים "four hundreds and fifty [450] prophets of Baal," 1 Kgs 18:19), especially in lists (e.g. גְמַלִּים אַרְבַּע מֵאוֹת שְׁלֹשִׁים וַחֲמִשָּׁה "four hundreds thirty and five [435] camels," Neh 7:68; נֶפֶשׁ שְׁבַע מֵאוֹת אַרְבָּעִים וַחֲמִשָּׁה "seven hundreds forty and five [745] persons," Jer 52:30).

With multiword numbers, the noun may accompany each separate digit. These discrete NPs may be joined together to quantify a lone entity. This construction is commonly used in describing someone's age or an extended interval of years. For example, Seth's lifetime is measured with the aggregate of two numbers each followed by the same noun שָׁנָה "year": שְׁתֵּים עֶשְׂרֵה שָׁנָה וּתְשַׁע מֵאוֹת שָׁנָה "twelve year and nine hundreds year" or "912 years" (Gen 5:8). The noun morphosyntax of each NP adheres to the expectations of the individual cardinal numbers. "Twelve years" (שְׁתֵּים עֶשְׂרֵה שָׁנָה) is feminine absolute followed by the singular noun, and "900 years" (תְּשַׁע מֵאוֹת שָׁנָה) is absolute with the singular noun. The repeated noun may follow two cardinal compounds (Gen 5:6; 11:19; 1 Kgs 6:1), as well as three cardinal compounds (Gen 23:1; 25:7).

> Gen 5:6
>
> חָמֵשׁ שָׁנִים וּמְאַת שָׁנָה
>
> five years and one hundred years [105 years]

> Gen 11:19
>
> תֵּשַׁע שָׁנִים וּמָאתַיִם שָׁנָה
>
> nine years and two hundred year [209 years]

1 Kgs 6:1

שְׁמוֹנִים שָׁנָה וְאַרְבַּע מֵאוֹת שָׁנָה

eighty year and four hundreds year [480 years]

Gen 23:1

מֵאָה שָׁנָה וְעֶשְׂרִים שָׁנָה וְשֶׁבַע שָׁנִים

one hundred year and twenty year and seven years [127 years]

Gen 25:7

מְאַת שָׁנָה וְשִׁבְעִים שָׁנָה וְחָמֵשׁ שָׁנִים

one hundred year and seventy year and five years [175 years]

Often for multiword numbers with three separate digits, the ones and tens are grouped together into a compound with a single noun and linked with a discrete hundreds NP (Gen 5:23; 5:18).

Gen 5:23

חָמֵשׁ וְשִׁשִּׁים שָׁנָה וּשְׁלֹשׁ מֵאוֹת שָׁנָה

five and sixty year and three hundreds year [365 years]

Gen 5:18

שְׁתַּיִם וְשִׁשִּׁים שָׁנָה וּמְאַת שָׁנָה

two and sixty year and one hundred year [162 years]

Infrequently, the tens and hundreds form a NP separate from the ones digit NP (Gen 47:28).

Gen 47:28

שֶׁבַע שָׁנִים וְאַרְבָּעִים וּמְאַת שָׁנָה

seven years and forty and one hundred year [147 years]

7.9.4.1.9 Higher than One Thousand. The numbers above one thousand are multiword compounds. They are composed of a combination of the previously discussed cardinal numbers. The morphosyntax of multiword number NPs aligns with that of these numbers.

The following examples serve to illustrate the wide range of large numbers. The digits are predominately arranged from largest to smallest but may alternatively be ordered smallest to largest. These numbers consist of an additive numeral with two (1 Kgs 5:12; Ezra 2:39; Judg 17:3; 2 Chr 12:3), three (Ezra 2:37; Num 4:40), or more elements (Ezra 2:7; Dan 12:12). The counted entity is often omitted. Each digit is separated by *waw* (1 Kgs 5:12; Ezra 2:39; Judg 17:3; 2 Chr 12:3; Num 4:40), or *waw* is used with the final numeral (Ezra 2:37; 2:7; Dan 12:12).

1 Kgs 5:12

חֲמִשָּׁה וָאָלֶף

five and one thousand [1,005]

Ezra 2:39

אֶלֶף וְשִׁבְעָה עָשָׂר

one thousand and seventeen [1,017]

Ezra 2:37

אֶלֶף חֲמִשִּׁים וּשְׁנָיִם

one thousand, fifty, and two [1,052]

Judg 17:3

אֶלֶף־וּמֵאָה הַכֶּסֶף

one thousand and one hundred [1,100] (pieces of) silver

2 Chr 12:3

בְּאֶלֶף וּמָאתַיִם רֶכֶב

one thousand and two hundred [1,200] chariots

Ezra 2:7

אֶלֶף מָאתַיִם חֲמִשִּׁים וְאַרְבָּעָה

one thousand, two hundred, fifty, and four [1,254]

Dan 12:12

אַשְׁרֵי הַמְחַכֶּה וְיַגִּיעַ לְיָמִים אֶלֶף שְׁלֹשׁ מֵאוֹת שְׁלֹשִׁים וַחֲמִשָּׁה

Blessed is the one who tarries and reaches one thousand, three hundreds, thirty, and five [1,335] days.

Num 4:40

אַלְפַּיִם וְשֵׁשׁ מֵאוֹת וּשְׁלֹשִׁים

two thousand and six hundreds and thirty [2,630]

Numbers larger than three thousand include the thousands digit as the multiplying unit (e.g., 12 × 1,000), such as 2 Chronicles 1:14, or as the ten-thousands unit (e.g., 20 × 10,000), such as Neh 7:70. These are combined with additive numbers to indicate the lower thousands (Ezra 2:69), hundreds (1 Chr 29:7), tens (Ezra 2:64), and ones digits (Jer 52:28).

2 Chr 1:14

וּשְׁנַיִם־עָשָׂר אֶלֶף פָּרָשִׁים

twelve thousand [12,000] horsemen

Neh 7:70

זָהָב דַּרְכְּמוֹנִים שְׁתֵּי רִבּוֹת

two ten-thousands [20,000] gold coins

Ezra 2:69

שֵׁשׁ־רִבֹּאות וָאָֽלֶף

six ten-thousands and one thousand [61,000]

1 Chr 29:7

וּנְחֹשֶׁת רִבּוֹ וּשְׁמוֹנַת אֲלָפִים כִּכָּרִים

ten thousand and eight thousands [18,000] bronze talents

Ezra 2:64

אַרְבַּע רִבּוֹא אֲלָפִים שְׁלֹשׁ־מֵאוֹת שִׁשִּׁים

four ten-thousand, two thousand, three hundreds, sixty [42,360]

Jer 52:28

יְהוּדִים שְׁלֹשֶׁת אֲלָפִים וְעֶשְׂרִים וּשְׁלֹשָׁה

three thousands and twenty and three [3,023] Jews

For even larger numbers, a compound additive (e.g., 100 + 20 and 7 + 50), as with 1 Chr 12:38 and Num 2:31, or a multiplicative number (e.g., 6 × 100) may precede the thousands digit (Num 31:32). The multiplying unit—typically אֶלֶף "thousand"—may be repeated for each higher digit like the repetition of the counted entity with multiword numbers (see §7.9.4.1.8). So 675,000 is construed as the aggregate of שֵׁשׁ־מֵאוֹת אֶלֶף "six hundreds thousand [600,000]," וְשִׁבְעִים אֶלֶף "seventy thousand [70,000]," and וַחֲמֵשֶׁת־אֲלָפִים "five thousands [5,000]" (Num 31:32).

1 Chr 12:38

מֵאָה וְעֶשְׂרִים אֶלֶף

one hundred and twenty thousand [120,000]

Num 2:31

מְאַת אֶלֶף וְשִׁבְעָה וַחֲמִשִּׁים אֶלֶף וְשֵׁשׁ מֵאוֹת

one hundred thousand and seven and fifty thousand and six hundred [157,600]

Num 31:32

צֹאן שֵׁשׁ־מֵאוֹת אֶלֶף וְשִׁבְעִים אֶלֶף וַחֲמֵשֶׁת־אֲלָפִים

six hundreds thousand and seventy thousand and five thousands [675,000] sheep

These large thousands are also combined with lower additive numbers (2 Chr 26:13; Num 26:51). The numerals usually are listed in descending orders of magnitude.

2 Chr 26:13

חֵיל צָבָא שְׁלֹשׁ מֵאוֹת אֶלֶף וְשִׁבְעַת אֲלָפִים וַחֲמֵשׁ מֵאוֹת

three hundreds thousand and seven thousands and five hundreds [307,500] troop force

Num 26:51

שֵׁשׁ־מֵאוֹת אֶלֶף וָאָלֶף שְׁבַע מֵאוֹת וּשְׁלֹשִׁים

six hundreds thousand and one thousand seven hundreds and thirty [601,730]

7.9.4.2 Ordinal Numbers

An <u>ordinal number</u> represents an arrangement of entities in a sequence. The ordered list in 1 Chronicles 27 outlines David's twelve military divisions by the month of the year that each named commander served.

1 CHRONICLES 27	VERSE
עַל הַמַּחֲלֹקֶת הָרִאשׁוֹנָה לַחֹדֶשׁ הָרִאשׁוֹן יָשָׁבְעָם בֶּן־זַבְדִּיאֵל	v. 2
Jashobeam ben-Zabdiel was over **the first division** for **the first month**.	
וְעַל מַחֲלֹקֶת । הַחֹדֶשׁ הַשֵּׁנִי דּוֹדַי הָאֲחוֹחִי	v. 4
Dodai the Ahohite was over a division for **the second month**.	
שַׂר הַצָּבָא הַשְּׁלִישִׁי לַחֹדֶשׁ הַשְּׁלִישִׁי בְּנָיָהוּ בֶן־יְהוֹיָדָע הַכֹּהֵן רֹאשׁ	v. 5
The third army commander was Benaiah ben-Jehoiada, the high priest, for **the third month**.	
הָרְבִיעִי לַחֹדֶשׁ הָרְבִיעִי עֲשָׂה־אֵל אֲחִי יוֹאָב	v. 7
The fourth was Asael, Joab's brother, for **the fourth month**.	
הַחֲמִישִׁי לַחֹדֶשׁ הַחֲמִישִׁי הַשַּׂר שַׁמְהוּת הַיִּזְרָח	v. 8
The fifth was commander Shamhuth, the Izrahite, **for the fifth month**.	
הַשִּׁשִּׁי לַחֹדֶשׁ הַשִּׁשִּׁי עִירָא בֶן־עִקֵּשׁ הַתְּקוֹעִי	v. 9
The sixth was Ira ben-Ikkesh, the Tekoite, for **the sixth month**.	
הַשְּׁבִיעִי לַחֹדֶשׁ הַשְּׁבִיעִי חֶלֶץ הַפְּלוֹנִי מִן־בְּנֵי אֶפְרָיִם	v. 10
The seventh was Helez, the Pelonites from the Ephraimites, for **the seventh month**.	
הַשְּׁמִינִי לַחֹדֶשׁ הַשְּׁמִינִי סִבְּכַי הַחֻשָׁתִי לַזַּרְחִי	v. 11
The eighth was Sibbecai, the Hushathite of Zerah, for **the eighth month**.	
הַתְּשִׁיעִי לַחֹדֶשׁ הַתְּשִׁיעִי אֲבִיעֶזֶר הָעֲנְּתֹתִי לַבֶּן । יְמִינִי	v. 12
The ninth was Abiezer, the Anathothite of Benjamin, for **the ninth month**.	
הָעֲשִׂירִי לַחֹדֶשׁ הָעֲשִׂירִי מַהְרַי הַנְּטוֹפָתִי לַזַּרְחִי	v. 13
The tenth was Maharai, the Netophathite of Zerah, for **the tenth month**.	

1 CHRONICLES 27	VERSE
עַשְׁתֵּי־עָשָׂר֙ לְעַשְׁתֵּי־עָשָׂ֣ר הַחֹ֔דֶשׁ בְּנָיָ֖ה הַפִּרְעָתוֹנִ֑י מִן־בְּנֵ֖י אֶפְרָ֑יִם	v. 14
Eleven was Benaiah, the Pirathonite from the Ephraimites, for **the eleventh month**.	
הַשְּׁנֵ֤ים עָשָׂר֙ לִשְׁנֵ֣ים עָשָׂ֣ר הַחֹ֔דֶשׁ חֶלְדַּ֥י הַנְּטוֹפָתִ֖י לְעָתְנִיאֵ֑ל	v. 15
Twelve was Heldai, the Netophathite of Othniel, for **the twelfth month**.	

BH ordinals are adjectives, agreeing in gender, number, and definiteness with their modifying noun. The attributive ordinal הָרִאשׁוֹן "first" matches the gender of its head noun (Jer 25:1), the number (Exod 34:1, Gen 41:20), and definiteness (Exod 40:2). The numeral אֶחָד "one" may also represent the initial element in a sequence (Exod 40:2).[99] An indefinite ordinal serves as a predicate (Isa 48:12).

Jer 25:1

הִ֗יא הַשָּׁנָ֣ה הָרִֽאשֹׁנִ֔ית לִנְבוּכַדְרֶאצַּ֖ר מֶ֥לֶךְ בָּבֶֽל

That is **the first year** (F) of Nebuchadnezzar, King of Babylon.

Exod 34:1

וְכָתַבְתִּי֙ עַל־הַלֻּחֹ֔ת אֶת־הַדְּבָרִ֔ים אֲשֶׁ֥ר הָי֛וּ עַל־הַלֻּחֹ֥ת הָרִאשֹׁנִ֖ים אֲשֶׁ֥ר שִׁבַּֽרְתָּ

I will write on the tablets the words which were on **the first tablets** (MP) which you broke.

Gen 41:20

וַתֹּאכַ֣לְנָה הַפָּר֗וֹת הָרַקּ֛וֹת וְהָרָע֑וֹת אֵ֣ת שֶׁ֤בַע הַפָּרוֹת֙ הָרִֽאשֹׁנ֔וֹת הַבְּרִיאֹֽת

The thin and sick cows ate the **first** seven fat **cows** (FP).

Exod 40:2

בְּיוֹם־הַחֹ֥דֶשׁ הָרִאשׁ֖וֹן בְּאֶחָ֣ד לַחֹ֑דֶשׁ תָּקִ֕ים אֶת־מִשְׁכַּ֖ן אֹ֥הֶל מוֹעֵֽד

In **the first month** (def.) on the first [day] of that month, you will erect the tabernacle, the tent of meeting.

Isa 48:12

אֲנִ֣י רִאשׁ֔וֹן אַ֖ף אֲנִ֥י אַחֲרֽוֹן

I am **first**. I am also **last**.

The initial and final ordinals are built from the nouns, רֹאשׁ "head" and אַחַר "back." The other nine ordinals, two through ten, are formed from the basic form of the cardinal numbers with the noun pattern (קְטִילִי).[100]

---

[99] See, also, יֹום אֶחָד "first day" (Gen 1:5), שֵׁם הָאֶחָד "name of the first [river]" (Gen 2:11), שֵׁם הָאַחַת "name of the first [midwife]" (Exod 1:15).

[100] The cardinal numbers one through ten can also be used like ordinals to orient the years of a sovereign's reign: שְׁנַת אַחַת "first year," שְׁנַת שְׁתַּיִם "second year," שְׁנַת שָׁלֹשׁ "third year," שְׁנַת אַרְבַּע "fourth year" (but also, שְׁנַת הָרְבִעִית Jer 28:1; 46:2; 51:59), שְׁנַת חָמֵשׁ "fifth year," שְׁנַת־שֵׁשׁ

SOURCE/ROOT	ORDINAL	M	F	CARDINAL
רֹאשׁ "head"	"first"	רִאשׁוֹן	רִאשֹׁנָה	אֶחָד "one"
(שׁנ(י	"second"[101]	שֵׁנִי	שֵׁנִית	שְׁנַיִם "two"
שׁלשׁ	"third"	שְׁלִישִׁי	שְׁלִישִׁית	שְׁלֹשָׁה "three"
רבע	"fourth"	רְבִיעִי	רְבִיעִית	אַרְבָּעָה "four"
חמשׁ	"fifth"	חֲמִישִׁי	חֲמִישִׁית	חֲמִשָּׁה "five"
שׁדשׁ	"sixth"	שִׁשִּׁי	שִׁשִּׁית	שִׁשָּׁה "six"
שׁבע	"seventh"	שְׁבִיעִי	שְׁבִיעִית	שִׁבְעָה "seven"
שׁמן	"eighth"	שְׁמִינִי	שְׁמִינִית	שְׁמֹנָה "eight"
תשׁע	"ninth"	תְּשִׁיעִי	תְּשִׁיעִית	תִּשְׁעָה "nine"
עשׂר	"tenth"	עֲשִׂירִי	עֲשִׂירִית	עֲשָׂרָה "ten"
אַחַר "back"	"last"	אַחֲרוֹן	אַחֲרֹנָה	——

No special forms exist for the ordinals above ten. Cardinal numbers are used instead.[102] Most commonly, the ordinal function is found with the years of a sovereign's reign (Neh 5:14) and the days of the month (Exod 12:18). The date formula may assume the noun יוֹם "day" (Neh 6:15).

Neh 5:14

מִשְּׁנַת עֶשְׂרִים וְעַד שְׁנַת שְׁלֹשִׁים וּשְׁתַּיִם לְאַרְתַּחְשַׁסְתְּא הַמֶּלֶךְ שָׁנִים שְׁתֵּים עֶשְׂרֵה אֲנִי וְאַחַי לֶחֶם הַפֶּחָה לֹא אָכַלְתִּי

From **the twentieth** year to **the thirty-second** year of King Artaxerxes— for twelve years—I and my brothers did not eat the governmental food.

"sixth year," שְׁנַת־שֶׁבַע "seventh year" (but also, שְׁנַת הַשְּׁבִיעִית Ezra 7:8), שְׁנַת שְׁמֹנֶה "eighth year," שְׁנַת־תֵּשַׁע "ninth year" (but also, שְׁנַת הַתְּשִׁיעִית 2 Kgs 17:6; 25:1), שְׁנַת הָעֲשִׂרִית "tenth year."

[101] A plural form of שֵׁנִי "second" is found in the description of Noah's ark describing the level between the "lower" and "third" deck: תַּחְתִּיִּם שְׁנִיִּם וּשְׁלִשִׁים תַּעֲשֶׂהָ "You shall make it with lower, second, and third (stories)" (Gen 6:16).

[102] The ordinals הַגּוֹרָל הָרִאשׁוֹן "the first lot" through הָעֲשִׂרִי "tenth" are listed in 1 Chr 24:7–11, followed by the cardinals עַשְׁתֵּי עָשָׂר "eleven" through אַרְבָּעָה וְעֶשְׂרִים "twenty-four" in verses 12–18, to indicate the order of the heads of the Levitical families. Similar sequences are found in 1 Chr 25:9–31 and 27:2–15.

Exod 12:18

בָּרִאשֹׁן בְּאַרְבָּעָה֩ עָשָׂ֨ר י֤וֹם לַחֹ֨דֶשׁ֙ בָּעֶ֔רֶב תֹּאכְל֖וּ מַצֹּ֑ת עַ֠ד י֣וֹם הָאֶחָ֧ד וְעֶשְׂרִ֛ים
לַחֹ֖דֶשׁ בָּעָֽרֶב׃

In the first [month] on **the fourteenth day** of the month in the evening,
you shall eat unleavened bread until **the twenty-first day** of the month in
the evening.

Neh 6:15

וַתִּשְׁלַם֙ הַֽחוֹמָ֔ה בְּעֶשְׂרִ֥ים וַחֲמִשָּׁ֖ה לֶאֱל֑וּל לַחֲמִשִּׁ֥ים וּשְׁנַ֖יִם יֽוֹם׃

The wall was completed in fifty-two days **on the twenty-fifth [day]** of
Elul.

7.9.4.3 Fractions

A <u>fraction</u> expresses the numerical ratio of a part to the whole. It represents this
portion as the quotient of two numbers—the first specifies the given number of
parts and the second indicates the whole number of parts. For instance, the fraction
two-thirds (2/3) includes two shares of a three-part whole.

BH fractions are typically represented as one part of a multipart whole. Ordinal
numerals (see above §7.9.4.2) can express this relationship: שְׁלִשִׁית "third part"
(2 Sam 18:2), רְבִיעִית "fourth part" (Num 15:4–5), and חֲמִישִׁית "fifth part" (Gen
47:24).

The fraction, חֲצִי "one-half" (1 Kgs 16:21), is connected to the verb חָצָה "divide." The ordinal שֵׁנִי "two" is not used for this purpose.[103]

1 Kgs 16:21

אָ֧ז יֵחָלֵ֛ק הָעָ֥ם יִשְׂרָאֵ֖ל לַחֵ֑צִי חֲצִ֨י הָעָ֜ם הָיָ֗ה אַחֲרֵ֤י תִבְנִ֤י בֶן־גִּינַת֙ לְהַמְלִיכ֔וֹ וְהַחֲצִ֖י
אַחֲרֵ֥י עָמְרִֽי

Then the people of Israel were divided **in half: half** the people followed
Tibni ben-Ginath to make him king, and **half** followed Omri.

Other fractional numerals have forms related to their respective whole numbers:
שְׁלִשִׁיָּה "one-third" (Isa 19:24), רֹבַע and רֶבַע "a quarter" (1 Sam 9:8), חֹמֶשׁ "one-
fifth" (Gen 47:26), and מַעֲשֵׂר "tenth" (Ezek 45:11, 14) or עִשָּׂרוֹן "tenth" (Exod
29:40).

Exod 29:40

וְעִשָּׂרֹ֨ן סֹ֜לֶת בָּל֨וּל בְּשֶׁ֤מֶן כָּתִית֙ רֶ֣בַע הַהִ֔ין וְנֵ֕סֶךְ רְבִיעִ֥ת הַהִ֖ין יָ֑יִן לַכֶּ֖בֶשׂ הָאֶחָֽד׃

One-tenth [1/10th] of semolina mixed with **one quarter** hin of pressed
oil along with a libation of **one-fourth** hin wine [shall be offered] for the
first lamb.

---

[103] The noun, תָּוֶךְ "middle," can indicate a central point measured by area (Num 35:5) or distance
(Judg 15:4).

Multipart fractions (Num 15:6) are rare, but they appear to be arranged as construct forms שְׁנֵי עֶשְׂרֹנִים "two-tenth parts" (also Lev 23:13; 24:5; Num 15:6; 28:9, 12, 20; 29:9, 14).

Num 15:6

לְאַ֗יִל תַּעֲשֶׂ֥ה מִנְחָ֛ה סֹ֖לֶת **שְׁנֵ֣י עֶשְׂרֹנִ֑ים** בְּלוּלָ֥ה בַשֶּׁ֖מֶן **שְׁלִשִׁ֥ית** הַהִֽין

For the ram, you shall make a grain offering [consisting of] **two-tenths** [an *ephah* of] semolina with **one-third** a *hin* of oil.

7.9.4.4 Multipliers

A multiplicative numeral, or simply <u>multiplier</u>, indicates the replication of an entity by a designated amount. English uses several expressions as multipliers: once, twice, thrice, dual, double, triple, quadruple, etc. The cardinals sequenced with the word *time(s)* and the morpheme *-fold* also convey this notion: *one time, two times, three times*, etc., and *onefold, twofold, threefold*, etc.

Hebrew similarly expresses multipliers in various ways. A single instance is פַּעַם "once, one time" (Judg 16:28). The dual numeral is מִשְׁנֶה "twice" (Exod 16:5)—after וּמִשְׁנֶה־כֶּסֶף or before כֶּסֶף מִשְׁנֶה "double silver" the nominal (Gen 43:12, 15)—or כֶּפֶל (Job 41:5) and כִּפְלַיִם (Job 11:6) "double."[104] The cardinal שְׁנַיִם "two" may also serve as a multiplier (Exod 22:3).

Judg 16:28

וְחַזְּקֵ֨נִי נָ֜א אַ֣ךְ **הַפַּ֤עַם** הַזֶּה֙ הָאֱלֹהִ֔ים

Would you God strengthen me yet this **once**?

Exod 16:5

וְהָיָה֙ בַּיּ֣וֹם הַשִּׁשִּׁ֔י וְהֵכִ֖ינוּ אֵ֣ת אֲשֶׁר־יָבִ֑יאוּ וְהָיָ֣ה **מִשְׁנֶ֔ה** עַ֥ל אֲשֶֽׁר־יִלְקְט֖וּ י֥וֹם ׀ יֽוֹם׃

On the sixth day, they would prepare what they took in, and it would be **double** according to what they gathered day by day.

Exod 22:3

אִֽם־הִמָּצֵא֩ תִמָּצֵ֨א בְיָד֜וֹ הַגְּנֵבָ֗ה מִשּׁ֧וֹר עַד־חֲמ֛וֹר עַד־שֶׂ֖ה חַיִּ֑ים **שְׁנַ֖יִם** יְשַׁלֵּֽם׃

If a stolen ox, donkey, or sheep is found alive in his possession, he must pay back **double**.

The dual forms of other cardinals can designate multipliers. These include אַרְבַּעְתָּיִם "fourfold" (2 Sam 12:6) and שִׁבְעָתָיִם "sevenfold" (Ps 12:7).[105] Elsewhere the cardinal is used (Lev 26:24) or a mixture of these (Gen 4:24).

2 Sam 12:6

וְאֶת־הַכִּבְשָׂ֖ה יְשַׁלֵּ֣ם **אַרְבַּעְתָּ֑יִם**

He must pay back the ewe-lamb **fourfold**.

---

[104] The dual noun, כִּלְאַ֖יִם "two kinds," could be included as an analogous multiplier (Lev 19:19).

[105] See also Gen 4:15, 24; Isa 30:26.

Ps 12:7

אִמְרֹות יְהוָה אֲמָרֹות טְהֹרֹות כֶּסֶף צָרוּף בַּעֲלִיל לָאָרֶץ מְזֻקָּק **שִׁבְעָתָיִם**׃

Yahweh's words are pure words, like silver refined in an earthen crucible, purified **seven times.**

Lev 26:24

וְהִכֵּיתִי אֶתְכֶם גַּם־אָנִי **שֶׁבַע** עַל־חַטֹּאתֵיכֶם׃

I, even I, will strike you **seven times** according to your sins.

Gen 4:24

כִּי **שִׁבְעָתַיִם** יֻקַּם־קָיִן וְלֶמֶךְ **שִׁבְעִים וְשִׁבְעָה**׃

If Cain is avenged **sevenfold**, then Lamech **seventy-seven times**.

The noun פַּעַם "time" is used as a multiplier with cardinal numbers. These include a פַּעַם אֶחָת "one time" (Josh 6:3), פַּעַם וּשְׁתָּיִם "a time or two" (Neh 13:20), פַּעֲמַיִם "two times" (Gen 27:36), שָׁלֹשׁ פְּעָמִים "three times" (Exod 23:17), שֶׁבַע פְּעָמִים "seven times" (Gen 33:3; 1 Kgs 18:43), מֵאָה פְעָמִים "one hundred times" (2 Sam 24:3), and אֶלֶף פְּעָמִים "a thousand times" (Deut 1:11).

Josh 6:3

וְסַבֹּתֶם אֶת־הָעִיר כֹּל אַנְשֵׁי הַמִּלְחָמָה הַקֵּיף אֶת־הָעִיר **פַּעַם אֶחָת**

Encircle the city with all the army—go around the city **one time.**

Neh 13:20

וַיָּלִינוּ הָרֹכְלִים וּמֹכְרֵי כָל־מִמְכָּר מִחוּץ לִירוּשָׁלִָם **פַּעַם וּשְׁתָּיִם**

A time or two, the traders and sellers of all merchandise stayed overnight outside of Jerusalem.

Gen 27:36

הֲכִי קָרָא שְׁמֹו יַעֲקֹב וַיַּעְקְבֵנִי זֶה **פַעֲמַיִם**

Isn't it because his name is called Jacob, he has tricked me in this same way **twice!**

2 Sam 24:3

וְיֹוסֵף יְהוָה אֱלֹהֶיךָ אֶל־הָעָם כָּהֵם וְכָהֵם **מֵאָה פְעָמִים**

Yahweh your God will add to the people more and more, **one hundred times.**

The plural nouns, יָדֹות "hands" (Gen 43:34), רְגָלִים "feet" (Exod 23:14), מֹנִים "occasion" (Gen 31:7), and שְׁעָרִים "measures" (Gen 26:12), are also used for counting multiples.

Gen 43:34

וַתֵּרֶב מַשְׂאַת בִּנְיָמִן מִמַּשְׂאֹת כֻּלָּם **חָמֵשׁ יָדוֹת**

The portion of Benjamin was **five times** greater than all of their portions.

Exod 23:14

שָׁלֹשׁ רְגָלִים תָּחֹג לִי בַּשָּׁנָה

Three times in the year you shall celebrate a feast for me.

Gen 31:7

וְהֶחֱלִף אֶת־מַשְׂכֻּרְתִּי **עֲשֶׂרֶת מֹנִים**

He changed my wages **ten times**.

Gen 26:12

וַיִּזְרַע יִצְחָק בָּאָרֶץ הַהִוא וַיִּמְצָא בַּשָּׁנָה הַהִוא **מֵאָה שְׁעָרִים**

Isaac sowed in that land, and he reaped **one hundred times** in that year.

7.9.4.5 Distributives

A <u>distributive</u> numeral refers to the number of entities in a group or class. A group of two is a צֶמֶד "pair" (1 Kgs 19:19). A distributive can combine with a cardinal to enumerate the number of groups, for instance, וַחֲמֵשׁ מֵאוֹת צֶמֶד־בָּקָר "five hundred pairs [or teams] of cattle" (Job 1:3). Some plural cardinal numbers appear to have specialized distributive usages to designate military divisions as in Exod 18:21. These corps include companies of ten (עֲשָׂרֹת), fifty (חֲמִשִּׁים), one hundred (מֵאוֹת), and one thousand (אֲלָפִים). The passive verb, חֲמֻשִׁים "be grouped in fifties," also designates a similar notion (Josh 1:14).

1 Kgs 19:19

וְהוּא חֹרֵשׁ שְׁנֵים־עָשָׂר **צְמָדִים** לְפָנָיו

He was ploughing with twelve **pairs** [of yoked oxen] in front of him.

Exod 18:21

וְשַׂמְתָּ עֲלֵהֶם **שָׂרֵי אֲלָפִים** שָׂרֵי **מֵאוֹת** שָׂרֵי **חֲמִשִּׁים** וְשָׂרֵי **עֲשָׂרֹת**

You shall appoint over them commanders of **groups of one thousand**, commanders of **groups of one hundred**, commanders of **groups of fifty**, and commanders of **groups of ten**.

Josh 1:14

וְאַתֶּם תַּעַבְרוּ **חֲמֻשִׁים** לִפְנֵי אֲחֵיכֶם כֹּל גִּבּוֹרֵי הַחַיִל

But all the army warriors will cross over **in groups of fifty** before your brothers.

Other expressions can denote similar distributive meanings. The first type is a number followed by the preposition לְ- "of, per" and another number designate the group size. The distributive is אַחַת לְשָׁלֹשׁ שָׁנִים "one per three years" (1 Kgs

10:22). Elsewhere a single entity can compose a set, as with שְׁנֵי הָעֹמֶר לָאֶחָד "two sheaves for each [i.e., apiece]" (Exod 16:22) or אַרְבָּעָה פָנִים לְאֶחָת "four faces per one" (Ezek 1:6).

1 Kgs 10:22

אַחַת לְשָׁלֹשׁ שָׁנִים תָּבוֹא | אֳנִי תַרְשִׁישׁ
Once every three years, the fleet of Tarshish arrived.

Exod 16:22

וַיְהִי | בַּיּוֹם הַשִּׁשִּׁי לָקְטוּ לֶחֶם מִשְׁנֶה שְׁנֵי הָעֹמֶר לָאֶחָד
On the sixth (day) they gathered double food, **two sheaves per one [each]**.

Ezek 1:6

וְאַרְבָּעָה פָנִים לְאֶחָת וְאַרְבַּע כְּנָפַיִם לְאַחַת לָהֶם:
They had **four faces each** and **four wings each**.

The distributive is elsewhere expressed by the repetition of a noun phrase (Exod 16:5), the duplication of a cardinal number (Gen 7:2; 1 Kgs 18:13), or a repeated noun phrase with a cardinal number (Josh 3:12).

Exod 16:5

וְהָיָה בַּיּוֹם הַשִּׁשִּׁי וְהֵכִינוּ אֵת אֲשֶׁר־יָבִיאוּ וְהָיָה מִשְׁנֶה עַל אֲשֶׁר־יִלְקְטוּ יוֹם | יוֹם:
On the sixth day, they would prepare what they took in, and it would be double according to what they gathered **day (by) day**.

Gen 7:2

מִכֹּל | הַבְּהֵמָה הַטְּהוֹרָה תִּקַּח־לְךָ שִׁבְעָה שִׁבְעָה אִישׁ וְאִשְׁתּוֹ
You shall take some of the clean animals, **seven pairs** [lit. **seven (by) seven**], each and its mate.

1 Kgs 18:13

וָאַחְבִּא מִנְּבִיאֵי יְהֹוָה מֵאָה אִישׁ חֲמִשִּׁים חֲמִשִּׁים אִישׁ בַּמְּעָרָה
I hid one hundred of the prophets of Yahweh, **fifty men** [lit. **fifty-fifty**] **per cave**.

Josh 3:12

וְעַתָּה קְחוּ לָכֶם שְׁנֵי עָשָׂר אִישׁ מִשִּׁבְטֵי יִשְׂרָאֵל אִישׁ־אֶחָד אִישׁ־אֶחָד לַשָּׁבֶט:
Now take twelve men from the tribes of Israel, **one** [lit. **each one (by) each one**] for each tribe.

7.9.5 Measure Words

Accurate measurement is a clear ethical standard in the Old Testament (Lev 19:36; Deut 25:15). Through the prophecy of Ezekiel, Yahweh sanctions and regulates honest dealings. He warns the leaders of Israel to enact trustworthy transactions, even setting the standard of the market (Ezek 45:10–12). The regulated measure for both dry (בַּת "*bath*") and liquid (אֵיפָה "*ephah*") amounts is a known magnitude (חֹמֶר "*homer* capacity").

Ezek 45:10–11

מֹאזְנֵי־צֶדֶק וְאֵיפַת־צֶדֶק וּבַת־צֶדֶק יְהִי לָכֶם: הָאֵיפָה וְהַבַּת תֹּכֶן אֶחָד יִהְיֶה לָשֵׂאת מַעְשַׂר הַחֹמֶר הַבַּת וַעְשִׂירִת הַחֹמֶר הָאֵיפָה אֶל־הַחֹמֶר יִהְיֶה מַתְכֻּנְתּוֹ:

You shall have just scales—a fair *ephah* **dry-measure** and a fair *bath* **liquid-measure**. The *ephah* and the *bath* shall be a fixed quantity: the *bath* according to the capacity of one-tenth of a *homer* and the *ephah* according to one-tenth of a *homer*. Each proportion shall be based on the *homer* **capacity**.

A <u>measure word</u> is a type of noun <u>classifier</u> that when combined with a numeral indicates an amount. Generally, measure words are count nouns and represent standardized or customary units of measurement for certain entities, particularly noncount nouns (see §7.5.3). These units measure weight, liquid and dry volume, length, and area. Several measure words represent container capacity (אֵיפָה "pot," מֶרְקָחָה "vessel," כְּלִי "basket," סַל "bottle, jar," בַּקְבֻּק "jar," נֵבֶל "*ephah*-container"), anthropic units (קֹמֶץ "handful," אַמָּה "cubit," זֶרֶת "span," טֶפַח "handbreadth (four fingers)," אֶצְבַּע "finger"), agronomic components (עֹמֶר "sheaf," עֲרֵמָה "heap," קָנֶה "rod, reed," צֶמֶד "acre," חֶלְקָה "plot"), or foodstuff (כִּכָּר "loaf of bread," פַּת "piece").[106]

MEASURE WORDS	MEASURED ITEMS
WEIGHT	
שֶׁקֶל "shekel," כִּכָּר "talent," גֵּרָה "gerah," מָנֶה "mina," מֶרְקָחָה "pot"	בַּרְזֶל "gold," בַּרְזֶל "iron," נְחוּשָׁה "copper, bronze," כֶּתֶם "gold," פַּז "refined gold," סָגוּר "gold," חָרוּץ "gold," בְּדִיל "tin; plummet, lead weight," עֹפֶרֶת "lead," סַפִּיר "lapis-lazuli," לְבוֹנָה "frankincense," כַּרְכֹּם "saffron," קִנָּמוֹן "cinnamon," נֵרְדְּ "nard," מֹר "myrrh," גַּד "coriander"

---

[106] For more information on the archaeological data, see Raz Kletter, "Vessels and Measures: The Biblical Liquid Capacity System," *IEJ* 64 (2014): 22–37.

MEASURE WORDS	MEASURED ITEMS
WEIGHT	
DRY VOLUME	
קֹמֶץ "handful," סַל "basket," חַלָּה "cake," כִּכָּר "loaf," פַּת "piece," בַּקְבֻּק "bottle, jar," עֲרֵמָה "heap," סְאָה "seah-measure," אֵיפָה "ephah-measure," חֹמֶר "homer-measure," כֹּר "cor-measure," לֶתֶךְ "lethech-measure," עֹמֶר "sheaf," קַב "kab-measure"	לֶחֶם "food; bread," דְּבַשׁ "honey," סֹלֶת "fine flour," מֶלַח "salt," קֶמַח "flour," מָן "manna," נֹפֶת "honey," מַאֲכָל "food," בַּר "grain; produce," דֶּשֶׁא "grass," יְבוּל "produce," שֶׁבֶר "grain," אָבִיב "ears (of grain)," דָּגָן "grain," פְּרִי "fruit, produce; offspring," אֹכֶל "food;" חָצִיר "grass;" אָבִיב "barley ears;" דְּבִיֹונִים/חריייונים "dung"
LIQUID VOLUME	
בַּת "bath-measure," הִין "hin-measure," חֹק "portion," כֹּר "cor-measure," לֹג "log-measure," חֹמֶר "homer-measure," נֵבֶל "jar"	יַיִן "wine," חָלָב "milk," תִּירֹושׁ "new wine," עָסִיס "sweet wine," שֵׁכָר "alcoholic beverage," יִצְהָר "oil," שֶׁמֶן "oil"
LENGTH	
אַמָּה "cubit," קָנֶה "rod, reed," זֶרֶת "span," טֶפַח "handbreadth (four fingers)," אֶצְבַּע "finger"	אֹרֶךְ "length," רֹחַב "width," קֹומָה "height," גֹּבַהּ "height," עֳבִי "thickness," פֵּאָה "side," דֶּרֶךְ "route"
AREA	
צֶמֶד "acre," חֶלְקָה "plot"	שָׂדֶה "field," כֶּרֶם "vineyard"

The quantity of the measure word may be indicated by morphology (2 Kgs 7:1), a cardinal number (1 Sam 17:4–5), or another numeral (Num 15:5). The measured item is in apposition either before or after the measure word. The cardinal number modifies the measure word and not the noncount entity. For instance, the feminine number שֵׁשׁ "six" agrees with the gender of the measure word אַמֹּות "cubits" and not the masculine referent גֹּבַהּ "height" or the Philistine warrior Goliath (1 Sam 17:4–5).

2 Kgs 7:1

כָּעֵת ׀ מָחָר סְאָה־סֹלֶת בְּשֶׁקֶל וְסָאתַיִם שְׂעֹרִים בְּשֶׁקֶל בְּשַׁעַר שֹׁמְרֹון

At this time tomorrow at the gate of Samaria, **a seah** of semanola will be exchanged for a shekel and **two seahs** of barley for a shekel.

1 Sam 17:4–5

וַיֵּצֵא אִישׁ־הַבֵּנַיִם מִמַּחֲנֹות פְּלִשְׁתִּים גָּלְיָת שְׁמֹו מִגַּת גָּבְהֹו שֵׁשׁ אַמֹּות וָזָרֶת׃

וְכוֹבַע נְחֹשֶׁת עַל־רֹאשׁוֹ וְשִׁרְיוֹן קַשְׂקַשִּׂים הוּא לָבוּשׁ וּמִשְׁקַל הַשִּׁרְיוֹן **חֲמֵשֶׁת־אֲלָפִים שְׁקָלִים** נְחֹשֶׁת:

The champion-warrior emerged from the Philistine encampment—his name was Goliath from Gath. His height was **six cubits and a span**. He had a bronze helmet on his head and wore scale armor. The weight of the armor was **five thousand shekels** of bronze.

Num 15:5

וְיַיִן לַנֶּסֶךְ **רְבִיעִית הַהִין** תַּעֲשֶׂה עַל־הָעֹלָה

You shall present upon the whole burnt offering **a quarter *hin*** of wine as a libation.

The measure word can be implicit for certain items. The weight שֶׁקֶל "shekel" is assumed (Gen 20:16), as well as אֵיפָה "*ephah*" (Lev 14:21), כִּכָּר "loaf" or חַלָּה "cake" (1 Sam 10:3–4; 1 Sam 21:4), and אַמָּה "cubit" (Exod 27:11).[107]

Gen 20:16[108]

הִנֵּה נָתַתִּי **אֶלֶף** כֶּסֶף לְאָחִיךְ

I hereby give your brother **one thousand** [shekels of] silver!

Lev 14:21[109]

וְאִם־דַּל הוּא וְאֵין יָדוֹ מַשֶּׂגֶת וְלָקַח כֶּבֶשׂ אֶחָד אָשָׁם לִתְנוּפָה לְכַפֵּר עָלָיו **וְעִשָּׂרוֹן** סֹלֶת אֶחָד בָּלוּל בַּשֶּׁמֶן לְמִנְחָה וְלֹג שָׁמֶן:

If he is impoverished without sufficient means, he shall take one lamb as a guilt offering of the wave offering to make atonement for himself along with **one-tenth** [*ephah* of] semolina mixed with oil as a grain offering and one log of oil.

1 Sam 10:3–4

וּמְצָאוּךָ שָּׁם שְׁלֹשָׁה אֲנָשִׁים עֹלִים אֶל־הָאֱלֹהִים בֵּית־אֵל אֶחָד נֹשֵׂא| שְׁלֹשָׁה גְדָיִים וְאֶחָד נֹשֵׂא **שְׁלֹשֶׁת כִּכְּרוֹת** לֶחֶם וְאֶחָד נֹשֵׂא נֵבֶל־יָיִן וְשָׁאֲלוּ לְךָ לְשָׁלוֹם וְנָתְנוּ לְךָ **שְׁתֵּי**־לֶחֶם וְלָקַחְתָּ מִיָּדָם:

Three men will find you there going up to God at Bethel: one carrying three goats, one carrying **three loaves** of bread, and one carrying a jar of wine. They will inquire about your well-being and give to you **two** [loaves of] bread. You should accept them.

---

107 Joüon-Muraoka §142n.
108 Compare to אַרְבַּע מֵאֹת שֶׁקֶל־כֶּסֶף "four hundred shekels of silver" (Gen 23:15).
109 Compare to עֲשִׂירִת הָאֵיפָה סֹלֶת "one-tenth *ephah* of semolina" (Lev 5:11).

1 Sam 21:4[110]

חֲמִשָּׁה־לֶחֶם תְּנָה בְיָדִי אוֹ הַנִּמְצָא

Give me **five** [cakes of] bread or whatever can be found.

Exod 27:11[111]

וְכֵן לִפְאַת צָפוֹן בָּאֹרֶךְ קְלָעִים מֵאָה אֹרֶךְ

Likewise, the length of the curtains should be **one hundred** [cubits] long along the north side.

Finally, the measure word may describe a more inexact unit of length or thickness, such as a horizonal layer: שְׁלֹשָׁה טוּרִים גָּזִית "three courses of ashlar stone" (1 Kgs 7:12).

In conclusion, the morphosyntax and semantics of BH noun phrases can be quite complex. The student should pay careful attention to the standard morphological properties and note where certain lexemes deviate from the regular patterns. The sections on the various numbers may best be referenced as needed in reading. The next chapter explores the ways in which NPs are combined with adjectives and participles.

7.10 EXERCISES

Provide the missing lexical form, first-person suffix form, and/or the base (noun pattern) for each of the following nouns.

1	LEXEME	SUFFIXED (VOCALIC)	BASE FORM
a.		מַלְכִּי	*malk
b.	אֶרֶץ		
c.		טַעְמִי	
d.			*bayt

2	LEXEME	SUFFIXED (VOCALIC)	BASE FORM
a.	נֶדֶר		
b.			*šibr ('grain')
c.		פְּרִי	
d.	פֶּשַׁע		*pišʿ

---

[110] Compare to חַלַּת לֶחֶם אַחַת "one cake of bread" (2 Sam 6:19).
[111] Compare to מֵאָה בָאַמָּה אֹרֶךְ "one hundred cubits long" (Exod 27:9).

2	LEXEME	SUFFIXED (VOCALIC)	BASE FORM
e.	אֹכֶל		

3	LEXEME	SUFFIXED (VOCALIC)	BASE FORM
a.		מְלָכַי	*malakīm
b.	אֲרָצוֹת		
c.		כֹּהֲנִי	*kāhin
d.	גֹּבַח		
e.		מִכְרוֹ	

4	LEXEME	SUFFIXED (VOCALIC)	BASE FORM
a.		מַאֲכָלִי	
b.	מַמְלָכָה		
c.		צִדְקָתִי	*ṣidaqat
d.			*mišpaṭ
e.	עֵבְדוּת		

Translate the following Hebrew sentences into English. Give the inflection of the highlighted nouns. Describe the syntactic function of each.

5.   עֲלֵיהֶם **עוֹף־הַשָּׁמַיִם** יִשְׁכּוֹן מִבֵּין עֳפָאיִם יִתְּנוּ־קוֹל׃ (Ps 104:12)

6.   וְ**רוּחַ** נְשָׂאַתְנִי וַתְּבִיאֵנִי כַשְׂדִּימָה אֶל־הַגּוֹלָה בַּמַּרְאֶה בְּ**רוּחַ אֱלֹהִים**
(Ezek 11:24)

7.   וְנִלְחַמְתִּי אֲנִי אִתְּכֶם בְּ**יָד** נְטוּיָה וּבִ**זְרוֹעַ** חֲזָקָה וּבְ**אַף** וּבְחֵמָה וּבְ**קֶצֶף** גָּדוֹל׃
(Jer 21:5)

Translate. Describe the form and syntax of the highlighted numbers.

8. רְאוּ כִּי־יְהוָה֙ נָתַ֣ן לָכֶ֣ם הַשַּׁבָּ֔ת עַל־כֵּ֠ן ה֣וּא נֹתֵ֧ן לָכֶ֛ם בַּיּ֥וֹם **הַשִּׁשִּׁ֖י** לֶ֣חֶם יוֹמָ֑יִם שְׁב֣וּ ׀ אִ֣ישׁ תַּחְתָּ֗יו אַל־יֵ֥צֵא אִ֛ישׁ מִמְּקֹמ֖וֹ בַּיּ֥וֹם **הַשְּׁבִיעִֽי**׃ (Exod 16:29)

9. וּפָקַדְתִּ֨י עֲלֵיהֶ֜ם **אַרְבַּ֧ע** מִשְׁפָּח֗וֹת נְאֻם־יְהוָה֙ אֶת־הַחֶ֣רֶב לַהֲרֹ֔ג וְאֶת־הַכְּלָבִ֖ים לִסְחֹ֑ב וְאֶת־ע֧וֹף הַשָּׁמַ֛יִם וְאֶת־בֶּהֱמַ֥ת הָאָ֖רֶץ לֶאֱכֹ֥ל וּלְהַשְׁחִֽית׃ (Jer 15:3)

10. וַתֹּ֣אמֶר אֵלָ֗יו אֵ֚יךְ תֹּאמַ֣ר אֲהַבְתִּ֔יךְ וְלִבְּךָ֖ אֵ֣ין אִתִּ֑י זֶ֣ה **שָׁלֹ֤שׁ** פְּעָמִים֙ הֵתַ֣לְתָּ בִּ֔י וְלֹא־הִגַּ֣דְתָּ לִּ֔י בַּמֶּ֖ה כֹּחֲךָ֥ גָדֽוֹל׃ (Judg 16:15)

Translate from English to Hebrew.

11. King Solomon his son paid four gold shekels for the bread and jar of wine.

12. I know that the place is here on Mount Sinai. My good ear hears the report day by day, and my (two) eyes see the way to my grave.

13. The Midianite clan went out and gathered 4,500 baskets of manna for their children.

14. The lord's servant has unclean lips. He does not know the word of God or fear God.

15. Now all these will happen on the tenth day. Then you will say Yahweh is more powerful than two thousand men.

Guided Reading: Prov 8:22–31

22 יְהוָה קָנָנִי רֵאשִׁית דַּרְכּוֹ קֶדֶם מִפְעָלָיו מֵאָז: 23 מֵעוֹלָם נִסַּכְתִּי מֵרֹאשׁ מִקַּדְמֵי־אָרֶץ: 24 בְּאֵין־תְּהֹמוֹת חוֹלָלְתִּי בְּאֵין מַעְיָנוֹת נִכְבַּדֵּי־מָיִם: 25 בְּטֶרֶם הָרִים הָטְבָּעוּ לִפְנֵי גְבָעוֹת חוֹלָלְתִּי: 26 עַד־לֹא עָשָׂה אֶרֶץ וְחוּצוֹת וְרֹאשׁ עָפְרוֹת תֵּבֵל: 27 בַּהֲכִינוֹ שָׁמַיִם שָׁם אָנִי בְּחוּקוֹ חוּג עַל־פְּנֵי תְהוֹם: 28 בְּאַמְּצוֹ שְׁחָקִים מִמָּעַל בַּעֲזוֹז עִינוֹת תְּהוֹם: 29 בְּשׂוּמוֹ לַיָּם| חֻקּוֹ וּמַיִם לֹא יַעַבְרוּ־פִיו בְּחוּקוֹ מוֹסְדֵי אָרֶץ: 30 וָאֶהְיֶה אֶצְלוֹ אָמוֹן וָאֶהְיֶה שַׁעֲשֻׁעִים יוֹם| יוֹם מְשַׂחֶקֶת לְפָנָיו בְּכָל־עֵת: 31 מְשַׂחֶקֶת בְּתֵבֵל אַרְצוֹ וְשַׁעֲשֻׁעַי אֶת־בְּנֵי אָדָם:

VOCABULARY AND NOTES

Verse 22

קָנָנִי	Qal	SC 3MS + 1CS SF	קנה	"create"
רֵאשִׁית		N.FS		"beginning"
קֶדֶם		N.MS		"prior; before" (PREP)
מִפְעָלָיו		N.MP + 3MS SF	מִפְעָל	"deed"
מֵאָז		ADV		"from long ago"

Verse 23

נִסַּכְתִּי	Niphal	SC 1CS	נסך	"be consecrated"

Verse 24

תְּהֹמוֹת		N.FP		"abyss"
חוֹלָלְתִּי	Polal	SC 1CS	חיל	"be birthed"
מַעְיָנוֹת		N.FP		"spring"
נִכְבַּדֵּי	Niphal	PTCL MP CSTR	כבד	"make heavy"

Verse 25

בְּטֶרֶם		PREP		"before"
הָטְבָּעוּ	Hophal	SC 3CP	טבע	"be sunk"
גְבָעוֹת		N.FP		"hill"

Verse 26

חוּצוֹת		N.MP		"outside"

עֲפָרוֹת		N.MP		"dust; soil"
תֵּבֵל		N.FS		"world; earth"

Verse 27

הֲכִינוֹ	Hiphil	INF CSTR + 3MS SF	כון	"establish"
חוּקּוֹ	Qal	INF CSTR + 3MS SF	חוק	"inscribe; carve"
חוּג		N.MS		"vault, horizon"

Verse 28

אַמְּצוֹ	Piel	INF CSTR + 3MS SF	אמץ	"make firm"
שְׁחָקִים		N.MP		"sky, cloud"
מִמַּעַל		PREP		"above"
עֲזוֹז	Qal			"be strong"

Verse 29

שׂוּמוֹ	Qal	INF CSTR + 3MS suff	שׂים	
חֻקּוֹ		N.MS + 3MS SF		"limit, boundary"
מוֹסְדֵי		N.MP CSTR		"foundation"

Verse 30

אֶצְלוֹ		PREP + 3MS SF		"beside"
אָמוֹן		N.MS		"artisan (אָמָן)"
שַׁעֲשֻׁעִים		N.MP		"delight"
מְשַׂחֶקֶת	Piel	PTCL FS	שׂחק	"jest; play"

//////////////

PRONOUNS, ADJECTIVES, AND PARTICIPLES

P ronouns, adjectives, and participles share many morphological and syntactical features. Functionally, pronouns restate previously mentioned entities. Adjectives describe or predicate various qualities or circumstances. Participles, much like adjectives, involve description but do so as actions, events, or verbal states. Designated as <u>verbal adjectives</u>, participles are considered a hybrid word class. Because of their morphosyntactic and functional similarities, pronouns, adjectives, and participles are discussed together in this chapter.

8.1 GOING DEEPER WITH PARTICIPLES

The opening chapters of the book of Joshua present the initial stages of Israel's encroachment into Canaan. The first campaign takes place against the fortified city of Jericho. Joshua—a spy himself—sends scouts to the city for reconnaissance. The spies are taken in and protected by Rahab who knows of Yahweh's powerful deeds on behalf of his people. The people of Canaan fear attack, as word of the Israelite advance spreads throughout the countryside. The captain of the army of Yahweh appears to Joshua at the end of chapter 5 in a pattern resembling Yahweh's appearance to Moses at the burning bush. He is instructed to remove his sandals because he is on holy ground (5:15).

Joshua 6:1 shifts scenes to the city of Jericho, depicting conditions from inside enemy lines ahead of Israel's advance. Typically, Hebrew narrative continues the main line of the story with consecutive forms: *wayyiqtol* forms for perfective

351

aspect and *wəqātal* forms for imperfective aspect. However, Josh 6:1 utilizes a series of four predicate participles to describe the status of the city:

Josh 6:1

וִירִיחוֹ סֹגֶרֶת וּמְסֻגֶּרֶת מִפְּנֵי בְּנֵי יִשְׂרָאֵל אֵין יוֹצֵא וְאֵין בָּא:

Now Jericho **was closed** and **had been closed off** from before Israel; no one **was exiting**, and no one **was entering**.

One commentator notes that "the Hebrew syntax appears to go to great lengths to avoid the normal consecution of tenses."[1] The ancient versions have handled the first two participles in different ways.

Targum Jonathan

וִירִיחוֹ אֲחִידָא וּמְתַקְּפָא מִן קֳדָם בְּנֵי יִשְׂרָאֵל

Now Jericho was **closed off** and **fortified** from before the sons of Israel.[2]

Syriac Peshitta

> *w'yrḥw 'ḥyd' ḥwt mn qdm bny 'sryl*
> Now Jericho was **closed off** from before the sons of Israel.

Septuagint

> Καὶ Ιεριχω συγκεκλεισμένη καὶ ᾠχυρωμένη
> And Jericho was **closed** and **fortified**

Vulgate

> *Hericho autem clausa erat atque munita, timore filiorum Israël*
> Now Jericho was **closed up** and **fortified** by fear of the sons of Israel.

A similar variety of interpretations exist in most modern translations as well:

CSB	Now Jericho was **strongly fortified** because of the Israelites.
NASB	Now Jericho was **tightly shut** because of the sons of Israel.
ESV	Now Jericho was **shut up inside and outside** because of the people of Israel.
RSV	Now Jericho was **shut up from within and from without** because of the people of Israel.
NJB	Now, Jericho had **shut** and **barricaded** its gates (against the Israelites).
KJV	Now Jericho was **straitly shut up** because of the children of Israel.
NLT	Now the **gates of** Jericho were **tightly shut** because the people were afraid of the Israelites.

---

[1] Trent C. Butler, *Joshua*, WBC 7 (Waco, TX: Word, 1983), 65.

[2] Targum Tosefta to the Prophets expands this verse considerably: וירִיחוֹ אֲחִידָא בְּדַשִׁין דְּפַרְזְלָא וּמְתַקְּפָא וּמְתָאֲחִדָא בְּעַבְרִין דִּנְחָשָׁא "Now Jericho was closed off with doors of iron and fortified and closed off with bars of bronze."

NIV Now the **gates of** Jericho were **securely barred** because of the Israelites.

Most of the versions divide into two main approaches: those that translate סֹגֶרֶת וּמְסֻגֶּרֶת as two words (e.g., "shut" and "barricaded"), and those that translate them together with an intensive meaning (e.g., "strongly fortified" and "tightly shut"). A third, less common interpretation adds the notion of gates being barred, which goes back as early as the Targum Tosefta to the Prophets, which appears to expand the shorter Targum Jonathan.[3]

The two Hebrew participles themselves occur as two stems of the root סגר "to close" (*Qal* and *Pual*). One of the interpretive problems concerns the fact that the *Qal* of this root elsewhere appears to be transitive (i.e., Jericho closed X), even though most translations render the clause intransitively (i.e., Jericho was closed). The *Qal* indicates the act of shutting things such as doors and wounds, or even enclosing someone.[4] This latter usage is attested in Exod 14:3 in conjunction with a prepositional phrase עֲלֵיהֶם "over them."

Exod 14:3

נְבֻכִים הֵם בָּאָרֶץ סָגַר עֲלֵיהֶם הַמִּדְבָּר

They are wandering aimlessly in the land; the wilderness **is enclosed upon them**.

The meaning of סגר here appears to be intransitive, in the sense of "enclosed upon," with no mention of an object undergoing the act of closing. On the other hand, the transitive meaning of the *Qal* could simply refer to shutting the gates of Jericho as they did just before the spies escaped in Josh 2:5 (הַשַּׁעַר לִסְגּוֹר) and 7 (הַשַּׁעַר סָגָרוּ), in which case the gates are elided here in Josh 6:1.

A second interpretive issue concerns the syntactical function of the participles in the larger narrative setting. The clauses preceding and following Josh 6:1 contain consecutive preterite constructions, which are typical in Hebrew narrative prose. This verse, however, fronts the subject "Jericho," which is predicated by these two participles—סֹגֶרֶת and מְסֻגֶּרֶת. The participles are subsequently defined by two additional participial clauses: אֵין יוֹצֵא וְאֵין בָּא "there was no one exiting or entering." Earlier scholars proposed that verse 1 signals a source division between J and E.[5] Others believe it to be an editorial insertion, and thus an intrusive element in the narrative.[6] Richard Hess calls it a "stylistic intrusion," posing a "narrative obstacle"

---

[3] See previous note.

[4] See examples in BDB, 688; *HALOT*, s.v. "סגר," 742–43.

[5] E.g., H. Holzinger, *Das Buch Josua* (Tübingen: Mohr, 1901), 15–19; Otto Eissfeldt, *Hexateuch-Synopse: Die Erzählung der fünf Bücher Mose und des Buches Josua mit dem Anfange des Richterbuches in ihre vier Quellen zerlegt und in deutscher Übersetzung dargeboten samt einer in Einleitung und Anmerkungen gegebenen Begründung* (Leipzig: Hinrichs, 1922), 210–14. For a fuller discussion of the source-critical analysis of this text, see Thomas B. Dozeman, *Joshua 1–12*, AB 6B (New Haven: Yale University Press, 2015), 316–20.

[6] See C. F. Keil and F. Delitzsch, *Joshua, Judges, Ruth, 1 and 2 Samuel*, vol. 2 of *Commentary on the Old Testament* (repr. Peabody, MA: Hendrickson, 2001), 47; C. J. Goslinga, *Joshua, Judges,*

reminiscent of Jericho as a physical obstacle for Israel's possession of the land.[7] It is rather common for participles to function predicatively with fronted subjects in narrative prose as a means of signaling new or background information. As Mark Smith explains, this construction represents a departure from the main narrative, providing new information that is somehow significant for subsequent developments in the narrative.[8] In this case, the predicate participle explains the constrained conditions that had developed in Jericho just before Israel's advance. It demonstrates the level of anxiety among its residents consistent with what Rahab reported to the spies earlier (Josh 2:9–11).[9] As Richard D. Nelson asserts, Joshua 6 constitutes "a self-contained plot unit," beginning with background information in the form of a circumstantial clause and ending with a summary statement in verse 27.[10]

This example illustrates the way in which Hebrew utilizes the predicate participle to add depth to the story. We will discuss this usage more fully in the treatment of the predicate participle below (§8.6.3).

8.2 CHAPTER OBJECTIVES

This chapter discusses the morphology and syntax of pronouns, adjectives, verbal adjectives, and participles. It also outlines various morphological and semantic features distinguishing nouns and adjectives as distinct grammatical categories.

8.3 INTRODUCTION

It is common for beginning grammars to introduce students to pronouns and adjectives at roughly the same time. Treatments of adjective syntax helpfully illustrate the predicate position with the independent personal pronouns as subject (e.g., הוּא רַע "he/it is evil"). One sees a correlation between pronouns and adjectives in the use of the third-person independent pronouns as far demonstratives. Demonstrative pronouns agree with the word they modify in number, gender, and definiteness, as in הָאִישׁ הַהוּא "that man" and הָעִיר הַהִיא "that city." This usage corresponds with the syntax of attributive adjectives. The pronoun also features prominently in the syntax of verbless clauses, particularly the tripartite structure with the third-person independent pronoun in the copular position (e.g., יהוה הוּא הָאֱלֹהִים "Yahweh is God"). It is logical to consider adjectives and participles in a single chapter,

---

Ruth, Bible Student's Commentary (Grand Rapids: Zondervan, 1987), 66–68.

[7] Richard S. Hess, *Joshua: An Introduction and Commentary*, Tyndale Old Testament Commentary 6 (Downers Grove, IL: InterVarsity, 1996), 128.

[8] Mark S. Smith, "Grammatically Speaking: The Participle as a Main Verb of Clauses (Predicative Participle) in Direct Discourse and Narrative in Pre-Mishnaic Hebrew," in *Sirach, Scrolls, and Sages*, ed. T. Muraoka and John F. Elwolde, STDJ 33 (Leiden: Brill, 1999), 291.

[9] As Robert G. Boling describes the comment, "The story begins well past the beginning of action, a favorite narrative device." See *Joshua*, AB 6 (Garden City, NY: Doubleday, 1982), 205.

[10] Richard D. Nelson, *Joshua: A Commentary*, OTL (Louisville: Westminster John Knox, 1997), 90.

categorizing the latter form as a verbal adjective. Such an identification, however, must account for the finer morphological and semantic distinction between *Qal* active participles (fientive roots) and verbal adjectives proper (stative roots).

8.4 PRONOUNS

8.4.1 Morphology and Usage

Biblical Hebrew attests a fully productive set of independent personal pronouns. Independent personal pronouns provide the morphological basis for the pronominal elements throughout the language. They are attached to nouns, prepositions, and verbal roots (as highlighted below). Pronouns are marked for person (first, second, and third) and gender (in the second and third persons), as well as number (singular and plural).

PG	N	INDEPENDENT PERSONAL PRONOUN	SUBJECT SC	SUBJECT PC	OBJECT SUFFIX	GENITIVE/ POSSESSIVE SUFFIX	PREPOSITION SUFFIX
3M		הוא	כָּתַב	יִכְתֹּב	־הוּ, ־ֶ֫נּוּ, ־ֹו, אֹתֹו	־ֹו, ־ָיו	־ֹו, ־ָיו
3F		הִיא	כָּתְבָה	תְּכְתֹּב	־ָהּ, ־ֶ֫הָ, אֹתָהּ	־ָהּ, ־ֶ֫יהָ	־ָהּ, ־ֶ֫יהָ
2M	S	(ה)אַתָּ	כָּתַבְתָּ	תְּכְתֹּב	־ךָ, אֹתְךָ	־ךָ, ־ֶ֫יךָ	־ךָ, ־ֶ֫יךָ
2F		אַתְּ	כָּתַבְתְּ	תְּכְתְּבִי	־ָךְ, אֹתָךְ	־ֵךְ, ־ַיִךְ	־ָךְ, ־ַיִךְ
1C		אָנֹכִי/אֲנִי	כָּתַבְתִּי	אֶכְתֹּב	־נִי, אֹתִי	־ִי, ־ַי	־ִי, ־ַי
3M		הֵם/הֵמָּה	כָּתְבוּ	יִכְתְּבוּ	־ם, אֹתָם	־ָם, ־ֵיהֶם	־ָם, ־ֵיהֶם
3F		הֵנָּה	—	תִּכְתֹּבְנָה	־ן, אֹתָן	־ָן, ־ֵיהֶן	־ָן, ־ֵיהֶן
2M	P	אַתֶּם	כְּתַבְתֶּם	תִּכְתְּבוּ	־כֶם, אֶתְכֶם	־כֶם, ־ֵיכֶם	־כֶם, ־ֵיכֶם
2F		אַתֵּנָה / אַתֵּן	כְּתַבְתֶּן	תִּכְתֹּבְנָה	אֶתְכֶן	־כֶן, ־ֵיכֶן	־כֶן, ־ֵיכֶן
1C		אֲנַ֫חְנוּ	כָּתַבְנוּ	נִכְתֹּב	־נוּ, אֹתָנוּ	־ֵ֫נוּ, ־ֵינוּ	־ֵ֫נוּ, ־ֵינוּ

Independent personal pronouns most commonly occur as subjects of verbless or verbal clauses. Morphological adaptations of the pronouns are either prefixed or suffixed to verbs to create the verbal inflection. In addition to pronominal subjects, another set of pronominal elements can be suffixed to verbal forms that function as the object of the verbal phrase. Some verbs may take two different pronominal elements in a single form:

PC	אֶשְׁמְרֵם	I will guard **them**.
SC	שְׁמַרְתִּיהָ	I guarded **her**.

Pronominal suffixes with nouns mark the possessive. Different morphological forms are attached to singular nouns and plural nouns. Plural nouns generally contain a *yod* as part of the suffix. Singular and plural nouns with 1CS pronominal suffixes are distinguished by the vowel with the *yod* (i.e., ◌ַי-, vs. ◌ִי-).

PLURAL NOUNS	SINGULAR NOUNS
חַרְבוֹתָיו "his swords"	חַרְבּוֹ "his sword"
כַּסְפֶּיהָ "her (pieces of) silver"	חַרְבָּהּ "her sword"
רַגְלֶיךָ "your [MS] feet"	חַרְבְּךָ "your [MS] sword"
חֹמֹתַיִךְ "your [FS] walls"	כַּסְפֵּךְ "your [FS] silver"
עֲצָמַי "my bones"	כַּסְפִּי "my silver"
חַרְבֹתֵיהֶם or חַרְבוֹתָם "their [M] swords"	חַרְבָּם "their [M] sword"
יַלְדֵיהֶן "their [F] children"	נַחֲלָתָן "their [F] inheritance"
דִּבְרֵיכֶם "your [MP] words"	חַרְבְּכֶם "your [MP] sword"
גִּלּוּלֵיכֶן "your [FP] idols"	יֶדְכֶן "your [FP] hand"
בְּנֹתֵינוּ "our daughters"	כַּסְפֵּנוּ "our silver"

Prepositions also take pronominal suffixes corresponding to nominal suffixes, with some prepositions taking the singular type and others the plural type (see further §11.4.1):

PLURAL NOUN TYPES	SINGULAR NOUN TYPES
עַל "on, upon"	בְּ "in"
עָלָיו upon him/it	בּוֹ in him/it
עָלֶיהָ upon her/it	בָּהּ in her/it
עָלֶיךָ upon you (MS)	בְּךָ in you (MS)
עָלַיִךְ upon you (FS)	בָּךְ in you (FS)
עָלַי upon me	בִּי in me

PLURAL NOUN TYPES	SINGULAR NOUN TYPES
תַּחַת "under"	עִם "with"
תַּחְתֵּיהֶם under them (MP)	עִמָּם with them (MP)
תַּחְתֵּיהֶן under them (FP)	עִמָּן with them (FP)
תַּחְתֵּיכֶם under you (MP)	עִמָּכֶם with you (MP)
תַּחְתֵּיכֶן under you (FP)	עִמָּכֶן with you (FP)
תַּחְתֵּינוּ under us	עִמָּנוּ with us

A special use of the noun נֶפֶשׁ "soul, life" with pronominal suffixes has been taken to indicate reflexivity: נַפְשׁוֹ "himself" (lit., "his soul/life"), נַפְשָׁהּ "herself," נַפְשִׁי "myself," and so on (e.g., Deut 4:9).

Deut 4:9

רַק הִשָּׁמֶר לְךָ וּשְׁמֹר נַפְשְׁךָ מְאֹד פֶּן־תִּשְׁכַּח אֶת־הַדְּבָרִים אֲשֶׁר־רָאוּ עֵינֶיךָ
Only be on guard and watch **yourself** carefully, lest you forget the things your eyes have seen.

Many grammarians propose that נֶפֶשׁ + pronominal suffix seems to suggest the force of an independent pronoun, as in Gen 49:6. The reflexive usage is common in later Rabbinic Hebrew.

Gen 49:6

בְּסֹדָם אַל־תָּבֹא נַפְשִׁי בִּקְהָלָם אַל־תֵּחַד כְּבֹדִי
Let **me** not enter into their counsel, let my glory not unite with their assembly.

Such uses, however, may represent a possessive NP, as in "my soul" or perhaps "my life," rather than a reflexive pronoun. In the above example, for instance, the verb is 3FS, which may be understood as "let not my soul enter." This interpretation matches the poetic parallel of the possessive pronoun in the next line, "let not my glory unite." The meaning of נֶפֶשׁ is admittedly difficult, as is the case with most terms associated with the human constitution and metaphysical realities.[11] Furthermore, reflexivity in BH, whereby actions are carried out in the interests of the actor, is clearly indicated by certain verbal stems (e.g., *Hitpael*) as opposed to reflexive pronouns (see §4.8.4).

Pronominal suffixes are not limited to genitival functions. They attach to particles, such as הִנֵּה, אֵין, יֵשׁ, or עוֹד, and function as subjects of clauses. Examples include:

---

[11] For more on the meaning of West Semitic *npš*, see Matthew McAffee, *Life and Mortality in Ugaritic: A Lexical and Literary Study*, EANEC 7 (University Park, PA: Eisenbrauns, 2019), 67–124.

Gen 16:1

הִנָּ֤ךְ הָרָה֙ וְיֹלַ֣דְתְּ בֵּ֔ן וְקָרָ֥את שְׁמ֖וֹ יִשְׁמָעֵֽאל

Look, you are pregnant and will bear a son and call his name Ishmael.

Exod 5:10

אֵינֶ֛נִּי נֹתֵ֥ן לָכֶ֖ם תֶּֽבֶן

I am not giving you straw.

Deut 13:4

הֲיִשְׁכֶ֗ם אֹהֲבִים֙ אֶת־יְהוָ֣ה אֱלֹהֵיכֶ֔ם בְּכָל־לְבַבְכֶ֖ם וּבְכָל־נַפְשְׁכֶֽם

Whether **you** love Yahweh your God with all your heart and with all your soul.

1 Kgs 1:4

הִנֵּ֗ה עֹֽדָךְ֙ מְדַבֶּ֣רֶת שָׁ֖ם עִם־הַמֶּ֑לֶךְ וַאֲנִי֙ אָב֣וֹא אַחֲרַ֔יִךְ

Look, while you are there speaking with the king, I will enter behind you.

Independent personal pronouns sometimes occur in verbal clauses, even though finite verbs are already marked with pronominal subjects. Since the added pronoun in such contexts is redundant, this usage may be used to highlight the one doing the action over the action itself or mark a change of focus in the narrative or direct discourse. English translations tend to represent this construction with the addition of a reflexive pronoun (e.g., Josh 1:6).

Josh 1:6

חֲזַ֖ק וֶאֱמָ֑ץ כִּ֣י **אַתָּ֗ה** תַּנְחִיל֙ אֶת־הָעָ֣ם הַזֶּ֔ה אֶת־הָאָ֕רֶץ אֲשֶׁר־נִשְׁבַּ֥עְתִּי לַאֲבוֹתָ֖ם
לָתֵ֥ת לָהֶֽם:

Be strong and courageous, for you **yourself** will make this people possess the land that I swore to their fathers to give them.

The statement emphasizes that it is Joshua, not the recently deceased Moses (v. 1), who will lead the people of Israel into the land of promise. Later in Joshua, the 3FS independent pronoun similarly precedes a finite verb in a narrative comment (Josh 2:6). This takes place after Rahab's speech to the men looking for the Hebrew spies. She explains that she did not know where they went, but that if they pursued after the men quickly, they might be able to locate them. The narrative then explains:

Josh 2:6

וְהִ֖יא הֶעֱלָ֣תַם הַגָּ֑גָה וַֽתִּטְמְנֵ֖ם

But **she** had taken them up to the roof and hid them.

8.4.2 Independent Pronouns and Verbless Clauses

The independent pronouns more commonly serve as subjects of verbless predicate constructions. Independent pronouns can function as the subject of predicate adjectives and often occur in second position (i.e., PRED–SUBJ, e.g., Isa 31:2).

Isa 31:2

וְגַם־הוּא חָכָם֒

And also, **he** is wise.

The pronoun can also serve as the subject of nominal predicates (1 Sam 15:29).

1 Sam 15:29

כִּי לֹא אָדָם הוּא

For **he** is not a man.

Any independent pronoun (first, second, or third singular and plural) can appear as the subject of these kinds of predicate constructions, in either PRED–SUBJ or SUBJ–PRED positions:

First Person

Josh 9:8

עֲבָדֶיךָ אֲנַחְנוּ

We are your servants. (PRED–SUBJ)

Josh 5:14

לֹא כִּי אֲנִי שַׂר־צְבָא־יְהוָה

No, but **I** am the commander of the army of Yahweh. (SUBJ–PRED)

Second Person

2 Sam 15:19

כִּי־נָכְרִי אַתָּה וְגַם־גֹּלֶה אַתָּה לִמְקוֹמֶךָ

For **you** are a foreigner and **you** are also an exile from your place. (PRED–SUBJ)

2 Sam 12:7

אַתָּה הָאִישׁ

You are the man! (SUBJ–PRED)

In the simplest of terms, predicates offer a description of the subject and can do so as adjectives, nouns, or even prepositional phrases. According to Francis I. Andersen, definite predicates *identify* a definite subject (i.e., *identification* verbless clause). These clauses are usually ordered SUBJ–PRED and answer the question, "Who or what is the subject?" If a predicate is indefinite, however, the clause *classifies* the definite subject (i.e., *classification* verbless clause). It answers the question, "What is the subject like?" The usual word order for classification clauses is PRED–SUBJ.[12] As Andersen explains, "When both S and P are definite, the predicate has total semantic overlap with the subject; that is, each has exactly the same referent . . . When S is definite and P is indefinite . . . the predicate has partial semantic overlap with the subject, that is, it refers to the general class of the subject."[13]

Biblical Hebrew attests a special use of third-person independent pronouns in verbless clauses. Scholars often call this use a tripartite verbless clause because it contains three elements: a subject, a predicate, and a third-person independent pronoun. The pronoun is sometimes called pleonastic in light of its syntactical redundancy, but it may be considered to be a copula. Two general orders are attested for this construction: (1) the pronoun is in medial position, or (2) the pronoun takes final position.[14]

Medial Position

Gen 42:6

וְיוֹסֵף הוּא הַשַּׁלִּיט עַל־הָאָרֶץ

Joseph **was** ruler over the land.

Final Position

Isa 1:13

קְטֹרֶת תּוֹעֵבָה הִיא לִי

Incense **is** an abomination to me.

More complex arrangements of this tripartite structure are possible as well, as in Deut 10:17.

Deut 10:17

כִּי יְהוָה אֱלֹהֵיכֶם הוּא אֱלֹהֵי הָאֱלֹהִים

For Yahweh your God **is** the God of gods.

Scholars differ in their analysis of this construction. One approach interprets the pronoun as a copula. The term *copula* refers to the predicative link or connection between subject and predicate. It comes from Latin *copulatio*, meaning "coupling, joining, linking."[15] In the Indo-European languages this link is designated by a verb (e.g., "to be") as in the English assertion "God is holy" and in Greek the verb εἰμι, as in οὗτος γάρ ἐστιν ὁ νόμος καὶ οἱ προφῆται "this **is** the law and the prophets" (Matt 7:12). A commonly cited example from Hebrew is,

---

[12] Andersen, *Hebrew Verbless Clause*, 32; summarized and described in *IBHS* §§8.4.1a; 8.4.2a; 16.3.3a.

[13] Andersen, 32.

[14] See Cynthia L. Miller, "Pivotal Issues in Analyzing the Verbless Clause," in *The Verbless Clause in Biblical Hebrew: Linguistic Approaches*, ed. Cynthia L. Miller, LSAWS 1 (Winona Lake, IN: Eisenbrauns, 1999), 13–14.

[15] See the description of the term "copula" in Gideon Goldenberg, *Studies in Semitic Linguistics: Selected Writings* (Jerusalem: Magnes, 1998), 157.

יהוה **הוא** הָאֱלֹהִים
Yahweh (SUBJ) **is** (COP) God (PRED).

Unlike English, Hebrew does not require the predicative link to be marked explicitly, but it can do so syntactically, as in טוֹב **הוא** "he (is) good," that is, "he (definite subject pronoun) is good (indefinite predicate)." In other words, a copula is not necessary for predication in Hebrew. The same is true for Greek, which also formulates <u>bipartite</u> (i.e., without εἰμι) predicate constructions like ἀγαθὸς ὁ ἄνθρωπος "The man *is* good." Tamar Zewi suggests that the copula represents a secondary development in the Indo-European languages, which she asserts for the Semitic languages as well. At the classical stage of the Semitic languages the copula was nonexistent.[16] However, the copula's absence at the earliest stages of a given language does not actually settle the issue, if indeed a copula develops at a later stage. The fact that Hebrew can express predication with or without the third-person pronoun cannot furnish justification for denying its copular function.

Nevertheless, several scholars have sought alternative explanations for the pronoun in this tripartite construction. They suggest that all such examples simply mark <u>extraposition</u>—the pronoun either resumes or anticipates an extrapositioned subject, and thus functions as the subject or predicate of the clause.[17] This approach renders the above example as,

יהוה **הוא** הָאֱלֹהִים
Yahweh (extrapositioned SUBJ), **he** (resumptive PRO) [is] God (PRED).

A more explicit way of rendering the extrapositioned subject is, "*As for* Yahweh, he *is* God." This usage is sometimes called *casus pendens*, a Latin phrase meaning "hanging/suspended case." It refers to a fronted subject standing outside the clause (i.e., hanging or suspended) that is further defined by the clause.

Rejecting the copular analysis, S. R. Driver interprets the tripartite verbless clause as an example of *casus pendens*. He cites an example from Gen 34:21 where the pronoun occurs in final position:

Gen 34:21

הָאֲנָשִׁים הָאֵלֶּה שְׁלֵמִים הֵם אִתָּנוּ
These men—**they** are at peace with us.

Driver argued that the pronoun does not express a copula but rather resumes the fronted topic (i.e., הָאֲנָשִׁים הָאֵלֶּה "these men" as *casus pendens*).[18] Gideon

---

[16] Tamar Zewi, "The Definition of the Copula and the Role of the 3rd Independent Personal Pronouns in Nominal Sentences of Semitic Languages," *Folia Linguistica Historica* 17 (1996): 42–43. Zewi references the studies of O. Jespersen, *The Philosophy of Grammar* (London: Allen & Unwin, 1924), 131–32; J. Lyons, *Introduction to Theoretical Linguistics* (Cambridge: Cambridge University Press, 1968), 322–23; and P. H. Matthews, *Syntax* (Cambridge: Cambridge University Press, 1981), 116–17.

[17] As formulated by Geoffrey Khan, "Some Aspects of the Copula in Northwest Semitic," in *Biblical Hebrew in Its Northwest Semitic Setting: Typological and Historical Perspectives*, ed. Steven E. Fassberg and Avi Hurvitz (Winona Lake, IN: Eisenbrauns, 2006), 155.

[18] Driver, *Treatise*, 293–94.

Goldenberg follows Driver, asserting that the tripartite constructions attested in Semitic (Hebrew, Aramaic, Arabic, and Ethiopic) are "structurally various sorts of extrapositional constructions, in which the predicate is a nominal sentence with one of the members being the pronoun referring to the extrapositive subject."[19] Zewi, like Driver and Goldenberg, maintains that the tripartite formula, SUBJ–PRED–PRO, involves a resumptive pronoun, not a true copula, whereby the nominal construction indicates extraposition.[20] She outlines three different clausal types for this construction:

Type 1 (clause of classification)
definite SUBJ–PRO–indefinite PRED

Song 6:8

שִׁשִּׁים הֵמָּה מְלָכוֹת

Sixty, they are queens.

Type 2 (clause of identification)
definite SUBJ–PRO–definite PRED

Num 16:7

וְהָיָה הָאִישׁ אֲשֶׁר־יִבְחַר יְהוָה הוּא הַקָּדוֹשׁ

The man whom Yahweh chooses; he will be the holy one.

Type 3 (clause of classification)
definite SUBJ–indefinite PRED–PRO

Gen 40:18

הַסַּלִּים שְׁלֹשֶׁת יָמִים הֵם

The baskets, three days are they.

Another non-copular proposal has been advanced by T. Muraoka, who stresses the emphatic force of the pronoun in these environments.[21] He outlines three structural types with the pronoun as copula: two medial positions (SUBJ–COP–PRED and PRED–COP–SUBJ) and one final position (SUBJ–PRED–COP). The SUBJ–COP–PRED type denotes "selective-exclusive," which singles out the subject for emphasis and contrasts it from other constituents.[22] One example of this type is Deut 4:35.

Deut 4:35

יְהוָה הוּא הָאֱלֹהִים אֵין עוֹד מִלְּבַדּוֹ

Yahweh, **he** is God; there is no other beside him.

---

[19] Goldenberg, *Studies in Semitic Linguistics*, 165.

[20] Zewi, "Definition of the Copula," 47–49.

[21] T. Muraoka, *Emphatic Words and Structures in Biblical Hebrew* (Leiden: Brill, 1985), 68–69. Muraoka believes his study supports the conclusions of Driver, GKC (§141g–h), and Joüon-Muraoka (§154i–j), since they all acknowledge the emphatic force of the pronoun in this construction.

[22] Muraoka, 72–73. He concedes that this construction may be understood as *casus pendens* or extraposition as well.

The selective-exclusive aspect emphasizes that Yahweh is the God of Israel, in stark contrast to all others who would draw Israel's allegiance. The SUBJ–COP–PRED type, according to Muraoka, shows the original "demonstrative force" of third-person pronouns. It indicates that "S[ubject] is emphasized by being isolated, and at the same time C[opula], which resumes S, receives prominence after a pause or by being isolated in its turn."[23] This type corresponds to Zewi's Type 2 (identification clause) mentioned above. The SUBJ–PRED–COP type, simply denotes the predicate's description of the subject (i.e., classification clause), so that "the predicate (and consequently the nominal phrase as a whole) is emphasized by C following it."[24] Muraoka advances Exod 3:5 as an example. Here, God solemnly reminds Moses regarding the nature of the ground on which he stood.

Exod 3:5

הַמָּקוֹם אֲשֶׁר אַתָּה עוֹמֵד עָלָיו אַדְמַת־קֹדֶשׁ הוּא

The place on which you are standing **is** holy ground.

The last tripartite type is PRED–COP–SUBJ, whose meaning is much the same as PRED–SUBJ–COP, only in this case the emphasis is placed upon the predicate and not the nominal phrase as a whole.

Geoffrey Khan compares the Biblical Hebrew tripartite pronominal structure with similar constructions in Modern Neo-Aramaic. He divides the clausal types into those whose pronoun is placed after the second nominal (Zewi's Type 3) and those whose pronoun falls after the first nominal (Zewi's Types 1 and 2). His typological comparisons lead to the conclusion that the pronoun functions in one of two ways: (1) when the pronoun follows the second nominal it expresses the prominence of new information related to the predicate, or (2) when the pronoun follows the first nominal it can either convey prominence of the preceding nominal as a predicate expressing new information or as a predicate itself expressing contrastive focus.[25] Khan's formulation of the tripartite verbless clause recognizes the difficulty of explaining these constructions exclusively as extraposition or *casus pendens*. One of the main difficulties is when a third-person pronoun follows second-person pronominal elements in a clause.[26] For instance, Zewi cites the following example from 2 Samuel 7 in support of her Type 1 extraposition:

2 Sam 7:28

אַתָּה־הוּא הָאֱלֹהִים

You are God.

As Khan rightly notes, the third-person pronoun cannot indicate extraposition or function as the resumptive pronoun of the second-person אַתָּה. Instead, the third-person copula in such environments may have "arisen by grammatical

---

[23] Muraoka, 73.
[24] Muraoka, 75.
[25] Khan, "Some Aspects of the Copula," 169.
[26] See also John Cook, "The Hebrew Participle and Stative," *JNSL* 34 (2008): 8 n. 10.

concord with the predicate rather than with the subject."[27] In fact, typological comparisons for the rise of the copula exist in the Northeastern Neo-Aramaic dialects, which may offer parallels for a similar development in Biblical Hebrew.[28]

Khan stops short of affirming the establishment of a pronominal copula in BH but instead describes the situation as transitional. The third-person pronoun in certain syntactical environments shifts away from its pronominal usage to a copular function. His discussion provides a judicious assessment of the status of the copula. Nonetheless, the evidence from BH supports the fact that the copula existed as a component of verbless clause syntax. We find no reason to deny its presence in the language.

8.5 ADJECTIVES

The basic notion of the adjective is description. Adjectives describe or modify nominals in a variety of ways. The referentiality of the adjective is always external to itself, in that the description refers to some other entity. This feature is distinct from nominals since their referentiality is always internal. Nouns designate their named entity. For example, the English noun "apple" refers to the item that is identified by the name "apple." If we wanted to further designate that it is a "green apple," the adjective "green" refers to the external entity "apple" being further characterized as a certain color. The same is true of Hebrew nouns and adjectives. The Hebrew noun עֵץ "tree" is self-referential. It refers to the class of plants identified as "tree." We could be even more specific. We can name a particular type of tree within the broader class of tree, specifying, for instance, אַלּוֹן "oak" or שִׁטָּה "acacia." Each of these nouns identifying different types of trees could be further modified with an adjective as a property: עֵץ גָּדוֹל "a large tree," אַלּוֹן מָלֵא "a full oak," or הַשִּׁטָּה הַחֲזָקָה "the strong acacia (tree/wood)."

A longstanding tradition among grammars of Western language groups the adjective as a subset of the noun. This idea can be traced back to one of the earliest known grammars of the Western world. Sometime during the second century BC, Dionysius Thrax in his Greek grammar identified all adjectives under the category "derivative noun."[29] This view of the adjective is also reflected in recent linguistic approaches that have likewise made it a subcategory of nouns. Chomsky's generative grammar, for instance, assumes that grammatical categories constitute one

---

[27] Khan, "Some Aspects of the Copula," 172.

[28] Khan, 172–73.

[29] See the translation of Thrax's grammar in Thos. Davidson, "The Grammar of Dionysios," *Journal of Speculative Philosophy* 8 (1874): esp. 331–32. A derivative noun is defined as "one which derives its origin from another noun, as γαιήιος (earth-born)." Thrax further subdivided derivative nouns into seven classes: patronymics, possessives, comparatives, diminutives, nominals, superlatives, and verbals. Interestingly, Thrax gave participles a separate category, noting they share properties of both nouns and verbs (336). In general, he identified the following parts of speech: noun, verb, participle, article, pronoun, preposition, adverb, and conjunction (331–39).

of two types: substantives (consisting of nouns and adjectives) or predicates (consisting of verbs and adjectives).[30] Hebrew grammars follow a similar approach in denying the adjective's status as an independent component of Hebrew grammar.[31] Joshua Blau suggests that "the line between substantives and adjectives is rather blurred." He goes so far as to say that the evidence in Biblical Hebrew and the Semitic languages contradicts "a strict separation of substantives and adjectives."[32] Blau criticizes Burkhart Kienast, who argues for a distinct classification between substantives and adjectives based on Akkadian morphology.[33] Other commonly cited grammars such as Joüon-Muraoka and *IBHS* similarly group the adjective as a subcategory of the noun.[34]

Cynthia Miller-Naudé and Jacobus A. Naudé have explored the identity of Hebrew adjectives from the perspective of morphology and syntax, in the end affirming that the adjective deserves its own lexical categorization independent of nouns and predicates.[35] More specifically, they suggest that the very evidence utilized to demonstrate the singularity of nouns and adjectives is only superficial and not indicative of their sameness.[36] H. H. Hardy II similarly notes that although "the morphologies of both are similar, nouns and adjectives differ in their inflections and usage."[37] Amikam Gai affirms the morphological distinctions between the two and argues that they should be treated as two separate categories of grammar.[38] We will take a similar approach in our treatment of adjectives in the following sections.

8.5.1 Gender and Number

One of the ways in which nouns and adjectives are distinct is with respect to gender. Gender for nouns is lexically determined and exhibits morphological diversity. Adjectives, on the other hand, mark gender morphologically. Another way of illustrating this point is to say that unlike adjectives, a noun is either masculine or

---

[30] According to Chomsky's formulation, there are "two categories of traditional grammar: substantive ([+N]), including nouns and adjectives, and predicate ([+V]), including verbs and adjectives." See Noam Chomsky, *Lectures on Government and Binding: The Pisa Lectures*, Studies in Generative Grammar 9 (Berlin: de Gruyter, 1993), 48. For a fuller discussion of various approaches to the adjective in linguistics (e.g., generative, functional, or cognitive perspectives), see Cynthia L. Miller-Naudé and Jacobus A. Naudé, "Is the Adjective Distinct from the Nouns as a Grammatical Category in Biblical Hebrew?" *Die Skriflig* 50 (2016): 1–3.

[31] Miller-Naudé and Naudé, "Is the Adjective Distinct," 1.

[32] Blau, 260.

[33] Burkhart Kienast, *Historische semitische Sprachwissenschaft: Mit Beiträgen von Erhart Graefe (Altaegyptisch) und Gene B. Gragg (Kuschitisch)* (Weisbaden: Harrassowitz, 2001), 71–80.

[34] Joüon and Muraoka state: "The noun in Hebrew and Semitic grammar includes not only the substantive but also the adjective, for in its formation and inflection the adjective does not differ from the substantive" (Joüon-Muraoka §86); Waltke and O'Connor note "the marginal character of the adjective" (*IBHS*, 255 n. 1), citing the work of G. Bergsträsser, *Introduction to the Semitic Languages*, trans. Peter T. Daniels (Winona Lake, IN: Eisenbrauns, 1983), 8.

[35] They follow the linguistic theory of M. C. Baker, *Lexical Categories: Verbs, Nouns, Adjectives* (Cambridge: Cambridge University Press, 2003).

[36] Miller-Naudé and Naudé, "Is the Adjective Distinct," 2.

[37] H. H. Hardy II, *Exegetical Gems*, 36.

[38] Amikam Gai, "The Category 'Adjective' in Semitic Languages," *JSS* 40 (1995): 1–9.

feminine but not both. For example, the noun עֵץ "tree" is masculine and forms its plural as עֵצִים "trees." The noun חָכְמָה "wisdom" on the other hand, is feminine, forming its plural as חָכְמוֹת. Even in those cases where noun endings do not correspond with their grammatical gender, a given noun is still analyzed as either masculine or feminine. The noun עִיר "city" is intrinsically feminine even though it does not end in הָ- and despite its plural form עָרִים "cities." The same is true for nouns exhibiting mixed morphologies, as in the feminine noun אֶרֶץ "land" and the masculine מָקוֹם "place," whose plurals are formed with the feminine plural marker, אֲרָצוֹת "lands" and מְקֹמוֹת "places."

Adjectives generate four base forms that are all inflected for gender and number. We may illustrate this feature with the Hebrew adjective זָקֵן "old."

F	M	
זְקֵנָה "old woman"	זָקֵן "old man"	S
זְקֵנוֹת "old women"	זְקֵנִים "old men"	P

Every adjective can potentially produce these four forms. Substantives, however, can only produce two forms (or three if attested in the dual). Nouns are marked for number but not gender.

M NOUN REGULAR	F NOUN REGULAR	M NOUN	IRREGULAR	F NOUN IRREGULAR	F NOUN IRREGULAR	
עַם "people"	תּוֹרָה "teaching"	אָב "father"	אֵם "mother"	אִשָּׁה "woman"	יָד "hand"	S
עַמִּים "peoples"	תּוֹרוֹת "teachings"	אָבוֹת "fathers"	אִמּוֹת "mothers"	נָשִׁים "women"	יָדִים "hands"	P
					יָדַיִם "(two) hands"	D

The gender of nouns is lexically conditioned. Gai identifies this feature of adjectives as "gender inflection," or more specifically, "grammatical-structural inflection." As he states: "the adjective is subjected to formal rules of inflection, identical with those affecting other inflectional systems in the languages, mainly that of the verb and the pronominal."[39] Verbs are affixed and prefixed with pronominal elements that are marked for number and gender.[40] Independent pronouns and pronominal suffixes attach to nouns and likewise mark both number and gender. These inflectional features mirror the adjectives and are distinct from the more limited inflectional capabilities of nouns. In terms of grammatical gender, noun morphology is relative (as outlined in the chart above) but semantically absolute.

---

[39] Gai, 2.
[40] For a discussion of the morphology of suffix and prefix conjugations, see above §§ 5.6.1 and 5.7.1

Conversely, the gender of adjectives is morphologically determined but lexically dependent upon the substantive referent.

As Gai explains, the inflectional features of the adjective provide grammatical demarcations that are meant to align and even signal the inherent gender of the substantives they modify in various ways.[41] They offer an external means of identifying the gender of substantives whose morphology may obscure grammatical gender. This function of the adjective resembles that of verbs (i.e., subject nouns agree with the gender of the verb) and pronouns (i.e., their gender will match the antecedent). The morphology of pronouns and adjectives always corresponds to the grammatical gender of the entities to which they refer or which they modify. Thus, the ending ∅ occurs for all adjectives modifying masculine singular nouns (e.g., Josh 21:45).

Josh 21:45

לֹא־נָפַל דָּבָר מִכֹּל הַדָּבָר הַטּוֹב אֲשֶׁר־דִּבֶּר יְהוָה אֶל־בֵּית יִשְׂרָאֵל
No word from every **good word** that Yahweh spoke to the house of Israel failed.

The ending ‑ִים is affixed to all adjectives modifying masculine plural nouns (e.g., Prov 23:8), even masculine nouns whose plural is formed with ‑וֹת (e.g., Neh 9:13).

Prov 23:8

וְשִׁחַתָּ דְּבָרֶיךָ הַנְּעִימִים
You will vomit your **pleasant** words.

Neh 9:13

וַתִּתֵּן לָהֶם מִשְׁפָּטִים יְשָׁרִים וְתוֹרוֹת אֱמֶת חֻקִּים וּמִצְוֹת טוֹבִים
You gave them **upright judgments** and instructions of truth, statutes and **good commandments**.

The accented ending ‑ָה accompanies all adjectives modifying feminine singular nouns, irrespective of the noun's formal ending. Examples include:

Josh 6:5

יָרִיעוּ כָל־הָעָם תְּרוּעָה גְדוֹלָה
All the people will raise **a great shout**.

Gen 10:12

וְאֶת־רֶסֶן בֵּין נִינְוֵה וּבֵין כָּלַח הִוא הָעִיר הַגְּדֹלָה׃
Resen between Ninevah and Calah, that is, **the great city**.

Finally, the ending ‑וֹת always appears with adjectives modifying feminine plural nouns.

---

[41] Gai, "The Category 'Adjective' in Semitic Languages," 2.

Amos 8:13

בַּיּ֣וֹם הַה֗וּא תִּ֠תְעַלַּפְנָה הַבְּתוּלֹ֧ת הַיָּפ֛וֹת וְהַבַּחוּרִ֖ים בַּצָּמָֽא׃

In that day **the beautiful virgins** and the choice men will faint with thirst.

Ezra 10:44

כָּל־אֵ֕לֶּה נָֽשְׂא֖וּ נָשִׁ֣ים נָכְרִיּ֑וֹת

All these had taken **foreign wives**.

Like nominals, adjectives are morphologically marked for singular and plural number. However, adjectives are unlike nominals in that they do not mark the dual. Plural adjectives are used to modify dual nouns. The following example is illustrative:

Ps 18:28

כִּֽי־אַ֭תָּה עַם־עָנִ֣י תוֹשִׁ֑יעַ וְעֵינַ֖יִם רָמ֣וֹת תַּשְׁפִּֽיל׃

For you rescue an afflicted people, but you bring low **exalted eyes**.

Miller-Naudé and Naudé suggest that this morphological feature further distinguishes adjectives from nouns.[42] Even nouns sometimes fail to indicate the dual morphologically. For instance, dual nouns in construct are no longer distinguishable from plural construct nouns. Genesis 27:22 illustrates this feature poignantly.

Gen 27:22

הַקֹּל֙ ק֣וֹל יַעֲקֹ֔ב וְהַיָּדַ֖יִם יְדֵ֥י עֵשָֽׂו

The voice is the voice of Jacob, but **the hands** are **the hands of** Esau.

Furthermore, the number of times markedly dual nouns are modified by an adjective in the HB is rather meager with only three occurrences.[43] Hebrew instead prefers to modify dual nouns by way of construct constructions, like רוּם־עֵינַ֫יִם "haughtiness of eyes" (Prov 21:4), or וּגְל֣וּי עֵינָ֑יִם "uncovered of eyes" (Num 24:4), more than attributive constructions, like וְעֵינַ֖יִם רָמ֣וֹת "exalted eyes" (Ps 18:28, cited above). Nonetheless, the observation of Miller-Naudé and Naudé holds true. The fact that this construction is so infrequent may signal a certain hesitancy to produce attributive constructions with duals because adjectives do not themselves have dual endings.

The four inflectional forms of the adjective (MS, MP, FS, FP) are fully productive, unlike nouns, which produce either masculine forms or feminine forms but never both. Miller-Naudé and Naudé note that this limitation is commonly misrepresented in grammars by citing the example סוּס "horse."

---

[42] Miller-Naudé and Naudé, "Is the Adjective Distinct," 4.

[43] Isa 42:7; Ps 18:28; Dan 8:3.

F	M	
סוּסָה "mare"	סוּס "horse"	S
סוּסוֹת "mares"	סוּסִים "horses"	P

This word gives the impression that nouns are fully productive, just like adjectives. However, such is not the case for every noun, which necessitates an alternative explanation.[44] Quite simply, these terms may in fact be analyzed as two lexically distinct nouns, one referring to "stallion," a male horse (סוּס), the other referring to "mare," a female horse (סוּסָה), both of which are inflected for number (סוּסִים and סוּסוֹת).[45]

8.5.2 Adjectival Patterns

One further way of distinguishing nouns and adjectives morphologically is to consider nominal patterns versus adjectival patterns. Grammarians are generally skeptical about the ability of nominal patterns to offer a distinction between nouns and adjectives in the Semitic languages. Waltke and O'Connor note, "The noun class in Hebrew does not rigidly distinguish adjectives from substantives."[46] From the perspective of Semitic grammar more broadly, S. Moscati observed that "the distinctions between noun and adjective, concrete and abstract, are not always apparent from a purely thematic point of view." He continues, "While in some case differentiation and opposition may be recognized (particularly in Akkadian), by and large these patterns occur indiscriminately."[47]

The overlap between nouns and adjectives broadly speaking is without question, yet the way in which this overlap is often framed may overstate the situation somewhat. This observation stems from the reality that Hebrew (and other Semitic languages) apparently reserved certain vocalization patterns for classes of words. We outlined the nominal internal and affixal patterns in chapter 7 (§§7.6.1.1 and 7.6.1.2). Alongside these well-established nominal patterns, Hebrew also attests several patterns predominantly reserved for adjectives.

A common adjectival pattern is *qātēl* (< historical **qatil*), which is used to denote verbal adjectives like יָבֵשׁ "dry," טָמֵא "unclean," אָשֵׁם "guilty," and many others. Even though this category overwhelmingly consists of verbal adjectives, it also attests a few nouns, seemingly limited to body-part names such as יָרֵךְ "thigh"

---

[44] One might propose אָדָם as another example of a fully productive noun (i.e., אָדָם, אֲדָמָה, אֲדָמוֹת). However, אָדָם "humanity" and אֲדָמָה "ground" are notionally distinct and thus represent two different nouns. Furthermore, although the plural of אֲדָמָה is אֲדָמוֹת, the plural form *אֲדָמִים is not attested. The bare noun can be used for an individual or more generally the human species (§7.1), elsewhere the construct is used, בְּנֵי אָדָם (Ezek 31:14; Prov 8:31) or בְּנֵי־הָאָדָם (Gen 11:5; Eccl 3:19) "son of humanity."

[45] Miller-Naudé and Naudé, "Is the Adjective Distinct," 4.

[46] *IBHS* §5.2h.

[47] Sabatino Moscati, *An Introduction to the Comparative Grammar of the Semitic Languages: Phonology and Morphology*, Porta Linguarum Orientalium (Wiesbaden: Harrassowitz, 1980), 77.

and כָּתֵף "shoulder." Another verbal adjective pattern is *qōtēl* (historical *qātil), functioning as the *Qal* active participle of fientive verbs (see below). Attributive participles describe the entity they modify (e.g., הָעֵץ הַצֹּמֵחַ "the sprouting tree" in Exod 10:5). A substantivized participle, such as שׁוֹמֵר "one who guards," places the focus on the entity whose activity is characterized by that of the underlying verbal root (i.e., "the person whose behavior is characterized as guarding"). Other scholars emphasize its nominal semantics, simply calling such forms "agent nouns."[48] Admittedly, some of these forms do not attest underlying verbal roots in the *Qal*, such as כֹּהֵן "priest." Others have such a nominal force that their underlying verbal quality is no longer prominent, as in שׁוֹפֵט "judge, ruler." Many scholars therefore conclude that the distinction between noun and (verbal) adjective is unsustainable. Nonetheless, the underlying verbal *adjectival* identity of the *qōtēl* pattern in BH is overwhelmingly prevalent.

Other adjectival patterns include *qatīl and *qatūl, which in BH produce *qātîl* and *qātûl* patterns, respectively. The *qātîl* adjectives include צָעִיר "small, insignificant," חָסִיד "kind," חָמִיץ "seasoned," and תָּמִים "complete, blameless." The ordinals for numbers three through ten follow this pattern with the accompanying adjectival suffix ִי-, as in שְׁלִישִׁי "fifth," רְבִיעִי "fourth," and so on (see §7.9.4.2). Some words with this pattern have apparently become <u>substantivized</u>, such as יָמִין "right (hand or side)" and חָצִיר "(something) green." The familiar noun נָבִיא "prophet" is also from this class, for which no derived verb is known in Hebrew. Scholars have appealed to Akkadian *nabû(m)* meaning "to name, call, proclaim" as an external parallel for this word.[49] Akkadian also attests the adjective *nabû* meaning "called," which may support the idea that נָבִיא represents another nominalized adjective having developed from "called" to "one (divinely) called" in Hebrew.[50] This pattern functioned as a G stem passive participle in Aramaic, as in כְּתִיב "written."[51] Biblical Hebrew, however, utilized the adjectival pattern *qātûl* (*qatū) for the *Qal* passive participle, as in כְּכָל־הַכָּתוּב בּוֹ "according to all that is written in it" (Josh 1:8).

The Hebrew pattern *qittēl* (historical *qattil) indicates bodily defects, such as אִלֵּם "dumb," עִוֵּר "blind," פִּסֵּחַ "lame," or more general notions of deformity, such as עִקֵּשׁ "crooked." The initial /i/ vowel of the Hebrew pattern developed by way of <u>attenuation</u> (*qattil > *qittil > *qittēl*).

Another highly productive adjectival pattern in BH is *qattîl* (historical *qattīl), with doubled second radical and long /i/ vowel in the second syllable. Scholars identify these adjectives as having intensive meanings.[52] The following examples are common: צַדִּיק "most righteous," אַדִּיר "most powerful," שַׁלִּיט "domineering,"

---

[48] E.g., Edward Lipiński, *Semitic Languages: Outline of Comparative Grammar*, OLA 80 (Leuven: Peeters, 1997), 211.

[49] *CAD*, 11:32.

[50] See the discussion in H.-P. Müller, "נָבִיא," *TDOT* 9:132–33.

[51] See Rosenthal, *Grammar of Biblical Aramaic*, 65.

[52] Moscati, *Comparative Grammar*, 79; Lipiński, *Semitic Languages*, 213.

and חַנִּין "most gracious" (but only used of God).[53] The pattern *qāṭôl* (historical *qaṭāl*) is frequently employed to produce adjectives related to many stative verbs.[54] One commonly attested *qāṭôl* adjective קָדוֹשׁ "holy," as well as גָּדוֹל "large, great," טָהוֹר "clean, pure," קָטֹן "small," and שָׁלוֹשׁ "three." This pattern is not limited to adjectives, given its frequent use for nouns (e.g., מָקוֹם "place," שָׁלוֹם "well-being, peace," אָדוֹן "lord, master," לָשׁוֹן "tongue").

Less common adjectival patterns are attested as well. Prefixed *'alep* forms are sometimes used for elative adjectives, such as אַכְזָב "deceptive" or אַכְזָר "cruel, fierce."[55] Forms with reduplicated second and third radicals are commonly utilized for adjectives throughout West Semitic. For instance, the Hebrew adjective יְרַקְרַק (*qaṭalṭal*) occurs meaning "greenish, pale green."[56]

Nominals and adjectives are not always distinguished by patterns, however. Some noun patterns like *qāṭāl* (e.g., דָּבָר "word, thing"; historical *qaṭal*) attest adjectives as well (e.g., חָדָשׁ "new," חָכָם "wise," רָשָׁע "wicked"). Similarly, one finds adjectives reflecting the nominal *qal* pattern with geminate roots (e.g., עַם "people," הַר "mountain," גַּן "garden"; historical *qall*), such as דַּל "low, weak," רַב "many," רַע "evil," מַר "bitter."

8.5.3 Definiteness

Adjectives indicate definiteness in one of three ways. Substantive adjectives are attested with or without the article. In the former case, the article adds a particularizing force: טוֹבָה "a good woman" versus הַטּוֹבָה "the good woman." Attributive adjectives have the article if the noun it is modifying is definite: מֶלֶךְ רַע "an evil king" or הַמֶּלֶךְ הָרַע "the evil king." Predicate adjectives are always indefinite. Other ways of marking definiteness for adjectives also occur. Like nominals, adjectives appear in the construct state whereby they are bound to a following noun. Construct phrases are common for substantive adjectives, as in the following example (Josh 1:14):

> Josh 1:14
> כֹּל גִּבּוֹרֵי הַחַיִל
> all **the great in** strength

Attributive adjectives occur in the construct state as well. In the following two examples, the construct forms of the adjectives are bound to a noun that further describes the quality of the adjective. In both cases, the entire noun phrase describes the preceding noun:

---

[53] For examples, see BDB, 337.
[54] H. Ringgren, "קדשׁ," *TDOT*, 12:528.
[55] Moscati, *Comparative Grammar*, 80. See also BDB, 469, 470.
[56] Moscati, *Comparative Grammar*, 79. See also BDB, 439.

2 Sam 14:27

הִיא הָיְתָה אִשָּׁה יְפַת מַרְאֶה

She was a woman **beautiful of** appearance.

1 Kgs 1:6

וְגַם־הוּא טוֹב־תֹּאַר מְאֹד

He also was exceedingly **handsome of** appearance.

Adjectives also indicate definiteness in the pronominal state. The pronominal state is formed by attaching pronominal suffixes to nouns. This feature is especially common for nominalized adjectives like זָקֵן "elder" (e.g., Judg 8:14).

Judg 8:14

אֶת־שָׂרֵי סֻכּוֹת וְאֶת־זְקֵנֶיהָ

the chiefs of Succoth and **its elders**

Other substantive adjectives can appear in the pronominal state as well.

1 Sam 2:35

וְהִתְהַלֵּךְ לִפְנֵי־מְשִׁיחִי כָּל־הַיָּמִים

He will walk before **my anointed one** all the days.

Ps 35:17

הָשִׁיבָה נַפְשִׁי מִשֹּׁאֵיהֶם מִכְּפִירִים יְחִידָתִי

Restore my soul from their devastations,

From lions **my only** (soul).

Ps 125:5

וְהַמַּטִּים עֲקַלְקַלּוֹתָם יוֹלִיכֵם יְהוָה אֶת־פֹּעֲלֵי הָאָוֶן

As for those turning aside to **their crooked ways**,

Yahweh will lead them with the doers of iniquity.

8.5.4 Adjectival Syntax

The adjective commonly functions in one of three ways: attributive, substantive, and predicate. Other uses of the adjective include comparative, superlative/elative, intensive, and adverbial.

8.5.4.1 Attributive

Attributive adjectives function as modifiers of nouns. They agree with the nouns they modify in number, gender, and definiteness. We have already discussed gender and number agreement (see §8.5.1). If the modified noun is indefinite, the adjective will be indefinite as well. Examples include:

Deut 1:46

וַתֵּשְׁבוּ בְקָדֵשׁ יָמִים רַבִּים

You dwelt in Kadesh **for many days**.

Josh 6:5

יָרִיעוּ כָל־הָעָם תְּרוּעָה גְדוֹלָה

All the people raised **a great shout**.

Definite nouns are modified by definite adjectives (e.g., Josh 7:9).

Josh 7:9

וּמַה־תַּעֲשֵׂה לְשִׁמְךָ הַגָּדוֹל

What will you do **for your great name**?

Definiteness is also marked with the construct and pronominal states. Attributive adjectives are separated from the noun they modify when that noun is in construct with another noun. In such cases, the attributive adjective occurs at the end of the construct phrase, agreeing in number, gender, and definiteness with the head noun:

Judg 2:7

אֲשֶׁר רָאוּ אֵת כָּל־מַעֲשֵׂה יְהוָה הַגָּדוֹל אֲשֶׁר עָשָׂה לְיִשְׂרָאֵל

Because they saw all **the great work** of Yahweh which he did for Israel.

2 Chr 17:2

וַיִּתֶּן־חַיִל בְּכָל־עָרֵי יְהוּדָה הַבְּצֻרוֹת

He placed a troop in all **the fortified cities** of Judah.

Nouns in the pronominal state usually require an attributive adjective to be marked with the article.

Neh 9:35

וּבְטוּבְךָ הָרָב אֲשֶׁר־נָתַתָּ לָהֶם

and with your great goodness which you gave them

1 Chr 24:31

אָחִיו הַקָּטָן

his younger brother

2 Chr 6:32

לְמַעַן שִׁמְךָ הַגָּדוֹל וְיָדְךָ הַחֲזָקָה וּזְרוֹעֲךָ הַנְּטוּיָה

for the sake of **your great name**, **your strong hand**, and your outstretched arm

In poetic texts, however, the article is sometimes omitted, as in the following example from Psalm 18:

Ps 18:18

יְצִילֵנִי מֵאֹיְבִי **עָז**

He rescued me from **my strong enemy**.

Attributive adjectives typically follow the modified noun, as in each of the examples listed above. Less frequently the adjective precedes the noun, in which cases the adjectival quality is stressed over the noun.

Gen 17:14

וְעָרֵל ׀ זָכָר אֲשֶׁר לֹא־יִמּוֹל אֶת־בְּשַׂר עָרְלָתוֹ וְנִכְרְתָה הַנֶּפֶשׁ הַהִוא מֵעַמֶּיהָ

As for **an uncircumcised male** who has not circumcised the flesh of his foreskin, that person will be cut off from his[57] people.

Prov 7:26

כִּי־**רַבִּים חֲלָלִים** הִפִּילָה וַעֲצֻמִים כָּל־הֲרֻגֶיהָ׃

For **many pierced** she brings down,

Numerous are all her slain.[58]

8.5.4.2 Substantive

Substantive adjectives are nominalized adjectives. They function as a noun and are either indefinite or definite. The following contexts exemplify indefinite substantive adjectives:

Deut 1:39

וּבְנֵיכֶם אֲשֶׁר לֹא־יָדְעוּ הַיּוֹם **טוֹב וָרָע**

and your sons who do not know today any **good** or **evil**

Ps 37:35

רָאִיתִי **רָשָׁע עָרִיץ** וּמִתְעָרֶה כְּאֶזְרָח רַעֲנָן׃

I have seen **a wicked [person], a ruthless [person]**,

He exposes himself like a luxuriant native tree.

Ps 51:21

אָז תַּחְפֹּץ זִבְחֵי־צֶדֶק עוֹלָה **וְכָלִיל**

Then you would delight in sacrifices of righteousness, in a whole burnt offering or **a perfect [offering]**.

---

[57] The pronoun is feminine since its antecedent is the feminine noun נֶפֶשׁ "soul." It could be translated, "that *soul* will be cut off from *its* people."

[58] Joüon and Muraoka note that this attributive position is limited to the adjective רַב when it is used in the sense of "many" as opposed to "great" (Joüon-Muraoka §141b). Waltke and O'Connor reason that its tendency to be fronted may stem from its affinity with numerals, which also may precede the counted noun (*IBHS* §14.3.1b). However, the above example from Gen 17:14 demonstrates that this position is not confined to רַב, even if רַב more commonly precedes the modified noun. The example from Prov 7:26 appears to place the focus of the statement on the fact that the adulterous woman has many victims. The parallel line also places the adjective עצמים as the first member of verbless clause: "*Numerous* (PRED ADJ) are all her slain (SUBJ)."

Definite substantive adjectives are prefixed with the article:

Exod 30:15

הֶעָשִׁיר לֹא־יַרְבֶּה וְהַדַּל לֹא יַמְעִיט מִמַּחֲצִית הַשָּׁקֶל

The rich shall not contribute more and **the poor** shall not contribute less than half of the shekel.

Deut 12:28

כִּי תַעֲשֶׂה הַטּוֹב וְהַיָּשָׁר בְּעֵינֵי יְהוָה אֱלֹהֶיךָ

for you will do **that which is good** and **upright** in the eyes of Yahweh your God

Substantive adjectives in the pronominal state are definite semantically:

Gen 22:16

כִּי יַעַן אֲשֶׁר עָשִׂיתָ אֶת־הַדָּבָר הַזֶּה וְלֹא חָשַׂכְתָּ אֶת־בִּנְךָ אֶת־יְחִידֶךָ

Because you have done this thing and have not withheld your son, **your only one**.

Similarly, substantive adjectives in the construct state are definite, as in the following passages:

Exod 28:3

וְאַתָּה תְּדַבֵּר אֶל־כָּל־חַכְמֵי־לֵב אֲשֶׁר מִלֵּאתִיו רוּחַ חָכְמָה

You shall say to all **the wise of** heart whom I have filled with a spirit of wisdom.

Ps 7:11

מָגִנִּי עַל־אֱלֹהִים מוֹשִׁיעַ יִשְׁרֵי־לֵב:

My shield is by God, who rescues the **upright in** heart.

8.5.4.3 Predicate

Predicate adjectives assert something about the subject of the clause.[59] Predicate adjectives usually precede the subject, exhibiting agreement in number and gender, but not definiteness. The predicate is indefinite though the subject is always definite. In the following example from Deuteronomy 1, the subject is also modified by a relative clause:

Deut 1:14

טוֹב־הַדָּבָר אֲשֶׁר־דִּבַּרְתָּ לַעֲשׂוֹת

Good is the thing you have spoken to do.

In Josh 2:17 the predicate adjective is modified by a genitive phrase (with מִן preposition) that is also modified by a relative clause:

---

[59] *IBHS* §14.3.2.

Josh 2:17

נְקִיִּם אֲנַחְנוּ מִשְּׁבֻעָתֵךְ הַזֶּה אֲשֶׁר הִשְׁבַּעְתָּנוּ

We are **guiltless** from this oath which you have sworn to us.

The above examples contain additional modification of what is being asserted about the subject, all of which follows the PRED–SUBJ construction. Sometimes modifiers of the predicate adjective can precede the PRED–SUBJ construction, which resultantly draw the focus of the clause as in Ps 33:1.

Ps 33:1

לַיְשָׁרִים נָאוָה תְהִלָּה

For the upright praise is **fitting**.

Verbless clauses consisting of PRED–SUBJ order are by default non-aspectual/ temporal; they simply assert some quality or condition of the subject irrespective of the time or duration of that quality or condition. Hebrew can add an aspectual/ temporal component to predicate adjective constructions by use of the verb היה. For instance, the consecutive preterite with a predicate adjective makes a perfective assertion about a past condition:

1 Sam 2:17

וַתְּהִי חַטַּאת הַנְּעָרִים גְּדוֹלָה מְאֹד אֶת־פְּנֵי יְהוָה

The sin of the young men **was** very **great** before Yahweh.

The narrative context of 1 Sam 2:17 indicates that the sin of Eli's sons had become exceedingly great during their tenure in the Shiloh temple. The same aspectual/ temporal qualification is possible with the non-verb-initial suffix conjugation of היה:

Gen 13:6

כִּי־הָיָה רְכוּשָׁם רָב וְלֹא יָכְלוּ לָשֶׁבֶת יַחְדָּו

For their possessions **were great** and they were not able to dwell together.

Imperfective assertions occur with the prefix conjugation of היה and typically denote a condition that has not yet come into effect but will be in the future:

Gen 44:10

וְאַתֶּם תִּהְיוּ נְקִיִּם

You **shall be innocent**.

2 Sam 2:26

הֲלוֹא יָדַעְתָּה כִּי־מָרָה תִהְיֶה בָּאַחֲרוֹנָה

Do you not know that **it will be bitter** in the end?

The subject of predicate adjectives is sometimes formed by attaching a pronominal suffix to certain particles. The presentative particle הִנֵּה "behold, look" is commonly used in such constructions:

Gen 16:11

הִנָּךְ הָרָה וְיֹלַדְתְּ בֵּן

Look, you are **pregnant** and will bear a son.

The same construction occurs with other particles as well, such as עוֹד "again, still":

2 Sam 18:14

עוֹדֶנּוּ חַי בְּלֵב הָאֵלָה

He was still **alive** in the heart of the tree.

8.5.4.4 Comparative

Comparative adjectives provide the ability to relate the quality of two entities in terms of degree (e.g., *better, wiser, stronger, older,* and *younger*). Comparative adjectives in English add the morpheme -*er* to the adjective (e.g., *old* becomes *older*) and are followed by the word *than* and the noun with which the comparison is being made (e.g., *John is older than Maya*). Biblical Greek is similar to English in its comparative morpheme -τερ- attached to certain adjectives, such as ἰσχυρός "powerful," which becomes ἰσχυρότερος "**more** powerful."[60] Unlike English and Greek, BH does not have a unique comparative morpheme but instead attaches the preposition מִן "from, away from" to the noun or pronoun to draw a comparison. We can observe this usage in the following examples:

Hos 2:9

אֵלְכָה וְאָשׁוּבָה אֶל־אִישִׁי הָרִאשׁוֹן כִּי טוֹב לִי אָז מֵעָתָּה

I will go and return to my first husband, for it was **better** for me then **than now**.

The comparative adjective often appears in the attributive position:

Deut 1:28

עַם גָּדוֹל וָרָם מִמֶּנּוּ

a people **greater and taller than we**

Judg 1:13

עָתְנִיאֵל בֶּן־קְנַז אֲחִי כָלֵב הַקָּטֹן מִמֶּנּוּ

Othniel, son of Kenaz, **the younger brother** of Caleb

It can occur as a predicate:

Judg 8:2

הֲלוֹא טוֹב עֹלְלוֹת אֶפְרָיִם מִבְצִיר אֲבִיעֶזֶר

Are not the gleanings of Ephraim **better than** the harvest of Abiezer?

---

[60] For more on the Greek comparative adjectives, see Andreas J. Köstenberger, Benjamin L. Merkle, and Robert L. Plummer, *Going Deeper with New Testament Greek: An Intermediate Study of the Grammar and Syntax of the New Testament* (Nashville: B&H Academic, 2016), 171–72.

1 Sam 1:8

הֲלֹוא אָנֹכִי טֹוב לָךְ מֵעֲשָׂרָה בָּנִים

Am I not **better** to you **than** ten sons?"

In some cases, the comparative מִן is omitted in situations that are contextually comparative.

Gen 1:16

וַיַּעַשׂ אֱלֹהִים אֶת־שְׁנֵי הַמְּאֹרֹת הַגְּדֹלִים אֶת־הַמָּאֹור **הַגָּדֹל** לְמֶמְשֶׁלֶת הַיֹּום וְאֶת־הַמָּאֹור **הַקָּטֹן** לְמֶמְשֶׁלֶת הַלַּיְלָה

God made two great luminaries: **the greater** luminary to rule the day and **the smaller** luminary to rule the night.

Gen 19:31

וַתֹּאמֶר הַבְּכִירָה אֶל־**הַצְּעִירָה**

The firstborn said to **the younger**.

Gen 48:14

וַיִּשְׁלַח יִשְׂרָאֵל אֶת־יְמִינֹו וַיָּשֶׁת עַל־רֹאשׁ אֶפְרַיִם וְהוּא **הַצָּעִיר** וְאֶת־שְׂמֹאלֹו עַל־רֹאשׁ מְנַשֶּׁה

He stretched out his right hand and placed (it) upon the head of Ephraim, that is **the younger**, and his left hand upon the head of Manasseh.

Another type of comparison occurs when the adjective is followed by a noun prefixed with the inseparable preposition -כְּ:

1 Sam 2:2

אֵין־קָדֹושׁ כַּיהוה

There is no one **as holy as Yahweh**.

The nuance of this usage expresses a comparison indicating "X is similar to Y" rather than "X is a degree in quality more than Y."

8.5.4.5 Superlative

Superlative adjectives identify the outstanding quality of one entity among three or more entities in its class. Grammarians sometime distinguish the attributive, comparative, and superlative adjectives according to the following schema:[61]

DEGREE OF COMPARISON	
absolute	wise
comparative	wiser
superlative	wisest

---

[61] Adapted from *IBHS* §14.4.

The superlative use of the adjective usually occurs as definite.

Gen 42:13

וְהִנֵּה הַקָּטֹן אֶת־אָבִינוּ הַיּוֹם וְהָאֶחָד אֵינֶנּוּ

Look, **the youngest** is with our father today, and one is no more.

Sometimes the superlative adjective is in the attributive position:

Gen 43:34

וְהָבִיאוּ אֶת־אֲחִיכֶם הַקָּטֹן אֵלַי וְאֵדְעָה כִּי לֹא מְרַגְּלִים אַתֶּם

Bring **your youngest brother** to me that I may know that you are not spies.

The class of a given superlative is often designated by the בְּ preposition, meaning "the X-*est* in/among Y":

Judg 6:15

הִנֵּה אַלְפִּי הַדַּל בִּמְנַשֶּׁה וְאָנֹכִי הַצָּעִיר בְּבֵית אָבִי

Look, my family is **the least** in Manasseh, and I am **the smallest** in the house of my father.

The superlative constructions can also indicate class genitivally by way of a construct chain, meaning "the X-*est* of Y":

Gen 24:2

וַיֹּאמֶר אַבְרָהָם אֶל־עַבְדּוֹ זְקַן בֵּיתוֹ הַמֹּשֵׁל בְּכָל־אֲשֶׁר־לוֹ

Abraham said to his servant, **the eldest** of his house who oversees all that belongs to him.

1 Sam 8:14

וְאֶת־שְׂדוֹתֵיכֶם וְאֶת־כַּרְמֵיכֶם וְזֵיתֵיכֶם הַטּוֹבִים יִקָּח וְנָתַן לַעֲבָדָיו׃

The best of your fields, vineyards and olive groves he will take and give to his servants.

Similarly, the superlative comparison may occur with מִכֹּל, meaning "the X-*est* of all Y," which appears to intensify the supreme quality of the superlative:

1 Sam 9:21

וּמִשְׁפַּחְתִּי הַצְּעִרָה מִכָּל־מִשְׁפְּחוֹת שִׁבְטֵי בִנְיָמֵן

[Is not] my clan **the least of** all the clans of the tribes of Benjamin?

The adverb מְאֹד "very" plus the adjective provides another means of expressing superlatives in Hebrew, as in the familiar description of God's creation activity at end of the sixth day (Gen 1:31).

Gen 1:31

וַיַּרְא אֱלֹהִים אֶת־כָּל־אֲשֶׁר עָשָׂה וְהִנֵּה־טוֹב מְאֹד

God saw all that he had made and look, it was **exceedingly good**.

Other examples include:

Num 11:33

וַיַּ֤ךְ יְהוָה֙ בָּעָ֔ם מַכָּ֖ה רַבָּ֥ה מְאֹֽד

Yahweh struck the people with an **exceedingly great** plague.

Joel 2:11

וַֽיהוָ֗ה נָתַ֤ן קוֹלוֹ֙ לִפְנֵ֣י חֵיל֔וֹ כִּ֥י רַ֛ב מְאֹ֖ד מַחֲנֵ֑הוּ

Yahweh utters his voice before his army, for his camp is **exceedingly great**.

Zech 14:14

וְנִבְקַע֩ הַ֨ר הַזֵּיתִ֜ים מֶחֶצְי֗וֹ מִזְרָ֤חָה וָיָ֙מָּה֙ גֵּ֣יא גְּדוֹלָ֣ה מְאֹ֔ד

The Mount of Olives will be split in half from east to west by **an exceedingly great** valley.

Sometimes the superlative is indicated by repetition, as in the well-known example from Isaiah's call narrative:

Isa 6:3

וְקָרָ֨א זֶ֤ה אֶל־זֶה֙ וְאָמַ֔ר קָד֧וֹשׁ׀ קָד֛וֹשׁ קָד֖וֹשׁ יְהוָ֣ה צְבָא֑וֹת

This one calls out to the other: "**Holy, holy, holy** is Yahweh of armies!"

8.5.4.6 Intensification (with הָלַךְ)

The root הלך is combined with adjectives in certain contexts to indicate an intensification of the adjectival quality or condition. For example, the *Qal* participle of הלך is combined with חָזֵק "strong" and דַּל "weak" to depict the strengthening of David's position in Israel in contrast with the weakening of Saul's dynasty:

2 Sam 3:1

וְדָוִד֙ הֹלֵ֣ךְ וְחָזֵ֔ק וּבֵ֥ית שָׁא֖וּל הֹלְכִ֥ים וְדַלִּֽים

Now David **was growing stronger**, but the house of Saul **was growing weaker**.

The infinitive absolute occurs as a cognate accusative in combination with the adjective קָרֵב to indicate approaching movement:

2 Sam 18:25

וַיֵּ֥לֶךְ הָל֖וֹךְ וְקָרֵֽב

He came **nearer and nearer**.

8.5.5 Adjectives and Nouns: Syntactical Distinctions

In addition to morphological differences, nouns and adjectives are distinct in their syntactical functions. Miller-Naudé and Naudé offer several syntactical arguments, in addition to the morphological ones noted above, demonstrating this distinction by applying the linguistic approach of M. C. Baker to BH.[62] The similarities between a noun (e.g., "goodness") and a substantive adjective (e.g., "the good") are only superficial, according to Baker. Nouns are lexical identifiers, meaning that they refer to persons, things, or situations. Syntactically, they function as subjects, objects, or compliments. Adjectives, on the other hand, are not "inherently referential," even though they can function in ways that are similar to nouns (e.g., substantive adjectives). Nonetheless, as Baker argues, there are three syntactical features of adjectives that distinguish them from nouns, which Miller-Naudé and Naudé apply to Hebrew as follows.

First, only the adjective can appear as an attributive modifier of a noun. Nouns cannot modify other nouns attributively as adjectives can. Instead, nouns modify other nouns through various construct phrases or in apposition (i.e., restating a noun with an added quality or identification).

Second, adjectives can occur as the complement of "degree heads," whereas nouns cannot. Examples of degree heads in English are "so," "too," "as," "how." Miller-Naudé and Naudé note the Hebrew degree head מָה "how," which can occur with adjective or verbal constructions (stative or non-stative), but never with nouns. They cite the following examples:

Ps 31:20

מָה רַב־טוּבְךָ אֲשֶׁר־צָפַנְתָּ לִּירֵאֶיךָ

How great (ADJ) is your goodness which you have treasured up for those who fear you.

Ps 3:2

יְהוָה מָה־רַבּוּ צָרָי

O Yahweh, **how** my adversaries **have increased** (stative verb).

Finally, nouns are inherently referential, while adjectives are not. In other words, nouns identify persons, places, or things, whereas adjectives describe the qualities or characteristics of some other entity, but they cannot identify the entity itself. For example, in English we can use the adjective *good* substantively as *the good*, but we must supply the assumed entity that is being modified—*the good* [thing], *the good* [quality], *the good* [person]. Hebrew works in the same way. A substantive adjective with the article may have the appearance of a noun, but beneath the surface it always references what Miller-Naudé and Naudé call a "null (or zero) noun." We can illustrate this point with the following example from the book of Judges:

Judg 15:18

וְעַתָּה אָמוּת בַּצָּמָא וְנָפַלְתִּי בְּיַד הָעֲרֵלִים

But now will I die of thirst and fall into the hand of **the uncircumcised**?

---

[62] Miller-Naudé and Naudé, "Is the Adjective Distinct," 4–8; M. C. Baker, *Lexical Categories: Verbs, Nouns, Adjectives* (Cambridge: Cambridge University Press, 2003), 23–94.

Without the broader context of this statement, one would assume that "uncircumcised" must mean "uncircumcised *individuals*." The broader context of the Samson episodes further clarifies that the "uncircumcised *Philistines*" are in view (Judg 14:3). The familiar refrain from Judges that "everyone did evil in the eyes of the Lord" offers another example:

Judg 6:1

וַיַּעֲשׂוּ בְנֵי־יִשְׂרָאֵל הָרַע בְּעֵינֵי יְהוָה

The sons of Israel did **the evil** in the eyes of Yahweh.

The referent of "the evil" in this context is the kind of practice that falls outside what is prescribed in Torah, or what is "evil *conduct*" in Yahweh's estimation. Miller-Naudé and Naudé summarize this syntactical phenomenon in this way: "when an adjective occurs with the definite article (or in another definite construction in Biblical Hebrew), it is necessary either to reconstruct a null noun from the previous discourse context or to use a generic common noun such as *people* or *one*."[63] They outline three syntactical ramifications of the non-referentiality of adjectives in Biblical Hebrew:[64]

1. Adjectives cannot serve as pronoun antecedents, while nouns can.
2. Adjectives cannot be modified by relative clauses, while nouns can.
3. Adjectives cannot function as augments of verbs, while nouns can.

8.6 PARTICIPLES AND VERBAL ADJECTIVES

8.6.1 Morphology

The Hebrew participles are <u>verbal adjectives,</u> in that they possess both verbal and adjectival qualities. In the *Qal* stem Hebrew distinguishes between fientive and stative verbal adjectives. Fientive verbs attest both active and passive forms, while stative verbal adjectives attest two vowel patterns, resulting in a set of four forms:[65]

	ACTIVE	PASSIVE
Fientive	קוֹטֵל (*qātil*)	קָטוּל (*qatūl*)
Stative 1	קָטֵל (*qatil*)	∅
Stative 2	קָטֹל (*qatul*)	∅

---

[63] Miller-Naudé and Naudé, "Is the Adjective Distinct," 6.
[64] Miller-Naudé and Naudé, 7.
[65] This formulation is adapted from the presentation of the Ugaritic verbal adjective in Bordreuil and Pardee, *Manual of Ugaritic*, 57.

These forms are not fully productive in that not every root can attest to both an active and a passive form. The distinction between *qatil and *qatul adjectives is lexically conditioned, as in כָּבֵד "heavy," שָׂמֵחַ "glad," versus יָכֹל "able," יָגֵר "afraid." The alternating stative patterns are primarily morphological in nature, both of which describe a state of being.

The primary stative verbal adjective in Hebrew is essentially identical to the *qatil adjective. The masculine singular form is identical to the 3MS *Qal* stative verb, though its inflected forms are distinct. For example, the adjective זָקֵן attests זָקֵן "old man," זְקֵנִים "old men," and זְקֵנוֹת "old women," as well as a variety of construct and suffixal forms (זִקְנֵי, זְקֵנָיו, etc.). The adjective appears to be fully adapted into the finite verb paradigm (e.g., the suffix conjugation: זָקְנָה "she is old," זָקַנְתְּ "you are old," זָקַנְתִּי "I am old"). We also find the consecutive preterite וַיִּזְקַן "he was old" (2 Chr 24:15). Outside of these forms, it is difficult to distinguish between the verbal adjective and the *Qal* stative. For instance, Gen 18:12 וַאדֹנִי זָקֵן "My lord is old" is ambiguous. זָקֵן could be analyzed as the 3MS *Qal* stative SC verb or the MS verbal adjective functioning as a predicate. It is more common for predicate adjectives to precede their subject, which might lead one to expect וְזָקֵן אֲדֹנִי if it is the adjective.

FINAL VOWELS IN SEMITIC

Historically speaking, the two adjective forms would have had different endings.[66] Suffix conjugation verbs had a final /a/ vowel, while the verbal adjective would have ended with one of three case vowels in the singular, or one of two for the plural.[67]

VERBAL ADJECTIVE FORMS WITH RECONSTRUCTED FINAL VOWELS

	M		F	
	S	P	S	P
NOM	zaqinu	zaqinūma	zaqinatu	zaqinātu
GEN	zaqini	zaqinīma	zaqinati	zaqināti
ACC	zaqina		zaqinata	

[66] Blau, 225.

[67] On the reconstruction of case vowels in Hebrew, see Pardee, "Vestiges du système casuel," 113–21.

The situation attested in Biblical Hebrew is akin to that of Akkadian, which attests a fully productive paradigm for verbal adjectives. The following forms of the verbal adjective *damiq-* "good" exhibit morphological similarity with the Hebrew *qatil* adjective:[68]

	M		F	
	S	P	S	P
NOM	*damqum*	*damqūtum*	*damiqtum*	*damqātum*
GEN	*damqim*	*damqūtim*	*damiqtim*	*damqātim*
ACC	*damqam*		*damiqtam*	

The language has also expanded the *qatil* adjective into a number of finite verbs inflected for gender, number, and person, identified as *Qal* statives as discussed in chapter 3 (§3.7.1).

The *Qal* stem is the only stem that attests to both active and passive participial forms. The *Qal* active participle is formed with the long /o/ in the first syllable (written *plene* or defectively) and *ṣere* in the second: קוֹטֵל/קֹטֵל.[69]

The *Qal* active participles are attested for transitive and intransitive verbs but do not occur for stative verbs. The *Qal* participial counterpart for statives roots is the **qatil* verbal adjective (e.g., עָרֵל "uncircumcised," טָמֵן "unclean," מָלֵא "full"). The *Qal* passive participle is formed with the pattern: קָטוּל. The derived stems have a single participial form whose semantics correspond to that of the verbal stem (*Niphal* as passive, *Piel* as factitive, *Hiphil* as causative, etc.).[70]

8.6.2 Semantics

At the outset of this section, we introduce the participle descriptively as a verbal adjective. However, other scholars emphasize that it shares the verbal and nominal qualities of the *qōtēl* pattern. In the classic presentation of this approach,

---

[68] The following chart adapted from Huehnergard, *Grammar of Akkadian*, 26.

[69] The morphology of the *Qal* active participle requires us to give attention to the phonological development known as the Canaanite shift. Across the Canaanite languages (i.e., Hebrew, Phoenician, Moabite, Ammonite) there exists evidence for the sound shift *ā to ō (see Joshua Fox, "A Sequence of Vowel Shifts in Phoenician and Other Languages," *JNES* 55 [1996]: 40). The evidence goes back at least as early as the Amarna Canaanite texts from fourteenth century BC and possibly even earlier. See Zellig S. Harris, *Development of the Canaanite Dialects: An Investigation in Linguistic History*, American Oriental Series 16 (New Haven: American Oriental Society, 1939), 44; W. Randall Garr, *Dialect Geography of Syria-Palestine, 1000–586 B.C.E.* (Winona Lake, IN: Eisenbrauns, 2004), 30–32. For example, the G stem active participle in Aramaic is vocalized in Biblical Aramaic as *qātēl*. For the root יהב "to give," the participle is יָהֵב "the one giving" (Dan 2:21). Aramaic did not undergo the Canaanite shift and thus preserves the historically long /a/ of the first syllable (realized in the Tiberian vocalization as *qāmeṣ*). The Akkadian G stem participle likewise attests long /a/ in the first syllable (*pārisum, pārisim, pārisam*, etc.). The *Qal* active participle, however, attests long /o/ in the initial syllable, evincing the sound shift *ā to ō. We may therefore reconstruct the historic form of the *Qal* active participle as **qātil*.

[70] For more on the semantics of the verbal stems, see chapter 3.

E. Sellin examines all occurrences of the participle and categorized them according to verbal versus nominal uses.[71] Gesenius's grammar presents the participle as occupying a place somewhere between the noun and the verb, "most nearly related to the adjective."[72]

Benjamin Kedar-Kopfstein attempts to move beyond the emphasis on nominal versus verbal aspects of the participle by focusing on the semantics of the *qōtēl* pattern.[73] The emphasis in earlier studies on the syntactical function of the participle has led to the verbal/nominal opposition problem. If, however, one focuses on the semantic aspects of a given verb in relation to the various uses of the participle, such opposition disappears. The perceived variety in the participle's usage stems from the semantic character of individual verbs. He assumes the verbal/nominal dichotomy as fact and proposes that the *qōtēl* pattern originated as one of many other nominal patterns. He explains that the *qōtēl* pattern "annexed the function of an active participle and was subsequently absorbed by this function."[74] The existence of the competing *qātēl* (verbal adjective) pattern proves this development for Kedar-Kopfstein, since *qōtēl* never served as the sole participial form in Hebrew. The stative patterns, *qātōl* and *qātēl*, have existed alongside *qōtēl*.

When a given participle exhibits both nominal and verbal semantic qualities, Kedar-Kopfstein claims that it is the result of the semantic characteristics of the verb. For instance, a verb expressing an activity that in certain environments indicates a particular vocation may become a term for that profession, like יֹצֵר "potter" or זוֹנָה "prostitute." Other verbs, according to Kedar-Kopfstein, express "qualities or permanent occupations that are considered characteristic of the subject," again producing a <u>substantive</u> noun in words like חוֹטֵא "sinner" or עוֹשֵׁק "oppressor."[75] Kedar-Kopfstein develops a continuum of semantic meaning for participles ranging from class *a* to class *i*.[76] The semantics of class *a* is closer to nominals, and class *i* verbals:

---

[71] E. Sellin, *Die verbal-nominale Doppelnatur der hebräischen Participien und Infinitive und ihre darauf beruhende verschiedene Construktion* (Leipzig: Fock, 1889).

[72] GKC §116a.

[73] Benjamin Kedar-Kopfstein, "Semantic Aspects of the Pattern Qôtēl," *Hebrew Annual Review* 1 (1977): 155–76.

[74] Kedar-Kopfstein, "Pattern Qôtēl," 156.

[75] Kedar-Kopfstein, 158.

[76] Kedar-Kopfstein, 160.

PARTICIPLE SEMANTICS									
NOMINAL								VERBAL	
CLASS	A	B	C	D	E	F	G	H	I
Example	שׂוֹרֵק "choice vine"	רוֹזֵן "prince"	כּוֹרֵם "vine dresser"	כּוֹבֵס "fuller"	שׁוֹפֵט "judge"	שׂוֹנֵא "enemy"	קוֹנֶה "buyer"	יוֹקֵד "burning"	נוֹטֵן "giving"
Formal Features	no radical cognates		derived from nouns	connected with verbal root in derived stem	identical with participle of the Qal				
									verbal
Signifi- cation	substantive denoting object		profession, term of agent				Perma-nent activity	Tem-porary activity	attributively denoted action	predicative denoting action

Another influential study of the Hebrew participle emphasizes the opposition between its nominal and verbal qualities, offering a historical explanation via language change. Amnon Gordon explains, "The participle can appear as fulfilling both functions, nominal and verbal, in which case I refer to it as an "intermediate" form, as its Hebrew name (*benoni* "one in the middle") implies; or it may fulfill a nominal function with no verbal overtones."[77] Although the "intermediate" nature of the participle has been proposed by earlier scholars, as Gordon notes, his work offers a full-fledged study in an effort to establish this view further.[78] He explains the intermediate quality of the participle by stating that it is somewhere between the verbal notion of "he/she/they are doing the action" and the nominal notion of "he/she/they who do the action."[79] Gordon's analysis does not distinguish between nouns and adjectives, as the above discussion has attempted to maintain, but identifies its origin as a noun. At the earliest stages of BH, the participle experienced a transition from a nominal to a mixed form that expanded its function to that of a verb through the process of reanalysis. He traces this development into Mishnaic Hebrew and concludes his analysis with an examination of Modern Hebrew. The intermediate nature of the participle on display in Classical Biblical Hebrew

---

[77] Amnon Gordon, "The Development of the Participle in Biblical, Mishnaic, and Modern Hebrew," *Afroasiatic Linguistics* 8 (1982): 12.

[78] Gordon ("Development of the Participle," 14) mentions G. Bergsträsser, *A Grammar of the Hebrew Language*, trans. M. Ben Asher (Jerusalem: Magnes, 1926), 425; GKC §116a; F. R. Blake, *A Resurvey of Hebrew Tenses* (Rome: Pontifical Biblical Institute, 1951), 28–30; T. Givón, "The Drift from VSO to SVO in Biblical Hebrew: the Pragmatics of Tense-Aspect," in *Mechanism of Syntactic Change*, ed. Charles Li (Austin: University of Texas Press, 1977), 209.

[79] Gordon, "Development of the Participle," 5.

eventually gave way to a more tensed usage in Late Biblical Hebrew, which led to a decrease in its intermediary function.[80]

Other scholars continue to refine the basic position that participles involved a mixture of nominal and verbal qualities.[81] Again, an underlying assumption of these studies that emphasize the intermediate nature of the participle is that the adjective be classified as a subset of nouns. We argue in this chapter for a tripartite view of the language consisting of nouns, verbs, and adjectives. John Cook applies this framework to participles and verbal adjectives as a means of avoiding the participles classification as an intermediate or mixed form. He does so by appealing to recent studies on the typology of adjectives and "intransitive predication."[82] He adopts the fourfold categorization of intransitive predication proposed by Leon Stassen: event (e.g., *John walks*), class (e.g., *John is a carpenter*), location (e.g., *John is in the kitchen*), and property (e.g., *John is tall*).[83] Cook illustrates the prototypical encoding strategies for the Hebrew verbal (event type), nominal (class type), and locative (location type) clauses:

Prototypical Verbal (event)

Gen 22:6

וַיֵּלְכוּ שְׁנֵיהֶם יַחְדָּו

The two of them walked together.

Prototypical Nominal (class) *Zero Copula*

Josh 22:34

יְהוָה הָאֱלֹהִים

Yahweh is God.

Pronominal Copula

2 Kgs 19:15

אַתָּה־הוּא הָאֱלֹהִים

You are God.

---

[80] Gordon, 46. In Mishnaic Hebrew its verbal qualities become more pronounced, though intermediate functions still occur. By the time of Modern Hebrew, the intermediate function has disappeared altogether, with polarized verbal and nominal functions firmly fixed in the language.

[81] See also J. W. Dyk, *Participles in Context: A Computer-Assisted Study of Old Testament Hebrew* (Amsterdam: VU University Press, 1994); F. I. Andersen and A. D. Forbes, "The Participle in Biblical Hebrew and the Overlap of Grammar and Lexicon," in *Milk and Honey: Essays on Ancient Israel and the Bible in Appreciation of the Judaic Studies Program at the University of California, San Diego*, ed. S. Malena and D. Miano (Winona Lake, IN: Eisenbrauns, 2007), 185–212.

[82] Cook, "Hebrew Participle and Stative," 1–19.

[83] Leon Stassen observes that the first three categories have "prototypical encoding strategies," while the fourth category does not but draws from the other three. See *Intransitive Predication*, Oxford Studies in Typology and Linguistic Theory 17 (Oxford: Clarendon, 1997), 12.

Particle Copula
   Judg 6:13
   וְיֵשׁ יְהוָה עִמָּנוּ
   Yahweh is with us.

Prototypical Locative (less frequent in Hebrew)
   Gen 6:4
   הַנְּפִלִים הָיוּ בָאָרֶץ
   The Nephilim were in the land.

The central question Cook seeks to answer regarding the Hebrew participle is: What encoding strategies does Biblical Hebrew use for predicate adjectives and are they the same for stative and participle adjectives?[84] He draws several conclusions. First, adjectives (property type) are encoded in the same manner as nominals (class type) as outline above. Second, the same encoding strategy is applied to participles as well. Verbal adjectives, however, follow what Cook calls a split strategy, since the verbal adjective can take either verbal or adjectival morphology. He cites the following examples:[85]

a. Zero Copula
Adjective:
   Gen 29:31
   וְרָחֵל עֲקָרָה
   Rachel was barren.

Participle:
   1 Kgs 13:1
   וְיָרָבְעָם עֹמֵד עַל־הַמִּזְבֵּחַ
   Jeroboam was standing beside the altar.

b. Pronominal Copula
Adjective:
   Lam 1:18
   צַדִּיק הוּא יְהוָה
   Yahweh is righteous.

Participle:
   Deut 31:3
   יְהוֹשֻׁעַ הוּא עֹבֵר לְפָנֶיךָ
   Joshua is crossing over before you.

---

[84] Cook, "Hebrew Participle and Stative," 9.
[85] Cook, 10–11.

c. Verbal Copula

Adjective:

Gen 11:30

וַתְּהִי שָׂרַי עֲקָרָה

Sarai was barren.

Participle:

2 Kgs 9:14

וְיוֹרָם הָיָה שֹׁמֵר בְּרָמֹת גִּלְעָד

Joram was guarding at Ramoth-Gilead.

d. Particle Copula

Participle:

Gen 43:4

אִם־יֶשְׁךָ מְשַׁלֵּחַ אֶת־אָחִינוּ אִתָּנוּ

If you are sending our brother with us.

The split strategy of verbal adjectives results in verbal, verbal adjective, and verbal copula constructions. Again, Cook offers these examples:

a. Verbal

Gen 48:10

וְעֵינֵי יִשְׂרָאֵל כָּבְדוּ מִזֹּקֶן

The eyes of Israel were heavy from old age.

b. Verbal Adjective (Zero Copula)

Exod 17:12

וִידֵי מֹשֶׁה כְּבֵדִים

The hands of Moses were heavy.

c. Verbal Adjective (+ Verbal Copula)

Gen 50:9

וַיְהִי הַמַּחֲנֶה כָּבֵד מְאֹד

The camp was exceedingly heavy.

Participles differ from standard adjectives and verbal adjectives in being able to demarcate event predicates (e.g., "he is crossing over"; "he is sending"), and they are not limited to properties or states (e.g., "she is barren"; "he is old"). This distinction may contribute to the confusion regarding the intermediate nature of participles and the penchant to analyze them as verbs whenever they take an object. The typological approach rather demonstrates a shift between verbal and nominal constructions whereby participles can function as predicates in nominal predicate constructions. This ability is a feature of all adjectives, as outlined above, and demonstrates that participles and verbal adjectives are best classified with adjectives, thus avoiding the imprecise categorization of the participle as a hybrid form—sometimes nominal and sometimes verbal.[86]

The semantic feature of verbal adjectives comes from their derivation as stative roots, which refer to qualities or characteristics (e.g., כָּבֵד "heavy," זָקֵן "old," טָמֵא "unclean," יָרֵא "fearsome"). This aspect distinguishes these forms from *Qal* participles, which are largely associated with <u>fientive</u> or action roots (הָלַךְ "walking," יָדַע "knowing," עֹבֵד "serving, working," יָצָא "going out"). This situation changes once we move outside the *Qal*. The semantics of the roots correlate with the semantics of the stems in which they are attested. Not every root is attested in every stem.[87] Outside the *Qal*, the semantic diversity of participles only increases. What does not change, however, is the ability of adjectival syntactical categories to provide a framework for understanding the usage of the participle across the stems.[88]

8.6.3 Syntactical Function

Participles and verbal adjectives fall within the broader class of adjectives. For this reason, our treatment of verbal adjective and participle usage follows the basic parameters of adjectival usage outlined earlier in this chapter. They include attributive, substantival, and predicate functions. Adverbial constructions are discussed at the end of this section.

---

[86] Cook, "Hebrew Participle and Stative," 12.

[87] For more on the semantics of the Hebrew stems, see chapter 4.

[88] Such an approach does not deny the semantic challenges that many *qōtēl* forms pose, as Kedar-Kopstein's study successfully demonstrates. For instance, how do we account for the existence of *qōtēl* forms for which a fientive meaning is no longer operative or for which no verbal root is attested? In the case of professional terms like שֹׁפֵט, for instance, it is reasonable to conclude that the profession of carrying out the activity of the root שׁפט eventually developed into a specific occupation. For this root in particular, the occupational notion of a שֹׁפֵט "deliverer, governor," takes on its own specialized meaning beyond the simple notion of "judge" associated with the verbal root. Or, how might we explain the existence of *qōtēl* terms with no accompanying verbal root? It is also possible that the usefulness of the *qōtēl* pattern as a term of profession led to the production of new *qōtēl* profession terms with no corresponding verbal root, like כֹּהֵן "priest." Even with this term, however, there was a need to verbalize the activity of "serving as a כֹּהֵן," for which purpose the *Piel* denominative כִּהֵן "to function as a priest" was presumably created. The *qōtēl* pattern apparently competes with the historical *nomen professionis* (i.e., profession noun) *qattāl* pattern in the Semitic languages. Once the Canaanite shift *ā to ō occurred, the *qattāl* (BH *qattōl*) pattern may have been losing ground to *qōtēl*. Even though the *Qal* participle also endured the same Canaanite shift (*qātil > qōtēl*), it continued to maintain its morphological distinction from other similar patterns (like verbal adjective *qātēl*); whereas the change from *qattāl* to *qattōl* did not. The morphological inconsistency of the Semitic *nomen professionis* in Hebrew may have contributed to the adaptation of the *Qal* participle *qōtēl* for expressing professional activity. Its origins as a verbal adjective for fientive/action verbs makes this possibility a logical development. The evidence for *nomen professionis* is mixed in Hebrew, attesting to one of two patterns: (1) *qattāl > qittôl* (with Canaanite shift), as in גִּבּוֹר "mighty man, warrior" and שִׁכּוֹר "drunkard;" (2) *qattāl > qattāl* (without Canaanite shift), as in גַּנָּב "thief," חַטָּא "sinner," and חָרָשׁ "artisan." The latter development without the vowel shift from *ā > ō resulted in confusion with the nominal pattern *qattal > qattāl*, as in אַיָּל "deer," חַטָּא "sinful," and יַבָּשָׁה "dry ground." It is unknown why the vowel shift did not occur for some professional terms, but it resulted in potential confusion with other commonly attested patterns. See BL §67hγ–nγ.

8.6.3.1 Attributive

The attributive function of adjectives involves the description or qualification of a noun. Verbal adjectives routinely occur in the attributive position, agreeing with the modified noun in number, gender, and definiteness. Attributive adjectives usually follow the nouns they modify. Leviticus 5:2 shows the verbal adjective טָמֵא "unclean" modifying indefinite nouns that are either masculine or feminine:

Lev 5:2

אֹו נֶפֶשׁ אֲשֶׁר תִּגַּע בְּכָל־דָּבָר טָמֵא אֹו בְנִבְלַת חַיָּה טְמֵאָה אֹו בְּנִבְלַת בְּהֵמָה
טְמֵאָה אֹו בְּנִבְלַת שֶׁרֶץ טָמֵא וְנֶעְלַם מִמֶּנּוּ וְהוּא טָמֵא וְאָשֵׁם׃

Or if a person touches any **unclean thing** (M)—whether an **unclean animal** (F) carcass, or **an unclean beast** (F) carcass, or an **unclean swarming** (M) carcass—even when it is concealed from him, he is unclean, and he is guilty.

Similarly, עָיֵף "weary" modifies אֶרֶץ "land" in Isa 32:2.

Isa 32:2

כְּפַלְגֵי־מַיִם בְּצָיֹון כְּצֵל סֶלַע־כָּבֵד בְּאֶרֶץ עֲיֵפָה

like streams of water in a dry land, like the shade of a great rock **in a weary land**

The proper name Philistines takes a definite verbal adjective in Judg 14:3.

Judg 14:3

הַאֵין בִּבְנֹות אַחֶיךָ וּבְכָל־עַמִּי אִשָּׁה כִּי־אַתָּה הֹולֵךְ לָקַחַת אִשָּׁה מִפְּלִשְׁתִּים
הָעֲרֵלִים

Is there not a woman among the daughters of your brothers or among any of my people that you are going to take a woman **from the uncircumcised Philistines**?

The participle also functions attributively, but the semantics of the participle is such that the attributive qualifier is a verbal action. For example, the *Niphal* participle describes King Saul's attendants as stationed at his side:

1 Sam 22:17

וַיֹּאמֶר הַמֶּלֶךְ לָרָצִים הַנִּצָּבִים עָלָיו

And the king spoke **to the attendants who were stationed** beside him.

The young men sent out to survey the land of Canaan are defined by their surveying activity, expressed in this context with a *Piel* participle:

Josh 2:1

וַיִּשְׁלַח יְהֹושֻׁעַ־בִּן־נוּן מִן־הַשִּׁטִּים שְׁנַיִם־אֲנָשִׁים מְרַגְּלִים חֶרֶשׁ לֵאמֹר לְכוּ רְאוּ
אֶת־הָאָרֶץ וְאֶת־יְרִיחֹו

Joshua, son of Nun, secretly sent two **surveying men** from Shittim, saying, "Go, see the land, especially Jericho."

These two spies are referenced again in Josh 6:22 with a definite attributive construction:

Josh 6:22

וְלִשְׁנַ֨יִם הָאֲנָשִׁ֤ים הַֽמְרַגְּלִים֙ אֶת־הָאָ֔רֶץ אָמַ֣ר יְהוֹשֻׁ֗עַ בֹּ֚אוּ בֵּית־הָאִשָּׁ֣ה הַזּוֹנָ֔ה

וְהוֹצִ֨יאוּ מִשָּׁ֤ם אֶת־הָֽאִשָּׁה֙ וְאֶת־כָּל־אֲשֶׁר־לָ֔הּ כַּאֲשֶׁ֖ר נִשְׁבַּעְתֶּ֥ם לָֽהּ׃

To the two **men who had surveyed** the land Joshua said: "Go to the house of the woman harlot and bring out from there the woman and all who belong to her, as you swore to her."

The *Hiphil* participle describes the activity of Yahweh's messenger in 2 Sam 24.

2 Sam 24:17

וַיֹּאמֶר֩ דָּוִ֨ד אֶל־יְהוָ֜ה בִּרְאֹת֣וֹ ׀ אֶת־הַמַּלְאָ֣ךְ ׀ הַמַּכֶּ֣ה בָעָ֗ם וַיֹּ֙אמֶר֙ הִנֵּ֨ה אָנֹכִ֤י חָטָ֙אתִי֙

וְאָנֹכִ֣י הֶעֱוֵ֔יתִי וְאֵ֥לֶּה הַצֹּ֖אן מֶ֣ה עָשׂ֑וּ תְּהִ֨י נָ֤א יָדְךָ֙ בִּ֔י וּבְבֵ֥ית אָבִֽי׃

David spoke to Yahweh when he saw **the messenger striking** the people and said, "Look, I myself have sinned and I myself have committed iniquity, but as for these sheep, what have they done? Please, let your hand be against me and the house of my father."

8.6.3.2 Substantive

The substantive position constitutes an independent use of the adjective as a nominal. Substantivized verbal adjectives and participles fill the same slot as nouns, having the potential to serve as subjects and objects of verbal clauses, or as nominal modifiers in a variety of construct and prepositional phrases. This syntactical function is usually marked by the addition of the article.[89] Verbal adjectives describe states or conditions, so that the focus then shifts to the one possessing those qualities rather than the qualities themselves. For participles, the article places the focus on the actor doing the action, rather than the action itself. It is important to clarify, however, that substantivized participles do not actually transform into nouns since, like all adjectives, they are not self-referential. The participle still requires a null referent, such as "*one* who does X."[90]

a. Subject of a Verb

Isaiah 28:16

הַֽמַּאֲמִ֖ין לֹ֥א יָחִֽישׁ

The one believing will not make haste.

---

[89] See Joüon-Muraoka §154fc n. 5.

[90] This observation is not intended to ignore the challenges of professional terms that have adopted the *Qal* active participle pattern, as outlined above.

Ezek 39:15

וְעָבְר֣וּ הָעֹבְרִים֮ בָּאָרֶץ֒ וְרָאָה֙ עֶ֣צֶם אָדָ֔ם וּבָנָ֥ה אֶצְל֖וֹ צִיּ֑וּן עַ֣ד קָבְר֤וּ אֹתוֹ֙ הַֽמְקַבְּרִ֔ים אֶל־גֵּ֖יא הֲמ֥וֹן גּֽוֹג׃

Those passing by will pass through the land and see the bone of a man and build it as a monument, until **those burying** have buried it in the valley of Hamon-Gog.

Amos 5:13

לָכֵ֗ן הַמַּשְׂכִּ֛יל בָּעֵ֥ת הַהִ֖יא יִדֹּ֑ם כִּ֛י עֵ֥ת רָעָ֖ה הִֽיא׃

Therefore, **those acting prudently** at that time will be silent, for it is an evil time.

b. Object of a Verb

Exod 12:32

וּפָסַ֤ח יְהוָה֙ עַל־הַפֶּ֔תַח וְלֹ֤א יִתֵּן֙ הַמַּשְׁחִ֔ית לָבֹ֥א אֶל־בָּתֵּיכֶ֖ם לִנְגֹּֽף

Yahweh will pass over the doorway and not allow **the one destroying** to enter into their house to strike (you).

c. Second Member of a Construct Phrase

2 Kgs 14:6

וְאֶת־בְּנֵ֥י הַמַּכִּ֖ים לֹ֣א הֵמִ֑ית כַּכָּת֣וּב בְּסֵ֣פֶר תּֽוֹרַת־מֹשֶׁ֗ה אֲשֶׁר־צִוָּ֨ה יְהוָ֜ה לֵאמֹ֗ר לֹא־יוּמְת֨וּ אָב֤וֹת עַל־בָּנִים֙ וּבָנִים֙ לֹא־יוּמְת֣וּ עַל־אָב֔וֹת כִּ֛י אִם־אִ֥ישׁ בְּחֶטְא֖וֹ יָמֻֽתוּ׃

The sons **of those who were slaying** he did not put to death according to what is written in the book of the Torah of Moses which Yahweh commanded saying, "Fathers shall not be put to death for sons, and sons shall not be put to death for fathers, but only shall a man be put to death for his own guilt."

d. Object of a Preposition

Isa 29:21

מַחֲטִיאֵ֤י אָדָם֙ בְּדָבָ֔ר וְלַמּוֹכִ֥יחַ בַּשַּׁ֖עַר יְקֹשׁ֑וּן וַיַּטּ֥וּ בַתֹּ֖הוּ צַדִּֽיק׃

They cause a person to err in word, and lay a snare **for the one adjudicating** at the gate, and have turned aside the righteous in emptiness.

e. Vocative

Isa 51:1

שִׁמְע֥וּ אֵלַ֛י רֹ֥דְפֵי צֶ֖דֶק מְבַקְשֵׁ֥י יְהוָ֑ה

Listen to me, O **those pursuing** righteousness, **those seeking** Yahweh.

f. Apposition

1 Sam 14:6

וַיֹּאמֶר יְהוֹנָתָן אֶל־הַנַּעַר | **נֹשֵׂא** כֵלָיו לְכָה וְנַעְבְּרָה אֶל־מַצַּב הָעֲרֵלִים הָאֵלֶּה

Jonathan said to the young man, **bearer** of his armor, "Come, let us cross
over to the garrison of these uncircumcised men."

g. Substantive Used as Subject without an Article

Jonah 2:9

מְשַׁמְּרִים הַבְלֵי־שָׁוְא חַסְדָּם יַעֲזֹבוּ׃

Those who observe the futility of idols will forsake their loyalty.

There are several instances in Biblical Hebrew where a definite participle appears to function as a predicate. As we have outlined above for the adjective more generally, the syntax for predicate adjectives requires them to be indefinite, as in הוּא טוֹב "he is good," or הָאָרֶץ יָפָה "the land is beautiful." By definition, a participle marked as definite cannot occupy the predicate adjective position. However, substantival participles can and do occupy the predicate position of a nominal clause. The following examples are noteworthy:

Gen 2:13

וְשֵׁם־הַנָּהָר הַשֵּׁנִי גִּיחוֹן הוּא **הַסּוֹבֵב** אֵת כָּל־אֶרֶץ כּוּשׁ׃

The name of the second river is Gishon: it is **the one flowing throughout**
all the land of Cush.

Deut 31:8

וַיהוָֹה הוּא | **הַהֹלֵךְ** לְפָנֶיךָ

Yahweh is **the one going** before you.

Josh 23:3 (cf. 23:10)

וְאַתֶּם רְאִיתֶם אֵת כָּל־אֲשֶׁר עָשָׂה יְהוָה אֱלֹהֵיכֶם לְכָל־הַגּוֹיִם הָאֵלֶּה מִפְּנֵיכֶם כִּי
יְהוָה אֱלֹהֵיכֶם הוּא **הַנִּלְחָם** לָכֶם׃

You have seen all that Yahweh your God has done to all these nations
from before you, for Yahweh your God is **the one fighting** for you.

2 Sam 20:24

וִיהוֹשָׁפָט בֶּן־אֲחִילוּד **הַמַּזְכִּיר**

Jehoshaphat, son of Ahilud, was **the one recording**.

In each example, the article requires us to analyze the form as a substantive participle functioning as a predicate nominative. The outcome of this analysis is that the expression places the focus on the individual or entity who is doing the activity rather than the activity itself, "It is X who/which does Y." In many instances this construction takes a pronominal copula, as in Gen 2:13, Deut 31:8, and Josh 23:3, but it is not required, as 2 Sam 20:24 demonstrates. This distinction is brought into sharper focus when one compares a similar expression constructed as a predicate adjective. For example, 1 Samuel offers a helpful contrast for the example of Deut 31:8 from above:

1 Sam 25:28

שָׂא נָא לְפֶשַׁע אֲמָתֶךָ כִּי עָשֹׂה־יַעֲשֶׂה יְהוָה לַאדֹנִי בַּיִת נֶאֱמָן כִּי־מִלְחֲמוֹת יְהוָה
אֲדֹנִי נִלְחָם וְרָעָה לֹא־תִמָּצֵא בְךָ מִיָּמֶיךָ:

Please, forgive the transgression of your maidservant, for Yahweh will indeed make for my lord a firm dynasty, for Yahweh my Lord is **fighting** the battles and evil will not be found in you all your days.

The predicate construction simply asserts that Yahweh is fighting on David's behalf to establish the Davidic dynasty. In contrast, the expression in Josh 23:3 emphasizes that Yahweh himself is the one fighting the Canaanite nations on behalf of Israel. A similar contrast emerges in 1 Kings:

1 Kgs 4:3

אֱלִיחֹרֶף וַאֲחִיָּה בְּנֵי שִׁישָׁא סֹפְרִים יְהוֹשָׁפָט בֶּן־אֲחִילוּד הַמַּזְכִּיר:

Elihoreph and Ahijah, sons of Shisha, were scribes; Jehoshaphat, son of Ahilud was **the one recording**.

Elihoreph and Ahijah are functioning as scribes, but the focus is shifted to Jehoshaphat who is the one recording what is happening.

1 Kgs 3:3

וַיֶּאֱהַב שְׁלֹמֹה אֶת־יְהוָה לָלֶכֶת בְּחֻקּוֹת דָּוִד אָבִיו רַק בַּבָּמוֹת הוּא מְזַבֵּחַ וּמַקְטִיר:

Solomon loved Yahweh by walking in the statutes of David his father, only at the high places he was **sacrificing** and **burning incense**.

The example from 1 Kgs 3:3, however, simply describes the actions of Solomon by using a typical predicate adjective construction—he was sacrificing and burning incense—and does not focus on the fact that Solomon is the one doing the activity as opposed to someone else.

These examples highlight the difficulty in identifying the subject of verbless clauses when both constituents are definite. Ellen van Wolde discusses this problem in terms of the degree of definiteness between two given constituents in a verbless clause. She notes that one of the clausal constituents is taken as the starting point and provides the focus of the clause, while the other constituent offers information about the topic of focus.[91] Identifying which constituent functions as

---

[91] Van Wolde, "Verbless Cause," 330–33. A similar approach has been proposed by Eugen van Ness Goetchinus for Greek equative verbal clauses. He notes that when two nominative nouns are connected by an equative verb (e.g., εἰμί, γίνομαι), "the more definite of the two is the subject." He outlines the following parameters: (a) if one of the two nouns is a proper name, it is the subject; (b) if only one of the nouns has the article, it is the subject; (c) if both nouns are equally definite (or indefinite), the one with the narrower reference is the subject; (d) if one of the two nouns has been referenced in the immediate context, it is the subject; (e) if the clause contains a pronoun, it is the subject. See *The Language of the New Testament* (New York: Scribner, 1965), 58–59. Similarly, Daniel

the starting point or subject when both exhibit some level of definiteness requires one to consider definiteness as a continuum or degree of definiteness. Van Wolde proposes maximal definiteness versus minimal definiteness as two poles on a continuum. Proper nouns are considered maximally definite, while definite nouns, demonstrative articles, definite numerals, and nouns with direct object marker אֵת are somewhat less definite. Moving in the other direction on the continuum, independent pronouns, nouns with pronominal suffixes, indefinite nouns, and indefinite numerals are closer to indefiniteness, whereas clitic pronouns and zero anaphora are maximally indefinite. She outlines this continuum as follows:

DEFINITENESS MAXIMAL

↑

proper noun (person or place names)

definite noun

demonstrative article

definite numeral

noun with direct object marker אֵת

independent pronoun

noun with pronominal suffix

indefinite noun

indefinite numeral

clitic pronoun

↓   zero anaphora

DEFINITENESS MINIMAL

Van Wolde eschews the terms "subject" and "predicate" as inadequate as a means of accounting for the syntactical features of Hebrew verbless clauses. Instead, she distinguishes "given" versus "new" information. Given elements have already been introduced in the context and are therefore more readily identified by the reader. Given information therefore tends to be less definite. Newly introduced elements are unfamiliar to the reader and are typically marked as more definite, necessitating that they be defined by the more "known" element of the clause. When the given, less definite element is in the first position, it marks continuity with the surrounding context. When a new, more definite element occurs in the first

---

Wallace has adapted the approach of Lane McGaughy (*Toward a Descriptive Analysis of* εἶναι *as a Linking Verb in New Testament Greek*, SBL Dissertation Series 6 [Missoula, MT: Society of Biblical Literature, 1972], 68–72), who criticizes Goetchius's criteria for indiscriminately mixing categories: (a) and (b) are grammatical, (d) is contextual, and (c) is semantic. McGaughy offers three rules: (1) the subject is a pronoun; (2) the subject is articular; and (3) the subject is a proper name. Wallace adds the following "pecking order" reminiscent of van Wolde's continuum: (1) the pronoun has the greatest priority, and (2) articular nouns and proper names appear to have equal priority; if both occur, word order may determine which constituent has priority. See Daniel B. Wallace, *Greek Grammar beyond the Basics: An Exegetical Syntax of the New Testament* (Grand Rapids: Zondervan, 1996), 44.

position, it indicates a break in the topic chain and garners new focus. Regardless of the problems with the terminology "subject" and "predicate," we still must decide which element to place in the subject slot and which one to mark as predicate. According to van Wolde's framework, the given, less definite word corresponds to the traditional subject, which is defined by the new, more definite word in the predicate position.[92] If we apply this logic to the above examples of the substantive participles, all the articular participles are in the subject slot:

Deut 31:8

וַיהוָ֣ה ה֗וּא | הַהֹלֵ֣ךְ לְפָנֶ֔יךָ

The one going before you is Yahweh.

Josh 23:3

יְהוָ֤ה אֱלֹֽהֵיכֶם֙ ה֣וּא הַנִּלְחָ֣ם לָכֶ֑ם

The one fighting for you is Yahweh your God.

2 Sam 20:4

וִיהוֹשָׁפָ֥ט בֶּן־אֲחִיל֖וּד הַמַּזְכִּֽיר

The one recording was Jehoshaphat, son of Ahilud.

In each of these examples, the articular participles are less definite than the proper name, according to van Wolde's continuum, and thus constitute given information. The proper names further identify or qualify each known entity. The one walking before the Israelites (Deut 31:8) or fighting for them (Josh 23:3) is identified as Yahweh. The person recording in 2 Sam 20:4 is identified as Jehoshaphat. The more definite proper names in these examples occur in the first position and therefore mark a break in the topic chain. The example from Gen 2:13, however, places the more definite element in the second position. The independent personal pronoun is less definite than the articular participle.

Gen 2:13

ה֥וּא הַסּוֹבֵ֕ב אֵ֖ת כָּל־אֶ֥רֶץ כּֽוּשׁ

It is **the one flowing throughout** all the land of Cush.

When the known entity is in first position, it marks topic continuity. Here, the articular infinitive describes the river Gihon identified in the preceding clause.

Van Wolde is critical of the "classification" versus "identification" model outlined in many grammars. However, van Wolde's approach is not entirely inconsistent with the classification versus identification framework as espoused by Andersen, since the main opposition is between Definite SUBJ–Indefinite PRED (classification) and Definite SUBJ–Definite PRED (identification) type clauses.[93] Van Wolde's analysis rather focuses on the identification clause to order the priority of each constituent on a continuum of lesser to maximal definiteness.

---

[92] As applied in Hardy, *Exegetical Gems*, 159–60.
[93] See Andersen, *Hebrew Verbless Clause*.

8.6.3.3 Predicate

The predicate position allows verbal adjectives and participles to function verbally. The stative quality of verbal adjectives means that they assert some quality or characteristic of the subject. This usage is already illustrated for predicate adjectives above. The participle, on the other hand, renders actions as opposed to states or conditions, which results in the predication of ongoing/imperfective action. This usage should be distinguished from substantive participles functioning as predicates of nominal clauses (i.e., predicate nominative).

Num 5:3

וְלֹא יְטַמְּאוּ אֶת־מַחֲנֵיהֶם אֲשֶׁר אֲנִי שֹׁכֵן בְּתוֹכָם

They shall not defile their camp where I am **dwelling** in their midst.

The meaning of this predicate construction with the *Qal* participle stresses the ongoing reality that Yahweh continually dwells amid Israel and results in the people's need to maintain purity within the camp. We note from this example that the subject comes before the participle, which here is a 1CS independent personal pronoun. The same is true of the 2MS pronoun in Genesis 13:

Gen 13:15

כִּי אֶת־כָּל־הָאָרֶץ אֲשֶׁר־אַתָּה רֹאֶה לְךָ אֶתְּנֶנָּה וּלְזַרְעֲךָ עַד־עוֹלָם:

For all the land which you are **seeing** I will give to you and your seed forever."

The word order of predicate participial clauses can be either SUBJ–PRED or PRED–SUBJ. The SUBJ–PRED position places the focus on identifying the actor, while PRED–SUBJ places the focus on the action being done by the actor.

a. SUBJ–PRED

Num 13:19

וּמָה הָאָרֶץ אֲשֶׁר־**הוּא** יֹשֵׁב בָּהּ הֲטוֹבָה הִוא אִם־רָעָה וּמָה הֶעָרִים אֲשֶׁר־**הוּא**
יוֹשֵׁב בָּהֵנָּה הַבְּמַחֲנִים אִם בְּמִבְצָרִים:

How is the land in which **he** [i.e. the people] **dwells**? Is [the land] good or bad? And how are the cities in which **he** [the people] **dwells**? Are [the cities] encampments or fortifications?

b. PRED–SUBJ

Judg 3:24

וַיֹּאמְרוּ אַךְ מֵסִיךְ **הוּא** אֶת־רַגְלָיו בַּחֲדַר הַמְּקֵרָה

They said, "Surely **he is covering** his feet in the cool chamber."

Verbal adjectives also exhibit both SUBJ–PRED and PRED–SUBJ word order, though its preference appears to be for the latter:[94]

---

[94] This preference may stem from the fact that the masculine singular forms resemble the *Qal* stative SC, which would favor verb-initial syntax. Whenever the *qātēl* pattern occurs with an

a. SUBJ–PRED

Gen 42:18

זֹאת עֲשׂוּ וִחְיוּ אֶת־הָאֱלֹהִים **אֲנִי יָרֵא**

Do this and live. **I fear** God.

1 Kgs 11:22

וַיֹּאמֶר לוֹ פַרְעֹה כִּי מַה־**אַתָּה חָסֵר** עִמִּי וְהִנְּךָ מְבַקֵּשׁ לָלֶכֶת אֶל־אַרְצֶךָ

Pharaoh said to him, "What do **you lack** from me that, look, you are seeking to go to your own land?"

b. PRED–SUBJ

Exod 7:27

וְאִם־**מָאֵן אַתָּה** לְשַׁלֵּחַ הִנֵּה אָנֹכִי נֹגֵף אֶת־כָּל־גְּבוּלְךָ בַּצְפַרְדְּעִים

If **you refuse** to send (them) away, I will strike all your region with frogs.

Josh 22:19

וְאַךְ אִם־**טְמֵאָה אֶרֶץ** אֲחֻזַּתְכֶם עִבְרוּ לָכֶם אֶל־אֶרֶץ אֲחֻזַּת יְהוָה אֲשֶׁר שָׁכַן־שָׁם
מִשְׁכַּן יְהוָה וְהֵאָחֲזוּ בְּתוֹכֵנוּ

Indeed, if **the land** of your possession **is unclean**, cross over into the land
of the possession of Yahweh where the dwelling of Yahweh resides and
take possession among us.

Like other adjectives, the subject of verbal adjectives and participles can occur
as a pronominal suffix attached to particles, such as הִנֵּה, אֵין, or עוֹד:

a. הִנֵּה

Num 24:14

וְעַתָּה **הִנְנִי הוֹלֵךְ** לְעַמִּי לְכָה אִיעָצְךָ אֲשֶׁר יַעֲשֶׂה הָעָם הַזֶּה לְעַמְּךָ בְּאַחֲרִית הַיָּמִים:

Now **look, I am going** to my people. Come, I will advise you as to what
this people will do to your people in the coming days.

b. אֵין

2 Kgs 17:34

אֵינָם יְרֵאִים אֶת־יְהוָה **וְאֵינָם עֹשִׂים** כְּחֻקֹּתָם וּכְמִשְׁפָּטָם וְכַתּוֹרָה וְכַמִּצְוָה אֲשֶׁר
צִוָּה יְהוָה אֶת־בְּנֵי יַעֲקֹב

They do not fear Yahweh, and **they do not act** according to their statutes,
their judgments, the law, or the commandment that Yahweh commanded
the sons of Jacob.

---

independent pronoun other than the 3MS, the form has to be analyzed as a verbal adjective, however,
as in מָאֵן אַתָּה "you are refusing."

c. עוֹד

1 Kgs 1:14

הִנֵּה **עוֹדָךְ מְדַבֶּרֶת** שָׁם עִם־הַמֶּלֶךְ וַאֲנִי אָבוֹא אַחֲרַיִךְ וּמִלֵּאתִי אֶת־דְּבָרָיִךְ:

Look, **while you are speaking** there with the king, I will go after you and confirm your words.

In a few instances, the predicate construction of the participle omits the subject, as in the following two examples from 1 Samuel:

1 Sam 6:3

אִם־**מְשַׁלְּחִים** אֶת־אֲרוֹן אֱלֹהֵי יִשְׂרָאֵל אַל־תְּשַׁלְּחוּ אֹתוֹ רֵיקָם

If (you) are **sending away** the ark of the God of Israel, do not send it away empty.

1 Sam 15:12

בָּא־שָׁאוּל הַכַּרְמֶלָה וְהִנֵּה **מַצִּיב** לוֹ יָד

Saul has gone to Carmel and look, (he) is **setting up** his own monument.

In all the predicate examples mentioned thus far, the time referent of the verbal adjectives or participles must be inferred from their context. The example from 1 Kgs 10:24 occurs in the context of a historical narration of what was happening at the time of Solomon's reign: וְכָל־הָאָרֶץ מְבַקְשִׁים אֶת־פְּנֵי שְׁלֹמֹה "All the earth *was* seeking the face of Solomon." The predicate participle allows the writer to report on the event vividly, showing the progressive nature of their coming to seek the wisdom of Solomon. This passage also shows what many scholars identify as background information to the narrative foreground of the story—whenever the baseline of the narrative sequence is interrupted by nonsequential constructions, it introduces circumstantial information.[95]

1 KINGS 10:23–26			
V.	**NARRATIVE FOREGROUND**	**NARRATIVE BACKGROUND**	**TRANSLATION**
23	**וַיִּגְדַּל** הַמֶּלֶךְ שְׁלֹמֹה ...		King Solomon **increased** ...
24		וְכָל־הָאָרֶץ מְבַקְשִׁים אֶת־פְּנֵי שְׁלֹמֹה ...	**Now all the land was seeking** the face of Solomon ...
25		וְהֵמָּה **מְבִאִים** אִישׁ מִנְחָתוֹ ...	Each one **brought** his gift ...

---

[95] See §5.8.1.

1 KINGS 10:23–26			
V.	NARRATIVE FOREGROUND	NARRATIVE BACKGROUND	TRANSLATION
26a	וַיֶּאֱסֹ֣ף שְׁלֹמֹה֮ רֶ֣כֶב וּפָרָשִׁים֒ ...		Solomon **gathered** chariotry and horsemen ...
26b	וַיְהִי־ל֗וֹ אֶ֤לֶף וְאַרְ־ בַּע־מֵא֣וֹת רֶ֔כֶב ...		**He had** 1,400 chariots ...
26c	וַיַּנְחֵם֙ בְּעָרֵ֣י הָרֶ֔כֶב ...		**He left** them in chariot cities ...

Driver comments briefly on the participle's use in circumstantial clauses, which he likewise describes as communicating narrative background and which are formally marked with fronted subjects.[96] The usage is technically a subcategory of the predicate participle. In another sense, the circumstantial participle could also be described as adverbial since it further defines the action of the main verb by indicating the circumstances in which it occurs. Circumstantial clauses in English are often introduced with words like *when*, *as*, or *while*. In Hebrew, the circumstantial participle describes the verb's contemporaneous circumstances rather than sequential or conjunctive verbal action. This usage resembles the more common adverbial function of the participle in Greek.[97] The most extensive treatment of the Hebrew circumstantial participle is found in Amnon Gordon's broader study of the participle in Biblical, Mishnaic, and Modern Hebrew.[98] The following examples illustrate the Hebrew circumstantial participle.

1 Sam 6:13

וּבֵית שֶׁמֶשׁ **קֹצְרִים** קְצִיר־חִטִּים בָּעֵמֶק וַיִּשְׂאוּ אֶת־עֵינֵיהֶם

As the household of Shemesh were **reaping** the wheat harvest in the valley, they lifted their eyes.

1 Sam 9:27

הֵמָּה **יֹרְדִים** בִּקְצֵה הָעִיר וּשְׁמוּאֵל אָמַר אֶל־שָׁאוּל

While they were **going** down to the end of the city, Samuel said to Saul.

Neh 2:6

וַיֹּ֩אמֶר֩ לִ֨י הַמֶּ֜לֶךְ וְהַשֵּׁגַ֣ל | **יוֹשֶׁ֣בֶת** אֶצְל֗וֹ

And the king said to me *as* the queen was **sitting** beside him.

---

[96] Driver, *Treatise*, 166 (and 159).
[97] See discussions in Wallace, *Greek Grammar*, 622–40; Köstenberger, Merkle, and Plummer, *New Testament Greek*, 327–35.
[98] Gordon, "Development of the Participle," 15–17.

Hebrew is also able to mark explicitly predicate verbal adjectives and participles for aspect with the addition of the auxiliary verb היה. This use of the participle is sometimes called <u>periphrastic</u>, similar to Greek periphrastic constructions consisting of the verb εἰμι + the participle and Aramaic periphrastic construction, הוה + participle. Hebrew periphrastic constructions cease to offer background information, but instead they incorporate predicate verbal adjectives and participles into the foreground of the narrative baseline in the case of third-person expressions. This construction is also common in direct discourse (i.e., first and second person). The suffix conjugation and consecutive preterite forms of היה mark perfective aspect, while the prefix conjugation and *wəqātal* mark imperfective.[99]

a. Perfective Constructions

2 Kgs 4:1

וְאַתָּ֣ה יָדַ֔עְתָּ כִּ֣י עַבְדְּךָ֗ הָיָ֤ה יָרֵא֙ אֶת־יְהוָ֔ה

You did not know that your servant was **fearful** of Yahweh.

Deut 9:22

וּבְתַבְעֵרָה֙ וּבְמַסָּ֔ה וּבְקִבְרֹ֖ת הַֽתַּאֲוָ֑ה מַקְצִפִ֥ים הֱיִיתֶ֖ם אֶת־יְהוָֽה׃

At Taberah, Massah, and Kibroth-Hattaavah **you were provoking** Yahweh.

Judg 16:21

וַֽיְהִ֥י טוֹחֵ֖ן בְּבֵ֥ית האסורים[100]

He was grinding at the prison house.

b. Imperfective Constructions

Lev 15:26

וְכָֽל־הַכְּלִ֗י אֲשֶׁ֧ר תֵּשֵׁ֛ב עָלָ֖יו טָמֵ֣א יִהְיֶ֑ה כְּטֻמְאַ֖ת נִדָּתָֽהּ

Any vessel upon which she sits will be **unclean** according to the uncleanness of her impurity.

Deut 16:15

כִּ֣י יְבָרֶכְךָ֞ יְהוָ֣ה אֱלֹהֶ֗יךָ בְּכֹ֤ל תְּבוּאָֽתְךָ֙ וּבְכֹל֙ מַעֲשֵׂ֣ה יָדֶ֔יךָ וְהָיִ֖יתָ אַ֥ךְ שָׂמֵֽחַ

For Yahweh your God will bless you in all your labor and in all the work of your hands, so that **you will be** wholly **joyful**.

Deut 28:29

וְהָיִ֜יתָ מְמַשֵּׁ֣שׁ בַּֽצָּהֳרַ֗יִם כַּאֲשֶׁ֨ר יְמַשֵּׁ֤שׁ הָעִוֵּר֙ בָּאֲפֵלָ֔ה

You will be groping at noonday as a blindman gropes in darkness.

---

[99] For more on these conjugations, see chapter 4.

[100] *Ketiv*: הָאֲסִירִים.

There are other uses of the auxiliary verb היה that fall outside the confines of the above description. Some *Qal* active participles have functionally become professional terms, as mentioned above, and thus occur as predicate nominatives. Sometimes these constructions are likewise marked apsectually, as in the notation regarding the occupations of Cain and Abel:

Gen 4:2

וַיְהִי־הֶ֫בֶל רֹ֫עֵה צֹאן וְקַ֫יִן הָיָה עֹבֵד אֲדָמָה

Abel **was a tender of** sheep, but Cain **was a worker of** the ground.

8.7 ADVERBIAL ADJECTIVES

Hebrew adjectives and verbal adjectives are also able to function adverbially. In this adverbial function, adjectives further define/describe the verbal action in much the same way that they modify nouns attributively. The following examples illustrate this usage for adjectives in general.

Adjectives

Gen 15:2

וְאָנֹכִי הוֹלֵךְ עֲרִירִי

I go along **childless**.

Gen 42:30

דִּבֶּר הָאִישׁ אֲדֹנֵי הָאָ֫רֶץ אִתָּ֫נוּ קָשׁוֹת

The man, the lord of the land, spoke with us **harshly**.

Ps 15:2

הוֹלֵךְ תָּמִים וּפֹעֵל צֶ֫דֶק וְדֹבֵר אֱמֶת בִּלְבָבוֹ׃

the one who walks **blamelessly** and who practices righteousness and who speaks in his heart

Verbal Adjectives

2 Sam 16:14

וַיָּבֹא הַמֶּ֫לֶךְ וְכָל־הָעָם אֲשֶׁר־אִתּוֹ עֲיֵפִים וַיִּנָּפֵשׁ שָׁם׃

The king and all the people with him arrived **weary**, and he was refreshed.

2 Sam 18:25

וַיֵּ֫לֶךְ הָלוֹךְ וְקָרֵב

He came nearer and **nearer** (lit. coming and **approaching**).

Isa 20:2

וַיַּ֫עַשׂ כֵּן הָלֹךְ עָרוֹם וְיָחֵף

And he did so, going along naked and **barefoot**.

The last two examples occur in conjunction with the infinitive absolute. We discuss the nature of the infinitive absolute in chapter 9, where we define it as a nonfinite verbal form that can function both verbally and nominally. In these cases, the verbal adjective adjoined to an infinitive absolute may result in its mirroring the nominal function of the infinitive absolute as an adverbial accusative (see §9.6.1).

This chapter surveyed the meaning and function of pronouns, adjectives, and participles. Sometimes these grammatical categories overlap in their semantic and syntactical properties. Nonetheless, students will find the threefold uses of the adjective a helpful means of mapping the morphosyntactic diversity. These function as attributive, substantival, and predicate.

8.8 EXERCISES

Translate the following Hebrew sentences into English. Identify the morphological pattern and syntactical function of the adjectives in the following verses.

1. מֵקִים מֵעָפָר דָּל מֵאַשְׁפֹּת יָרִים אֶבְיוֹן לְהוֹשִׁיב עִם־נְדִיבִים וְכִסֵּא כָבוֹד יַנְחִלֵם
כִּי לַיהוָה מְצֻקֵי אֶרֶץ וַיָּשֶׁת עֲלֵיהֶם תֵּבֵל: (1 Sam 2:8)

2. וְלוֹ־הָיָה בֵן וּשְׁמוֹ שָׁאוּל בָּחוּר וָטוֹב וְאֵין אִישׁ מִבְּנֵי יִשְׂרָאֵל טוֹב מִמֶּנּוּ מִשִּׁכְמוֹ
וָמַעְלָה גָּבֹהַּ מִכָּל־הָעָם: (1 Sam 9:2)

3. צַהֲלִי וָרֹנִּי יוֹשֶׁבֶת צִיּוֹן כִּי־גָדוֹל בְּקִרְבֵּךְ קְדוֹשׁ יִשְׂרָאֵל: (Isa 12:6)

4. הוֹלֵךְ תָּמִים וּפֹעֵל צֶדֶק וְדֹבֵר אֱמֶת בִּלְבָבוֹ: (Ps 15:2)

5. גַּם מִזֵּדִים חֲשֹׂךְ עַבְדֶּךָ אַל־יִמְשְׁלוּ־בִי אָז אֵיתָם וְנִקֵּיתִי מִפֶּשַׁע רָב: (Ps 19:14)

Translate the following sentences. Identify the morphological stem and syntactical function of the participles in the following verses.

6. וְהָאָרֶץ הָיְתָה תֹהוּ וָבֹהוּ וְחֹשֶׁךְ עַל־פְּנֵי תְהוֹם וְרוּחַ אֱלֹהִים מְרַחֶפֶת עַל־פְּנֵי הַמָּיִם: (Gen 1:2)

7. לֵךְ אֶל־פַּרְעֹה בַּבֹּקֶר הִנֵּה יֹצֵא הַמַּיְמָה וְנִצַּבְתָּ לִקְרָאתוֹ עַל־שְׂפַת הַיְאֹר וְהַמַּטֶּה אֲשֶׁר־נֶהְפַּךְ לְנָחָשׁ תִּקַּח בְּיָדֶךָ: (Exod 7:15)

8. כִּי כָּל־אֹכֵל חֵלֶב מִן־הַבְּהֵמָה אֲשֶׁר יַקְרִיב מִמֶּנָּה אִשֶּׁה לַיהוָה וְנִכְרְתָה הַנֶּפֶשׁ הָאֹכֶלֶת מֵעַמֶּיהָ: (Lev 7:25)

9. כִּי אָנֹכִי מֵת בָּאָרֶץ הַזֹּאת אֵינֶנִּי עֹבֵר אֶת־הַיַּרְדֵּן וְאַתֶּם עֹבְרִים וִירִשְׁתֶּם אֶת־הָאָרֶץ הַטּוֹבָה הַזֹּאת: (Deut 4:22)

Translate the following verse. Apply van Wolde's continuum of definiteness to the following participial clause as a means of identifying the subject from the predicate.

10. הֵם הַמְדַבְּרִים אֶל־פַּרְעֹה מֶלֶךְ־מִצְרַיִם לְהוֹצִיא אֶת־בְּנֵי־יִשְׂרָאֵל מִמִּצְרָיִם הוּא מֹשֶׁה וְאַהֲרֹן: (Exod 6:27)

Translate from English to Hebrew

11. I am not a beast. I am your servant, king of Israel.

12. Moses lifted his hands to heaven to conquer the foreign city.

13. The rich are not wise or upright. They are not greater than the poor.

14. I am sitting in the house of God. I am fearing him with my whole heart.

15. The one judging the people seeks the elders and prophets.

Guided Reading: Ezek 18:1–13

1 וַיְהִי דְבַר־יְהוָה אֵלַי לֵאמֹר: 2 מַה־לָּכֶם אַתֶּם מֹשְׁלִים אֶת־הַמָּשָׁל הַזֶּה עַל־אַדְמַת יִשְׂ־
רָאֵל לֵאמֹר אָבוֹת יֹאכְלוּ בֹסֶר וְשִׁנֵּי הַבָּנִים תִּקְהֶינָה: 3 חַי־אָנִי נְאֻם אֲדֹנָי יְהוִה אִם־יִהְיֶה
לָכֶם עוֹד מְשֹׁל הַמָּשָׁל הַזֶּה בְּיִשְׂרָאֵל: 4 הֵן כָּל־הַנְּפָשׁוֹת לִי הֵנָּה כְּנֶפֶשׁ הָאָב וּכְנֶפֶשׁ הַבֵּן
לִי־הֵנָּה הַנֶּפֶשׁ הַחֹטֵאת הִיא תָמוּת: 5 וְאִישׁ כִּי־יִהְיֶה צַדִּיק וְעָשָׂה מִשְׁפָּט וּצְדָקָה: 6 אֶל־
הֶהָרִים לֹא אָכָל וְעֵינָיו לֹא נָשָׂא אֶל־גִּלּוּלֵי בֵּית יִשְׂרָאֵל וְאֶת־אֵשֶׁת רֵעֵהוּ לֹא טִמֵּא וְאֶל־
אִשָּׁה נִדָּה לֹא יִקְרָב: 7 וְאִישׁ לֹא יוֹנֶה חֲבֹלָתוֹ חוֹב יָשִׁיב גְּזֵלָה לֹא יִגְזֹל לַחְמוֹ לְרָעֵב יִתֵּן
וְעֵירֹם יְכַסֶּה־בָּגֶד: 8 בַּנֶּשֶׁךְ לֹא־יִתֵּן וְתַרְבִּית לֹא יִקָּח מֵעָוֶל יָשִׁיב יָדוֹ מִשְׁפַּט אֱמֶת יַעֲשֶׂה
בֵּין אִישׁ לְאִישׁ: 9 בְּחֻקּוֹתַי יְהַלֵּךְ וּמִשְׁפָּטַי שָׁמַר לַעֲשׂוֹת אֱמֶת צַדִּיק הוּא חָיֹה יִחְיֶה נְאֻם
אֲדֹנָי יְהוִה: 10 וְהוֹלִיד בֵּן־פָּרִיץ שֹׁפֵךְ דָּם וְעָשָׂה אָח מֵאַחַד מֵאֵלֶּה: 11 וְהוּא אֶת־כָּל־אֵלֶּה
לֹא עָשָׂה כִּי גַם אֶל־הֶהָרִים אָכָל וְאֶת־אֵשֶׁת רֵעֵהוּ טִמֵּא: 12 עָנִי וְאֶבְיוֹן הוֹנָה גְּזֵלוֹת גָּזָל
חֲבֹל לֹא יָשִׁיב וְאֶל־הַגִּלּוּלִים נָשָׂא עֵינָיו תּוֹעֵבָה עָשָׂה: 13 בַּנֶּשֶׁךְ נָתַן וְתַרְבִּית לָקַח וָחָי לֹא
יִחְיֶה אֵת כָּל־הַתּוֹעֵבוֹת הָאֵלֶּה עָשָׂה מוֹת יוּמָת דָּמָיו בּוֹ יִהְיֶה:

VOCABULARY AND NOTES

Verse 2

מֹשְׁלִים	Qal				"quote a proverb"
מָשָׁל		N.MS			"proverb; saying"
בֹסֶר		N.MS			"unripe (i.e., sour) grapes" [collective]
שִׁנֵּי		N.FP CSTR			"tooth"
תִּקְהֶינָה	Qal	PC 3FP		קהה	"be sensitive"

Verse 4

Hebrew	Stem	Parsing	Root	Gloss
הֵן		INTJ		"behold" (הִנֵּה)
נְפָשׁוֹת		N.FP		"life, person"
הֵנָּה		IPP 3FP		"they"
חֹטֵאת	Qal	ACT PTCL FS	חטא	
תָּמוּת	Qal	PC 3FS	מות	

Verse 5

Hebrew	Stem	Parsing	Root	Gloss
צְדָקָה		N.FS		"righteousness" (ADJ צַדִּיק)

Verse 6

Hebrew	Stem	Parsing	Root	Gloss
גִּלּוּלֵי		N.MP CSTR		"idol"
רֵעֵהוּ		N.MS + 3MS SF	רֵעַ	"neighbor"
טִמֵּא	Piel	SC 3MS	טמא	"defile"
נִדָּה		N.FS		"menstruation; impurity"

Verse 7

Hebrew	Stem	Parsing	Root	Gloss
יוֹנֶה	Hiphil	PC 3MS	ינה	"treat violently"
חֲבֹלָתוֹ		N.FS + 3MS SF		"(debt) collateral"
חוֹב		N.MS		"debt"
יָשִׁיב	Hiphil			"give back"
גְּזֵלָה		N.FS		"plunder"
יִגְזֹל	Qal			"seize, rob"
רָעֵב		ADJ.MS		"hungry" (person)
עֵירֹם		ADJ.MS		"naked" (person)
יְכַסֶּה	Piel PC	3MS	כסה	"cover"

Verse 8

Hebrew	Stem	Parsing	Root	Gloss
נֶשֶׁךְ		N.MS		"interest" [on money]
תַּרְבִּית		N.FS		"profit" [on food]
עָוֶל		N.MS		"injustice"
אֱמֶת		N.FS		"truth"

Verse 9

Hebrew	Stem	Parsing	Root	Gloss
חֻקּוֹתַי		N.FP + 1CS SF	חֻקָּה	"statute"

יֵהָלֵךְ	*Piel*	PC 3MS	הלך בְּ-	"walk in; follow"
חָיָה	*Qal*	INF ABS	חיה	

Verse 10

הוֹלִיד	*Hiphil*	SC 3MS	ילד	"beget"
פָּרִיץ		N.MS		"criminal"
שֹׁפֵךְ	*Qal*			"shed" (+ דָם "blood")
אָח		INTJ		"alas!" (not אָח "brother")

Verse 12

עָנִי		ADJ.MS		"poor, afflicted"
אֶבְיוֹן		ADJ.MS		"needy"
הוֹנָה	*Hiphil*	SC 3MS	ינה	
חֲבֹל		N.MS		"pledge" (חֲבֹלָתוֹ in v. 7)
תּוֹעֵבָה		N.FS		"abomination"

Verse 13

מוֹת	*Qal*	INF ABS	מות	
יוּמָת	*Hophal*	PC 3MS		"be killed"

//////////////

CHAPTER 9

INFINITIVES AND TEMPORAL CLAUSES

The grammar of Hebrew infinitives is significantly different than in English. Unlike the English infinitive *to write*, the base form of the Hebrew verb is not the infinitive, לִכְתֹּב "to write." This distinction is held by the third masculine singular form of the *Qal* suffix conjugation, כָּתַב "he wrote." Also, Hebrew infinitives have several specialized uses that are not found in English. They function to mark verbal prominence, to replace finite verbs, to explain a prior concept, and to provide a temporal setting. Very few of these uses are congruent with the English infinitive, so special attention should be paid to the functional differences. Even so, the infinitives overlap morphosyntactically with imperatives in both languages. Hebrew and English infinitives share similarities in syntax as nominalizers that take objects and adverbial modifiers and in semantics as representing non-indicative modalities.

9.1 GOING DEEPER WITH INFINITIVES

The opening chapters of 1 Samuel portray the rise of the lad Samuel to his special role as Yahweh's prophet while at the same time recount Eli's tragic demise. We are most familiar with Yahweh's pronouncement of judgment against Eli's house by the mouth of the young prophet Samuel. Currently under the authority of Eli in the Shiloh temple, Samuel relays the message to his mentor that judgment awaits his household. Samuel was not the first to declare this unfavorable oracle to Eli, however.

1 Samuel 2 outlines the sins of Eli's sons, the infamous Hophni and Phinehas. They are introduced as בְּנֵי בְלִיָּעַל "sons of Belial" (v. 12). The narrative chronicles their brute force in selfishly demanding the choicest of the temple offerings from those who offered them (vv. 13–17) and openly committing sexual misconduct

409

with female temple attendants (v. 22). Eli makes a feeble attempt to rebuke their reprehensible behavior, but it goes unheeded, thus portraying Eli as doing too little too late to curtail the wickedness that had taken root in the Shiloh cult.

In the midst of the narrative, an anonymous אִישׁ־אֱלֹהִים "man of God" approaches the elderly Eli with a message of rebuke. Kyle McCarter notes the parallel reference to an anonymous "man of God" in 1 Kgs 13:1–3 who delivers God's word of judgment against Jeroboam.[1] The context in that passage is similar to this one in signaling the doom of Jeroboam's dynasty. The oracle against Eli's household may be divided into the following sections:

1. Role of the priestly office (vv. 27–28).
2. Dereliction of the priestly office (v. 29).
3. Sentence against the priestly officers (vv. 30–34, 36).
4. Provision of a faithful priest (v. 35).

As commentators have observed, this pronouncement speaks to God's plan for the future of the Israelite priesthood, despite the failure of the Elide era. The oracle speaks to its eventual elimination (1 Kgs 2:26–27) and future replacement with the faithful priesthood of Zadok (2 Sam 15:24–37), whose line served as priests in Jerusalem up until the exile.[2]

For the purposes of this chapter, we are interested in the outline of priestly duties in the first section of the oracle. The speech contains a series of infinitival forms illustrating a variety of functions discussed in this chapter.

1 Sam 2:27–28

וַיָּבֹא אִישׁ־אֱלֹהִים אֶל־עֵלִי וַיֹּאמֶר אֵלָיו כֹּה אָמַר יְהֹוָה הֲנִגְלֹה נִגְלֵיתִי אֶל־בֵּית אָבִיךָ
בִּהְיוֹתָם בְּמִצְרַיִם לְבֵית פַּרְעֹה: וּבָחֹר אֹתוֹ מִכָּל־שִׁבְטֵי יִשְׂרָאֵל לִי לְכֹהֵן לַעֲלוֹת
עַל־מִזְבְּחִי לְהַקְטִיר קְטֹרֶת לָשֵׂאת אֵפוֹד לְפָנָי וָאֶתְּנָה לְבֵית אָבִיךָ אֶת־כָּל־אִשֵּׁי
בְּנֵי יִשְׂרָאֵל:

A man of God came unto Eli and said to him, "Thus says Yahweh: I have **indeed** revealed myself to the household of your father **when they were** in Egypt in the household of Pharaoh, and **chose** him from all the tribes of Israel as my priest, **to make offerings** on my altar, **to burn** incense, (and) **to take up** an ephod before me, and I set for the household of your father all the fire offerings of the sons of Israel."

We note the following infinitive absolute and infinitive construct forms scattered throughout this oracle:

Infinitive Absolute

הֲנִגְלֹה נִגְלֵיתִי

וּבָחֹר

---

[1] P. Kyle McCarter Jr., *I Samuel*, AB 8 (Garden City, NY: Doubleday, 1980), 92.
[2] David T. Tsumura, *The First Book of Samuel*, NICOT (Grand Rapids: Eerdmans, 2007), 165; McCarter, *I Samuel*, 92–93.

Infinitive Construct

בִּהְיוֹתָם

לַעֲלוֹת

לְהַקְטִיר

לָשֵׂאת

The first infinitive absolute serves to intensify the force of the finite verb נִגְלֵיתִי "I revealed myself," a use sometimes called the tautological infinitive (see §9.6.1 below). It is common for the infinitive in such environments to mirror the stem of the finite verb as it does here (*Niphal* SC + *Niphal* INF ABS). The interpretive force of the infinitive underlines the certainty of Yahweh's previous disclosure to and commissioning of the Elide line, heightening the presumptuous nature of its current state of affairs. The following infinitive construct predicates a temporal clause (PREP בְּ + INF CSTR היה + Subj SF ם-) specifying the timeframe of the divine disclosure: "when they were in Egypt." A new clause is signaled by the *waw* + *Qal* infinitive absolute. The infinitive absolute subsumes the person, number, and aspect of the finite verbal unit to which it is adjoined. The intensification of the tautological infinitive therefore applies to its adjoined infinitive—just as Yahweh indeed revealed himself to the Elide household, his calling it to priestly service was likewise certain. The remaining infinitive constructs function adverbially and define the priestly responsibilities as threefold: (1) making offerings on the altar, (2) burning incense, and (3) bearing the priestly ephod.

9.2 CHAPTER OBJECTIVES

This chapter describes the form and function of infinitives. Two infinitives are classified based on their grammatical properties. Their morphology is compared first (§9.4). The various functions of infinitives construct (§9.5) and infinitives absolute (§9.6) are described in the following sections. These latter sections focus on the syntax and semantics of each form.

9.3 INTRODUCTION

The BH verb paradigm includes several nonfinite forms. Participles and infinitives are examples of nonfinite verbs that are not fully inflected for tense, aspect, or modality.[3] While these forms lack some characteristics of finite verbs, other features are shared with adjectives and nouns. Defying rigid classification, infinitives and participles are defined with "squishy" grammatical categories. If one pictures

---

[3] The infinitive is found more than seven thousand times in the Hebrew Bible. It occurs nearly twice as many times as the imperative and almost in as many verses as the participle. For a further discussion of participles, see chapter 8.

the prototypically structured word classes as circumscribed circles, the nonfinite forms occupy the fuzzy shared boundaries of verbs, adjectives, and nouns (see figure). In this way, they can be described as having qualities of "verbiness" and "nouniness."[4] More traditional approaches label them as verbal adjectives and verbal nouns using hybrid word class designations. According to such descriptions, the infinitive is qualified semantically as a verbal noun, meaning that it exhibits qualities characteristic of both verbs and nouns. To put it another way, one could say that the morphology of the infinitives is identifiably nominal, while their usage corresponds with the function of both nouns and verbs.[5] While these lexical categories can be helpful as broad descriptors or heuristics, they do not indicate to what degree or in what way the words resemble verbs, adjectives, or nouns.

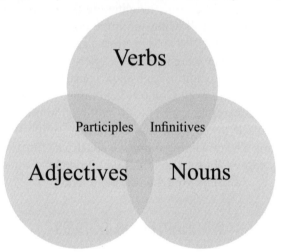

We describe the properties of infinitives in light of their morphology, syntax, and semantics. Morphologically, we distinguish two mostly distinct forms, כְּתֹב and כָּתוֹב, for verbal roots in the *Qal* stem (§9.4). They are described as the infinitive construct and the infinitive absolute based on their formal similarity to the construct and absolute nominal morphology (לְשׁוֹן and לָשׁוֹן "tongue").[6] This formal distinction is unique to Biblical Hebrew among the Northwest Semitic languages.[7] Syntactically, an infinitive is the head of a nominal or verbal predicate. Within the predicate, the infinitive may form grammatical relations analogous to a verb with a subject, complements, and adverbs, including other infinitives. Semantically,

---

[4] Adjectives similarly resist many of these prototypical word class boundaries as discussed previously (§8.5). See Hans-Jürgen Sasse, "Scales between Nouniness and Verbiness," in *Language Typology and Language Universals*, ed. Martin Haspelmath et al., Handbooks of Linguistics and Communication Science 20.1 (Berlin: de Gruyter, 2001), 495–509.

[5] Bordreuil and Pardee, *Manual of Ugaritic*, 56.

[6] GKC §45a.

[7] Observe, however, that the infinitive absolute has been proposed for both Phoenician (see Stanislav Segert, *Grammar of Phoenician and Punic*, 124) and Ammonite (see Kent P. Jackson, *The Ammonite Language of the Iron Age* [Chico, CA: Scholars Press, 1983], 10, 16), as already noted in *IBHS* §35.1a n. 2.

infinitives construct can express a range of non-indicative or temporal notions (§9.5), and infinitives absolute can pragmatically highlight a finite verb or serve as a replacement for a finite verb (§9.6).

9.4 INFINITIVE MORPHOLOGY

Gesenius described infinitives construct and absolute as exhibiting a shorter and longer form respectively. According to his analysis, the shorter infinitive (construct) is used in connection with pronominal suffixes or prepositions, can govern a substantive in the genitive or accusative, and can be dependent upon substantives as a genitive or verbs as an object. On the other hand, Gesenius described the longer infinitive (absolute) as emphasizing the abstraction of the verbal idea, irrespective of the subject or object of the verbal action.[8]

Students often struggle to understand the meaning of the terms "construct" and "absolute" as applied to Hebrew infinitives. This terminology suggests that the difference between the two is that one is the construct verbal noun while the other is the absolute. The following discussion shows that the infinitive construct and absolute are most likely two, historically distinct forms that developed independently of one another.[9] The designation "absolute" corresponds to the resemblance of *qātôl* infinitives to nouns functioning in the absolute state. As defined in chapter 7, the absolute state of nouns is the lexical or dictionary form. It can stand as the last member of a construct chain, or it can stand alone. The construct state, however, is bound to another noun, serving as the head noun of the construct chain following it (see §7.6.2.3). The infinitive construct is likewise able to take pronominal suffixes and prepositions, whereas the infinitive absolute does not.[10]

9.4.1 Qal Infinitive Construct

The Masoretic vocalization of the *Qal* infinitive construct indicates a reduced vowel in the first syllable and a *ḥolem* (i.e., long *o*) in the second (e.g., כְּתֹב "writing"). The historical base of this form was **qutul-*, which is also the pattern for some nouns like בְּכֹר "firstborn," written defectively or *plene* (i.e., בְּכוֹר) and בָּמֳתֵי "high

---

[8] GKC §45a.

[9] See also *IBHS* §35.1b. Joshua Fox raises the possibility that the infinitive construct **qutul* may have arisen as a development from the infinitive absolute **qatāl*, but in the end rejects it as unlikely. According to this argument, the construct state of **qatāl* would have been *qətôl*. One could therefore argue that "one of the uses of the infinitive construct is for the construct state, and that two infinitive forms, 'infinitive construct' *qətôl* and 'infinitive absolute' *qātôl*, were then syntactically differentiated." However, Fox makes the following observations that challenge this reconstruction: (1) the uses of the two infinitives are significantly different, (2) the short /o/ of the suffixal forms (e.g., כָּתְבָם) is not easily derived from the short /a/ of **qatāl* (see below), and (3) the derived stems maintain distinct patterns for the infinitive construct and infinitive absolute (as treated below). See Joshua Fox, *Semitic Noun Patterns*, HSS 59 (Winona Lake, IN: Eisenbrauns, 2003), 208. For a defense of this view, see Jerzy Kuryłowicz, "La nature des procès dits 'analogiques'," *Acta Linguistica* 5 (1949): 30–31.

[10] Similarly, see Joüon-Muraoka §49a n. 6.

places" found only as the plural construct form in MT.[11] The reduction of the first vowel to *shewa* in this pattern is consistent in both the noun and verbal noun. We reconstruct a historical development whereby final case vowels were lost, resulting in an absolute form with a lengthened vowel in the final, stressed syllable (i.e., **qutulu > *qutul > qətōl*). Comparative evidence for this historical base exists in Arabic *qutul*, a rare *maṣdar* (i.e., verbal noun) pattern attested for intransitive *qatala* verbs.[12] Even though Hebrew *qutul* nouns and infinitives construct have identical historical bases, they attest distinct vowel patterns when suffixes are attached, as in the following examples:

	NOUN	INF CSTR
ABS	בְּכוֹר/בְּכֹר	כְּתֹב
SF	בְּכוֹרֵיהֶם, בְּכוֹרוֹ, בְּכֹרִי	כָּתְבֶם, כָּתְבָה

A further observation involves the visual similarity of the *Qal* infinitive construct with the *Qal* imperative:

Qal INF CSTR   *Qal* IMPV
קְטֹל   קְטֹל

The *Qal* imperative pattern **qutul* existed alongside two others, one with the theme vowel *a* (**qatal*), and the other with the theme vowel *i* (**qitil*). Certain III-guttural roots do however distinguish the infinitive construct and imperative morphologically:

Qal INF CSTR   *Qal* IMPV
שְׁלֹחַ   שְׁלַח
שְׁמֹעַ   שְׁמַע

This distinction is maintained in other stems as well, as in the *Niphal* infinitive construct הִשָּׁבֵעַ and imperative הִשָּׁמַע. Joshua Blau observes that these forms and the frequency of *plene* spellings (e.g., כְּתוֹב, לֶאֱסוֹר) offer evidence that the vowel of the second syllable must have been lengthened from an originally short vowel once final vowels were lost.[13] Morphological distinction is also detected in environments involving aspirated *bgdkpt* consonants. Spirantization in the following

---

[11] See further H. H. Hardy II and Benjamin D. Thomas, "Another Look at Biblical Hebrew *bɔmɔ* 'High Place'," *VT* 62 (2012): 175–88. Note that the historical vowels were limited to *a*, *i*, and *u*, either short or long. Historical *u*-vowel was realized in Biblical Hebrew in the following ways: *qibbuṣ* in closed unaccented syllable with doubled consonant (e.g., רֻבּוֹ), *qames-ḥaṭup* in closed unaccented syllable (e.g., חָכְמָה), *holem* in open and closed syllables (e.g., אֹזֶן, בְּכֹר), *shewa* in unaccented open syllables, and *ḥatep-qames* in open pro-pretonic syllables (e.g., קֳדָשִׁים).

[12] Thackston, *Koranic and Classical Arabic*, 66; Fox, *Semitic Noun Patterns*, 204.

[13] Blau, 213.

infinitive construct forms indicates the presence of the proto-*u vowel before the second root consonant:

לִבְדּוֹק	"to mend"	(e.g., 2 Chr 34:10)
לִצְבֹא	"to wage war"	(Num 4:23)
בִּנְפֹל	"in (his) fall"	(Isa 30:25)

Joshua Fox concludes that these forms prove "that there was a proto-vowel before C_2 at some stage, and that the infinitive construct is not formed directly from the imperfect base -*qtōl*." On the other hand, non-spirantized forms like לִשְׁכַּב (e.g., 2 Sam 11:13) represent an analogical extension of the prefix conjugation morphology to that of the infinitive construct.[14]

Morphological variations of the *Qal* infinitive construct do occur, however. We qualify these variations according to four categories: (1) feminine formations, (2) variant /a/ and /i/ patterns, (3) various weak verb alterations, and (4) pronominal suffix variations.[15]

First, the infinitive is routinely attested with the nominal feminine suffix, either with the *mater* pattern הָ- or various ת- patterns:

הָ-

לְרָחְצָה	"for washing"	(Exod 40:30)
לְטָמְאָה	"for becoming unclean"	(Lev 15:32)

ת-

לָשֶׁבֶת	"to dwell"	(Gen 13:6)
יְכֹלֶת	"to be able"	(Num 14:16)
לִקְרַאת	"to call"	(Gen 15:10)
לָשֵׂאת	"to lift up"	(Exod 38:7)

The second group of forms shows variation in the quality of the initial vowel. Since the non-suffixal form of the infinitive construct reduces this vowel to *shewa* (e.g., שְׁמֹר), the variation only appears with suffixes. The most common vowel of the suffixal form is *qameṣ-ḥaṭup* (i.e., short /o/), as in the two feminine forms with הָ- listed above, which is the expected vowel for a *qutul* base. Sometimes, however, the vowel of the first syllable alternates to /i/ and /a/:

i-vowel

רִבְעִי	"my lying down"	(Ps 139:3)
לְשִׁכְנוֹ	"for his dwelling"	(Deut 12:5)
בְּשִׁבְרִי	"in my breaking"	(Lev 26:26)

---

[14] Fox, *Semitic Noun Patterns*, 207.

[15] This morphological variation is not limited to the *Qal* but applies to pronominal suffixes of all stems. For convenience we are treating this morphological feature here, while our fuller discussion of infinitive morphology occurs below.

a-vowel

לְאַהֲבָה   "to love"   (Deut 10:12, 15; 11:13)

A second vowel variation occurs in the second syllable, where the Masoretes use an /a/ vowel. The expected realization of the historical /u/ in the second syllable of the *qutul* base is *holem* (e.g., כְּתֹב) or *qames-hatup* for forms with *maqqep* and certain suffixal forms:

מְלָךְ־מֶלֶךְ	"reigning of the king"	(Gen 36:31)
לֶאֱכָל־לֶחֶם	"for eating bread"	(Gen 37:25)
לְשָׁמְרָךְ	"for your keeping"	(Exod 23:20)

Nevertheless, certain roots attest short /a/ in the second syllable:

לִשְׁכַּב	"to lay"	(Gen 39:10)
בִּשְׁפַל	"in becoming low"	(Eccl 12:4)

These *a* and *i*-vowel variations in the first and second syllables of the *Qal* infinitive construct provide vestigial evidence of earlier *qitil* and *qatal* infinitives that once existed alongside the infinitive *qutul*.[16] This situation parallels similar developments in the imperative and prefix conjugation.[17]

The third category of morphological variation is associated with weak verb vocalic changes. For example, III-weak verbs often form the infinitive construct with the addition of the feminine plural תֹ- ending:

רְאוֹת	"to see"	(Exod 10:28)
עֲשׂוֹת	"to do"	(Gen 2:4)
עֲלוֹת	"to go up"	(Gen 32:25)
לִחְיוֹת	"to live"	(Ezek 33:12)

The feminine plural suffix is not the only way of forming in the infinitive construct in III-weak verbs, since masculine and feminine singular forms are also attested— רְאֹה:ראה MS (Gen 48:11), רְאֲוָה FS (Ezek 28:17); עֲשֹׁה:עשה MS (Gen 50:2), עֲשֹׂתוֹ FS + SF (Gen 41:32).

---

[16] See BL §43; Blau, 226–27.
[17] For the imperative historical morphology, see §6.5.1. On the prefix conjugation, see §5.7.1.

WEAK VERB VARIATIONS OF THE INFINITIVE CONSTRUCT

Other weak verb variations also relate to the situation just described involving *qutul, *qitil, and *qatal infinitives.

לָתֵת (√נתן) – The first *nun* and third *yod* are lost. The *ṣere* likely results from the earlier *qitil base. The final ת is the feminine morpheme.

לָרֶשֶׁת (√ירש) – This I-weak pattern attests a segholate pattern with ת. The suffixal form לְרִשְׁתָּהּ shows an /i/ vowel under the ר, which is consistent with certain *wəqātal* forms (e.g., וִירִשְׁתֶּם, Deut 4:1). The pausal form of the infinitive construct, however, shows an /a/ vowel: לָרָשֶׁת (Neh 9:23). The imperative attests רֵשׁ with *ṣere* (1 Kgs 21:15), but רָשׁ in pause (Deut 2:24) and the feminine form יְרָשָׁה (Deut 23:23). An /a/ theme vowel consistently occurs in the prefix conjugation as well: יִירַשׁ (Ps 25:13). These morphological permutations are complicated by the I-weak consonant. The prefix conjugation indicates a *yaqtal base, which corresponds to a *qatal imperative and infinitive construct. The forms of the infinitive construct with *ḥireq* must therefore have arisen from the pattern of I-weak root consonant.

לֶכֶת (√הלך) – The infinitive construct of this root follows two different patterns: (1) לֶכֶת (with preposition: לָלֶכֶת) and (2) הֲלָךְ (with *maqqep*: ־הֲלָךְ). The second pattern is less common, but it mirrors the situation existing for the prefix conjugation, which also attests two morphological patterns: (1) תֵּלֵךְ ,יֵלֵךְ, etc. and (2) אֶהֲלָךְ ,יְהֲלָךְ (sometimes with *patah*: תְּהֲלַךְ). The imperative does so as well: (1) לֵךְ (with *maqqep*: ־לֶךְ), לְכָה (pausal form: לֵכָה) and (2) הֲלוֹךְ ,הִלְכוּ. The preference for pattern 1 shows that this I-ה root adopted the morphology of I-weak roots (cf. יָשַׁב). The meagerly attested pattern 2 indicates the underlying base of the imperative and infinitive construct of הלך must have been *qutul.

דַּעַת (√ידע) – The ת- feminine formation can occur with the preposition ל (e.g., לָדַעַת) or pronominal suffixes (e.g., דַּעְתִּי, Deut 9:24). The infinitive construct of this root also attests an alternate feminine form with ◌ָה-, but with *ṣere* in the first syllable: דֵּעָה (Exod 2:4). An /a/ theme vowel is consistent throughout the prefix conjugation (יֵדַע, Isa 7:16) and the imperative (דַּע, Gen 20:7). The יֵדַע prefix conjugation pattern (as opposed to יִירַשׁ) is characteristic of I-*waw* roots. The underlying base of the infinitive דַּעַת is *qatal.

The fourth morphological variation involves a discrepancy in pronominal suffixes. The following chart outlines the alternate suffixal forms:

	PRO SF 1		PRO SF 2	
3FS	־ָהּ	בְּלִדְתָּהּ "when she bore" (Gen 38:5)	־ֶ֫נָּה, ־ֶ֫נָּה	לְיַחְמֵ֫נָּה "to make it conceive" (Gen 30:41) בֹּאָ֫נָה "its coming" (Jer 8:7)
1CS	־ִי	בְּשׁוּבִי "when I come" (Judg 8:9)	־ֵ֫נִי	לַהֲמִיתֵ֫נִי "to put me to death" (1 Sam 28:9)

We discuss proposals regarding the function of these alternate suffixes below.

9.4.2 Qal Infinitive Absolute

Unlike the infinitive construct, the infinitive absolute does not take suffixes of any kind: gender, number, or pronominal. It only rarely appears as the object of a preposition. Grammarians often describe this form as independent (i.e., absolute), both morphologically and functionally.

The vocalization of the *Qal* infinitive absolute in Hebrew consists of an /a/ vowel in the first syllable and an /o/ vowel in the second: כָּתוֹב. The historical development of the vowel in the second syllable demonstrates the phonological shift of historically long /a/ to long /o/, also known as the Canaanite shift.[18] (The original vowels developed along the following lines: **qatālu > *qatāl > qatōl*.) The infinitive absolute can also be written defectively as כָּתֹב or *plene* as כָּתוֹב.

COMPARATIVE SEMITICS AND THE HEBREW INFINITIVE ABSOLUTE

The comparative situation indicates that the Hebrew infinitive absolute parallels the infinitival forms attested in other Semitic languages. In Akkadian, for instance, the G stem infinitive takes the nominal pattern *parās*, only occurring in the masculine singular (e.g., *kašādum* "arriving").[19] The same nominal pattern *qatāl* is attested for the Ugaritic infinitive as well, as in the following example from the Kirta epic: *w yqrb b šal (ša'āli) krt* "he approached while asking Kirta" (*KTU* 1.14 I:37–38). It is apparent that Hebrew reserved the *qatāl* pattern common to other languages for the limited functions of the infinitive absolute.[20] In contrast, the functions of the *qatāl* infinitive in Ugaritic correspond broadly to the uses of both the infinitive absolute and the infinitive construct in Hebrew.[21]

---

[18] See the discussion of this shift as it relates to the *Qal* participle in §8.6.1.

[19] See Huehnergard, *Grammar of Akkadian*, 17, 337.

[20] Bordreuil and Pardee, *Manual of Ugaritic*, 56.

[21] See Huehnergard, *Introduction to Ugaritic*, 60. Daniel Sivan states that Ugaritic attests both an infinitive construct and an infinitive absolute. See *A Grammar of the Ugaritic Language*, Handbook of Oriental Studies 28 (Atlanta: SBL, 2001), 123. However, it may be more accurate to say that the Ugaritic infinitive fulfills the functions of the two independent Hebrew infinitive forms, since Ugaritic only attests one infinitive form.

9.4.3 Infinitive Morphology and the Derived Stems

The forms of the infinitive absolute in the derived stems are not always consistent in their distinction from the infinitive construct. We may outline the attested forms as follows:

	QAL	NIPHAL	PIEL	HITPAEL	HIPHIL
INF CSTR	קְטֹל (=IMPV) קְטוֹל	הִקָּטֵל (=IMPV)	קַטֵּל (=IMPV)	הִתְקַטֵּל (=IMPV)	הַקְטִיל
INF ABS	קָטוֹל קָטֹל	הִקָּטֵל (=IMPV) נִקְטוֹל/נִקְטֹל	קַטֵּל (=IMPV) קַטּוֹל/קַטֹּל	הִתְקַטֵּל (=IMPV)	הַקְטֵל (=IMPV) הַקְטֵיל הַקְטִיל

Much like the infinitive construct in the *Qal*, the infinitives construct of the derived stems are often patterned like the imperative. It is likely that this feature is analogical to the *Qal*, irrespective of the underlying historical distinctions between the *Qal* infinitive construct and the imperative (see above).

The *Niphal* infinitive construct, for instance, usually takes the form of the imperative:

Exod 22:3

אִם־הִמָּצֵא תִמָּצֵא בְיָדוֹ הַגְּנֵבָה

If what is stolen is **indeed** found in his possession

This tendency is not uniform, however. Sometimes the form is vocalized with an /o/ theme vowel in contexts that clearly indicate its function as an infinitive absolute:

Lev 7:18

וְאִם הֵאָכֹל יֵאָכֵל מִבְּשַׂר־זֶבַח שְׁלָמָיו בַּיּוֹם הַשְּׁלִישִׁי לֹא יֵרָצֶה הַמַּקְרִיב אֹתוֹ

If **indeed** some of the flesh of his *zebaḥ šəlāmāyw* is eaten on the third day, the one offering it will not be accepted.

2 Sam 17:11

כִּי יָעַצְתִּי הֵאָסֹף יֵאָסֵף עָלֶיךָ כָל־יִשְׂרָאֵל מִדָּן וְעַד־בְּאֵר שֶׁבַע

For I have counseled: all Israel must **surely** be gathered to you from Dan to Beersheba.

A third variation of the *Niphal* infinitive absolute is similar to the suffix conjugation (נִקְטַל) and participle (נִקְטָל), but instead takes a long /o/ theme vowel (i.e., נִקְטוֹל):

Gen 31:30

וְעַתָּה הָלֹךְ הָלַכְתָּ כִּי־נִכְסֹף נִכְסַפְתָּה לְבֵית אָבִיךָ לָמָּה גָנַבְתָּ אֶת־אֱלֹהָי:

Now, you ran off because you **indeed** longed for the house of your father. Why have you stolen my gods?

Judg 11:25

הֲרוֹב רָב֙ עִם־יִשְׂרָאֵ֔ל אִם־נִלְחֹ֥ם נִלְחַ֖ם בָּֽם

Has he indeed striven with Israel, or **indeed** fought with them?

The development of the /o/-type forms may have arisen on analogy to the *Qal* infinitive absolute (i.e., נִקְטֹל ~ קָטֹל). The appearance of /o/ in forms like הֵאָסֹף cited above is likely a bleeding over of the נִקְטֹל type, perhaps secondarily distinguished from the infinitive construct and imperative form הִקָּטֵל.[22] Such distinctions are not consistently maintained.

The distribution of the *Piel* infinitival forms exhibits similar characteristics. As in the *Qal* and *Niphal*, the *Piel* infinitives construct and absolute as a rule adopt the morphology of the *Piel* imperative (קַטֵּל):

Num 22:17

כִּי־כַבֵּ֤ד אֲכַבֶּדְךָ֙ מְאֹ֔ד

For I will **indeed** honor you exceedingly.

Jer 39:18

כִּ֤י מַלֵּ֨ט אֲמַלֶּטְךָ֙ וּבַחֶ֖רֶב לֹ֣א תִפֹּ֑ל

For I will **certainly** rescue you, and you will not fall by the sword.

The *Piel* infinitive absolute attests an alternative pattern, however, once again with an /o/ theme vowel resembling the *Qal* infinitive absolute:

Josh 24:10

וְלֹ֥א אָבִ֖יתִי לִשְׁמֹ֣עַ לְבִלְעָ֑ם וַיְבָ֤רֶךְ בָּרוֹךְ֙ אֶתְכֶ֔ם וָאַצִּ֥ל אֶתְכֶ֖ם מִיָּדֽוֹ׃

I was not willing to listen to Balaam. He **indeed** blessed you, and I delivered you from his hand.

1 Kgs 19:10

קַנֹּ֨א קִנֵּ֜אתִי לַיהֹוָ֣ה ׀ אֱלֹהֵ֣י צְבָא֗וֹת

I was **exceedingly** zealous for Yahweh, God of armies.

We even find one example of a *Pual* infinitive absolute with /o/:

Gen 40:15

כִּֽי־גֻנֹּ֣ב גֻּנַּ֔בְתִּי מֵאֶ֖רֶץ הָעִבְרִ֑ים

For I was **indeed** stolen away from the land of the Hebrews.

Again, the vestigial /o/ vowel preserved in these *Piel* and *Pual* infinitive absolute forms represents a similar development to that of the *Qal* and is applied to the *Niphal* (i.e., *qattālu > *qattōl*).[23]

---

[22] Gesenius explains the nature of נִפְטוֹל as bearing "the same relation as the קָטוֹל to קָטַל in the *Qal*" (GKC §51k). He reconstructs the long /o/ as originating from historically long /a/ analogical to the long /a/ of the *Qal* infinitive absolute (i.e., *niqtālu). See also BL §44y–z.

[23] See GKC §52a; BL §45o.

The *Hiphil* stem similarly attests some distinction between construct and absolute forms of the infinitive. The imperative of the *Hiphil* is formed by attaching the prefix *ha-* and theme vowel is *ṣere* (i.e. הַקְטֵל) rather than the characteristic *ḥireq-yod* vowel (e.g. suffix conjugation הִקְטִיל and prefix conjugation יַקְטִיל).[24] In contrast to the imperative, the infinitive construct most often maintains the *ḥireq-yod*: הַקְטִיל.

Num 9:19

וּבְהַאֲרִיךְ הֶעָנָן עַל־הַמִּשְׁכָּן יָמִים רַבִּים וְשָׁמְרוּ בְנֵי־יִשְׂרָאֵל אֶת־מִשְׁמֶרֶת יְהוָה וְלֹא יִסָּעוּ:

When the cloud **lingered** over the dwelling place for many days, the sons of Israel would keep the charge of Yahweh and not set out.

Sometimes the consonantal text did not have the *yod* in such forms, yet the Masoretes would still vocalize with *ḥireq*:

Jer 32:32

עַל כָּל־רָעַת בְּנֵי־יִשְׂרָאֵל וּבְנֵי יְהוּדָה אֲשֶׁר עָשׂוּ לְהַכְעִסֵנִי

On account of all the evil of the sons of Israel and the sons of Judah that they did **to provoke me**.

Third-weak verbs in the *Hiphil* mark the infinitive construct with an וֹת- ending (e.g., לְהַשְׁקוֹת), as is the case for the *Qal* infinitive construct. The *Hiphil* infinitive absolute, however, maintains a final *ṣere* vowel with ה- *mater*. The *Qal* infinitive absolute similarly maintains the ה- *mater*, but with *ḥolem*.

	QAL	HIPHIL
IMPV	עֲלֵה	הַעַל
INF CSTR	עֲלוֹת	הַעֲלוֹת
INF ABS	עָלֹה	הַעֲלֵה

Geminate *Hiphil* verbs do not mark any distinction between the imperative, infinitive construct, or infinitive absolute. For instance, we have the infinitive construct לְהָפֵר (√פרר "to break") in 2 Sam 17:14, the infinitive absolute הָפֵר in Prov 15:22, and the imperative הָפֵר in Ps 85:5. The potential addition of the preposition לְ on the infinitive construct, however, does allow for a distinction between it and the imperative.

As with the other derived stems, the *Hiphil* routinely utilizes the imperative form for the infinitive absolute:

---

[24] On the morphology of the *Hiphil* more generally, see §4.9.1.

Exod 8:24

רַק הַרְחֵק לֹא־תַרְחִיקוּ לָלֶכֶת הַעְתִּירוּ בַּעֲדִי

Only you must **certainly** not journey too far. Make supplication on my behalf.

Twice the infinitive construct form with *ḥireq-yod* appears with an infinitive absolute usage (Josh 4:3; 9:20). Nineteen *Hiphil* infinitives absolute occur with *yod* and are vocalized by the Masoretes with *ṣere*:

Amos 9:8

אֶפֶס כִּי לֹא הַשְׁמֵיד אַשְׁמִיד אֶת־בֵּית יַעֲקֹב נְאֻם־יְהוָה

Nonetheless, I will not **utterly** destroy the house of Jacob, declares Yahweh.[25]

9.5 INFINITIVE CONSTRUCT

The infinitive construct shares some grammatical categories with verbs and some relational features with nouns. Even though widely considered a verbal noun, its morphosyntactic properties diverge significantly from nouns (§9.5.1). The infinitive construct is perhaps best classified as a nominalizing nonfinite verb. As a nonfinite verb, it serves as the head of an embedded clause (§9.5.2). As a nominalizer, the embedded clause functions as a nominal predicate in a main clause like a nonverbal participant (§9.5.3).

The similarities and differences involved in the morphosyntax of the infinitive construct can be observed by comparing the word class features of verbs, adjectives, and nouns. Parsing is the method of describing the grammatical categories of a word. Hebrew verbs are parsed based on stem, conjugation, person, gender, number, and root. Participles are akin to verbs, but they include state (absolute, construct, or pronominal) and are not inflected for person. Adjectives are identical to participles except they do not distinguish stem. The infinitive construct is construed with different stems (e.g., *Qal*, *Piel*, *Hiphil*, etc.), but it is unmarked for all the other categories. Nouns and pronouns are classed with gender, number, and state. Pronouns additionally inflect for person. Most Hebrew words can be associated with a derivational root.

---

[25] The remaining occurrences with *ṣere-yod* are: Deut 15:14; Josh 6:3; Judg 1:28; 1 Kgs 9:25; Neh 7:3; Isa 59:4; Jer 3:15; 7:5; 10:5; 23:32; 25:3; 35:15; 36:16; 44:4, 17, 25; Job 34:35; Prov 27:14.

	WORD CLASS	STEM	PERSON	GENDER	NUMBER	STATE	ROOT
כָּתַב	Verb (SC)	Qal	3	M	S	——	כתב "write"
תְּחַזֵּק	Verb (PC)	Piel	2	M	S	——	חזק "be strong"
הַשְׁמִיעוּ	Verb (IMPV)	Hiphil	(2)	M	P	——	שמע "listen"
מִתְהַלֶּכֶת	Participle	Hitpael	——	F	S	ABS/CSTR	הלך "walk"
יָפָה	Adjective	——	——	F	S	ABS	יפה "be beautiful"
שְׁפֹט	Infinitive Construct	Qal	——	——	——	——[26]	שפט "judge"
מִכְתָּב	Noun	——	——	M	S	CSTR	כתב "write"
אַתְּ	Pronoun	——	2	F	S	——	——

Title of table: **PARSING HEBREW WORD CLASSES**

A cursory comparison of these data shows that the infinitive construct has little in common with the inflection of nouns. The stem inflection categorizes it closer to participles and finite verbs. Despite these similarities, the infinitive construct serves to nominalize a predicate. Nominalization is the process or result by which the functional category of a word or phrase becomes a noun. It is often a result of morphological transformation or inflection. For example, English derivational suffix -ment is used to nominalize the verb to judge as a derived noun judgment. The English gerund uses the derivational suffix -ing as its nominalizing formative.

A further note (and chart) helps to clarify the similarities and differences between the Hebrew infinitive construct and its translation equivalents in English. The use of the infinitive construct often resembles that of English infinitives and gerunds, but the lack of formal overlap can cause confusion. In Hebrew, the infinitive construct (e.g., כְּתֹב, דַּעַת) may be translated with either the English infinitive (e.g., write, know) or the gerund (e.g., writing, knowing) depending on its syntax. On the other hand, the English -ing form serves as both the active participle and the gerund (e.g., writing, knowing), but the Hebrew participle has its own unique form and syntax (e.g., כֹּתֵב, יֹדֵעַ). Finally, the English base verb form (e.g., write, know) is used with infinitives, imperatives, present tense, and some modal auxiliaries, while different verbal forms indicate each of these functions in Hebrew.

---

[26] See above (§9.4.1) for a morphological description of the infinitive construct with pronominal suffixes. The nomenclature of infinitive construct and infinitive absolute, however, should not be confused for inflected states. These descriptors have to do with identifying the difference in the two morphosyntactic forms.

HEBREW AND ENGLISH NONFINITE VERB COMPARISON		
INFINITIVE	GERUND	PARTICIPLE
write	writing	
know	knowing	
INFINITIVE CONSTRUCT		ACTIVE PARTICIPLE
כְּתֹב		כֹּתֵב
דֵּעַת		יֹדֵעַ

9.5.1 Infinitive Construct and Derived Nouns

Many morphosyntactic characteristics resist categorizing the infinitive construct strictly as a noun or a verb. Grammarians use the term <u>verbal noun</u> to indicate its hybrid nature.[27] However, this nomenclature is less than ideal. When comparing its morphosyntax and semantics, the infinitive construct has demonstrably more properties of "verbiness" than "nouniness." Its noun features are severely restricted. Furthermore, Hebrew employs a wide range of derivational strategies apart from the infinitive construct to form derived (or deverbal) nominals. These non-infinitive-construct forms are fully incorporated as nouns. Only a very few cases of infinitives construct can truly be considered hybrid verbal nouns.

First, the morphosyntax of infinitive construct is mostly verbal. Unlike a noun, infinitives construct are inflected with verbal stems and semantics: שְׁמֹעַ "hear(ing)" (*Qal*), הִשָּׁמַע "be(ing) heard" (*Niphal*), and הַשְׁמִעַ "proclaim(ing)" (*Hiphil*). The infinitive construct takes verbal complementation often with אֵת (1 Kgs 5:14) and adverbial modifiers (Gen 13:6) rather than construct phrases and adjectives like nouns. And it denotes a verbal—albeit nominalized—action (see the full description below, §9.5.3).

> 1 Kgs 5:14
>
> וַיָּבֹאוּ מִכָּל־הָעַמִּים לִשְׁמֹעַ אֵת חָכְמַת שְׁלֹמֹה
>
> Some from all peoples came **to hear** Solomon's wisdom.

> Gen 13:6
>
> וְלֹא־נָשָׂא אֹתָם הָאָרֶץ לָשֶׁבֶת יַחְדָּו
>
> The land could not support them **to dwell** together.

Second, the infinitive construct is construed with a derived noun pattern, but it exhibits extremely limited nominal morphosyntax. The form of the *Qal* infinitive construct is comprised of several noun patterns, such as **qutul*, **qatal*, and **til-t*

---

[27] E.g., Fox, *Semitic Noun Patterns*, 26–29. Also, see Joüon-Muraoka §§40b, 65a; *IBHS* §§20.1g, 36.1.1a; *BHRG* §15.6; GKC §§83, 115.

(see above).[28] Analogous to the forms of the Arabic *masdar*, the Hebrew infinitive construct does not have a single unique pattern in the simple stem (*Qal* ~ Form I) but takes a standard form with the derived stems. The infinitive construct takes (mostly) nominal pronominal suffixes and functions syntactically as a nominal element in a phrase or clause. However, the infinitive construct does not conform to most morphosyntactic features of nouns. It does not have gender. It does not inflect for number. It cannot be prefixed with the definite article or the object marker אֵת. It cannot be modified by adjectives, demonstratives, numerals, or relatives. Apposition is not permitted. It cannot be replaced or referred to with a pronominal element. All modification must follow the infinitive construct.

MORPHOSYNTACTIC FEATURES OF THE INFINITIVE CONSTRUCT			
	VERB	INFINITIVE CONSTRUCT	NOUN
INFLECTION			
Stem	+	+	−
Gender	+	−	+
Number	+	−	+
Construct/Absolute State	−	−	+
Pronominal Suffixes	+	+	+
MODIFICATION			
Adverb	+	+	−
Complement	+	+	−
Definite	−	−	+
Adjective	−	−	+
Demonstrative	−	−	+
Numeral	−	−	+
Relative	−	−	+
Apposition	−	−	+
Pronoun Reference	−	−	+

Third, other action nouns are derived from verbs besides the infinitive construct, and without exception these deverbal nouns are fully incorporated into nominal morphosyntax. Deverbal nouns function in like manner to isolated nouns and are

---

[28] The most common infinitive construct pattern **qutul* is a rare noun pattern in Semitic (Fox, *Semitic Noun Patterns*, 203–8), but it does occur with some Hebrew lexemes (see, Fox, *Semitic Noun Patterns*, 205, and Hardy and Thomas, "Biblical Hebrew *bɔmɔ*," 175–88). Fox (205–8) also discusses the other action noun patterns related to the Hebrew infinitive construct.

not grammatically restricted like the infinitive construct. English verbal nouns may provide some grounds for comparison. The English derivational suffix *-er* is used to form agent nouns (e.g., *writer, knower*). Hebrew uses a participle or noun pattern in similar ways (e.g., כֹּתֵב "writer" < *qātil* or יָדַע "expert" < *qattāl*). The English *-ing* form can designate a gerund or verbal noun (e.g., *writing, knowing*) as can other derivational suffixes (e.g., *inscription, knowledge*). Hebrew nouns take a number of forms in Hebrew (e.g., כְּתָב, כְּתֹבֶת, מִכְתָּב, דֵּעָה, דַּע, מַדָּע). These lexemes are inflected for gender, number, and state, and they function with standard noun modifiers.

HEBREW VERBAL NOUNS			
AGENT NOUN	**DEVERBAL NOUN**	**DEVERBAL NOUN**	**DEVERBAL NOUN**
כֹּתֵב "writer"[29]	כְּתָב "writing"	כְּתֹבֶת "writing, imprint"	מִכְתָּב "writing, inscription"
יָדַע "expert"	דֵּעָה "knowing"	דַּע "knowledge"	מַדָּע "knowledge"

Fourth, a small class of <u>verbal nouns</u> share identical forms with the infinitive construct, and an even smaller number assume some of the morphosyntactic properties of the nonfinite verb. Two examples are found with the root ידע "know." The first דַּעַת is the expected *Qal* infinitive construct form of a I-weak verb with a final-radical guttural (< *tal-t*).[30] The form is identical for the infinitive construct "know(ing)" and the verbal noun "knowledge." The diachronic details are obscured, but most likely the noun should be understood to have derived from the infinitive construct. The nonfinite verb is used to describe the impetus for exiling humanity from the garden of Eden (Gen 3:22). The infinitive construct "knowing" takes a compound object, טוֹב וָרָע "good and evil." The definite verbal noun "knowledge" is exemplified in 1 Kgs 7:14. The earlier descriptions of the infamous tree in Genesis, however, demonstrate a definite noun with the same verbal complement: עֵץ הַדַּעַת טוֹב וָרָע "the tree of the knowing good and evil" (2:9, 17).[31] The verbal noun in Jer 22:16 also takes an object complement אֹתִי "me."

Gen 3:22

הֵן הָאָדָם הָיָה כְּאַחַד מִמֶּנּוּ לָדַעַת טוֹב וָרָע
The man has become like one of us **knowing** good and evil.

---

[29] Typically, a writer is סֹפֵר "scribe" in Hebrew. It may serve as an agent nominal pattern (Isa 10:1; Jer 32:12). Other agent-noun patterns are available, such as *qattāl* (e.g. דַּיָּן "judge").

[30] Compare other R1 weak verbs with the monosyllabic *til-t* (לֶדֶת, רֶשֶׁת, רֶדֶת, צֶקֶת, צֵאת, לֶכֶת, שֶׁבֶת, תֵת), but not all these roots follow this patterning (יְרְאָה, סְפוֹת, יְסֹד, יְכֹלֶת).

[31] See also the similar usage with the participle, כֵּאלֹהִים יֹדְעֵי טוֹב וָרָע "like God knowing of good and evil" (Gen 3:5).

1 Kgs 7:14

וַיִּמָּלֵ֗א אֶת־הַֽחָכְמָ֤ה וְאֶת־הַתְּבוּנָה֙ וְאֶת־הַדַּ֔עַת לַעֲשֹׂ֥ות כָּל־מְלָאכָ֖ה בַּנְּחֹֽשֶׁת

He was filled with the wisdom, the understanding, and **the knowledge** to do every work in bronze.

Jer 22:16

דָּ֛ן דִּין־עָנִ֥י וְאֶבְיֹ֖ון אָ֣ז טֹ֑וב הֲלֹוא־הִ֛יא הַדַּ֥עַת אֹתִ֖י

He came to the defense of the poor and impoverished, then it was upright. Is this not **knowing** me?

These few homophonous examples complicate our ability to generalize strict distinctions between some derived noun forms and the infinitive construct. How the hybrid instances are categorized, though, can reveal the grammatical assumptions of the organizer. All Hebrew lexicons give separate entries for the infinitive construct and verbal noun of דַּעַת, but a second derivative of the same verb ידע demonstrates dissimilar morphosyntactic and semantic assumptions. The form דֵּעָה is not registered as an infinitive construct form in *DCH* (4:99–110), but it is listed as a noun (2:456).[32] BDB only lists it as a verbal form.[33] *HALOT* includes the form with the verb with only one example (Exod 2:4),[34] and the other examples are listed elsewhere with a unique lexeme דֵּעָה labeled "special inf(initive)."[35] Several instances (1 Sam 2:3; Ps 73:11; Isa 28:9) appear to be nominal and several others more verbal (Exod 2:4; Isa 11:9; and maybe Jer 3:15).

9.5.2 Infinitive Construct as a Nonfinite Verb

The infinitive construct is a <u>nonfinite verb</u>. As a clausal head, it has the morphosyntactic and semantic properties of a verb but is nonfinite and impersonal.[36] The infinitive construct is construed with different stems (e.g., *Qal*, *Niphal*, *Piel*). It may take complements and subjects. It can be modified by adverbial adjuncts including other infinitives construct. And semantically it conveys an action. Unlike a finite verb, the infinitive construct is not overtly marked for tense, aspect, or modality; neither does it inflect for person, number, or gender.[37] The finite and personal notions, however, are determined from context or are designated independent of the infinitive form. Yet, on account of these unmarked features, an infinitive construct only infrequently governs a main clause predicate on its own (see further §9.5.3).

---

[32] Isaiah 11:9 is not found with the verb ידע, but Exod 2:4 is listed under meaning 7 of the *Qal* (4:100).

[33] BDB, 393.

[34] *HALOT*, s.v. "ידע I," 390.

[35] *HALOT*, s.v. "דֵּעַת," 228.

[36] For a generativist's case that the infinitive construct should be considered clausal, that is, more verbal than nominal, see Edit Doron, "The Infinitive in Biblical Hebrew," in *Linguistic Studies on Biblical Hebrew*, ed. Robert D. Holmstedt, SSLL 102 (Leiden: Brill, 2021), 160–65.

[37] Doron argues the infinitive can in fact indicate various TAM notions based on its construction type. See Doron, "Infinitive in Biblical Hebrew," 151–60.

The infinitive construct selects most of its grammatical relations like a finite verb. Regarding its word order, it is strictly forward branching. All its clause constituents follow the nonfinite verb complex, and only the negation בִּלְתִּי may precede it (Exod 9:17; see §10.7).

Exod 9:17

עוֹדְךָ מִסְתּוֹלֵל בְּעַמִּי לְבִלְתִּי שַׁלְּחָם:

You are still being condescending against my people in **not** sending them out.

The semantic role of agent, the doer of the action (or SUBJ), can be assumed from the previous elements (e.g., פִּיהָ לָקַחַת "its mouth receive[d]," Gen 4:11).[38] Instead, it may be specified as the element ordinarily immediately following the infinitive construct either as a noun phrase (Judg 18:31) or a pronominal suffix (1 Sam 25:16).[39]

Gen 4:11

וְעַתָּה אָרוּר אָתָּה מִן־הָאֲדָמָה אֲשֶׁר פָּצְתָה אֶת־פִּיהָ לָקַחַת אֶת־דְּמֵי אָחִיךָ מִיָּדֶךָ:

Now you are cursed on behalf of **the ground** that opened **its mouth to receive** your brother's blood from your hand.

Judg 18:31

כָּל־יְמֵי הֱיוֹת בֵּית־הָאֱלֹהִים בְּשִׁלֹה

all the days [when] **the house of God was** in Shiloh.

1 Sam 25:16

כָּל־יְמֵי הֱיוֹתֵנוּ עִמָּם רֹעִים הַצֹּאן

all the days of **our being** with them herding the sheep.

The patient (i.e., OBJ) is expressed as a NP (Gen 2:4), initiated by an object marker (Gen 13:16), or as a pronominal suffix (Exod 2:14). Only one pronominal suffix is ever attached to the verb, but a second pronominal can be expressed with the object marker (Gen 38:5).

Gen 2:4

בְּיוֹם עֲשׂוֹת יְהוָה אֱלֹהִים אֶרֶץ וְשָׁמָיִם

In the day of Yahweh God **making the earth and heavens**

Gen 13:16

אִם־יוּכַל אִישׁ לִמְנוֹת אֶת־עֲפַר הָאָרֶץ

If someone can **count the dust of the earth**

---

[38] For nonfinite verbs with no overt lexical subject, the predicate should be considered null PRO rather than subjectless. Doron, "Infinitive in Biblical Hebrew."

[39] Some examples show flexibility in the position of the subject, e.g., לְבִלְתִּי הַכּוֹת־אֹתוֹ כָּל־מֹצְאוֹ "so that **anyone finding him** would not smite him" (Gen 4:15).

Exod 2:14

הַלְהָרְגֵ֙נִי֙ אַתָּ֣ה אֹמֵ֔ר כַּאֲשֶׁ֥ר הָרַ֖גְתָּ אֶת־הַמִּצְרִ֑י

"Are you thinking of **killing me**," he said, "just as you killed the Egyptian?"

Gen 38:5

בְלִדְתָּ֥הּ **אֹתֽוֹ**

when she birthed **him**.

Most pronominal suffixes attached to the infinitive construct can be subjective or objective. In the case of the 1CS forms, the morphology of subjective and objective suffixes is different, following the pronominal suffix paradigm of verbs and nouns. The verbal suffix נִי◌- is always objective (1 Kgs 18:9), and the nominal suffix י◌- is most commonly subjective (Jer 12:15).

1 Kgs 18:9

מֶ֣ה חָטָ֔אתִי כִּֽי־אַתָּ֗ה נֹתֵ֧ן אֶֽת־עַבְדְּךָ֛ בְּיַד־אַחְאָ֖ב לַהֲמִיתֵֽנִי

How have I sinned that you are putting your servant under the authority of Ahab **to execute me**?

Jer 12:15

וְהָיָ֗ה אַחֲרֵי֙ **נָתְשִׁ֣י** אוֹתָ֔ם אָשׁ֖וּב וְרִֽחַמְתִּ֑ים

After **I uproot** them, I will return and cherish them.

Adverbial modifiers typical follow these constituents, including other infinitives construct (Deut 8:2).

Deut 8:2

וְזָכַרְתָּ֣ אֶת־כָּל־הַדֶּ֗רֶךְ אֲשֶׁ֨ר הֹלִֽיכֲךָ֜ יְהוָ֧ה אֱלֹהֶ֛יךָ זֶ֛ה אַרְבָּעִ֥ים שָׁנָ֖ה בַּמִּדְבָּ֑ר לְמַ֨עַן
עַנֹּֽתְךָ֜ **לְנַסֹּֽתְךָ֗** **לָדַ֜עַת** אֶת־אֲשֶׁ֧ר בִּֽלְבָבְךָ֛ הֲתִשְׁמֹ֥ר מִצְוֹתָ֖יו אִם־לֹֽא׃

Remember this whole forty-year journey in the wilderness that Yahweh your God has led you so as to humble you **to test you to know** what was in your heart whether you would observe his commandments or not.

Semantically, the infinitive construct expresses a range of non-indicative verbal notions. Primary among these volitional semantics is the deontic idea of possibility or potentiality. Constructions with prepositions indicate result (לְמַ֫עַן) or purpose (-לְ) and commonly encode volition. Deuteronomy 8:2 (above) shows both in the sequence, לְמַ֫עַן עַנֹּֽתְךָ לְנַסֹּֽתְךָ "so that he might humble you for the purpose that he might test you." Other TAM notions are often encoded in the broader narrative frames. For instance, the non-indicative temporal form וְהָיָה אַחֲרֵי (wǝqātal) indicates the yet-to-be realized action נָתְשִׁי "I will uproot" in a posteriority relationship with the main verbal sequence (Jer 12:15). In 1 Kgs 18:9, the ongoing and impending execution of Obadiah is indicated by the preceding participle predicate אַתָּה נֹתֵן . . . לַהֲמִיתֵ֫נִי "you are giving [authority] . . . to execute me." The context of the main clause indicates other irrealis notions.

9.5.3 Nominalization of the Infinitive Construct

An infinitive construct may form grammatical relations with subsequent elements to form a type of embedded clausal unit. Analogous to a finite verb, these relations include subjects, complements, and adverbs, as well as other infinitives (§9.5.2). Unlike a finite verb, the syntactic unit headed by the nonfinite verb functions as a nominalized participant in a main clause and not as main clause predication.

A functionalist vantagepoint explains this distinction as the difference between a nominal predicate and a verbal predicate. Kees Hengeveld provides the following definitions of these prototypical functions:

> A *nominal* predicate is a predicate which, without further measures being taken, can be used as the head of a term.
>
> A *verbal* predicate is a predicate which, without further measures being taken, has a predicative use *only*.[40]

In Hebrew, the infinitive construct functions as the head of a nominal predicate, and a finite verb governs verbal predicates. The nominal predicate does not require the addition of another element to nominalize it. The verbal predicate necessitates a nominalizing construction as its "further measures," according to Hengeveld's definitions. The nominal predicate is headed by an infinitive construct, לֶכְתְּךָ אֶת־הַמִּדְבָּר הַגָּדֹל הַזֶּה, and serves as the complement of the verb יָדַע in Deut 2:7. At 1 Sam 14:3, the verbal predicate, הָלַךְ יוֹנָתָן, requires the nominalizing particle כִּי (§10.4.2.2).

Deut 2:7

יָדַע לֶכְתְּךָ אֶת־הַמִּדְבָּר הַגָּדֹל הַזֶּה
[God] knows **your journey** in this great wilderness.

1 Sam 14:3

וְהָעָם לֹא יָדַע כִּי הָלַךְ יוֹנָתָן
The people did not know **that** Jonathan had gone.

As part of a noun phrase, the nominal predicate can function like any other nominal constituent. It can resemble a noun in a construct phrase (קוֹל עַנּוֹת "a voice of singing," Exod 32:18; עֵת בֹּא־דְבָרוֹ "time of the coming of his word," Ps 105:19) or a noun with suffixes (עֵת בֹּאָנָה "time of her coming," Jer 8:7; also, עֵת לִדְתָּנָה "time of their birthing," Job 39:2).

Within the main clause, the nominal predicate may function as a clause participant. It can constituent a subject (Exod 14:12) or compound subject (1 Sam 29:6). The infinitive construct can be a verbal complement (Exod 4:24) or compound complement (Ps 139:2).

---

[40] Kees Hengeveld, *Non-Verbal Predication: Theory, Typology, Diachrony* (Berlin: de Gruyter, 1992), 58. These definitions build on the foundational work of functional grammarian Simon C. Dik, *The Theory of Functional Grammar* (Dordrecht: Foris, 1989).

Exod 14:12

כִּי טוֹב לָנוּ֙ **עֲבֹד** אֶת־מִצְרַ֔יִם מִמֻּתֵ֖נוּ בַּמִּדְבָּֽר

Serving Egypt is better for us than our dying in the wilderness.

1 Sam 29:6

כִּֽי־יָשָׁ֣ר אַתָּ֗ה וְט֤וֹב בְּעֵינַי֙ **צֵאתְךָ֤ וּבֹאֲךָ֙** אִתִּ֣י בַּֽמַּחֲנֶ֔ה

Certainly, you are upright. **Your leaving** and **entering** with me into battle is good in my eyes.

Exod 4:24

וַיְבַקֵּ֖שׁ הֲמִיתֽוֹ

[Yahweh] sought **his demise**.

Ps 139:2

אַתָּ֣ה יָ֭דַעְתָּ **שִׁבְתִּ֣י** **וְקוּמִ֑י**

You know **my sitting** and **my standing**.

The infinitive can be a prepositional complement (1 Sam 15:22) and adverbal modifier (Exod 2:18). The nominal predicate can also be used with an existential (Exod 32:18).

1 Sam 15:22

הַחֵ֤פֶץ לַֽיהוָה֙ בְּעֹל֣וֹת וּזְבָחִ֔ים **כִּשְׁמֹ֖עַ** בְּק֣וֹל יְהוָ֑ה הִנֵּ֤ה שְׁמֹ֙עַ֙ מִזֶּ֣בַח ט֔וֹב לְהַקְשִׁ֖יב מֵחֵ֥לֶב אֵילִֽים׃

Does Yahweh desire whole burnt offerings and sacrifices **as much as obeying** Yahweh's voice? Listen: obedience is better than sacrifice—to pay attention more than the fat of rams.

Exod 2:18

מַדּ֛וּעַ מִהַרְתֶּ֥ן **בֹּ֖א** הַיּֽוֹם

Why have you hastened **in arriving** today?

Exod 32:18

אֵ֥ין קוֹל֙ **עֲנ֣וֹת** גְּבוּרָ֔ה וְאֵ֥ין ק֖וֹל **עֲנ֣וֹת** חֲלוּשָׁ֑ה

There is no sound of **singing** triumph, and there is no sound of **singing** defeat.

A small number of verbs, including יסף "do again, continue," יכל "be able," and חלל "begin," repeatedly appear sequenced with an infinitive construct as a complement. These strings resemble serial verb constructions (e.g., Exod 10:29).[41]

---

[41] See Martin Haspelmath, "The Serial Verb Construction: Comparative Concept and Cross-Linguistic Generalizations," *Language and Linguistics* 17, no. 3 (2016): 291–319. For a book-length treatment, see Alexandra Y. Aikhenvald and R. M. W. Dixon, *Serial Verb Constructions: A Cross-Linguistic Typology* (Oxford and New York: Oxford University Press, 2006).

These constructions are not standardized in Biblical Hebrew, and the form with the preposition is also evidenced (e.g., Gen 38:26).[42]

Exod 10:29

לֹא־אֹסֵף עוֹד רְאוֹת פָּנֶיךָ

I will never again **see** your face.

Gen 38:26

וְלֹא־יָסַף עוֹד לְדַעְתָּה

He did not continue **to know her** anymore.

Two specialized constructions are worth mentioning on account of their frequency in Biblical Hebrew. They encode irrealis and temporal notions signaled by their use in fixed formations.

9.5.3.1 Irrealis Usages

The most common nominal predicate usage involves a preposition followed by the infinitive construct, which designates various modalities. This construction accounts for more than two-thirds of all infinitive construct occurrences. It can express contingency (necessity, possibility), evidentiality (inferential), volition (hope), or deontic modality (purpose, result). The prepositions include -לְ "to, for," -בְּ "in, when," לְמַעַן "so that, in order that," and בַּעֲבוּר "on account of, because of." Deuteronomy 6:23 exemplifies the two most commonplace sequences: the first begins with לְמַעַן and the second with -לְ. The first expresses the deontic modality indicating the result of Yahweh's deliverance from Egypt. The second signals the purpose of bringing the people into the promised land. Exodus 9:16 provides two other examples indicating evidentiality with בַּעֲבוּר and result again with לְמַעַן.

Deut 6:23

וְאוֹתָנוּ הוֹצִיא מִשָּׁם לְמַעַן הָבִיא אֹתָנוּ לָתֶת לָנוּ אֶת־הָאָרֶץ אֲשֶׁר נִשְׁבַּע לַאֲבֹתֵינוּ׃

He led us out from there **so that he would bring** us **to give** us the land that was sworn to our fathers.

Exod 9:16

וְאוּלָם בַּעֲבוּר זֹאת הֶעֱמַדְתִּיךָ בַּעֲבוּר הַרְאֹתְךָ אֶת־כֹּחִי וּלְמַעַן סַפֵּר שְׁמִי בְּכָל־הָאָרֶץ׃

However, on account of this [reason] I have appointed you: **so that you would experience** my strength and **so that** my name **would be renowned** in all the earth.

9.5.3.2 Temporal Usages

The second most frequently attested infinitive construct sequence indicates temporality. These expressions are largely made up of a temporal preposition (e.g., עַד

---

[42] For יכל, compare the different forms at Exod 2:3 and Gen 13:6. For חלל, compare Deut 2:25 and Gen 6:1.

"until," Exod 10:26; אַחֲרֵי "after," Deut 12:30; לִפְנֵי "before," Mal 3:23; see further §11.4.3.4) or time word (e.g., יוֹם "day," Deut 9:24) followed by the nominal predicate. They can be a part of a clause as an adverbial modifier. Frequently, they follow the main verb phrase, but they can start a clause (Gen 2:17).

Exod 10:26

וַאֲנַחְנוּ לֹא־נֵדַע מַה־נַּעֲבֹד אֶת־יְהוָה עַד־בֹּאֵנוּ שָׁמָּה

But we will not know how we might serve Yahweh **until we arrive** there.

Deut 12:30

הִשָּׁמֶר לְךָ פֶּן־תִּנָּקֵשׁ אַחֲרֵיהֶם אַחֲרֵי הִשָּׁמְדָם מִפָּנֶיךָ

Be on your guard lest you be lured after them even **after they are destroyed** from before you.

Mal 3:23

הִנֵּה אָנֹכִי שֹׁלֵחַ לָכֶם אֵת אֵלִיָּה הַנָּבִיא לִפְנֵי בּוֹא יוֹם יְהוָה הַגָּדוֹל וְהַנּוֹרָא:

Astonishingly, I am sending you the prophet Elijah **before the coming of** the great and fearsome day of Yahweh!

Deut 9:24

מַמְרִים הֱיִיתֶם עִם־יְהוָה מִיּוֹם דַּעְתִּי אֶתְכֶם:

You have been rebelling against Yahweh **ever since I have known** you!

Gen 2:17

כִּי בְּיוֹם אֲכָלְךָ מִמֶּנּוּ מוֹת תָּמוּת

For you will certainly die **when you eat** from it.

As discussed in a previous section (§9.5.2), this construction may be used as a way of creating the setting of an ensuing clausal sequence. The basic structure begins with a sequential conjugation of the verb היה "to be." Ordinarily וַיְהִי is used with narrative sequences (e.g., Num 7:1; 11:25), and וְהָיָה with non-narrative sequences (e.g., Deut 17:18). The prepositional or nominal phrase with the infinitive construct follows as an adverbial modifier for this frame. The main event sequence then begins with a clause that contains the sequential conjugation *wayyiqtol* (e.g., Num 7:1) or *wǝqātal* (e.g., Deut 17:18) and corresponds to the initial היה frame.

Num 7:1

וַיְהִי בְּיוֹם כַּלּוֹת מֹשֶׁה לְהָקִים אֶת־הַמִּשְׁכָּן וַיִּמְשַׁח אֹתוֹ וַיְקַדֵּשׁ אֹתוֹ וְאֶת־כָּל־כֵּלָיו וְאֶת־הַמִּזְבֵּחַ וְאֶת־כָּל־כֵּלָיו

When Moses finished erecting the tabernacle, **he anointed** it **and sanctified** it along with all its furnishings, the altar, and all its accoutrements.

Num 11:25

וַיְהִי כְּנוֹחַ עֲלֵיהֶם הָרוּחַ וַיִּתְנַבְּאוּ וְלֹא יָסָפוּ

As the spirit **rested** on them, **they prophesied** but did not continue [to prophesy].

Deut 17:18

וְהָיָה כְשִׁבְתּוֹ עַל כִּסֵּא מַמְלַכְתּוֹ וְכָתַב לוֹ אֶת־מִשְׁנֵה הַתּוֹרָה הַזֹּאת עַל־סֵפֶר
מִלִּפְנֵי הַכֹּהֲנִים הַלְוִיִּם:

When he assumes the throne of his kingdom, **he shall write** for himself a copy of this instruction on a scroll in the presence of the Levitical priests.

The initial construction serves as the temporal or circumstantial setting of the following main event sequence. Before the beginning of the main sequence, though, other clauses may intervene providing relevant material, that is, so-called background or antecedent information (e.g., Deut 5:23).

Deut 5:23

וַיְהִי כְּשָׁמְעֲכֶם אֶת־הַקּוֹל מִתּוֹךְ הַחֹשֶׁךְ וְהָהָר בֹּעֵר בָּאֵשׁ וַתִּקְרְבוּן אֵלַי כָּל־רָאשֵׁי
שִׁבְטֵיכֶם וְזִקְנֵיכֶם:

When you heard the voice from the midst of the darkness—**while the mountain was ablaze with fire**—you approached me with your tribal leaders and your elders.

Several variations occur. The main event can be initiated with *yiqtol* instead of a sequential form. This situation often occurs with nonsequential, offline, or habitual events (e.g., יֵרֵד "it would fall" at Num 11:9) or independent didactive statements not in a sequence (e.g., תָּרִימוּ "you shall offer" at Num 15:19).

Num 11:9

וּבְרֶדֶת הַטַּל עַל־הַמַּחֲנֶה לָיְלָה יֵרֵד הַמָּן עָלָיו

When the dew would fall on the camp at night, the manna **would fall** on it.

Num 15:19

וְהָיָה בַּאֲכָלְכֶם מִלֶּחֶם הָאָרֶץ תָּרִימוּ תְרוּמָה לַיהוָה:

When you eat from the food of the land, **you should offer** an offering to Yahweh.

At times, the initial frame with the verb היה is omitted. In such cases, the TAM of the nominal predicate is determined by the verb of the following main event. Narrative setting is indicated with *wayyiqtol* (e.g., Gen 27:34) and non-narrative with *wəqātal* (e.g., Deut 23:12; also, Num 11:9 above). In comparison to the clause internal adverbial modifier of Gen 2:17 (above), the serpent uses the clause sequence in Gen 3:5 to enact Eve's recounting of God's instruction (3:3).[43]

Gen 27:34

כִּשְׁמֹעַ עֵשָׂו אֶת־דִּבְרֵי אָבִיו **וַיִּצְעַק** צְעָקָה גְּדֹלָה וּמָרָה עַד־מְאֹד

As Esau **heard** his father's words, **he exclaimed** with an exceedingly loud and bitter cry.

Deut 23:12

וְהָיָה לִפְנוֹת־עֶרֶב יִרְחַץ בַּמָּיִם **וּכְבֹא** הַשֶּׁמֶשׁ **יָבֹא** אֶל־תּוֹךְ הַמַּחֲנֶה׃

Prior to evening, he should wash with water, and **as** the sun **sets**, **he may reenter** into the camp.

Gen 3:5

כִּי יֹדֵעַ אֱלֹהִים כִּי בְּיוֹם **אֲכָלְכֶם** מִמֶּנּוּ **וְנִפְקְחוּ** עֵינֵיכֶם וִהְיִיתֶם כֵּאלֹהִים יֹדְעֵי טוֹב וָרָע׃

For God knows that **when you eat** from it, your eyes **will be opened**, and you will be like gods knowing good and evil.

The main sequence may even switch between *wayyiqtol* and *wəqātal* forms. The result is a habitual situation. Numbers 10:35–36 provides such an example of enacting a repeated pattern of behavior as the people followed the ark away from the mountain of Yahweh (vv. 33–34).

Num 10:35–36

ז[44] **וַיְהִי בִּנְסֹעַ הָאָרֹן וַיֹּאמֶר** מֹשֶׁה קוּמָה ׀ יְהוָה וְיָפֻצוּ אֹיְבֶיךָ וְיָנֻסוּ מְשַׂנְאֶיךָ מִפָּנֶיךָ׃
וּבְנֻחֹה יֹאמַר שׁוּבָה יְהוָה רִבְבוֹת אַלְפֵי יִשְׂרָאֵל׃ ז

When the ark set out, Moses **said**: "Arise, Yahweh, so that your enemies scatter and your opponents flee from you." **Then whenever it would stop, he would say**: "Return, Yahweh, the myriad thousands of Israel."

9.6 INFINITIVE ABSOLUTE

The infinitive absolute functions in one of two ways: as a nominal or a verbal. As a nonfinite verb, the infinitive absolute sometimes acts as a nominal predicate whereby it is nominalized as an adverb. At other times it functions as a verbal predicate in its verbalizing role as a replacement for a finite verbal form.[45]

---

[43] It is intriguing to note that the rabbinic text, Avot of Rabbi Natan (1:5), puts the responsibility of creating the expanded instruction in Genesis 3 on the man rather than the woman as a way to fence the Torah (סיג לתורה).

[44] In the MT, an inverted *nun* occurs at the beginning and end of Numb 10:35–36 and brackets the eighty-five letters of this passage. See Yeivin, *Tiberian Masorah*, #81.

[45] The terminology "nominal predicate" and "verbal predicate" comes from Hengeveld, *Non-Verbal Predication*, 58. Galia Hatav similarly defines the infinitive absolute as "a non-finite verb

Scholars have described the function of the infinitive absolute in a variety of ways in light of the heuristic categorization "verbal noun." Joüon and Muraoka simply divide its usage into nominal and verbal, with nominal being the most common of the two. Apart from the less common nominal functions like subject, object, or predicate, they identify its main function to be an "accusative of the internal object," which can occur in both prepositive (most common) and postpositive positions.[46] This function is sometimes called the paronomastic infinitive. The term highlights that the infinitive absolute often intensifies an infinitive or finite verbal form from the same root and gives the impression of a wordplay.[47] Other grammarians call this function a tautological infinitive (from Greek ταυτολογία "same word").[48] We prefer this later descriptor. Psalm 40:2 illustrates a prepositive position tautological infinitive:

Ps 40:2

קַוֺּה קִוִּיתִי יְהוָה

I **indeed** waited for Yahweh.

According to Joüon and Muraoka, "this linguistic process allows Hebrew to express certain emphatic nuances in a subtle way."[49] In much the same way that Hebrew can front a clause constituent to indicate a topicalizing force, the prepositive position reinforces the focus on the verbal action. Gesenius likewise stressed the so-called emphatic force of the infinitive absolute in such environments, as a means of emphasizing "the idea of the verb in the abstract." This notion conveys the action of the verb "without any regard to the agent or to the circumstances of time and mood under which it takes place."[50] In a study focusing on the infinitive absolute, Muraoka says it is used for "emphasis with various nuances" in "giving the verbal idea in abstract."[51] Similarly, Waltke and O'Connor also describe the infinitive absolute as expressing verbal action in the abstract, or more specifically, "bare verbal action or state in the abstract."[52]

---

form in all of its occurrences, deprived of temporal and agreement features as well as clitics." See "The Nature of the Infinitive Absolute," in *Linguistic Studies on Biblical Hebrew*, ed. Robert D. Holmstedt, SSLL 102 (Leiden: Brill, 2021), 125.

[46] Joüon-Muraoka §123d.

[47] See Muraoka, *Emphatic Words*, 86, citing the earlier work of H. Reckendorf, *Über Paronomasie in den semitischen Sprachen* (Giessen: Töpelmann, 1909), 100–26; *IBHS* §35.3.1.

[48] See Gideon Goldenberg, "Tautological Infinitive," *Israel Oriental Studies* 1 (1971): 36–85; Yoo-Ki Kim, *The Function of the Tautological Infinitive in Classical Biblical Hebrew* (Winona Lake, IN: Eisenbrauns, 2009); Galia Hatav, "The Infinitive Absolute and Topicalization of Events in Biblical Hebrew," in *Advances in Biblical Hebrew Linguistics: Data, Method, and Analyses*, ed. Adina Moshavi and Tania Notarius (Winona Lake, IN: Eisenbrauns, 2017), 185–207.

[49] Joüon and Muraoka §123d.

[50] GKC §113a.

[51] Muraoka, *Emphatic Words*, 91–92.

[52] They subdivide its nominal uses into two main categories: (1) "absolute complement to a clause" functioning as a nominative, and (2) "adverbial complement" functioning as an accusative (*IBHS* §35.3.1.). The absolute complement function corresponds to analyses that have drawn attention to the infinitive absolute's emphatic effect on the main verb, but they qualify that it involves an intensification of the verbal force of the action and not necessarily the semantics of the verbal root

In a recent study on the infinitive absolute, Galia Hatav criticizes these approaches for their inability to account for all uses. She takes issue with the nomenclature "infinitive," instead preferring to call this Hebrew form "a non-finite verb form" that is "deprived of temporal and agreement features as well as clitics."[53] She analyzes all uses outlined in previous studies and attempts to offer a system-wide framework. Following other studies informed by <u>Generative Grammar</u>, Hatav defines the infinitive absolute as a "root phrase whose function is to name the eventuality of the verb in question."[54] Hatav's assessment is that the infinitive absolute serves as the "citation" or "lexical concept" of the verb and provides "the bundle of the lexical properties of that verb." Or, using the description of Gesenius, it is "the idea of the verb *in the abstract.*"[55]

Hatav admits that her proposal to see the infinitive absolute as a root phrase works well for its usage in contexts where it is attached to a finite clause, but it is less obvious in explaining its use as an independent verbal expression (e.g., in the place of an imperative).[56] In contrast, Edit Doron focuses her analysis of the infinitive absolute on its function as an independent stand-in for a finite verbal form. She affirms the infinitival nature of the Hebrew infinitive generally but defines it in terms of its ability to function in different types of clausal constructions. The two broader clausal constructions she analyzes are (1) infinitival clauses with imperatival force (i.e., infinitive absolute), and (2) infinitival clauses allowing pronominal clitics (i.e., the infinitive construct).[57] Doron sees the infinitive absolute as "the citation form of the verb" having adverbial uses without augmentation. As an adverbial, the infinitive absolute can either modify the finite verbal form itself (i.e., the tautological infinitive) or the verbal phrase as a whole.[58] Her framework stresses that the functional category of the infinitive absolute is mood due to its lack of tense/aspect inflection. This distinction leads Doron to conclude that the

---

itself. They note that the focus of earlier grammarians on the semantic distinction between prepositive position (= intensification) and postpositive position (= duration) is not altogether consistent (cf. GKC, §113r, which describes this position as expressing "the long *continuance* of an action"). What remains consistent, nonetheless, is that both positions always express intensification. The nuance of continuance may instead be lexically conditioned by certain verbal roots, such as הלך, which often qualifies the verbal action in terms of continuation. Waltke and O'Connor cite the work of Riekert on the infinitive absolute in Genesis in their critique of the pre- versus post-positional semantic distinction. S. J. P. K. Riekert, "The Structural Patterns of Paronomastic and Co-ordinated Infinitives Absolute in Genesis," *JNSL* 7 (1979): 69–83.

[53] Hatav, "Infinitive Absolute," 125.

[54] Hatav, 125. By root she means the irreducible lexical element carrying the "encyclopedic meaning" of the triconsonantal unit.

[55] Hatav, 130.

[56] Hatav, 135.

[57] On the function of the infinitive construct, see §9.5.1 above.

[58] Doron, "Infinitive in Biblical Hebrew," 150–52. Note that she assumes the existence of one infinitive in Biblical Hebrew with two distinct functions: the infinitive construct function and the infinitive absolute function. Doron does not, however, justify this claim morphologically, but only syntactically. In light of the morphological difficulties involved in deriving the construct form *qatōl* from infinitive *qātōl* (see §9.4.1 above), we prefer to reconstruct two morphologically distinct forms with complementary functions.

imperatival use of the infinitive absolute is more generic than the finite volitive forms, qualifying its force as "a general obligation, not restricted to any particular time and place."[59] However, as we will observe in the examples below, the ability of the infinitive absolute to function in environments resembling third-person volitional expressions with explicit subjects would seem to challenge this assessment.

These studies do not question the functional categories of usage traditionally espoused for the infinitive absolute. Rather, they reflect an interest in finding a satisfactory means of explaining its function comprehensively on the basis of linguistic criteria. The studies of both Hatav and Doron have moved this discussion along considerably, even though each proposal sustains gaps in its explanatory power. Doron leaves aside the adverbial uses and rather focuses on its clausal function, particularly its use as an imperative. Defining these imperatival uses as "generic" with no temporal anchor to the speech act is helpful.[60] This proposal is therefore limited to the independent functions of the infinitive absolute without regard to its various roles within the clause. Hatav suggests that her "root phrase" theory may account for the infinitive absolute's imperatival function of the commands in the Decalogue as "the pure eventuality that is to be performed by every person at all times."[61] This assessment resembles Doron's "generic" interpretation. However, a generic or universal construal of the infinitive's force in such environments is not reflective of its appearance in indicative statements, which are quite specific in terms of space and time (see below).

Leaving aside these unresolved questions for the moment, we simply understand the infinitive absolute to be a nonfinite verbal form that can function in one of two ways: as a nominal predicate or as a verbal predicate. The remainder of this section will outline its usage according to this broadly construed framework.[62]

9.6.1 Nominal Predicate Uses

Clausal nominal use. As a nominalized verbal predicate, the infinitive absolute can fill the noun slot of a given clause. Grammarians rightly observe, however, that this function is not its most common function in Biblical Hebrew.[63]

a. Subject of Finite Verb

Isa 57:20

וְהָרְשָׁעִים כַּיָּם נִגְרָשׁ כִּי הַשְׁקֵט לֹא יוּכָל

The wicked are like the driven sea, for **making quietness** is not possible.

---

[59] Doron, "Infinitive in Biblical Hebrew," 152 n. 8.
[60] Doron, 151–52.
[61] Hatav, "Infinitive Absolute," 137.
[62] We will revisit the work of Doron and Hatav in our summary observations regarding the verbal predicate uses of the infinitive absolute.
[63] See Joüon-Muraoka §123b; *IBHS* §35.3.3a.

Job 6:25

וּמַה־יּוֹכִיחַ **הוֹכֵחַ** מִכֶּם

What does **proof** from you prove?

b. Subject of Predicate Clause

1 Sam 15:23

כִּי חַטַּאת־קֶסֶם מֶרִי וְאָוֶן וּתְרָפִים **הַפְצַר**

For rebellion is the sin of divination, and **presumption** is iniquity and idolatry.

Job 25:2

הַמְשֵׁל וָפַחַד עִמּוֹ

Exercising dominion and dread are with him.

c. Object of a Finite Verb

Isa 7:16

כִּי בְּטֶרֶם יֵדַע הַנַּעַר **מָאֹס** בָּרָע **וּבָחֹר** בַּטּוֹב תֵּעָזֵב הָאֲדָמָה

For before the lad knows **refusing** the evil and **choosing** the good, the land will be forsaken.

Hab 3:2

בְּרֹגֶז **רַחֵם** תִּזְכּוֹר

In wrath remember **showing compassion**.

Job 9:18

לֹא־יִתְּנֵנִי **הָשֵׁב** רוּחִי

He will not grant me **return** of my breath.

d. Predicate Nominative

Ps 17:5

תָּמֹךְ אֲשֻׁרַי בְּמַעְגְּלוֹתֶיךָ

My steps are **holding fast** to your paths.

Hos 4:2

אָלֹה וְכַחֵשׁ וְרָצֹחַ וְגָנֹב וְנָאֹף

[There is] cursing, deceiving, murdering, stealing, and committing adultery.

e. Genitival Phrase

Isa 4:4

בְּרוּחַ מִשְׁפָּט וּבְרוּחַ **בָּעֵר**

With a spirit of judgment and with a spirit of **burning**.

Prov 21:16

אָדָ֗ם תּוֹעֶ֥ה מִדֶּ֣רֶךְ **הַשְׂכֵּ֑ל** בִּקְהַ֖ל רְפָאִ֣ים יָנֽוּחַ

A man erring from the way **of insight** will rest in the assembly of the *Rəpā'îm*.

f. Object of a Preposition

2 Kgs 13:17

וְהִכִּיתָ֧ אֶת־אֲרָ֛ם בַּאֲפֵ֖ק עַד־**כַּלֵּֽה**

You shall strike the Arameans at Aphek until (their) **end**.

Joüon and Muraoka consider this last use of the infinitive absolute as the object of a preposition extremely rare and perhaps suspect.[64] Nonetheless, this function is a logical extension of the infinitive absolute's nominalization that makes them theoretically able to fill the role of regular nouns, which are often governed by prepositions.

g. Apposition

1 Sam 3:12

בַּיּ֤וֹם הַהוּא֙ אָקִ֣ים אֶל־עֵלִ֔י אֵ֛ת כָּל־אֲשֶׁ֥ר דִּבַּ֖רְתִּי אֶל־בֵּית֑וֹ **הָחֵ֖ל וְכַלֵּֽה**׃

In that day I will raise up against Eli all that I spoke unto his house, (its) **beginning** and **ending**.

h. Adverbial Accusative

One of the more common nominal functions of the infinitive absolute is an adverbial accusative. Nouns serve several adverbial functions, such as temporal, locational, and manner. An extremely wooden English translation of such an adverbial function of a noun often requires the addition of a preposition, as in the following example:

Ps 58:2

מֵישָׁרִ֗ים תִּשְׁפְּט֑וּ בְּנֵ֣י אָדָֽם

Do you humans judge [with] **uprightness**?

The following sample of infinitive absolute constructions exhibit the same adverbializing force as adverbial accusative nouns. An extremely wooden translation of this nuance could add a preposition, as in "the waters receded . . . [with] going and returning," but perhaps the meaning would be best understood as "the waters receded continually" (Gen 8:3). Elsewhere, an English participle can connote the adverbial sense (Gen 12:9; 21:16; Exod 30:36; 1 Sam 6:12; 17:16).

Gen 8:3

וַיָּשֻׁ֧בוּ הַמַּ֛יִם מֵעַ֥ל הָאָ֖רֶץ **הָל֣וֹךְ וָשׁ֑וֹב**

The waters receded from upon the earth, **going and receding**.

---

[64] Joüon-Muraoka §123c. Note the suggestion that עַד־כַּלֵּה has become an adverb (cf. 2 Chr 24:10).

Gen 12:9

וַיִּסַּע אַבְרָם הָלוֹךְ וְנָסוֹעַ הַנֶּגְבָּה

Abram set out, **going and setting out** toward the Negeb.

Gen 21:16

וַתֵּלֶךְ וַתֵּשֶׁב לָהּ מִנֶּגֶד הַרְחֵק כִּמְטַחֲוֵי קֶשֶׁת

She went and sat down opposite him, **at a distance of** about the shot of a
bow.

Exod 30:36

וְשָׁחַקְתָּ מִמֶּנָּה הָדֵק

You shall beat some of it **making it fine.**

1 Sam 6:12

בִּמְסִלָּה אַחַת הָלְכוּ הָלֹךְ וְגָעוֹ

On one highway they (the cows) went, **walking and lowing.**

1 Sam 17:16

וַיִּגַּשׁ הַפְּלִשְׁתִּי הַשְׁכֵּם וְהַעֲרֵב וַיִּתְיַצֵּב אַרְבָּעִים יוֹם:

The Philistines approached **morning and evening** and stationed themselves forty days.

Intensification. The intensification function of the infinitive absolute reflects that
of the so-called adverbial accusative. This usage is also called the paronomastic
or tautological infinitive. The difference between the adverbial accusative and the
intensification usage is that the former functions on the clause level, while the
latter is limited to the verbal action itself. Grammarians sometimes identify this
accusative usage as an internal accusative, or what Ernst Jenni called "an inner
object."[65] It demarcates the intensification of the verbal action's force rather than
its lexical meaning.

In most cases the tautological infinitive intensifies a finite verb of the same root
and stem in either prepositive or postpositive positions:

a. Prepositive Position

Gen 3:4

וַיֹּאמֶר הַנָּחָשׁ אֶל־הָאִשָּׁה לֹא־מוֹת תְּמֻתוּן:

The serpent said to the woman, "You will **surely** not die." (*Qal* with *Qal*)

Gen 16:10

וַיֹּאמֶר לָהּ מַלְאַךְ יְהֹוָה הַרְבָּה אַרְבֶּה אֶת־זַרְעֵךְ

The messenger of Yahweh said to her, "I will **certainly** multiply your
seed." (*Hiphil* with *Hiphil*)

---

[65] *IBHS,* §35.3.1a; Jenni, *Lehrbuch,* 117–18.

Exod 4:14

יָדַ֗עְתִּי כִּי־דַבֵּ֥ר יְדַבֵּ֖ר הֽוּא

I know that he speaks **well**. (*Piel* with *Piel*)

b. Postpositive Position

Num 11:15

וְאִם־כָּ֣כָה ׀ אַתְּ־עֹ֣שֶׂה לִּ֗י הָרְגֵ֤נִי נָא֙ הָרֹ֔ג

If you treat me in this way, please kill me **indeed**. (*Qal* with *Qal*)

The tautological infinitive can intensify a finite verb of the same root but with a different stem:

Exod 21:22

עָנ֖וֹשׁ יֵעָנֵ֑שׁ

He will **certainly** be fined. (*Qal* infinitive with *Niphal* verb)

Another group of tautological infinitives modify a finite verb with a different verbal root. This usage often involves certain verbal roots that can specify a certain kind of verbal intensification. We note the following examples:

a. הלך – Continuation

Gen 12:9

וַיִּסַּ֣ע אַבְרָ֔ם הָל֥וֹךְ וְנָס֖וֹעַ הַנֶּֽגְבָּה׃

Abram set out, **continuing** and setting out for the Negeb.

This infinitive also regularly occurs with a finite verbal form of הלך, perhaps indicating "to go continually" or "with continuation." Examples include:

Judg 4:24

וַתֵּ֜לֶךְ יַ֤ד בְּנֵֽי־יִשְׂרָאֵל֙ הָל֣וֹךְ וְקָשָׁ֔ה עַ֖ל יָבִ֣ין מֶֽלֶךְ־כְּנָֽעַן

The hand of the sons of Israel **continued** to increase in dominance over Jabin, king of Canaan.

2 Sam 5:10

וַיֵּ֥לֶךְ דָּוִ֖ד הָל֣וֹךְ וְגָד֑וֹל וַיהוָ֛ה אֱלֹהֵ֥י צְבָא֖וֹת עִמּֽוֹ׃

David went along **continuing** in greatness, and Yahweh, God of armies was with him.

b. רבה – Increase

Gen 41:49

וַיִּצְבֹּ֨ר יוֹסֵ֥ף בָּ֛ר כְּח֥וֹל הַיָּ֖ם הַרְבֵּ֣ה מְאֹ֑ד עַ֛ד כִּי־חָדַ֥ל לִסְפֹּ֖ר כִּי־אֵ֥ין מִסְפָּֽר׃

Joseph stored up with very **great increase** grain like the sand of the sea until he ceased to count, for it was without number.

Josh 13:1

וְהָאָרֶץ נִשְׁאֲרָה הַרְבֵּה־מְאֹד לְרִשְׁתָּהּ

The land remains with very **much** to possess.

1 Kgs 10:10

וַתִּתֵּן לַמֶּלֶךְ מֵאָה וְעֶשְׂרִים ׀ כִּכַּר זָהָב וּבְשָׂמִים הַרְבֵּה מְאֹד

She gave to the king one hundred and twenty *kikkars* of gold and (she gave) balsam at a very **great quantity**.

2 Kgs 10:18

אַחְאָב עָבַד אֶת־הַבַּעַל מְעָט יֵהוּא יַעַבְדֶנּוּ הַרְבֵּה

Ahab served Baal a little. Jehu will serve him **with increase**!

c. יטב – Excellence

Deut 17:4

וְדָרַשְׁתָּ הֵיטֵב

You shall seek **with excellence** (lit., "with doing well," or perhaps "diligently").

2 Kgs 11:18

וְאֶת־צַלְמָיו שִׁבְּרוּ הֵיטֵב וְאֵת מַתָּן כֹּהֵן הַבַּעַל הָרְגוּ לִפְנֵי הַמִּזְבְּחוֹת

His [Baal] images they smashed **thoroughly** and Mattan, priest of Baal, they slaughtered before the altars.

9.6.2 Verbal Predicate Uses

The infinitive absolute can function as a verbal predicate in two types of settings: (1) the infinitive is adjoined to another verbal form and mirrors the function of the corresponding verb, and (2) the infinitive functions independently with the force of a finite verb.

Adjoined to Other Verbal Forms. The first category of examples involves infinitives absolute adjoined to finite verbs. The context of these infinitives indicate that they continue the aspectual features of the head verb and likewise assume its subject.

Exod 8:11

וַיַּרְא פַּרְעֹה כִּי הָיְתָה הָרְוָחָה וְהַכְבֵּד אֶת־לִבּוֹ

Pharaoh saw that there was relief and **weighed down** his heart. (following *wayyiqtol*)

Lev 25:14

וְכִי־תִמְכְּרוּ מִמְכָּר לַעֲמִיתֶ֔ךָ א֥וֹ קָנֹ֖ה מִיַּ֣ד עֲמִיתֶ֑ךָ

When you make a sale to your neighbor or **buy** from the hand of your neighbor (following prefix conjugation)

1 Sam 25:26

אֲשֶׁ֣ר מְנָעֲךָ֤ יְהוָה֙ מִבּ֣וֹא בְדָמִ֔ים וְהוֹשֵׁ֥עַ יָדְךָ֖ לָ֑ךְ

In that Yahweh kept you from going in bloodshed and **rescued** you by your hand. (following suffix conjugation)

The infinitive absolute can also mirror nonfinite verbs, including the infinitive construct in the following example:

Exod 32:6

וַיֵּ֤שֶׁב הָעָם֙ לֶאֱכֹ֣ל וְשָׁת֔וֹ וַיָּקֻ֖מוּ לְצַחֵֽק

The people sat down to eat and **drink** and arose to make amusement.

Replacement for Other Verbal Forms. The second category of uses are independent in nature, appearing to stand in place of finite verbal forms. The most common independent use of the infinitive absolute in Hebrew is the imperative.

a. Imperative

Exod 13:3

וַיֹּ֨אמֶר מֹשֶׁ֜ה אֶל־הָעָ֗ם זָכ֞וֹר אֶת־הַיּ֤וֹם הַזֶּה֙ אֲשֶׁ֨ר יְצָאתֶ֤ם מִמִּצְרַ֙יִם֙ מִבֵּ֣ית עֲבָדִ֔ים

Moses said, "**Remember** this day that you came out from Egypt, from the house of slavery."

Exod 20:8

זָכ֛וֹר אֶת־י֥וֹם הַשַּׁבָּ֖ת לְקַדְּשֽׁוֹ׃

Remember the Sabbath day by sanctifying it.

Deut 5:12

שָׁמ֣וֹר אֶת־יוֹם֙ הַשַּׁבָּ֔ת לְקַדְּשׁ֑וֹ

Observe the day of the Sabbath by sanctifying it.

Num 4:2

נָשֹׂ֗א אֶת־רֹאשׁ֙ בְּנֵ֣י קְהָ֔ת מִתּ֖וֹךְ בְּנֵ֥י לֵוִֽי

Take the headcount of the sons of Kohath from the midst of the sons of Levi.

Deut 1:16

שָׁמֹ֤עַ בֵּין־אֲחֵיכֶם֙ וּשְׁפַטְתֶּ֣ם צֶ֔דֶק בֵּֽין־אִ֥ישׁ וּבֵין־אָחִ֖יו וּבֵ֥ין גֵּרֽוֹ

Hear between your brothers and judge rightly between a man and his brother and his sojourner.

Deut 31:26

לָקֹחַ אֵת סֵפֶר הַתּוֹרָה הַזֶּה

Take the book of this instruction.

b. Third-Person Volitive Expressions

On a few occasions, the infinitive absolute occurs in environments that appear to reflect third-person volitional expressions.

Gen 17:10

הִמּוֹל לָכֶם כָּל־זָכָר

Every male of yours **is to be circumcised**.

Lev 6:7

וְזֹאת תּוֹרַת הַמִּנְחָה הַקְרֵב אֹתָהּ בְּנֵי־אַהֲרֹן לִפְנֵי יְהוָה אֶל־פְּנֵי הַמִּזְבֵּחַ:

This is the law of the *minḥâ*: the sons of Aaron **are to offer** it before Yahweh in front of the altar.

Num 15:35

מוֹת יוּמַת הָאִישׁ רָגוֹם אֹתוֹ בָאֲבָנִים כָּל־הָעֵדָה מִחוּץ לַמַּחֲנֶה

The man must certainly be put to death. All the assembly **must stone** him with stones outside the camp.

c. Indicatives

Rarely, the infinitive absolute can function as an indicative verb. The fact that these forms occur with explicitly stated subjects supports analyzing them functionally as finite verbs. We can illustrate this usage from Ecclesiastes, where the infinitive is followed by the 1CS independent pronoun, presumably the subject of the infinitive:[66]

Eccl 4:2

וְשַׁבֵּחַ אֲנִי אֶת־הַמֵּתִים שֶׁכְּבָר מֵתוּ מִן־הַחַיִּים אֲשֶׁר הֵמָּה חַיִּים עֲדֶנָה:

I praised the dead who were already dead more than the living who were still alive.

This construction in Hebrew can also occur in third-person expressions, such as the use of the *Niphal* infinitive absolute in Esther:

---

[66] This function of the infinitive absolute parallels the well-established narrative use of the infinitive absolute in Phoenician inscriptions. The Karatepe Inscription attests this usage multiple times, including examples where the 1CS independent pronoun immediately follows the infinitive:

KAI 26 I:3–4, 6

l'b wl'm yḥw 'nk 'yt dnnym yrḥb 'nk 'rṣ 'mq 'dn . . . wml' 'nk 'qrt p'r

As a father and mother, **I enlivened** the Danunians. **I enlarged** the land of the plain of 'Adana . . . **I filled** the granaries of *Pa'ar*.

On these lines, see François Bron, *Recherches sur les inscriptions phéniciennes de Karatepe*, Hautes Études Orientales 11 (Genève: Droz, 1979), 36–44.

Esth 3:13

וְנִשְׁל֨וֹחַ סְפָרִ֜ים בְּיַ֣ד הָרָצִים֮ אֶל־כָּל־מְדִינ֣וֹת הַמֶּ֒לֶךְ֒

Letters **were sent** by the hand of the couriers into all the provinces of the king.

The ability of the infinitive absolute to function as an independent verbal form may have derived from the tendency to adjoin it to finite verbal forms. In these contexts, the semantics of the head finite verb are subsumed by the adjoined non-finite verb (i.e., infinitive absolute), which expresses the lexical meaning of the root in the abstract, according to Gesenius, or as the root phrase/clause, according to Hatav and Doron. English does something similar when two verbs are connected by the coordinating conjunction "and" with the same subject. The subject is nonobligatory: "He entered the store and bought groceries." This example is not exact, however, since the second verb is also marked for past tense. In Hebrew, the adjoined infinitive absolute contains neither tense nor person or number, which are determined by its finite verbal head. The independent usage simply removes the verbal abstraction (i.e., the infinitive absolute) from its adjoined environment, repurposing this nonfinite verb in certain finite verbal contexts. The propensity in Biblical Hebrew to use this form as an imperative may have arisen on analogy with the imperative, which is not marked for person, only number and gender. In other words, second-person imperatival statements do not require an explicit subject, enabling the infinitive absolute to provide a stylistic alternative to the imperative. In Biblical Hebrew, this function was expanded to include third-person volitional expressions, which do require an explicit subject. Once this syntactical adaptation of the infinitive absolute occurred, it allowed for other possibilities for finite verbal usage. Its adaptation to indicative statements once again required the inclusion of an explicit subject in the form of a noun or pronoun, depending on the grammatical person of the statement (i.e., 1, 2, or 3 person).

The morphosyntax of the Hebrew infinitive is complex and multifaceted. Part of the challenge for students of Biblical Hebrew is that its functions do not parallel the usage of the English infinitive. This chapter has examined the morphological features of the infinitive construct and the infinitive absolute and has systematically catalogued their diversity of functions throughout the Hebrew Bible.

9.7 EXERCISES

Translate the following Hebrew sentences into English. Identify every infinitive construct and infinitive absolute, analyzing its syntactical function.

1. וַיְהִ֞י בְּצֵ֤את נַפְשָׁהּ֙ כִּ֣י מֵ֔תָה וַתִּקְרָ֥א שְׁמ֖וֹ בֶּן־אוֹנִ֑י וְאָבִ֖יו קָֽרָא־ל֥וֹ בִנְיָמִֽין׃
(Gen 35:18)

2. וּבְבֹא מֹשֶׁה אֶל־אֹהֶל מוֹעֵד לְדַבֵּר אִתּוֹ וַיִּשְׁמַע אֶת־הַקּוֹל מִדַּבֵּר אֵלָיו מֵעַל הַכַּפֹּרֶת אֲשֶׁר עַל־אֲרֹן הָעֵדֻת מִבֵּין שְׁנֵי הַכְּרֻבִים וַיְדַבֵּר אֵלָיו: (Num 7:89)

3. וְזֹאת הַמִּצְוָה הַחֻקִּים וְהַמִּשְׁפָּטִים אֲשֶׁר צִוָּה יְהוָה אֱלֹהֵיכֶם לְלַמֵּד אֶתְכֶם לַעֲשׂוֹת בָּאָרֶץ אֲשֶׁר אַתֶּם עֹבְרִים שָׁמָּה לְרִשְׁתָּהּ: (Deut 6:1)

4. וְעַתָּה יִשְׂרָאֵל מָה יְהוָה אֱלֹהֶיךָ שֹׁאֵל מֵעִמָּךְ כִּי אִם־לְיִרְאָה אֶת־יְהוָה אֱלֹהֶיךָ לָלֶכֶת בְּכָל־דְּרָכָיו וּלְאַהֲבָה אֹתוֹ וְלַעֲבֹד אֶת־יְהוָה אֱלֹהֶיךָ בְּכָל־לְבָבְךָ וּבְכָל־ נַפְשֶׁךָ: (Deut 10:12)

5. וַיִּשְׁלַח הַמֶּלֶךְ וַיִּקְרָא לְשִׁמְעִי וַיֹּאמֶר אֵלָיו הֲלוֹא הִשְׁבַּעְתִּיךָ בַיהוָה וָאָעִד בְּךָ לֵאמֹר בְּיוֹם צֵאתְךָ וְהָלַכְתָּ אָנֶה וָאָנָה יָדֹעַ תֵּדַע כִּי מוֹת תָּמוּת וַתֹּאמֶר אֵלַי טוֹב הַדָּבָר שָׁמָעְתִּי: (1 Kgs 2:42)

6. וַיֹּאמֶר מְשָׁרְתוֹ מָה אֶתֵּן זֶה לִפְנֵי מֵאָה אִישׁ וַיֹּאמֶר תֵּן לָעָם וְיֹאכֵלוּ כִּי כֹה אָמַר יְהוָה אָכֹל וְהוֹתֵר: (2 Kgs 4:43)

7. בְּלֶכְתָּם יֵלֵכוּ וּבְעָמְדָם יַעֲמֹדוּ וּבְהִנָּשְׂאָם מֵעַל הָאָרֶץ יִנָּשְׂאוּ הָאוֹפַנִּים לְעֻמָּתָם כִּי רוּחַ הַחַיָּה בָּאוֹפַנִּים: (Ezek 1:21)

8. וַיֹּאמֶר לְהַשְׁמִידָם לוּלֵי מֹשֶׁה בְחִירוֹ עָמַד בַּפֶּרֶץ לְפָנָיו לְהָשִׁיב חֲמָתוֹ מֵהַשְׁחִית: (Ps 106:23)

9. וַיהוָה שָׁב אֶת־ שְׁבִית אִיּוֹב בְּהִתְפַּלְלוֹ בְּעַד רֵעֵהוּ וַיֹּסֶף יְהוָה אֶת־כָּל־אֲשֶׁר
לְאִיּוֹב לְמִשְׁנֶה: (Job 42:10)

10. כִּי טוֹב אֲמָר־לְךָ עֲלֵה הֵנָּה מֵהַשְׁפִּילְךָ לִפְנֵי נָדִיב אֲשֶׁר רָאוּ עֵינֶיךָ: (Prov 25:7)

Translate from English to Hebrew.

11. Yahweh God gave us his instruction so that we might truly live with wisdom in the world.

12. The children of Israel refused to go to the mountain but returned to their tents for fear of the fire increasing more and more.

13. Samuel truly prophesied to King Saul to not offer the sacrifice.

14. Pharaoh continued to give an evil report to the people until they left Egypt.

15. When they remembered to carefully do the commandments, the inhabitants of Jerusalem rose early and obeyed Moses's words that he commanded them.

Guided Reading: Deut 5:6–21

6 אָנֹכִי יְהוָה אֱלֹהֶיךָ אֲשֶׁר הוֹצֵאתִיךָ מֵאֶרֶץ מִצְרַיִם מִבֵּית עֲבָדִים: 7 לֹא יִהְיֶה־לְךָ אֱלֹהִים אֲחֵרִים עַל־פָּנָי: 8 לֹא־תַעֲשֶׂה־לְךָ פֶסֶל כָּל־תְּמוּנָה אֲשֶׁר בַּשָּׁמַיִם מִמַּעַל וַאֲשֶׁר בָּאָרֶץ מִתַּחַת וַאֲשֶׁר בַּמַּיִם מִתַּחַת לָאָרֶץ: 9 לֹא־תִשְׁתַּחֲוֶה לָהֶם וְלֹא תָעָבְדֵם כִּי אָנֹכִי יְהוָה אֱלֹהֶיךָ אֵל קַנָּא פֹּקֵד עֲוֹן אָבוֹת עַל־בָּנִים וְעַל־שִׁלֵּשִׁים וְעַל־רִבֵּעִים לְשֹׂנְאָי: 10 וְעֹשֶׂה חֶסֶד לַאֲלָפִים לְאֹהֲבַי וּלְשֹׁמְרֵי מִצְוֹתָו: 11 לֹא תִשָּׂא אֶת־שֵׁם־יְהוָה אֱלֹהֶיךָ לַשָּׁוְא כִּי לֹא יְנַקֶּה יְהוָה אֵת אֲשֶׁר־יִשָּׂא אֶת־שְׁמוֹ לַשָּׁוְא: 12 שָׁמוֹר אֶת־יוֹם הַשַּׁבָּת לְקַדְּשׁוֹ כַּאֲשֶׁר צִוְּךָ יְהוָה אֱלֹהֶיךָ: 13 שֵׁשֶׁת יָמִים תַּעֲבֹד וְעָשִׂיתָ כָּל־מְלַאכְתֶּךָ: 14 וְיוֹם הַשְּׁבִיעִי שַׁבָּת לַיהוָה אֱלֹהֶיךָ לֹא תַעֲשֶׂה כָל־מְלָאכָה אַתָּה וּבִנְךָ־וּבִתֶּךָ וְעַבְדְּךָ־וַאֲמָתֶךָ וְשׁוֹרְךָ וַחֲמֹרְךָ וְכָל־בְּהֶמְתֶּךָ וְגֵרְךָ אֲשֶׁר בִּשְׁעָרֶיךָ לְמַעַן יָנוּחַ עַבְדְּךָ וַאֲמָתְךָ כָּמוֹךָ: 15 וְזָכַרְתָּ כִּי־עֶבֶד הָיִיתָ בְּאֶרֶץ מִצְרַיִם וַיֹּצִאֲךָ יְהוָה אֱלֹהֶיךָ מִשָּׁם בְּיָד חֲזָקָה וּבִזְרֹעַ נְטוּיָה עַל־כֵּן צִוְּךָ יְהוָה אֱלֹהֶיךָ לַעֲשׂוֹת אֶת־יוֹם הַשַּׁבָּת: 16 כַּבֵּד אֶת־אָבִיךָ וְאֶת־אִמֶּךָ כַּאֲשֶׁר צִוְּךָ יְהוָה אֱלֹהֶיךָ לְמַעַן יַאֲרִיכֻן יָמֶיךָ וּלְמַעַן יִיטַב לָךְ עַל הָאֲדָמָה אֲשֶׁר־יְהוָה אֱלֹהֶיךָ נֹתֵן לָךְ: 17 לֹא תִּרְצָח: 18 וְלֹא תִּנְאָף: 19 וְלֹא תִּגְנֹב: 20 וְלֹא־תַעֲנֶה בְרֵעֲךָ עֵד שָׁוְא: 21 וְלֹא תַחְמֹד אֵשֶׁת רֵעֶךָ וְלֹא תִתְאַוֶּה בֵּית רֵעֶךָ שָׂדֵהוּ וְעַבְדּוֹ וַאֲמָתוֹ שׁוֹרוֹ וַחֲמֹרוֹ וְכֹל אֲשֶׁר לְרֵעֶךָ:

VOCABULARY AND NOTES[67]

Verse 6				
הוֹצֵאתִיךָ	*Hiphil* SC	1CS + 2MS SF	יצא	

Verse 7				
אֲחֵרִים		ADJ.MP		"other"

Verse 8				
פֶסֶל		N.MS		"idol"
תְּמוּנָה		N.FS		"form"
מַעַל		N.MS		"above"

Verse 9				
תִשְׁתַּחֲוֶה	*Hištaphel*			"worship"
תָעָבְדֵם	*Hophal*	PC 2MS + 3MP SF	עבד	"serve" (*Qal*; תַּעֲבֹד; Deut 7:16)
קַנָּא		ADJ.MS		"jealous"
עֲוֹן		N.MS CSTR		"iniquity"

---

[67] Two cantillation traditions are marked starting with the final word of v. 6 through v. 19.

שְׁלֵשִׁים		ADJ.MP		"third generation"
רִבֵּעִים		ADJ.MP		"fourth generation"
שֹׂנְאָי	*Qal*	ACT PTCL MP + 1CS SF	שׂנא	"hate"

Verse 10

אֹהֲבַי	*Qal*	ACT PTCL MP + 1CS SF	אהב	
שֹׁמְרֵי	*Qal*	ACT PTCL MP CSTR	שׁמר	
מִצְוֹתָו		N.MP + 3MS SF	מִצְוָה	"commandment" (*qere* מִצְוֹתַי + 1 CS SF)

Verse 11

שָׁוְא		N.MS		"emptiness"
יְנַקֶּה	*Piel*	PC 3MS	נקה	"acquit"

Verse 12

שָׁמוֹר	*Qal*	INF ABS	שׁמר	
שַׁבָּת		N.FS		"Sabbath"
קַדְּשׁוֹ	*Piel*	INF CSTR + 3MS SF	קדשׁ	"make honor"
צִוְּךָ	*Piel*	SC 3MS + 2MS SF	צוה	

Verse 13

מְלַאכְתֶּךָ		N.FS + 2MS SF	מְלָאכָה	"work; occupation"

Verse 14

שְׁבִיעִי		ADJ.MS		"seventh"
בִּתֶּךָ		N.FS + 2MS SF	בַּת	
אֲמָתֶךָ		N.FS + 2MS SF	אָמָה	"female servant"
שׁוֹרְךָ		N.MS + 2MS SF	שׁוֹר	"ox"
חֲמֹרְךָ		N.MS + 2MS SF	חֲמוֹר	"donkey"
בְּהֶמְתֶּךָ		N.FS + 2MS SF	בְּהֵמָה	"cattle"
גֵּרְךָ		N.MS + 2MS SF	גֵּר	"immigrant"
יָנוּחַ	*Qal*			"rest"
כָּמוֹךָ		PREP + 2MS		"like"

Verse 15

וַיֹּצִאֲךָ	*Hiphil*	CP 3MS + 2MS SF	יצא	
חֲזָקָה		ADJ.FS		"strong"
זְרֹעַ		N.FS		"arm"
נְטוּיָה	*Qal*	PASS PTCL FS	נטה	"stretch out"

Verse 16

כַּבֵּד	*Piel*	INF ABS (or IMPV MS)	כבד	"honor"
אִמֶּךָ		N.FS + 2MS SF	אֵם	

יַאֲרִיכֻן	*Hiphil*	PC 2MP	אַרך	"lengthen"
יִיטַב	*Qal*			"prosper"

Verse 17

תִּרְצָח	*Qal*			"murder"[68]

Verse 18

תִּנְאָף	*Qal*			"commit adultery"

Verse 19

תִּגְנֹב	*Qal*			"steal"

Verse 20

רֵעֲךָ		N.MS + 2MS SF	רֵעַ	"neighbor"
עֵד		N.MS		"witness"

Verse 21

תַחְמֹד	*Qal*			"desire"
תִתְאַוֶּה	*Hitpael*	PC 2MS	אוה	"wish for"

---

[68] The initial letter of the verb is marked with both *rafe* and *dagesh* (vv. 17–19) signaling two different pronunciations.

///////////////

CHAPTER 10

CONJUNCTIONS, ADVERBS, AND OTHER PARTICLES

A great deal of communication relies substantially on supposition and impli-cature. Speakers assume their audience shares essential concepts and knows their context. The audience likewise presumes standard conventions are shared with the speaker. For instance, the statement, *here is my house, but now I live over there*, brings together notions of location, time, possession, and object. These can be un-derstood even if the deictic position (*here, over there, now*, see §7.9.2.3) is different for the speaker and audience, or if the house is owned by a landlord rather than the individual speaking (*my, I*), or if the domicile (*house*) is the primary site of dwell-ing (*live*). Misunderstandings can occur when the presumptions are inaccurate, or conventions are not standardized and lack clarity. Communication may also fail if topics switch opaquely. The abridged statement, *here is my house; I live over there*, appears to provide contradictory information. In conversation, however, a gaffe in expression can be corrected by a simple question: *Do you mean you don't live there anymore?* However, some other forms of communication—like the written word—do not allow for more explanation. Conjunctions and adverbs can serve to mitigate this kind of confusion. In the original statement, for example, the conjunction *but* and adverb *now* are placed at the beginning of the second clause to signal that the second clause is temporally present and contrasts with what comes before.

10.1 GOING DEEPER WITH PARTICLES

In the wake of the dedication of the temple at Jerusalem, Yahweh appears to Solo-mon. The night vision is described starting at 2 Chr 7:12. He cautions the king that the mere presence of the sanctuary does not guarantee blessing (Jer 7:3–8) and describes the conditions for the people's prayers to be heard in the newly constructed dwelling place (see Solomon's request, 2 Chr 6:39).

2 Chr 7:12

וַיֵּרָא יְהוָה אֶל־שְׁלֹמֹה בַּלָּיְלָה וַיֹּאמֶר לוֹ שָׁמַעְתִּי אֶת־תְּפִלָּתֶךָ וּבָחַרְתִּי בַּמָּקוֹם הַזֶּה לִי לְבֵית זָבַח:

Yahweh appeared to Solomon that night and said to him: "I have heard your prayer and chose this place as my house of sacrifice."

Three instances of divine retribution are then outlined in the following verse (2 Chr 7:13). These "covenant curses" are instigated through drought, locusts, or disease. Each of these circumstances is initiated with the particle, הֵן or אִם, and linked with the conjunction *waw*. In the first instance, two clauses depict the cause, הֵן אֶעֱצֹר הַשָּׁמַיִם וְלֹא־יִהְיֶה מָטָר "If I should close the heavens and no rain comes." The second and third include a single clause each.

2 Chr 7:13

הֵן אֶעֱצֹר הַשָּׁמַיִם וְלֹא־יִהְיֶה מָטָר וְהֵן־אֲצַוֶּה עַל־חָגָב לֶאֱכוֹל הָאָרֶץ וְאִם־אֲשַׁלַּח דֶּבֶר בְּעַמִּי:

If I should close the heavens and no rain comes, **or if** I command the locust to devour the land, **or if** I send pestilence on my people.

For many modern readers, it is unbelievable and even repugnant to consider that tragedy is caused by divine justice. Most would consider a plague the result of a natural disaster. Yet, Yahweh claims that he orchestrates these dreadful events. The broader context of the passage allows for some clarity. God's people are experiencing a covenant curse on account of their evil deeds. Yahweh is sending disaster with the purpose of motivating their repentance. The principle assumes that Israel experiences cursing while in the land of blessing, only when Israel has abandoned their covenant responsibilities (Leviticus 26; Deuteronomy 27). The result of catastrophe would undoubtedly cause Israel to call out to God. It should be noted that the same explanation cannot be extended to New Testament Christians suffering difficulty (John 9). National and territorial blessing is not promised in the same manner as Israel.

In 2 Chr 7:14, Yahweh urges his people not merely to ask for rescue but to consider their ways and seek absolution. Four conditions are required for granting a reprieve to those called by God's name. The people must humble themselves, pray, seek his face, and repent (v. 14). These obligations are linked with conjunctions and similar verbal conjugations. Four PC verbs are preceded by a *waw*. This series indicates the simple coordination of ideas. The fifth clause, however, signals a shift to the apodosis.

2 Chr 7:14

וְיִכָּנְע֣וּ עַמִּ֡י אֲשֶׁ֣ר נִֽקְרָא־שְׁמִ֣י עֲלֵיהֶם֩ וְיִֽתְפַּֽלְל֨וּ וִיבַקְשׁ֤וּ פָנַי֙ וְיָשֻׁ֙בוּ֙ מִדַּרְכֵיהֶ֣ם הָרָעִ֔ים
וַאֲנִי֙ אֶשְׁמַ֣ע מִן־הַשָּׁמַ֔יִם וְאֶסְלַח֙ לְחַטָּאתָ֔ם וְאֶרְפָּ֖א אֶת־אַרְצָֽם׃

Should my people upon whom my name is called **humble themselves,
pray, seek** my face, and **repent** from their evil ways, **then I** will hear
from heaven, forgive their sin, and heal their land.

The apodosis is initiated with a nonobligatory independent personal pronoun
and the shift to first person (וַאֲנִי "then I"). Yahweh promises to respond not with
continued judgment but merciful action and restoration. Should the people doubt
God's ready attentiveness, he ends with two clauses beginning with the temporal
adverb עַתָּה "now, presently." Yahweh occupies the temple and is near to his people in the here and now. And his presence is enduring.

2 Chr 7:15–16

עַתָּ֗ה עֵינַי֙ יִהְי֣וּ פְתֻח֔וֹת וְאָזְנַ֖י קַשֻּׁב֑וֹת לִתְפִלַּ֖ת הַמָּק֣וֹם הַזֶּֽה׃ וְעַתָּ֗ה בָּחַ֤רְתִּי וְהִקְדַּ֙שְׁתִּי֙
אֶת־הַבַּ֣יִת הַזֶּ֔ה לִהְיוֹת־שְׁמִ֥י שָׁ֖ם עַד־עוֹלָ֑ם וְהָי֨וּ עֵינַ֧י וְלִבִּ֛י שָׁ֖ם כָּל־הַיָּמִֽים׃

Now my eyes are open, and my ears are attentive to prayer from this
place. **And now** I have chosen and sanctified this house so that my name
will be there forever, and my eyes and heart will be there always.

The visionary voice communicates a clear progression of Yahweh's interaction
with his people. The clauses move from judgment to repentance and reinstatement.
Each new situation is signaled with clause linkers and various other linguistic cues.
Close attention to the semantics of just a small number of frequently used function
words can help to understand the discourse relationships.

10.2 CHAPTER OBJECTIVES

This chapter describes a wide range of conjunctions, adverbs, and other particles.
These elements generally are used in communication to clarify or relate words,
phrases, clauses, and other discourse units.

10.3 INTRODUCTION

This chapter focuses on words that primarily express grammatical functions rather
than lexical (or what some have dubbed denotative) meanings. A grammatical function can signal a structural relationship (syntax), a contextual notion (pragmatics),
existence, or a number of speech acts.[1] These grammatical relations are grouped
together as <u>function words</u>. Function words elicit syntactic and semantic connections within clauses, between clauses, and in larger discourse units. In traditional

---

[1] Determiners, pronouns, and quantifiers have been discussed in previous chapters.

grammar, function words include those lexemes not circumscribed in the word class categories of noun, adjective, or verb. Semitic grammarians often refer to this catchall group as <u>particles</u>, which include conjunctions (§10.4), adverbs (§10.5), conjunctive adverbs (§10.6), negations (§10.7), interrogatives (§10.8), pragmatic markers (§10.9), existentials (§10.10), and direct object markers (§10.11). Prepositions are discussed in chapter 11.

Function words are common, <u>polysemous</u> words. Of the fifteen most repeated lexemes in the Hebrew Bible, eleven are function words, including the top six.[2] Their frequency restricts the total number of unique function words in languages.[3] Knowing these terms has tremendous payoff because they are so common. On a semantic level, function words often signal different connotations—many of which have overlapping nuances. The result is that function words are polysemous. Unlike nouns and verbs, the multifunctionality limits the reader's ability to rely upon word-for-word substitutions from the source to the target language. For example, every instance of Hebrew וֹ cannot be glossed with the simple English connective (*and*). It commonly indicates an explanation (*that is*; *namely*), contrast (*but*; *however*), topicalization (*now*), result (*so*), cause (*for*; *because*), adverb (*even*; *also*), conditional (*if*), sequential (*then*), comitative (*with*), restrictive (*even so*; *yet*), correlative (*both . . . and*), or even a dummy or null word that is best, at times, left untranslated. It is better to understand the many functions of a grammatical word like וֹ, consider its use in context, and decide the overlapping function most equivalent in the target language. The following treatment details the principal grammatical words in Biblical Hebrew and their multivalent functions.

10.4 CONJUNCTIONS

A <u>conjunction</u> is a function word that expresses a semantic relationship linking two or more conjoins of like syntactic constituency. <u>Conjoins</u> (sometimes called conjuncts) are elements of similar constituent rank, such as words, phrases, clauses, propositions, or even larger discourse units. Conjoins need not employ a conjunction; they may simply be sequenced asyndetically. If a conjunction is used, it indicates an overt syntactic and semantic relation between the conjoined elements. Conjunctions can be divided between linkers that encode either coordination or subordination. <u>Coordination</u> assumes the conjoins are syntactically independent.

---

[2] The six most common BH words are -וֹ, -הַ, -לְ, -בְּ, אֵת, and מִן. The other five function words in the top fifteen lexemes include עַל, אֶל, אֲשֶׁר, כִּי, and -כְּ.

[3] It is often claimed that function words are a closed set while content words are open. While function words are more constrained than other lexemes, new grammatical relations do emerge through the normal course of language evolution, often emerging from a preexisting open-set word (grammaticalization). Yet, it is more likely that a function word takes on an ancillary meaning (polysemy) than a new function word is innovated. For examples, see H. H. Hardy II, *The Development of Biblical Hebrew Prepositions*, ANEM 28 (Atlanta: SBL, 2022). By comparison, content words are more readily added to languages.

English examples include *and*, *or*, and *but*. <u>Subordination</u> indicates syntactical dependency—that is to say, one serves as a constituent of the other. English examples include *while*, *if*, *when*, *as*, *because*, and *that*. At times, the distinction between coordination and subordination is not altogether clear, and certain linkers may function in either capacity.

The English examples below may help to distinguish the basic differences. Example (1a) demonstrates covert or asyndetic conjunction between two clauses (<u>parataxis</u>). The conjoins represent equal constituency; no semantic relationship is expressed. The clauses could be reordered without any explicit change in meaning or syntactic dependency. Implicit differences, however, can often be inferred. Other examples include the additive coordinating conjunction *and* (1b), which joins the two clauses semantically but does not specify the syntactic relationship. The conjoins are interchangeable (i.e., *Sarah ate a burger, and I drank a soda*) without a necessary change in meaning or structure. In example (1c), the conjunction *while* is subordinating. It expresses both the temporal relation and embedded syntax. The second clause modifies and is dependent on the main clause (<u>hypotaxis</u> or underneath agreement). The semantics and syntax are explicitly changed should the conjoins be exchanged (i.e., *Sarah ate a burger while I drank a soda*).

(1a)   I drank a soda. Sarah ate a burger.
(1b)   I drank a soda, **and** Sarah ate a burger.
(1c)   I drank a soda **while** Sarah ate a burger.

10.4.1 Coordination

A <u>coordinator</u> (or coordinating conjunction) is a linker that produces the grammatical relationship of overt coordination. The coordinated elements share constituency without any marked syntactic subordination, and a new syntactic unit is created from the conjoined expression. When the conjoins are clauses, the outcome is a <u>coordinating clause</u>.

Three main syntactic characteristics circumscribe this class of function words. First, a coordinator links elements of similar constituency—words with words, phrases with phrases, and clauses with clauses, including subordinating clauses (see §10.4.2).[4] Second, a coordinator is conjoin initial. No constituent element

---

[4] Scholars disagree on the degree to which the elements must be symmetrical; see Cynthia L. Miller, "The Pragmatics of Waw as a Discourse Marker in Biblical Hebrew Dialogue," *ZAH* 12, no. 2 (1999): 166n6; Bo Isaksson, "Subordination: Biblical Hebrew," in *EHLL* 6:657–64. E. Cowper and V. DeCaen ("Biblical Hebrew: A Formal Perspective on the Left Periphery," *Toronto Working Papers in Linguistics* 38 [2017]: 1–33) alternatively suggest a model of asymmetric coordination. Jesse R. Scheumann argues that the structure of coordination is hierarchical and the coordinator ן- encodes sub-constituents as a defective head. See Scheumann, "A Syntactic Analysis of Phrasal Coordination in Biblical Hebrew" (PhD diss., University of the Free State Bloemfontein, 2020).

or linker may precede a coordinator.[5] Third, a coordinator can allow for multiple coordinated conjoins.

Hebrew has two primary coordinators -וְ and אֹו. Syntactically, the former functions as an additive and the latter as an alternative (Lev 12:8). The coordinator may link elements that are contiguous or noncontiguous.[6] In Gen 31:43, -וְ coordinates a string of clauses in the first part of the speech, and אֹו connects the nonadjacent PPs. The semantics of these functions are described in the following sections.

Lev 12:8

וְאִם־לֹא תִמְצָא יָדָהּ דֵּי שֶׂה וְלָקְחָה שְׁתֵּי־תֹרִים אֹו שְׁנֵי בְּנֵי יֹונָה אֶחָד לְעֹלָה וְאֶחָד לְחַטָּאת

If [the woman giving birth] does not own enough sheep, she may take [for the offering] **two** turtledoves **or two** doves—**one** for a whole-brunt offering **and one** for a sin-offering.

Gen 31:43

וַיַּעַן לָבָן וַיֹּאמֶר אֶל־יַעֲקֹב הַבָּנֹות בְּנֹתַי וְהַבָּנִים בָּנַי וְהַצֹּאן צֹאנִי וְכֹל אֲשֶׁר־אַתָּה רֹאֶה לִי־הוּא וְלִבְנֹתַי מָה־אֶעֱשֶׂה לָאֵלֶּה הַיֹּום אֹו לִבְנֵיהֶן אֲשֶׁר יָלָדוּ׃

Laban answered and said to Jacob: "The daughters are my daughters, **and the children** are my children, **and the flock** is my flock, **and everything** which you see belongs to me. What should I do today for these my daughters[7] **or** for the children they carried?"

Several other function words can be added to these two primary coordinators. They may be characterized by some but not all the above properties. These are discussed as correlatives (§10.4.1.3) and other conjunctions (§10.4.1.4).

10.4.1.1 -וְ Coordinator

The -וְ coordinator functions as a <u>proclitic</u> and takes various forms (i.e., <u>allophones</u>) depending on the phonology of the prefixed word. The most common is -וְ. It takes the corresponding full vowel when the vowel of the following syllable is a composite *shewa* (e.g., וַאֲנִיֹּות, וֶאֱמֶת, וַחֲזַק). The composite *shewa* is elided with some א-initial words (e.g., וֵאלֹהִים). The coordinator becomes -וִי for words starting with initial *yod-shewa* syllables (e.g., וִירוּשָׁלַם and וִיהִי). For words with one syllable or initial accent, the pretonic vowel may change to *qames* (e.g., וָשֶׂה or תֹהוּ וָבֹהוּ) or *patah* -וַ with certain consecutive forms. When preceding the labial consonants ב, מ, and פ or most syllables with a *shewa*, -וּ is the expected form (e.g., רֶכֶב וּפָרָשִׁים, חֻקִּים וּמִשְׁפָּטִים, בָּנִים וּבָנֹות).

---

[5] Robert Holmstedt, "Critical at the Margins: Edge Constituents in Biblical Hebrew," *KUSATU* 17 (2014): 143.

[6] This phenomenon may be understood by employing ellipsis and/or fronting. See the discussion of "split coordination" with -וְ in Scheumann, "Syntactic Analysis," 91–115.

[7] The demonstrative pronoun could refer to the sheep of the flock. Laban lists these previously. The change in order and number agreement suggests that the daughters are the more likely referent.

The additive coordinator creates a new grammatically plural constituent from the compound elements. The conjoined constituent may serve in any syntactic position: subject (Gen 31:44), verb phrase (twice in Song 2:10), object (Eccl 3:17), prepositional phrase (Ps 104:23), infinitive (Deut 8:6), and adverb (Isa 54:3).

Gen 31:44

וְעַתָּ֕ה לְכָ֛ה נִכְרְתָ֥ה בְרִ֖ית אֲנִ֥י וָאָֽתָּה

And now, come let us—**me and you**—cut a covenant.

Song 2:10

עָנָ֥ה דוֹדִ֖י וְאָ֣מַר לִ֑י ק֥וּמִי לָ֛ךְ רַעְיָתִ֥י יָפָתִ֖י וּלְכִי־לָֽךְ׃

My love **answered and said** to me: "**Arise**, my darling my beauty, **and come**."

Eccl 3:17

אָמַ֤רְתִּֽי אֲנִי֙ בְּלִבִּ֔י אֶת־הַצַּדִּיק֙ וְאֶת־הָ֣רָשָׁ֔ע יִשְׁפֹּ֖ט הָאֱלֹהִ֑ים

I said in my heart: "God will judge **the righteous and the wicked**."

Ps 104:23

יֵצֵ֣א אָדָ֣ם לְפָעֳל֑וֹ וְֽלַעֲבֹ֖דָת֣וֹ עֲדֵי־עָֽרֶב׃

Humanity goes out **to his work and to his labor** until evening.

Deut 8:6

וְשָׁ֣מַרְתָּ֔ אֶת־מִצְוֺ֖ת יְהוָ֣ה אֱלֹהֶ֑יךָ לָלֶ֥כֶת בִּדְרָכָ֖יו וּלְיִרְאָ֥ה אֹתֽוֹ׃

Keep the commandments of Yahweh your God **to walk** in his ways **and to fear** him.

Isa 54:3

יָמִ֥ין וּשְׂמֹ֖אול תִּפְרֹ֑צִי

You will spread out **south and north**.

Other grammatical elements can also be coordinated with -וְ, including adjectives (Gen 18:18), subordinators (Num 27:16–17), interrogatives (1 Sam 30:13), interjections (אָמֵ֥ן וְאָמֵֽן), deictic markers (Exod 2:12), preposition complements (Gen 1:14), and even the *nomen rectum* of a construct phrase (Num 31:54). The only limitation appears to be that the coordinator cannot accommodate suffixed elements (e.g., בֵּיתִ֥י וָךְ** "the house of me and you") without another linked lexeme (e.g. אֹתִ֥י וְאֹתָֽךְ).

Gen 18:18

וְאַ֨בְרָהָ֔ם הָי֧וֹ יִֽהְיֶ֛ה לְג֥וֹי גָּד֖וֹל וְעָצ֑וּם

Abraham will certainly become a **great and mighty** nation.

Num 27:16–17

יִפְקֹד יְהוָה אֱלֹהֵי הָרוּחֹת לְכָל־בָּשָׂר אִישׁ עַל־הָעֵדָה: אֲשֶׁר־יֵצֵא לִפְנֵיהֶם וַאֲשֶׁר יָבֹא לִפְנֵיהֶם וַאֲשֶׁר יוֹצִיאֵם וַאֲשֶׁר יְבִיאֵם וְלֹא תִהְיֶה עֲדַת יְהוָה כַּצֹּאן אֲשֶׁר אֵין־לָהֶם רֹעֶה:

May Yahweh the God breathing into all flesh appoint a man over the community **who** will go out before them, **who** will go in before them, **who** will lead them out, **and who** will lead them in so that Yahweh's community will not be like the flock without their shepherd.

1 Sam 30:13

וַיֹּאמֶר לוֹ דָוִד לְמִי־אַתָּה וְאֵי מִזֶּה אָתָּה
David said to him: "**To whom** do you belong? **And where** are you from?"

Exod 2:12

וַיִּפֶן כֹּה וָכֹה וַיַּרְא כִּי אֵין אִישׁ
He turned **here and here** and did not see anyone.

Gen 1:14

וְהָיוּ לְאֹתֹת וּלְמוֹעֲדִים וּלְיָמִים וְשָׁנִים:
They will be for signs and for assembly times and **for days and years**.

Num 31:54

וַיִּקַּח מֹשֶׁה וְאֶלְעָזָר הַכֹּהֵן אֶת־הַזָּהָב מֵאֵת שָׂרֵי הָאֲלָפִים וְהַמֵּאוֹת
Moses and Eleazar the priest took the gold from the commanders of **the thousands and of the hundreds**.

With more than two conjoins, the -וְ may connect each element (Deut 6:5), may only be present with the final element (2 Chr 6:37), or may be intermittent (Gen 43:11).[8] A combination of these strategies may also be used to form nestled groups (Gen 46:7).

Deut 6:5

וְאָהַבְתָּ אֵת יְהוָה אֱלֹהֶיךָ בְּכָל־לְבָבְךָ וּבְכָל־נַפְשְׁךָ וּבְכָל־מְאֹדֶךָ:
You should love Yahweh your God **with all your heart and with all your person and with all your muchness**.

2 Chr 6:37

חָטָאנוּ הֶעֱוִינוּ וְרָשָׁעְנוּ
We have sinned, done wrong, **and** acted wickedly.

---

[8] Scheumann, "Syntactic Analysis," 91–115.

Gen 43:11

קְח֞וּ מִזִּמְרַ֤ת הָאָ֙רֶץ֙ בִּכְלֵיכֶ֔ם וְהוֹרִ֥ידוּ לָאִ֖ישׁ מִנְחָ֑ה מְעַ֤ט צֳרִי֙ **וּמְעַ֣ט דְּבַ֔שׁ נְכֹאת**
וָלֹ֖ט בָּטְנִ֥ים וּשְׁקֵדִֽים

Take some of the land's choice produce in your packs and bring [them]
down to the man as a gift: **a measure of balsam and some honey, gum**
resin and myrrh, pistachios and almonds.

Gen 46:7

בָּנָ֞יו **וּבְנֵ֤י בָנָיו֙** אִתּ֔וֹ בְּנֹתָ֥יו **וּבְנ֣וֹת בָּנָ֗יו וְכָל־זַרְע֔וֹ** הֵבִ֥יא אִתּ֖וֹ מִצְרָֽיְמָה׃

His sons **and his grandsons** with him, his daughters **and his grand-**
daughters, and all his offspring entered with him into Egypt.

From a semantic perspective, -וְ is the least marked conjunction. It is difficult, if
not impossible, to summarize its prototypical semantics. Functionally, -וְ represents
a multiplicity of senses. The coordinator is most commonly additive (*and*) but also
may function as an adverbial (*even; also*), causative (*for; because*), comitative
(*with*), concessive (*although*), conditional (*if*), contrastive (*but; however*), expla-
native (*that is; namely*), restrictive (*even so; yet*), result (*so*), sequential (*and then*),
similarity (*as*), successive (*then*), topical (*now*), or another propositional connective. Some discourse situations can restrict its meaning (e.g., *wəqātal, wayyiqtol,*
אִם ... וְ-), but context is the ultimate determiner of its situational meaning. In
the most general terms, the truth or falsity of the statement is communicable to all
conjoins. If the statement is true for one element, it is true for the others.

10.4.1.2 אוֹ Coordinator

The alternative coordinator אוֹ creates a conjoined set in which one (and only
one) of the elements is intended to substitute as the constituent. The conjoins most
often represent symmetrical constituency. The coordinated constituent may serve
in any syntactic position: subject (Jer 23:33), verb phrases (Job 13:22), object
(Exod 21:20), prepositional phrase (Gen 24:49), infinitive (Lev 5:4), and adverb
(2 Kgs 13:19). When linking more than two conjoins—in contrast to the additive
coordinator -וְ—each noninitial element must be headed by אוֹ.

Jer 23:33

וְכִי־יִשְׁאָלְךָ֩ הָעָ֨ם הַזֶּ֜ה **אֽוֹ־הַנָּבִ֤יא אֽוֹ־כֹהֵן֙**

If **this people or the prophet or a priest** asks you

Job 13:22

וּ֭קְרָא וְאָנֹכִ֣י אֶֽעֱנֶ֑ה **אֽוֹ־אֲ֝דַבֵּ֗ר** וַהֲשִׁיבֵֽנִי׃

Call and **I will reply, or should I speak** and bring me back!

Exod 21:20

וְכִי־יַכֶּה֩ אִ֨ישׁ אֶת־עַבְדּ֜וֹ א֤וֹ אֶת־אֲמָתוֹ֙ בַּשֵּׁ֔בֶט וּמֵ֖ת תַּ֣חַת יָד֑וֹ נָקֹ֖ם יִנָּקֵֽם׃

If a man strikes **his male or female servant** with his staff and [the servant] dies by his hand, the servant shall certainly be avenged.

Gen 24:49

וְ֠עַתָּה אִם־יֶשְׁכֶ֨ם עֹשִׂ֜ים חֶ֧סֶד וֶאֱמֶ֛ת אֶת־אֲדֹנִ֖י הַגִּ֣ידוּ לִ֑י וְאִם־לֹ֕א הַגִּ֣ידוּ לִ֔י וְאֶפְנֶ֥ה עַל־יָמִ֖ין א֥וֹ עַל־שְׂמֹֽאל׃

Now if you are planning to show kindness and faithfulness to my lord, tell me! But if not, tell me so that I can turn away **to the right or to the left**.

Lev 5:4

נֶ֡פֶשׁ כִּ֣י תִשָּׁבַע֩ לְבַטֵּ֨א בִשְׂפָתַ֜יִם לְהָרַ֣ע ׀ א֣וֹ לְהֵיטִ֗יב לְ֠כֹל אֲשֶׁ֨ר יְבַטֵּ֧א הָאָדָ֛ם בִּשְׁבֻעָ֖ה

If a person swears unthinkingly with his lips **to do evil or to do good** concerning anything which a human may speak unthinkingly in an oath

2 Kgs 13:19

וַיֹּ֨אמֶר֙ לְהַכּ֜וֹת חָמֵ֤שׁ אוֹ־שֵׁשׁ֙ פְּעָמִ֔ים אָ֛ז הִכִּ֥יתָ אֶת־אֲרָ֖ם עַד־כַּלֵּ֑ה וְעַתָּ֕ה שָׁלֹ֥שׁ פְּעָמִ֖ים תַּכֶּ֥ה אֶת־אֲרָֽם׃

He said: "Had you struck [the ground] **five or six times**, then you would have completely struck down Aram. But now, you will only strike down Aram three times."

Other grammatical elements can be coordinated with אוֹ. These include adjectives (Lev 21:18), subordinators (Exod 21:33), interrogatives (Job 16:3), deictic markers (Eccl 11:6), quantified NPs (Lev 11:32), and the *nomen rectum* of a construct phrase (Deut 4:16; see also 17:6).

Lev 21:18

כִּ֥י כָל־אִ֛ישׁ אֲשֶׁר־בּ֥וֹ מ֖וּם לֹ֣א יִקְרָ֑ב אִ֤ישׁ עִוֵּר֙ א֣וֹ פִסֵּ֔חַ א֥וֹ חָרֻ֖ם א֥וֹ שָׂרֽוּעַ׃

For no one who has a disfigurement shall approach—**a blind or lame or mutilated or deformed man**.

Exod 21:33

וְכִֽי־יִפְתַּ֨ח אִ֜ישׁ בּ֗וֹר א֠וֹ כִּֽי־יִכְרֶ֥ה אִ֛ישׁ בֹּ֖ר וְלֹ֣א יְכַסֶּ֑נּוּ וְנָֽפַל־שָׁ֥מָּה שּׁ֖וֹר א֥וֹ חֲמֽוֹר׃

When someone opens a cistern **or when** someone digs a cistern and does not cover it, and an ox or donkey falls into it.

Job 16:2b–3

מְנַחֲמֵ֖י עָמָ֣ל כֻּלְּכֶֽם׃ הֲקֵ֥ץ לְדִבְרֵי־ר֑וּחַ א֥וֹ מַה־יַּ֝מְרִֽיצְךָ֗ כִּ֣י תַעֲנֶֽה׃

All of you are toilsome commiserators! **Will** windy words ever end? **Or** what pains you that you keep responding?

Eccl 11:6

הֲזֶה אוֹ־זֶה

Will it be this one **or** this one?

Lev 11:32

יִטְמָא מִכָּל־כְּלִי־עֵץ אוֹ בֶגֶד אוֹ־עוֹר אוֹ שָׂק

It shall be unclean—every article of wood **or** clothing **or** hide **or** sack.

Deut 4:16

תַּבְנִית זָכָר אוֹ נְקֵבָה

An image of a male **or** of a female

Semantically, אוֹ is more marked than the -וְ coordinator. Most of its functions are similar to the logic connective OR (∨). For true statements, the clause is true for one conjoin. The other conjoins are not likewise true. Typically, only one conjoin is intended to substitute as the constituent, but it is not necessarily the case in all instances that this conjoin is true to the exclusion of all the other options. In the below example (Exod 4:11), there are two coordinating sequences. The first involves the two questions (מִי . . . אוֹ מִי). It is not an either-or situation—Yahweh is the answer for both! The second coordination similarly designates the various attributes that God imparts to humanity (אִלֵּם . . . חֵרֵשׁ . . .). Again, each is not exclusive. Yahweh is in ultimate control of every physical condition, and he gives speech to even those with heavy mouths and tongues (vv. 10–12).

Exod 4:11

מִי שָׂם פֶּה לָאָדָם אוֹ מִי־יָשׂוּם אִלֵּם אוֹ חֵרֵשׁ אוֹ פִקֵּחַ אוֹ עִוֵּר הֲלֹא אָנֹכִי יְהוָה׃

Who imparted a mouth to humanity? **Or** who imparts muteness **or** deafness **or** sightedness **or** blindness? Is it not I, Yahweh?

10.4.1.3 Correlatives

The correlative conjunctions are two or more sequenced linkers used to form a single constituent. English and Hebrew correlatives head each conjoin as the initial element. Two Hebrew linking sequences include the exclusive alternative correlatives אוֹ . . . אוֹ "either . . . or," and the inclusive additive correlatives, גַּם . . . וְגַם "both . . . and." In the former case, one and only one element is true if the statement is true. In the latter, all elements are true if the statement is true. While the coordinators אוֹ and -וְ can be used in like fashion, these correlative series are explicitly marked for exclusivity and inclusivity.

The syntax of the correlatives is like that of the previously described coordinators with the addition of the extra element. Two (or more) exclusive alternatives are conjoined using a series of אוֹ correlations. The conjoins are typically symmetrical. They are commonly VPs or NPs. In 1 Sam 26:10–11, David swears that he would not kill God's anointed leader. Rather he sets out two alternatives for Saul's death: either he will die of old age, or he will die in battle. Another instance of correlative אוֹ is found in the goring ox passage (Exod 21:28–32). The punishment is equivalent regardless of the gender of the victim (v. 29). In the situation where reparations are required, justice is similarly meted out impartially regardless of the victim's age or gender (v. 31). A series of more than two conjoins is found in Num 9:22. The NPs describe three temporal alternatives as various intensifying lengths of time (two days, a month, or years) that the Israelites would encamp in the wilderness and wait on the cloud.

1 Sam 26:10

חַי־יְהוָה כִּי אִם־יְהוָה יִגָּפֶנּוּ **אוֹ**־יוֹמוֹ יָבוֹא וָמֵת **אוֹ** בַמִּלְחָמָה יֵרֵד וְנִסְפָּה

By the life of Yahweh, if Yahweh shall strike him down: **either** his day will come and he will die, **or** in battle he will go down and be carried away.

Exod 21:29–31

וְאִם שׁוֹר נַגָּח הוּא מִתְּמֹל שִׁלְשֹׁם וְהוּעַד בִּבְעָלָיו וְלֹא יִשְׁמְרֶנּוּ וְהֵמִית אִישׁ **אוֹ** אִשָּׁה הַשּׁוֹר יִסָּקֵל וְגַם־בְּעָלָיו יוּמָת: אִם־כֹּפֶר יוּשַׁת עָלָיו וְנָתַן פִּדְיֹן נַפְשׁוֹ כְּכֹל אֲשֶׁר־יוּשַׁת עָלָיו: **אוֹ**־בֵן יִגָּח **אוֹ**־בַת יִגָּח כַּמִּשְׁפָּט הַזֶּה יֵעָשֶׂה לּוֹ:

If an ox has gored previously—and its master had been warned but did not watch it—and kills a man or woman, the ox shall be stoned to death and also its master should be killed. If a restitution is imposed on him, he shall pay the ransom for his life according to everything imposed on him. **Whether** it gores a son **or** gores a daughter, it is to be done to him according to this commandment.

Num 9:22

אוֹ־יֹמַיִם **אוֹ**־חֹדֶשׁ **אוֹ**־יָמִים בְּהַאֲרִיךְ הֶעָנָן עַל־הַמִּשְׁכָּן לִשְׁכֹּן עָלָיו יַחֲנוּ בְנֵי־יִשְׂרָאֵל

Whether two days, **or** a month, **or** years—whenever the cloud stayed on the tabernacle—the Israelites would encamp.

The inclusive additive correlatives גַם . . . וְגַם function similarly. Correlatives conjoin prepositional phrases (as in 1 Sam 2:26), NPs (as in 1 Sam 12:14), or VPs (as in Gen 24:44).

1 Sam 2:26

וְהַנַּעַר שְׁמוּאֵל הֹלֵךְ וְגָדֵל וָטוֹב גַּם עִם־יְהוָה וְגַם עִם־אֲנָשִׁים:

The boy Samuel lived and matured, and he became reputable **with both** Yahweh **and** people.

1 Sam 12:14

אִם־תִּירְאוּ אֶת־יְהוָה וַעֲבַדְתֶּם אֹתוֹ וּשְׁמַעְתֶּם בְּקֹלוֹ וְלֹא תַמְרוּ אֶת־פִּי יְהוָה וִהְיִתֶם
גַּם־אַתֶּם וְגַם־הַמֶּלֶךְ אֲשֶׁר מָלַךְ עֲלֵיכֶם אַחַר יְהוָה אֱלֹהֵיכֶם׃

If you fear Yahweh, serve him, obey his voice, and do not rebel against Yahweh's command, then you all—**both** you **and** the king who rules over you—will follow faithfully after Yahweh your God.

Gen 24:44

גַּם־אַתָּה שְׁתֵה וְגַם לִגְמַלֶּיךָ אֶשְׁאָב

As for you, drink, **and additionally**, I will draw [water] for your camels.

10.4.1.4 Other Conjunctions

Three other clause conjunctions are noteworthy and appear frequently. The lexemes כִּי, אִם, and פֶּן link two or more conjoined clauses.[9] They primarily link clauses rather than other constituent types, have other non-conjunctive functions, or do not adhere exactly to the characteristics outlined for primary coordinators.

These conjunctions operate at the front edge of a clause, but other elements may come before. The coordinators -וְ or אוֹ can precede to link a sequence of other similar conjoins or larger discourse elements (e.g., אוֹ כִי at Lev 15:25; וְאִם at Prov 30:32; אוֹ אִם at 1 Kgs 21:6; וּפֶן at Deut 12:3). Other function words (e.g., כִּי אִם at Eccl 4:10; גַּם אִם at Eccl 4:11; רַק אִם at 2 Chr 33:8) or vocatives (בְּנִי אִם at Prov 1:10; יהוה אֱלֹהַי אִם at Ps 7:4; וְאַתָּה אִם at 2 Chr 7:17) may also be prior.

Semantically, כִּי, אִם, and פֶּן designate syntactic dependency of the clause with a conjoined clause either before or after it. The conjunction כִּי commonly expresses cause/grounds (Gen 12:10), result (Deut 31:23), and circumstances (Deut 6:25), as well as concessive (Deut 29:18), asseverative (Deut 5:25), or adversative relationships (Deut 5:3).

Gen 12:10

וַיֵּרֶד אַבְרָם מִצְרַיְמָה לָגוּר שָׁם כִּי־כָבֵד הָרָעָב בָּאָרֶץ

Abram went down toward Egypt to sojourn there **because** the famine was severe in the land.

Deut 31:23

חֲזַק וֶאֱמָץ כִּי אַתָּה תָּבִיא אֶת־בְּנֵי יִשְׂרָאֵל אֶל־הָאָרֶץ

Be strong and firm **so that** you can lead the Israelites into the land.

---

[9] Several other conjunctions may also be identified, but they are quite infrequent. These include: אוּלָם "however; although," אִלּוּ "even if," הֵן "if" (rarely), לָהֵן "therefore," לוּ "if," לוּלֵא "unless; if not," and לוּלֵא "unless."

Deut 6:25

וּצְדָקָה תִּהְיֶה־לָּנוּ **כִּי**־נִשְׁמֹר לַעֲשׂוֹת אֶת־כָּל־הַמִּצְוָה הַזֹּאת לִפְנֵי יְהוָה אֱלֹהֵינוּ
כַּאֲשֶׁר צִוָּנוּ:

Righteousness will be ours **if** we are careful to do every single commandment before Yahweh our God just as he commanded us.

Deut 29:18

שָׁלוֹם יִהְיֶה־לִּי **כִּי** בִּשְׁרִרוּת לִבִּי אֵלֵךְ

Peace will be mine **even though** I walk with a stubborn heart.

Deut 5:25

וְעַתָּה לָמָּה נָמוּת **כִּי** תֹאכְלֵנוּ הָאֵשׁ הַגְּדֹלָה הַזֹּאת

Now for what do we die? **Surely** this massive blaze will devour us!

Deut 5:3

לֹא אֶת־אֲבֹתֵינוּ כָּרַת יְהוָה אֶת־הַבְּרִית הַזֹּאת **כִּי** אִתָּנוּ אֲנַחְנוּ אֵלֶּה פֹה הַיּוֹם כֻּלָּנוּ
חַיִּים:

Yahweh initiated this covenant not just with our fathers **but** with us, we
who are here today, all of us who are alive.

The linker אִם indicates the protasis, *if*-clause, of a conditional (Gen 18:30).[10] The
apodosis, *then*-clause, can be asyndetic (1 Chr 28:9) or connected with a -וְ coordinator (2 Sam 15:33).[11]

Gen 18:30

לֹא אֶעֱשֶׂה **אִם**־אֶמְצָא שָׁם שְׁלֹשִׁים

I will not do it **if** I find thirty [righteous].

1 Chr 28:9

אִם־תִּדְרְשֶׁנּוּ יִמָּצֵא לָךְ **וְאִם**־תַּעַזְבֶנּוּ יַזְנִיחֲךָ לָעַד

If you seek him, [then] he will be found for you, but **if** you abandon him,
[then] he will reject you forever.

2 Sam 15:33

אִם עָבַרְתָּ אִתִּי וְהָיִתָ עָלַי לְמַשָּׂא

If you travel along with me, **then** you will be a burden to me.

---

[10] A condition may also be introduced with כִּי (e.g., 2 Kgs 4:29, כִּי־תִמְצָא אִישׁ לֹא תְבָרְכֶנּוּ וְכִי־יְבָרֶכְךָ
אִישׁ לֹא תַעֲנֶנּוּ "**If** you encounter a man, do not greet him, **and if** a man greets you, do not answer him.")

[11] Some conditionals—especially in certain subgenres—contain unmarked protases and apodoses.
Proverbs 29:14 is one such example: מֶלֶךְ שׁוֹפֵט בֶּאֱמֶת דַּלִּים כִּסְאוֹ לָעַד יִכּוֹן "[If] a king judges the poor
faithfully, [then] his throne will be established forever." Such asyndetic relationships must be reck-
oned through context.

Finally, פֶּן is a prohibitive or apprehensive akin to English *lest* (Exod 1:10).[12]

Exod 1:10

הָבָה נִתְחַכְּמָה לֹו פֶּן־יִרְבֶּה

Look here! Let us deal shrewdly with [Israel], **lest** they multiply!

The function word אִם can also serve in a similar manner as a contrastive. This use often is found in a clause initiated with a yes-no question (see §10.8) to elicit an *either . . . or* situation (Josh 5:13). In addition, it is found with the sequence אִם־לֹא (Deut 8:2). The particle may precede both alternatives (without a coordinator, Exod 19:13, or with a coordinator, Josh 24:15).

Josh 5:13

הֲלָנוּ אַתָּה אִם־לְצָרֵינוּ

Are you for us **or** for our enemies?

Deut 8:2

הֲתִשְׁמֹר מִצְוֹתָו אִם־לֹא

Will you keep his commandments, **or not**?

Exod 19:13

לֹא־תִגַּע בֹּו יָד כִּי־סָקֹול יִסָּקֵל אֹו־יָרֹה יִיָּרֶה אִם־בְּהֵמָה אִם־אִישׁ לֹא יִחְיֶה

A hand shall not touch him because he will be stoned with stones or speared with spears—**whether** beast **or** human, neither shall live.

Josh 24:15

בַּחֲרוּ לָכֶם הַיֹּום אֶת־מִי תַעֲבֹדוּן אִם אֶת־אֱלֹהִים אֲשֶׁר־עָבְדוּ אֲבֹותֵיכֶם אֲשֶׁר בְּעֵבֶר הַנָּהָר וְאִם אֶת־אֱלֹהֵי הָאֱמֹרִי אֲשֶׁר אַתֶּם יֹשְׁבִים בְּאַרְצָם וְאָנֹכִי וּבֵיתִי נַעֲבֹד אֶת־יְהוָה

Choose today for yourselves who you will serve, **either** the gods that your fathers served beyond the River [Euphrates] **or** the Amorite gods. But as for me and my house, we will serve Yahweh!

The specific function of כִּי and אִם as temporal subordinators (*when*) with the narrative frames, וַיְהִי and וְהָיָה, are discussed below (§10.4.2.3). At times, כִּי and אִם function as complementizers (§10.4.2.2).

10.4.2 Subordination

Unlike coordination, subordination involves syntactical dependency. A subordinator, or subordinating conjunction, is a function word that expresses a syntactic relationship that makes an embedded clause (also called a subordinating clause) into

---

[12] Frantisek Lichtenberk, "Apprehensional Epistemics," in *Modality in Grammar and Discourse*, ed. Joan Bybee and Suzanne Fleischman, Typological Studies in Language 32 (Amsterdam: Benjamins, 1995), 293–327.

a constituent member of another clause. The embedded clause contains its own predication and serves a subordinate role as related to the <u>matrix clause</u>.[13] Subordinators are clause initial and may signal various semantic relations—many analogous to other function words. More than one subordinated clause may be linked together using a coordinator. In such cases, the coordinator must come before the subordinator (e.g., וַאֲשֶׁר, אוֹ כִי, or וְעַד) and never the inverse order.

Subordinators may be organized into three main categories—relativizers (§10.4.2.1), complementizers (§10.4.2.2), or adverbializers (§10.4.2.3). Each type is characterized by its syntactic function in the matrix clause as an adnominal, nominal, or adverbial. A relativizer embeds a clause with the constituency of a noun or adjective modifying a nominal head. A complementizer indicates the embedded clause serves as the complement of a verb or preposition. An adverbializer modifies the matrix verb as an adverb. The final section (§10.4.2.4) describes other constructions that express clause subordination.

10.4.2.1 Relativizer

A <u>relativizer</u> is a type of subordinator that creates an embedded clause (i.e., <u>relative clause</u>) assigning it the constituency of an adnominal in the matrix clause. The most frequent Hebrew subordinator is the relative אֲשֶׁר.[14] This lexeme occurs nearly 5,500 times.

Semantically, the embedded clause describes an appositional nominal, which must precede the relativizer. This word is referred to as the <u>head</u> of the relative clause (or traditionally antecedent). The head serves both as a matrix-clause constituent and as an embedded-clause constituent.[15] In the following examples (2a, 3a), the second conjoins can be expressed as embedded clauses using the relativizer *that*. The resulting embedded clauses (2b, 3b) describe the head noun *soda* in the matrix clause. In both instances, the coreferential pronoun *it* is deleted from the embedded clause.

(2a)	I drank a soda. **It** wasn't fizzy.
(2b)	I drank **a soda that** ___ wasn't fizzy.
(3a)	I drank a soda. Sarah purchased **it**.
(3b)	I drank **a soda that** Sarah purchased ___.

Hebrew relative clauses work mostly in like manner. The relativizer is clause initial and follows a nominal constituent in a matrix clause. It does not take any

---

[13] See Holmstedt, *Relative Clause*. He uses the term "pivot constituent" in place of subordinator (see e.g., 7).

[14] The terms *relative* or *relative particle* are commonly used as a general word class designation—analogous to *subordinator*—without reference to functional type. That is to say, the relative אֲשֶׁר may function as a relativizer, a complementizer, or part of an adverbializer compound. These latter designations are based on its matrix clause constituency as an adnominal, nominal, or adverbial.

[15] Holmstedt, *Relative Clause*, 102–4.

grammatical agreement with its head beyond syntactic proximity.[16] The embedded clause requires, at minimum, predication. In Gen 21:23b, two relativizers describe the head nouns, חֶסֶד and אֶרֶץ. The first relative elaborates that covenant faithfulness has been accomplished between the speaker and addressee. The second clarifies that the location includes the address's present residence.

Gen 21:23b

כַּחֶסֶד אֲשֶׁר־עָשִׂיתִי עִמְּךָ תַּעֲשֶׂה עִמָּדִי וְעִם־הָאָרֶץ אֲשֶׁר־גַּרְתָּה בָּהּ׃

According to **the covenant-faithfulness₁ that₁** I have done (___₁) with you, you shall do with me and with **the land₂ that₂** you have sojourned **in** (**it₂**)

The two diagrams show the constituency of the head in the embedded clauses:

Genesis 21:23b: Embedded Clause 1

				PREP
				+
			REL - - -	NP (MS)
עִמְּךָ	[אֶת־הַחֶסֶד]	עָשִׂיתִי	אֲשֶׁר	כַּחֶסֶד
PREP		VERB (1CS)		
+				
PRO (2MS)	NP (MS) - - - - - - - - - REL			

Genesis 21:23b: Embedded Clause 2

			PREP
			+
		REL - - - -	NP (FS)
בָּהּ	גַּרְתָּה	אֲשֶׁר	עִם הָאָרֶץ
PREP	VERB (2MS)		
+			
PRO (3FS) - - - - - - - - - - - REL			

When the head is the subject of the embedded clause, no independent constituent is included in the embedded clause (e.g., Gen 15:7).[17] The embedded constituent is often but not always omitted when it is the object of the embedded clause as with חֶסֶד "covenant-faithfulness" (e.g., the first relative clause of Gen 21:23b above as compared to 2 Sam 9:7: עָשֹׂה אֶעֱשֶׂה עִמְּךָ חֶסֶד "I will certainly do covenant-faithfulness with you"). With certain constructions—particularly when

---

[16] Also, Hebrew, unlike English, does not mark the difference between nonrestrictive and restrictive relative clauses.

[17] An exceedingly small number of exceptions may be noted. See, for instance, Num 14:8, אֶרֶץ אֲשֶׁר־הִוא זָבַת חָלָב וּדְבָשׁ׃ "a land which it is flowing with milk and honey."

the head functions as the complement of a preposition or a genitive formative—a resumptive pronoun is used to specify the constituency of the head in the embedded clause (e.g., the second relative clause of Gen 21:23b above with בָּהּ and also Deut 8:9). With location heads, the resumption is signaled in the embedded clause by the adverb שָׁם (e.g., Deut 4:14, along with the object of the infinitive construct).

Gen 15:7

אֲנִי יְהוָה אֲשֶׁר הוֹצֵאתִ֫יךָ מֵאוּר כַּשְׂדִּים

I am Yahweh **who** (**I**) **brought** you out from Ur of the Chaldeans.

Genesis 15:7: Embedded Clause

				PRED (MS)	
					SUBJ (1CS)
		REL	– – – – –		(1CS)
מֵאוּר כַּשְׂדִּים	הוֹצֵאתִיךָ	אֲשֶׁר	יְהוָה		אֲנִי
PREP + NP	VERB (1CS) + OBJ (2MS)	– – – – REL			

Deut 8:9

אֶרֶץ אֲשֶׁר אֲבָנֶיהָ בַרְזֶל וּמֵהֲרָרֶיהָ תַּחְצֹב נְחֹשֶׁת

a land that its rocks are iron and from **its** mountains you can mine copper.

Deut 4:14

בָּאָ֫רֶץ אֲשֶׁר אַתֶּם עֹבְרִים שָׁמָּה לְרִשְׁתָּהּ

in **the land that** you are crossing over **to [there]** in order **to possess it**.

The other primary relativizer is -שֶׁ◌. It occurs only 139 times, mostly in Ecclesiastes, Song of Songs, and the fifth book of the Psalter.[18] Its functions are parallel to אֲשֶׁר. In Song 1:6 and Ruth 2:21, the initial nouns are further described with the relatives (שֶׁלִּי and אֲשֶׁר־לִי "that belongs to me").[19] The former is used as the

---

[18] See further Holmstedt's distribution summary (Holmstedt, *Relative Clause*, 225–29 [§7.3]).

[19] The first part of Song 1:6 (אַל־תִּרְאֻ֫נִי שֶׁאֲנִי שְׁחַרְחֹ֫רֶת שֶׁשֱּׁזָפַ֫תְנִי הַשָּׁ֑מֶשׁ) provides a syntactic parallel to אֲשֶׁר in Gen 15:7. The head may be identified with the immediately preceding 1CS verbal complement, and the pronoun is repeated to clarity its function in both the successive embedded clauses. See the similar conclusion of Holmstedt that "Song 1:6 . . . can be much more simply understood as a relative clause modifying the 1CS clitic pronoun attached to the preceding verb" in *Relative Clause*, 215–16 n. 1. In the previous verse (Song 1:5), the speaker describes her physical appearance,

typical genitive construction in later Hebrew. Both these lexemes can also function as complementizers (see §10.4.2.2).

Song 1:6

כַּרְמִי שֶׁלִּי לֹא נָטָרְתִּי

I have not kept watch over **my vineyard**.

Ruth 2:21

עִם־הַנְּעָרִים אֲשֶׁר־לִי תִּדְבָּקִין

You should stay near to **my servants**.

Other relativizers include the lexemes מִי and מָה, which designate personal and nonpersonal heads.[20]

10.4.2.2 Complementizer

A <u>complementizer</u> is a type of subordinator that designates an embedded clause as a complement of a matrix-clause constituent.[21] The complementizer is clause initial, heads its embedded clause, and does not have a separate head/antecedent in the matrix clause. Like relativizers, Hebrew complementizers are invariable. Unlike relativizers, complementizers have constituency only in the matrix clause and not the embedded clause, and resumptive pronouns are not used in the embedded clause. In example (4a), the complement of the verb *saw* is *Sarah*, and the following relative clause provides an adnominal description of the complement. The complement of the verb *saw* in example (4b), however, is the embedded clause headed by *that*. This example designates the action Sarah took as the object of the matrix-clause verb.

(4a)   I saw <u>Sarah</u> who purchased a burger.
(4b)   I saw <u>that</u> Sarah purchased a burger.

Hebrew כִּי and אֲשֶׁר are the most common complementizers. Less frequently, the relative -שֶׁ◌ designates a complement clause. These complementizers are regularly found with verbs of cognition (i.e., ידע, זכר, בין, אמן; e.g., Deut 29:15; Eccl 1:17; Jonah 4:2), communication (i.e., אמר, נגד, ענה, שבע, שמע, e.g., Judg 6:16 with direct speech; Neh 13:22; Eccl 8:14), and observation (i.e., ראה, e.g., Exod 3:4; 1 Sam 18:15; Eccl 3:18).[22]

שְׁחוֹרָה אֲנִי וְנָאוָה בְּנוֹת יְרוּשָׁלִַם "I am dark (skinned) and beautiful, O Daughters of Jerusalem." See the recent discussion of these metaphors in Brian P. Gault, *Body as Landscape, Love as Intoxication: Conceptual Metaphors in the Song of Songs*, Ancient Israel and Its Literature 36 (Atlanta: SBL, 2019), 67–73. Her self-consciousness regarding her increased melanin appears to incite obloquy, so she proscribes: "Do not stare at me and my darkened skin that the sun has burned."

[20] Holmstedt suggests the relative function extends to the definite article and demonstrative pronouns; see *Relative Clause*, 64–68 (§3.2.1), 69–77 (§3.2.3).

[21] It should be noted that the term *complementizer* may be used more broadly in some settings for any nominalizing constituent.

[22] This discussion excludes examples with prepositions. See §10.4.2.3.

Deut 29:15

כִּי־אַתֶּם יְדַעְתֶּם אֵת אֲשֶׁר־יָשַׁבְנוּ בְּאֶרֶץ מִצְרָיִם וְאֵת אֲשֶׁר־עָבַרְנוּ בְּקֶרֶב הַגּוֹיִם
אֲשֶׁר עֲבַרְתֶּם:

For **you know that** we dwelt in the land of Egypt **and that** we traveled
through the nations which you traveled.

Eccl 1:17

יָדַעְתִּי שֶׁגַּם־זֶה הוּא רַעְיוֹן רוּחַ
I know that this too is a vapory longing.

Jonah 4:2

כִּי יָדַעְתִּי כִּי אַתָּה אֵל־חַנּוּן וְרַחוּם אֶרֶךְ אַפַּיִם וְרַב־חֶסֶד וְנִחָם עַל־הָרָעָה
For **I know that** you are a God of grace, compassion, long-suffering,
prolific loyalty, and comforting in disaster.

Judg 6:16

וַיֹּאמֶר אֵלָיו יְהוָה כִּי אֶהְיֶה עִמָּךְ
Yahweh **said** to him **that**: "I am with you."

Neh 13:22

וָאֹמְרָה לַלְוִיִּם אֲשֶׁר יִהְיוּ מִטַּהֲרִים וּבָאִים שֹׁמְרִים הַשְּׁעָרִים לְקַדֵּשׁ אֶת־יוֹם הַשַּׁבָּת
I said to the Levites **that** they should purify and go guard the gates to
sanctify the Sabbath date.

Eccl 8:14

אָמַרְתִּי שֶׁגַּם־זֶה הָבֶל
I said that this too is futility.

Exod 3:4

וַיַּרְא יְהוָה כִּי סָר לִרְאוֹת
Yahweh **saw that** he turned to have a look.

1 Sam 18:15

וַיַּרְא שָׁאוּל אֲשֶׁר־הוּא מַשְׂכִּיל מְאֹד
Saul **saw that** he was exceedingly successful.

Eccl 3:18

וְלִרְאוֹת שְׁהֶם־בְּהֵמָה הֵמָּה לָהֶם
[This happens] **to see** for themselves **that** they are animals.

The conjunction אִם can be used as a verbal complement with ראה "see" (Ps
139:24) and נגד "tell" (Job 38:18, also v. 4).

Ps 139:24

וּרְאֵ֗ה אִם־דֶּֽרֶךְ־עֹ֥צֶב בִּ֑י

See **whether** a hurtful way is in me.

Job 38:18

הֲ֭הִתְבֹּנַנְתָּ עַד־רַחֲבֵי־אָ֑רֶץ הַ֝גֵּ֗ד אִם־יָדַ֥עְתָּ כֻלָּֽהּ

Tell [me] **what** you know of all this!

10.4.2.3 Adverbializer

An <u>adverbializer</u> is a type of subordinator that designates an intra-clausal, adverbial relation. It links a matrix-clause verb to an embedded clause functioning like an adverb.[23] Adverbializers initiate an embedded clause and characteristically designate temporal, logical, or comparative relations. English marks temporal clauses with adverbializers like *while, when, after, before* (5a), and *until* (5b) as well as conditional, comparative, and causal examples such as *if* (5c), *(just) as* (5d), and *because* (5e).

(5a)   Sarah goes to the store [**while/when/after/before**] she talks on the phone.
(5b)   Sarah does not go to the store **until** she talks on the phone.
(5c)   Sarah may cause an accident **if** she talks on the phone.
(5d)   Sarah talks to her dog **just as** she talks on the phone.
(5e)   Sarah caused an accident **because** she talks on the phone.

Crosslinguistically, adverbializers are often derived from prepositions and result in polysemous lexemes. A similar multifunctional situation exists in BH. Prepositions are used as adverbializers when followed immediately by a clause or a complementizer with predication.[24] The adverbializer may come before (Lev 25:48), in the middle (Lev 13:55), or after the matrix verb it modifies (Josh 7:8).

Lev 25:48

אַחֲרֵ֣י נִמְכַּ֔ר גְּאֻלָּ֖ה תִּהְיֶה־לּ֑וֹ

After he is sold, he may be redeemed.

---

[23] Adverbial clauses are evidenced in many of the world's languages. See Sandra A. Thompson and Robert E. Longacre, "Adverbial Clauses," in *Grammatical Categories and the Lexicon, vol. 3 of Language Typology and Syntactic Description*, ed. Timothy Shopen (Cambridge: Cambridge University Press, 1985), 171–234. Some scholars, however, have used the similar term "adverbializer" to indicate a morphological element that produces an adverb from another constituent; e.g., Orin Gensler, "Why Semitic Adverbializers (Akkadian -*iš*, Syriac -*ā'īt*) Should Not Be Derived from Existential * *īt*," *JSS* 45 (2000): 233–65. Such elements are described here as affixes with an adverbial function.

[24] On the historical development of these constructions, see Boyd and Hardy, "Hebrew Adverbialization," 33–51.

Lev 13:55

וְרָאָה הַכֹּהֵן אַחֲרֵי| הֻכַּבֵּס אֶת־הַנֶּגַע

The priest should inspect the infected area **after it was washed**.

Josh 7:8

בִּי אֲדֹנָי מָה אֹמַר אַחֲרֵי אֲשֶׁר הָפַךְ יִשְׂרָאֵל עֹרֶף לִפְנֵי אֹיְבָיו

O Lord, what can I say **after Israel turned away in the presence of its enemies**?

Multiword adverbializer clauses are typically headed by the relative אֲשֶׁר (Ps 119:49), but sometimes כִּי is used (Ps 139:14). Other adverbializers are used directly with clauses and do not require coordination with another subordinator. These include: בְּטֶרֶם "before," בִּלְעֲדֵי "except," בַּעֲבוּר "so that; for the sake of," and לְמַעַן "so that."

Ps 119:49

זְכֹר־דָּבָר לְעַבְדֶּךָ עַל אֲשֶׁר יִחַלְתָּנִי

Remember the word to your servant **because** you have given me hope.

Ps 139:14

אוֹדְךָ עַל כִּי נוֹרָאוֹת נִפְלֵיתִי

I will praise you **because** I am miraculously created in remarkable ways.

The adverbializers can be organized semantically. Spatial and temporal relationships, like בְּטֶרֶם "before," and אַחֲרֵי "after," are quite common. Other contingency relations designate cause (יַעַן "because"), result (לְמַעַן "so that"), basis (עַל אֹדֹת "on account of"), or exception (אַךְ "except"). A few relations indicate manner or process, such as כְּמוֹ "like, as" and תַּחַת אֲשֶׁר "instead."

ADVERBIALIZERS BY CONSTRUCTION AND RELATION SEMANTICS	
ADVERBIALIZER + CLAUSE	PREP + REL + CLAUSE
Space/Time Relations	
אַחַר "after"	אַחַר אֲשֶׁר "after"
אַחֲרֵי "after"	אַחֲרֵי אֲשֶׁר "after"
אֶל "toward"	אֶל אֲשֶׁר "toward"
———	אֶת אֲשֶׁר "with"
———	בַּאֲשֶׁר "when, while"
———	כַּאֲשֶׁר "when, while"
בְּטֶרֶם "before" (time only)	———
———	לַאֲשֶׁר "to, for"

ADVERBIALIZERS BY CONSTRUCTION AND RELATION SEMANTICS	
ADVERBIALIZER + CLAUSE	PREP + REL + CLAUSE
עַד "until"	עַד אֲשֶׁר "until"
עַל "when; because"	עַל אֲשֶׁר "when; because"
	עַל כִּי "because"
Contingency Relations	
אַךְ "except"	אַךְ אֲשֶׁר "except"
בִּלְעֲדֵי "except"	——
בַּעֲבוּר "so that; for the sake of"	——
יַעַן "because"	יַעַן אֲשֶׁר "because; since; so that"
כְּפִי "because"	כְּפִי אֲשֶׁר "because"
לְמַעַן "so that"	——
מִן "from; because"	מֵאֲשֶׁר "from, because"
עַל אֹדֹת "on account of; about"	עַל־אֹדוֹת אֲשֶׁר "because"
Manner/Process Relations	
כְּמוֹ "like, as"	כַּאֲשֶׁר "like, as"
——	תַּחַת אֲשֶׁר "instead"

10.4.2.4 Clausal Subordination

A wide range of constructions can express subordination between complete clauses. These transitional constructions include many of the same prepositions, conjunctions, and adverbializers discussed previously. The subordinating structures typically provide semantic information about the setting of the discourse. Very commonly, they represent temporal, circumstantial, concessive, or conditional notions within the event sequence of narrative or discourse.

The basic structure begins with a sequential conjugation of the verb היה "to be." The form וַיְהִי expresses a past time sequence, and וְהָיָה a non-past time sequence. The setting information follows this framing verb as part of the initial subordinate clause. In some instances, the framing verb may be missing. The main event sequence continues with a following clause that contains the corresponding form—typically the sequential conjugation *wayyiqtol* or *wəqātal*. Other clauses may intervene between the initial frame and the main clause. These provide additional nonsequential information.

PAST TIME SEQUENCE	NON-PAST TIME SEQUENCE
(Subordinating Clause with וַיְהִי)	(Subordinating Clause with וְהָיָה)
+	+
Setting Information (e.g., temporal, circumstantial, conditional)	
+	+
Main Clause (*wayyiqtol*)	Main Clause (*wəqātal*)

The semantics of the setting information are consistent with many of the sub-ordinating elements discussed in the previous sections. For instance, -בְּ regularly signals general time, כַּאֲשֶׁר and -כְּ contemporaneous time, מִן approximate time, and אַחֲרֵי/אַחַר posterior time (§11.4.3.4). Circumstantial and conditional constructions are often initiated with אִם. The relativizer כִּי serves mostly as a temporal. Other rarer constructions are also found.

In the most basic structure, a temporal NP provides the setting information. The subordinating clause can be as simple as וַיְהִי הַיּוֹם (Job 1:6) or וְהָיָה הַיּוֹם (Exod 12:14) indicating a timeframe.[25]

Job 1:6

וַיְהִי הַיּוֹם וַיָּבֹאוּ בְּנֵי הָאֱלֹהִים לְהִתְיַצֵּב עַל־יְהוָה

On the (appointed) day, the sons of God arrived to present themselves to Yahweh.

Exod 12:14

וְהָיָה הַיּוֹם הַזֶּה לָכֶם לְזִכָּרוֹן וְחַגֹּתֶם אֹתוֹ חַג לַיהוָה

On this day as a memorial for you, you must commemorate it as a festival to Yahweh.[26]

More frequently, the subordinating clause employs a prepositional phrase. The initial clause of Josh 24:29 signals a jump in narrative time from Joshua disbanding the Israelite army in the previous verse (v. 28) and his death. Exodus 16:5 prescribes how Israel is to prepare the manna on the sixth day in anticipation of the Sabbath during the wilderness journey. Second Samuel 14:26 indicates the protracted timeframe, during which Absalom would regularly cut his hair. The main clause (וְגִלְּחוֹ) follows an embedded clause.

Josh 24:29

וַיְהִי אַחֲרֵי הַדְּבָרִים הָאֵלֶּה וַיָּמָת יְהוֹשֻׁעַ בִּן־נוּן עֶבֶד יְהוָה

After these things, Joshua son of Nun, Yahweh's servant, died.

---

[25] See also 1 Sam 1:4; 14:1; 2 Kgs 4:8, 11, 18; Job 1:13; 2:1.

[26] In Exodus 12, the instructions for the Passover in Egypt pause at this point and turn to the enactment of the subsequent remembrance of this deliverance (vv. 14–20). Afterwards, the description of Moses's commands continues in v. 21. The clausal subordination in v. 14 signals the shift, and the initial *wayyiqtol* of v. 21 (וַיִּקְרָא) indicates the narrative resumption.

Exod 16:5

וְהָיָה בַּיּוֹם הַשִּׁשִּׁי וְהֵכִינוּ אֵת אֲשֶׁר־יָבִיאוּ

On the sixth day, they shall prepare whatever they gather.

2 Sam 14:26

וְהָיָה מִקֵּץ יָמִים ׀ לַיָּמִים אֲשֶׁר יְגַלֵּחַ כִּי־כָבֵד עָלָיו וְגִלְּחוֹ

Year after year, whenever he needed to cut his head because it was so heavy, **he would shave it**.

Additional nonsequential information may be placed between the initial subordinating clause and the main clause. Leviticus 9:1–2a adds an asyndetic clause (קָרָא מֹשֶׁה לְאַהֲרֹן וּלְבָנָיו וּלְזִקְנֵי יִשְׂרָאֵל) further describing the background events of the timeframe (בַּיּוֹם הַשְּׁמִינִי). Jeremiah 41:4–5 includes an added comment with an infinitive phrase (לְהָמִית אֶת־גְּדַלְיָהוּ) and a nonconsecutive verb phrase (וְאִישׁ לֹא יָדָע). Nearly two entire verses of background information intervene between the temporal clause (וַיְהִי בַּיּוֹם הַהוּא) and main clause (וַיִּקְרָא) of 1 Sam 3:2–4. The additional setting conditions position Eli and Samuel in different locations using participle clauses (וּשְׁמוּאֵל שֹׁכֵב בְּהֵיכַל יְהֹוָה אֲשֶׁר־שָׁם אֲרוֹן אֱלֹהִים and וְעֵלִי שֹׁכֵב בִּמְקֹמוֹ), indicate Eli's failing eyesight (וְעֵינָיו הֵחֵלּוּ כֵהוֹת לֹא יוּכַל לִרְאוֹת), and describe the waning evening hour (וְנֵר אֱלֹהִים טֶרֶם יִכְבֶּה).

Lev 9:1–2a

וַיְהִי בַּיּוֹם הַשְּׁמִינִי קָרָא מֹשֶׁה לְאַהֲרֹן וּלְבָנָיו וּלְזִקְנֵי יִשְׂרָאֵל: וַיֹּאמֶר אֶל־אַהֲרֹן

On the eighth day—when Moses had called together Aaron, his sons, and the elders of Israel—he **said** to Aaron:

Jer 41:4–5

וַיְהִי בַּיּוֹם הַשֵּׁנִי לְהָמִית אֶת־גְּדַלְיָהוּ וְאִישׁ לֹא יָדָע: וַיָּבֹאוּ אֲנָשִׁים מִשְּׁכֶם מִשִּׁלוֹ וּמִשֹּׁמְרוֹן שְׁמֹנִים

On the second day after killing Gedaliah while no one yet knew, eighty men **arrived** from Shechem, Shiloh, and Samaria.

1 Sam 3:2–4

וַיְהִי בַּיּוֹם הַהוּא וְעֵלִי שֹׁכֵב בִּמְקֹמוֹ וְעֵינָיו הֵחֵלּוּ כֵהוֹת לֹא יוּכַל לִרְאוֹת: וְנֵר אֱלֹהִים טֶרֶם יִכְבֶּה וּשְׁמוּאֵל שֹׁכֵב בְּהֵיכַל יְהֹוָה אֲשֶׁר־שָׁם אֲרוֹן אֱלֹהִים: וַיִּקְרָא יְהוָה אֶל־שְׁמוּאֵל

On that day—while Eli was lying down in his place, now his eyes had begun to dim and he was unable to see, meanwhile the lamp of God had not yet subsided, and Samuel was lying down in the temple of Yahweh where the ark of God was—Yahweh **spoke** to Samuel.

Returning to the initial setting clause, the subordinating preposition may be followed by a nonfinite verb. The verbal semantics, particularly TAM, are inferred from the framing verb and the following main clause. The subordinating clause of

2 Sam 11:16 describes the circumstances of Joab arranging for Uriah's death at the order of the king. In Josh 3:13, the priests' approach to the Jordan river is assured to prompt the watery diversion.

2 Sam 11:16

וַיְהִ֗י בִּשְׁמ֤וֹר יוֹאָב֙ אֶל־הָעִ֔יר וַיִּתֵּן֙ אֶת־א֣וּרִיָּ֔ה אֶל־הַמָּקוֹם֙ אֲשֶׁ֣ר יָדַ֔ע כִּ֥י אַנְשֵׁי־חַ֖יִל
שָֽׁם:

When Joab beset the city, **he put** Uriah at the place where he knew that armed men were there.

Josh 3:13

וְהָיָ֡ה כְּנ֣וֹחַ כַּפּ֣וֹת רַגְלֵ֣י הַכֹּהֲנִ֡ים נֹשְׂאֵי֩ אֲר֨וֹן יְהוָ֜ה אֲד֤וֹן כָּל־הָאָ֙רֶץ֙ בְּמֵ֣י הַיַּרְדֵּ֔ן מֵ֣י
הַיַּרְדֵּ֗ן יִכָּ֣רֵת֔וּן הַמַּ֥יִם הַיֹּרְדִ֖ים מִלְמָ֑עְלָה וְיַעַמְד֖וּ נֵ֥ד אֶחָֽד:

As soon as the soles of the feet of the priests carrying the ark of Yahweh, lord of all the earth, **rest** on the water of the Jordan, the waters of the Jordan **will be cut off**, that is, the waters flowing downstream, **and they will stand still** as one mass.

The subordinating clause may contain an adverbializer with a finite verb. In 1 Sam 8:1 and Exod 17:11, temporal and circumstantial settings are initiated with כַּאֲשֶׁר. The embedded verbs correspond to the conjugation of the initial framing verb and the main clause: *qātal* with *wayyiqtol* (וַיְהִי) and *yiqtol* with *wəqātal* (וְהָיָה). The second sentence of Exod 17:11 does not repeat the initial framing verb (וְהָיָה).

1 Sam 8:1

וַיְהִ֕י כַּאֲשֶׁ֥ר זָקֵ֖ן שְׁמוּאֵ֑ל וַיָּ֧שֶׂם אֶת־בָּנָ֛יו שֹׁפְטִ֖ים לְיִשְׂרָאֵֽל:

When Samuel had grown old, he made his sons Israel's judges.

Exod 17:11

וְהָיָ֗ה כַּאֲשֶׁ֨ר יָרִ֥ים מֹשֶׁ֛ה יָד֖וֹ וְגָבַ֣ר יִשְׂרָאֵ֑ל וְכַאֲשֶׁ֥ר יָנִ֛יחַ יָד֖וֹ וְגָבַ֥ר עֲמָלֵֽק:

As long as Moses raised his hand, then Israel would prevail, **but whenever** he rested his hand, then Amalek would prevail.

Conditional or circumstantial clauses may be signaled with אִם in the subordinating clause. Deuteronomy 28:1 presents the setting of Yahweh's exaltation of the people.

Deut 28:1

וְהָיָ֗ה אִם־שָׁמ֤וֹעַ תִּשְׁמַע֙ בְּקוֹל֙ יְהוָ֣ה אֱלֹהֶ֔יךָ לִשְׁמֹ֤ר לַעֲשׂוֹת֙ אֶת־כָּל־מִצְוֹתָ֔יו אֲשֶׁ֛ר
אָנֹכִ֥י מְצַוְּךָ֖ הַיּ֑וֹם וּנְתָ֨נְךָ֜ יְהוָ֤ה אֱלֹהֶ֙יךָ֙ עֶלְי֔וֹן עַ֖ל כָּל־גּוֹיֵ֥י הָאָֽרֶץ:

If (*or:* in as much as) you dutifully obey the voice of Yahweh your God to carefully do all his commandments that I am commanding you today, **then** Yahweh your God **will highly exalt you** above all the nations of the earth.

First Kings 11:38 provides a sequence of three clauses embedded with the frame
(וְהָיָה אִם) as the apodosis of the conditional. And the protasis (וְהָיִיתִי עִמָּךְ) follows.

1 Kgs 11:38

וְהָיָה אִם־תִּשְׁמַע אֶת־כָּל־אֲשֶׁר אֲצַוֶּךָ וְהָלַכְתָּ בִדְרָכַי וְעָשִׂיתָ הַיָּשָׁר בְּעֵינַי לִשְׁמוֹר
חֻקּוֹתַי וּמִצְוֹתַי כַּאֲשֶׁר עָשָׂה דָּוִד עַבְדִּי וְהָיִיתִי עִמָּךְ

If you obey all that I will command you, you walk in my ways, and you
do right in my eyes to keep my statutes and my commandments just as
David my servant did, **then I will be** with you.

The conjunction כִּי is used with a finite verb in the subordinating clause to indicate the temporal or circumstantial setting. David sacrifices as the ark moved
from the home of Obed-Edom to the city of David. Second Samuel 6:13 describes
the setting of the ark's ritual procession (וַיְהִי כִּי) that habituated David's joy and
sacrifice. All three verbs indicate completed events. The suffix conjugation (צָעֲדוּ)
entails the setting information, and וַיִּזְבַּח resumes the main narrative. In Judg 12:5,
the setting of the exchange between the fleeing Ephraimites and the Gileadites is
imperfective with both the framing verb (וְהָיָה כִּי) and the subordinating clauses
(אֶעֱבֹרָה and יֹאמְרוּ). The main narrative verbs, however, are *wayyiqtol* before and
after (וַיֹּאמְרוּ and וַיִּלְכֹּד).

2 Sam 6:13

וַיְהִי כִּי צָעֲדוּ נֹשְׂאֵי אֲרוֹן־יְהוָה שִׁשָּׁה צְעָדִים וַיִּזְבַּח שׁוֹר וּמְרִיא:

Whenever those carrying the ark of Yahweh **marched** six steps, **he sacri-
ficed** an ox and a fatling.

Judg 12:5

וַיִּלְכֹּד גִּלְעָד אֶת־מַעְבְּרוֹת הַיַּרְדֵּן לְאֶפְרָיִם וְהָיָה כִּי יֹאמְרוּ פְּלִיטֵי אֶפְרַיִם אֶעֱבֹרָה
וַיֹּאמְרוּ לוֹ אַנְשֵׁי־גִלְעָד הַאֶפְרָתִי אַתָּה וַיֹּאמֶר לֹא

The Gileadites captured fords of the Jordan into Ephraim. **When** the
Ephraimite deserters **would say**, "Let me cross," the Gileadites **asked**
him, "Are you an Ephraimite?" He said, "No."

Some constructions begin without the initial frame (וַיְהִי or וְהָיָה). In these situations, the bare subordinating structure comes first, and the main clause follows with
the sequential verb. Hosea 1:2 initiates the temporal setting for Yahweh's command to marry Gomer with a noun in construct with a finite verb (דִּבֶּר). Genesis
22:4 begins with the subordinating string (בַּיּוֹם הַשְּׁלִישִׁי), and it continues the main
narrative events with the clause (וַיִּשָּׂא אַבְרָהָם אֶת־עֵינָיו). Esther 2:1–2 includes
initial subordinating clauses as the setting for the narrative. The first indicates the
event timeframe (אַחַר הַדְּבָרִים הָאֵלֶּה), and the second provides the circumstance
(כְּשֹׁךְ חֲמַת הַמֶּלֶךְ אֲחַשְׁוֵרוֹשׁ). As with the previous examples, additional clauses
may intervene before the main discourse to provide background information. The
clause (זָכַר אֶת־וַשְׁתִּי וְאֵת אֲשֶׁר־עָשָׂתָה וְאֵת אֲשֶׁר־נִגְזַר עָלֶיהָ) is probably best to

be considered part of the setting. The narrative would then begin with the king's attendants suggesting the search for a new queen (וַיֹּאמְרוּ).

Hos 1:2

תְּחִלַּת דִּבֶּר־יְהוָה בְּהוֹשֵׁעַ וַיֹּאמֶר יְהוָה אֶל־הוֹשֵׁעַ

At the beginning when Yahweh spoke with Hosea, Yahweh **said** to Hosea.

Gen 22:4

בַּיּוֹם הַשְּׁלִישִׁי וַיִּשָּׂא אַבְרָהָם אֶת־עֵינָיו

On the third day, Abraham **lifted** his eyes.

Esth 2:1–2

אַחַר הַדְּבָרִים הָאֵלֶּה כְּשֹׁךְ חֲמַת הַמֶּלֶךְ אֲחַשְׁוֵרוֹשׁ זָכַר אֶת־וַשְׁתִּי וְאֵת אֲשֶׁר־עָשָׂתָה
וְאֵת אֲשֶׁר־נִגְזַר עָלֶיהָ: וַיֹּאמְרוּ נַעֲרֵי־הַמֶּלֶךְ מְשָׁרְתָיו

After these things **as** King Ahasuerus's anger **subsided**, he reminisced about Vashti, what she had done, and what was decided concerning her, the king's personal servants **said** . . .

10.5 ADVERBS

Adverbs generally consist of a variety of constructions that modify verbs, adjectives, clauses, or other adverbs. Their syntax is largely described as functioning within a clause or discourse unit (§10.5.1). And they provide different types of semantic information to the modified construction (§10.5.2).

10.5.1 Syntax of Adverbs

The syntax of adverbs is circumscribed by several propensities. They can be added to a constituent without changing its syntactic status in a clause. Multiple adverbs can occur in the same clause. Their scope can apply to different elements, constituents, entire clauses, propositions, or discourse units. Albeit flexible, the position of adverbs is proximate to the modified unit. And their constituency is optional or nonobligatory—that is, they are adjuncts.

A comparison of similar strings from two consecutive verses exhibits several of these characteristics of adverbs. Joshua 1:6–7 includes two repeated compounded commands, חֲזַק וֶאֱמָץ (see also, Deut 31:7, 23; Josh 1:9, 18; 1 Chr 22:13; 28:20). The second verse adds an initial clause linker (§10.6.3) and a modifier after the verb. Neither of these is a required clause constituent. Yet their inclusion provides important semantic information. At the beginning of the first clause, רַק "only; nevertheless" indicates a modal restriction, and the adverb מְאֹד "very" amplifies the degree of importance of the preceding command.

Josh 1:6

חֲזַק וֶאֱמָץ

Be strong and courageous.

Josh 1:7

רַק חֲזַק וֶאֱמַץ מְאֹד לִשְׁמֹר לַעֲשׂוֹת כְּכָל־הַתּוֹרָה אֲשֶׁר צִוְּךָ מֹשֶׁה עַבְדִּי

Nevertheless, be strong and **very** courageous to carefully do every instruction that my servant Moses commanded you.

The category of adverb represents an assortment of single and compound morphemes, lexemes, phrases, and clauses. Only a few lexemes are pure adverbs, like מְאֹד. Derivational adverbs can be formed with various suffixes (e.g., directive *he*, ◌ָם-, ◌ִית-). Several deictic and interrogative elements also serve in similar ways. And specific phrase and clause constructions are discussed elsewhere as having adverbial functions (nouns, chapter 7; adjectives and participles, chapter 8; infinitives, chapter 9; adverbializers, §10.4.2.3; prepositional phrases, chapter 11).

10.5.2 Adverbial Semantic Functions

Adverbs can express a range of semantic functions. In Josh 1:7 above, the adverb מְאֹד describes the verb amplifying its quantity or degree. Adverbs may describe another clause constituent within the realms of space, time, process, respect, contingency, association, modality, or degree.[27]

ADVERB SEMANTICS	
Space	position, direction, distance
Time	position, duration, frequency, relationship
Process	manner, means, instrument, agentive
Respect	measure, focus
Contingency	cause, reason, purpose, result, condition, concession
Association	comparison, contrast, equative
Modality	emphasis, approximation, restriction
Quantity	degree, intensification, diminution

The most common simple and derivational adverbs can be categorized using these broad semantic frames.

10.5.2.1 Space

Spatial adverbs describe position, direction, or distance with respect to elements in the clause. The altitudinal adverbs, מַעְלָה "above, upwards," and מַטָּה "below, downwards," designate the direction of the verbal motion (Deut 28:43). Both are

---

[27] For English examples of these descriptive categories, see Quirk et al., *Comprehensive Grammar*, 479–500.

commonly a part of prepositional phrases with *lamed* (i.e., לְמֶעְלָה, see Prov 15:24; and לְמַטָּה). The suffix on each is the directive *he* (see also מִמַּעַל).

Deut 28:43

הַגֵּר אֲשֶׁר בְּקִרְבְּךָ יַעֲלֶה עָלֶיךָ מַעְלָה מָּעְלָה וְאַתָּה תֵרֵד מַטָּה מָּטָּה:

The immigrant in your midst will arise **higher and higher** above you, but you will descend **lower and lower**.

Prov 15:24

אֹרַח חַיִּים לְמַעְלָה לְמַשְׂכִּיל לְמַעַן סוּר מִשְּׁאוֹל מָטָּה:

The path of life is **upward** for the insightful so that he may turn away from Sheol **below**.

The direction *backward* can be expressed with אֲחֹרַנִּית (also אַחֲרוֹן), and *front-ward* with רִאשׁוֹן (also רֵאשִׁית "first"). The former is found in Isa 38:8 (and 2 Kgs 20:9–11). There, the shadow advances along the reverse course as a divine sign to Hezekiah.

Isa 38:8

הִנְנִי מֵשִׁיב אֶת־צֵל הַמַּעֲלוֹת אֲשֶׁר יָרְדָה בְמַעֲלוֹת אָחָז בַּשֶּׁמֶשׁ אֲחֹרַנִּית עֶשֶׂר מַעֲלוֹת

I am making the sun's shadow that descends Ahaz's steps to return **backward** ten steps.

The positions פְּנִימָה "inside" (2 Chr 29:18), חוּצָה "outside" (Deut 23:14), and סָבִיב "around" (Ps 3:7) are also adverbs of space.

2 Chr 29:18

וַיָּבוֹאוּ פְנִימָה אֶל־חִזְקִיָּהוּ הַמֶּלֶךְ

They entered **inside** to King Hezekiah.

Deut 23:14

וְהָיָה בְּשִׁבְתְּךָ חוּץ וְחָפַרְתָּה בָהּ וְשַׁבְתָּ וְכִסִּיתָ אֶת־צֵאָתֶךָ

When you defecate **outside**, you shall dig a hole, return, and cover over your excrement.

Ps 3:7

לֹא־אִירָא מֵרִבְבוֹת עָם אֲשֶׁר סָבִיב שָׁתוּ עָלָי:

I will not fear the multitudes of nations that **all around** stand against me.

Deictic adverbs indicate locality in reference to the speaker. The near and far deixis is marked with פֹּה "here" (also פוֹ) and שָׁם "there." Several other words combine these notions with directional meanings or elements. Direction toward the deictic center is indicated with הֲלֹם "hither; to here" and הֵנָּה "hither, to here." Direction outward is signified by שָׁמָּה "thither, to there" and הָלְאָה "yonder; beyond."

10.5.2.2 Time

Temporal adverbs signal time with respect to the occasion of the discourse. Time is relative to the speaker's present. The men of Succoth reject Gideon's demand for food at the current moment, עַתָּה "now, at present" (Judg 8:6). Previous time may be nonspecific, טֶרֶם "before (time); still, not yet" (Gen 2:4b–5), or may exhibit a more specific relationship to the present, תְּמוֹל "previously, yesterday" and/or שִׁלְשׁוֹם "in the past, three days ago" (2 Sam 3:17). Subsequent time may be marked with אָז "then" (Judg 13:21), מָחָר "tomorrow, in the future" (Exod 13:14), and עוֹלָם "a long time, forever" (Ps 61:8). The adverb אָז "at that time" can also specify past time, as with Gen 12:6. The collocation מֵעוֹלָם "from long ago" likewise indicates past time.

Judg 8:6

הֲכַף זֶבַח וְצַלְמֻנָּע **עַתָּה** בְּיָדֶךָ כִּי־נִתֵּן לִצְבָאֲךָ לָחֶם׃

Are Zebah and Zalmunna **presently** in your hands that we shall give your army bread?

Gen 2:4b–5

בְּיוֹם עֲשׂוֹת יְהוָה אֱלֹהִים אֶרֶץ וְשָׁמָיִם׃ וְכֹל ׀ שִׂיחַ הַשָּׂדֶה **טֶרֶם** יִהְיֶה בָאָרֶץ וְכָל־עֵשֶׂב הַשָּׂדֶה **טֶרֶם** יִצְמָח

When Yahweh God made the earth and the heavens—now it was **before** every plant of the field would be in the land and **before** every grass of the field would sprout.

2 Sam 3:17

גַּם־תְּמוֹל גַּם־שִׁלְשֹׁם הֱיִיתֶם מְבַקְשִׁים אֶת־דָּוִד לְמֶלֶךְ עֲלֵיכֶם

Both yesterday and the day before, you have been seeking David to be king over you.

Judg 13:21

וְלֹא־יָסַף עוֹד מַלְאַךְ יְהוָה לְהֵרָאֹה אֶל־מָנוֹחַ וְאֶל־אִשְׁתּוֹ **אָז** יָדַע מָנוֹחַ כִּי־מַלְאַךְ יְהוָה הוּא׃

Yahweh's messenger did not manifest himself again to Manoah or his wife. Manoah knew **then** that he was Yahweh's messenger.

Exod 13:14

וְהָיָה כִּי־יִשְׁאָלְךָ בִנְךָ **מָחָר** לֵאמֹר מַה־זֹּאת וְאָמַרְתָּ אֵלָיו בְּחֹזֶק יָד הוֹצִיאָנוּ יְהוָה מִמִּצְרַיִם מִבֵּית עֲבָדִים׃

When your son asks you **in the future**, "What is this?" You should say to him: "With mighty strength, Yahweh brought us out from Egypt from the house of slavery!"

Ps 61:8

יֵשֵׁב עוֹלָם לִפְנֵי אֱלֹהִים

He will dwell **a long time** before God.

Gen 12:6

וְהַכְּנַעֲנִי אָז בָּאָרֶץ

The Canaanites **at that time** were in the land.

Duration or frequency of time is portrayed with יוֹמָם "daily" and לַיְלָה "nightly" (1 Sam 25:16) as well as תָּמִיד "continually" (Ps 72:15) and continuance עוֹד "still, yet" (Ps 84:5). The adverb פִּתְאֹם "suddenly" (כִּי־פִתְאֹם יָקוּם אֵידָם "for destruction will come suddenly," Prov 24:22) indicates the immediacy of events. The adverbial function of ordinals and recurrence lexemes (פַּעַם) could be included as well.

1 Sam 25:16

חוֹמָה הָיוּ עָלֵינוּ גַּם־לַיְלָה גַּם־יוֹמָם כָּל־יְמֵי הֱיוֹתֵנוּ עִמָּם רֹעִים הַצֹּאן׃

They were a wall over us both **nightly** and **daily**—every day we were with them tending the flock.

Ps 72:15

וְיִתְפַּלֵּל בַּעֲדוֹ תָמִיד כָּל־הַיּוֹם יְבָרֲכֶנְהוּ

May prayer be said for him **constantly**; every day may blessing be his.

Ps 84:5

אַשְׁרֵי יוֹשְׁבֵי בֵיתֶךָ עוֹד יְהַלְלוּךָ

Blessed are those dwelling in your house **still** praising you!

10.5.2.3 Process

An adverb may specify how an action occurs. The adverb יַחְדָּו (also יַחַד) can indicate unity of action, association, inclusivity, degree, or proximity. For instance, Israel responds in unison in Exod 19:8. An action done in a related way is designated with כֵּן (Esth 4:16) or כֹּה (also, כָּכָה).

Exod 19:8

וַיַּעֲנוּ כָל־הָעָם יַחְדָּו

All the people answered **together**.

Esth 4:16

גַּם־אֲנִי וְנַעֲרֹתַי אָצוּם כֵּן

Both I and my servants will fast **in the same manner**.

Manner and means may also be indicated by an adverb, as with קֹדְרַנִּית (קֹדְרַנִּית) "we have walked in a mournful way," Mal 3:14), חִנָּם (חִנָּם חָפְרוּ לְנַפְשִׁי) "for nothing they dug a pit for my life," Ps 35:7), רֵיקָם (וְרֵיקָם הֱשִׁיבַנִי יְהוָה) "Yahweh brought me back empty," Ruth 1:21), and מְהֵרָה (לָנוּ מְהֵרָה וְהוֹשִׁיעָה אֵלֵינוּ עֲלֵה) "Come to us swiftly and save us," Josh 10:6).

10.5.2.4 Contingency

Adverbial contingency enacts conditionality or exigency upon the modified element. These adverbs are concerned with cause, reason, purpose, result, condition, or concession. Various contingent notions are found with גַם (Isa 48:7–8).

Isa 48:7–8

עַתָּה נִבְרְאוּ וְלֹא מֵאָז וְלִפְנֵי־יוֹם וְלֹא שְׁמַעְתָּם פֶּן־תֹּאמַר הִנֵּה יְדַעְתִּין: **גַּם לֹא־שָׁמַעְתָּ**
גַּם לֹא יָדַעְתָּ גַּם מֵאָז לֹא־פִּתְּחָה אָזְנֶךָ

They have been created right now and not previously. Before today, you have not heard [of them], so that you could not say, "Certainly I knew them," **even though** you had neither heard **nor** known, [and] previously your ear was not **even** open.

The reason may be interrogated with a question word. The interrogative adverb מַדּוּעַ commonly inquires after purpose or reason (Jer 14:19).

Jer 14:19

הֲמָאֹס מָאַסְתָּ אֶת־יְהוּדָה אִם־בְּצִיּוֹן גָּעֲלָה נַפְשֶׁךָ **מַדּוּעַ** הִכִּיתָנוּ וְאֵין לָנוּ מַרְפֵּא
Have you utterly rejected Judah? Or has your soul so despised Zion? **Why** do you strike us? Where is our healing?

10.5.2.5 Association

Adverbs can indicate various associative notions. The additive adverb גַם specifies accompaniment (Num 13:28) and repetition (Gen 3:6). (For the sequence גַם . . . וְגַם "both . . . and," see §10.4.1.3.) It can also be used to denote result (Josh 24:18), contrast (Exod 7:23), and contingency (see above).

Num 13:28

אֶפֶס כִּי־עַז הָעָם הַיֹּשֵׁב בָּאָרֶץ וְהֶעָרִים בְּצֻרוֹת גְּדֹלֹת מְאֹד **וְגַם־יְלִדֵי** הָעֲנָק רָאִינוּ
שָׁם:

However, the people dwelling in the land are strong, the cities are very impressively fortified, and **in addition** we saw the descendants of Anak there.

Gen 3:6

וַתִּתֵּן **גַּם־לְאִישָׁהּ** עִמָּהּ וַיֹּאכַל
She gave **also** to her husband with her, and he ate.

Josh 24:18

וַיְגָ֣רֶשׁ יְהוָ֗ה אֶת־כָּל־הָעַמִּ֜ים וְאֶת־הָאֱמֹרִ֛י יֹשֵׁ֥ב הָאָ֖רֶץ מִפָּנֵ֑ינוּ **גַּם־אֲנַ֙חְנוּ֙** נַעֲבֹ֣ד אֶת־יְהוָ֔ה כִּי־ה֖וּא אֱלֹהֵֽינוּ׃

Yahweh expelled all the peoples as well as the Amorites living in the land from before us, **therefore** we will serve Yahweh because he is our God.

Exod 7:23

וַיִּ֣פֶן פַּרְעֹ֔ה וַיָּבֹ֖א אֶל־בֵּית֑וֹ וְלֹא־שָׁ֥ת לִבּ֖וֹ **גַּם־לָזֹֽאת**׃

Pharaoh turned and entered his house and did not take to heart **even** on account of this.

10.5.2.6 Modality

Modal adverbs can amplify the validity of a statement. The most common emphatic marker is מְאֹד "very." Other amplifiers include אָמְנָם "truly, really" (אָכֵן/אָמֵן), "indeed, surely" (Exod 2:14), and the asseverative function of אַךְ (Deut 16:15).

Exod 2:14

אָכֵ֖ן נוֹדַ֥ע הַדָּבָֽר

The matter is **surely** known.

Deut 16:15

וְהָיִ֖יתָ **אַ֥ךְ** שָׂמֵֽחַ

You will **certainly** have joy.

The adverbs גַּם and אַף can add emphasis to nonverbal constituents. This construction commonly occurs when גַּם or אַף is sequenced with independent personal pronouns. They serve to highlight the subjects (Judg 8:31), objects (Gen 27:34), and even preposition complements (Gen 4:26). The usages of גַּם־אֲנִי and אַף־אֲנִי in Lev 26:23–24 and 26:27–28 appear as basic equivalents. Another possible analysis is to consider the function as a pragmatic construction to mark focus.

Judg 8:31

יָלְדָה־לּ֖וֹ **גַם־הִ֑יא** בֵּ֑ן

She—**even she**—bore him a son.

Gen 27:34

בָּרֲכֵ֥נִי **גַם־אָ֖נִי** אָבִֽי

Bless me—**even me**—my father!

Gen 4:26

וּלְשֵׁ֣ת **גַּם־הוּא֮** יֻלַּד־בֵּ֒ן

A son was born to Seth—**even him**.

Lev 26:23–24

וְאִם־בְּאֵ֫לֶּה לֹא תִוָּסְר֣וּ לִ֔י וַהֲלַכְתֶּ֥ם עִמִּ֖י קֶֽרִי: וְהָלַכְתִּ֧י **אַף־אֲנִ֛י** עִמָּכֶ֖ם בְּקֶ֑רִי וְהִכֵּיתִ֤י אֶתְכֶם֙ **גַּם־אָ֔נִי** שֶׁ֖בַע עַל־חַטֹּאתֵיכֶֽם:

If by means of these, you do not accept my discipline but live discordantly with me, I—**even I**—will live with you in discord, and **it will be me** who strikes you seven times according to your sins.

Lev 26:27–28

וְאִם־בְּזֹ֕את לֹ֥א תִשְׁמְע֖וּ לִ֑י וַהֲלַכְתֶּ֥ם עִמִּ֖י בְּקֶֽרִי: וְהָלַכְתִּ֤י עִמָּכֶם֙ בַּחֲמַת־קֶ֔רִי וְיִסַּרְתִּ֤י אֶתְכֶם֙ **אַף־אָ֔נִי** שֶׁ֖בַע עַל־חַטֹּאתֵיכֶֽם:

If by means of this you do not obey me but live with me in discord, I will live with you in heated discord, and **it will be me** who disciplines you seven times according to you sins.

The restrictive semantic function is a limiting factor or opposition. Examples include some uses of אַךְ (Judg 16:28) and רַק (Gen 6:5).

Judg 16:28

וְחַזְּקֵ֨נִי נָ֜א אַ֣ךְ הַפַּ֤עַם הַזֶּה֙ הָאֱלֹהִ֔ים
Strengthen me **just** this once, O God.

Gen 6:5

וְכָל־יֵ֫צֶר֙ מַחְשְׁבֹ֣ת לִבּ֔וֹ רַ֥ק רַ֖ע כָּל־הַיּֽוֹם
Every intention of his heart's thoughts was **only** evil always.

10.5.2.7 Quantity

The semantic notion of degree measures or assesses a gradable quality of the modified element on an imagined gradient. The degree may be intensified or diminished, as with 2 Kgs 10:18. It may instead involve relative goodness (Gen 40:16) and badness (Ps 109:7).

2 Kgs 10:18

אַחְאָ֕ב עָבַ֥ד אֶת־הַבַּ֖עַל **מְעָ֑ט** יֵה֖וּא יַעַבְדֶ֥נּוּ **הַרְבֵּֽה**
Ahab served Baal **a little**; Jehu will serve him **a lot**.

Gen 40:16

וַיַּ֥רְא שַׂר־הָאֹפִ֖ים כִּ֣י **ט֣וֹב** פָּתָ֑ר
The chief baker saw that he interpreted **positively**.

Ps 109:7

בְּהִשָּׁ֣פְט֔וֹ יֵצֵ֣א **רָשָׁ֑ע** וּתְפִלָּת֗וֹ תִּהְיֶ֥ה לַחֲטָאָֽה:
When he is judged, he will leave **badly**, and his prayer will become sin.

10.6 CONJUNCTIVE ADVERBS

Conjunctive adverbs consist of adverbs that link clauses. Rather than modifying a particular element or discourse unit, they create a semantic relationship between two classes more akin to a conjunction.[28] English *however, nevertheless, therefore, furthermore, still,* and *thus* are examples. This word class is rarely exclusive. Most of these Hebrew lexemes function in some contexts as ordinary adverbs (§10.5), and they are not always easily distinguished from conjunctions (see §10.4).

Hebrew conjunctive adverbs are identified by position and semantics. They may head any clause type except relative clauses. Only conjunctions and other adverbs may precede a conjunctive adverb in a clause. The scope of a conjunctive adverb applies to the entire clause. The semantics include result, inference, addition, apposition, contrast, or concession. For our purposes, the conjunctive adverbs are organized into three semantic groupings: result, addition, and contrast.

10.6.1 Result

Conjunctive adverbs, such as לָכֵן, עַל־כֵּן, and עַתָּה, express the semantic relationship of result or inference between two clauses. The conjunctive adverb heads the discourse unit that serves as the effect or consequence of another. As with most implicatures, the result clause can be logical or temporal—or both—by nature. In English, similar linkers include *therefore, consequently, so,* and the logical connector *then.* The connective result usually follows the evidential statement.

Almost all examples of לָכֵן are conjunctive adverbs. It is the most exclusive lexeme of this word class.[29] Judges 10:13 provides a typical example. The second clause, headed by לָכֵן, explains the result or consequence of Israel's continual idolatry. In some instances, a cause-effect discourse unit starts with the adverbializer יַעַן and is resolved with the לָכֵן unit (Num 20:12).

> Judg 10:13
>
> וְאַתֶּם עֲזַבְתֶּם אוֹתִי וַתַּעַבְדוּ אֱלֹהִים אֲחֵרִים לָכֵן לֹא־אוֹסִיף לְהוֹשִׁיעַ אֶתְכֶם:
> You abandoned me and served other gods **therefore** I will not again deliver you.

---

[28] Some scholars label this class as linking adverbs; see e.g., Douglas Biber, Stig Johansson, Geoffrey Leech, Susan Conrad, and Edward Finegan, *Longman Grammar of Spoken and Written English* (Harlow: Pearson, 1999), 763–65. For English examples of these semantic relationships, see 875–79.

[29] The exceptional example in Zech 11:7 is likely a textual error.

Num 20:12

יַעַן לֹא־הֶאֱמַנְתֶּם בִּי לְהַקְדִּישֵׁנִי לְעֵינֵי בְּנֵי יִשְׂרָאֵל לָכֵן לֹא תָבִיאוּ אֶת־הַקָּהָל הַזֶּה אֶל־הָאָרֶץ אֲשֶׁר־נָתַתִּי לָהֶם:

Because you did not trust me to sanctify me in the eyes of the children of Israel, **therefore** you will not take this assembly into the land which I have given them.

The lexicalized prepositional phrase עַל־כֵּן similarly expresses inferential semantics as a conjunctive adverb. For instance, עַל־כֵּן is used in Ps 25:8 to connect a verbless clause and a verbal clause. The first clause is the premise, and the entailment is linked by the conjunctive adverb.

Ps 25:8

טוֹב־וְיָשָׁר יְהוָה **עַל־כֵּן** יוֹרֶה חַטָּאִים בַּדָּרֶךְ:

Yahweh is good and upright **therefore** he can teach sinners the way.

The adverb עַתָּה in some instances functions as a conjunctive adverb indicating result or inference. In Hos 10:2, Israel's idolatry and divided heart demands the acknowledgment of sin. The second clause expresses this consequence. The temporal connotation is not completely missing in every instance of עַתָּה as effects naturally follow in time.[30] The people express their wish to Samuel for a king because of his senescence (1 Sam 8:5).

Hos 10:2

חָלַק לִבָּם **עַתָּה** יֶאְשָׁמוּ

Their heart is divided **consequently** they must redress their guilt.

1 Sam 8:5

הִנֵּה אַתָּה זָקַנְתָּ וּבָנֶיךָ לֹא הָלְכוּ בִּדְרָכֶיךָ **עַתָּה** שִׂימָה־לָּנוּ מֶלֶךְ לְשָׁפְטֵנוּ כְּכָל־הַגּוֹיִם

See here, you are old, and your sons do not walk in your ways, **so** appoint us a king to judge us like all the nations.

10.6.2 Addition

The notion of addition may be expressed with the conjunctive adverbs אַף, גַּם, and עוֹד. English *in addition*, *also*, *furthermore* function in similar manner. Many instances of אַף "also" are conjunctive adverbs. The actions of bowing down and worship are unmistakably linked with the connective as with Isa 46:6.

---

[30] In some instances, the temporal circumstance may rightly infer a logical result (*post hoc ergo propter hoc*): עָשִׂיתִי לְמִימֵי קֶדֶם וִיצַרְתִּיהָ עַתָּה הֲבֵיאתִיהָ "I produced and fashioned it in ancient days. Now I have made it arrive" (2 Kgs 19:25). Temporal and logical connectives may be linked explicitly as וְעַתָּה לָכֵן (Jer 32:36; 42:15).

Isa 46:6

יִשְׂכְּרוּ צוֹרֵף וְיַעֲשֵׂהוּ אֵל יִסְגְּדוּ **אַף־יִשְׁתַּחֲוּוּ**

They will hire a metalsmith, and he will make it into a god. They will bow down; **also**, they will worship it.

Two other lexemes are used occasionally as conjunctive adverbs. Some cases of גַם are additive or appositive. These may occur with a preceding *waw* (Josh 7:11) or without a *waw* (2 Sam 12:27). A small number of clause-initial uses of עוֹד are conjunctive. Jehoshaphat's pride led him to remove the places of false worship as opposed to many of his fellow kings (2 Chr 17:6).

Josh 7:11

חָטָא יִשְׂרָאֵל **וְגַם** עָבְרוּ אֶת־בְּרִיתִי אֲשֶׁר צִוִּיתִי אוֹתָם

Israel has sinned, **and what's more**, they have transgressed my covenant which I commanded them.

2 Sam 12:27

נִלְחַמְתִּי בְרַבָּה **גַּם**־לָכַדְתִּי אֶת־עִיר הַמָּיִם

I fought against Rabbah; **also**, I captured its water supply.

2 Chr 17:6

וַיִּגְבַּהּ לִבּוֹ בְּדַרְכֵי יְהוָה **וְעוֹד** הֵסִיר אֶת־הַבָּמוֹת וְאֶת־הָאֲשֵׁרִים מִיהוּדָה׃

He prided his heart in the ways of Yahweh, and **furthermore**, he removed the high places and Asherahs from Judah.

10.6.3 Contrast

Contrastive semantic relationships—similar to English *however, on the other hand, otherwise*—can be signaled by some instances by רַק, אֲבָל, and אַךְ. The adversative אֲבָל is primarily used as a conjunctive adverb. In 1 Kgs 1:42, Adonijah welcomes Jonathan son of Abiathar to his coronation feast (see vv. 9, 25) and alleges an auspicious report (וְטוֹב תְּבַשֵּׂר "you must bring good news"). The retort (v. 43) is anything but favorable and is signaled as such beginning with אֲבָל.

1 Kgs 1:43

וַיַּעַן יוֹנָתָן וַיֹּאמֶר לַאֲדֹנִיָּהוּ **אֲבָל** אֲדֹנֵינוּ הַמֶּלֶךְ־דָּוִד הִמְלִיךְ אֶת־שְׁלֹמֹה׃

Jonathan answered and said to Adonijah, "**On the contrary**, our lord King David has made Solomon king."

The particle רַק designates a contrast or poses an exception. A small number of instances link discourse units as with Exod 8:25. A similar condition is communicated with אַךְ as a contrastive conjunctive adverb (Num 36:6).

Exod 8:25

הִנֵּה אָנֹכִי יוֹצֵא מֵעִמָּךְ וְהַעְתַּרְתִּי אֶל־יְהֹוָה וְסָר הֶעָרֹב מִפַּרְעֹה מֵעֲבָדָיו וּמֵעַמּוֹ
מָחָר רַק אַל־יֹסֵף פַּרְעֹה הָתֵל לְבִלְתִּי שַׁלַּח אֶת־הָעָם לִזְבֹּחַ לַיהוָה

Straightaway! I am leaving you. I will petition Yahweh, and the swarms
will depart tomorrow away from Pharaoh, his servants, and his people;
however, Pharaoh must not again behave deceptively not to allow the
people to go sacrifice to Yahweh.

Num 36:6

זֶה הַדָּבָר אֲשֶׁר־צִוָּה יְהוָה לִבְנוֹת צְלָפְחָד לֵאמֹר לַטּוֹב בְּעֵינֵיהֶם תִּהְיֶינָה לְנָשִׁים אַךְ
לְמִשְׁפַּחַת מַטֵּה אֲבִיהֶם תִּהְיֶינָה לְנָשִׁים:

This is the word which Yahweh commanded for Zelophehad's daughters:
They may have husbands according to what is good in their eyes; **however**, they must have husbands according to the family clan of their father.

In a very small number of cases, a clause will begin with more than one of these
lexemes. It is unlikely that such instances should be understood as conjunctive
adverbs. For example, Num 12:2 sequences a yes-no interrogative (§10.8) with
the two lexemes (רַק and אַךְ). The speech of Miriam and Aaron does not appear
to provide a response to a prior discourse unit. The particles should instead be
understood as an exclusive adverb, "Does Yahweh solely (רַק) speak with Moses,"
and a restrictive adverb, "Does Yahweh speak just (אַךְ) with Moses" (Num 12:2).

Num 12:2

וַיֹּאמְרוּ הֲרַק אַךְ־בְּמֹשֶׁה דִּבֶּר יְהוָה הֲלֹא גַּם־בָּנוּ דִבֵּר

They said: "Does Yahweh **solely** speak **just** with Moses, or does he speak
also with us?"

10.7 NEGATIONS

Negatives serve to invert the semantics of the following constituent. Negation
operates with verbs, nouns, adjectives, adverbs, and prepositions. A negator may
immediately precede any of these constituents or be the first element of a clause.
Some may also serve as a single word response to a question. The principle negators are לֹא, אֵין, בִּלְתִּי, אַל, and אֶפֶס. These are discussed from least to most marked.

NEGATORS	TYPES OF NEGATED CONSTITUENT
לֹא	Any
אֵין	Existential, Participle, Infinitive Construct, Noun, Adjective, Preposition, Adverb, Response
(לְ)בִלְתִּי	Infinitive Construct, Noun, Adjective, Finite Verb, Preposition, Response

NEGATORS	TYPES OF NEGATED CONSTITUENT
אַל	Injunctive Verb, Noun, Response
אֶפֶס	Existential, Response

10.7.1 לֹא

The least marked negator is לֹא. The vast majority of its more than five thousand tokens are used to negate finite verbs. It often signals a simple counterfactual with a suffix conjugation (Gen 4:9) or prefix conjugation verb (Gen 15:4).

Gen 4:9

וַיֹּאמֶר יְהוָה אֶל־קַיִן אֵי הֶבֶל אָחִיךָ וַיֹּאמֶר **לֹא יָדַעְתִּי** הֲשֹׁמֵר אָחִי אָנֹכִי:

Yahweh said to Cain, "Where is Abel your brother?" He responded, "**I do not know**. Am I my brother's guardian?"

Gen 15:4

וְהִנֵּה דְבַר־יְהוָה אֵלָיו לֵאמֹר **לֹא יִירָשְׁךָ** זֶה

Yahweh's word came to him, saying: "This one **will not inherit your** (household)."

The negators can help distinguish between the real and irrealis finite verbs. The indicative is typically signaled with לֹא, while אַל functions with the volitional modality (see further below). Proverbs 27:1 features the injunctive with אַל followed by the indicative with לֹא (cf. Jas 4:13–14).

Prov 27:1

אַל־תִּתְהַלֵּל בְּיוֹם מָחָר כִּי **לֹא־תֵדַע** מַה־יֵּלֶד יוֹם:

Do not boast in tomorrow because **you do not know** what a day will bring.

Noun phrases (לֹא יוֹם אֶחָד "not a single day," Num 11:19), pronouns (לֹא אַתֶּם, Judg 21:22), demonstratives (לֹא זֶה, Gen 44:5; לֹא־זֹאת, Jer 2:17), adjectives (לֹא־טוֹב, Gen 2:18), and adverbs (לֹא־כֵן, Gen 48:18; לֹא עַתָּה, Num 24:17) can all be negated with לֹא. The negation is used less frequently with infinitives construct (לוֹא לִזְרוֹת וְלוֹא לְהָבַר "neither to scatter nor to sift," Jer 4:11), conjoined with prepositions (בְּלֹא כַכָּתוּב "not according to what is written," 2 Chr 30:18) as an existential (לֹא מִלִּבִּי "it was not from my heart," Num 16:28).

The negation can invert the meaning of an entire clause. It precedes both independent (לֹא יֵעָקֵב יֵאָמֵר עוֹד שִׁמְךָ "Never again will your name be called Jacob," Gen 32:29) and relative clauses (לֹא אֲשֶׁר יִרְאֶה הָאָדָם "not what people see," 1 Sam 16:7). It can serve as a one-word negative response (לֹא כִּי אֶת־יְהוָה נַעֲבֹד "No! Rather we will serve Yahweh!" Josh 24:21) or to reject a negative assertion (לֹא תוּכְלוּ לַעֲבֹד אֶת־יְהוָה "No longer will you be able to serve Yahweh," Josh 24:19). It may be also used with a yes-no interrogative to anticipate a positive answer:

Num 12:2

וַיֹּאמְרוּ הֲרַק אַךְ־בְּמֹשֶׁה דִּבֶּר יְהוָה הֲלֹא גַם־בָּנוּ דִבֵּר

They challenged: "Does Yahweh only speak with Moses? **Does he not also speak** with us?"

10.7.2 אֵין

The negator אֵין is principally used as an existential marker (§10.10). It provides a negative null subject for a verbless clause. The predicate constituent may be an adjective (קָדוֹשׁ), prepositional phrase (בִּלְתֶּךָ), or noun (צוּר) as in 1 Sam 2:2. The predicate may also be a participle (Prov 26:20). A pronominal suffix can be attached to the negator to indicate the person, gender, and number of the subject. The 1CS suffix (אֵינֶנִּי) indicates that the speaker is the doer of the participle action (Deut 4:22).

1 Sam 2:2

אֵין־קָדוֹשׁ כַּיהוָה כִּי אֵין בִּלְתֶּךָ וְאֵין צוּר

None is holy like Yahweh because **there is none** except you and **there is no** rock like our God.

Prov 26:20

וּבְאֵין נִרְגָּן יִשְׁתֹּק מָדוֹן

When **there is no** grumbling, strife grows silent.

Deut 4:22

אֵינֶנִּי עֹבֵר אֶת־הַיַּרְדֵּן

I am not crossing the Jordan.

10.7.3 בִּלְתִּי(לְ)

The negator לְבִלְתִּי is mostly used to negate the infinitive construct. The *lamed* of the negation is not repeated with the following infinitive (Deut 4:21). Other phrases are negated without the preposition, consequently the lexeme is listed as בִּלְתִּי in most dictionaries. The rarer forms, לְבְלִי and בַּל, are related etymologically and functionally.

Deut 4:21

וַיִּשָּׁבַע לְבִלְתִּי עָבְרִי אֶת־הַיַּרְדֵּן וּלְבִלְתִּי־בֹא אֶל־הָאָרֶץ הַטּוֹבָה אֲשֶׁר יְהוָה אֱלֹהֶיךָ נֹתֵן לְךָ נַחֲלָה

He swore **to not allow me to cross** the Jordan and **to not allow me to enter** the good land that Yahweh your God is giving to you as an inheritance.

Noun phrases can be negated with בִּלְתִּי (בִּלְתִּי סָרָה "unceasing," Isa 14:6). Elsewhere it is used like a negative existential (עַד־בִּלְתִּי שָׁמַיִם "until the heavens are nothing," Job 14:12) and for exceptions (בִּלְתִּי כָלֵב "not Caleb," Num 32:12).

Prepositional phrases may also be negated as with Exod 22:19. Occasionally, בִּלְתִּי is found with finite verbs (Exod 20:20). It is used once as a negative response.[31]

Exod 22:19

זֹבֵחַ לָאֱלֹהִים יָחֳרָם בִּלְתִּי לַיהוָה לְבַדּוֹ

The one sacrificing to the gods—**except to Yahweh alone**—is to be destroyed.

Exod 20:20

אַל־תִּירָאוּ כִּי לְבַעֲבוּר נַסּוֹת אֶתְכֶם בָּא הָאֱלֹהִים וּבַעֲבוּר תִּהְיֶה יִרְאָתוֹ עַל־פְּנֵיכֶם לְבִלְתִּי תֶחֱטָאוּ

Do not fear because God has come so as to test you and so that you will reverence him **rather than sin**.

10.7.4 אַל

The negator אַל functions mostly to give prohibitive injunctions. With a second-person jussive conjugation verb, the collocation is the primary way to issue a negative command (1 Kgs 13:22).[32] With more deferential force, the third-person jussive form (1 Sam 22:15) or combination אַל־נָא (Num 10:31) is used.

1 Kgs 13:22

אַל־תֹּאכַל לֶחֶם וְאַל־תֵּשְׁתְּ מָיִם

Do not eat bread and **do not drink** water.

1 Sam 22:15

אַל־יָשֵׂם הַמֶּלֶךְ בְּעַבְדּוֹ דָבָר בְּכָל־בֵּית אָבִי

May the king **not ascribe** anything to his servant among all my father's household.

Num 10:31

אַל־נָא תַּעֲזֹב אֹתָנוּ

Please don't leave us!

An elliptical verb may be implied with וְאַל "but not" used after an imperative:

Joel 2:13

וְקִרְעוּ לְבַבְכֶם וְאַל־בִּגְדֵיכֶם

Tear your heart, **but** [tear] **not** your garments.

---

[31] The response to the questions in Isa 10:3–4: וּמַה־תַּעֲשׂוּ "What will you do?," עַל־מִי תָנוּסוּ "To whom will you flee?," and וְאָנָה תַעֲזְבוּ "Where will you leave?" is בְּלְתִּי "nothing, nobody, nowhere."

[32] The short and long prefix conjugations are only differentiable with certain forms of third-weak, middle-weak, and *Hiphil* stem verbs. Some jussive forms have an initial accent as with לֹא־תֹאכַל לֶחֶם וְלֹא־תִשְׁתֶּה שָׁם מָיִם "You must not eat bread or drink water there" (1 Kgs 13:17) but not with לֹא־תֹאכַל לֶחֶם וְלֹא תִשְׁתֶּה־מָיִם "You must not eat bread or drink water" (v. 9). אַל is found with forms that are distinguishable (e.g. תֵּשְׁתְּ), as well as those that are not (e.g. תֹּאכַל).

The negator אַל is used with several other constituents.[33] Possibly one of the less intuitive examples is as a response. It serves to affirm a negative command. For instance, Lot responds to the divine warning not to tarry from fleeing Sodom (Gen 19:17) with the clear affirmation אַל־נָא אֲדֹנָי "Certainly not, Lord!" (v. 18).

Gen 19:17

הִמָּלֵט עַל־נַפְשֶׁךָ **אַל־תַּבִּיט** אַחֲרֶיךָ **וְאַל־תַּעֲמֹד** בְּכָל־הַכִּכָּר הָהָרָה הִמָּלֵט פֶּן־תִּסָּפֶה

Run for it! **Neither look** behind you **nor stay** in any of the vicinity. Run lest you be destroyed.

10.7.5. אֶפֶס

The negator אֶפֶס is rare. It is mostly used in parallel constructions with the semantically similar negative existential אֵין (Isa 45:6).[34] It also can function as an elliptical negative response (Amos 6:10).

Isa 45:6

אֶפֶס בִּלְעָדַי אֲנִי יְהוָה וְאֵין עוֹד

There is none except me—I am Yahweh and there is no other.

Amos 6:10

וְאָמַר לַאֲשֶׁר בְּיַרְכְּתֵי הַבַּיִת הַעוֹד עִמָּךְ וְאָמַר **אָפֶס**

Someone calls to another inside the house: "Is there anyone with you?" And he responds: "**Nobody!**"

10.8 QUESTIONS

Questions specify a particular type of answer. Different function words and constructions are used to illicit certain responses. A <u>Wh-question</u> includes an interrogative pronoun that anticipates an assumed referent. These <u>interrogatives</u> function like pronouns and are clause initial. They are used in the place of the questioned item. The basic forms are מַה, מִי (with the consonant doubled, and מֶה or מָה following gutturals), אֵי (or אֵין, אָן, אֵיפֹה), אֵיךְ (or אֵיכָה), אָנָה, and מַדּוּעַ (also לָמָה and לָמֶה). They inquire as to a person (*who?*), a nonpersonal entity (*what?*), a location (*where?*), a manner (*how?*), a time (*when?*), and a reason (*how?* or *why?*). Ecclesiastes 8:4 describes the nature of authority and power by rhetorically asking who can question how a monarch behaves. Proverbs 30:4 contains six questions asking four *who*-queries (מִי) and two *what*-queries (מַה).

---

[33] Several times, it negates a noun phrase (Ps 83:2; Prov 27:2); once it negates an adverb (Job 24:25).

[34] It can be compounded to form the preposition בְּאֶפֶס with a function like the privative בְּלִי "without" (e.g., בְּאֶפֶס עֵצִים תִּכְבֶּה־אֵשׁ "Without wood, a fire is extinguished," Prov 26:20).

Eccl 8:4

וּמִי יֹאמַר־לוֹ מַה־תַּעֲשֶׂה

Who may say to [a king]: "**What** are you doing?"

Prov 30:4

מִי עָלָה־שָׁמַיִם ׀ וַיֵּרַד מִי אָסַף־רוּחַ ׀ בְּחָפְנָיו מִי צָרַר־מַיִם ׀ בַּשִּׂמְלָה מִי הֵקִים
כָּל־אַפְסֵי־אָרֶץ מַה־שְּׁמוֹ וּמַה־שֶּׁם־בְּנוֹ כִּי תֵדָע:

Who has ascended to heaven and descended? **Who** has gathered the wind into his palms? **Who** has bundled the waters into a cloak? **Who** has erected all the ends of the earth? **What** is his name, and **what** is his son's name? Surely you know!

Prepositions can attach to the interrogatives to specify the constituency of the pronoun. Jonah 1:8 includes לְמִי "to whom" and מֵאַיִן "from where," and Isa 40:18 asks אֶל־מִי "to whom?"

Jonah 1:8

לְמִי־הָרָעָה הַזֹּאת לָנוּ מַה־מְּלַאכְתְּךָ וּמֵאַיִן תָּבוֹא מָה אַרְצֶךָ וְאֵי־מִזֶּה עַם אָתָּה

Because of whom is this disaster ours? **What** is your business? **From where** are you travelling? **What** is your land? **From which** people are you?

Isa 40:18

וְאֶל־מִי תְּדַמְּיוּן אֵל וּמַה־דְּמוּת תַּעַרְכוּ לוֹ:

To whom can you compare God? **What** kind of image can you prepare of him?

Yes-no questions and alternative questions can be marked by intonation or the clause-initial morpheme -הֲ, often called the interrogative *he*. A yes-no question anticipates the answer is either the affirmative or negative. It may be initiated by intonation, usually clause final rising (2 Sam 18:29), or with the clause-initial morpheme -הֲ (v. 32). A response can signal a question where it is not explicitly marked in a preceding clause (Gen 27:24).

2 Sam 18:29

וַיֹּאמֶר הַמֶּלֶךְ שָׁלוֹם לַנַּעַר לְאַבְשָׁלוֹם

The king said: "**My boy Absalom is well?**"

2 Sam 18:32

וַיֹּאמֶר הַמֶּלֶךְ אֶל־הַכּוּשִׁי הֲשָׁלוֹם לַנַּעַר לְאַבְשָׁלוֹם

The king said to the Cushite: "**Is my boy Absalom well?**"

Gen 27:24

וַיֹּאמֶר אַתָּה זֶה בְּנִי עֵשָׂו וַיֹּאמֶר **אָנִי**

[Isaac] said, "You are my son Esau?"
[Jacob] responded: "**I am**."

The answer כֵּן is never used as the affirmative in Biblical Hebrew, rather the response restates part (Gen 29:5) or all the question as an indicative clause (Gen 43:27–28). The negative response may simply be indicated with a bare negator (לֹא in 2 Kgs 20:10; אָ֫יִן in Judg 4:20) or the negated indicative clause (Gen 18:28).

Gen 29:5

וַיֹּאמֶר לָהֶם הַיְדַעְתֶּם אֶת־לָבָן בֶּן־נָחוֹר וַיֹּאמְרוּ **יָדָעְנוּ**׃

He said to him: "Do you know Laban ben Nahor?" They said: "**We know**."

Gen 43:27–28

וַיֹּאמֶר הֲשָׁלוֹם אֲבִיכֶם הַזָּקֵן אֲשֶׁר אֲמַרְתֶּם הַעוֹדֶנּוּ חָי וַיֹּאמְרוּ שָׁלוֹם לְעַבְדְּךָ
לְאָבִינוּ עוֹדֶנּוּ חָי

He said: "Is your elderly father whom you mentioned **well**? **Is he still living**?" They said: "Your servant, our father, is **well. He is still living**."

2 Kgs 20:10

וַיֹּאמֶר יְחִזְקִיָּהוּ נָקֵל לַצֵּל לִנְטוֹת עֶשֶׂר מַעֲלוֹת **לֹא** כִּי יָשׁוּב הַצֵּל אֲחֹרַנִּית עֶשֶׂר
מַעֲלוֹת׃

Hezekiah said: "Is it easier for a shadow to extend ten steps? **No**! Let the shadow go backwards ten steps."

Judg 4:20

וְאָמַר הֲיֵשׁ־פֹּה אִישׁ וְאָמַרְתְּ **אָיִן**

Should he ask, "Is there someone here?" Then say: "**There is not**."

Gen 18:28

הֲתַשְׁחִית בַּחֲמִשָּׁה אֶת־כָּל־הָעִיר וַיֹּאמֶר **לֹא אַשְׁחִית** אִם־אֶמְצָא שָׁם אַרְבָּעִים
וַחֲמִשָּׁה

"**Will you destroy** the entire city on behalf of five?" He said: "**I will not destroy** if I find forty-five [righteous] there."

Yes-no rhetorical questions are often signaled with the interrogative *he*. The initial morpheme -הֲ presumes a negative answer (Gen 18:14), while הֲלֹא affirms it is true (1 Sam 1:8).[35] While Elkanah expresses what he views as a truism in 1 Sam 1:8, the narrator implies the opposite is in fact true based on Hannah's lack of response to her husband and eventual vow (see v. 11).

---

[35] For the development of הֲלוֹא/הֲלֹא, see Matthew McAffee, "A Reassessment of the Hebrew Negative Interrogative Particle *hlʾ*," *JAOS* 135 (2015): 115–30.

Gen 18:14

הֲיִפָּלֵא מֵיהוָה דָּבָר

Is anything impossible with Yahweh?

(Response: Anything is possible with Yahweh.)

1 Sam 1:8

וַיֹּאמֶר לָהּ אֶלְקָנָה אִישָׁהּ חַנָּה לָמֶה תִבְכִּי וְלָמֶה לֹא תֹאכְלִי וְלָמֶה יֵרַע לְבָבֵךְ הֲלוֹא

אָנֹכִי טוֹב לָךְ מֵעֲשָׂרָה בָּנִים:

Elkanah her husband asked her: "Hannah, why are you weeping and not eating? Why is your heart distraught? **Am I not** better to you than ten sons?"

(Response: No, you are not better to me than ten sons.)

An <u>alternative question</u> presents two or more options and anticipates one of the expressed choices is the answer. The different possibilities can be signaled with אִם (Num 13:20). A simple either-or question may end with אִם־לֹא (Num 11:23). This construction is employed as a type of indirect question as in Exod 16:4.

Num 13:20

וּמָה הָאָרֶץ הַשְּׁמֵנָה הִוא אִם־רָזָה הֲיֵשׁ־בָּהּ עֵץ אִם־אַיִן

What about the land—is it bountiful **or bare**? Are there trees **or nothing**?

Deut 8:2

הֲתִשְׁמֹר מִצְוֹתָיו אִם־לֹא

Will you keep my commandments, **or not**?

Exod 16:4

הִנְנִי מַמְטִיר לָכֶם לֶחֶם מִן־הַשָּׁמָיִם וְיָצָא הָעָם וְלָקְטוּ דְּבַר־יוֹם בְּיוֹמוֹ לְמַעַן אֲנַסֶּנּוּ

הֲיֵלֵךְ בְּתוֹרָתִי אִם־לֹא

I plan to rain down bread from heaven for you: the people should go out and gather a day's amount. In so doing, I will test whether they walk according to my instruction, **or not**?

10.9 REACTION SIGNALS

Certain utterances encode or elicit extemporaneous reactions. <u>Reaction signals</u> are a large, open class or set of lexemes and sounds that are traditionally called <u>interjections</u> (or exclamations).[36] English examples include *wow, tsk, ick, ouch, please, psst, shh, hey,* and *aha.* They are meant to embody feelings, emotions, desires, perceptions, or cognitive states. Their pragmatic function can overlap with some

---

[36] See Neal R. Norrick, "Interjections as Pragmatic Markers," *Journal of Pragmatics* 41 (2009): 866–91.

vocatives as "attention getters."[37] A number function like discourse markers or adverbs, but they stand outside of the normal syntax of a clause. They are not assigned clause or phrase constituency.

Hebrew reaction signals indicate feelings (joy, sorrow), desires (silence, desperation, entreaty), perceptions (approval, disapproval), or cognitive states (warning, shock, surprise).

10.9.1 Joy (הֶאָח)

The feeling of mirth or joy can be signaled with the הֶאָח particle. In Ezek 26:2, the city-state of Tyre celebrates the downfall of Jerusalem with the initial blissful cry. Yahweh responds that Tyre will itself be left in ruins (vv. 3–5).

Ezek 26:2.

בֶּן־אָדָם יַעַן אֲשֶׁר־אָמְרָה צֹּר עַל־יְרוּשָׁלַ͏ִם הֶאָח נִשְׁבְּרָה דַּלְתוֹת הָעַמִּים נָסֵבָּה אֵלַי אִמָּלְאָה הָחֳרָבָה:

Human, on account of the fact that Tyre said concerning Jerusalem: "**Hooray!** The doors of the people are shattered. It has been handed over to me. Let me be filled. It is destroyed."

10.9.2 Sorrow (אֲהָהּ)

The emotion of regret, distress, or sorrow is heightened with אֲהָהּ. When Gideon comprehends that he has been in the presence of Yahweh's divine messenger, he acknowledges that he will die (Judg 6:22). The prophet expresses regret and fear on account of his lack of maturity (Jer 1:6). Both examples begin with an attention-getting signals and the vocative, naming the addressee.

Judg 6:22

וַיֹּאמֶר גִּדְעוֹן אֲהָהּ אֲדֹנָי יְהוִה כִּי־עַל־כֵּן רָאִיתִי מַלְאַךְ יְהוָה פָּנִים אֶל־פָּנִים:
Gideon said: "**Oh no**, Lord Yahweh! Because of this [I realize that] I have seen the angel of Yahweh face to face!"

Jer 1:6

וָאֹמַר אֲהָהּ אֲדֹנָי יְהוִה הִנֵּה לֹא־יָדַעְתִּי דַּבֵּר כִּי־נַעַר אָנֹכִי:
I said: "**Alas**, Lord Yahweh! Really?! I do not know how to speak because I am a mere youth."

10.9.3 Silence (הַס)

The desire to enact quiet and still is expressed by הַס. Upon Ehud's promise of a clandestine rumor, King Eglon clears his chambers to listen attentively (Judg

---

[37] This observation comes from Young Bok Kim (personal communication). See further, Biber et al., *Longman Grammar*, 1112–13.

3:19). Similarly, the one responsible for clearing a house of dead bodies must be restrained (Amos 6:10).

Judg 3:19

וַיֹּאמֶר דְּבַר־סֵתֶר לִי אֵלֶיךָ הַמֶּלֶךְ וַיֹּאמֶר הָס וַיֵּצְאוּ מֵעָלָיו כָּל־הָעֹמְדִים עָלָיו

He said, "I have a secret for you, King." He said, "**Shh!**" Then all his aides left him.

Amos 6:10

וְאָמַר לַאֲשֶׁר בְּיַרְכְּתֵי הַבַּיִת הַעוֹד עִמָּךְ וְאָמַר אָפֶס וְאָמַר הָס כִּי לֹא לְהַזְכִּיר בְּשֵׁם יְהוָה׃

He will say to the one in the back of the house, "Is anyone there with you?" He will reply, "None." And he will say, "**Hush!** Careful, don't mention Yahweh's name."

10.9.4 Desperation (בִּי)

In various desperate circumstances, the particle בִּי may be used to request attention. Aaron pleads for his sister whose skin became white like snow and was about to die. He intercedes for forgiveness following their challenge to Moses's prophetic authority (Num 12:11). In 1 Sam 1:26, Hannah reminds Eli of her desperation in asking for Yahweh's miraculous intervention to give her a child. She commits Samuel to God's service in response to answering her prayer.

Num 12:11

וַיֹּאמֶר אַהֲרֹן אֶל־מֹשֶׁה בִּי אֲדֹנִי אַל־נָא תָשֵׁת עָלֵינוּ חַטָּאת אֲשֶׁר נוֹאַלְנוּ וַאֲשֶׁר חָטָאנוּ׃

Aaron said to Moses, "**I beg you**, my lord, do not hold against us the offense which we foolishly did and sinned."

1 Sam 1:26

וַתֹּאמֶר בִּי אֲדֹנִי חֵי נַפְשְׁךָ אֲדֹנִי אֲנִי הָאִשָּׁה הַנִּצֶּבֶת עִמְּכָה בָּזֶה לְהִתְפַּלֵּל אֶל־יְהוָה׃

She said, "**Pardon**, my lord, on your life, my lord, I am the woman who was standing with you right here [previously] praying to Yahweh."

10.9.5 Entreaty (נָא)

The particle of entreaty (נָא, נָא־, or נָּא־) typically accompanies a verb. Volitional verbs are most common (Gen 12:13).[38] In rare instances, it may be independent (Exod 33:18) or even repeated (Num 12:13). And it can follow other function words (e.g., אַל־נָא, Gen 33:10; אִם־נָא, Gen 30:27; אִם־יֶשְׁךָ־נָּא, Gen 24:42). As a reaction signal, it is intended to elicit a sympathetic response as a polite request.

---

[38] For the use of נָא as a volitional particle, see §6.8.

Several English idioms can designate a similar deferential expression, including
kindly, *cordially*, *graciously*, *please*, *humbly*, and *I beg you*.

Gen 12:13

אִמְרִי־**נָא** אֲחֹתִי אָתְּ

I beg you, say, "You are my sister."

Exod 33:18

וַיֹּאמַר הַרְאֵנִי **נָא** אֶת־כְּבֹדֶךָ:

He said, "Show me your glory, **please**."

Num 12:13

וַיִּצְעַק מֹשֶׁה אֶל־יְהוָה לֵאמֹר אֵל **נָא** רְפָא **נָא** לָהּ:

Moses cried out to Yahweh: "God, **kindly**, would you **graciously** heal
her?"

10.9.6 Approval (אָמֵן)

Affirmation may be given with the reaction signal, אָמֵן. It may be used to initiate
a true statement as with 1 Kgs 1:36. Elsewhere it may end an assertion or serve as
a verifying response (Neh 8:6).

1 Kgs 1:36

וַיַּעַן בְּנָיָהוּ בֶן־יְהוֹיָדָע אֶת־הַמֶּלֶךְ וַיֹּאמֶר | **אָמֵן** כֵּן יֹאמַר יְהוָֹה אֱלֹהֵי אֲדֹנִי הַמֶּלֶךְ:

Benaiah son of Jehoiada answered the king and said, "**Yes!** May it be as
Yahweh the God of my lord the king says."

Neh 8:6

וַיְבָרֶךְ עֶזְרָא אֶת־יְהוָה הָאֱלֹהִים הַגָּדוֹל וַיַּעֲנוּ כָל־הָעָם **אָמֵן** | **אָמֵן** בְּמֹעַל יְדֵיהֶם
וַיִּקְּדוּ וַיִּשְׁתַּחֲוֻ לַיהוָה אַפַּיִם אָרְצָה:

Ezra blessed Yahweh the great God, and all the people answered, "**Amen,
amen**," while lifting their hands. They knelt and worshiped Yahweh with
their faces on the ground.

10.9.7 Disapproval (חָלִילָה)

To refuse a claim, the particle חָלִילָה introduces a disapproving declaration. The
rejection of Job's friends is strengthened by his outcry against them (Job 27:5).
In Gen 18:25, Abraham declares incredulity that God would treat righteous and
wicked people in like manner.

Job 27:5

חָלִילָה לִּי אִם־אַצְדִּיק אֶתְכֶם עַד־אֶגְוָע לֹא־אָסִיר תֻּמָּתִי מִמֶּנִּי:

Certainly not! I will never admit you are right even till the day I die;
I will not allow my integrity to be taken from me.

Gen 18:25

חָלִ֙לָה֙ לְּךָ֜ מֵעֲשֹׂ֣ת ׀ כַּדָּבָ֣ר הַזֶּ֗ה לְהָמִ֤ית צַדִּיק֙ עִם־רָשָׁ֔ע וְהָיָ֥ה כַצַּדִּ֖יק כָּרָשָׁ֑ע
No way that you would do this matter: killing the righteous with the wicked. Then it would be the same for the righteous and wicked.

10.9.8 Warning (הוֹי or אוֹי)

The similar attention-getters, אוֹי and הוֹי, express cognitive states brought about by external threats. Both particles can indicate mental distress (Isa 6:5) or emotional lament (Jer 22:18), and the latter can also be used to attract attention (Zech 2:10).

Isa 6:5

וָאֹמַ֞ר אֽוֹי־לִ֣י כִֽי־נִדְמֵ֗יתִי כִּ֣י אִ֤ישׁ טְמֵֽא־שְׂפָתַ֙יִם֙ אָנֹ֔כִי וּבְתוֹךְ֙ עַם־טְמֵ֣א שְׂפָתַ֔יִם
אָנֹכִ֖י יוֹשֵׁ֑ב כִּ֗י אֶת־הַמֶּ֛לֶךְ יְהוָ֥ה צְבָא֖וֹת רָא֥וּ עֵינָֽי׃
I said: "**Woe** to me for I am silenced because I am a man with unclean lips, and I am living among a people with unclean lips and because my eyes have seen King Yahweh of Hosts."

Jer 22:18

לֹא־יִסְפְּד֣וּ ל֔וֹ ה֥וֹי אָחִ֖י וְה֣וֹי אָח֑וֹת
They will not grieve for him [in the vein of]: "**Goodbye**, dear brother!" and "**Rest in peace**, my sister!"

Zech 2:10

ה֣וֹי ה֗וֹי וְנֻ֛סוּ מֵאֶ֥רֶץ צָפ֖וֹן נְאֻם־יְהוָ֑ה כִּ֞י כְּאַרְבַּ֧ע רוּח֣וֹת הַשָּׁמַ֛יִם פֵּרַ֥שְׂתִּי אֶתְכֶ֖ם
נְאֻם־יְהוָֽה׃
Hey, listen up! Flee from the land of the north, declares Yahweh, for I have scattered you like the four winds of heaven, declares Yahweh.

10.9.9 Shock (אָנָּא)

The particle אָנָּא can indicate the feeling of shock over the gravity of a situation. Examples from Exod 32:31 and Jonah 1:14 present a reaction to dire, solemn circumstances of idolatry and execution.

Exod 32:31

וַיָּ֧שָׁב מֹשֶׁ֛ה אֶל־יְהוָ֖ה וַיֹּאמַ֑ר **אָ֣נָּ֗א** חָטָ֞א הָעָ֤ם הַזֶּה֙ חֲטָאָ֣ה גְדֹלָ֔ה וַיַּעֲשׂ֥וּ לָהֶ֖ם אֱלֹהֵ֥י
זָהָֽב׃
Moses returned to Yahweh and said: "**Oy vey!** This nation has sinned gravely, and they made themselves golden gods."

Jonah 1:14

וַיִּקְרְא֨וּ אֶל־יְהֹוָ֜ה וַיֹּאמְר֗וּ אָנָּ֤ה יְהֹוָה֙ אַל־נָ֣א נֹאבְדָ֗ה בְּנֶ֙פֶשׁ֙ הָאִ֣ישׁ הַזֶּ֔ה

They called to Yahweh and said: "**Oy vey!** Yahweh, let us not perish because of this man's life!"

10.9.10 Surprise (הִנֵּה or רְאֵה)

The most common attention-getter enacts a cognitive state of <u>mirativity or surprise</u>. A mirative marks an utterance as newsworthy.[39] You might think of a town crier (*step right up!*), a newspaper hawker (*extra, extra read all about it*), or clickbait titles (*five foods nutritionists know help to lose weight*) as forms of attention getting. Hebrew attention-getters include הִנֵּה, הֵן, and sometimes רְאֵה. They can be combined with other lexemes and commonly with pronominal elements (e.g., with the 1CS as הִנְנִי or הִנֵּנִי).[40] The particle may be situated anywhere within a clause, but commonly it initiates the newsworthy material. Most instances are found in reported speech (1 Sam 14:8).[41] But it can highlight information in narrative prose (Exod 3:2), didactic discourse (Lev 13:5), and even poetry (Ps 7:15).

1 Sam 14:8

וַיֹּ֙אמֶר֙ יְה֣וֹנָתָ֔ן הִנֵּ֛ה אֲנַ֥חְנוּ עֹבְרִ֖ים אֶל־הָאֲנָשִׁ֑ים

Jonathan said: "**Here's the plan**, we will cross over to the men."

Exod 3:2

וַ֠יֵּרָא מַלְאַ֨ךְ יְהֹוָ֥ה אֵלָ֛יו בְּלַבַּת־אֵ֖שׁ מִתּ֣וֹךְ הַסְּנֶ֑ה וַיַּ֗רְא וְהִנֵּ֤ה הַסְּנֶה֙ בֹּעֵ֣ר בָּאֵ֔שׁ
וְהַסְּנֶ֖ה אֵינֶ֥נּוּ אֻכָּֽל׃

Yahweh's messenger appeared to him in the fiery flare from within the bush, and he took a look. **Marvel of marvels!** The bush was on fire, but it was not burned up.

Lev 13:5

וְרָאָ֣הוּ הַכֹּהֵן֮ בַּיּ֣וֹם הַשְּׁבִיעִי֒ וְהִנֵּ֤ה הַנֶּ֙גַע֙ עָמַ֣ד בְּעֵינָ֔יו לֹֽא־פָשָׂ֥ה הַנֶּ֖גַע בָּע֑וֹר וְהִסְגִּיר֧וֹ
הַכֹּהֵ֛ן שִׁבְעַ֥ת יָמִ֖ים שֵׁנִֽית׃

The priest will examine him on the seventh day. If **indeed** the malady remains unchanged without spreading on his skin, the priest shall quarantine him seven more days.

---

[39] Cynthia L. Miller-Naudé and C. H. J. van der Merwe, "הִנֵּה and Mirativity in Biblical Hebrew," *HS* 52 (2011): 53–81.

[40] The first two are related forms but should be distinguished from the independent personal pronouns, הֵנָּה and הֵן "they." The last is homophonous with the *Qal* imperative MS of ראה "see."

[41] Cynthia L. Miller, *The Representation of Speech in Biblical Hebrew Narrative: A Linguistic Analysis*, HSM 55 (Atlanta: Scholars, 1996).

Ps 7:15

הִנֵּה יְחַבֶּל־אָוֶן וְהָרָה עָמָל וְיָלַד שָׁקֶר׃

Beware! The wicked labor with misfortune; he conceives mischief and gives birth to deceit.

While not independent of the verbal notion of seeing or beholding, these particles only necessitate the cognitive eye as a metaphor for recognizing something unique, unusual, or unexpected. A sense of suddenness (i.e., surprise) can be included but is not always necessitated (cf. Gen 1:31 and 6:12).[42]

Gen 1:31

וַיַּרְא אֱלֹהִים אֶת־כָּל־אֲשֶׁר עָשָׂה וְהִנֵּה־טוֹב מְאֹד

God saw all he made, and **wow** was it very pleasing.

Gen 6:12

וַיַּרְא אֱלֹהִים אֶת־הָאָרֶץ וְהִנֵּה נִשְׁחָתָה

God saw the earth, and **wow** was it ruined.

The same particle can also indicate deixis as a presentative (1 Sam 3:4) or a combination of these notions (Exod 2:6).

1 Sam 3:4

וַיִּקְרָא יְהוָה אֶל־שְׁמוּאֵל וַיֹּאמֶר הִנֵּנִי׃

Yahweh called to Samuel, and he responded, "**I'm right here!**"

Exod 2:6

וַתִּפְתַּח וַתִּרְאֵהוּ אֶת־הַיֶּלֶד וְהִנֵּה־נַעַר בֹּכֶה

She opened [the basket] and saw the child. **There** was a little boy crying!

10.10 EXISTENTIALS

An existential posits the existence of its referent. The main predication of an existential clause does not include a finite verb. It functions analogously to the verb הָיָה with an assumed (or null) subject, but it does not mark time, aspect, or modality. Normally, the complement immediately follows the function word and serves as its implicit existence parameter.

The existential is expressed with יֵשׁ, and the nonexistential with אֵין. Job 33:32–33 uses both. The negative existential occurs four times more often than the positive existential in BH.

---

42 See further Hardy, *Exegetical Gems*, 194–96.

Job 33:32–33

אִם־יֵשׁ־מִלִּין הֲשִׁיבֵנִי דַּבֵּר כִּי־חָפַצְתִּי צַדְּקֶךָ׃ אִם־אַיִן אַתָּה שְׁמַע־לִי הַחֲרֵשׁ
וַאֲאַלֶּפְךָ חָכְמָה׃

If **there are** words, answer me. Speak so that I can take pleasure in your righteousness. If **there are not** [words], you listen to me! Be silent so that I can teach you wisdom.

Overt referents can be expressed with pronominal suffixes, often with participles (Exod 5:10; Deut 13:4).

Exod 5:10

כֹּה אָמַר פַּרְעֹה אֵינֶנִּי נֹתֵן לָכֶם תֶּבֶן
Pharaoh has stated: "**I am not giving** straw to you."

Deut 13:4

הֲיִשְׁכֶם אֹהֲבִים אֶת־יְהוָה אֱלֹהֵיכֶם בְּכָל־לְבַבְכֶם וּבְכָל־נַפְשְׁכֶם
Will you be loyal to Yahweh your God with all your heart and with all your person?

10.11 OBJECT MARKERS

Three constructions can signal a verb complement or object. Complements may be marked with a proclitic אֵת (Eccl 12:1; Deut 24:9; Gen 49:29), a prefixed ־לְ (Exod 32:13; Ps 25:7b),[43] or a verb pronominal suffix (Jer 15:15).[44] Within the same clause, complements may be marked using different constructions (Ps 132:1).

Eccl 12:1

וּזְכֹר אֶת־בּוֹרְאֶיךָ בִּימֵי בְּחוּרֹתֶיךָ
Remember **your Creator** in your youthful years.

Deut 24:9

זָכוֹר אֵת אֲשֶׁר־עָשָׂה יְהוָה אֱלֹהֶיךָ לְמִרְיָם
Remember **what** Yahweh your God did to Miriam.

Gen 49:29

קִבְרוּ אֹתִי אֶל־אֲבֹתָי
Bury **me** with my fathers.

---

[43] The preposition ־לְ can be used to mark a dative (§11.4.3.5), namely, an indirect object, as with 1 Sam 1:5 **וּלְחַנָּה** יִתֵּן מָנָה אַחַת אַפָּיִם כִּי אֶת־חַנָּה אָהֵב וַיהוָה סָגַר רַחְמָהּ "He would give a double portion **to Hannah** because he loved Hannah, but Yahweh had closed her womb").

[44] See §3.6.3 on completion and valency.

Exod 32:13

זְכֹר לְאַבְרָהָם֩ לְיִצְחָק וּלְיִשְׂרָאֵל

Remember **Abraham, Isaac, and Israel**.

Ps 25:7

חַטֹּאות נְעוּרַ֗י ׀ וּפְשָׁעַי֮ אַל־תִּזְכֹּר כְּחַסְדְּךָ֥ זְכָר־לִי־אַ֑תָּה לְמַעַן טוּבְךָ֥ יְהוָֽה׃

According to your covenant love, do not remember my youthful sins and transgressions; Remember **me**—will you?—because of your goodness, Yahweh!

Jer 15:15

אַתָּ֤ה יָדַ֙עְתָּ֙ יְהוָ֔ה זָכְרֵ֥נִי וּפָקְדֵ֖נִי

As for you, Yahweh, you know: **Remember me and visit me!**

Ps 132:1

זְכוֹר־יְהוָ֥ה לְדָוִ֑ד אֵ֣ת כָּל־עֻנּוֹתֽוֹ

Yahweh, remember **David** [and] **all his hardships**.

COMPARING THE TWO FUNCTIONS OF אֶת

The lexical form of the object marker אֶת (אֵת־) is homophonous with the comitative preposition אֶת (אֵת־). The forms with pronominal suffixes, however, are different.

OBJECT MARKER		PREPOSITION		
P	**S**	**P**	**S**	
אֹתָ֫נוּ	אֹתִי	אִתָּ֫נוּ	אִתִּי	1C
אֶתְכֶם	אֹתְךָ (pausal: אֹתָ֑ךְ)	אִתְּכֶם	אִתְּךָ (pausal: אִתָּ֑ךְ)	2M
—	אֹתָךְ	—	אִתָּךְ	2F
אֹתָם (or אֶתְהֶם)	אֹתוֹ	אִתָּם	אִתּוֹ	3M
אֶתְהֶן	אֹתָהּ	—	אִתָּהּ	3F

Some complements lack overt marking. These include deictic markers (Isa 46:8), relative clauses (Mic 6:5), indefinite nominals (Deut 32:7), and even definite nominals (Mal 3:22, and above Ps 25:7a).

Isa 46:8

זִכְרוּ־זֹ֔את

Remember **this**.

Mic 6:5

עַמִּי זְכָר־נָא מַה־יָּעַץ בָּלָק מֶלֶךְ מוֹאָב

My people, remember well **what Balak, king of Moab, recommended**.

Deut 32:7

זְכֹר יְמוֹת עוֹלָם

Remember **bygone times**.

Mal 3:22

זִכְרוּ תּוֹרַת מֹשֶׁה עַבְדִּי

Remember **my servant Moses's instruction**.

In prototypical clauses, the subject is a known, animate entity. An object, however, can have similar semantic and pragmatic qualities. Overt complement marking helps to differentiate between subjects and objects when both are identified and animate.[45] An example is Gen 27:41 where עֵשָׂו and יַעֲקֹב could serve as the subject or object of the verb. Like the accusative case, overt marking serves to designate the complement, אֶת־יַעֲקֹב. The plural constituents (מִצְרַיִם and בְּנֵי יִשְׂרָאֵל) in Exod 1:13 are similarly discerned. English, of course, encodes subject/object constituency through word order.

Gen 27:41

וַיִּשְׂטֹם עֵשָׂו אֶת־יַעֲקֹב עַל־הַבְּרָכָה אֲשֶׁר בֵּרְכוֹ אָבִיו

Esau resented **Jacob** because of the blessing his father gave him.

Exod 1:13

וַיַּעֲבִדוּ מִצְרַיִם אֶת־בְּנֵי יִשְׂרָאֵל בְּפָרֶךְ:

The Egyptians worked **the Israelites** ruthlessly.

In clauses with two objects, the overt marker אֵת typically designates the direct object. Other indirect objects and object complements are either unmarked or part of prepositional phrases (e.g., dative -לְ, see §11.4.3.5).[46] Judges 8:31 indicates אֶת־שְׁמוֹ "his name" as the patient of the ditransitive verb, while אֲבִימֶלֶךְ is the attributive object complement. In Jer 9:10, the first clause marks the secondary object with -לְ and the second is unmarked. Both direct objects have proclitic אֵת.

Judg 8:31

וַיָּשֶׂם אֶת־שְׁמוֹ אֲבִימֶלֶךְ

He named **his name** Abimelech

---

[45] See the discussion of Judith Aissen, "Differential Object Marking: Iconicity vs. Economy," *Natural Language and Linguistic Theory* 21 (2003): 435–83.

[46] Other complement constructions may also serve in similar ways, e.g., וְאֶתֶּנְךָ לִבְרִית עָם לְאוֹר גּוֹיִם "I will make you [to be] a covenant for people, a light for the nations" (Isa 42:6).

Jer 9:10

וְנָתַתִּי אֶת־יְרוּשָׁלַ͏ִם לְגַלִּים מְעוֹן תַּנִּים וְאֶת־עָרֵי יְהוּדָה אֶתֵּן שְׁמָמָה מִבְּלִי יוֹשֵׁב׃

I will make **Jerusalem** rubble [and] a den of jackals, and I will make **the Judean cities** a desolation [and] unlivable.

In some clauses with de-agentified verbs, the object is not always "promoted" to become the subject. The agent of the action in Gen 17:5 is unspecified with the *Niphal* verb יִקָּרֵא "it is called." However, instead of the patient taking on the constituency of the subject, שִׁמְךָ "your name" remains overtly marked as the direct object, and the proper name remains the unmarked object complement.

Gen 17:5

וְלֹא־יִקָּרֵא עוֹד אֶת־שִׁמְךָ אַבְרָם

Your name will no longer be called Abram.

Crosslinguistically, variability in object-marking constructions is common in the world's languages. This phenomenon is referred to as Differential Object Marking and is recognized in more than 300 other languages including Amharic, Basque, Catalan, Estonian, Kannada, Korean, Mongolian, Persian, Pintjatjara, Spanish, Tamil, and Turkish.[47] In Biblical Hebrew, the tendency to mark certain objects, especially with אֵת, correlates to higher levels of definiteness and animacy.[48] These qualities are syntactically, semantically, and pragmatically determined.[49] Bekins suggests that the level of definiteness and animacy may be understood based on the following gradients:[50]

Definiteness Scale
Pronoun > Proper Noun > Definite NP > Indefinite specific NP > Nonspecific NP

Animacy Scale
Human > Animate > Inanimate

So, for instance, the highest level would be a pronoun designating a human. The expectation is that such objects would be more likely to have overt marking. An inanimate, nonspecific NP would most likely not be explicitly marked as a complement.

---

[47] Georg Bossong, "Animacy and Markedness in Universal Grammar," *Glossologia* 2–3 (1983): 7–20. Also, Georg Bossong, *Empirische Universalienforschung: Differentielle Objektmarkierung in den neuiranischen Sprachen* (Tübingen: Narr, 1985).

[48] Bekins, *Transitivity and Object Marking.*

[49] W. R. Garr suggests that affectedness also plays a role in the use of the object marker ("Affectedness, Aspect, and Biblical *'et*," *ZAH* 4.2 [1991]: 119–34). Geoffrey Khan ("Object Markers and Agreement Pronouns in Semitic Languages," *BSOAS* 47 [1984]: 468–500) points to the broader notion of individuation, following the transitivity parameters of Paul Hopper and Sandra A. Thompson ("Transitivity in Grammar and Discourse," *Language* 56.2 [1980]: 251–99).

[50] See, e.g., Peter Bekins, "The Use of Differential Object Marking in Northwest Semitic," *KUSATU* 20 (2016): 3–50.

In conclusion, function words do a variety of important tasks. And they can function in more than one way. Because of their frequency, readers should learn—or, at least, know where to find quickly—the most common terms and functions. Familiarity with function words allows one to read more fluently and understand the relationship between the component parts of a discourse. We now turn our attention to a final group of particles in chapter 11: prepositions.

10.12 EXERCISES

Translate the following Hebrew sentences into English. Identify and define the function of each conjunction, adverb, and particle.

1. עַד אֲשֶׁר־יָנִיחַ יְהוָה ׀ לַאֲחֵיכֶם כָּכֶם וְיָרְשׁוּ גַם־הֵמָּה אֶת־הָאָרֶץ אֲשֶׁר־יְהוָה אֱלֹהֵיכֶם נֹתֵן לָהֶם וְשַׁבְתֶּם לְאֶרֶץ יְרֻשַּׁתְכֶם וִירִשְׁתֶּם אוֹתָהּ אֲשֶׁר ׀ נָתַן לָכֶם מֹשֶׁה עֶבֶד יְהוָה בְּעֵבֶר הַיַּרְדֵּן מִזְרַח הַשָּׁמֶשׁ: (Josh 1:15)

2. וְאֶקְחָה פַת־לֶחֶם וְסַעֲדוּ לִבְּכֶם אַחַר תַּעֲבֹרוּ כִּי־עַל־כֵּן עֲבַרְתֶּם עַל־עַבְדְּכֶם וַיֹּאמְרוּ כֵּן תַּעֲשֶׂה כַּאֲשֶׁר דִּבַּרְתָּ: (Gen 18:5)

3. וַיֹּאמֶר יוֹאָשׁ לְכֹל אֲשֶׁר־עָמְדוּ עָלָיו הַאַתֶּם ׀ תְּרִיבוּן לַבַּעַל אִם־אַתֶּם תּוֹשִׁיעוּן אוֹתוֹ אֲשֶׁר יָרִיב לוֹ יוּמַת עַד־הַבֹּקֶר אִם־אֱלֹהִים הוּא יָרֶב לוֹ כִּי נָתַץ אֶת־מִזְבְּחוֹ: (Judg 6:31)

4. הִוָּסְרִי יְרוּשָׁלַ͏ִם פֶּן־תֵּקַע נַפְשִׁי מִמֵּךְ פֶּן־אֲשִׂימֵךְ שְׁמָמָה אֶרֶץ לוֹא נוֹשָׁבָה: (Jer 6:8)

5. וְאִם־פָּשֹׂה תִפְשֶׂה הַמִּסְפַּחַת בָּעוֹר אַחֲרֵי הֵרָאֹתוֹ אֶל־הַכֹּהֵן לְטָהֳרָתוֹ וְנִרְאָה שֵׁנִית אֶל־הַכֹּהֵן: (Lev 13:7)

6. וַיָּ֤פֶץ יְהוָ֨ה אֹתָ֥ם מִשָּׁ֖ם עַל־פְּנֵ֣י כָל־הָאָ֑רֶץ וַֽיַּחְדְּל֖וּ לִבְנֹ֥ת הָעִֽיר: עַל־כֵּ֞ן קָרָ֤א שְׁמָהּ֙ בָּבֶ֔ל כִּי־שָׁ֛ם בָּלַ֥ל יְהוָ֖ה שְׂפַ֣ת כָּל־הָאָ֑רֶץ וּמִשָּׁם֙ הֱפִיצָ֣ם יְהוָ֔ה עַל־פְּנֵ֖י כָּל־הָאָֽרֶץ: (Gen 11:8–9)

7. וְאִ֣ם׀ תֵּלֵ֣ךְ בִּדְרָכַ֗י לִשְׁמֹ֤ר חֻקַּי֙ וּמִצְוֺתַ֔י כַּאֲשֶׁ֥ר הָלַ֖ךְ דָּוִ֣יד אָבִ֑יךָ וְהַאֲרַכְתִּ֖י אֶת־ יָמֶֽיךָ: (1 Kgs 3:14)

8. כִּ֣י מִֽי־יוֹדֵעַ֩ מַה־טּ֨וֹב לָֽאָדָ֜ם בַּֽחַיִּ֗ים מִסְפַּ֛ר יְמֵי־חַיֵּ֥י הֶבְל֖וֹ וְיַעֲשֵׂ֣ם כַּצֵּ֑ל אֲשֶׁ֣ר מִֽי־ יַגִּ֣יד לָֽאָדָ֔ם מַה־יִּהְיֶ֥ה אַחֲרָ֖יו תַּ֥חַת הַשָּֽׁמֶשׁ: (Eccl 6:12)

9. וְרָאִיתִי֩ אֲנִ֨י דָנִיֵּ֤אל לְבַדִּי֙ אֶת־הַמַּרְאָ֔ה וְהָאֲנָשִׁים֙ אֲשֶׁ֣ר הָי֣וּ עִמִּ֔י לֹ֥א רָא֖וּ אֶת־ הַמַּרְאָ֑ה אֲבָ֗ל חֲרָדָ֤ה גְדֹלָה֙ נָפְלָ֣ה עֲלֵיהֶ֔ם וַֽיִּבְרְח֖וּ בְּהֵחָבֵֽא: (Dan 10:7)

10. וְהָיָ֣ה׀ בַּיּ֣וֹם הַה֗וּא לֹֽא־יוֹסִ֨יף ע֜וֹד שְׁאָ֤ר יִשְׂרָאֵל֙ וּפְלֵיטַ֣ת בֵּֽית־יַעֲקֹ֔ב לְהִשָּׁעֵ֖ן עַל־ מַכֵּ֑הוּ וְנִשְׁעַ֗ן עַל־יְהוָ֛ה קְד֥וֹשׁ יִשְׂרָאֵ֖ל בֶּאֱמֶֽת: (Isa 10:20)

Translate from English to Hebrew.

11.   When she returned to her family, Sarah followed after God in both the land of Canaan and the land of Egypt.

12.   If they guard the city and the field that belonged to my father, then I will see that they love me because they kept Yahweh's commandment.

13. King David said to them: "On the seventh day, you shall lift your hands upwards and also worship Yahweh."

14. Then the water under the earth rose above the mountains so that it covered all the land for forty days.

15. Oh my, do you know to not make an image? Certainly, no image exists for God creator of all.

Guided Reading: Mal 1:1–10

1 מַשָּׂא דְבַר־יְהוָה אֶל־יִשְׂרָאֵל בְּיַד מַלְאָכִי: 2 אָהַבְתִּי אֶתְכֶם אָמַר יְהוָה וַאֲמַרְתֶּם בַּמָּה אֲהַבְתָּנוּ הֲלוֹא־אָח עֵשָׂו לְיַעֲקֹב נְאֻם־יְהוָה וָאֹהַב אֶת־יַעֲקֹב: 3 וְאֶת־עֵשָׂו שָׂנֵאתִי וָאָשִׂים אֶת־הָרָיו שְׁמָמָה וְאֶת־נַחֲלָתוֹ לְתַנּוֹת מִדְבָּר: 4 כִּי־תֹאמַר אֱדוֹם רֻשַּׁשְׁנוּ וְנָשׁוּב וְנִבְנֶה חֳרָ־בוֹת כֹּה אָמַר יְהוָה צְבָאוֹת הֵמָּה יִבְנוּ וַאֲנִי אֶהֱרוֹס וְקָרְאוּ לָהֶם גְּבוּל רִשְׁעָה וְהָעָם אֲשֶׁר־זָעַם יְהוָה עַד־עוֹלָם: 5 וְעֵינֵיכֶם תִּרְאֶינָה וְאַתֶּם תֹּאמְרוּ יִגְדַּל יְהוָה מֵעַל לִגְבוּל יִשְׂרָאֵל: 6 בֵּן יְכַבֵּד אָב וְעֶבֶד אֲדֹנָיו וְאִם־אָב אָנִי אַיֵּה כְבוֹדִי וְאִם־אֲדוֹנִים אָנִי אַיֵּה מוֹרָאִי אָמַר | יְהוָה צְבָאוֹת לָכֶם הַכֹּהֲנִים בּוֹזֵי שְׁמִי וַאֲמַרְתֶּם בַּמֶּה בָזִינוּ אֶת־שְׁמֶךָ: 7 מַגִּישִׁים עַל־מִזְבְּחִי לֶחֶם מְגֹאָל וַאֲמַרְתֶּם בַּמֶּה גֵאַלְנוּךָ בֶּאֱמָרְכֶם שֻׁלְחַן יְהוָה נִבְזֶה הוּא: 8 וְכִי־תַגִּשׁוּן עִוֵּר לִזְבֹּחַ אֵין רָע וְכִי תַגִּישׁוּ פִּסֵּחַ וְחֹלֶה אֵין רָע הַקְרִיבֵהוּ נָא לְפֶחָתֶךָ הֲיִרְצְךָ אוֹ הֲיִשָּׂא פָנֶיךָ אָמַר יְהוָה צְבָאוֹת: 9 וְעַתָּה חַלּוּ־נָא פְנֵי־אֵל וִיחָנֵּנוּ מִיֶּדְכֶם הָיְתָה זֹּאת הֲיִשָּׂא מִכֶּם פָּנִים אָמַר יְהוָה צְבָאוֹת: 10 מִי גַם־בָּכֶם וְיִסְגֹּר דְּלָתַיִם וְלֹא־תָאִירוּ מִזְבְּחִי חִנָּם אֵין־לִי חֵפֶץ בָּכֶם אָמַר יְהוָה צְבָאוֹת וּמִנְחָה לֹא־אֶרְצֶה מִיֶּדְכֶם:

VOCABULARY AND NOTES

Verse 1

מַשָּׂא		N.MS	"pronouncement""
מַלְאָכִי	PN		"Malachi"

Verse 2

וַאֲהַבְתָּנוּ	*Qal wəqātal*	2MS + 1CP SF	אהב	"love, be faithful"
עֵשָׂו		PN		"Esau"
וָאֹהַב	*Qal*	CP 1CS	אהב	

Verse 3

שָׂנֵאתִי	*Qal*			"hate, reject"
וָאָשִׂים	*Qal*	CP 1CS	שׂים	
שְׁמָמָה		N.FS		"waste; devastation"
תַּנּוֹת		N.FP		"jackal"

Verse 4

אֱדוֹם		PN		"Edom"
רֻשַּׁשְׁנוּ	*Pual*	SC 1CP	רשׁשׁ	"be leveled"
חֳרָבוֹת		N.FP		"ruin; desolation"
צְבָאוֹת		N.FP		"army" [used as a title with יהוה]
הֵמָּה		IPP MP		"they"
אֶהֱרוֹס	*Qal*	PC 1CS	הרס	"tear down"
רִשְׁעָה		N.FS		"wickedness"
זַעַם	*Qal*			"curse"

Verse 5

| תִּרְאֶינָה | *Qal* | PC 3FP | ראה | |
| יִגְדַּל | *Qal* | | | "be great" |

Verse 6

יְכַבֵּד	*Piel*	PC 3MS	כבד	"honor"
אַיֵּה		INTR		"where?"
מוֹרָאִי		N.MS + 1CS SF		"fear; reverence"
בּוֹזֵי	*Qal*	ACT PTCL MP CSTR	בזה	"despise"
בָּזִינוּ	*Qal*	SC 1CP	בזה	

Verse 7

מַגִּישִׁים	*Hiphil*	PTCL.MP	נגשׁ	"bring near"
מְגֹאָל	*Pual*	PTCL.MS	גאל	"be defiled"
גֵּאַלְנוּךָ	*Piel*	SC 1CP + 2MS SF	גאל	"defile"
שֻׁלְחַן		N.MS		"table"

Verse 8

Hebrew	Stem	Parsing	Root	Gloss
תַּגִּשׁוּן	*Hiphil*	PC 2MP		
עִוֵּר		ADJ.MS		"blind (animal)"
זְבֹחַ	*Qal*			"slaughter; sacrificial slaughter"
פִּסֵּחַ		ADJ.MS		"lame"
חֹלֶה	*Qal*			"be sick"
פֶּחָתֶךָ		N.MS		"governor" (פֶּחָה)
יִרְצְךָ	*Qal*	PC 3MS + 2MS	רצה	"be pleased with"

Verse 9

Hebrew	Stem	Parsing	Root	Gloss
חַלּוּ	*Piel*	IMPV MP	חלה	"appease"
וִיחָנֵּנוּ	*Qal*	PC 3MS + 1CP	חנן	"show favor"
מִכֶּם		+ 2MP SF	מִן	

Verse 10

Hebrew	Stem	Parsing	Root	Gloss
יִסְגֹּר	*Qal*			"shut"
דְלָתַיִם		N.FD		"door"
תָאִירוּ	*Hiphil*	PC 2MP	אור	"ignite (a fire)"
חִנָּם		ADV		"vainly"
חֵפֶץ		N.MS		"pleasure"
אֶרְצֶה	*Qal*	PC 1CS	רצה	

CHAPTER 11

///////////////

PREPOSITIONS

The smallest elements of language can often have great impact on the meaning of a sentence. There is a significant difference whether one says, *let's meet beside the building*, or *let's meet away from the building*, as opposed to *let's meet on the building*. In each, the only variation is a preposition. Yet, they indicate different meeting spots or proposed locations. In contrast, a temporal preposition could specify a meeting time, *let's meet in an hour* or *let's meet for an hour*. Other relations can indicate logical notions, such as purpose, even when using the same preposition, *let's meet for dinner*. These constructions provide much more information than simply the bare discourse unit, *let's meet*. Prepositions serve to specify a relationship between information in a discourse unit like *let's meet* and the element that follows it, *the building, an hour*, or *dinner*. Multiple expressions can also be linked: *let's meet beside the building in an hour for dinner*.

11.1 GOING DEEPER WITH PREPOSITIONS

In the Decalogue, the first command seems to be a straightforward declaration of Israelite monotheism. Since Yahweh identifies himself as Israel's one and only liberator from Egyptian slavery, they are expected to pledge exclusive fealty to him as their sovereign Lord. Exodus 20:3 and Deut 5:7 read identically, beginning לֹא יִהְיֶה־לְךָ אֱלֹהִים אֲחֵרִים "You shall not have other gods." The negative directive establishes allegiance to Yahweh and excludes other divine usurpers.

The command ends with a prepositional phrase. The full command reads: לא יהיה לך אלהים אחרים על פני. English translations render the preposition in several different ways:

CSB	Do not have other gods **besides me**.
CEV	Do not worship any god **except me**.
KJV	Thou shalt have no other gods **before me**.
NIV	You shall have no other gods **before me**.
NLT	You must not have any other god **but me**.

The English preposition *besides* (CSB) implies addition. Yahweh is exclusively God. Other gods are not to be added. The phrase *except me* (CEV) excludes Yahweh from the prohibition on the worship of any god. Outside of updating the archaic verb auxiliary (*shalt*), the NIV follows the KJV exactly. The expression *before me* seems to indicate priority, erecting Yahweh as the foremost deity. Finally, the contrastive conjunction *but* (NLT) allows for only one God.

The Hebrew prepositional phrase is not regularly used in this way in other biblical passages. In fact, other constructions could more explicitly convey similar connotations. The exclusionary relationship is designated with מִבַּלְעָדַי "apart from me" or זוּלָתִי "except me" (Isa 45:21). The sense of sole representative may be signaled with וְאֵין עוֹד "none other" (Isa 45:6) or לְבַדּוֹ "by himself" (Exod 22:19). The preeminence of God is expressed as גָדוֹל יְהוָה מִכָּל־הָאֱלֹהִים "Yahweh is greater than all the gods" (Exod 18:11). And the contrastive is אֶפֶס אֱלֹהִים "but God" in Isa 45:14.

The construction עַל פְּנֵי almost without exception communicates notions of space. Most commonly, it indicates the location in the presence of something or someone (e.g., וַיְכַהֵן אֶלְעָזָר וְאִיתָמָר **עַל־פְּנֵי** אַהֲרֹן אֲבִיהֶם "Eleazar and Ithamar served as priest **in the presence of** their father Aaron," Num 3:4). The phrase can function like a cardinal direction as an extension from the anthropomorphic orientation (e.g., עֲלֵה אֶל־הַר הָעֲבָרִים הַזֶּה הַר־נְבוֹ אֲשֶׁר בְּאֶרֶץ מוֹאָב אֲשֶׁר **עַל־פְּנֵי** יְרֵחוֹ "Climb Mount Nebo in the Abarim hills, which is in the land of Moab **east of** [in front of] Jericho," Deut 32:49). Elsewhere, it can locate an entity on the surface of an object (e.g., וַתֵּלֶךְ הַתֵּבָה **עַל־פְּנֵי** הַמָּיִם "the ark went **along the surface of** the waters," Gen 7:18). This spatial orientation appears to be extended metaphorically to the priority of one son over another in Deut 21:16.

> Deut 21:16
>
> לֹא יוּכַל לְבַכֵּר אֶת־בֶּן־הָאֲהוּבָה **עַל־פְּנֵי** בֶן־הַשְּׂנוּאָה הַבְּכֹר
>
> He should not treat as the firstborn his loved wife's son **over** his hated wife's son.

Turning our attention back to the Decalogue command, the prepositional phrase עַל־פְּנֵי most likely signals one of the locative senses, either "in my presence" or "over me."[1] It is tempting to understand the latter spatial notion as a metaphor

---

[1] The strange extra vowel on this word and double cantillation pointing indicates two different reading traditions. One reads the form as pausal, עַל־פְּנֵי, while the other does not, עַל־פְּנֵי. The Masoretes represent both options.

for priority, like Deut 21:16.[2] After all, God does not possess a physical face with eyes or a mouth unless his presence is a metonym for cultic space. And Yahweh certainly is to be given prominence over any other god. This meaning, however, is limited to only one other example.

The proximal sense "in my presence" provides more comparable evidence. While Yahweh is without a corporeal body in the Hebrew Bible, his presence is real. Exodus 33 provides several important texts concerning human engagement with God's presence, that is, his face. Moses enters the tent to meet with Yahweh and speaks "face to face" (פָּנִים אֶל־פָּנִים, v. 11). In the subsequent exchange, God promises: פָּנַי יֵלֵכוּ וַהֲנִחֹתִי לָךְ "My presence (face) will go, and I will bring you rest" (v. 14, also see v. 15 and Exod 32:1, 23). In response to Moses's request to see God's glory (כְּבֹדֶךָ, Exod 33:18), a provision is made for his goodness to pass before Moses's face (עַל־פָּנֶיךָ, v. 19). However, God acknowledges that Moses would not live if he saw his face (לֹא תוּכַל לִרְאֹת אֶת־פָּנָי "You are not able to see my face," vv. 20, 23). This interaction suggests that God manifests himself in physical space, but one only approaches his presence by an exclusive and restricted invitation.

The Decalogue commandment would then be understood as proscribing the placement of other gods, idols, and images in proximity of his presence. Most immediately, the golden calf incident (Exod 32) challenged Yahweh's prohibition. Similar warnings are conveyed throughout the biblical books. Foreign gods are excluded from Israel's possession and veneration (Ps 81:10). The erection of stone images is prohibited in the land (Lev 26:1). Elsewhere, idolatry often involves setting up detestable representations in God's house (Jer 7:30; 32:34). Their removal is obligatory for repentance (Jer 4:1).

It is tempting to be confused on account of the polysemy of prepositions and other function words. How does one adjudicate the many possible options and their explicit and implicit meanings? While these occasions might seem overwhelming and often are not easily deciphered, we must start with understanding the possibilities. This chapter serves as a starting point and one that seeks to provide more than the simple glosses of an introductory grammar.

11.2 CHAPTER OBJECTIVES

This chapter discusses the wide range of grammatical relationships expressed with Hebrew prepositions. Careful attention is given to the ways that Hebrew prepositions create semantic links between elements within clauses. Prepositions are particularly difficult to understand on account of their polysemy and because similar functions are grouped with different lexemes in different languages. Some may be tempted to conclude that preposition meaning is unknowably arbitrary and variable. The following discussion argues for a conceptually driven approach rather

---

[2] Such an understanding is one possible interpretation of the KJV/NIV *before me*, even though most English readers would probably select the notion of priority.

than a more lexeme-based description. This approach explains the basic relations in language that are embodied in human experience. This knowledge produces shared patterns and processes onto which additional relationships may be mapped and extended.

11.3 INTRODUCTION

This chapter focuses on the function words commonly called *prepositions*. They signal grammatical relations within clauses and discourse units. They indicate both syntactic and semantic relations. Traditionally, prepositions belong to the category of particles, which includes several other lexemes (see chapter 10).

11.4 PREPOSITIONS

Prepositions construct grammatical relationships between various discourse types. They function both in the syntactic and semantic realms of language. These BH function words precede a required participant (i.e., a complement or prepositional object)—thus the term *pre*position.[3] The syntactic links created by prepositions indicate semantic notions such as place, time, movement, evaluation, interest, instrument, or process. The following sections detail the morphology (§11.4.1), syntax (§11.4.2), and semantics (§11.4.3) of these function words.

11.4.1 Preposition Morphology

Most Hebrew grammars categorize prepositions according to their morphology and etymology. Three groups can be identified by the morphological characteristics—primary, secondary, and multiword prepositions.[4] These classifications provide convenient groupings for identifying the morphosyntactic differences of prepositions along with evidence showing their development and etymology.[5] This threefold categorization, however, does not correlate with the semantic groupings of prepositions.

---

[3] Other languages have *post*positions (e.g. Turkish) or a mixture of both types (e.g. German).

[4] For more details, see H. H. Hardy II, *The Development of Biblical Hebrew Prepositions*, ANEM 28 (Atlanta: SBL Press, 2022). This grouping overlaps but is not identical to the threefold opposition of simple, compound, and complex prepositions (*IBHS* §11.1.2). Simple prepositions are discrete lexemes; compound prepositions conjoin more than one simple preposition; and complex prepositions include a preposition combined with at least one other non-preposition element. The latter two categories are included here as multiword prepositions.

[5] See, e.g., BL, 634–47. Other similar approaches may be found in Semitic languages. See Brockelmann, *Grundriss*, 1:494–99; Rainer Voigt, "Die Präpositionen im Semitischen—Über Morphologisierungsprozesse im Semitischen," in *Tradition and Innovation: Norm and Deviation in Arabic and Semitic Linguistics*, ed. Lutz Edzard and Mohammed Nekroumi (Wiesbaden: Harrassowitz, 1999), 22.

11.4.1.1 Primary Prepositions

Primary prepositions are mostly composed of one or two consonant morphemes. The "primary" notion refers to their etymological origin. These prepositions do not conform to an identifiable Hebrew root and base pattern. Principal examples are ־לְ, ־בְּ, ־כְּ, אֵת, עִם, and מִן. Their expanded forms are also included: בְּמוֹ, לְמוֹ, כְּמוֹ, ־עִמָּד, and מִנִּי.[6] Eight others may also be added to this number: אֶל, בְּלִי, מוּל, עַד, עַל, בִּלְתִּי, זוּלַת, and טֶרֶם. In sum, these fourteen lexemes do not have definitive Hebrew roots and bases.

Several primary prepositions may be derived from various lexemes or roots, but their complete etymologies are debated. For instance, originating third-weak roots have been proposed for אֶל, עַד, and עַל. This suggestion is based at least in part on the independent lexemes found in poetic passages, אֱלֵי, עֲדֵי, and עֲלֵי, and their corresponding pronominal forms.[7] The privatives בְּלִי and בִּלְתִּי are undoubtedly related to the negative בַּל "not"; זוּלַת may originate from a middle-weak root not found in BH; and מוּל has been traced back to the noun מוֹל "front."[8] Finally, the triradical preposition טֶרֶם does not have a related BH root.[9]

PRIMARY PREPOSITIONS		
ONE CONSONANT	TWO CONSONANT	THREE CONSONANT
־לְ	אֶל	בִּלְתִּי
־בְּ	אֵת	זוּלַת
־כְּ	בְּלִי	טֶרֶם
	מוּל	
	מִן	
	עַד	
	עַל	
	עִם	

---

[6] Twice in Isa 30:11, the form is מִנִּי, possibly on analogy of the third-weak long forms (אֱלֵי, עֲדֵי, and עֲלֵי).

[7] Several grammars present these independent long forms as evidence for an originating triradical, third-weak root structure (e.g., G. R. Driver, "Problems of Semitic Grammar," *ZDMG* 91 [1937]: 343–51; GKC §103n; Blau, 284–85). We suggest these forms are frozen expanded forms, based on similar comparative Semitic forms (Kienast, *Historische semitische Sprachwissenschaft*, 175), or possibly on analogy to the Northwest Semitic plural construct and pronominal forms (Hardy, *Biblical Hebrew Prepositions*, §2.2).

[8] Some have alternatively suggested origins from the Hebrew root מול "circumcision" or אול "strong; front"; see e.g., Justus Olshausen, *Lehrbuch der hebräischen Sprache*, 2 vols. (Braunschweig: Vieweg 1861), §223c. No etymological source is clear or agreed upon widely.

[9] Once, the form is בטרום, but it is read as בְּטֶרֶם in MT manuscripts (Ruth 3:14).

The three one-consonant primary prepositions attach directly to the following lexeme, while the others can be independent. <u>Inseparable prepositions</u> must be written attached to the following word (e.g., כַּגּוֹיִם, בְּבֵיתֶךָ, לַעֲשֹׂת), a pronominal suffix (e.g., כְּמוֹךָ, בָּהֶם, לִי), or an expanding morpheme (e.g., כְּמוֹ, בְּמוֹ, לְמוֹ).[10] The preposition מִן usually functions like an inseparable preposition. In 89 percent of its occurrences, the final *nun* of the lexeme combines as either מִ◌ or מֵ- depending on the following consonant (e.g., מִבַּיִת or מֵאֶרֶץ). The pronominal forms show analogous assimilation (e.g., מִנִּי, מִכֶּם, מֵהֶם, מֵהֵנָּה) or exhibit reduplication, *min* + *mi(n)* + pronominal suffix (e.g., מִמֶּנּוּ, מִמֶּנָּה, מִמֵּךְ, מִמְּךָ, מִמֶּנִּי).[11] Otherwise, the preposition may be joined without assimilation to a following word using a *maqqep* (מִן־).[12] The independent form is found in only three instances (Exod 2:7; Job 38:1; 40:6).

The two- and three-consonant lexemes are considered <u>separable prepositions</u>. Independent forms exist for all these prepositions, but some like מִן may be connected phonologically to the following word with *maqqep*. Five prepositions (אֶל, אֵת, עַד, עִם, עַל) occur more frequently with a *maqqep* than without one.[13] The forms are evenly split for בְּלִי. Three prepositions (בִּלְתִּי, מוּל, אֵצֶל) are much more commonly written without the *maqqep*.[14] The one instance of טֶרֶם with *maqqep* may be analyzed as a conjunction (Isa 65:24).

Most primary prepositions have forms with pronominal suffixes. Type 1 suffixes are connected directly to most of the primary prepositions (see chart below). Some of these lexemes take alternative forms with the pronominals. Notice the obscured consonant doubling (אֵת, מִן, עִם), the lengthened base (כְּמוֹ-), and the subtle vowel differences (אֵת, זוּלַת). Type 2 suffixes are attached with a linking particle, which is related to the long poetic forms (אֱלֵי, עֲדֵי, and עֲלֵי) and on analogy with the plural nouns (e.g., דִּבְרֵיהֶם "their words"). While the entire pronominal paradigm is important to recognized, the different forms are seen by comparing the prepositions with vowel-only, consonant-vowel, and consonant-vowel-consonant suffixes.

---

[10] The poetic forms also occur with *maqqep* (כְּמוֹ־, בְּמוֹ־, לְמוֹ־). A number of phonological changes take place when the inseparable forms combine with words beginning with a *shewa*, an accented syllable, or a definite article (*BHRG* §39.1.2).

[11] Rare alternate forms include first person (מֶנִּי), second-person masculine (מִמֶּךָ), third person (מִנְּהוּ, מִנֶּה), and third plural (M מֶהֶמָּה, מִנְהֶם, and F מֵהֵן).

[12] The form מִן is joined with *maqqep* in about 11 percent of the instances of non-pronominal prepositional phrases.

[13] The percentage of the forms with *maqqep* is 67 percent for אֵת, 76 percent for עַד, 84 percent for עִם, 84 percent for עַל, and 99 percent for אֶל (including the expanded form אֱלֵי־).

[14] The forms without *maqqep* comprise 98 percent of the 42 occurrences of אֵצֶל, 97 percent of the 35 occurrences of מוּל, and 83 percent of the 111 occurrences of בִּלְתִּי.

PRIMARY PREPOSITIONS WITH PRONOMINAL SUFFIXES			
TYPE 1 PRONOMINAL SUFFIXES			
	BASE FORM	**VOCALIC SUFFIX**	**CV SUFFIX**	**CVC SUFFIX**
‎-לְ	‎-ל	‎לוֹ[15] ‎לִי	‎לָנוּ	‎לָהֶם
‎-בְּ	‎-ב	‎בּוֹ ‎בִּי	‎בָּנוּ	‎בָּהֶם (or ‎בָּם)
‎-כְּ	‎-כְּמוֹ	‎כָּמֹהוּ ‎כָּמוֹנִי	‎כָּמֹנוּ	‎כְּמוֹהֶם
‎אֵת	‎-אֹת	‎אֹתוֹ ‎אֹתִי	‎אֹתָנוּ	‎אֶתְכֶם
‎מִן	‎-(נ)מִ ‎-(נ)מִמֶּ	‎(מִנִּי) ‎מִמֶּנִּי	‎(מִנֶּהוּ ,מֶנְהוּ) ‎מִמֶּנּוּ	‎מֵהֶם (מֵהֵמָּה , ‎(מִנְהֶם
‎עִם	‎-עִמָּ ‎-עִמָד	‎עִמִּי ‎עִמָדִי	‎עִמָּנוּ ————	‎עִמָּם ‎(עִמָּהֶם)
‎בִּלְתִּי	‎-בִּלְתּ	‎בִּלְתִּי	‎בִּלְתֶּךָ	————
‎זוּלַת	‎-זוּלָת	‎זוּלָתָה ‎זוּלָתִי	‎זוּלָתֶךָ	————

TYPE 2 PRONOMINAL SUFFIXES			
	BASE FORM	**VOCALIC SUFFIX**	**CV SUFFIX**	**CVC SUFFIX**
‎אֶל	‎-אֵלַי	‎אֵלָי ‎אֵלַי	‎אֵלֵינוּ	‎אֲלֵיהֶם
‎עַד	‎-עָדַי	‎עָדָיו ‎עָדַי	‎עָדֶיהָ	‎עָדֵיכֶם
‎עַל	‎-עָלַי	‎עָלָיו ‎עָלַי	‎עָלֵינוּ	‎עֲלֵיהֶם

---

[15] In poetic passages, the form is often ‎לָמוֹ.

11.4.1.2 Secondary Prepositions

Secondary prepositions entail a known triconsonantal root and a derivational base. Secondary prepositions may be traced to construct-state nouns, which originally headed an adverbial NP. For instance, the preposition סָבִיב indicates the location around an entity (e.g., Neh 12:28). Its root is סבב "to surround" and the noun pattern is *qatīl*.[16] It originates from the construct state of the noun סָבִיב "environ(s)" (see Amos 3:11). Eleven prepositions conform to these classification requirements, אַחַר (אַחֲרֵי), אֵצֶל, בֵּין, בַּעַד, חֵלֶף, יַעַן, נֶגֶד, נֹכַח, עֵקֶב, סָבִיב, and תַּחַת. Their etymologies may be summarized as follows:

ETYMOLOGY OF SECONDARY PREPOSITIONS		
PREPOSITION	ROOT	BASE (NOUN PATTERN)
(אַחֲרֵי) אַחַר	אחר	*qattal-(ay)*
אֵצֶל	אצל	*qitl*
בֵּין	בין	*qatl*
בַּעַד	בעד[17]	*qatl*
חֵלֶף	חלף	*qitl*
יַעַן	ענה[18]	*yaqtil*
נֶגֶד	נגד	*qitl*
נֹכַח	נכח	*qutl*
עֵקֶב	עקב	*qitl*
סָבִיב	סבב	*qatīl*
תַּחַת	תחת	*qatl*

The secondary prepositions are mostly comprised of separable or independent lexemes. Six of these prepositions are connected to the following word using *maqqep* in Tiberian Hebrew. Each of these is rare. The largest ratio of conjoined forms to independent forms (בַּעַד : בַּעַד־) is less than one to five. In the case of

---

[16] Fox, *Semitic Noun Patterns*, 187–96.

[17] No BH verb exists from this root; however, √*B'D* is attested in several Semitic languages, including Syriac "to depart; be distant," Palmyrene "to remove, cede (property)," Arabic "remove; be far off," Old South Arabian "to take, carry away," and Geʿez "to separate." Cognate function words are found in Ugaritic (*b'd* "behind; for"), Aramaic (*b'd* "after"), Arabic (*ba'du* "after"), and Old South Arabian (*b'd(n)* "after"). The BH noun בַּעַד "price" is likely unrelated etymologically.

[18] This preposition may originate as a noun or possibly a verb (Hardy, *Biblical Hebrew Prepositions*, §3.1.7). In either case, the root would be connected to the third-weak verb realized in BH as the lexeme ענה "to answer."

אֵצֶל- only one example exists (Isa 19:19). Five prepositions are not joined with *maqqep* at all. These are סָבִיב, עֵקֶב, נֹכַח, יַעַן, חֵלֶף.

SECONDARY PREPOSITIONS WITH *MAQQEP*	
PREPOSITION	PERCENTAGE OF FORMS WITH **MAQQEP**
בְּעַד	15.4%
בֵּין	14.6%
אַחֲרֵי[19]	13.9%
תַּחַת	7.6%
נֶגֶד	3%
אֵצֶל	2.4%
סָבִיב, עֵקֶב, נֹכַח, יַעַן, חֵלֶף	0%

Eight secondary prepositions have forms with pronominal objects. For the most part, these prepositions take either type 1 or type 2 suffixes. The chart below outlines the basic breakdown and forms of the secondary prepositions. Type 1 pronominal suffixes are used with נֶגֶד, בְּעַד, בֵּין, אֵצֶל, and נֹכַח, and type 2 pronominal suffixes with אַחֲרֵי, סָבִיב, and תַּחַת. The form בֵּין displays a mixture of these types.[20] No pronominal forms exist with חֵלֶף, יַעַן, or עֵקֶב.

SECONDARY PREPOSITIONS WITH PRONOMINAL SUFFIXES				
TYPE 1 PRONOMINAL SUFFIXES				
	BASE FORM	VOCALIC SUFFIX	CV SUFFIX	CVC SUFFIX
אֵצֶל	אֵצֶל-	אֶצְלִי	—	אֶצְלָם
בֵּין	בֵּין- בֵּינוֹת-	בֵּינִי	בֵּינֵינוּ[21] בֵּינוֹתֵינוּ	בֵּינֵיהֶם בֵּינוֹתָם
בְּעַד	בַּעַד-	בַּעֲדִי[22]	בַּעֲדֵנוּ[23]	בַּעֲדָם
נֶגֶד	נֶגֶד-	נֶגְדִּי	נֶגְדְּךָ	נֶגְדָּם
נֹכַח	נִכְחַ-	נִכְחוֹ	—	—

---

[19] The biform אַחַר is not written with *maqqep*.
[20] See Blau, 284–85.
[21] The type 1 form בֵּינֵנוּ occurs once at Josh 22:25.
[22] The form בַּעֲדֵנִי occurs once at Ps 139:11.
[23] The type 2 form בַּעֲדֵינוּ occurs once at Amos 9:10.

SECONDARY PREPOSITIONS WITH PRONOMINAL SUFFIXES				
TYPE 2 PRONOMINAL SUFFIXES				
	BASE FORM	VOCALIC SUFFIX	CV SUFFIX	CVC SUFFIX
אַחַר (אַחֲרֵי)	אַחֲרֵי-	אַחֲרָיו אַחֲרַי	אַחֲרֵינוּ	אַחֲרֵיהֶם
סָבִיב	סְבִיב- סְבִיבוֹת-	סְבִיבָיו²⁴ סְבִיבוֹתַי	סְבִיבֶיךָ סְבִיבֹתֵינוּ	——— סְבִיבֹתֵיהֶם
תַּחַת	תַּחַת- תַּחְתְּ-	תַּחְתָּיו²⁵ תַּחְתִּי	תַּחְתֵּינוּ תַּחְתֵּנִי	תַּחְתֵּיהֶם תַּחְתָּם

11.4.1.3 Multiword Prepositions

Multiword prepositions are <u>polymorphic</u>. These composite strings are composed of more than one discrete consecutive lexeme and function as a unit to modify a single complement. Several different combinations can be identified—namely compound and complex prepositions.[26] Some grammars use the terms compound and complex interchangeably to refer to this class of prepositions. The following discussion distinguishes between these as distinct kinds of multiword prepositions based on their constitute parts.

A <u>compound preposition</u> includes a sequence of two or more identifiable prepositions with a composite function. English examples include *into*, *within*, *without*, and *onto*. Hebrew compounds may aggregate two prepositions, such as מֵעִם joining מִן and עִם; three prepositions, such as מֵעַל לְ- joining מִן, עַל, and לְ-; or rarely four prepositions, such as לְמִתַּחַת לְ- joining לְ-, מִן, תַּחַת, and לְ-. No compound preposition contains more than four discrete prepositions.

Compound prepositions include combinations of primary prepositions and at most one secondary preposition. For instance, מֵאַחַר contains מִן and אַחַר (see chart below). They can also include a negation as a compositional element: בִּבְלִי- (only with *maqqep*), בְּלֹא, בַּל־עָלֶיךָ (Ps 16:2), בַּל־עִמָּךְ (Prov 23:7), and בִּלְעֲדֵי (see עֲדֵי + בַּל + מִן as מִבַּלְעֲדֵי).[27] The most common preposition used in these strings is מִן. It is found with twelve of the eighteen most frequent compounds.

---

[24] Usually the form is סְבִיבוֹתָיו, but סביבתו occurs in 1 Sam 26:5, 7.

[25] The type 1 form תַּחְתּוֹ occurs much less frequently.

[26] See *IBHS* §11.1.2b. A third composite category of compound-complex prepositions exists. These include strings of multiple prepositions and noun phrases functioning together.

[27] Several other compound prepositions exist but are mostly limited to static expressions. These include כְּבָרִאשֹׁנָה "as previously," מִלְמַעְלָה "under(neath)," עַד לְ- "unto" (LBH), עַד־כַּמֶּה "for how many," עַד־לְמֵרָחוֹק "unto a far distance" (LBH), and עַד־מִן "unto from."

COMPOUND PREPOSITIONS	
PREP + PREP	
אֶל־אַחֲרֵי	אֶל + אַחֲרֵי
בִּבְלִי	בְּ- + בְּלִי
בְּלֹא	בְּ- + לֹא
בִּלְעֲדֵי	בַּל + עֲדֵי
כְּעַל	כְּ- + עַל
לִבְלִי	לְ- + בְּלִי
לְמִן	לְ- + מִן-
(מֵאַחַר or מִן־אַחֲרֵי) מֵאַחֲרֵי	מִן + אַחֲרֵי
מֵאֵצֶל	מִן + אֵצֶל
מֵאֵת	מִן + אֵת
מִבְּלִי	מִן + בְּלִי
מִבְּעַד	מִן + בְּעַד
מֵעַל	מִן + עַל
מֵעִם	מִן + עִם
מִתַּחַת	מִן + תַּחַת
PREP + PREP + PREP	
מִבַּלְעֲדֵי	מִן + בַּל + עֲדֵי
מִבַּעַד לְ-	מִן + בַּעַד + לְ-
מֵעַל לְ-	מִן + עַל + לְ-
PREP + PREP + PREP + PREP (RARELY ATTESTED)	
לְמִתַּחַת לְ-	לְ- + מִן + תַּחַת + לְ-
עַד־מִתַּחַת לְ-	עַד + מִן + תַּחַת + לְ-

A <u>complex preposition</u> consists of the concatenation of at least one preposition and a content word operating as a lexicalized unit or chunk. The content word is a nominal element. In most cases, the content item is used outside of the lexicalized string as an independent word. English complex prepositions include *aside from, by means of, by way of, in front of, in regard to, on top of, prior to, with respect to,* and *with reference to.*[28] The content elements are *side, means, way, front, regard, top, prior, respect,* and *reference.*

Complex prepositions operate as a fixed unit, and the compositional elements cannot be modified individually. If, for instance, the nominal element is quantified or qualified, the usage is betrayed as a prepositional phrase rather than a complex preposition. The first example (1a) contains a complex-preposition phrase: [(*in front of*) PREP *the café*] PP. The latter two examples do not include complex prepositions. Examples (1b, 1c) are composed of multiple nested prepositional phrases: [*in*PREP *the (rear) front* {*of*PREP *the café*} PP]PP.

(1a)   She met a friend in front of (i.e., outside) the café.
(1b)   She met a friend in the front (i.e., inside) of the café.
(1c)   She met a friend in the rear front (i.e., a portion of the inside) of the café.

A number of English prepositions are written as single words but have detectable complex or compound origins: *aboard* (*a-* "on" + *board*), *across* (*a-* + *cross*), *alongside* (*a-* + *long* + *side*), *before* (*be-* "by" + *fore*), *behind* (*be-* + *hind*), *below* (*be-* + *low*), *beneath* (*be-* + *neath*), *beside* (*be-* + *side*), *inside, instead, outside, throughout, underneath*. These strings have lost any association with their original compositional elements (e.g., *alongside* ≠ *on the longer side*; *below* ≠ *by the lowest*; *underneath* ≠ *under beneath*). Unfortunately, word division in BH rarely helps to identify a complex preposition as compared to a prepositional phrase. Frequency of use and semantic shift provide better indication of their fixed nature as a lexicalized unit.

Hebrew complex prepositions contain at least one preposition combined with the nominal element. They must be fixed strings. As with the English examples discussed above, the nominal element of complex prepositions cannot be modified or quantified. Complex prepositions aggregate two elements. There are no clear cases of three-element complex prepositions.[29] The string typically includes a primary preposition and a nominal—such as לִפְנֵי from -לְ and the construct form of פָּנִים "face." The nominal element takes the construct form with non-pronominal complements. Examples include: דֵּי, עֲבוּר, פִּי, תּוֹךְ, יַד, יָעִינֵי, פְּנֵי, and דְּבַר (see the most common examples in the chart below). A few nominal elements are not evidenced outside of the fossilized string (e.g., עֻמָּה, גְּלַל, מַעַן). The complex preposition לִקְרַאת includes the infinitive construct form of קְרָא "meet."

---

[28] See further Sebastian Hoffmann, *Grammaticalization and English Complex Prepositions: A Corpus-Based Study, Routledge Advances in Corpus Linguistics 7* (London: Routledge, 2006).

[29] The only possible candidate is -לְ מָחוּץ with the relational function of "outside" (see below, §11.4.3.3).

COMPLEX PREPOSITIONS	
PREP + NP	
בְּאֶפֶס	בְּ- + אֶפֶס
בִּגְלַל	בְּ- + *גָּלָל
בְּדִי	בְּ- + דִּי
בַּעֲבוּר	בְּ- + עֲבוּר
בְּפִי	בְּ- + פֶּה
בְּקֶרֶב	בְּ- + קֶרֶב
בְּתוֹךְ	בְּ- + תָּוֶךְ
כְּדֵי	כְּ- + דִּי
כְּפִי	כְּ- + פֶּה
לְיַד	לְ- + יָד
לְמַעַן	לְ- + *מַעַן
לְעֵינֵי	לְ- + עֵינִים
לְעֻמַּת	לְ- + *עֻמָּה
לִפְנֵי	לְ- + פָּנִים
לִקְרַאת	לְ- + קְרַאת
מִדֵּי	מִן + דִּי
מִמַּעַל	מִן + מַעַל
מִפְּנֵי	מִן + פָּנִים
עַל־דְּבַר	עַל + דְּבַר
עַל אֹדוֹת	עַל + אֹדוֹת
עַל־פִּי	עַל + פֶּה
עַל־פְּנֵי	עַל + פָּנִים

Pronominal suffixes may be attached to the nominal element of complex preposi-tions. These include either type 1 or type 2 suffixes. Generally, the suffixed forms pattern after those of its corresponding nominal form.

COMPLEX PREPOSITIONS WITH PRONOMINAL SUFFIXES				
TYPE 1 PRONOMINAL SUFFIXES				
	NOMINAL FORM	**VOCALIC SUFFIX**	**CV SUFFIX**	**CVC SUFFIX**
בְּתוֹךְ	תּוֹךְ	בְּתוֹכוֹ בְּתוֹכִי	בְּתוֹכֵנוּ	בְּתוֹכָם
TYPE 2 PRONOMINAL SUFFIXES				
	NOMINAL FORM	**VOCALIC SUFFIX**	**CV SUFFIX**	**CVC SUFFIX**
לִפְנֵי	פָּנִים	לְפָנָיו לְפָנַי	לְפָנֵינוּ	לִפְנֵיהֶם

More rarely, three or even four sequential elements create complex or more precisely described as <u>compound-complex prepositions</u>. These chains usually include the sequences PREP + NP + PREP, PREP + PREP + NP, and PREP + PREP + NP + PREP. The chart represents only a sampling of these multiword prepositions:

COMPOUND-COMPLEX PREPOSITIONS	
PREP + PREP + NP	
מִלִּפְנֵי	מִן + לִפְנֵי (לְ- + פָּנִים)
מִלְּעֻמַּת	מִן + לְ- + עֻמָּה
כִּלְעֻמַּת	כְּ- + לְ- + עֻמָּה
PREP + NP + PREP	
לְמַטָּה לְ-	לְ- + מַטָּה + לְ-
מִבֵּית לְ-	מִן + בַּיִת + לְ-
מִמַּעַל לְ-	מִן + מַעַל + לְ-
PREP + PREP + NP + PREP	
אֶל מִחוּץ לְ-	אֶל + מִן + חוּץ + לְ-

Several multiword prepositions may be combined to their complements with a *maqqep*. Common examples include:

MULTIWORD PREPOSITIONS WITH *MAQQEP*			
מִן	לְ-	כְּ-	בְּ-
מֵאֵת־	לְבַד־	כְּפִי־	בְּיוֹם־
מִפְּנֵי־	לְיַד־		בְּקֶרֶב־

MULTIWORD PREPOSITIONS WITH *MAQQEP*			
מֵעַל־	לְמַעַן־		בְּתוֹךְ־
	לְפִי־		
	לִפְנֵי־		
	לִקְרַאת־		

11.4.2 Preposition Syntax

The syntax of prepositions operates on both the phrase and clause level. A preposition heads a <u>prepositional phrase</u> with an obligatory complement that in traditional grammar is called a <u>prepositional object</u>. The PP correlates to a specific element and function within the clause or serves to connect more than one clause.

On the phrase level, Hebrew prepositions are transitive, and the complement directly follows the preposition. The preposition cannot be "stranded" as with some English constructions (e.g., *Look what I have to put up with!*).[30] As exemplified in Isa 62:7, the preposition complement can be a pronominal suffix (לוֹ), a VP (עַד־יְכוֹנֵן, and also the following expression beginning with עַד־יָשִׂים), or a NP (בָּאָרֶץ).[31]

The complement may include an embedded clause (Hos 5:15) or infinitive (Exod 19:24).

Isa 62:7

וְאַל־תִּתְּנוּ דֳמִי לוֹ עַד־יְכוֹנֵן וְעַד־יָשִׂים אֶת־יְרוּשָׁלִַם תְּהִלָּה בָּאָרֶץ׃

Do not give **to him** rest **until he establishes and gives** Jerusalem praise **in the earth**.

Hos 5:15

אֵלֵךְ אָשׁוּבָה אֶל־מְקוֹמִי עַד אֲשֶׁר־יֶאְשְׁמוּ וּבִקְשׁוּ פָנָי

I will go (and) turn back to my place **until they acknowledge (their) guilt and seek my face**.

Exod 19:24

וְהַכֹּהֲנִים וְהָעָם אַל־יֶהֶרְסוּ לַעֲלֹת אֶל־יְהוָה

The priests and the people should not break through **to go up** toward Yahweh.

---

[30] A very small number of contradictory examples may be cited. But these likely represent textual corruption (Hardy, *Exegetical Gems*, 7–12) or other rare grammatical aberrations (Hardy, *Biblical Hebrew Prepositions*, §3.2.3.4). Also, some secondary prepositions may function as independent adverbial NPs (see, e.g., Hardy, *Biblical Hebrew Prepositions*, §§3.2–3.3).

[31] The intra-clausal function is discussed further as part of the adverbializer section (§10.4.2.3).

To express multiple complements with the same preposition, the preposition is typically repeated with each new complement. Isaiah 62:7 links two prepositions (עַד־יְכוֹנֵן וְעַד־יָשִׂים "until he will establish and set") to indicate a compound modifier. Jeremiah 44:10 has two examples of repeated prepositions with different complements. The first group compound with the preposition -בְּ modifies the main verb, and the second is לִפְנֵי within the embedded clause.

Jer 44:10

וְלֹא יָרְאוּ וְלֹא־הָלְכוּ בְתוֹרָתִי וּבְחֻקֹּתַי אֲשֶׁר־נָתַתִּי לִפְנֵיכֶם וְלִפְנֵי אֲבוֹתֵיכֶם

They have neither feared nor followed **in my instruction or statutes** that I gave **before you and your fathers**.

In constructions with multiple prepositions and a shared complement, compound (or compound-complex) prepositions are used. Each prepositional element designates one relational notion with the same complement (2 Kgs 5:27). The relations remain discrete but create a rightward branching structure. The PP מִלְּפָנָיו compounds the complex preposition לִפְנֵי with the third masculine singular pronominal suffix ("before him") and the preposition מִן ("from").

2 Kgs 5:27

וַיֵּצֵא מִלְּפָנָיו מְצֹרָע כַּשָּׁלֶג

He left **from before him** as one afflicted with a skin disease like snow.

On the clause level, prepositions link the embedded complement to a NP or a VP. This relationship is signaled syntactically by placing the PP as near as possible to the modified element. In Exod 29:29, the first PP (לְאַהֲרֹן) follows and is an attributive modifier of the NP (בִּגְדֵי הַקֹּדֶשׁ), and the other two PPs (לְבָנָיו and אַחֲרָיו) relate to the verb (יִהְיוּ). Elsewhere, the PP can precede the verb it modifies (Exod 28:40). When describing a NP, the PP typically follows it and can function as a predicate (Lev 2:3) or an attributive constituent (1 Chr 6:39). These functions are usually differentiated by the clause syntax. The relative particle may also be used to denote the attributive function (e.g., אֲשֶׁר לְאַהֲרֹן at Exod 29:29).

Exod 29:29

וּבִגְדֵי הַקֹּדֶשׁ אֲשֶׁר לְאַהֲרֹן יִהְיוּ לְבָנָיו אַחֲרָיו

The holy clothes, which [belong] **to Aaron**, will [belong] **to his sons after him**.

Exod 28:40

וְלִבְנֵי אַהֲרֹן תַּעֲשֶׂה כֻתֳּנֹת

You will make the tunics **for Aaron's sons**.

Lev 2:3

וְהַנּוֹתֶרֶת מִן־הַמִּנְחָה לְאַהֲרֹן וּלְבָנָיו

The leftovers from the offering [belong] **to Aaron and his sons**.

1 Chr 6:39

וְאֵ֣לֶּה מוֹשְׁבוֹתָ֞ם לְטִֽירוֹתָ֤ם בִּגְבוּלָ֔ם לִבְנֵ֥י אַהֲרֹ֖ן לְמִשְׁפַּ֥חַת הַקְּהָתִ֑י

These are their dwelling places **for their encampments** in their territory
[which belong] **to the sons of Aaron** to the Kohathite clan.

Most adverbial modifiers are verb adjacent. The PP may come before (Exod 31:17) or after (Gen 2:2) the verb. It can be more distant from the verb, but in such cases it follows more commonly than precedes (Exod 16:29).

Exod 31:17

וּבַיּוֹם֙ הַשְּׁבִיעִ֔י שָׁבַ֖ת וַיִּנָּפַֽשׁ

But **on the seventh day**, he ceased and was refreshed.

Gen 2:2

וַיִּשְׁבֹּת֙ בַּיּ֣וֹם הַשְּׁבִיעִ֔י מִכָּל־מְלַאכְתּ֖וֹ אֲשֶׁ֥ר עָשָֽׂה

He ceased **on the seventh day** from all his work which he had done.

Exod 16:29

אַל־יֵ֥צֵא אִ֛ישׁ מִמְּקֹמ֖וֹ בַּיּ֥וֹם הַשְּׁבִיעִֽי

A man must not depart from his place **on the seventh day**.

Hebrew can designate a direct object, indirect object, and object complement within the same clause using certain function words. The direct object can be a pronominal or nominal element with the verb or an object marker. The indirect object is often the complement of a dative preposition like -לְ. The object complement is typically an indefinite NP and unmarked. In Gen 48:4, הָאָ֣רֶץ הַזֹּ֔את comprises the direct object, לְזַרְעֲךָ֥ indicates the indirect object, and אֲחֻזַּ֥ת עוֹלָֽם is the object complement. The PP אַחֲרֶ֖יךָ further specifies the preceding NP (זַרְעֲךָ֥ אַחֲרֶ֖יךָ "your offspring after you"). The word order is not determinative. The main verb of Gen 13:15 includes an object suffix that refers to the fronted element (כָּל־הָאָ֛רֶץ אֲשֶׁר־אַתָּ֥ה רֹאֶ֖ה), and the compound indirect object is found split up before (לְךָ֣) and after the verb (לְזַרְעֲךָ֖).

Gen 48:4

וְנָתַתִּ֞י אֶת־הָאָ֧רֶץ הַזֹּ֛את לְזַרְעֲךָ֥ אַחֲרֶ֖יךָ אֲחֻזַּ֥ת עוֹלָֽם

I will give this land **to your future offspring** after you as a permanent possession.

Gen 13:15

כִּ֧י אֶת־כָּל־הָאָ֛רֶץ אֲשֶׁר־אַתָּ֥ה רֹאֶ֖ה לְךָ֣ אֶתְּנֶ֑נָּה וּֽלְזַרְעֲךָ֖ עַד־עוֹלָֽם׃

For I will give all the land that you see **to you** and **to your offspring** permanently.

With certain verb-particle combinations, the preposition marks a verbal complement. Some common examples include נגע "touch" with -בְּ (Gen 3:3), בחר "choose" with -בְּ (1 Sam 16:8), and זנה "prostitute" with אַחֲרֵי (Judg 8:33). For many lexemes, specific prepositions signal unique verbal semantics. One oft-cited example is שָׁמַע "hear." With -בְּ the verb connotes obedience as in Exod 19:5.

Gen 3:3

וְלֹא תִגְּעוּ בּוֹ

You should not touch **it**.

1 Sam 16:8

וַיֹּאמֶר גַּם־בָּזֶה לֹא־בָחַר יְהוָה

He said: "Also Yahweh has not chosen **this** [son]."

Judg 8:33

וַיִּזְנוּ אַחֲרֵי הַבְּעָלִים

They fornicated **with the baals**.[32]

Exod 19:5

וְעַתָּה אִם־שָׁמוֹעַ תִּשְׁמְעוּ בְּקֹלִי וּשְׁמַרְתֶּם אֶת־בְּרִיתִי וִהְיִיתֶם לִי סְגֻלָּה מִכָּל־הָעַמִּים

Now, if you steadfastly **obey my voice** and keep my covenant, you will be my possession out of all the peoples.

11.4.3 Preposition Semantics

Prepositions form semantic and syntactical links between various phrase types and clauses. From a semantic point of view, Hebrew prepositions fall into two groups: prepositions with a singular function and compound prepositions with composite functions. The second group is comprised of a combination of more than one function with a shared complement.

The semantic function of prepositions is best understood within a cognitive linguistic approach. Ronald Langacker describes semantic function as profiling the relationship of varying degrees of participant prominence. The most prominent participant, called the <u>Trajector</u> [TR], "is construed as being located, evaluated, or described."[33] The preposition links the TR to a second participant, called the <u>Landmark</u> [LM]. The landmark carries secondary focus as a point of reference or ground for the TR.[34] In traditional grammar, the LM is identified as the object of a preposition. In example (2a), the preposition *over* locates the clause prominent participant, *the ram* [TR] with respect to the physical place, *the wall* [LM]. Example (2b) stations the ram within a temporal framework, *at night*. The preposition *because of* (2c) provides a reason for the ram's departure. In example (2d), *like* compares the actions of two related entities, *the ram* [TR] and *the sheep* [LM]. In the latter two examples, the TR is best understood as the situation, event, or state

---

[32] The idiom זנה אחרי "prostitute after" is a euphemism for false worship or idolatry.

[33] Langacker, *Cognitive Grammar*, 70.

[34] Ellen van Wolde, *Reframing Biblical Studies: When Language and Text Meet Culture, Cognition, and Context* (Winona Lake, IN: Eisenbrauns, 2009), 105–7.

being described and not merely the entity (*the ram*).[35] With spatiotemporal expressions, such as seen in the first two examples, the TR is often seen as a mutable entity, while the LM is comparably inert or stationary.

(2a)   The ram jumps over the wall.
(2b)   The ram lies down at night.
(2c)   The ram flees because of the storm.
(2d)   The ram eats grass like the sheep.

The same framework describes the semantic function of <u>complex prepositions</u>. In Gen 1:6, the principal participant is a physical entity, רָקִיעַ "firmament, vault, hemisphere," and it is situated in relationship to הַמָּיִם "the water(s)." The preposition בְּתוֹךְ designates a locative relationship indicating the TR as "amid, in the midst of, or within" the LM.

> Gen 1:6
>
> יְהִי רָקִיעַ **בְּתוֹךְ** הַמָּיִם
> Let a firmament [TR] be **amid** the water [LM].

The resulting situation is that הָרָקִיעַ forms a spatial division in reference to the waters above and the waters below (Gen 1:7).

With <u>compound prepositions</u>, multiple spatial relations can govern a shared LM. In example (3), the pouring event is located using the function *in* for the inside of a container (*the cup*) or the complex preposition *in front of* to indicate the orientation of coffee pouring with respect to the cup. A third option involves the compound preposition *into*. The noncontradictory spatial functions (*in* and *to*) orient the TR with reference to the container in two ways. The compound provides both the resulting location (*in*) and the event direction (*to*) of the LM (*the cup*).

(3)   The coffee is poured (in, in front of, into) the cup.

The Hebrew compound preposition מִתַּחַת designates two spatial relationships of the shared LM in Gen 1:9. The second element תַּחַת specifies the waters situated beneath the firmament. These are the waters that were divided by הָרָקִיעַ "the firmament" in verses 6–7. The first element מִן indicates the source location of the TR (יִקָּווּ הַמַּיִם).

> Gen 1:9
>
> יִקָּווּ הַמַּיִם **מִתַּחַת** הַשָּׁמַיִם אֶל־מָקוֹם אֶחָד
> Let the waters [TR] **from below** the heavens [LM] be amassed to one place.

Most prepositions exhibit <u>polysemy</u>, that is, they can represent distinct semantic functions. Each specific meaning depends on the conceptual structure of the

---

[35] See Andrea Tyler and Vyvyan Evans, *The Semantics of English Prepositions: Spatial Scenes, Embodied Meaning and Cognition* (Cambridge: Cambridge University Press, 2003), 226.

participants, usage context, and material embodiment.[36] In example (4), a human individual (*the merchant*) is described as taking a journey. The English preposition *on* specifies the relationship of a LM to that event. It may indicate a locative (*on the path*), an instrument (*on foot*), or a temporal situation (*on the Sabbath*). These dissimilar functions depend on the nature of the LM as a place, mechanism, or time, as well as the knowledge that the TR is an animate agent.

(4)   The merchant travels on (the path, foot, the Sabbath).

It should be noted that while the variability of LMs is limitless (e.g., *the river, horseback, the first of the month*), the semantic variation of the preposition is limited to a discrete number of functions.[37]

Preposition functions may be related at the conceptional level to a semantic network of related but distinct meanings. The related meanings can be circumscribed within the framework of principled polysemy.[38] Distinct meanings are understood as deriving from an original or primary spatial sense. The primary spatial configuration can be schematized using a prototype or image schema.[39]

Through usage-based extension, other associated meanings are created and incorporated within the speakers' mental lexicon. In the case of the English preposition *on*, the image schema indicates the basic locative relationship using a two-dimensional arrangement of a TR as above and touching the LM.

Image Schema for English Preposition *on*

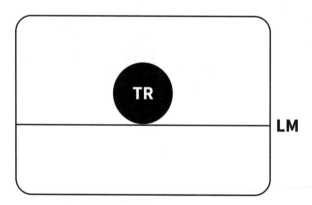

[36] Tyler and Evans, *English Prepositions*, 2–4.

[37] The replacement of the merchant with a different subject—for example, the word—would limit the LM possibilities and the semantics of the preposition.

[38] Tyler and Evans, *English Prepositions*, 37–38.

[39] The term "proto-scene" is sometimes used (Tyler and Evans, 45–54). See the updated discussion of "image schema" in Vyvyan Evans, "The Perceptual Basis of Spatial Representation," in *Language, Cognition and Space: The State of the Art and New Directions*, ed. Vyvyan Evans and Paul Chilton (Sheffield: Equinox, 2010), 21–50. Other similar models are also called image schemas; see e.g., George Lakoff, *Women, Fire, and Dangerous Things: What Categories Reveal about the Mind* (Chicago: University of Chicago Press, 1987).

The instrumental and temporal functions of the preposition are assumed to have derived from this spatial sense through on-line usage with non-spatial TRs or LMs. The associated meanings extend the metaphor of the physical relationship into such realms as agency and time. Location in space is used analogically to indicate the relational foundation of an instrument LM (e.g., *on foot*) or the temporal position of an event LM (e.g., *on the Sabbath*).

Although different prepositions can be used interchangeably in the same syntactic position, their semantics should not be considered arbitrary or identical. Example (5) positions the TR (*the paper*) in different locations based on the semantic domain of the function word in reference to the same LM (*the desk*). The preposition *on* describes the TR as adjoining the top of the LM. The spatial preposition *in* designates the LM as a container. The preposition *at* is a generic locative, indicating proximity. The location of the paper is different depending on the semantics of each preposition.

(5)   The paper is (on, in, at) the desk.

Separate prepositional phrases can be sequenced to specify different aspects of the TR with relation to various LMs. These series must involve complementary reference points and orientations. Example (6) situates the meeting event within several temporal frameworks. The preposition *on* designates a day, *in* a time frame, *at* a quantified time, *during* an interval, and *for* a duration.

(6)   Let's meet on (Monday, the first of month) in (the evening, an hour) at (5 p.m., dusk) during (the Holiday Break) for (ten minutes).

A sequence of prepositions cannot produce incongruous conceptual situations. That is to say, the prepositions must be noncontradictory if referring to the same LM (7a, 7c), but they may be the opposite or matching with different LMs (7b, 7d).

(7a)   *Let's meet after class before class.
(7b)   Let's meet after class before dinner.
(7c)   *Let's meet in front of the coffee shop behind the coffee shop.
(7d)   Let's meet in front of the coffee shop in front of the mailbox.

11.4.3.1 Semantic Functions of Prepositions by Relationship Type

Learning the seemingly countless number of meanings for each preposition is a difficult task for language learners. Most beginning students identify each preposition by a few English glosses as they did with nouns and verbs. For example, -לְ means "to" or "for," and -בְּ is explained as "in," "with," and "at."[40] These

---

[40] The following examples are taken from *BHRG* §39; *IBHS* §11; David J. A. Clines, ed., *The Dictionary of Classical Hebrew*, 6 vols. (Sheffield, UK: Sheffield Academic, 1993–2011); Ernst Jenni, *Die hebräischen Präpositionen*, 3 vols. (Stuttgart: Kohlhammer, 1992–2000); van Wolde, *Reframing Biblical Studies*.

glosses—while helpful when first acquiring translation facility—can be frustrat-ingly restricting or even lead to false inferences about the semantic relationships of prepositions when reading.

Several issues must be addressed in order to understand the semantic function(s) of Hebrew prepositions. First, English glosses almost never overlap uniquely with any one Hebrew preposition. Both -בְּ and עַל are commonly glossed "on," -לְ and אֶל "to," four prepositions אֶל, אֵצֶל, אֶת, and עַל "beside," and at least five preposi-tions -בְּ, עִם, אֶת, -לְ, and אֶל "with." Second, the long lists of preposition meanings found in most BH grammars and dictionaries are not arbitrary but represent an interconnected semantic network.[41] The inseparable preposition -בְּ alone is de-scribed as "in, inside, within, among, into, on, onto, upon, through, by, at, during, throughout, when, whenever, if, with, on account of, because of, for, by means of, by, of, as, than, according to, at the cost of, in exchange of, despite, in respect of, concerning, about, against, over, in charge of, from, after, to, when."[42]

Such variety can give the impression that prepositions can mean almost any-thing. But most functions can be understood as having developed from a small number of core meanings and extended through contextual and embodied usage. Third, the semantics can be the opposite of one's English expectations. The con-trasting prepositions לִפְנֵי and אַחֲרֵי indicate the spatial locations "in front of" and "behind," but the temporal orientations are "prior to" and "subsequent to," respec-tively.[43] These realities produce a confusing array of seemingly unrelatable mean-ings and glosses that only account for some functions of the prepositions.

To provide a different approach, this section attempts to place comparable rela-tional categories together. Following insights from cognitive semantics, we begin by defining the motion events of spatial verbs (§11.4.3.2). Prepositions often in-dicate similar and supplemental spatial relations (§11.4.3.3). These spatial rela-tionships are grouped using contrasting and similar dyads. The pairs—wherever possible—are organized into a cohesive locative schema. The temporal (§11.4.3.4)

---

[41] Hardy, *Biblical Hebrew Prepositions*.

[42] DCH 2, s.v. "בְּ," 82–86.

[43] English spatiotemporal orientation represents contrasting expressions depending on their as-sumed dietic center. Past time may be referred to as what is behind the speaker or before the present moment. Future time is designated as what is in front of the speaker or after the present moment. In Hebrew, the speaker is the dietic center of the temporal metaphors, but the orientation of the speaker is the reverse of the modern Western person. English speakers face the future as their primary tem-poral orientation. We journey through time facing forward. Hebrew speakers face the past, moving through time backwards. Hebrew speakers mirror this orientation in their representation of cardinal direction. North is not primary for ancient Semitic peoples. The facing direction is rather east—the location of the sun's rising (מִזְרָח) or exiting (מוֹצָא). The words, קַדוּמִים "ancient times," קָדִים "east (side)," קֶדֶם "east; past time," קַדְמָה "origin, former time," קֶדְמוֹן "east," קַדְמוֹן "eastern; former," and קַדְמֹנִי "eastern; former," are related to the verb קדם "be in front (of)." The opposite direction is the location of the sun's setting (מַעֲרָב) or entering (מָבוֹא). To the speaker, that direction is אחר "be be-hind" as with the lexemes: אָחוֹר "west, behind; future," אַחֲרוֹן "western; last, latter," אַחֲרִית "future." The cardinal directions, south and north, correspond to יָמִין "right (hand)" and "left."

The Hebrew cardinal directions are also signaled with geographical terms: יָם "sea, west," נֶגֶב "Ne-gev, south" (also תֵּימָן "Teman, south" and דָּרוֹם "south [wind]"), and צָפוֹן "Zaphon, north."

and logical functions (§11.4.3.5) are outlined, where possible, with analogous parings. Most lexicons provide a traditional listing of various glosses for each lexeme (including our Appendix B: Biblical Hebrew Vocabulary).

11.4.3.2 Motion in Space

Describing motion through space (and time) may seem to be a straightforward, universal task of language; however, languages encode various aspects of movement in vastly different ways. To describe this diversity across the world's languages, Leonard Talmy categorizes <u>motion events</u> using five semantic components: figure, motion, path, ground, and manner.[44] In both examples (8a, 8b), the figure is the plural subject, the motion is GO, the path is THROUGH, the ground is RIVER, and the manner is ON FOOT.

(8a)   They walked through the river.

(8b)   Ps 66:6

בְּנָהָר יַעַבְרוּ בְרָגֶל
They crossed the river on foot.

The verb in each example is notably different although generally indicating the motion GO. English *walk* is a <u>manner-conflating</u> verb. The motion event assumes the manner of movement (i.e., GO ON FOOT). In contrast, Hebrew עבר "cross (over)" is a <u>path-conflating</u> action. It supposes that the motion event entails a path (THROUGH). The verb עבר assumes the path over or through a location (i.e., the ground RIVER). In the case of Ps 66:6, the location is specified using a separate prepositional phrase בְּנָהָר "inside the river."[45] In both examples, the unexpressed verb path (8a) or manner (8b) can be designated with an adjunct phrase, or <u>satellite</u>. The path, THROUGH THE RIVER, is expressed in (8a), and the manner is בְרָגֶל "on foot" (8b).

English verbs rarely convey their path of motion. This semantic component is primarily encoded using a preposition (e.g., *walk to, come into*) or particle (e.g., *go up, fall down*).[46] Because of this, English is typologically considered a <u>satellite-framing</u> language. The satellites can create opposite semantics with the same verb. For instance, the movement into a location with the verb *go* is specified by *go in* while motion out of a location is *go out*.

---

[44] Leonard Talmy, "Semantics and Syntax of Motion," in *Syntax and Semantics*, ed. John P. Kimball (New York: Academic Press, 1975), 4:181–238; Talmy, "Lexicalization Patterns: Semantic Structure in *Lexical Forms*," in *Grammatical Categories and the Lexicon*, vol. 3 of *Language Typology and Syntactic Description*, ed. Timothy Shopen (Cambridge: Cambridge University Press, 1985), 57–149.

[45] The preposition elsewhere is not required (e.g. Deut 2:28).

[46] Judith Huber, *Motion and the English Verb: A Diachronic Study* (New York: Oxford University Press, 2017).

Satellite Framing with English *Go*

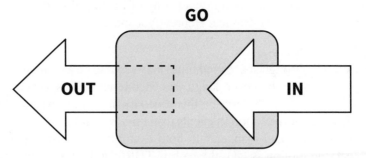

Hebrew can be classified generally as a <u>verb-framing</u> language. It encodes specific paths of movement as part of the lexical semantics of its many path-conflating verbs.[47] For instance, the verb בָּא specifies the movement of an animate agent into a bounded or contained space (i.e., "enter"). The reverse motion, יָצָא is the progress away from a circumscribed locale (i.e., "exit").

Verb-Framing Verbs in Hebrew

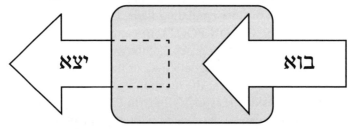

Hebrew motion verbs orient along a vertical, horizontal, or geographical path. The up-down orientation (e.g., עלה "ascend"; ירד "descend") indicates topographical altitude or egocentric/allocentric elevation. Motions resulting in anthropoidal posture can also indicate change in vertical position (e.g., קום "arise"; שכב "recline"; ישב "stay"). The horizontal orientations denote progress-regress (e.g., אשר "advance"; שוב "return") or the direction toward-away/aside (e.g., פנה "turn toward"; סור "turn away"). The geographical orientations comprise motion in relation to a goal (e.g., בוא "enter"; קרב "approach"), source (e.g., יצא "exit"; נסע "depart"), a particular path (e.g., עבר "cross"; גור "sojourn"), or rotation around a central location (e.g., סבב "circumscribe").

---

[47] Leonard Talmy, *Toward a Cognitive Semantics*, 2 vols. (Cambridge, MA: MIT Press, 2000).

MOTION EVENTS WITH PATH	
VERB	**MOTION + PATH**
Vertical	
עלה "ascend"	"go up"
ירד "descend"	"go down"
קום "arise"	"stand up"
שכב "recline"	"lie down"
ישב "stay"	"sit down"
Horizontal	
אשר "advance" (also, עתק)	"go forward"
שוב "return"	"go backward"
פנה "turn" (also, קרא "meet, encounter")	"turn toward"
סור "turn" (also, נטה "deviate")	"turn away"
Geographical	
בוא "enter" (also אתה)	"go in"
יצא "exit"	"go out"
קרב "approach" (also נגש)	"go near"
נסע "depart" (also, עזב)	"go away"
עבר "cross"	"go over/through"
גור "sojourn"	"go about"
סבב "circumscribe"	"go around" (rotational)

Some Hebrew motion verbs are manner conflating rather than path conflating. These include הלך "walk, travel," דרך "thread," רוץ "run," עוף "fly," or רכב "ride." Hebrew verbs may designate the path or manner of the motion event using prepositions, suffixes, and adverbs as "satellites." Various satellites indicate the path of motion with a verb like הלך "walk, travel." Similar to English *go*, movement to a locality and movement originating from a locality can be indicated by preposition adjuncts.

Satellite Framing with Hebrew הלך

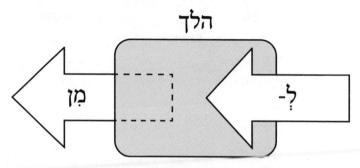

Another difference involves the assumed reference point of English and Hebrew motion events. English uses <u>egocentric</u> deixis (see §7.9.2). Motion verbs are relative to the speaker, such as *go/come in* or *go/come out*. That is to say, the motion events orient the speaker's location with respect to the movement: *I go to work on Mondays* (i.e., the speaker is assumed not to be at the work location) compared to *I come to work on Mondays* (i.e., the speaker is assumed to be at the work location). In BH, motion verbs are not speaker oriented. They use a reference point that is an <u>allocentric</u> entity or locality (LM). The movement pathways orient using inside-outside, up-down, front-behind, and toward-away from the deictic center (i.e., the ground or LM).

The ground or LM of path-conflating motion verbs may be assumed from context (1 Sam 31:7), or it may be made explicit using a direct object (1 Chr 19:15), a directive suffix (1 Chr 19:15), or a preposition (Jonah 3:4).

1 Sam 31:7

וַיַּעַזְבוּ אֶת־הֶעָרִים וַיָּנֻסוּ וַיָּבֹאוּ פְלִשְׁתִּים וַיֵּשְׁבוּ בָּהֶן

They abandoned **the cities** and fled. Then the Philistines entered [**the cities**] and dwelt in them.

1 Chr 19:15 (cf. 2 Sam 10:14)

וַיָּבֹאוּ הָעִירָה וַיָּבֹא יוֹאָב יְרוּשָׁלָ͏ִם

They entered **the city**, then Joab entered **Jerusalem**.

Jonah 3:4

וַיָּחֶל יוֹנָה לָבוֹא בָעִיר מַהֲלַךְ יוֹם אֶחָד

Jonah began **to enter the city** one day's journey.

Other examples include circumscribed physical locations such as a region/territory (Num 22:36), a camp/community (Deut 23:11), the interior of a city (1 Sam 9:14), a tent (Gen 31:33), a room/chamber (Judg 3:23–24), the forest (1 Sam 14:26), and the grave (1 Kgs 13:22).

Num 22:36

וַיִּשְׁמַע בָּלָק כִּי בָא בִלְעָם וַיֵּצֵא לִקְרָאתוֹ אֶל־עִיר מוֹאָב אֲשֶׁר עַל־גְּבוּל אַרְנֹן אֲשֶׁר
בִּקְצֵה הַגְּבוּל׃

Balak heard that Balaam arrived [**in his territory**], so he went out [**from his capital city**] to meet him at the city of Moab, which was on the boundary of the Arnon at the far limit of his border.

Deut 23:11

וְיָצָא אֶל־מִחוּץ לַמַּחֲנֶה לֹא יָבֹא אֶל־תּוֹךְ הַמַּחֲנֶה

[The unclean man] must exit [**the camp**] toward the outside of the camp—he may not reenter [**the camp**] toward the inside of camp.

1 Sam 9:14

וַיַּעֲלוּ הָעִיר הֵמָּה בָּאִים בְּתוֹךְ הָעִיר וְהִנֵּה שְׁמוּאֵל יֹצֵא לִקְרָאתָם לַעֲלוֹת הַבָּמָה

They went up to the city. As they were entering **into the interior of the city**, Samuel was just leaving [**the interior of the city**] to meet them heading to the high pace.

Gen 31:33

וַיֵּצֵא מֵאֹהֶל לֵאָה וַיָּבֹא בְּאֹהֶל רָחֵל׃

[Laban] exited **Leah's tent** and entered **Rachel's tent**.

Judg 3:23–24

וַיֵּצֵא אֵהוּד הַמִּסְדְּרוֹנָה וַיִּסְגֹּר דַּלְתוֹת הָעֲלִיָּה בַּעֲדוֹ וְנָעָל׃ וְהוּא יָצָא וַעֲבָדָיו בָּאוּ

Ehud exited [**the chamber**] through the privy. He had shut the doors of the roof chamber behind him and bolted [them]. Once he had gone out [**the chamber**], his servants entered [**the chamber**].

1 Sam 14:26

וַיָּבֹא הָעָם אֶל־הַיַּעַר

The people entered **the forest**.

1 Kgs 13:22

לֹא־תָבוֹא נִבְלָתְךָ אֶל־קֶבֶר אֲבֹתֶיךָ

Your corpse will not enter **your ancestors' grave**.

A number of metaphorical or idiomatic uses also present inanimate agents as moving toward the locality of God (Jonah 2:8), a person (Hos 13:13), a siege (2 Kgs 25:2), or a time (Isa 63:4).

Jonah 2:8

וַתָּבוֹא אֵלֶיךָ תְּפִלָּתִי אֶל־הֵיכַל קָדְשֶׁךָ

My prayer entered **to you** in your holy temple.

Hos 13:13

חֶבְלֵי יוֹלֵדָה יָבֹאוּ לוֹ

The pains of labor will enter **him**.

2 Kgs 25:2

וַתָּבֹא הָעִיר בַּמָּצוֹר

The city enters **the siege**.

Isa 63:4

וּשְׁנַת גְּאוּלַי בָּאָה

The year of my revenge **comes** (lit. "**enters [time]**").

Regardless of the framing assumptions, additional prepositions can be used to indicate other spatial, path, or manner notions. It is important to understand the orientations of both the verbs and prepositions. They can, at times, seem to present conflicting meanings.[48] In Deut 28:7, for example, Israel's enemies are said to יצא "go out" for war. The motion verb provides implicit locative reference to their unspecified homelands. The movement path and direction are specified with prepositional phrases. The enemies are unified along one route (בְּדֶרֶךְ אֶחָד) and directed toward an encounter with the people of Israel (אֵלֶיךָ). Their assured defeat, however, results in the inversion of this directional motion (יָנוּסוּ "they flee") from the location of Israel (לְפָנֶיךָ "before you"). Rather than simply reversing course, the enemies abscond indiscriminately using multiple avenues of escape (בְּשִׁבְעָה דְרָכִים).

Deut 28:7b

בְּדֶרֶךְ אֶחָד יֵצְאוּ אֵלֶיךָ וּבְשִׁבְעָה דְרָכִים יָנוּסוּ לְפָנֶיךָ:

On one path [your enemies] will march out **toward you**, but on seven paths they will flee **before you**.

The collocation of verb and satellite may be seen as similar to a number of path-conflating verbs in Hebrew. A sample of these include:

MOTION VERB + SATELLITES		
SEMANTICS	MOTION VERB WITH SATELLITES	PATH-CONFLATING MOTION VERBS
movement within a locality	הלך בָּאֶרֶץ	גור
movement as far as a locality	הלך עַד־עִיר	——
movement to a locality	הלך לְאֶרֶץ	בוא
movement away from a locality	הלך מֵאֶרֶץ	יצא

---

[48] H. H. Hardy II, "The Table of Grammar: לקראת as Test Case," *Journal for Semitics* 29, no. 2 (2020): 1–16.

MOTION VERB + SATELLITES		
SEMANTICS	MOTION VERB WITH SATELLITES	PATH-CONFLATING MOTION VERBS
movement along or over a locality	הלך עַל־דֶּרֶךְ	עבר
movement around a locality	הלך סָבִיב לַמִּזְבֵּחַ	סבב
motion toward a locality/entity	הלך אַרְצָה הלך אֶל־אֶרֶץ	קרב
movement in front of an entity	הלך לִפְנֵי הָעָם	——
movement following an entity	הלך אַחֲרֵי הָעָם	——

The individual preposition relations (i.e., satellites) are outlined in the next section.

11.4.3.3 Spatial Relations of Prepositions

Spatial prepositions indicate the position of a TR with respect to a LM. These spatial relationships are often extended metaphorically to temporal and other non-spatial situations. As much as possible, the following organization outlines contrastive orientations by using pairs of prepositions.

ABOVE ~ BELOW. The prepositions עַל and תַּחַת indicate the opposite spatial positions of the TR and LM. עַל expresses that the TR is spatially positioned higher than the LM. The relation corresponds to English *above* or *over*.[49] The TR may or may not touch the LM on the upper side. The antonymic location is found with תַּחַת. It signals that the TR is lower than the LM (i.e., English *below* or *under*). The image schemas represent the basic spatial notions of each of these prepositions.

Image Schema for Hebrew עַל

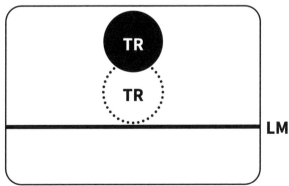

---

[49] Vyvyan Evans and Andrea Tyler, "Applying Cognitive Linguistics to Pedagogical Grammar: The English Prepositions of Verticality," *Revista Brasileira de Linguistica Aplicada* 5, no. 2 (2004): 11–42.

Image Schema for Hebrew תַּחַת

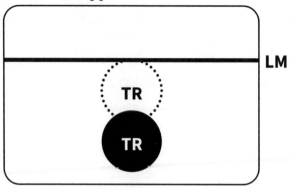

LM

Absalom's ill-fated insurrection provides a disastrous illustration of his presage attractiveness being his ultimate undoing (2 Sam 14:25–26). Second Samuel 18:9 situates the mule passing under the oak branches, while the rider is above the mule.[50] The result is that Absalom's head is at branch level, his heavy hair is ostensibly trapped in the tree, and he is discovered and slayed.

> 2 Sam 18:9
>
> וְאַבְשָׁלוֹם רֹכֵב עַל־הַפֶּרֶד וַיָּבֹא הַפֶּרֶד תַּחַת **שׂוֹבֶךְ** הָאֵלָה הַגְּדוֹלָה
>
> Absalom was riding **on the mule**, and the mule went[51] **under the branches** of the large oak tree.

The phrase עַל־פְּנֵי has several specialized usages. Commonly, this collocation can designate the space opposite the facing position of the LM—not simply orthogonal to the horizon—as seen in the horizontal two-dimensional image schema.[52] In three dimensions, the preposition references the space above or below depending on the facing direction of the LM as up or down.

Image Schema for Hebrew עַל־פְּנֵי (Horizontal Facing)

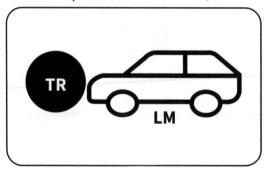

---

[50] Languages represent the spatial idiom in different ways to indicate the position of a rider with respect to an equine, e.g., English *He rode on a horse*; French *Il monte à cheval;* Arabic *yrkb ḥiṣānan;* German *Er reitet auf einem Pferd*; and Russian *Он едем на лошади.*

[51] The path-conflating verb (§11.4.3.2) indicates that Absalom's path probably was through the forest (הַיַּעַר), and it anticipates the same outcome of his army (see v. 8).

[52] See van Wolde, *Reframing Biblical Studies*, 153–68.

Image Schema for Hebrew עַל־פְּנֵי (Up Facing)

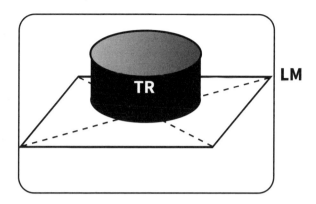

Image Schema for Hebrew עַל־פְּנֵי (Down Facing)

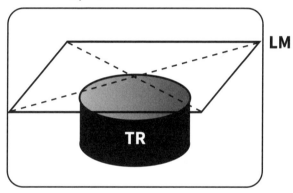

For instance, the TR orientation may be located horizontally in front of, beside, or opposite the LM (2 Sam 15:18). The TR may be situated vertically upwards (over) when the LM is facing up (Job 5:10) or even downwards ("underneath" or "beneath") when the LM is embodied as facing downward (Gen 1:20).

2 Sam 15:18

שֵׁשׁ־מֵאוֹת אִישׁ אֲשֶׁר־בָּאוּ בְרַגְלוֹ מִגַּת עֹבְרִים עַל־פְּנֵי הַמֶּלֶךְ

The six hundred men who arrived with him from Gath passed by **in front of the king**.

Job 5:10

הַנֹּתֵן מָטָר עַל־פְּנֵי־אָרֶץ וְשֹׁלֵחַ מַיִם עַל־פְּנֵי חוּצוֹת

He provides rain **upon the earth** and sends water **upon the pastures**.

Gen 1:20

וְעוֹף יְעוֹפֵף עַל־הָאָרֶץ **עַל־פְּנֵי** רְקִיעַ הַשָּׁמָיִם

Let the birds fly above the land **underneath (i.e. on the face of)** the heavenly firmament.

The composite meaning "on the face of" (Josh 7:6) indicates contact with the ground (i.e., facedown). Elsewhere contact with various body parts may be indicated with עַל without regard for an explicit vertical orientation (Lev 14:14; Gen 45:14).

Josh 7:6

וַיִּקְרַע יְהוֹשֻׁעַ שִׂמְלֹתָיו וַיִּפֹּל **עַל־פָּנָיו** אַרְצָה לִפְנֵי אֲרוֹן יְהוָה עַד־הָעֶרֶב

Joshua tore his clothes and fell **on his face** to the ground before the ark of Yahweh until evening.

Lev 14:14

וְלָקַח הַכֹּהֵן מִדַּם הָאָשָׁם וְנָתַן הַכֹּהֵן **עַל־תְּנוּךְ** אֹזֶן הַמִּטַּהֵר הַיְמָנִית **וְעַל־בֹּהֶן** יָדוֹ הַיְמָנִית **וְעַל־בֹּהֶן** רַגְלוֹ הַיְמָנִית:

The priest will take some of the blood of the guilt offering and put [it] **on the lobe** of the right ear of the one being purified, **on the thumb** of his right hand, and **on the big toe** of his right foot.

Gen 45:14

וּבִנְיָמִן בָּכָה **עַל־צַוָּארָיו**

Benjamin wept **on [Joseph's] neck.**

Similarly, the preposition -בְּ can indicate that the TR is physically adjacent to the LM. This spatial orientation is similar to the English *on* preposition. And like English *on* and Hebrew עַל־פְּנֵי, the attachment indicated by -בְּ is typically situated vertically above (Image Scheme 1) or below (Image Scheme 2), but it may also be horizontal (Image Scheme 3).

Image Schema 1 for Hebrew -בְּ "on"

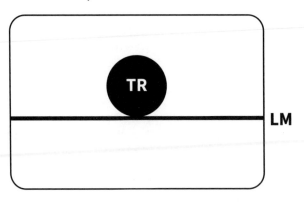

Image Schema 2 for Hebrew -בְּ "on"

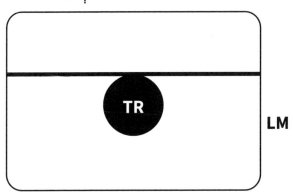

Image Schema 3 for Hebrew -בְּ "on"

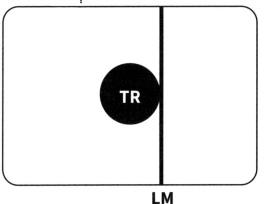

These relations are exemplified in the following examples. Elijah is commanded to stand on the mountain in 1 Kgs 19:11. Note that in Exod 12:11 the preposition -בְּ is used in two different ways. The first employs adjacency, בְּרַגְלֵיכֶם "on your feet," and the second instance is containment, בְּיֶדְכֶם "in your hand." The adjoining surface would be the bottom of the feet: the sandals are under the LM. First Samuel 31:10 demonstrates the horizontal position to the city wall (בְּחוֹמַת בֵּית שָׁן).

1 Kgs 19:11

צֵא וְעָמַדְתָּ בָהָר לִפְנֵי יְהוָה
Head out and stand **on the mountain** before Yahweh.

Exod 12:11

נַעֲלֵיכֶם בְּרַגְלֵיכֶם וּמַקֶּלְכֶם בְּיֶדְכֶם
Your sandals are **on your feet**. Your walking stick is in your hand.

1 Sam 31:10

וְאֶת־גְּוִיָּתוֹ תָּקְעוּ בְּחוֹמַת בֵּית שָׁן
His body they suspended **on the wall** of Beth-shan.

INSIDE ~ OUTSIDE. The semantic notion of containment delimits whether a TR is circumscribed or enclosed by a LM. The preposition -בְּ can designate a container (LM) for an object (TR). The image schema can be represented as the TR bounded by the LM.

Image Schema for Hebrew -בְּ "in"

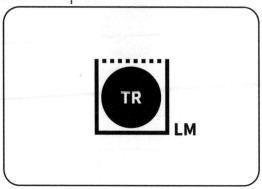

This spatial situation is illustrated by baskets (דּוּדִים) used as a container for the severed heads of Ahab's heirs in 2 Kgs 10:7.

2 Kgs 10:7

וַיִּקְחוּ אֶת־בְּנֵי הַמֶּלֶךְ וַיִּשְׁחֲטוּ שִׁבְעִים אִישׁ וַיָּשִׂימוּ אֶת־רָאשֵׁיהֶם֙ **בַּדּוּדִים** וַיִּשְׁלְחוּ אֵלָיו יִזְרְעֶאלָה:

They took the king's sons and slaughtered all seventy men. Then they put their heads [TR] **in baskets** [LM] and sent them to him at Jezreel.

The LM may have clear delimited physical boundaries—like houses or the walls of a city (Isa 56:5), a jar or jug (1 Kgs 17:12), or a body part (Gen 2:7)—or the enclosed space may have more imagined perimeters—like the heavens (Gen 11:4), land (Gen 12:6), fire (Isa 37:19), or groups of people (Deut 4:27).

Isa 56:5

וְנָתַתִּי לָהֶם בְּבֵיתִי וּבְחוֹמֹתַי֙ יָד וָשֵׁם טוֹב מִבָּנִים וּמִבָּנוֹת
I will give [eunuchs] a memorial and name better than sons and daughters **in houses and in walls**.

1 Kgs 17:12

חַי־יְהוָה אֱלֹהֶיךָ אִם־יֶשׁ־לִי מָעוֹג כִּי אִם־מְלֹא כַף־קֶמַח֙ **בַּכַּד** וּמְעַט־שֶׁמֶן **בַּצַּפָּחַת**
As Yahweh your God lives, if only I had a loaf, but rather a mere handful of flour is **in the jar** and only a little oil is **in the jug**!

Gen 2:7

וַיִּפַּח בְּאַפָּיו נִשְׁמַת חַיִּים וַיְהִי הָאָדָם לְנֶפֶשׁ חַיָּה
He blew the breath of life **in his nostrils**, and the man became a living person.

Gen 11:4

וְרֹאשׁוֹ **בַשָּׁמַיִם**

The [tower's] pinnacle shall be **in the heavens**.

Gen 12:6

וְהַכְּנַעֲנִי אָז **בָּאָרֶץ**

The Canaanites were at that time **in the land**.

Isa 37:19

וְנָתֹן אֶת־אֱלֹהֵיהֶם **בָּאֵשׁ**

[The Assyrians] have put their gods **in the fire**.

Deut 4:27

וְהֵפִיץ יְהוָה אֶתְכֶם **בָּעַמִּים** וְנִשְׁאַרְתֶּם מְתֵי מִסְפָּר **בַּגּוֹיִם** אֲשֶׁר יְנַהֵג יְהוָה אֶתְכֶם
שָׁמָּה:

Yahweh will scatter you **among the nations**, and you will remain as few
in number **within the nations** where Yahweh will drive you.

The preposition -בְּ also designates a TR that may not be entirely enclosed. In the
gruesome scene of Sisera's death (Judg 4:21), three instances of the preposition
are found as indicating the partial encompassing LMs. The first entails the peg and
hammer held in Jael's hand. The second and third usages share the same TR. The
peg is said to penetrate Sisera's head into the ground beneath as he slept. Both his
temple and the ground serve as partial enclosures (LMs)—neither surrounds the
entirely of the TR.[53]

Judg 4:21

וַתִּקַּח יָעֵל אֵשֶׁת־חֶבֶר אֶת־יְתַד הָאֹהֶל וַתָּשֶׂם אֶת־הַמַּקֶּבֶת **בְּיָדָהּ** וַתָּבוֹא אֵלָיו
בַּלָּאט וַתִּתְקַע אֶת־הַיָּתֵד **בְּרַקָּתוֹ** וַתִּצְנַח **בָּאָרֶץ**

Jael, Heber's wife, took the tent-peg and the hammer **in her hand** and
entered [the tent] surreptitiously toward him. She skewered the peg **in his
temple** and pierced **into the ground**.

The spatial relationship can be further specified as distant from the boundaries
of the container. Two complex prepositions provide collocations indicating interior
localities. The preposition בְּקֶרֶב indicates that the TR is viewed as completely interior or surrounded by the LM (Isa 5:25), and בְּתוֹךְ orients the TR inside the middle
region of the LM (Mic 2:12). Several examples use these two in parallel semantic
and syntactic usages (e.g., Gen 18:24; Amos 3:9).

---

[53] A similar example is found with הַמַּרְצֵעַ "the awl" that is to be וּבַדֶּלֶת "put in the ear
and in the door" in Deut 15:17. וְנָתַתָּה בְאָזְנוֹ וּבַדֶּלֶת

Isa 5:25

עַל־כֵּן חָרָה אַף־יְהוָֹה בְּעַמּוֹ וַיֵּט יָדֹו עָלָיו וַיַּכֵּהוּ וַיִּרְגְּזוּ הֶהָרִים וַתְּהִי נִבְלָתָם כַּסּוּחָה
בְּקֶרֶב חוּצֹות

Therefore, Yahweh's anger burned against his people. He stretched out his hand against them and struck them. The mountains quaked, and their corpses were like waste **within the streets**.

Mic 2:12

יַחַד אֲשִׂימֶנּוּ כְּצֹאן בָּצְרָה כְּעֵדֶר **בְּתֹוךְ הַדָּבְרֹו**

I will put them together like sheep in a pen and a flock **inside its pasture**.

The antonymic relationship—external to a container—is rarer but can be designated with the multipart string, -לְ מִחוּץ "outside." The locality can be a city (Gen 19:16) or other enclosing structure, such as the tabernacle curtain (Exod 26:35).

Gen 19:16

וַיֹּצִאֻהוּ וַיַּנִּחֻהוּ מִחוּץ לָעִיר

They brought him out and sat him **outside the city**.

Exod 26:35

וְשַׂמְתָּ אֶת־הַשֻּׁלְחָן מִחוּץ לַפָּרֹכֶת

You shall put the table **outside the curtain**.

While בְּתֹוךְ indicates an encompassing LM, סָבִיב circumscribes an exterior distal locality where the TR is equally distant from the LM on several sides (Gen 41:48). Rarely, if ever, does סָבִיב serve as a path preposition like English *around*.[54]

Gen 41:48

וַיִּקְבֹּץ אֶת־כָּל־אֹכֶל| שֶׁבַע שָׁנִים אֲשֶׁר הָיוּ בְּאֶרֶץ מִצְרַיִם וַיִּתֶּן־אֹכֶל בֶּעָרִים אֹכֶל
שְׂדֵה־הָעִיר אֲשֶׁר סְבִיבֹתֶיהָ נָתַן בְּתֹוכָהּ:

During the seven years, he gathered all the food in the land of Egypt and stored the provisions in the cities—the food [harvested] from the fields **around each city** he deposited inside each.

SOURCE ~ GOAL. The prepositions מִן and -לְ express source and goal locations. Neither necessarily imply motion or the actualization of the path from or to the LM, unlike directional prepositions such as מִפְּנֵי "away from" and אֶל "toward" (see below). They merely orient the TR with respect to an origin locality (i.e., source) or a spatial objective (i.e., goal). When combined with verbs of motion stipulating manner or path trajectories, the prepositions can specify beginning or end points of a path with respect to a LM. The image schemas may be construed as:

---

[54] Seth Lindstromberg, *English Prepositions Explained* (Amsterdam: Benjamins, 2010), 133–39.

Image Schema for Hebrew מִן

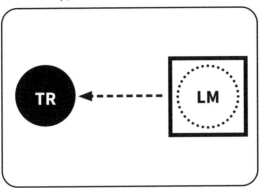

Image Schema for Hebrew -לְ

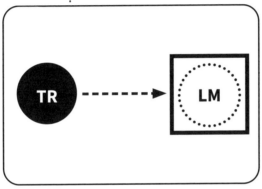

The source, or spatial origin, of a TR is designated by מִן "from, out (of)." Even if the path of motion is in opposite directions vertically, the LM is the source (Exod 32:1; Gen 13:1). Likewise, the spatial objective (i.e., goal) is indicated by -לְ "to" (2 Sam 11:8; 1 Sam 25:35).

Exod 32:1

וַיַּרְא הָעָם כִּי־בֹשֵׁשׁ מֹשֶׁה לָרֶדֶת מִן־הָהָר

The people saw that Moses delayed in coming down **from the mountain**.

Gen 13:1

וַיַּעַל אַבְרָם מִמִּצְרַיִם הוּא וְאִשְׁתּוֹ וְכָל־אֲשֶׁר־לוֹ וְלוֹט עִמּוֹ הַנֶּגְבָּה:

Abraham went up **from Egypt**—along with his wife, possessions, and Lot with him—toward the Negev.

2 Sam 11:8

וַיֹּאמֶר דָּוִד לְאוּרִיָּה רֵד לְבֵיתְךָ

David said to Uriah: "Go down **to your house**."

1 Sam 25:35

וְלָהּ אָמַ֥ר עֲלִ֖י לְשָׁל֣וֹם לְבֵיתֵ֑ךְ

He said to her: "Go up in peace **to your house**."

The preposition עַד depicts the remotest boundary of the TR extending to the LM. The LM itself can even be incorporated into the extent, that is, approaching and including the greatest extent. The far limit may be an expansion verticality (Ps 57:11) or extension with horizonal motion (2 Sam 15:32).

Ps 57:11

כִּי־גָדֹ֣ל עַד־שָׁמַ֣יִם חַסְדֶּ֑ךָ וְעַד־שְׁחָקִ֣ים אֲמִתֶּֽךָ׃

For your covenant-love extends **up to the heavens**, and your faithfulness **up to the clouds**.

2 Sam15:32

וַיְהִ֤י דָוִד֙ בָּ֣א עַד־הָרֹ֔אשׁ אֲשֶׁר־יִשְׁתַּחֲוֶ֥ה שָׁ֖ם לֵאלֹהִ֑ים וְהִנֵּ֤ה לִקְרָאתוֹ֙ חוּשַׁ֣י הָאַרְכִּ֔י
קָר֣וּעַ כֻּתָּנְתּ֔וֹ וַאֲדָמָ֖ה עַל־רֹאשֽׁוֹ׃

When David had arrived **upon the precipice** where he would worship God, astonishingly Hushai the Archite approached him with his tunic in tatters and dust on his head.

The far extent can also be paired with a beginning limit. The source preposition מִן often serves with עַד to indicate these binary limits.

Image Schema for Hebrew עַד . . . מִן "from (out of) LM₁ unto LM₂"

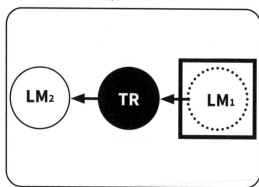

Israel journeyed eleven days to their camp site in the Zin wilderness (Deut 1:2). The initial point of departure was Sinai, and the trip terminated at Kadesh-Barnea. Elsewhere, the priests were to have pants that extended from their hips to their thighs, covering their nakedness (Exod 28:42).

Deut 1:2

אַחַ֨ד עָשָׂ֥ר יוֹם֙ מֵֽחֹרֵ֔ב דֶּ֖רֶךְ הַר־שֵׂעִ֑יר עַ֖ד קָדֵ֥שׁ בַּרְנֵֽעַ׃

It was eleven days **from Horeb** by way of Mount Seir **unto Kadesh-Barnea**.

Exod 28:42

וְעֲשֵׂה לָהֶם מִכְנְסֵי־בָד לְכַסּוֹת בְּשַׂר עֶרְוָה מִמָּתְנַיִם וְעַד־יְרֵכַיִם יִהְיוּ׃

Make them linen undergarments to cover their naked flesh—they were **from the waist to the thighs**.

AWAY FROM ~ TOWARD

Related to מִן and -לְ, <u>directional prepositions</u> signal the route of the TR without any assumptions about the actual source or goal.[55] The preposition מִפְּנֵי can indicate farther and farther movement in the direction away from a LM, and the actual beginning point need not be the LM. In the case of the more frequent preposition אֶל, it denotes motion nearer in the direction toward a LM; however, the goal may or may not be attained. The image schemas for מִפְּנֵי and אֶל envisage the path of motion either pointed from or to the LM. The incremental change of position is required, but the TR need not extend to the ultimate goal or the originating source. The directive *he* and complex preposition לִקְרַאת function similarly to אֶל.

Image Schema for Hebrew אֶל

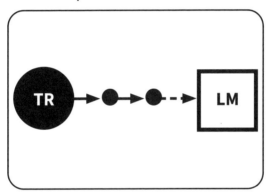

Image Schema for Hebrew מִפְּנֵי

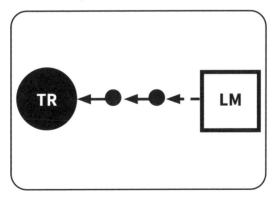

---

[55] Lindstromberg, *English Prepositions Explained*, 29–50.

In Gen 3:8, the collocation מִפְּנֵי describes the action of the man and woman isolating themselves away from God, who was moving about the garden. Noah's family (Gen 7:7) and Moses and Aaron (Num 20:6) arrive at a LM they withdrew from indicated by אֶל and מִפְּנֵי. Finally, the prayer gesture of outstretched hands (Exod 9:29; 2 Chr 6:13) indicates the direction of movement and possibly the orientation of the supplicant's palms but not the attainment of the LM!

Gen 3:8

וַיִּתְחַבֵּא הָאָדָם וְאִשְׁתּוֹ מִפְּנֵי יְהוָה אֱלֹהִים בְּתוֹךְ עֵץ הַגָּן׃

The man and his wife hid themselves **away from Yahweh God** among the tree(s) in the garden.

Gen 7:7

וַיָּבֹא נֹחַ וּבָנָיו וְאִשְׁתּוֹ וּנְשֵׁי־בָנָיו אִתּוֹ אֶל־הַתֵּבָה מִפְּנֵי מֵי הַמַּבּוּל׃

Noah along with his sons, his wife, and his sons' wives entered the ark **away from the floodwaters.**

Num 20:6

וַיָּבֹא מֹשֶׁה וְאַהֲרֹן מִפְּנֵי הַקָּהָל אֶל־פֶּתַח אֹהֶל מוֹעֵד

Moses and Aaron went **away from the congregation** toward the entrance of the tent of meeting.

Exod 9:29

וַיֹּאמֶר אֵלָיו מֹשֶׁה כְּצֵאתִי אֶת־הָעִיר אֶפְרֹשׂ אֶת־כַּפַּי אֶל־יְהוָה

Moses said to him: "When I leave the city, I will stretch out my hands **toward Yahweh.**"

2 Chr 6:13

וַיִּבְרַךְ עַל־בִּרְכָּיו נֶגֶד כָּל־קְהַל יִשְׂרָאֵל וַיִּפְרֹשׂ כַּפָּיו הַשָּׁמָיְמָה

He knelt on his knees before all the Israelite congregation and stretched out his hands **toward heaven.**

Path prepositions relate movement through space along specific routes (i.e., English *across*, *through*).[56] Unlike the previously mentioned functions, however, path prepositions indicate the trajectory of the motion event. They are closely correlated to verbs of movement but provide distinct functional information regarding spatial orientation.[57] The functions, as defined by Tyler and Evans, distinguish that the TR is located along "a contiguous series of spatial points" with respect to the LM. They further state that "the concept of path requires a particular spatial goal, which is achieved by being connected to a spatial source by virtue of a series of contiguous points."[58]

---

[56] Talmy, *Toward a Cognitive Semantics*, 180–85.

[57] Vyvyan Evans and Andrea Tyler, "Rethinking English 'Prepositions of Movement': The Case of *To* and *Through*," *Belgian Journal of Linguistics* 18 (2004): 247–70.

[58] Tyler and Evans, *Semantics of English Prepositions*, 217–18.

While these series of points create a linear route, the pathway need only connect the source and goal. It does not have to form a straight line over the shortest distance between the points; that is to say, the path may follow an arc, spiral, or crisscross pattern.

The path function בְּעַד indicates motion through the interior structure of a LM. An entrance and exit point exterior to the LM is assumed. The image scheme is structured in two-dimensional space.

Image Schema for Hebrew בְּעַד

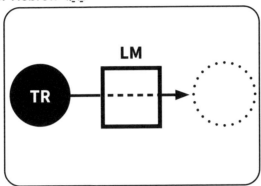

In 2 Kgs 1:2, King Ahaziah enters and exits the window as described using בְּעַד. The head of Sheba was similarly delivered to Joab through (בְּעַד) the wall of Abel Beth-Maacah on the wise counsel of an unnamed woman (2 Sam 20:21). Finally, the preposition בְּתוֹךְ occasionally indicates a comparable path function (2 Chr 23:20).

2 Kgs 1:2

וַיִּפֹּל אֲחַזְיָה בְּעַד הַשְּׂבָכָה בַּעֲלִיָּתוֹ אֲשֶׁר בְּשֹׁמְרוֹן וַיָּחַל

Ahaziah fell **through the lattice window** of his upper-floor room in Samaria and was injured.

2 Sam 20:21

וַתֹּאמֶר הָאִשָּׁה אֶל־יוֹאָב הִנֵּה רֹאשׁוֹ מֻשְׁלָךְ אֵלֶיךָ בְּעַד הַחוֹמָה

The woman said to Joab: "Watch! His head will be thrown to you **through/over the wall**."

2 Chr 23:20

וַיּוֹרֶד אֶת־הַמֶּלֶךְ מִבֵּית יְהוָה וַיָּבֹאוּ בְּתוֹךְ־שַׁעַר הָעֶלְיוֹן בֵּית הַמֶּלֶךְ וַיּוֹשִׁיבוּ אֶת־הַמֶּלֶךְ עַל כִּסֵּא הַמַּמְלָכָה

He brought down the king from the house of Yahweh. Then they entered the king's house **through the upper gate** and sat the king on the throne of the kingdom.

IN FRONT OF ~ BEHIND. The forward- and rearward-facing position of a LM can locate a proximate TR using direction in space. These relations are indicated by so-called <u>projective prepositions</u>. In BH, the <u>point of view</u> is intrinsic to the LM, that is, the orientation is arranged according to its assumed front and back.

The frontal projective is primarily signaled with לִפְנֵי, and אַחַר/אַחֲרֵי is the back.[59] The image schemas can be envisioned as:

Image Schema for Hebrew לִפְנֵי

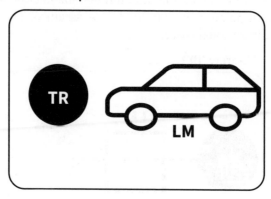

Image Schema for Hebrew אַחַר/אַחֲרֵי

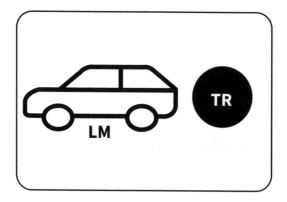

The preposition לִפְנֵי assumes the LM is oriented in the same direction as its supposed front (Esth 4:6), face (Lev 19:14), or forward movement (Judg 9:39). Analogous spatial senses are found with נֶגֶד, נֹכַח, קֶדֶם, and אֵת.

> Esth 4:6
>
> וַיֵּצֵא הֲתָךְ אֶל־מָרְדֳּכָי אֶל־רְחוֹב הָעִיר אֲשֶׁר לִפְנֵי שַׁעַר־הַמֶּלֶךְ:
>
> Hathach went out to Mordecai at the city square **in front of the King's Gate**.

---

[59] These terms may also be used for <u>egocentric</u> direction in reference to the static location facing the rising sun. The resulting orientation לִפְנֵי is an analog to the cardinal direction east. The use of the opposite direction (i.e., 180 degrees) is found in Deut 11:30 (מְבוֹא הַשָּׁמֶשׁ) הֲלֹא־הֵמָּה בְּעֵבֶר הַיַּרְדֵּן אַחֲרֵי דֶּרֶךְ "Are they not in the region beyond the Jordan River, **west of the road**, at the setting of the sun?").

Lev 19:14

לֹא־תְקַלֵּל חֵרֵשׁ וְלִפְנֵי עִוֵּר לֹא תִתֵּן מִכְשֹׁל

Do not curse the deaf or put a stumbling block **in front of the blind**.

Judg 9:39

וַיֵּצֵא גַּעַל לִפְנֵי בַּעֲלֵי שְׁכֶם וַיִּלָּחֶם בַּאֲבִימֶלֶךְ

Gaal went out **in front of the residents of Shechem** and fought with Abimelech.

The backwards or rear projective preposition is אַחַר/אַחֲרֵי (Num 3:23). The preposition בַּעַד can also indicate a similar location.

Num 3:23

מִשְׁפְּחֹת הַגֵּרְשֻׁנִּי **אַחֲרֵי הַמִּשְׁכָּן** יַחֲנוּ יָמָּה:

The clans of the Gershonites were to camp **behind the tabernacle** on the west.

SPATIAL PROXIMITY. Prepositions can indicate a range of proximal locations. The TR may be understood as *near*, *by*, or *close to* the LM. For entities with one or more identifiable sides, adjoining proximity can be designated as *next to* or *adjacent to*, and those in more remote vicinity can be designated as *beside*.[60]

Several BH prepositions locate a TR in spatial proximity to the LM. Most common is אֵצֶל which may indicate near or adjacent proximity to the LM. Naboth's vineyard is described as close to Ahab's palace in the background clause (1 Kgs 21:1) and then further stipulated as adjacent in the dialogue of the next verse with the verb קָרוֹב (1 Kgs 21:2).

1 Kgs 21:1

כֶּרֶם הָיָה לְנָבוֹת הַיִּזְרְעֵאלִי אֲשֶׁר בְּיִזְרְעֶאל **אֵצֶל** הֵיכַל אַחְאָב מֶלֶךְ שֹׁמְרוֹן

Naboth the Jezreelite possessed a vineyard in Jezreel **beside (next to)** the palace of King Ahab of Samaria.

1 Kgs 21:2

וַיְדַבֵּר אַחְאָב אֶל־נָבוֹת ׀ לֵאמֹר ׀ תְּנָה־לִּי אֶת־כַּרְמְךָ וִיהִי־לִי לְגַן־יָרָק כִּי הוּא קָרוֹב **אֵצֶל** בֵּיתִי

Ahab spoke to Naboth: "Give me your vineyard so that I can possess it for a vegetable garden because it is close **by my house**."

The image schema illustrates the proximity of אֵצֶל with the solid circle and the adjoining location with the dotted circle.

---

60 Lindstromberg, *English Prepositions Explained*, 152–54.

Image Schema for Hebrew אֵצֶל

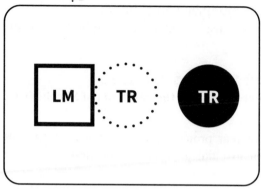

The comitative preposition אֶת "with" can, at times, specify a connection to a locality, corresponding to אֵצֶל (Ezek 43:7b–8a). And אֶל and מִצַּד may indicate similar proximities.

> Ezek 43:7b–8a
>
> וְלֹא יְטַמְּאוּ עוֹד בֵּית־יִשְׂרָאֵל שֵׁם קָדְשִׁי הֵמָּה וּמַלְכֵיהֶם בִּזְנוּתָם וּבְפִגְרֵי מַלְכֵיהֶם
>
> בָּמוֹתָם: בְּתִתָּם סִפָּם **אֶת־סִפִּי** וּמְזוּזָתָם **אֵצֶל** מְזוּזָתִי וְהַקִּיר בֵּינִי וּבֵינֵיהֶם
>
> The house of Israel will no longer defile my holy name—they or their kings—with their infidelity or their kings' corpses at their high places when they put their threshold **near** my threshold and their doorpost **beside** my doorpost with only a wall between me and them.

The complex prepositions, עַל יֶרֶךְ and לְעֻמַּת, are typically used to indicate adjacent localities. The latter construction can even be used to indicate a proximate location corresponding to several points equidistant from the LM, much like English *alongside*. The image schema is arranged as matching positions along parallel lines.

Image Schema for Hebrew לְעֻמַּת

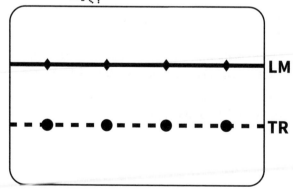

This usage is found with the description of Saul's kinsman, Shimei, shadowing David along the mountain path and tormenting him on account of his bloodlust:

2 Sam 16:13

וַיֵּ֨לֶךְ דָּוִ֤ד וַאֲנָשָׁיו֙ בַּדָּ֔רֶךְ וְשִׁמְעִ֗י הֹלֵ֞ךְ בְּצֵ֤לַע הָהָר֙ **לְעֻמָּת֔וֹ**

David and his men traveled on the road, but Shimei was going on the side of mountain **alongside him.**

BETWEEN. Two (or more) LMs can serve as extremities that orient the TR in the area delimited by them. The image schema limits the TR with respect to two LMs.[61]

Image Schema for Hebrew בֵּין . . . וּבֵין

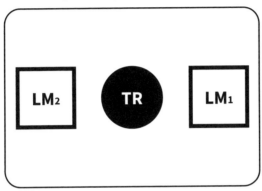

As with English *between* and *among*, BH בֵּין can specify a location amid a plural (1 Sam 26:13) or dual LM (Judg 15:4).

1 Sam 26:13

וַיַּעֲבֹ֤ר דָּוִד֙ הָעֵ֔בֶר וַיַּעֲמֹ֥ד עַל־רֹאשׁ־הָהָ֖ר מֵרָחֹ֑ק רַ֥ב הַמָּק֖וֹם **בֵּינֵיהֶֽם**׃

David crossed to the other side and stood on the faraway mountaintop with a considerable distance **between them.**

Judg 15:4

וַיֵּ֣לֶךְ שִׁמְשׁ֔וֹן וַיִּלְכֹּ֖ד שְׁלֹשׁ־מֵא֣וֹת שׁוּעָלִ֑ים וַיִּקַּ֣ח לַפִּדִ֗ים וַיֶּ֤פֶן זָנָב֙ אֶל־זָנָ֔ב וַיָּ֨שֶׂם לַפִּ֥יד אֶחָ֛ד **בֵּין־שְׁנֵ֥י הַזְּנָב֖וֹת בַּתָּֽוֶךְ**׃

Samson went and captured three hundred foxes. Then he took torches, positioned [each pair of foxes] tail-to-tail, and tied a torch midway **between each pair of tails.**

Unlike the English sequence *between* LM₁ *and* LM₂, BH repeats the preposition with the subsequent LMs (Gen 17:2) or indicates a subsequent LM with לְ- (Ezek 41:18).

---

[61] Joost Zwarts ("'Between' Constructions in Biblical Hebrew," *Linguistics in the Netherlands* 38, no. 1 [2021]: 163–78) suggests a similar notion of spatial "betweenness" using a convex hull as "the smallest convex region that contains both [LMs]" (171).

Gen 17:2

וְאֶתְּנָה בְרִיתִי בֵּינִי וּבֵינֶךָ

I will establish my covenant **between me and you**.

Ezek 41:18

וְתִמֹרָה֙ בֵּין־כְּרוּב לְכְרוּב

There was a palm tree **between each cherub**.

The relation בֵּין can also create a perceived space separating the LMs. The resulting separation may be understood as physical or conceptual:

Mic 4:3

וְשָׁפַט בֵּין עַמִּים רַבִּים

He will judge **among many nations**.

11.4.3.4 Temporal Relations of Prepositions

Many expressions used to describe time develop from spatial notions. Humans almost universally connect movement through space and time. The metaphors of traversing locations extend to temporal progress. These locative descriptions are applied to idioms of time (e.g., *time ran out, an hour goes by quickly, finish the year, a day is coming*) and preposition relations (e.g., *out of time, in an hour, at noon, over a year, from day to day*). Locality and time also correlate in BH.

The following section discusses the marking of simultaneous time, temporal duration, and various kinds of ordered events. Most commonly, time is an enclosing container, and the event happenings are conceptualized as being encompassed within it. Intervals and durations of location and time can be expressed in like manner. Initial and terminal relationships correspond to source and goal locations. Anterior and posterior time are signaled by the forward and backward prepositions. As much as possible, the temporal relations are presented using the previously discussed contrasting locative dyads (§11.4.3.3).

GENERAL, APPROXIMAL, and CONTEMPORANEOUS TIME

Simultaneous settings may be described using several different prepositions. The constructions range from expressing general notions of time to approximal and contemporaneous periods. In these instances, the event framed by the verb can be understood as the TR, and time expression is the LM. Many of these constructions are closely related to other adverbial modifiers.

The preposition -בְּ is the least marked of the temporal relations. Analogous to the -בְּ "inside" spatial relationship, the LM encompasses the TR. The preposition -בְּ serves to frame the event in simultaneous time.[62] Beyond simply envisioning the event as taking place bounded by the LM, additional specification is not provided. And no overt antonym exists. This versatile relation is found with nearly

---

[62] *BHRG* §39.6.2.

all expressions of time (Josh 5:10) and events (Deut 13:10) but only rarely with time deixis (Lev 16:30). It is found with several compound prepositions—בְּיוֹם and בְּעֵת—used as general temporal relations (i.e., *when*).[63] In contrast, temporal deixis is normally construed with an adverb (e.g., הַיּוֹם "today," אֶתְמוֹל "yesterday," עַתָּה "now," אָז "then").[64] English requires an assortment of words to render this wide range of uses, including *in*, *on*, *at*, and *during*.

Josh 5:10

וַיַּעֲשׂוּ אֶת־הַפֶּסַח בָּאַרְבָּעָה עָשָׂר יוֹם לַחֹדֶשׁ בָּעֶרֶב בְּעַרְבוֹת יְרִיחוֹ

They observed the Passover **on the fourteenth day** of the month **in the evening** on the plains around Jericho.

Deut 13:10

כִּי הָרֹג תַּהַרְגֶנּוּ יָדְךָ תִּהְיֶה־בּוֹ בָרִאשׁוֹנָה לַהֲמִיתוֹ וְיַד־כָּל־הָעָם בָּאַחֲרֹנָה:

Surely you must kill [an idolator]—your hand will be against him **at the beginning** to execute him, and the hand of the people **at the end**.

Lev 16:30

כִּי־בַיּוֹם הַזֶּה יְכַפֵּר עֲלֵיכֶם לְטַהֵר אֶתְכֶם מִכֹּל חַטֹּאתֵיכֶם לִפְנֵי יְהוָה תִּטְהָרוּ:

For **on this day**, he will make atonement for you to purify you, you will be clean from all your sins before Yahweh.

While -בְּ designates a broad temporal period, approximal time (*about, around*) is more strictly represented with -כְּ (Gen 18:10) or מִן (Judg 14:8).

Gen 18:10

וַיֹּאמֶר שׁוֹב אָשׁוּב אֵלֶיךָ כָּעֵת חַיָּה וְהִנֵּה־בֵן לְשָׂרָה אִשְׁתֶּךָ

He said: "I will certainly return to you **near to the time of life**, and Sarah your wife will have a son."

Judg 14:8

וַיָּשָׁב מִיָּמִים לְקַחְתָּהּ

He returned **after some time** to marry her.

On the opposite end of the spectrum, the preposition -כְּ marks contemporaneity with an infinitive construct (Exod 9:29) or a NP (Josh 6:15). This timeframe is directly proximate to the events of the main clause (i.e., *meanwhile, as soon as, while, when, at*).[65] The collocation relative כַּאֲשֶׁר functions similarly with a verb phrase to indicate a contemporary event (Gen 18:33).

---

[63] Hardy, *Exegetical Gems*, 147–50.
[64] See further Kingham, "Biblical Hebrew Time Phrases," 497–545.
[65] *BHRG* §39.10.4.

Exod 9:29

בְּצֵאתִי אֶת־הָעִיר אֶפְרֹשׁ אֶת־כַּפַּי אֶל־יְהוָה הַקֹּלוֹת יֶחְדָּלוּן וְהַבָּרָד לֹא יִהְיֶה־עוֹד לְמַעַן תֵּדַע כִּי לַיהוָה הָאָרֶץ

As I leave the city, I will spread out my hands to Yahweh. The thunder will stop, and the hail will be no more so that you might know that the land belongs to Yahweh.

Josh 6:15

וַיַּשְׁכִּמוּ כַּעֲלוֹת הַשַּׁחַר וַיָּסֹבּוּ אֶת־הָעִיר כַּמִּשְׁפָּט הַזֶּה שֶׁבַע פְּעָמִים

They arose early **at dawn** and encircled the city seven times according to this commandment.

Gen 18:33

וַיֵּלֶךְ יְהוָה כַּאֲשֶׁר כִּלָּה לְדַבֵּר אֶל־אַבְרָהָם

Yahweh left **as soon as** he finished speaking to Abraham.

When preceded by וַיְהִי (Exod 16:10) or וְהָיָה (Exod 16:5), these expressions serve as the temporal backbone of narrative (see §10.4.2.4).

Exod 16:10

וַיְהִי כְּדַבֵּר אַהֲרֹן אֶל־כָּל־עֲדַת בְּנֵי־יִשְׂרָאֵל וַיִּפְנוּ אֶל־הַמִּדְבָּר וְהִנֵּה כְּבוֹד יְהוָה נִרְאָה בֶּעָנָן׃

While Aaron spoke to all the congregation of the children of Israel, they faced the wilderness, and immediately the glory of Yahweh appeared in the cloud.

Exod 16:5

וְהָיָה בַּיּוֹם הַשִּׁשִּׁי וְהֵכִינוּ אֵת אֲשֶׁר־יָבִיאוּ וְהָיָה מִשְׁנֶה עַל אֲשֶׁר־יִלְקְטוּ יוֹם ׀ יוֹם׃

It would happen on the sixth day [of each week], they would prepare what they gathered, and it would be twice what they collected each of the other days.

The narrative frame (וַיְהִי) can be elided in some temporal expressions, while the PP functions alone to designate simultaneous time:

Gen 22:4

בַּיּוֹם הַשְּׁלִישִׁי וַיִּשָּׂא אַבְרָהָם אֶת־עֵינָיו וַיַּרְא אֶת־הַמָּקוֹם מֵרָחֹק׃

On the third day, Abraham lifted his eyes and saw the place from a distance.

DURATION

Several prepositions signal duration. The preposition -לְ can indicate a narrow (2 Sam 11:1) or more broad time period (Isa 40:8). Other compounds (e.g., בְּתוֹךְ at 1 Kgs 3:20; בְּקֶרֶב at Hab 3:2) similarly designate durative notions of time.

2 Sam 11:1

וַיְהִי֩ לִתְשׁוּבַ֨ת הַשָּׁנָ֜ה לְעֵ֣ת ׀ צֵ֣את הַמַּלְאֹכִ֗ים וַיִּשְׁלַ֣ח דָּוִ֡ד אֶת־יוֹאָב֩ וְאֶת־עֲבָדָ֨יו עִמּ֜וֹ וְאֶת־כָּל־יִשְׂרָאֵ֗ל

During springtime (i.e., the return) **of the year when kings campaign**, David sent out Joab along with his servants and all Israel.

Isa 40:8

יָבֵ֥שׁ חָצִ֖יר נָ֣בֵֽל צִ֑יץ וּדְבַר־אֱלֹהֵ֖ינוּ יָק֥וּם לְעוֹלָֽם׃

The grass dries up, the blossoms wither, but the word of our God stands **forever**.

The preposition עַד designates similar temporal notions, either by itself (Judg 16:2) or as a distant limit (*until, up to, as far as*) often in conjunction with an initial limit marked by (Isa 9:6).

Judg 16:2

וַיָּסֹ֜בּוּ וַיֶּאֶרְבוּ־ל֤וֹ כָל־הַלַּ֙יְלָה֙ בְּשַׁ֣עַר הָעִ֔יר וַיִּֽתְחָרְשׁ֥וּ כָל־הַלַּ֖יְלָה לֵאמֹ֑ר **עַד־א֥וֹר הַבֹּ֖קֶר** וַהֲרַגְנֻֽהוּ

They encircled [the city] and lay in ambush for [Samson] all night at the gate of the city, saying: "**At morning light**, we will kill him!"

Isa 9:6

מֵעַתָּה֙ **וְעַד־עוֹלָ֔ם** קִנְאַ֛ת יְהוָ֥ה צְבָא֖וֹת תַּעֲשֶׂה־זֹּֽאת

From now until forever, the zeal of Yahweh of armies will do this.

Analogous to its spatial usage, temporal בֵּין "between" can indicate a time bounded by two LMs. This usage is limited to the twilight interval "between the two nights" (בֵּין הָעַרְבָּֽיִם)—that is, between sunset and dusk (e.g., Exod 12:6).

Exod 12:6

וְהָיָ֤ה לָכֶם֙ לְמִשְׁמֶ֔רֶת עַ֣ד אַרְבָּעָ֥ה עָשָׂ֛ר י֖וֹם לַחֹ֣דֶשׁ הַזֶּ֑ה וְשָׁחֲט֣וּ אֹת֗וֹ כֹּ֛ל קְהַ֥ל עֲדַת־יִשְׂרָאֵ֖ל **בֵּ֥ין הָעַרְבָּֽיִם**׃

You should keep watch over [the Passover lamb] until the fourteenth day of this month, and then the entire assembled Israelite congregation shall slaughter [it] **at twilight**.

INITIAL ~ TERMINUS

The preposition מִן can indicate an initial time, and -לְ is used for a temporal terminus. The LM is frequently a time period (Exod 19:11) or an extremity (Isa 37:26). The sequence of מִן followed by עַד indicates a duration with the commencement and the termination as LMs (1 Sam 12:2). The source and goal can even function together as a merism designating a temporal duration (Ps 96:2).

Exod 19:11

וְהָיוּ נְכֹנִים לַיּוֹם הַשְּׁלִישִׁי כִּי | **בַּיּוֹם הַשְּׁלִישִׁי** יֵרֵד יְהוָה לְעֵינֵי כָל־הָעָם עַל־הַר סִינָי

They must be prepared **by the third day** for Yahweh will descend on the third day before the eyes of all the people upon Mount Sinai.

Isa 37:26

הֲלוֹא־שָׁמַעְתָּ לְמֵרָחוֹק אוֹתָהּ עָשִׂיתִי **מִימֵי קֶדֶם** וִיצַרְתִּיהָ

Have you not heard? From far away, I made it **from ancient days** and formed it.

1 Sam 12:2

וַאֲנִי הִתְהַלַּכְתִּי לִפְנֵיכֶם **מִנְּעֻרַי עַד־הַיּוֹם הַזֶּה**

I have walked before you **since my youth until this day**.

Ps 96:2

שִׁירוּ לַיהוָה בָּרֲכוּ שְׁמוֹ בַּשְּׂרוּ **מִיּוֹם־לְיוֹם** יְשׁוּעָתוֹ:

Sing to Yahweh. Bless his name. Announce his salvation **from day to day**.

ANTERIOR ~ POSTERIOR

The preposition pair, טֶרֶם/לִפְנֵי and אַחֲרֵי/אַחַר, forms a temporal dyad. Anterior time is indicated with לִפְנֵי "before" and (בְּ)טֶרֶם "before, not yet." Posterior references use אַחַר or אַחֲרֵי "after":

Josh 10:14

וְלֹא הָיָה כַּיּוֹם הַהוּא **לְפָנָיו וְאַחֲרָיו** לִשְׁמֹעַ יְהוָה בְּקוֹל אִישׁ

There has been none like that day **before it or after it** that God heeded a man's voice.

11.4.3.5 Logical Relations of Prepositions

Many prepositions serve a wide variety of logical functions in addition to their spatial and temporal relationships. These semantic notions provide analytical relations centered on the correlation between the TR and LM. Major functions include adversative, benefactive, causative, comitative, comparative, dative, equative, exchange, instrumental, manner, partitive, possessive, privative, and purpose relations. The following list should not be considered exhaustive but exemplary of this diversity. As with the previous sections, the organization is grouped according to similar relations. The descriptions are brief, and the exemplars are limited to one per preposition. A Hebrew lexicon should be consulted for a more comprehensive listing of the variety of usages for each preposition, and numerous grammatical studies provide more details.[66]

---

[66] See, e.g., Hardy, *Biblical Hebrew Prepositions*.

ADVERSATIVE

The <u>adversative</u> indicates a contrast or opposition. English *against* functions in a similar way. This notion is expressed with -בְּ (Deut 7:24), לִקְרַאת (1 Sam 17:21), and עַל (Gen 50:20).

Deut 7:24

לֹא־יִתְיַצֵּב אִישׁ **בְּפָנֶיךָ** עַד הִשְׁמִדְךָ אֹתָם

No one will stand **against your face** until you destroy them.

1 Sam 17:21

וַתַּעֲרֹךְ יִשְׂרָאֵל וּפְלִשְׁתִּים מַעֲרָכָה **לִקְרַאת מַעֲרָכָה**:

Israel and the Philistines arrayed for battle rank **against rank**.

Gen 50:20

וְאַתֶּם חֲשַׁבְתֶּם **עָלַי** רָעָה אֱלֹהִים חֲשָׁבָהּ לְטֹבָה לְמַעַן עֲשֹׂה כַּיּוֹם הַזֶּה לְהַחֲיֹת עַם־רָב:

While you planned evil **against me**, God planned it for good to orchestrate this day to bring life to many people.

BENEFACTIVE

The LM receives the benefit of the expression whether intended or not. The semantic role of beneficiary overlaps significantly with the idea of an <u>indirect object</u> (see <u>dative</u> below). The <u>benefactive</u> (English *to, for*) is often signaled by the prepositions -לְ (Deut 2:34–35), אֶל (Judg 8:14), or עִם (Gen 24:12).

Deut 2:34–35

לֹא הִשְׁאַרְנוּ שָׂרִיד: רַק הַבְּהֵמָה בָּזַזְנוּ **לָנוּ**

We did not leave a survivor—we plundered only the cattle **for ourselves**.

Judg 8:14

וַיִּכְתֹּב **אֵלָיו** אֶת־שָׂרֵי סֻכּוֹת וְאֶת־זְקֵנֶיהָ שִׁבְעִים וְשִׁבְעָה אִישׁ

[The young man] wrote down **for him** [the names] of the leaders of Succoth and its seventy-seven elders.

Gen 24:12

וַעֲשֵׂה־חֶסֶד **עִם אֲדֹנִי** אַבְרָהָם

Do covenant-love **for my lord**, Abraham.

CAUSATIVE

The LM indicates the cause, ground, or reason for a proposition. This <u>causative</u> notion is expressed by a large number of prepositions, including בִּגְלַל, -בְּ, אֶל, אַחֲרֵי

(Gen 12:13), בַּעֲבוּר (Gen 12:13), בְּעַד, -לְ, לְנֹכַח, מִן, מִפְּנֵי (Gen 36:7), עַל (Gen 27:41), עֵקֶם, and תַּחַת (1 Sam 24:20).

Gen 12:13

אִמְרִי־נָא אֲחֹתִי אָתְּ לְמַעַן יִיטַב־לִי **בַעֲבוּרֵךְ** וְחָיְתָה נַפְשִׁי **בִּגְלָלֵךְ**

Say you are my sister so that it may be well for me **on account of you** and my life will be saved **on account of you**.

Gen 36:7

וְלֹא יָכְלָה אֶרֶץ מְגוּרֵיהֶם לָשֵׂאת אֹתָם **מִפְּנֵי מִקְנֵיהֶם**

The land of their sojournings is not able to sustain them **because of their cattle**.

Gen 27:41

וַיִּשְׂטֹם עֵשָׂו אֶת־יַעֲקֹב **עַל־הַבְּרָכָה** אֲשֶׁר בֵּרֲכוֹ אָבִיו

Esau resented Jacob **because of the blessing** his father gave him.

1 Sam 24:20

וַיהוָה יְשַׁלֶּמְךָ טוֹבָה **תַּחַת הַיּוֹם הַזֶּה** אֲשֶׁר עָשִׂיתָה לִי

May Yahweh repay you with good **on account of this day** on which you have done [good] to me.

COMITATIVE

The <u>comitative</u> designates the LM as accompanying the TR. The LM expresses a nonobligatory participant of the clause. Notions of shared proximity are common, but physical propinquity is not required. Several prepositions can signal this relation, including -בְּ (Exod 10:9), אֵת (2 Kgs 3:7), עִם (Ps 73:23), בְּתוֹךְ (Jer 41:8), and אֶל (1 Sam 14:34).

Exod 10:9

בִּנְעָרֵינוּ וּבִזְקֵנֵינוּ נֵלֵךְ

We will go **with our young and old**.

2 Kgs 3:7

הֲתֵלֵךְ **אִתִּי** אֶל־מוֹאָב לַמִּלְחָמָה

Will you go **with me** to Moab to fight?

Ps 73:23

וַאֲנִי תָמִיד **עִמָּךְ**

I am always **with you**.

Jer 41:8
וַיֶּחְדַּ֕ל וְלֹ֥א הֱמִיתָ֖ם **בְּת֥וֹךְ אֲחֵיהֶֽם**
He stopped and did not kill them **with their brothers**.

1 Sam 14:34
וְלֹא־תֶחֶטְא֥וּ לַיהוָ֖ה לֶאֱכֹ֣ל **אֶל־הַדָּ֑ם**
Do not sin against Yahweh by eating [the sacrifice] **with the blood**.

COMPARATIVE

The comparative relation indicates correspondence in quality (Deut 4:32), quantity (Ps 38:5), or relative degree (Exod 16:5) to the LM. These relations are found with -כְּ, מִן, and עַל.

Deut 4:32
הֲנִֽהְיָ֗ה **כַּדָּבָ֤ר הַגָּדוֹל֙** הַזֶּ֔ה א֖וֹ הֲנִשְׁמַ֥ע **כָּמֹֽהוּ**
Has there ever been anything **like this great thing**? Or has anything **like it** ever been heard?

Ps 38:5
כִּ֣י עֲ֭וֺנֹתַי עָבְר֣וּ רֹאשִׁ֑י כְּמַשָּׂ֥א כָ֝בֵ֗ד יִכְבְּד֥וּ **מִמֶּֽנִּי׃**
For my iniquities submerge my head; like a heavy burden they are too weighty **for me**.

Exod 16:5
וְהָיָ֣ה מִשְׁנֶ֔ה **עַ֥ל** אֲשֶֽׁר־יִלְקְט֖וּ י֥וֹם ׀ יֽוֹם
[The portion gathered on the sixth day] will be two times **more than** what they collected each of the other days.

DATIVE

The dative relation indicates the direction or recipient of the TR. The -לְ can mark a LM as an indirect object (Ps 119:110). The semantic roles of the LM can include the benefactor, the recipient, the possessor, or the experiencer with a particular interest in the action as with the so-called ethical dative (Gen 12:1).[67]

Ps 119:110
נָתְנ֬וּ רְשָׁעִ֣ים פַּ֣ח **לִ֑י**
The wicked have set a trap **for me**.

[67] Jacobus Naudé, "The Syntactical Status of the Ethical Dative in Biblical Hebrew," *Journal for Semitics* 9 (1997): 129–65.

Gen 12:1

לֶךְ־לְךָ מֵאַרְצְךָ וּמִמּוֹלַדְתְּךָ וּמִבֵּית אָבִיךָ אֶל־הָאָרֶץ אֲשֶׁר אַרְאֶךָּ

Go **yourself** from your land, your family, and your father's household to
the land that I will show you.

EQUATIVE

The equative or descriptive relation indicates similarity, likeness, or identity. Related functions include notions of reidentification, reclassification, explicative, and
specification. Common descriptive functions include with -לְ (Exod 12:14) and -בְּ
(Gen 5:1). These notions may at times be indistinguishable from the comparative
(e.g., Gen 1:26).

Exod 12:14

וְהָיָה הַיּוֹם הַזֶּה לָכֶם לְזִכָּרוֹן

This day will be for you **(as) a remembrance.**

Gen 5:1

בְּיוֹם בְּרֹא אֱלֹהִים אָדָם בִּדְמוּת אֱלֹהִים עָשָׂה אֹתוֹ

When God created humanity, he made [humankind] **in the image of God.**

Gen 1:26

נַעֲשֶׂה אָדָם בְּצַלְמֵנוּ כִּדְמוּתֵנוּ

Let us make humanity **in our likeness as our image.**

EXCHANGE

Exchange represents the value or worth of the TR in relation to the LM. This relation is sometimes referred to as price. The prepositions -בְּ, בַּעֲבוּר (Amos 8:6),
and חֵלֶף (Num 18:21) are used. Additionally, תַּחַת takes a similar sense in the *lex
talionis* passages (Exod 21:23–25; also, in vv. 26–27 and Lev 24:20, but נֶפֶשׁ בְּנֶפֶשׁ
in Deut 19:21).

Amos 8:6

לִקְנוֹת בַּכֶּסֶף דַּלִּים וְאֶבְיוֹן בַּעֲבוּר נַעֲלָיִם

[We] will acquire the poor **for silver** and the needy **for a pair of sandals.**

Num 18:21

וְלִבְנֵי לֵוִי הִנֵּה נָתַתִּי כָּל־מַעֲשֵׂר בְּיִשְׂרָאֵל לְנַחֲלָה חֵלֶף עֲבֹדָתָם

I gave the Levites the entire tithe of Israel as an inheritance **for their
service.**

Exod 21:23–25

וְאִם־אָסוֹן יִהְיֶה וְנָתַתָּה נֶפֶשׁ תַּחַת נָפֶשׁ: עַיִן תַּחַת עַיִן שֵׁן תַּחַת שֵׁן יָד תַּחַת יָד
רֶגֶל תַּחַת רֶגֶל: כְּוִיָּה תַּחַת כְּוִיָּה פֶּצַע תַּחַת פֶּצַע חַבּוּרָה תַּחַת חַבּוּרָה:

If there is injury, then you must assess a life **for** life, eye **for** eye, tooth **for** tooth, hand **for** hand, foot **for** foot, burn **for** burn, wound **for** wound, [and] blow **for** blow.

INSTRUMENTAL (MEANS)

The LM can express the stimulus or physical object (LM) used to do the TR. An <u>in-strumental</u> notion often indicates a weapon or other device with -בְּ (1 Sam 17:45), מִן (Gen 9:11), -לְ (Exod 17:13).

1 Sam 17:45

אַתָּה בָּא אֵלַי בְּחֶרֶב וּבַחֲנִית וּבְכִידוֹן וְאָנֹכִי בָא־אֵלֶיךָ בְּשֵׁם יְהוָה צְבָאוֹת

You came to me **with a sword, spear, and javelin**, but I came to you with the name of Yahweh of armies.

Gen 9:11

וְלֹא־יִכָּרֵת כָּל־בָּשָׂר עוֹד מִמֵּי הַמַּבּוּל

All flesh will not be cut off again **by flood waters**.

Exod 17:13

וַיַּחֲלֹשׁ יְהוֹשֻׁעַ אֶת־עֲמָלֵק וְאֶת־עַמּוֹ לְפִי־חָרֶב:

Joshua defeated Amalek and his people **with the edge of the sword**.

MANNER

The <u>manner</u> function indicates how the TR is accomplished or carried out. It is also described as mode or means (English *according to*). These prepositions include -לְ (Isa 11:3), אַחַר (Ps 73:24), עַל (Lev 5:22), and several etymologically related compound prepositions (כְּפִי at Lev 25:52, לְפִי at Josh 18:4, עַל פִּי at Num 26:56). When the LM is an inanimate object, the function is often called the <u>instrumental</u> (see above).

Isa 11:3

וְלֹא־לְמַרְאֵה עֵינָיו יִשְׁפּוֹט וְלֹא־לְמִשְׁמַע אָזְנָיו יוֹכִיחַ

He will judge not **according to the sight of** his eyes, and he will decide not **according to the hearing of** his ears.

Ps 73:24

בַּעֲצָתְךָ תַנְחֵנִי וְאַחַר כָּבוֹד תִּקָּחֵנִי:

With your counsel you guide me,
And **according to glory** you lead me.

Lev 5:22

וְנִשְׁבַּ֤ע **עַל־שֶׁ֙קֶר֙** עַל־אַחַ֔ת מִכֹּ֥ל אֲשֶׁר־יַעֲשֶׂ֛ה הָאָדָ֖ם לַחֲטֹ֥א בָהֵֽנָּה

[If someone] swears **in manner of a lie** according to anything a person might do to sin by them.

PARTITIVE

The <u>partitive</u> relation denotes a subset of the LM. English *some of* and *from* have similar functions. Partitives are signaled with מִן (Deut 1:25) or -בְּ (Prov 9:5).

Deut 1:25

וַיִּקְח֤וּ בְיָדָם֙ **מִפְּרִ֣י הָאָ֔רֶץ** וַיּוֹרִ֖דוּ אֵלֵ֑ינוּ

They took **some fruit of the land** in their hand and brought [it] to us.

Prov 9:5

לְכ֣וּ לַחֲמ֣וּ **בְֽלַחֲמִ֑י** וּ֜שְׁת֗וּ **בְּיַ֣יִן** מָסָֽכְתִּי׃

Come, eat **some of my food**, and drink **some wine** that I have blended.

POSSESSIVE

The <u>possessive</u> indicates the LM is the possessor of the TR. The common preposition -לְ serves to indicate attributive or inalienable qualities (Exod 16:25) as well as alienable possession (1 Sam 1:2). A parallel function is found with the accompaniment notion of עִם (Job 12:13).

Exod 16:25

אִכְלֻ֥הוּ הַיּ֖וֹם כִּֽי־שַׁבָּ֥ת הַיּ֖וֹם **לַיהוָ֑ה**

Eat it today because today is a Sabbath **belonging to Yahweh**.

1 Sam 1:2

וְל֜וֹ שְׁתֵּ֣י נָשִׁ֗ים שֵׁ֤ם אַחַת֙ חַנָּ֔ה וְשֵׁ֥ם הַשֵּׁנִ֖ית פְּנִנָּ֑ה וַיְהִ֤י **לִפְנִנָּה֙** יְלָדִ֔ים **וּלְחַנָּ֖ה** אֵ֥ין יְלָדִֽים׃

Now **[Elkanah] had** two wives—one named Hannah and a second named Peninnah—and **Peninnah had** children, but **Hannah had** no children.

Job 12:13

עִמּ֖וֹ חָכְמָ֣ה וּגְבוּרָ֑ה **ל֝֗וֹ** עֵצָ֥ה וּתְבוּנָֽה׃

Wisdom and strength **belong to him**; counsel and understanding **are his**.

PRIVATIVE

The <u>privative</u> notion expresses the loss, absence, or removal of the LM. This relation is found with מִן (Prov 20:3) and בְּאֶ֫פֶס (Dan 8:25).

Prov 20:3

כָּבוֹד לָאִישׁ שֶׁבֶת מֵרִיב

Honor belongs to the one abstaining **from accusation**.

Dan 8:25

וּבְאֶפֶס יָד יִשָּׁבֵר

But **without a hand**, he will be broken.

PURPOSE

<u>Purpose</u> describes the LM as the intended consequence, goal, or result of the action. This relation is most commonly seen with -לְ and an infinitive construct verb (e.g., Exod 3:8). Other prepositions indicating purpose or result are לְמַעַן (Gen 12:13) and בַּעֲבוּר (Exod 19:9).

Exod 3:8

וָאֵרֵד לְהַצִּילוֹ ׀ מִיַּד מִצְרַיִם וּלְהַעֲלֹתוֹ מִן־הָאָרֶץ הַהִוא אֶל־אֶרֶץ טוֹבָה וּרְחָבָה אֶל־אֶרֶץ זָבַת חָלָב וּדְבָשׁ

I came down **to rescue [my people]** from the Egyptians and **to bring them up** out of that land to a pleasant and expansive land flowing with milk and honey.

Gen 12:13

אִמְרִי־נָא אֲחֹתִי אָתְּ לְמַעַן יִיטַב־לִי בַעֲבוּרֵךְ וְחָיְתָה נַפְשִׁי בִּגְלָלֵךְ

Say you are my sister **so that** it may be well for me on account of you and my life will be saved on account of you.

Exod 19:9

הִנֵּה אָנֹכִי בָּא אֵלֶיךָ בְּעַב הֶעָנָן בַּעֲבוּר יִשְׁמַע הָעָם בְּדַבְּרִי עִמָּךְ וְגַם־בְּךָ יַאֲמִינוּ לְעוֹלָם

Incredibly I am coming to you in a dense cloud **with the result that** the people will hear when I speak with you, and also, they will believe in you forever.

Readers would do well to focus their attention on learning words that happen frequently. Nearly every verse has a preposition. Their significance to exegesis cannot be overstated, even though their functions are often understudied. The meanings are constrained and can be determined in their context with reference to other usages and understanding the cognitive situation. We hope this chapter will serve as a reference point as you read more and more Hebrew texts and hone your understanding of these important and common linguistic structures.

11.5 EXERCISES

Translate the following verses into English and analyze the semantics of the prepositions.

1. וְזָכַרְתִּי אֶת־בְּרִיתִי אֲשֶׁר בֵּינִי וּבֵינֵיכֶם וּבֵין כָּל־נֶפֶשׁ חַיָּה בְּכָל־בָּשָׂר וְלֹא־יִהְיֶה עוֹד הַמַּיִם לְמַבּוּל לְשַׁחֵת כָּל־בָּשָׂר: (Gen 9:15)

2. וַנִּשְׁמַע וַיִּמַּס לְבָבֵנוּ וְלֹא־קָמָה עוֹד רוּחַ בְּאִישׁ מִפְּנֵיכֶם כִּי יְהוָה אֱלֹהֵיכֶם הוּא אֱלֹהִים בַּשָּׁמַיִם מִמַּעַל וְעַל־הָאָרֶץ מִתָּחַת: (Josh 2:11)

3. וַיֹּאמֶר דָּוִד אֶל־אָכִישׁ אִם־נָא מָצָאתִי חֵן בְּעֵינֶיךָ יִתְּנוּ־לִי מָקוֹם בְּאַחַת עָרֵי הַשָּׂדֶה וְאֵשְׁבָה שָּׁם וְלָמָּה יֵשֵׁב עַבְדְּךָ בְּעִיר הַמַּמְלָכָה עִמָּךְ: (1 Sam 27:5)

4. וְהָיָה אִם־תִּשְׁמַע אֶת־כָּל־אֲשֶׁר אֲצַוֶּךָ וְהָלַכְתָּ בִדְרָכַי וְעָשִׂיתָ הַיָּשָׁר בְּעֵינַי לִשְׁמוֹר חֻקּוֹתַי וּמִצְוֹתַי כַּאֲשֶׁר עָשָׂה דָּוִד עַבְדִּי וְהָיִיתִי עִמָּךְ וּבָנִיתִי לְךָ בַיִת־ נֶאֱמָן כַּאֲשֶׁר בָּנִיתִי לְדָוִד וְנָתַתִּי לְךָ אֶת־יִשְׂרָאֵל: (1 Kgs 11:38)

5. מֵעֹצֶר וּמִמִּשְׁפָּט לֻקָּח וְאֶת־דּוֹרוֹ מִי יְשׂוֹחֵחַ כִּי נִגְזַר מֵאֶרֶץ חַיִּים מִפֶּשַׁע עַמִּי נֶגַע לָמוֹ: (Isa 53:8)

6. וְהָיְתָה לִי לְשֵׁם שָׂשׂוֹן לִתְהִלָּה וּלְתִפְאֶרֶת לְכֹל גּוֹיֵי הָאָרֶץ אֲשֶׁר יִשְׁמְעוּ אֶת־כָּל־ הַטּוֹבָה אֲשֶׁר אָנֹכִי עֹשֶׂה אֹתָם וּפָחֲדוּ וְרָגְזוּ עַל כָּל־הַטּוֹבָה וְעַל כָּל־הַשָּׁלוֹם אֲשֶׁר אָנֹכִי עֹשֶׂה לָּהּ (Jer 33:9)

7. וּבְלֶכֶת הַחַיּוֹת יֵלְכוּ הָאוֹפַנִּים אֶצְלָם וּבְהִנָּשֵׂא הַחַיּוֹת מֵעַל הָאָרֶץ יִנָּשְׂאוּ הָאוֹפַנִּים: (Ezek 1:19)

8. לֵךְ מִנֶּגֶד לְאִישׁ כְּסִיל וּבַל־יָדַעְתָּ שִׂפְתֵי־דָעַת: (Prov 14:7)

9. אֲשֶׁר חֹטֶא עֹשֶׂה רָע מְאַת וּמַאֲרִיךְ לוֹ כִּי גַּם־יוֹדֵעַ אָנִי אֲשֶׁר יִהְיֶה־טּוֹב לְיִרְאֵי הָאֱלֹהִים אֲשֶׁר יִירְאוּ מִלְּפָנָיו: (Eccl 8:12)

10. וְאַל־תְּכַס עַל־עֲוֺנָם וְחַטָּאתָם מִלְּפָנֶיךָ אַל־תִּמָּחֶה כִּי הִכְעִיסוּ לְנֶגֶד הַבּוֹנִים: (Neh 3:37)

Translate from English to Hebrew.

11. Naomi spoke to her, saying: "Ruth, arise, go into Boaz's field. Gather food while walking behind the men. Bring it back to me, and we shall eat together."

12. The priest went to the camp from the field. He entered into the tabernacle and offered the sacrifice on top of the altar in the fire.

13. Jacob left the Aramean lands with all his family and possessions, traveled through Canaan, and arrived at Bethel. He fell on his face before Esau.

14. Between evening and morning, God gave some fruit of the trees to the man for food, which is better than the grass of the field.

15. You and the people shall observe my statute this day by going to Jerusalem so that you may remember Yahweh your God. This festival shall be for you a commemoration.

Guided Reading: Gen 3:8–21

8 וַיִּשְׁמְע֡וּ אֶת־ק֠וֹל יְהוָ֨ה אֱלֹהִ֜ים מִתְהַלֵּ֤ךְ בַּגָּן֙ לְר֣וּחַ הַיּ֔וֹם וַיִּתְחַבֵּ֨א הָֽאָדָ֜ם וְאִשְׁתּ֗וֹ מִפְּנֵי֙ יְהוָ֣ה אֱלֹהִ֔ים בְּת֖וֹךְ עֵ֥ץ הַגָּֽן׃ 9 וַיִּקְרָ֛א יְהוָ֥ה אֱלֹהִ֖ים אֶל־הָֽאָדָ֑ם וַיֹּ֥אמֶר ל֖וֹ אַיֶּֽכָּה׃ 10 וַיֹּ֕אמֶר אֶת־קֹלְךָ֥ שָׁמַ֖עְתִּי בַּגָּ֑ן וָאִירָ֛א כִּֽי־עֵירֹ֥ם אָנֹ֖כִי וָאֵחָבֵֽא׃ 11 וַיֹּ֕אמֶר מִ֚י הִגִּ֣יד לְךָ֔ כִּ֥י עֵירֹ֖ם אָ֑תָּה הֲמִן־הָעֵ֗ץ אֲשֶׁ֧ר צִוִּיתִ֛יךָ לְבִלְתִּ֥י אֲכָל־מִמֶּ֖נּוּ אָכָֽלְתָּ׃ 12 וַיֹּ֖אמֶר הָֽאָדָ֑ם הָֽאִשָּׁה֙ אֲשֶׁ֣ר נָתַ֣תָּה עִמָּדִ֔י הִ֛וא נָֽתְנָה־לִּ֥י מִן־הָעֵ֖ץ וָאֹכֵֽל׃ 13 וַיֹּ֨אמֶר יְהוָ֧ה אֱלֹהִ֛ים לָאִשָּׁ֖ה מַה־זֹּ֣את עָשִׂ֑ית וַתֹּ֙אמֶר֙ הָֽאִשָּׁ֔ה הַנָּחָ֥שׁ הִשִּׁיאַ֖נִי וָאֹכֵֽל׃ 14 וַיֹּאמֶר֩ יְהוָ֨ה אֱלֹהִ֥ים ׀ אֶֽל־הַנָּחָשׁ֮ כִּ֣י עָשִׂ֣יתָ זֹּאת֒ אָר֤וּר אַתָּה֙ מִכָּל־הַבְּהֵמָ֔ה וּמִכֹּ֖ל חַיַּ֣ת הַשָּׂדֶ֑ה עַל־גְּחֹנְךָ֣ תֵלֵ֔ךְ וְעָפָ֥ר תֹּאכַ֖ל כָּל־יְמֵ֥י חַיֶּֽיךָ׃ 15 וְאֵיבָ֣ה ׀ אָשִׁ֗ית בֵּֽינְךָ֙ וּבֵ֣ין הָֽאִשָּׁ֔ה וּבֵ֥ין זַרְעֲךָ֖ וּבֵ֣ין זַרְעָ֑הּ ה֚וּא יְשׁוּפְךָ֣ רֹ֔אשׁ וְאַתָּ֖ה תְּשׁוּפֶ֥נּוּ עָקֵֽב׃ 16 אֶֽל־הָאִשָּׁ֣ה אָמַ֗ר הַרְבָּ֤ה אַרְבֶּה֙ עִצְּבוֹנֵ֣ךְ וְהֵֽרֹנֵ֔ךְ בְּעֶ֖צֶב תֵּֽלְדִ֣י בָנִ֑ים וְאֶל־אִישֵׁךְ֙ תְּשׁ֣וּקָתֵ֔ךְ וְה֖וּא יִמְשָׁל־בָּֽךְ׃ 17 וּלְאָדָ֣ם אָמַ֗ר כִּֽי־שָׁמַעְתָּ֮ לְק֣וֹל אִשְׁתֶּךָ֒ וַתֹּ֙אכַל֙ מִן־הָעֵ֔ץ אֲשֶׁ֤ר צִוִּיתִ֙יךָ֙ לֵאמֹ֔ר לֹ֥א תֹאכַ֖ל מִמֶּ֑נּוּ אֲרוּרָ֤ה הָֽאֲדָמָה֙ בַּֽעֲבוּרֶ֔ךָ בְּעִצָּבוֹן֙ תֹּֽאכֲלֶ֔נָּה כֹּ֖ל יְמֵ֥י חַיֶּֽיךָ׃ 18 וְק֥וֹץ וְדַרְדַּ֖ר תַּצְמִ֣יחַֽ לָ֑ךְ וְאָכַלְתָּ֖ אֶת־עֵ֥שֶׂב הַשָּׂדֶֽה׃ 19 בְּזֵעַ֤ת אַפֶּ֙יךָ֙ תֹּ֣אכַל לֶ֔חֶם עַ֤ד שֽׁוּבְךָ֙ אֶל־הָ֣אֲדָמָ֔ה כִּ֥י מִמֶּ֖נָּה לֻקָּ֑חְתָּ כִּֽי־עָפָ֣ר אַ֔תָּה וְאֶל־עָפָ֖ר תָּשֽׁוּב׃ 20 וַיִּקְרָ֧א הָֽאָדָ֛ם שֵׁ֥ם אִשְׁתּ֖וֹ חַוָּ֑ה כִּ֛י הִ֥וא הָֽיְתָ֖ה אֵ֥ם כָּל־חָֽי׃ 21 וַיַּ֩עַשׂ֩ יְהוָ֨ה אֱלֹהִ֜ים לְאָדָ֧ם וּלְאִשְׁתּ֛וֹ כָּתְנ֥וֹת ע֖וֹר וַיַּלְבִּשֵֽׁם׃

VOCABULARY AND NOTES

Verse 8

מִתְהַלֵּךְ	*Hitpael*	PTC MS	הלך	"walk about"
גָּן		N.MS		"garden"
לְרוּחַ הַיּוֹם		idiom		"wind/breeze of the day"

וַיִּתְחַבֵּא	Hitpael	CP 3MS	חבא	"keep oneself hidden"

Verse 9

אַיֶּכָּה		INTR (אַיִן) + 2 MS SF		"where are you?"

Verse 10

וָאִירָא	Qal	CP 1CS	ירא	
עֵירֹם		ADJ.MS		"naked"
אֵחָבֵא	Niphal	CP 1CS	חבא	"hide"

Verse 11

הִגִּיד	Hiphil	SC 3MS	נגד	"command"
צִוִּיתִיךָ	Piel	SC 1CS + 2MS SF	צוה	
בִּלְתִּי		NEG		"no"

Verse 12

נָתַתָּה	Qal	SC 2MS	נתן	
עִמָּדִי		PREP + 1CS SF		"with; beside" (עִם)
הִוא		IPP 3FS		"she" (qere הִיא)
וָאֹכֵל	Qal	CP 1CS	אכל	

Verse 13

נָחָשׁ		N.MS		"snake"
הִשִּׁיאַנִי	Hiphil	SC 3MS + 1CS SF	נשא	"deceive"

Verse 14

אָרוּר	Qal	PASS PTCL MS	ארר	"cursed"
בְּהֵמָה		N.FS		"beast; cattle"
חַיַּת		N.FS CSTR		"animal; living organism"
גְּחֹנְךָ		N.MS + 2MS SF		"belly"
תֵלֵךְ	Qal	PC 2MS	הלך	
עָפָר		N.MS		"dust"

Verse 15

אֵיבָה		N.FS		"enmity"
אָשִׁית	Qal	PC 1CS	שׁית	
זַרְעָה		N.MS + 3FS SF		"offspring"
יְשׁוּפְךָ	Qal	PC 3MS + 2MS SF	שׁוף	"bruise"
תְּשׁוּפֶנּוּ	Qal PC	2MS + 3MS SF	שׁוף	
עָקֵב				"heel"

Verse 16

הַרְבָּה	*Hiphil*	INF ABS	רבה	"make great"
אַרְבֶּה	*Hiphil*	PC 1CS	רבה	
עִצְּבוֹנֵךְ		N.MS + 2FS SF		"labor"
הֵרֹנֵךְ		N.MS + 2FS		"pregnancy"
עֶצֶב		N.MS		"toil"
תֵּלְדִי	*Qal*	PC 2FS	ילד	
תְּשׁוּקָתֵךְ		N.FS + 2FS SF		"desire"
יִמְשָׁל	*Qal*			"rule"

Verse 17

אָדָם		PN		"Adam"
אִשְׁתֶּךָ		N.FS + 2MS		"wife"
בַּעֲבוּרֶךָ		PREP + 2MS		"on account of you"
תֹּאכֲלֶנָּה	*Qal* PC	2MS + 3FS SF	אכל	

Verse 18

קוֹץ		N.MS		"thorn"
דַרְדַּר		N.MS		"thistle"
תַּצְמִיחַ	*Hiphil*	PC 3FS	צמח	"produce"
וְאָכַלְתָּ	*Qal wəqātal*	2MS	אכל	
עֵשֶׂב		N.MS		"plant(s)"

Verse 19

זֵעַת		N.FS CSTR		"sweat"
אַפֶּיךָ		N.MD + 2MS SF	אַף	
שׁוּבְךָ	*Qal*	INF CSTR + 2MS SF	שׁוּב	
מִמֶּנָּה		מִן + 3FS SF		
לֻקָּחְתָּ	*Qal*	passive SC 2MS	לקח	"be taken"

Verse 20

חַוָּה		PN		"Eve"
הָיְתָה	*Qal*	SC 3FS	היה	
חָי		ADJ		"living"

Verse 21

כָּתְנוֹת		N.FP		"tunic"
עוֹר		N.MS		"skin"
וַיַּלְבִּשֵׁם	*Hiphil*	CP 3MS + 3MP SF	לבשׁ	"clothe"

/////////////////

TEXTUAL CRITICISM

1. METHOD OF TEXTUAL CRITICISM

In this section,[1] we will describe a method for analyzing a textual problem and then walk through a specific problem in Isa 53:11. Each problem in the text is different and usually requires its own solution, but working through an example in detail will provide a general orientation and approach to work through subsequent problems encountered in the text.

1.1 Method for Hebrew Bible Textual Criticism

Any method of textual criticism is founded upon two types of evidence: external and internal. The former describes the actual evidence according to its various witnesses, while the internal evidence seeks to answer what ancient scribes and translators probably copied or did not copy.

1.2 External Evidence

This step is probably the most objective. At the end of this step, one will have collected all the readings in their different ancient languages and grouped all these witnesses according to the *Hebrew* readings of the text, as opposed to the language of any Ancient Version. That is, the text critic will make a decision about the Hebrew parent text behind each Ancient Version and then group all witnesses underneath a respective Hebrew reading.

OFTEN PROVIDE VARIANTS TO 𝔐	GENERALLY AGREE WITH 𝔐
Qumran Manuscripts (𝔔)	Theodotion (θ′)
Hebrew Parent Text of Old Greek (𝔊)	Aquila (α′)
Samaritan Pentateuch (𝔪)	Symmachus (σ′)

---

[1] This lesson is authored by John D. Meade.

OFTEN PROVIDE VARIANTS TO 𝔐	GENERALLY AGREE WITH 𝔐
	Vulgate (𝒱)
	Peshitta (𝒮)
	Targum (𝒯)

The external evidence for each reading must be weighed or evaluated and not merely counted. That is, the reading with the most quantitative support will not necessarily be the original text. Based on the general description of the witnesses in chapter 2, it might be clear by now that generally proto-𝔐 was the parent text of θ′, α′, σ′, 𝒱, 𝒮, and 𝒯. Thus, one could group θ′, α′, σ′, 𝒱, 𝒮, and 𝒯 under 𝔐+ when all of these witnesses agree, and we could count them all as one witness. When any one of these witnesses diverges from 𝔐, one will then consider that witness weightier because it has diverged from the normal grouping (e.g., §2.4.1.4, Isa 7:11 where θ′ α′ σ′ probably diverged from 𝔐). Similarly, when 𝒮 agrees exclusively with 𝔊, one must remember that at times 𝒮 was influenced by 𝔊, and therefore 𝔊 (𝒮) may only count as one witness. There are times when 𝒱 depends on θ′, α′, and σ′, and in those cases 𝒱 is not an independent witness. Thus, textual critics evaluate witnesses according to their tendencies and do not merely count them.

At the end of this step, one will summarize the evidence and present what reading appears to have the stronger external evidence, that is, the stronger base of witnesses. But the original reading is not usually determined by external evidence without consulting the internal evidence.

1.3 Internal Evidence[2]

The basic question for the textual critic to answer here is: Which reading best explains how the others arose? The reading that can answer that question is probably the original text because it assumes that secondary readings can be explained by the one reading whose origin cannot be explained unless it is the original.

There are two other crucial internal rules or canons for determining this: (1) the more difficult reading is preferable (*difficilior lectio potior*), and (2) the shorter reading is preferable (*brevior lectio potior*). The more difficult reading is usually the original reading since it assumes that a scribe would be more likely to copy a text in a familiar way rather than in a difficult or unfamiliar way. That is, between two readings, the harder of the two is more likely to be the original reading, while the easier one is likely the one the scribe introduced in an attempt to smooth out the difficult text. The difficulty might be grammatical, lexical, historical, stylistic, or theological. But one needs to beware that the more difficult reading is not an impossible, bizarre, or gibberish reading caused by a scribal accident. That reading must be set aside.

The shorter reading is usually the original reading due to the tendency of scribes to expand their texts through glosses, conflations, dittography, simple expansions, and explications. Thus, a text that shows care to copy its source and not expand

---

[2] See McCarter, *Textual Criticism*, 72–74 for a brief discussion.

upon it is preferred as the original. But a major exception to this rule is the common error of haplography or parablepsis, which shortens the text by accident, and therefore in these cases the longer text is preferable (cf. §2.3.3.3.4 above).

A textual critic should be suspicious of readings that offer stylistic improvements, modernized or updated readings, simplified or trivialized readings, and readings that attempt to resolve alleged contradictions or smooth out difficulties. These criteria further unpack the two main canons; essentially, the smoother, easier reading is suspect compared to the more difficult one that remains appropriate to the context of the passage.

Once one has reasoned which reading gave rise to the others, one should declare which reading is the original according to the internal evidence.

1.4 Making a Textual Decision

Once both the external and internal evidence have been considered for a particular problem, one must choose the most likely original reading, give reasons for rejecting the other reading(s), and explain the relationship of all the readings as far as it is possible to do so according to the canons mentioned above. These canons include: Which reading best explains how the others arose? Which reading is more difficult than the others (*lectio difficilior*), and therefore which reading(s) would the scribe be more likely to change? Was there a shorter reading (*lectio brevior*) which may explain how a longer reading arose? Or was the shorter reading caused by the scribal mistake of haplography or parablepsis, creating an erroneous shorter text?

Theoretically, it is possible that none of the readings could yield a credible solution, and the original may need to be reconstructed by internal probability (i.e., what would the author have written?), such that the textual critic would need to emend or correct the text. An emended reading should not be used to validate the interpretation of the passage as a whole, since this would involve circular reasoning. This use of the term "conjectural emendation" does not refer to choosing a text other than 𝔐 as sometimes is popularly thought. Rather, choosing a better Hebrew text other than 𝔐 is simply a decision between known witnesses. There are decisions which theorize based upon the available evidence that a certain reading existed in the original text and is no longer attested in any known manuscript. This emended text is one not found in any of the textual witnesses and comes from the intuition of the textual critic. We should not confuse a proper "conjectural emendation" (i.e. a reading based on the so-called counsel of despair with no manuscript evidence) with a textual critic choosing a better Hebrew reading than 𝔐.

2. GUIDED EXAMPLE: ISAIAH 53:11—HE WILL SEE LIGHT OR HE WILL SEE?

In Isa 53:11, there is a problem over whether the original text had the word אור "light" or not. The *BHS* apparatus notes that, "1QIsa^ab 𝔊 have 'light,' but ראה = רוה 'to drink'." This note does not accurately describe the evidence for the problem and incorporates an emendation not supported in any of the sources. Although

BHQ promises a more accurate apparatus, the *BHS* apparatus is full of problems, and thus the student is encouraged to go deeper by tracking down the readings from the editions of the Ancient Versions and proceed to reconstruct problems as presented below. One must get control over the sources before proposing solutions. Logos and Accordance software has made it easier to acquire the necessary sources in digital formats. I will first list the witnesses in original script, supply a simple English translation for them, and provide further information about where the student can find each of these readings for future problems.

2.1 Listing of Witnesses

𝔐 (A)[3]	יִרְאֶה יִשְׂבָּע
	he will see, he will be satisfied
𝔐 (L)[4]	יִרְאֶה יִשְׂבָּע
	he will see, he will be satisfied
𝔐 (Kennicott)[5]	No variants
𝔐 (de Rossi)[6]	No variants
1QIsa[a][7]	יראה אור וישבע
	He will see light and be satisfied

---

[3] Images of the Aleppo Codex were digitized in 2002 by Ardon Bar Hama. See barhama.com, accessed September 23, 2022, https://barhama.com/ajaxzoom/viewer/viewer.php?zoomDir=/pic/Aleppo WM/&example=viewer5. The student will have to work at finding the text among the images.

[4] Codex Leningrad is the base text of the fifth edition of *BHS*. One can now access images of Codex Leningrad on Sefaria.org: https://www.sefaria.org/sheets/300725?lang=bi. Thus, for our problem, find Isaiah 53:11 in Sefaria's Tanakh feature, click on 53:11, and find and click "Manuscripts" under the "Resources" heading for the verse. You are then looking at the page in Codex Leningrad in which Isa 53:11 appears (https://manuscripts.sefaria.org/leningrad-color/BIB_LENCDX_F241A.jpg). One can also view images of the codex here: https://archive.org/stream/Leningrad_Codex/Leningrad#mode/2up.

[5] Kennicott, *Vetus Testamentum Hebraicum*, 2:69.

[6] Giovanni Bernardo de Rossi, *Variae lectiones Veteris Testamenti: ex immensa manuscriptorum editorumque codicum congerie haustae et ad Samaritanum textum, ad vetustissimas versiones, ad accuratiores sacrae criticae fontes ac leges examinatae,* 4 vols. (Parmae: Ex Regio Typographeo, 1784–1788), 3:51.

[7] For the DSS, the student must be able to access volume 39 of Discoveries in the Judean Desert series (Emanuel Tov, *Introduction and Indexes*, DJD 39 [Oxford: Clarendon, 2002]), which contains the indices. There are several indices in this work, but most important for the student is "The Index of Passages in the 'Biblical Texts'" (185–201), which shows all texts contained in the DSS. For Isa 53:11, see page 193, where 1QIsa[b] is listed as containing text from 53:1–12 and 4QIsa[d] is listed as containing text from 53:8–12. It is assumed that 1QIsa[a] contains the whole book with few lacunae.

Now that we have identified three DSS that are relevant to our problem, we still need to find the texts to record the readings. Using the same DJD index volume, turn to the "Categorized List of the 'Biblical Texts'" (165–83). Under lists from Qumran, look up Isaiah (171–72) and find that 1QIsa[a] and 1QIsa[b] are the first two manuscripts listed on page 171, and 4QIsa[d] is found on the same page. Since the publication of the indices, DJD 32 has been published in two parts so you will want to look at Part 1 to find the readings. For 4QIsa[d], look at DJD 15. For 1QIsa[a], turn in DJD 32 Part 1 to pages 88–89 and find line 19 for the reading with אור. For 1QIsa[b], turn in the same volume to pages 140–41 and find line 22 for the reading with אור. For 4QIsa[d], turn in DJD 15 to page 83 (Plate XIV fragment 11 column 2) and find line 20 for the reading with אור[ר] ושבע. Also, for 1QIsa[a], I encourage students to explore the manuscript online here: The Israel Museum, "The Digitized Dead Sea Scrolls," http://

1QIsa[b]	יראה אור י[שבע] He will see light, he will [be satisfied
4QIsa[d]	יראה או[ר]ושבע He will see lig[ht]and be satisfied
𝔊[8]	δεῖξαι αὐτῷ φῶς To show him light
θ'[9]	ὄψεται ἐμπλησθήσεται He will see, he will be filled
α'	ὄψεται ἐμπλησθήσεται He will see, he will be filled
σ'	ὄψεται χορτασθήσεται He will see, he will be filled
𝔙[10]	videbit et saturabitur He will see and be satisfied
𝔖[11]	nḥz᾽ wnsb῾ He will see and be satisfied
𝔗[12]	יחזון בפורענות סנאיהון יסבעון They shall see the retribution of their adversaries. They shall be satisfied...

dss.collections.imj.org.il/isaiah. Likewise, for 4QIsa[d], one can view its fragments here: https://www.deadseascrolls.org.il/explore-the-archive/manuscript/4Q58-1.

[8] For the Old Greek version, the student should not use Rahlfs's edition but the Göttingen *Septuaginta* volumes (see below for a list of the volumes that have been published). *Isaias* is edited by Joseph Ziegler and contains our reading on page 323 in the top line (see the image: Isaiah 53 in the Göttingen Septuaginta Critical Edition, §2.4.1.2). When there is no Göttingen volume, one must use Rahlfs. One can access Liddell, Scott, and Jones's Greek Lexicon (LSJ) online via Logeion (https://logeion.uchicago.edu/lexidium) or download the app to one's mobile device. T. Muraoka's *A Greek-English Lexicon of the Septuagint* is also helpful at this stage.

[9] The readings of "the Three" should be retrieved from the Second Apparatus (the apparatus below the solid horizontal line) of the Göttingen volumes where possible (there is no II App in the Psalms volume). This second apparatus is the most up-to-date repository of the readings of Theodotion, Aquila, and Symmachus. Where there is no Göttingen volume, the student must consult the earlier edition by Field (see below for editions of the Three). In Ziegler's *Isaias* volume, the readings to the Three appear on page 323, on the fourth line of the Second Apparatus. For this text, manuscripts Q and 86 contain relevant readings to our problem (see the image: Isaiah 53 in the Göttingen Septuaginta Critical Edition, §2.4.1.2).

[10] For Jerome's Latin Vulgate, the student will need to access the fifth edition of Weber and Gryson, page 1152. If one does not read Latin, make sure to consult Whitaker's Words online (http://archives.nd.edu/words.html) or download William Whitaker's Words app for your mobile device. This tool will help one parse Latin words and provide a gloss for the word. One will also want to use the Latin lexica available on Logeion online (https://logeion.uchicago.edu/lexidium) or download the app to one's mobile device.

[11] No doubt, accessing the Syriac Peshitta's readings will prove the most challenging. The Leiden Peshitta for Isa 53:11 can be found on page 97 in the last line. The student can look up the text of the Peshitta online at the Comprehensive Aramaic Lexicon (http://cal.huc.edu/searching/CAL_search_page.html). If one clicks on "Text Browse" > "Syriac" > "Submit," then one can find the various works composed in Syriac including "P Is." Once one clicks on "P Is," one can scroll the text by chapter and verse. All the words are morphologically tagged, and the links take one to lexical entries. Furthermore, English translations of the Peshitta are now available through Gorgias Press's *Antioch Bible* series, and students are encouraged to consult this translation as they work in the Peshitta.

[12] The text of the Aramaic Targums is best accessed in Alexander Sperber's four volume *The Bible in Aramaic*. Isaiah 53:11 appears in volume III on the top of page 109. Again, one can look up the text

2.2. Determination of Exemplars and Parent Texts

1ᴄ̣Isaᵃ 1ᴄ̣Isaᵇ 4ᴄ̣Isaᵈ

ᴄ̣ preserves three texts reading "he will see light." But it is not the number of witnesses that is important here since one weighs the witnesses, not merely counts them. First, of the three scrolls, most scholars believe that 1ᴄ̣Isaᵇ (and 4ᴄ̣Isaᵈ to a slightly lesser degree) represent proto-𝔐; that is, their text reflects the consonantal layer of 𝔐 in almost every detail.[13] Thus, when they disagree with 𝔐 on a word-level variant, the textual critic should take note of it. Second, 1ᴄ̣Isaᵃ does not follow proto-𝔐 in spelling and textual character as closely, but here it does contain the additional word in agreement with the other two manuscripts.

𝔊

According to Hatch and Redpath's *Concordance to the Septuagint*, 𝔊-Isaiah uses φῶς "light" some 30×.[14] Most often, the Greek term renders אוֹר "light," but on a couple of occasions (4:5; 50:10), the term renders נֹגַהּ "bright light."[15] Thus, the translator's Hebrew text probably had אוֹר in it, and he rendered the word with his normal equivalent. Since ᴄ̣ shows that at this time there are Hebrew manuscripts with אוֹר, the translator's parent text probably contained the word. Thus, in the evaluation below, 𝔊 will be grouped under the Hebrew reading reflecting אוֹר.

θ′ α′ σ′

The Three usually translate a text like proto-𝔐 literally; thus when they agree on a missing word, their Hebrew parent text probably did not contain it. At this particular place, the reading in the Second Apparatus of the Göttingen Edition is uncharacteristically difficult to understand, for it is not clear whether the Three have φῶς or not. Only checking the manuscripts can confirm that the Three's text lacks the key word.[16] The Three are the earliest witnesses to the reading without אוֹר.

---

of the Targums online at the Comprehensive Aramaic Lexicon (http://cal.huc.edu/searching/CAL_search_page.html). If one clicks on "Text Browse" > "Palestinian Aramaic" > "Submit," then one can find the various works composed in this dialect of Aramaic including "TgJ Is." Once one clicks on "TgJ Is," one can scroll the text by chapter and verse. The words are morphologically tagged, and the links take one to lexical entries. Furthermore, English translations of the Aramaic Targums are now available through Liturgical Press's *The Aramaic Bible* series, and students are encouraged to consult this translation as they work in the Targums.

[13] Tov, *Textual Criticism*, 31–32; see also Emanuel Tov, *Textual Criticism of the Hebrew Bible*, 4th ed. (Minneapolis: Fortress, 2022), 124.

[14] Edwin Hatch and Henry A. Redpath, *A Concordance to the Septuagint and the Other Greek Versions of the Old Testament (Including the Apocryphal Books)*, 2nd ed. (Grand Rapids: Baker, 1998), 1451.

[15] The *Concordance* can be freely downloaded here: https://archive.org/details/concordancetosep00hatc_0/mode/2up.

[16] For the relevant reading in Ra 86, see folio 112v at DVL (Digivatlib), accessed September 23, 2022, https://digi.vatlib.it/view/MSS_Barb.gr.549; and commentary by John D. Meade at Meade,

ט ס ת

These three Ancient Versions usually follow proto-𝔐 as they do here. Their Hebrew text most probably lacked the word אור "light." ת's בפורענות סנאיהון "retribution of their adversaries" probably does not reflect a text with a direct object. Rather the targumists supplied a contextual complement to ease the literary and grammatical difficulty presented by proto-𝔐.

2.3 Summary and Evaluation of the External Evidence

The summary of the extant readings must be done in Hebrew. For this problem, this step poses little challenge since 𝔔 provides the variant reading in Hebrew.[17] The two textual choices with evidence are as follows:

HEBREW READING	TRANSLATION	WITNESSES
יראה אור	He will see light	1𝔔Isaᵃ 1𝔔Isaᵇ 4𝔔Isaᵈ 𝔊
יראה	He will see	𝔐+ (= θ′ α′ σ′ ט ס ת)

The addition of אור in 𝔔 and the Hebrew text behind 𝔊 is found in independent sources. At Qumran, there was not an impulse to create a single standard text and the three relevant witnesses are not all proto-𝔐. The Hebrew text behind 𝔊 would have been in Alexandria, and its text also included אור. Thus, these independent witnesses must go back to a common source preserving the original אור. The reading of 𝔐+ appears to have a wide base of witnesses, but the base is deceptive. When we weigh these witnesses and do not simply count them, the witnesses are not independent but have a common source in proto-𝔐. Thus, the external evidence for this problem favors the additional word, but the internal evidence will need to decide the question.

2.4 Evaluation of the Internal Evidence

On internal grounds, the reading of 𝔐+ with its lack of direct object for the verb is grammatically difficult, and thus one could argue that a text with an object is a secondary facilitation to a difficult text. 𝔐+ also represents the shorter text, which 𝔔 and 𝔊 could have augmented secondarily.

On the other hand, the idiom "to see light" in Hebrew means "to have life" (cf. Job 3:16; Ps 36:10), and contextually, the resurrection of the innocent Servant could be his vindication for his vicarious suffering and death. Furthermore, in some Hebrew scripts of DSS, אור resembles the הא- ending of the previous word

---

"'He Will See Light' in Isaiah 53:11," Evangelical Textual Criticism (blog), April 10, 2020, https://evangelicaltextualcriticism.blogspot.com/2020/04/he-will-see-light-in-isaiah-5311.html.

[17] There will be textual problems that will require more work to arrive at a retroversion from Greek to the putative Hebrew parent text. But patiently using Hatch and Redpath to determine Greek-Hebrew translation equivalents and other studies on translation technique can be helpful in this process.

and even the beginning of the following word ו־ in 1QIsaᵃ. Thus, an accidental copyist mistake could account for the shorter reading. Also, perhaps a theological reason could be found for the omission of אור in 𝔐.[18]

The internal evidence favors the reading of "he will see light."

2.5 Conclusion

No textual decision is pure and simple, but the external and internal evidence for this problem probably support the reading "he will see light." Many English translations such as the NIV ("he will see the light of life") and the CSB ("he will see light") reflect the addition, while the ESV continues to read with 𝔐 ("he shall see"). Thus, the longer reading is the original text.

3. KEY TAKEAWAYS

Ancient texts, including the Bible, underwent modification for various reasons. Textual criticism is the discipline that gathers all of the ancient copies and ancient versions of a book in order to produce an edition without the common copying errors in it. The key topics of the chapter include a thorough introduction to all of the witnesses of the Hebrew Bible and a method for solving textual problems. Along the way, we detailed the steps of textual criticism and the typical mistakes committed by scribes. These are listed below in summary fashion.

KEY STEPS TO TEXTUAL CRITICISM

- Gather relevant textual witnesses for the problem
- List them and provide English translations for them
- Group witnesses according to the Hebrew parent text
- Evaluate External Evidence based on any unexpected agreements (e.g., Aquila agrees with 𝔊 against 𝔐)
- Evaluate Internal Evidence
- Make a decision on the original text and update translation of the text if necessary

TYPICAL SCRIBAL MISTAKES
- Spelling conventions
- Similarities of consonants (e.g., ך/ד)
- Longer additions and omissions
- Large-Scale Differences

---

[18] *CTAT*, 2:406.

4 BIBLIOGRAPHY

4.1 Hebrew Editions

Biblia Hebraica Quinta. Edited by Adrian Schenker et al. Stuttgart: Deutsche Bibelgesellschaft, 2004–. (Published fascicles include: Genesis, Leviticus, Deuteronomy, Judges, Minor Prophets, Proverbs, Megilloth, Ezra and Nehemiah.)

Biblia Hebraica Stuttgartensia. 5th ed. Edited by Karl Elliger and Wilhelm Rudolph. Stuttgart: Deutsche Bibelgesellschaft, 1997.

Discoveries in the Judaean Desert. Volumes 1–40. Oxford: Clarendon, 1955–2010.

Kennicott, Benjamin. *Vetus Testamentum Hebraicum: cum variis lectionibus.* 2 vols. Oxford: Clarendon, 1776, 1780. (Online: vol. 1: https://archive.org/details/vetustestamentum01kenn; vol. 2: https://archive.org/details/vetustestamentum02kenn.)

Leon Levy Dead Sea Scrolls Digital Library. https://www.deadseascrolls.org.il/?locale=en_US.

Rossi, Giovanni Bernardo de. *Variae lectiones Veteris Testamenti: ex immensa manuscriptorum editorumque codicum congerie haustae et ad Samaritanum textum, ad vetustissimas versiones, ad accuratiores sacrae criticae fontes ac leges examinatae.* 4 vols. Parmae: Ex Regio Typographeo, 1784–1788. (Online: vol. 1: https://books.google.com/books?id=0pCCcWkPG8cC&source=gbs_similarbooks; vol. 2: https://books.google.com/books/about/Variae_lectiones_Veteris_Testamenti_ex_i.html?id=v60WAAAAQAAJ; vol. 3: https://books.google.com/books?id=4_mQ8F9fxx0C&printsec=frontcover&source=gbs_ge_summary_r&cad=0#v=onepage&q&f=false; vol. 4: https://books.google.com/books?id=1K0WAAAAQAAJ&source=gbs_similarbooks.)

See also Drew Longacre, OTTC: A Blog for Old Testament Textual Criticism. Longacre has collected numerous links to online digital manuscripts and editions. http://oldtestamenttextualcriticism.blogspot.com/p/online-digital-images.html.

4.2 Greek Editions

Field, Frederick. *Origenis Hexaplorum Quae Supersunt.* 2 vols. Oxford: Clarendon, 1875. Repr. Hildesheim: Olms, 1964. (Online: vol. 1: http://archive.org/details/origenhexapla01unknuoft; vol. 2: http://archive.org/details/origenhexapla02unknuoft)

Gentry, Peter John, ed. *Ecclesiastes.* SVTG 11.2. Göttingen: Vandenhoeck & Ruprecht, 2019.

Hanhart, Robert, ed. *Esdrae Liber I.* 2nd ed. SVTG 8.1. Göttingen: Vandenhoeck & Ruprecht, 1991.

————, ed. *Esdrae Liber II*. SVTG 8.2. Göttingen: Vandenhoeck & Ruprecht, 1993.

————, ed. *Esther*. 2nd ed. SVTG 8.3. Göttingen: Vandenhoeck & Ruprecht, 1983.

————, ed. *Iudith*. SVTG 8.4. Göttingen: Vandenhoeck & Ruprecht, 1979.

————, ed. *Maccabaeorum Liber II*. 2nd ed. SVTG 9.2. Göttingen: Vandenhoeck & Ruprecht, 1976.

————, ed. *Maccabaeorum Liber III*. 2nd ed. SVTG 9.3. Göttingen: Vandenhoeck & Ruprecht, 1960, 1980.

————, ed. *Paralipomenon Liber II*. SVTG 7.2. Göttingen: Vandenhoeck & Ruprecht, 2014.

————, ed. *Tobit*. SVTG 8.5. Göttingen: Vandenhoeck & Ruprecht, 1983.

Kappler, Werner, ed. *Maccabaeorum Liber I*. 2nd ed. SVTG 9.1. Göttingen: Vandenhoeck & Ruprecht, 1967.

Meade, John D. *A Critical Edition of the Hexaplaric Fragments of Job 22–42*. Leuven: Peeters, 2020.

Quast, Udo, ed. *Ruth*. SVTG 4.3. Göttingen: Vandenhoeck & Ruprecht, 2006.

Rahlfs, Alfred, ed. Psalmi cum Odis. 2nd ed. SVTG 10. Göttingen: Vandenhoeck & Ruprecht, 1979.

Rahlfs, Alfred, and Robert Hanhart, eds. *Septuaginta: Id est Vetus Testamentum graece iuxta LXX Interpretes*. Rev. ed. Stuttgart: Deutsche Bibelgesellschaft, 2006 (also known as Rahlfs-Hanhart edition).

The Hexapla Institute. www.hexapla.org.

Wevers, John W., ed. *Deuteronomium*. SVTG 3.2. Göttingen: Vandenhoeck & Ruprecht, 1977.

————, ed. *Exodus*. SVTG 2.1. Göttingen: Vandenhoeck & Ruprecht, 1991.

————, ed. *Genesis*. SVTG 1. Göttingen: Vandenhoeck & Ruprecht, 1974.

————, ed. *Leviticus*. SVTG 2.2. Göttingen: Vandenhoeck & Ruprecht, 1986.

————, ed. *Numeri*. SVTG 3.1. Göttingen: Vandenhoeck & Ruprecht, 1982.

Ziegler, Joseph, ed. Duodecim Prophetae. 3rd ed. SVTG 13. Göttingen: Vandenhoeck & Ruprecht, 1984.

————, ed. *Ezechiel*. 2nd ed. SVTG 16.1. Göttingen: Vandenhoeck & Ruprecht, 977.

————, ed. *Ieremias, Baruch, Threni, Epistula Ieremiae*. 2nd ed. SVTG 15. Göttingen: Vandenhoeck & Ruprecht, 1976.

————, ed. *Iob*. SVTG 11.4. Göttingen: Vandenhoeck & Ruprecht, 1982.

————, ed. *Isaias*. 3rd ed. SVTG 14. Göttingen: Vandenhoeck & Ruprecht, 1983.

————, ed. *Sapientia Iesu Filii Sirach*. 2nd ed. SVTG 12.2. Göttingen: Vandenhoeck & Ruprecht, 1980.

————, ed. Sapientia Salomonis. 2nd ed. SVTG 12.1. Göttingen: Vandenhoeck & Ruprecht, 1980.

————, ed. *Susanna, Daniel, Bel et Draco*. 2nd ed. SVTG 16.2. Göttingen: Vandenhoeck & Ruprecht, 1999.

4.3 Latin Editions

Weber, Robert, and Roger Gryson, eds. *Biblia Sacra iuxta vulgatam versionem.* 5th ed. Stuttgart: Deutsche Bibelgesellschaft, 2007.

4.4 Syriac Editions

Kiraz, George, et al., eds. *The Antioch Bible.* Piscataway, NJ: Gorgias, 2012–.
Romeny, Bas ter Haar, et al., eds. *The Old Testament in Syriac according to the Peshitta Version.* Leiden: Brill, 1973–.

4.5 Aramaic Editions

Comprehensive Aramaic Lexicon. http://cal.huc.edu/searching/CAL_search_page.html.
McNamara, Martin J. *Aramaic Bible.* 19 vols. Collegeville: Liturgical Press, 1987–2008.
Sperber, Alexander. *The Bible in Aramaic Based on Old Manuscripts and Printed Texts.* 4 vols. Leiden: Brill, 1959–1968.

///////////////////

SEMANTIC ANALYSIS

1. SEMANTICS DEFINED

Semantics is the study of meaning. Understanding the meaning of morphemes, lexemes, and phrases—dubbed <u>lexical semantics</u>—requires investigating what that signifier intends to signify.[1] Lexical semantics investigates the relationship of a signifier (lexical unit) to the signified (referenced entity). Beyond simple referentiality, meaning also involves <u>entailment</u> and various other implicit concepts or implicatures. The Hebrew word עֵינַיִם, for instance, signifies human or animal eyes—that is, the body part. Further, it can entail the concepts of sight and vision.[2] It can also imply notions of wisdom, knowledge, opinions, or even feelings.

WHAT DOES *WORD* MEAN?

Although the concept *word* provides for a convenient nomenclature in everyday speech, linguists have struggled to define what a word is. Some have proposed it is something circumscribed as a semantic unit (meaning), a prosodic unit (phonology), or even a graphic unit (orthography).

Words only have meaning as part of a cultural and syntactical context. Since words are instantiated within a cultural product called language and are not universal signs or essential concepts, their range of meaning must be related to the conceptual world and use of the speakers. These relations connect a word or phrase

---

[1] D. A. Cruse, *Lexical Semantics* (Cambridge: Cambridge University Press, 1986). For the issues involved in formal semantics and the various logical aspects of meaning, see Thomas Ede Zimmermann and Wolfgang Sternefeld, *Introduction to Semantics. An Essential Guide to the Composition of Meaning* (Berlin: de Gruyter, 2013).

[2] For a discussion of this word in Genesis, see Hardy, *Exegetical Gems*, 13–21.

with its referenced entity or entities. A lexical unit is best described by outlining its various contextual usages. Usage includes relationships to other related lexemes, semantic networks, and morphosyntactic affiliations.

Word studies explore both the general meanings (semantic range) of a certain lexeme and the relationship of its usage to other elements. To accomplish this task, one studies the usages of a certain lexeme in general (*langue*)—including <u>paradigmatic</u> relationships, semantic fields, and morphosyntactic characteristics—and the <u>syntagmatic</u> relationship of specific usages to other clause and discourse elements (*parole*). Once the basic lexical semantics are stipulated, one can discuss the specific sense of a word in any given context.

> A "word study" could involve a simple search of a lexicon or dictionary. Or it could entail a careful analysis of every morphological form, syntactic function, context, translation, cultural data, and related lexemes. Regardless of the specific process, word studies fall under the rubric of semantics. When done properly, semantic analysis seeks to identify the meaning and connotation of a lexical unit.

At a very basic level, lexical study requires examining the use of a word in each context and grouping similar usages together to create a classification network. These groupings enable the identification of various connections between the different categories of usage. Mapping related words, including both synonyms and antonyms, and examining their translation value in different languages offers further specification.

One should avoid several common misconceptions about meaning. First, meaning does not necessarily equal translation value. Words do not have identical semantic ranges in any two languages. Hebrew חֶסֶד may have some similar notions as English *loyalty*, but it is not identical in meaning or usage. A Hebrew market would not have a *ḥesed*-program for frequent shoppers. Second, not all the general meanings of a word are relevant to a specific usage. The Hebrew verb פקד has a wide range of meanings, including "visit," "pay attention to," "carefully inspect," "tend," "look for," "examine," "count," "assign," "punish," "harm," "put in charge of," "muster," "deposit," "determine," "command," "keep," and "afflict." All of these meanings are not operative in a passage like Gen 21:1 (וַיהוָה פָּקַד אֶת־שָׂרָה "Now Yahweh ____ Sarah"). Third, one cannot import the origins (etymology) of a word into all occasions of a word. The Hebrew verb חטא can mean "miss," "do wrong," "sin," and "be liable." But the meaning in an instance like Exod 32:30 (אַתֶּם חֲטָאתֶם חֲטָאָה גְדֹלָה) does not mean: "you have *missed* a great sin." Fourth, every use of the same word does not have the same meaning—context determines specific meaning. Hebrew לָשׁוֹן identifies the body part "tongue" in one context (Judg 7:5) but may elsewhere refers to "language" (Deut 28:49). Fifth, words constructed on similar roots or forms do not always have obvious semantic connections. The meaning of מַלְאָךְ "messenger" is not necessarily connected with מְלָאכָה "work," as in Gen 2:2 (וַיְכַל אֱלֹהִים בַּיּוֹם הַשְּׁבִיעִי מְלַאכְתּוֹ). Sixth, similar spelling or sounding roots are not always related. Hebrew מִדְבָּר "wilderness" is derived from a different root than דָּבָר "word." One should not try to connect these meanings as part of describing the semantic range of either word.

2. SEMANTIC ANALYSIS METHODOLOGY

The following list outlines a method for conducting the semantic analysis of a Hebrew lexeme. The first set of steps (a–f) provides a guide to the collection and organization of the basic data. Not every word will incorporate the steps in the same way.

    (a) Use one or more Hebrew dictionaries to find basic properties of the lexeme (e.g., *DCH*, *HALOT*, *BDB*). Include part of speech, gender, root, pattern, and declension. Note any differences.

    (b) Outline other morphologically similar words using at least two Hebrew dictionaries. Provide the meaning of each and the relation to the lexeme. Do they have a shared root or similar context?

    (c) Detail each use of the lexeme in a given corpus (e.g., Pentateuch, historical books, the Prophets, etc.). Translate each verse and note the syntax (the semantic roles or phrase relationships) and the context (literary and cultural).

    (d) Describe related terms and ideas in each context. What verbs are used? What other lexemes comprise similar, opposite, accompanying, or parallel meanings? Are there frequently used associated term or phrases?

    (e) Provide a semantic network of the closest terms. Designate the semantic relationships (e.g., synonym, antonym, paronym, homonym, hyponym, hypernym, contextually-related/neighbor-of, type-of, part-of, parallelism).

    (f) Group together similar usages and note differences.

  The information gathered from the above steps allows one to describe the semantics of the lexeme in a selected passage. The following eight instructions are helpful in arranging the semantic study into a written form.

    (1) Summarize the semantic domain (range of usages) of the lexeme in the chosen corpus (e.g., Pentateuch).

    (2) Categorize similar meanings and group the references into a dictionary-like entry.

    (3) Discuss the particular contexts that offer clues to its usage and meaning.

    (4) Describe the relationship between associated concepts, words, and phrases. What synonyms, or near synonyms, are used? How is this word used differently than other similar concepts? How are other terms or concepts related to this grouping?

    (5) Consider the ancient historical and cultural context, including what this word may signify for the original audience situated around the ancient

world of the text. Consult a standard Bible dictionary for assistance (e.g., *Anchor Bible Dictionary, IVP Dictionary of the OT*).

(6) Give the translation values for the usages in the LXX and three more "literal" English translations. Discuss the different nuances of these translations and your semantic categorization.

(7) Consider the use of the term in a subset of the Bible (e.g., Torah, Book of the Twelve) or single book. Are there any *exegetically significant* connections between the usages of this term within the book?

(8) Finally, detail the usages found in the passage and each meaning. Make an overt statement of meaning for the usage under consideration. Provide the reasons for this assessment, including its importance for the overall interpretation of the passage.

3. OTHER WORD STUDY RESOURCES

Botterweck, G. Johannes, ed. *Theological Dictionary of the Old Testament*. 17 Vols. Grand Rapids: Eerdmans, 1974–2021.

Harris, R. Laird, et al., eds. *Theological Wordbook of the Old Testament*. Chicago: Moody, 2003.

Jenni, Ernst, and Claus Westermann, *Theological Lexicon of the Old Testament*. 3 Vols. Translated by Mark E. Biddle. Peabody, MA: Hendrickson, 1997.

VanGemeran, Willem, ed., *New International Dictionary of Old Testament Theology and Exegesis*. 5 Vols. Grand Rapids: Zondervan, 1997.

4. SEMANTIC CASE STUDY: לֵבָב, לֵב "HEART"

The word לֵב "heart" occurs 601 times in BH, while its biform לֵבָב occurs 252 times. The following case study treats both related words together.[3] In most cases, לֵב(ב) refers to the human mind as the cognitive center of one's existence (i.e., mind, thought) and thus serves both an emotional and intellectual function. A second meaning for לֵב(ב) can indicate "vitality" or "vital force," often in contexts where it is strengthened or renewed. Third, לֵב(ב) denotes human volition, "will" or "desire," commonly appearing in contexts where it refers to desire toward or resistance against a certain course of action. Finally, this Hebrew word can indicate "midst" or "inside," most often with regard to the chest area. We outline the usage of Hebrew לֵב(ב) as follows:

---

[3] H.-J. Fabry observes that there is no discernable difference between the two forms, but that their usage appears to be stylistic, with לֵב occurring more frequently in earlier literature and לֵבָב more common in later literature. Fabry, "לֵב," *TDOT* 7:407. Our analysis also affirms their sameness in meaning.

1. Heart (organ)/chest/midst
2. Vitality/life force
3. Will/desire
4. Mind/thought
   a. Cognitive/intellectual activity
   b. Emotional activity— the heart acting emotionally

We will summarize the developments of this Hebrew lexeme and highlight several important examples from each of the four major categories.

Heart (organ)/chest/midst

The basic meaning of Hebrew (לֵב) is the visceral organ known in English as the heart.[4] The clearest example of this meaning is found in Hos 13:8 in an oracle condemning Ephraim's idolatry: אֶפְגְּשֵׁם כְּדֹב שַׁכּוּל וְאֶקְרַע סְגוֹר לִבָּם "I will encounter them like a bear robbed of its cubs, and I will tear out the enclosure of **their lēb**."[5] The "enclosure of the heart" must refer to the thoracic cavity in which the viscera was located, and thus yields a rough parallel to Ugaritic *lb* in *KTU* 1.39:8 denoting an animal "heart" offered up in flames to the gods. Psalm 38:11 describes the movement of the לֵב as the physical organ. In this example, לֵב is parallel to כֹּחַ "strength:"

Ps 38:11

לִבִּי סְחַרְחַר עֲזָבַנִי כֹחִי

My lēb palpitates, **my strength** forsakes me.

The root סחר refers to the act of wandering about carrying out one's business (often as a merchant/trader) with the factitive likely suggesting a state movement.[6] In this case it is a violent throbbing in the chest.[7]

More than likely the human organ meaning developed into "chest" as a reference to the physical cavity housing the heart. Evidence for this meaning is found in Exod 28:29–30. Aaron carries the names of the twelve sons of Israel in the breast piece of judgment "upon his *lēb*" (עַל־לִבּוֹ). In this example, the locale of the "heart" is the external chest area where the symbolic piece would have rested.[8] Also, ritual mourning involves beating upon one's chest (מְתֹפְפֹת עַל־לִבְבֵהֶן) in Nah 2:8.[9] A similar designation occurs in 2 Sam 18:4 where Joab took three javelins and

---

[4] Fabry's caution that "the OT scarcely ever used *lēb* for the 'heart' as a physical organ" is too restrictive (*TDOT* 7:411).

[5] The word סְגוֹר is a derivative of the root סגר meaning "to shut, close" (see BDB, 689), whose verbal noun here denotes the "enclosure" or "chest cavity" of the physical heart. Cf. Fritz Stolz's translation, "covering of the heart" (Stolz, "לֵב," *TLOT* 2:638).

[6] See BDB, 695.

[7] *HALOT*, s.v. "סחר," 750.

[8] Cf. 2 Kgs 28:30.

[9] Cf. *KTU* 1.5 VI:21 and 1.6 I:5 where ʿAnatu mourns for Baʿlu by tilling her *lb* like a garden (see above).

"thrust them into Absalom's *lēb* (לֵב) while he was still alive and hiding in the midst (לֵב) of the tree."[10] The point of this description is not that Joab pierced the blood pumping organ of Absalom, but rather that he pierced the javelins deep into his chest area inflicting a fatal wound.[11]

The semantic range of (לֵבָב) as "chest" was extended to include the innermost part of inanimate objects. Absalom, whose "heart" was pierced by Joab, was said to be hiding in the לֵב of the tree when Joab discovered him (2 Sam 18:4). This language can also describe the sea as a designation for the locale of the tumultuous deeps within it: קָפְאוּ תְהֹמֹת בְּלֶב־יָם "the deeps congealed in the *lēb* of the sea" (Exod 15:8).[12] The uppermost recesses of the heavens are once described as having a לֵב "heart" in Deut 4:11 (וְהָהָר בֹּעֵר בָּאֵשׁ עַד־לֵב הַשָּׁמַיִם "the mountain was burning with fire to the *lēb* of the heavens").

Therefore, we may conclude that (לֵב)ב must have originally referred to the human blood-pumping organ located beneath the chest. As a derived physical meaning, the (לֵבָב) designates the outer chest area due to its close proximity to the organ beneath it and eventually expanded to include the inner part of physical entities (e.g., a tree, the sea, the heavens). We find unconvincing H. L. Ginsberg's suggestion that (לֵב)ב also meant "throat" in contexts where it is depicted as speaking.[13] All of the examples Ginsberg lists are better explained as references to the "mind" speaking (with the verb הגה), which is a well-established idiom for this word in Hebrew.[14]

Vitality/vital force

The (לֵב)ב can also designate the vitality/life force of humans and animals. Before looking at specific examples, it is worth considering how this meaning would have developed within the language. As Hebrew usage originally designated the internal organ housed within the chest cavity of both humans and animals, it is reasonable to posit that "vitality" is directly tied to the perceived physical strength or weakness of the organ.[15]

For instance, the vital force of individuals is revived or refreshed by the physical nourishment of food and drink. In Gen 18:5 Abraham urges the three men who visited him to stay and eat: "Sustain (סַעֲדוּ) your *lēb*; after you may go on." The root סעד means "to support"[16] or perhaps, metaphorically in this case, "to feed one's

---

[10] See also 2 Kgs 9:24 where Jehu strikes Joram between the shoulders so that the arrow "went out from his *leb*," which probably indicates that the arrow went into the midst of his back and protruded his chest area.

[11] H. L. Ginsberg, "Heart," in *Encyclopedia Judaica*, ed. Fred Skolnik and Michael Berenbaum, 2nd ed. (Detroit: Macmillan, 2007), 8:508; contra Stolz, *TLOT*, 2:638, who calls this example a "cardiac injury."

[12] See Prov 23:34; 30:19; Ezek 27:4, 25–27; 28:2, 8; Ps 46:3.

[13] Ginsberg, *Encyclopedia Judaica*, 8:509, similarly critiqued by Stolz, *TLOT*, 2:638–39.

[14] Isa 33:18; Pss 19:15; 49:4; Job 8:10; Eccl 5:1. See below.

[15] See Ps 38:11 where לִבִּי "my heart" is parallel with כֹחִי "my strength" (cited above).

[16] See BDB, 703.

vitality." The same notion appears in Judg 19:8 in the Levite's retrieval of his concubine when her father presses him: "Please, sustain (סְעָד־נָא) your *lēbāb*," after which the narrative states that the two of them ate. This idea applies to the strength of an animal, so that a man of valor is compared to the לֵב of a lion: "Even he who is valiant, whose *lēb* is like the lion's *lēb*, will indeed melt" (2 Sam 17:10).[17] One's vital force can waste away, commonly expressed in the idiom utilizing the verb מסס "to melt" with (לֵב(ב) as subject. Following the Israelites' debilitating defeat at Ai, the narrative states: וַיִּמַּס לְבַב־הָעָם וַיְהִי לְמָיִם "the people's *lēbāb* melted and became as water" (Josh 7:5). All such examples occur amidst moments of crisis that have a paralyzing effect on individuals, thus liquefying their vital energy.[18]

Will/desire

Biblical Hebrew (לֵב(ב) indicates the will or desire of individuals. (לֵב(ב) expresses this meaning in contexts where individuals are moved to respond to an external or internal influence, either negatively (compliance) or positively (resistance). The will is sometimes swayed in terms of allegiance, which is aptly demonstrable in David's ability to regain the loyalty of the elders of Judah after Absalom's death: "And he inclined the *lēbāb* of all the men of Judah as one man" (2 Sam 19:15). The positive notion of the will can also express an internal compulsion, as in the case of one's free desire to give an offering: מֵאֵת כָּל־אִישׁ אֲשֶׁר יִדְּבֶנּוּ לִבּוֹ תִּקְחוּ אֶת־תְּרוּמָתִי "From everyone whose *lēb* compels him you may receive my contribution" (Exod 25:2).[19] The opposite of such generosity is evident when the will is bad: נָתוֹן תִּתֵּן לוֹ וְלֹא־יֵרַע לְבָבְךָ בְּתִתְּךָ לוֹ "You must indeed give. Do not let your *lēbāb* act badly when you give to him" (Deut 15:10).[20]

One of the most prominent examples of the will's resistance to external influence occurs in the heart of Pharaoh motif in Exodus 4–15.[21] The לֵב of Pharaoh stands in opposition to the command of Yahweh to release the people of Israel from bondage. In a series of exchanges between Moses and Pharaoh, the narrative describes the will of the Egyptian king as "strong" (חזק) and "heavy/dull/unmoved" (כבד),[22] which then leads both Pharaoh and Yahweh to "strengthen," "weigh down," and "harden" (קשׁה) his will even more against Yahweh's command.[23] The outcome

---

[17] Cf. the comparison made between the *npš* of Môtu and *npš lbʾim* "the *npš* of a lion" (*KTU* 1.5 I:14). Here, however, *npš* does not mean "vitality," as is common for *npš* elsewhere in Ugaritic (e.g., *KTU* 1.6 III:19; 1.17 I:36; 1.18 IV:25; 1.19 IV:36, 39; 2.33:23), but rather "throat."

[18] See also Deut 1:28; 7:5; Josh 2:11; 5:1. Similar idioms also include "failing (נפל) *lēb*" (1 Sam 17:32) and "weakness (רכך) of *lēb(āb)*" (Deut 20:3, 8; Lev 19:17; 26:36).

[19] Cf. Exod 35:5, 21, 22, 26, 29.

[20] Not to be confused with the idiom "bad *lēb(āb)*," meaning "sad" (see below).

[21] On this motif, see McAffee, "Pharaoh in Exodus 4–15," 331–54; Jonathan Grossman, "The Structural Paradigm of the Ten Plagues Narrative and the Hardening of Pharaoh's Heart," *VT* 64 (2014): 588–610.

[22] Exod 7:13, 14, 22; 8:19(15); 9:7, 35.

[23] Exod 4:21; 7:3; 8:15(11), 32(28); 9:12, 34; 10:1, 20, 27; 11:10; 13:15; 14:4, 8, 17.

of this battle of the gods is that the will of Pharaoh and his servants is "changed" (יהפך) toward the people of Israel.[24]

Other uses of (ב)לֵב for "will" indicate a defection of loyalty wherein the will is said to be turned away from something. The majority of such examples come from covenant contexts in which the people of Israel are in danger of turning their will away from Yahweh. In Deut 29:17, for instance, the people are warned of the individual or clan in their midst "whose *lēbāb* is turning away this day from Yahweh our God to serve the gods of those nations." Similarly, it is said of Solomon that when he was old his wives "turned away his *lēbāb* after other gods" (1 Kgs 11:4). Conversely, a person can redirect his will back to Yahweh by "inclining" (נטה) it as Moses instructs Israel: "Now remove the foreign gods that are in your midst and incline your *lēbāb* to Yahweh your God" (Josh 24:23).

Returning our attention to 1 Kgs 11:4, we see that the narrative explains that the will of Solomon was not "completely with Yahweh his God" (שָׁלֵם עִם־יְהוָה אֱלֹהָיו) as the will of David his father was.[25] The will as "whole" suggests undivided loyalty, or as it is elsewhere stated, again of David, that he walked "with integrity of *lēbāb* and uprightness" (בְּתָם־לֵבָב וּבְיֹשֶׁר) (1 Kgs 9:4).[26] The idiom "with all one's *lēb(āb)*" also falls in this category, as in the case of Jehu who did not walk in the Torah of Yahweh "with all his *lēbāb*" (בְּכָל־לְבָבוֹ) (2 Kgs 10:31), that is, with a complete sense of loyalty.

Many uses of (ב)לֵב occur in parallel with נֶפֶשׁ, "with all one's *lēb(āb)* and being." This merism becomes a technical expression of covenant loyalty.[27] The paradigmatic example of this usage is the Shema, which arranges these two anthropological terms with כל "all, every": "You shall love Yahweh your God with all your *lēbāb*, with all your *nepeš*, and with all your might" (Deut 6:5). The guiding principle of the Shema concerns the allegiance of Yahweh's covenant members, and the sphere in which that allegiance is to be demonstrated is the total person and his associations.[28] To love God with all one's heart certainly means to exercise

---

[24] Exod 14:5.

[25] Cf. 2 Kgs 20:3: Hezekiah states that he walked before Yahweh "in faithfulness and with a whole *lēbāb*" (בֶּאֱמֶת וּבְלֵבָב שָׁלֵם).

[26] There are differing opinions about the nature of David's heart, particularly his description as a "man after God's own *lēbāb*" (1 Sam 13:14). The Hebrew phrase is כִּלְבָבוֹ "according to his *lēbāb*." P. Kyle McCarter proposed that the meaning of this statement indicates that David was the man God sought according to his mind (i.e., the man he had in mind to be king in contrast to Saul as the choice of the people), and not that David was an extraordinary man of godliness (McCarter, *I Samuel*, 226). Recently, however, Benjamin M. Johnson has argued persuasively against McCarter in favor of the traditional interpretation that this expression refers to the character of David ("The Heart of Yahweh's Chosen One in 1 Samuel," *JBL* 131 [2012]: 455–66). A major issue underlying these two proposals is how one interprets לבב (1): according to his "will" = a man whose "will" is devoted to the "will" of Yahweh, or (2) according his "mind/thought" = the man whom God chooses. Texts that speak of David's (ב)לֵב being "whole" or "with integrity" would tend to support the former option, that is, that David's "will" was entirely devoted to the ways of Yahweh.

[27] Cf. Deut 4:29; 6:5; 10:12; 11:13, 18; 13:4; 26:16; 30:2, 6, 10; Josh 22:5; 23:14; 1 Sam 2:35 (of Yahweh); 1 Kgs 2:4; 8:48; 2 Kgs 23:3, 25.

[28] On the meaning of the Hebrew verb אהב according to its ancient Near Eastern covenant background, see William L. Moran, "The Ancient Near Eastern Background of the Love of God in

loyal devotion with all one's desire/will.[29] The New Testament evangelists Matthew and Mark expand this formula to include both "heart" (καρδία) and "mind" (διανοία).[30] Moshe Weinfeld points to later developments in Jewish thought in which (ב)לֵב was associated with the term דַּעַת "understanding," thus yielding a precedence for this expansion.[31] In the covenant formula "with all one's lēb(āb) and being," however, (ב)לֵב may simply denote the broader semantics of the term, including both "will" and "mind/thought." In other words, the entire orientation encompasses one's allegiance to God up to the deepest recesses of the inner person.[32] This observation leads us to consider the final category of usage for Hebrew (ב)לֵב as "mind/thought."

Mind/thought

The largest category of usage for Hebrew (ב)לֵב is "mind/thought." Most lexical studies of this term have typically devised an additional category for its emotive aspects, but it is better to treat the emotive sense as a subset of "mind/thought."[33]

This term generally denotes the inner cognitive processes of human individuals. The idea becomes clear in the following example from Deuteronomy where the lexeme occurs with the verb ידע: "Know with your lēbāb that as a man disciplines his son Yahweh your God is disciplining you" (Deut 8:5). Similarly, Samuel tells Saul that he will eat with him and that on the next day he will tell him "everything that is in your lēbāb" (וְכֹל אֲשֶׁר בִּלְבָבְךָ) (1 Sam 9:19). An exalted (ב)לֵב indicates lofty ideas about one's worth, so that the future Israelite king is urged to carefully observe the statutes of God "so as to not lift up his lēbāb (רוּם־לְבָבוֹ) above his brothers" (Deut 17:20).[34] Just before Samuel anoints David as the next king of Israel, Yahweh reminds him that "man looks with the eyes (לַעֵינַיִם), but Yahweh sees the lēbāb (לַלֵּבָב)" (1 Sam 16:7).[35] Each of these examples refer to cognition.

Several idioms occur involving Hebrew (ב)לֵב as "mind/thought." To set (שׂית/שׂים) something to mind means to ponder or consider it, as David pondered the words

---

Deuteronomy," *CBQ* 25 (1963): 77–87; cf. Moshe Weinfeld, "Covenant Terminology in the Ancient Near East and Its Influence on the West," *JAOS* 93 (1973): 191–3.

[29] Patrick D. Miller defines it as "an undivided loyalty, both good and evil impulses." See *Deuteronomy*, Interpretation (Louisville: Westminster John Knox, 1990), 103.

[30] Matt 22:37; Mark 12:30.

[31] Weinfeld, *Deuteronomy 1–11*, AB 5 (New York: Doubleday, 1991), 338–39. Weinfeld cites the LXX as translating לבב as διανοία here, but actually it reads καρδία.

[32] Jeffrey H. Tigay states that it "refers to the interior of the body, conceived of as the seat of thought, intention, and feeling." See *Deuteronomy*, The JPS Torah Commentary (Philadelphia: Jewish Publication Society, 1996), 77.

[33] See Stolz's categories (d) psychological aspects, (e) intellectual functions, and (f) all dimensions of human existence (*TLOT*, 2:639–40). Fabry lists categories (3) affective center (elemental emotions, individual emotions, wrath, and love/hate/gratitude) and (4) noetic center (cognition, memory, wisdom, and confusion/folly) (*TDOT* 7:414–23). Waltke comes closest to our divisions, devising three overall categories of usage for the human (ב)לֵב: emotion, thought, or will (*TWOT*, "(ב)לֵב," 466).

[34] Cf. 2 Kgs 14:10.

[35] Cf. 1 Kgs 8:39.

of the Philistine king Achish (1 Sam 21:3) or as Pharaoh failed to do in response to the plagues of Yahweh (Exod 7:23).[36] The (לֵב) is commonly construed with terms of speaking (e.g., דבר, אמר), which indicates internal speech whereby a person speaks in his mind (i.e., speaking to one's heart)[37] or external speech—someone verbalizes what is on his mind.[38] Another related idiom is to place something into the (לֵב) of someone else, as God placed it in Solomon's mind (נָתַן אֱלֹהִים בְּלִבּוֹ) to listen to divine wisdom (1 Kgs 10:24). A human being can also speak in such a way that it reaches the innermost recesses (mind/thought) of the individual. In these cases, (לֵב) indicates an emotional/intimate connection. For example, Shechem, son of Hamor, loved Jacob's daughter Dinah and "spoke to the *lēb* of the young woman" (Gen 34:3). The idea seems to be that a person speaks "deeply" to someone (i.e., speech that comforts, speech that convinces).[39] A person's (לֵב) can be "stolen" when someone acts deceptively, thus keeping knowledge about intentions out of the other person's mind.[40]

Numerous passages refer to those "skillful (חכם) of *lēb(āb)*"[41] who are essentially skilled artisans. The expression "breadth/width of *lēb(āb)*" describes someone possessing intellectual acumen.[42] The opposite is to be "lacking (חסר) of *lēb(āb)*" as it is routinely said of the fool in the book of Proverbs.[43] A related idiom is the capacity to produce plans in one's (לֵב). The prophet Nathan instructs David to go ahead and do "all that is in your *lēbāb*" (2 Sam 7:3) as it related to his intention to build a temple for Yahweh.[44]

In certain contexts, the mind can become numb and unresponsive as it did for Jacob when his sons told him Joseph was still alive (Gen 45:26). It can die (וַיָּמָת לִבּוֹ) and become like stone as in the case of Nabal (1 Sam 25:37).[45] In Isa 6:10 the prophet is commanded to make the (לֵב) of the people dull (הַשְׁמֵן לֵב־הָעָם). In other cases, it denotes a component of the internal self (conscience?) that can strike the broader thoughts of the individual. Two examples come from the life of David, and both describe his realization that he had sinned: once against King Saul (1 Sam 24:6)

---

[36] Cf. Exod 9:21; 1 Sam 4:13; 9:20; 25:25; 2 Sam 13:20, 33; 18:3; 19:20.

[37] Gen 8:21; 17:17; 24:45; 27:41; 1 Sam 1:13; 27:1; 1 Kgs 12:26.

[38] Judg 16:18.

[39] Gen 50:21; Judg 19:3; 2 Sam 19:8.

[40] When Jacob "steals the mind of Laban" in Gen 31:20. See also 2 Sam 15:6 where Absalom "steals" the hearts of the men of Israel away from his father David. This particular idiom, however, may instead reflect the meaning "will/favor" discussed above—he stole the favor of the people from his father.

[41] Exod 31:6; 35:25, 35; 36:1, 2, 8; 1 Kgs 3:12.

[42] 1 Kgs 5:9.

[43] I.e., "lacking *lēb(āb)*" (Prov 6:32; 7:7; 9:4, 16; 10:13; 11:12; 12:11; 15:21).

[44] Cf. Gen 6:5; 1 Kgs 8:17, 18; 12:33.

[45] We do not find convincing the idea that this example describes a physical heart attack, as Stolz has suggested (*TLOT*, 2:638). Furthermore, his contention that "medical knowledge concerning the heart" was necessarily absent in Israel and in surrounding cultures (citing J. Hempel, "Heilung als Symbol und Wirklichkeit," *NAWG* 3 [1958]: 253) is not entirely valid. For one, there seems to have been a fairly sophisticated medical knowledge about this human organ in Egyptian thought; see Robert K. Ritner, "The Cardiovascular System in Ancient Egyptian Thought," *JNES* 65 (2006): 99–109.

and once against Yahweh in the unauthorized census, "David's *lēb* struck him (וַיַּ֤ךְ לֵב־דָּוִד֙ אֹת֔וֹ) after he had thus numbered the people" (2 Sam 24:10).

Finally, a large category of idioms constructed with the (לְ)בָב as "mind/thought" portray emotional processes. In each case, the (לֵ)בָב is acting in some way that produces emotions, whether good or bad, and is accompanied by various modifiers expressing emotive processes. A "good (טוב) *lēb(āb)*" indicates happy feelings,[46] while a "bad (רע) *lēbāb*" means the individual is sad.[47] Undesirable feelings such as a "trembling (חרד) *lēb*" for emotional distress[48] or "stumbling (מִשְׁכוֹל) of *lēb*" indicating regret[49] are attested. What is important to observe about these emotive aspects is that they require qualifiers, therefore suggesting that, according to Hebrew thought, feelings were conceived as a function of the mind so that cognition and emotion arise from the same anthropological source.[50]

No one word can perfectly capture every facet of semantic analysis. Nonetheless, our treatment of (לֵ)בָב illustrates an application of the method outlined above and serves as a guide for students to consult as they conduct their own semantic analysis of Hebrew words.

---

[46] E.g., Deut 28:28; Judg 16:25; 18:20; 19:6, 9, 22; 1 Sam 25:36; 2 Sam 13:28; 1 Kgs 8:66; 21:7.

[47] 1 Sam 1:8.

[48] E.g., 1 Sam 4:13; 28:5. Cf. "dread (פחד) of *lēbāb*" (Deut 28:67).

[49] 1 Sam 25:31.

[50] For this reason, we have not devised a separate category of usage for "emotion" as other lexicographers have done; note Fabry's categories (3) "affective center" and (4) "noetic center" in *TDOT*, 7:414–23.

SYNTACTIC ANALYSIS

Syntax is the study of how morphemes, lexemes, phrases, and clauses are put together into larger discourse units. On the most basic level, syntactic studies describe how these elements are arranged and the relationships that construct meaning. The last century or so has produced a large corpus of theoretical approaches to syntax. These theories advance very different ways to investigate syntactic structures and to understand the fundamental interaction between syntax and semantics.[1] Yet, a basic analysis of Hebrew word order and grammatical relationships can be fruitful regardless of one's theoretical assumptions.

This approach focuses on clause-level syntax in BH narrative. It begins with isolating the essential constituent of each clause and describing the order. The exercise of identifying the main clause elements is vital to understanding basic syntax. Beyond this application, word order variation can reveal subtle clause emphases, parallelism, pragmatic information like topicalization, and discourse features like backgrounding.

CLAUSES AND SENTENCES

A clause expresses a proposition and contains, at least, a predicate and an implied or expressed subject. The predicate may include a verb phrase—that is, a verb, objects, and modifiers—or be verbless. Multiple clauses can be linked to form a sentence.

Most Hebrew clauses rely on VO word order. The object [O] follows the verb [V] (e.g., Jonah 1:3). Subjects [S], when expressed, may come before or after the verb (v. 5) and usually precede the object (vv. 4, 10). In clauses with a consecutive form (*wayyiqtol* or *wəqātal*), the expected word order is VSO. Modifying elements [M] typically follow the verb. Most short modifiers are found next to the verb (v. 6), and longer modifying phrases come at the end of the clause (vv. 4, 8).

---

[1] Giorgio Graffi, *200 Years of Syntax. A Critical Study* (Amsterdam: Benjamins, 2001).

Jonah 1:3

וַיִּתֵּן שְׂכָרָהּ

He paid its fare.

Jonah 1:5

וַיִּירְאוּ הַמַּלָּחִים . . . וְיוֹנָה יָרַד אֶל־יַרְכְּתֵי הַסְּפִינָה

The **mariners** were afraid. . . . But **Jonah** had gone down into the bowels of the ship.

Jonah 1:4

וַיהֹוָה הֵטִיל רוּחַ־גְּדוֹלָה אֶל־הַיָּם

Now **Yahweh** threw a great wind into the sea.

Jonah 1:10

כִּי־יָדְעוּ הָאֲנָשִׁים כִּי־מִלִּפְנֵי יְהוָה הוּא בֹרֵחַ

For **the men** knew that **he** was fleeing from before Yahweh.

Jonah 1:6

וַיִּקְרַב אֵלָיו רַב הַחֹבֵל

The ship captain approached **him**.

Jonah 1:8

וַיִּפֹּל הַגּוֹרָל עַל־יוֹנָה

The lot fell **on Jonah**.

Unlike the strict word order of English clauses, the order of constituents is flexible in Biblical Hebrew. Almost any constituent can be reordered to focus on that clause element. For example, the object may come before the verb (v. 9).[2] This arrangement can be used to highlight an important aspect of the clause.

Jonah 1:9

וְאֶת־יְהֹוָה אֱלֹהֵי הַשָּׁמַיִם אֲנִי יָרֵא

I fear Yahweh the God of heaven.

The addition of a subject to a clause with a finite verb can indicate a shift in topic. Since Hebrew finite verbs include the basic grammatical information about their subjects, their presence is nonobligatory.[3] Jonah 1:4 begins with an expressed subject and a nonconsecutive verb. It signals a contrast with Jonah's activities in

---

[2] A constituent is rarely interrupted. The final relative clause of v. 9 (אֲשֶׁר־עָשָׂה אֶת־הַיָּם וְאֶת־הַיַּבָּשָׁה) may demonstrate an unusual separation. One would expect the object to follow the verb before the relative (i.e., אֲנִי יָרֵא אֲשֶׁר־עָשָׂה אֶת־הַיָּם וְאֶת־הַיַּבָּשָׁה). The object (אֱלֹהֵי הַשָּׁמַיִם) is fronted while the relative remains in its expected location. This augmentation produces the appearance of a divided complement.

[3] The subject is not optional for clauses with nonfinite verbs, for example: כִּי הַיָּם הוֹלֵךְ וְסֹעֵר "For the sea was really storming" (v. 11).

verse 3 by shifting the topic to Yahweh to focus on his reaction to the prophet's insubordination. The narrative continues with the onset of a storm. The last clause highlights the result on the ship. In the ensuing narrative of verse 5, the sailors' dire distress and heavenward plea is contrasted with Jonah's disinterested descent. The change in verbal form and the fronting of the subject highlights this juxtaposition.

Jonah 1:4

וַיהוָ֡ה הֵטִ֣יל רֽוּחַ־גְּדוֹלָה֮ אֶל־הַיָּם֒ וַיְהִ֤י סַֽעַר־גָּדוֹל֙ בַּיָּ֔ם וְהָ֣אֳנִיָּ֔ה חִשְּׁבָ֖ה לְהִשָּׁבֵֽר

Now **Yahweh** threw a great wind into the sea. A great storm came on the sea, and **the ship** threatened to break apart.

Jonah 1:5

וְיוֹנָ֗ה יָרַד֙ אֶל־יַרְכְּתֵ֣י הַסְּפִינָ֔ה

But **Jonah** had gone down into the bowels of the ship.

Verbless clauses include a predicate without an overt verb. The verbless clause identifies salvation as Yahweh's reaction to waywardness and rebellion. The order of the subject and predicate may signal an identifying or classifying relationship. Francis I. Andersen suggests that definite NP predicates identify the subject with the basic word order Subject–Predicate [S–P].[4] These clauses indicate who or what is being identified (Exod 6:2). At the end of Jonah's prayer (2:10), the question is what God will do in response to contrition.

Jonah 2:10

יְשׁוּעָ֖תָה לַֽיהוָֽה

Salvation is Yahweh's.

Exod 6:2

אֲנִ֖י יְהוָֽה

I am Yahweh

An indefinite predicate, on the other hand, classifies its subject and has the opposite order, Predicate–Subject [P–S]. A classification clause expresses what the subject is like. Jonah's response to the sailor's questions follows this descriptive pattern (Jonah 1:9).

Jonah 1:9

עִבְרִ֥י אָנֹ֖כִי

I am a Hebrew.

---

[4] Andersen, *Hebrew Verbless Clause*. See the helpful summary and examples in *IBHS* §8.4.

CASE STUDY: JONAH 1

The exegetical value of investigating clause word order is evident when combined with other pragmatic observations and discourse relationships.[5] We suggest students practice on a narrative passage of their choosing and follow five basic steps:

1. Divide the verses into clauses (and translate).
2. Diagram the basic clause constituents (Subjects, Verbs, Objects, Modifiers).
3. Describe each constituent that does not follow the expected word order, that is, any marked or highlighted elements.
4. Determine the function of the clause linkers.
5. Detail the discourse type (e.g., Mainline Narrative, Background, Direct Discourse)

In the following example, we summarize the basic arrangement and discourse features of Jonah 1. The mainline narrative is positioned on the right. These clauses indicate foregrounded sequenced events. Direct discourse, background, and various non-narrative (discursive) clauses are to the left of this column. In the outermost columns, a simple ordered set is used to outline the elements of each clause (e.g., S–V–O–M; in the following chart N represents Negation, and Voc Vocative).

JONAH 1 SYNTACTIC ANALYSIS			
OTHER ELEMENTS		**MAINLINE NARRATIVE**	
Discourse (Yahweh to Jonah)		¹וַיְהִי֙ דְּבַר־יְהֹוָ֔ה אֶל־יוֹנָ֥ה בֶן־אֲמִתַּ֖י	V–S–M–M
V	²ק֥וּם	לֵאמֹֽר:	
V–M	לֵ֤ךְ אֶל־נִֽינְוֵ֙ה הָעִ֣יר הַגְּדוֹלָ֔ה		
V–M	וּקְרָ֣א עָלֶ֑יהָ		
V–S–M	כִּֽי־עָלְתָ֥ה רָעָתָ֖ם לְפָנָֽי:		

---

[5] For a helpful guide to introduce various issues in text linguistics, see Matthew H. Patton and Frederic Clarke Putnam, *Basics of Hebrew Discourse: A Guide to Working with Hebrew Prose and Poetry* (Grand Rapids: Zondervan, 2019). See further Walter R. Bodine, ed., *Discourse Analysis of Biblical Literature: What It Is and What It Offers* (Atlanta: Scholars, 1995). Also, compare the studies collected in Ellen van Wolde, ed., *Narrative Syntax and the Hebrew Bible: Papers of the Tilburg Conference 1996* (Leiden: Brill, 1997).

JONAH 1 SYNTACTIC ANALYSIS		
OTHER ELEMENTS	**MAINLINE NARRATIVE**	
Background	³ וַיָּ֤קָם יוֹנָה֙ לִבְרֹ֣חַ תַּרְשִׁ֔ישָׁה	V–S–M
S–V–O–M ⁴וַֽיהוָ֗ה הֵטִ֤יל רֽוּחַ־גְּדוֹלָה֙ אֶל־הַיָּ֔ם	מִלִּפְנֵ֖י יְהוָ֑ה	
	וַיֵּ֣רֶד יָפ֗וֹ	V–M
	וַיִּמְצָ֤א אָנִיָּ֣ה ׀ בָּאָ֣ה תַרְשִׁ֔ישׁ	V–O–M
	וַיִּתֵּ֣ן שְׂכָרָ֗הּ	V–O
	וַיֵּ֤רֶד בָּהּ֙ לָב֤וֹא עִמָּהֶם֙ תַּרְשִׁ֔ישָׁה מִלִּפְנֵ֖י יְהוָֽה:	V–M–M
Background	⁽⁴⁾ וַֽיהוָ֗ה הֵטִ֤יל סַֽעַר־גָּד֖וֹל בַּיָּ֑ם	V–S–M
S–V–M ⁽⁴⁾וְהָ֣אֳנִיָּ֔ה חִשְּׁבָ֖ה לְהִשָּׁבֵֽר:		
Background	⁵ וַיִּֽירְא֣וּ הַמַּלָּחִ֗ים	V–S
S–V–M ⁽⁵⁾וְיוֹנָ֗ה יָרַד֙ אֶל־יַרְכְּתֵ֣י הַסְּפִינָ֔ה	וַֽיִּזְעֲקוּ֮ אִ֣ישׁ אֶל־אֱלֹהָיו֒	V–M
	וַיָּטִ֨לוּ אֶת־הַכֵּלִ֜ים אֲשֶׁ֤ר בָּֽאֳנִיָּה֙ אֶל־הַיָּ֔ם לְהָקֵ֖ל מֵֽעֲלֵיהֶ֑ם	V–O–M
	⁽⁵⁾ וַֽיִּשְׁכַּ֖ב	V
	וַיֵּֽרָדַֽם:	V
Discourse (Captain to Jonah)	⁶ וַיִּקְרַ֤ב אֵלָיו֙ רַ֣ב הַחֹבֵ֔ל	V–M–O
S–P ⁽⁶⁾מַה־לְּךָ֣ נִרְדָּ֑ם	וַיֹּ֥אמֶר ל֖וֹ	V–M
V קוּם		
V–M קְרָ֣א אֶל־אֱלֹהֶ֔יךָ		
V–S–M אוּלַ֞י יִתְעַשֵּׁ֧ת הָאֱלֹהִ֛ים לָ֖נוּ		
N–V וְלֹ֥א נֹאבֵֽד:		
Discourse (Sailors to Themselves):	⁷ וַיֹּאמְר֞וּ אִ֣ישׁ אֶל־רֵעֵ֗הוּ	V–M
V ⁽⁷⁾לְכוּ֙		
V–O וְנַפִּ֣ילָה גֽוֹרָל֔וֹת		
V–M וְנֵ֣דְעָ֔ה בְּשֶׁלְּמִ֛י הָרָעָ֥ה הַזֹּ֖את לָ֑נוּ		
	⁽⁷⁾ וַיַּפִּ֖לוּ גּֽוֹרָל֑וֹת	V–O
	וַיִּפֹּ֥ל הַגּוֹרָ֖ל עַל־יוֹנָֽה:	V–S–M

JONAH 1 SYNTACTIC ANALYSIS			
OTHER ELEMENTS		**MAINLINE NARRATIVE**	
Discourse (Sailors to Jonah)		8 וַיֹּאמְרוּ אֵלָיו	V–M
V-M-M	‏(8) הַגִּידָה־נָּא לָנוּ בַּאֲשֶׁר לְמִי־ הָרָעָה הַזֹּאת לָנוּ		
P-S	מַה־מְּלַאכְתְּךָ		
M-V	וּמֵאַיִן תָּבוֹא		
P-S	מָה אַרְצֶךָ		
PS	וְאֵי־מִזֶּה עַם אָתָּה:		
Discourse (Jonah to Sailors)		‏9 וַיֹּאמֶר אֲלֵיהֶם	V–M
P-S	‏(9) עִבְרִי אָנֹכִי		
O-S-V	וְאֶת־יְהוָה אֱלֹהֵי הַשָּׁמַיִם אֲנִי יָרֵא		
V-O	אֲשֶׁר־עָשָׂה אֶת־הַיָּם וְאֶת־הַיַּבָּשָׁה:		
Discourse (Sailors to Jonah)		‏10 וַיִּירְאוּ הָאֲנָשִׁים יִרְאָה גְדוֹלָה	V–S–M
		וַיֹּאמְרוּ אֵלָיו	V–M
O–V	‏(10) מַה־זֹּאת עָשִׂיתָ		
Background			
V–S–O	‏(10) כִּי־יָדְעוּ הָאֲנָשִׁים כִּי־מִלִּפְנֵי יְהוָה הוּא בֹרֵחַ		
V–M	כִּי הִגִּיד לָהֶם:		
Discourse (Sailors to Jonah)		‏11 וַיֹּאמְרוּ אֵלָיו	V–M
O–V–M	‏(11) מַה־נַּעֲשֶׂה לָּךְ		
V–S–M	וְיִשְׁתֹּק הַיָּם מֵעָלֵינוּ		
Background			
S–V	‏(11) כִּי הַיָּם הוֹלֵךְ וְסֹעֵר:		
Discourse (Jonah to Sailors)		‏12 וַיֹּאמֶר אֲלֵיהֶם	V–M
V	‏(12) שָׂאוּנִי		
V-O-M	וַהֲטִילֻנִי אֶל־הַיָּם		
V-S-M	וְיִשְׁתֹּק הַיָּם מֵעֲלֵיכֶם		
V-S-O	כִּי יוֹדֵעַ אָנִי כִּי בְשֶׁלִּי הַסַּעַר הַגָּדוֹל הַזֶּה עֲלֵיכֶם:		

JONAH 1 SYNTACTIC ANALYSIS	
OTHER ELEMENTS	**MAINLINE NARRATIVE**
Background	¹³ וַיַּחְתְּרוּ הָאֲנָשִׁים לְהָשִׁיב V–S–M
N–V ⁽¹³⁾ וְלֹא יָכֹלוּ	אֶל־הַיַּבָּשָׁה
Background	
S–V–M ⁽¹³⁾ כִּי הַיָּם הוֹלֵךְ וְסֹעֵר עֲלֵיהֶם:	
Discourse (Sailors to Yahweh)	¹⁴ וַיִּקְרְאוּ אֶל־יְהוָה V–M
Voc–V–M ⁽¹⁴⁾ אָנָּה יְהוָה אַל־נָא נֹאבְדָה	וַיֹּאמְרוּ V
בְּנֶפֶשׁ הָאִישׁ הַזֶּה	
N–V–M–O וְאַל־תִּתֵּן עָלֵינוּ דָּם נָקִיא	
S–Voc–M– כִּי־אַתָּה יְהוָה כַּאֲשֶׁר חָפַצְתָּ	
V עָשִׂיתָ:	
	וַיִּשְׂאוּ אֶת־יוֹנָה ¹⁵ V–S–M–O
	וַיְטִלֻהוּ אֶל־הַיָּם V–O–M
	וַיַּעֲמֹד הַיָּם מִזַּעְפּוֹ: V–O
	וַיִּירְאוּ הָאֲנָשִׁים יִרְאָה גְדוֹלָה ¹⁶ V–S–M–O
	אֶת־יְהוָה
	וַיִּזְבְּחוּ־זֶבַח לַיהוָה V–O–M
	וַיִּדְּרוּ נְדָרִים: V–O

APPENDIX A

CONTINUING WITH HEBREW

Think back to your last road trip. Maybe you were a young teen heading out West with your grandparents to see the Grand Canyon. Or you hiked with friends in the Appalachian Mountains. Perhaps it was a leisurely drive down the Pacific Coast Highway with your Labrador hanging out the passenger window. How you or your travel companions prepared for the journey (or maybe didn't prepare) is instructive for thinking wisely about your next steps with Hebrew.

Learning Hebrew is like taking a trip. Most of the trip's joy depends on either pure luck or judicious planning. Few of us have the innate compass to succeed on a whim. So, assuming you don't want to wing it, ask yourself five basic questions about continuing your Hebrew trek:

1. What is your desired destination?
2. Why is it important to go there?
3. How do you get there?
4. Who else is traveling or has traveled along this way?
5. What do you need to take with you?

Let us look at each in more detail.

WHAT IS YOUR DESIRED DESTINATION?

Like many students first starting to learn Hebrew at college or seminary, your original destination may have been to survive the first year of a grammar course or arrive at the end of this textbook. You did it. You are there. Take a moment and consider that accomplishment. You have spent months learning a foreign writing system, odd sounding sounds, unfamiliar vocabulary, seemingly unending paradigms, wearisome rules of grammar, and endless exceptions to those rules. But despite all those challenges, you have succeeded in reading the Bible that Jesus read! Of course, there is a lot more Hebrew to read and know. But remember you didn't know a *kap* from a *pataḥ* only a little while ago. You found the motivation to keep going even when you botched a quiz, forgot an "easy" vocabulary word, or jumbled the vowel reduction rules for the twentieth time. You arrived at this goal, but—and this is a *big* "but"—your Hebrew journey doesn't end here.

The pertinent question is now: What's next? What will you do with this newly honed skill and awareness? We discuss a few tangible next steps below, but this query is an opportunity to consider the place of Hebrew in your life. After more than a year of study, consider how you have changed and perhaps how your path may be altered on account of your effort and study. To echo the aphorism of the Heraclitean philosophers: *everything flows* (κινεῖται καὶ ῥεῖ . . . τὰ πάντα, quoted by Plato in *Cratylus* 402a) or more popularly remembered as "No one steps in the same river twice." Things are not as they once were.

Let us suggest three possible destinations to consider. Each of these goals is attainable for you. They are listed in order of consequence and increasing commitment.

Meditate and Pray (Parts of) the Hebrew Bible

Our Lord prayed the words of Scripture with his last breaths. According to Matt 27:46, his final comfort was Ps 22:2. The Hebrew of this verse reads:

אֵלִי אֵלִי לָמָה עֲזַבְתָּנִי

My God, my God, why have you abandoned me?

In our times of greatest need and failures, God invites us to cry out to him by name:

עַד־אָנָה יְהוָה תִּשְׁכָּחֵנִי נֶצַח

"How long, Yahweh? Will you forget me forever?" (Ps 13:2).

Through tears, we might echo the faithful command of Neh 8:10:

וְאַל־תֵּעָצֵבוּ כִּי־חֶדְוַת יְהוָה הִיא מָעֻזְּכֶם

"Do not be grieved for the joy of Yahweh is your refuge."

Christians daily repeat the faithful words of Rahab echoed in the creeds:

יְהוָה אֱלֹהֵיכֶם הוּא אֱלֹהִים בַּשָּׁמַיִם מִמַּעַל וְעַל־הָאָרֶץ מִתָּחַת

"Yahweh your God is God in the heavens above and on the earth below" (Josh 2:11).

The faithful bring to mind the greatest commandment:

שְׁמַע יִשְׂרָאֵל יְהוָה אֱלֹהֵינוּ יְהוָה אֶחָד (Deut 6:4).

God's declaration of his self-proclaimed character requires deep reflection:

יְהוָה। יְהוָה אֵל רַחוּם וְחַנּוּן אֶרֶךְ אַפַּיִם וְרַב־חֶסֶד וֶאֱמֶת (Exod 34:6).

These foundational words can be on your lips, but only if you are committed to memorize and learn them.

Use Electronic Tools Wisely

Beyond meditation and prayer, Bible students should want to engage wisely with the overwhelming data available online and in electronic tools. Information is never self-interpreting. Even the morphological data embedded within your electronic Hebrew Bible are built on certain assumptions. It must be sifted and mediated upon carefully. And the pressures of time and individual responsibilities will always require abbreviated learning. If electronic tools are available, we would be wise to use them to the extent they are functional and helpful. They can speed up research, help faulty memories, and point to valuable resources. Yet, a sage interpreter must learn the intended use of each tool, the value of each instrument, and the limits of its effectiveness.

Read the Hebrew Bible Fluently

This destination is *undeniably* attainable. The proof is that you are reading this sentence! You likely don't remember, but you once could not read English. You worked hard to learn English words, the different ways letters are written, and the proper way to put together phrases. And now, you can read fluently. While the process likely looked different than learning Hebrew, you have a proven track record of success. You can do it again.

Your response may be to think that none of the listed destinations is possible for you. They sound too lofty. Possibly they are. However, please take each as a pre-planned excursion. You can alter the path along the way. Whatever you do, do not finish this chapter without considering where you might go next. The busyness of life and the pressures of the immediate will distract you from the important, if you fail to have a destination.

WHY IS IT IMPORTANT TO GO THERE?

This question is possibly most critical of all. While our actions are certainly motivated by a range of factors, if you do not have vibrant motivation and clear reasons, there is little hope that you will continue reading Hebrew.

Let us suggest three incentives. First, continuing Hebrew can help you to *know God more*. It is not possible to know a person who you have never engaged. If you do not listen to someone's words whether written or aloud, you do not know that person. Can you imagine only ever speaking to your spouse through an interpreter? You can skip that intermediary and go straight to the source. Christian theologians refer to special revelation as how God chooses to disclose himself. The Bible holds primary place in our endeavor to know who God is and how he acts in the world.

Two-thirds of the Christian's Bible is written in Hebrew. What would your relationships look like if you ignored more than half of what a friend said?

Second, continuing Hebrew can help you *build assurance* in your faith. While you might uphold the truthfulness of the Scriptures, such an affirmation is not the same as knowing the Scriptures' truth. From the earliest days of the Church, Christians have heard or asked particularly difficult questions about the place of the Hebrew Bible in the lives of New Testament believers. Many of these are of concern even in our modern times. Questions can bring doubt upon the meaning, purpose, or veracity of the Bible. It might be tempting to ignore these misgivings. But rarely does ignorance solve difficult problems. We encourage the opposite approach. Pray fervently. Seek understanding. Learn deeply.

Third, continuing Hebrew can help you gain *wisdom for life*. As we learn God's word, our understanding of his creation increases, our reverence for his instructions intensifies, and our care for our neighbor grows. The Scriptures guide us into true living and truly living. They show us God's world through God's word. What a worthy and worthwhile endeavor!

HOW DO YOU GET THERE?

We have five suggestions based on the advice of previous Hebrew travelers.

Start with a proper self-evaluation. Be kind but honest with yourself. What has been most difficult thing about learning Hebrew? Where have I seen the most improvement? What resources are available in this task? What motivations, incentives, or disciplines will best support the journey?

Begin with a head start. If you are an undergraduate or graduate student, take another course. Your program may not require any more Hebrew classes. But remember the curriculum is the minimum requirement for the degree. It is the starting place. So, join a reading course or group. Find others to encourage. Give yourself a bit more structured time before striking out on your own.

Commit to study from the Hebrew text when teaching or preaching. If you take on the humbling task to interpret and teach the word of God, does it not make sense to use the capability and skills you have learned to do it to the best of your abilities? You would not expect that the person translating your Bible merely looked at another English version. So too, you can engage God's word using Hebrew. Your listeners may never know Hebrew, but they will value your expertise and trust your faithful study.

Use daily time to read Hebrew. Make it a routine. Five minutes. Ten minutes. The number of minutes matters less than the frequency. Regular day-to-day reading is fundamental. You may not feel much is happening, but the trip is measured as you look back over a week, month, year, and decade. By covering only *one verse* a day in a year, you can read any of the books in the Minor Prophets as well as Song of Songs, Ruth, Lamentations, Esther, Ecclesiastes, Ezra, or a twelve-chapter sequence in the Torah. *Three verses* a day open the books of Leviticus, Deuteronomy, Proverbs, Job, and any of the remaining historical books. Practicing a daily reading of *five verses* enables you to cover any biblical book or more than seventy percent of the Psalms in only one year.

Use Sunday (or another day weekly) to focus on longer reading times as a way to rest from weekly duties and typical distractions.

Who Else Is Traveling or Has Traveled along This Way?

Even the best made plans will need to change from time to time. We may even face an unforeseen detour. These are moments to pause, reset, and restart. Don't give up. It is more likely your trip will get back on course if you are traveling with someone.

Consider how you can build accountability into your trip. Who is in front of you along the way who can answer questions and encourage you? Who might be interested in learning Hebrew that you can help start? Bring someone along. Don't do it alone.

TRAVEL TIPS

1. Find others and get together to read in person or via video.
2. Use online resources like www.dailydoseofhebrew.com or a podcast that discuss the biblical text.
3. Look for a weeklong or weekend class in person or online to continue learning from a scholar or tutor.
4. Be encouraged by others. Several recent resources highlight the rewards of studying the biblical languages.[1]
5. Last of all: don't give up the journey. Keep reading, reading, reading Hebrew. It is worth it.

WHAT DO YOU NEED TO TAKE WITH YOU?

Beyond prioritizing small amounts of time, continuing with the discipline of reading, and finding encouraging strategies, such as reading with others, a few specialized tools will help with your adventure. A corresponding bibliography follows the text at the end of this chapter.

---

[1] Catherine L. McDowell and Philip H. Towner, *The Rewards of Learning Greek and Hebrew: Discovering the Richness of the Bible in Its Original Languages* (Peabody, MA: Hendrickson, 2021). Adam J. Howell, Benjamin L. Merkle, and Robert L. Plummer, *Hebrew for Life: Strategies for Learning, Retaining, and Reviving Biblical Hebrew* (Grand Rapids: Baker Academic, 2020).

Hebrew Bibles

The complete scholarly Hebrew Bible is called *Biblia Hebraica Stuttgartensia* [*BHS*]. It is in the process of being replaced by *Biblia Hebraica Quinta* [*BHQ*], but only some of the individual books are published (see further details in Guided Lesson א: Textual Criticism). The essentially same Hebrew text, based on the Firkovich Codex (B 19A), is used in all major printed and electronic editions.[2] The differences relate to how the notes are handled. The *BHS* and *BHQ* have text-critical notations. An electronic edition may be synced with a morphological database. Each of the three reader's Bibles have various vocabulary and morphology notes. Think of the comparison between a CSB Study Bible, the CSB mobile app, and a CSB Reference Bible. The text is the same, but the accompanying material is different.

Readers/Text Commentaries

Several books provide help as you read certain books or portions of books. They can be considered guided readers or text commentaries. The volumes in the Baylor Handbook on the Hebrew Bible Series, for instance, are organized by biblical book.

Grammars

As you read, you will want to refresh your grammar at every level. One of the best ways is to look back at your beginning grammar or pick up another one. A few concise grammars are also available. They can be used alongside this volume. Once you master these presentations, the advanced grammars are helpful for reference. Most have scripture and topic indices and are searchable as electronic versions. Some are in the public domain and can be accessed online. The miscellaneous grammar tools describe Hebrew parallelism, linguistic studies, accents, and the Masorah.

Vocabulary Guides, Lexicons, Word Studies

Learning Hebrew vocabulary is an ongoing challenge. These tools help readers prioritize knowing words, seek for information about forms and references, and provide the greater context of their use.

---

[2] See §1.6.2.

BIBLIOGRAPHY

HEBREW BIBLES

Brown, A. Philip, II, and Bryan W. Smith, eds. *A Reader's Hebrew Bible.* Grand Rapids: Zondervan, 2008.

Elliger, Karl, and Willhelm Rudolph. *Biblia Hebraica Stuttgartensia.* 5th ed. Stuttgart: Deutsche Bibelgesellschaft, 1997.

The Hebrew Old Testament, Reader's Edition. Wheaton, IL: Crossway, 2021.

Vance, Donald R., George Athas, Wilhelm Rudolph, and Yael Avrahami, eds. *Biblia Hebraica Stuttgartensia: A Reader's Edition.* Peabody, MA: Hendrickson, 2015.

READERS/TEXT COMMENTARIES

Chisholm, Robert B. *A Workbook for Intermediate Hebrew: Grammar, Exegesis, and Commentary on Jonah and Ruth.* Grand Rapids: Kregel Academic, 2006.

Hardy, H. H., II. *Exegetical Journeys from Biblical Hebrew.* Grand Rapids: Baker Academic, 2024.

Kline, Jonathan G. *A Proverb a Day in Biblical Hebrew.* Peabody, MA: Hendrickson Academic, 2019.

Meyers, Pete, and Jonathan G. Kline. *A Hebrew Reader for the Psalms: 40 Beloved Texts.* Peabody, MA: Hendrickson Academic, 2021.

Van Pelt, Miles, and Gary D. Practico. *Graded Reader of Biblical Hebrew. A Guide to Reading the Hebrew Bible.* 2nd ed. Grand Rapids: Zondervan Academic, 2020.

BAYLOR HANDBOOKS ON THE HEBREW BIBLE SERIES

Baker, David W., with Jason A. Riley. *Genesis 37–50: A Handbook on the Hebrew Text.* Waco, TX: Baylor University Press, 2015.

Bandstra, Barry. *Genesis 1–11: A Handbook on the Hebrew Text.* Waco, TX: Baylor University Press, 2008.

Eddinger, Terry W. *Malachi: A Handbook on the Hebrew Text.* Waco, TX: Baylor University Press, 2012.

Garrett, Duane A. *Amos: A Handbook on the Hebrew Text.* Waco, TX: Baylor University Press, 2008.

Holmstedt, Robert D. *Ruth: A Handbook on the Hebrew Text.* Waco, TX: Baylor University Press, 2010.

Holmstedt, Robert D., and John Screnock. *Esther: A Handbook on the Hebrew Text*. Waco, TX: Baylor University Press, 2015.

Holmstedt, Robert D., John A. Cook, and Phillip S. Marshall. *Qoheleth: A Handbook on the Hebrew Text*. Waco, TX: Baylor University Press, 2017.

Robson, James E. *Deuteronomy 1–11: A Handbook on the Hebrew Text*. Waco, TX: Baylor University Press, 2015.

Rogland, Max. *Haggai and Zechariah 1–8: A Handbook on the Hebrew Text*. Waco, TX: Baylor University Press, 2016.

Tully, Eric J. *Hosea: A Handbook on the Hebrew Text*. Waco, TX: Baylor University Press, 2018.

GRAMMARS (BEGINNING)

Cook, John A., and Robert D. Holmstedt. *Beginning Biblical Hebrew: A Grammar and Illustrated Reader*. Grand Rapids: Baker Academic, 2013.

Fuller, Russell T., and Kyoungwon Choi, *Invitation to Biblical Hebrew. A Beginning Grammar*. Grand Rapids: Kregel Academic, 2006.

Garrett, Duane A., and Jason S. DeRouchie. *A Modern Grammar for Biblical Hebrew*. Nashville: B&H Academic, 2009.

Hackett, Jo Ann. *A Basic Introduction to Biblical Hebrew*. Peabody, MA: Hendrickson, 2010.

Kelley, Page H. *Biblical Hebrew: An Introductory Grammar*. Grand Rapids: Eerdmans, 1992.

Kutz, Karl V., and Rebekah L. Josberger. *Learning Biblical Hebrew: Reading for Comprehension: An Introductory Grammar*. Bellingham, WA: Lexham, 2018.

Lambdin, Thomas O. *Introduction to Biblical Hebrew*. New York: Scribner, 1971.

Pratico, Gary D., and Miles V. Van Pelt. *Basics of Biblical Hebrew*. 3rd ed. Grand Rapids: Zondervan, 2019.

Ross, Allen P. *Introducing Biblical Hebrew*. Grand Rapids: Baker Academic, 2001.

Seow, C. L. *A Grammar for Biblical Hebrew*. Rev. ed. Nashville: Abingdon, 1995.

GRAMMARS (CONCISE)

Arnold, Bill T., and John H. Choi. *A Guide to Biblical Hebrew Syntax*. 2nd ed. Cambridge: Cambridge University Press, 2018.

Hardy, H. H., II. *Exegetical Gems from Biblical Hebrew: A Refreshing Guide to Grammar and Interpretation*. Grand Rapids: Baker Academic, 2019.

Long, Gary A. *Grammatical Concepts 101 for Biblical Hebrew*. 2nd ed. Grand Rapids: Baker Academic, 2013.

Van Pelt, Miles V. *Biblical Hebrew: A Compact Guide*. 2nd ed. Grand Rapids: Zondervan, 2019.

Williams, Ronald J. *Williams' Hebrew Syntax*, 3rd ed. Revised and expanded by John C. Beckman. University of Toronto, 2007.

GRAMMARS (INTERMEDIATE/ADVANCED)

Bauer, Hans, and Pontus Leander. *Historische Grammatik der hebräischen Sprache des Alten Testamentes*. Halle: Niemeyer, 1922.

Blau, Joshua. *Phonlogy and Morphology of Biblical Hebrew*. LSAWS 2. Winona Lake, IN: Eisenbrauns, 2010.

Davidson, Andrew B. *Introductory Hebrew Grammar Hebrew Syntax*. 3rd ed. Edinburgh: T&T Clark, 1902.

Fuller, Russell T., and Kyoungwon Choi. *Invitation to Biblical Hebrew Syntax: An Intermediate Grammar*. Grand Rapids: Kregel Academic, 2017.

Gesenius' Hebrew Grammar. Edited and revised by E. Kautzsch and A. E. Cowley. Oxford: Clarendon, 1910.

Holmstedt, Robert D. *Biblical Hebrew Syntax: A Linguistic Introduction*. Grand Rapids: Baker Academic, 2022.

Joüon, Paul, and T. Muraoka. *A Grammar of Biblical Hebrew*. 2nd ed. Subsidia Biblica 27. Rome: Pontifical Biblical Institute, 2006.

Khan, Geoffrey. *The Tiberian Pronunciation Tradition of Biblical Hebrew*, 2 vols. Cambridge Semitic Languages and Cultures. Cambridge: Open Book, 2020.

Merwe, Christo H. J. van der, Jacobus A. Naudé, and Jan H. Kroeze. *A Biblical Hebrew Reference Grammar*. 2nd ed. London: Bloomsbury Academic, 2017.

Reymond, Eric D. *Intermediate Biblical Hebrew Grammar: A Student's Guide to Phonology and Morphology*. Resources for Biblical Study 58. Atlanta: SBL, 2018.

Waltke, Bruce K., and Michael P. O'Connor. *An Introduction to Biblical Hebrew Syntax*. Winona Lake, IN: Eisenbrauns, 1990.

GRAMMARS (MISCELLANEOUS)

Berlin, Adele. *The Dynamics of Biblical Parallelism*. Grand Rapids: Eerdmans, 2007.

Kelley, Page H., Daniel S. Mynatt, and Timothy G. Crawford. *The Masorah of Biblia Hebraica Stuttgartensia: Introduction and Annotated Glossary*. Grand Rapids: Eerdmans, 1998.

Noonan, Benjamin J. *Advances in the Study of Biblical Hebrew and Aramaic: New Insights for Reading the Old Testament*. Grand Rapids: Zondervan Academic, 2020.

Futato, Mark. *Basics of Hebrew Accents*. Grand Rapids: Zondervan Academic, 2020.

Park, Sung Jin. *The Fundamentals of Hebrew Accents: Divisions and Exegetical Roles beyond Syntax.* Cambridge: Cambridge University Press, 2020.

Scott, William R. *A Simplified Guide to BHS.* 4th ed. D & F Scott, 2007.

Yeivin, Israel. *Introduction to the Tiberian Masorah.* Translated and edited by E. J. Revell. Masoretic Studies 5. Missoula, MT: Scholars Press, 1980.

VOCABULARY GUIDES

Landes, George M. *Building Your Biblical Hebrew Vocabulary: Learning Words by Frequency and Cognate.* 2nd ed. Atlanta: SBL, 2001.

Osborne, William R., and Russell L. Meek. *A Book-by-Book Guide to Biblical Hebrew.* Peabody, MA: Hendrickson Academic, 2019.

Pratico, Gary D., and Miles Van Pelt. *The Vocabulary Guide to Biblical Hebrew and Aramaic.* 2nd ed. Grand Rapids: Zondervan, 2019.

LEXICONS

Clines, David, ed. *The Concise Dictionary of Classical Hebrew.* Sheffield: Sheffield Academic, 2009.

Klein, Ernest. *A Comprehensive Etymological Dictionary of the Hebrew Language for Readers of English.* Jerusalem: University of Haifa, 1987.

Koehler, Ludwig, and Walter Baumgartner. *The Hebrew and Aramaic Lexicon of the Old Testament.* 2 vols. Translated and edited by M. E. J. Richardson. Leiden: Brill, 2001.

Brown, Francis, Samuel R. Driver, and Charles A. Briggs. *A Hebrew and English Lexicon of the Old Testament.* Rev. ed. Oxford: Oxford University Press, 1980.

WORD STUDY RESOURCES

Botterweck, G. Johannes, ed. *Theological Dictionary of the Old Testament.* 17 Vols. Grand Rapids: Eerdmans, 1974–2021.

Harris, R. Laird, et al., eds. *Theological Wordbook of the Old Testament.* Chicago: Moody, 2003.

Jenni, Ernst, and Claus Westermann. *Theological Lexicon of the Old Testament.* 3 Vols. Translated by Mark E. Biddle. Peabody, MA: Hendrickson, 1997.

VanGemeran, Willem, ed. *New International Dictionary of Old Testament Theology and Exegesis.* 5 Vols. Grand Rapids: Zondervan, 1997.

/////////////

APPENDIX B

BIBLICAL HEBREW VOCABULARY

Learning vocabulary is a challenge. Instructors and students know that they must do it. But few would say it is enjoyable and certainly not easy. Some recent insights from the field of Second Language Vocabulary Acquisition (SLVA) suggest ways to improve the traditional method of learning vocabulary.[1] We apply a few of these ideas to the following lists. The wordlists are divided into groups of seven or eight words. Each list should be learned separately. Once one group is mastered, the student is encouraged to move to the next list. And the student should review the prior lists frequently.

The following comprises all lexemes that occur in the Hebrew Bible forty times or more. The vocabulary includes 898 entries.[2] Most beginning textbooks cover the majority of the first 238 words, occurring more than 200 times. These are listed first as a group. The remaining 660 lexemes are separated into 90 wordlists.

These wordlists can be learned in any number of arrangements. Let us suggest three scenarios:

Scenario A: Learn Words Occurring 65× or more in 15 weeks (one semester). Three wordlists should be mastered per week of the semester (Wordlists 1–45). The total number of words would be 344.

---

[1] Many of these methods are discussed in Jeremy Paul Thompson, "Learning Biblical Hebrew Vocabulary: Insights from Second Language Vocabulary Acquisition," PhD diss., University of Stellenbosch, 2011.

[2] The definitions are derived from H. H. Hardy II, *The Comprehensive Biblical Hebrew and Aramaic Glossary.* Copyright H. H. Hardy II and used with permission.

Scenario B: Learn Words Occurring 40× or more in 15 weeks (one semester). The wordlist should be divided into 15 groups. Six wordlists should be mastered per week of the semester.

Scenario C: Learn Words Occurring 40× or more in 30 weeks (two semesters). The wordlist should be divided into 30 groups. Three wordlists should be mastered per week of the semester.

LEXEMES OCCURRING 200× OR MORE
IN ORDER OF FREQUENCY

1)   וְ   and; also; but; so; then

2)   הַ   the

3)   לְ   to, toward; for; in regard to; of, about

4)   בְּ   in, on, at; with; through; among; when; in exchange for

5)   אֵת   (marker of the direct object)

6)   מִן   from; of; on account of; beside; above; than; since

7)   יהוה   Yahweh

8)   עַל   on; toward; beside; against; according to; more than; before; because

9)   אֶל   toward; against; according to; concerning

10)   אֲשֶׁר   who; which; that

11)   כֹּל   all, every; entirety; whole

12)   אמר   *Qal:* say | *Niphal:* be said; be called | *Hiphil:* declare

13)   לֹא   no, not

14)   בֵּן   Son

15)   כִּי   for; because; that; when; if; indeed

16)   היה   *Qal:* be; become; happen; occur | *Niphal:* be; occur; flee

17)   כְּ   like, as, similar to, according to, about

18)   עשׂה   *Qal:* do; make, create; obtain | *Niphal:* be done; be made | *Pual:* be created

19)   אֱלֹהִים   god, deity

20)   בוא   *Qal:* enter, come in | *Hiphil:* bring in; lead in | *Hophal:* be brought

21)   מֶלֶךְ   king

22)   יִשְׂרָאֵל   Israel

23)   אֶרֶץ   earth, land, ground

24) יוֹם day; daylight; lifetime; year

25) אִישׁ man, human; husband

26) פָּנֶה face; front

27) בַּיִת house; family

28) נתן *Qal*: give; set, put | *Qal* passive: be given; be put | *Niphal*: be
given; be put, be set

29) עַם people; nation

30) זֶה this; here

31) יָד hand

32) הלך *Qal*: go, come; walk; behave | *Niphal*: vanish | *Piel*: go; walk |
Hitpael: walk to and fro | *Hiphil*: bring; lead

33) דָּבָר word; speech; thing

34) הוּא he

35) ראה *Qal*: see; reveal; perceive, understand; select | *Qal* passive: be
seen | *Niphal*: become visible; appear | *Hitpael*: face one an-
other | *Hiphil*: show | *Hophal*: be shown

36) עַד until; during; upon

37) אָב father

38) שׁמע *Qal*: hear, listen; obey | *Niphal*: be heard (of); be obeyed | *Piel*:
cause to hear | *Hiphil*: cause to hear; make proclamation

39) דבר *Qal*: speak | *Niphal*: speak with one another | *Piel*: speak | *Pual*:
be spoken | *Hitpael*: converse

40) עִיר city; district

41) ישב *Qal*: sit; dwell; remain, stay | *Niphal*: be inhabited | *Piel*: inhabit |
Hiphil: cause to sit; cause to dwell | *Hophal*: be made to dwell

42) יצא *Qal*: go out; come out | *Hiphil*: lead out | *Hophal*: be led out

43) שׁוּב *Qal*: return, turn back | *Hiphil*: cause to return; bring back |
Hophal: be brought back | *Polel*: bring back; restore

44) דָּוִד David

45) אִם if; if only; not; whether; unless

46) הִנֵּה behold! lo!

47) עִם with; toward

48) אֶחָד one; a(n)

49) לקח *Qal*: take; receive | *Qal* passive: be taken | *Niphal*: be taken away
| *Hitpael*: take hold of oneself

50) ידע *Qal*: know | *Niphal*: be known | *Piel*: cause to know | *Pual*: be
known | *Hitpael*: make oneself known | *Hiphil*: make known |
Hophal: be made known | *Poel*: be caused to know

51) עַיִן eye; spring

52) אֵת with; beside

53) עלה Qal: go up, climb, ascend | Niphal: arise, go up; be exalted | Hit-
pael: raise up | Hiphil: lead up; bring up | Hophal: be brought
up

54) שָׁנָה year

55) אֲנִי I

56) שֵׁם name

57) שלח Qal: send (out, away); stretch out | Niphal: be sent | Piel: let go;
send out | Pual: be sent off | Hiphil: let loose

58) מות Qal: die; perish | Hiphil: kill | Hophal: be killed | Polel: kill

59) שָׁם there; then

60) יְהוּדָה Judah

61) אכל Qal: eat, consume | Qal passive: devoured | Niphal: be eaten |
Hiphil: feed

62) עֶבֶד slave; servant

63) אֵין there is not; not, no

64) אִשָּׁה woman; wife

65) אָדוֹן lord, master; husband

66) גַם also; even

67) שְׁנַיִם two

68) מֹשֶׁה Moses

69) נֶפֶשׁ soul; life; person, living being; self; desire, passion

70) מָה what? how?

71) אַתָּה You

72) כֹּהֵן Priest

73) הַ (interrogative particle)

74) אֵלֶּה These

75) כֵּן thus; so; then

76) אַל no, not

77) קרא Qal: call; proclaim, read | Niphal: be called; be mentioned |
Pual: be called

78) דֶּרֶךְ way; road; journey; custom, manner

79) אַחַר behind; after; afterward

80) מִצְרַיִם Egypt; Egyptians

81) נשא Qal: lift; carry; take | Niphal: be carried; be elevated | Piel: raise
up | Hitpael: raise oneself | Hiphil: bring up

82)	יְרוּשָׁלֵם	Jerusalem
83)	אָח	brother; fellow
84)	קוּם	*Qal*: arise; stand	*Piel*: confirm, establish	*Hiphil*: lift up; raise, erect, establish	*Hophal*: be set up	*Polel*: raise up	*Hitpolel*: rise up
85)	שָׁלֹשׁ	Three
86)	לֵב	heart; mind; disposition; will
87)	רֹאשׁ	head; top; chief; beginning
88)	בַּת	daughter
89)	שִׂים	*Qal*: put, place, set (up); arrange; establish	*Qal* passive: be set (up)	*Hiphil*: set oneself	*Hophal*: be placed
90)	מַיִם	water
91)	מֵאָה	hundred
92)	כֹּה	thus; here; now
93)	הֵם	they
94)	גּוֹי	people; nation
95)	הַר	mountain, hill; hill country
96)	עבר	*Qal*: pass over, cross; traverse	*Niphal*: be crossed	*Piel*: bring across	*Hiphil*: bring over
97)	אָדָם	man, person; humanity
98)	גָּדוֹל	great
99)	עמד	*Qal*: stand; take a stand; abide	*Hiphil*: station; set; appoint	*Hophal*: be placed
100)	תַּחַת	below; underneath; instead of
101)	חָמֵשׁ	five
102)	קוֹל	sound; voice
103)	נכה	*Niphal*: be struck	*Piel*: smite	*Pual*: be smitten	*Hiphil*: strike, smite	*Hophal*: be killed; be beaten
104)	פֶּה	mouth; opening
105)	צוה	*Piel*: command	*Pual*: be commanded
106)	ילד	*Qal*: bear; give birth	*Qal* passive: be born	*Niphal*: be born	*Piel*: midwife	*Hitpael*: declare one's lineage	*Hiphil*: beget	*Hophal*: be born
107)	אֶלֶף	thousand
108)	עֶשֶׂר	ten
109)	שֶׁבַע	seven, group of seven
110)	הִיא	she
111)	עוֹד	still; yet; again; besides; duration

112) טוֹב good; desirable; usable; kind

113) צָבָא army, troops; war; warfare

114) קֹדֶשׁ holiness, sacredness, apartness

115) שׁמר *Qal*: keep; watch over; guard | *Niphal*: be guarded | *Piel*: revere | *Hitpael*: keep away

116) מצא *Qal*: find; obtain | *Niphal*: be found | *Hiphil*: attain; present

117) אַרְבַּע four

118) עוֹלָם long time; future

119) עַתָּה now

120) נפל *Qal*: fall; lie | *Hitpael*: lie prostrate | *Hiphil*: cause to fall; apportion | *Pilel*: fall

121) מִי who?

122) מִשְׁפָּט judgment; case; claim

123) רַב great

124) שָׁמַיִם heaven, sky; heavens

125) שַׂר ruler; prince; officer

126) תָּוֶךְ midst

127) חֶרֶב sword

128) בֵּין between; interval

129) שָׁאוּל Saul; Shaul

130) נָא surely; please

131) כֶּסֶף silver; money

132) מִזְבֵּחַ altar

133) מָקוֹם place; locality

134) יָם sea

135) זָהָב gold

136) ירד *Qal*: go down; descend | *Hiphil*: bring down; send down; prostrate | *Hophal*: be brought down; be taken down

137) רוּחַ spirit; breath; wind

138) בנה *Qal*: build | *Niphal*: be built

139) אֵשׁ fire

140) נְאֻם utterance

141) שַׁעַר gate

142) נגד *Hiphil*: tell, announce, declare | *Hophal*: be told

143) דָּם blood

144) אָנֹכִי I

145) רַע evil; bad; depravity; poor

146) לֵוִי　Levi

147) מלך　*Qal*: reign; be king | *Hiphil*: make to be king; install as king | *Hophal*: become king

148) יַעֲקֹב　Jacob

149) אֹהֶל　tent

150) אַהֲרֹן　Aaron

151) סָבִיב　circuit; surroundings

152) עֶשֶׂר　ten

153) עֵץ　tree; timber, wood; forest

154) ברך　*Qal*: blessed; praised | *Niphal*: be blessed | *Piel*: bless; praise | *Pual*: be blessed; be praised | *Hitpael*: be blessed

155) כְּלִי　vessel; utensil; article, thing

156) שָׂדֶה　field, pasture, land

157) אוֹ　or; either

158) מִלְחָמָה　battle; war

159) ירא　*Qal*: fear | *Niphal*: be feared; be honored | *Piel*: make afraid; terrify

160) ענה　*Qal*: answer, reply, respond | *Niphal*: be answered | *Hiphil*: give an answer; made to answer

161) נָבִיא　prophet

162) רָעָה　evil, wickedness, calamity

163) מִשְׁפָּחָה　clan; family

164) פקד　*Qal*: assign a position; remember; investigate; muster; miss; punish; number | *Niphal*: be assigned a position; be missing | *Piel*: muster | *Pual*: be caused to miss; be numbered | *Hitpael*: be mustered | *Hiphil*: establish; entrust; deposit | *Hophal*: be visited; be deposited; be made an overseer

165) מְאֹד　muchness; strength, power; abundance; exceedingly, very

166) לֶחֶם　food; bread

167) סור　*Qal*: turn aside; retreat | *Hiphil*: remove | *Hophal*: be removed | *Polel*: be turned aside

168) חַטָּאת　sin; sin offering

169) עֵת　time; occasion

170) שְׁלֹמֹה　Solomon

171) פְּלִשְׁתִּי　Philistine

172) חזק　*Qal*: be strong; strengthen | *Piel*: make strong; strengthen | *Hitpael*: seize; keep hold of | *Hiphil*: prove oneself strong

173) כָּרַת *Qal*: cut off, cut down | *Qal* passive: be cut down | *Niphal*: be cut off; be eliminated | *Hiphil*: exterminate | *Hophal*: be exterminated

174) עָבַד *Qal*: labor, work; serve | *Qal* passive: be worked | *Niphal*: be cultivated | *Hiphil*: make to serve | *Hophal*: be made to serve

175) עֹלָה whole burnt offering

176) חיה *Qal*: live; revive | *Piel*: allow to live; bring back to life | *Hiphil*: keep alive; revive

177) אֹיֵב enemy

178) בְּרִית covenant; contract

179) חֹדֶשׁ month; new moon

180) אַתֶּם you

181) קרב *Qal*: approach, come near | *Niphal*: be brought | *Piel*: bring near | *Hiphil*: bring near; join; offer

182) אַף nose; anger

183) שֵׁשׁ six

184) צֹאן small cattle; flock; sheep and/or goats

185) פַּרְעֹה Pharaoh

186) אֶבֶן stone; rock

187) לְמַעַן in order that; for the sake of; on account of

188) בָּשָׂר flesh; meat

189) מִדְבָּר pasture; wilderness

190) חַי life; lifetime

191) רָשָׁע wicked, guilty

192) בָּבֶל Babel (Babylon); Babylonia

193) לֵבָב heart; mind; will

194) מַטֶּה staff; tribe

195) רֶגֶל foot

196) מלא *Qal*: fill; be full | *Niphal*: be filled; be accomplished | *Piel*: fill; accomplish, complete | *Pual*: be filled | *Hitpael*: amass oneself

197) אַמָּה cubit; forearm

198) חֶסֶד faithfulness, loyalty; kindness; goodness

199) חַיִל strength; wealth; army

200) גְּבוּל border, boundary; territory; mountain

201) נַעַר young man, lad; servant

202) חטא *Qal*: sin; offend; miss | *Piel*: purify; bear a loss | *Hitpael*: purify oneself | *Hiphil*: cause to sin

203) שָׁלוֹם peace; welfare; wholeness

204)	אֵל	god, deity
205)	מַעֲשֶׂה	work, labor; deed; accomplishment
206)	ירשׁ	*Qal*: take possession of; inherit	*Niphal*: be impoverished	*Piel*: possess	*Hiphil*: cause to possess; inherit; dispossess
207)	זֶרַע	seed; offspring; sowing
208)	לַיְלָה	Night
209)	קֶרֶב	midst; among; inward part
210)	בקשׁ	*Piel*: seek; require; consult	*Pual*: be sought
211)	זכר	*Qal*: remember	*Niphal*: be remembered	*Hiphil*: make known; mention
212)	כתב	*Qal*: write	*Niphal*: be written	*Piel*: write repeatedly
213)	מוֹעֵד	appointed time; meeting; assembly place
214)	תּוֹרָה	instruction; law
215)	אֲדָמָה	earth; land
216)	נַחֲלָה	possession; property; inheritance
217)	אֵם	mother
218)	כון	*Niphal*: be firm, be established; endure	*Hiphil*: establish; make firm	*Hophal*: be established	*Polel*: establish	*Polal*: be established	*Hitpolel*: be established
219)	יְהוֹשׁוּעַ	Joshua
220)	אהב	*Qal*: love; like	*Niphal*: lovable	*Piel*: love
221)	שׁתה	*Qal*: drink	*Niphal*: be drunk
222)	בֶּגֶד	garment; clothing
223)	נטה	*Qal*: stretch out; spread out, extend; bow	*Niphal*: be stretched out	*Hiphil*: stretch; extend
224)	יסף	*Qal*: add	*Niphal*: be added	*Hiphil*: increase; add
225)	מַחֲנֶה	encampment, camp
226)	עזב	*Qal*: leave; forsake; loose	*Qal* passive: be desolate	*Niphal*: be abandoned
227)	בֹּקֶר	morning
228)	נצל	*Niphal*: deliver oneself, escape; be delivered	*Piel*: deliver; spoil	*Hitpael*: strip oneself	*Hiphil*: take away; rescue	*Hophal*: be snatched
229)	שׁכב	*Qal*: lie (down); sleep	*Niphal*: be lain	*Pual*: be lain	*Hiphil*: make to lie down	*Hophal*: be laid down
230)	יוֹסֵף	Joseph
231)	מַלְאָךְ	messenger
232)	מִנְחָה	gift, tribute; offering

233) כלה *Qal*: stop, be finished, perish | *Piel*: bring to an end, complete | *Pual*: be finished

234) צַדִּיק just, righteous

235) שׁפט *Qal*: judge, rule | *Niphal*: plead, dispute; be judged | *Poel*: judge

236) אֲרוֹן ark; chest

237) אסף *Qal*: gather; remove | *Niphal*: be gathered | *Piel*: glean | *Pual*: be gathered | *Hitpael*: gather oneself

238) כָּבוֹד glorious; glory; honor

LEXEMES OCCURRING 199× TO 40×

Wordlist 1		
	כַּף	palm; sole; bowl
	רום	*Qal*: be high; be exalted	*Hiphil*: lift (up); erect; contribute	*Hophal*: be taken off	*Polel*: raise; exalt	*Polal*: raise; exalt	*Hitpolel*: exalt oneself
	יכל	*Qal*: be able; endure; prevail
	שֶׁמֶן	fat, oil
	חָצֵר	court; enclosure
	בְּהֵמָה	beast; cattle
	שֵׁבֶט	rod, staff, scepter; tribe

Wordlist 2		
	אֹזֶן	ear
	רֵעַ	companion; neighbor; friend
	סֵפֶר	document; letter; scroll
	יַרְדֵּן	Jordan
	שבע	*Qal*: swear	*Niphal*: swear an oath	*Hiphil*: cause to swear an oath
	אבד	*Qal*: perish; be destroyed	*Piel*: destroy	*Hiphil*: exterminate
	מִצְוָה	commandment
	בָּקָר	cattle, herd, ox

Wordlist 3		
	גלה	*Qal*: uncover; go into exile	*Niphal*: show; reveal	*Piel*: uncover	*Pual*: rebuke	*Hitpael*: expose oneself	*Hiphil*: exile	*Hophal*: be exiled
	רִאשׁוֹן	first; beginning
	אֶפְרַיִם	Ephraim
	מוֹאָב	Moab

זָקֵן elder; old person

שָׂפָה lip; language; edge

יֹשַׁע *Niphal*: be saved | *Hiphil*: deliver, save; assist

Wordlist 4

רבה *Qal*: increase; be great | *Piel*: make increase | *Hiphil*: make numerous; make great

אַבְרָהָם Abraham

שׁאל *Qal*: ask, inquire | *Niphal*: ask for oneself | *Piel*: inquire carefully; beg | *Hiphil*: grant a request

חוה *Hištaphel*: bow down; worship

לחם *Qal*: fight | *Niphal*: engage in battle

קדשׁ *Qal*: be set apart, be consecrated | *Niphal*: show oneself sacred; be sanctified | *Piel*: set apart, dedicate; sanctify, honor | *Pual*: be dedicated | *Hitpael*: consecrate oneself; keep oneself holy; be observed as holy | *Hiphil*: set apart, devote, consecrate

בִּנְיָמִן Benjamin

בחר *Qal*: choose; examine | *Niphal*: be chosen

Wordlist 5

בין *Qal*: understand; discern | *Niphal*: be discerning | *Hiphil*: have understanding | *Polel*: take care of | *Hitpolel*: get understanding

דּוֹר generation; time period

הרג *Qal*: kill; slay | *Qal* passive: be killed | *Niphal*: be killed

רעה *Qal*: shepherd, graze; pasture; feed

מְלָאכָה work; occupation

אַחֵר (an)other; later

דרשׁ *Qal*: seek; investigate | *Niphal*: be sought

Wordlist 6

פֶּתַח opening, doorway, entrance

חוּץ outside; street

סבב *Qal*: turn about; go around; surround | *Niphal*: turn oneself around; surround | *Piel*: change | *Hiphil*: turn; reverse | *Hophal*: be turned; be surrounded | *Poel*: encompass; surround

טמא *Qal*: be(come) unclean | *Niphal*: defile oneself | *Piel*: defile | *Pual*: be defiled | *Hitpael*: defile oneself | *Hotpaal*: be defiled

זֶבַח   ritual sacrifice

בַּעַל   lord, master, owner; husband; Baal

בַּד   part; member; alone; except

אַיִל   ram; ruler

Wordlist 7	אַךְ	surely; only; however
	נוס	*Qal*: flee; escape | *Hiphil*: cause to flee | *Polel*: be driven
	גִּבּוֹר	strong, mighty; hero
	צְדָקָה	righteousness
	שׂמח	*Qal*: rejoice, be glad | *Piel*: be made glad | *Hiphil*: allow to rejoice
	שֵׁנִי	second
	צִיּוֹן	Zion
Wordlist 8	מָוֶת	death
	רֹב	multitude, greatness
	צָפוֹן	north; Mount Zaphon
	כסה	*Qal*: cover; forgive | *Niphal*: be covered | *Piel*: cover | *Pual*: be covered | *Hitpael*: cover oneself
	נֶגֶד	before; front; opposite
	אַשּׁוּר	Asshur; Assyria
	שׂנא	*Qal*: hate | *Niphal*: be(come) hated | *Piel*: hate
	נגע	*Qal*: touch; strike; reach | *Niphal*: be stricken; be defeated | *Piel*: strike | *Pual*: be stricken | *Hiphil*: cause to touch; extend
Wordlist 9	עֵדָה	assembly
	חָכְמָה	wisdom
	מְנַשֶּׁה	Manasseh
	שבר	*Qal*: shatter; break | *Niphal*: be broken | *Piel*: shatter; break apart | *Hiphil*: cause to break forth; be born | *Hophal*: be broken
	שְׁמֹנֶה	eight
	הלל	*Piel*: praise | *Pual*: be praised | *Hitpael*: be praised
	נסע	*Qal*: pull out; pull up; depart | *Niphal*: be pulled up; be removed | *Hiphil*: lead out; remove

Wordlist 10	יוֹאָב	Joab
	עֲבֹדָה	work
	רדף	*Qal*: pursue | *Niphal*: disappear; be pursued | *Piel*: chase | *Pual*: be chased away | *Hiphil*: cause to pursue
	חנה	*Qal*: encamp; besiege; decline
	שחת	*Niphal*: be spoiled | *Piel*: ruin, destroy, annihilate | *Hiphil*: destroy | *Hophal*: be ruined
	שֶׁ-	which, that; since, because
	כְּמוֹ	like; as; when
	אָז	then; since
Wordlist 11	יַיִן	wine
	מַעַל	above
	יָמִין	right hand
	שְׁמוּאֵל	Samuel
	מִשְׁכָּן	abode, dwelling place
	נְחֹשֶׁת	copper, bronze
	קרא	*Qal*: meet; happen, encounter | *Niphal*: happen to be; be met | *Hiphil*: cause to happen
Wordlist 12	יֵשׁ	there is
	סוּס	horse
	חָכָם	wise, experienced; skillful
	נַחַל	wadi; stream; trench
	פתח	*Qal*: open | *Niphal*: be opened | *Piel*: loosen; free | *Hitpael*: loosen oneself
	חלל	*Niphal*: be defiled | *Piel*: profane; defile | *Pual*: be profaned | *Hiphil*: begin | *Hophal*: be begun
	כִּסֵּא	seat; throne
	שֶׁמֶשׁ	sun
Wordlist 13	עֶרֶב	evening; sunset
	מִסְפָּר	number
	נוח	*Qal*: rest; repose | *Hiphil*: cause to rest; satisfy; leave | *Hophal*: be given rest
	זבח	*Qal*: slaughter; sacrificial slaughter | *Piel*: sacrifice

פָּנָה *Qal*: turn | *Piel*: prepare; remove; turn away | *Hiphil*: turn; make to turn; *Hophal*: be turned

אַף also; even

פַּר bull

Wordlist 14 פֶּן lest; perhaps

קָבַר *Qal*: bury | *Niphal*: be buried | *Piel*: bury | *Pual*: be buried

שָׁאַר *Qal*: remain | *Niphal*: be left over | *Hiphil*: leave over

חוֹמָה wall; fortifications

חֹק ordinance, regulation; rule, prescription; limit, boundary

נָשִׂיא prince

שָׁכַן *Qal*: dwell | *Piel*: make to dwell | *Hiphil*: establish; cause to settle

יִרְמְיָהוּ Jeremiah

Wordlist 15 קָבַץ *Qal*: gather; collect | *Niphal*: assemble | *Piel*: gather together | *Pual*: be gathered | *Hitpael*: gather together

אֱמֶת truth; faithfulness

כֹּחַ power, strength

אֲרָם Aram

חֲצִי half

חֵמָה heat; wrath, rage; venom

שָׁלַךְ *Hiphil*: cast, throw | *Hophal*: be cast; be thrown

Wordlist 16 בּוֹשׁ *Qal*: be ashamed | *Hiphil*: put to shame | *Hitpolel*: be ashamed

נָגַשׁ *Qal*: draw near; approach | *Niphal*: approach | *Hitpael*: draw oneself near | *Hiphil*: bring near | *Hophal*: be brought near

קָהָל assembly, congregation

עֶצֶם bone; skeleton

גָּדַל *Qal*: grow up; become strong; become great | *Piel*: raise; let grow; make great | *Pual*: be grown | *Hitpael*: boast | *Hiphil*: enlarge

בְּכֹר firstborn

אוֹר light

לכד   *Qal*: take control; capture, seize | *Niphal*: be taken; be captured | *Hitpael*: struggle together

Wordlist 17	אֲנַחְנוּ	we
	רֶכֶב	chariot
	נָהָר	stream, river
	פְּרִי	fruit, produce; offspring
	חַי	living; alive
	צֶדֶק	righteous, righteousness
	אָחוֹת	sister

Wordlist 18

יָשָׁר   smooth; straight; pleasing

תּוֹעֵבָה   abomination

פַּעַם   foot; pace, footstep; time, occurrence

מַמְלָכָה   kingdom, dominion; sovereignty; reign

יטב   *Qal*: be good; be pleasing; go well | *Hiphil*: deal well with; do good to

שפך   *Qal*: pour (out); shed | *Qal* passive: be poured out | *Niphal*: be shed; be poured out | *Hitpael*: pour oneself out

קָדוֹשׁ   sacred, holy

לְשׁוֹן   tongue; language

Wordlist 19

שלם   *Qal*: be finished; be completed; come to an end; keep quiet | *Piel*: fulfill, repay; complete | *Pual*: be requited | *Hiphil*: bring to completion; make peace | *Hophal*: be at peace

שׂרף   *Qal*: burn (up) | *Niphal*: be burned | *Pual*: be burned

בטח   *Qal*: trust | *Hiphil*: rely upon

נבא   *Niphal*: prophesy | *Hitpael*: rage

קטר   *Piel*: burn up | *Pual*: be burned up | *Hiphil*: offer up in smoke | *Hophal*: be offered up in smoke

מִגְרָשׁ   open land, outskirts; pasture

כבד   *Qal*: be heavy; be honored | *Niphal*: make heavy | *Piel*: make heavy, glorify | *Pual*: be honored | *Hitpael*: make oneself heavy; honor oneself | *Hiphil*: make heavy; cause to honor

Wordlist 20	בכה	*Qal*: weep | *Piel*: weep
	שֶׁקֶר	deception, deceit; disappointment
	בִּלְתִּי	no, not
	עַמּוּד	pillar, column
	חשׁב	*Qal*: think; account; devise | *Niphal*: be reckoned | *Piel*: think of; plan; compute | *Hitpael*: consider oneself
	ידה	*Hitpael*: praise | *Hiphil*: confess
	שַׁבָּת	Sabbath
	כָּנָף	wing; extremity, edge
Wordlist 21	עָפָר	dust; soil
	נֶגֶב	Negev; southern territory; south
	אַבְשָׁלוֹם	Absalom
	רַק	only; still; however; but
	שֹׁמְרוֹן	Samaria
	יִצְחָק	Isaac
	נחם	*Niphal*: regret, be sorry; console oneself | *Piel*: comfort | *Pual*: be comforted | *Hitpael*: repent; be comforted; have compassion
Wordlist 22	כֶּבֶשׂ	lamb
	ספר	*Qal*: write; count | *Niphal*: be counted | *Piel*: announce, report; count | *Pual*: be told
	עַמּוֹן	Ammon
	בָּמָה	hill; high place
	יתר	*Niphal*: be left over, remain (over) | *Hiphil*: leave (over); excel
	שְׁלִישִׁי	third
	בְּעַד	behind; about; on behalf of
	תָּמִיד	continually
Wordlist 23	יָרָבְעָם	Jeroboam
	גאל	*Qal*: redeem; avenge; act as a kinsman-redeemer | *Niphal*: be redeemed
	רוץ	*Qal*: run | *Hiphil*: cause to run; drive away | *Polel*: dash back and forth

חֻקָּה	statute	
מַרְאֶה	appearance	
גִּלְעָד	Gilead	
כפר	*Qal*: cover | *Piel*: make atonement; appease | *Pual*: be atoned (for) | *Hitpael*: be atoned (for)	

Wordlist 24

שכח	*Qal*: forget | *Niphal*: be forgotten | *Piel*: cause to forget | *Hitpael*: be forgotten | *Hiphil*: make to forget
רֹחַב	breadth, width
רָעָב	hunger; famine
מְעַט	little; few
אֱדוֹם	Edom
הֵן	if, whether; behold
יַעַן	because of; because, on account of
עוֹר	skin

Wordlist 25

שרת	*Piel*: serve
שְׁבִיעִי	seventh
עֵשָׂו	Esau
רעע	*Qal*: be evil; be bad | *Niphal*: suffer | *Hiphil*: treat badly; do evil
שבע	*Qal*: be satiated | *Niphal*: be satisfied | *Piel*: satisfy | *Hiphil*: satisfy
לבש	*Qal*: put on; wear | *Pual*: be clothed | *Hiphil*: clothe
חַיָּה	animal; living organism

Wordlist 26

חֲמוֹר	male donkey
אמן	*Niphal*: be faithful | *Hiphil*: believe (in)
טָהוֹר	pure; clean
יֶתֶר	rest; remainder
יַחְדָּו	together
אֹרֶךְ	length
שִׂמְחָה	joy, gladness; mirth
מלט	*Niphal*: escape | *Piel*: allow to escape; deliver | *Hitpael*: escape | *Hiphil*: give birth; deliver

Wordlist 27	חָלָל	pierced
	טהר	*Qal*: be clean; pure | *Piel*: cleanse | *Pual*: be cleansed | *Hitpael*: cleanse oneself
	הפך	*Qal*: turn; overturn; change | *Niphal*: be overthrown; be changed | *Hitpael*: to transform oneself; to turn around repeatedly | *Hophal*: be turned
	אַחְאָב	Ahab
	כְּנַעַן	Canaan
	חרה	*Qal*: be(come) hot; be(come) angry | *Niphal*: be angry (with) | *Hitpael*: be anxious | *Hiphil*: kindle
	פֶּשַׁע	transgression; crime
Wordlist 28	קָצֶה	end, extremity
	חֵלֶב	fat
	עֵבֶר	opposite side; region beyond a body of water
	שמם	*Qal*: be desolate; be appalled | *Niphal*: be desolated; be appalled | *Hiphil*: devastate; ravage; show horror | *Hophal*: be desolate | *Poel*: cause horror | *Hitpolel*: be appalled; cause oneself ruin
	גֵּר	sojourner
	כֶּרֶם	vineyard
	זְרוֹעַ	arm; forearm; shoulder; strength, force
	כְּרוּב	cherub
Wordlist 29	תָּמִים	complete, sound
	מַלְכוּת	royalty; dominion; reign; kingdom
	יֶלֶד	child; boy; youth
	שמד	*Niphal*: be destroyed; be exterminated | *Hiphil*: exterminate
	עֵצָה	counsel, advice
	דֶּלֶת	door; tablet
	יְהוּדִי	Judean, Jew, Jewish
Wordlist 30	שׁית	*Qal*: put, place, set; appoint, fix | *Qal* passive: be imposed
	שׁיר	*Qal*: sing | *Hophal*: be sung | *Polel*: sing
	שֶׁקֶל	shekel; weight

טָמֵא unclean

דַּעַת understanding; knowledge

אֱמֹרִי Amorite

עָנָן cloud

שֶׁלֶם peace offering

| Wordlist 31 | לָמַד | *Qal*: learn | *Piel*: teach | *Pual*: be taught; be skillful |

פֵּאָה corner; side, edge; region

רָחוֹק distant, far; distance

קנה *Qal*: create; acquire, buy | *Niphal*: be bought | *Hiphil*: sell

הָמוֹן sound, murmur, roar; crowd

פלל *Piel*: intervene | *Hitpael*: make intercession (for)

גור *Qal*: live as a foreigner | *Hitpolel*: stay as a foreigner

| Wordlist 32 | עֵדוּת | testimony |

כַּשְׂדִּים Chaldean; Chaldea

פֹּה here

יְהוֹשָׁפָט Jehoshaphat

יְהוֹנָתָן Jonathan

זָכָר man; male

סתר *Niphal*: hide oneself; be hidden | *Piel*: hide | *Pual*: be hidden | *Hitpael*: hide oneself | *Hiphil*: hide; conceal

קלל *Qal*: be light; be slight; be swift | *Niphal*: be esteemed lightly; appear swift, trifling | *Piel*: curse | *Pual*: be cursed | *Hiphil*: make light | *Pilpel*: shake back and forth | *Hitpalpel*: shake oneself

| Wordlist 33 | עזר | *Qal*: help | *Niphal*: be helped | *Hiphil*: help |

סגר *Qal*: shut; close | *Niphal*: be shut; shut oneself | *Piel*: hand over | *Pual*: be shut up | *Hiphil*: deliver

מהר *Niphal*: hasten | *Piel*: act hastily

משל *Qal*: rule | *Hiphil*: cause to have dominion over

חֹשֶׁךְ darkness

קָרְבָּן offering

הֵיכָל palace; temple

עָנִי   poor, needy; afflicted, humble

Wordlist 34	עוּר	*Qal*: be awake | *Niphal*: be awakened | *Hiphil*: wake up | *Polel*: awaken; disturb | *Hitpolel*: arise; stir oneself up
	מכר	*Qal*: sell | *Niphal*: be sold | *Hitpael*: sell oneself
	שׁחט	*Qal*: slaughter | *Niphal*: be slaughtered
	שׁוֹר	ox, bovine; cattle
	ענה	*Qal*: become low; be downcast | *Niphal*: be afflicted; humble oneself | *Piel*: humble; afflict | *Pual*: be humiliated | *Hitpael*: humble oneself | *Hiphil*: afflict
	אוֹת	sign; omen; miracle
	אוֹצָר	treasure; treasury, storehouse
	מִשְׁמֶרֶת	guard, watch; charge

Wordlist 35	נֶגַע	illness; plague; wound
	גּוֹרָל	lot
	תֵּשַׁע	nine
	רכב	*Qal*: mount; ride | *Hiphil*: cause to ride
	יְשׁוּעָה	salvation
	שִׁיר	song
	תְּפִלָּה	prayer
	חנן	*Qal*: show favor; be gracious | *Piel*: make gracious | *Hitpael*: plead (for compassion) | *Hophal*: be shown compassion | *Poel*: have compassion

Wordlist 36	אָוֶן	trouble; sorrow; disaster
	קֶשֶׁת	bow
	מִקְנֶה	commodities
	בַּרְזֶל	iron
	תְּרוּמָה	offering
	עֹז	strength, might
	נַעֲרָה	young girl; maidservant
	קָרוֹב	close, nearby

Wordlist 37	קֶרֶן	horn
	ערך	*Qal*: arrange; set in order | *Hiphil*: confront

חלה   *Qal*: be(come) weak; become ill | *Niphal*: be made sick | *Piel*: appease | *Pual*: be made weak | *Hitpael*: make oneself sick | *Hiphil*: make sick | *Hophal*: be made sick, be wounded

מִקְדָּשׁ   sanctuary

עֵז   goat

חִזְקִיָּהוּ   Hezekiah

סֶלָה   musical term

נצב   *Niphal*: station oneself, take a stand; be stationed | *Hiphil*: station; erect; establish | *Hophal*: be fixed

Wordlist 38   שָׁלָל   prey, spoil, plunder

זעק   *Qal*: cry (out); call (for help) | *Niphal*: be called together | *Hiphil*: summon; make a proclamation

מאס   *Qal*: reject | *Niphal*: be rejected

מִזְרָח   sunrise; east

בֵּית־אֵל   Bethel

כְּנַעֲנִי   Canaanite

אֶרֶז   cedar

פלא   *Niphal*: be wonderful; be miraculous | *Piel*: fulfill a vow | *Hitpael*: do a wondrous act | *Hiphil*: do wonderfully

Wordlist 39   בַּל   no, not

אסר   *Qal*: bind; capture | *Niphal*: be bound | *Pual*: be captured

חפץ   *Qal*: delight (in); have pleasure (in)

חֶרְפָּה   reproach, taunt

צוּר   rock, hill, mountain

הֶבֶל   vanity; breath

קִיר   wall

אֶלְעָזָר   Eleazar

Wordlist 40   גָּד   Gad

שׁוֹפָר   horn, shophar

רחץ   *Qal*: wash; bathe | *Pual*: be washed | *Hitpael*: wash oneself

רְאוּבֵן   Reuben

בֶּטֶן stomach; womb

מַדּוּעַ why?

עוֹף birds; insects

בְּרָכָה blessing

Wordlist 41	גִּבְעָה	hill
	לְבָנוֹן	Lebanon
	שׁבת	*Qal*: stop; cease; rest | *Niphal*: finish | *Hiphil*: put an end to; remove
	שֻׁלְחָן	table
	בּוֹר	cistern, well
	צַר	enemy
	כְּסִיל	fool
	חֵן	grace, favor
Wordlist 42	צָרָה	need
	נבט	*Piel*: look | *Hiphil*: look upon, behold
	ריב	*Qal*: quarrel, strive; conduct a lawsuit | *Hiphil*: rebel
	משׁח	*Qal*: smear, anoint | *Niphal*: be anointed
	לין	*Qal*: stay the night; dwell | *Hitpolel*: dwell
	זָר	strange; unauthorized, prohibited; unknown
	דָּן	Dan
	קָדִים	east; east wind
Wordlist 43	רפא	*Qal*: heal | *Niphal*: be(come) healed | *Piel*: heal | *Hitpael*: be healed
	תקע	*Qal*: thrust; blow; clap | *Niphal*: be blown
	עֵד	witness
	כִּכָּר	talent, weight measurement; round district; loaf
	אֲבִימֶלֶךְ	Abimelech
	קֵץ	end; border
	קֶבֶר	grave; sepulcher
	פרשׂ	*Qal*: spread (out); stretch out | *Niphal*: be scattered | *Piel*: spread out; scatter

Wordlist 44	כָּתֵף	shoulder; side
	צלח	*Qal*: prosper, succeed | *Hiphil*: be successful
	כשל	*Qal*: stumble, stagger; totter | *Niphal*: stagger | *Piel*: devour | *Hiphil*: cause to stumble; make weak | *Hophal*: overthrown
	חֵלֶק	portion, share; territory
	אֲחֻזָּה	possession; property
	פוץ	*Qal*: scatter, disperse | *Niphal*: be scattered | *Hiphil*: scatter
	שְׁאֵרִית	rest, remainder; remnant
	חֲלוֹם	dream
Wordlist 45	אִשֶּׁה	fire offering
	שכם	*Hiphil*: arise, do early
	נצח	*Niphal*: be enduring | *Piel*: inspect; direct
	תפש	*Qal*: hold, seize; wield | *Niphal*: be seized | *Piel*: cause to grasp
	טוֹבָה	welfare; benefit; good
	גֶּבֶר	male; person
	שְׁאוֹל	underworld, afterlife; Sheol
	עֵמֶק	valley; plain
Wordlist 46	תמם	*Qal*: be(come) complete; be innocent | *Hitpael*: show oneself blameless | *Hiphil*: finish, complete
	אחז	*Qal*: grasp; seize | *Niphal*: be caught | *Hophal*: fasten
	יְאֹר	stream, canal; the Nile
	קרע	*Qal*: tear, rip up | *Niphal*: be torn
	ברח	*Qal*: flee; go through | *Hiphil*: chase; pass through
	אֵלִיָּהוּ	Elijah
	יָרֵא	fear
	מָלֵא	full
Wordlist 47	שִׁפְחָה	maidservant
	ארר	*Qal*: curse | *Qal* passive: cursed | *Niphal*: be cursed | *Piel*: curse
	אַתְּ	you

אַבְנֵר   Abner

דרך   *Qal*: tread; march | *Hiphil*: cause to tread

רִיב   dispute; plea

חַג   feast, festival; procession

Wordlist 48	חֶבְרוֹן	Hebron
	נְבוּכַדְ־רֶאצַּר	Nebuchadnezzar
	שׁקה	*Pual*: be watered	*Hiphil*: give a drink; cause to drink; irrigate
	נצר	*Qal*: guard; watch; keep
	קָנֶה	reed, stalk
	סֶלַע	rock; cliff
	גְּבוּרָה	strength, might
Wordlist 49	אַבְרָם	Abram
	דּוֹד	beloved, lover; uncle
	אֵצֶל	beside
	אַחֲרִית	end; future; descendants
	קֶדֶם	front; east; before
	אֵיךְ	how?
	אֶבְיוֹן	poor, needy
Wordlist 50	אֵילָם	porch
	בָּשָׁן	Bashan
	בִּלְעָם	Bileam
	אַלּוּף	chief
	עֲרָבָה	desert, steppe
	נֶסֶךְ	libation; drink-offering
	פדה	*Qal*: ransom	*Niphal*: be ransomed	*Hiphil*: allow to be ransomed	*Hophal*: be ransomed
Wordlist 51	בער	*Qal*: burn, consume	*Piel*: kindle; consume, devour	*Pual*: be kindled	*Hiphil*: burn up; destroy
	זנה	*Qal*: commit fornication; act like a harlot	*Pual*: be whorish	*Hiphil*: commit fornication

שָׂכַל   *Qal*: have success | *Hiphil*: consider; contemplate

מָרְדְּכַי   Mordecai

מָגֵן   shield

קְטֹרֶת   smoke; incense

חָמָס   violence, wrong

Wordlist 52   נֶ֫דֶר   vow

מִדְיָן   Midian

יכח   *Niphal*: argue; adjudicate | *Hitpael*: rebuke, punish; decide | *Hiphil*: argue | *Hophal*: be reproved

בְּלִי   no, not; failure; ending, destruction

אָסָא   Asa

נטע   *Qal*: plant | *Niphal*: be planted

יֵהוּא   Jehu

Wordlist 53   אֹ֫רַח   way, path; behavior

נחל   *Qal*: possess | *Piel*: apportion | *Hitpael*: receive as a possession | *Hiphil*: give as a possession; cause to inherit | *Hophal*: made to possess

אֱלִישָׁע   Elisha

אֱלוֹהַּ   god, deity

יבש   *Qal*: be(come) dry; dry up | *Piel*: dry (up) | *Hiphil*: cause to dry up

אִיּוֹב   Job

רֵיחַ   odor, scent

Wordlist 54   תְּהִלָּה   praise; praise song, psalm

רחק   *Qal*: be distant; distance | *Piel*: remove; be far | *Hiphil*: remove; depart

שדד   *Qal*: deal violently with; devastate | *Qal* passive: be destroyed | *Niphal*: be devastated | *Piel*: do violence; destroy | *Pual*: be devastated | *Poel*: devastate

אֶ֫דֶן   base, pedestal

פָּרָשׁ   horse, steed

יְרִחוֹ   Jericho

מִזְמוֹר   psalm; melody

Wordlist 55	יָעַץ	*Qal*: advise, counsel | *Niphal*: consult; decide | *Hitpael*: consult together
	צָרַר	*Qal*: bind, tie up; wind up; be cramped | *Pual*: be tied up | *Hiphil*: make narrow; cause distress
	פָּעַל	*Qal*: make, do
	חָזָק	strong; firm; mighty
	יַעַר	wood, forest; thicket
	רָצוֹן	favor; (good)will
	רְבִיעִי	fourth
Wordlist 56	אָמָה	maid; female slave
	טֶרֶם	not yet; even; before
	צָעַק	*Qal*: cry (out); call | *Niphal*: be called | *Piel*: cry aloud | *Hiphil*: call together
	זרע	*Qal*: sow | *Niphal*: be sown | *Pual*: be sown | *Hiphil*: yield
	מַחֲשָׁבָה	thought; plan; intent
	שְׁמָמָה	waste; devastation
	צִדְקִיָּהוּ	Zedekiah
Wordlist 57	חֵץ	arrow
	אֶסְתֵּר	Esther
	כעס	*Qal*: be vexed; be angry | *Piel*: anger | *Hiphil*: vex, provoke anger
	חדל	*Qal*: cease; refrain from
	גֶּפֶן	vine
	חזה	*Qal*: see
	שֵׁן	tooth; ivory; fork prong
Wordlist 58	עָמָל	trouble; labor, toil
	חלק	*Qal*: divide, apportion; share | *Niphal*: be divided | *Piel*: divide; scatter | *Pual*: be divided | *Hitpael*: apportion among themselves | *Hiphil*: take possession
	אַלְמָנָה	widow
	גָּמָל	camel
	יְרִיעָה	curtain
	שָׁוְא	emptiness, vanity

	הָמָן	Haman
Wordlist 59	דְּבַשׁ	honey
	לָבָן	Laban
	שְׂמֹאל	left, leftward; north
	מִדָּה	length; measurement
	עֶרְוָה	nakedness
	דבק	Qal: cling, hold | Pual: be joined | Hiphil: get hold of; cause to stick | Hophal: made to cling to
	אבה	Qal: want; be willing
Wordlist 60	קָטֹן	small, young; insignificant
	מָרוֹם	top, high, upward; elevated; heavens
	סֹלֶת	fine flour
	מַצָּה	matzah; unleavened bread
	חָדָשׁ	new; fresh
	מְדִינָה	province
	חתת	Qal: be shattered | Niphal: be dismayed | Piel: dismay | Hiphil: shatter
Wordlist 61	רנן	Qal: give a ringing cry; cry aloud; praise | Piel: cry out; exult | Pual: be exultant | Hiphil: cause to exult; rejoice
	יצק	Qal: pour out; cast; flow | Hiphil: pour into | Hophal: be poured out
	סֹפֵר	scribe
	צֵל	shadow
	לְמוֹ	to, toward; for; in regard to; of, about
	עֶלְיוֹן	upper; height
	צָדוֹק	Zadok
Wordlist 62	יֹאשִׁיָּהוּ	Josiah
	שָׂעִיר	male goat; buck
	מדד	Qal: measure | Niphal: be measured | Piel: measure out | Hitpolel: stretch oneself over
	מָחָר	tomorrow; future
	הוֹי	ah! alas!

	רֵאשִׁית	beginning; chief
	אַחֲרוֹן	behind; future
Wordlist 63	קֶרֶשׁ	board, plank
	יוֹמָם	daytime; by day
	יְהוֹיָדָע	Jehoiada
	הַרְבֵּה	much, many
	נַפְתָּלִי	Naphtali
	נדח	*Niphal*: be scattered | *Pual*: be scattered | *Hiphil*: drive away; scatter | *Hophal*: be frightened away
	עֲבוּר	produce, yield
Wordlist 64	בקע	*Qal*: break open; cleave | *Niphal*: break forth; split | *Piel*: splinter; break up | *Pual*: be broken; burst | *Hitpael*: be burst; be cleft | *Hiphil*: break through; assault | *Hophal*: be assaulted
	תעה	*Qal*: err; wander | *Niphal*: be led astray | *Hiphil*: cause to err
	כבס	*Qal*: wash | *Piel*: wash | *Pual*: be washed
	מוּסָר	discipline, correction
	חרם	*Hiphil*: ban; devote; exterminate | *Hophal*: be utterly destroyed
	נשׂג	*Hiphil*: reach, collect; produce
	נכר	*Niphal*: disguise oneself | *Piel*: deface | *Hitpael*: act as a stranger; distinguish oneself | *Hiphil*: recognize; acknowledge
Wordlist 65	רַב	officer
	רְחַבְעָם	Rehoboam
	טַבַּעַת	signet ring; ring
	בְּתוּלָה	virgin
	שְׁבִי	captivity; captives
	פַּחַד	dread, fear; trembling
	אֵפֹד	ephod
Wordlist 66	גָּאוֹן	exaltation, majesty; height
	אֱמוּנָה	firmness; fidelity

	תִּפְאֶרֶת	glory, beauty
	קָצִיר	harvest; harvesting
	פֶּסַח	Passover
	תְּכֵלֶת	purple (wool)
	בגד	*Qal*: deal treacherously
Wordlist 67	נגף	*Qal*: strike; smite	*Niphal*: be struck; be smitten	*Hitpa-el*: stumble
	מַעֲלָה	stair; pilgrimage
	מִשְׁקָל	weight
	יָהּ	Yah
	נְבֵלָה	carcass; corpse
	חֶבֶל	cord, rope
	עַד	future time; long time
Wordlist 68	יצב	*Hitpael*: take a stand; station oneself
	חִתִּי	Hittite
	גִּלּוּל	idol
	יִשְׁמָעֵאל	Ishmael
	דַּל	poor; helpless
	ברא	*Qal*: create	*Niphal*: be created
	סלח	*Qal*: forgive, pardon	*Niphal*: be forgiven
Wordlist 69	סמך	*Qal*: lay; support; rest	*Niphal*: support oneself	*Piel*: refresh
	רצה	*Qal*: take pleasure (in); be pleased (with)	*Niphal*: be acceptable	*Hitpael*: make oneself acceptable
	לִשְׁכָּה	room, chamber; hall
	שַׂק	sack; sackcloth
	שַׁדַּי	Shaddai
	חֲנִית	spear
	אֹמֶר	speech; word
Wordlist 70	הֵנָּה	they
	אַיֵּה	where?
	מַכָּה	wound; plague

רחם   *Qal*: love | *Piel*: have compassion | *Pual*: show compassion; be compassionate

פרר   *Hiphil*: break; frustrate | *Hophal*: be broken; be frustrated

חרש   *Qal*: be deaf | *Hitpael*: keep oneself silent | *Hiphil*: keep silent

אַרְיֵה   lion

Wordlist 71   מָתְנַיִם   loins

יוֹאָשׁ   Joash

חיל   *Qal*: be in labor; tremble | *Hiphil*: cause to tremble | *Hophal*: be birthed | *Polel*: bring on labor pains | *Polal*: be birthed | *Hitpolel*: writhe

רצח   *Qal*: kill, slay, murder | *Niphal*: be slain | *Piel*: murder, assassinate | *Pual*: murder

הֵנָּה   here, there; to here; now

גיל   *Qal*: rejoice

שְׁכֶם   Shechem

Wordlist 72   שבה   *Qal*: take captive, deport | *Niphal*: be deported

קוה   *Qal*: wait, hope | *Piel*: wait, hope (for)

רָחֵל   Rachel

צפה   *Qal*: spread out; arrange | *Piel*: overlay | *Pual*: be overlaid

שֶׂה   sheep; goat

קָטָן   small, young, unimportant

אָסָף   Asaph

Wordlist 73   מִשְׁכָּב   bed

רפה   *Qal*: sink; release | *Niphal*: be released | *Piel*: weaken | *Hitpael*: be slackened | *Hiphil*: let go; abandon

נָכְרִי   foreign

אָשָׁם   guilt, trespass; guilt offering

קוֹמָה   height

ירה   *Hiphil*: teach

פגע   *Qal*: meet; encounter, fall upon | *Hiphil*: cause to encounter; assail

Wordlist 74	מָאֵן	*Piel*: refuse
	דֶּבֶר	plague
	פרץ	*Qal*: break (through, out, open, up); split; spread | *Niphal*: spread | *Pual*: be broken down | *Hitpael*: break away
	קשב	*Qal*: incline | *Hiphil*: pay attention (to)
	מִשְׁתֶּה	drink; drinking, feast
	עצר	*Qal*: restrain, stop; detain | *Niphal*: be restrained
	נֹחַ	Noah
Wordlist 75	יַחַד	unity; community
	נְעוּרִים	youth; early life
	עִמָּד	at; with; beside; against
	סָרִיס	eunuch; official
	חֲמִישִׁי	fifth
	אוּלַי	perhaps; may be
	זמר	*Piel*: sing, make music; praise
Wordlist 76	גרש	*Qal*: cast out; drive out | *Niphal*: be cast out | *Piel*: drive out | *Pual*: be driven out
	יצר	*Qal*: form; fashion | *Niphal*: be formed | *Pual*: be formed | *Hophal*: be formed
	מִגְדָּל	tower
	זְבוּלוּן	Zebulun
	אַשְׁרֵי	blessed, happy
	שֶׁבֶר	breaking; crushing; fracture; breach
	מֶרְכָּבָה	chariot
Wordlist 77	יִרְאָה	fear; terror
	רוע	*Hiphil*: shout; cheer | *Polal*: be jubilant | *Hitpolel*: shout in jubilation
	נֵר	lamp
	מַשָּׂא	load, burden
	חָלָב	milk
	מרה	*Qal*: be disobedient; be rebellious | *Hiphil*: behave disobediently; behave rebelliously

	קָשַׁר	Qal: bind; conspire against | Niphal: be bound up | Piel: tie (on) | Pual: be bound together, be copulating | Hitpael: conspire together (against)
Wordlist 78	נָקִי	clean; free; blameless
	בלל	Qal: confuse, confound; mix | Hitpolel: mix oneself
	אָשֵׁר	Asher
	חלץ	Qal: prepare for battle; draw out; withdraw | Niphal: be equipped; be delivered | Piel: tear out; rescue | Hiphil: equip
	מוֹשָׁב	seat; dwelling; assembly
	בָּלָק	Balak
	שִׁמְעוֹן	Simeon
Wordlist 79	בָּחוּר	young man
	שִׁמְעִי	Shimei
	נקה	Qal: clean | Niphal: be clean; be free | Piel: free; acquit
	חגר	Qal: gird (on)
	נֵצַח	eminence, perpetuity; splendor
	בזז	Qal: plunder | Niphal: be plundered | Pual: be plundered
	אֹכֶל	food
Wordlist 80	גִּבְעָה	Gibea
	הרה	Qal: conceive; become pregnant | Qal passive: be conceived | Poel: conceive, devise
	אֶפֶס	end; extremity
	נָגִיד	leader; ruler
	יחל	Niphal: wait | Piel: await | Hiphil: wait
	רְחֹב	open plaza
	אור	Qal: be light; shine | Niphal: be lit up | Hiphil: cause to shine; give light
Wordlist 81	יִשָּׂשכָר	Issachar
	קִנְאָה	jealousy; zeal
	פשט	Qal: dash away; put off | Piel: strip | Hitpael: strip oneself | Hiphil: strip (off)
	הרס	Qal: break; tear down | Niphal: ruined | Piel: ruin

נִיחוֹחַ	soothing, appeasement
מְנוֹרָה	menorah; lamp stand
מָתַי	when?

Wordlist 82	תְּבוּאָה	yield; income
	יָפֶה	beautiful; fair
	שְׁבוּת	captivity; deportation
	מַעֲלָל	deed; practice
	נתץ	*Qal*: pull down; break down | *Qal* passive: be broken up | *Niphal*: be pulled down | *Piel*: tear down | *Pual*: be torn down
	גּוֹלָה	exiles; exile
	יסד	*Qal*: establish; found | *Niphal*: be founded | *Piel*: found | *Pual*: be founded | *Hophal*: be founded

Wordlist 83	יוֹנָתָן	Jonathan
	כִּנּוֹר	lyre; zither
	אֱנוֹשׁ	man, person; humanity
	לוּחַ	tablet; (writing) board
	מַחֲלֹקֶת	division; portion
	בדל	*Niphal*: withdraw; be separated | *Hiphil*: separate; divide
	יָתוֹם	orphan

Wordlist 84	שׁקט	*Qal*: be quiet; be at peace | *Hiphil*: keep peace
	בזה	*Qal*: despise | *Niphal*: be despised | *Hiphil*: make despicable
	נָתָן	Nathan
	זוב	*Qal*: flow
	יִשַׁי	Jesse
	נוע	*Qal*: totter; tremble; quiver | *Niphal*: be tossed about | *Hiphil*: shake; toss about
	אָן	where? to where?

Wordlist 85	בֶּטַח	security
	צֹר	Tyre
	תְּבוּנָה	understanding

	חָרְבָּה	waste, ruin; desolation
	שָׁנִי	scarlet
	אָחָז	Ahaz
	חָרוֹן	anger
Wordlist 86	אָחוֹר	back; rear, posterior
	בְּרִיחַ	bar; lock
	בֵּית לֶחֶם	Bethlehem
	מְעָרָה	cave
	טַף	children
	צדק	*Qal*: be just; be right | *Niphal*: be justified | *Piel*: justify | *Hitpael*: justify oneself | *Hiphil*: declare righteous; do justice
	כָּבֵד	heavy, weighty, numerous
Wordlist 87	יְחִזְקִיָּהוּ	Hezekiah
	אזן	*Hiphil*: listen
	יְבוּסִי	Jebusite
	צַוָּאר	neck; back of the head
	גַּן	garden
	אמץ	*Qal*: be strong | *Piel*: make firm; strengthen | *Hitpael*: prove to be strong | *Hiphil*: prove to be strong
	מוט	*Qal*: shake; totter | *Niphal*: be shaken; be made to totter | *Hiphil*: drop, let fall | *Hitpolel*: be tossed about; reel
Wordlist 88	בלע	*Qal*: swallow | *Niphal*: be swallowed | *Piel*: engulf
	פשע	*Qal*: transgress; rebel, revolt | *Niphal*: be offended
	רגז	*Qal*: tremble; quake; excite | *Hitpael*: excite oneself | *Hiphil*: cause to quake; make to be excited
	תוֹלֵעָה	worm
	אֲשֵׁרָה	Asherah; asherah pole
	צִפּוֹר	bird
	רַחֲמִים	compassion
Wordlist 89	אֵיפָה	ephah (dry measurement)
	גִּלְגָּל	Gilgal

דָּגָן grain

עוד *Hiphil*: witness; admonish | *Hophal*: be warned

מְרָרִי Merari; Merarite

מִצְפָּה Mizpah

בַּד poll; shoot

Wordlist 90

יסר *Qal*: instruct; admonish | *Niphal*: be instructed | *Piel*: teach; rebuke | *Hiphil*: chasten | *Nitpael*: be corrected

נטש *Qal*: leave; forsake; give up | *Niphal*: be forsaken; be let go | *Pual*: be abandoned

חמל *Qal*: spare, have compassion

גנב *Qal*: steal | *Niphal*: be stolen | *Piel*: steal | *Pual*: be stolen (away) | *Hitpael*: steal away; leave stealthily

צֵלָע rib, side

אֵי where?

עֹל yoke

//////////////

APPENDIX C

ENGLISH TO HEBREW CATALOGUE

above	מֵעַל	before	לִפְנֵי
according	עַל כְּ-	behind	אַחֲרֵי
after	אַחַר	believe	אמן
again	עוֹד	belong	לְ-
Ahab	אַחְאָב	Benjamin	בִּנְיָמִן
all	כֹּל	Bethel	בֵּית־אֵל
also	אַף, גַּם	better than	טוֹב מִן
altar	מִזְבֵּחַ	between	בֵּין
among	בְּ-, קֶרֶב	blood	דָּם
angry	חרה	boat	אֳנִיָּה
appeared	ראה	Boaz	בֹּעַז
Aramean	אֲרַמִּי	both	גַּם
arise	עלה, קום	bread	לֶחֶם
arrive	בוא	bring back	שׁוב
at	בְּ-	call	קרא
attack	צרר, נכה	camp	מַחֲנֶה
back	גֵּו	Canaan	כְּנַעַן
basket	סַל	capture	לכד
be	היה	carry	נשׂא
beast	בְּהֵמָה	child	בֵּן, יֶלֶד
because	כִּי	city	עִיר
become	היה	clan	אֶלֶף, מִשְׁפָּחָה

655

cloud	עָנָן	follow	רדף
command	צוה	food	אֹכֶל
commandment	מִצְוָה	for	לְ-
commemoration	זִכָּרוֹן	foreign	נָכְרִי
conquer	תפשׂ	forty	אַרְבָּעִים
continue	יסף	four	אַרְבַּע
cover	כסה	from	מִן
cow	פָּרָה	fruit	פְּרִי
creator	קֹנֶה	gather	קבץ, אסף
dark	עָב, עֲרָפֶל	get up early	שכם
David	דָּוִד	give	נתן
day	יוֹם	go	הלך
defeat	חלשׁ	God	אֱלֹהִים
defile	חלל, טמא	gold	זָהָב
do	עשׂה	good	טוֹב
dwell	ישׁב	grass	עֵשֶׂב, דֶּשֶׁא
each	כֹּל	grave	קֶבֶר
ear	אֹזֶן	greater than	גָּדוֹל מִן
earth	אֲדָמָה, אֶרֶץ	guard	שמר
eat	אכל	hand	יָד
Egypt	מִצְרַיִם	happen	קרא
elder	זָקֵן	hate	שׂנא
enemy	אֹיֵב	he	הוּא
enter	בוא	hear	שמע
Esau	עֵשָׂו	heart	לֵב, לֵבָב
evening	עֶרֶב	heaven	שָׁמַיִם
evil	רַע	here	פֹּה
exist	יֵשׁ	honey	דְּבַשׁ
eye	עַיִן	Hoshea	הוֹשֵׁעַ
face	פָּנִים	house	בַּיִת
fall	נפל	I	אָנֹכִי, אֲנִי
family	מִשְׁפָּחָה	if	אִם, אִלּוּ
father	אָב	image	צֶלֶם, פֶּסֶל
favor	חֵן	in	בְּ-
fear	ירא	increasing	רבב
festival	חַג	inhabitant	ישׁב
field	שָׂדֶה	instruction	תּוֹרָה
fill	מלא	into	אֶל
fire	אֵשׁ	Israel	יִשְׂרָאֵל

it	הִיא, הוּא	offer	קרב, עלה
Jacob	יַעֲקֹב	on	בְּ-, עַל
jar	צַפַּחַת, כַּד	one	אֶחָד
Jerusalem	יְרוּשָׁלַם	or	אוֹ
Joshua	יְהוֹשׁוּעַ	overflow	צוף, שטף
judge	שׁפט	pay	שבר
keep	שׁמר	people	עַם, גּוֹי
kill	קטל, הרג	Pharaoh	פַּרְעֹה
king	מֶלֶךְ	pitch	כֹּפֶר
know	ידע	place	מָקוֹם
land	אֶרֶץ	please	אָנָּא, נָא
left	שְׂמֹאל	poor	אֶבְיוֹן, עָנִי
lie down	שׁכב	possession	יְרֻשָּׁה, מִקְנֶה
lift	נשׂא	powerful	עָזוּז, חָזָק
lip	שָׂפָה	priest	כֹּהֵן
listen	שׁמע	prophesy	נבא
live	חיה	prophet	נָבִיא
living beings	נֶפֶשׁ חָיָה	pure	טָהוֹר
lord	אָדוֹן	pursue	רדף
love	אהב	refuse	מָאַס
maidservant	נַעֲרָה, שִׁפְחָה	remember	זכר
make	עשׂה	report	שְׁמוּעָה, מַאֲמָר
man	אָדָם, אִישׁ	return	שׁוּב
manna	מָן	rich	עָשִׁיר
Midianite	מִדְיָנִי	right	יְשָׁרָה
milk	חָלָב	righteous	צַדִּיק
mind	לֵבָב, לֵב	rise	קום
morning	בֹּקֶר	rise early	שׁכם
Moses	מֹשֶׁה	Ruth	רוּת
mother	אֵם	sacrifice	קָרְבָּן, זֶבַח
mountain	הַר	Samuel	שְׁמוּאֵל
name	שֵׁם	Sarah	שָׂרָה
Naomi	נָעֳמִי	Saul	שָׁאוּל
nation	גּוֹי, עַם	save	ישׁע
no	אַל, לֹא	say	אמר
Noah	נֹחַ	saying	לֵאמֹר
now	עַתָּה	see	ראה
obey	שׁמע	seek	דרשׁ, בקשׁ
observe	שׁמר	servant	עֶבֶד

serve	עבד	through	בְּ-
seventh	שְׁבִיעִי	to	לְ-
she	הִיא	together	יַחְדָּו
shekel	שֶׁקֶל	top	מָרוֹם, רֹאשׁ
silver	כֶּסֶף	travel	הלך
Sinai	סִינַי	trees	עֵץ, עֵצָה
sit	ישׁב	tribe	אַמָּה, מַטֶּה
slaughter	טבח, שׁחט	two	שְׁנַיִם
so	כֵּן	unclean	טָמֵא
Solomon	שְׁלֹמֹה	under	תַּחַת
some	מִן	until	עַד
son	בֵּן	upright	יְשָׁרָה
soul	נֶפֶשׁ	upwards	מָרוֹם
speak	דבר	vessel	כְּלִי
spirit	רוּחַ	walk	הלך
statute	חֹק	wash	רחץ, כבס
strike	נכה	water	מַיִם
strong	עַז, גִּבּוֹר	way	דֶּרֶךְ, אֹרַח
tabernacle	מִשְׁכָּן	we	אֲנַחְנוּ
take	לקח	what	מָה
teach	למד	when	כִּי, בְּ-
temple	הֵיכָל	while	כִּי, כְּ-
tent	אֹהֶל	whole	כֹּל
tenth	עֲשִׂירִי	wilderness	מִדְבָּר
than	מִן	wine	יַיִן
that	כִּי, אֲשֶׁר	wisdom	חָכְמָה
then	אָז	wise	חָכָם
there is	יֵשׁ	with	עִם
these	אֵלֶּה	word	מִלָּה, דָּבָר
they	הֵם	world	תֵּבֵל
this	זֶה	worship	עבד
those	הֵם	Yahweh	יהוה
thousand	אֶלֶף	you	אַתָּה

APPENDIX D

GLOSSARY

Abecedary refers to ancient documents (often clay tablets) containing a successive list of the alphabet.

Ablaut (see **Apophony**)

Absolute state is the lexical or dictionary form of a noun. It is used as the final element of a construct phrase or by itself (see **Construct state**).

Abstract nouns specify nonphysical referents.

Acrophony refers to the practice of associating the sound of a letter with the initial sound of its name.

Additive numbers are multiword numerals that add to calculate a total amount.

Adjectives are a category of lexemes (**Word class**) that describe states (e.g., *green*) or emotions (e.g., *sad*) of entities. They are more time-stable than verbs but less so than nouns (see **Substantives**).

Adjuncts (**Satellites** or **Obliques**) are optional clause constituents that are not obligatory (or core) **Constituents**, e.g., **Adverbs**, **Conjunctions**, and **Prepositional phrases**. They are not counted in **Valency**.

Adverbializers are a type of subordinator that designates an intra-clausal, adverbial relation. They link a matrix-clause verb to an embedded clause functioning like an adverb.

Adversative relation indicates the semantic notion of contrast or opposition (e.g., English *against*).

Affixes (namely **Prefixes**, **Suffixes**, and **Infixes**) include derivative or inflectional morphemes that convey semantic-syntactic information.

Agent is a semantic description of the doer, initiator, or direct cause of the action or event. The performer of the verbal action is often animate (e.g., a person) but may be inanimate (e.g., a force or instrument).

Aktionsart (see **Situation aspect**)

Allocentric means having one's focus outside oneself. Allocentric **Deixis** points to an external, non-speaker oriented entity or locality (**Landmark**) that serves as a deictic reference point (cf. **Egocentric**). In BH, motion verbs are not speaker oriented. They use a reference point that is an **Allocentric** entity or locality. The movement pathways orient using inside-outside, up-down, front-behind, and toward-away from the deictic center.

Allophone is one of two or more variant pronunciations of the same phoneme in a language.

Alphabetic script is a significant innovation of the Semitic-speaking world that developed a limited number of written signs (22–30) to represent the phonetic values of language.

Alphasyllabary (or *abugida*) is a writing system that represents CV sequences with a single sign.

Alternative question presents two options and often anticipates one of the expressed choices as the answer.

Alveolar ("little cavity") is a sound articulated by placing the tip of the tongue on the ridge of the mouth behind the teeth (e.g., /s/).

Ambitransitive describes verbs that may or may not take direct objects; that is, they can be constructed as either transitive (e.g., *I watched*) or intransitive (e.g., *I watched the game*).

Anaphoric use of a pronoun refers to a previously mentioned noun.

Anarthrous and **Arthrous** specify the absence and presence of a definite article, respectively.

Animate nouns refer to living entities, whereas **Inanimate nouns** refer to nonliving objects.

Antecedent (see **Head**)

Anticausative verbs do not specify the cause of the action, even though the action assumes volitional agency (i.e., a **Causer**). While the causer of the verbal action or event is not a core constituent, other constituents (**Agent, Causee**, etc.) may be included.

Antonyms are lexemes with opposite meanings.

Apocopation (verb: *apocopate*) is a phonetic process yielding the loss of a consonant (e.g. the *he* of the article as with בַּבַּיִת from בְּהַבַּיִת).

Apophony (**Ablaut** or **Vowel gradation**) is a morphological change or alternation of a word's internal vowel.

Apotropaic is a kind of magic intended to ward off evil or malevolent spirits.

Apposition describes two or more elements with the same constituent function and referent. The elements are typically contiguous.

Archive is a collection of written materials.

Arguments (or **Complements**) are obligatory clause elements that complete a **Predicate**.

Aspect, or viewpoint aspect, describes the speaker's or author's portrayal of a verbal action (e.g., perfective or imperfective), focusing on the extent or duration of action rather than the timeframe of the action.

Aspiration refers to consonants pronounced with an accompanying exhale of breath (i.e., aspirate); IPA [○ʰ]. In Hebrew the aspirated consonants are the *bgdkpt* letters which may be pronounced with or without aspiration: [bʰ], [gʰ], [dʰ], etc.

Asseverative function adds affirmative emphasis.

Asyndetic refers to coordination without the use of coordinating conjunctions.

Atelic verbs express action without regard to the end or goal (i.e., *telos*) of the action.

Attenuation refers to the historical phonological vowel change from /a/ to /i/ under certain conditions (e.g., **qattil > *qittil > qittēl*).

Auxiliary verbs are a part of verb phrases (e.g., English *will, do, have, shall*) that designate various verbal information, such as **TAM**, not specified by the lexical verb.

Avalent describes **Impersonal** verb clauses that do not require any arguments and have zero valency (e.g., *it rains*).

Background describes non-mainline clauses in narrative, providing circumstantial or other information that is necessary for understanding the story (see **Foreground**).

Base is a historical reconstruction of the underlying morphological framework indicating a word's essential consonantal-vowel pattern. Hebrew grammarians utilize the root קטל transcribed as *qtl* for representing these reconstructions, and an asterisk is used to denote a reconstructed form (e.g., **qattāl, *yiqtol*).

Benefactive notion indicates the LM receives the benefit of an expression whether intended or not. It may be signaled by a preposition (e.g., *to, for*).

Binyanim (see **Stem**)

Bipartite verbless clauses consists of only two syntactic constituents, a subject and predicate, without a **Copula** (e.g., הוא טוב "he (is) good") (see **Tripartite verbless clause**).

Bivalent verbs are transitive, taking two **Constituents** (e.g. *she closes the door*).

Cardinal number designates a numerical amount of a countable entity.

Casus pendens is a Latin phrase meaning "hanging/suspended case." It refers to a fronted subject standing outside prototypical clause syntax (i.e., hanging or suspended) yet is defined by the clause.

Causation denotes a semantic property wherein a cause element brings about a consequent action or a resulting state. The causative notion is expressed by a large number of Hebrew prepositions wherein the LM can indicate the cause, ground, or reason for a proposition.

Causative verb indicates the **Causer** as an expressed agentive participant of the action.

Causee is the clause participant that that is the agent or doer of the action and is entailed by the **Causer**.

Causer brings about or prompts an action or event carried out by an agent (**Causee**) and serves the semantic role often as the grammatical subject.

Clause constituent is a component of a sentence (i.e., **Subject**, **Object**, etc.).

Clauses express a proposition and contain, at least, a predicate and an implied or expressed subject. The predicate may include a verb phrase—that is, a verb, objects, and modifiers—or be verbless.

Collective nouns are morphologically singular but refer to an assemblage of entities. Some collectives may have singular or plural forms and can be enumerated with cardinal numbers.

Comitative notion indicates that the LM accompanies in proximity or function.

Common gender does not formally distinguish grammatical gender as **Masculine** or **Feminine**.

Common nouns specify nonspecific entities with lexical meaning.

Comparative notion indicates that the LM corresponds in quality, quantity, or relative degree.

Complementizer is a type of subordinator that designates an embedded clause as a complement of a matrix clause constituent.

Complements are required or expected constituents of a linguistic expression (cf. **Adjuncts**).

Completion (or **Semantic transitivity**) indicates a semantic notion whether the endpoint of an action is identified. It is indicated by the presence of a verbal **Argument**.

Complex prepositions consist of the linking together (i.e., concatenation) of at least one preposition and a content word operating as a lexicalized unit or chunk.

Compound-complex prepositions consist of a sequence of three or even four prepositional elements.

Compound prepositions consist of a sequence of two or more identifiable prepositions with a composite function.

Concessive function expresses a condition or a circumstance that is contrary to the statement of the main clause (e.g. English: *although, in spite of*).

Concrete nouns signify physical referents (see **Abstract nouns**).

Conjoins (or **Conjuncts**) are coordinated elements of similar constituent rank, such as words, phrases, clauses, propositions, or even larger discourse units.

Conjugations describe the morphological patterns comprising prefixes and suffixes that together with a root create either a finite or nonfinite verb.

Conjunction (or linker) is a function word that expresses a semantic relationship between two or more conjoins of like syntactic constituency (see **Coordination** and **Subordination**).

Conjunctive adverbs are linkers that connect clauses syntactically and semantically. Rather than modifying a particular clause element like adverbs, they create a relationship between two larger discourse units more akin to a **Conjunction**.

Conjuncts (see **Conjoins**)

Constituents include core elements of clauses, such as the **subject** and **object**.

Construct phrases are nominal expressions in which a head noun is morphologically bound to at least one other contiguous noun that forms a genitive relationship (or construct chain). The final noun is described as the **absolute state**, and all non-final elements are **Construct state**.

Construct state is the morphologically distinct form of a noun (or other nominal element) found in the non-final position of a **Construct phrase**.

Continuous aspect expresses an action in process or in an ongoing state.

Contronym (or auto-antonym) is a single word with opposite meanings.

Conversive theory states that past (i.e., SC) and future (i.e., PC) forms could be "converted" into the opposite tense by attaching a *waw*.

Coordination is a type of conjunction in which the conjoins are syntactically independent.

Coordinator (or coordinating conjunction) is a linker (e.g., *and*, *or*, and *but*) that produces the grammatical relationship of overt **Coordination**. The coordinated elements (**Conjoins**) share constituency without any marked syntactic subordination, and a new syntactic unit is created from the conjoined expression.

Copula is a pleonastic element, often a pronoun or verb *hyh*, that may mark the nexus between a subject and predicate in a verbless clause.

Core constituents include the subject, object, or indirect object.

Countability is a characteristic of nouns that entails counting.

Count nouns can be construed with either singular or plural forms and can be subdivided based on their semantic and grammatical properties relating to plurality (see **Noncount nouns**).

Customary (see **Frequentative**)

Dative notion indicates that the LM is an **Indirect object** (semantically the **Experiencer**) of an action.

De-agentifying removes the semantic role of causer, doer, or instigator (i.e., **agent**) from a clause.

De-agentive refers to the fact that clauses with certain verb types do not stipulate an agent.

Definiteness describes the semantic property of the degree to which a nominal referent is identifiable or distinguishable.

Deixis designates an extralinguistic discourse setting, often expressing proximity or immediacy, that is, place or time. The adjective form is *deictic*.

Demonstratives are determiners that point to the relative setting of a known referent. The reference point is determined from the perspective of the speaker (personal **Deixis**) or the context of the situation (discourse **Deixis**).

Denominative (or denominal) verbs are derived from nouns or nominals.

Deontic modality (or event modality) deals with events or situations that are not yet realized but are asserted as potential in the mind of the speaker. They are not necessarily what will actually become reality (see **Modality**).

Determiners are words or morphemes that combine in noun phrases to

specify the contextual reference, the deictic orientation, and/or the quantity of another constituent.

Diachronic refers to linguistic development through time in contrast to **Synchronic**, which refers to development within a particular time.

Diglossia describes two languages spoken in a single social context.

Directional prepositions signal the route of the TR with respect to the LM without reference necessarily to the originating source or eventual goal.

Discourse situation involves information about the speaker, addressee, and their locations in relation to each other as portrayed in an account.

Distributive events repeat a given action in different spatial locations and/or temporal contexts (e.g., *Sam examined each word*).

Ditransitive verbs (e.g., *tell*, *give*) require two objects or arguments (e.g., *Tim gave Sarah₁ a dog₂*).

Dynamism is a property of a verb that conveys a situation as a non-static, mutable event or as a static, immutable event (see **Fientivity** and **Stativity**). The semantic difference may be represented by the English verbs *do* (non-static or **fientivity**) and *be* (static or **stativity**).

Egocentric deixis points to a speaker-oriented entity or locality (**Landmark**) that serves as a deictic reference point (see **Allocentric**).

Entailment involves the aspects of meaning beyond simple referentiality, such as implicit concepts or implicatures.

Epicene nouns lack grammatical distinction of gender.

Epistemic modality (or propositional modality) refers to the speaker's attitude toward or knowledge about the truth or factuality of the proposition being asserted.

Epistolary refers to literary works written in the form of a letter.

Equative or descriptive relation indicates similarity, likeness, or identity.

Exchange (or price) notion represents the value or worth of the TR in relation to the LM.

Experiencer is the semantic patient undergoing the effect of the action (see **Dative**).

Extraposition (see *Casus pendens*) refers to a fronted (i.e., extrapositioned) element which stands outside the structure of the clause and which is restated within the clause with a pronoun (e.g., *As for Yahweh, he is God*).

Factitive verbs indicate actions that result in a state.

Feminine gender (see **Gender**)

Fientivity (or **Fientive** verbs) designate active or dynamic situations and can be either transitive or intransitive.

Finite verbs are those forms inflected for **TAM**, person (1, 2, or 3), gender (M or F), and number (S or P).

First-weak verbs (see **Weak verbs**)

Foreground constitutes the focus or main line of narrative prose or discourse (see **Background**).

Fractions express the numerical ratio of a part to the whole.

Frequentative verbs express an event or action that takes place multiple times or is repeated over time under certain conditions. It is also called iterative, habitual, or customary.

Fricative consonants are articulated by forcing air through a narrow channel of the mouth (e.g., *th*, *ph*).

Fronted (see **Extraposition**)

Function words elicit syntactic and semantic connections within clauses, between clauses, and in larger discourse units. In traditional grammar, function words include those lexemes not circumscribed in the word class categories of noun, adjective, or verb. Semitic grammarians often refer to this catchall group as **Particles**, which include conjunctions, adverbs, conjunctive adverbs, negations, interrogatives, pragmatic markers, existentials, and direct object markers.

Geminate roots have identical R2 and R3 consonants (designated ע״ע).

Gender describes a lexical and grammatical property of nouns.

Hebrew nouns are generally categorized into either **Masculine** or **Feminine** subclasses.

Gnomic perfect (or proverbial perfect) describes an action, event, or circumstances as a whole.

Grammatical concord refers to the morphosyntactic relationship between two words that match in grammatical categories, for instance a noun and adjective in a noun phrase or a subject and verb within a clause.

Habitual (see **Frequentative**)

Head (or **Antecedent**) is the element of a phrase that could by itself substitute for the entire phrase.

Heterographs are distinct lexemes that are pronounced similarly but spelled differently.

Heuristic device offers a simplified summary of a concept that is sufficient for an elementary level introduction but not adequate for advanced understanding.

Hieroglyphs are pictorial representations of sounds, syllables, or entire words (e.g., Egyptian hieroglyphics).

Homographs are distinct lexemes that are spelled similarly but are not necessarily pronounced identically.

Homoioarcton ("similar beginning") occurs when a scribal copyist omits text between words with similar beginnings.

Homoioteleuton ("similar ending") occurs when a scribal copyist omits text between words with similar endings.

Homonyms are distinct lexemes that are pronounced and spelled similarly.

Homophones are distinct lexemes that are pronounced similarly but may or may not be spelled identically.

Hollow verbs (see **Weak Verbs**)

Hypotaxis is covert or asyndetic subordination between two clauses (see **Parataxis**).

Image schema (or **Prototype**) is the schematization of a primary spatial configuration.

Imperfective aspect presents an event in part or as an incomplete action.

Impersonal verbs express action that does not have a clear agent.

Inanimate nouns (see **Animate nouns**).

Inchoative aspect expresses the beginning of a state, action, or event.

Indefinite subject is used when the verb has a nonspecific or unknown agent.

Indicative is the mood of declaration or portrayal of realis.

Indirect object is a kind of secondary complement that semantically indicates the recipient, beneficiary, or direction of the verb (see **Dative**).

Individuative nouns designate a distinct semantic referent. Most may be pluralized to indicate more than one entity.

Inflection refers to the various forms of a word that do not change its part of speech or basic meaning. This variation commonly includes an affix change and expresses different grammatical categories (e.g., gender, number, case).

Ingressive (or **Inchoative**) aspect denotes the initiation or beginning of a state, event, or action.

Inseparable prepositions are function words attached to the following word (e.g., בְּבֵית), a pronominal suffix (e.g., לִי), or an expanding morpheme (e.g., כְּמוֹ).

Instrumental relation often indicates a weapon or other device. The LM can express the stimulus or physical object used to do the TR.

Intensive action refers to progressive events that are escalating in degree.

Internal object is an object that is implied and need not be expressed.

Interrogative is a question.

Intransitive verbs lack objects (e.g., *he runs*).

IPA (International Phonetic Alphabet) provides a technical system of phonetic symbols derived from Latin script for a written representation of the sounds of languages.

Irrealis portrays actions or situations that are not actualized but that exist in the mind of the speaker as potential (see **Realis**).

Isomorphic ("equal form") refers to a correspondence of form or structure.

Iterative (or **Frequentative**) events include a repetitive action at different, disconnected times (e.g., *he rewatched the video again and again*) or segments (e.g., *they chitchatted back and forth*).

Iterative aspect (or semelfactive) expresses a repeated event or action in a single occasion.

Landmark (**LM**) carries secondary focus as a point of reference or ground for the **Trajector** (**TR**).

Lemma is the dictionary or base form of a word (e.g., *hit*).

Lexemes are the basic lexical units of a word (e.g., *hit, hits, hitting*).

Lexical semantics is the study of the meaning of morphemes, lexemes, or phrases and requires investigating what that signifier intends to signify.

Lingua franca (plural: *linguae francae*) is a language adopted by speakers of different languages for purposes of exchange (lit. "bridge language").

Linkers (see **Conjunctions**)

Logogram is a sign or character used to represent a word or phrase (e.g., $ = *dollar*).

Manner function indicates how the TR is accomplished or carried out. It is also described as mode or means (English *according to*). When the LM is an inanimate object, the function may be the **Instrumental**.

Manner-conflating verbs entail a type of movement (i.e., "go on foot"). English *walk* is a manner-conflating verb (see **Path-conflating**).

Marked forms (i.e., markedness) have specialized meaning and form and are often less common than **Unmarked forms**.

Masculine gender (see **Gender**)

Masorah generally refers to the various scribal activities of the Masoretes. It can refer specifically to the Masoretic notes preserved in codices such as M^L (11th cent.) or the Aleppo Codex (10th cent.).

Mater lectionis is a consonant letter representing a vowel sound (e.g., ו and י).

Matrix clause (or main clause) is a clause that is not syntactically dependent upon or subordinate to another clause.

Measure words are **Count nouns** and represent standardized or customary units of measurement for certain entities, particularly **Noncount nouns**.

Mediopassive describes the combined **Middle** and **Passive** voice semantics of the *Niphal*.

Memation refers to the suffixal addition of the Hebrew consonant *mem*.

Metathesis refers to the inversion of the sequence of sounds.

Middle voice indicates that the subject of the verb undergoes or experiences the verbal action to some degree.

Mirativity is a cognitive state of surprise and marks an utterance as newsworthy.

Modality (see **Mood**)

Mood (or **Modality**) refers to the relation of the verbal action to reality.

Morphosyntax describes the relationship between morphemes and their syntactical function.

Multiplier (or **multiplicative numeral**) indicates the replication of an entity by a designated amount. English uses several expressions as multipliers: *once, twice, thrice, dual, double, triple, quadruple*.

Multiword prepositions are polymorphic strings, comprised of more than one discrete consecutive lexeme and function as a unit to modify a single complement (see **Compound prepositions**, **Complex prepositions**, and **Compound-complex prepositions**).

Nominal is a descriptor for a word functioning like a noun.

Nominalization is the process or result by which the functional category of a word or phrase becomes a noun.

Noncount nouns cannot be quantified with a cardinal number except with a **Measure word** and do not take plural morphemes (see **Count nouns**).

Nonfinite verbs include infinitives and participles. As a clause head, they have the morphosyntactic and semantic properties of a verb but are not marked for **Person** and do not indicate **TAM**.

Nonrestrictive relative clauses provide an optional description of a syntactic **Head**.

Noun class is a description that organizes nouns with similar semantic and grammatical characteristics.

Noun phrase is a syntactic categorization of one or more lexemes functioning as a noun.

Nouns designate words that refer to time-stable, concrete objects (e.g., persons, places, things) or abstract entities. These entities serve as the primary actors, participants, and concepts in the communication of events and ideas.

Number distinguishes grammatical entities that are viewed as either singular (*he/she/it*) or plural (*they*).

Numerals specify amounts.

Object is a syntactic description of the constituent that completes an action or event.

Object complement is the secondary object in a clause that serves as a predicate of the direct object.

Obliques (see **Adjuncts**)

Ordinal number represents an ordered arrangement of entities in a sequence.

Palimpsest refers to a repurposed ancient manuscript with traces of an initial text that has been erased or scraped off and overlayed with a secondary text.

Parablepsis ("looking beside") is a scribal error involving the copyist looking aside and accidentally skipping a portion of the text.

Paradigmatic relations include associated lexemes that exhibit some degree of interchangeability (see **Syntagmatic**).

Parataxis is a covert or asyndetic coordination between two clauses (see **Hypotaxis**).

Paronomastic infinitives intensify an infinitive or finite verbal form from the same root and give the impression of a wordplay. Some call this function a **Tautological** infinitive (Greek ταυτολογία "same word").

Parsing is the method of describing the grammatical categories of a word. Hebrew finite verbs are parsed based on stem, conjugation, person, gender, number, and root.

Participles, much like adjectives, involve description but do so via verbal action. As hybrid words, they are designated **Verbal adjectives.**

Particles are lexemes that are not otherwise categorized as nouns, adjectives, or verbs. Examples include conjunctions, adverbs, conjunctive adverbs, negations, interrogatives, pragmatic markers, existentials, and direct object markers (see **Function words**).

Partitive relation involves a subset of the LM.

Part of speech (see **Word class**)

Passive voice situates the subject as the patient which undergoes an action or is acted upon.

Path-conflating verbs entail a path of movement. English *enter* is a path-conflating verb (see **Manner-conflating verb**).

Path prepositions relate movement through space along specific routes (i.e., English *across*, *through*).

Patient is a semantic description of the receiver of an action or the constituent being acted upon. In active clauses (e.g., *Tom hit the ball*), the agent (*Tom*) holds the syntactic role of the subject; whereas the patient (*the ball*) is the **object** or **Complement**. Passive clauses typically designate the patient as the subject (e.g., *The ball was hit*).

Perfective aspect presents an event as a whole or as a completed action.

Performative refers to circumstances in which an utterance performs an action or brings about an event.

Periphrastic refers to the use of auxiliary verb to predicate verbal adjectives and participles for aspect (e.g., *he is going*).

Person refers to the grammatical distinction between the speaker (first person: *I*), the one being addressed (second person: *you*) and all other participants (third person: *he, she, it, they*).

Pharyngeal is a consonant primarily articulated by placing the root of the tongue against the throat or pharynx (e.g., ח).

Phonation refers to the articulation of linguistic sounds.

Phoneme is a perceptually distinct unit or segment of sound in a specific language.

Phrasal head is the primary member of a phrase or phrasal unit.

Phrasal units combine words into noun phrases, verb phrases, clauses, etc.

Pictograph (see **Hieroglyph**)

Pluractionality (see **Verbal plurality**)

Plural-only nouns do not have a singular form.

Polysemy (or coexpression) refers to words that can represent distinct semantic functions.

Possessive function indicates the LM is the possessor of the TR.

Postalveolar is a sound articulated by placing the tip of the tongue on the back of the ridge of the mouth behind the teeth (e.g., *sh*).

Postpositive position means a constituent comes after another constituent.

Pragmatics is the study of meaning embedded in the context of utterances.

Predicate is the obligatory part of the clause that says something about the **Subject**.

Prepositional object is the obligatory element of the PP, which correlates to a specific element and function within the clause (see **Landmark**).

Prepositional phrase (PP) is a phrase headed by a preposition.

Prepositions construct syntactic and semantic relationships between various discourse types and are positioned before a required participant (i.e., a **Complement** or **Prepositional object**).

Prepositive position means an element comes before another element.

Price (see **Exchange**)

Principled polysemy is a semantic network at the conceptional level of related but distinct meanings. Distinct meanings are understood as deriving from primary senses.

Privative notion expresses the loss, absence, or removal of the LM.

Proclitic is an element whose stress falls to a following word. In Hebrew, proclitics are often marked with *maqqep* (e.g., אֶת־הַמֶּלֶךְ).

Progression involves a sequential development from one unit in a series to the next.

Progressive aspect is an event that expresses a durative, dynamic action.

Pronominal state describes a noun with the pronominal suffix (e.g., אַרְצִי "my land").

Proper nouns (i.e., names) refer to specific entities.

Purpose describes a relation that is produced as the intended consequence, goal, or result.

Quadraliteral/quadraconsonantal are verbal roots consisting of four **Radicals**.

Quantifier designates a nonspecific quantity of a set of items.

Radicals are the three (rarely two or four) consonants that constitute the verbal root, often described as R1, R2, and R3.

Reaction signals (i.e., **Interjections** or **Exclamations**) are utterances that encode or elicit extemporaneous reactions. They are a large, open class or set of lexemes and sounds.

Realis portrays situations that are actualized or brought about in real life circumstances (see **Irrealis**).

Reciprocality denotes a shared action (or event) between multiple agents. For example, *they watched each other*.

Reflexive conveys an action in which the agent and patient are coreferential.

Relativizer is a type of subordinator that assigns an embedded clause the constituency of adnominal in the matrix clause. Semantically, the embedded clause describes an appositional nominal, which precedes the relativizer.

Restrictive relative clauses define the meaning of a NP with necessary information about its referent.

Resultative refers to a causative verb where the occasioned situation is fientive or dynamic (see **Factitive**).

Resumptive pronoun occurs in a relative clause restating something about its antecedent. It is used to specify the constituency of the head in an embedded clause.

Root refers to the abstract consonantal structure made up of between two and four consonants (**Radicals**) and carries the basic semantic information.

Satellite-framing language is a typological description of verbs where satellites can create different semantics with the same verb—the movement into a location is specified by *go in* while motion out of a location is *go out* (see **Verb-framing**).

Satellites (see **Adjuncts**)

Second-weak verbs (or **Hollow** verbs) (see **Weak verbs**)

Segholate nouns originate from the structure, *CVCC*, where *V* is an original short **a-*, **i-*, or **u*-class vowel (e.g., מֶלֶךְ).

Semantic roles (or **Thematic relations**) indicate the ways in which the clause participants are involved with an action or event.

Semantics is the study of the meaning. Understanding the meaning of morphemes, lexemes, or phrases—dubbed **Lexical semantics**—requires investigating what that signifier intends to signify.

Semantic situations refer to the characteristics of verbs that encode their situational meaning (i.e. grammatical voice, dynamism, completion, causation, and plurality). Semantic situation overlaps with *Aktionsart*.

Separable prepositions are two- and three-consonant prepositions that do not form a unit with the following word.

Situation aspect (or *Aktionsart*) refers to a range of semantic characteristics involved in a verbal action (see **Semantic situations**).

Stativity (or stative verb) expresses non-dynamic states of being, describing a characteristic (e.g., *the man is heavy*), an external circumstance (e.g., *the animal dies*), or an emotional/rational status (e.g., *the child knows*).

Stem designates the distinct consonant and vowel patterning of the root that structure the basic verbal building blocks of syntax and semantics (i.e., *Qal, Niphal, Piel, Pual, Hitpael, Hiphil*). Some grammarians identify the stems as **Binyanim** (בִּנְיָנִים).

Strong verbs are the regular verb roots consisting of three non-weak root consonants, or radicals (see **Weak verbs**).

Subject is a syntactic element that exhibits morphological agreement with the verb and is described in a clause.

Subordinating clause (relative clause or embedded clause) is a clause that functions as a constituent member of another clause (see **Matrix clause**).

Subordination indicates syntactic dependency between constructions; that is to say, one conjoin serves as a constituent of the other.

Subordinator (or subordinating conjunction) is a function word that expresses a syntactic relationship that makes an embedded clause (or **Subordinating clause**) into a constituent member of another.

Substantive refers to a noun or a grammatical organization of **nouns** and **adjectives**.

Suppletion involves a morphological pattern change within a paradigm.

Synchronic (see **Diachronic**)

Synonymity comprises the semantic equivalence with different words or constructions (e.g., *I will write*; *I am going to write*).

Syntagmatic relations include the combining of associated clause elements in specific usage patterns as collocations (see **Paradigmatic**).

TAM refers to **Tense**, **Aspect**, and **Mood/Modality**.

Tense connotes the idea of time or temporality.

Theme vowel is the vowel of the second syllable of BH verbs.

Third-weak verbs (or so-called third-*he* verbs) (see **Weak verbs**)

Topicalization is the syntactical means by which the topic of a clause is established.

Topic shift designates a new topic that is discontinuous from the preceding focus or topic.

Trajector (TR) is a semantic function that profiles a prominent element as being located, evaluated, or described in relation to a **Landmark** (LM).

Transitive verbs have at least one **argument**. The complement is the receiver of the verbal action.

Transitivity concerns the obligation of an object constituent (see **Completion**).

Triliteral (see **Triradical**)

Tripartite verbless clause is a clause with at least three constituents: a subject, a predicate, and a independent pronoun serving as a **Copula**, for example הָאִישׁ טוֹב הוּא "the man is good" (cf. **Bipartite verbless clause**).

Triradical are verbal roots consisting of three radicals (see **Radical**).

Trivalent verbs (e.g., *put, give*) are transitive and can designate up to three obligatory constituents.

Univalent verbs have one clause constituent other than the verb.

Unmarked forms (see **Marked forms**).

Unvoiced consonants are pronounced without the use of the vocal chords (e.g., unvoiced *p* vs. **Voiced** *b*).

Urtext is a German word for "original text."

Uvular is a consonant articulated by placing the back of the tongue against the uvula (i.e., the soft part of the palate above the throat) (e.g., *q*).

Valency describes the number of obligatory or core constituents, or valents, in a clause.

Verbal adjectives (see **Participles**).

Verbal nouns (or gerunds) are verb forms that possess both verbal and nominal qualities.

Verb-framing language is a typological description where verbs encode specific paths of movement as part of their lexical semantics (see **Satellite-framing**).

Verb phrase is a syntactic categorization of one or more lexemes functioning as a single predicate.

Verb plurality (or **Pluractionality**) involves the semantic notion of multiplicity of an event.

Verbs designate words that refer to less time-stable actions, events, and states. They organize the elements of a clause (**Subject**, **Object**, **Adjuncts**) into units of meaning.

Voice (or **Diathesis**) describes a morphosyntactic property of verbs that correlates between the semantic roles and the syntactic functions of the clause constituents.

Voiced consonants are pronounced with the vibration of the vocal chords (e.g., voiced *d* versus **Unvoiced** *t*).

Volitive forms mainly concern deontic or event **Modality** in that they involve the speaker's desire that a given situation or event take place.

Vorlage indicates the assumed predecessor to another text (e.g., the parent Hebrew text of the Old Greek Septuagint).

Vowel gradation (see **Apophony**)

Weak verbs are the irregular verb roots consisting of one or more weak radicals (e.g., I-weak, middle-weak or hollow, and III-weak or third-*he*) (see **Strong verb**).

Wh-question is an interrogative in which the initial interrogative pronoun anticipates an assumed referent.

Word classes (or **Parts of speech**) are the lexical categories used to classify words.

Yes-no questions anticipate the answer to the interrogative is either affirmative or negative.

BIBLIOGRAPHY

/////////////////

Abegg, Martin, Peter Flint, and Eugene Ulrich. *The Dead Sea Scrolls Bible: The Oldest Known Bible Translated for the First Time into English*. New York: HarperCollins, 1999.

Abusch, Tzvi, John Huehnergard, and Piotr Steinkeller, eds. *Lingering over Words: Studies in Ancient Near Eastern Literature in Honor of William F. Moran*. HSS 37. Atlanta: Scholars Press, 1990.

Adam, Klaus-Peter. "'And He Behaved Like a Prophet among Them' (1Sam 10:11b): The Depreciative Use of נבא *Hitpael* and the Comparative Evidence of Ecstatic Prophecy." *Die Welt des Orients* 39 (2009): 3–57.

Aḥituv, Shmuel. *Echoes from the Past: Hebrew and Cognate Inscriptions from the Biblical Period*. Jerusalem: Carta, 2008.

Aikhenvald, Alexandra Y., and R. M. W. Dixon. *Serial Verb Constructions: A Cross-Linguistic Typology*. Oxford: Oxford University Press, 2006.

Aissen, Judith. "Differential Object Marking: Iconicity vs. Economy." *Natural Language and Linguistic Theory* 21 (2003): 435–483.

Aitken, James K., ed. *T&T Clark Companion to the Septuagint*. London: T&T Clark, 2015.

Albrektson, Bertil. "Reflections on the Emergence of a Standard Text of the Hebrew Bible." Pages 49–65 in *Congress Volume: Göttingen 1977*. Edited by J. A. Emerton. VTSup 29. Leiden: Brill, 1978.

Albright, William F. "The Early Alphabetic Inscriptions from Sinai and their Decipherment." *BASOR* 110 (1948): 6–22.

Andersen, Francis I. *The Hebrew Verbless Clause in the Pentateuch*. JBLMS 14. Nashville: Abingdon, 1970.

———. *The Sentence in Biblical Hebrew*. The Hague: Mouton, 1974.

Andersen, Francis I., and A. D. Forbes. "The Participle in Biblical Hebrew and the Overlap of Grammar and Lexicon." Pages 185–212 in *Milk and Honey: Essays on Ancient Israel and the Bible in Appreciation of the Judaic Studies Program at the University of California, San Diego*. Edited by S. Malena and D. Miano. Winona Lake, IN: Eisenbrauns, 2007.

Andrason, Alexander, and Juan-Pablo Vita. "The YQTL-Ø 'Preterite' in Ugaritic Epic Poetry." *ArOr* 85 (2017): 345–87.

Annus, Amar. "On the Origin of Watchers: A Comparative Study of the Antediluvian Wisdom in Mesopotamian and Jewish Traditions." *Journal for the Study of the Pseudepigrapha* 19 (2010): 277–320.

Aussant, Emilie. "To Classify Words: Western and Indian Grammatical Approaches." Pages 213–35 in *Sanskrit Syntax: Selected Papers Presented at the Seminar on Sanskrit Syntax and Discourse Structures, 13–15 June 2013, Université Paris Diderot, with an Updated and Revised Bibliography by Hans Henrich Hock.* Edited by Peter M. Scharf. Providence, RI: The Sanskrit Library, 2015.

Austin, J. L. *How to Do Things with Words.* 2nd ed. Edited by J. O. Urmson and Marin Sbisa. Cambridge: Harvard University Press, 1962.

Avigad, Nahman, and Benjamin Sass. *Corpus of West Semitic Stamp Seals.* Jerusalem: Israel Exploration Society, 1997.

Bache, Carl. "Aspect and Aktionsart: Towards a Semantic Distinction." *Journal of Linguistics* 18 (1982): 57–72.

Baden, Joel S. *The Composition of the Pentateuch: Renewing the Documentary Hypothesis.* New Haven: Yale University Press, 2012.

———. "Hithpael and Niphal in Biblical Hebrew: Semantic and Morphological Overlap." *VT* 60 (2010): 34–35.

Baker, Mark. *Lexical Categories: Verbs, Nouns, Adjectives.* Cambridge: Cambridge University Press, 2003.

Baker, Mark, and William Croft. "Lexical Categories: Legacy, Lacuna, and Opportunity for Functionalists and Formalists." *Annual Review of Linguistics* 3 (2017): 179–197.

Baltes, P. B., and N. J. Smelser, eds. *International Encyclopedia of the Social & Behavioral Sciences.* Amsterdam: Pergamon, 2001.

Bar-Asher, M. "The Gender of Nouns in Biblical Hebrew." *Semitics* 6 (1978): 1–14.

Baranowski, Krzystof J. "The Biblical Hebrew *wayyiqtol* and the Evidence of the Amarna Letters from Canaan." *JHS* 16 (2016): 1–18.

Barkay, Gabriel. "The Priestly Benediction on Silver Plaques from Ketef Hinnom in Jerusalem." *Tel Aviv* 19 (1992): 139–92.

———, Marilyn J. Lundberg, Andrew G. Vaughn, and Bruce Zuckerman. "The Amulets from Ketef Hinnom: A New Edition and Evaluation." *BASOR* 334 (2004): 41–71.

Barr, James. "A New Look at Kethibh-Qere." Pages 19–37 in *Remembering All the Way: A Collection of Old Testament Studies Published on the Occasion of the Fortieth Anniversary of the Oudtestamentisch Werkgezelschap in Nederland.* Edited by A. S. van der Woude. Oudtestamentisch Stüdien 21. Leiden: Brill, 1981.

———. "Textual Criticism: Hebrew Bible." Pages 363–71 in vol. 2 of *The Oxford Encyclopedia of Biblical Interpretation.* Edited by Steven L. McKenzie. Oxford: Oxford University Press, 2013.

Barrera, Julio Trebolle. "Kings (MT/LXX) and Chronicles: The Double and Triple Textual Tradition." Pages 483–501 in *Reflection and Refraction: Studies in Biblical Historiography in Honour of A. Graeme Auld.* Edited by Robert Rezetko, Timothy H. Lim, and W. Brian Aucker. *VTSup* 113. Leiden: Brill, 2007.

Barth, Jacob. "Das passive Qal und seine Participien." Pages 145–53 in *Jubelschrift zum Siebzigsten Geburtstag des Dr. Israel Hildesheimer.* Berlin: Engel, 1980.

Barthélemy, Dominique. *Critique textuelle de l'Ancien Testament.* 5 vols. Göttingen: Vandenhoeck Ruprecht, 1982–2015.

———. *Studies in the Text of the Old Testament: An Introduction to the Hebrew Old Testament Text Project.* Winona Lake, IN: Eisenbrauns, 2012.

Barthélemy, Dominique et al., eds. *Preliminary and Interim Report on the Hebrew Old Testament Text Project.* 5 vols. New York: United Bible Society, 1973–1980.

Bauer, Hans, and Pontus Leander. *Historische Grammatik der hebräischen Sprache des Alten Testamentes.* Halle: Niemeyer, 1922. Repr. Hildesheim: Olms, 1962.

Beckman, John C. "Toward the Meaning of the Biblical Hebrew *Piel* Stem." PhD diss., Harvard University, 2015.

Bekins, Peter. "Definiteness and the Definite Article." Pages 28–33 in *Where Shall Wisdom Be Found? A Grammatical Tributer to Professor Stephen A. Kaufman.* Edited by Hélène M. Dallaire, Benjamin J. Noonan, and Jennifer E. Noonan. Winona Lake, IN: Eisenbrauns, 2017.

———. *Transitivity and Object Marking in Biblical Hebrew: An Investigation of the Object Preposition 'et.* HSS 64. Winona Lake, IN: Eisenbrauns, 2014.

———. "The Use of Differential Object Marking in Northwest Semitic." *KUSATU* 20 (2016): 3–50.

Bergsträsser, Gotthelf. *A Grammar of the Hebrew Language* (Hebrew). Translated by M. Ben Asher. Jerusalem: Magnes, 1926.

———. *Hebräische Grammatik: Mit Benutzung der von E. Kautzsch bearbeiteten 28, Auflage von Wilhelm Gesenius' hebräischer Grammatik.* Leipzig: Vogel, 1918.

———. *Introduction to the Semitic Languages.* Translated by Peter T. Daniels. Winona Lake, IN: Eisenbrauns, 1983.

Biber, Douglas, Stig Johansson, Geoffrey Leech, Susan Conrad, and Edward Finegan. *Longman Grammar of Spoken and Written English.* Harlow: Pearson, 1999.

Black, David A. *Linguistics for Students of New Testament Greek: A Survey of Basic Concepts and Application.* 2nd ed. Grand Rapids: Baker, 1995.

Blake, Frank R. "The Internal Passive in Semitic." *JAOS* 22 (1901): 45–54.

———. *A Resurvey of Hebrew Tenses.* Rome: Pontifical Biblical Institute, 1951.

Blass, Fiedrich, Albert Debrunner, Robert W. Funk. *A Greek Grammar of the New Testament and Other Early Christian Literature.* Rev. ed. Chicago: University of Chicago Press, 1961.

Blau, Joshua. *Phonology and Morphology of Biblical Hebrew.* LSAWS 2. Winona Lake, IN: Eisenbrauns, 2010.

Block, Daniel I. *Judges, Ruth.* NAC 6. Nashville: B&H, 1999.

Bodine, Walter R., ed. *Discourse Analysis of Biblical Literature: What It Is and What It Offers.* Atlanta: Scholars Press, 1995.

Boling, Robert G. *Joshua.* AB 6. Garden City, NY: Doubleday, 1982.

Bordreuil, Pierre, and Dennis G. Pardee. *A Manual of Ugaritic.* LSAWS 3. Winona Lake, IN: Eisenbrauns, 2009.

———. "Textes alphabétiques en ougaritique." Pages 341–48 in *Études ougaritiques 1: Travaux 1985–1995.* Edited by M. Yon and D. Arnaud. Ras Shamra-Ougarit 14. Paris: Éditions Recherche sur les Civilisations, 2001.

Bordreuil, Pierre, and Dennis Pardee, with Robert Hawley. *Une bibliothèque au sud de la ville. Textes 1994–2002 en cunéiforme alphabétique de la maison d'Ourtenou.* Ras Shamra-Ougarit 18. Paris: Maison de l'Orient et de la Méditerranée, 2012.

Bossong, Georg. "Animacy and Markedness in Universal Grammar." *Glossologia* 2–3 (1983): 7–20.

———. *Empirische Universalienforschung: Differentielle Objektmarkierung in den neuiranischen Sprachen.* Tübingen: Narr, 1985.

Böttcher, Friedrich. *Ausführliches Lehrbuch der hebräischen Sprache.* Leipzig: Barth, 1866.

Botterweck, G. Johannes, ed. *Theological Dictionary of the Old Testament.* 17 vols. Grand Rapids: Eerdmans, 1975–2021.

Boyd, Samuel L. *Language Contact, Colonial Administration, and the Construction of Identity in Ancient Israel: Constructing the Context for Contact.* HSS 66. Leiden: Brill, 2021.

Boyd, Samuel L., and H. H. Hardy II. "Hebrew Adverbialization, Aramaic Language Contact, and *mpny 'šr* in Exodus 19:18." Pages 33–51, in *Studies in Semitic Language Contact.* Edited by Aaron Butts. SSLL 82. Leiden: Brill, 2015.

Boyd, Steven W. "The Binyamin (Verbal Stems)." Pages 85–125, in *Where Shall Wisdom Be Found? A Grammatical Tribute to Professor Stephen A. Kaufman.* Edited by Hélène M. Dallaire, Benjamin J. Noonan, and Jennifer E. Noonan. Winona Lake, IN: Eisenbrauns, 2017.

Bravmann, M. M. "Notes on the Forms of the Imperative in Hebrew and Arabic." *JQR* 42 (1951): 51–56.

Breuer, Mordechai. *The Biblical Text in the Jerusalem Crown Edition and Its Sources in the Masora and Manuscripts.* Jerusalem: Keren Ha-Masora, 2003.

Brockelmann, Carl. *Grundriss der vergleichenden Grammatik der semitischen Sprachen*. 2 vols. Berlin: Reuther & Reichard, 1908–1913. Repr. Hildesheim: Olms, 1961.

Bron, François. *Recherches sur les inscriptions phéniciennes de Karatepe*. Hautes Études Orientales 11. Genève: Droz, 1979.

Brotzman, Ellis R., and Eric J. Tully. *Old Testament Textual Criticism: A Practical Introduction*. Grand Rapids: Baker, 2016.

Brown, A. Philip, II, and Bryan W. Smith. *A Reader's Hebrew Bible*. Grand Rapids: Zondervan, 2008.

Brown, Francis, S. R. Driver, and Charles A. Briggs. *A Hebrew and English Lexicon of the Old Testament with an Appendix Containing the Biblical Aramaic Based on the Lexicon of William Gesenius as Translated by Edward Robinson*. Oxford: Clarendon, 1906.

Burkitt, F. C. "The Hebrew Papyrus of the Ten Commandments." *JQR* 15 (1903): 392–408.

Butler, Trent C. *Joshua*. WBC 7. Waco, TX: Word, 1983.

Callaway, Mary C. "Canonical Criticism." Pages 142–55 in *To Each Its Own Meaning: An Introduction to Biblical Criticisms and Their Application*. Edited by Stephen R. Haynes and Steven L. McKenzie. Philadelphia: WJK, 1999.

Caplice, Richard, with Daniel Snell. *Introduction to Akkadian*. 4th ed. Rome: Pontifical Biblical Institute, 2002.

Carbajosa, Ignacio. "Peshitta." Pages 262–77 in vol. 1A of *Textual History of the Bible: The Hebrew Bible*. Edited by Armin Lange and Emanuel Tov. Leiden: Brill, 2016.

Carr, David M. *The Formation of the Hebrew Bible: A New Reconstruction*. Oxford: Oxford University Press, 2011.

Charpin, Dominique. *Reading and Writing in Babylon*. Translated by Jane Marie Todd. Cambridge: Harvard University Press, 2011.

Chiesa, Bruno. "Textual History and Textual Criticism of the Hebrew Old Testament." Pages 257–72 in vol. 1 of *The Madrid Qumran Congress. Proceeding of the International Congress on the Dead Sea Scrolls Madrid 18–21 March 1991*. Edited by Julio Trebolle Barrera and Luis Vegas Montaner. STDJ 11. Leiden: Brill, 1992.

Childs, Brevard S. *The Book of Exodus*. OTL. Louisville: WJK, 1974.

———. *Introduction to the Old Testament as Scripture*. Philadelphia: Fortress, 1979.

Chomsky, Noam. *Lectures on Government and Binding: The Pisa Lectures*. Studies in Generative Grammar 9. Berlin: de Gruyter, 1993.

Christiansen, Brent. "A Linguistic Analysis of the Biblical Particle *nā'*: A Test Case." *VT* 59 (2009): 379–93.

Clines, David J. A., ed. *The Dictionary of Classical Hebrew*. 6 vols. Sheffield: Sheffield Academic, 1993–2011.

Coakley, J. F. *Robinson's Paradigms and Exercises in Syriac Grammar*. 5th ed. Oxford: Oxford University Press, 2002.

Cohen, Chaim. "The Enclitic *mem* in Biblical Hebrew: Its Existence and Initial Discovery." Pages 231–60 in *Sefer Moshe: The Moshe Weinfeld Jubilee Volume*. Edited by Chaim Cohen, Avi Hurvitz, and Shalom M. Paul. Winona Lake, IN: Eisenbrauns, 2004.

Coleman, Stephen. *The Biblical Hebrew Transitivity Alternation in Cognitive Linguistic Perspective*. Abhandlungen für die Kunde des Morgenlandes 114. Wiesbaden: Harrassowitz, 2018.

Comprehensive Aramaic Lexicon. https://cal.huc.edu/.

Comrie, Bernard. *Aspect: An Introduction to the Study of Verbal Aspect and Related Problems*. Cambridge Textbooks in Linguistics. Cambridge: Cambridge University Press, 1976.

Cook, John A. "The Hebrew Participle and Stative." *JNSL* 34 (2008): 1–19.

———. *Time and the Biblical Hebrew Verb: The Expression of Tense, Aspect, and Modality in Biblical Hebrew*. LSAWS 7. Winona Lake, IN: Eisenbrauns, 2012.

Corbett, G. G. *Number*. Cambridge: Cambridge University Press, 2000.

Cowper, E., and V. DeCaen. "Biblical Hebrew: A Formal Perspective on the Left Periphery." *Toronto Working Papers in Linguistics* 38 (2017): 1–33.

Cox, Claude. "Septuagint." Pages 175–81 in vol. 1C of *Textual History of the Bible: The Hebrew Bible*. Edited by Armin Lange and Emanuel Tov. Leiden: Brill, 2017.

———. "Some Things Biblical Scholars Should Know about the Septuagint." *Restoration Quarterly* 56.2 (2014): 85–97.

Crawford, Sidnie White. "Samaritan Pentateuch." Pages 166–75 in vol. 1A of *Textual History of the Bible: The Hebrew Bible*. Edited by Armin Lange and Emanuel Tov. Leiden: Brill, 2016.

Creason, Stuart A. "Aramaic." Pages 391–426 in *The Cambridge Encyclopedia of the World's Ancient Languages*. Edited by Roger D. Woodard. Cambridge: Cambridge University Press, 2004.

———. "Semantic Classes of Hebrew Verbs: A Study of *Aktionsart* in the Hebrew Verbal System." Ph.D. diss., The University of Chicago, 1995.

Cross, Frank M. "The Development of the Jewish Scripts." Pages 133–202 in *The Bible and the Ancient Near East: Essays in Honor of William Foxwell Albright*. Edited by G. Ernest Wright. Winona Lake, IN: Eisenbrauns, 1979.

———. "The Evolution of the Proto-Canaanite Alphabet." *BASOR* 134 (1954): 15–24.

———. "An Old Canaanite Inscription Recently Found at Lachish." *Tel Aviv* 11 (1984): 71–76.

———. "The Oldest Manuscripts from Qumran." *JBL* 74 (1955): 147–72.

Cruse, D. A. *Lexical Semantics*. Cambridge: Cambridge University Press, 1986.

Dallaire, Hélène. *The Syntax of Volitives in Biblical Hebrew and Amarna Canaanite Prose.* LSAWS 9. Winona Lake, IN: Eisenbrauns, 2014.

———. "The Syntax of Volitives in Northwest Semitic Prose." PhD diss., Hebrew Union College, 2002.

Darnell, John Coleman, F. W. Dobbs-Allsopp, Marilyn J. Lundberg, P. Kyle McCarter, Bruce Zuckerman, and Colleen Manassa. "Two Early Alphabetic Inscriptions from the Wadi el-Ḥôl: New Evidence for the Origin of the Alphabet from the Western Desert of Egypt." *The Annual of the American Schools of Oriental Research* 59 (2005): 63–124.

Davidson, Andrew B. *Introductory Hebrew Grammar Hebrew Syntax.* 3rd ed. Edinburgh: T&T Clark, 1902.

Davidson, Thomas. "The Grammar of Dionysios Thrax." *Journal of Speculative Philosophy* 8 (1874): 326–39.

Davies, Graham. I., ed. *Ancient Hebrew Inscriptions: Corpus and Concordance.* 2 vols. Cambridge: Cambridge University Press, 1991–2004.

———. "A Note on the Etymology of hištaḥawāh." *VT* 29 (1979): 493–95.

Davila, J. R. "Text-Type and Terminology: Genesis and Exodus as Test Cases." *RevQ* 16 (1993): 3–37.

DeCean, Vincent J. J. "Ewald and Driver on Biblical Hebrew 'Aspect': Anteriority and the Orientalist Framework." *ZAH* 9 (1996): 126–51.

Dempster, Stephen G. "The Old Testament Canon, Josephus, and Cognitive Environment." Pages 321–61 in *The Enduring Authority of the Christian Scriptures.* Edited by D. A. Carson. Grand Rapids: Eerdmans, 2016.

Demsky, Aaron. "An Iron Age IIA Alphabetic Writing Exercise from Khirbet Qeiyafa." *IEJ* 62 (2012): 186–99.

de Rossi, Giovanni Bernardo. *Variae lectiones Veteris Testamenti: ex immensa manuscriptorum editorumque codicum congerie haustae et ad Samaritanum textum, ad vetustissimas versiones, ad accuratiores sacrae criticae fontes ac leges examinatae.* 4 vols. Parmae: Ex Regio Typographeo, 1784–1788.

de Waard, Jan. *A Handbook on Isaiah.* Winona Lake, IN: Eisenbrauns, 1997.

———. *A Handbook on Jeremiah.* Winona Lake, IN: Eisenbrauns, 2003.

Dhont, Marieke. *Style and Context of Old Greek Job.* JSJSup 183. Leiden: Brill, 2017.

Dik, Simon C. *The Theory of Functional Grammar.* Dordrecht: Foris, 1989.

Dines, Jennifer M. *The Septuagint.* London: T&T Clark, 2004.

Dobbs-Allsopp, F. W. "Biblical Hebrew Statives and Situation Aspect." *JSS* 45 (2000): 21–53.

Dobbs-Allsopp, F. W., J. J. M. Roberts, C. L. Seow, and R. E. Whitaker. *Hebrew Inscriptions: Texts from the Biblical Period of the Monarchy with Concordance.* New Haven, CT: Yale University Press, 2005.

Donnelly-Lewis, Brian. "The Khirbet Qeiyafa Ostracon: A New Collation Based on the Multispectral Images, with Translation and Commentary," *BASOR* 388 (2022): forthcoming.

Doron, Edit. "The Infinitive in Biblical Hebrew." Pages 144–68 in *Linguistic Studies on Biblical Hebrew*. Edited by Robert D. Holmstedt. SSLL 102. Leiden: Brill, 2021.

Dotan, Aron, ed. *Biblia Hebraica Leningradensia*. Peabody, MA: Hendrickson, 2001.

———. "Masorah." Pages 609–56 in vol. 13 of *Encyclopedia Judaica*. 2nd ed. Edited by Fred Skolnik and Michael Berenbaum. Detroit: Macmillan, 2007.

Dotan, Aron, and Nurit Reich. *Masora Thesaurus: A Complete Alphabetic Collection of the Masora Notes in the Leningrad Codex*. Altamonte Springs: Oak Tree Software, 2014.

Dowty, David. *Word Meaning and Montague Grammar: The Semantics of Verbs and Times in Generative Semantics and in Montague's PTQ*. Studies in Linguistics and Philosophy 7. Dordrecht: Kluwer, 1979.

Dozeman, Thomas B. *Joshua 1–12*. AB 6B. New Haven: Yale University Press, 2015.

Dressler, Wolfgang. *Studien zur verbalen Pluralität: Iterativum, Distributivum, Durativum, Intensivum in der allgemeinen Grammatik, im Lateinischen und Hethitischen*. Vienna: Böhlau im Kommission, 1968.

Driver, G. R. "Problems of Semitic Grammar." *ZDMG* 91 (1937): 343–51.

Driver, S. R. *A Treatise on the Use of the Tenses in Hebrew*. 3rd ed. Oxford: Clarendon, 1892.

Dyk, J. W. *Participles in Context: A Computer-Assisted Study of Old Testament Hebrew*. Amsterdam: VU University Press, 1994.

Ego, Beate. "Targumim." Pages 239–61 in vol. 1A of *Textual History of the Bible: The Hebrew Bible*. Edited by Armin Lange and Emanuel Tov. Leiden: Brill, 2016.

Eissfeldt, Otto. *Hexateuch-Synopse: Die Erzählung der fünf Bücher Mose und des Buches Josua mit them Anfange des Richterbuches in ihre vier Quellen zerlegt und in deutscher Übersetzung dargeboten samt einer in Einleitung und Anmerkungen gegebenen Begründung*. Leipzig: Hinrichs, 1922.

Elgvin, Torleif, Menachem Kister, Timothy Lim, Bilhah Nitzan, Stephen Pfann, Elisha Qimron, Lawrence H. Schiffman, Annette Steudel, eds. *Qumran Cave 4. The Sapiential Texts, Part 1*. DJD 15. Oxford: Clarendon, 1997.

Elliger, Karl, and Wilhelm Rudolph, eds. *Biblica Hebraica Stuttgartensia*. 5th ed. Stuttgart: Deutsche Bibelgesellschaft, 1997.

Emerton, J. A. "The Etymology of *hištaḥawāh*." *Oudtestamentische Studiën* 20 (1977): 41–55. Repr. in pages 83–96 in *Studies on the Language and Literature of the Bible: Selected Works of J. A. Emerton*. Edited by Graham Davies and Robert Gordon. VTSup 165. Leiden: Brill, 2015.

Evans, Vyvyan. "The Perceptual Basis of Spatial Representation." Pages 21–50 in *Language, Cognition and Space: The State of the Art and New Directions*. Edited by Vyvyan Evans and Paul Chilton. Sheffield: Equinox, 2010.

Evans, Vyvyan, and Andrea Tyler. "Applying Cognitive Linguistics to Pedagogical Grammar: The English Prepositions of Verticality." *Revista Brasileira de Linguística Aplicada* 5.2 (2004): 11–42.

———. "Rethinking English 'Prepositions of Movement': The Case of *To* and *Through*." *Belgian Journal of Linguistics* 18 (2004): 247–70.

Ewald, Georg August Heinrich von. *A Grammar of the Hebrew Language of the Old Testament*. Translated by John Nicholson. London: Whittaker, 1836.

———. *Grammatica critica linguae Arabicae*. 2 vols. Leipzig: Hahn, 1831–1833.

Faber, A. "Second Harvest: šibbolet Revisited (Yet Again)." *JSS* 37 (1992): 1–10.

Fassberg, Steven E. *A Grammar of Palestinian Targum Fragments from the Cairo Genizah*. HSS 38. Atlanta: Scholars, 1990.

———. "The Lengthened Imperative קָטְלָה in Biblical Hebrew." *HS* 40 (1999): 1–13.

———. *Studies in the Syntax of Biblical Hebrew* (Hebrew). Jerusalem: Magnes, 1994.

Fassi Fehri, Abdelkader. "Verbal Plurality, Transitivity, and Causativity." Pages 151–85 in *Research in Afroasiatic Grammar 2: Selected Papers from the Fifth Conference on Afroasiatic Languages, Paris, 2000*. Edited by Jacqueline Lecarme. Philadelphia: Benjamins, 2003.

Ferguson, Anthony Michael. "A Comparison of the Non-Aligned Texts of Qumran to the Masoretic Text." PhD diss., The Southern Baptist Theological Seminary, 2018.

Fernández Marcos, Natalio. *The Septuagint in Context: Introduction to the Greek Versions of the Bible*. Translated by Wilfred G. E. Watson. Leiden: Brill, 2000.

Filip, Hana. "Aspectual Class and Aktionsart." Pages 1186–217 in *Semantics: An International Handbook of Natural Language Meaning*. Edited by Claudia Maienborn, Klaus von Heusinger and Paul Portner. Berlin: de Gruyter, 2011.

Finsterbusch, Karin. "Other Texts." Pages 265–68 in vol. 1B of *Textual History of the Bible: The Hebrew Bible*. Edited by Armin Lange and Emanuel Tov. Leiden: Brill, 2017.

Fitzmyer, Joseph A. *A Guide to the Dead Sea Scrolls and Related Literature*. Rev. ed. Grand Rapids: Eerdmans, 2008.

Fox, Joshua. *Semitic Noun Patterns*. HSS 52. Winona Lake, IN: Eisenbrauns, 2003.

———. "A Sequence of Vowel Shifts in Phoenician and Other Languages." *JNES* 55 (1996): 37–47.

Freedman, David Noel, ed. *Anchor Yale Bible Dictionary*. 6 vols. New York: Doubleday, 1992.

Friedersdorf, Conor. "Reading, Writing, and Thinking Online: An Interview with Alan Jacobs." *The Atlantic*. June 8, 2010. https://www.theatlantic.com/projects/ideas-2010/archive/2010/06/reading-writing-and-thinking-online-an-interview-with-alan-jacobs/57807/.

Friedman, Matti. *The Aleppo Codex: A True Story of Obsession, Faith, and the Pursuit of an Ancient Bible*. Chapel Hill, NC: Algonquin, 2012.

Friedrich, J., and W. Röllig. *Phönizisch-Punische Grammatik*. 3rd ed. Edited by M. G. Amadasi Guzzo. AnOr 55. Rome: Pontifical Biblical Institute, 1999.

Fruyt, Michèle, Michel Mazoyer, and Dennis Pardee, eds. *Grammatical Case in the Languages of the Middle East and Europe Acts of the International Colloquium Variations, Concurrence et Évolution des cas dans divers domaines linguistiques, Paris, 2–4 April 2007*. SAOC 64. Chicago: The Oriental Institute, 2011.

Gai, Amikam. "The Category 'Adjective' in Semitic Languages." *JSS* 40 (1995): 1–9.

Galil, G. "The Hebrew Inscription from Khirbet Qeiyafa/Netaʿim." *UF* 41 (2009): 193–242.

Gane, Roy E. *Old Testament Law for Christians: Original Context and Enduring Application*. Grand Rapids: Baker Academic, 2017.

Gardiner, Alan. "The Egyptian Origin of the Semitic Alphabet." *Journal of Egyptian Archaeology* 3 (1916): 1–16.

———. "Sinai Script and the Origin of the Alphabet." *Palestine Exploration Fund Quarterly Statement* (1929): 48–55.

Garr, W. Randall. "Affectedness, Aspect, and Biblical *ʾet*." *Zeitschrift für Althebraistik* 4.2 (1991): 119–34.

———. *Dialect Geography of Syria-Palestine, 1000–586 B.C.E.* Winona Lake, IN: Eisenbrauns, 2004.

Garr, W. Randall, and Steven E. Fassberg, eds. *A Handbook of Biblical Hebrew*. 2 vols. Winona Lake, IN: Eisenbrauns, 2016.

Gault, Brian P. *Body as Landscape, Love as Intoxication: Conceptual Metaphors in the Song of Songs*. Ancient Israel and Its Literature 36. Atlanta: SBL, 2019.

Gensler, Orin. "Why Semitic Adverbializers (Akkadian *-iš*, Syriac *-āʾīt*) Should Not Be Derived from Existential * *ʾīt*." *JSS* 45 (2000): 233–65.

Gentry, Peter J., ed. *Ecclesiastes*. SVTG 11.2. Göttingen: Vandenhoeck & Ruprecht, 2019.

———. "Pre-Hexaplaric Translations, Hexapla, Post-Hexaplaric Translations." Pages 211–35 in vol. 1A of *Textual History of the Bible: The Hebrew Bible*. Edited by Armin Lange and Emanuel Tov. Leiden: Brill, 2016.

———. "Propaedeutic to a Lexicon of the Three: The Priority of a New Critical Edition of Hexaplaric Fragments." *Aramaic Studies* 2.2 (2004): 145–74.

———. "The Septuagint and Origen's Hexapla." Pages 191–206 in *The T&T Clark Handbook of Septuagint Research*. Edited by William A. Ross and W. Edward Glenny. London: Bloomsbury T&T Clark, 2021.

———. "The System of the Finite Verb in Classical Biblical Hebrew." *HS* 39 (1998): 7–39.

———. "The Text of the Old Testament." *JETS* 52 (2009): 19–45.

Gentry, Peter J., and John D. Meade. "MasPsᵃ and the Early History of the Hebrew Psalter." Pages 113–45 in *From Scribal Error to Rewriting: How Ancient Texts Could and Could Not Be Changed*. Edited by Anneli Aejmelaeus, Drew Longacre, and Natia Mirotadze. Göttingen: Vandenhoeck & Ruprecht, 2020.

Ginsberg, H. L. "Heart." Pages 508–9 in vol. 8 of *Encyclopedia Judaica*. 2nd ed. Edited by Fred Skolnik and Michael Berenbaum. Detroit: Macmillan, 2007.

———. "The Rebellion and Death of Baʿlu." *Or* 5 (1936): 161–98.

Ginsburg, Christian D. *The Massorah Compiled from Manuscripts. Alphabetically and Lexically Arranged*. 4 vols. London, 1880–1905.

Givón, Talmy, ed. *Discourse Syntax*. Syntax and Semantics 12. New York: Academic Press, 1979.

———. "The Drift from VSO to SVO in Biblical Hebrew: the Pragmatics of Tense-Aspect." Pages 181–255 in *Mechanism of Syntactic Change*. Edited by Charles Li. Austin: University of Texas Press, 1977.

———. *On Understanding Grammar*. Rev. ed. Amsterdam: Benjamins, 2018.

———. *Syntax: An Introduction*. Amsterdam: Benjamins, 2001.

Glanville, Peter John. *The Lexical Semantics of the Arabic Verb*. Oxford: Oxford University Press, 2018.

Goetchius, Eugene Van Ness. *The Language of the New Testament*. New York: Scribner, 1965.

Goetze, Albrecht. "The So-Called Intensive of the Semitic Languages." *JAOS* 62 (1942): 1–8.

Gogel, Sandra Landis. *A Grammar of Epigraphic Hebrew*. Atlanta: Scholars Press, 1998.

Goldenberg, Gideon. *Studies in Semitic Linguistics: Selected Writings*. Jerusalem: Magnes, 1998.

———. "Tautological Infinitive." *Israel Oriental Studies* 1 (1971): 36–85.

Goldfajn, Tal. *Word Order and Time in Biblical Hebrew Narrative*, Oxford Theological Monographs. Oxford: Clarendon, 1998.

Goldwasser, Orly. "Canaanites Reading Hieroglyphs: Horus is Hathor? The Invention of the Alphabet in Sinai." *Ägypten und Levante* 16 (2006): 121–60.

———. "The Miners who Invented the Alphabet: A Response to Christopher Rollston." *Journal of Ancient Egyptian Interconnections* 4.3 (2012): 9–22.

Gordis, Robert. *The Biblical Text in the Making: A Study of the Kethib-Qere*. 2nd ed. New York: KTAV, 1971.

Gordon, Amnon. "The Development of the Participle in Biblical, Mishnaic, and Modern Hebrew." *Afroasiatic Linguistics* 8 (1982): 121–79.

Gordon, Cyrus H. *Ugaritic Textbook: Grammar, Texts in Transliteration, Cuneiform Selections, Glossary, Indices*. Rev. ed. AnOr 38. Rome: Pontifical Biblical Institute, 1998.

Goshen-Gottstein, Moshe H. *The Aleppo Codex*. Jerusalem: Magnes, 1976.

———. "Hebrew Biblical Manuscripts: Their History and Their Place in the HUBP Edition." *Biblica* 48 (1967): 253–74.

———, ed. *The Hebrew University Bible. The Book of Isaiah*. Jerusalem: Magnus, 1995.

———. *Mikraot Gedolot. Biblia Rabbinica: A Reprint of the 1525 Venice Edition*. Jerusalem: Makor, 1972.

———. "The System of Verbal Stems in the Classical Semitic Languages." Pages 70–91 in *Proceedings of the International Conference on Semitic Studies Held in Jerusalem, 19–23 July 1965*. Jerusalem: The Israel Academy of Sciences and Humanities, 1969.

———. "The Textual Criticism of the Old Testament: Rise, Decline, Rebirth." *JBL* 102 (1983): 365–99.

Goshen-Gottstein, Moshe H., and Shemaryahu Talmon, eds. *The Hebrew University Bible. The Book of Ezekiel*. Jerusalem: Magnus, 2004.

Goslinga, C. J. *Joshua, Judges, Ruth*. Bible Student's Commentary. Grand Rapids: Zondervan, 1987.

Graffi, Giorgio. *200 Years of Syntax. A Critical Study*. Amsterdam: Benjamins, 2001.

Grafton, Anthony, and Megan Williams. *Christianity and the Transformation of the Book: Origen, Eusebius, and the Library of Caesarea*. Cambridge: Harvard University Press, 2006.

Graves, Michael. "Vulgate." Pages 278–88 in vol. 1A of *Textual History of the Bible: The Hebrew Bible*. Edited by Armin Lange and Emanuel Tov. Leiden: Brill, 2016.

Greenberg, Joseph. "The Last Stages of Grammatical Elements: Contractive and Expansive Desemanticization." Pages 301–14 in *Approaches to Grammaticalization*. Edited by E. Traugott and B. Heine. Amsterdam: Benjamins, 1991.

Greenstein, Edward L. "Forms and Functions of the Finite Verb in Ugaritic Narrative Verse." Pages 75–102 in *Biblical Hebrew in Its Northwest Semitic Setting: Typology and Historical Perspectives*. Edited by Steven E. Fassberg and Avi Hurwitz. Winona Lake, IN: Eisenbrauns, 2006.

———. "On the Prefixed Preterite in Biblical Hebrew." *HS* 29 (1988): 7–17.

Greenwood, Kyle, ed. *Since the Beginning: Interpreting Genesis 1 and 2 through the Ages*. Grand Rapids: Baker Academic, 2018.

Gropp, Douglas M. "The Function of the Finite Verb in Classical Biblical Hebrew." *Hebrew Annual Review* 13 (1991): 45–62.

Grossman, Jonathan. "The Structural Paradigm of the Ten Plagues Narrative and the Hardening of Pharaoh's Heart." *VT* 64 (2014): 588–610.

Gzella, Holger. "Voice in Classical Hebrew against Its Semitic Background." *Or* 78 (2009): 292–325.

Hackett, Jo Ann. *A Basic Introduction to Biblical Hebrew*. Peabody, MA: Hendrickson, 2010.

———. "Yaqtul and a Ugaritic Incantation Text." Pages 111–17 in *Language and Nature: Papers Presented to John Huehnergard on the Occasion of His 60th Birthday*. Edited by Rebecca Hasselbach and Naʿama Pat-El. SAOC 67. Chicago: The Oriental Institute, 2012.

Halpern, Baruch. "Sacred History and Ideology: Chronicles' Thematic Structure-Indications of an Earlier Source." Pages 35–54 in *The Creation of Sacred Literature*. Edited by Richard E. Friedman. Near Eastern Studies 22. Berkeley: University of California Press, 1981.

Hamilton, G. J. "The Development of the Early Alphabet." PhD diss., Harvard University, 1985.

Haran, Menahem. "Archives, Libraries, and the Order of the Biblical Books." *JANES* 22 (1993): 51–61.

———. "Book-Scrolls at the Beginning of the Second Temple Period: The Transitions from Papyrus to Skins." *HUCA* 54 (1983): 111–22.

———. "Book-Size and the Device of Catch-Lines in the Biblical Canon." *JJS* 36 (1985): 1–11.

Hardy, H. H., II. "Comparative-Historical Linguistics." in *Linguistics for Hebraists*. Edited by R. Holmstedt and J. Cook. LSAWS. Winona Lake, IN: Eisenbrauns, forthcoming.

———. *The Development of Biblical Hebrew Prepositions*. ANEM 28. Atlanta: SBL, 2022.

———. *Exegetical Gems from Biblical Hebrew: A Refreshing Guide to Grammar and Interpretation*. Grand Rapids: Baker Academic, 2019.

———. "The Table of Grammar: לקראת as Test Case." *Journal for Semitics* 29.2 (2020): 1–16.

Hardy, H. H., II, and Benjamin Thomas. "Another Look at Biblical Hebrew *bɔmɔ* 'High Place'." *VT* 62.2 (2012): 175–88.

Harris, R. Laird, Archer, Gleason L., and Bruce K. Waltke, eds. *Theological Wordbook of the Old Testament*. 2 vols. Chicago: Moody, 1980.

Harris, Zellig S. *Development of the Canaanite Dialects: An Investigation in Linguistic History*, American Oriental Series 16. New Haven: American Oriental Society, 1939.

Haspelmath, Martin. "The Serial Verb Construction: Comparative Concept and Cross-Linguistic Generalizations." *Language and Linguistics* 17.3 (2016): 291–319.

———. "Word Classes and Parts of Speech." Pages 16538–45 in *International Encyclopedia of the Social & Behavioral Sciences*. Edited by P. B. Baltes and N. J. Smelser. Amsterdam: Pergamon, 2001.

Haspelmath, Martin, Ekkehard König, Wulf Oesterreicher, and Wolfgang Raible, eds. *Language Typology and Language Universals*. Handbooks of Linguistics and Communication Science 20.1. Berlin: de Gruyter, 2001.

Hasselbach, Rebecca "Agreement and the Development of Gender in Semitic." *ZDMG* 164 (2014): 33–66, 319–44.

Hatav, Galia. "Anchoring World and Time in Biblical Hebrew." *Journal of Linguistics* 40 (2004): 491–526.

———. "The Infinitive Absolute and Topicalization of Events in Biblical Hebrew." Pages 185–207 in *Advances in Biblical Hebrew Linguistics: Data, Method, and Analyses*. Edited by Adina Moshavi and Tania Notarius. Winona Lake, IN: Eisenbrauns, 2017.

———. "The Nature of the Infinitive Absolute." Pages 125–43 in *Linguistic Studies on Biblical Hebrew*. Edited by Robert D. Holmstedt. SSLL 102. Leiden: Brill, 2021.

———. "Past and Future Interpretation of Wayyiqtol." *JSS* 56 (2011): 85–109.

Hatch, Edwin, and Henry A. Redpath. *A Concordance to the Septuagint and the Other Greek Versions of the Old Testament (Including the Apocryphal Books)*. 2nd ed. Grand Rapids: Baker, 1998.

Hawley, Robert. "Apprendre a ecrire a Ougarit: une typologie des abecedaires." Pages 215–32, in *D'Ougarit à Jérusalem: Recueil d'études épigraphiques et archéologiques offert à Pierre Bordreuil*. Edited by Carole Roche. Orient & Méditerranée 2. Paris: De Boccard, 2008.

The Hebrew Old Testament, Reader's Edition. Wheaton, IL: Crossway, 2021.

Heimerdinger, Jean-Marc. *Topic, Focus and Foreground in Ancient Hebrew Narratives*. JSOTSup 295. Sheffield: Sheffield Academic, 1999.

Heine, Bernd, and Tania Kuteva. *World Lexicon of Grammaticalization*. Cambridge: Cambridge University Press, 2002.

Hempel, J. "Heilung als Symbol und Wirklichkeit." *NAWG* 3 (1958): 237–314.

Hendel, Ronald S. "In the Margins of the Hebrew Verbal System." *ZAH* 9 (1996): 152–81.

———. "Sibilants and *šibbōlet* (Judges 12:6)." *BASOR* 301 (1996): 69–75.

Hendel, Ronald S., and Jan Joosten. *How Old Is the Hebrew Bible? A Linguistic, Textual, and Historical Study*. New Haven: Yale University Press, 2018.

Hengeveld, Kees. *Non-Verbal Predication: Theory, Typology, Diachrony*. Berlin: de Gruyter, 1992.

Herbert, E. D., and Emanuel Tov, eds. *The Bible as Book: The Hebrew Bible and the Judean Desert Discoveries*. London: British Library, 2002.

Hess, Richard S. *Joshua: An Introduction and Commentary*. Tyndale Old Testament Commentary 6. Downers Grove, IL: InterVarsity, 1996.

———. "Splitting the Adam: The Usage of 'ādām in Genesis i–v." Pages 1–15 in *Studies in the Pentateuch*. Edited by J. Emerton. VTSup 41. Leiden: Brill, 1990.

Hetzron, Robert. "Hebrew." Pages 192–209 in *The Major Languages of South Asia, the Middle East, and Africa*. Edited by Bernard Comrie. London: Routledge, 1987.

Hillers, Delbert R. "Some Performative Utterances in the Bible." Pages 757–66 in *Pomegranates and Golden Bells: Studies in Biblical, Jewish, and Near Eastern Ritual, Law, and Literature in Honor of Jacob Milgrom*. Edited by

David P. Wright, David Noel Freedman, and Avi Hurvitz. Winona Lake, IN: Eisenbrauns, 1995.

Hoffman, Adina, and Peter Cole. *Sacred Trash: The Lost and Found World of the Cairo Geniza.* New York: Schocken, 2011.

Hoffmann, Sebastian. *Grammaticalization and English Complex Prepositions: A Corpus-Based Study.* Routledge Advances in Corpus Linguistics 7. London: Routledge, 2006.

Hoftijzer, J., and K. Jongeling. *Dictionary of the North-West Semitic Inscriptions.* 2 vols. Leiden: Brill, 1995.

Höflmayer, Felix, Haggai Misgav, Lyndelle Webster, and Katharina Streit. "Early Alphabetic Writing in the Ancient Near East: the 'Missing Link' from Tel Lachish." *Antiquity* 95 (2021): 705–19.

Holmstedt, Robert D. "Critical at the Margins: Edge Constituents in Biblical Hebrew." *KUSATU* 17 (2014): 109–56.

———. *Linguistic Studies on Biblical Hebrew.* SSLL 102. Leiden: Brill, 2021.

———. *The Relative Clause in Biblical Hebrew.* LSAWS 10. Winona Lake, IN: Eisenbrauns, 2016.

Holmstedt, Robert, and J. Cook, eds. *Linguistics for Hebraists.* LSAWS. Winona Lake, IN: Eisenbrauns, forthcoming.

Holzinger, H. *Das Buch Josua.* Tübingen: Mohr, 1901.

Hopper, Paul. "Aspect and Foregrounding in Discourse." Pages 231–41 in *Discourse Syntax.* Edited by T. Givón. Syntax and Semantics 12. New York: Academic Press, 1979.

Hopper, Paul, and Sandra A. Thompson. "Transitivity in Grammar and Discourse." *Language* 56.2 (1980): 251–99.

Hornkohl, Aaron D. "Transitional Biblical Hebrew." Pages 31–42 in *Periods, Corpora, and Reading Traditions.* Vol. 1 of *A Handbook of Biblical Hebrew.* Edited by W. Randall Garr and Steven E. Fassberg. Winona Lake, IN: Eisenbrauns, 2016.

Hornkohl, Aaron D., and Geoffrey Khan, eds. *New Perspectives in Biblical and Rabbinic Hebrew.* Cambridge Semitic Languages and Cultures 7. Cambridge: Open Book, 2021.

Hough, Carole, ed. *The Oxford Handbook of Names and Naming.* Oxford: Oxford University Press, 2016.

Howell, Adam J., Benjamin L. Merkle, and Robert L. Plummer. *Hebrew for Life: Strategies for Learning, Retaining, and Reviving Biblical Hebrew.* Grand Rapids: Baker Academic, 2020.

Huber, Judith. *Motion and the English Verb: A Diachronic Study.* New York: Oxford University Press, 2017.

Huehnergard, John. "Biblical Hebrew Nominal Patterns." Pages 25–64 in *Epigraphy, Philology, and the Hebrew Bible: Methodological Perspectives on Philological and Comparative Study of the Hebrew Bible in Honor of Jo*

Ann Hackett. Edited by Jeremy M. Hutton and Aaron D. Rubin. ANEM 12. Atlanta: Society of Biblical Literature, 2015.

———. "A Dt Stem in Ugaritic?" *UF* 17 (1986): 402.

———. "The Early Hebrew Prefix-Conjugations." *HS* 29 (1988): 19–23.

———. *A Grammar of Akkadian*. 3rd ed. HSS 45. Winona Lake, IN: Eisenbrauns, 2011.

———. "Historical Phonology and the Hebrew *Piel*." Pages 209–29 in *Linguistics and Biblical Hebrew*. Edited by W. R. Bodine. Winona Lake, IN: Eisenbrauns, 1992.

———. *An Introduction to Ugaritic*. Peabody, MA: Hendrickson, 2012.

———. "Proto-Semitic." Pages 49–79 in *The Semitic Languages*. 2nd ed. Edited by John Huehnergard and Naʿama Pat-El. London: Routledge, 2019.

———. *Ugaritic Vocabulary in Syllabic Transcription*. Rev. ed. HSS 32. Winona Lake, IN: Eisenbrauns, 2008.

Irvine, Judith. "Strategies of Status Manipulation in the Wolof Greeting." Pages 167–91 in *Explorations in the Ethnography of Speaking*. Edited by Richard Bauman and Joel Sherzer. Cambridge: Cambridge University Press, 1974.

Isaksson, Bo. "Subordination: Biblical Hebrew." *EHLL* 3:657–64.

Jackson, Kent P. *The Ammonite Language of the Iron Age*. Chico, CA: Scholars Press, 1983.

Jenni, Ernst. *Das hebräische Pi'el: Syntaktisch-semasiologische Untersuchung einer Verbalform im Alten Testament*. Zurich: EVZ Verlag, 1968.

———. *Die hebräischen Präpositionen*. 3 vols. Stuttgart: Kohlhammer, 1992–2000.

———. *Lehrbuch der hebräischen Sprache des Alten Testaments*. Basil: Helbing and Lichtenhahn, 1981.

———. "Höfliche Bitte im Alten Testament." Pages 1–16 in *Congress Volume: Basel, 2001*. Edited by A. Lemaire. VTSup 92. Leiden: Brill, 2002.

Jenni, Ernst, Claus Westermann, and Mark E. Biddle, eds. *Theological Lexicon of the Old Testament*. 3 vols. Peabody, MA: Hendrickson, 1997.

Jerusalem Crown, The Bible of the Hebrew University of Jerusalem. Jerusalem: Ben-Zvi Printing, 2000.

Jespersen, Otto. *The Philosophy of Grammar*. London: Allen & Unwin, 1924.

Jobes, Karen H. *Invitation to the Septuagint*. 2nd ed. Grand Rapids: Baker Academic, 2015.

Johnson, Benjamin M. "The Heart of Yahweh's Chosen One in 1 Samuel." *JBL* 131 (2012): 455–66.

Jones, Ethan C. "Hearing the 'Voice' of the Niphal: A Response to Ellen van Wolde." *JSOT* 45 (2021): 291–308.

Joosten, Jan. "Do the Finite Verbal Forms in Biblical Hebrew Express Aspect?" *JANES* 29 (2002): 49–70.

———. "The Lengthened Imperative with Accusative Suffix in Biblical Hebrew." *ZAW* 111 (1999): 423–26.

———. "The Long Form of the Prefixed Conjugation Referring to the Past in Biblical Hebrew Prose." *HS* 40 (1999): 15–26.

Joüon, Paul, and T. Muraoka. *A Grammar of Biblical Hebrew*. 2nd ed. Subsidia Biblica 27. Rome: Pontifical Biblical Institute, 2006.

Juhás, Peter. *Die biblisch-hebräische Partikel נָא im Lichte der antiken Bibelübersetzungen: unter besonderer Berücksichtigung ihrer vermuteten Höflichkeitsfunktion*. SSN 67. Leiden: Brill, 2017.

Kappler, Werner, ed. *Maccabaeorum Liber II*. SVTG 9.2. Göttingen: Vandenhoeck & Ruprecht, 2008.

Kaufman, Stephen A. "An Emphatic Plea for Please." *Maarav* 7 (1991): 195–98.

———. "Semitics: Directions and Re-Directions." Pages 273–82 in *The Study of the Ancient Near East in the Twenty-First Century: The William Foxwell Albright Centennial Conference*. Edited by Jerrold S. Cooper and Glenn M. Schwartz. Winona Lake, IN: Eisenbrauns, 1996.

Kawashima, Robert S. "'Orphaned' Converted Tense Forms in Classical Biblical Hebrew Prose." *JSS* 55 (2010): 11–35.

Kedar-Kopfstein, Benjamin. "Semantic Aspects of the Pattern Qôtēl." *Hebrew Annual Review* 1 (1977): 155–76.

Keil, C. F., and and F. Delitzsch. *Joshua, Judges, Ruth, 1 and 2 Samuel*. Vol. 2 of *Commentary on the Old Testament*. Repr. Peabody, MA: Hendrickson, 2001.

Kelley, Page H. *Biblical Hebrew: An Introductory Grammar*. Grand Rapids: Eerdmans, 1992.

Kelley, Page H., Daniel S. Mynatt, and Timothy G. Crawford. *The Masorah of Biblia Hebraica Stuttgartensia: Introduction and Annotated Glossary*. Grand Rapids: Eerdmans, 1998.

Kelly, Thomas Forrest. *The Role of the Scroll: An Illustrated Introduction to Scrolls in the Middle Ages*. New York: Norton, 2019.

Kemmer, Suzanne. *The Middle Voice*. Typological Studies in Language 23. Amsterdam: Benjamins, 1993.

Kennicott, Benjamin. *Vetus Testamentum Hebraicum: cum variis lectionibus*. 2 vols. Oxford: Clarendon, 1776, 1780. (Online: vol. 1: https://archive.org /details/vetustestamentum01kenn; vol. 2: https://archive.org/details/vetustesta mentum02kenn.)

Khan, Geoffrey, ed. *Encyclopedia of Hebrew Language and Linguistics*. 4 vols. Leiden: Brill, 2013.

———. "Object Markers and Agreement Pronouns in Semitic Languages." *BSOAS* 47 (1984): 468–500.

———. "Some Aspects of the Copula in Northwest Semitic." Pages 155–76 in *Biblical Hebrew in Its Northwest Semitic Setting: Typological and Historical Perspectives*. Edited by Steven E. Fassberg and Avi Hurvitz. Winona Lake, IN: Eisenbrauns, 2006.

———. *The Tiberian Pronunciation Tradition of Biblical Hebrew*. 2 vols. Cambridge Semitic Languages and Cultures 1. Cambridge: Open Book, 2020.

Kienast, Burkhart. *Historische semitische Sprachwissenschaft: Mit Beiträgen von Erhart Graefe (Altaegyptisch) und Gene B. Gragg (Kuschitisch)*. Weisbaden: Harrassowitz, 2001.

Kim, Dong-Hyuk. *Early Biblical Hebrew, Late Biblical Hebrew, and Linguistic Variability: A Sociolinguistic Evaluation of the Linguistic Dating of Biblical Texts*. VTSup 156. Leiden: Brill, 2013.

Kim, Yoo-Ki. *The Function of the Tautological Infinitive in Classical Biblical Hebrew*. Winona Lake, IN: Eisenbrauns, 2009.

Kingham, Cody. "Parts of Speech in Biblical Hebrew Time Phrases: A Cognitive-Statistical Analysis." Pages 497–545 in *New Perspectives in Biblical and Rabbinic Hebrew*. Edited by Aaron Hornkohl and Geoffrey Khan. Cambridge Semitic Languages and Cultures 7. Cambridge: Open Book, 2021.

Kittel, Rudolf, ed. *Biblia Hebraica*, 3rd ed. Stuttgart: Württembergische Bibelanstalt, 1937.

Kletter, Raz. "Vessels and Measures: The Biblical Liquid Capacity System." *IEJ* 64 (2014): 22–37.

Kline, Meredith G. "Divine Kingship and Sons of God in Genesis 6:1–4." *Westminster Theological Journal* 24 (1962): 187–204.

Knoppers, Gary. "The Synoptic Problem? An Old Testament Perspective." *BBR* 19.1 (2009): 11–34.

Koschmieder, Erwin. "Zu den Grundfragen der Aspekttheorie." *IF* 53 (1935): 280–300.

Köstenberger, Andreas J., Benjamin L. Merkle, and Robert L. Plummer. *Going Deeper with New Testament Greek: An Intermediate Study of the Grammar and Syntax of the New Testament*. Nashville: B&H Academic, 2016.

Kouwenberg, N. J. C. *The Akkadian Verb and Its Semitic Background*. Languages of the Ancient Near East. Winona Lake, IN: Eisenbrauns, 2010.

———. *Gemination in the Akkadian Verb*. Assen: Van Gorcum, 1997.

———. *Introduction to Old Assyrian*. Munster: Zaphon, 2019.

Kuryłowicz, Jerzy. "La nature des procès dits 'analogiques'." *Acta Linguistica* 5 (19449): 15–37.

Labat, René. *Manuel d'Épigraphie Akkadiene: Signes, Syllabaire, Idéogrammes*. 6th ed. Paris: Geuthner, 1995.

Labov, William. "The Transformation of Experience in Narrative Syntax." Pages 354–96 in *Language in the Inner City*. Edited by William Labov. Philadelphia: University of Pennsylvania Press, 1972.

Lakoff, George. *Women, Fire, and Dangerous Things: What Categories Reveal about the Mind*. Chicago: The University of Chicago Press, 1987.

Lam, Joseph. "The Invention and Development of the Alphabet." Pages 189–201 in *Visible Language: Inventions of Writing in the Ancient Middle East and Beyond*. Edited by Christopher Woods with Emily Teeter and Geoff Emberling. Oriental Institute Museum Publications 32. Chicago: The Oriental Institute, 2010.

Lambdin, T. O. *Introduction to Biblical Hebrew.* New York: Scribner, 1971.

———. "The Junctural Origin of the West Semitic Definite Article." Pages 315–33 in *Near Eastern Studies in Honor of William Foxwell Albright.* Edited by H. Goedicke. Baltimore: Johns Hopkins Press, 1971.

Lambert, Mayer. "L'Emploi du nifal en Hébreu." *Revue des études Juives* 41 (1900): 196–214.

———. *Traité de grammaire hébraïque.* Paris: Presses universitaires de France, 1946.

Lane, Edward William. *An Arabic-English Lexicon.* London: Williams and Norgate, 1863–93.

Langacker, Ronald W. *Cognitive Grammar: A Basic Introduction.* Oxford: Oxford University Press, 2008.

Lange, Armin. "Ancient and Late Ancient Hebrew and Aramaic Jewish Texts." Pages 112–65 in vol. 1A of *Textual History of the Bible: The Hebrew Bible.* Edited by Armin Lange and Emanuel Tov. Leiden: Brill, 2016.

———. "'Nobody Dared to Add to Them, to Take from Them, or to Make Changes,' (Josephus, Ag. Ap. 1.42): The Textual Standardization of Jewish Scriptures in Light of the Dead Sea Scrolls." Pages 105–26 in *Flores Florentino: Dead Sea Scrolls and Other Early Jewish Studies in Honour of Florentino García Martínez.* Edited by A. Hilhorst, É. Puech, and E. J. C. Tigchelaar. JSJSup 122. Leiden: Brill, 2007.

Lange, Armin, and Emanuel Tov, eds. *Textual History of the Bible: The Hebrew Bible. 3 vols.* Leiden: Brill, 2016–2017.

Lehmann, Reinhard G. "27–30–22–26 – How Many Letters Needs an Alphabet? The Case of Semitic." Pages 11–52 in *The Idea of Writing: Writing Across Borders.* Edited by Alex de Voogt and Joachim Friedrich Quack. Leiden: Brill, 2012.

Lemke, Werner. "The Synoptic Problem in the Chronicler's History." *HTR* 58.4 (1965): 349–63.

Leon Levy Dead Sea Scrolls Digital Library. https://www.deadseascrolls.org.il.

Levin, Beth, and Malka Rappaport Hovav. *Unaccusativity: At the Syntax-Lexical Semantics Interface.* Cambridge, MA: MIT Press, 1995.

Levin, Beth. *English Verb Classes and Alternations.* Chicago: University of Chicago Press, 1993.

Li, Charles, ed. *Mechanism of Syntactic Change.* Austin: University of Texas Press, 1977.

Lichtenberk, Frantisek. "Apprehensional Epistemics." Pages 293–327 in *Modality in Grammar and Discourse.* Edited by Joan Bybee and Suzanne Fleischman. Typological Studies in Language 32. Amsterdam: Benjamins, 1995.

Liddell, H. G., R. Scott, and H. S. Jones. *A Greek-English Lexicon with a Revised Supplement.* 9th ed. Edited By E. A. Barber. Oxford: Clarendon, 1996.

Lindenberger, James M. *Ancient Aramaic and Hebrew Letters.* 2nd ed. Writings from the Ancient World 14. Atlanta: Society of Biblical Literature, 2003.

Lindstromberg, Seth. *English Prepositions Explained*. Rev. ed. Amsterdam: Benjamins, 2010.

Lipiński, Edward. *Semitic Languages: Outline of Comparative Grammar*. OLA 80. Leuven: Peeters, 1997.

Lipka, Leonhard. "Causatives and Inchoatives in English and their Treatment in Recent Lexicographic Practice." *Studia Anglica Posnaniensia* 14 (1982): 3–16.

Lipschits, Oded, and David S. Vanderhooft. *The Yehud Stamp Impressions: A Corpus of Inscribed Impressions from the Persian and Hellenistic Periods in Judah*. Winona Lake, IN: Eisenbrauns, 2011.

Logeion Lexion. https://logeion.uchicago.edu/lexidium.

Longacre, Drew. "The Parting of the Ways of Old and New Testament Textual Criticism: Deconstructing a Disciplinary Division." Pages 87–111 in *Written for Our Instruction: Essays in Honor of William Varner*. Edited by Abner Chou and Christian Locatell. Dallas: Fontes, 2021.

———. "Reconsidering the Date of the En-Gedi Leviticus Scroll (EGLev): Exploring the Limitations of the Comparative-Typological Paleographic Method." *Textus* 27 (2018): 44–84.

Longacre, Robert E. *Joseph: A Story of Divine Providence: A Text Theoretical and Textlinguistic Analysis of Genesis 37 and 39–40*. Winona Lake, IN: Eisenbrauns, 1989.

Lunn, Nicholas. "Differentiating Intensive and Abstract Plural Nouns in Biblical Hebrew." *JNSL* 42.1 (2016): 81–99.

Lyons, John. *Introduction to Theoretical Linguistics*. Cambridge: Cambridge University Press, 1968.

———. *Semantics*. Cambridge: Cambridge University Press, 1977.

Mankowski, Paul V. *Akkadian Loanwords in Biblical Hebrew*. HSS 47. Leiden: Brill, 2000.

Marcus, David. *The Masorah of the Former Prophets in the Leningrad Codex*. 5 vols. Texts and Studies 3. Piscataway, NJ: Gorgias, 2017–21.

———. "Ridiculing the Ephraimites: The Shibboleth Incident (Judg 12:6)." *Maarav* 8 (1992): 95–105.

Mathews, K. A. *Genesis 1–11:26*. NAC 1A. Nashville: B&H, 1996.

Matthews, P. H. *Syntax*. Cambridge: Cambridge University Press, 1981.

McAffee, Matthew. "The Heart of Pharaoh in Exodus 4–15." *BBR* 20 (2010): 331–54.

———. *Life and Mortality in Ugaritic: A Lexical and Literary Study*. EANEC 7. University Park, PA: Eisenbrauns, 2019.

———. "A Reassessment of the Hebrew Negative Interrogative Particle *hlʾ*." *JAOS* 135 (2015): 115–30.

McCarter, P. Kyle, Jr. *1 Samuel*. AB 8. Garden City, NY: Doubleday, 1980.

———. *Textual Criticism: Recovering the Text of the Hebrew Bible*. Philadelphia: Fortress, 1986.

McDowell, Catherine L., and Philip H. Towner. *The Rewards of Learning Greek and Hebrew: Discovering the Richness of the Bible in Its Original Languages.* Peabody, MA: Hendrickson, 2021.

McFall, Leslie. *The Enigma of the Hebrew Verbal System: Solutions from Ewald to the Present Day.* Sheffield: Almond, 1982.

McGaughy, Lane C. *Toward a Descriptive Analysis of* Εἶναι *as a Linking Verb in New Testament Greek.* SBL Dissertation Series 6. Missoula, MT: Society of Biblical Literature, 1972.

McLauren, Dougald, III, "Defining Collective Nouns: How Cognitive Linguistics Helps Biblical Hebrew Grammarians." *Journal for Semitics* 30.2 (2021): 1–15.

Meade, John D. "Masoretic Text." Pages XX–XXX in *Dictionary of the Bible and Ancient Media.* Edited by Chris Keith. London: Bloomsbury T&T Clark, 2016.

———. "The Relationship of Peshitta Qoheleth to Greek Ecclesiastes." Pages 343–78 in *Like Nails Firmly Fixed (Qoh 12:11): Essays on the Text and Language of the Hebrew and Greek Scriptures, Presented to Peter J. Gentry on the Occasion of His Retirement.* Edited by Phillip S. Marshall, John D. Meade, and Jonathan Kiel. Contributions to Biblical Exegesis and Theology 115. Leuven: Peeters, 2022.

Meade, John D., and Peter J. Gentry. "Evaluating Evaluations: the Commentary of *BHQ* and the Problem of הוֹלֵלוֹת in Ecclesiastes 1:17." Pages 197–217 in *Sophia-Paideia: Sapienza e Educazione (Sir 1,27): Miscellanea di studi offerti in onore del prof. Don Mario Cimosa.* Edited by G. Bonney and R. Vicent. Nuova Biblioteca di Scienze Religiose 34. Rome: Libreria Ateneo Salesiano, 2012.

Mengden, Ferdinand von. *Cardinal Numerals: Old English from a Cross-Linguistic Perspective.* Topics in English Linguistics. Berlin: de Gruyter, 2010.

Mettinger, Tryggve N. D. *King and Messiah: The Civil and Sacral Legitimation of the Israelite Kings.* Coniectanea Biblica Old Testament Series 8. Lund: CWK Gleerup, 1976.

Metzger, Bruce, and Bart D. Ehrman. *The Text of the New Testament: Its Transmission, Corruption, and Restoration.* 4th ed. Oxford: Oxford University Press, 2005.

Meyer, Rudolf. *Hebräische Grammatik.* 3rd ed. Berlin: de Gruyter, 1972.

Millard, Alan R. "The Ostracon from the Days of David Found at Khirbet Qeiyafa." *Tyndale Bulletin* 62 (2011): 1–13.

Miller, Cynthia L. "Pivotal Issues in Analyzing the Verbless Clause." Pages 3–17 in *The Verbless Clause in Biblical Hebrew: Linguistic Approaches.* Edited by Cynthia L. Miller. LSAWS 1. Winona Lake, IN: Eisenbrauns, 1999.

———. "The Pragmatics of Waw as a Discourse Marker in Biblical Hebrew Dialogue." *ZAH* 12.2 (1999): 165–91.

———. "Reported Speech." PhD diss., University of Chicago, 1993.

———. *The Representation of Speech in Biblical Hebrew Narrative: A Linguistic Analysis.* HSM 55. Atlanta: Scholars Press, 1996.

Miller-Naudé, Cynthia L., and C. H. J. van der Merwe. "הִנֵּה and Mirativity in Biblical Hebrew." *HS* 52 (2011): 53–81.

Miller-Naudé, Cynthia L., and Jacobus A. Naudé. "Is the Adjective Distinct from the Nouns as a Grammatical Category in Biblical Hebrew?" *Die Skriflig* 50 (2016): 1–9.

———. "The Participle and Negation in Biblical Hebrew." *KUSATU* 19 (2015): 165–99.

Miller, Patrick D. *Deuteronomy.* Interpretation. Louisville: WJK, 1990.

Moran, William L. "The Ancient Near Eastern Background of the Love of God in Deuteronomy." *CBQ* 25 (1963): 77–87.

———. "Early Canaanite *yaqtula.*" *Or* 29 (1960): 1–19.

———. "The Hebrew Language in Its Northwest Semitic Background." Pages 197–218 in *The Bible and the Ancient Near East: Essays in Honor of William Foxwell Albright.* Edited by G. Ernest Wright. Garden City, NY: Doubleday, 1961.

Morrow, William S. *An Introduction to Biblical Law.* Grand Rapids: Eerdmans, 2017.

Moscati, Sabatino. *An Introduction to the Comparative Grammar of the Semitic Languages: Phonology and Morphology.* Porta Linguarum Orientalium. Wiesbaden: Harrassowitz, 1980.

Moshavi, Adina. "Indefinite Numerical Construct Phrases in Biblical Hebrew." *JSS* 63 (2018): 99–123.

Muraoka, Takamitsu. *Emphatic Words and Structures in Biblical Hebrew.* Leiden: Brill, 1985.

———. *A Greek-English Lexicon of the Septuagint.* Leuven: Peeters, 2009.

Muraoka, Takamitsu, and J. F. Elwolde, eds. *The Hebrew of the Dead Sea Scrolls and Ben Sira, Proceedings of a Symposium Held at Leiden University, 11–14 December 1995.* STDJ 26. Leiden: Brill, 1997.

Naudé, Jacobus A. "The Interpretation and Translation of the Biblical Hebrew Quantifier *kol.*" *Journal for Semitics* 20.2 (2011): 408–21.

———. "The Syntactical Status of the Ethical Dative in Biblical Hebrew." *Journal for Semitics* 9 (1997): 129–65.

———. "Syntactic Patterns of Quantifier Float in Biblical Hebrew." *HS* 52 (2011): 121–36.

Naveh, Joseph. "Scripts and Inscriptions in Ancient Samaria." *IEJ* 48 (1998): 91–100.

Nelson, Richard D. *Joshua: A Commentary.* OTL. Louisville: WJK, 1997.

Netzer, Yael. "Quantifier." *EHLL* 3:311–15.

Newsome, James D. *A Synoptic Harmony of Samuel, Kings, and Chronicles: With Related Passages from Psalms, Isaiah, Jeremiah, and Ezra.* Eugene, OR: Wipf & Stock, 1986.

Niccacci, Alviero. "Basic Facts and Theory of the Biblical Hebrew Verb System in Prose." Pages 167–202 in *Narrative Syntax and the Hebrew Bible: Papers of the Tilburg Conference 1996.* Edited by Ellen van Wolde. Leiden: Brill, 1997.

———. "An Integrated Verb System for Biblical Hebrew Prose and Poetry." Pages 99–127 in *Congress Volume Ljubljana 2007.* Edited by A. Lemaire. VTSup 133. Leiden: Brill, 2010.

———. "Problematic Points that Seem to Contradict a Coherent System of Biblical Hebrew Syntax in Poetry." *KUSATU* 15 (2013): 77–94.

———. *The Syntax of the Verb in Classical Hebrew Prose.* Translated by W. G. E. Watson. JSOTSup 86. Sheffield: JSOT Press, 1990.

Nihan, Christophe. "Textual Fluidity and Rewriting in Parallel Traditions: The Case of Samuel and Chronicles." *Journal of Ancient Judaism* 4.2 (2013): 186–209.

Noonan, Benjamin J. *Non-Semitic Loanwords in the Hebrew Bible: A Lexicon of Language Contact.* LSAWS 14. University Park, PA: Eisenbrauns, 2019.

Norrick, Neal R. "Interjections as Pragmatic Markers." *Journal of Pragmatics* 41 (2009): 866–91.

Notarius, Tania. "Narrative Tenses in Archaic Hebrew in the North-West Semitic Linguistic Context." Pages 237–59 in *Neue Beiträge zur Semitistik.* Edited by Viktor Golinets, Hanna Jenni, Hans-Peter Mathys, and Samuel Sarasin. Münster: Ugarit-Verlag, 2015.

Nougayrol, Jean. "Textes suméro-accadiens des archives et bibliothèques privées d'Ugarit." Pages 1–446 in *Ugaritica V.* Edited by Charles Virolleaud, Jean Nougayrol, Emmanuel Laroche, and Andrée Herdner. Bibliothèque Archéologique et Historique 80; Mission de Ras Shamra 16. Paris: Imprimerie Nationale, 1968.

Olmo Lete, Gregorio del, and Joaquín Sanmartín. *A Dictionary of the Ugaritic Language in the Alphabetic Tradition.* 3rd rev. ed. Translated by Wilfred G. E. Watson. Handbook of Oriental Studies, Section 1: The Near and Middle East 112. Leiden: Brill, 2015.

Olshausen, Justus. *Lehrbuch der hebräischen Sprache.* 2 vols. Braunschweig: Vieweg, 1861.

Orlinsky, H. M. "The Origin of the Kethib-Qere System: A New Approach." Pages 184–92 in *Congress Volume Oxford 1959.* Edited by G. W. Anderson, P. A. H. de Boer, G. R. Castellino, Henri Cazelles, E. Hammershaimb, H. G. May, and W. Zimmerli. VTSup 7. Leiden: Brill, 1960.

Palmer, F. R. *Mood and Modality.* 2nd ed. Cambridge Textbooks in Linguistics. Cambridge University Press, 2001.

Pardee, Dennis G. "The Biblical Hebrew Verbal System in a Nutshell." Pages 285–317 in *Language and Nature: Papers Presented to John Huehnergard on the Occasion of His 60th Birthday*. Edited by Rebecca Hasselbach and Naʿama Pat-El. SAOC 67. Chicago: The Oriental Institute, 2012.

———. "The 'Epistolary Perfect' in Hebrew Letters." *BN* 22 (1983): 34–40.

———. *Handbook of Hebrew Letters*. SBL Sources for Biblical Study 15. Chico, CA: Scholars Press, 1982.

———. "Judicial Plea from Meṣad Ḥashavyahu (Yavneh-Yam): A New Philological Study." *Maarav* 1 (1978): 33–66.

———. Review of *An Introduction to Biblical Hebrew Syntax*, by Bruce K. Waltke and Michael Patrick O'Connor. *JNES* 53 (1994): 150–53.

———. Review of *The Anterior Construction in Classical Hebrew*, by Ziony Zevit. *JANES* 60 (2001): 308–12.

———. Review of *Canaanite in the Amarna Tablets*, by Anson F. Rainey. *JNES* 58 (1999): 313–17.

———. "The Ugaritic Alphabetic Cuneiform Writing System in the Context of Other Alphabetic Systems." Pages 181–200 in *Studies in Semitic and Afroasiatic Linguistics Presented to Gene B. Gragg*. Edited by Cynthia L. Miller. SAOC 60. Chicago: The Oriental Institute, 2007.

———. "Vestiges du système casuel entre le nom et le pronom suffixe en hébreu biblique." Pages 113–21 in *Grammatical Case in the Languages of the Middle East and Europe: Acts of the International Colloquium "Variations, Concurrence et Évolution des cas dans divers domaines linguistiques," Paris, 2–4 April 2007*. Edited by Michèle Fruyt, Michel Mazoyer, and Dennis Pardee. SAOC 64. Chicago: The Oriental Institute, 2011.

Pardee, Dennis G., and Robert M. Whiting. "Aspects of Epistolary Verbal Usage in Ugaritic and Akkadian." *BSOAS* 50 (1987): 1–31.

Pariente, Itsik. "On the Formation of the Tiberian Hebrew Imperatives: Evidence from Spirantization." *HS* 45 (2004): 71–77.

Parker, Simon B. "Possession Trance and Prophecy in Pre-Exilic Israel." *VT* 28 (1978): 271–85.

Patton, Matthew H., and Frederic Clarke Putnam. *Basics of Hebrew Discourse: A Guide to Working with Hebrew Prose and Poetry*. Grand Rapids: Zondervan, 2019.

Peterson, Eugene. *A Long Obedience in the Same Direction: Discipleship in an Instant Society*. Rev. ed. Downers Grove, IL: IVP, 2000.

Petrie, W. M. Flinders. *Seventy Years of Archaeology*. New York: Holt, 1932.

Picus, Daniel. "Reading Regularly: The Liturgical Reading of Torah in its Late Antique Material World." Pages 217–32 in *Material Aspects of Reading in Ancient and Medieval Cultures: Materiality, Presence and Performance*. Edited by Anna Krauß, Jonas Leipziger, and Friederike Schücking-Jungblut. Materiale Textkulturen 26. Berlin: de Gruyter, 2020.

Polzin, Robert. *Late Biblical Hebrew: Toward an Historical Typology of Biblical Hebrew Prose*. HSM 12. Missoula, MT: Scholars Press, 1976.

Pope, Marvin H. *Job*. AB 15. New York: Doubleday, 1965.

Porter, Stanley E. *Idioms of the Greek New Testament*. 2nd ed. Biblical Languages: Greek 2. Sheffield: Sheffield Academic, 1994.

———. *Verbal Aspect in the Greek of the New Testament, with Reference to Tense and Mood*. Studies in Biblical Greek. New York: Lang, 1989.

Pratico, Gary D., and Miles V. Van Pelt. *Basics of Biblical Hebrew Grammar*. Grand Rapids: Zondervan, 2001.

Qimron, Elisha. *The Hebrew of the Dead Sea Scrolls*. HSS 29. Winona Lake, IN: Eisenbrauns, 1986.

Quirk, Randolph, Sidney Greenbaum, Geoffrey Leech, and Jan Svartvik. *A Comprehensive Grammar of the English Language*. London: Longman, 1985.

Rabin, Chaim, Shemaryahu Talmon, and Emanuel Tov, eds. *The Hebrew University Bible. The Book of Jeremiah*. Jerusalem: Magnes, 1989.

Rahlfs, Alfred. *Septuaginta: Id est Vetus Testamentum Graece iuxta LXX Interpretes*. Stuttgart: Württembergische Bibelanstalt, 1935.

Rahlfs, Alfred, and Robert Hanhart, eds. *Septuaginta: Id est Vetus Testamentum graece iuxta LXX Interpretes*. Rev. ed. Stuttgart: Deutsche Bibelgesellschaft, 2006.

Rainey, Anson F. "The Ancient Hebrew Prefix Conjugation in the Light of Amarna Canaanite." *HS* 27 (1986): 4–19.

———. *Canaanite in the Amarna Tablets: A Linguistic Analysis of the Mixed Dialect Used by Scribes from Canaan*. 4 vols. Leiden: Brill, 1996.

———. "The Prefix Conjugation Patterns of Early Northwest Semitic." Pages 407–20 in *Lingering over Words: Studies in Ancient Near Eastern Literature in Honor of William F. Moran*. Edited by Tzvi Abusch, John Huehnergard, and Piotr Steinkeller. HSS 37. Atlanta: Scholars Press, 1990.

Rand, Michael. "Fientivity, Transitivity, and Stem Vowel Variation in Byzantine *Piyyuṭ*." *JQR* 93 (2003): 471–95.

Reckendorf, H. *Über Paronomasie in den semitischen Sprachen*. Giessen: Töpelmann, 1909.

Rendsburg, Gary A. "The Ammonite Phoneme /Ṯ/." *BASOR* 269 (1988): 73–79.

———. *Diglossia in Ancient Hebrew*. American Oriental Series 72. New Haven, CT: American Oriental Society, 1990.

———. *Israelian Hebrew in the Book of Kings*. Occasional Publications of the Department of Near Eastern Studies and the Program of Jewish Studies, Cornell University 5. Bethesda, MD: CDL, 2002.

———. *Linguistic Evidence for the Northern Origin of Selected Psalms*. SBLMS 43. Atlanta: Scholars Press, 1990.

———. "More on Hebrew Šibbōlet." *JSS* 33 (1988): 255–58.

Rendtorff, Rolf. *The Old Testament: An Introduction*. Philadelphia: Fortress, 1989.

Renz, Johannes, and Wolfgang Röllig. *Handbuch der althebräischen Epigraphik.* 3 vols. Darmstadt: Wissenschaftliche, 1995–2003.

Revell, E. J. "Logic of Concord with Collectives in Biblical Narrative." *Maarav* 9 (2002): 61–91.

———. "The System of the Verb in Standard Biblical Prose." *HUCA* 60 (1989): 1–37.

Reymond, Eric. D. "The Passive Qal in the Hebrew of the Second Temple Period, Especially as Found in the Wisdom of Ben Sira." Pages 1110–27 in *Sibyls, Scriptures, and Scrolls: John Collins at Seventy.* Edited by Joel Baden, Hindy Najman, and Eibert Tigchelaar. JSJSup 175. Leiden: Brill, 2016.

———. *Qumran Hebrew: An Overview of Orthography, Phonology, and Morphology.* Resources for Biblical Study 76. Atlanta: SBL, 2014.

Riekert, S. J. P. K. "The Struct Patterns of Paronomastic and Co-ordinated Infinitives Absolute in Genesis." *JNSL* 7 (1979): 69–83.

Ritner, Robert K. "The Cardiovascular System in Ancient Egyptian Thought." *JNES* 65 (2006): 99–109.

Robertson, A. T. *Grammar of the Greek New Testament in the Light of Historical Research.* 3rd ed. London: Dorian, 1919.

Rofé, Alexander. *Introduction to the Literature of the Hebrew Bible.* Jerusalem: Simor, 2009.

Rollston, Christopher A. "Scribal Education in Ancient Israel: The Old Hebrew Epigraphic Evidence." *BASOR* 344 (2006): 47–74.

———. *Writing and Literacy in the World of Ancient Israel: Epigraphic Evidence from the Iron Age.* Atlanta: SBL, 2010.

Rosenthal, Franz. *A Grammar of Biblical Aramaic.* 7th ed. Porta Linguarum Orientalium 5. Wiesbaden: Harrassowitz, 2006.

Ross, Allen P. *Introducing Biblical Hebrew.* Grand Rapids: Baker Academic, 2001.

Ryder, Stuart A. *The D-Stem in Western Semitic.* The Hague: Mouton, 1974.

Salvesen, Alison, ed. *Origen's Hexapla and Fragments.* Tübingen: Mohr Siebeck, 1998.

Sanders, Seth L. *The Invention of Hebrew.* Urbana: University of Illinois Press, 2011.

———. "Performatives Utterances and Divine Language in Ugaritic." *JNES* 63 (2004): 161–81.

Sarna, Nahum. "The Order of the Books." Pages 407–13 in *Studies in Jewish Bibliography, History and Literature in Honor of I. Edward Kiev.* Edited by Charles Berlin. New York: KTAV, 1971.

Sass, Benjamin. "The Genesis of the Alphabet and Its Development in the Second Millennium B.C.—Twenty Years Later." *De Kêmi à Birīt Nāri* 2 (2005): 147–66.

Sasse, Hans-Jürgen. "Scales between Nouniness and Verbiness." Pages 495–509 in *Language Typology and Language Universals.* Edited by Martin Haspelmath, Ekkehard König, Wulf Oesterreicher, and Wolfgang Raible.

Handbooks of Linguistics and Communication Science 20.1. Berlin: de Gruyter, 2001.

Scanlin, Harold P. *The Dead Sea Scrolls & Modern Translations of the Old Testament*. Wheaton, IL: Tyndale, 1993.

Schenker, Adrian, et al, eds. *Biblia Hebraica Quinta*. Stuttgart: Deutsche Bibelgesellschaft, 2004–.

Scheumann, Jesse R. "A Syntactic Analysis of Phrasal Coordination in Biblical Hebrew." PhD diss., University of the Free State Bloemfontein, 2020.

Schmid, Konrad. *The Old Testament: A Literary History*. Minneapolis: Fortress, 2012.

Schniedewind, William M. *How the Bible Became a Book: The Textualization of Ancient Israel*. Cambridge: Cambridge University Press, 2004.

Schwartz, Baruch J. "How the Compiler of the Pentateuch Worked: the Composition of Genesis 37." Pages 263–78 in *The Book of Genesis: Composition, Reception, and Interpretation*. Edited by Craig A. Evans, Joel H. Lohr, and David L. Petersen. VTSup 152. Leiden: Brill, 2012.

Schwarz, Glenn M. "Non-Cuneiform Writing at Third-Millennium Umm el-Marra, Syria: Evidence of an Early Alphabetic Tradition?" *Pasiphae: rivista di filologia e antichità egee* 15 (2021): 255–66.

Scott, William R. *A Simplified Guide to BHS: Critical Apparatus, Masora, Accents, Unusual Letters, and Other Markings*. 3rd ed. Richland Hills, TX: BIBAL, 1987.

Screnock, John. "Some Oddities of Ancient Hebrew Numeral Syntax." *HS* 61 (2020): 23–44.

———. "The Syntax of Cardinal Numerals in Judges, Amos, Esther, and 1QM." *JSS* 63 (2018): 125–54.

———. "The Syntax of Complex Adding Numerals and Hebrew Diachrony." *JBL* 137 (2018): 789–819.

Segal, Moses H. "Mišnaic Hebrew and Its Relation to Biblical Hebrew and to Aramaic." *JQR* 20 (1908): 647–737.

Segert, Stanislav. *A Basic Grammar of the Ugaritic Language*. Berkeley: University of California Press, 1984.

———. *A Grammar of Phoenician and Punic*. Munich: Beck, 1976.

Sellin, E. *Die verbal-nominal Doppelnatur der hebräischen Participien und Infinitive und ihre darauf beruhende verschiedene Construktion*. Leipzig: Fock, 1889.

Sharp, Granville. *A Letter to a Learned Friend Respecting Some Particularities of the Hebrew Syntax*. London: Vernor and Hood, 1803.

Shibatani, Maysayoshi. *Passive and Voice*. Typological Studies in Language 16. Amsterdam: Benjamins, 1998.

Shulman, Ahouva. "The Particle נָא in Biblical Hebrew Prose." *HS* 40 (1999): 57–82.

———. "The Use of Modal Verb Forms in Biblical Hebrew Prose." PhD diss., University of Toronto, 1996.

Siebenthal, Heinrich von. "'Collectives' in Ancient Hebrew: A Closer Look at the Semantics of an Intriguing Noun Category." *KUSATU* 10 (2009): 67–81.

Siebesma, P. A. *The Function of the Niph'al in Biblical Hebrew: In Relationship to Other Passive-Reflexive Verbal Stems and to the Pu'al and Hoph'al in Particular*. SSN 28. Assen: Van Gorcum, 1991.

Sivan, Daniel. *A Grammar of the Ugaritic Language*. Handbook of Oriental Studies 28. Atlanta: SBL, 2001.

———. "The Internal Passive of G-Stems in Northwest Semitic Languages" (Hebrew). Pages 47–56 in *Mas'at Aharon: Linguistic Studies Presented to Aaron Dotan*. Edited by M. Bar-Asher and C. E. Cohen. Jerusalem: Bialik, 2009.

Smith, Mark S. "Grammatically Speaking: The Participle as a Main Verb of Clauses (Predicative Participle) in Direct Discourse and Narrative in Pre-Mishnaic Hebrew." Pages 278–332 in *Sirach, Scrolls, and Sages*. Edited by T. Muraoka and John F. Elwolde. STDJ 33. Leiden: Brill, 1999.

———. *The Origins and Development of the* Waw-*Consecutive: Northwest Semitic Evidence from Ugarit to Qumran*. HSS 39. Atlanta: Scholars Press, 1991.

Smoak, Jeremy D. *The Priestly Blessing in Inscription and Scripture*. New York: Oxford University Press, 2016.

Smoak, Jeremy, and William Schniedewind. "Religion at Kuntillet ʿAjrud." *Religions* 10.3 (2019): 1–18.

Smyth, Herbert Weir. *Greek Grammar*. Revised by Gordon Messing. Cambridge: Harvard University Press, 1956.

Sperber, Alexander. *The Bible in Aramaic*. 4 vols. Leiden: Brill, 1992.

Sprengling, Martin. *The Alphabet: Its Rise and Development from the Sinai Inscriptions*. Oriental Institute Communications 12. Chicago: University of Chicago Press, 1931.

Stackert, Jeffery. "Pentateuchal Coherence and the Science of Reading." Pages 253–68 in *The Formation of the Pentateuch: Bridging the Academic Cultures of Europe, Israel, and North America*. Edited by Jan C. Gertz, Bernard M. Levinson, Dalit Rom-Shiloni, and Konrad Schmid. FAT 111. Tübingen: Mohr Siebeck, 2016.

Staps, Camil. "A Case Study of Reciprocal Middles in Biblical Hebrew: The Niphal of לחם." *Or* 87 (2018): 159–83.

Stassen, Leon. *Intransitive Predication*. Oxford Studies in Typology and Linguistic Theory 17. Oxford: Clarendon, 1997.

Steiner, Richard L. "On the Dating of Hebrew Sound Changes (*ḫ > ḥ and *ġ > ʿ) and Greek Translations (2 Esdras and Judith)." *JBL* 124 (2005): 229–67.

Stevenson, W. B. *Grammar of Palestinian Jewish Aramaic*. 2nd ed. Oxford: Clarendon, 1967.

Streck, Michael P. Review of *Ugaritische Grammatik*, by J. Tropper. *ZDMG* 152 (2002): 185–92.

Suchard, Benjamin D. *The Development of the Biblical Hebrew Vowels*. SSLL 99. Leiden: Brill, 2020.

Talmy, Leonard. "Lexicalization Patterns: Semantic Structure in Lexical Forms." Pages 57–149 in *Grammatical Categories and the Lexicon. Vol. 3 of Language Typology and Syntactic Description*. Edited by Timothy Shopen. Cambridge: Cambridge University Press, 1985.

———. "Semantics and Syntax of Motion." Pages 181–238 in vol. 4 of *Syntax and Semantics*. Edited by John P. Kimball. New York: Academic Press, 1975.

———. *Toward a Cognitive Semantics*. 2 vols. Cambridge, MA: MIT Press, 2000.

Tawil, Hayim. *Akkadian Lexicon Companion for Biblical Hebrew*. Brooklyn: KTAV, 2009.

Taylor, John R. *Cognitive Grammar*. Oxford: Oxford University Press, 2002.

Teeter, David Andrew. *Scribal Laws: Exegetical Variation in the Textual Transmission of Biblical Law in the Late Second Temple Period*. FAT 92. Tübingen: Mohr Siebeck, 2014.

Thackston, W. M. *An Introduction to Koranic and Classical Arabic*. Bethesda, MD: IBEX, 1994.

The Text & Canon Institute. www.textandcanon.org.

Thompson, Jeremy Paul. "Learning Biblical Hebrew Vocabulary: Insights from Second Language Vocabulary Acquisition." PhD diss., University of Stellenbosch, 2011.

Thompson, Sandra A., and Robert E. Longacre. "Adverbial Clauses." Pages 171–234 in *Grammatical Categories and the Lexicon. Vol. 3 of Language Typology and Syntactic Description*. Edited by Timothy Shopen. Cambridge: Cambridge University Press, 1985.

Tice, Brian. *A Letter Respecting Some Particularities of the Hebrew Syntax*. Grand Rapids: MJR Press, 2017.

Tigay, Jeffrey H. *Deuteronomy*. The JPS Torah Commentary. Philadelphia: Jewish Publication Society, 1996.

Tov, Emanuel. "The Biblical Texts from the Judean Desert—An Overview and Assessment." Pages 128–54 in *Hebrew Bible, Greek Bible and Qumran: Collected Essays*. TSAJ 121. Tübingen: Mohr Siebeck, 2008.

———. *Introduction and Indexes*. DJD 39. Oxford: Clarendon, 2002.

———. "The Ketiv/Qere Variations in Light of the Manuscripts from the Judean Desert." Pages 197–205 in *The Hebrew Bible, Greek Bible, and Qumran: Collected Essays*. TSAJ 121. Tübingen: Mohr Siebeck, 2008.

———. "A Modern Textual Outlook Based on the Qumran Scrolls." *HUCA* 53 (1982): 11–27.

———. "'Proto-Masoretic,' 'Pre-Masoretic,' 'Semi-Masoretic,' and 'Masoretic': A Study in Terminology and Textual Theory." Pages 31–52 in *Found in Translation: Essays on Jewish Biblical Translation in Honor of Leonard J. Greenspoon*. Edited by James W. Barker, Anthony LeDonne, and Joel N. Lohr. West Lafayette, IN: Purdue University Press, 2018.

———. *Revised Lists of the Texts from the Judaean Desert*. Leiden: Brill, 2010.

———. "Septuagint." Pages 191–210 in vol. 1A of *Textual History of the Bible: The Hebrew Bible*. Edited by Armin Lange and Emanuel Tov. Leiden: Brill, 2016.

———. *Textual Criticism of the Hebrew Bible*. 3rd ed. Minneapolis: Fortress, 2012.

Trebolle Barrera, Julio C. "Kings (MT/LXX) and Chronicles: The Double and Triple Textual Tradition." Pages 483–501 in *Reflection and Refraction: Studies in Biblical Historiography in Honour of A. Graeme Auld*. Edited by Robert Rezetko, Timothy H. Lim, and W. Brian Aucker. VTSup 113. Leiden: Brill, 2007.

Tropper, Josef. "Das letzte Zeichen des ugaritischen Alphabets." *UF* 27 (1995): 505–28.

———. *Ugaritische Grammatik*. 2nd ed. AOAT 273. Münser: Ugarit-Verlag, 2012.

Trovato, Paolo. *Everything You Always Wanted to Know about Lachmann's Method: A Non-Standard Handbook of Genealogical Textual Criticism in the Age of Post-Structuralism, Cladistics, and Copy-Text*. Padova: Libreriauniversitaria, 2014.

Tsevat, Matitiahu. *A Study of the Language of the Biblical Psalms*. JBL Monograph Series 9. Philadelphia: SBL, 1955.

Tsumura, David T. *The First Book of Samuel*. NICOT. Grand Rapids: Eerdmans, 2007.

Tyler, Andrea, and Vyvyan Evans. *The Semantics of English Prepositions: Spatial Scenes, Embodied Meaning and Cognition*. Cambridge: Cambridge University Press, 2003.

Ulrich, Eugene. *The Dead Sea Scrolls and the Developmental Composition of the Bible*. Leiden: Brill, 2015.

Ulrich, Eugene, and Peter W. Flint, eds. *Qumran Cave 1:II, The Isaiah Scrolls*. 2 vols. DJD 32. Oxford: Clarendon, 2010.

Vance, Donald R., George Athas, Wilhelm Rudolph, and Yael Avrahami. *Biblia Hebraica Stuttgartensia: A Reader's Edition*. Peabody, MA: Hendrickson, 2014.

VanderKam, James C. *The Dead Sea Scrolls and the Bible*. Grand Rapids: Eerdmans, 2012.

Van Dyke Parunak, H. "Discourse Implications of Resumption in Hebrew אשר Clauses: A Pre-liminary Assessment from Genesis." Pages 101–16 in *Literary Structure and Rhetorical Strategies in the Hebrew Bible*. Edited by L. J. de Regt, J. de Waard, and J. P. Fokkelman. Winona Lake, IN: Eisenbrauns, 1996.

van Keulen, P. S. F. *Two Versions of the Solomon Narrative: An Inquiry into the Relationship between MT 1 Kgs. 2–11 and LXX 3 Reg. 2–11*. VTSup 104. Leiden: Brill, 2005.

Van Langendonck, Willy, and Mark Van de Velde. "Names and Grammar." Pages 20–33 in *The Oxford Handbook of Names and Naming*. Edited by Carole Hough. Oxford: Oxford University Press, 2016.

van Liere, Frans. *An Introduction to the Medieval Bible*. Cambridge: Cambridge University Press, 2014.

Van Seters, John. "The Chronicler's Account of the Temple-Building: A Continuity Theme." Pages 99–114 in *Changing Perspectives I: Studies in the History, Literature and Religion of Biblical Israel*. London: Routledge, 2011.

van Wolde, Ellen, ed. *Narrative Syntax and the Hebrew Bible: Papers of the Tilburg Conference 1996*. Leiden: Brill, 1997.

———. "The Niphal as Middle Voice and Its Consequence for Meaning." *JSOT* 43 (2019): 453–78.

———. *Reframing Biblical Studies: When Language and Text Meet Culture, Cognition, and Context*. Winona Lake, IN: Eisenbrauns, 2009.

———. "The Verbless Cause and Its Textual Function." Pages 321–36 in *The Verbless Clause in Biblical Hebrew: Linguistic Approaches*. Edited by Cynthia L. Miller. LSAWS 1. Winona Lake, IN: Eisenbrauns, 1999.

Verheij, Arian J. C. *Bits, Bytes, and Binyanim: A Quantitative Study of Verbal Lexeme Formations in the Hebrew Bible*. OLA 93. Leuven: Peeters, 2000.

———. *Verbs and Numbers: A Study of the Frequencies of the Hebrew Verbal Tense Forms in the Books of Samuel, Kings, and Chronicles*. SSN 28. Assen: Van Gorcum, 1990.

Voigt, Rainer. "Die Präpositionen im Semitischen—Über Morphologisierungsprozesse im Semitischen." Pages 22–43 in *Tradition and Innovation: Norm and Deviation in Arabic and Semitic Linguistics*. Edited by Lutz Edzard and Mohammed Nekroumi. Wiesbaden: Harrassowitz, 1999.

von Soden, Wolfram, with Werner R. Mayer. *Grundriss der akkadischen Grammatik*. 3rd ed. AnOr 33. Rome: Pontifical Biblical Institute, 1995.

Vriezen, T. C., and A. S. van der Woude. *Ancient Israelite and Early Jewish Literature*. Translated by Brian Doyle. Leiden: Brill, 2005.

Wallace, Daniel B. *Greek Grammar beyond the Basics: An Exegetical Syntax of the New Testament*. Grand Rapids: Zondervan, 1996.

Waltke, Bruce K. *Genesis: A Commentary*. Grand Rapids: Zondervan, 2001.

Watts, J. Wash. *A Survey of Syntax in the Hebrew Old Testament*. Grand Rapids: Eerdmans, 1964.

Watts, Richard J. *Politeness*, Key Topics in Sociolinguistics. Cambridge: Cambridge University Press, 2003.

Weber, Robert, and Roger Gryson. *Biblia Sacra iuxta vulgatam versionem*. 5th ed. Stuttgart: Deutsche Bibelgesellschaft, 2007.

Weil, Gérard E. *Massorah Gedolah iuxta codicem Leningradensem B 19 a*. 4 vols. Rome: Pontifical Biblical Institute, 1971.

Weinfeld, Moshe. "Covenant Terminology in the Ancient Near East and Its Influence on the West." *JAOS* 93 (1973): 190–99.

———. *Deuteronomy 1–11*. AB 5. New York: Doubleday, 1991.

Weinrich, Harald. *Tempus: Besprochene und erzählte Welt*. 4th ed. Stuttgart: Beck, 1985.

Weitzman, Michael P. "Peshitta, Septuagint, and Targum." Pages 51–84 in *VI Symposium Syriacum 1992: University of Cambridge, Faculty of Divinity, 30 August–2 September, 1992*. Edited by René Lavenant. Rome: Pontifical Biblical Institute, 1994.

———. *The Syriac Version of the Old Testament: An Introduction*. Cambridge: Cambridge University Press, 1999.

Wevers, John W. "The Use of Versions for Text Criticism: The Septuagint." Pages 15–24 in *La Septuaginta en la investigacion contemporanea (V Congreso de la IOSCS)*. Edited by Natalio Fernández Marcos. Madrid: CSIC, 1985.

Whitaker's Words. University of Notre Dame Archives. https://archives.nd.edu/words.html.

Williams, Ronald J. "The Passive Qal Theme in Hebrew." Pages 43–50 in *Essays on the Ancient Semitic World*. Edited by J. W. Wevers and D. B. Redford. Toronto: University of Toronto Press, 1970.

———. *Williams' Hebrew Syntax*. 3rd ed. Revised and expanded by John C. Beckman. Toronto: University of Toronto Press, 2007.

Williamson, Hugh G. M. *Isaiah 6–12: A Critical and Exegetical Commentary*. New York: Bloomsbury, 2018.

Wilson-Wright, Aren. "From Persepolis to Jerusalem: A Reevaluation of Old-Persian-Hebrew Contact in the Achaemenid Period." *VT* 65 (2015): 152–67.

———. "The Word for 'One' in Proto-Semitic." *JSS* 59 (2014): 1–13.

Wilt, Timothy. "A Sociolinguistic Analysis of *nā'*." *VT* 46 (1996): 237–55.

Woodhouse, R. "The Biblical Shibboleth Story in the Light of Late Egyptian Perceptions of Semitic Sibilants: Reconciling Divergent Views." *JAOS* 123 (2003): 271–90.

———. "Hebrew Šibbōlet 'Ear of Grain; (Olive) Branch' and 'Stream, Torrent, Flood': An Etymological Appraisal." *Studia Etymologica Cracoviensia* 7 (2002): 172–89.

Woods, Christopher, Emily Teeter, and Geoff Emberling, eds. *Visible Language: Inventions of Writing in the Ancient Middle East and Beyond*. Oriental Institute Museum Publications 32. Chicago: The Oriental Institute, 2015.

Wright, W. *A Grammar of the Arabic Language*. Cambridge: Cambridge University Press, 1896.

Würthwein, Ernst. *The Text of the Old Testament: An Introduction to the Biblia Hebraica*. 3rd ed. Revised and expanded by Alexander Achilles Fischer. Translated by Erroll F. Rhodes. Grand Rapids: Eerdmans, 2014.

Yeivin, Israel. *Introduction to the Tiberian Masorah*. Translated and edited by E. J. Revell. Masoretic Studies 5. Missoula, MT: Scholars Press, 1980.

Young, Ian. "The Biblical Scrolls from Qumran and the Masoretic Text: A Statistical Approach." Pages 81–139 in *Feasts and Fasts: A Festschrift in Honour of Alan David Crown*. Edited by Marianne Dacy, Jennifer Dowling and Suzanne Faigan. Mandelbaum Studies in Judaica 11. Sydney: Mandelbaum, 2005.

Young, Ian, Robert Rezetko, and Martin Ehrensvärd. *Linguistic Dating of Biblical Texts*. 2 vols. London: Equinox, 2008.

Zatelli, I. "I prodromi della definizione di verbo performativo nelle grammatiche tradizionali dell'ebraico biblico." Pages 690–97 in *Semitic and Assyriological Studies Presented to Pelio Fronzaroli by Pupils and Colleagues*. Edited by Paolo Marrassini. Wiesbaden: Harrassowitz, 2003.

Zevit, Ziony. *The Anterior Construction in Classical Hebrew*. SBLMS 50. Atlanta: Scholars Press, 1998.

Zewi, Tamar. "The Definition of the Copula and the Role of the 3rd Independent Personal Pronouns in Nominal Sentences of Semitic Languages." *Folia Linguistica Historica* 17 (1996): 41–55.

Ziegler, Joseph, ed. *Sapientia Iesu Filii Sirach*. 2nd ed. SVTG 12.2. Göttingen: Vandenhoeck & Ruprecht, 1980.

Ziegler, Joseph, ed. *Isaias*. SVTG 14. Göttingen: Vandenhoeck & Ruprecht, 1939.

Zimmermann, Thomas Ede, and Wolfgang Sternefeld. *Introduction to Semantics. An Essential Guide to the Composition of Meaning*. Berlin: de Gruyter, 2013.

Zwarts, Joost. "'Between' Constructions in Biblical Hebrew." *Linguistics in the Netherlands* 38.1 (2021): 163–78.

NAME INDEX

//////////////

A

Abegg, Martin *28*

Adam, Kluas-Peter *154–55*

Aḥituv, Shmuel *22*

Aikhenvald, Alexandra Y. *431*

Aissen, Judith *507*

Albrektson, Bertil *43*

Albright. William F. *8, 11*

Andersen, Francis. I. *206, 309, 359–60, 387, 397, 603*

Anderson, G. W. *39, 43*

Andrason, Alexander *207*

Annus, Amar *176*

Aussant, Emilie *275*

Austin, J. L. *194*

Avigad, Nahman *22*

B

Bache, Carl *88*

Baden, Joel S. *108, 154–55, 248*

Baker, Mark *276, 365, 381*

Baltes, P. B. *275*

Baranowski, Krzystof J. *207*

Bar-Asher, M. *108, 285*

Barkay, Gabriel *25*

Barr, James *42, 44*

Barthélemy, Dominique *47, 50, 57, 65–66, 71*

Barth, Jacob *108*

Beckman, John C. *146–49, 194*

Bekins, Peter *78, 308, 508*

Bergsträsser, Gotthelf *211, 365, 386*

Berlin, Charles *24*

Biber, Douglas *488, 499*

Black, David A. *87*

Blake, Frank R. *108–9, 386*

Blass, Fiedrich *87*

Blau, Joshua *130, 152–53, 156–58, 178–79, 198, 231–32, 287, 365, 365–66, 383, 414, 416, 519, 523*

Block, Daniel I. *5*

Bodine, Walter R. *604*

Boling, Robert G. *354*

Bordreuil, Pierre *15, 129, 140–41, 152–53, 156, 158, 209, 382, 412, 418*

Bossong, Georg *508*

Böttcher, Friedrich *108*

Botterweck, G. Johannes *592*

Boyd, Samuel L. *18, 21, 473*

Boyd, Steven W. *91–92, 130, 132*

Bravmann, M. M. *229*

Breuer, Mordechai *35*

Brockelmann, Carl *231, 518*

Bron, Framçois *445*

Brotzman, Ellis R. *46, 68*

Brown, A. Philip, II *32*

Burkitt, F. C. *31*

Butler, Trent C. *352*

C

Callaway, Mary C. *24*

Caplice, Richard *255*

Carbajosa, Ignacio *71*

Carr, David M.   26
Charpin, Dominique   14, 24
Chiesa, Bruno   28, 53
Childs, Brevard   24, 117
Chomsky, Noam   364–65
Christiansen, Brent   261–63
Cohen, Chaim   20
Coleman, Stephen   102
Cole, Peter   31
Comrie, Bernard   88, 92, 178–79
Conrad, Susan   488
Cook, John A.   88, 178, 182–83, 188, 199,
    363, 387–88
Corbett, G. G.   95
Cowper, E.   457
Cox, Claude   61–62
Crawford, Sidnie W.   50, 52
Creason, Stuart   87, 157, 178
Croft, William   276
Cross, Frank M.   8–9, 11, 18–19
Cruse, D. A.   589

D

Dallaire, Hélène   92, 239, 245, 308
Darnell, John C.   8–13
Davidson, Thomas   364
Davies, Graham I.   22, 157, 166
Davila, J. R.   28
DeCaen, V.   457
DeCean, Vincent   178
Delitzsch, F.   353
Dempster, Stephen G.   31
Demsky, Aaron   13
de Rossi, Giovanni B.   580
de Waard, Jan   57, 65, 69, 72, 306
Dhont, Marieke   62
Dik, Simon C.   430
Dines, Jennifer M.   31, 61
Dixon, R.   431
Dobbs-Allsopp, F. W.   18, 22, 178, 195
Donnelly-Lewis, Brian   13
Doron, Edit   427–28, 437–38, 446
Dotan, Aron   32–33, 35, 39

Dowty, David   87
Dozeman, Thomas B.   353
Dressler, Wolfgang   95, 148–49
Driver, G. R.   519
Driver, S. R.   178, 182, 361–62, 401
Dyk, J. W.   387

E

Ego, Beate   72
Ehrensvärd, Martin   20
Ehrman, Bart D.   31
Eissfeldt, Otto   353
Elliger, Karl   32, 36
Elwolde, J. F.   22, 354
Emberling, Geoff   8, 10
Emerton, J. A.   157
Evans, Craig A.   248
Evans, Vyvyan   533–34, 543, 554

F

Fabry, H.-J.   592–93, 597, 599
Fassberg, Steven E.   20, 152–53, 158, 207,
    238–41, 255, 260
Fassi Fehri, Abdelkader   148
Ferguson, Anthony M.   53
Filip, Hana   88
Finegan, Edward   488
Finsterbusch, Karen   60
Fitzmyer, Joseph A.   27
Flint, Peter   28
Forbes, A. D.   387
Fox, Joshua   384, 413–15, 424–25, 522
Freedman, David N.   194
Friedersdorf, Conor   23
Friedman, Matti   32
Friedman, Richard E.   26
Friedrich, J.   139, 157
Fruyt, Michéle   278

G

Gai, Amikam   365–66
Galil, G.   13
Gane, Roy E.   77, 203

Gaon, Saadin *180*
Gardiner, Alan *8–9, 11*
Garr, W. Randall *20, 211, 384, 508*
Gault, Brian P. *471*
Gensler, Orin *473*
Gentry, Peter J. *47–48, 54, 58, 64, 68–69, 71–73, 178, 183, 205, 255, 258*
Ginsberg, H. L. *211, 594*
Ginsburg, Christian D. *35*
Givón, Talmy *206, 276, 386*
Glanville, Peter J. *129*
Goetchinus, Eugen van Ness *395*
Goetze, Albretcht *141–43*
Goldenberg, Gideon *360–62, 436*
Goldfajn, Tal *178, 180–81*
Goldwasser, Orly *8–9, 11–12*
Gordis, Robert *38, 43–44*
Gordon, Amnon *386–87, 401*
Gordon, Cyrus H. *140, 207*
Gordon, Robert *157*
Goshen-Gottstein, Moshe *25, 28, 31, 32, 33, 119*
Goslinga, C. J. *353*
Graffi, Giorgio *601*
Grafton, Anthony *69*
Graves, Michael *70*
Greenberg, Joseph *148*
Greenstein, Edward L. *207, 210*
Greenwood, Kyle *271*
Gropp, Douglas M. *178, 251*
Gryson, Roger *581*
Gzella, Holger *126*

H

Hackett, Jo Ann *204, 207–8, 291*
Halpern, Baruch *26*
Hamilton, G. J. *9*
Hamilton, Victor P. *163*
Haran, Menahem *24, 30*
Hardy, H. H., II *16, 21, 102, 211, 365, 397, 414, 425, 456, 473, 504, 518–19, 522, 529, 536, 542, 561, 564, 589, 619*
Harris, R. Laird *592*

Harris, Zellig S. *384*
Haspelmath, Martin *275, 412, 431*
Hasselbach, Rebecca *178, 207, 323*
Hatav, Galia *178, 184, 435–38, 446*
Hatch, Edwin *582–83*
Hawley, Robert *15, 140*
Heimerdinger, Jean-Marc *206*
Heine, Bernd *134, 148*
Hempel, J. *598*
Hendel, Ronald S. *4–5, 19, 56, 72, 185*
Hengeveld, Kees *430, 435*
Herbert, E. D. *28*
Hess, Richard S. *273, 353–54*
Hetzron, Robert *178*
Hillers, Delbert R. *194*
Hoffman, Adina *31*
Hoffmann, Sebastian *526*
Höflmayer, Felix *13*
Holmstedt, Robert D. *16, 306, 427, 436, 458, 468, 470–71*
Holzinger, H. *353*
Hopper, Paul *205, 508*
Hornkohl, Aaron D. *20, 184, 281*
Hough, Carole *282*
Hovav, Malka *91*
Howell, Adam J. *613*
Huber, Judith *537*
Huehnergard, John *7, 139–40, 141, 152, 166, 178, 180, 187, 196, 197, 207, 238, 240, 255, 291, 384, 418*

I

Irvine, Judith *249*
Isaksson, Bo *457*

J

Jackson, Kent P. *412*
Jenni, Ernst *xxi, 135, 143–44, 146, 149, 159, 242–43, 441, 535, 592*
Jespersen, O. *361*
Jobes, Karen H. *31*
Johansson, Stig *488*
Johnson, Benjamin M. *596*

Jones, Ethan C. *133*
Jones, H. S. *581*
Joosten, Jan *19, 56, 72, 178, 182–83, 241*
Joüon, Paul *xix, 97, 119, 130, 154, 157, 167, 187, 194, 197, 204, 229, 238–39, 241, 258, 259, 278, 297, 308, 345, 362, 365, 374, 392, 413, 424, 436, 438, 440*
Juhás, Peter *262–63*

K

Kahn, Geoffrey *44, 364*
Kappler, Werner *30*
Kaufman, Stephen A. *92, 148, 239–42, 260, 262, 308*
Kautzsch, E. *211*
Kawashima, Robert S. *205*
Kedar-Kopfstein, Benjamin *385*
Keil, C. F. *353*
Kelley, Page H. *34, 204*
Kelly, Thomas F. *23*
Kemmer, Suzanne *90*
Kennicott, Benjamin *58, 580*
Khan, Geoffrey *32, 108, 184, 281, 361, 363–64, 508*
Kienast, Burkhart *365, 519*
Kim, Dong-Hyuk *20*
Kim, Yoo-Ki *436*
Kim, Young Bok *499*
Kingham, Cody *281, 561*
Kittel, Rudolf *32*
Kletter, Raz *343*
Kline, Meredith G. *176*
Knoppers, Gary *26*
Koschmieder, Erwin *194*
Köstenberger, Andreas J. *377, 401*
Kouwenberg, N. *129, 147–50, 159*
Kuryłowicz, Jerzy *413*
Kuteva, Tania *134*

L

Labat, René *14*
Labov, William *205*
Lam, Joseph *10, 20, 155, 211, 247*

Lambdin, Thomas O. *135, 174, 186, 204, 205, 212, 215–16, 240, 260–61*
Lambert, Mayer *108, 239, 241*
Langacker, Ronald W. *276, 285, 532*
Lange, Armin *48–49, 53, 60, 67*
Leech, Geoffrey *488*
Lehmann, Reinhard G. *15*
Lemke, Werner *26*
Lete, Gregorio *157*
Levin, Beth *91*
Lichtenberk, Frantisek *467*
Liddell, H. G. *581*
Lim, Timothy *26*
Lindenberger, James M. *27*
Lindstromberg, Seth *550, 553, 557*
Lipiński, Edward *370*
Lipka, Leonhard *94*
Lipschits, Oded *22*
Longacre, Drew *48, 54*
Longacre, Robert E. *205–6, 473*
Lundberg, Marilyn J. *25*
Lunn, Nicholas *300*
Lyons, John *90, 316, 361*

M

Mankowski, Paul V. *21*
Marcos, Natalio F. *31, 37, 72*
Marcus, David *6, 35*
Mathews, Kenneth A. *176, 271*
Mayer, Werner R. *141, 255*
Mazoyer, Michel *278*
McAffee, Matthew *8, 15, 115, 118, 357, 497, 595*
McCarter, P. Kyle, Jr. *56, 65, 410, 578, 596*
McDowell, Catherine L. *613*
McFall, Leslie *179, 182–84, 187, 196, 205*
McLauren, Dougald, III *288*
Meade, John D. *xv, 45, 48, 54, 71, 73, 577, 582*
Merkle, Benjamin L. *377, 401, 613*
Mettinger, Tryggve *254*
Metzger, Bruce *31*
Millard, Alan R. *13*

Miller, Cynthia   *14, 205, 225–26, 360, 457, 503*
Miller, Patrick D.   *597*
Miller-Naudé, Cynthia   *317, 365–66, 368–69, 380–82, 503*
Moran, William L.   *196, 209, 212, 254–55, 258, 596*
Morrow, William S.   *77, 203*
Moscati, Sabatino   *369, 370, 371*
Moshavi, Adina   *323, 436*
Müller, H.-P.   *370*
Muraoka, Takamitsu   *22, 97, 119, 130, 154, 157, 167, 194, 197, 229, 238–39, 241, 258–59, 278, 297, 308, 345, 354, 362–63, 365, 374, 392, 413, 424, 436, 438, 440, 581*

N

Naudé, Jacobus   *316–17, 365, 368–69, 380–81, 567*
Naveh, Joseph   *19*
Nelson, Richard D.   *354*
Netzer, Yael   *316*
Newsome, James D.   *26*
Niccacci, Alverio   *178, 179–80, 181, 206, 215–17*
Nihan, Christophe   *26*
Noonan, Benjamin J.   *21, 92, 308*
Noonan, Jennifer E.   *92, 308*
Norrick, Neal R.   *498*
Notarius, Tania   *207–9, 436*
Nougayrol, Jean   *139*

O

O'Connor, Michael P.   *88, 143–44, 146, 149–50, 154, 159, 165, 186, 193, 199, 208, 212, 214, 216, 237, 239, 246, 260, 365, 369, 374, 436–37*
Olshausen, Justus   *519*
Orlinski, Harry M.   *39, 43*
Orlinsky. H. M.   *39, 43*

P

Palmer, F. R.   *185*
Pardee, Dennis G.   *14–17, 25, 129, 139–40, 152, 156, 158, 178, 182–83, 186, 194–97, 206, 208–9, 211, 212, 214, 216–17, 278, 382–83, 412, 418*
Pariente, Itsik   *231–32*
Parker, Simon B.   *154*
Patton, Matthew H.   *604*
Peterson, Eugene   *xii*
Petrie, W. M. Flinders   *8*
Picus, Daniel   *23*
Plummer, Robert L.   *377, 401, 613*
Polzin, Robert   *21*
Pope, Marvin H.   *163*
Porter, Stanley E.   *87*
Pratico, Gary D.   *204*
Propp, William   *79*
Putnam, Frederic C.   *604*

Q

Qimron, Elisha   *44, 56, 258*
Quack, J. F.   *15*
Quirk, Randolph   *316, 481*

R

Rabin, Chaim   *33*
Rahlfs, Alfred   *66, 73, 581*
Rainey, Anson F.   *139, 196–97, 208–9*
Rand, Michael   *101–3*
Reckendorf, H.   *436*
Redford, D. B.   *108*
Redpath, Henry A.   *582–83*
Reich, Nurit   *35*
Rendsburg, Gary A.   *4–5, 20*
Rendtorff, Rolf   *24*
Renz, Johannes   *22*
Revell, E. John   *178–79, 240, 288*
Reymond, Eric D.   *22, 108–9, 127, 211*
Rezetko, Robert   *20, 26*
Riekert, S.   *437*
Ringgren, H.   *371*

Ritner, Robert K. *598*
Robertson, A. T. *87*
Rofé, Alexander *26*
Röllig, Wolfgang *22, 139, 157*
Rollston, Christopher A. *8, 18*
Rosenthal, Franz *139, 152, 370*
Ross, Allen P. *204*
Rudolph, Wilhelm *32, 36*
Ryder, Stuart A. *143, 148*

S

Salvesen, Alison *31*
Sanders, Paul *49*
Sanders, Seth L. *18, 194*
Sanmartín, Joaquín *157*
Sarna, Nahum *24*
Sass, Benjamin *8, 22*
Sasse, Hans-Jürgen *412*
Scanlin, Harold P. *27*
Schenker, Adrian *32, 36*
Scheumann, Jesse R. *457–58, 460*
Schmid, Konrad *26*
Schniedewind, William M. *59, 284*
Schroeder, N. W. *182*
Schwartz, Baruch J. *248*
Schwartz, Glenn M. *12*
Scott, R. *581*
Scott, William R. *34*
Screnock, John *320, 322–23, 325, 327*
Segal, Moses H. *21*
Segert, Stanislav *139–40, 157, 412*
Sellin, E. *385*
Sharp, Granville *205*
Shibatani, Maysayoshi *89*
Shulman, Ahouva *225, 241, 260–62*
Siebesma, P. A. *129*
Sivan, Daniel *108, 418*
Smelser, N. J. *275*
Smith, Bryan W. *32*
Smith, Mark S. *210–11, 354*
Smoak, Jeremy D. *25, 284*
Smyth, Herbert W. *195*
Snell, Daniel *255*

Sperber, Alexander *581*
Sprengling, Martin *11*
Stackert, Jeffery *248*
Staps, Camil *136*
Stassen, Leon *387*
Steiner, Richard L. *17*
Sternefeld, Wolfgang *589*
Stolz, Fritz *593–94, 597–98*
Streck, Michael P. *238*
Suchard, Benjamin D. *197*

T

Talmon, Shemaryahu *33*
Talmy, Leonard *537, 538, 554*
Tawil, Hayim *21*
Taylor, John R. *276*
Teeter, David A. *53, 67*
Teeter, Emily *8, 10*
Thackston, W. M. *139, 141, 152, 414*
Thomas, Benjamin D. *414, 425*
Thompson, Jeremy P. *619*
Thompson, Sandra A. *473, 508*
Tice, Brian *205*
Tigay, Jeffery H. *597*
Tov, Emanuel *28–29, 33, 44, 47, 52–55, 60, 67, 68, 580, 582*
Towner, Philip H. *613*
Trebolle Barrera, Julio C. *26, 28, 58*
Tropper, Josef *16, 140, 152, 158, 207, 238*
Trovato, Paolo *46*
Tsevat, Mattitahu *239*
Tsumura, David T. *410*
Tully, Eric J. *46, 68*
Tyler, Andrea *533–34, 543, 554*

U

Ulrich, Eugene *28, 67*

V

Vance, Donald R. *32*
Vanderhooft, David S. *22*
VanderKam, James C. *28*
Van de Velde, Mark *282*

Van Dyke Parunak, H. *306*
van der Woude, A. S. *24*
VanGemeran, Willem *592*
van Keulen, P. S. F. *26*
Van Langendonck, Willy *282*
Van Pelt, Miles V. *204*
van Sder Merwe, C. H. J. *503*
Van Seters, John *26*
van Wolde, Ellen *133, 179, 205, 309–10,*
    395–97, 405, 532, 535, 544, 604
Vaughn, Andrew G. *25*
Verheij, Arian J. C. *21, 119*
Vita, Juan-Pablo *207*
Voigt, Rainer *518*
von Ewald, G. *181–82, 187, 196, 205, 229,*
    239
von Mengden, Ferdinand *320*
von Siebenthal, Heinrich *287*
von Soden, Wolfram *141, 255*
Vriezen, T. C. *24*

W

Wallace, Daniel *396, 401*
Waltke, Bruce K. *50, 88, 143–44, 146,*
    149–50, 154, 159, 165, 176, 186, 193,
    199, 208, 212, 214, 216, 237, 239, 246,
    260, 365, 369, 374, 436, 437, 597
Watts, J. Wash *204, 226*
Watts, Richard J. *226*
Weber, Robert *581*
Webster, Daniel *8*
Weil, Gérard E. *37–38*

Weinfeld, Moshe *20, 597*
Weinrich, Harald *179, 205*
Weitzman, Michael P. *71*
Wells, Bruce *77*
Westbrook, Raymond *77*
Westermann, Claus *592*
Wevers, John W. *72, 108*
Williams, Megan *69*
Williams, Ronald J. *108, 192, 194, 204, 304*
Williamson, Hugh G. M. *70*
Wilson-Wright, Aren *21, 324*
Wilt, Timothy *261*
Woodard, Roger D. *157*
Woodhouse, R. *4*
Woods, Christopher *8, 10*
Wright, David P. *194*
Wright, G. Ernest *212*
Wright, W. *238*
Würthwein, Ernst *23, 38*

Y

Yeivin, Israel *35, 435*
Young, Ian *20–21, 29*

Z

Zatelli, I. *194*
Zevit, Ziony *178, 181–82*
Zewi, Tamar *361–63*
Ziegler, Joseph *30, 581*
Zimmermann, Thomas *589*
Zuckerman, Bruce *25*
Zwarts, Joost *559*

SUBJECT INDEX

////////////////

abecedary   *15*

abjad   *15*

absolute state   *301–2, 323, 314*

acrophony   *11–12*

adjective   *94, 101, 187, 276, 278, 283, 288–89,*
    312, 322, 364–404

  adverbial   *403–4*

  attributive   *371–74, 391*

  comparative   *377–78*

  intensification   *380*

  predicate   *375–77*

  substantive   *371–2, 374–75, 381*

  superlative   *378–80*

  verbal   *See participle*

adjunct   *80, 89–92, 95, 304, 480, 537–39*

adverb   *92, 96, 294, 304, 313–15, 412, 480–87*

  of association   *481, 485–86*

  of contingency   *481, 485*

  of modality   *481, 486–87*

  of process   *481, 484–85*

  of quantity   *481, 487*

  of space   *481–82*

  of time   *481, 483–84*

  conjunctive   *488–91*

  locative   *313–14*

  temporal   *314–16, 483–84*

adverbializer   *468, 473–75, 488*

adversative   *565*

Aktionsart   *87–88*

allocentric   *538, 540*

allophone   *458*

alphasyllabary   *15*

anaphor   *281, 396*

anarthrous   *307*

animacy scale   *508*

antecedent   *468, 471*

anticausative   *88–91, 129–33*

apodosis   *192–93, 203, 211–12, 257, 466, 479*

apotropaic   *25*

apposition   *279, 304–7, 344, 394, 425, 440,*
    468

Aramaic Square Script   *18–19, 39, 42*

argument   *91–98, 103–4, 126, 380*

arthrous   *307*

aspect   *80, 87–88, 96, 173–88, 205–7, 213–14,*
    376, 402

  frequentative   *145–46, 179, 199–200*

  habitual   *88, 95, 176, 179, 199, 292, 434*

  imperfective   *174–75, 178–79, 183, 187,*
    199–201, 214, 352

  perfective   *174–79, 188, 402*

  progressive   *199*

  situation. *See Aktionsart*

  viewpoint   *88, 182*

  perfect, epistolary   *195–96*

asseverative   *465, 486*

asyndetic   *456–57, 466, 477*

atelic   *147*

attenuation   *156, 370*

background   *180, 205–7, 214–17, 400–402,*
    434, 477–79, 601, 604–7

base. *See* noun pattern

benefactive   *130, 565*

binyanim. *See* stem, verb

717

casus pendens   *361–3*
causation   *80, 88, 93–95, 144, 158–59*
causativity   *120, 159*
clause   *77–78, 80, 84–99, 121, 174, 211, 262,*
   277–80, 304, 306, 437, 455–58, 465–81,
   488–91, 529–32, 601–4
   circumstantial   *206, 209, 261, 354,*
      400–401, 475–79
   of classification   *359–63, 397, 603*
   conditional   *186, 212, 257*
   dependent. *See* clause, embedded
   embedded   *306, 422, 467–81, 529–30*
   of identification   *359–63, 381, 397*
   matrix   *468–73*
   nominal. *See* clause, verbless
   relative   *214, 277–78, 306, 375, 382,*
      468–71, 488, 506–7
   restrictive and nonrestrictive relative   *255,*
      306–7
   temporal   *174, 214, 409–11, 422, 432–35*
   subordinate. *See* clause, embedded
   verbless   *190–91, 205, 309, 354–55,*
      359–64, 376, 395–98, 489, 493–4, 603
   verbless, bipartite   *361*
   verbless, tripartite   *360–63*
comitative   *456, 461, 506, 558, 564, 566–67*
command   *185–86, 203–4, 223–26, 232–37,*
   240–43, 248–54, 260
   indirect   *252–53*
   infinitive absolute as   *237, 438, 444–45*
   negative   *203–4, 248–50, 260, 494–95*
   positive   *203, 249–50*
complementizer   *468, 471–73*
completion   *88, 92–93, 96–97, 103, 146*
concessive   *461, 465, 475*
conjoin   *456–68*
conjugation, verb   *21, 80, 83–84, 118–19*
   cohortative   *185, 197–98, 215–17, 223–24,*
      239–41, 245–46, 254–61
   imperative. *See* command
   imperative, long   *238–43, 255, 262*
   jussive   *40, 157, 185, 196–204, 215, 217,*
      223–24, 229, 243–54, 494

jussive, third-person   *244–46, 251–55*
prefix   *83–4, 100–102, 123, 173–218*
*qatal   *100–101, 124, 187, 197, 199, 214,*
   231, 371, 414–17
*qatāl   *371, 413, 418*
*qatil   *100–101, 187, 214, 369, 383–84*
*qatul   *100–101, 108, 187, 214, 382–83*
*qatūl   *370, 382*
*qātil   *292–93, 370, 382, 390, 426*
*qitil   *231, 414–17*
*qutal   *108*
*qutul   *197, 231, 238, 413–17*
suffix   *83–4, 100–102, 123, 173–218*
volitive   *157, 185–86, 197–98, 215–18,*
   223–63
waw conjugations   *21, 119, 204–18*
wayyiqtol   *21, 119, 174–75, 177–85, 198,*
   204–18, 435, 461, 475–79, 601
wəqatāl   *21, 119, 175–85, 198, 204–18,*
   211–18, 435, 461, 475–79, 601
X+*qātal*   *174–76, 180–81, 211–18*
X+*yiqtol*   *211–18*
*yaqtal   *100–101, 417*
*yaqtil   *100–101, 157, 198*
*yaqtul   *100–101, 196–98, 207–11, 214*
*yaqtulØ   *100, 196–98, 207–11, 243–45,*
   254–55
*yaqtula   *196–98, 254–55*
*yaqtulu   *100, 196–98, 207–11, 231,*
   243–45, 254–55
conjunct. *See* conjoin
conjunction   *212, 446, 453–80, 488*
constituent   *80, 86–87, 89, 92–94, 121–22,*
   302–5, 309, 395–7, 430, 456–9, 468
construct phrase   *300–318, 371–73, 393, 430,*
   459–62
construct state   *301–2, 371, 413, 522*
constructio ad sensum   *287–88*
conversive theory   *181*
coordination   *456–67*
coordinator   *457–68*
copula   *103, 280, 354, 359–64, 387–89*
de-agentive   *78–80, 89–91, 108*

definiteness   *301–2, 307–10, 371–73, 395–97, 508*

definiteness continuum   *309–10, 395–97*

deixis   *310–16, 482, 504, 540, 560*

demonstrative   *278, 309–16, 396, 425, 492*

determiner   *307–16*

diathesis. *See* voice

diglossia   *20*

discourse situation   *312–13, 461*

distributive   *88, 95, 179, 305, 317, 341–43*

dynamism   *88, 91–94, 96–98, 126*

egocentric   *538–40*

epicene   *295*

ethical dative   *567–68*

exchange   *536, 568–69*

existential   *491–95, 504–5*

extraposition   *361–64*

factitive   *88, 93–94, 116, 127–28, 141–50, 159, 384, 593*

fientivity   *87–88, 91–94, 97–105, 126–35, 159–61, 187–88, 382, 390*

focus   *175–76, 358, 363, 394–95, 398, 486, 602–3*

foreground   *180, 205–6, 215–17, 400–402, 603–4*

fraction   *338–39*

framing verb   *475–79*

fronting. *See* foreground

function word   *455–509, 518*

gnomic perfect   *190*

grammatical concord   *285, 287–88, 300, 363–64*

halaḥam   *15*

head   *277, 294, 300–306, 316–18, 412–13, 427, 430, 468–71, 488*

Hebrew words

   אֲהָהּ   *499*

   אוֹ   *458, 461–65, 468*

   אוֹי   *502*

   אַחֲרֵי / אַחַר   *336–37, 474–76, 522–25, 543, 556–57, 564, 569*

   אֵין   *317, 353, 357, 399, 491–495, 504, 516*

   אַךְ   *474–75, 486–87, 490–91*

אַל   *244–46, 248–53, 260, 491–95*

אֶל   *103–4, 456, 474, 496, 519–21, 525, 528, 536, 542–43, 550, 553–54, 558, 565–67*

אִם   *260–61, 545, 461–62, 465–67, 472, 476, 478–79, 498, 500*

אָמֵן   *459, 486, 501*

אָנָּא   *502–3*

אֶפֶס   *491–92, 495, 527, 570*

אֵצֶל   *106, 520, 522–23, 525, 536, 557–58*

אֲשֶׁר   *306–7, 456, 468–76*

אֵת   *62, 121, 308–9, 396, 425–26, 456, 505–9, 519–21, 525, 536, 556, 558, 566*

בְּ   *174, 411, 432, 456, 474, 535–36, 542, 546–50, 560*

בִּגְלַל   *527, 565–66*

בִּי   *500*

בְּיוֹם   *561*

בֵּין   *522–23, 559–60, 563*

בִּלְעֲדֵי   *474–75, 516, 524–25*

בַּעֲבוּר   *432, 474–75, 527, 566, 586, 571*

בַּעַד   *522–25, 555–57, 566*

בְּעֵת   *561*

בְּתוֹךְ   *527–28, 549–50, 555, 562, 566*

גַּם   *68, 463–65, 485–87, 489–91*

הָאָח   *499*

הוֹי   *502*

הִנֵּה   *503–4*

הַס   *499–500*

וְ   *456–67*

וְהָיָה   *174, 214, 429, 433, 467, 475–79, 562*

וַיְהִי   *98, 138, 174–75, 214, 433, 458, 467, 475–79, 562*

חָלִילָה   *501–2*

יַעַן   *474–75, 488, 522–23*

כְּ   *307, 456, 474–78, 519–21, 525–28, 561–62, 567*

כַּאֲשֶׁר   *474–76, 561*

כִּי   *174–75, 192–93, 430, 456, 465–68, 471, 475–76, 479*

כְּפִי   *475, 527–28, 569*

לְ 97–99, 280, 417, 421, 456, 507, 519–21, 524–29, 531–32, 535–36, 540–42, 550–53, 562–71

לֹא 203, 224, 246–47, 260, 317, 491–93

לְבִלְתִּי 491, 493–94

לְמַעַן 429, 432, 474–75, 529, 571

לְעֻמַּת 527, 558–59

לִפְנֵי 433, 526–30, 536, 556, 564

לִקְרַאת 526–27, 565

מִחוּץ לְ 528, 550

מִן 319–23, 375, 377–78, 456, 475–76, 519–30, 540, 550–53, 561, 563, 566–67, 569–70

מִפְּנֵי 527, 550, 553–54, 566

נָא 34, 228, 232, 239–40, 244, 258–63, 494–95, 500–501

סָבִיב 482, 522–24, 543, 550

עַד 314, 433–34, 468, 475, 519–25, 529–30, 542, 552–53, 563–65

עַל 20, 73, 81, 353, 356, 456, 519–21, 524–27, 536, 543–44, 546, 565–67, 569–70

עַל אֹדֹת 474–75

עַל יֶרֶךְ 558

עַל פִּי 527, 569

עַל־פְּנֵי 516–17, 527, 544–46

עַל־כֵּן 488–89

עִם 357, 519–21, 524–25, 536, 565–66, 570

עַתָּה 40, 314–15, 455, 483, 488–89, 561

פֶּן 465–67

רְאֵה 503–4

שֶׁ 470–72

תַּחַת 357, 475, 522–25, 533, 543–44, 566, 568

Hieroglyph, Egyptian 8–13

hypotaxis 457

image schema 534, 543–559

inchoate. See ingressive

incipient. See ingressive

indicative 157, 185, 196–198, 217, 225, 254, 445–46, 492, 497

infinitive

  absolute, infinitive 128–29, 237, 318, 380, 404, 410–13, 418–422, 435–46

  construct, infinitive 82, 128–29, 410–18, 422–35, 491, 493, 561, 571

  tautological 411, 435–38, 441–42

ingressive 117, 129–30, 134–35, 137, 200, 208

instrumental 535, 564, 569–70

intensive 88, 96, 141–50, 353, 370

interjection. See reaction signal

interrogative. See question

irrealis, or nonreal 42, 185–86, 192–93, 199–201, 211, 257, 262, 432, 492

iterative 88, 95, 148–49, 199–200

ketiv-qere 22, 35, 38–44, 245–46

Kuntillet ʿAjrud 18, 284

Landmark [LM] 532

languages

  Akkadian 6–7, 13–14, 16, 21, 120, 123–24, 140–43, 147, 156, 158–59, 166, 187, 195, 255, 370, 384, 418

  Ammonite 7, 384

  Arabic 6–7, 15–17, 31, 61, 108, 124, 129, 139–41, 152, 156, 158, 166, 238–39, 414, 425

  Aramaic 3, 6–7, 15, 17–19, 27, 31, 38, 61, 64, 124, 139, 152, 157–58, 370, 420, 587

  Armenian 31, 61, 586–87

  Canaanite 7, 13–18, 140, 196, 212, 255, 418

  Coptic 31, 61

  Eblaite 7, 14

  Edomite 7

  Ethiopian 7, 15, 31, 61, 123–24

  Ethiopic 7, 31, 61

  Georgian 31, 61

  Geʿez 7, 15

  Gothic 61

  Greek 31, 45, 61–62, 73, 108, 129, 173, 189, 191, 195, 277, 302, 360–61, 364, 377, 401–2, 587

  Hebrew, Archaic Biblical 19–20, 208

  Hebrew, Babylonian 32, 47

  Hebrew, Classical Biblical 19–21

  Hebrew, Epigraphic 21–22

Hebrew, Late Biblical   *19–20, 22*
Hebrew, Palestinian   *32, 47*
Hebrew, Rabbinic   *21, 31–34, 357*
Hebrew, Standard Biblical   *19–21*
Hebrew, Tiberian   *xxiii, 17, 32, 44, 47, 100, 108, 522*
Hebrew, Transitional Biblical   *19–20*
Latin   *31, 60–61, 119, 129, 360, 587*
Moabite   *7, 384*
Old Church Slavonic   *31, 61*
Phoenician   *7, 17–18, 139, 157, 384, 445*
Proto-Semitic   *xxiii, 18, 120*
Sabaic   *7*
Semitic, Central   *7, 123*
Semitic, East   *7, 14*
Semitic, Northwest   *6–7, 14, 44, 194, 197, 412*
Semitic, West   *7, 11, 15–16, 255, 371*
South Arabian, Modern   *7*
South Arabian, Old   *7*
Syriac   *6–7, 15, 31, 60–61, 69, 587*
Ugaritic   *7, 13–17, 120, 129, 139–41, 151, 156–58, 195, 207, 209, 212, 238, 240, 418, 593*
lingua franca   *6, 18*
linker. *See* conjunction
manner   *87, 440, 474–75, 481, 484, 495, 550, 569–70*
manner-conflating verbs   *537–542*
marked   *83, 97, 129, 148, 177–82, 188, 241, 243–45, 278, 280, 294–95, 355, 358, 366, 368, 373, 394–96, 427, 446*
Masorah finalis   *33–38*
Masorah magna   *33–38, 37*
Masorah marginalis   *33–38*
Masorah parva   *33–38, 37*
measure word   *285–86, 320, 342–46*
mirativity   *503–4*
modality   *80–81, 185–86, 432, 481, 486–87, 492*
  deontic   *185–86, 429, 432*
  epistemic   *185*
modifier
  adnominal   *468, 471*

adverbial   *426, 429, 433–35, 531*
mood. *See* modality
morphosyntax   *77, 302, 321–23, 331–32, 424–25*
multiplier   *327, 339–41*
negation   *428, 491–95*
nomen professionis   *292, 390*
nomina unitatis   *290*
nominal   *105–6, 143–45, 277–82, 293, 306, 359–64, 369–71, 384–90, 412*
nominalization   *423*
nonverbal sentence   *179–80, 215–17*
noun   *105–7, 271–320, 412, 422–27*
  abstract   *284–85*
  affix, noun   *293–94*
  agent   *370, 426*
  animate   *86, 280, 507–598*
  collective   *287–90*
  common   *274, 281–86, 298, 307, 382*
  concrete   *284–85*
  count   *281, 284–89, 320, 343*
  derivation, noun   *364*
  dual   *84, 299–300, 368*
  gender, noun   *80, 277, 280–81, 294–97, 309*
  inanimate   *86, 507–598*
  individuative   *281, 287–90*
  inflection   *294–302, 425*
  mass. *See* noncount noun
  name. *See* proper noun
  noncount   *281, 284–89, 320, 343*
  noun class   *281–90, 369*
  noun phrase   *277–281*
  number, noun   *287, 294, 297–300*
  pattern, noun   *291–94, 298, 371, 424–26, 522*
    *qatil   *101, 383–84*
    *qatīl   *370*
    *qātil   *292–3, 370, 426*
    *qatl   *291–92, 522*
    *qatul   *101, 383–84*
    *qatūl   *370*
    *qattāl   *292–3, 390, 426*
    *qittil   *292–3, 370*

qitl 291–92, 522
qutl 291–92, 522
plural-only 286–87
prefix, noun 293–94
proper 281–83, 396, 508
segholate 291–92, 298
state, noun 300–302
substantives 276, 364–67
suffix, noun 293–94
verbal 424–27
number, grammatical 83–85, 95, 121, 272–74, 277, 284–90, 297–300, 310–11, 365–69, 425–26
numeral 277–78, 307–8, 316, 320–46, 396, 425
  additive number 323–35
  cardinal number 285, 288–89, 320–44
  distributive number 317, 341–42
  ordinal number 294, 324, 335–38, 370
object 78, 80, 84, 89–92, 97–98, 103–5, 121–22, 146–50, 277–81
  complement, object 103–5, 280, 507–8
  direct 103–5, 146–47, 309, 396, 507–8, 531
  indirect 103–5, 122, 280, 309, 531, 565–67
  internal 92, 105, 436
  marker, object 62, 121, 308–11, 396, 425, 505–9, 531
  prepositional 79, 99, 103, 440, 529
Paleo-Hebrew script 18–19, 25
paradigmatic 105, 590
parataxis 457
paronomastic infinitive. See tautological infinitive
participle 382–92, 398–404, 412
particle 232, 275–76, 357, 376–77, 388–89, 399, 453–509, 537
path-conflating verbs 537–44
performative 193–96, 253–54
periphrastic 402
phrasal units 277
phrase 92, 104, 214, 277–80, 300–319, 423–25
pictograph 11–13

pluractionality 95–96
pluralis maiestatis 287
polysemy 173, 517, 533–34
  principled 533–34
possessive 281, 355–57, 570
pragmatics 455
preformative 100, 123, 128–29
preposition 515–72
  complex 525–26, 533
  compound 524–25, 533
  compound-complex 528–30
  multiword 524–29
  polymorphic 524
  primary 519–21, 524
  secondary 522–24
prepositional phrase 89, 103, 122, 304, 359, 494, 526, 529–71
privative 519, 570–71
proclitic 458, 505–7
pronominal state 301–2, 372–75
pronominal suffix 39–41, 240–41, 283, 291, 316, 322, 356–58, 396, 415–18, 425, 428–29, 493, 505–6, 520–24, 527–530
pronoun 38–40, 90, 136–37, 186, 272–74, 281–82, 310, 351–67, 396–98, 422–25, 445–46, 455, 468, 486, 492, 508
  interrogative 495–96
  resumptive 306, 361–63, 469–71
protasis 78, 192–93, 203, 211, 257, 260, 466, 479
prototype. See image schema
qere perpetuum 38, 43
quantifier 278, 282–83, 289, 316–20
question 359, 463, 467, 485, 491–93, 495–98
  alternative 467, 491–93, 496–97
  interrogative *he* 496–97
  wh-question 495
  yes-no question. See alternative question
reaction signal 498–504
realis, or real 185–86
reciprocality 88, 96, 129–30, 135–36, 152–53
reflexivity 88–93, 96–97, 105, 123–30, 136–37, 152–55, 167–68, 357–58

relative   *175–76, 213–14, 277–78, 306,*
   375–76, 382, 425, 468–72, 474, 530, 561
relative clause. *See* clause
relativizer   *468–71, 476*
result   *87–88, 186, 216–17, 255, 258, 423,*
   429, 432, 456, 461, 465, 474, 481, 485,
   488–89, 571
resultative   *93–94, 130, 135, 144–45, 159, 200*
root
   geminate   *82, 166–67, 371, 421*
   hollow   *81–82, 185, 243–45*
   middle weak. *See* hollow root
   quadriconsonantal   *82–83*
   quadriliteral. *See* quadriconsonantal
   strong   *81, 197*
   weak   *81–82, 100, 106, 157, 166–67, 185,*
      197–98, 207–210, 243–46, 254, 416–17,
      421, 426, 519
root phrase   *437–38*
satellite   *537, 542*
satellite framing   *537–40*
script
   alphabetic   *7–13*
   cuneiform   *13–17*
   Old Hebrew   *18–19, 50*
semantics   *80, 91–92, 168, 177–78, 217, 281,*
   305–6, 384–90, 411–12, 481, 532–43,
   589–91
semantic roles or thematic relations   *80,*
   86–89, 109, 128, 302–4, 591
   agent   *78–79, 86–99, 108, 129–36, 142,*
      147, 150, 158–59, 164, 302, 428, 534
   causee   *86–87, 93–94*
   causer   *79, 86–87, 90–94, 121, 129–31*
   experiencer   *87, 567*
   force   *86, 481, 569*
   instrument   *86, 481, 534–35, 569*
   patient   *78–79, 86–96, 108, 129–36,*
      146–47, 153, 302–3, 428, 507–8
Sinaitic Inscriptions   *8*
stative   *78, 80, 91–94, 97–98, 100–103,*
   116–18, 126–27, 134–35, 142–43, 146–47,
   161, 187, 381–85, 398

stativity   *77, 88, 91–94, 214*
stem vowel   *99–102, 166*
stem, verb   *115–68*
   C, or *Hiphil*   *109, 116–27, 130–31, 144–45,*
      149, 152, 155–68, 198, 229–30, 419–24
   Cp, or *Hophal*   *78–79, 108, 119–20,*
      125–27, 155, 164–65
   D, or *Piel*   *108, 116–27, 137–55, 158–63*
   derived   *109, 119, 122–28, 168, 229, 419*
   distribution. *See* frequency, stem
   Dp, or *Pual*   *78, 108–9, 119–21, 125–27,*
      137, 150–51, 420
   frequency, stem   *124–25*
   G, or *Qal*   *96–107, 137*
   Gp, or *Qal* passive   *108–9, 127, 134*
   Grundstamm   *96*
   L, or *Poel*   *124, 166–68*
   N, or *Niphal*   *78–79, 108–9, 119–20,*
      122–37, 154–55, 229–30, 414, 419–20
   R, or *Pilpel*   *124, 166–67*
   RL, or *Polel*   *124, 166–68*
   Semitic, comparative   *124, 129, 187*
   tD, or *Hitpael*   *119–28, 136–37, 155–57,*
      229–30
subject   *78–95, 121–22, 129–36, 278–81*
subordination   *456–57, 467–75*
subordinator   *459, 462, 467–74*
syntagmatic   *590*
syntax   *xv, 77, 80, 119, 186, 308, 354, 372,*
   412, 457, 480, 529, 601
TAM   *88, 173, 177, 429, 434, 477*
tense   *80, 88, 173, 177–85*
   converted   205
   prophetic future   191–92
   future   173, 178–80, 196, 205
   nonpast   *199*
   narrative   *179*
   past   *173, 178–83, 188, 199, 205*
   present   *173, 178–80*
texts and manuscripts   *22*
   Aleppo Codex   *32–34, 49, 54, 580*
   Aquila   *47, 67–70, 577*

Aramaic Targums *41, 47, 72–74, 352, 582–3, 587*

Biblia Hebraica Quinta *32, 37–38, 580, 585, 614–15*

Biblia Hebraica Stuttgartensia *32, 36, 580, 585, 614–15*

Cairo Fustat Genizah *48, 120, 158*

Dead Sea Scrolls *27–29, 47, 52–60, 577, 580–85*

En-Gedi *27–28, 52, 54*

Greek versions, post-hexaplaric *67–70*

Greek Versions, pre-hexaplaric *47, 67–70*

Hexapla *63, 67–70, 587*

Latin Vulgate *47, 70–71, 73, 352, 578, 581, 587*

Leningrad Codex, or Firkovich B 19a *32–34, 36, 49, 580, 585, 614*

Masada *27–28, 52, 54–55*

Masoretic Text *28–29, 32–44, 47–50, 577–78, 585*

Naḥal Ḥever *27–28, 52, 54*

Naḥal Sdeir *27–28, 52, 54*

Naḥal Ṣeʿelim *27–28, 52, 54*

Nash Papyrus *31*

Old Greek. *See* Septuagint

Quinta *47, 68*

Qumran, Khirbet *27, 29, 47, 52 Samaritan Pentateuch 28, 47, 50–52, 577*

Septuagint *19, 31, 41, 47, 61–67, 352, 577, 585–86*

Septuagint, Göttingen *586*

Sexta *47, 68*

Symmachus *47, 67–70, 577*

Syriac Peshitta *41, 47, 71–72, 352, 578, 581, 587*

Syro-Hexapla *69, 71*

Theodotion *47, 67–70, 577*

Wadi Murabbaʿat *27–28, 52, 54*

Textual Criticism *19, 28, 45–74, 577–87*

theme vowel *99–102, 120, 150, 155–57, 164, 187, 198, 229–31, 414, 417–21*

topic *85–86, 175, 361, 395–97, 601–2*

topicalization *85–86, 456, 601*

Trajector [TR] *532, 554*

transitivity *80, 87–88, 92–93, 103–4, 126, 146–50*

  ambitransitivity *88, 92–93, 104–5*

  ditransitivity *88, 92–93, 97, 103–4, 507*

  intransitivity *88, 90–93, 97–98, 103–4, 116–17, 129–30, 133–34, 142–51, 158–65, 353*

unmarked *83, 86, 259, 427, 507–8*

valency *80, 88, 92–94, 103–5, 126, 159*

  avalent *93, 98, 126*

  bivalent *93, 126*

  trivalent *93, 126*

  univalent *93, 126*

verb *77*

  affix, verb *80–3*

  auxiliary *89–94, 130, 402–3*

  causative *90–93, 164*

  clause-initial *183, 211*

  denominative *106–7*

  finite *119–21, 177, 180, 280, 358, 383–84, 409–13*

  gender, verb *80, 83–86, 121, 177*

  impersonal *92–93, 98–99, 427*

  infix, verb *80, 120, 152*

  non-clause-initial *211*

  nonfinite *119, 177, 180, 411–12, 422–28, 435, 446*

  number, verb *80, 83–86, 121, 177*

  person, verb *80, 83–86, 121, 177*

  plurality, verb. *See* pluractionality

  sequence, verb *174–75, 186, 205–6, 214–17, 240, 251, 259, 400, 429–35, 475–76*

voice *80, 87–90, 92, 126*

  active *88–92, 96*

  mediopassive *90, 129–30*

  middle *88, 90, 105, 131*

  passive *88–90, 150*

  reflexive *88–90, 97*

volitive *157, 177, 185–87, 197–98, 215–18, 223–63, 445*

volitive sequence *214–17, 240, 251, 259*

word class *275–77, 321, 351, 412, 422–23, 456, 488*

SCRIPTURE INDEX

//////////////////

Genesis

1   253
1:1   35, 180, 308
1:2   181, 405
1:3   253
1:4   181
1:5   181, 336
1:6   253, 533
1:7   533
1:9   271, 533
1:11   253, 271
1:11–12   272
1:12   271
1:14   253, 263, 459–60
1:16   378
1:20   253, 545–46
1:22   253
1:24   253, 271, 308
1:25   271
1:26   253, 272, 274, 568
1:26–28   272, 274
1:27   271, 274
1:27–28   272
1:28   177, 272, 274
1:29   181
1:29–30   272
1:31   379, 504
2:2   306–7, 531, 590
2–3   273
2:4   416, 428
2:4b–5   483

2:5   98
2:6   212
2:7   548
2:11   336
2:13   394, 397
2:17   433, 435
2:18   492
3   435
3:3   306, 435, 531–32
3:4   441
3:5   426, 435
3:6   297, 485
3:8   152, 554
3:8–21   574
3:9   304
3:20   104, 279–81
3:22   218, 426
4:1   97, 183
4:2   403
4:3   214, 319–20
4:8   65
4:9   492
4:11   428
4:12   247
4:14   215
4:15   111, 339, 428
4:24   339–40
4:26   486
5:1   27, 568
5:4   160
5:6   331
5:8   331

5:18   332
5:23   332
6   174, 177
6:1   108, 174–75, 432
6:1–4   177
6:2   174
6:2–3   175
6:3   175
6:4   176, 183, 300, 388
6:5   177, 487, 598
6:7   308
6:9   152, 309
6:12   504
6:16   337
7:2   342
7:7   554
7:11   131
7:15   322
7:18   516
7:24   331
8:1   160
8:3   440
8:6   97
8:13   330
8:21   598
9:3   103
9:11   569
9:15   572
9:29   316
10:12   367
10:28–13:9   48
11:3   64

11:3–4   64
11:4   548–49
11:5   369
11:8–9   510
11:19   331
11:30   389
11:31   169
12:1   567–68
12:4   145
12:5   84, 86, 103
12:6   103, 483, 484,
   548–49
12:9   440, 441–42
12:10   85, 465
12:11   214, 259
12:13   98–99, 259,
   500–501, 566, 571
13   398
13:1   86, 551
13:6   376, 415, 424, 432
13:14   232
13:15   398, 531
13:16   428
13:17   152
14:11–13   85
14:14–17   85
14:16   86
14:17   86
14:18   145
14:18–19   85
14:18–20   84–85
14:18b   85
14:19   85
14:20   85
14:21–24   85
15:1   245
15:2   403
15:4   492
15:6   213
15:7   469–70
15:10   415
15:18   195
16:1   358

16:2   176
16:10   441
16:11   377
17:1b–2   216
17:2   559–60
17:5   103, 508
17:10   445
17:14   374
17:16   184
17:17   598
18:3   260
18:4   105
18:5   33, 509, 594
18:10   561
18:12   383
18:14   497–98
18:18   459
18:21   262
18:24   549
18:25   501–2
18:28   497
18:30   245, 466
18:32   245
18:33   146, 561–62
19:8   245, 256
19:12–13   313
19:14   231
19:16   550
19:17   245, 495
19:31   378
20:7   417
20:9   201
20:16   345
21:1   590
21:5   326–27
21:12   245
21:16   210, 440–41
21:17   245
21:22   214
21:23   238, 469–70
22:1   214
22:3   163–64
22:4   479–80, 562

22:6   387
22:12   245
22:16   375
23:1   331–32
23:11   195
23:15   345
24:1   97
24:2   379
24:8   246
24:12   565
24:31   199
24:42   500
24:44   464–65
24:45   598
24:49   461–62
24:55   34
24:56   245
25:7   331–32
25:23   109
25:28   98
26:2   245
26:12   340–41
26:24   245
26:26   97
27:12   317–18
27:19   239
27:22   309, 368
27:24   496–97
27:31   226
27:34   434–35, 486
27:36   340
27:37   169
27:40   215
27:41   507, 566, 598
28:2   283
28:14   241
29:5   497
29:8   200
29:22   135–36
29:27   319
29:31   388
29:32   200
30:2   99

30:8 *120*
30:27 *500*
30:41 *418*
31:7 *340–41*
31:20 *598*
31:30 *419*
31:31 *98*
31:33 *540–41*
31:35 *245*
31:36 *99*
31:38 *319, 326*
31:40 *100*
31:41 *319, 322*
31:43 *458*
31:44 *459*
32:8 *99*
32:25 *416*
32:28 *132*
32:29 *492*
32:31 *132*
33:3 *340*
33:10 *500*
34:3 *598*
34:5 *213*
34:21 *361*
35:2 *155*
35:9 *132*
35:10 *132*
35:17 *245*
35:18 *446*
35:21 *22*
36:7 *566*
36:8 *282*
36:31 *416*
37 *248*
37:3 *103*
37:3–4 *218*
37:15 *307*
37:17 *223, 257*
37:19 *223*
37:20 *223*
37:21b *224*
37:21b–22a *227*

37:22 *224, 234, 245, 249*
37:25 *416*
37:27 *224, 245, 251*
37:33 *109, 152*
37:35 *70*
38 *224*
38:5 *418, 428–29*
38:11 *201*
38:14 *154*
38:26 *432*
39:7 *238, 242*
39:9 *201*
39:10 *306, 416*
39:12 *242*
39:19 *99*
40:14 *162, 259*
40:15 *150, 420*
40:16 *487*
40:18 *362*
41:5 *4*
41:6 *4*
41:14 *105*
41:17 *4*
41:20 *336*
41:22 *4*
41:23 *4*
41:24 *4*
41:26 *4*
41:27 *4*
41:32 *416*
41:39 *162*
41:48 *550*
41:49 *442*
42:1 *152–53*
42:4 *163*
42:6 *360*
42:13 *379*
42:18 *399*
42:22 *245*
42:30 *403*
42:36 *202*
42:37 *241–42*
42:38 *70*

43:2 *234, 318–19*
43:4 *389*
43:8 *224*
43:11 *233, 460–61*
43:12 *339*
43:15 *339*
43:16 *233*
43:23 *245*
43:27–28 *497*
43:31 *105*
43:34 *340–41, 379*
44:4 *226*
44:5 *492*
44:10 *376*
44:15 *201*
44:16 *153*
44:18 *99, 228, 245*
44:23–46:20 *48*
44:29 *70*
44:31 *70*
44:33 *252*
44:34 *202*
45:4 *258*
45:5 *245*
45:9 *245*
45:14 *546*
45:17 *233*
45:20 *245*
45:24 *245*
45:26 *598*
46:1 *283*
46:3 *245, 248*
46:7 *460–61*
47:4 *258*
47:14 *99, 283*
47:17–50:23 *48*
47:24 *338*
47:26 *338*
47:28 *332*
47:31 *64*
48 *5*
48:4 *531*
48:10 *389*

48:11 *416*
48:14 *378*
48:18 *492*
49:2–27 *20*
49:4 *245, 248*
49:6 *245, 357*
49:8–12 *224*
49:13 *20*
49:17 *20*
49:18 *146*
49:22 *20*
49:26 *20*
49:29 *505*
50:2 *416*
50:6 *237*
50:9 *389*
50:15 *202*
50:19 *245*
50:20 *565*
50:21 *245, 598*
50:22 *330*

Exodus

1:10 *467*
1:13 *507*
1:14 *64*
1:15 *322, 336*
1:16 *108, 149*
2:3 *432*
2:4 *417, 427*
2:6 *504*
2:7 *520*
2:12 *314, 459–60*
2:14 *162, 428–29, 486*
2:14–3:21 *48*
2:18 *431*
3:2 *503*
3:3 *257, 262*
3:4 *471–72*
3:5 *245, 306–7, 363*
3:8 *571*
3:19–20 *213*
3:20 *181, 213*

4–10 *313*
4–11 *116*
4–15 *116, 118, 595*
4:9 *134, 218*
4:10 *318*
4:11 *463*
4:14 *99, 442*
4:15 *213*
4:21 *595*
4:23 *313*
4:24 *430–31*
4:31 *162*
5:1 *234, 313*
5:2 *202*
5:3 *256, 258*
5:7 *64*
5:8 *64*
5:9 *169*
5:10 *358, 505*
5:14 *315–16*
5:16 *64*
5:18 *64*
6:2 *603*
6:4 *160*
6:11 *313*
6:16 *330*
6:18 *331*
6:27 *405*
7:1 *97*
7:3 *595*
7:13 *117, 595*
7:13–14 *110*
7:14 *595*
7:15 *405*
7:16 *313*
7:19 *284*
7:22 *595*
7:23 *485, 486, 598*
7:26 *313*
7:27 *399*
8:1 *284*
8:11 *117–18, 144, 157, 443*

8:15 *118, 595*
8:16 *198, 313*
8:17 *163*
8:19 *595*
8:24 *422*
8:25 *245, 490–91*
8:32 *595*
9:1 *313*
9:7 *595*
9:12 *117, 142, 595*
9:13–14 *313*
9:14 *313*
9:16 *432*
9:17 *428*
9:18 *304–5, 315*
9:18–13:2 *48*
9:21 *598*
9:24 *245*
9:29 *554, 561–62*
9:34 *595*
9:35 *595*
10:1 *595*
10:3 *72, 313*
10:5 *370*
10:7 *313*
10:9 *566*
10:19 *289*
10:20 *595*
10:26 *433*
10:27 *595*
10:28 *245, 416*
10:29 *431–32*
11:10 *595*
12 *476*
12:6 *563*
12:9 *245*
12:11 *547*
12:14 *476, 568*
12:14–20 *476*
12:18 *337, 338*
12:21 *231, 476*
12:25 *215*
12:32 *393*

13:2–16:1 48
13:3 444
13:14 483
13:15 214, 595
13–16 49
14:3 353
14:4 595
14:5 596
14:8 595
14:12 430–31
14:13 245, 315
14:14 136, 199
14:17 595
15 49
15:1 200, 210, 257
15:1–18 20
15:2 209
15:5 20, 199
15:7 20
15:8 20, 594
15:10 20
15:11 20
15:16 20
15:20 157
15:25 163
15:26 203
16:4 202, 288, 498
16:5 339, 342, 476–77, 562, 567
16:10 562
16:12 96–97
16:19 245, 252
16:21 98
16:22 342
16:25 570
16:26 59
16:29 245, 348, 531–32
17:4 96–97
17:5–18:14 48
17:11 215, 478
17:12 389
17:13 569
17:14 27

18:11 319, 516
18:20 306–7
18:21 325, 341
19:5 532
19:8 484
19:9 571
19:10 170
19:11 563, 564
19:13 467
19:15 245
19:24 529
20 237
20:1–21 204
20:2–17 27
20:3 515
20:8 237, 444
20:11 59
20:12 234
20:16 204
20:17 51
20:17a 50–51
20:18 51
20:19 245
20:20 245, 494
20:22–23:33 203
20:24 203
21:11 323
21:20 461–62
21:22 442
21:23–25 568–69
21:28–29 78
21:28–30 77
21:28–32 464
21:28a 78
21:28b 78
21:29 186
21:29–31 464
21:33 97, 462
22:3 339, 419
22:4 39, 247
22:11 165
22:12 109
22:19 494, 516

22:26–27 25
23:1 204, 245
23:7 245
23:10 203
23:14 340–41
23:17 72, 340
23:20 416
23:21 245
23:29 240
24:7 27
24:24 250
25:2 595
26:35 550
27:9 346
27:11 345–46
28:3 375
28:10 323
28:29–30 593
28:40 530
28:42 552, 553
29:29 530
29:40 338
29:44 304
30:15 375
30:36 440–41
31:6 598
31:17 531
32 517
32:1 517, 551
32:6 444
32:10 99
32:11 99
32:13 505
32:18 430–31
32:19 142
32:22 245
32:23 517
32:30 590
32:31 502
33 517
33:6 153
33:15 245
33:18 500–501, 517

33:19 *517*
33:20 *72*
33:22 *215*
34:1 *336*
34:3 *245*
34:6 *610*
34:24 *72*
34:28 *27*
35:2 *59*
35:5 *595*
35:21 *595*
35:22 *595*
35:25 *598*
35:26 *595*
35:29 *595*
35:35 *598*
36:1 *598*
36:2 *598*
36:4 *306*
36:6 *245*
36:8 *598*
37:17 *309*
38:7 *415*
39:17 *305*
40:2 *336*
40:12 *105*
40:30 *415*
45:9 *216*

Leviticus

1:4–5 *263*
2:3 *530*
4:7 *134*
4:23 *165*
5:2 *391*
5:4 *461–62*
5:11 *345*
5:16 *252*
5:22 *569–70*
6:3 *102*
6:7 *445*
6:21 *109*
7:14 *320*

7:18 *419*
7:25 *405*
9:1–2 *477*
9:1–2a *477*
9:2 *234*
10:9 *245*
11:32 *111, 462–63*
11:43 *136–37, 245*
12:8 *458*
13:5 *503*
13:7 *509*
13:55 *473–74*
14:8 *105*
14:8–9 *105*
14:9 *105*
14:14 *546*
14:21 *345*
14:41 *134*
15:12 *109*
15:25 *465*
15:26 *402*
15:32 *415*
16:2 *245*
16:22 *163*
16:30 *561*
18:24 *245*
19:4 *245*
19:14 *556–57*
19:17 *595*
19:19 *339*
19:23 *323*
19:29 *245*
19:31 *245*
19:36 *342*
21:18 *462*
22:16 *158*
23:13 *339*
23:30 *145*
24:5 *339*
24:20 *568*
25:14 *444*
25:21 *323*
25:36 *245*

25:48 *473*
25:52 *569*
26 *454*
26:1 *517*
26:23–24 *486–87*
26:24 *339–40*
26:26 *415*
26:27–28 *486–87*
26:36 *595*

Numbers

1:2 *27*
2:31 *334*
3 *331*
3:4 *145, 516*
3:23 *557*
3:46 *331*
4:2 *444*
4:18 *245*
4:23 *415*
4:40 *332–33*
5:2 *216*
5:3 *398*
6:18 *105*
6:24–26 *25*
7:1 *218, 433*
7:89 *447*
8:19 *258*
9:18 *200*
9:19 *421*
9:22 *464–65*
10:16–35 *48*
10:31 *494*
10:35–36 *435*
10:36 *329*
11:4–6 *320*
11:9 *434*
11:15 *442*
11:19 *492*
11:19–20 *321*
11:23 *498*
11:25 *433–34*
11:31 *314*

11:32   *315*
11:33   *99, 380*
12:2   *491, 493*
12:4   *323*
12:9   *99*
12:11   *500*
12:12   *245*
12:13   *500–501*
13:2   *216*
13:18   *318*
13:19   *398*
13:20   *498*
13:28   *297, 485*
14:8   *469*
14:9   *245*
14:16   *415*
14:22   *311*
14:35   *312*
14:42   *245*
15:4–5   *338*
15:5   *344–45*
15:6   *339*
15:13   *311*
15:19   *434*
15:35   *445*
16:7   *362*
16:13   *154*
16:15   *245, 249, 317–18*
16:26   *245*
16:28   *492*
16:30   *70*
18:21   *568*
19:1–10   *265*
20:6   *554*
20:12   *488–89*
20:18–21   *282*
20:28   *158–59*
20:29   *279–81*
21:14   *27*
21:16   *283*
21:34   *245*
22:6   *150, 239*
22:17   *420*

22:19   *247*
22:23   *163*
22:25   *132*
22:28   *311*
22:36   *540–41*
23:7–10   *20*
23:10   *251*
23:15   *314*
23:18–24   *20*
23:19   *317*
24:3–9   *20*
24:4   *368*
24:14   *399*
24:16–19   *20*
24:17   *492*
24:18   *282*
24:19   *247*
25:3   *99*
25:9   *39*
26:2   *27*
26:51   *334–35*
26:56   *569*
27:16–17   *459–60*
28:9   *339*
28:12   *339*
28:20   *339*
29:9   *339*
29:14   *339*
31:2   *34, 232*
31:32   *334*
31:46   *290*
31:54   *459–60*
32:5   *245*
32:10   *99*
32:12   *493*
32:13   *99*
33:46   *283*
33:47   *283*
35:5   *338*
36:6   *490–91*

Deuteronomy

1   *375*

1:2   *552*
1:10   *59*
1:11   *340*
1:14   *375*
1:16   *444*
1:19   *312*
1:21   *245*
1:25   *570*
1:28   *377, 595*
1:39   *374*
1:46   *373*
2:5   *245*
2:7   *319, 430*
2:9   *245*
2:9–3:12   *48*
2:19   *245*
2:24   *417*
2:25   *432*
2:34–35   *565*
3:2   *245*
3:26   *245*
4:1   *417*
4:5   *122*
4:9   *357*
4:10   *121*
4:11   *59, 594*
4:13   *27*
4:14   *470*
4:16   *462, 463*
4:21   *493*
4:22   *405, 493*
4:26   *195*
4:27   *548–49*
4:29   *596*
4:32   *567*
4:35   *362*
4:41   *210*
5   *237*
5:1–6:1   *59*
5:3   *465, 466*
5:6   *449*
5:6–21   *27, 204, 449*
5:7   *515*

5:12   *59, 237, 444*
5:19   *449*
5:23   *434*
5:25   *465, 466*
6:1   *34, 447*
6:4   *235, 610*
6:4–9   *xi*
6:5   *460, 596*
6:15   *99*
6:23   *432*
6:25   *465–66*
7:1   *288*
7:4   *99, 109*
7:5   *595*
7:7   *319–20*
7:9   *25–26*
7:16   *449*
7:24   *565*
8:2   *429, 467, 498*
8:5   *597*
8:5–10   *59*
8:6   *459*
8:9   *470*
9:4   *245*
9:7   *245*
9:22   *402*
9:24   *417, 433*
9:26   *245*
9:27   *245*
10:4   *103–4*
10:12   *416, 447, 596*
10:15   *416*
10:17   *360*
11:10   *205*
11:13   *416, 596*
11:17   *99, 145*
11:18   *596*
11:29a   *51*
11:30   *51*
12:3   *311, 465*
12:5   *415*
12:23–24   *134*
12:24   *134*

12:27   *134*
12:28   *375*
12:29   *198*
12:30   *433*
13:3   *256*
13:4   *358, 505, 596*
13:10   *561*
13:16   *40*
14:22   *306*
14:28   *323*
15:10   *595*
15:14   *422*
15:16   *102*
15:17   *549*
16:15   *402, 486*
17:4   *443*
17:18   *27, 433–34*
17:20   *597*
18:9–14   *70*
18:16   *245–46*
18:22   *278*
19:7   *305*
19:9   *323*
19:21   *568*
20:3   *245, 595*
20:5   *252*
20:8   *595*
21:3   *109*
21:4   *109*
21:6   *105*
21:8   *245*
21:15   *306*
21:16   *516–17*
23:11   *540–41*
23:12   *97, 434–35*
23:14   *482*
23:23   *417*
24:9   *505*
25:7   *102*
25:11   *322*
25:15   *342*
26:16   *596*
27   *454*

27:1–3a   *51*
27:1–7   *51*
27:4   *51, 215*
27:4–7   *51*
28:1   *478*
28:7   *542*
28:7b   *542*
28:8   *247*
28:21   *158, 247*
28:28   *599*
28:29   *402*
28:36   *247*
28:43   *481–82*
28:49   *590*
28:58   *27*
28:61   *27*
28:67   *599*
29:15   *471–72*
29:17   *596*
29:18   *465–66*
29:20   *27*
29:21   *27*
29:27   *27*
30:2   *596*
30:5   *170*
30:6   *596*
30:10   *27, 596*
30:14   *xi*
31:1   *57*
31:3   *388*
31:6   *245*
31:7   *480*
31:8   *394–95, 397*
31:11   *xi, 72*
31:19   *231*
31:23   *465, 480*
31:24   *27*
31:26   *27, 445*
32   *208*
32:1–43   *20*
32:7   *506–7*
32:8   *208, 247*
32:8–20   *208*

32:10   *186*
32:13   *33*
32:18   *209, 247, 250*
32:45   *57*
32:49   *311, 312, 516*
32:50   *48*
33:13–17   *5*
33:17   *326–27*
33:23   *69*

Joshua

1:1   *110*
1:2   *110*
1:3   *110*
1:4   *110*
1:5   *110*
1:6   *358, 481*
1:6–7   *480*
1:7   *245, 481*
1:8   *27, 210, 370*
1:9   *245, 480*
1:14   *341, 371*
1:15   *509*
1:18   *480*
2:1   *391*
2:5   *353*
2:6   *358*
2:9–11   *354*
2:11   *572, 595, 610*
2:17   *375–76*
3:4   *245*
3:5   *153*
3:12   *342*
3:13   *131, 478*
4:3   *422*
4:6   *311*
4:14   *151*
5:1–2   *60*
5:9   *312*
5:10   *561*
5:11   *311, 595*
5:13   *467*
5:14   *359*

5:15   *351*
6   *354*
6:1   *351–53*
6:3   *340, 422*
6:5   *288, 367, 373*
6:15   *561–62*
6:20   *288*
6:22   *392*
6:26   *311*
7:3   *245*
7:5   *595*
7:6   *546*
7:8   *473–74*
7:9   *373*
7:11   *490*
7:19   *245, 263*
7:21   *286*
8:1   *245*
8:4   *245*
8:31   *27*
8:34   *27*
8:34–35   *xi, 60*
9:8   *183, 359*
9:12   *154*
9:13   *154*
9:20   *422*
10:6   *245, 485*
10:8   *245*
10:12   *210*
10:14   *564*
10:19   *245*
10:25   *245*
10:26   *287*
11:6   *245, 305*
13:1   *443*
14:11   *314–15*
14:15   *289*
16:5–17:18   *5*
18:4   *569*
18:4–9   *27*
19:30   *329*
19:49–50   *5*
20:4   *311–12*

21:6   *325*
21:19   *325*
21:32   *305*
21:33   *325*
21:45   *316–17, 367*
22   *5*
22:3   *319*
22:5   *596*
22:19   *245, 399*
22:22   *245–46*
22:25   *523*
22:34   *387*
23:3   *394–95, 397*
23:6   *27*
23:14   *316–17, 596*
24:10   *420*
24:15   *467*
24:16   *27*
24:18   *485–86*
24:21   *492*
24:23   *596*
24:26   *27*
24:29   *476*

Judges

1   *36–38*
1:2   *97*
1:3   *37–38*
1:13   *377*
1:28   *422*
1:29   *5*
2:1   *184, 205, 208*
2:7   *373*
2:9   *5*
2:15   *189*
2:19   *200*
3:6   *170*
3:19   *500*
3:23–24   *540–41*
3:24   *398*
3:26–29   *6*
4:4   *305*
4:18   *245*

4:19   *318*
4:20   *497*
4:21   *549*
4:24   *442*
5:1–30   *20*
5:4   *98*
5:17   *5*
6:1   *382*
6–8   *5*
6:13   *388*
6:15   *379*
6:16   *471–72*
6:18   *245*
6:20   *134*
6:22   *499*
6:23   *245*
6:31   *509*
6:39   *99, 245*
7:3   *252*
7:5   *590*
7:24–25   *6*
8:1–3   *5*
8:2   *377*
8:6   *483*
8:9   *418*
8:14   *372, 565*
8:24   *256*
8:31   *486, 507*
8:33   *531–32*
9:6   *135–36*
9:8   *230, 238*
9:14   *230*
9:16   *158*
9:29   *238*
9:33   *198*
9:39   *556–57*
9:53   *308*
10:6–12:7   *5*
10:13   *488*
11:6   *38*
11:21   *311*
11:25   *420*
11:32–33   *6*

12   *4–6*
12:4   *5*
12:5   *5, 479*
12:5b–6   *4*
12:6   *4*
13:4   *245*
13:7   *245*
13:14   *245, 252–53*
13:21   *483*
14:3   *382, 391*
14:8   *561*
15:1   *257*
15:2   *240*
15:4   *338, 559*
15:18   *381*
16:2   *563–64*
16:10   *258*
16:15   *348*
16:18   *598*
16:21   *402*
16:25   *149, 165, 599*
16:27   *97*
16:28   *339, 487*
17:3   *195, 332–33*
18:9   *245*
18:20   *599*
18:25   *245*
18:31   *428*
19:3   *598*
19:6   *599*
19:8   *595*
19:9   *260, 599*
19:20   *245*
19:22   *599*
19:23   *245*
20:4   *283*
21:22   *492*
21:24   *152*

Ruth

1:8   *40*
1:20   *245*
1:21   *485*

2:11   *34*
2:21   *470–71*
3:3   *245*
3:4–5   *34*
3:11   *245*
3:12   *34*
3:14   *245, 519*
3:15   *287*
3:17   *34, 245*

1 Samuel

1:1   *183*
1:2   *570*
1:3–4   *219*
1:4   *476*
1:5   *505*
1:7   *210*
1:8   *378, 497–98, 599*
1:13   *598*
1:14   *154*
1:16   *245*
1:20   *104–5*
1:26   *500*
2   *409*
2:1–10   *20*
2:2   *378, 493*
2:3   *245, 427*
2:8   *404*
2:10   *247*
2:17   *376*
2:20   *253*
2:26   *464*
2:27   *46*
2:27–28   *410*
2:35   *162, 372, 596*
3:2   *189*
3:2–4   *477*
3:4   *104, 504*
3:5   *104*
3:6   *104–5*
3:12   *440*
3:14   *155*
3:17   *245*

4:6   *190*
4:13   *42, 316, 598–99*
4:20   *152, 245*
5:1   *189*
5:6   *42*
5:9   *42*
5:12   *42*
6:3   *245, 400*
6:4   *42*
6:5   *42*
6:9   *193, 212*
6:12   *440–41*
6:13   *401*
7:8   *245, 249*
7:12   *308*
7:16   *145*
8:1   *104, 478*
8:5   *191, 489*
8:11–12   *136*
8:14   *379*
8:20   *136*
9:2   *404*
9:6   *256*
9:8   *338*
9:9   *205*
9:10   *256*
9:14   *540–41*
9:16   *315*
9:19   *597*
9:20   *245, 598*
9:21   *379*
9:27   *401*
10:3   *314*
10:3–4   *345*
10:5   *247*
10:8   *249–50*
10:13   *154*
10:25   *27*
11:1   *230*
12:2   *563–64*
12:14   *464–65*
12:20   *245, 264*
13:14   *596*

13:15   *65*
14:1   *476*
14:3   *430*
14:6   *394*
14:8   *503*
14:14   *326*
14:18   *239*
14:26   *540–41*
14:27   *42*
14:32   *42*
14:34   *566–67*
14:36   *131, 245–46*
15:12   *400*
15:22   *431*
15:23   *439*
15:24   *98*
15:29   *359*
16:7   *245, 492, 597*
16:8   *531–32*
16–18   *67*
17:4–5   *344–45*
17:6   *134*
17:10   *38*
17:16   *440–41*
17:21   *565*
17:28   *311, 318–19*
17:32   *245, 595*
17:45   *569*
18:1   *41*
18:10   *154*
18:15   *471–72*
18:17   *245*
18:21   *240*
19:4   *245*
19:10   *133*
20:2   *41*
20:3   *245*
20:38   *245*
21:3   *245, 278–81, 598*
21:4   *345–46*
21:15   *154*
21:16   *201*
22:15   *245, 494*

22:17   *391*
22:18   *330*
22:23   *245*
23:2   *201*
23:17   *245*
24:6   *598*
24:18   *104–5*
24:19   *39*
24:20   *566*
25:8   *264*
25:10   *227*
25:16   *428, 484*
25:25   *245, 598*
25:26   *444*
25:28   *395*
25:31   *599*
25:35   *551–52*
25:36   *599*
25:37   *598*
26:3   *180*
26:5   *524*
26:7   *524*
26:9   *245*
26:10   *464*
26:10–11   *463*
26:13   *559*
26:20   *245*
27:1   *598*
27:5   *572*
27:9   *202*
28:5   *599*
28:9   *418*
28:13   *245*
28:15   *136*
28:20   *317*
29:6   *430–31*
29:10   *98*
30:6   *22*
30:13   *459–60*
31:7   *540*
31:10   *547*

2 Samuel

1:20 *245*
2:26 *376*
2:31 *330*
3:1 *56, 380*
3:2 *56*
3:12 *230*
3:17 *145, 315–16, 483*
3:20 *325–26*
3:29 *245*
3:31 *305*
5:3 *279–80, 305*
5:10 *442*
6:12 *305*
6:13 *479*
6:16 *304–5*
6:19 *346*
6:20 *135*
7 *363*
7:3 *598*
7:9 *258*
7:16 *162*
7:18 *305*
7:28 *363*
7:29 *150*
8:3 *34*
8:8 *305*
8:10 *305*
8:11 *305*
9:1 *217*
9:5 *305*
9:7 *245, 469*
10:14 *540*
11:1 *562–63*
11:1–1 Kgs 2:11 *68*
11:8 *551*
11:13 *415*
11:15 *27*
11:16 *478*
11:25 *245*
12:6 *339*
12:7 *359*
12:11 *311–12*

12:27 *490*
12:31 *64*
13:2 *154*
13:5 *154*
13:6 *154*
13:12 *245*
13:13 *160*
13:20 *245, 598*
13:21 *305*
13:21–22 *66*
13:26 *245*
13:28 *245, 599*
13:33 *245, 251, 598*
13:37 *42*
14:2 *154, 245*
14:15 *262*
14:18 *245*
14:25–26 *544*
14:26 *476–77*
14:27 *372*
15:6 *598*
15:18 *545*
15:19 *359*
15:24–37 *410*
15:32 *552*
15:33 *466*
16:1 *319–20*
16:5 *305*
16:6 *305*
16:13 *559*
16:14 *403*
16:16 *254*
16:23 *34*
17:10 *595*
17:11 *419*
17:12 *40*
17:14 *319, 421*
17:16 *245*
17:17 *305*
17:21 *305*
18:2 *338*
18:3 *328, 598*
18:4 *593, 594*

18:9 *544*
18:14 *377*
18:18 *162*
18:19 *237*
18:22b–23 *237*
18:23 *237*
18:25 *380, 403*
18:27 *310–11*
18:29 *496*
18:31 *154*
18:32 *496*
19:8 *598*
19:12 *305*
19:15 *595*
19:17 *305*
19:20 *245, 598*
20:4 *397*
20:10 *134*
20:15 *283*
20:21 *555*
20:24 *394*
21:9 *39, 323*
22:5–20 *208*
23:18–19 *323*
24 *392*
24:2 *21*
24:3 *340*
24:10 *599*
24:17 *392*

1 Kings

1:1 *305*
1:1–10 *112*
1:2 *305*
1:4 *358*
1:5 *154*
1:6 *372*
1:13 *305*
1:14 *400*
1:17 *226*
1:28 *305*
1:31 *305*
1:32 *305*

1:36   *501*
1:37   *40, 305*
1:38   *305*
1:42   *490*
1:43   *305, 490*
1:47   *305*
2:4   *596*
2:9   *245*
2:11   *68*
2:15   *162*
2:16   *245*
2:20   *245*
2:26–27   *410*
2:30   *309*
2:42   *447*
3:3   *395*
3:12   *598*
3:14   *56, 510*
3:16   *19, 210*
3:20   *562*
3:26   *245*
3:27   *21*
4:3   *395*
5:9   *598*
5:12   *332*
5:14   *424*
5:25   *287*
6:1   *331, 332*
7:12   *346*
7:14   *426–27*
8:1   *247*
8:17   *598*
8:18   *598*
8:35   *219*
8:39   *597*
8:48   *40, 596*
8:56   *278*
8:57   *245, 253, 264*
8:65   *325*
8:66   *599*
9:4   *596*
9:7   *163*
9:16   *103–4*

9:25   *422*
10:10   *443*
10:14   *330*
10:22   *342*
10:23–26   *400*
10:24   *400, 598*
11:1   *278–81*
11:4   *596*
11:22   *399*
11:38   *479, 572*
11:39   *318*
11:41   *27*
12:26   *598*
12:33   *598*
13:1   *388*
13:1–3   *410*
13:3   *134*
13:7   *69*
13:17   *494*
13:22   *494, 540–41*
13:26   *279–80*
14:2   *154*
14:11   *289*
14:19   *27*
16:2–3   *111*
16:20   *27*
16:21   *338*
16:22   *103*
16:25   *210*
16:27   *27*
17:12   *548*
17:13   *245*
18:9   *429*
18:13   *342*
18:19   *331*
18:21   *279–81*
18:40   *245*
18:43   *340*
19:2   *315*
19:7   *97*
19:10   *420*
19:11   *547*
19:19   *341*

20:6   *315*
20:8   *245*
20:11   *245*
20:16   *329*
20:25   *38*
20:31   *259–60*
20:32   *252*
20:40   *314*
21:1   *557*
21:2   *257, 557*
21:6   *465*
21:7   *599*
21:9–10   *27*
21:15   *417*
21:27   *169*
22:8   *245*
22:30   *154*
22:39   *27*
22:45   *27*

2 Kings

1:2   *555*
1:15   *245*
2:18   *245*
2:23   *227*
3:4   *305*
3:7   *566*
4:1   *402*
4:3   *245*
4:8   *476*
4:11   *476*
4:16   *245*
4:18   *476*
4:24   *245*
4:29   *466*
4:43   *447*
5:6   *27, 196*
5:18   *34*
5:27   *530*
6:9   *313*
6:16   *245*
6:27   *245*
6:28   *315*

6:28b–29 *315*
7:1 *315, 344*
7:18 *315*
8:4 *238*
8:25 *324*
9:14 *389*
9:15 *245*
9:16 *283*
9:24 *594*
10:1–7 *26*
10:2–3 *27*
10:6 *27, 315*
10:7 *548*
10:18 *443, 487*
10:19 *161, 245*
10:21 *131*
10:25 *245, 250*
10:31 *596*
11:1 *145*
11:10 *305*
11:15 *245*
11:18 *443*
12:8 *245*
12:18 *210*
13:3 *99*
13:12 *27*
13:17 *440*
13:19 *461–62*
14:6 *27, 393*
14:10 *597*
14:15 *27*
14:18 *319*
14:28 *27*
15:15 *27*
17:6 *337*
17:34 *399*
18:26 *6–7, 245*
18:28 *7*
18:29 *245*
18:30 *245*
18:31 *245*
18:32 *245*
19:6 *245*

19:8–14 *26*
19:10 *245*
19:10–13 *27*
19:15 *387*
19:25 *489*
20:3 *596*
20:9–11 *482*
20:10 *497*
20:20 *27*
21:24 *304*
22:8 *27*
22:11 *27*
22:35 *165*
23:3 *596*
23:18 *245*
23:21 *27*
23:25 *596*
23:31 *329*
24:14 *328*
25:1 *337*
25:2 *541–42*
25:24 *245*
28:30 *593*

1 Chronicles

2:22 *329*
6:39 *530–31*
9:1 *27*
12:38 *334*
13:10 *99*
15:29 *305*
17:16 *305*
18:10 *305*
18:11 *305*
19:15 *540*
21 *27*
21:2 *21*
21:24 *305*
22:13 *480*
24:6 *27*
24:7–11 *337*
24:12–18 *337*
24:31 *373*

25:9–31 *337*
27 *335*
27:2–15 *337*
27:24 *305*
27:31 *305*
28:9 *466*
28:20 *480*
29:7 *333–34*
29:9 *305*
29:24 *305*
29:27 *330*

2 Chronicles

1:14 *333*
2:3–16 *26*
2:11–15 *27*
2:12 *196*
2:15 *133*
6:13 *554*
6:32 *373*
6:37 *460*
6:39 *454*
7:12 *453–54*
7:13 *454*
7:14 *454–55*
7:15–16 *455*
7:17 *465*
12:3 *332–33*
13:22 *27*
14:12 *319*
17:2 *373*
17:6 *490*
18:29 *154*
20:17 *170*
21:12 *27*
21:12–15 *27*
23:20 *555*
24:10 *440*
24:15 *383*
25:10 *99*
26:13 *334–35*
27:7 *27*
28:3 *162*

28:20 *103*
29:18 *482*
30:5 *27*
30:18 *492*
32:17 *26*
32:18 *7*
32:27 *319*
33:8 *465*
34:10 *415*
34:30–31 *27*
35:4 *27*
36:22–23 *27*

Ezra

1:1–4 *27*
1:8 *323*
2:4–5 *330*
2:7 *332–33*
2:37 *332–33*
2:39 *332–33*
2:64 *333–34*
2:69 *333–34*
4:7 *6*
4:11–16 *27*
4:17–22 *27*
5:7–17 *27*
7:8 *337*
7:12–26 *27*
7:16 *158*
8:31 *27*
8:35 *330*
10:44 *368*

Nehemiah

1:4 *245*
1:5 *25–26*
2:6 *401*
3:37 *573*
4:4 *319*
4:13 *319*
5:14 *337*
6:6–7 *27*
6:15 *337–38*

6:17 *26*
6:19 *26*
7:3 *422*
7:5 *27*
7:31–32 *330*
7:68 *331*
7:70 *333*
8:1–18 *27*
8:6 *501*
8:8 *xi*
8:10 *610*
9:3 *27*
9:13 *367*
9:23 *417*
9:35 *373*
10:1–2 *27*
12:22–23 *27*
12:28 *522*
13:1 *27*
13:20 *340*
13:22 *471–72*
13:24 *7*
13:28 *240*

Esther

1:1 *330*
1:19 *27*
2:1–2 *479–80*
2:7 *162*
2:23 *27*
3:9 *27*
3:12 *27*
3:13 *163, 446*
4:6 *556*
4:8 *27*
4:16 *484*
6:1–2 *27*
6:6 *319*
8:5 *27*
8:8 *27*
8:9 *27*
8:17 *154*
9:29 *312*

Job

1:1–8 *220*
1:3 *341*
1:6 *476*
1:10 *40*
1:13 *476*
1:19 *190*
1:22 *188*
2:1 *476*
3:13 *99–100*
3:16 *583*
5:10 *545*
6:25 *439*
7:20 *65*
8:10 *594*
9:18 *439*
10:17 *250*
11:6 *339*
12:13 *570–71*
13:22 *461*
13:27 *250*
14:7 *133, 134*
14:12 *493*
14:21 *135*
15:33 *247*
16:2b–3 *462*
16:3 *462*
16:6 *257*
16:9 *109*
16:13 *134*
18:9 *247*
18:12 *247*
20:23 *247*
20:26 *247*
20:28 *247*
21:4 *102*
21:22 *122*
22:28 *198*
23:9 *245–46*
23:11 *245–46*
24:14 *247*
24:25 *247, 495*
25:2 *439*

27:5   144, 501
27:8   247
27:22   247
29:13   62
29:24a–30:1   62
31:28   193
32:2   99, 144
33:11   247
33:21   247
33:27   247
33:28   41
33:32–33   504–5
34:11   157
34:35   422
34:37   247
35:7   144
36:2   319
36:14   247
36:15   247
37:4   247
37:5   247
38:1   520
38:4   472
38:18   472–73
38:24   247
39:2   430
39:26   247
40:6   520
40:8–9   250
40:9   250
41:5   339
42:10   448

Psalms

1:1   188
1:3   169
2:7   191
3   242
3:2   381
3:6   190
3:7   482
3:8   192, 242
5   242

5:2   239, 243
5:3   238
5:11   236
6:3   236
6:4   190
6:9   235
7:4   465
7:11   375
7:15   503
9:18   70
10:12   232
11:3   193
12:4   198
12:7   339–40
13:2   610
13:6   104
15:2   403–4
16:2   524
16:11   165
17:5   439
17:6   236
18   373
18:12   247
18:18   374
18:28   368
19:14   404
19:15   594
22:2   610
24:6   40
25:6   236
25:7   506
25:7a   506
25:7b   505
25:8   489
25:9   247
25:13   417
29   171
29:2   236
31:20   381
33:1   376
34:10   233
34:14–15   233
35:7   484

35:17   372
36:7   34
36:10   583
36:12   300
37:35   374
38:5   567
38:11   593–94
39:4   161
39:13   238
40:2   436
42:5–6   219
42:6   235
44:21–22   193, 211
46:3   594
47:4   247
49:4   594
49:5   246
51:6   190
51:21   374
55:15   146
55:17   205
56:14   152
57:11   552
58:2   440
58:5   247
58:10   98
61:8   483–84
64:9   205
66:6   537
68:9   98
68:15   98
68:26   34
68:31   102
69:3   4
69:7   146
71:20   41
71:21   250
72:15   484
73:11   427
73:23   566
73:24   569
74:6   40
74:15   130–31

78:26 *247*
81:10 *517*
82:8 *264*
83:2 *495*
83:15 *162*
84:5 *484*
85:5 *421*
85:14 *247*
91:4 *247*
93:1 *102*
94:23 *205*
95:6 *236*
96:2 *563–64*
100:3 *41*
103:2 *235*
103:22 *235*
104:12 *347*
104:20 *250*
104:23 *459–60*
105:19 *430*
105:28 *41*
106:23 *447*
106:38 *134*
106:40 *99*
107:29 *247*
107:33 *247*
107:35 *247*
109:7 *487*
119:31 *161*
119:49 *474*
119:110 *567*
119:130 *xii*
119:171 *157*
122:8 *262*
125:5 *372*
132:1 *150, 505–6*
139:2 *430–31*
139:3 *415*
139:11 *523*
139:14 *474*
139:24 *472–73*
140:3 *317*
144:12 *150–51*

145 *58*
145:13–14 *58*
147:18 *247*

Proverbs

1:7 *191*
1:8 *233*
1:10 *465*
1:11 *234*
1:18 *200*
1:22 *191*
4:1–2 *192*
6:18 *300*
6:32 *598*
7:7 *598*
7:26 *374*
8:22–31 *349*
8:31 *369*
9:4 *598*
9:5 *570*
9:16 *598*
10:13 *598*
10:27 *102*
11:12 *598*
12:11 *598*
12:26 *247*
13:7 *154*
14:7 *573*
15:21 *598*
15:22 *421*
15:24 *482*
15:25 *247*
17:17 *98*
20:3 *570–71*
21:4 *368*
21:16 *440*
21:29 *42*
23:7 *524*
23:8 *367*
23:19 *149*
23:31 *152*
23:32 *102*
23:34 *594*

24:22 *484*
25:6 *304*
25:7 *448*
25:16 *233*
26:20 *493, 495*
27:1 *492*
27:2 *495*
27:14 *422*
27:27 *319*
29:14 *466*
30:4 *495–96*
30:19 *594*
30:32 *465*
31:30 *154*

Ecclesiastes

1:14 *62*
1:17 *73, 471–72*
2:4 *161*
2:7 *319*
2:12 *64*
3:17 *459*
3:18 *471–72*
3:19 *369*
4:2 *445*
4:10 *465*
4:11 *465*
5:1 *594*
5:5 *71*
5:6 *319*
5:16 *64, 319*
6:11 *319*
6:12 *510*
7:16 *319*
7:29 *289*
8:4 *496*
8:10 *155*
8:12 *573*
8:14 *471, 472*
9:18 *319*
10:11 *102*
11:6 *462, 463*
12:1 *505*

12:4   *416*
12:7   *247*
12:9   *151, 319*
12:12   *319*

Song of Songs

1:4   *231*
1:5   *470*
1:6   *470–71*
2:10   *21, 459*
6:8   *362*

Isaiah

1:12   *71–72*
1:13   *360*
1:18   *264*
1:20   *109*
2:11   *192*
3:9   *104–5*
4:4   *439*
5:2   *111, 210*
5:19   *219*
5:25   *99, 549–50*
6:3   *380*
6:5   *502*
6:10   *598*
6:11   *317–18*
7:1   *189*
7:3   *235*
7:11   *69, 578*
7:16   *417, 439*
7:18   *282, 284*
8:8   *109*
9:5   *184, 206*
9:6   *205, 563*
9:8   *305, 316–17*
10:1   *426*
10:3–4   *494*
10:4   *56*
10:20   *510*
10:32   *39*
11:3   *569*
11:4   *70*

11:9   *192, 427*
12:1   *247*
12:4   *198*
12:6   *404*
14:6   *493*
14:14   *155*
14:29   *63*
18:2   *314*
18:7   *314*
19:18   *7*
19:19   *523*
19:24   *338*
20:2   *403*
22:1   *316*
23:10   *56*
24:6   *319*
25:8   *284*
26:19   *288–89*
27:6   *247*
28:9   *427*
28:10   *319*
28:13   *319*
28:16   *392*
29:11   *311*
29:13   *151*
29:21   *393*
30:8   *231*
30:11   *519*
30:25   *415*
30:26   *339*
30:33   *319*
31:2   *359*
32:2   *391*
33:18   *594*
34:17   *151*
37:19   *548–49*
37:26   *563–64*
38:8   *482*
40:7–8   *57*
40:8   *57, 562–63*
40:18   *496*
40:30   *137*
40–66   *20*

41:2   *247*
41:23   *245*
41:28   *245–46*
42:6   *245, 507*
42:7   *368*
42:18   *279–80*
44:17   *153*
45:6   *495, 516*
45:14   *516*
45:21   *516*
46:6   *489–90*
46:8   *506*
48:7–8   *485*
48:12   *336*
49:9   *231*
50:2   *247*
51:1   *393*
51:3   *205*
53   *63, 581*
53:8   *56, 572*
53:11   *577, 579–81*
54:3   *459*
56:5   *548*
57:6   *134*
57:20   *438*
58:10   *250*
59:4   *422*
62:7   *529–30*
63:3   *247*
63:4   *541–42*
65:6   *27*
65:17   *162*
65:20   *326–27*
65:24   *520*
66:5   *144*

Jeremiah

1:3   *324*
1:6   *499*
1:18   *191*
2:15   *219*
2:17   *492*
3:15   *279–81, 422, 427*

3:25   *264*
4:1   *517*
4:11   *492*
4:31   *154*
6:7   *35*
6:8   *509*
6:12   *246*
6:15   *137*
6:21   *137*
7:3–8   *454*
7:5   *422*
7:13   *163*
7:30   *517*
7:33   *288*
8:7   *418, 430*
9:10   *507–8*
10:5   *422*
10:13   *319*
10:18   *70*
11:23   *304*
12:15   *429*
12:17   *203*
13:10   *312*
14:19   *485*
15:3   *348*
15:15   *505*
20:7   *103*
21:5   *347*
22:16   *426–27*
22:18   *502*
22:30   *27*
23:32   *422*
23:33   *65, 461*
25:1   *336*
25:3   *329, 422*
25:13   *27*
25:30   *133*
28:1   *336*
29:1–29   *27*
29:4–23   *27*
29:26–28   *27*
31:18   *150*
31:33   *311*

31:37   *34*
32:10–12   *27*
32:12   *426*
32:32   *421*
32:34   *517*
32:36   *489*
33:9   *572*
35:15   *422*
36:16   *422*
38:25   *264*
39:18   *420*
41:4–5   *477*
41:8   *566–67*
42:15   *489*
44:4   *422*
44:10   *530*
44:17   *422*
44:24   *235*
44:25   *422*
46:2   *336*
47:2   *289*
49:8   *164*
50:20   *150*
50:29   *34*
51:3   *34*
51:59   *336*
51:60–64   *27*
52:28   *333–34*
52:30   *331*

Lamentations

1:18   *388*
2:15   *310*
3:50   *247*
4:1   *155*
4:5   *20*

Ezekiel

1:6   *342*
1:14   *70*
1:19   *573*
1:21   *447*
2:9–10   *27*

3:3   *249*
3:20   *219*
5:16   *245*
11:24   *347*
14:7   *247*
16:15   *247*
18:1–13   *406*
18:3   *281*
26:2   *499*
27:4   *594*
27:16   *71*
27:25–27   *594*
28:2   *594*
28:8   *594*
28:17   *416*
29:3   *283*
29:4   *284*
31:14   *369*
31:15   *70*
31:16   *70*
31:17   *70*
32:19   *164*
33:12   *416*
36:9   *109*
38:8   *165*
39:15   *393*
40:10   *314*
41:18   *559–60*
43:7b–8a   *558*
45:10–11   *343*
45:10–12   *343*
45:11   *338*
45:14   *338*
46:12   *132*
46:22   *164*
48:14   *247*
48:16   *34*

Daniel

1:9   *603*
2:4   *6*
2:21   *384*
8:3   *368*

8:12   *247*
8:25   *570–71*
9:4   *25–26*
9:19   *70*
9:25   *250*
10:7   *510*
11:4   *247*
11:10   *247*
11:16   *247*
11:17   *247*
11:18   *247*
11:19   *247*
11:25   *247*
11:28   *247*
11:30   *247*
12:5–7   *282*
12:7   *316*
12:12   *332–33*

Hosea

1:2   *479–80*
2:9   *377*
4:2   *439*
5:14   *109*
5:15   *529*
6:1   *247*
8:51   *99*
9:15   *245–47*
10:2   *489*
11:4   *245–46*
13:8   *593*
13:13   *541–42*

Joel

2:2   *247*
2:11   *380*
2:13   *494*
2:20   *247*
4:14   *306*

Amos

3:9   *549*
3:11   *522*

4:7   *169*
5:13   *393*
6:10   *495, 500*
7:17   *151*
8:6   *568*
8:11   *163*
8:13   *297, 368*
9:6   *134*
9:8   *422*
9:10   *523*

Jonah

1   *604*
1:3   *601–2*
1:4   *206, 601–3*
1:5   *133, 601–3*
1:6   *601–2*
1:8   *496, 601–2*
1:9   *602–3*
1:10   *601–2*
1:14   *502–3*
2:8   *541*
2:9   *394*
2:10   *603*
3:4   *540*
4:2   *471–72*
4:11   *290*

Micah

2:12   *549–50*
3:4   *247*
3:6   *98*
3:12   *35*
4:3   *560*
6:5   *506–7*
6:7   *328*
7:10   *247*

Nahum

2:7   *132*
2:8   *593*
3:11   *247*

Habakkuk

1:5   *155*
2:3   *247*
3:2   *439, 562*

Zephaniah

1:2   *245*
1:3   *245*
1:17   *134*

Haggai

1:6   *318*

Zechariah

1:7   *324*
1:13   *306*
2:10   *502*
4:10   *305*
5:6   *46*
7:3   *319*
7:14   *98*
8:17   *103*
9:5   *247*
10:8   *20*
11:7   *488*
14:14   *380*

Malachi

1:1–10   *511*
1:6   *144*
1:8   *228, 263*
2:7   *202*
3:10   *160*
3:14   *484*
3:22   *506*
3:23   *433*

Matthew

5:17   *30*
7:12   *30, 360*
11:13   *30*

22:30 *176*
22:37 *597*
22:40 *30*
27:46 *610*

Mark

12:25 *176*
12:30 *597*
16:8 *46*
16:9 *46*
16:9–20 *46*
16:20 *46*

Luke

16:16 *30*
16:29 *30*
16:31 *30*
24:44 *30*

John

4 *52*
6:68 *xii*
9 *454*
9:22 *189*

Acts

13:15 *30*
24:14 *30*
28:23 *30*

Romans

3:21 *30*

Colossians

3:16 *xii*

Hebrews

7:4 *85*

James

4:13–14 *492*

1 Peter

3:19–20 *176*

2 Peter

2:4 *176*

Jude

6–7 *176*

THE JEWISH

COOKBOOK

LEAH KOENIG

THE JEWISH

COOKBOOK

FOREWORD BY JULIA TURSHEN

LEGEND 7

FOREWORD 8

SALADS, SPREADS,
PICKLES & STARTERS

68

INTRODUCTION

10

SOUPS & STEWS

120

BREAKFAST

14

VEGETABLES
& GRAINS

152

BREADS

44

FRITTERS & SAVORY PASTRIES

182

DUMPLINGS, NOODLES & KUGELS

218

MAIN DISHES

244

CAKES, COOKIES & SWEET PASTRIES

314

CONFECTIONS & PUDDINGS

376

CONDIMENTS, SPICES & DRINKS

394

INDEX 424

DAIRY-FREE

GLUTEN-FREE

VEGAN

VEGETARIAN

5 INGREDIENTS OR LESS

30 MINUTES OR LESS

FOREWORD

It is very humbling to be asked to set the table for what follows in these pages. I have also asked myself if I am the right person for the job since I have never been a particularly religious or regularly practicing Jew (I've always felt most aligned with the "ish" in *Jewish*). Yet, so much of the work I do as a cookbook author, a home cook, and a member of my family and various communities is tied to my Jewish identity. That identity is informed by two Jewish adages. The first is the idea that an enemy is someone whose story you just don't know yet. The other is the idea of *tikkun olam* or the notion of repair—of doing work to improve the world and using our time here to leave the world better than we found it. These neighborly values help me navigate the world and the food within it.

Leah Koenig stepped up to the proverbial plate to write *The Jewish Cookbook*, this incredible collection of Jewish recipes. The sheer variety of recipes goes a long way to show that Jewish food is all about the people who cook it and what's been handed down and held onto. In this book, Leah shows us that Jewish food is not defined by place, but by spirit, culture, and faith in so many senses of the word. Unlike just about every other cuisine in the world, Jewish food is not distinguished by geography. It is a diasporic cuisine, which means it's also defined by resilience, adaptability and infinite adjustments, longing and remembering, and often homesickness—even if home is no longer. In a way, every meal a Jew eats, wherever they are in the world, is an attempt to get back to somewhere.

For those of us who hold Jewish food sacred, this perpetual hunger for home gives us much in common with others who have been forced to leave wherever they call home. There is empathy at the Jewish table for refugees across the world who cook as a way to stay tethered and does not stop within the religion. It extends to enslaved Africans who wove seeds into their braided hair to keep with them a part of where they were taken, to displaced Palestinians who cook dishes like *maqluba* and hummus sprinkled with za'atar as a way to continue their culture, and to survivors of natural disasters in places like Puerto Rico, who continue to pass on their recipes even when they've lost everything. Food reminds us who we are and where we come from.

The diasporic quality of Jewish food, and the empathy it brings with it, also means that Jewish food, when it's at its best, is for everyone. After all, sharing Jewish food is the only way it continues. And when we share it, extraordinary things can happen. Enemies can share stories and relationships can shift. While a bowl of chicken soup might not be the answer to world peace, it can be an invitation to a dinner table and to a conversation. It can be a safe place to have uncomfortable dialogue. It can be a place for *tikkun olam* in action.

This book is full of recipes for those types of meals and many others, too. It contains so much history, covering so many peoples and geographies, in one place. It takes you from Morocco to Mexico to Montreal, from the Upper West Side to London and beyond. Diving into it makes me, the granddaughter of Jewish bakery owners on one side and grain millers on the other, feel very seen and connected (see the Breads chapter, especially the New York-Style Bagels on page 58). It also makes me feel so excited for all the foods that aren't yet in my family repertoire, like the Groundnut Stew (page 246) from the Abayudaya, the small Jewish community in Eastern Uganda. I can't wait to make the Plum Dumplings (page 224) for my mother, who is partial to anything made with the fruit, and I am especially tempted by the potato dough that encases the dumplings. I thought I knew everything there was to know about split pea soup until I read the recipe for Spiced Split Pea Stew (page 249), otherwise known as *kik wot* by the Ethiopian Jews who make it. I could keep going, but you have the whole book in front of you.

The Jewish food I know is Ashkenazi. It is the collection of recipes and dishes that made their way in boats from Eastern Europe and landed in places like Brooklyn, where my grandparents ran their bread bakery for decades. Things like challah bread brushed with eggs so it turns beautifully bronze. And chicken in the pot and fat slices of brisket, thick potato pancakes that are a vehicle for sour cream more than anything, and cold borscht poured over a hot boiled potato. Things like dessert tables piled with honey cake, coconut macaroons, and *teiglachs* (as close as Jews get to French croquembouches).

For me, Jewish food is less everyday food and more food for occasions and holidays, for births and deaths and all of the significant moments in between. As a cookbook author constantly in search of recipes that will excite people, I am so comforted by the repetition of holiday foods and the reliability of expecting the same dishes every year on certain days. Along with the familiar flavors are also the same prayers and songs. There are the same candlesticks that my grandmother packed in her suitcase when she fled the pogroms. The repetition also makes it clear both how much has changed, and how important it is to hold onto things that make us feel connected to something bigger and steadier than any of us individuals.

When I look around my holiday tables now, the people have changed. There are incredible additions like my wife and sister-in-law, other new family members, and all of the pets and babies that come with them. There are also notable absences. Holidays give us all a moment to remember everyone who used to sit with us. Meals let us see what is ahead as much as they encourage us to look back. Using a meal to remember is when Jewish food feels most transcendent. I never knew my maternal grandparents who ran the bakery, but I think about them often and feel most closely connected when I get to hold things that once belonged to them—the candlesticks and so on—and cook the foods they prepared. Asking about my grandparents, knowing their stories and telling them to keep the stories and lesson alive, reminds me that answers about how we can move forward often appear if we look backwards. Their bakery, Ratchick's, was culturally Jewish but it wasn't kosher. They specialized in bread, cakes, and cookies. They made things they grew up with rather than fancy pastries. They made the kinds of things that families bought as part of their routines. The bakery was part of its neighborhood's fabric.

My grandparents always had what were called *pushkes* on the bakery counter, small collection boxes where customers could leave extra change for local organizations that served the community. The pushkes made it easy for customers who had something to give to give. This sense of giving back didn't start in the bakery.

When my grandmother was a young girl in Odessa, her family's bakery also served as a community oven. Neighbors would leave pots of meat in the morning to cook all day in the bakery's oven and then pick them up later. When she was just a child, my grandmother would move some of the meat from the wealthy families' pots and sneak it into the pots that didn't have as much. I like to believe my grandmother was Robin Hood.

One day much later in life, my grandmother was walking down the street in Brooklyn to go to work at her bakery. She recognized the television set that two teenagers were carrying down the block. It was hers. They had just stolen it from her apartment. She went right up to them, told them to return it, and then said she was going to take them to the bakery to feed them. I am going to repeat that: my grandmother's answer to confronting the young boys who stole from her was to feed them. Her answer was to heal something that was broken and not to break it down even more.

When I think about how food can play a role in social justice—in reminding us all that we are each others' neighbors—I think about my grandmother and how, even when she didn't have much, she always gave. I think about how she used food to feed and support her family, but also to be part of her community.

And that to me is Jewish food. It's my grandparents' bakery and my own holiday table. It's the food in this book. It's recipes like the 400-odd that follow that tell us who we come from and introduces us to so many other people, too. Jewish food is food that gives, that pulls up another chair to the table. Jewish food asks if you've had enough to eat because there's always enough, and it ensures that you have seconds, thirds, and leftovers to take with you so that it never, ever, ends.

Julia Turshen

INTRODUCTION

Enjoying Jewish food is simple—describing it is more complex. As a Jewish food writer and cookbook author who leads cooking classes and demonstrations around the globe, I am regularly asked, "How do you define Jewish food?" My answer is always the same: "That depends entirely on whom you ask."

Jewish food is as varied as Jewish culture, which has flourished all over the world and has absorbed local customs from a range of places and peoples. Invite someone with Eastern European ancestry, like me, to describe an iconic Jewish meal, and she will likely speak in reverent tones of brisket and matzo ball soup, or blintzes and cheesecake, latkes and applesauce. A similar question posed to a Jew of Moroccan descent will elicit equally fond descriptions of rich chicken or lamb tagines and *chraime*—fish poached in spicy tomato sauce. A Jew hailing from Turkey, meanwhile, might offer up flaky *bourekas*, savory hand pie–like pastries, and *sutlach*, a sweet, milky pudding thickened with rice flour, as dishes evocative of Jewish cuisine.

In addition to its rich and multiple heritages, Jewish cuisine includes festive dishes eaten for celebration and commemoration, as well as the everyday fare that sustains Jewish communities throughout the week. For a religiously observant Eastern European family on Friday night (the Sabbath, or *Shabbat*), Jewish cuisine might mean challah, roast chicken, and apple cake, while on a weekday it might mean corned beef on rye bread with a pickle, or a bowl of egg noodles folded with creamy curd cheese. A culturally Jewish American family, meanwhile, may serve brisket and matzo ball soup for a Passover seder, and yet eat cheeseburgers at a summer barbecue.

As disparate as these definitions of Jewish food are, they are all accurate expressions of how Jewish people eat today. Jewish communities throughout the centuries have lived, cooked, and shared festive meals, forming a cuisine that is both intensely regional and profoundly global. It is as personal and specific as the spread of dishes found on a single table, and as expansive and varied as the entirety of the Jewish Diaspora. As Jewish communities moved—and move they have many times throughout the centuries, sometimes by choice but often under threat of religious persecution—they adopted food customs from neighboring cuisines, and adapted beloved dishes to the flavors of their new homes, creating localized variations of canonical dishes. In doing so, they carved out their cuisine's particular contours, creating food traditions that were both a part of and apart from their locales.

That is why in Mexico City, which has a significant Jewish community with Eastern European ancestry, one might find matzo ball soup simmered with smoky chili peppers and topped with cilantro (coriander), minced onion, and avocado—seasonings common to Mexican cooking. It is also why the stuffed tomatoes eaten by Jews in Calcutta (many of whom originally hailed from Syria and Iraq) are fragrant with fresh ginger, a hallmark of Indian cuisine. And it is why challah, the classic Shabbat bread, has been repurposed as the base for custardy French toast in Jewish American delicatessens.

JEWISH CUISINE AROUND THE WORLD

The history of Jewish cuisine stretches back 3,500 years to biblical times, when the ancient Israelites lived and farmed in mostly one region. During that time, their existence was closely tied to the land. They ate olives and grapes and pressed them into oil and wine; boiled dates into rich syrup; ate freshly plucked figs; planted fields with barley, wheat, and legumes; milked goats and sheep to make cheese; and foraged for wild greens and garlic.

After the Diaspora, when Israelites were exiled from their ancestral homeland some two thousand years ago, a new era of Jewish cuisine began. Jewish communities fanned out from the Middle East to places near and far. These communities were bound together by a shared basic set of liturgy and laws. They were also deeply influenced by the customs, people, and ingredients found in their new homes, and differences evolved between them over time. Over the centuries, a few primary threads of Jewish culture and cuisine developed based on several primary geographic regions where Jews settled.

Ashkenazi Jews have roots around the Rhine River (now western Germany and eastern France), and eventually spread across Eastern and Central Europe—everywhere from Poland, Lithuania, and Russia to Austria, Hungary, and Romania. Ashkenazi cuisine was shaped by a climate that was too cold for growing crops during half of the year. It was also formed in many places by poverty, and the great skill home cooks cultivated to create nourishing delicacies out of meager means. Despite areas of overlap between different regions, it is by no means monolithic. The vast array of dumplings enjoyed by Czech and Hungarian Jews, for example, is not shared elsewhere with the same fervor. And German Jews make a unique variation of challah called *berches* that is softened with mashed potato instead of egg.

Sephardi Jews are rooted in the Iberian Peninsula. For generations, Jewish, Catholic, and Muslim communities lived side by side in relative peace, cross-pollinating one another's cultures, ideas, and recipes. But after the Spanish Inquisition in the late fifteenth century, Jews either fled in exile or were forced to convert to Catholicism. Many resettled in Mediterranean countries like Greece, Turkey, and Italy; in Bulgaria and elsewhere in the Balkans; Amsterdam (where Jews were involved in the spice trade); the Middle East (especially Syria, Egypt, Iraq, Lebanon); and North Africa (Tunisia, Morocco, Libya). As a result, there is an even wider variance within Sephardi cuisine than Ashkenazi cuisine. Much of it is shaped by relatively warm climates, access to a great variety of fresh ingredients, and heavy culinary influence from the Ottoman Empire.

Mizrahi Jews trace their ancestry to Middle Eastern countries like Syria, Yemen, Egypt, Iraq, and Iran (Persia), and North African countries including Morocco, Libya, Tunisia, and Algeria. These ancient communities predated the Spanish Inquisition, and the influx of Sephardi Jews from Spain and Portugal to the region that followed. Jews who hail from parts of Central Asia located along the winding Silk Road—including Uzbekistan (Bukhara), Azerbaijan, and Georgia—are also categorized as Mizrahi, since they descended from biblical-era Middle Eastern communities. There is a fair amount of overlap between Mizrahi and Sephardi cuisines, including an emphasis on produce, bold spices, rice, and couscous.

Beyond these three broadly defined regions of Jewish cuisine there also exist outlying communities. Rome, for example, welcomed an influx of Sephardi Jews after the Spanish Inquisition and a community of Libyan Jews in the late twentieth century, but has also been home to a significant Jewish community since ancient times. The original Roman Jews, who are often identified as *Italkim*, settled in Rome as early as the second century BCE, and many of their descendants still live there today. The Bene Israel Jews of Mumbai and the Beta Israel Jews of Ethiopia are two prime illustrations of communities that maintained their own histories and, for many generations, were largely cut off from the rest of the global Jewish world. (The majority of both of those communities resettled in Israel in the second half of the twentieth century.) Eastern Uganda, meanwhile, is also home to a small Jewish community called Abayudaya, which was founded in the early twentieth century.

Over the past 150 years, Jewish geographic boundaries have blurred and mixed even more significantly. In the late nineteenth and early twentieth centuries, the United States and Canada witnessed a massive influx of Jews from Central and Eastern Europe. In North America, Jewish cuisine—which largely, though not exclusively, is Ashkenazi cuisine—took on its own contours. It was there that the modern Jewish delicatessen was born and the trifecta of bagels, lox, and cream cheese was first enjoyed.

Meanwhile, South Africa, Australia, and parts of Latin and South America became vibrant hubs of Jewish life. In South Africa and Australia, Eastern Europe–hailing communities tend to hold tightly to their traditional dishes, while incorporating local ingredients and flavors. Many Latin and South American Jewish communities stretch back centuries and are home to both Ashkenazi and Sephardi Jews.

Israel has also evolved into a veritable melting pot of cultures and cuisines. Jews from all corners of the globe have made their homes there, and rub shoulders as neighbors. It is common to find families where one side is, say, Polish or Lithuanian and the other Moroccan, Turkish, or Syrian. Meanwhile, Israeli Jews pull significant influence from their Palestinian and other Arab neighbors, incorporating and adapting both cooking techniques and dishes. The result is the rapidly evolving, regionally driven, exciting hodgepodge that is modern Israeli cuisine.

For the home cook, this constant motion of the Jewish people creates endless stories to explore and the delicious mosaic of global Jewish cuisine enjoyed today by Jews and non-Jews alike.

CHEFS AND NOUVEAU JEWISH CUISINE

The heart of traditional Jewish cooking begins in the family kitchen. It is there, over the slap of challah dough being kneaded against a wooden table, or the rush of fragrant steam escaping from a ceramic tagine, that generations of home cooks shaped the diverse canon of Jewish cuisine. Of course, kosher restaurants and bakeries have existed for centuries, to serve religious Jewish communities worldwide. But in recent decades, a new generation of restaurant chefs has begun to play an increasingly defining role in both the celebration and evolution of Jewish food far beyond Jewish communities.

This new crop of chefs has brought Jewish cooking into the international spotlight. While the main focus of this cookbook remains home cooking, it would be incomplete without an acknowledgment of these chefs' contributions. So throughout these pages are recipes from contemporary and innovative chefs and restaurants around the world.

There are stalwarts like the historic smoked fish purveyor Russ & Daughters in New York City (page 421), which opened a restaurant in honor of its 100th birthday and has breathed new life and flavor into its multigenerational legacy. Their Super Heebster bagel—topped with whitefish and baked salmon salad, wasabi-infused roe, and horseradish-dill cream cheese—is just one delicious example of Old World meets new innovation. There are delicatessens—like Wexler's Deli in Los Angeles (page 109) or Wise Sons with locations in San Francisco and Tokyo (page 27)—that are reimagining classic deli fare with artisanal meats and pickles cured in-house and creative updates like a Reuben sandwich with roasted mushrooms.

There are modern Middle Eastern–inspired restaurants like Zahav in Philadelphia see page 311), Safta in Denver (page 57), and Yotam Ottolenghi's empire (page 137) in London. In Israel, a generation of classically trained chefs, including Uri Scheft (page 343) and Eyal Shani (page 169), has lovingly mined their own families' culinary heritages to delicious effect. These have helped familiarize diners and cooks with an entire pantry's worth of ingredients—preserved lemons, pomegranate molasses, and za'atar, just to name a few.

Additionally, in Europe and elsewhere, chefs are exploring Jewish cuisine and, in a sense, reclaiming a rich cultural history that was largely lost in the Holocaust. In Frankfurt, for example, restaurants like Maxie Eisen (page 125 have introduced pastrami to a new generation of fans. In Krakow, chef Aleksander Baron marries traditional Eastern European flavors—duck schmaltz, sorrel—with fine dining at Zoni (page 233).

Collectively, these chefs have broadened the appeal of Jewish cuisine both within and beyond the Jewish community—imbuing it with a sense of vibrancy and relevance in a way only chefs can. In turn, they have inspired Jewish home cooks to innovate and experiment more freely their own kitchens. As a result, Jewish cuisine has, in recent years, stepped onto the global gastronomic stage.

COLLECTING AND CATALOGING JEWISH CUISINE

Today, as ever, Jewish food is constantly evolving as Jewish people continue to relocate, as imported ingredients become increasingly available, and as our modern world and social media continue to build bridges between geographically disparate communities.

To write a cookbook attempting to represent the entirety of Jewish cuisine is, then, an act of humility. My goal in crafting this book was to illuminate as many types of Jewish kitchens and tables around the world as possible. I sought to shine a light on the dishes that sustain Jews around the world during the week and those that delight them on Shabbat and the holidays. I delved into the depths of historical cookbooks and delicatessen menus.

And thanks to the generosity of numerous cooks who welcomed me into their homes, I peeked into treasured recipe boxes and cooked alongside the true experts of Jewish cuisine. As I researched, I encountered many regional twists on dishes I thought I already knew well. There was a Hungarian take on noodle kugel, which embellishes the sweet pudding with poppy seeds and decadent pockets of jam. There was an Italian recipe for charoset that includes roasted chestnuts, and another from Yemen that favors sesame seeds. In many cases, I had to make difficult decisions about how many and which variations to include. After all, Jewish food is not only regional, it changes from family to family, with each cook often insisting that he or she holds the secret for the most authentic and delicious recipes.

I was also introduced to dozens of recipes. Learning about each of these dishes felt miraculous—for example, the sweet egg meringue called *jaban* that Moroccan Jews eat at the close of Passover; a dish of sautéed zucchini (courgette) peels called *kaskarikas* that Turkish Jews make to avoid wasting food; or the Eastern European-descended cheese bagel, or *baygelach,* that can be found in Montreal's Jewish bakeries. This stunning global diversity, tucked away like the glistening seeds of a pomegranate waiting to be unwrapped, served as a reminder of why, after spending so much time immersed in the subject of Jewish food, I never tire of it. My hope is that through these pages, I can share this profound sense of wonder and discovery with you.

My own definition for Jewish cuisine, which I have honed over the past decades of immersing myself professionally and personally in the subject, is that it includes any dish that holds cultural, sacred, or ritual significance to the Jewish communities (and their friends) that cook and eat it. What that looks like in practice is not the same today as it will be tomorrow. So no matter how thoroughly or carefully researched I have aimed to be, I can only hope this book is an adequate snapshot of this special food culture as it stands today. Fortunately, with a cuisine that is at once rooted in centuries of tradition and is as vast as our own culinary imaginations, the future is destined to be just as delicious.

JEWISH HOLIDAYS AND FOOD TRADITIONS

Jewish cuisine can be divided into two categories: foods eaten during the week, and those served on Shabbat and the holidays. The latter category is vastly larger than the former—partly because Shabbat is celebrated every week, and there are many holidays throughout the year, and partly because Shabbat and holiday meals tend to be festive, communal affairs where home cooks pull out all the stops. Every Jewish community has its own repertoire of dishes and customs that make a holiday feel complete. But there are commonalities shared across most Jewish holiday meals. Family and friends—some from down the block and others from half a world away—gather together around a festively set table. Candles are often lit to signal the holiday's beginning. Blessings over wine and bread may be recited. As conversation begins to flow, a parade of warming dishes is set on the table. And in some families, singing together at a holiday meal is almost as central as the food. Enjoyed with community and ritual, the dishes one eats on a holiday are bound to be memorable. Since Jewish holidays are based on the Hebrew calendar, their timing shifts a bit from year to year in the Western calendar. Here is a brief breakdown of the major Jewish holidays, with their approximate dates.

★ SHABBAT
Every Friday at sunset through Saturday at sundown

Shabbat celebrates the seventh day of biblical creation and is a day of rest. Observant Jews abstain from driving, using electricity, and cooking. As a result, many traditional Shabbat dishes can be made ahead and served cold or at room temperature. Alternatively, some dishes are set to cook before the holiday begins and are ready for lunch the following day. Three festive meals can be served: Shabbat dinner on Friday evening, Shabbat lunch midday on Saturday, and/or *seudah shlishit,* a "third meal" on Saturday afternoon. Stews and braised meats are common main dishes.

★ ROSH HASHANAH
Early fall, September/October

Rosh Hashanah, or "the head of the year" in Hebrew, is the spiritual beginning of the Jewish year, and is colloquially known as the Jewish New Year. It launches the autumnal festival season called the High Holidays, and is a time of great joy and contemplation. It's traditional to share meals with family during the holiday, and eat symbolic foods—most notably apples dipped in honey—meant to usher in a sweet and fortuitous year ahead.

★ YOM KIPPUR
Week after Rosh Hashanah, September/October

Yom Kippur, or the Day of Atonement, is a solemn holiday where Jews request forgiveness for any wrongdoings, and is marked by a 25-hour fast. Yom Kippur's period of abstinence is preceded by a significant meal and capped off, after nightfall, with a celebratory spread. Ashkenazi Jews tend to serve breakfast and brunch fare like bagels and lox, coffee cake, and noodle kugels. Other communities have their own break-fast foods like *harira,* a hearty noodle and legume soup eaten by Moroccan Jews, or the crustless quiches called *jibn* served by Syrian Jews.

★ SUKKOT
Several days after Yom Kippur, usually October

Sukkot marks the forty years the Israelites wandered in the desert after leaving enslavement in ancient Egypt. It also marks a period of autumnal harvest. Observant families celebrate by building a temporary outdoor dwelling called a *sukkah,* which serves as their dining room during the holiday. Stuffed foods and other dishes that highlight the season's abundance are typically served.

✱ HANUKKAH
Usually December

Hanukkah, also known as the Festival of Lights, honors the rededication of the Temple in Jerusalem after the Maccabees (a small Judean army) recaptured it from the ancient Greeks. In the story, the Maccabees found only enough oil in the Temple's ruins to light its menorah for one night, but the light miraculously lasted for eight nights. Deep-fried foods—everything from Ashkenazi potato latkes to the fried chicken enjoyed by Italian Jews—and other dishes that feature oil are traditional celebrations.

✱ TU BISHVAT
Usually January

Known as the New Year of the Trees, Tu Bishvat marks the switch from one year's tree crops to the next. This holiday has transformed into an annual fête for trees and everything that grows on their branches. People eat apricots, apples, figs, plums, dates, olives, and other tree fruits. There is also a custom of eating foods made with wheat, barley, dates, grapes, figs, pomegranates, and olives (for more on the significance of these seven species, see page 381).

✱ PURIM
February/March

Purim celebrates a biblical story about the heroism of Queen Esther, the Jewish Queen of Persia who saved her people from destruction at the hands of Haman, a vizier intent on eliminating Persia's Jews. On Purim, people gather to read the *megillah* (scroll) of Esther's story, dress up in costumes, hold boisterous parties at night, and enjoy a lavish *seudah* (meal) the following day, featuring foods that resemble Haman (see page 339). They also customarily share gifts of food—often hamantaschen or other small sweets—with friends and give to charity.

✱ PASSOVER
March/April

One of the most widely observed holidays on the Jewish calendar, Passover celebrates the Israelites' exodus from enslavement in ancient Egypt. On the first of eight nights, people gather with friends and family for a seder, a ritual meal and storytelling recounting the Passover story and includes a lavish feast. Jews traditionally do not eat *chametz* (leavened foods made from wheat, barley, oats, rye, and spelt) throughout the weeklong holiday, and instead enjoy unleavened matzo. This tradition derives from the Passover story, which tells how when the Jews left ancient Egypt, they did so in haste. The bread dough they had prepared did not have time to rise, so they carried it on their backs where it baked, unleavened, in the hot sun. Some observant Jews from Ashkenazi backgrounds also avoid corn, rice, legumes, and other foods that resemble *chametz*, called *kitniyot*.

✱ SHAVUOT
May/June

Shavuot evokes the moment when God revealed the Torah to the Israelites at Mount Sinai. It also marks the end of the barley harvest and the beginning of the wheat harvest in ancient Israel. Observant Jews customarily stay up all night studying texts, and some communities have a tradition of eating foods made with dairy—things like cheesecake and blintzes.

KOSHER TRADITIONS

Kashrut (kosher) refers to the Jewish dietary laws outlined in the Torah and the Talmud, the two primary texts of Judaism. Throughout history, these traditions have shaped the way Jewish people cook and eat. The word means "fit" in Hebrew and to keep kosher is, in essence, the set of rules that govern what is and is not fit for consumption, according to Jewish law. There are many minutiae for those who keep kosher, but the basic laws:

- prohibit milk and meat to be cooked together in the same dish or served at the same meal;
- prohibit the consumption of certain animal species, including pigs, shellfish, some birds, insects, and any mammal that does not both chew its cud and have cloven hooves;
- require that animals permitted for consumption be slaughtered in a specific manner; and
- forbid the consumption of blood.

Because of the restriction against consuming milk and meat together, traditional Jewish recipes tend to be classified as "dairy" (made with milk or other dairy products), "meat" (made with beef, chicken, lamb, or other kinds of meat), or "parve" (made solely with eggs, fish, grains, produce, or other neutral ingredients that can be served alongside either meat or dairy foods).

Throughout history, many Jewish home cooks have adapted dishes to be kosher. Greek Jews, for example, top the meaty eggplant casserole moussaka with a layer of dairy-free béchamel. Kosher-keeping Jews in Alsace, France, meanwhile, enjoy the traditional onion and cheese-covered flatbread *tarte flambée* with sautéed mushrooms instead of diced pork fat. One could argue that the laws of keeping kosher exist at the heart of all Jewish cuisine. That said, different communities and individuals maintain their own relationship to keeping kosher, and there is a strong tradition of ignoring kosher laws as there is to adhering to them. Strictly observant Jews adhere as closely possible, both in their own homes and beyond. Less observant people might take a more flexible approach, or find meaning in the laws without following each detail (as in the American Jewish tradition of eating Chinese food on Christmas, where it is almost certain there will be pork and shellfish consumed). Some people are entirely indifferent, while others openly reject it, and view doing so as part of their Jewish identities. Regardless of this personal variance of observance, it is impossible to imagine a Jewish cuisine in absence of these traditions.

INTRODUCTION

BREAKFAST

HUEVOS HAMINADOS

These eggs turn luxuriously creamy and take on gorgeous mahogany color and rich flavor after an overnight slow-cooker bath. Thrifty Sephardi home cooks traditionally saved the skins from onions used during the week to make *huevos haminados* for Shabbat morning. If you are starting the recipe with fresh onions, remove the skins and then store the "skinned" onions in a zip-top bag in the refrigerator until needed, up to 2 weeks.

Serves: 6–12
Preparation time: 10 minutes
Cooking time: 8–12 hours

- Skins from 5 large onions, rinsed
- 6–12 eggs, in the shell
- 2 tablespoons coffee grounds (not instant)
- 1 tablespoon distilled white vinegar
- 2 tablespoons extra-virgin olive oil

Lay the onion skins in the bottom of a slow cooker. Nestle the eggs in the skins and top with the coffee grounds, vinegar, and olive oil. Add water to cover by 2 inches (5 cm). Set the slow cooker to low and let the eggs cook for 8–12 hours (less time for lighter, milder-tasting eggs, more time for darker, more intensely flavored eggs). Remove the eggs from the slow cooker with a slotted spoon and rinse under cold water. Serve warm, at room temperature, or cold.

TOMATO SCRAMBLED EGGS

Tomato and egg scrambles, called *menemen*, are beloved by Turks (including Turkish Jews) and typically served as part of a larger breakfast spread of cheese, pita, sliced vegetables, and olives. The dish gets its name from a small village just outside the city of Smyrna. Some versions include finely chopped bell pepper, so feel free to add that into the mix along with the onions.

Serves: 2 or 3
Preparation time: 5 minutes
Cooking time: 15 minutes

- 3 tablespoons extra-virgin olive oil
- 1 small onion, finely chopped
- 2 garlic cloves, finely chopped
- ½ teaspoon Aleppo pepper or crushed pepper flakes
- 1 teaspoon dried oregano
- 1 can (14½ oz/411 g) diced (chopped) tomatoes, drained
- 1 teaspoon kosher salt, plus more as needed
- Freshly ground black pepper
- 4 eggs
- Crumbled feta cheese, for serving (optional)

In a medium saucepan, heat the oil over medium heat. Add the onion and garlic and cook, stirring occasionally, until softened and lightly browned, 6–8 minutes. Add the Aleppo pepper and oregano and cook, stirring, until fragrant, about 1 minute. Add the drained tomatoes (discard the juice or reserve for another use), salt, and a generous amount of black pepper and cook, stirring occasionally, until thickened, about 5 minutes.

Meanwhile, in a bowl, whisk together the eggs and a pinch of salt. Add the eggs to the tomato mixture and cook, stirring almost constantly, until the eggs are scrambled and just barely set. Remove from the heat and divide onto plates. Serve hot, sprinkled with feta, if desired.

Huevos Haminados

SHAKSHUKA

This North African dish of eggs poached in spicy tomato sauce has gained widespread popularity. This version is on the mild side, so increase the Aleppo pepper or serve with Harissa (page 409), if desired.

Serves: 2
Preparation time: 10 minutes
Cooking time: 25 minutes

- 3 tablespoons extra-virgin olive oil, plus more for serving
- 1 medium onion, finely chopped
- 2 medium red or yellow bell peppers, sliced into thin strips
- 5 garlic cloves, thinly sliced
- 1 teaspoon smoked paprika
- 1 teaspoon onion powder
- ½ teaspoon Aleppo pepper or ¼ teaspoon crushed pepper flakes
- 1 can (28 oz/795 g) diced (chopped) tomatoes
- 4 tablespoons tomato paste (purée)
- 1 teaspoon kosher salt, plus more as needed
- ¼ teaspoon freshly ground black pepper
- 4 eggs
- 2 oz (55 g) crumbled feta cheese (optional)
- Za'atar and fresh cilantro (coriander), for serving

In a large frying pan, heat the oil over medium heat. Add the onion and bell peppers and cook, stirring occasionally, until softened, 6–8 minutes. Add the garlic, smoked paprika, onion powder, and Aleppo pepper and cook, stirring, until fragrant, about 2 minutes.

Stir in the diced (chopped) tomatoes, tomato paste (purée), salt, and black pepper. Bring to a simmer and cook, stirring occasionally, until the mixture thickens slightly, about 10 minutes. Taste and stir in additional salt, if desired.

Using the back of a spoon, create 4 shallow wells in the sauce. Break one egg into each well. Cover the pan and cook, basting the eggs once or twice with the sauce, until the whites are set and the yolks are still soft, about 5 minutes.

Remove from the heat and sprinkle with the feta, if desired. Scatter za'atar and cilantro (coriander) over the top and drizzle with a little more oil. Serve hot.

MALAWACH

Malawach—a flaky fried bread that resembles scallion pancakes in texture—is an everyday dish for Yemenite Jews. It is typically eaten with S'chug (page 411), and Grated Tomato Relish (page 411), but can also be topped with a drizzle of honey.

Serves: 8
Preparation time: 45 minutes, plus resting and chilling
Cooking time: 20 minutes

- 3¾ cups (525 g) all-purpose (plain) flour
- ⅓ cup (65 g) sugar
- 2½ teaspoons kosher salt
- Vegetable oil, for greasing the work surface
- 1 stick (4 oz/115 g) unsalted butter, samneh, or ghee, at room temperature, plus more for frying

In a stand mixer fitted with the paddle attachment, whisk together the flour, sugar, and salt. With the machine on low speed, add 1 cup (240 ml/8 fl oz) water and beat until the dough begins to come together. Switch to the dough hook and knead until the dough is smooth, about 5 minutes. Cover the bowl with a tea towel and let rest for 30 minutes.

Line a large baking sheet with parchment paper. Spread a couple of teaspoons of oil on a flat work surface. Divide the dough into 8 equal pieces. Working with 1 piece of dough at a time, flatten it into a large, very thin rectangle. Spread 1 tablespoon (15 g) butter evenly over the top of the dough. Starting from a long edge, roll the dough up like a jelly roll (Swiss roll), then coil the roll onto itself and place on the prepared baking sheet. Cover with plastic wrap (cling film) and continue the process with the remaining dough and butter. Refrigerate the dough coils until fully chilled, at least 4 hours or up to overnight.

Remove the dough from the refrigerator and use a rolling pin to flatten the coils into 8-inch (20 cm) rounds.

In a large nonstick frying pan, heat about 1 teaspoon butter over medium heat. Add a dough round and cook, turning once, until golden brown on both sides, 1–2 minutes per side. Repeat with the remaining rounds.

Shakshuka

DESAYUNO: THE SEPHARDI BRUNCH TRADITION

Sephardi Jews have a unique connection to brunch, particularly on Shabbat. Called *desayuno* ("breakfast" in Spanish), this meal is traditionally served in the mid- to late morning on Saturdays, just after religious services.

Desayuno meals are casual and feature parve and dairy foods, rather than the heavier meat dishes served later in the day at lunch. And because there is a prohibition against active cooking on Shabbat, the dishes served tend to be recipes that can be prepared in advance, and foods that taste good cold or at room temperature. Flaky *bourekas* (pages 212–214) and *bulemas* (page 206) filled with eggplant, spinach, cheese,

or potato are de rigueur *desayuno* fare, as are the overnight eggs, Huevos Haminados (page 16), and the sesame seed–coated *biscochos* (Sesame Seed Cookie Rings, page 354). Egyptian Jews are likely to serve *ful medames* (Stewed Fava Beans, page 21), while Turkish and Greek Jews might include Stuffed Grape Leaves (page 110).

The spread is typically rounded out with yogurt and jams, fruit, olives, and cheese. A small glass of ouzo or arak (anise-flavored liquor) for sipping would not be out of place. Regardless of what is on the table, this Jewish brunch sets a relaxed and celebratory mood for Shabbat afternoon.

TOASTED PITA AND SCRAMBLED EGGS

Mizrahi cuisine includes a category of recipes called *fatoot* that are made with stale flatbread that gets ripped and repurposed into something thrifty and delicious. (Fittingly, the word *fatoot* is Arabic for "crumbled.") Yemenite Jews serve this dish, called *fatoot samneh*, of torn pita toasted in *samneh* (clarified butter) and scrambled with eggs on Friday mornings, when preparations for Shabbat are underway and a quick, satisfying meal is needed. Like Matzo Brei (page 21), it can be served sweet or savory. Either way, the toasty, fragrant pita and creamy scrambled eggs make it a satisfying breakfast worth remembering when there is extra pita lying about.

Serves: 2–4
Preparation time: 5 minutes
Cooking time: 10 minutes

- 4 tablespoons samneh, ghee, or unsalted butter
- 2 pita breads (6 inch/15 cm), ripped into small pieces
- 4 eggs, lightly beaten
- ¼ teaspoon kosher salt, plus more as needed
- Honey or S'chug (page 411) and Hilbeh (page 409), for serving

In a medium frying pan, melt the *samneh* over medium heat. Add the pita pieces and cook, stirring occasionally, until toasted and lightly browned, about 5 minutes.

Meanwhile, in a medium bowl, whisk together the eggs and salt. Pour the eggs over the toasted pita and cook, stirring constantly, until the eggs are just set. Taste and add more salt, if desired. Divide onto plates and serve drizzled with honey or dolloped with *s'chug* or *hilbeh*.

MATZO BREI

Matzo brei (rhymes with "fry") might best be described as Passover-friendly French toast—a puffed, tender jumble of crumbled matzo that gets softened and bound with egg, then fried in butter or vegetable oil. The dish dates back to the turn of the twentieth century in America, and has become a ubiquitous menu item at Jewish delicatessens across the country. It can be served savory with a sprinkle of salt, or sweet with jam, maple syrup, or cinnamon sugar.

Serves: 4
Preparation time: 5 minutes
Cooking time: 10 minutes

- 5 sheets unsalted matzo, broken into 2-inch (5 cm) pieces
- 3 eggs
- ½ teaspoon kosher salt
- 4 tablespoons (60 g) unsalted butter or ¼ cup (60 ml/2 fl oz) vegetable oil
- Optional toppings: flaky sea salt, fruit preserves, cinnamon sugar, maple syrup

Spread the matzo pieces in an even layer in a large baking dish. Add 1 cup (240 ml/8 fl oz) warm tap water and gently stir until the matzo is moistened. Let stand until the matzo softens, 1–2 minutes, then pour off excess water.

In a medium bowl, whisk together the eggs and salt. Pour the egg mixture over the softened matzo and stir to combine.

In a large nonstick frying pan, melt the butter over medium heat. Add the matzo and egg mixture and press it into an even layer with a flat spatula. Cook, undisturbed, until the bottom is golden brown and the mixture sets, about 5 minutes. Flip the matzo brei and continue cooking until the second side is golden, 4–5 minutes.

Transfer the matzo brei to a serving platter or plates. Serve immediately with desired toppings on the side.

STEWED FAVA BEANS

One of Egypt's national dishes, these creamy, stewed fava beans (broad beans)—called *ful medames*—are eaten throughout the day. Jewish families often serve them for Shabbat lunch as part of a mezze spread. At breakfast, they are delicious topped with a fried egg.

Serves: 6
Preparation time: 15 minutes, plus soaking
Cooking time: 3 hours

- 2 cups (340 g) dried small fava beans (broad beans)
- 2 teaspoons baking soda (bicarbonate of soda)
- ¼ cup (60 ml/2 fl oz) extra-virgin olive oil
- ¼ cup (60 ml/2 fl oz) fresh lemon juice
- 2 teaspoons ground cumin
- ¼ teaspoon cayenne pepper
- 2 garlic cloves, minced or pushed through a press
- 1 teaspoon kosher salt, plus more as needed

For serving:
- Sliced hard-boiled eggs
- Extra-virgin olive oil, for drizzling
- Plain yogurt
- Minced fresh flat-leaf parsley
- Lemon wedges

Place the fava beans (broad beans) and baking soda (bicarb) in a large bowl and cover with water by at least 2 inches (5 cm). Cover the bowl with a tea towel and soak for at least 8 hours, or overnight. Drain the water, rinse the beans, and drain again.

Place the beans in a large saucepan and add water to cover by several inches. Bring to a boil over high heat. Reduce the heat to medium, partially cover, and simmer, stirring occasionally, until they are very soft and beginning to fall apart, 2–2½ hours. (Add water to the pot as necessary if it begins to look dry during cooking.)

When the beans are tender, pour off any excess liquid from the pan, leaving a few tablespoons, and use the back of a spoon to mash some of the beans into a paste consistency. Add the oil, lemon juice, cumin, cayenne, garlic, and salt and toss well. Taste and add more salt, if desired.

Serve the beans: Transfer the beans to a wide, shallow serving dish. Arrange sliced eggs around the sides, then drizzle with a little olive oil, dollop with yogurt, and sprinkle with parsley. Pass extra lemon wedges alongside for squeezing.

SALAMI AND EGGS

Sometimes, the simplest dishes are the most satisfying. This combination of sharp, savory salami and eggs, served either scrambled or as an omelet, was the in-a-hurry breakfast, and often dinner, for Ashkenazi American Jews. In some families, it was known as a specialty of fathers. It also became, and remains, a regular menu item at Jewish delicatessens. Start with medium-firm beef sausage, and serve the dish as is or dressed up with a smear of yellow mustard and a side of rye or pumpernickel toast.

Serves: 2 or 3
Preparation time: 5 minutes
Cooking time: 20 minutes

• 2 tablespoons vegetable oil
• 1 small onion, finely chopped
• 2 inches (5 cm) kosher salami, cut into thin rounds or matchsticks
• 6 eggs
• ½ teaspoon kosher salt
• ½ teaspoon freshly ground black pepper

In a medium nonstick frying pan, heat the oil over medium heat. Add the onion and cook, stirring occasionally, until softened and lightly browned, 6–8 minutes. Add the salami and cook, stirring occasionally, until lightly browned and sizzling, about 5 minutes.

Meanwhile, in a bowl, whisk together the eggs, salt, and pepper.

Pour the eggs over the fried salami, reduce the heat to medium-low, and cook undisturbed for 30 seconds. Use a silicone spatula to push the cooked egg from the bottom of the pan in several places, allowing the uncooked egg to spill toward the bottom. Cover the pan and let cook until the eggs are just set and no longer runny on top, 4–5 minutes.

Remove from the heat and transfer the omelet to a serving plate. Slice into wedges and serve.

LOX, EGGS, AND ONIONS

Commonly called a LEO, this savory scramble of eggs with browned onions and salty bits of lox (or more commonly smoked salmon) is a popular item on Jewish delicatessen menus. It is also easy to make at home for breakfast, brunch, or even dinner.

Serves: 6
Preparation time: 10 minutes
Cooking time: 15 minutes

• 2 tablespoons (30 g) unsalted butter
• 1 large red onion, finely chopped
• ½ teaspoon sugar
• ¾ teaspoon kosher salt, plus more as needed
• ¼ teaspoon freshly ground black pepper
• 10 eggs
• ½ teaspoon onion powder
• 3 oz (85 g) Lox (page 24) or smoked salmon, finely chopped
• Crème fraîche and finely chopped fresh dill, for garnish

In a large frying pan, melt the butter over medium heat. When bubbling, add the onion, sugar, and a sprinkle of salt and cook, stirring occasionally, until softened and lightly browned, 7–10 minutes.

Meanwhile, in a medium bowl, whisk together the eggs, onion powder, salt, and pepper until fully combined and slightly frothy. Pour the egg mixture over the onions and cook, stirring often with a silicone spatula, until the eggs are just barely set.

Remove the pan from the heat and stir in the lox. Divide the eggs onto plates and serve dolloped with crème fraîche and sprinkled with dill.

AARON ISRAEL AND SAWAKO OKOCHI

SHALOM JAPAN
·
310 SOUTH 4TH STREET
BROOKLYN, NY
USA

Aaron Israel and Sawako Okochi are the husband-and-wife team behind Shalom Japan, a popular Brooklyn restaurant that highlights the chefs' respective Jewish and Japanese roots. Their dishes are at once sophisticated and playful, including many that fuse their two backgrounds like matzo ball ramen and *sake kasu* challah.

MATZO BREI WITH IKURA AND CRÈME FRAÎCHE

This take on the classic Passover dish matzo brei is dolloped with crème fraîche and topped with briny Japanese salmon roe.

Serves: 2
Preparation time: 15 minutes
Cooking time: 10 minutes

For the matzo brei:
· 3 sheets unsalted matzo, broken into 1-inch (2.5 cm) pieces
· 1 cup (240 ml/8 fl oz) whole milk
· 2 eggs
· 1 tablespoon sugar
· ¼ teaspoon ground cinnamon
· ¼ teaspoon kosher salt
· ⅛ teaspoon freshly ground black pepper
· 2 tablespoons (30 g) unsalted butter

For the topping:
· ½ cup (120 g) crème fraîche
· Grated zest of 1 lemon
· 1 tablespoon fresh lemon juice
· ⅛ teaspoon kosher salt
· Ikura (Japanese salmon roe), for serving

Make the matzo brei: Spread the matzo pieces in an even layer in a medium baking dish. Add the milk and gently stir until the matzo is moistened. Let stand until the matzo softens, 1–2 minutes, then pour off and discard excess liquid.

In a medium bowl, whisk together the eggs, sugar, cinnamon, salt, and pepper. Pour the egg mixture over the softened matzo and stir to combine. In a nonstick medium frying pan, heat the butter over medium heat. Add the matzo mixture and spread it evenly in the pan with a spatula. Cook until the bottom is golden brown, about 5 minutes. Carefully flip and cook the other side until golden brown, about 3 minutes. Transfer to a serving plate.

Make the topping: In a small bowl, mix together the crème fraîche, lemon zest, lemon juice, and salt.

To serve, spoon the seasoned crème fraîche on top of the matzo brei and top with *ikura* to taste. Serve immediately.

★ STAR RECIPE

PASTRAMI HASH

Jewish delicatessens across North America serve up this savory jumble of fried meat and potatoes. In America, the meat of choice is typically deli-style pastrami or corned beef, while Canadian delis use smoked meat. Either way, it is delicious, and even better topped with a poached or fried egg. Meat lovers can increase the pastrami-to-potato ratio as desired.

Serves: 6
Preparation time: 20 minutes
Cooking time: 30 minutes

• 2 lb (910 g) red or Yukon Gold potatoes, peeled and cut into ½-inch (1.25 cm) pieces
• 6 tablespoons vegetable oil
• 1 large sweet onion, finely chopped
• 1 red bell pepper, finely chopped
• 4 garlic cloves, thinly sliced
• ¾ teaspoon kosher salt, plus more as needed
• Freshly ground black pepper
• ¼-lb (115 g) thick-cut pastrami, cut into bite-size pieces
• Snipped chives, for serving

Bring a large saucepan filled with water to a boil over high heat. Add the potato pieces and cook, stirring occasionally, until tender but not falling apart, 8–10 minutes. Drain well.

Meanwhile, in a large frying pan, heat 4 tablespoons of the oil over medium-high heat. Add the onion, bell pepper, garlic, and a pinch of salt and cook, stirring occasionally, until softened and lightly browned, about 10 minutes.

Reduce the heat under the frying pan to medium. Add the remaining 2 tablespoons oil, the cooked potatoes, salt, and a generous amount of pepper. Cook, stirring occasionally, until the potatoes are golden brown, 8–10 minutes.

Add the pastrami and cook, stirring occasionally, until warmed through, 2–3 minutes. Remove from the heat and serve hot, sprinkled with chives.

LOX

Scandinavian-style salt-cured salmon called lox (which is the Americanized version of the Yiddish word for "salmon," *laks*) has become one of the most beloved foods within American Ashkenazi cuisine. It is typically very thinly sliced and draped on top of a bagel (pages 58–60) also spread with cream cheese. The optional smoked salt in this recipe adds a hint of smoky flavor, which many people have come to associate with salt-brined lox, but is actually only found in smoked salmon varieties like Nova.

Serves: 8
Preparation time: 15 minutes, plus curing

• ⅔ cup (110 g) kosher salt
• ½ cup (100 g) sugar
• 1 tablespoon smoked salt (optional)
• 1½–2 lb (680–910 g) skin-on salmon fillet, rinsed and thoroughly patted dry

In a large bowl, mix together the kosher salt, sugar, and smoked salt (if using).

Stretch a double layer of plastic wrap (cling film) into a shallow baking dish large enough to hold the salmon, letting the wrap hang over the edges of the dish by several inches. Sprinkle with half of the salt mixture. Using a sharp knife, make a few shallow cuts on the skin side of the salmon and place it, flesh side up, on top of the salt mixture. Cover with the remaining salt mixture.

Fold the plastic wrap ends around the salmon and cover snugly with additional plastic wrap. Refrigerate for 48–72 hours, turning the package once a day and using fingers to redistribute the brine. Drain off any liquid that accumulates in the dish. When ready, the salmon should feel firm to the touch at the thickest part.

Unwrap the salmon and rinse the fillet well under water, discarding any brine in the baking dish. Use a sharp knife to thinly slice the lox against the grain.

BREAKFAST

Pastrami Hash

THE APPETIZING SHOP

Walking into a nonkosher certified delicatessen today, one is likely find a novel's worth of choices on the menu. In one section, there are the meats—served cured, smoked, and piled high on sandwiches, dried into garlicky sausages, or braised in rich gravy. In another section, there are bagel sandwiches slathered with cream cheese and draped with smoked fish, or fried latkes and sautéed dumplings dolloped with sour cream.

But at kosher delicatessens, bagels and cream cheese are not on the menu. Since, according to kosher law, milk and meat are not allowed to be eaten together at the same meal, delicatessens traditionally stuck to meat. The dairy delights, meanwhile, could be found at the "appetizing shop"— the curiously named retail establishment, and New York City culinary institution, that is home to all types of smoked and pickled fish, as well as other foods served with bagels.

In the early twentieth century, the appetizing shop reigned as the counterpart to the delicatessen—a place where New Yorkers jostled at the counter for lox and sable, herring, cream cheese, and baked farmer cheese. (These foods thrived in Jewish communities outside of New York, but the term "appetizing" never gained traction elsewhere.)

New York was once home to dozens of appetizing shops, but many closed as supermarkets started carrying cream cheese and smoked fish in their dairy cases. A few stalwarts still carry on the tradition, most notably Russ & Daughters, which has thrived on Manhattan's Lower East Side since 1914, and Barney Greengrass, on the Upper West Side since 1908. In recent years, a few new appetizing-focused shops have opened, including Shelsky's in Brooklyn and Schmaltz Appetizing in Toronto. Find out more about Russ & Daughters on page 421.

CHREMSLACH

While these petite matzo-meal fritters have fallen out of favor in recent decades, they were once an Ashkenazi mainstay on Passover. Studded with raisins and almonds, with crisp outsides and tender middles, they are worth revisiting.

Serves: 6
Preparation time: 15 minutes
Cooking time: 25 minutes

- 3 sheets matzo
- ½ cup (70 g) raisins
- ¼ cup (35 g) whole almonds, finely chopped
- 3 eggs
- ⅓ cup (40 g) matzo meal
- ⅓ cup (65 g) sugar, plus more for serving
- 1 teaspoon ground cinnamon
- 1 teaspoon finely grated lemon zest
- 1 tablespoon fresh lemon juice
- ¼ teaspoon kosher salt
- Vegetable oil, for frying
- Honey, for serving

Add the matzo sheets to a small baking dish and cover with warm water. Soak for 10 minutes then squeeze completely dry and place in a medium bowl. Add the raisins, almonds, eggs, matzo meal, sugar, cinnamon, lemon zest, lemon juice, and salt and mix well to combine.

In a large frying pan, heat ¼ inch (6 mm) oil over medium heat. Line a large plate with a few layers of paper towels. Working in batches of 5–6, spoon the batter by the rounded tablespoonful into the oil, pressing down gently with the back of the spoon to flatten. Fry, turning once, until golden brown on both sides, 3–4 minutes. Transfer the fritters to the paper towels to drain. Serve warm or at room temperature, drizzled with honey or dusted with sugar.

EVAN BLOOM, ARI BLOOM, AND LEO BECKERMAN

WISE SONS JEWISH DELICATESSEN

•

MULTIPLE LOCATIONS
SAN FRANCISCO, CA
USA

WISE SONS JEWISH DELICATESSEN

•

MARUNOUCHI BUILDING
B1F
MUNOUCHI CHIYODA-KU
TOKYO, JAPAN

Evan Bloom, Ari Bloom, and Leo Beckerman are co-founders of Wise Sons Jewish Delicatessen—an artisanal deli and Ashkenazi comfort-food restaurant based in San Francisco with a location in Tokyo.

EVERYTHING ONION DIP

This creamy sour cream and yogurt-based dip is reminiscent of a savory everything bagel. Caramelized onions give it a rich flavor while a mix of sesame, poppy, and caraway seeds lend a pop of crunch. Serve it alongside bagel chips or crudités.

Serves: 4–6
Preparation time: 15 minutes, plus chilling
Cooking time: 25 minutes

• 2 tablespoons extra-virgin olive oil, plus more for serving
• 1 onion, finely chopped
• 1 garlic clove, finely chopped
• ½ teaspoon kosher salt, plus more as needed
• ¼ teaspoon sugar
• 1½ teaspoons sesame seeds
• ¾ teaspoon poppy seeds
• ½ teaspoon caraway seeds
• ½ cup (120 g) sour cream
• ½ cup (120 g) whole-milk Greek yogurt
• Roughly chopped fresh dill and flat-leaf parsley, for serving

In a medium frying pan, heat the oil over medium heat. Add the onion and cook until softened and lightly browned, 6–8 minutes. Add the garlic, salt, and sugar. Reduce the heat to medium-low and cook, stirring often, until the onion is golden brown, 10–15 minutes. Add the sesame seeds, poppy seeds, and caraway seeds and cook, stirring, until fragrant, 1–2 minutes. Remove from the heat and let cool.

In a medium bowl, stir together the sour cream and yogurt. Add the cooled onion mixture. (Use a rubber spatula to scrape in any oil or seeds clinging to the bottom of the pan.) Mix well, then taste and add more salt, if desired. Transfer to a serving bowl, cover, and refrigerate to allow the flavors to develop, for at least 2 hours and up to 1 day. (The longer the mixture sits, the more flavorful it gets.) Before serving, drizzle with a little more oil and sprinkle generously with dill and parsley.

PASTRAMI LOX

In recent years, salmon cured with traditional pastrami spices has become popular at delicatessens across America. It is deceptively easy to make at home, and has a wonderfully complex flavor thanks to the addition of flinty smoked paprika, herbaceous coriander, and sweet allspice. Sliced thin and paired with bagels (pages 58–60) and cream cheese, it makes an unforgettable brunch or Yom Kippur break-fast meal.

Serves: 8
Preparation time: 15 minutes, plus curing

• 1 tablespoon black peppercorns
• 1 tablespoon coriander seeds
• 3 tablespoons smoked paprika
• 2 teaspoons mustard powder
• 2 teaspoons garlic powder
• ½ teaspoon ground allspice
• ⅔ cup (110 g) kosher salt
• ½ cup (100 g) sugar
• 1½–2 lb (680–910 g) skin-on salmon fillet, rinsed and thoroughly patted dry

In a small, dry frying pan, toast the peppercorns and coriander seeds over medium heat, shaking the pan occasionally, until they begin to pop, 1–2 minutes. Transfer to a plate to cool, then add to a mortar and pestle or spice grinder and coarsely crush.

In a large bowl, mix together the crushed spices, the smoked paprika, mustard powder, garlic powder, allspice, salt, and sugar.

Stretch a double layer of plastic wrap (cling film) into a shallow baking dish large enough to hold the salmon, letting the wrap hang over the edges of the dish by several inches. Sprinkle with half of the salt mixture. Using a sharp knife, make a few shallow cuts on the skin side of the salmon and place it, flesh side up, on top of the salt mixture. Cover with the remaining salt mixture.

Fold the plastic wrap ends around the salmon and cover snugly with additional plastic wrap. Refrigerate for 48–72 hours, turning the package once or twice a day and using fingers to redistribute the brine. Drain off any liquid that accumulates in the dish. When ready, the salmon should feel firm to the touch at the thickest part.

Unwrap the salmon and rinse the fillet well under water, discarding any brine in the baking dish. Use a sharp knife to thinly slice the lox against the grain.

Pastrami Lox

CHEESE BLINTZES

Blintzes—crepe-thin pancakes stuffed with sweet or savory fillings, rolled into tidy parcels, and then pan-fried until golden—are an Eastern European delicacy. Immigrants from that region brought blintzes with them to America, where they quickly caught on. Blintzes filled with everything from kasha to sauerkraut to potato (you can use the filling from the Potato Bourekas on page 212 for this version) remain popular at Jewish deli-catessens and diners. Today, Ashkenazi Jews typically serve cheese-filled blintzes on Shavuot, when eating dairy foods is de rigueur. Cheese blintzes were tradition-ally filled with thick farmer cheese, but you can also use easier-to-find ricotta. Serve the fried blintzes topped with a dollop of sour cream and a drizzle of Blueberry Sauce (page 395) or Strawberry Sauce (page 394).

Makes: about 18 blintzes
Preparation time: 30 minutes, plus resting
Cooking time: 35 minutes

For the batter:
• 1¾ cups (415 ml/14 fl oz) milk
• 5 eggs
• 4 tablespoons sugar
• 2 cups all-purpose (plain) flour
• teaspoon vanilla extract
• ½ teaspoon kosher salt

For the filling:
• 2 cups (480 g) farmer cheese or ricotta cheese
• 4 oz (115 g) cream cheese, at room temperature
• 4 tablespoons powdered (icing) sugar
• ½ teaspoon vanilla extract
• ½ teaspoon finely grated lemon zest (optional)
• About 1½ sticks (6 oz/170 g) unsalted butter, for frying

Make the blintz batter: In a food processor, combine the milk, eggs, sugar, flour, vanilla, and salt and process, scraping down the sides of the bowl as necessary, until smooth. The batter should be the consistency of heavy cream. Let the batter rest at room temperature for at least 30 minutes.

Meanwhile, make the filling: In a small bowl, stir together the farmer cheese, cream cheese, powdered (icing) sugar, vanilla, and lemon zest (if using) until combined. Cover and refrigerate until ready to use.

Cook the blintz wrappers: In a 7- to 8-inch (18 to 20 cm) nonstick frying pan, melt about 1 teaspoon butter over medium heat. Once hot, pour ¼ cup (60 g) of batter into the pan. Immediately pick up the pan and swirl it in all directions to coat the bottom evenly with a thin layer of batter. Cook until the bottom is golden and the center is just dry, about 1 minute. (Do not flip the blintz wrapper.) Remove the wrapper with a spatula and place it on a piece of parchment paper. Continue making the wrappers, stacking them in between small sheets of parchment as you go. You should end up with about 18 wrappers.

To fill the wrappers, spoon 2 heaping tablespoons of the filling onto the lower third of each wrapper, leaving ½ inch (1.25 cm) at the bottom. Fold that ½ inch up over the filling, then fold in each side toward the center. Roll the blintz up and away from you, tucking the filling inside a neat package. Lay the filled blintz, seam side down, on a plate and continue the process with the remaining wrappers and filling.

In a large frying pan, heat about 1 tablespoon (15 g) butter over medium heat. Working in batches, place the blintzes, seam side down, in the pan and cook, turning once, until golden brown on both sides, 1–2 minutes per side. Remove from the pan and let cool on a plate while continuing to fry the remaining blintzes. Serve warm or at room temperature.

Cheese Blintzes

PASSOVER BLINTZES

Wheat flour is forbidden during the week of Passover, so this holiday-friendly version of blintzes relies instead on potato starch. The resulting blintz wrappers are light and delicate, but stand up well to either a sweet cheese or savory potato filling. Top them with sour cream and, if filled with cheese, with a dollop of sweet-tart jam.

Serves: 4–6
Preparation time: 30 minutes
Cooking time: 35 minutes

- ¾ cup (135 g) potato starch
- 4 eggs
- 1 tablespoon sugar
- ½ teaspoon kosher salt
- Vegetable oil, for frying
- Filling from Potato Bourekas (page 212) or Cheese Blintzes (page 30)

In a large bowl, whisk together the potato starch and 1 cup (240 ml/8 fl oz) water until the starch is dissolved. Beat in the eggs, sugar, and salt until a loose batter forms.

In a 7- to 8-inch (18 to 20 cm) nonstick frying pan, heat about 1 teaspoon vegetable oil over medium heat. Once hot, pour ¼ cup (60 g) of the batter into the pan. Immediately pick up the pan and swirl it in all directions to coat the bottom evenly with a thin layer of batter. Cook until the bottom is golden and the center is just dry, 1–2 minutes. (Do not flip.) Carefully remove the wrapper with a spatula and place it on a large plate or baking sheet. Continue making wrappers with the remaining batter.

To fill the wrappers, spoon 2 heaping tablespoons of desired filling onto the lower third of the wrapper, leaving ½ inch (1.25 cm) at the bottom. Fold that ½ inch up over the filling, then fold in each side toward the center. Roll the blintz up and away from you, tucking the filling inside a neat package. Lay the filled blintz, seam side down, on a plate and continue with the remaining wrappers and filling.

In a large frying pan, heat about 1 tablespoon oil over medium heat. Working in batches, place 5–6 blintzes, seam side down, in the pan and cook, turning once, until golden brown on both sides, 1–2 minutes per side. Remove from the pan and let cool on a plate while continuing to fry the remaining blintzes. Serve warm or at room temperature.

MATZO COFFEE

This simple and old-school Passover breakfast is a bit of an acquired taste, but worth trying. The recipe can easily be scaled up to serve more people, and the sugar and half-and-half (single cream) levels should be adjusted to taste. Start with very hot, very fresh coffee and serve it with a spoon for scooping up the velvety-soft matzo pieces.

Serves: 1
Preparation time: 5 minutes

- 1 teaspoon half-and-half (single cream)
- 1 teaspoon sugar
- 1 sheet matzo, crumbled into 2-inch (5 cm) pieces
- 1 cup (240 ml/8 fl oz) freshly brewed coffee (not espresso)

In a large mug, stir together the half-and-half (single cream) and sugar. Add as many of the matzo pieces as comfortably fit in the mug. Pour the coffee on top and stir gently. Serve immediately.

LAUREL KRATOCHVILA

FINE BAGELS
•
**WARSCHAUER STRASSE 74
BERLIN, GERMANY**

Laurel Kratochvila is the proprietor of Fine Bagels, an artisanal bagel and pastry shop in Berlin. Originally from the United States, but with Jewish baking roots that stretch back four generations to Warsaw, Kratochvila's bagels include both traditional (sesame seed, salt, everything) and innovative (za'atar, rosemary sea salt) flavors.

CRÈME D'AMANDES CHALLAH PERDU

This recipe is Kratochvila's take on the French dish *pain perdu*. Slices of challah French toast get an extra step of caramelization and a layer of baked-on almond cream that gives them the decadent flavor of an almond croissant.

Serves: 6–8
Preparation time: 30 minutes
Cooking time: 45 minutes

For the almond cream:
• 1 stick (4 oz/115 g) unsalted butter, at room temperature
• ½ cup (100 g) sugar
• ¾ cup (90 g) almond flour (ground almonds)
• 2 eggs
• ¼ teaspoon almond extract

For the French toast:
• 8 eggs
• 2 cups (475 ml/16 fl oz) whole milk
• 2 teaspoons vanilla extract
• ½ teaspoon kosher salt
• Unsalted butter, for frying
• 1 lb (455 g) loaf challah, cut into slices 1 inch (2.5 cm) thick
• Sugar, for sprinkling

• Sliced (flaked) almonds, for sprinkling
• Powdered (icing) sugar, for dusting

Make the almond cream: In a stand mixer fitted with the paddle attachment, beat the butter on medium speed until completely smooth, about 3 minutes. Add the sugar and beat at medium speed, scraping down the sides of the bowl as necessary, until fully incorporated. Beat in the almond flour, then beat in the eggs 1 at a time, followed by the almond extract. Increase the speed to high and beat until light in color and completely smooth, about 4 minutes. Transfer the mixture to a piping bag (if the almond cream will be piped on top of the toast), or simply set the bowl aside (if the cream will be spooned).

Make the French toast: Line a large baking sheet with parchment paper and set aside. In a medium bowl, whisk together the eggs, milk, vanilla, and salt. In a large nonstick frying pan, heat 1 tablespoon (15 g) butter over medium heat. Working in batches of 2, dip the challah slices on both sides into the egg mixture, then add to the pan. Fry, flipping once, until golden brown on both sides, 2–3 minutes per side. Sprinkle both pieces evenly with about ½ teaspoon sugar and fry for 1 minute longer. Flip and repeat the sugar sprinkling and frying on the other side. Transfer the fried challah slices to the prepared baking sheet. Repeat with the remaining slices of challah, adding more butter to the pan as necessary. Allow the fried challah pieces to cool completely while preheating the oven.

Preheat the oven to 350°F (180°C/Gas Mark 4).

Once the fried challah is cool, pipe or spoon an even layer of the almond cream on top of each piece of toast, leaving about a ½-inch (1.25 cm) border on all sides (the cream will spread during baking). Sprinkle the tops with the sliced (flaked) almonds. Bake until the topping is golden brown and gently puffed, 7–8 minutes. Remove from the oven and transfer to a serving platter. Lightly dust with powdered (icing) sugar and serve hot.

MATZO MEAL PANCAKES

Fluffy matzo meal pancakes, sometimes called *bubaleh* (a Yiddish term of endearment), make a convincing Passover-friendly alternative to traditional flour-based pancakes. Serve them fresh from the frying pan topped with sour cream and jam, maple syrup, or a hefty sprinkle of cinnamon sugar.

Serves: 4
Preparation time: 10 minutes
Cooking time: 25 minutes

- 1 cup (130 g) matzo meal
- 1 tablespoon sugar
- 1 teaspoon baking powder
- 1 teaspoon kosher salt
- 2 eggs, lightly beaten
- 1½ cups (355 ml/12 fl oz) milk or water, plus more as needed
- Vegetable oil, for frying

In a large bowl, whisk together the matzo meal, sugar, baking powder, and salt. Add the eggs and milk and whisk until combined. Let stand 5 minutes to allow the matzo meal to absorb the liquid. The mixture should be thick but pourable. If necessary, whisk in a little more milk until the desired consistency is reached.

In a large nonstick frying pan, heat about 2 teaspoons of oil over medium heat. Working in batches of 3–4, pour the batter by the ¼ cup (60 g) into the frying pan, nudging gently into rounds. Cook until tiny bubbles appear on the surface, 1–2 minutes. Flip and continue cooking until golden brown on both sides, another 1–2 minutes. Transfer the cooked pancakes to a large plate and serve immediately.

CHALLAH FRENCH TOAST

Day-old challah makes an ideal base for French toast. It is no surprise, then, that Jewish delicatessens across America serve rich, custardy French toast made from the classic Shabbat bread. For an autumnal treat, start with the Sephardi *pan de calabaza* (Yeasted Pumpkin Bread, page 52).

Serves: 2 or 3
Preparation time: 10 minutes
Cooking time: 10 minutes

- 6 eggs
- ¾ cup (175 ml/6 fl oz) milk
- ½ teaspoon kosher salt
- 6 slices (1 inch/2.5 cm thick) Challah (page 46) or Yeasted Pumpkin Bread (page 52)
- 2 tablespoons (30 g) unsalted butter
- Maple syrup and ground cinnamon, for serving

In a shallow dish, whisk together the eggs, milk, and salt. Working in batches, lay the bread slices in the egg mixture and let sit, turning once, until soaked through, about 2 minutes per side.

In a large frying pan, melt about 1 tablespoon (15 g) butter over medium heat until foaming. Fry half of the bread slices, flipping once, until golden brown on both sides, 2–3 minutes per side. Repeat with another 1 tablespoon (15 g) butter and the remaining bread slices. Serve immediately, drizzled with maple syrup and sprinkled with a little cinnamon.

Matzo Meal Pancakes

CHEESE DANISH

Originating in Austria, these yeasted pastries, which are typically filled with cheese or fruit, became wildly popular in America during the mid-twentieth century. For decades, they were a mainstay at Jewish bakeries as well as in diners and coffee shops. They have since fallen from ubiquity but are still served after a bris ceremony and on Sunday mornings. This recipe yields a tender, almost cookielike dough that provides a delicious vessel for the sweet and lemony cream cheese filling. For a puffier Danish, substitute 1 pound (455 g) of store-bought frozen puff pastry. After thawing, roll, cut, and bake it according to this recipe's directions.

Makes: about 20 pastries
Preparation time: 40 minutes, plus resting
Cooking time: 20 minutes

For the dough:
- 1 packet (¼ oz/7 g) active dry yeast (2¼ teaspoons)
- ½ cup (100 g) plus 1 teaspoon sugar
- ⅓ cup (75 ml/2½ fl oz) milk, warmed (110°F/43°C)
- 3–3¼ cups (420–455 g) all-purpose (plain) flour, plus more for rolling
- 1 teaspoon kosher salt
- 2 eggs
- 1 stick (4 oz/115 g) unsalted butter, at room temperature
- ¼ cup (60 g) sour cream, at room temperature

For the filling:
- 12 oz (340 g) cream cheese, at room temperature
- ½ cup (60 g) powdered (icing) sugar
- 1 egg yolk (reserve the white for egg wash)
- 1 tablespoon all-purpose (plain) flour
- ½ teaspoon finely grated lemon zest
- 1 teaspoon vanilla extract
- ⅛ teaspoon kosher salt
- About ½ cup (180 g) raspberry or apricot jam (optional)

Make the dough: In a stand mixer fitted with the paddle attachment, combine the yeast, 1 teaspoon of the sugar, and warmed milk and let sit until foamy, 5–10 minutes. Meanwhile, in a bowl, whisk together 3 cups (420 g) of the flour, the remaining ½ cup (100 g) sugar, and the salt.

Add the eggs, butter, sour cream, and flour mixture to the bubbling yeast mixture and beat at low speed (increasing to medium when the flour is incorporated) until a soft and pliable but not sticky dough forms. If needed, sprinkle in up to 4 tablespoons additional flour, 1 tablespoon at a time, to reach the desired consistency. (You might not use all the flour.) Form the dough into a ball and place it back in the stand mixer bowl. Cover the bowl with a clean tea towel and let rest for 1 hour.

Meanwhile, make the filling: In a medium bowl, beat together the cream cheese, powdered (icing) sugar, egg yolk, flour, lemon zest, vanilla, and salt. Refrigerate until needed.

Preheat the oven to 375°F (190°C/Gas Mark 5). Line 2 large sheet pans with parchment paper.

Working with about half of the dough at a time (leaving the other half covered in the bowl), roll out the dough into a large square or rectangle, about ¼ inch (6 mm) thick. Use a knife to trim off any ragged ends. Cut the dough into about 4-inch (10 cm) squares. Spoon a rounded tablespoon of the cream cheese filling into the center of one square. If desired, nestle 1 teaspoon jam in the center of the filling. Fold one corner of the pastry to the center, then fold in the opposite corner, overlapping the first corner and press firmly to seal where they meet. Lay the filled pastry on the sheet pan and repeat with the remaining dough and filling. Whisk the reserved egg white with 1 teaspoon water and brush the pastries with a little egg wash.

Bake, rotating the pans halfway through baking, until puffed and golden brown, 15–20 minutes.

BLUEBERRY BUNS

In the 1920s, a Polish Jewish immigrant to Canada named Annie Kaplansky started selling small, yeasted buns stuffed with blueberries at her bakeshop, Health Bread Bakery. The tender, fruit-filled pastry had roots in Eastern Europe (a similar sweet called *jagodzianki* is still enjoyed in Poland today), but quickly became a hallmark of Toronto's Jewish cuisine. Soon, other Jewish bakeries across the city started selling the buns, too, helping to shape generations of culinary memories for Toronto's Jewish community.

Makes: about 2 dozen pastries
Preparation time: 50 minutes
Cooking time: 20 minutes

- 1 packet (¼ oz/7 g) active dry yeast (2¼ teaspoons)
- ½ cup (100 g) plus 1 teaspoon sugar
- ⅔ cup (150 ml/5 fl oz) warm water (110°F/43°C)
- 3¼–3½ cups (455–490 g) all-purpose (plain) flour, plus more for kneading and rolling
- ¾ teaspoon kosher salt
- ¼ cup (60 ml/2 fl oz) vegetable oil, plus more for greasing the bowl
- 3 eggs
- 1 teaspoon vanilla extract
- Double recipe Blueberry Sauce (page 395)
- Coarse sugar, for topping

In a large bowl, stir together the yeast, 1 teaspoon of the sugar, and the water and let sit until bubbling and frothy, 5–10 minutes.

Meanwhile, in a medium bowl, whisk together 3¼ cups (455 g) of the flour, the remaining ½ cup (100 g) sugar, and the salt.

Whisk the oil, 2 of the eggs, and the vanilla into the yeast and water mixture until combined. Add the flour mixture and stir until a shaggy dough begins to form. Turn the dough out onto a lightly floured surface and knead well, adding up to 4 tablespoons additional flour, as necessary, until a supple, slightly sticky dough forms, about 10 minutes. (The kneading can also be done in a stand mixer with a dough hook, 5–7 minutes.) Grease a large bowl with about 1 teaspoon oil, add the dough, and turn to coat. Cover with a tea towel and let sit in a warm place until doubled in size, about 1½ hours.

Line 2 large baking sheets with parchment paper. Pinch off golf ball–size pieces of dough and, on a lightly floured surface, pat and press into 4-inch (10 cm) rounds. (Keep any remaining dough covered, so it does not dry out.) Spoon 1 heaping tablespoon blueberry sauce into the center of each round. Bring the sides of the rounds up to meet each other, tucking the filling inside and pinching along the seam to seal. Gently form the sealed buns into ovals and place, seam side down, on the prepared baking sheets, leaving about 1 inch (2.5 cm) space in between.

In a small bowl, beat the remaining egg with 1 teaspoon water for an egg wash. Brush the tops of the buns with the egg wash (you will not use all of it). Sprinkle the tops generously with coarse sugar and then let them rest while the oven preheats.

Preheat the oven to 375°F (190°C/Gas Mark 5). Bake until golden brown and puffed, 15–20 minutes. (It is okay if some of the blueberry filling leaks out during baking.) Transfer the buns to wire racks to cool. Serve warm or at room temperature. Serve any extra blueberry sauce on the side to drizzle on top.

SCHNECKEN

Tasting like a cross between a sticky bun and rugelach, these glazed, nut- and currant-filled pastries check all the indulgence boxes. The word *schnecken* means "snails" in German. They are sweet enough to be served for dessert, but really shine as a breakfast pastry.

Makes: about 2 dozen pastries
Preparation time: 40 minutes, plus rising
Cooking time: 25 minutes

For the dough:
• 1 packet (¼ oz/7 g) active dry yeast (2¼ teaspoons)
• ½ cup (100 g) plus 1 teaspoon sugar
• ¼ cup (60 ml/2 fl oz) warm water (110°F/43°C)
• 3½–4 cups (490–560 g) all-purpose (plain) flour, plus more for kneading and rolling
• ½ teaspoon kosher salt
• ¾ cup (175 ml/6 fl oz) milk
• 1 egg, lightly beaten
• 1 teaspoon vanilla extract
• 1 teaspoon finely grated lemon zest
• 4 oz (115 g) cream cheese, cut into pieces, at room temperature
• 1 teaspoon vegetable oil

For the filling:
• 1½ cups (155 g) pecan halves, roughly chopped
• 1¼ sticks (5 oz/140 g) unsalted butter, at room temperature
• 1¼ cups (225 g) light brown sugar
• 2 teaspoons ground cinnamon
• 1 cup (140 g) dried currants or raisins

For the caramel glaze:
• 1 stick (4 oz/115 g) unsalted butter, melted
• 1 cup (180 g) light brown sugar
• ¼ teaspoon kosher salt

Make the dough: In a large bowl, stir together the yeast, 1 teaspoon of the sugar, and the warm water. Let sit until foaming, 5–10 minutes.

In a second bowl, whisk together 3½ cups (490 g) flour, the remaining ½ cup (100 g) sugar, and the salt.

Stir the milk, egg, vanilla, and lemon zest into the yeast mixture. Add the flour mixture and stir until a wet dough comes together.

Turn the dough out onto a floured surface. Knead well, adding the softened cream cheese pieces a few at a time, and adding enough additional flour (up to ½ cup/70 g) to achieve a supple, slightly tacky dough, about 10 minutes. (The kneading can also be done in a stand mixer with a dough hook, 5–7 minutes.) Grease a large bowl with the oil, add the dough, and turn to coat. Cover the bowl with plastic wrap (cling film) or a clean tea towel and let sit in a warm place until doubled in size, 1½–2 hours.

Meanwhile, make the filling: In a food processor, combine the pecans, butter, brown sugar, and cinnamon and pulse, scraping down the sides of the bowl as necessary, until a smooth paste forms.

Preheat the oven to 375°F (190°C/Gas Mark 5).

Meanwhile, make the caramel glaze: In a medium bowl, stir together the melted butter, brown sugar, and salt. Divide the glaze evenly between two 9 × 13-inch (23 × 33 cm) baking dishes, smoothing across the bottom of each.

Gently punch down the dough, turn out onto a floured surface, and divide in half, keeping 1 piece covered in the bowl while working with the remaining piece. Roll out the dough into a large rectangle ¼ inch (6 mm) thick.

Evenly spread half of the filling over the dough, leaving a ¼-inch (6 mm) border around the edges. Evenly sprinkle half of the currants over the top. Starting at one of the long ends, roll the dough up tightly like a jelly roll (Swiss roll). Using a sharp knife, cut the roll crosswise into 1-inch (2.5 cm) segments. Transfer the rolls to one of the baking dishes, nestling each one into the glaze. Repeat the process with the remaining dough, filling, and currants, fitting them into the second baking dish.

Bake, rotating the dishes front to back halfway through, until golden brown and cooked through, 20–25 minutes.

Meanwhile, line 2 large baking sheets with parchment paper.

Remove the baking dishes from the oven and let sit until the glaze stops actively bubbling, 2–3 minutes. Invert the *schnecken* onto the prepared baking sheets, spooning any extra glaze left in the baking dish on top. Let cool slightly and serve warm.

Schnecken

COILED CINNAMON BUNS

These coiled Dutch pastries, called *zeeuwse bolussen*, were first developed by Sephardi Jews who fled Spain and Portugal for Amsterdam during the Spanish Inquisition. They taste similar to American-style cinnamon rolls, though not iced and more subtly sweet overall. They are traditionally served for breakfast spread with a thick layer of softened butter. To warm the milk for the dough, heat it in a microwave in 30-second intervals until it feels hot to the touch, but isn't boiling.

Makes: about 15 buns
Preparation time: 40 minutes, plus resting
Cooking time: 10 minutes

- 1 packet (¼ oz/7 g) active dry yeast (2¼ teaspoons)
- 4 tablespoons plus 1 teaspoon sugar
- 1 cup (240 ml/8 fl oz) milk, warmed (110°F/43°C)
- 3–3½ cups (420–490 g) all-purpose (plain) flour
- ¾ teaspoon kosher salt
- 1 egg
- 1 stick (4 oz/115 g) unsalted butter, cut into chunks, at room temperature
- 1 cup (180 g) light brown sugar
- 1 tablespoon ground cinnamon

In a stand mixer fitted with the paddle attachment, combine the yeast, 1 teaspoon of the sugar, and warmed milk and let sit until foamy, 5–10 minutes.

Meanwhile, in a bowl, whisk together 3 cups (420 g) of the flour and the salt.

Add the egg and remaining 4 tablespoons sugar to the yeast mixture and beat on low until combined. Add the flour mixture and beat until the dough just comes together. (It will still be wet and sticky at this point.) Switch to a dough hook and add the butter pieces. Knead at medium speed, adding up to ½ cup (70 g) additional flour as needed, until the dough is soft and supple. (You might not use all the flour.) Remove bowl from the stand mixer, cover with a tea towel, and let rest for 15 minutes.

Meanwhile, line a large baking sheet with parchment paper. In a large bowl, whisk together the brown sugar and cinnamon until fully combined.

Pull off a 2-ounce (55 g) piece of dough (slightly larger than a golf ball), roll into a ball, roll in the cinnamon-sugar mixture, and place on the prepared baking sheet. Continue with the remaining dough. Cover and let rest for 20 minutes.

Preheat the oven to 450°F (230°C/Gas Mark 8).

Working with 1 ball of dough at a time, roll into a 7-inch (18 cm) rope. Roll the rope again in the cinnamon sugar. Starting from one end, coil the roll onto itself, tucking the final end underneath, and place it back on the baking sheet. Continue with remaining dough balls and cinnamon sugar mixture. Cover lightly and let rest for 20 more minutes.

Bake until puffed and cooked through, about 10 minutes. (Watch carefully to make sure the sugar doesn't burn.) Transfer the buns to a wire rack to cool. Serve warm and store leftovers, well wrapped, at room temperature for up to 3 days or in the freezer for up to 3 months. Reheat and refresh leftovers in the toaster (mini) oven or oven.

JACHNUN

Like a croissant but denser, this slow-cooked Yemenite pastry is traditionally served on Shabbat morning with hard-boiled eggs and a variety of fresh and spicy condiments. The dough (called *ajin*) is stretched as thinly as possible, slathered with clarified butter (*samneh*), then tightly rolled and steamed overnight at a low temperature to yield a hearty morning dish that tastes like pure comfort. To make *jachnun* dairy-free, spread the dough with additional vegetable oil instead of *samneh* or butter. It will not be quite as moist or flavorful, but will still be delicious.

Serves: 6
Preparation time: 35 minutes, plus resting
Cooking time: 10 hours

- 3 cups (420 g) all-purpose (plain) flour,
  plus more for kneading
- 2 tablespoons sugar
- ½ teaspoon baking powder
- 2 teaspoons kosher salt
- ¼ cup (60 ml/2 fl oz) vegetable oil
- Samneh, ghee, or softened unsalted butter,
  at room temperature, for spreading
- 6 eggs, in the shell (optional)
- Grated Tomato Relish (page 411), Hilbeh (page 409),
  and S'chug (page 411), for serving

In a large bowl, combine the flour, sugar, baking powder, salt, oil, and 1 cup (240 ml/8 fl oz) water and stir until the dough begins to come together. Turn the dough out onto a lightly floured surface and knead until supple, about 10 minutes. (The kneading step can also be done in a stand mixer with a dough hook until the desired consistency is reached, 5–7 minutes.) Shape the dough into a ball and place back into the bowl. Cover the bowl and let rest at room temperature for 1 hour. (The dough can also be refrigerated overnight. Let it come to room temperature before proceeding.)

Divide the dough into 6 equal balls. Working on an oiled surface with 1 ball of dough at a time (keeping the others covered), press and roll it out into a large, very thin rectangle. The dough should be translucent, and it is okay if it rips in a few places.

Spread about 2 teaspoons of *samneh* over the surface, then fold the dough over itself into thirds (like folding a letter). Roll out the dough again in both directions to make another large, thin rectangle. Starting at one of the short ends, roll up the rectangle like a jelly roll (Swiss roll). Cut a square of parchment paper just big enough to cradle the roll and place the dough in the center, then add to the bottom of a slow cooker. Repeat the process with the remaining dough, adding more oil to the rolling surface as necessary, and tucking each dough roll into a parchment square before adding to the slow cooker.

If desired, nestle eggs into the slow cooker. Cover all of the dough rolls and the eggs (if using) with another piece of parchment paper, to help facilitate steaming. Cover the slow cooker and cook on low until the dough is caramelized and flaky and the eggs are well browned, about 8 hours. Remove the *jachnun* bundles and eggs from the slow cooker (discarding the parchment), and serve hot or warm with the eggs, tomato relish, *hilbeh*, and *s'chug* alongside.

CHEESE BAGELS

This horseshoe-shaped pastry likely has roots in Eastern Europe, but today is closely associated with Montreal's Jewish community. There, the breakfast pastries, called either cheese bagels or *bagelach*, come filled with lightly sweetened farmer cheese. They are sold at kosher bakeries and also prepared by home cooks—either way, they make a decadent treat for breakfast or brunch.

Makes: 6 large pastries
Preparation time: 30 minutes
Cooking time: 30 minutes

- 1 lb (455 g) farmer cheese
- 1 egg yolk (reserve the white for egg wash)
- 2 tablespoons all-purpose (plain) flour, plus more for rolling
- ⅓ cup (65 g) sugar
- ½ teaspoon finely grated lemon zest
- 1 teaspoon vanilla extract
- ¼ teaspoon kosher salt
- 1 sheet frozen puff pastry, thawed

Preheat the oven to 350°F (180°C/Gas Mark 4). Line a large baking sheet with parchment paper.

In a bowl, mix together the farmer cheese, egg yolk, flour, sugar, lemon zest, vanilla, and salt until fully combined.

On a lightly floured surface using a lightly floured rolling pin, roll out the puff pastry into a 12 × 18-inch (30 × 46 cm) rectangle. Spread half of the cheese filling in a thick line along one of the long sides of the pastry, leaving about a ½-inch (1.25 cm) border. Roll the dough over the filling (like making a jelly roll/Swiss roll) one time, just far enough to encase the filling inside the dough. Run a sharp knife along the edge of the roll to trim off the remaining dough and set the trimmed dough aside. Cut the filled roll crosswise into 3 equal-size shorter rolls. Curve each roll into a U shape and place on the prepared baking sheet. Repeat with the reserved strip of dough and the remaining filling to make 3 more pastries. Evenly brush the tops of the filled pastries with a little of the reserved egg white (you might not use all of it).

Bake, rotating the baking sheet front to back halfway through, until puffed and golden brown, about 30 minutes. Transfer the pastries to wire racks to cool.

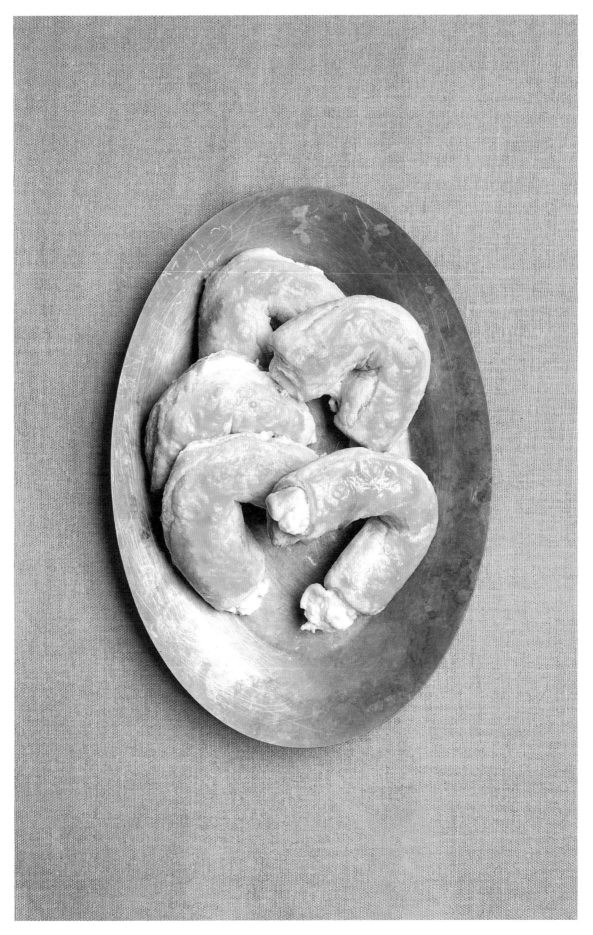

Cheese Bagels

BREADS

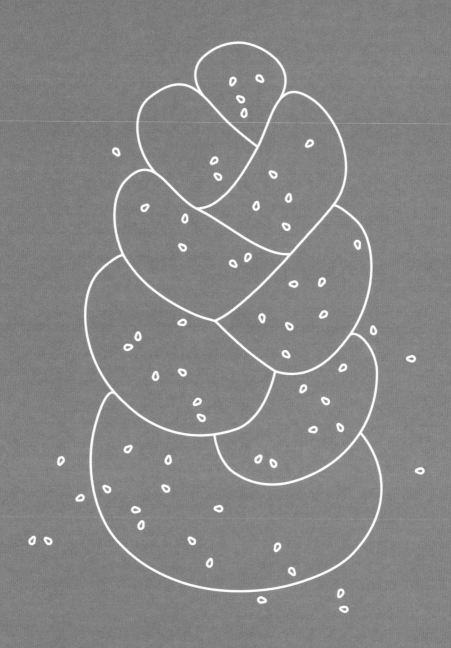

CHALLAH

Arguably one of the most universally recognized Jewish breads, these braided (plaited), egg-enriched loaves are comfortingly tender and rich. They are traditionally served by Ashkenazi Jews as the ritual bread on Shabbat and holidays, but leftovers also make delicious Challah French Toast (page 34) on Sunday mornings. On Rosh Hashanah, many families add raisins to their challah to infuse a bit of extra sweetness for the New Year. (For more information on challah, see facing page.)

Makes: 2 loaves
Preparation tIme: 25 minutes, plus rising
Cooking time: 35 minutes

• 1 tablespoon active dry yeast
• ½ cup (100 g) plus 1 teaspoon sugar
• 1 cup (240 ml/8 fl oz) warm water (110°F/43°C)
• 4½–5 cups (630–700 g) all-purpose (plain) flour, plus more for kneading and rolling
• 1½ teaspoons kosher salt
• ⅓ cup (75 ml/2½ fl oz) vegetable oil, plus more for greasing the bowl
• 3 eggs
• 1 cup (140 g) raisins, soaked in water for 5 minutes and drained (optional)
• Sesame seeds or poppy seeds, for topping (optional)

In a very large bowl, stir together the yeast, 1 teaspoon of the sugar, and the warm water. Let sit until foaming, 5–10 minutes.

Meanwhile, in a separate large bowl, whisk together 4½ cups (630 g) of the flour, the remaining ½ cup (100 g) sugar, and the salt.

Add the oil and 2 of the eggs to the yeast mixture and whisk to combine. Add the flour mixture and raisins (if using) and stir until a shaggy dough begins to form. Turn the dough out onto a lightly floured surface and knead well, adding up to ½ cup (70 g) more flour, a little at a time, as necessary until a supple, elastic dough forms, about 10 minutes. (The kneading can also be done in a stand mixer with a dough hook, 5–7 minutes.) Grease a large bowl with about 1 teaspoon of oil, add the dough, and turn to coat. Cover with plastic wrap (cling film) or a clean tea towel and let sit in a warm place until doubled in size, about 2 hours.

Line a large baking sheet with parchment paper. Gently deflate the dough with the heel of your hand and divide in half. Divide each dough half into thirds and roll each third into a long rope. Pinch the top of 3 ropes together and braid (plait), pinching at the bottom to seal. Place the braided loaf on the prepared baking sheet. Repeat the process with the remaining 3 ropes.

Meanwhile, preheat the oven to 375°F (190°C/ Gas Mark 5).

Whisk the remaining egg in a small bowl and brush the loaves with one coat of egg wash. (Set the remaining egg wash aside in the fridge.) Cover the loaves loosely with lightly greased parchment paper and let rise for another 30 minutes.

Uncover the loaves and brush with a second coat of egg wash. Sprinkle with sesame or poppy seeds, if desired, and bake until deep golden brown and cooked through, or until an instant-read thermometer inserted in the center of the loaf registers 195°F (90°C), 30–35 minutes. Transfer the loaves to a wire rack to cool for 15 minutes before slicing. Revive leftovers by reheating them briefly in an oven or toaster (mini) oven.

CHALLAH AND THE SHABBAT TABLE

The Shabbat table holds ample symbolic weight on top of its freshly pressed tablecloth and four sturdy legs. After the destruction of the Holy Temple in Jerusalem, the rabbis of the time transferred many of the rites once performed there (blessing wine, lighting candles, etc.) to the home. At the center of the domestic ritual is bread—loaves meant to represent the "showbreads" that were once placed on the altar in divine offering. Many families sprinkle salt over challah after reciting the blessings—a practice that directly connects back to the Temple.

Shabbat tables are usually graced with two (or more) loaves of bread, called *lechem mishneh*, which symbolizes the double portion of manna the ancient Israelites gathered before Shabbat while wandering in the wilderness. For many families, *lechem mishneh* refers to challah—thick, eggy loaves twisted into braids (plaits) and baked until bronzed outside and pillowy soft within.

For centuries, challah did not have a specific form, but in the fifteenth century in Austria and southern Germany, Jews adopted the shape of a Teutonic solstice bread, braided to resemble the hair of a malevolent demon called Bertcha or Holle. Jewish families dropped the solstice and demon references, but kept the braided loaves, vaulting them to the center of Shabbat and holiday celebrations. Originally made without eggs (see Potato Challah, 49), challah dough eventually got enriched with eggs as it spread throughout Europe.

There are many ways to braid challah dough. The most common form is a three-strand braid, but some people prefer to make loaves with more strands, to shape the dough into a spiral, or even to make small, knotted rolls. Here are a few basic techniques:

3-STRAND BRAID: Divide the dough into 3 equal pieces and roll each piece into a long rope. Lay the ropes side by side and pinch at the top to connect. Grab the rope on the right and cross it over the middle rope. (That now becomes the middle rope.) Take the rope on the left and cross it over the middle rope. (That now becomes the middle rope.) Continue braiding in that fashion until you reach the bottom of the ropes. Pinch the bottom to connect and gently transfer the braid to a prepared baking sheet.

4-STRAND BRAID: Divide the dough into 4 equal pieces and roll each piece into a long rope. Lay the ropes side by side and pinch at the top to connect. Grab the rope furthest to the right and weave it toward the left weaving over the rope closest to it, under the following rope, and over the final rope. Continue braiding in this fashion, always starting with the rope furthest to the right and weaving over, under, over, until you reach the bottom of the ropes. Pinch the bottom to connect and gently transfer the braid to a prepared baking sheet.

6-STRAND BRAID: Divide the dough into 6 equal pieces and roll each piece into a long rope. Lay the ropes side by side and pinch at the top to connect. Grab the rope furthest to the right and weave it toward the left passing over 2 ropes, under 1 rope, and over the final 2 ropes. Continue in this fashion, always starting with the rope furthest to the right, until you reach the bottom of the ropes. Pinch the bottom to connect and gently transfer the braid to a prepared baking sheet.

ROUND/SPIRAL: Roll the dough into a long rope, about 24 inches (60 cm) long. Coil the rope in on itself and place in a lightly greased, round baking pan, tucking the end underneath. This loaf, which is commonly used on Rosh Hashanah, will take slightly longer to bake than a traditional braid.

ROLLS/KNOTS: Pinch off small handfuls of dough and roll into ropes 6–7 inches (15–18 cm) long. Tie the ropes into single knots and place on baking sheets. Rolls will take slightly less time to bake than a traditional braid.

KUBANEH

On Saturday mornings, Yemenite Jews serve this majestic, pull-apart yeast bread, as part of a Shabbat breakfast spread. Slathered with butter (traditionally clarified butter, called *samneh*) and baked overnight in a very low oven, the dough caramelizes and gains a rich, mahogany color. Serve the bread with quartered hard-boiled eggs or Huevos Haminados (page 16), S'chug (page 411), and Grated Tomato Relish (page 411).

Serves: 6
Preparation time: 45 minutes
Cooking time: 8 hours

- 1 packet (¼ oz/7g) active dry yeast (2¼ teaspoons)
- ⅓ cup (65 g) plus 1 teaspoon sugar
- 1¼ cups (295 ml/10 fl oz) warm water (110°F/43°C)
- 3½–3¾ cups (490–525 g) all-purpose (plain) flour
- 1½ teaspoons kosher salt
- 15 tablespoons (215 g) unsalted butter, samneh, or ghee, at room temperature
- Vegetable oil, for greasing the work surface

In a stand mixer fitted with the paddle attachment, stir together the yeast, 1 teaspoon of the sugar, and the warm water. Let sit until foaming, 5–10 minutes.

Meanwhile, in a large bowl, whisk together 3½ cups (490 g) flour, the remaining ⅓ cup (65 g) sugar, and the salt.

Add the flour mixture to the water mixture and beat at low speed until the dough comes together. Switch to a dough hook and knead, adding up to ¼ cup (35 g) additional flour, a little at a time, as necessary until a supple, elastic dough forms, 7–8 minutes. (You might not need all the additional flour.) Cover the bowl with a tea towel and let rest until doubled in size, about 1 hour.

Spread 2 tablespoons of the butter evenly around the bottom and sides of a 9-inch (23 cm) round springform pan. Next, spread a couple of teaspoons of oil on a flat work surface. Gently deflate the dough with the heel of your hand, then divide into 6 equal pieces. Working on the oiled surface with one piece of dough at a time, use your hands and fingers to stretch it into a large, very thin rectangle. (It is okay if it tears in a couple of spots.) Spread 2 tablespoons of the softened butter evenly over the top. Starting at one of the long sides, roll the dough up like a jelly roll (Swiss roll), then coil it onto itself, tucking the end underneath. Place the spiral in the prepared pan, then repeat with the remaining dough and butter, arranging the coils like a flower in the pan. Spread the remaining tablespoon of butter on top, then loosely cover the pan with a tea towel and let the dough coils rise until they reach the top of the pan, about 30 minutes.

Meanwhile, preheat the oven to 225°F (110°C/Gas Mark ¼).

Cover the pan with foil and bake until deeply golden brown and caramelized, about 8 hours.

POTATO CHALLAH

The traditional German Shabbat and festival bread, called *berches*, looks just like the egg-enriched challah that Eastern European Jews eat, but contains no eggs in the dough. Instead, mashed potatoes help give the braided (plaited) loaves their soft, downy texture. *Berches* is also sometimes called *vasser challah* (Yiddish for "water challah") to distinguish it from *eier* (egg) challah. To make the bread completely vegan, skip the egg wash and brush the loaves instead with 1 tablespoon barley malt syrup mixed with 2 teaspoons warm water. Some Jewish families in Brazil and other parts of South America add mashed yuca (cassava) root to their challah dough.

Makes: 2 loaves
Preparation time: 25 minutes, plus rising
Cooking time: 30 minutes

- ½ lb (225 g) Yukon Gold potato (about 1 medium), peeled and cut into chunks
- 1 tablespoon active dry yeast
- ⅓ cup (65 g) plus 1 teaspoon sugar
- ¾ cup (175 ml/6 fl oz) warm water (110°F/43°C)
- 4–4½ cups (560–630 g) all-purpose (plain) flour, plus more for kneading
- 1½ teaspoons kosher salt
- ½ cup (120 ml/4 fl oz) vegetable oil, plus more for greasing the bowl
- 1 egg, beaten
- Poppy seeds (optional)

Bring a small saucepan filled with water to a boil over high heat. Add the potato chunks and cook until tender, about 15 minutes. Drain well, then mash with a potato masher until completely smooth. Set aside.

In a very large bowl, stir together the yeast, 1 teaspoon of the sugar, and the warm water. Let sit until foaming, 5–10 minutes.

Meanwhile, in a separate large bowl, whisk together 4 cups (560 g) flour, the remaining ⅓ cup (65 g) sugar, and the salt.

Add the oil and mashed potato to the yeast mixture and whisk until fully combined. Add the flour mixture and stir with a wooden spoon until a shaggy dough begins to form. Turn the dough out onto a lightly floured surface and knead well, adding only enough more flour (up to ½ cup/70 g), a little at a time, until a supple, elastic dough forms, about 10 minutes. (The kneading can also be done in a stand mixer with a dough hook, 5–7 minutes.) Grease a large bowl with about 1 teaspoon of oil, add the dough, and turn to coat. Cover the bowl with plastic wrap (cling film) or a clean tea towel and let sit in a warm place until doubled in size, 1–2 hours.

Line a large baking sheet with parchment paper. Gently deflate the dough with the heel of your hand and divide in half. Divide each dough half into thirds and roll each third into a long rope. Pinch the top of 3 ropes together and braid (plait), pinching at the bottom to seal. Place the braided loaf on the prepared baking sheet. Repeat the process with the remaining 3 ropes.

Preheat the oven to 375°F (190°C/Gas Mark 5).

Meanwhile, brush the tops of the loaves with a coat of egg wash. Cover loaves loosely with lightly greased parchment paper and let rise for another 30 minutes.

Uncover the loaves and brush with a second coat of egg wash. Sprinkle with poppy seeds, if desired, and bake until deep golden brown and cooked through, or an instant-read thermometer inserted in the center of a loaf registers 195°F (90°C), 25–30 minutes. Transfer the loaves to a wire rack to cool for at least 30 minutes before slicing.

SPICED HONEY BREAD

The word *dabo* simply means "bread" in Amharic and can refer to many different types of bread eaten in Ethiopia. But for Ethiopian Jews, it usually refers to this spiced, honey-sweetened wheat bread eaten on Shabbat and holidays. Throughout the week, injera (the spongy flatbread made from teff flour) is employed to scoop up split pea stews like *kik wot* (Spiced Split Pea Stew, page 249) and the fiery chicken dish, Doro Wot (page 274)—so the use of wheat flour helps set *dabo* apart as special. *Dabo* is relatively simple to make, but tastes best when it proofs for an extended time. Start the dough the night before and let it rise overnight in the fridge. The soft, subtly sweet loaf is worth the wait.

Makes: 1 round loaf
Preparation time: 30 minutes, plus rising
Cooking time: 45 minutes

- 1 packet (¼ oz/7g) active dry yeast (2¼ teaspoons)
- 1 teaspoon sugar
- 1½ cups (355 ml/12 fl oz) warm water (110°F/43°C)
- 4½ cups (630 g) all-purpose (plain) flour, plus more for kneading
- 2 teaspoons kosher salt
- 1 teaspoon nigella seeds (black caraway)
- ¾ teaspoon ground cardamom
- ¾ teaspoon ground coriander
- ⅓ cup (115 g) honey
- ¼ cup (60 ml/2 fl oz) vegetable oil, plus more for greasing

In a very large bowl, stir together the yeast, sugar, and warm water. Let sit until foaming, 5–10 minutes.

Meanwhile, in a separate large bowl, whisk together the flour, salt, nigella seeds, cardamom, and coriander.

Add the honey and oil to the yeast mixture and whisk to combine. Add the flour mixture and stir until a shaggy dough begins to form. Turn the dough out onto a lightly floured surface and knead well, adding a little more flour, 1 tablespoon at a time, as necessary until a supple but relatively sticky dough forms, about 10 minutes. (The kneading can also be done in a stand mixer with a dough hook, 5–7 minutes.) Grease a large bowl with about 1 teaspoon of oil, add the dough, and turn to coat. Cover the bowl with plastic wrap (cling film) or a clean tea towel and refrigerate for at least 8 hours, or up to 24.

Line the bottom of a 9-inch (23 cm) round springform pan with a round of parchment paper. Lightly grease the parchment paper and the sides of the pan with oil. Remove the dough from the fridge and gently deflate with the heel of your hand (do not overwork it). Transfer the dough to the springform pan and gently press it to fill the bottom. Cover the pan with foil (fully covered, but not tight) and let the dough rise for 2 hours.

Preheat the oven to 375°F (190°C/Gas Mark 5).

Bake, covered, for 35 minutes, then uncover the pan and continue baking until the bread is puffed, golden brown, and an instant-read thermometer inserted in the center of the loaf registers 195°F (90°C), 5–10 minutes. Transfer the pan to a wire rack and let the bread cool for 30 minutes, then unmold and let the bread continue cooling directly on the rack.

MICHAEL SHEMTOV

BUTCHER & BEE
•
1085 MORRISON DRIVE
CHARLESTON, SC
USA

BUTCHER & BEE
•
902 MAIN STREET
NASHVILLE, TN
USA

Michael Shemtov owns several eateries in the American South, including the Middle Eastern–inspired sandwich shop and restaurant Butcher & Bee. With locations in downtown Charleston and East Nashville, Butcher & Bee pulls from Shemtov's own Israeli heritage with a focus on locally sourced ingredients and sustainably raised meats.

RICE CHALLAH

Shemtov's rice challah, which enriches the traditional Ashkenazi Shabbat bread with both rice flour and cooked white rice, pays homage to the historical tradition in the Carolinas of adding rice to breads. The resulting challah is wonderfully tender and moist.

Makes: 2 loaves
Preparation time: 25 minutes, plus rising
Cooking time: 50 minutes

- ⅓ cup (65 g) long-grain rice
- 1 packet (¼ oz/7 g) active dry yeast (2¼ teaspoons)
- 3 tablespoons honey
- ¾ cup (175 ml/6 fl oz) warm water
- 3 cups (420 g) bread flour (strong white flour)
- 1 cup (140 g) rice flour
- 2½ teaspoons kosher salt
- 3 eggs
- 6 tablespoons (85 g) unsalted butter or nonhydrogenated margarine, at room temperature, cut into small pieces
- Vegetable oil, for greasing the bowl
- Egg wash: 1 egg beaten with 1 teaspoon water

Fill a small saucepan with water and bring to a boil over high heat. Add the rice and cook, stirring occasionally, until just cooked through with a little bite remaining, 10–15 minutes. Drain and set aside to cool.

In the bowl of a stand mixer fitted with the paddle attachment, combine the yeast, honey, and warm water and let stand until foaming, 5–10 minutes.

Meanwhile, in a large bowl, whisk together the bread flour, rice flour, and salt.

Add the eggs to the yeast mixture and beat on low to combine. Add the flour mixture and the butter pieces and beat on low, scraping down the sides of the bowl as necessary, until just combined. Switch to the dough hook and knead at medium speed until the dough is supple and elastic, 5–7 minutes. Add the cooked and cooled rice and beat until just combined. (The dough will feel sticky and moist at this point.) Pull out the dough and form into a ball. Rub about 1 teaspoon of oil around the bottom of the mixer bowl and return the dough to the bowl, turning to coat with oil. Cover the bowl and let rise until nearly doubled in size, 1–1½ hours.

Line a large baking sheet with parchment paper. Gently deflate the dough with the heel of your hand and divide in half. Divide each dough half into thirds and roll each third into a long rope. Pinch the top of 3 ropes together and braid (plait), pinching at the bottom to seal. Place the braided (plaited) loaf on the lined baking sheet. Repeat the process with the remaining 3 ropes. Cover the loaves loosely with lightly greased parchment paper and let rise for 30 minutes.

Meanwhile, preheat the oven to 350°F (180°C/Gas Mark 4).

Brush the loaves with an even layer of the egg wash (you will not use all of it). Bake until deep golden brown and cooked through, or until an instant-read thermometer inserted in the center of a loaf registers to 195°F (90°C), 30–35 minutes. Remove from the oven and transfer to a wire rack to cool for 30 minutes before slicing.

YEASTED PUMPKIN BREAD

Sephardi Jews traditionally eat foods made with pumpkin and squash on Rosh Hashanah, when they hold symbolic significance (page 248). Jewish traders also played a major role in spreading the New World gourd across the Mediterranean during the time of Columbus, and Sephardi cuisine continues to utilize pumpkin in many baked goods, jams, and other dishes today. This tender, gently spiced bread, called *pan de calabaza*, can be shaped in a spiral for Rosh Hashanah, baked in a loaf pan, or formed into rolls. But this recipe's sunset-colored challah-style braid (plait) is particularly beautiful. Serve it on an autumnal Shabbat or at any fall meal. The leftovers make outstanding Challah French Toast (page 34).

Makes: 2 loaves
Preparation time: 25 minutes, plus rising
Cooking time: 35 minutes

• 1 packet (¼ oz/7g) active dry yeast (2¼ teaspoons)
• ½ cup (100 g) plus 1 teaspoon sugar
• 1 cup (240 ml/8 fl oz) warm water (110°F/43°C)
• 4½–5 cups (630–700 g) all-purpose (plain) flour,
  plus more for kneading
• ¾ teaspoon ground cinnamon
• ½ teaspoon ground cardamom
• ½ teaspoon ground ginger
• 2 teaspoons kosher salt
• ½ cup (130 g) canned unsweetened pumpkin purée
• ¼ cup (60 ml/2 fl oz) vegetable oil, plus more for
  greasing the bowl
• 2 eggs

In a very large bowl, stir together the yeast, 1 teaspoon of the sugar, and the warm water. Let sit until foaming, 5–10 minutes.

Meanwhile, in a separate large bowl, whisk together 4½ cups (630 g) flour, the remaining ½ cup (100 g) sugar, the cinnamon, cardamom, ginger, and salt.

Add the pumpkin purée, oil, and 1 of the eggs to the yeast mixture and whisk to combine. Add the flour mixture and stir until a shaggy dough begins to form. Turn the dough out onto a lightly floured surface and knead well, adding up to ½ cup (70 g) more flour, a little at a time, as necessary until a supple, elastic dough forms, about 10 minutes. (The kneading can also be done in a stand mixer with a dough hook, 5–7 minutes.) Grease a large bowl with about 1 teaspoon of oil, add the dough, and turn to coat. Cover with plastic wrap (cling film) or a clean tea towel and let sit in a warm place until doubled in size, about 2 hours.

Line a large baking sheet with parchment paper. Gently deflate the dough with the heel of your hand and divide in half. Divide each dough half into thirds and roll each third into a long rope. Pinch the top of 3 ropes together and braid (plait), pinching at the bottom to seal. Place the braided loaf on the prepared baking sheet. Repeat the process with the remaining 3 ropes.

Preheat the oven to 375°F (190°C/Gas Mark 5).

Meanwhile, whisk the remaining egg in a small bowl and brush the loaves with a coat of egg wash. (Set the remaining egg wash aside in the fridge.) Cover the loaves loosely with lightly greased parchment paper and let rise for another 30 minutes.

Uncover the loaves and brush with a second coat of egg wash. Bake until deep golden brown and cooked through, or until an instant-read thermometer inserted in the center of the loaf registers 195°F (90°C), 30–35 minutes. Transfer the loaves to a wire rack to cool for 15 minutes before slicing. Revive leftovers by reheating them briefly in an oven or toaster (mini) oven.

Yeasted Pumpkin Bread

SOUR CREAM BISCUITS

Hungarian Jews serve these golden, sour cream–enriched biscuits, called *pogacsa*, thickly spread with softened butter and jam or drizzled with honey. The crosshatched top gives the pastry a distinctively regal look.

Makes: about 30 biscuits
Preparation time: 30 minutes
Cooking time: 20 minutes

- 3 cups (420 g) all-purpose (plain) flour, plus more for rolling
- 1½ teaspoons baking powder
- 1¼ teaspoons kosher salt
- ⅓ cup (40 g) powdered (icing) sugar
- ¾ cup (180 g) sour cream
- 2 sticks (8 oz/225 g) unsalted butter, cut into pieces, at room temperature
- 3 eggs
- 2–3 tablespoons milk

Preheat the oven to 375°F (190°C/Gas Mark 5). Line 2 large baking sheets with parchment paper.

In a medium bowl, whisk together the flour, baking powder, salt, and powdered (icing) sugar.

In a stand mixer fitted with the paddle attachment, beat the sour cream and butter at medium speed until fluffy. Add 2 of the eggs and 2 tablespoons milk and beat until combined. Add the flour mixture and beat at low speed, until a slightly tacky dough comes together. If the dough appears dry, add the remaining 1 tablespoon milk. Gather the dough into a ball.

Roll out the dough until it is ½ inch (1.25 cm) thick. Using a sharp knife, score a crosshatch pattern in the top of the dough, then use a 2-inch (5 cm) round biscuit or cookie cutter to cut out rounds. Place the biscuits on the prepared baking sheets, leaving about ¼ inch (6 mm) space in between them. Gather dough scraps and repeat.

In a bowl, whisk the remaining egg and lightly brush the tops of each biscuit with the egg wash. Bake until golden brown, 18–20 minutes. Transfer the biscuits to a wire rack. to cool.

PITA

Pita is likely the best known Middle Eastern flatbread. When sliced in half, it reveals a pocket perfect for stuffing. It is also a staple of the mezze table and the ideal vehicle for swiping up dips and spreads.

Makes: 8 large pitas
Preparation time: 25 minutes, plus rising
Cooking time: 25 minutes

- 1 packet (¼ oz/7 g) active dry yeast (2¼ teaspoons)
- 1 teaspoon sugar
- 1 cup (240 ml/8 fl oz) warm water (110°F/43°C)
- 2½–2¾ cups (350–385 g) bread flour (strong white flour), plus more for kneading
- 1½ teaspoons kosher salt
- 2 tablespoons extra-virgin olive oil, plus more for greasing the bowl

In a medium bowl, stir together the yeast, sugar, and warm water. Stir in ¼ cup (35 g) of the flour and let sit until bubbling and frothy, about 15 minutes.

Meanwhile, in a large bowl, whisk together 2¼ cups (315 g) flour and the salt. Whisk the oil into the yeast mixture, then make a well in the dry ingredients and pour in the wet. Stir until the dough begins to form, then transfer the dough to a lightly floured surface. Knead, adding up to ¼ cup (35 g) additional flour as needed, until the dough is supple and slightly tacky, 8–10 minutes. Grease a large bowl, add the dough, and turn to coat. Cover the bowl with a tea towel and let rise until doubled in size, 1–1½ hours.

Preheat the oven to 475°F (245°C/Gas Mark 9) and place a large baking sheet inside to heat.

Gently deflate the dough and divide into 8 equal pieces. Roll each piece into a ball, place on a flat surface, and cover with a damp tea towel to rest for 10 minutes. Working on a lightly floured surface, roll the ball into a 6-inch (15 cm) round. Gently transfer the round of dough to the preheated baking sheet. Bake about 2 minutes. Then flip and continue baking until lightly golden brown, another 1–2 minutes. Repeat with the remaining dough.

Sour Cream Biscuits

RYE BREAD

The darling of the Jewish delicatessen, rye bread is arguably the most important bread in the Ashkenazi canon aside from Challah (page 46). Rye bread means different things to different people, ranging from the dense, dark, sour loaves of Eastern Europe to molasses-enriched pumpernickel and the white flour–lightened soft rye loaves that have become the standard in America. This loaf falls somewhere in the middle—sturdy crusted with a moist and tender crumb and fragrant caraway seeds threaded through each slice. Serve it piled with pastrami or Corned Beef (page 292), or topped with Egg Salad (page 94), Tuna Salad (page 85), Danish Herring Salad (page 88), or a dollop of Black Radish and Onion Relish (page 72).

Makes: 1 loaf
Preparation time: 25 minutes, plus rising and cooling
Cooking time: 50 minutes

For the sponge:
• 1 teaspoon active dry yeast
• 1 teaspoon sugar
• 1¼ cups (295 ml/10 fl oz) warm water (110°F/43°C)
• 1 tablespoon molasses
• ½ cup (70 g) bread flour (strong white flour)
• ½ cup (60 g) dark rye flour

For the dough:
• 1½ cups (210 g) bread flour (strong white flour)
• ¾ cup (85 g) dark rye flour
• 1½ teaspoons caraway seeds, plus more for topping
• 1½ teaspoons kosher salt
• Vegetable oil for greasing the bowl
• Cornmeal, for the baking sheet

Make the sponge: In a large bowl, whisk together the yeast, sugar, warm water, molasses, bread flour, and rye flour until completely smooth and the consistency of pancake batter.

Make the dough: In a separate bowl, whisk together the bread flour, rye flour, caraway seeds, and salt. Pour the dough mixture on top of the sponge (do not mix), cover the bowl with a tea towel, and let sit at room temperature until the mixture is bubbling, about 2 hours.

Transfer the sponge and dough to the bowl of a stand mixer fitted with the paddle attachment and beat on low, scraping down the sides of the bowl, until a shaggy dough forms. Switch to a dough hook and knead at medium speed until the dough is supple and smooth, 7–10 minutes. Grease the bottom of a large bowl with about 1 teaspoon of vegetable oil. Gather up the dough and form it into a ball, then place it into the greased bowl and turn to coat. Cover the bowl with a tea towel and let rise until doubled in size, 1½–2 hours.

Sprinkle a large baking sheet with cornmeal. Gently deflate the dough with the heel of your hand, shape into a squat oval, and place on the prepared baking sheet. Cover the dough loosely with a piece of plastic wrap (cling film) and let it rise until puffed, 1–1½ hours.

30 minutes before baking, preheat the oven to 450°F (230°C/Gas Mark 8).

Using a sharp knife, make a vertical slash ¼ inch (6 mm) deep down the center of the loaf and sprinkle with additional caraway seeds. Place 4–5 ice cubes in a small baking dish and place on the bottom of the oven, to create steam. Immediately slide in the loaf and close the oven door. Bake for 15 minutes, then reduce the temperature to 400°F (200°C/Gas Mark 6) and continue baking until bread is golden brown, 30–35 minutes. Transfer the bread to a wire rack to cool for at least 30 minutes before slicing.

ALON SHAYA

SABA
•
5757 MAGAZINE STREET
NEW ORLEANS, LA
USA

SAFTA
•
3330 BRIGHTON
BOULEVARD
DENVER, CO
USA

Alon Shaya is a James Beard Award–winning chef who was born in Israel, raised in Philadelphia, and now lives in New Orleans. He was formerly the executive chef and partner of three celebrated New Orleans restaurants: Domenica, Pizza Domenica, and Shaya. In 2017, he founded Pomegranate Hospitality and currently helms two inventive Middle Eastern eateries: Saba, in New Orleans, and Safta, in Denver.

SCHMALTZY CORN BREAD WITH ALEPPO PEPPER

This schmaltz-enriched corn bread is at once savory, sweet, and tender with a hint of spice and delightfully crackly edges. Ghee (clarified butter) can be susbtituted for the schmaltz, and almond milk and margarine for the milk and butter.

Serves: 6–8
Preparation time: 15 minutes
Cooking time: 30 minutes

- 1 cup (240 ml/8 fl oz) almond milk or whole milk
- 4 tablespoons (60 g) nonhydrogenated margarine or unsalted butter, melted
- 1 egg
- 1¼ cups (175 g) medium or coarsely ground cornmeal
- 1 cup (140 g) all-purpose (plain) flour
- ½ cup (100 g) sugar
- 1 teaspoon baking powder
- 1½ teaspoons Aleppo pepper
- ¾ teaspoon kosher salt
- ½ cup (70 g) fresh or thawed frozen corn kernels
- ¼ cup (60 g) Schmaltz (page 410) or ghee (clarified butter)
- 3 tablespoons cane syrup or honey

Preheat the oven to 400°F (200°C/Gas Mark 6).

In a large bowl, whisk together the almond milk, melted margarine, and egg until combined. (The mixture might appear a bit lumpy, but will smooth out.)

In a medium bowl, whisk together the cornmeal, flour, sugar, baking powder, Aleppo pepper, and salt. Fold in the corn kernels. Add the cornmeal mixture to the wet mixture and stir until a thick batter forms.

In a 9-inch (23 cm) cast-iron skillet (or other ovenproof frying pan), heat the schmaltz over high heat, swirling the pan to evenly coat the bottom with fat. It will start to bubble, then sizzle, then smoke. As soon as it begins to smoke, scrape the batter into the hot skillet and smooth it into an even layer. Transfer immediately to the oven and bake until the corn bread is golden along the edges and set in the center, 20–25 minutes. Remove from the oven and drizzle or brush the cane syrup evenly over the top. Serve warm.

NEW YORK–STYLE BAGELS

Bagels are ubiquitous in the United States today, but New York City will always be their spiritual home. Brought over by Eastern European immigrants, the "roll with a hole" caught on quickly. In Europe, bagels were eaten as part of a meal or as a snack, and rarely adorned with much in the way of toppings. It was only after they arrived in New York that people began slicing bagels, spreading them with tangy cream cheese, and draping them with velvety slices of Lox (page 24). Aficionados will insist that true bagels are always boiled in water before getting baked, yielding chewy crusts and tender insides.

Makes: 12 bagels
Preparation time: 25 minutes, plus resting
Cooking time: 25 minutes

- 1 packet (¼ oz/7 g) active dry yeast (2¼ teaspoons)
- 2 teaspoons sugar
- 1½ cups (355 ml/12 fl oz) warm water (110°F/43°C)
- 4 cups (560 g) bread flour (strong white flour), plus more for kneading
- 2 tablespoons kosher salt
- 1 tablespoon barley malt syrup or brown rice syrup
- Vegetable oil, for greasing the bowl
- 1 tablespoon baking soda (bicarbonate of soda)
- 1 egg, beaten
- Sesame seeds, poppy seeds, or Everything Bagel Spice Mix (page 416), for topping

In a medium bowl, stir together the yeast, sugar, and warm water and let sit until bubbling and frothy, 5–10 minutes.

Meanwhile, in a large bowl, stir together the flour and 1 tablespoon of the salt.

Stir the barley malt syrup into the yeast and water mixture, then make a well in the dry ingredients and pour in the wet. Stir until the dough begins to form, then transfer the dough to a lightly floured surface and knead the dough, adding in a little more flour 1 tablespoon at a time, as needed, until supple but slightly sticky, 8–10 minutes. (The kneading can also be done in a stand mixer with a dough hook, 5–7 minutes.) Grease a large bowl with about 1 teaspoon oil, add the dough, and turn to coat. Cover the bowl with a tea towel and let rise until slightly puffed, about 30 minutes.

Gently deflate the dough with the heel of your hand, turn it out onto a flat surface, and divide into 12 equal pieces. Working with 1 piece at a time (keeping the others covered), roll it into an 8-inch (20 cm) rope. Wrap the rope around your hand, bringing the ends together, then roll your hand back and forth a few times against a flat surface to seal the ends. Lay the bagel on a clean tea towel (to prevent sticking) while continuing with the remaining dough. Cover the bagels with another tea towel and let rest for 15 minutes.

Meanwhile, preheat the oven to 450°F (230°C/Gas Mark 8). Line a large baking sheet with parchment paper.

In a large pot, combine 10 cups (2.4 liters/2½ qt) water, the baking soda (bicarb), and remaining 1 tablespoon salt and bring to a boil over high heat. Reduce the heat to medium and keep at a gentle simmer. Working in batches of 4, gently drop the bagels into the simmering water. Cook for 30 seconds on each side and transfer with a slotted spoon to the prepared baking sheet.

Lightly brush the tops of the bagels with the beaten egg (you will not use all of it) and top with a generous sprinkle of seeds. Bake, rotating the baking sheet front to back halfway through, until the bagels are golden brown and cooked through, 16–18 minutes. Transfer the bagels to a wire rack to cool.

MONTREAL-STYLE BAGELS

Montreal has a bagel tradition and style all its own. There, at the iconic 24-hour bakeries Fairmount and St-Viateur, the bagels are petite and lightly sweet, thanks to the bath they take in honey-sweetened water before getting baked in wood-fired ovens. Visitors to Montreal often come home with a dozen bagels to keep in the freezer for whenever the mood strikes, but this version comes close to the real thing.

Makes: 15 bagels
Preparation time: 25 minutes, plus resting
Cooking time: 25 minutes

- 1 packet (¼ oz/7 g) active dry yeast (2¼ teaspoons)
- 2 tablespoons plus 1 teaspoon sugar
- 1½ cups (355 ml/12 fl oz) warm water (110°F/43°C)
- 5 cups (700 g) all-purpose (plain) flour, plus more for kneading
- 2 teaspoons kosher salt
- ⅓ cup (115 g) plus ¼ cup (85 g) honey
- 2 tablespoons vegetable oil, plus more for greasing the bowl
- 2 egg yolks
- ½ cup (70 g) sesame seeds
- ½ cup (70 g) poppy seeds

In a large bowl, stir together the yeast, 1 teaspoon sugar, and warm water and let sit until bubbling and frothy, 5–10 minutes.

Meanwhile, in a medium bowl, whisk together the flour and salt.

Whisk the remaining 2 tablespoons sugar, ¼ cup (85 g) honey, oil, and egg yolks into the yeast and water mixture. Adding 1 cup (140 g) at a time, stir the flour mixture into the wet ingredients until you have a sticky dough that holds together. Transfer the dough to a work surface and knead, sprinkling over more flour as necessary, until it is supple and elastic, about 5 minutes. Grease a large bowl with about 1 teaspoon of oil, place dough in the bowl, and turn to coat. Cover with a tea towel or plastic wrap (cling film) and allow to rise for 30 minutes.

While the dough is rising, in a large pot, whisk the remaining ⅓ cup (115 g) honey into 10 cups (2.4 liters/ 2½ qt) water and bring to a boil over medium-high heat.

Punch down the dough and divide it into 15 equal balls. Working on a lightly floured surface with one ball of dough at a time (keep the others covered), roll it into a 10- to 12-inch (25 to 30 cm) rope. Wrap the rope around your hand, bringing the ends together, then roll your hand back and forth a few times against the flat surface to seal the ends. There should be an approximately 1-inch (2.5 cm) hole (or larger) in the center of the bagel.

Preheat the oven to 450°F (230°C/Gas Mark 8). Line 2 large baking sheets with parchment paper.

When the water is boiling, slip 3–4 bagels into the water and boil for 1 minute, flipping halfway through. (The bagels should quickly float to the surface. If they stick to the bottom of the pot, gently nudge them free with a wooden spoon.) Remove the boiled bagels from the pot with a slotted spoon and place on a plate until cool enough to handle. Repeat with the remaining bagels.

Spread the sesame seeds on one plate and the poppy seeds on another. Press about half of the boiled bagels into the sesame seeds on both sides, and the other half into the poppy seeds. Lay the seeded bagels on the prepared baking sheet.

Bake, flipping the bagels and rotating the baking sheets front to back halfway through, until golden brown, 18–20 minutes. Transfer to a wire rack to cool.

JERUSALEM BAGELS

In the Old City of Jerusalem, it is hard to miss the vendors selling stacks of these elongated, sesame-strewn rings, sometimes called *baygaleh*, which usually come with za'atar for dipping. Often still warm from the oven, they make an exquisite breakfast. Palestinian in origin, the bagels are now ubiquitous in Jerusalem and throughout Israel. The milk powder gives the dough a lovely hint of sweetness and soft texture, so do not skip it. Use the leftover powder to make the Indian Jewish sweet milk fritters, Gulab Jamun (page 360).

Makes: 6 large bagels
Preparation time: 30 minutes, plus rising
Cooking time: 20 minutes

- 1 packet (¼ oz/7 g) active dry yeast (2¼ teaspoons)
- 1 tablespoon plus 1 teaspoon sugar
- 1¼ cups (295 ml/10 fl oz) warm water (110°F/43°C)
- 4 cups (560 g) all-purpose (plain) flour, plus more as needed
- 1½ tablespoons milk powder
- 1½ teaspoons kosher salt, plus more for sprinkling
- ¼ cup (60 ml/2 fl oz) vegetable oil, plus more for greasing the bowl
- 1 egg, beaten
- Sesame seeds, for sprinkling

In a large bowl, stir together the yeast, 1 teaspoon of the sugar, and the warm water. Let sit until foaming, 5–10 minutes.

In a separate large bowl, whisk together the flour, remaining 1 tablespoon sugar, milk powder, and salt.

Stir the oil into the yeast mixture, then add the flour mixture. Stir until a shaggy dough begins to form. Turn the dough out onto a lightly floured surface and knead well, adding a little more flour, as needed, until a supple and smooth dough forms, about 10 minutes. (The kneading can also be done in a stand mixer fitted with a dough hook, 5–7 minutes.) Grease a large bowl with about 1 teaspoon of oil, add the dough, and turn to coat. Cover the bowl with plastic wrap (cling film) or a tea towel and let rise until doubled in size, 1½–2 hours.

Preheat the oven to 375°F (190°C/Gas Mark 5). Line 2 large baking sheets with parchment paper.

Gently deflate the dough with the heel of your hand and divide into 6 equal parts. Working with one piece at a time, roll the dough into long ropes about 1½ feet (45 cm) long. Shape into elongated ovals, pinching firmly at the seal, and place on the prepared baking sheets.

Brush the tops of the bagels lightly and evenly with the beaten egg (you will not use all of it) and sprinkle with sesame seeds and more salt. Let rise for 15 minutes.

Bake, rotating the baking sheets front to back halfway through, until golden brown and cooked through, about 20 minutes. Transfer the bagels to wire racks to cool. Serve warm or at room temperature, and reheat leftovers in the oven or toaster (mini) oven until warmed through.

Jerusalem Bagels

BIALYS

These saucer-shaped rolls tend to get lumped together with bagels, but they are entirely their own entity. Unlike a bagel, one typically does not slice a bialy. And instead of a smattering of seeds across the top, they have a small indentation in the center that comes dotted with softened onions and poppy seeds. Originally baked in Bialystok, Poland, where they were called *Bialystoker kuchen* in Yiddish, they also enjoyed widespread popularity in New York City in the late nineteeth through mid-twentieth centuries. (A few bakeries still make them today, though they have somewhat fallen by the wayside.) These bialys have a pizza crust–like chew and include a generous amount of savory onion and poppy seed filling. They are best eaten the day they are made, but leftovers can be revived in a toaster or toaster (mini) oven. Either way, spread them thickly with softened butter or cream cheese for a perfect handheld breakfast or snack.

Makes: 12 bialys
Preparation time: 35 minutes, plus rising
Cooking time: 35 minutes

- 1 packet (¼ oz/7 g) active dry yeast (2 ¼ teaspoons)
- 1 teaspoon sugar
- 1½ cups (355 ml/12 fl oz) warm water (110°F/43°C)
- 4 cups (560 g) all-purpose (plain) flour, plus more as needed
- 1 tablespoon plus ¼ teaspoon kosher salt
- 3 tablespoons vegetable oil, plus more for greasing the bowl
- 1 large onion, very finely chopped
- 2½ teaspoons poppy seeds

In a medium bowl, stir together the yeast, sugar, and water and let sit until bubbling and frothy, 5–10 minutes.

Meanwhile, in a large bowl, stir together the flour and 1 tablespoon of the salt.

Stir 1 tablespoon of the oil into the yeast and water mixture, then make a well in the dry ingredients and pour in the wet. Stir until the dough begins to form, then transfer the dough to a lightly floured surface and knead the dough, adding in a little more flour 1 tablespoon at a time, as needed, until supple but slightly sticky, 8–10 minutes. (The kneading can also be done in a stand mixer with a dough hook, 5–7 minutes.) Grease a large bowl with about 1 teaspoon vegetable oil, add the dough, and turn to coat. Cover the bowl with a damp tea towel and let rise until doubled in size, 1½–2 hours.

Meanwhile, in a medium frying pan, heat the remaining 2 tablespoons oil over medium heat. Add the onion, the remaining ¼ teaspoon salt, and about 1 teaspoon water. Cover and cook, stirring occasionally, until very soft and lightly browned, about 10 minutes. Uncover and stir in the poppy seeds. Remove from the heat and let cool slightly.

Preheat the oven to 425°F (220°C/Gas Mark 6). Line 2 large baking sheets with parchment paper. Divide the dough into 12 equal pieces (about 75 g each) and roll into balls. Working on a lightly floured surface with 1 ball of dough at a time (keep the others covered), pat into a round 4 inches (10 cm) in diameter. Use your fingers to press a small indentation in the center. Place the shaped bialys on the prepared baking sheets. Dividing evenly, spoon a little of the onion and poppy seed mixture into each indentation.

Bake, rotating the baking sheets halfway through, until golden brown and cooked through, 15–18 minutes. Transfer the bialys to wire racks to cool.

LAUREL KRATOCHVILA

FINE BAGELS
·
WARSCHAUER STRASSE 74
BERLIN, GERMANY

Laurel Kratochvila is the proprietor of Fine Bagels, an artisanal bagel and pastry shop in Berlin. Originally from the United States, but with Jewish baking roots that stretch back four generations to Warsaw, Kratochvila makes bagels that include both traditional (sesame seed, salt, everything) and innovative (za'atar, rosemary sea salt) flavors.

BALTIC RYE BAGEL

This take on bagels harnesses the dark, sweet, and sour flavors of Latvian black bread. They taste wonderful spread with cream cheese or butter and fruit jam, and also pair perfectly with pickled fish.

Makes: 10 bagels
Preparation time: 25 minutes, plus rising
Cooking time: 25 minutes

• ¾ cup (105 g) golden raisins (sultanas)
• 3 cups (420 g) bread flour (strong white flour)
• 1 cup (120 g) dark rye flour
• 1 packet (¼ oz/7 g) active dry yeast (2¼ teaspoons)
• 2 teaspoons kosher salt
• 1 tablespoon unsweetened cocoa powder
• 1 tablespoon caraway seeds
• 1 teaspoon instant espresso powder
• ½ teaspoon ground fennel seeds
• 1 tablespoon plus 1 teaspoon molasses
• 1 tablespoon plus 1 teaspoon barley malt syrup
• 2 tablespoons apple cider vinegar
• 1¼ cups (295 ml/10 fl oz) warm water (110°F/43°C)
• Vegetable oil, for greasing the bowl
• 1 tablespoon kosher salt
• ½ cup (70 g) barley malt syrup

In a medium bowl, combine the golden raisins (sultanas) with warm tap water to cover. Soak for 15 minutes, then drain and set aside.

In a stand mixer fitted with the paddle attachment, combine the bread (strong) flour, rye flour, yeast, salt, cocoa powder, caraway, espresso powder, and fennel. Beat on low until just combined. Add the molasses, barley malt, cider vinegar, warm water, and drained raisins. Beat until the dough just comes together. It will be a fairly firm dough. Switch to the dough hook and knead on low speed until the dough springs back when pressed, 5–7 minutes. Remove the dough and form into a ball. Grease the bowl with about 1 teaspoon oil, return dough to the bowl, and turn to coat the dough with oil. Cover the bowl and let rise until lightly puffed, about 1 hour.

Line a large baking sheet with parchment paper. Gently deflate the dough with the heel of your hand and divide into 10 equal pieces. Form the dough into loose balls and place on the baking sheet. Cover with a damp cloth and let rise for 15 more minutes.

Working with 1 ball of dough at a time (keeping the others covered), roll it into a rope 8 inches (20 cm) long. Wrap the rope around your hand, bringing the ends together, then roll your hand back and forth a few times against a flat surface to seal the ends. Place the formed bagels back on the lined baking sheet. Cover loosely with plastic wrap (cling film) and refrigerate for at least 12 hours, and up to 1 day.

When ready to bake, preheat the oven to 400°F (200°C/Gas Mark 6).

Meanwhile, in a medium saucepan, stir together about 10 cups (2.4 liters/2½ qt) water with the salt and barley malt and bring to a boil over high heat. Working in batches of 3 or 4, gently drop the bagels into the boiling water. Cook for 30 seconds on each side, then use a slotted spoon to transfer the boiled bagels back to the baking sheet.

When all of the bagels are boiled, transfer the baking sheet to the oven and bake until the bagels are firm but a little springy when pressed, 12–14 minutes. Transfer the bagels to a wire rack to cool.

ADJARULI KHACHAPURI

There are many different types of cheese-filled breads and savory pastries in Georgian cuisine, which are traditionally baked in a large clay oven called a *toné*. Among the most decadent is *adjaruli khachapuri*, an elongated bread boat filled with a pool of melted cheese, butter, and often an egg. Georgian Jews created dairy-freebean-filled (Kidney Bean–Filled Bread, page 66) and potato-filled versions of *khachapuri*.

Serves: 4–6
Preparation time: 30 minutes, plus rising
Cooking time: 20 minutes

• 1 packet (¼ oz/7 g) active dry yeast (2¼ teaspoons)
• 1 teaspoon sugar
• 1 cup (240 ml/8 fl oz) warm water (110°F/43°C)
• 2½–2¾ cups (350–385 g) all-purpose (plain) flour, plus more for kneading and rolling
• 1 teaspoon kosher salt
• ¼ cup (60 ml/2 fl oz) vegetable oil, plus more for greasing and brushing
• 3 cups (240 g) shredded mozzarella cheese
• 8 oz (225 g) feta cheese, crumbled
• 2–4 eggs
• 2 tablespoons (30 g) unsalted butter, cut into small pieces

In a medium bowl, stir together the yeast, sugar, and water and let sit until foaming and frothy, about 5 minutes.

Meanwhile, in a large bowl, whisk together 2½ cups (350 g) flour and the salt.

Add the oil to the yeast and water mixture and stir to combine. Make a well in the center of the flour mixture and pour in the wet ingredients. Stir with a wooden spoon until the dough comes together, then turn the dough out onto a floured surface and knead well, adding up to ¼ cup (35 g) additional flour, 1 tablespoon at a time as needed, until dough is smooth and supple, about 10 minutes. You may not need all of the additional flour. (The kneading can also be done in a stand mixer fitted with a dough hook, 5–7 minutes.) Grease a large bowl with about 1 teaspoon of oil, add the dough, and turn to coat. Cover with plastic wrap (cling film) or a tea towel and let sit in a warm place until doubled in size, 1–1½ hours.

Preheat the oven to 500°F (260°C/Gas Mark 10). Line 2 large baking sheets with parchment paper.

In a medium bowl, stir together the mozzarella and feta. Gently deflate the dough with the heel of your hand and divide into 2 equal balls. On a floured surface using a floured rolling pin, roll one of the balls into a thin round about 12 inches (30 cm) in diameter. Spread the dough with half of the cheese mixture, leaving a ½-inch (1.25 cm) border. Roll up one side of the round toward the center (like a jelly roll/Swiss roll), stopping a little bit less then halfway. Roll up the opposite side in the same manner. Pinch the ends on one side and twist the ends a few times to seal. Repeat on the other side, forming a boat shape with the filling exposed in the middle. Repeat with the remaining dough and filling.

Carefully transfer the filled dough boats to the prepared baking sheets. Brush the dough with a little oil and bake until puffed and lightly golden, 12–14 minutes. Gently crack 1–2 eggs into each dough boat and continue cooking until the whites are just set, 3–4 minutes.

Remove from the oven and sprinkle the top of each dough boat with half of the butter. Drag and swirl a butter knife through the filling, breaking the yolk and mixing the filling together. Serve immediately.

Adjaruli Khachapuri

KIDNEY BEAN–FILLED BREAD

Georgian Jews created a dairy-free, bean-filled version of the country's famous stuffed breads, called *lobiani*, so they could be enjoyed with meat meals. Non-Jewish Georgians adopted the bread, adding butter and bacon to the filling—but the entirely vegan bean filling is perfectly delicious with no additional flavoring.

Serves: 4
Preparation time: 35 minutes, plus rising
Cooking time: 45 minutes

For the dough:
- 1 packet (¼ oz/7 g) active dry yeast (2¼ teaspoons)
- 1 teaspoon sugar
- 1 cup (240 ml/8 fl oz) warm water (110°F/43°C)
- 2½–3 cups (350–420 g) all-purpose (plain) flour, plus more for kneading and rolling
- 1 teaspoon kosher salt
- ¼ cup (60 ml/2 fl oz) vegetable oil, plus more for greasing

For the filling:
- ¼ cup (60 ml/2 fl oz) vegetable oil, plus more for brushing
- 1 onion, finely chopped
- 2 garlic cloves, finely chopped
- ¼ teaspoon ground coriander
- ¼ teaspoon cayenne pepper (optional)
- 1 can (15 oz/425 g) kidney beans, rinsed and drained
- ¾ teaspoon kosher salt
- Extra-virgin olive oil, for topping (optional)

Make the dough: In a medium bowl, stir together the yeast, sugar, and water and let sit until foaming and frothy, about 5 minutes.

Meanwhile, in a large bowl, whisk together 2½ cups (350 g) flour and the salt.

Add the oil to the yeast and water mixture and stir to combine. Make a well in the center of the flour mixture and pour in the wet ingredients. Stir with a wooden spoon until the dough comes together, then turn the dough out onto a floured surface and knead well, adding up to ½ cup (70 g) additional flour, 1 tablespoon at a time as needed, until dough is smooth and supple, about 10 minutes. You may not need all of the additional flour. (The kneading can also be done in a stand mixer fitted with a dough hook, 5–7 minutes.) Grease a large bowl with about 1 teaspoon of oil, add the dough, and turn to coat. Cover with plastic wrap (cling film) or a tea towel and let sit in a warm place until doubled in size, 1–1½ hours.

Meanwhile, make the filling: In a large frying pan, heat the oil over medium heat. Add the onion and garlic and cook, stirring occasionally, until softened and lightly browned, 6–8 minutes. Add the coriander and cayenne (if using) and cook, stirring, until fragrant, about 1 minute. Remove from the heat.

Place the kidney beans in a food processor and add the browned onions and garlic (and any oil remaining in the pan), and the salt. Pulse, scraping down the sides of the bowl as necessary, until a thick, chunky paste forms. Let the mixture cool to the touch.

Gently deflate the dough with the heel of your hand and divide into 4 equal pieces. Working on a lightly floured surface with one piece at a time (keeping the others covered), gently roll the dough into an 8-inch (20 cm) round ¼ inch (6 mm) thick. Spoon a scant ½ cup (100 g) of the cooled kidney bean filling into the center of the round, then gently stretch and wrap the dough around the filling, pinching to seal the bundle at the center. Turn the bundle over and gently press down to flatten, then roll it into a 7-inch (18 cm) round. (Press and roll carefully so the filling does not spill out.) Repeat with the remaining dough and filling, creating 4 filled dough rounds.

Heat a large nonstick frying pan over medium-low heat. Working in batches, fry the dough rounds until golden brown on each side, 5–7 minutes per side. Transfer to a serving plate and, if desired, brush the top of each cooked round with a little oil. Slice into wedges and serve immediately.

ONION AND POPPY SEED PLETZEL

Polish and Russian Jews favored this focaccia-like bread topped with browned onions and crunchy poppy seeds. In the early and mid-twentieth century, it was commonly found in American Jewish bakeries, where it was sometimes called onion board. The bread has fallen out of fashion, but is delicious and worth revisiting. Serve it spread with Chopped Chicken Liver (page 94), Mock Chopped Liver (page 98), or the paprika and caper-flavored cream cheese spread, *liptauer* (Paprika Cheese Spread, page 92).

Serves: 6–8
Preparation time: 30 minutes, plus rising
Cooking time: 25 minutes

- 1 packet (¼ oz/7 g) active dry yeast (2¼ teaspoons)
- 1 tablespoon sugar
- 1 cup (240 ml/8 fl oz) warm water (110°F/43°C)
- 2½–2¾ cups (350–385 g) bread flour (strong white flour), plus more for kneading
- 2 teaspoons kosher salt
- ¼ cup (60 ml/2 fl oz) plus 3 tablespoons vegetable oil, plus more for greasing the bowl
- 2 large red or yellow onions, finely chopped
- ½ teaspoon onion powder
- 1 egg, beaten
- 1 tablespoon poppy seeds

In a medium bowl, stir together the yeast, sugar, and water and let sit until foaming and frothy, about 5 minutes.

Meanwhile, in a large bowl, whisk together 2½ cups (350 g) flour and 1¼ teaspoons salt.

Add ¼ cup (60 ml/2 fl oz) of the oil to the yeast mixture and stir to combine. Make a well in the center of the flour mixture and pour in the wet ingredients. Stir with a wooden spoon until the dough comes together, then turn the dough out onto a floured surface and knead well, adding up to ¼ cup (35 g) additional flour, 1 tablespoon at a time as necessary, until the dough is smooth and supple, about 10 minutes. You may not need all of the additional flour. (The kneading can also be done in a stand mixer fitted with a dough hook, 5–7 minutes.) Grease a large bowl with about 1 teaspoon of oil, add the dough, and turn to coat. Cover with plastic wrap (cling film) or a tea towel and let sit in a warm place until nearly doubled in size, 1–1½ hours.

Meanwhile, in a large frying pan, heat the remaining 3 tablespoons oil over medium heat. Add the onions, cover, and cook, stirring occasionally, until softened, 10–15 minutes. Uncover and stir in the remaining ¾ teaspoon salt and the onion powder. If the bottom of the pan looks dry, stir in 1 teaspoon water. Continue cooking, stirring often, until golden brown, about 5 minutes. Remove from the heat and set aside to cool.

Preheat the oven to 425°F (220°C/Gas Mark 7). Line 2 large baking sheets with parchment paper.

Deflate the dough with the heel of your hand and divide into 2 equal pieces. Working with one piece of dough at a time, stretch and press the dough into large ovals, about ¼ inch (6 mm) thick. Transfer the dough to the prepared baking sheets and, using your fingertips, gently press indentations all over the surface. Loosely cover with lightly greased plastic wrap (cling film) or a tea towel and let rest until slightly puffed, about 30 minutes.

Gently brush the tops of each oval of dough with a thin, even layer of beaten egg. (You will not use all of it.) Divide the onion mixture equally between the ovals, spreading into an even layer. Dividing evenly, sprinkle the ovals with the poppy seeds.

Bake until golden brown and cooked through, 20–25 minutes. Transfer to a wire rack to cool slightly, then cut into squares or rectangles. Serve warm or at room temperature.

SALADS, SPREADS, PICKLES & STARTERS

ROASTED RED PEPPER SALAD

This simple, Moroccan pepper salad, called *piments rotis*, makes a colorful addition to a Shabbat or holiday mezze spread.

Serves: 6–8
Preparation time: 5 minutes, plus resting
Cooking time: 25 minutes

- 1 jar (24 oz/680 g) roasted red peppers, drained well and patted dry with paper towels
- ¼ teaspoon kosher salt, plus more as needed
- ¼ cup (60 ml/2 fl oz) extra-virgin olive oil, plus more as needed
- 3 garlic cloves, minced or pushed through a press

Slice the peppers into long, thin strips and place them in a large frying pan set over medium heat. Cook, stirring occasionally, until the peppers begin to release their liquid, about 5 minutes. Add the salt, reduce the heat to medium-low, and continue cooking until almost all of the liquid has evaporated, 10–15 minutes.

Add the oil and garlic and cook, stirring, until fragrant, 3–5 minutes. Remove from the heat and transfer to a serving dish. Let sit for at least 30 minutes to allow the flavors to meld. Taste and add a little more salt or oil, if desired.

MASHED EGGPLANT SALAD

Mashed eggplant (aubergine) salads, sometimes referred to as eggplant caviar, are ubiquitous across the lands once ruled by the Ottoman Empire, from Morocco to the Balkans and Ukraine. Each region had its own spin on the dish reflecting local ingredients and tastes. In Romania, Jews ate the dip (called *putlejela*) like their neighbors did—simply dressed with lemon juice, finely chopped onion, garlic, and sunflower oil, with sliced tomatoes and minced green peppers serving as a colorful garnish. Serve this dip straight up, or think of it as a canvas for flavor, adding a dash of smoked paprika, chili powder, dried mint, or a spoonful of mayonnaise.

Serves: 6
Preparation time: 15 minutes, plus cooling
Cooking time: 30 minutes

- 2 lb (910 g) eggplant (aubergine), about 2 medium
- 1 small onion, grated on the large holes of a box grater and squeezed dry
- 1 large garlic clove, minced or pushed through a press
- 2 tablespoons fresh lemon juice, plus more as needed
- 2 tablespoons vegetable oil
- 1 teaspoon kosher salt, plus more as needed
- ½ teaspoon freshly ground black pepper
- Sliced tomatoes and minced green bell pepper, for serving

Preheat the broiler (grill) and set the rack in its lowest position. Line a large sheet pan with foil.

Prick the eggplants (aubergines) in several places with a fork and lay on the pan. Broil (grill), turning every 5 minutes, until the skins burst and the flesh is completely soft, 25–30 minutes. Remove from the oven, carefully slit down the center, and place, slit side down, in a colander set in the sink to cool and drain.

Once cool enough to handle, peel off and discard the skin and transfer the eggplant pulp to a food processor. Pulse a few times until a chunky paste forms. (Alternatively, transfer the pulp to a large wooden cutting board and finely chop.) Transfer the eggplant to a bowl and add the onion, garlic, lemon juice, oil, salt, and pepper. Mash together with a fork until combined. Taste and add more lemon juice or salt, if desired.

Transfer to a serving bowl and serve at room temperature, surrounded with sliced tomatoes and small piles of minced bell pepper. Or cover and chill in the fridge (without the garnish) until ready to serve, up to 3 days. Garnish with the tomatoes and bell pepper just before serving.

RED PEPPER AND TOMATO RAGOUT

Hungarians universally love this late-summer spread, called *lecsó*, made from stewed red peppers and tomatoes. It is quite versatile—equally delicious spooned over scrambled eggs, the cornmeal porridge Mamaliga (page 167), or roasted chicken or fish. It can also be enjoyed straight from the bowl, topped with crumbled feta and paired with crusty bread. Some non-Jewish versions of *lecsó* are made with pork sausage. If desired, finely chopped beef sausage can be added as a substitute.

Serves: 8
Preparation time: 10 minutes
Cooking time: 35 minutes

- ¼ cup (60 ml/2 fl oz) vegetable oil or extra-virgin olive oil
- 2 medium onions, halved through the root and thinly sliced
- 3 large green or red bell peppers (about 1½ lb/680 g), sliced into strips ½ inch (1.25 cm) wide
- 1 teaspoon sugar
- ¾ teaspoon kosher salt, plus more as needed
- 1 tablespoon sweet paprika
- ½ teaspoon onion powder
- ¼ teaspoon cayenne pepper
- 2 tablespoons tomato paste (purée)
- 1 can (28 oz/795 g) diced (chopped) tomatoes
- Freshly ground black pepper

In a large saucepan, heat the oil over medium heat. Add the onions, peppers, sugar, and a generous pinch of salt and cook, stirring occasionally, until the vegetables soften, 15–20 minutes. Add the paprika, onion powder, and cayenne and cook, stirring, until fragrant, about 1 minute.

Stir in the tomato paste (purée), the diced (chopped) tomatoes, salt, and a generous amount of black pepper. Bring the mixture to a simmer, then reduce the heat to low, partially cover, and cook, stirring often, until the vegetables grow very tender and the mixture thickens, 10–15 minutes. Taste and adjust the salt and pepper, if desired. Remove from the heat and let cool to room temperature before serving.

MATBUCHA

Cooked tomato, pepper, and eggplant (aubergine) relishes are eaten throughout the Mediterranean and Middle East—particularly in the hot summer months. This saucy Moroccan version has become popular in Israel, where it is typically served as part of a mezze course. It is equally delicious warm or at room temperature served with challah or pita for dipping. It can also be spooned as a flavorful condiment over grilled or roasted fish, meat, chicken, or vegetables.

Serves: 8
Preparation time: 20 minutes
Cooking time: 35 minutes

- ¼ cup (60 ml/2 fl oz) plus 3 tablespoons extra-virgin olive oil
- 1 medium onion, finely chopped
- 2½ cups (200 g) cubes (½ inch/1.25 cm) peeled eggplant
- 2 medium red bell peppers, cut into ½-inch (1.25 cm) pieces
- 1 jalapeño, seeded and finely chopped
- 6 garlic cloves, thinly sliced
- 2 teaspoons light brown sugar
- 1 teaspoon kosher salt, plus more as needed
- 1 tablespoon sweet paprika
- 1 teaspoon onion powder
- ½ teaspoon Aleppo pepper, or more to taste
- Freshly ground black pepper
- 1 can (14½ oz/411 g) diced (chopped) tomatoes

In a large saucepan, heat ¼ cup (60 ml/2 fl oz) olive oil over medium heat. Add the onion, eggplant (aubergine), bell peppers, jalapeño, garlic, brown sugar, and a generous pinch of salt and cook, stirring occasionally, until the vegetables soften, about 15 minutes. Add the paprika, onion powder, and Aleppo pepper and cook, stirring, until fragrant, 1–2 minutes.

Stir in the tomatoes, the remaining 3 tablespoons oil, salt, and a generous amount of black pepper. Bring the mixture to a simmer, then reduce the heat to low, partially cover, and cook, stirring often, until the vegetables grow very tender and the mixture thickens, 10–15 minutes. A few times during the cooking process, mash the vegetables a bit with a potato masher or the back of a spoon. Taste and adjust the salt, black pepper, and Aleppo pepper, if desired. Remove from the heat and let cool slightly before serving.

BABA GHANOUJ

Middle Eastern cuisine is filled with mashed eggplant (aubergine) salads, but baba ghanouj—which combines roasted eggplant, tahini, lemon juice, and garlic—is likely the best known. The rich, tangy, and lightly smoky dip is originally Lebanese, and has become a central part of the Israeli table.

Serves: 6–8
Preparation time: 15 minutes, plus cooling
Cooking time: 30 minutes

• 2 lb (910 g) eggplant (aubergine), about 2 medium
• 1 large garlic clove, finely chopped
• 2 tablespoons fresh lemon juice, plus more as needed
• ⅓ cup (75 g) tahini
• 1 teaspoon kosher salt, plus more as needed
• ½ teaspoon ground cumin
• ½ teaspoon smoked paprika, plus more for serving
• Roughly chopped fresh flat-leaf parsley, for serving

Preheat the broiler (grill) and set the rack in its lowest position. Line a large sheet pan with foil.

Prick the eggplants (aubergines) in several places with a fork and lay on the pan. Broil (grill), turning every 5–10 minutes, until the skins burst and the flesh is completely soft, 25–30 minutes. Remove from the oven, carefully slit eggplants down the center and place, slit side down, in a colander set in the sink to cool and drain.

Once cool enough to handle, peel off and discard the skin. Transfer the eggplant flesh to a food processor and add the garlic. Pulse a few times until a chunky paste forms. Transfer the eggplant to a bowl and add the lemon juice, tahini, salt, cumin, and smoked paprika. Use a fork to mash and mix until well combined. Taste and add more lemon juice and salt, if desired.

Transfer to a serving dish and sprinkle with parsley and a little more smoked paprika.

BLACK RADISH AND ONION RELISH

This radish and onion relish, called *retach mit schmaltz* in Yiddish, is delightfully luscious and light. It was once a standard appetizer within Ashkenazi cuisine, but has unfortunately fallen out of fashion in recent decades. Serve it alongside Chopped Chicken Liver (page 94), or thickly spread on matzo, Challah (page 46), or Rye Bread (page 56). It can be made vegetarian by substituting a mild vegetable oil (like sunflower or safflower) for the Schmaltz (page 410), but will not be quite as savory or deeply flavored.

Serves: 6
Preparation time: 10 minutes, plus resting

• 1 lb (455 g) black radishes, peeled and quartered
• 1 small onion, peeled and quartered
• 6 tablespoons Schmaltz (page 410) or vegetable oil
• ½ teaspoon kosher salt, plus more as needed
• ½ teaspoon freshly ground black pepper

Grate the radishes and onion with the large holes of a box grater or the shredding disc of a food processor. Lay the grated radish and onion in a clean tea towel and squeeze out as much water as possible, then transfer to a large bowl.

Add the schmaltz, salt, and pepper and stir well to combine. Taste and add more salt, if desired. Transfer the mixture to a container, cover, and refrigerate for at least 2 hours to allow flavors to meld. The relish can be stored in the fridge for up to 1 week.

MICHAEL SHEMTOV

BUTCHER & BEE
•
1085 MORRISON DRIVE
CHARLESTON, SC
USA

BUTCHER & BEE
•
902 MAIN STREET
NASHVILLE, TN
USA

Michael Shemtov owns several eateries in the American South, including the Middle Eastern–inspired sandwich shop and restaurant Butcher & Bee. With locations in downtown Charleston and Nashville, Butcher & Bee pulls from Shemtov's own Israeli heritage with a focus on locally sourced ingredients and sustainably raised meats.

SPICY EGGPLANT AND HARISSA SALAD

This sultry fried eggplant (aubergine) salad is dressed with a spicy and refreshing mix of harissa and sherry vinegar, and finished with a shower of fresh herbs.

Serves: 6
Preparation time: 20 minutes
Cooking time: 40 minutes

• 3 lb (1.35 kg) eggplant (aubergine), about 3 medium, peeled cut into 1-inch (2.5 cm) chunks
• 3 tablespoons kosher salt, plus more as needed
• Vegetable oil, for deep-frying
• 4 garlic cloves, thinly sliced
• ½ cup (120 g) harissa, store-bought or homemade (page 409)
• 1½ tablespoons sherry vinegar
• 4 tablespoons finely chopped flat-leaf parsley, plus more for garnish
• 4 tablespoons finely chopped cilantro (fresh coriander), plus more for garnish

Toss the eggplant (aubergine) and salt together in a large colander. Place colander over a large bowl and let eggplant drain for 1 hour, then thoroughly pat the eggplant pieces dry with paper towels.

Line a large baking sheet with paper towels. Pour 2 inches (5 cm) vegetable oil in a large heavy pot, set over medium-high heat, and bring to 350°F (177°C) on a deep-fry thermometer. Working in batches and being careful not to overcrowd the pan, fry the eggplant pieces, stirring occasionally, until golden brown, 4–5 minutes per batch. Using a slotted spoon, transfer the fried eggplant to the baking sheet to drain. Add the sliced garlic to the last batch of eggplant, near the end of cooking, to allow it to crisp up.

In a large bowl, stir together the harissa, vinegar, parsley, and cilantro (coriander). Add the fried eggplant and garlic and toss well to coat. Let the mixture stand for 30 minutes, stirring occasionally, to allow the flavors to meld. Taste and add more salt, if needed. Serve at room temperature, sprinkled with more parsley and cilantro.

✴ STAR RECIPE

TOMATO AND ONION SALAD

This light, simple tomato salad, called *achik chuchuk*, is the perfect foil for the hearty meat and rice *plovs* (pilafs) ubiquitous to Bukharian Jewish cuisine. With so few ingredients in the mix, it is imperative to use in-season, perfectly ripe tomatoes and to slice the onions paper thin. Serve the salad as is, or dress it up with some chopped fresh cilantro (coriander) and a pinch of crushed pepper flakes.

Serves: 4–6
Preparation time: 10 minutes

- 1½ lb (680 g) tomatoes, sliced into ½-inch (1.25 cm) wedges
- ½ medium sweet onion, very thinly sliced
- 1 teaspoon red or white wine vinegar
- 1 tablespoon vegetable oil
- ½ teaspoon kosher salt, plus more as needed

In a medium bowl, combine the tomatoes, onion, vinegar, oil, and salt. Gently toss until just combined. Taste and add more salt, if desired. Let stand for 10 minutes to allow flavors to meld and the onions to mellow before serving.

GRILLED VEGETABLE SALAD

This Tunisian salad, called *mechouia*, can be served as part of a mezze spread or, when garnished with hard-boiled eggs, tuna, and olives, makes a delicious centerpiece for a light lunch or dinner. Cooking the vegetables on an outdoor grill (barbecue), which is the traditional way of making *mechouia*, imparts a lovely smoky flavor. But if you make it indoors under an oven broiler (grill), adding a bit of smoked paprika achieves similar results.

Serves: 6
Preparation time: 45 minutes
Cooking time: 35 minutes

- 4 medium red bell peppers (about 1½ lb/680 g)
- 4 medium tomatoes (about 1 lb/455 g)
- 2 medium red onions (about 1 lb/455 g), halved through the root
- 1 garlic clove, finely chopped
- ¼ teaspoon smoked paprika (optional)
- ¼ teaspoon crushed pepper flakes, plus more as needed
- ¾ teaspoon kosher salt, plus more as needed
- 2 teaspoons fresh lemon juice, plus more as needed
- 3 tablespoons extra-virgin olive oil
- For serving: quartered hard-boiled eggs, drained oil-packed tuna, pitted olives

Preheat an outdoor grill (barbecue) or the oven broiler (grill). If using the broiler, cover a large sheet pan with foil.

Wash and thoroughly dry the peppers and tomatoes and trim off the peppers' stems. Arrange them on the grill grates or on the sheet pan along with the onions. Grill or broil, turning and rotating the vegetables with a pair of tongs every 10 minutes, until they are blistered and very tender within, 15–20 minutes for the tomatoes, and 25–35 minutes for the peppers and onions. As the vegetables are ready, transfer them to a large paper bag and close it (to allow the vegetables to steam). Let the remaining vegetables continue cooking until ready.

Once all the vegetables are cooked and cooled, remove their skins (and the seeds from the peppers), cut into chunks, and place in a fine-mesh sieve to drain.

Transfer the drained vegetables to a food processor and add the garlic, smoked paprika (if using), pepper flakes, and salt. Pulse, scraping down the sides of the bowl often, until a chunky paste with some larger, textured pieces forms.

Transfer the mixture to a bowl and stir in the lemon juice and oil. Taste and add more pepper flakes, salt, or lemon juice, if desired.

Spread the mixture in a wide, shallow bowl. Arrange eggs, tuna, and olives around the side. Sprinkle with a little additional salt and serve at room temperature.

Tomato and Onion Salad

ORANGE AND OLIVE SALAD

The combination of sweet, juicy oranges and briny olives may seem unusual to unfamiliar palates, but this traditional Moroccan salad is a delicious study in contrasts. The wrinkled, velvet-textured olives can be found at specialty food shops. Feel free to substitute another favorite type of olive.

Serves: 6
Preparation time: 25 minutes

For the dressing:
- ¼ cup (60 ml/2 fl oz) extra-virgin olive oil
- ½ teaspoon finely grated lemon zest
- 1 tablespoon fresh lemon juice
- 1½ tablespoons honey
- 1 small garlic clove, minced or pushed through a press
- ½ teaspoon ground cumin
- ½ teaspoon kosher salt
- ½ small red onion, finely chopped

For the salad:
- 6 navel oranges
- 1 cup (160 g) oil-cured black olives, pitted and roughly chopped
- ⅓ cup (15 g) chopped fresh flat-leaf parsley

Make the dressing: In a medium bowl, whisk together the oil, lemon zest, lemon juice, honey, garlic, cumin, and salt. Add the red onion and stir to combine. Let rest for 15 minutes to allow the onion to soften and mellow.

Prepare the salad: Using a sharp serrated knife, slice off the ends of each orange. Stand an orange upright on one of its flat ends. Starting at the top, cut away the peel, following the curve of the fruit to the bottom and taking care to remove all the white pith and membrane. Continue in this manner around the fruit, until all the peel is gone. Lay the orange on its side and cut crosswise into slices ½ inch (1.25 cm) thick. Repeat with the rest of the oranges.

Arrange the orange slices on a serving platter. Scatter with the olives and parsley and drizzle evenly with the dressing.

FENNEL AND BLACK OLIVE SALAD

Tunisian Jews serve this fennel salad, called *salatat al-bisbas*, as part of a mezze spread. The mix of sweet fennel, briny olives, and spicy harissa is quite refreshing.

Serves: 6–8
Preparation time: 15 minutes

- 3 medium fennel bulbs (about 3 lb/1.35 kg)
- ½ cup (80 g) oil-cured black olives, pitted and roughly chopped
- 2 tablespoons distilled white vinegar
- 1 tablespoon red wine vinegar
- 3 tablespoons vegetable oil
- 1 teaspoon Harissa (page 409)
- ½ teaspoon kosher salt, plus more as needed
- ¼ teaspoon freshly ground black pepper, plus more as needed

Cut off the stalks and fronds from the fennel bulbs and reserve for another use. Halve each bulb (or quarter them if you like smaller pieces), remove the tough core, and slice very thinly. Transfer the fennel to a large bowl and scatter with the olives.

In a small bowl, whisk together the white vinegar, red wine vinegar, oil, harissa, salt, and pepper until combined and emulsified. Drizzle the vinegar mixture over the fennel and toss to coat. Taste and adjust the seasonings, if desired. Serve immediately.

BEET AND RED ONION SALAD

Popular throughout Balkan and Middle Eastern cuisines, simply dressed roasted-beet salads are a staple of the Shabbat mezze spread. Here, the softened red roots are tossed with a refreshing mix of cumin, red onion, and mint.

Serves: 8
Preparation time: 15 minutes
Cooking time: 1 hour

- 6 medium beets (about 2 lb/910 g total), trimmed and scrubbed
- 3 tablespoons red wine vinegar or fresh lemon juice
- 2 tablespoons extra-virgin olive oil
- ½ teaspoon ground cumin
- ½ teaspoon kosher salt, plus more as needed
- 1 tablespoon sugar (optional)
- ½ medium red onion, halved through the root and thinly sliced
- ½ cup (20 g) roughly chopped fresh mint leaves

Preheat the oven to 450°F (230°C/Gas Mark 8).

Wrap each beet tightly in foil and place in a baking dish. Roast until the beets are very tender, about 1 hour. Remove from the oven and let cool to the touch. Unwrap the beets and peel, then chop into ½-inch (1.25 cm) pieces.

In the bottom of a large bowl, whisk together the vinegar, oil, cumin, salt, and sugar (if using) until fully combined. Add the roasted beets, red onion, and about half of the mint and toss to combine. Taste and add more salt, if desired. Transfer to a serving bowl and sprinkle with the remaining mint.

BEETS WITH SOUR CREAM

Beets, sour cream, and fresh dill are a classic summer trio across Central and Eastern European Jewish cooking. This salad, which coats roasted beets in a creamy, herb-speckled dressing, would make ideal warm-weather picnic fare. It is also a good match for an Ashkenazi Shavuot table, where dairy-filled dishes are celebrated (see page 13).

Serves: 4–6
Preparation time: 15 minutes, plus chilling
Cooking time: 1 hour

- 6 medium beets (about 2 lb/910 g total), trimmed and scrubbed
- 1 small shallot, finely chopped
- 2 teaspoons red wine vinegar
- ½ cup (120 g) sour cream
- 2 tablespoons mayonnaise
- 1 tablespoon extra-virgin olive oil
- 2 teaspoons sugar
- ½ teaspoon kosher salt, plus more as needed
- ¼ teaspoon freshly ground black pepper
- ½ cup (25 g) finely chopped fresh dill, plus more for serving
- 5 radishes, thinly sliced (optional)

Preheat the oven to 450°F (230°C/Gas Mark 8).

Wrap each beet tightly in foil and place in a baking dish. Roast until the beets are very tender, about 1 hour. Remove from the oven and let cool to the touch. Unwrap the beets and peel, then chop into ½-inch (1.25 cm) pieces.

In the bottom of a large bowl, stir together the shallot and vinegar and allow to sit for 10 minutes, stirring occasionally, to soften the flavor of the shallot. Whisk in the sour cream, mayonnaise, oil, sugar, salt, and pepper until fully combined. Add the roasted beets, dill, and radishes (if using) and toss to combine. Taste and add more salt, if desired. Transfer to a serving bowl, cover, and refrigerate for at least 1 hour, or overnight, to allow the flavors to meld. Just before serving, sprinkle with a little more chopped dill.

CHOPPED TOMATO AND CUCUMBER SALAD

Variations of chopped tomato and cucumber salads are popular across the Middle East, including in Israel. They are typically served at breakfast with labneh and pita, or as part of a mezze spread. The Dijon and shallot in this version are unorthodox—but delicious—additions. The crisp, brightly flavored salad is also tasty when tucked into a pita alongside Falafel (page 194) or fried eggplant (aubergine) in Sabich (page 259).

Serves: 6–8
Preparation time: 25 minutes

For the dressing:
• ½ teaspoon finely grated lemon zest
• 2 tablespoons fresh lemon juice
• 2 tablespoons finely chopped shallot
• 1 teaspoon Dijon mustard
• 1 teaspoon red wine vinegar
• ¼ teaspoon kosher salt
• Freshly ground black pepper
• ¼ cup (60 ml/2 fl oz) extra-virgin olive oil

For the salad:
• 1 lb (455 g) tomatoes, seeded and finely chopped
• 1 lb (455 g) Persian (mini) cucumbers, finely chopped
• ½ small red onion, finely chopped
• 4 tablespoons finely chopped fresh flat-leaf parsley
• Kosher salt and freshly ground black pepper

Make the dressing: In a blender, combine the lemon zest, lemon juice, shallot, mustard, vinegar, salt, and a generous amount of pepper and purée until smooth. With the blender still running, slowly drizzle in the oil until emulsified. (The dressing can be made 1 day in advance and stored, covered, in the refrigerator.)

Assemble the salad: In a large bowl, combine the tomatoes, cucumbers, red onion, and parsley. Season lightly with salt and pepper. Drizzle the dressing over the salad and toss to combine. Serve immediately.

CARROT SALAD WITH CUMIN

This cooked carrot salad hails from Morocco. Perfumed with cumin and cinnamon and brightened with lemon zest and fresh parsley, it makes a delicious addition to a mezze spread.

Serves: 4–6
Preparation time: 20 minutes
Cooking time: 15 minutes

• 2 lb (910 g) carrots, halved lengthwise if thick, and sliced crosswise into ½-inch (1.25 cm) pieces
• ½ teaspoon finely grated lemon zest
• 2 tablespoons fresh lemon juice
• 3 tablespoons extra-virgin olive oil
• 1 tablespoon honey
• 2 garlic cloves, minced or pushed through a press
• 4 tablespoons chopped fresh flat-leaf parsley
• 1½ teaspoons ground cumin
• ½ teaspoon ground cinnamon
• ¼ teaspoon crushed pepper flakes
• ½ teaspoon kosher salt
• ¼ teaspoon finely ground black pepper

Bring a medium saucepan filled with water to a boil over high heat. Add the carrots, bring back to a boil, then reduce the heat to medium-low, cover, and cook until the carrots are tender but not mushy, 8–10 minutes. Drain, rinse with cold water, and drain again.

In a large bowl, whisk together the lemon zest, lemon juice, oil, honey, garlic, parsley, cumin, cinnamon, pepper flakes, salt, and black pepper. Add the cooked and drained carrots and toss well to combine. Let sit for 15 minutes before serving to allow the flavors to meld. Serve at room temperature or chilled.

Chopped Tomato and Cucumber Salad

FATTOUSH

This Levantine salad, which tosses bits of ripped, toasted pita into an herb- and vegetable-packed salad is popular throughout the Middle East, including in Israel. The dressing for this version is flavored with a refreshing mix of lemony ground sumac and tangy pomegranate molasses.

Serves: 6–8
Preparation time: 25 minutes

- 2 white pita breads (6-inch/15 cm diameter)
- ¼ cup (60 ml/2 fl oz) plus 2 teaspoons extra-virgin olive oil
- 1 tablespoon ground sumac, plus more for serving
- 2 tablespoons fresh lemon juice
- 2 tablespoons pomegranate molasses
- 1 large garlic clove, minced or pushed through a press
- ½ teaspoon kosher salt, plus more for serving
- ¼ teaspoon freshly ground black pepper
- 1 romaine heart, halved lengthwise and thinly sliced
- 2 medium tomatoes, seeded and chopped
- 3 Kirby (pickling) cucumbers, peeled, halved lengthwise, and sliced into half-moons
- 5 radishes, ends trimmed and thinly sliced
- 1 small bunch scallions (spring onions), white and green parts, thinly sliced
- ¼ cup chiffonade-cut fresh basil
- ¼ cup fresh mint leaves, coarsely torn

Preheat the oven to 400°F (200°C/Gas Mark 6).

Lay the pitas on a large baking sheet and drizzle or brush each pita with 1 teaspoon of the oil. Bake until completely dry and crisp, 10–15 minutes. Remove from the oven and let cool to the touch, then break into bite-size pieces. Set aside.

In a medium bowl, whisk together the sumac, lemon juice, pomegranate molasses, garlic, salt, and pepper. Whisking constantly, drizzle in the remaining ¼ cup (60 ml/2 fl oz) oil until combined and emulsified.

In a large bowl, mix together the romaine, tomatoes, cucumbers, radishes, scallions (spring onions), basil, and mint. Fold in the pita pieces. Drizzle the dressing over the salad and season with a little more salt and toss to combine. Serve immediately, sprinkled with more sumac.

COLESLAW

Jewish delicatessens worth their salt offer patrons a complimentary bowl of pickles and another of creamy coleslaw to nibble on while contemplating their orders. The salad's vinegary flavor and crunchy texture perfectly offset whatever mile-high meat sandwich one orders.

Serves: 6–8
Preparation time: 15 minutes, plus chilling

- 1 small head green cabbage (about 2 lb/910 g)
- 1 small carrot, peeled
- ¾ cup (240 g) mayonnaise
- 3 tablespoons apple cider vinegar
- ¼ cup (50 g) sugar
- 1½ teaspoons kosher salt
- ¼ teaspoon freshly ground black pepper
- 1 teaspoon celery seed

Quarter, core, and thinly shred the cabbage and add it to a large bowl. Using the large holes of a box grater or the shredding disc of a food processor, grate the carrot and add to the bowl.

In a medium bowl, whisk together the mayonnaise, vinegar, sugar, salt, pepper, and celery seed until thoroughly combined.

Drizzle the dressing over the vegetables and toss to fully coat. Cover and refrigerate for about 1 hour to allow the flavors to mellow and meld. Serve chilled. Store leftovers covered in the fridge for up to 3 days.

HEALTH SALAD

In the mid- to late-twentieth century, New York City's delicatessens introduced a mayonnaise-free cabbage salad meant to be a healthier alternative to traditional Coleslaw (page 80). Regardless of its purported health benefits, the vinegar- and oil-dressed slaw is refreshing and delicious. It tastes best when it has had a chance to rest and soften in the refrigerator for a couple of days, so plan to make it ahead.

Serves: 8
Preparation time: 15 minutes, plus chilling

- 1 small head green cabbage (about 2 lb/910 g)
- 1 tablespoon plus 1½ teaspoons kosher salt
- 1 small green or red bell pepper, quartered and thinly sliced
- 1 large carrot, peeled
- 1 large cucumber (about ½ lb/225 g), peeled, halved, and seeded
- ½ small sweet onion (like Vidalia), halved
- ¼ cup (60 ml/2 fl oz) vegetable oil
- ½ cup (120 ml/4 fl oz) distilled white vinegar
- ¼ cup (60 ml/2 fl oz) apple cider vinegar
- ⅓ cup (65 g) sugar
- ½ teaspoon freshly ground black pepper

Quarter, core, and thinly shred the cabbage and add it to a large bowl along with 1 tablespoon of the salt. Using your hands, squeeze and massage the cabbage and salt together until the cabbage softens and just begins to release some of its juices, 2–3 minutes. Add the bell pepper.

Using the large holes of a box grater or the shredding disc of a food processor, grate the carrot, cucumber, and onion and add to the bowl.

In a separate medium bowl, whisk together the oil, white vinegar, cider vinegar, sugar, remaining 1½ teaspoons salt, and black pepper until thoroughly combined.

Drizzle the dressing over the vegetables and toss to coat. Cover and refrigerate for at least 2 hours, or overnight, to allow the flavors to meld.

PICKLED CUCUMBER SALAD

Serve this Eastern European cucumber salad alongside Corned Beef (page 292), Hanukkah Fried Chicken (page 285), or any dish that would benefit from its sweet-tart flavor and refreshingly crisp-tender texture. For the best texture, slice the cucumbers and onion as thinly as possible.

Serves: 6–8
Preparation time: 10 minutes, plus resting

- 1 lb (455 g) Kirby (pickling) cucumbers or Persian (mini) cucumbers, scrubbed, patted dry, and very thinly sliced
- ½ medium red onion, halved and very thinly sliced
- ¼ cup (50 g) sugar
- ⅓ cup (75 ml/2½ fl oz) apple cider vinegar or rice vinegar
- 1 teaspoon dried dill
- 1 teaspoon kosher salt
- ¼ teaspoon crushed pepper flakes (optional)

Add the cucumbers and red onion to a large bowl. In a small bowl, whisk together the sugar, vinegar, dill, salt, and pepper flakes (if using) until the sugar dissolves. Pour the vinegar mixture over the cucumber and onion mixture and toss to combine. Let the salad sit for at least 1 hour, tossing occasionally, to allow the flavors to soften and meld. Or cover and refrigerate for up to 3 days. The longer the salad sits, the more pickled it will get.

BAZARGAN

Syrian Jews serve this tangy, herb-flecked grain salad as part of the mezze spread at Shabbat lunch. The dish's name references the bazaar—the bustling outdoor market where home cooks bought their spices and other ingredients. Bazargan is typically made with tamarind paste, which is common across Syrian cuisine. The sour paste can be found in Middle Eastern and international food markets, and online. Pomegranate Molasses (page 410) also makes a fine substitute.

Serves: 6–8
Preparation time: 10 minutes
Cooking time: 20 minutes

- ⅓ cup (30 g) walnut halves, roughly chopped
- ¼ cup (30 g) pine nuts
- 1¼ cups (200 g) fine or medium bulgur
- 2½ cups (590 ml/20 fl oz) boiling water
- 2 medium shallots, finely chopped
- 1 medium bunch flat-leaf parsley, stems trimmed and finely chopped
- 3 tablespoons tamarind paste or pomegranate molasses
- 1 tablespoon tomato paste (purée)
- 2 tablespoons honey
- 1 tablespoon fresh lemon juice
- 3 tablespoons extra-virgin olive oil
- 1 teaspoon ground cumin
- ½ teaspoon Aleppo pepper
- ½ teaspoon dried mint
- 1 teaspoon kosher salt, plus more as needed
- ½ teaspoon freshly ground black pepper
- Pomegranate seeds, for serving

In a small frying pan, toast the walnuts and pine nuts over medium-low heat, shaking pan occasionally, until fragrant and lightly browned, 5–7 minutes. Remove pan from the heat and let cool.

Combine the bulgur and the boiling water in a heatproof medium bowl and let sit until bulgur is tender but still slightly chewy, about 30 minutes. Drain well and transfer to a large bowl along with the shallots, parsley, and toasted walnuts and pine nuts.

In a medium bowl, whisk together the tamarind paste, tomato paste (purée), honey, lemon juice, oil, cumin, Aleppo pepper, mint, salt, and black pepper. Drizzle the dressing over the bulgur mixture and toss to combine. Taste and add more salt, if desired. Transfer to a serving bowl and sprinkle generously with pomegranate seeds.

TABBOULEH

This Levantine salad, which is widely eaten throughout the Middle East, is a vision of freshness—heaps of finely chopped parsley, mint, scallions (spring onions), and tomatoes dotted with softened bulgur. In America, home cooks tend to use a much higher ratio of bulgur to herbs, resulting in more of a grain salad. This version splits the difference, delicately balancing green and grain, and brightening the mix with plenty of lemon juice.

Serves: 6
Preparation time: 20 minutes, plus resting
Cooking time: 15 minutes

- ¾ cup (125 g) fine or medium bulgur
- 2 cups (475 ml/16 fl oz) boiling water
- 1½ lb (680 g) tomatoes (3–4 medium), seeded and finely chopped
- 2 Persian (mini) cucumbers, finely chopped
- 1 cup (50 g) finely chopped fresh flat-leaf parsley
- 1 cup (50 g) finely chopped fresh mint or cilantro, (coriander), from 1 large bunch
- 1 small bunch scallions (spring onions), white and green parts, thinly sliced
- Finely grated zest of 1 lemon
- ¼ cup (60 ml/2 fl oz) fresh lemon juice
- ¼ cup (60 ml/2 fl oz) extra-virgin olive oil
- 1½ teaspoons kosher salt
- ½ teaspoon freshly ground black pepper

Combine the bulgur and the boiling water in a heatproof bowl and let sit until the bulgur is tender but still slightly chewy, about 30 minutes. Drain well and transfer to a large bowl along with the tomatoes, cucumbers, parsley, mint, and scallions (spring onions).

In a small bowl, whisk together the lemon zest, lemon juice, oil, salt, and pepper. Add to the bulgur bowl and toss to combine. Serve immediately.

Bazargan

DILLED POTATO SALAD

Refreshing, just a bit tangy, and flecked with dill, this Eastern European–style potato salad makes a great addition to a picnic. Serve it alongside hard-boiled eggs and Lox (page 24).

Serves: 6–8
Preparation time: 10 minutes
Cooking time: 30 minutes

- 1½ lb (680 g) red or Yukon Gold potatoes, scrubbed and unpeeled
- 1 lb (455 g) Persian (mini) cucumbers, finely chopped
- ½ cup (25 g) finely chopped fresh dill
- 1 large garlic clove, minced or pushed through a press
- ½ teaspoon kosher salt, plus more as needed
- ½ teaspoon freshly ground black pepper
- 1 tablespoon distilled white vinegar or apple cider vinegar, plus more as needed
- 2 tablespoons vegetable oil

Place the potatoes in a large saucepan with water to cover by 2 inches (5 cm). Bring to a boil over high heat. Reduce the heat to medium-high and cook until potatoes are tender all the way through when pierced with a sharp knife, 20–30 minutes (longer for larger potatoes). Drain and let sit until cool enough to handle.

Peel the cooked potatoes and cut into ½-inch (1.25 cm) pieces. Add the potatoes to a large bowl along with the cucumbers, dill, garlic, salt, pepper, vinegar, and oil. Stir well to combine. Taste and add more salt or vinegar, if desired. Serve at room temperature or chilled.

CHICKPEA SALAD

Chickpea salads are a ubiquitous part of Sephardi mezze spreads across the Mediterranean and Middle East. Bright and fresh, this version is filled with chopped cucumber and bell peppers and flavored with cumin and fresh lemon juice. Starting with dried chickpeas enhances the salad's flavor, but canned chickpeas can be substituted. If desired, start with two 15-ounce (425 g) cans of chickpeas that have been rinsed, drained, and patted dry.

Serves: 6
Preparation time: 25 minutes, plus soaking
Cooking time: 1½ hours

- 1 cup (180 g) dried chickpeas
- 1 teaspoon baking soda (bicarbonate of soda)
- ½ medium red onion
- ½ teaspoon finely grated lemon zest
- ¼ cup (60 ml/2 fl oz) fresh lemon juice
- ¼ cup (60 ml/2 fl oz) extra-virgin olive oil
- 1 teaspoon dried oregano
- ½ teaspoon ground cumin
- ¾ teaspoon kosher salt
- ¼ teaspoon freshly ground black pepper
- 2 medium bell peppers (any color), finely chopped
- 1 large Persian (mini) cucumber, finely chopped
- ½ cup (25 g) finely chopped fresh parsley
- 4 oz (115 g) crumbled feta cheese (optional)

Place the chickpeas and baking soda (bicarb) in a large bowl and cover with water by at least 2 inches (5 cm). Cover the bowl with a tea towel and soak for at least 8 hours, or overnight. Drain the water, rinse the chickpeas, and drain again.

In a large saucepan, combine the chickpeas with water to cover by several inches. Bring to a boil over high heat, then reduce the heat to medium, partially cover, and simmer, stirring occasionally, until the chickpeas are very soft and beginning to burst from their skins, 1–1½ hours. If necessary, add more water while cooking to ensure the chickpeas stay fully covered. Drain well and set aside to cool.

In a large bowl, stir together the red onion, lemon zest, lemon juice, oil, oregano, cumin, salt, and pepper. Let the mixture sit for 15 minutes to allow the onions to mellow and soften.

Add the chickpeas, bell peppers, cucumber, parsley, and feta (if using) and toss to combine. Let stand 30 minutes before serving, stirring occasionally. Serve at room temperature.

TANGY WHITE BEAN SALAD

Originally hailing from Turkey, this vinegar- and sumac-flavored white bean salad is a staple of many Sephardi tables. Called *piyaz*, the salad is typically served with long-cooked eggs (Huevos Haminados, 16), but is equally tasty, and plenty substantial, served alone.

Serves: 8
Preparation time: 30 minutes, plus soaking
Cooking time: 1 hour

- 2 cups (360 g) dried white beans
  (e.g., navy, Great Northern, or cannellini)
- 2 teaspoons baking soda (bicarbonate of soda)
- ⅓ cup (75 ml/2½ fl oz) vegetable oil
- ½ cup (120 ml/4 fl oz) red wine vinegar
- 1½ teaspoons ground sumac
- 1 teaspoon kosher salt, plus more as needed
- ¼ teaspoon freshly ground black pepper,
  plus more as needed
- 1 large red onion, finely chopped
- 1 green bell pepper, finely chopped
- ½ lb (225 g) tomatoes, chopped
- 1 bunch scallions (spring onions), white and green parts,
  thinly sliced
- ½ cup (25 g) finely chopped fresh dill or parsley
- 4 peeled and halved Huevos Haminados (page 16)
  or hard-boiled eggs, for serving (optional)

Place the beans and baking soda (bicarb) in a large bowl and cover with water by at least 2 inches (5 cm). Cover the bowl with a tea towel and soak for at least 8 hours, or overnight. Drain the water, rinse the beans, and drain again.

In a large saucepan, combine the beans with water to cover by several inches. Bring to a boil over high heat, then reduce the heat to medium, partially cover, and simmer, stirring occasionally, until the beans are tender but not falling apart, 45–60 minutes (longer depending on the type of bean). If necessary, add more water while cooking to ensure the beans stay fully covered. Drain the beans, rinse with cool water, and drain again. Set aside to cool.

Meanwhile, in a large bowl, whisk together the oil, vinegar, sumac, salt, and pepper. Add the red onion and let sit (while the beans are cooking and cooling) to soften their flavor.

Add the drained, cooled beans to the bowl along with the bell pepper, tomatoes, scallions (spring onions), and dill. Toss to combine, then taste and add more salt and pepper, if desired. Transfer to a serving bowl and arrange the eggs (if using) around the side.

TUNA SALAD

This creamy spread is a staple of the Jewish delicatessen and any meal or gathering where bagels are served. To make a sandwich fit for the deli, toast two pieces of rye bread and spread them with mustard, then top with several spoonfuls of tuna salad, crisp lettuce, ripe tomato, and paper-thin slices of red onion.

Serves: 4
Preparation time: 10 minutes

- ⅓ cup (80 g) mayonnaise
- ½ teaspoon yellow mustard
- 1 teaspoon fresh lemon juice
- 1 tablespoon sweet relish (optional)
- ½ teaspoon kosher salt
- Freshly ground black pepper
- 2 cans (5 oz/142 g each) water-packed albacore
  tuna, drained
- 1 medium celery stalk, finely chopped
- 2 tablespoons finely chopped shallot or red onion

In a small bowl, whisk together the mayonnaise, mustard, lemon juice, relish (if using), salt, and a generous amount of pepper.

Add the drained tuna to a medium bowl and flake with a fork. Fold in the celery and shallot, followed by the mayonnaise mixture, stirring until fully combined. Taste and adjust the seasoning, if desired. Serve immediately or cover and chill in the refrigerator for up to 3 days.

BAKED SALMON SALAD

Baked salmon salad makes a satisfying sandwich filling or a spread for matzo or crackers. It tastes best made with fresh fish, and is a great way to repurpose leftover baked salmon. But an equivalent amount of drained canned salmon can be substituted. Some cooks add a couple of grated hard-boiled eggs to the mix as well.

Serves: 6
Preparation time: 20 minutes
Cooking time: 20 minutes

- 1 lb (455 g) salmon fillets, patted dry
- Extra-virgin olive oil, for brushing
- ½ teaspoon kosher salt, plus more as needed
- Freshly ground black pepper
- ½ cup (120 g) mayonnaise
- 2 teaspoons fresh lemon juice
- 1 celery stalk, finely chopped
- ½ small red onion, finely chopped
- 1 tablespoon finely chopped fresh dill or
  1 teaspoon dried

Preheat the oven to 400°F (200°C/Gas Mark 6). Line a large baking dish with parchment paper.

Brush the salmon fillets on both sides with a little oil and season lightly with salt and pepper. Place in the baking dish and bake until the fish is pale pink and cooked through, 15–20 minutes. When cool to the touch, use your fingers or a fork to flake the salmon into bite-size pieces. (Remove and discard any bones. If the salmon fillets were skin-on, remove and discard the skin.)

In a medium bowl, whisk together the mayonnaise and lemon juice to combine. Add the flaked salmon, celery, red onion, dill, salt, and a generous amount of pepper. Mix gently to combine. Serve at room temperature or chilled.

BLACK-EYED PEA SALAD

Just like with stewed *loubia* (Black-Eyed Pea Stew, page 248), this Middle Eastern black-eyed pea (bean) salad, called *salata loubia*, is traditionally served on Rosh Hashanah, with the peas symbolizing hopes for success and fertility in the New Year. The salad can be made completely raw, but sauteing the onion, celery, and bell pepper in oil softens its texture and flavor.

Serves: 6–8
Preparation time: 30 minutes, plus soaking
Cooking time: 1 hour 40 minutes

For the salad:
- 2 cups (360 g) dried black-eyed peas (beans)
- 2 teaspoons baking soda (bicarbonate of soda)
- 3 tablespoons extra-virgin olive oil
- 1 onion, finely chopped
- 2 celery stalks, finely chopped
- 1 green bell pepper, finely chopped
- 2 garlic cloves, finely chopped
- Kosher salt
- 20 cherry tomatoes, quartered
- ½ cup (25 g) finely chopped fresh flat-leaf parsley

For the dressing:
- 2 tablespoons red wine vinegar
- 1 tablespoon fresh lemon juice
- ⅓ cup (75 ml/2½ fl oz) extra-virgin olive oil
- 1 teaspoon ground cumin
- ¼ teaspoon kosher salt, plus more as needed
- ¼ teaspoon freshly ground black pepper

Make the salad: Place the black-eyed peas (beans) and baking soda (bicarb) in a large bowl and cover with water by about 2 inches (5 cm). Cover the bowl with a tea towel and soak at least 8 hours or overnight. Drain, rinse, and drain again.

In a medium saucepan, combine the soaked peas and water to cover by about 2 inches (5 cm). Bring to a boil over high heat, then reduce the heat to medium and cook, partially covered and stirring occasionally, until peas are tender, 1–1½ hours. Drain in a colander and set aside to cool, then transfer to a large bowl.

Meanwhile, in a large frying pan, heat the oil over medium heat. Add the onion, celery, bell pepper, garlic, and a generous pinch of salt and cook, stirring occasionally, until the vegetables soften but retain a bit of crunch, 8–10 minutes. Remove from the heat and let cool slightly.

Add the sautéed vegetables to the black-eyed peas along with the tomatoes and parsley.

Make the dressing: In a medium bowl, whisk together the vinegar, lemon juice, oil, cumin, salt, and pepper until fully combined. Pour the dressing over the salad and toss to combine. Taste and add more salt, if desired. Serve warm, at room temperature, or chilled.

SALADS, SPREADS, PICKLES & STARTERS

Baked Salmon Salad

SMOKED WHITEFISH SALAD

A staple of the Jewish appetizing case (see page 26), smoked whitefish salad is creamy and satisfying with a pleasant touch of smoke. Serve it piled on a bagel, or with crackers and crudités for dipping.

Serves: 4
Preparation time: 30 minutes

- 8 oz (225 g) smoked whitefish fillets
- 1 celery stalk, finely chopped
- 2 tablespoons finely chopped shallot
- 1 tablespoon finely chopped fresh dill
- ⅓ cup (80 g) mayonnaise
- 2 tablespoons sour cream (optional)
- ½ tablespoon fresh lemon juice, plus more as needed
- ¼ teaspoon kosher salt, plus more as needed
- ¼ teaspoon freshly ground black pepper

Remove and discard the skin from the whitefish fillets. Using fingers and a fork, gently flake the fish into small pieces, being careful to remove and discard all bones.

Add the flaked fish to a medium bowl along with the celery, shallot, dill, mayonnaise, sour cream (if using), lemon juice, salt, and pepper and stir gently to combine. Taste and add more lemon juice or salt, if desired. Serve chilled or at room temperature.

DANISH HERRING SALAD

South Africa's Jewish community (the majority of which originally hailed from Lithuania) is particularly partial to briny herring, serving it at virtually every holiday and special occasion. This salad steeps the fish in a sweet and tangy marinade with chopped apple and onion for crunch.

Serves: 4–6
Preparation time: 15 minutes, plus chilling

- 1 cup (240 ml/8 fl oz) tomato sauce (seasoned passata)
- ¾ cup (175 ml/6 fl oz) apple cider vinegar
- ½ cup (100 g) sugar
- ½ cup (120 ml/4 fl oz) vegetable oil
- 1 teaspoon Dijon mustard
- ¼ teaspoon freshly ground black pepper
- 6 matjes herring fillets, cut into ½-inch (1.25 cm) pieces
- 1 small apple, peeled and finely chopped
- 1 small onion, halved through the root and thinly sliced

In a large bowl, whisk together the tomato sauce, vinegar, sugar, oil, mustard, and pepper until fully combined. Add the herring pieces, apple, and onion and toss to fully coat. Cover the bowl and refrigerate for at least 24 hours before serving. Serve chilled.

CHOPPED HERRING PÂTÉ

The Yiddish name of this herring pâté, *forshmak*, literally translates as "before taste," giving away the dish's role as an appetizer. Some recipes add sautéed onion, then bake the mixture and serve it warm. The cold version is often served on Shabbat morning spread on Kichlach (page 339) or crackers.

Serves: 4–6
Preparation time: 15 minutes
Cooking time: 20 minutes

• 2 eggs
• 2 slices challah, crusts removed and torn into large pieces
• ½ cup (120 ml/4 fl oz) milk
• 2 matjes herring fillets, rinsed and patted dry
• 2 scallions (spring onions), white and green parts roughly chopped, plus more for garnish
• 1 large tart apple, peeled and roughly chopped
• ¼ cup (60 g) sour cream

Place the eggs in a small saucepan and cover with water by 1 inch (2.5 cm). Bring to a boil, uncovered, over high heat. As soon as the water boils, turn off the heat, cover the pan, and let sit for 20 minutes. Drain the eggs and cover with cold water to stop the cooking process. Peel the eggs and cut in half. Set aside.

Add the challah pieces to a small bowl and pour the milk over them. Let the bread soak for about 1 minute.

Squeeze the challah dry (discard the milk) and transfer to a food processor along with the eggs, herring fillets, scallions (spring onions), and apple. Pulse until a smooth paste forms. Transfer to a bowl and fold in the sour cream. Serve chilled or at room temperature, sprinkled with more scallions.

LOX SPREAD

A fixture of bagel shops and Yom Kippur break-fast gatherings, this creamy spread combines two of the most popular bagel toppings—cream cheese and lox. Cold-smoked Nova lox (which can be purchased at most supermarkets) is bright and briny, pairing effortlessly with the finely chopped cucumber and bright scallions (spring onions).

Serves: 6–8
Preparation time: 15 minutes, plus chilling

• 1 small Kirby (pickling) cucumber, peeled, seeded, and finely chopped
• 8 oz (225 g) cream cheese, at room temperature
• 2 teaspoons brine-packed capers, drained and chopped
• 2 scallions (spring onions), white and light-green parts, very thinly sliced
• ¼ teaspoon freshly ground black pepper
• 4 oz (115 g) Nova lox

Wrap the cucumber pieces in a clean tea towel and give a good squeeze to soften them and extract as much of their water as possible. Transfer the cucumbers to a medium bowl along with the cream cheese, capers, scallions (spring onions), and pepper.

Use the back of a fork to shred the lox into small pieces, then add to the bowl. Mash the ingredients together with the fork until blended. Transfer the lox spread to a serving bowl, cover, and refrigerate until well chilled, at least 6 hours, or overnight.

JEWISH DAIRY RESTAURANTS

Vegetarian restaurants may be commonplace today, but back in the early twentieth century, they were virtually nonexistent. One exception to the rule: the Jewish dairy restaurant. In accordance with Jewish dietary law (see page 13), which forbids consuming milk and meat together, kosher restaurants serving brisket and pot roast could not also serve dishes made with milk, cream, or cheese.

Instead, diners went to a dairy restaurant—establishments like Rappaport's, Ratner's, and Garden Cafeteria on New York City's Lower East Side that served dairy delights from Cheese Blintzes (page 30) and sour cream–topped Potato Latkes (page 184) to creamy Potato Soup (page 134) and savory Vegetable Cutlets with Mushroom Gravy (page 237) that were a predecessor to the modern veggie burger. These eateries were as much cultural institutions as they were delicious spots for lunch or dinner—bustling places frequented by families, businessmen, and stars of the stage and screen.

Most patrons of the dairy restaurant were not vegetarian themselves—they simply had a hankering for noodle kugel or a plate of fried dumplings. But a small subset of dairy restaurants in New York—and also in prewar Europe—espoused vegetarian values of health and animal rights. In 1930s Lithuania, a Jewish woman named Fania Lewando ran a successful vegetarian restaurant and wrote a cookbook that connected Jewish values and a meat-free diet. Vegetarian diners in New York could also dine at Schildkraut's—a kosher-style restaurant chain (and later vacation resort) that served meatloaf and mock meats made from nuts and vegetables, and implored diners to explore a vegetarian diet.

Though the heyday of the Jewish dairy restaurant ended with Ratner's closing in 2004, many dairy restaurant favorites from Mock Chopped Liver (page 98) to Noodles with Curd Cheese (page 230) are simple to make and enjoy at home.

EGG AND AVOCADO DIP

Although not a dish with significant Jewish lineage, egg and avocado dip has become a reliable staple of Australian Jews' Shabbat and holiday tables in recent decades. It is also enjoyed in America, particularly within religious Ashkenazi communities. The dip tastes like a cross between egg salad and guacamole, and makes a wonderful spread for sliced Challah (page 46) or matzo.

Serves: 6–8
Preparation time: 15 minutes
Cooking time: 20 minutes

- 3 eggs
- 2 large avocados, halved and pitted
- 2 teaspoons fresh lemon juice, plus more as needed
- ½ teaspoon kosher salt, plus more as needed
- 1 tablespoon mayonnaise
- ½ small red onion, finely chopped
- Sweet paprika, for serving

Place the eggs in a small saucepan and cover with water by 1 inch (2.5 cm). Bring to a boil, uncovered, over high heat. As soon as the water boils, remove from the heat, cover, and let sit for 20 minutes. Drain the eggs and cover with cold water to stop the cooking process. Peel the eggs, chop into ½-inch (1.25 cm) pieces, and set aside.

Scoop the avocado flesh into a medium bowl. Add the lemon juice, salt, and mayonnaise. Use a fork or a potato masher to mash into a chunky paste. Add the chopped eggs and red onion and gently fold to combine. Taste and add more salt and lemon juice, if desired. Transfer the mixture to a serving bowl and sprinkle with a little paprika. Serve immediately.

ASSAF GRANIT

MACHNEYUDA
•
BEIT YA'AKOV STREET 10
JERUSALEM, ISRAEL

THE PALOMAR
•
34 RUPERT STREET
LONDON, ENGLAND

YUDALE
•
BEIT YA'AKOV STREET 11
JERUSALEM, ISRAEL

THE BARBARY
•
16 NEAL'S YARD
LONDON, ENGLAND

BALAGAN
•
9 RUE D'ALGER
PARIS, FRANCE

COAL OFFICE
•
2 BAGLEY WALK
LONDON, ENGLAND

Assaf Granit is one of Israel's best-known chefs and television personalities. He is the co-owner of the award-winning restaurant Machneyuda in Jerusalem, and also co-owns restaurants in Paris (Balagan) and London (Palomar, Barbary, Coal Office).

SWEET AND SPICY FENNEL, ORANGE, AND OLIVE SALAD

The bright, crisp, and briny combination of fennel with oranges and olives already makes for an addictive salad. But a showering of meaty almonds plus Granit's harissa and *silan* (date honey)-spiked dressing brings the dish to another level.

Serves 8
Preparation time: 30 minutes

For the dressing:
• 2 tablespoons harissa
• 1 garlic clove, minced or pushed through a press
• 1 tablespoon plus 1 teaspoon white wine vinegar
• 1 ½ tablespoons silan (date honey)
• ½ teaspoon kosher salt, or more to taste
• ⅛ teaspoon freshly ground black pepper
• ⅓ cup vegetable oil

For the salad:
• 3 navel oranges
• 1 pound (454 g) fennel bulbs, quartered, cored, and thinly sliced
• 8 scallions (spring onions), white and light green parts, thinly sliced
• 1 cup (120 g) roasted, unsalted almonds, roughly chopped
• ¾ cup (120 g) kalamata olives, pitted and roughly chopped
• Kosher salt and freshly ground black pepper
• Plain, full fat yogurt, optional

Make the dressing:
Add the harissa, garlic, vinegar, silan, salt, and black pepper to a medium bowl and whisk to fully combine. While whisking, slowly drizzle in the vegetable oil until emulsified. Taste and add more salt, if desired.

Make the salad:
Peel and segment the oranges: Using a sharp serrated knife, slice off the ends of each orange. Stand one orange upright on one of its flat ends. Starting at the top, cut away at a section of the peel, following the curve of the fruit to the bottom and taking care to remove all the white pith. Continue in this manner around the fruit until all the peel is gone. Hold the peeled fruit in the palm of your hand and gently cut between the membranes to release the orange segments. Repeat process with the remaining oranges.

Add the orange segments, fennel, scallions (spring onions), almonds, and olives to a serving bowl and gently toss. Just before serving, season salad lightly with salt and pepper and drizzle with a generous amount of the dressing (reserving the remainder for another use), then toss to combine. Dollop salad in several places with a little yogurt, if desired, and serve immediately.

CHOPPED EGG AND ONION

Chopped egg and onion might be described as egg salad's more sophisticated cousin. It starts with the same base of chopped hard-boiled eggs, but the onions get caramelized before being folded into the mix. The result is rich, sultry, and gently sweet. The Ashkenazi dish is popular in Hungary, where it is referred to as *tsidó tojás*, literally "Jewish eggs." There, goose fat is typically used to soften the onions, adding an extra layer of savory flavor—but chicken schmaltz or vegetable oil work well, too. Serve it on hearty bread or on top of challah, crackers, or matzo.

Serves: 6
Preparation time: 10 minutes
Cooking time: 35 minutes

- 8 eggs
- 3 tablespoons vegetable oil or Schmaltz (page 410)
- 2 large onions, finely chopped
- 1 teaspoon sugar
- ½ teaspoon kosher salt, plus more as needed
- freshly ground black pepper
- 3 tablespoons mayonnaise
- ½ teaspoon yellow mustard
- 1 teaspoon sweet paprika, plus more for sprinkling
- ¼ teaspoon freshly ground black pepper

Place the eggs in a medium saucepan and cover with water by 1 inch (2.5 cm). Bring to a boil, uncovered, over high heat. As soon as the water boils, remove from the heat, cover, and let sit for 20 minutes. Drain the eggs and cover with cold water to stop the cooking process. Peel the eggs, cut them in half, and set aside.

Meanwhile, in a large frying pan set, heat the oil over medium heat. Add the onions, cover, and cook until they begin to soften, about 5 minutes. Uncover, stir in the sugar, a pinch of salt, and 1 tablespoon water and continue cooking, stirring often, until the onion takes on a golden color with some browned edges, 6–8 minutes more. Remove from the heat and set aside to cool slightly.

Add the cooked eggs and half of the cooled onion mixture to a food processor and pulse a few times to break everything up. Be careful not to overpulse—it should look textured and fluffy, not smooth or pasty. Transfer the mixture to a medium bowl and gently fold in the mayonnaise, mustard, paprika, reserved onions, salt, and pepper. Taste and adjust the seasonings, if desired.

PAPRIKA CHEESE SPREAD

This Central European cheese spread (called *liptauer* in Austria, *smirkás* in Slovakia, and *körözött* in Hungary) is traditionally made with either a soft sheep milk cheese called *bryndza* or with quark. This version substitutes the easier-to-find (and equally delicious) cream cheese, flavoring the mix with sweet paprika, briny capers, and a bit of grated onion. Creamy and deeply savory, *liptauer* is delicious spread over crackers or slices of challah, and makes a wonderful sandwich condiment.

Serves: 6
Preparation time: 10 minutes, plus chilling

- 8 oz (225 g) cream cheese, at room temperature
- 6 tablespoons (85 g) unsalted butter, at room temperature
- 2 tablespoons grated onion
- 1 tablespoon brine-packed capers, drained and finely chopped
- 1½ teaspoons sweet paprika, plus more for sprinkling
- 1 teaspoon yellow mustard
- ¼ teaspoon kosher salt

In a stand mixer fixed with the paddle attachment, combine the cream cheese, butter, onion, capers, paprika, mustard, and salt and beat at medium speed until well blended and fluffy, 2–3 minutes. Transfer to a serving dish, cover, and refrigerate until the flavors have developed and the spread is well chilled, at least 2 hours. Serve chilled, sprinkled with a little more paprika.

Chopped Egg and Onion

EGG SALAD

The Jewish delicatessen is best known for its pastrami and corned beef sandwiches, but egg salad—a deli menu standard in its own right—makes a worthy alternative. Traditionally, chopped egg salads were bound with schmaltz, but today mayonnaise is typically used. Heap this creamy, flavorful spread as high as you like atop rye bread or challah and, for the full delicatessen experience, serve with a half-sour pickle on the side.

Serves: 4
Preparation time: 15 minutes
Cooking time: 25 minutes

- 6 eggs
- 1 celery stalk, finely chopped
- ¼ cup (60 g) mayonnaise
- ½ teaspoon yellow mustard
- ½ teaspoon kosher salt, plus more as needed
- ⅛ teaspoon freshly ground black pepper

Place the eggs in a medium saucepan and cover with water by 1 inch (2.5 cm). Bring to a boil, uncovered, over high heat. As soon as the water boils, remove from the heat, cover, and let sit for 20 minutes. Drain the eggs and cover with cold water to stop the cooking process. Peel the eggs, finely chop them, and add to a large bowl.

Add the celery, mayonnaise, mustard, salt, and pepper to the bowl. Gently fold until fully combined. Taste and add more salt, if desired.

CHOPPED CHICKEN LIVER

Chopped liver (originally made with goose livers, but today mostly made with chicken livers) is a beloved appetizer within Ashkenazi Jewish cuisine—a thrifty dish that transforms a less desirable part of the bird into a deliciously rich dish. The livers are broiled and mashed with eggs, browned onions, and schmaltz to make a spread for crackers, matzo, or challah. Chopped liver, called *gehakte leber* in Yiddish, is traditionally served on Shabbat and Passover, and can also be found on the menu at most Jewish delicatessens.

Serves: 6–8
Preparation time: 15 minutes
Cooking time: 45 minutes

- 3 eggs
- 3–4 tablespoons Schmaltz (page 410) or vegetable oil
- 2 medium onions, finely chopped
- 1 lb (455 g) chicken livers, rinsed and patted dry
- 1 teaspoon kosher salt, plus more as needed
- Freshly ground black pepper

Place the eggs in a small saucepan and cover with water by 1 inch (2.5 cm). Bring to a boil, uncovered, over high heat. As soon as the water boils, remove from the heat, cover, and let sit for 20 minutes. Drain the eggs and cover with cold water to stop the cooking process. Peel the eggs, coarsely chop, and set aside.

Meanwhile, in a large frying pan, heat 3 tablespoons of the schmaltz over medium heat. Add the onions and cook, stirring occasionally and adding a splash of water if the pan begins to look dry, until softened and browned, 20–25 minutes. Remove from the heat and let cool.

Preheat the broiler (grill) and set the rack in the highest position. Lightly sprinkle the livers with salt on both sides and place on a sheet pan. Broil (grill), turning once, until light browned on both sides, 3–4 minutes per side. Remove from the broiler and rinse with cold water. Pat dry and set aside.

In a medium bowl, combine the eggs, broiled liver, and onions. Using a sturdy fork, mash into a chunky paste. Stir in the salt, a generous amount of pepper, and the remaining 1 tablespoon schmaltz, if needed to thin the mixture. Taste and add more salt and pepper, if desired. Cover the bowl and store in the fridge. Serve chilled or at room temperature.

ALEX RAIJ

LA VARA
•
268 CLINTON STREET
BROOKLYN, NY
USA

TXIKITO
•
240 9TH AVENUE
NEW YORK, NY
USA

**SAINT JULIVERT
FISHERIE**
•
264 CLINTON STREET
BROOKLYN, NY
USA

EL QUINTO PINO
•
401 WEST 24TH STREET
NEW YORK, NY
USA

Alex Raij is the founder, chef, and co-owner along with her husband, Eder Montero, of several restaurants in New York City, including the Michelin-starred La Vara—a Brooklyn-based restaurant that explores southern Spanish cuisine through the lens of its historic Jewish and Moorish influences.

PIPIRRANA SALAD

This Andalusian-inspired salad is updated with Middle Eastern ingredients—like *freekeh* (green wheat), tahini, and pomegranate molasses—and is reminiscent of many chopped salads enjoyed in Israel.

Serves: 8
Preparation time: 40 minutes
Cooking time: 45 minutes

• 2 teaspoons kosher salt, plus more as needed
• 1 cup (180 g) freekeh
• 6 small Persian (mini) cucumbers, peeled, seeded, and finely chopped
• 2 green bell peppers, finely chopped
• ½ bunch cilantro (coriander), leaves picked (stems discarded)

For the vinaigrette:
• ⅓ cup (75 ml/2½ fl oz) fresh lemon juice
• 2 garlic cloves, finely grated
• 1½ tablespoons pomegranate molasses
• 1½ teaspoons kosher salt
• 1 tablespoon Aleppo pepper
• ⅔ cup (150 ml/5 fl oz) extra-virgin olive oil

For the tahini yogurt:
• ½ cup (120 g) whole-milk Greek yogurt
• ⅓ cup (75 ml/2½ fl oz) lukewarm water
• 4 tablespoons tahini
• 2 tablespoons fresh lemon juice
• 1½ tablespoons pomegranate molasses
• 1 small garlic clove, roughly chopped
• 1 teaspoon kosher salt
• ⅛ teaspoon cayenne pepper
• 4 tablespoons extra-virgin olive oil, plus more for drizzling
• 1 tablespoon chopped fresh dill

In a medium saucepan, combine salt and 6 cups (1.4 liters/48 fl oz) water. Bring to a boil over high heat, then add the *freekeh*, reduce the heat to medium, and cook, partially covered and stirring occasionally, until tender, 40–45 minutes. Drain well and let cool completely.

In a large bowl, combine the cooled *freekeh*, cucumbers, bell peppers, and about half of the cilantro (coriander) leaves. Toss to combine and set aside.

Make the vinaigrette: In a blender, combine the lemon juice, garlic, pomegranate molasses, salt, and Aleppo pepper and blend until well combined. With the machine running, slowly add the olive oil until emulsified. Set aside.

Make the tahini yogurt: In a blender, blend the yogurt, water, tahini, lemon juice, pomegranate molasses, garlic, salt and cayenne until smooth. With the machine running, slowly add the olive oil until combined. Add the dill and blend briefly until just combined.

To assemble the salad, toss the *freekeh* and vegetable mixture with the desired amount of vinaigrette. Taste and add a little salt and more vinaigrette, if desired, then spread on a wide serving platter. Generously drizzle the top with tahini yogurt, sprinkle the salad with the remaining cilantro, and drizzle with a little more oil.

HUMMUS

This creamy Levantine spread is enjoyed throughout the Middle East, including in Israel, and in recent decades has come to enjoy widespread popularity in America, England, and elsewhere. The mixture of mashed chickpeas, nutty tahini, garlic, and lemon juice is eaten at all times of day, and is considered a staple of the mezze table. In the Middle East, it is often served with freshly made pita and slices of raw onion for dipping. For added crunch and toasty flavor, fry a handful of pine nuts in a little olive oil until lightly browned and fragrant, and sprinkle on top.

Serves: 6–8
Preparation time: 15 minutes

- 2 cans (15 oz/425 g each) chickpeas, drained (liquid reserved)
- ½ cup (110 g) tahini
- ⅓ cup (75 ml/2½ fl oz) extra-virgin olive oil, plus more for drizzling
- 1 large garlic clove, roughly chopped
- 3 tablespoons fresh lemon juice
- 1½ teaspoons kosher salt, plus more as needed
- ½ teaspoon ground cumin
- Sweet paprika, za'atar, and finely chopped fresh parsley, for serving

In a food processor, blend together the chickpeas, tahini, oil, garlic, lemon juice, salt, and cumin (if using), using a spatula to scrape down the sides of the bowl as necessary, until a chunky paste forms, about 1 minute.

With the motor running, slowly drizzle in up to ½ cup (120 ml) of the reserved chickpea liquid, until the hummus is smooth and creamy, 2–3 minutes. Taste and add more salt, if desired.

Transfer the hummus to a serving bowl and smooth with the back of a spoon; drizzle with a little more oil and sprinkle with paprika, za'atar, and parsley. Serve at room temperature.

SPICED SQUASH DIP

North African Jews, particularly those from Tunisia, enjoy this savory, squash- or pumpkin-based dip as part of the mezze course. Serve it thickly spread on bread or with crackers or toasted pita for dipping.

Serves: 6
Preparation time: 15 minutes
Cooking time: 1 hour

- 1 medium butternut squash (about 2 lb/910 g)
- 3 tablespoons plus 2 teaspoons extra-virgin olive oil
- 1 teaspoon ground cumin
- ½ teaspoon ground coriander
- ½ teaspoon sweet paprika
- 2 small garlic cloves, minced or pushed through a press
- 1 tablespoon Harissa (page 409), plus more as needed
- ½ teaspoon finely grated lemon zest
- 1 tablespoon fresh lemon juice
- ½ teaspoon kosher salt, plus more as needed
- Labneh or Greek yogurt, for serving (optional)
- Chopped fresh parsley or cilantro (coriander), for garnish

Preheat the oven to 400°F (200°C/Gas Mark 6). Line a large sheet pan with foil.

Halve the squash lengthwise. Scoop out the seeds and discard. Rub 1 teaspoon of oil evenly around each half and place the squash, cut side down, on the pan. Roast until very tender and a knife inserted into the squash cuts through easily, 50–60 minutes. Remove from the oven and let the squash cool to the touch. Scoop the flesh into a food processor and process until smooth. Set aside.

Heat a medium frying pan over medium-low heat. Add the cumin, coriander, and paprika and toast the spices, stirring constantly, until fragrant, about 2 minutes. Remove the pan from the heat and stir in the remaining 3 tablespoons oil and the garlic. Let sit for 10 minutes to allow flavors to meld.

Scrape the spiced oil into the mashed squash with a rubber spatula. Add the harissa, lemon zest, lemon juice, and salt and stir well to combine. Taste and stir in additional harissa and salt, if desired.

To serve, spread a thick layer of *labneh* (if using), on a serving dish, making a wide, shallow well in the *labneh* with the back of a spoon. Spoon a layer of the butternut squash mixture over the top and scatter with chopped parsley. Serve at room temperature.

HUMMUS WITH FAVA BEANS

Gild the lily by topping creamy hummus with a pile of tender, garlicky fava beans. This dish, called *hummus ful*, is often served with hard-boiled eggs and pickles alongside, and with pita and slices of raw onion for dipping. Look for canned fava beans (sometimes labeled *ful medames*) in international and Middle Eastern grocery stores, or online.

Serves: 6–8
Preparation time: 20 minutes, plus soaking
Cooking time: 2 hours

For the hummus:
- 1 cup (180 g) dried chickpeas
- 2 teaspoons baking soda (bicarbonate of soda)
- ½ cup (110 g) tahini
- ⅓ cup (75 ml/2½ fl oz) extra-virgin olive oil
- 1 large garlic clove, roughly chopped
- 3 tablespoons fresh lemon juice
- 1 teaspoon kosher salt, plus more as needed
- ½ teaspoon ground cumin (optional)

For the ful:
- 1 can (15 oz/425 g) fava beans (broad beans)
- 2 tablespoons extra-virgin olive oil
- 1 tablespoon fresh lemon juice, plus more as needed
- 1 garlic clove, minced or pushed through a press
- ½ teaspoon ground cumin
- ¼ teaspoon kosher salt, plus more as needed

For serving:
- Extra-virgin olive oil, for drizzling
- Sweet paprika, za'atar, and chopped fresh parsley

Make the hummus: Add the chickpeas and baking soda (bicarb) to a large bowl and cover with water by at least 2 inches (5 cm). Cover the bowl with a tea towel and soak for at least 8 hours, or overnight. Drain the water, rinse the chickpeas, and drain again.

In a large saucepan combine the chickpeas with water to cover by several inches. Bring to a boil over high heat, then reduce the heat to medium, partially cover, and simmer, stirring occasionally, until the chickpeas are very soft and beginning to burst from their skins, 1–1½ hours. If necessary, add more water while cooking to keep the chickpeas fully covered. Reserving the cooking liquid, drain the chickpeas.

In a food processor, combine the chickpeas, tahini, oil, garlic, lemon juice, salt, and cumin (if using) and blend, using a spatula to scrape down the sides of the bowl as necessary, until a chunky paste forms, about 1 minute.

With the motor running, slowly drizzle in up to ½ cup (120 ml/4 fl oz) of the reserved chickpea liquid, blending until the hummus is smooth and creamy, 2–3 minutes. Taste and add more salt, if desired. Set aside.

Make the *ful*: Add the fava beans (broad beans) with their liquid to a medium frying pan. Bring to a boil over medium heat and cook, stirring occasionally, until the beans are tender and the liquid mostly evaporates, about 10 minutes. Stir in the oil, lemon juice, garlic, cumin, and salt, using the back of the spoon to gently smash some of the fava beans. Taste and add more salt or lemon juice, if desired. Remove from the heat and let cool slightly.

To serve: Spread the hummus into a wide, shallow serving bowl and make a well in the center with the back of a spoon. Spoon the fava beans into the well, then drizzle with oil and sprinkle with paprika, za'atar, and parsley.

HUMMUS WITH SPICED MEAT

In this delightful hummus variation, called *hummus im basar*, the creamy chickpea spread is topped with spiced ground (minced) beef. Served with pita, it is a meal unto itself. Vegetarians can substitute 1 pound (455 g) meat-free crumbles for the ground beef, adding another couple of tablespoons of oil during cooking.

Serves: 6
Preparation time: 15 minutes
Cooking time: 15 minutes

- 2 tablespoons extra-virgin olive oil, plus more for drizzling
- 1 large onion, finely chopped
- 4 garlic cloves, finely chopped
- ¼ cup (30 g) pine nuts
- 1 teaspoon ground cumin
- ½ teaspoon ground cinnamon
- ½ teaspoon smoked paprika
- ½ teaspoon ground turmeric
- ½ teaspoon kosher salt, plus more as needed
- ¼ teaspoon freshly ground black pepper
- 1 lb (455 g) ground (minced) beef
- 1 teaspoon Harissa (page 409)
- Hummus (page 96)
- Za'atar and finely chopped fresh parsley or cilantro, for serving

In a large frying pan, heat the oil over medium heat. Add the onion and cook, stirring occasionally, until softened and lightly browned, 6–8 minutes. Add the garlic, pine nuts, cumin, cinnamon, smoked paprika, turmeric, salt, and pepper and stir until fragrant, about 1 minute. Add the ground (minced) beef and cook, breaking up the meat into small pieces with a spoon, until just cooked through, 4–5 minutes. Remove the pan from the heat and stir in the harissa.

Spoon the hummus onto a large serving plate and make a wide, shallow well in it with the back of a spoon. Mound the spiced beef into the well, then top with a generous sprinkle of za'atar and parsley, and a drizzle of additional olive oil.

MOCK CHOPPED LIVER

Chopped liver is so central to Ashkenazi Jewish cuisine that intrepid cooks created a vegetarian version that can be served with kosher dairy meals. By pairing chopped hard-boiled eggs, creamy beans or legumes, and fried onions, the pâté mimics the richness and deeply savory flavor of the original. In addition to being served in homes as a spread for challah, mock chopped liver was a staple at New York City's venerable dairy restaurants (page 90). If you prefer to start with your own lentils, soak and simmer ¾ cup (150 g) dried lentils to yield about the same amount as a 15-ounce (425 g) can.

Serves: 6–8
Preparation time: 20 minutes, plus chilling
Cooking time: 20 minutes

- 2 eggs
- 2 tablespoons vegetable oil
- 1 large onion, finely chopped
- 1 tablespoon light brown sugar
- ½ teaspoon kosher salt, plus more as needed
- 1 can (15 oz/425 g) brown lentils, rinsed and drained
- ½ cup (50 g) walnut halves
- 2 tablespoons mayonnaise
- 1 teaspoon sweet paprika
- ½ teaspoon onion powder
- ½ teaspoon freshly ground black pepper

Place the eggs in a small saucepan and cover with water by 1 inch (2.5 cm). Bring to a boil, uncovered, over high heat. As soon as the water boils, remove from the heat, cover, and let sit for 20 minutes. Drain the eggs and cover with cold water to stop the cooking process. Peel the eggs, quarter, and set aside.

Meanwhile, in a frying pan, heat the oil over medium heat. Add the onion, brown sugar, and a pinch of salt and cook, stirring occasionally, until softened and browned, 8–10 minutes. Remove from the heat and set aside to cool slightly.

In a food processor, combine the cooked eggs, cooled onion, lentils, walnuts, mayonnaise, paprika, onion powder, salt, and pepper and pulse until smooth, scraping down the sides of the bowl as necessary. Transfer to a medium bowl, cover, and refrigerate for at least 2 hours or overnight to let the flavors develop. Serve cold or at room temperature.

Hummus with Spiced Meat

SPINACH YOGURT DIP

Cold yogurt dips mixed with cooked vegetables—typically spinach, eggplant (aubergine), beets, or cucumber—are common across Persian cuisine. This spinach version, called *borani esfanaj*, is infused with dried mint and cinnamon and can be served with pita, challah, or any other bread during the mezze course. It also makes a great partner for crudités and is delicious on top of egg, fish, and vegetable dishes.

Serves: 8
Preparation time: 10 minutes, plus chilling
Cooking time: 20 minutes

• 10 oz (285 g) baby spinach, rinsed and drained, but not patted dry
• ¼ cup (60 ml/2 fl oz) vegetable oil
• 1 large onion, finely chopped
• 2 garlic cloves, minced or pushed through a press
• ½ teaspoon dried mint, plus more for serving
• ½ teaspoon ground cinnamon
• 2 cups (360 g) plain yogurt (not Greek)
• ¾ teaspoon kosher salt, plus more as needed
• ¼ teaspoon freshly ground black pepper
• Toasted walnuts, for serving

Add the baby spinach to a large saucepan set over medium-high heat. Cover and cook, stirring occasionally, until wilted, 2–4 minutes. Transfer the spinach to a colander to drain and cool to the touch, then squeeze out the excess water, coarsely chop, and set aside.

In a medium frying pan, heat the oil over medium heat. Add the onion and cook, stirring occasionally, until softened and golden brown, 10–15 minutes. Stir in the garlic, mint, and cinnamon and cook, stirring, until fragrant, about 1 minute. Add the wilted spinach and cook, stirring, until combined, 1–2 minutes. Remove from the heat and set aside to cool slightly.

In a medium bowl, whisk together the yogurt, salt, and pepper. Fold in the spinach and onion mixture until thoroughly combined. Cover and refrigerate for at least 2 hours, or up to 1 day, to allow the flavors to develop. Just before serving, taste and add more salt, if desired. Transfer to a serving dish and sprinkle with additional dried mint and toasted walnuts. Serve chilled.

MUHAMMARA

Syrian Jews serve this thick red pepper, walnut, and pomegranate relish with pita as part of an elaborate mezze spread on Shabbat and holidays. Muhammara's flavor is quite complex—a mix of sweetness from the peppers, tang from the Pomegranate Molasses (page 410), and richness from the ground walnuts. The dish gets its name from the Arabic word *hamra* (red) and can be served as a sauce alongside grilled meat or vegetables.

Serves: 6
Preparation time: 15 minutes
Cooking time: 5 minutes

• ½ cup (50 g) walnut halves
• 1 jar (7 oz/198 g) roasted red peppers, drained well and roughly chopped
• 1 small shallot, roughly chopped
• ⅓ cup (45 g) dried breadcrumbs
• 1 small garlic clove
• 1 teaspoon ground cumin
• ½ teaspoon crushed pepper flakes, plus more as needed
• ¼ teaspoon smoked paprika
• 2 teaspoons fresh lemon juice, plus more as needed
• 1 tablespoon Pomegranate Molasses (page 410)
• ½ teaspoon kosher salt, plus more as needed
• ⅓ cup (75 ml/2½ fl oz) extra-virgin olive oil, plus more for drizzling
• Fresh pomegranate seeds, for garnish

In a small dry frying pan, toast the walnuts over medium heat, shaking the pan occasionally, until fragrant and lightly browned, 5–7 minutes. Immediately transfer to a cutting board to cool enough to handle, then coarsely chop.

Add the walnuts to a food processor along with the roasted peppers, shallot, breadcrumbs, garlic, cumin, pepper flakes, smoked paprika, lemon juice, pomegranate molasses, and salt. Pulse until a chunky paste forms, scraping down the sides of the bowl as necessary. With the motor running, drizzle in the oil and purée until combined. Taste and add more salt, pepper flakes, and lemon juice, if desired.

Transfer the muhammara to a bowl and make a shallow well in the center with the back of a spoon. Sprinkle the pomegranate seeds in the well, then drizzle a little more oil on top.

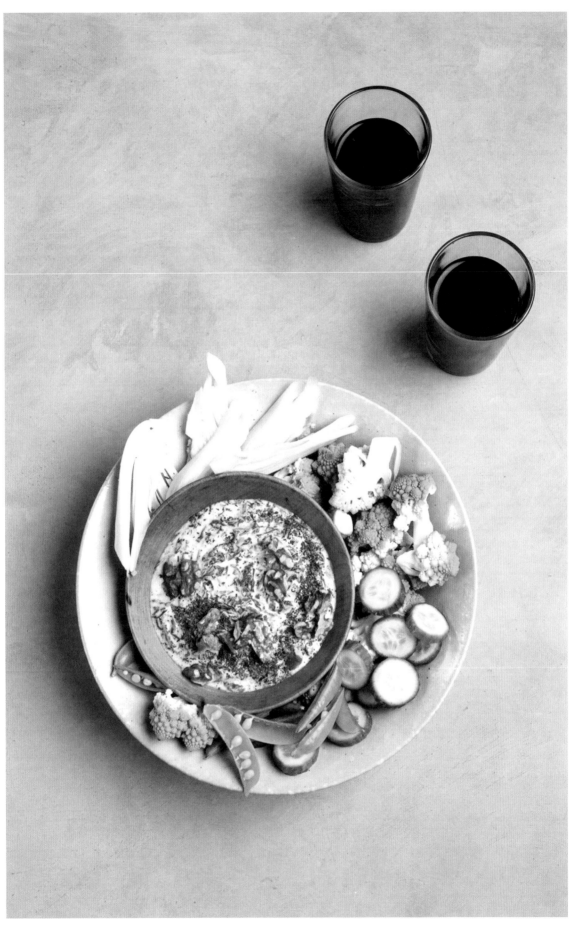

Spinach Yogurt Dip

SPINACH AND WALNUT PÂTÉ

In Georgia, pâtés called *pkhali* made from minced vegetables blended with a vinegary walnut purée are commonly served as a meal starter. In addition to the spinach used in this recipe, other vegetables including beets, green beans, and eggplant (aubergine) can be used as the base. Serve the creamy pâté with hearty bread or crackers for spreading or crudités for dipping.

Serves: 6–8
Preparation time: 20 minutes
Cooking time: 10 minutes

- 1½ cups (155 g) walnut halves, plus more for serving
- 1½ lb (680 g) baby spinach
- 1 small bunch cilantro (coriander), tough bottom stems removed
- 1 small bunch parsley, tough bottom stems removed
- 2 garlic cloves, roughly chopped
- ½ teaspoon sweet paprika
- ½ teaspoon ground turmeric
- ½ teaspoon ground fenugreek
- ¼ teaspoon cayenne pepper
- 1 teaspoon kosher salt
- ¼ cup (60 ml/2 fl oz) extra-virgin olive oil
- 1½ tablespoons apple cider vinegar
- Pomegranate seeds, for serving

In a small, dry frying pan, toast the walnuts over medium-low heat, shaking the pan occasionally, until fragrant and lightly browned, 5–7 minutes. Remove the pan from the heat and let walnuts cool.

Meanwhile, bring a large pot of water to a boil over high heat. Add the spinach and cook until wilted, about 30 seconds. Drain, rinse with cold water, and drain again, then squeeze out as much water as possible. Transfer the spinach to a food processor and pulse, scraping down the sides of the bowl as necessary, until smooth. Transfer the puréed spinach to a medium bowl.

Add the toasted walnuts to the food processor along with the cilantro, parsley, garlic, paprika, turmeric, fenugreek, cayenne, salt, oil, and vinegar and pulse until smooth. Add the walnut mixture to the spinach and mix well to thoroughly combine.

Transfer the mixture to a serving bowl and sprinkle with pomegranate seeds and more roughly chopped walnuts.

SAUERKRAUT

Naturally fermented cabbage has an effervescently sour flavor, and packs a probiotic punch that is great for digestive health. It is a great place to start for cooks looking to break into the world of lacto-fermentation. Serve this kraut on top of hot dogs, inside or alongside a knish (pages 198 and 213), in salads, or with any dish that could benefit from a boost of tangy flavor.

Makes: 1 quart (1 liter)
Preparation time: 30 minutes, plus fermenting

- 1 small head cabbage (about 2 lb/910 g), rinsed and tough outer leaves removed
- 1 tablespoon kosher salt, plus more as needed
- 1 teaspoon caraway seeds (optional)

Quarter and core the cabbage. Slice the quarters into very thin shreds. Add the shredded cabbage to a large bowl and sprinkle with the salt. Use your hands to gently massage the cabbage until it softens and releases liquid, 10–15 minutes. Add the caraway seeds (if using) and stir to combine.

Pack the cabbage and its liquid tightly into a clean, dry wide-mouth 1-quart (1-liter) glass jar. Press down firmly on the cabbage as you add it to the jar to release more liquid and press out any air bubbles. The liquid should fully cover the cabbage. If it does not, mix together 1 cup (240 ml/8 fl oz) water with 1 teaspoon kosher salt and pour it over until completely submerged.

Fill a smaller, clean jar or glass with water and place it in the widemouthed jar on top of the cabbage. (This will help keep the cabbage submerged under liquid while it ferments.) Cover with a towel and let sit at room temperature until fermented, 7–10 days. Remove the smaller glass jar and cover the wide-mouth jar with a lid. Refrigerate and enjoy for up to 9 months.

EVAN BLOOM, ARI BLOOM, AND LEO BECKERMAN

WISE SONS JEWISH
DELICATESSEN
•
MULTIPLE LOCATIONS
SAN FRANCISCO, CA
USA

WISE SONS JEWISH
DELICATESSEN
•
MARUNOUCHI BUILDING
B1F
MUNOUCHI CHIYODA-KU
TOKYO, JAPAN

Evan Bloom, Ari Bloom, and Leo Beckerman are co-founders of Wise Sons Jewish Delicatessen—an artisanal deli based in San Francisco with a location in Tokyo.

SMOKED WHITEFISH TARTINE WITH PICKLED MUSTARD SEEDS

This creative take on smoked whitefish salad layers the Ashkenazi spread on toasted pumpernickel or freshly fried latkes. A handful of peppery greens and a sprinkle of pickled mustard seeds perfectly offsets the creamy salad. The recipe makes more pickled mustard seeds than are needed for the tartines. Stir the extras into potato salad or spoon them onto roasted salmon.

Serves: 6
Preparation time: 25 minutes, plus chilling
Cooking time: 20 minutes

For the pickled mustard seeds:
• ½ cup distilled white vinegar
• ½ cup (100 g) sugar
• 2 teaspoons mustard powder
• 1 teaspoon smoked paprika
• ½ cup (80 g) yellow mustard seeds

For the tartine:
• 1 lb (455 g) smoked whitefish, bones removed and flaked into small pieces
• ½ medium red onion, finely chopped
• 1 large celery stalk, finely chopped
• ½ cup (120 g) whole-milk Greek yogurt or mayonnaise
• 2 teaspoons finely chopped fresh dill (stems okay), plus more for serving
• 2 teaspoons finely chopped flat-leaf parsley (stems okay)
• 2 tablespoons fresh lemon juice
• ⅛ teaspoon kosher salt
• ¼ teaspoon freshly ground black pepper
• Baby arugula or mustard greens, for serving
• Toasted pumpernickel bread or freshly fried Potato Latkes (page 184), for serving

Pickle the mustard seeds: In a medium saucepan, stir together the vinegar, ½ cup (120 ml/4 fl oz) water, the sugar, mustard powder, and smoked paprika. Bring to a boil over high heat, stirring often, then add the mustard seeds and reduce the heat to medium-low. Cook, stirring occasionally, until the seeds roughly double in size, about 10 minutes. Remove the pan from the heat and let cool, then transfer to a bowl, cover, and refrigerate until chilled, at least 2 hours or overnight.

Make the tartine: In a large bowl, combine the flaked whitefish, red onion, celery, yogurt, dill, parsley, lemon juice, salt, and pepper. Mix well to combine. Place a small handful of arugula on a slice of toasted pumpernickel or a latke. Top with a scoop of the whitefish salad, and sprinkle with some pickled mustard seeds and a little more dill.

KOSHER DILL PICKLES

Pickled vegetables are hugely popular across Jewish cuisine, but for Ashkenazi Jews no variety is better known or better loved than pickled cucumbers. These garlicky, dill-flecked cukes are a highlight of the Jewish delicatessen and easy enough to make at home when the summer cucumber crop is in full swing. Start with evenly sized cucumbers, to ensure they pickle at the same rate.

Makes: two 1-quart (1-liter) jars
Preparation time: 20 minutes, plus resting and chilling
Cooking time: 10 minutes

• ½ cup (120 ml/4 fl oz) distilled white vinegar
• ¼ cup (40 g) kosher salt
• 1 teaspoon coriander seeds
• 1 teaspoon black peppercorns
• 1 teaspoon mustard seeds
• 8–12 small or medium Kirby (pickling) cucumbers, scrubbed
• 6 garlic cloves, thinly sliced
• ½ small bunch dill, washed, patted dry, and tough stems trimmed off

In a medium saucepan, combine 4 cups (950 ml/32 fl oz) water, the vinegar, and salt. Bring to to a boil over medium-high heat, stirring to dissolve the salt, then remove from the heat and let cool slightly.

In a small bowl, stir together the coriander seeds, peppercorns, and mustard seeds. Pack as many cucumbers (vertically) as possible into two clean, dry 1-quart (1-liter) glass jars, sprinkling in the spice mixture and tucking in the garlic and dill as you go.

Divide the warm brine between the two jars, fully submerging the cucumbers. Let cool completely, then cover the jars with lids and refrigerate for 2–3 days before eating. Keep in the fridge for up to 2 weeks—the flavor will continue to develop over time.

PICKLED GREEN TOMATOES

Eastern European Jews pickled all sorts of summer produce, including the unharvested green tomatoes left on the vine at the end of the growing season. In America, some Jewish delis still serve pickled green tomatoes (along with cucumber pickles) as a perfect, tangy foil to their rich and meaty sandwiches. The key to success with these pickles is to start with firm tomatoes that can stand up to the brine without falling apart. So for this recipe, be certain to use unripe green tomatoes, rather than a juicy heirloom variety that happens to be green. Firm red plum tomatoes can also be substituted, though will not taste quite the same.

Makes: 1 quart (1 liter)
Preparation time: 15 minutes, plus resting and chilling
Cooking time: 10 minutes

• 1 cup (240 ml/8 fl oz) distilled white vinegar
• 1 tablespoon kosher salt
• 2 teaspoons sugar
• 1½ lb (680 g) unripe green tomatoes
• 2 garlic cloves, thinly sliced
• 2 bay leaves
• 1½ teaspoons black peppercorns

In a small saucepan, combine vinegar, 2 cups (475 ml/16 fl oz) water, the salt, and sugar. Bring to a boil over medium-high heat, stirring to dissolve the sugar and salt. Remove from the heat and let cool 10 minutes.

Trim about ½ inch (1.25 cm) off the stem end of each tomato, then slice into quarters. Add the garlic, bay leaves, and peppercorns to the bottom of a clean, dry 1-quart (1-liter) glass jar. Pack in as many of the tomato pieces as possible without squishing them too tightly. Pour the vinegar mixture over the top of the tomatoes to completely cover. Cover the jars with a tea towel and let stand at room temperature until the brine cools completely, about 2 hours. Cover the jar with a lid and refrigerate for up to 2 weeks. The tomatoes will be ready to eat after 1–2 days, and will continue to get more pickled the longer they sit.

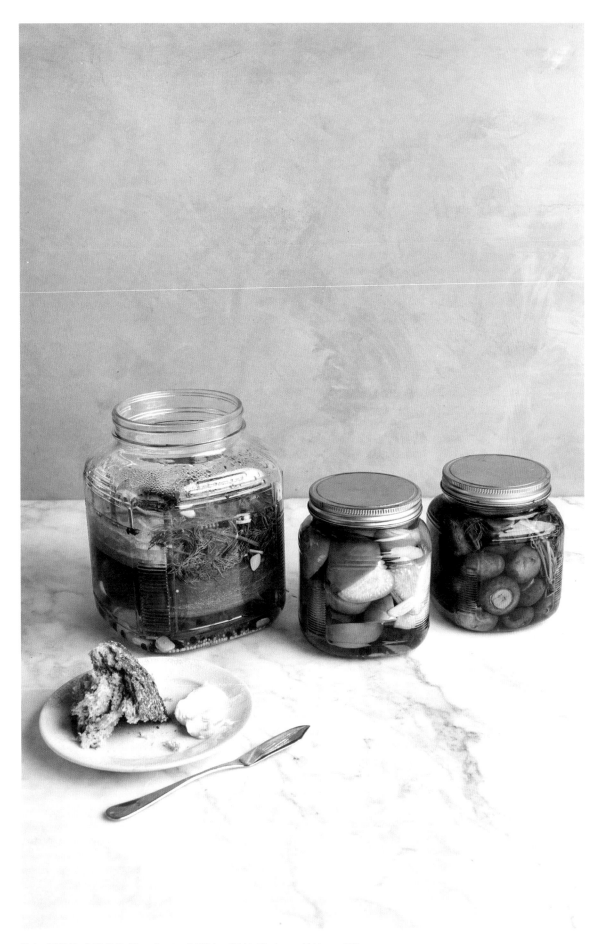

Kosher Dill Pickles (left), Pickled Green Tomatoes (middle), and Pickled Mushrooms (right; page 106)

PICKLING AND PRESERVING

For generations, Jewish communities across the world ate pickled and preserved foods out of necessity. In Eastern Europe, where the climate was too cold to grow crops half of the year, putting up crocks of pickles and sauerkraut or jarring sour cherries during the summer season ensured a family access to fruits and vegetables (and the nutrients they supplied) during the winter. Many families fermented beets in the early spring, creating a briny, tangy liquid called *rosl* that served as the base of Passover borscht. Others upcycled the lemony etrog (citron) used during the holiday of Sukkot (page 12), making jam from the peel to be enjoyed later in the year.

In warmer climates, where Sephardi and Mizrahi Jews typically hail from, transforming fruits like quince and pumpkin into jam, preserving lemon in salt, or pickling cauliflower and other vegetables helped these foods last before the advent of refrigeration. In both cases, these pickles and preserves became an integral part of the Jewish table—often served as part of an appetizer course, used to dress up salads and sandwiches, or eaten as a snack.

Apple Murabba (Apples in Syrup), page 401
Apricot Lekvar, page 400
Beet Eingemacht (Beet Jam), page 400
Beet Pickled Turnips, page 107
Candied Eggplant, page 402
Candied Quince, page 402
Kosher Dill Pickles, page 104
Pickled Green Tomatoes, page 104
Pickled Mushrooms, below
Preserved Lemons, page 116
Prune Lekvar, page 408
Pumpkin Jam, page 401
Sauerkraut, page 102
Turmeric-Pickled Cauliflower, page 107

PICKLED MUSHROOMS

Polish and Russian Jews traditionally make the most of mushroom season by pickling the caps in dill and garlic-scented brine (see the photo on the previous page). They are a common addition to appetizer spreads and also make tasty picnic fare. Other types of mushrooms can be substituted for the cremini (chestnut).

Makes: 1 quart (1 liter)
Preparation time: 10 minutes, plus resting and chilling
Cooking time: 20 minutes

• 2 lb (910 g) cremini (chestnut) mushrooms, cleaned
• 1 cup (240 ml/8 fl oz) distilled white vinegar
• 2 teaspoons kosher salt
• 1 bay leaf
• 2 garlic cloves, thinly sliced
• 2 large sprigs dill
• Vegetable oil, for topping

In a medium saucepan, combine the mushrooms with water to cover. Bring to a boil over high heat, then reduce the heat to medium and cook until tender, 5–10 minutes. Drain and set aside.

In a small saucepan, combine the vinegar, 1 cup (240 ml/ 8 fl oz) water, the salt, bay leaf, and garlic. Bring to a boil over high heat, stirring occasionally to dissolve the salt, then remove from the heat and let cool slightly.

Add the mushrooms to a clean, dry 1-quart (1-liter) glass jar, tucking the dill in between the mushrooms. Pour the warm brine on top to cover, then drizzle 1–2 teaspoons of oil on top, to help create a seal. Loosely cover the jar and let the brine come to room temperature. Cover tightly and refrigerate for at least 24 hours before serving. The flavor will continue to develop the longer the mushrooms are stored. Keep in the refrigerator for up to 1 month.

TURMERIC-PICKLED CAULIFLOWER

These Syrian cauliflower pickles get their golden hue from turmeric and a subtle touch of fiery heat from Aleppo pepper. They make a lovely, tangy addition to a mezze spread on Shabbat, and taste delicious tucked inside a pita with Falafel (page 194). Other vegetables including cabbage, turnips, firm tomatoes, and carrots, can be substituted for the cauliflower.

Makes: 1 quart (1 liter)
Preparation time: 15 minutes, plus resting and chilling
Cooking time: 10 minutes

- ¼ cup (60 ml/2 fl oz) distilled white or apple cider vinegar
- 2 tablespoons kosher salt
- 1 small head cauliflower (about 1½ lb/680 g), stem trimmed, cut into small florets
- 4 garlic cloves, smashed
- ½ teaspoon ground turmeric
- ½ teaspoon Aleppo pepper or ¼ teaspoon crushed pepper flakes

In a small saucepan, combine 2 cups (475 ml/16 fl oz) water, the vinegar, and salt and bring to a boil over medium heat, then remove from the heat.

Pack as many cauliflower florets as possible, along with the garlic, turmeric, and Aleppo pepper, into a clean, dry 1-quart (1-liter) glass jar. Pour as much brine as possible over the vegetables to cover (you may not need all of it), then press down to submerge the vegetables inside. Let the brine cool completely, then cover and refrigerate for up to 3 weeks. The cauliflower will be ready after 2–3 days, and will continue to take on a deeper pickled flavor as it sits. Serve chilled.

BEET-PICKLED TURNIPS

These Middle Eastern turnip pickles, called *turshi left*, get their rosy coloring and just a hint of sweetness from beets. They make a great addition to a mezze spread, and are also delicious tucked into Falafel (page 194) in pita.

Serves: 6–8
Preparation time: 10 minutes, plus resting and chilling
Cooking time: 10 minutes

- 2 tablespoons red wine vinegar
- 2 tablespoons apple cider vinegar
- 2 tablespoons kosher salt
- 1 teaspoon sugar
- 1 lb (455 g) turnips, peeled, quartered, and cut into slices ¼ inch (6 mm) thick
- 1 small beet, peeled, quartered, and cut into slices ¼ inch (6 mm) thick
- 4 garlic cloves, smashed
- 1 bay leaf
- ¼ teaspoon crushed pepper flakes
- 1 teaspoon extra-virgin olive oil

In a small saucepan, combine 2 cups (475 ml/16 fl oz) water, the red wine vinegar, apple cider vinegar, salt, and sugar. Bring to a boil over medium heat, then remove from the heat.

Pack the sliced turnips, beet, garlic, bay leaf, and pepper flakes into a clean, dry 1-quart (1-liter) glass jar. Pour as much brine as possible over the vegetables to cover (you may not need all of it). Let the brine cool completely, then drizzle oil on top. Cover the jar loosely and let sit for 3–5 days unrefrigerated, depending on how strong you like them. Cover and refrigerate for up to 3 weeks. Serve chilled, using tongs or a spoon (not fingers) to remove pickles from the jar.

SAUTÉED ZUCCHINI PEELS

It might seem odd to make a dish out of zucchini (courgette) peels without the flesh, but it is actually a wonderful example of culinary thrift. Turkish Jewish home cooks who were hesitant to throw anything away created this simple recipe, called *kaskarikas*, as a way of repurposing a pile of zucchini peels that would otherwise get tossed. It is a great dish to keep in mind during the height of summer, when the zucchini crop is overflowing. Serve it as part of a larger mezze spread, and use the peeled zucchini in the Crustless Spinach and Zucchini Quiche (page 252).

Serves: 2–4
Preparation time: 10 minutes
Cooking time: 10 minutes

- 6 medium zucchini (courgettes), about 2½ lb (1.1 kg), washed and dried
- 2 tablespoons extra-virgin olive oil
- 2 garlic cloves, finely chopped
- ⅓ cup (75 ml/2½ fl oz) tomato sauce (seasoned passata)
- ¼ teaspoon kosher salt, plus more as needed
- Finely chopped fresh dill and lemon wedges, for serving

Using a vegetable peeler or paring knife, thickly peel the zucchini (courgettes) leaving a little flesh attached to the peel. Cut the strips of peel into about 1-inch (2.5 cm) pieces. (Reserve the peeled zucchini for another use.)

In a medium saucepan, heat the oil over medium heat. Add the zucchini peels and cook, stirring occasionally, until softened, about 5 minutes. Add the garlic and cook, stirring, until fragrant, about 1 minute. Stir in the tomato sauce (seasoned passata) and salt and cook until just warmed through. Taste and add more salt, if desired.

Remove from the heat and transfer to a small serving dish. Serve warm or at room temperature, sprinkled with dill and with lemon wedges on the side for squeezing.

FRIED EGGPLANT SLICES

This Sephardi mezze classic, called *berenjena frita*, takes a while to prepare, but the mix of silky eggplant (aubergine) and bright herbs is completely worth the effort. Speed up preparation by using two separate pans to fry the eggplant simultaneously.

Serves: 8
Preparation time: 10 minutes, plus resting
Cooking time: 1 hour

- Extra-virgin olive oil, for frying
- 2 medium globe eggplants (aubergines), about 1½ lb (680 g) each, sliced into ¼-inch (6 mm) rounds
- ¼ cup (60 ml/2 fl oz) red wine vinegar
- ¼ cup (10 g) finely chopped fresh flat-leaf parsley
- 1 teaspoon dried oregano
- 4 garlic cloves, finely chopped
- Kosher salt, for sprinkling

In a large frying pan, heat ¼ inch (6 mm) oil over medium- high heat. Working in batches, add the eggplant (aubergine) slices to the hot oil and cook, turning once, until softened and lightly browned on both sides, 4–5 minutes per side.

Transfer half of the fried eggplant pieces to a medium baking dish. Sprinkle with half of the vinegar, parsley, oregano, garlic, and a little salt. Repeat with the remaining fried eggplant and remaining vinegar, parsley, oregano, and garlic. Sprinkle with more salt. Let sit at room temperature, basting occasionally with the juices in the baking dish, for 30 minutes. Or, cover and refrigerate overnight. Allow to come to room temperature before serving.

MICAH WEXLER

WEXLER'S DELI
•
MULTIPLE LOCATIONS
LOS ANGELES, CA
USA

Micah Wexler is the chef and co-owner, along with his business partner Michael Kassar, of Wexler's Deli, an artisanal delicatessen with multiple locations in Los Angeles. Prior to opening the deli, he and Kassar founded Mezze, which was a popular modern Middle Eastern restaurant also located in Los Angeles.

BEEF-STUFFED GRAPE LEAVES IN SPICED TOMATO SAUCE

This dish, which Wexler learned from his father, wraps a robustly spiced beef filling inside grape leaves and braises the parcels in a lemony tomato sauce until they are falling-apart tender.

Serves: 8
Preparation time: 1 hour
Cooking time: 2½ hours

- ⅓ cup (45 g) pine nuts
- ½ cup (120 ml/4 fl oz) extra-virgin olive oil
- 2 onions, finely chopped
- 2 lb (910 g) ground (minced) beef
- 1 tablespoon ground cinnamon
- 1 tablespoon ground coriander
- ¼ teaspoon ground allspice
- ¼ teaspoon ground cloves
- ¼ teaspoon ground nutmeg
- 1½ teaspoons kosher salt, plus more as needed
- ½ teaspoon freshly ground black pepper
- 5 garlic cloves, finely grated
- 2 tablespoons tomato paste (purée)
- 1 bunch flat-leaf parsley, finely chopped
- 1 bunch cilantro (coriander), finely chopped
- 1 jar (16 oz/454 g) grape (vine) leaves, drained
- 1 can (15 oz/425 g) tomato purée (passata)
- ½ cup (120 ml/4 fl oz) fresh lemon juice

In a small frying pan, toast the pine nuts over medium-low heat, stirring occasionally, until fragrant and lightly browned, 5–7 minutes. Remove from the heat and set aside to cool.

In a large frying pan, heat the oil over medium-high heat until smoking. Add the onions and cook, stirring occasionally until softened and slightly burned, 10–15 minutes. Remove the onions with a slotted spoon and transfer to a large bowl (leaving the oil in the pan).

Add the ground (minced) beef to the same pan along with the cinnamon, coriander, allspice, cloves, nutmeg, ¾ teaspoon of the salt, and the pepper. Cook, stirring occasionally, until the meat is just browned and fragrant, about 5 minutes. Add the garlic and tomato paste (purée) and cook, stirring, until fragrant, 1–2 minutes. Transfer the meat to the bowl with the onions. Add the pine nuts, parsley, and cilantro (coriander) to the bowl and set aside.

Using a small sharp knife, cut off the stems of the grape (vine) leaves, rinse under cold water, and lay the leaves around the rim of a colander to drain. Place 1 leaf, vein side up, on a flat surface and place 1 slightly rounded tablespoon of filling at the bottom of the leaf. Fold the bottom of the leaf over the filling, then fold each side in to the center. Starting at the bottom, roll the leaf upward, tucking the filling inside, and squeeze gently to seal. Gently place the sealed leaf, seam side down, in a large baking dish. Continue the filling and rolling process with the remaining leaves and filling.

Preheat the oven to 300°F (150°C/Gas Mark 2).

In a medium saucepan, combine the tomato purée (passata), 1½ cups (355 ml/12 fl oz) water, the lemon juice, and remaining ¾ teaspoon salt. Bring to a boil over high heat, stirring occasionally. Pour the tomato mixture over the filled grape leaves.

Cover the baking dish tightly with foil and bake until the grape leaves are very tender, about 2 hours. Serve hot or warm.

STUFFED GRAPE LEAVES

Sephardi and Mizrahi Jews serve tender stuffed grape leaves, called dolmades, filled with herbed rice (and sometimes meat) as part of a mezze spread on Shabbat and Sukkot. High-quality jarred grape leaves can be found in Middle Eastern and specialty grocery stores and also online.

Makes: about 2 dozen stuffed grape leaves
Preparation time: 45 minutes
Cooking time: 1 hour

- ⅓ cup (45 g) pine nuts
- ¼ cup (60 ml/2 fl oz) plus 3 tablespoons extra-virgin olive oil
- 1 medium onion, finely chopped
- 2 garlic cloves, finely chopped
- ½ kosher salt, plus more as needed
- 1 cup (200 g) long-grain white rice
- 1¾ cups (415 ml/14 fl oz) vegetable stock
- ⅓ cup (45 g) dried currants, soaked in water for 10 minutes and drained
- ½ cup (25 g) finely chopped fresh dill
- ½ cup (20 g) finely chopped fresh mint
- ½ teaspoon ground cinnamon
- Grated zest and juice of 1 lemon
- Freshly ground black pepper
- 1 jar (8 oz/225 g) grape (vine) leaves, rinsed and drained

In a small dry frying pan, toast the pine nuts over medium-low heat, stirring occasionally, until lightly browned, 5–7 minutes. Remove from the heat and let cool.

In a medium saucepan, heat 3 tablespoons the oil over medium heat. Add the onion, garlic, and a pinch of salt and cook, stirring occasionally, until softened, 6–8 minutes. Add the rice and cook, stirring, until toasty smelling, 1–2 minutes. Add ¾ cup (175 ml/6 fl oz) of the stock, reduce the heat to low, and cook, uncovered, until the liquid is nearly absorbed, 5–10 minutes. (The rice should be a little more than half-cooked at this point.) Remove the pan from the heat and stir in the pine nuts, currants, dill, mint, cinnamon, lemon zest, salt, and a generous amount of pepper. Let the mixture cool to the touch.

Meanwhile, bring a large pot of water to a boil. Add the grape (vine) leaves and boil until tender, 5–10 minutes. Drain the leaves, rinse with cold water, and drain again.

Place 1 leaf, vein side up and with the stem facing you, on a work surface and place 1 slightly rounded tablespoon of filling near the bottom of the leaf. Fold the bottom of the leaf over the filling, then fold each side in to the center. Starting at the bottom, roll the leaf upward, tucking the filling inside, and squeeze gently to seal. Repeat with the remaining leaves and filling.

Place the filled grape leaves in a single layer, seam side down, in a large Dutch oven (casserole) or wide-bottomed saucepan. Pour the remaining 1 cup (240 ml/8 fl oz) stock, remaining ¼ cup (60 ml/2 fl oz) oil, and lemon juice over the rolls. (If the liquid does not reach at least halfway up the sides of the rolls, add a little water or more stock.) Bring the mixture to a simmer over medium heat, then reduce the heat to low, and place an inverted, heatproof plate on top of the rolls to keep in place. Cover the pan and simmer until the grape leaves are tender when pierced with a fork, 35–40 minutes. Serve warm or at room temperature.

SALT-AND-PEPPER CHICKPEAS

Chickpeas are most closely associated with Sephardi and Mizrahi cuisines, but Ashkenazi Jews eat them, too, boiled and simply but generously seasoned with salt and pepper. Called either *arbes* ("peas" in Yiddish) or *nahit* ("chickpeas"), they are served as a snack on Purim in honor of the vegetarian diet Queen Esther was said to have eaten while living in ancient Persia. They also show up as an appetizer for Friday night dinner, on Saturday morning tables, and at life-cycle events like an engagement party.

Serves: 4–6
Prep time: 5 minutes, plus soaking
Cook time: 1½ hours

• 1 cup (180 g) dried chickpeas
• 2 teaspoons baking soda (bicarbonate of soda)
• 1 teaspoons kosher salt, plus more as needed
• Freshly ground black pepper

Add the chickpeas and baking soda (bicarb) to a large bowl and cover with water by at least 2 inches (5 cm). Cover the bowl with a tea towel and let soak for at least 8 hours (or overnight). Drain the water and rinse the chickpeas.

In a large pot, combine the chickpeas, water to cover by several inches, and salt. Bring to a boil over high heat, then reduce the heat to medium, partially cover, and simmer, stirring occasionally, until the chickpeas are very soft and bursting from their skins, about 1½ hours. If necessary, add more water while cooking to ensure the beans stay fully covered.

Drain the cooked beans well, blotting with a paper towel to soak up excess moisture, and transfer to a bowl. Season to taste with more salt and a generous amount of pepper. Serve warm.

FRIED HALLOUMI

This semihard brined cheese, typically made from a mix of goat and sheep milk, is popular across Greece, Turkey, and the Middle East. On its own, Halloumi is quite mild (think fresh mozzarella), but it has a high melting point that allows it to be fried or grilled into planks of salty, firm-but-gooey cheese bliss. In Israel, Halloumi is often served as part of a mezze course alongside hummus, pita, and Chopped Tomato and Cucumber Salad (page 78). It also tastes wonderful alongside fresh watermelon.

Serves: 4–6
Preparation time: 5 minutes
Cooking time: 5 minutes

• 8 oz (225 g) Halloumi cheese, cut into ½-inch (1.25 cm) planks and patted dry
• Exra-virgin olive oil, for brushing
• Lemon wedges, for serving

Heat a large frying pan or grill pan (griddle pan) over medium heat. Brush the cheese pieces on each side with a little oil and place on the hot pan. Cook, turning once, until browned on both sides, about 4 minutes total. Transfer the cheese to a serving dish and serve immediately, with lemon wedges for squeezing.

P'TCHA—JELLIED CALVES' FEET

Old World Ashkenazi cuisine includes a dish of garlicky jellied calves' feet called *p'tcha*. The labor-intensive recipe, which calls for thoroughly cleaning the feet and then boiling them for many hours, was sometimes served warm like a soup. But many families chilled it, which thickened the cooking liquid into aspic suspended with bits of meat and cartilage.

P'tcha is an example of Jewish poverty cuisine, where skilled home cooks transformed a less desirable (and therefore less expensive) part of an animal into a delicacy. And to this day, a small subset of Ashkenazi Jews maintains deep nostalgic affection for the dish. That said, it is fair to argue that there is no need to include a recipe for *p'tcha*—a dish that is no longer widely consumed and does not possess great comeback appeal—in a book aiming to capture Jewish cuisine in its contemporary moment. Let it be remembered, though, for its role in Jewish culinary history.

SWEET-AND-SOUR EGGS

Along with chopped liver and gefilte fish, sweet-and-sour carp was once a common Ashkenazi appetizer, or *forshpeis* in Yiddish. Some families also served a similar dish made with poached eggs, called *eiren zoyren*, as a thriftier alternative to fish. The flavorful sauce for both dishes is the same—a melted heap of caramelized onions and golden raisins (sultanas) that straddled the sweet-savory divide. This take on sweet-and-sour eggs is slightly updated for the contemporary palate. It uses red wine vinegar to add tartness to the sauce instead of the sour salt (citric acid) once favored by Eastern European Jewish households. It also poaches the eggs separately, instead of directly cooking them in the sauce, which allows for more precision and control over the finished dish. Serve the dish with thick slices of fresh challah for mopping up the sauce.

Serves: 6
Preparation time: 10 minutes
Cooking time: 45 minutes

For the sauce:
· 3 tablespoons vegetable oil
· 2 large sweet onions, halved through the root and thinly sliced
· ¼ cup (45 g) dark brown sugar
· ¼ cup (60 ml/2 fl oz) white wine or red wine vinegar
· 1½ teaspoons kosher salt
· ¼ teaspoon freshly ground black pepper
· ⅓ cup (45 g) golden raisins (sultanas)

For the eggs:
· ½ cup (120 ml/4 fl oz) distilled white vinegar
· 6 eggs

Make the sauce: In a large frying pan, heat the oil over medium heat. Add the onions and cook, stirring occasionally, until softened and lightly browned, 20–30 minutes. Add ½ cup (120 ml/4 fl oz) water, the brown sugar, vinegar, salt, pepper, and golden raisins (sultanas). Increase the heat to medium-high, bring mixture to a boil, and cook, stirring often, until the sauce thickens slightly, 3–5 minutes. Remove from the heat and set aside.

Make the eggs: In a medium saucepan, bring about 6 cups (1.4 liters/48 fl oz) water and the vinegar to a boil over high heat. Reduce the heat to medium-high heat. Using a large spoon, stir the water to create a whirlpool. Working in batches of 3, crack the eggs directly into the whirlpool and cook (do not stir) until the whites and yolks are just firm, about 5 minutes. Gently remove the eggs with a slotted spoon and transfer to a serving plate. Spoon the sauce on top and serve warm, at room temperature, or chilled.

MELANIE SHURKA

KUBEH
•
464 SIXTH AVENUE
NEW YORK, NY
USA

Melanie Shurka is the chef and owner along with her husband, David Ort, of Kubeh—a New York City–based restaurant that serves Middle Eastern small plates and specializes in *kubeh*, filled semolina-based dumplings.

ROASTED EGGPLANT WITH TAHINI AND POMEGRANATE

This dish, which is offered as a mezze option on Kubeh's menu, pairs softened wedges of eggplant (aubergine) with a sharp lemon dressing, rich tahini, and a bright pop of fresh pomegranate seeds.

Serves: 6
Preparation time: 30 minutes, plus chilling
Cooking time: 40 minutes

For the eggplant:
• 3 lb (1.35 kg) eggplant (aubergine), about 3 medium
• 2½ teaspoons kosher salt
• 1 cup (240 ml/8 fl oz) extra-virgin olive oil

For the lemon dressing:
• ½ cup (120 ml/4 fl oz) fresh lemon juice
• 3 tablespoons extra-virgin olive oil
• 1 teaspoon kosher salt

For the tahini dressing:
• ½ cup (110 g) tahini
• 2 tablespoons fresh lemon juice
• ½ teaspoon kosher salt
• ⅓–½ cup warm water (75 to 120 ml/2.5 to 4 fl oz)

For assembly:
• Pomegranate seeds, for serving
• Roughly chopped fresh flat-leaf parsley, for garnish

Prepare the eggplant (aubergine): Slice the eggplants crosswise into rounds ½ inch (1.25 cm) thick (keeping the skin on), and cut each round into quarters. Place the eggplant in a large bowl along with the salt and mix well. Line 2 large sheet pans with 2 layers of paper towels and divide the eggplant evenly between then. Transfer the pans to the refrigerator and allow to chill and drain, uncovered, for at least 3 and up to 6 hours.

Preheat the oven to 400°F (200°C/Gas Mark 6). Line two large sheet pans with parchment paper.

Transfer the eggplant pieces to a large bowl and add the olive oil. Gently massage the eggplant with your hands, to fully cover with oil. (It will look like too much oil, but the eggplant absorbs the excess while cooking.) Divide the eggplant onto the prepared sheet pans, spreading into a single layer on each pan. Roast, stirring occasionally, until golden brown and very tender, 30–40 minutes. Remove from the oven and let cool.

Meanwhile, make the lemon dressing: In a medium bowl, whisk together the lemon juice, olive oil, and salt. Set aside.

Make the tahini dressing: In a medium bowl, stir together the tahini, lemon juice, and salt. Slowly add warm water, stirring well after each addition, just until the mixture is creamy and thin enough to drizzle.

Assemble the salad: Transfer the cooked eggplant to a serving bowl. Sprinkle with a handful of pomegranate seeds and another handful of chopped parsley, then drizzle a generous amount of lemon dressing over top (reserving the rest for another use). Toss well, then drizzle the top with the desired amount of tahini dressing (reserving the rest). Sprinkle with more parsley and pomegranate seeds.

GEFILTE FISH

A staple of the Ashkenazi holiday table—particularly on passover—gefilte fish holds a key spot in the Jewish culinary canon. For more about its history and significance, see page 117.

Serves: 8
Preparation time: 20 minutes, plus cooling and chilling
Cooking time: 45 minutes

- 1 medium onion, roughly chopped
- 1 medium carrot, cut into chunks
- 1½ lb (680 g) whitefish fillets, skinned and cut into chunks
- ⅓ cup (45 g) matzo meal or dried breadcrumbs
- 2 eggs, lightly beaten
- 4 tablespoons finely chopped fresh dill
- 1 teaspoon kosher salt
- ¼ teaspoon freshly ground black pepper
- 1 teaspoon finely grated lemon zest (optional)
- Chrain (page 398), for serving

Preheat the oven to 350°F (180°C/Gas Mark 4). Line an 8 × 4-inch (20 × 10 cm) loaf pan with parchment paper, allowing the parchment to hang over by several inches on two opposite sides. Lightly grease the parchment paper.

In a food processor, pulse the onion and carrot until very finely chopped. Transfer the mixture to a large bowl. Tilt the bowl to pour off any liquid pooling at the bottom, but do not squeeze.

Add the fish to the food processor and pulse until it is finely chopped and begins to form into a ball. Add the fish to the vegetables along with the matzo meal, eggs, dill, salt, pepper, and lemon zest (if using). Mix well to combine.

Spoon the fish mixture into the prepared pan, gently smoothing the top with a spatula. Bake until golden brown around the edges, 40–45 minutes. (It is okay if some liquid pools at the top during baking.) Set the loaf pan on a wire rack to cool completely. If desired, cover and refrigerate until chilled, at least 2 hours.

Using the overhanging parchment, gently remove the chilled loaf and transfer to a cutting board to slice into pieces. Serve cold, topped with beet *chrain*.

GEFILTE FISH QUENELLES

Ingredients: see above

Make the fish mixture according to the method for Gefilte Fish then refrigerate for 30 minutes. Meanwhile, in a large soup pot, bring 3 quarts (2.8 liters) fish stock or vegetable stock to a boil over high heat. Reduce the heat to medium-low and keep at a simmer. Scoop out heaping tablespoons of the fish mixture and roll into egg-shaped patties. Gently drop the quenelles into the simmering stock. Cover the pot and cook until puffed, 30–35 minutes. Remove with a slotted spoon to a serving dish and spoon some of the stock on top. Let cool slightly, then cover the dish and refrigerate until chilled.

FRIED GEFILTE FISH

Ingredients: see above

Make the fish mixture according to the method for Gefilte Fish and set aside. In a large saucepan, heat 1 inch (2.5 cm) oil over medium heat. Line a large plate with paper towels. Spread enough matzo meal over a dinner plate to just cover the surface. Working in batches of 5–6, scoop heaping tablespoons of the fish mixture and, using moistened hands, form into balls. Roll the fish balls in the matzo meal to cover then fry, turning once, until golden brown all over and cooked through, 5–6 minutes. Drain on the paper towels.

Gefilte Fish

PRESERVED LEMONS

North African cuisines rely on salt-preserved lemons to add brightness and briny flavor to a wide variety of tagines and salads. The lemons take a month to fully cure, but can then be stored in the fridge for up to a year.

Makes: 1 quart (1 liter)
Preparation time: 15 minutes, plus curing

- Kosher salt
- 6–8 organic lemons, scrubbed and patted dry
- Juice of 3–5 additional lemons
- Optional add-ins: cinnamon stick, bay leaf, chilies, peppercorns

Sprinkle a ¼-inch (6 mm) layer of salt in the bottom of a clean, dry 1-quart (1-liter) glass jar with a tight-fitting lid.

Slice the tips off of each lemon and quarter lengthwise without cutting all the way through to the opposite side. Gently open each lemon and fill the crevices with about 1 tablespoon salt, then place in the jar. Press the lemons down as you go, packing them in as tightly as possible, with add-ins, if desired. When you can't fit any more lemons into the jar, pour over the additional lemon juice and press the lemons down until they are completely submerged. Cover the jar and let sit for 3 days at room temperature, turning the jar upside down occasionally.

Transfer the jar to the refrigerator and cure 3–4 weeks before using. Keep in the fridge for up to 1 year and use as needed.

CAPONATA ALLA GIUDIA

Before the Spanish Inquisition in the fifteenth century, parts of southern Italy (especially Sicily) were home to significant and vibrant populations of Jews. Since much of southern Italy was ruled by Spain at the time of the Inquisition, those communities were forced to flee. But while the region's Jewish life was effectively wiped out, much of their cuisine remained. Caponata, for example, is widely thought of as mainstream southern Italian fare, but Sicilian Jews first developed this sweet and sour eggplant (aubergine) relish as a dish that could be prepared before Shabbat and served at room temperature for Saturday lunch.

Serves: 8
Preparation time: 15 minutes, plus resting
Cooking time: 35 minutes

- ¼ cup (30 g) pine nuts
- Extra-virgin olive oil, for frying
- 1½ lb (680 g) eggplant (aubergine), peeled and cut into ½-inch (1.25 cm) pieces
- 1 large yellow onion, finely chopped
- 2 celery stalks, finely chopped
- 3 large garlic cloves, minced or pushed through a press
- 1¼ teaspoons kosher salt
- Freshly ground black pepper
- ¾ lb (340 g) tomatoes, peeled, seeded, and finely chopped
- 3 tablespoons apple cider vinegar
- 1 tablespoon sugar
- 2 tablespoons brine-packed capers, drained
- ⅓ cup (45 g) finely chopped pitted green olives
- ¼ cup (35 g) golden raisins (sultanas)
- Chopped fresh parsley, for garnish

In a small, dry frying pan, toast the pine nuts to over medium-low heat, shaking the pan occasionally, until fragrant and lightly browned, about 5 minutes. Transfer the pine nuts to a bowl to cool.

In a large frying pan, heat about ¼ inch (6 mm) oil over medium heat until shimmering. Add the eggplant (aubergine) pieces and cook, turning occasionally, until golden brown and softened but not mushy, about 10 minutes. Transfer the eggplant to a large bowl.

If the pan looks dry, add another tablespoon of oil. Add the onion, celery, garlic, and a generous pinch of salt and cook, stirring occasionally, until crisp-tender, about 5 minutes. Add the tomatoes, vinegar, sugar, capers, olives, golden raisins (sultanas), salt, and a generous amount of pepper. Cook, stirring occasionally, until the tomatoes soften, 6–8 minutes. Stir in the fried eggplant (with any residual oil from cooking) and pine nuts, cook until the mixture thickens slightly, about 5 minutes.

Remove from the heat and transfer to a serving bowl. Let stand for at least 30 minutes before serving to allow the flavors to meld. Taste and add salt, if desired. Serve at room temperature sprinkled with parsley.

GEFILTE FISH

Gefilte fish is one of the most contentious foods within Ashkenazi cuisine. Some people adore the chilled fish appetizer and can't imagine a Jewish holiday without it. Others find it utterly unpleasant. It is rare to find someone whose opinion exists in the middle of these two poles.

The word *gefilte* means "stuffed" in Yiddish, and gefilte fish was originally just that—finely chopped fish that got mixed with onions and matzo meal, stuffed back into the fish's skin, and then roasted. Eventually, that original preparation gave rise to the fish balls poached in fish broth that most people are familiar with today. And in recent decades, some home cooks have begun baking the fish mixture in loaf pans, which simplifies the preparation without sacrificing the final dish. Gefilte fish is traditionally made with carp, pike, and whitefish, but milder fish fillets

(cod, snapper, hake) work just as well while imparting a more delicate flavor.

There are several regional variations of the classic dish. Jews from the United Kingdom often fry the gefilte fish mixture, making crispy fish balls that resemble falafel. The practice stems back to the seventeenth century when Sephardi Jews settled in London, bringing their penchant for frying fish with them. And in Mexico, some cooks make gefilte fish a la Veracruzana (Veracruz-style), simmering the fish quenelles in a tomato sauce spiked with capers, oregano, and green olives. Recipes for gefilte fish quenelles and fried gefilte fish can be found on page 114. However it is made, the iconic Ashkenazi appetizer tastes best topped with a dollop of fiery prepared horseradish called *Chrain* (page 398).

FRIED FISH WITH CILANTRO-GARLIC SAUCE

Shabbat and holiday dinners in the Bukharian Jewish community invariably begin with this fried fish starter, called *mohibir'yon*. The sauce is traditionally very elemental, blending nothing more than fresh cilantro (coriander), garlic, salt, and water. If desired, dress it up with lemon zest or crushed pepper flakes, or substitute olive oil for some of the water.

Serves: 8
Preparation time: 25 minutes
Cooking time: 20 minutes

For the cilantro-garlic sauce:
• 1 large bunch cilantro (coriander), roughly chopped (leaves and stems)
• 3 garlic cloves, roughly chopped
• ½ teaspoon kosher salt, plus more as needed

For the fish:
• ½ cup (70 g) all-purpose (plain) flour
• 3 eggs
• Vegetable oil, for frying
• 8 trout or snapper fillets (4 oz/115 g each), patted dry with paper towels
• Kosher salt and freshly ground black pepper

Make the cilantro-garlic sauce: In a food processor, pulse the cilantro (coriander), garlic, and salt, scraping down the sides of the bowl as necessary, until finely chopped. Transfer to a bowl and stir in ½ cup (120 ml/4 fl oz) water to make a thick sauce. Taste and add more salt, if desired.

Cook the fish: Line a large plate with paper towels. Spread the flour onto a plate. Beat the eggs with a splash of water in a wide, shallow bowl (like a pie plate or a small baking dish). In a large frying pan, heat about ⅛ inch (3 mm) oil over medium heat. Season the fillets on both sides with a little salt and pepper. Working in batches, dredge the fillets in flour, tapping off the excess, then dip them in the egg, letting the extra drip off. Slip the battered fish into the hot oil and cook, flipping once, until cooked through and golden brown on both sides, about 3 minutes per side. Transfer the cooked fillets to the paper towels to drain.

Transfer the fish to a platter. Serve hot or warm, with cilantro-garlic sauce on the side for dipping or drizzling.

FIRST-COURSE FISH DISHES

Jewish communities across the globe tend to serve fish as a first course. The reason? Jewish dietary law includes a custom of not eating fish and meat at the same time. The custom is not held as strictly as the prohibition against serving milk and meat together, but is followed by religiously observant Jews. By serving fish first, the appetizer plates and forks can be cleared away, and diners can then enjoy meat during the rest of the meal.

Eastern Europe's Gefilte Fish (page 114) is arguably the most commonly known example of fish appetizers, but it is hardly the only one. There are variations on the gefilte theme, including Fried Gefilte Fish

(page 114) eaten in England, and South Africa's Curried Fish Balls (below). In Morocco, fish poached in spicy tomato sauce called Chraime (page 262) is often served as an appetizer. Bukharian Jews enjoy Fried Fish with Cilantro-Garlic Sauce (page 117) before the main meal, and the Jews of Calcutta eat *arook tahine*—scallion and ginger-scented fritters made with either fish or chicken—as a predinner nibble.

Of course, as is true with so many Jewish meals the world over, by the time the challah course and fish course are through, everyone is completely satiated, and must make room for the parade of dishes to follow.

CURRIED FISH BALLS

In South Africa, the Jewish community, which largely hails from Lithuania, developed this Passover and Shabbat appetizer. Balls of gefilte fish are pan-fried and then tossed with a sweet and tangy curry sauce in a wonderful mash-up of Eastern European, Malay, and Indian flavors that is unique to South Africa.

Serves: 6–8
Preparation time: 30 minutes, plus resting
Cooking time: 45 minutes

For the fish balls:
· 2 lb (910 g) firm fish fillets (sole, halibut, hake, snapper), skinned and cut into chunks
· 1 large onion, grated on the large holes of a box grater
· 1 large carrot, grated on the large holes of a box grater
· 2 eggs
· 2 tablespoons vegetable oil, plus more for frying
· ¼ cup (35 g) matzo meal or dried breadcrumbs
· 1 teaspoon kosher salt
· ¼ teaspoon freshly ground black pepper

For the curry sauce:
· 3 tablespoons vegetable oil
· 1 onion, halved through the root and thinly sliced
· 1½ tablespoons curry powder
· 1 teaspoon kosher salt, plus more as needed
· ½ teaspoon crushed pepper flakes
· 2 tablespoons light brown sugar
· 1½ cups (375 g) tomato sauce (seasoned passata)
· ⅓ cup (105 g) apricot jam

Make the fish balls: Working in batches if necessary, pulse the fish in a food processor until it is finely chopped and beginning to form a ball. Transfer to a large bowl and add the onion, carrot, eggs, oil, matzo meal, salt, and pepper. Mix well to combine. Cover the bowl and refrigerate for 30 minutes.

Meanwhile, make the curry sauce: In a large saucepan, heat the vegetable oil over medium heat. Add the onion and cook, stirring occasionally, until softened and lightly browned, 8–10 minutes. Add the curry powder, salt, and pepper flakes and cook, stirring, until fragrant, about 1 minute. Stir in the brown sugar, tomato sauce (seasoned passata), 1½ cups (355 ml/12 fl oz) water, and the jam. Bring the mixture to a low boil and cook, stirring occasionally, until slightly thickened, 5–10 minutes. Taste and add more salt, if needed. Keep warm.

To fry the fish balls, heat about ¼ inch (6 mm) oil in a large frying pan over medium heat. Line a large plate with paper towels. Form the fish mixture into 1-inch (2.5 cm) balls. Working in batches, fry them, turning as necessary, until browned all over and cooked through, 8–10 minutes. If they are browning too quickly, before the centers are cooked, nudge the heat down a little. Transfer the fried fish balls to the paper towels to drain, then add them to the curry sauce and gently toss to coat. Serve hot.

SALADS, SPREADS, PICKLES & STARTERS

Curried Fish Balls

SOUPS & STEWS

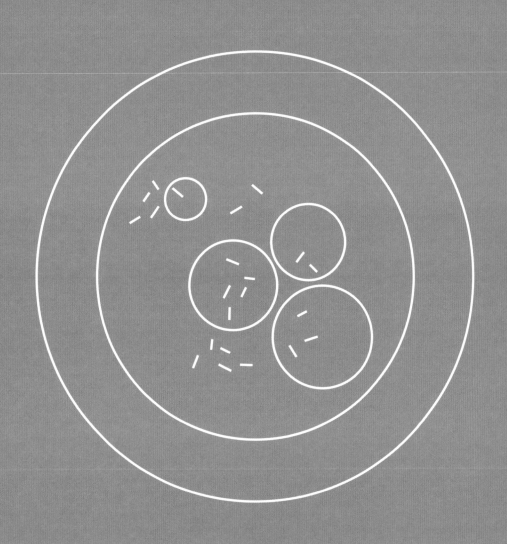

CHICKEN SOUP

This glistening soup is the undisputed crown jewel of Ashkenazi Jewish cuisine. Called everything from *goldene yoykh* (Yiddish for "golden broth") to Jewish penicillin (because of its healing qualities), it begins virtually every Shabbat and holiday dinner. Generations ago when resources were scarce for many Jewish families, chicken soup was almost always made with tough stewing hens that required many hours of boiling time. But when made with a standard broiler chicken, a full-flavored soup comes together quickly. In Mexico, some Jewish home cooks have begun to add regional flavors to the pot—to try a similar version, add 1 dried, seeded chipotle pepper along with the chicken and vegetables, and substitute fresh cilantro (coriander) for the dill. Garnish the soup at the table with finely chopped sweet onion, avocado, and more cilantro. Offer lime wedges alongside for squeezing. In either case, serve chicken soup with Passover-friendly egg noodles (page 226), Matzo Balls (page 220), or boiled Meat-Stuffed Kreplach (page 222).

Serves: 6–8
Preparation time: 15 minutes
Cooking time: 1½ hours

- 1 whole chicken (3½–4 lb/1.6–1.8 kg)
- 3 large carrots, halved crosswise
- 3 celery stalks, with leaves, halved crosswise
- 2 yellow onions, peeled and halved through the root
- 1 large parsnip, peeled and halved crosswise
- 6 garlic cloves, smashed
- ¼ cup (10 g) loosely packed fresh dill, with stems, plus more chopped dill for serving
- 1 tablespoon kosher salt
- Freshly ground pepper

Place the chicken, carrots, celery, onions, parsnip, garlic, and dill in a large soup pot and cover with cold water by 1 inch (2.5 cm). Bring to a boil over high heat, then reduce the heat to low. Gently simmer, partially covered, skimming off any foam that accumulates, until the chicken is very tender and falling off the bone, about 1½ hours. The soup should roll along at a very gentle simmer. If it starts to bubble too vigorously, turn the heat down a little.

Remove the chicken and vegetables from the pot and transfer to a cutting board and let cool to the touch. Strain the broth through a fine-mesh sieve into a large bowl. Return the strained broth to the pot.

Using your fingers, remove all the chicken meat from the bones and coarsely chop. (Discard the skin and bones.) Discard the dill. Slice the vegetables into bite-size pieces and return them to the pot with the chicken meat. Stir in salt and a generous amount of pepper. Taste and adjust seasoning, if desired. Divide into bowls and top with chopped dill. Serve hot.

SEMOLINA DUMPLINGS IN BEET SOUP

Iraqi and Kuridsh Jews make this tangy, bright-red beet soup with beef-filled semolina dumplings for Shabbat, holidays, and festive occasions. Called *marak kubbeh adom*, the spherical dumplings (*kubbeh* is Arabic for "ball") are related to a wide variety of Middle Eastern meat-filled dumplings, including the fried bulgur croquettes, Kibbeh (page 192).

Serves: 8
Preparation time: 1 hour
Cooking time: 1½ hours

For the kubbeh:
- 2 tablespoons vegetable oil
- 1 small onion, finely chopped
- 1½ teaspoons kosher salt, plus more as needed
- ½ lb (225 g) ground (minced) beef
- ½ cup (25 g) chopped fresh flat-leaf parsley, plus more for sprinkling
- 1½ teaspoons ground cumin
- ¾ teaspoon ground cinnamon
- ½ teaspoon ground allspice
- ¼ teaspoon freshly ground black pepper
- 2 cups (300 g) fine semolina, plus more for sprinkling
- 2 tablespoons all-purpose (plain) flour

For the soup:
- 3 tablespoons vegetable oil
- 1 large onion, finely chopped
- 2½ teaspoons kosher salt, plus more as needed
- 3 medium beets (about 1½ lb/680 g), peeled, quartered, and cut into thin slices
- 3 medium zucchini (courgettes), about 1 lb (455 g), peeled, halved, and cut into 1-inch (2.5 cm) pieces
- 4 large garlic cloves, thinly sliced
- 2 teaspoons sweet paprika
- 4 tablespoons tomato paste (purée)
- 8 cups (2 liters/2 qt) chicken or vegetable stock
- ¼ cup (60 ml/2 fl oz) fresh lemon juice
- 1 tablespoon red wine vinegar
- Freshly ground black pepper

Make the *kubbeh*: In a large saucepan, heat the vegetable oil over medium heat. Add the onion and a pinch of salt and cook, stirring occasionally, until soft and translucent, 7–8 minutes. Add the beef and cook, breaking up the meat into very small pieces with the back of a spoon, until the meat is browned, about 10 minutes. Stir in the parsley, cumin, cinnamon, allspice, ½ teaspoon salt, and pepper and cook, stirring, until fragrant, 1–2 minutes. Remove from the heat and set aside until cool enough to handle.

In a medium bowl, stir together the semolina, flour, and the remaining 1 teaspoon salt. Add 1 cup (240 ml/8 fl oz) water, stirring until completely combined. Cover the bowl and refrigerate for 30 minutes before forming the *kubbeh*.

Line a large baking sheet with parchment paper and sprinkle with a little semolina. Bring a large pot of water to a boil over medium-high heat. Using wet hands, pull off a rounded tablespoon of dough and roll it into a ball. Flatten the ball into a very thin round in the palm of your hand and place a rounded teaspoon of the meat mixture in the center. Close the dough around the meat (pinch off any excess dough), then gently roll the package in your palms to make a ball. Set aside on the prepared baking sheet.

Carefully transfer the filled *kubbeh* to the pot of boiling water. If they stick to the bottom of the pot, gently release with a spoon. Cover, reduce the heat to medium, and simmer until the *kubbeh* puff slightly and are fully cooked through, about 40 minutes.

Meanwhile, make the soup: In a large soup pot, heat the oil over medium heat. Add the onion and a pinch of salt and cook, stirring occasionally, until soft and translucent, 7–8 minutes. Add the beets, zucchini (courgettes), and garlic and continue cooking until they begin soften, 7–8 minutes. Stir in the paprika and tomato paste (purée) and cook, stirring, until fragrant, 1–2 minutes. Add the chicken stock and bring the soup to a boil. Reduce the heat to low, partially cover, and simmer for 30 minutes. Stir in the lemon juice, red wine vinegar, salt, and a generous amount of pepper.

Gently drop the cooked *kubbeh* into the soup, cover, and continue cooking for 10 minutes to warm through. Remove the pot from the heat. Taste and add more salt, if desired. Serve hot, sprinkled with additional parsley.

VEGETARIAN CHICKEN SOUP

Chicken soup is so central to Ashkenazi Jewish cuisine that vegetarians have developed meat-free approximations of the classic. A generous amount of olive oil provides the glistening golden broth typically provided by the chicken skin, while dried onion powder adds savory depth. Serve this soup with noodles, rice, or Matzo Balls (page 220).

Serves: 6
Preparation time: 20 minutes
Cooking time: 1 hour 45 minutes

- ¼ cup (60 ml/2 fl oz) extra-virgin olive oil, plus more as needed
- 2 large onions, quartered through the root
- 6 garlic cloves, roughly chopped
- 3 large carrots, cut into chunks
- 3 celery stalks, cut into chunks
- 1 large parsnip, peeled and cut into chunks
- 1 medium sweet potato (about ½ lb/225 g), peeled and cut into chunks
- 1 tablespoon onion powder
- 1½ teaspoons garlic powder
- ½ bunch dill, plus chopped dill for serving
- ½ bunch flat-leaf parsley
- 2 bay leaves
- 1½ tablespoons kosher salt, plus more as needed
- ½ teaspoon freshly ground black pepper

In a large soup pot, heat the oil over medium heat. Add the onions and garlic and cook, stirring occasionally, until softened and lightly browned, about 10 minutes. Add the carrots, celery, parsnip, sweet potato, onion powder, and garlic powder. Tie the dill and parsley bunches together at the stems with kitchen twine and add to the pot along with the bay leaves and 12 cups (2.8 liters/3 qt) water. Increase the heat to high and bring the soup to a boil. Reduce the heat to medium, partially cover, and cook, stirring occasionally, until the liquid has reduced by about a third, 1–1½ hours.

Remove the vegetables and strain the broth through a fine-mesh sieve into a large bowl. Return the broth to the pot and stir in the salt and pepper. Discard all of the vegetables and herbs except the carrots and celery. Cut those into bite-size pieces and return to the pot. Taste and if the soup is still a little thin, stir in a drizzle of additional oil and more salt, 1 teaspoon at a time. Serve hot, topped with chopped dill.

CHILLED BORSCHT

Tangy and refreshing, chilled borscht is the perfect antidote to a hot summer day. Ukrainian and Polish Jewish families used to ferment their own beet vinegar, called *rosl*, to add sour flavor, but apple cider vinegar makes a convincing substitute. To make the Polish variation called *chlodnik*, stir 1½ cups (355 ml/12 fl oz) buttermilk and two peeled and finely chopped Kirby (pickling) cucumbers into the borscht just before serving.

Serves: 6
Preparation time: 15 minutes, plus chilling
Cooking time: 1 hour

- 3 lb (1.35 kg) red beets, peeled and halved, or quartered if large
- 2 carrots, cut into large chunks
- 2 onions, quartered
- 2 bay leaves
- ¼ cup (60 ml/2 fl oz) apple cider vinegar
- 3 tablespoons sugar
- 1 tablespoon kosher salt, plus more as needed
- Boiled creamer (or other small) potatoes, sour cream, and chopped fresh dill, for serving

In a large pot, combine the beets, carrots, onions, 10 cups (2.4 liters/2½ qt) water, and bay leaves and bring to a boil over high heat. Reduce the heat to medium, partially cover, and cook until the beets are tender, about 1 hour.

Using a slotted spoon, remove the beets, carrots, onions, and bay leaves from the soup. If desired, strain the broth through a fine-mesh sieve and return to the pot. Discard the onions and bay leaves. Chop the carrots and about half of the beets and return to the pot. (Reserve the remaining cooked beets for another use.) Add the vinegar, sugar, and salt and stir well to combine. Taste and add more salt, if desired. Allow the soup to cool, then refrigerate until chilled, at least 4 hours.

To serve, add a couple of boiled potatoes to each bowl and ladle the soup on top. Garnish with a generous dollop of sour cream and a sprinkle of dill.

MAXIE EISEN
•
MUNCHENER STRASSE 18
FRANKFURT, GERMANY

STANLEY DIAMOND
•
OTTOSTRASSE 16-18
FRANKFURT, GERMANY

Brothers James and David Ardinast are co-owners of several restaurants including the pastrami-focused sandwich shop Maxie Eisen, the Jewish fine-dining spot Stanley Diamond, and the nouveau–Middle Eastern Bar Shuka, all based in Frankfurt. Together, they have helped introduce many Jewish dishes to contemporary German diners.

BRANDIED CHICKEN BOUILLON WITH LEMON-GINGER MATZO BALLS

The Ardinast brothers grew up eating their grandmother Adela's matzo ball soup, and created this homage that has become a signature dish at Maxie Eisen.

Serves: 6–8
Preparation time: 35 minutes, plus chilling
Cooking time: 2 hours 45 minutes

For the broth:
• 1 whole chicken (3½–4 lb/1.6–1.8 kg)
• 2 yellow onions, halved through the root
• 3 large carrots, halved crosswise
• 3 celery stalks, with leaves, halved crosswise
• 6 garlic cloves, smashed
• 1 sprig thyme
• 1 small bunch parsley (stems okay)
• 1 bay leaf
• 2 teaspoons black peppercorns
• 3 tablespoons brandy
• 1 tablespoon kosher salt, plus more as needed

For the matzo balls:
• 4 tablespoons vegetable oil
• 1 small onion, finely chopped
• 1 cup (105 g) matzo meal
• 1 teaspoon finely grated lemon zest
• 1 teaspoon grated fresh ginger
• 1 teaspoon kosher salt, plus more for boiling
• ¼ teaspoon freshly ground black pepper
• ⅛ teaspoon cayenne pepper
• 3 tablespoons finely chopped fresh parsley
• 4 eggs, lightly beaten
• 3 tablespoons seltzer (sparkling water)
• Chopped fresh parsley, for garnish

Make the broth: In a large soup pot, combine the chicken, onions, carrots, celery, garlic, thyme, parsley, bay leaf, and peppercorns. Pour the brandy on top, then cold water to cover by 1 inch (2.5 cm). Bring to a boil over high heat, then reduce the heat to medium-low. Gently simmer, partially covered, skimming off any foam that accumulates, until the chicken is very tender and falling off the bone, about 2 hours. The soup should roll along at a very gentle simmer. If needed, turn the heat down a little.

Carefully remove the chicken, vegetables, and herbs from the pot with tongs. (Discard the vegetables and herbs and reserve the boiled chicken for another use.) Strain the broth through a fine-mesh sieve lined with 2 layers of cheesecloth into a large bowl. (Discard any solids left in the strainer.) Return the strained broth back to the pot and stir in the salt. Taste and add more, if desired. Let the broth cool, then cover and refrigerate until needed.

Make the matzo balls: In a medium frying pan, heat the vegetable oil over medium heat. Add the onion and cook, stirring occasionally, until softened and lightly browned, 6–8 minutes. Remove from the heat and let cool slightly.

In a large bowl, mix together the matzo meal, lemon zest, ginger, salt, black pepper, cayenne, parsley, eggs, and seltzer (sparkling water) until fully combined. Fold in the onion, using a rubber spatula to scrape in any oil remaining in the frying pan. Cover the bowl and refrigerate for 1 hour to allow the matzo meal to soften.

When ready to cook, bring a large pot of generously salted water to a boil over high heat. Reduce the heat to medium and keep at a simmer. Moisten your hands with water, scoop out a rounded tablespoon of matzo ball batter, and roll it into a 1-inch (2.5 cm) ball. Drop into the simmering water, and repeat with remaining batter. Give the pot a gentle stir to release any matzo balls that may be sticking to the bottom. Cover the pot and simmer until the matzo balls are tender and puffed, 40–45 minutes. Remove the cooked matzo balls from the pot.

To serve, reheat the broth in a pot set over medium heat, stirring occasionally. Divide the broth among serving bowls and add 1–2 matzo balls per bowl. Sprinkle the soup with a little more fresh parsley.

AVGOLEMONO

Sauces and soups thickened with beaten eggs and gently soured with lemon juice are most popular in Greece, but beloved across many Mediterranean cuisines. Sephardi Jews serve avgolemono (literally "egg-lemon" in Greek) on Shabbat and to break the Yom Kippur fast—but it is simple enough to prepare for a weeknight dinner. The soup's creamy texture made without cream makes it particularly suitable for kosher meals. Vegetarians can replace the chicken stock with vegetable stock—though the soup's flavor will not be quite as rich or complex, it will still be delicious.

Serves: 6–8
Preparation time: 15 minutes
Cooking time: 30 minutes

- 2 tablespoons vegetable oil
- 1 small onion, finely chopped
- 1 celery stalk, finely chopped
- 1½ teaspoons kosher salt, plus more as needed
- 8 cups (2 liters/2 qt) chicken or vegetable stock, preferably homemade or low-sodium store-bought
- ⅔ cup (130 g) long-grained white rice, unrinsed
- 3 tablespoons cornstarch (cornflour)
- 3–4 tablespoons fresh lemon juice
- 4 egg yolks
- ½ teaspoon freshly ground black pepper, plus more as needed

In a large soup pot, heat the oil over medium heat. Add the onion, celery, and a pinch of salt and cook, stirring, until soft and translucent, 5–7 minutes. Add the stock to the pot, increase the heat to high, and bring to a boil. Stir in the rice, reduce the heat to medium, partially cover, and cook until the rice is completely tender, 15–20 minutes.

Meanwhile, in a medium bowl, whisk together the cornstarch (cornflour), 3 tablespoons lemon juice, the egg yolks, salt, and pepper until frothy.

Once the rice is cooked, slowly drizzle 1 cup (240 ml/ 8 fl oz) of the hot stock into the lemon and egg mixture, whisking constantly. Reduce the heat under the saucepan to medium-low and slowly stir the tempered egg mixture back into the saucepan. Continue cooking, stirring constantly, until thickened, about 5 minutes. Don't allow the mixture to boil, or the egg yolks could curdle. Remove the pan from the heat, taste and, if desired, stir in 1 more tablespoon lemon juice and additional salt and pepper, if desired. Serve hot.

Avgolemono

SWEET-AND-SOUR CABBAGE SOUP

Beet borscht is undoubtedly the most popular sweet-and-sour soup within the Ashkenazi soup canon. But this cabbage-based soup, called *krautsuppe* in German, is just as delicious. It is traditionally served during the cold winter months when a bright, savory potage is especially comforting.

Serves: 8
Preparation time: 15 minutes
Cooking time: 1 hour 50 minutes

- 3 tablespoons vegetable oil
- 2 lb (910 g) flanken or short ribs
- Kosher salt and freshly ground black pepper
- 2 large onions, halved through the root and thinly sliced
- 1 can (28 oz/795 g) diced (chopped) tomatoes
- 2 tablespoons tomato paste (purée)
- 8 cups (2 liters/2 qt) beef or vegetable stock
- 1 small cabbage (about 2 lb/910 g), core removed and finely shredded
- ¼ cup (45 g) light brown sugar
- ¼ cup (60 ml/2 fl oz) apple cider vinegar

In a large soup pot, heat 1 tablespoon of the oil over medium-high heat. Season the flanken on both sides with salt and pepper. Add to the pot and cook, flipping once, until seared on both sides, 6–8 minutes. Transfer to a plate and set aside.

Heat the remaining 2 tablespoons oil in the same pot. Add the onions and a generous pinch of salt and cook, stirring occasionally, until softened, about 10 minutes.

Return the browned flanken to the pot and add the diced tomatoes, tomato paste (purée), stock, and cabbage. Bring to a boil, then reduce the heat to medium-low, partially cover, and simmer until the vegetables and meat are tender, about 1½ hours. Stir in the brown sugar, vinegar, 2 teaspoons salt, and ½ teaspoon pepper.

Remove the pot from the heat. Take out the flanken and let cool to the touch. Cut the meat off the bones and chop into bite-size pieces. Return the meat to the soup pot. Taste and add a little more salt, if desired. Serve hot.

HOT BEET BORSCHT

Soured soups are hugely popular across Ukranian, Russian, Lithuanian, Polish, and Balkan cuisines—the bright and tangy flavors enlivening palates and spirits during the cold winter months. In America, the ruby-colored beet version of the soup is commonly associated with Jewish cuisine, since Jewish immigrants from those countries helped introduce it to American diners.

Serves: 8
Preparation time: 35 minutes
Cooking time: 1 hour 20 minutes

- 3 tablespoons vegetable oil
- 2 lb (910 g) flanken or short ribs
- Kosher salt and freshly ground black pepper
- 2 medium onions, halved through the root and thinly sliced
- 2 large carrots, thinly sliced
- 1 lb (455 g) beets, peeled and cut into ½-inch (1.25 cm) pieces
- 8 garlic cloves, finely chopped
- 2 tablespoons tomato paste (purée)
- 8 cups (1.9 liters/2 qt) beef or vegetable stock
- 3 cups (240 g) finely shredded cabbage
- 1 large Yukon Gold potato (about ½ lb/225 g), peeled and cut into ½-inch (1.25 cm) pieces
- 2 tablespoons fresh lemon juice
- 1 tablespoon red wine vinegar
- 1 teaspoon apple cider vinegar
- Chopped fresh dill, for serving

In a large soup pot, heat 1 tablespoon of the oil over medium-high heat. Season the flanken on both sides with salt and pepper. Add to the pot and cook, flipping once, until seared on both sides, 6–8 minutes. Transfer to a plate and set aside.

Heat the remaining 2 tablespoons oil in the same pot. Add the onions, carrots, beets, and a generous pinch of salt and cook, stirring occasionally, until softened, about 10 minutes. Add the garlic and tomato paste (purée) and cook, stirring, until fragrant, about 2 minutes.

Return the browned flanken to the pot along with the stock, cabbage, and potato. Bring to a boil, then reduce the heat to medium-low, partially cover, and simmer until the vegetables are very tender, about 1 hour. Stir in the lemon juice, red wine vinegar, apple cider vinegar, 2½ teaspoons salt, and ½ teaspoon pepper.

Remove the pot from the heat. Take out the flanken and let cool to the touch. Cut the meat off the bones and chop. Return the meat to the soup pot. Taste and add a little more salt, if desired. Serve hot, topped with chopped dill.

Sweet-and-Sour Cabbage Soup

MUSHROOM AND BARLEY SOUP

This soup may be homely, but its comforting mix of earthy mushrooms and plumped barley is remarkably delicious. Jewish families from Poland, Lithuania, and Ukraine served versions of the dish, called *krupnik*, for weeknight suppers, and immigrants from these countries brought it to America and Israel, where it remains popular today. A few ingredients in this variation stray from tradition (soy sauce, fresh thyme, cider vinegar), but help keep the soup exciting and robustly flavored for the contemporary palate.

Serves: 6–8
Preparation time: 25 minutes
Cooking time: 1 hour

- ½ oz (15 g) dried porcini mushrooms
- 1 cup (240 ml/8 fl oz) boiling water
- ⅓ cup (75 ml/2½ fl oz) extra-virgin olive oil
- 1 large yellow onion, finely chopped
- 2 large carrots, finely chopped
- 2 celery stalks, finely chopped
- 6 garlic cloves, finely chopped
- Kosher salt and freshly ground black pepper
- 1 lb (455 g) cremini (chestnut) or white button mushrooms, stemmed and thinly sliced
- 1 tablespoon chopped fresh thyme
- 1 bay leaf
- 1 tablespoon apple cider vinegar
- 2 tablespoons soy sauce or tamari, plus more as needed
- 7 cups (1.65 liters/56 fl oz) vegetable stock
- ½ cup (100 g) pearl barley, rinsed
- Chopped fresh flat-leaf parsley, for serving

Place the dried porcini in a heatproof bowl and cover with the boiling water. Let stand until tender, 15–20 minutes. Remove the mushrooms with a slotted spoon, rinse well, drain, and roughly chop. Strain the soaking liquid through a fine-mesh sieve or cheesecloth, reserving the liquid and discarding any sediment.

Meanwhile, in a large pot, heat the oil over medium heat. Add the onion, carrots, celery, garlic, and a pinch of salt and cook, stirring occasionally, until softened, 6–8 minutes. Add the porcini and cremini (chestnut) mushrooms and cook, stirring occasionally, until soft and lightly browned, 7–10 minutes.

Add the thyme, bay leaf, vinegar, soy sauce, reserved soaking liquid, stock, and barley. Increase the heat to medium-high and bring to a boil. Reduce the heat to medium-low, partially cover, and cook, stirring occasionally, until the barley is tender, about 40 minutes. Taste, then season with a generous amount of pepper and a little more soy sauce, if needed. Serve hot, topped with chopped parsley.

LENTIL SOUP

In the biblical story of dueling brothers Jacob and Esau, the elder son, Esau, sells his birthright to his younger brother, Jacob, for a few spoonfuls of "red stuff"—often interpreted to be a thick lentil stew. It is not surprising, then, that dishes featuring the humble pulse, including lentil soup, can be found across the entire global Jewish culinary cannon. This Eastern European–inspired version, called *linzen* in Yiddish, makes a hearty weeknight meal.

Serves: 6
Preparation time: 10 minutes
Cooking time: 45 minutes

- ¼ cup (60 ml) extra-virgin olive oil, plus more for drizzling
- 1 large onion, finely chopped
- 2 medium carrots, finely chopped
- 2 celery stalks, finely chopped
- 2 garlic cloves, finely chopped
- 1 teaspoon kosher salt, plus more as needed
- ½ teaspoon onion powder
- 1 teaspoon sweet paprika
- ½ teaspoon crushed red pepper flakes (optional)
- 2 tablespoons tomato paste (purée)
- 2 cups (400 g) red lentils, rinsed and drained
- 7 cups (1.65 liters/56 fl oz) vegetable stock
- Freshly ground black pepper
- Lemon wedges, for squeezing

In a large soup pot, heat the oil over medium heat. Add the onion, carrots, celery, garlic, and a pinch of salt and cook, stirring occasionally, until the vegetables soften, about 10 minutes. Add the onion powder, paprika, pepper flakes (if using), and tomato paste (purée) and cook, stirring, until fragrant, about 1 minute.

Add the lentils, stock, salt, and a generous amount of black pepper. Increase the heat to medium-high and bring the mixture to a simmer. Reduce the heat to medium-low, partially cover, and cook, stirring occasionally, until the lentils are tender and the soup thickens, 25–30 minutes. Taste and add more salt and pepper, if desired. Divide into bowls and serve hot, swirled with a little more oil and with lemon wedges on the side for squeezing.

HARIRA

This nourishing and deeply flavorful Moroccan soup comes brimming with legumes and lentils. Muslims traditionally serve it to break the nightly fast during the month of Ramadan, while Jews eat it to break the Yom Kippur fast. Many variations of harira include lamb (and you could certainly add some cubed lamb shoulder to the mix), but this version is complex and savory while remaining completely vegan. If a brothier soup is desired, decrease or omit the noodles.

Serves: 8
Preparation time: 15 minutes, plus soaking
Cooking time: 1½–2 hours

- 1 cup (180 g) dried chickpeas
- 2 teaspoons baking soda (bicarbonate of soda)
- ¼ cup (60 ml/2 fl oz) extra-virgin olive oil, plus more for drizzling
- 1 large onion, finely chopped
- 2 celery stalks, finely chopped
- 6 garlic cloves, finely chopped
- 1½ teaspoons kosher salt, plus more as needed
- 1 ½ teaspoons ground cumin
- 1 ½ teaspoons ground turmeric
- 1 teaspoon ground ginger
- 1 teaspoon onion powder
- ½ teaspoon ground cinnamon
- ½ teaspoon crushed pepper flakes
- Pinch of saffron, crushed
- 1 can (14½ oz/411 g) diced (chopped) tomatoes
- 8 cups (2 liters/2 qt) vegetable stock
- ¾ cup (150 g) dried brown, green, or French lentils, rinsed and drained
- ¼ teaspoon freshly ground black pepper
- 2 oz (55 g) angel hair pasta, broken into 1-inch (2.5 cm) pieces (about ¾ cup pieces)
- Lemon wedges, for serving

Place the chickpeas and baking soda (bicarb) in a large bowl and cover with cold water by at least 2 inches (5 cm). Cover the bowl with a tea towel and let the chickpeas soak overnight at room temperature. Drain, rinse, then drain well again.

In a large heavy-bottomed pot, heat the oil over medium heat. Add the onion, celery, garlic, and a pinch of salt and cook, stirring occasionally, until softened and lightly browned, 8–10 minutes. Stir in the cumin, turmeric, ginger, onion powder, cinnamon, pepper flakes, and saffron and cook, stirring, until fragrant, 1–2 minutes. Add the tomatoes and cook, stirring occasionally, until the mixture thickens, about 5 minutes.

Add the stock, drained chickpeas, lentils, salt, and black pepper. It will look like a lot of liquid, but will thicken as the beans swell and expand. Increase the heat to medium-high and bring mixture to a boil. Reduce the heat to medium-low, partially cover, and simmer, stirring occasionally, until the legumes are soft and creamy and the soup thickens, 1½–2 hours.

Just before serving, add the pasta and cook until softened, 2–5 minutes. Serve hot, drizzled with more olive oil and with lemon wedges on the side for squeezing. Store, covered, in the fridge, for up to 5 days. If the soup thickens too much, thin it with a little water or more stock while reheating it on the stove, and adjust salt as needed.

SOUPS & STEWS

SOUR CHERRY SOUP

Sweet, tart, creamy, and refreshing, chilled sour cherry soup (called *meggy leves* in Hungarian) is an Ashkenazi summertime treat. Sour cherries have a very short growing season, so buy a bundle when they appear at the farmers' market and make the most of their fleeting beauty. Frozen sour cherries, which are available at some specialty food markets, work well for this soup, too. But avoid the canned version, as it adds an unpleasant bitter taste to the soup.

Serves: 6
Preparation time: 25 minutes, plus chilling
Cooking time: 5 minutes

- 3 cups (420 g) fresh or thawed frozen sour cherries, pitted
- 1 cup (240 ml/8 fl oz) pure sour cherry juice (not from concentrate)
- ½ cup (100 g) sugar
- ¼ teaspoon kosher salt
- 2 cinnamon sticks
- 1 cup (240 ml/8 fl oz) heavy (whipping) cream
- Sour cream and ground cinnamon, for serving

In a medium saucepan, combine the cherries, cherry juice, 1 cup (240 ml/8 fl oz) water, sugar, salt, and cinnamon sticks and bring to a boil over medium-high heat. Reduce the heat to medium and simmer, stirring occasionally, for 5 minutes. Remove from the heat and transfer the soup to a nonreactive bowl. Let cool to room temperature, then cover and refrigerate until fully chilled, at least 2 hours or overnight.

Scoop about 1 cup (140 g) of the cherries out of the chilled soup and set aside. Add the heavy cream to the soup and use a hand blender to blend. Add the reserved whole cherries back to the soup and serve topped with sour cream and cinnamon.

SCHAV

The unique flavor of this summery Eastern European soup makes up for its humble appearance. Made from lemony-tart sorrel, which comes into season during the summer months, it is bracingly sour and refreshing. *Schav* is traditionally served chilled in bowls or glasses, with plenty of cool sour cream dolloped on top and hard-boiled eggs alongside as a hearty garnish. But it is also quite tasty served hot.

Serves: 4
Preparation time: 10 minutes, plus chilling
Cooking time: 45 minutes

- 4 tablespoons (60 g) unsalted butter
- 2 onions, finely chopped
- 1 teaspoon kosher salt, plus more as needed
- 1 teaspoon onion powder
- 2 medium russet (baking) potatoes (about 1 lb/455 g), peeled and cut into ½-inch (1.25 cm) pieces
- 5 cups (1.2 liters/40 fl oz) vegetable stock
- ¼ teaspoon freshly ground black pepper, plus more as needed
- ¾ lb (350 g) fresh sorrel, stems trimmed, leaves roughly chopped
- Chopped fresh chives, sour cream, and halved hard-boiled eggs, for serving

In a large saucepan, melt the butter over medium heat until foaming. Add the onions and a generous pinch of salt and cook, stirring occasionally, until softened, 8–10 minutes. Stir in the onion powder. Add the potatoes, stock, salt, and pepper. Increase the heat to medium-high and bring to a boil, then reduce the heat to low, cover, and cook until the potatoes are tender, 10–15 minutes. Uncover, stir in the sorrel leaves, and cook until wilted, 3–5 minutes. Taste and add more salt and pepper, if desired.

Remove the pan from the heat and let cool slightly. Transfer the pan to the fridge to chill, at least 3 hours or up to overnight. To serve, peel and quarter the hard-boiled eggs. Divide the soup into bowls and top with sour cream, chives, and hard-boiled egg.

Sour Cherry Soup

ORANGE SOUP

This soup, which is popular everyday fare in Israel, gets its name (*marak katom* in Hebrew) not from citrus fruit, but from the plethora of orange vegetables—typically carrots, sweet potatoes, and some variety of squash—that make up its base. It is delicious and satisfying all on its own, but even better swirled with a little yogurt and something spicy.

Serves: 6–8
Preparation time: 20 minutes
Cooking time: 40 minutes

- ¼ cup (60 ml/2 fl oz) extra-virgin olive oil
- 2 medium onions, finely chopped
- 4 garlic cloves, finely chopped
- 2-inch (5 cm) piece fresh ginger, peeled and finely chopped
- 1 medium butternut squash (about 2 lb/910 g), peeled, seeded, and cut into ½-inch (1.25 cm) pieces
- 2 lb (910 g) sweet potatoes, peeled and cut into ½-inch (1.25 cm) pieces
- ½ lb (225 g) carrots, cut into ½-inch (1.25 cm) rounds
- 2 cinnamon sticks
- 6 cups (1.4 liters/48 fl oz) vegetable stock, plus more as needed
- 1 tablespoon kosher salt, plus more as needed
- ½ teaspoon freshly ground black pepper
- Plain yogurt, Hawaij for Soup (page 415), or Harissa (page 409), for serving

In a large soup pot, heat the oil over medium-high heat. Add the onions, garlic, ginger, butternut squash, sweet potatoes, and carrots and cook, stirring occasionally, until the vegetables begin to soften, 15–20 minutes.

Add the cinnamon sticks and stock. Let the mixture come to a boil, then reduce the heat to medium-low, partially cover, and cook until the vegetables are very tender, about 15 minutes. Remove the pot from the heat and stir in the salt and pepper. Remove and discard the cinnamon sticks and let the soup cool slightly, then use a hand blender to blend until smooth and creamy. Taste and add more salt, if desired. If the soup looks too thick, stir in a little more stock. Serve hot, dolloped with yogurt and topped with *hawaij* or harissa.

POTATO SOUP

Potato soup was a weekday staple of the Eastern European Jewish diet, particularly during the winter months when home cooks had to make the most of a limited vegetable selection. This version of *kartofl zup*, as it is called in Yiddish, is aromatic, full flavored, and delightfully rich.

Serves: 6
Preparation time: 20 minutes
Cooking time: 30 minutes

- 3 tablespoons (45 g) unsalted butter
- 1 large onion, finely chopped
- 2 large leeks, white and light-green parts, thinly sliced
- 1 large carrot, finely chopped
- 1 medium parsnip, peeled and finely chopped
- 2 celery stalks, finely chopped
- 2 teaspoons kosher salt, plus more as needed
- 1 teaspoon dried dill, plus more for serving
- 4 medium russet (baking) potatoes (about 2 lb/910 g), peeled and cut into ½-inch (1.25 cm) pieces
- 5 cups (1.2 liters/40 fl oz) vegetable stock
- ½ teaspoon freshly ground black pepper, plus more as needed
- 1 cup (240 ml/8 fl oz) whole milk
- Sour cream, for serving

In a large soup pot, melt the butter over medium heat. Add the onion, leeks, carrot, parsnip, celery, and a generous pinch of salt and cook, stirring occasionally, until the vegetables soften, about 10 minutes. Stir in the dill.

Add the potatoes, stock, salt, and pepper. Increase the heat to medium-high and bring the mixture to a boil. Reduce the heat to medium-low, partially cover, and cook until the potatoes are very tender, 15–20 minutes.

Remove the pot from the heat and let cool for 5 minutes. Stir in the milk. Using a hand blender, blend the soup until smooth. Taste and add more salt and pepper, if desired. Divide into bowls and serve hot, topped with a dollop of sour cream and a sprinkle of dill.

Orange Soup

BEEF AND PAPRIKA GOULASH

Hungarian and Czech Jews share their non-Jewish neighbors' love of this savory, paprika-enriched beef stew. Serve it over egg noodles or as Czech Jews do, with fluffy Bread Dumplings (page 220) called *knedliky*.

Serves: 8
Preparation time: 15 minutes
Cooking time: 2 hours 20 minutes

• 3 tablespoons vegetable oil, plus more as needed
• 4 lb (1.8 kg) beef chuck, trimmed of excess fat and cut into 1-inch (2.5 cm) cubes
• 2 large onions, finely chopped
• 3 medium carrots, finely chopped
• 3 celery stalks, finely chopped
• 6 garlic cloves, thinly sliced
• 3 tablespoons all-purpose (plain) flour
• 1 tablespoon apple cider vinegar
• 4 cups (950 ml/32 fl oz) beef stock
• ⅓ cup (80 g) tomato paste (purée)
• 2 tablespoons sweet paprika (ideally Hungarian)
• ¼ teaspoon cayenne pepper
• 2 bay leaves
• 1 lb (455 g) Yukon Gold potatoes, peeled and cut into 1-inch (2.5 cm) pieces
• ½ teaspoon kosher salt, plus more as needed
• Freshly ground black pepper

In a large Dutch oven (casserole) or heavy-bottomed pot, heat the oil over medium-high heat. Working in batches, add the beef and cook, stirring occasionally, until lightly browned, about 5 minutes. Add a drizzle more oil if the pot begins to look dry. Remove the meat to a plate.

Reduce the heat to medium and add the onions, carrots, celery, and garlic to the pot. Cook, stirring occasionally, until softened and lightly browned, 8–10 minutes.

Add the flour and stir to coat vegetables, then stir in the vinegar, stock, ½ cup (120 ml/4 fl oz) water, tomato paste (purée), paprika, cayenne, bay leaves, and browned beef. Increase the heat to medium-high and bring to a boil. Reduce the heat to low, cover, and simmer until the meat is very tender, about 1½ hours.

Add the potatoes and continue cooking, partially covered, until the potatoes are tender and the stew thickens, 20–30 minutes. Add the salt and a generous amount of black pepper. Taste and stir in more salt, if needed. (Depending on the saltiness of your meat and broth, you may need none or quite a bit more.) Discard the bay leaves. Serve hot.

LAMB AND PEA SOUP

Ham and split pea soup is a popular dish across Australia, and some Jewish home cooks there began making a version with lamb, using smoked lamb bones to mimic the flavor of ham hocks. This version employs a bit of smoked paprika, which is easier to source than smoked bones, and gives the rich and hearty stew wonderful flavor.

Serves: 6–8
Preparation time: 15 minutes
Cooking time: 2 hours 30 minutes

• 3 tablespoons extra-virgin olive oil
• 1 large onion, finely chopped
• 2 medium carrots, sliced into ½-inch (1.25 cm) pieces
• 2 teaspoons kosher salt, plus more as needed
• ¾ teaspoon smoked paprika
• 2 cups (400 g) green split peas, rinsed and drained
• 1 lb (455 g) lamb bones
• 1 lb (455 g) lamb shoulder, cut into 1-inch (2.5 cm) pieces
• 6 cups (1.4 liters/48 fl oz) vegetable stock
• Freshly ground black pepper

In a large soup pot, heat the oil over medium heat. Add the onion, carrots, and a generous pinch of salt and cook, stirring occasionally, until the vegetables begin to soften, 8–10 minutes. Stir in the smoked paprika and cook, stirring, until fragrant, about 1 minute.

Add the split peas, lamb bones (if small, tie them into a cheesecloth bundle to make them easier to remove later), lamb shoulder, stock, and 4 cups (950 ml/32 fl oz) water. Increase the heat to medium-high and bring to a boil. Reduce the heat to low, partially cover, and simmer, stirring occasionally and skimming off the foam that accumulates on top as necessary, until the peas have disintegrated and the meat is very tender, about 2 hours. Remove and discard the lamb bones.

Stir in 2 teaspoons salt and a generous amount of pepper. Taste and adjust seasonings as desired. Serve hot, or refrigerate overnight and skim off and discard the fat that accumulates on top and reheat over medium-low heat.

YOTAM OTTOLENGHI

OTTOLENGHI
•
**MULTIPLE LOCATIONS
LONDON, ENGLAND**

NOPI
•
**21-22 WARWICK STREET
LONDON, ENGLAND**

ROVI
•
**59 WELLS STREET
LONDON, ENGLAND**

Yotam Ottolenghi is a widely acclaimed chef, restaurant owner, and cookbook author raised in Israel and living in London. His restaurants and books—particularly the James Beard Award–winning *Jerusalem: A Cookbook*, which he cowrote in 2012 with his Palestinian-born collaborator, Sami Tamimi—have helped introduce Middle Eastern dishes, ingredients, and cooking philosophies to a global audience.

YEMENI OXTAIL SOUP

This Yemenite soup is assertively flavored with cilantro (fresh coriander), cardamom, turmeric, copious amounts of garlic, and other spices. It is traditionally made with oxtail, which can be substituted with a mix of beef cheeks and short ribs.

Serves: 4–6
Preparation time: 30 minutes
Cooking time: 3½ hours

- 3½ lb (1.6 kg) bone-in oxtail pieces (ideally meaty pieces)
- 2 teaspoons kosher salt, plus more as needed
- ¼ teaspoon freshly ground black pepper, plus more as needed
- 3 tablespoons extra-virgin olive oil
- 2 bay leaves
- 1 bunch flat-leaf parsley, washed and patted dry
- 1 bunch cilantro (fresh coriander), washed and patted dry
- 3 tablespoons tomato paste (purée)
- 2 teaspoons ground coriander
- 2 teaspoons ground cumin
- 1½ teaspoons ground cardamom
- ½ teaspoon ground turmeric
- 1 can (14½ oz/411 g) diced (chopped) tomatoes
- 20 garlic cloves, peeled but whole
- 2 large waxy (boiling) potatoes, peeled and cut into 1-inch (2.5 cm) pieces
- 2 large carrots, halved lengthwise and cut crosswise into 2-inch (5 cm) lengths
- 1 medium onion, cut into 8 wedges
- 3 celery stalks, cut into 2-inch (5 cm) pieces
- 1 teaspoon superfine (caster) sugar
- 3 tablespoons fresh lemon juice
- S'chug, store-bought or homemade (page 411), for serving
- Lemon wedges, for serving

In a large bowl, toss together the oxtail pieces, ½ teaspoon of the salt, and pepper. In a large saucepan, heat 2 tablespoons of the olive oil over medium-high heat. Working in batches, sear the meat, turning often with tongs, until browned all over, 4–5 minutes per batch. Remove seared oxtail pieces to a plate while browning the remainder.

Once all of the meat is browned, return all of the oxtail to the pan, along with any cooking juices, and add 8 cups (2 liters/2 qt) water. Cover the saucepan, reduce the heat to medium, and simmer for 1½ hours, skimming any impurities off the surface, as necessary.

Tie the bay leaves, parsley, and cilantro (coriander) into a bundle with kitchen twine and add to the stew. Re-cover and simmer for 30 minutes, stirring occasionally.

In a small frying pan, heat the remaining 1 tablespoon oil over medium-high heat. Add the tomato paste (purée), ground coriander, cumin, cardamom, and turmeric and cook, stirring constantly, until fragrant, 1–2 minutes.

Add the spice mixture to the soup along with the diced (chopped) tomatoes (and their juices), garlic cloves, potatoes, carrots, onion, celery, sugar, remaining 1½ teaspoons salt, and a generous amount of pepper. Cover the saucepan and cook until the meat is falling off the bone and the vegetables are tender, about 1 hour. Remove and discard the herb bundle and stir in the lemon juice. Taste and add more salt and pepper, if desired.

Divide into bowls and serve hot, with *s'chug* and lemon wedges on the side.

BEAN, HERB, AND NOODLE STEW

Thick, hearty, and filled with beans and legumes, this stew is a rib-sticking delight. Called *aash-e reshteh*, it is traditionally served for Nowruz, the Persian New Year. Jewish families also serve it on Shabbat and Rosh Hashanah, and some families make it to celebrate a baby's first tooth. Wheat-based *reshteh* noodles can be found in specialty stores and online, but cooks can also substitute linguine in a pinch. The toppings—browned onions and garlic, fried mint, and thick yogurt—make the dish special, so don't skip them.

Serves: 8
Preparation time: 30 minutes, plus soaking
Cooking time: 1½ hours

For the soup:
- 1 cup (175 g) dried brown or green lentils
- ½ cup (90 g) dried chickpeas
- ½ cup (90 g) dried pinto beans
- 2 teaspoons baking soda (bicarbonate of soda)
- 2½ teaspoons kosher salt, plus more as needed
- 8 oz (225 g) reshteh noodles
- 2 tablespoons vegetable oil
- 1 large onion, finely chopped
- 1 lb (455 g) spinach, fresh or frozen, chopped
- 3 bunches scallions (spring onions), white and green parts, thinly sliced
- ½ cup (25 g) finely chopped fresh dill
- 1½ teaspoons ground turmeric
- 2 tablespoons fresh lemon juice
- Freshly ground black pepper

For the toppings:
- ½ cup (120 ml/4 fl oz) vegetable or olive oil
- 2 large onions, halved through the root and thinly sliced
- ¼ teaspoon ground turmeric
- Kosher salt
- 1 head garlic, cloves peeled and thinly sliced
- ¼ cup (10 g) dried mint
- Labneh or whole-milk Greek yogurt, for serving

Make the soup: Place the lentils, chickpeas, pinto beans, and baking soda (bicarb) in a large bowl and cover with water by at least 2 inches (5 cm). Cover the bowl with a tea towel and let soak at room temperature overnight. Drain and set aside.

Bring a large pot of salted water to a boil over high heat. Add the noodles and cook until tender, about 8 minutes (or use the times on the package). Reserving the cooking water, drain the noodles. Set both aside.

In the same large pot, heat the oil over medium heat. Add the onion and a pinch of salt and cook, stirring occasionally, until softened and lightly browned, 6–8 minutes. Add the soaked lentils, chickpeas, and pinto beans along with the spinach, scallions (spring onions), dill, and turmeric.

Gently pour enough of the reserved noodle cooking water over the top to cover the ingredients. If there isn't enough, add a bit of water. Increase the heat to medium-high and bring to a boil. Reduce the heat to low, partially cover, and cook, stirring occasionally, until the beans are soft and creamy and the mixture thickens, about 1½ hours. Stir in the lemon juice, salt, and a generous amount of pepper. Taste and adjust seasonings as desired.

While the soup is simmering, make the toppings:
In a large frying pan, heat ¼ cup (60 ml/2 fl oz) oil over medium-low heat. Add the onions, turmeric, and a pinch of salt and cook, stirring often, until softened and browned, 15–20 minutes. Transfer the onions and their oil to a serving bowl.

Add the remaining ¼ cup (60 ml/2 fl oz) oil to the pan and set it back over the heat. Add the garlic and a pinch of salt and cook, stirring often, until the garlic turns crispy, about 10 minutes. (Watch carefully so it does not burn.) Transfer the garlic to a second serving bowl, leaving a few tablespoons of oil in the pan. Add the mint to the pan and cook, stirring, until fragrant, 2–3 minutes. Transfer to a third serving bowl.

To serve, divide the cooked noodles into bowls and spoon the stew on top. Top with the cooked onions, garlic, and mint, and a generous dollop of *labneh*.

Bean, Herb, and Noodle Stew

BEEF AND CILANTRO SOUP

This Yemenite soup, called *marak temani*, can be made with either beef or chicken, but the beef version is particularly rich and satisfying. It gets its complex flavor from fresh cilantro (coriander) and *hawaij*, a turmeric-based spice mix used across Yemenite cooking. The soup is typically served on Shabbat, but would also make a delicious and hearty weeknight meal during the cold winter months.

Serves: 6–8
Preparation time: 15 minutes
Cooking time 2 hours 20 minutes

- ¼ cup (60 ml/2 fl oz) vegetable oil
- 2 medium onions, finely chopped
- 4 garlic cloves, thinly sliced
- 2 teaspoons kosher salt, plus more as needed
- 2½ teaspoons Hawaij for Soup (page 415)
- 2 beef soup bones (about ½ lb/225 g)
- 2 lb (910 g) beef chuck, cut into 1-inch (2.5 cm) cubes
- Freshly ground black pepper
- 1 bunch cilantro (coriander), stems okay, tied with kitchen string, plus more cilantro for serving
- 4 cups (950 ml/32 fl oz) beef stock
- 1 lb (455 g) Yukon Gold potatoes, peeled and cut into 2-inch (5 cm) pieces
- S'chug (page 411) and Hilbeh (page 409), for serving

In a large soup pot, heat the oil over medium heat. Add the onions, garlic, and a pinch of salt and cook, stirring occasionally, until softened and lightly browned, 10–15 minutes. Stir in the *hawaij* and cook, stirring, until fragrant, about 1 minute.

Add the soup bones, beef cubes, cilantro (coriander), stock, and 8 cups (2 liters/2 qt) water. Increase the heat to high and bring to a boil. Reduce the heat to medium-low, cover, and cook, stirring occasionally and skimming off any foam that accumulates at the top, for 1 hour 20 minutes.

Add the potatoes and continue cooking, partially covered, until the meat and potatoes are very tender, about 40 minutes. Remove and discard the cilantro bundle and stir in the salt and a generous amount of pepper. Taste and add more salt and pepper, if desired. Serve hot, sprinkled with more cilantro leaves and dolloped with *s'chug*. Or, allow to cool and refrigerate overnight. Skim off fat that accumulates at the top of soup, then reheat before serving.

RICE, LAMB, AND DRIED FRUIT STEW

The Bukharian Jews of Central Asia serve this hearty, slow-cooked stew, a relative of Cholent and Hamin (see page 147), on Saturdays for Shabbat lunch. Called *oshi savo*, the combination of lamb, dried fruit, rice, and tomatoes might seem unusual for those unfamiliar with it, but is deeply satisfying. If desired, beef can be substituted for the lamb.

Serves: 8
Preparation time: 20 minutes
Cooking time: 10 hours 15 minutes

- 2 tablespoons vegetable oil
- 2 onions, halved through the root and thinly sliced
- 1 lb (455 g) Yukon Gold potatoes, peeled and cut into 2-inch (5 cm) pieces
- 2 large carrots, cut into 2-inch (5 cm) pieces
- 1 cup (200 g) short-grain white or brown rice, rinsed and drained
- 1 cup (160 g) dried kidney beans
- 1½ lb (680 g) lamb shoulder, cut into 1-inch (2.5 cm) pieces
- 15 pitted prunes
- 6 eggs, in the shell (optional)
- 1 can (14½ oz/411 g) diced (chopped) tomatoes
- 2 teaspoons onion powder
- 2½ teaspoons kosher salt
- ½ teaspoon freshly ground black pepper

In a large frying pan, heat the oil over medium heat. Add the onions and cook, stirring occasionally, until softened and lightly browned, 10–15 minutes. Remove from the heat and transfer the onions to the bottom of a large slow cooker.

Layer the potatoes and carrots on top of the sautéed onions, then evenly pour the rice and kidney beans on top. Nestle the lamb, prunes, and eggs (if using), among the rice and beans.

In a medium bowl, stir together the diced (chopped) tomatoes with their juice, 1 cup (240 ml/8 fl oz) water, onion powder, salt, and pepper. Pour over the ingredients in the slow cooker. Add enough additional water to just cover the ingredients. Close the slow cooker's lid and cook on low, without stirring, until thick and stewy, 8–10 hours. Remove the eggs, peel, and place in a bowl. Serve alongside the hot stew.

BEEF AND SPELT STEW

German Jews are partial to this hearty, stick-to-your-ribs stew made with unripened (or "green kernel") spelt and enriched with beef bones and flanken. Traditionally, it was served as festive comfort food for Shabbat dinner or lunch, but it can be frozen in individual portions and easily thawed for weekday meals. *Gruenkern* can be found online (it comes both whole and ground—use whole for this recipe) or at international food stores.

Serves: 6–8
Preparation time: 25 minutes, plus soaking
Cooking time: 2 hours

- 1½ cups (250 g) whole gruenkern, rinsed and drained
- 2 tablespoons vegetable oil
- 2 large yellow onions, finely chopped
- 3 large carrots, finely chopped
- 2 teaspoons kosher salt, plus more as needed
- 1 lb (455 g) flanken or short ribs
- 1 lb (455 g) beef marrow bones
- 1½ lb (680 g) beef chuck, cut into 1-inch (2.5 cm) pieces
- Freshly ground black pepper

The night before making the soup: Add the *gruenkern* to a large bowl and cover with water by about 2 inches (5 cm). Cover with a tea towel and let sit at room temperature overnight. The following day, drain the *gruenkern* in a fine-mesh sieve, rinse, and drain again.

In a large soup pot, heat the oil over medium heat. Add the onions, carrots, and a generous pinch of salt and cook, stirring occasionally, until the vegetables begin to soften, 8–10 minutes.

Add the flanken, marrow bones, beef chuck, and soaked *gruenkern*. Cover with 12 cups (2.8 liters/3 qt) water and bring to a boil. Reduce the heat to low, partially covered, and simmer, stirring occasionally and skimming off the foam that accumulates on top as necessary, until the meat is very tender, about 2 hours.

Remove from the heat. Remove the flanken and bones with tongs and allow them to cool to the touch on a cutting board. Separate any meat from the flanken and add it back to the pot (discard the fat, gristle, and bones). Scoop out any marrow from the soup bones and add it to the pot (discard the bones).

Stir in 2 teaspoons salt and a generous amount of pepper. Taste and adjust seasonings as desired. Serve hot. Store covered in the fridge for up to 4 days. Reheat in a pot over medium-low heat.

KHARCHO

Fragrant with fenugreek and coriander and thickened with finely ground walnuts, this beef and rice soup is anything but ordinary. *Kharcho* is a mainstay of Georgian cuisine, including for Georgian Jews. The soup traditionally gets its tangy flavor from the sour plum paste called *tkemali*, but the more readily available tamarind paste and pomegranate molasses make worthy substitutes.

Serves: 6–8
Preparation time: 20 minutes
Cooking time: 2 hours 15 minutes

- ⅓ cup (30 g) walnut halves
- 3 tablespoons vegetable oil, plus more as needed
- 2 lb (910 g) beef chuck, trimmed of excess fat and cut into 1-inch (2.5 cm) cubes
- 2 large onion, finely chopped
- 2 carrots, finely chopped
- 4 garlic cloves, finely chopped
- ½ teaspoon kosher salt, plus more as needed
- 2 teaspoons sweet paprika
- 1 teaspoon ground fenugreek
- ¾ teaspoon ground coriander
- ½ teaspoon dried mint
- ½ teaspoon crushed pepper flakes
- 1 cup (240 g) canned crushed (finely diced) tomatoes
- 2 tablespoons tamarind paste or Pomegranate Molasses (page 409)
- 8 cups (1.9 liters/2 qt) beef or vegetable stock
- ¼ cup (50 g) long-grain white rice, rinsed well and drained
- Freshly ground black pepper
- Roughly chopped fresh cilantro (coriander) and dill, for serving

Pulse the walnuts in a food processor, scraping down the sides of the bowl once or twice, until nuts are finely ground with a few slightly larger pieces. Set aside.

In a large soup pot, heat the oil over medium-high heat. Working in batches, add the beef and cook, stirring occasionally, until lightly browned, about 5 minutes. Add a drizzle more oil if the pot begins to look dry. Transfer the beef to a plate.

Reduce the heat to medium and add the onion, carrots, garlic, and a pinch of salt to the pot. Cook, stirring occasionally, until softened and lightly browned, 8–10 minutes. Add the paprika, fenugreek, coriander, mint, and pepper flakes and cook, stirring, until fragrant, about 1 minute.

Stir in the tomatoes, tamarind paste, browned beef, and stock. Increase the heat to medium-high and bring to a boil. Reduce the heat to low, cover, and cook, stirring occasionally, until the beef is very tender, about 1½ hours.

Stir in the ground walnuts, rice, salt, and a generous amount of black pepper. Continue cooking, covered, until the rice is tender, about 20 minutes. Taste and add more salt and pepper, if desired. (The amount of salt needed will depend on how salty the beef and stock are.) Serve hot, sprinkled with chopped cilantro (coriander) and dill.

Kharcho

CHOLENT

For many religiously observant Ashkenazi Jews, no Shabbat lunch is complete without *cholent* (see page 147). There is no hard-and-fast recipe for *cholent*; Hungarians add plenty of paprika, while Romanians sometimes include chick-peas. Some Australian cooks stir in Vegemite, while American cholent makers might add barbecue sauce.

Serves: 8–10
Preparation time: 20 minutes
Cooking time: 12 hours

- 1 large onion, cut into 1-inch (2.5 cm) chunks
- 1 lb (455 g) Yukon Gold potatoes, peeled and cut into 2-inch (5 cm) chunks
- ½ lb (225 g) sweet potatoes, peeled and cut into 2-inch (5 cm) chunks
- ½ lb (225 g) carrots, cut into 2-inch (5 cm) pieces
- 6 garlic cloves, chopped
- 1 cup (200 g) pearl barley
- 1 cup (160 g) dried kidney or pinto beans (or a mix)
- 1 lb (455 g) beef marrow bones
- 1½ lb (680 g) beef chuck, cut into 1-inch (2.5 cm) pieces
- 2 tablespoons honey
- 2 tablespoons tomato paste (purée)
- 2 teaspoons smoked paprika
- 1 teaspoon onion powder
- 2½ teaspoons kosher salt
- ½ teaspoon freshly ground black pepper

Layer the onion, potatoes, sweet potatoes, carrots, and garlic in the bottom of a large slow cooker. Pour the barley and beans over the vegetables, then layer on the marrow bones and beef.

In a medium bowl, whisk together the honey, tomato paste (purée), smoked paprika, onion powder, salt, pepper, and 1 cup (240 ml/8 fl oz) water until fully combined. Pour over the ingredients in the slow cooker, then add enough water to just cover the meat, beans, and vegetables. (Do not stir.) Close the slow cooker's lid and cook on low until thick and stewy, 10–12 hours. Serve hot.

VEGETARIAN CHOLENT

Traditional Shabbat stews typically simmer overnight—a technique that helps to tenderize tough cuts of meat. This robustly flavored meat-free stew, however, can be made in a regular pot and served right away.

Serves: 8
Preparation time: 30 minutes
Cooking time: 1 hour 15 minutes

- ¼ cup (60 ml/2 fl oz) extra-virgin olive oil
- 2 large onions, finely chopped
- 2 medium carrots, sliced into ½-inch (1.25 cm) rounds
- 1 lb (455 g) baby potatoes, scrubbed and halved if thick
- 1 lb (455 g) sweet potato, peeled and cut into 1-inch (2.5 cm) pieces
- 6 large garlic cloves, thinly sliced
- 2 teaspoons chili powder
- 1 teaspoon onion powder
- 1 teaspoon smoked paprika
- 1 can (15 oz/425 g) kidney beans, rinsed and drained
- 1 can (15 oz/425 g) pinto beans, rinsed and drained
- ½ cup (100 g) pearl barley
- 3 tablespoons soy sauce or tamari
- 2 tablespoons tomato paste (purée)
- 2 tablespoons honey
- 5 cups (1.2 liters/40 fl oz) vegetable stock, plus more as needed
- ½ teaspoon freshly ground black pepper

In a large pot, heat the oil over medium heat. Add the onions, carrots, potatoes, sweet potato, and garlic and cook, stirring occasionally, until they begin to soften, about 15 minutes. Add the chili powder, onion powder, and smoked paprika and cook, stirring, until fragrant, about 1 minute.

Add the kidney beans, pinto beans, barley, soy sauce, tomato paste (purée), honey, stock, and pepper. Increase the heat to high and bring to a boil. Reduce the heat to medium-low, partially cover, and cook until the barley and vegetables are tender and the liquid thickens into a stew, 45–60 minutes. If the liquid reduces too much before the vegetables are fully tender, thin with a little more stock. Serve hot or warm.

Cholent

LAGMAN SOUP

Lagman is the Bukharian word for "noodles" (closely related to Chinese lo mein), and this meaty, cumin- and coriander-spiced soup traditionally comes brimming with chewy, hand-pulled wheat noodles. Look for long fresh noodles in Asian markets or international grocery stores. If you cannot find them, thick-cut noodles like linguine or udon can be substituted.

Serves: 6–8
Preparation time: 25 minutes
Cooking time: 2 hours 20 minutes

- 3 tablespoons vegetable oil, plus more as needed
- 2 lb (910 g) boneless beef or lamb shoulder, trimmed of excess fat and cut into 1-inch (2.5 cm) cubes
- 2 large onions, finely chopped
- 1 red bell pepper, cut into ½-inch (1.25 cm) pieces
- 2 carrots, cut into ½-inch (1.25 cm) pieces
- 4 garlic cloves, thinly sliced
- 1 teaspoon kosher salt, plus more as needed
- 2 tablespoons tomato paste (purée)
- 1½ teaspoons ground cumin
- 1 teaspoon sweet paprika
- 1 teaspoon ground coriander
- ½ teaspoon crushed pepper flakes
- 1 can (14½ oz/411 g) diced (chopped) tomatoes
- 4 cups (950 ml/32 fl oz) beef or vegetable stock
- 2 small russet (baking) potatoes, peeled and cut into ½-inch (1.25 cm) pieces
- 1 turnip, peeled and cut into ½-inch (1.25 cm) pieces
- Freshly ground black pepper
- 1 lb (455 g) fresh noodles, linguine, or udon
- Roughly chopped fresh cilantro (coriander), for serving

In a large soup pot, heat the oil over medium-high heat. Working in batches, add the beef and cook, stirring occasionally, until lightly browned, about 5 minutes. Add a drizzle more oil if the pot begins to look dry. Transfer the beef to a plate.

Reduce the heat to medium and add the onions, bell pepper, carrots, garlic, and a pinch of salt to the pot. Cook, stirring occasionally, until just beginning to soften, 6–8 minutes. Add the tomato paste (purée), cumin, paprika, coriander, and pepper flakes and cook, stirring, until fragrant, about 1 minute.

Stir in the diced tomatoes, beef stock, and 4 cups (950 ml/32 fl oz) water. Increase the heat to medium-high and bring to a boil. Reduce the heat to low, cover, and cook, stirring occasionally, until the beef is very tender, about 1½ hours.

Add the potatoes, turnip, salt, and a generous amount of black pepper and cook, covered, until the vegetables are tender, about 30 minutes. Taste and add more salt and pepper, if needed. (The amount of salt needed will depend on how salty the beef and stock are.)

Meanwhile, fill a large saucepan with water and add a generous pinch of salt. Bring to a boil over high heat. Add the noodles and cook, following the timing guidelines on the package. Drain the noodles, and rinse with cold water.

Add the desired amount of noodles to a bowl and ladle the soup on top. Serve hot, sprinkled with cilantro (coriander).

CHOLENT AND HAMIN:
A SHABBAT STEW BY ANY OTHER NAME

Shabbat food—the foods eaten from sunset on Friday through nightfall on Saturday—vary widely from region to region and country to country. But many Jewish communities share a tradition of serving warm, long-simmered stews for Shabbat lunch. There is a reason for this culinary consistency. Religiously observant Jews do not actively cook over flame or with electricity throughout the duration of Shabbat. Many Shabbat lunch dishes can be prepared in advance and served either cold or at room temperature. But these stews, which are set over very low heat before Shabbat begins and allowed to passively simmer until lunch the following day, became the answer for how to have a proper meal on Saturday without violating Jewish law.

This low and slow cooking technique likely originated in the ancient Middle East with a porridge of cracked wheat and lamb called *harisa* (not to be confused with the chili paste, harissa). The dish spread with traders to Spain, where the name changed to *hamin* (which means "warm" in Aramaic) and other ingredients like fava beans (broad beans) or chickpeas were added to the grains and meat. Sometime in the Middle Ages, the dish traveled to France, where it is called *schalet* (likely from the Old French word for "warm," *chalt*). It then spread to Germany and Eastern Europe where, through a bit of linguistic gymnastics, it became *tsholnt*, then *cholent*. Along the way, ingredients were changed to reflect the local tastes of wherever the dish was being prepared.

These Shabbat stews were traditionally made in covered pots set on late Friday afternoons in the dying embers of the hearth and allowed to cook in the residual heat until the following day. Later, they were set in very low-temperature ovens. The resulting "overnight stew" was thick and very well browned—a texture and flavor that, for many, came to symbolize the essence of Shabbat afternoon. When electric slow cookers came into existence, they revolutionized cholent making by giving cooks a bit more control over the timing and intensity of the stew's heat source without breaking the Jewish laws. But even today they remain hearty and purposefully overcooked. (Some cholent lovers claim that the near-burnt and crusty bits along the perimeter of the slow cooker or pot are the best part.)

Many less observant and secular Jews grew up without ever tasting cholent, *hamin*, or any of its cousins. After all, people who do not follow the Jewish law of abstaining from active cooking on Shabbat have little need for such a dish. But for those who were raised on it, and who ate it most weeks of the year, it is a deeply comforting and nostalgic dish. And considering the role these Shabbat stews have played in sustaining the Jewish people throughout the centuries, it is fair to argue that they are among the most central and important recipes within Jewish cuisine.

Hamin is a close cousin to Ashkenazi Cholent (page 144), but typically uses different spices and includes rice or wheat berries instead of barley. A related recipe, *adafina*, groups the various ingredients in cheesecloth bundles, cooking them together in one pot, but serving them in separate dishes. Most recipes for *hamin* and *adafina* include whole eggs. The eggs boil overnight, taking on the stew's rich flavor and becoming tasty morsels all their own.

CHICKEN HAMIN WITH BUCATINI

Like other Shabbat stews (see page 147), this dish, *hamin macaroni,* cooks overnight, and is traditionally served at Saturday lunch. Any thick, long pasta will work in this dish, but bucatini holds up perfectly to the low and slow cooking.

Serves: 6
Preparation time: 15 minutes
Cooking time: 8 hours 15 minutes

• 1 lb (455 g) bucatini pasta
• 3 tablespoons vegetable oil
• 2 large onions, halved through the root and thinly sliced
• 8 garlic cloves, thinly sliced
• Kosher salt and freshly ground black pepper
• ½ teaspoon ground turmeric
• ½ teaspoon ground cinnamon
• ¼ teaspoon ground cardamom
• 2 medium Yukon Gold or red potatoes (about 1 lb/455 g), peeled and sliced into ½-inch (1.25 cm) rounds
• 3 lb (1.35 kg) bone-in, skin-on chicken drumsticks and thighs, patted dry
• 6 eggs, in the shell (optional)
• ½ cup (120 ml/4 fl oz) chicken stock

Bring a large pot of salted water to a boil over high heat. Add the pasta and cook, stirring occasionally, until just short of tender, 7–8 minutes. (Do not overcook.) Drain well, transfer to a large bowl, and set aside.

Preheat the oven to 225°F (110°C/Gas Mark ¼).

In a large Dutch oven (casserole), heat the oil over medium-high heat. Add the onions, garlic, and a generous sprinkle of salt and pepper and cook, stirring occasionally, until softened and golden brown, 7–10 minutes. Stir in the turmeric, cinnamon, and cardamom, then remove from the heat. Transfer the onion mixture to the bowl of cooked pasta, and stir to coat the pasta.

Arrange the potato slices in a single layer in the bottom of the Dutch oven. Sprinkle with a little salt and top with about three-quarters of the onion-coated pasta. Generously season the chicken pieces on both sides with salt and pepper and arrange in the Dutch oven. Top with the remaining pasta, then nestle the eggs (if using) on top.

Pour in the stock, cover, and place in the oven. Bake until the chicken is falling off the bone and the pasta has browned on top, 6–8 hours. Serve the eggs on the side.

HAMIN

Sephardi and Mizrahi Jews typically begin preparing this hearty Shabbat stew on Friday afternoon. Beans or legumes, meat, and grains are mixed in a slow cooker or Dutch oven and allowed to simmer at a low temperature until lunch the following day.

Serves: 8–10
Preparation time: 20 minutes
Cooking time: 12 hours

• 2 onions, halved through the root and thinly sliced
• 1 lb (455 g) Yukon Gold potatoes, peeled and cut into 1½-inch (4 cm) pieces
• 1 lb (455 g) carrots, cut into 2-inch (5 cm) pieces
• 8 garlic cloves, thinly sliced
• ¾ cup (135 g) wheat berries (whole grain wheat)
• 1 cup (180 g) dried chickpeas
• 1 lb (455 g) beef marrow bones
• 1½ lb (680 g) beef chuck, cut into 1-inch (2.5 cm) pieces
• 6 eggs, in the shell
• 2 tablespoons honey
• 2 tablespoons tomato paste (purée)
• 1½ teaspoons ground cumin
• 1½ teaspoons smoked paprika
• 1½ teaspoons sweet paprika
• ½ teaspoon ground cinnamon
• ¼ teaspoon crushed pepper flakes
• 2½ teaspoons kosher salt, plus more as needed
• ½ teaspoon freshly ground black pepper

Layer the onions, potatoes, carrots, and garlic in the bottom of a large slow cooker. Pour the wheat berries (whole grain wheat) and chickpeas over the vegetables, then layer on the marrow bones and beef. Nestle the eggs throughout the pot, taking care so they don't break.

In a medium bowl, whisk together the honey, tomato paste (purée), cumin, smoked paprika, sweet paprika, cinnamon, pepper flakes, salt, pepper, and 1 cup (240 ml/8 fl oz) water until fully combined. Pour over the ingredients in the slow cooker, then add just enough water to cover the meat, chickpeas, and vegetables. (Do not stir.) Close the slow cooker's lid and cook on low until thick and stewy, 10–12 hours. Serve hot.

Chicken Hamin with Bucatini

WHITE BEAN AND MEATBALL STEW

This savory stew, which comes packed with creamy white beans, spinach, herbs, and robustly spiced meatballs (or sometimes sausage), is central to Tunisian Jewish cuisine. Called *t'fina pakaila*, it is traditionally served on Shabbat, Rosh Hashanah, and Sukkot, and is especially delicious spooned over couscous.

Serves: 8
Preparation time: 20 minutes
Cooking time: 2 hours

For the meatballs:
- 1 lb (455 g) ground (minced) beef
- 1 medium onion, grated
- ¼ cup (35 g) dried breadcrumbs
- 1 tablespoon ground cumin
- 1 teaspoon ground cinnamon
- 1 teaspoon smoked paprika
- ½ teaspoon ground coriander
- ½ teaspoon ground turmeric
- ½ teaspoon onion powder
- 2 teaspoons kosher salt
- ½ teaspoon freshly ground black pepper
- 2 eggs, lightly beaten
- 2 tablespoons extra-virgin olive oil

For the stew:
- ¼ cup (60 ml/2 fl oz) extra-virgin olive oil
- 1½ lb (680 g) beef flanken or short ribs, cut into pieces along the bone
- Kosher salt and freshly ground black pepper
- 1 large yellow onion, finely chopped
- 8 garlic cloves, chopped
- 5 cups (1.2 liters/40 fl oz) beef or chicken stock
- 1 can (15 oz/425 g) white beans, rinsed and drained
- 5 oz (140 g) baby spinach leaves
- ½ cup (20 g) finely chopped fresh mint
- ½ cup (20 g) finely chopped fresh cilantro (coriander)
- Harissa (page 409), for serving

Make the meatballs: In a large bowl, combine the beef, grated onion with its liquid, breadcrumbs, cumin, cinnamon, smoked paprika, coriander, turmeric, onion powder, salt, pepper, and eggs and mix with your hands to combine. Form the meat mixture into tightly rolled 1-inch (2.5 cm) balls, setting them aside. You should end up with about 35 meatballs.

In a large saucepan, heat the oil over medium-high heat. Working in batches, add the meatballs and cook, gently turning, until browned on all sides, about 4 minutes. Transfer the browned meatballs to a plate and refrigerate until needed.

Make the stew: Scrape up any debris from the bottom of the saucepan the meatballs were cooked in and wipe it clean. Add the olive oil and heat over medium-high heat. Season the flanken pieces with salt and pepper and cook, turning, until browned on all sides, 6–8 minutes. Transfer the browned meat to a plate. Add the onion and garlic to the saucepan and cook, stirring, until softened, 6–8 minutes. Return the meat to the saucepan along with the stock and bring to a boil. Reduce the heat to medium-low, cover, and cook until the beef is tender, about 1 hour.

Add the meatballs and white beans, increase the heat to medium, and simmer, uncovered, until the meatballs are cooked through, 8–10 minutes. Stir in the spinach, mint, and cilantro (coriander) and cook until the spinach wilts, about 2 minutes. Taste and add additional salt and pepper, if needed. Serve hot, swirled with harissa to taste.

White Bean and Meatball Stew

VEGETABLES
& GRAINS

TSIMMES

The Yiddish expression *"machan a tsimmes"* translates loosely to "make a fuss over," and this root vegetable and dried fruit stew follows suit. It is not terribly complicated to make, but it jumbles many sweet and tangy flavors together into one dish. Ashkenazi Jews traditionally serve tsimmes as a side dish on Shabbat and also Rosh Hashanah and Sukkot, when autumn's carrots and sweet potatoes are in peak season. It can be made vegetarian, like the dish below, or with meat (Tsimmes with Flanken, facing page).

Serves: 8
Preparation time: 25 minutes
Cooking time: 1 hour

- 1 lb (455 g) carrots, cut into 1-inch (2.5 cm) pieces
- 2 lb (910 g) sweet potatoes, peeled and cut into 1½-inch (4 cm) pieces
- 2 tablespoons vegetable oil
- ⅓ cup (60 g) light brown sugar
- ½ cup (120 ml/4 fl oz) orange juice
- 1 tablespoon fresh lemon juice
- 1 teaspoon ground ginger
- 1 tablespoon finely chopped fresh ginger
- 1½ teaspoons ground cinnamon
- 1½ teaspoons kosher salt
- 1 cup (180 g) dried apricots
- 1 cup (180 g) pitted prunes

Fill a large Dutch oven (casserole) or other ovenproof pot with water and bring to a boil over high heat. Add the carrots and sweet potatoes and cook until tender, but not completely soft, about 15 minutes. Drain well, rinse with cool water, and drain again. Return the carrots and sweet potatoes to the Dutch oven and set aside.

Preheat the oven to 350°F (180°C/Gas Mark 4).

In a large bowl, whisk together the oil, brown sugar, orange juice, lemon juice, ground ginger, fresh ginger, cinnamon, and salt until combined. Add the apricots and prunes to the vegetables in the Dutch oven and pour liquid mixture over top. Cover and bake until very tender, 25–30 minutes. Gently stir the mixture and continue cooking, uncovered, until the juices thicken into a syrup, about 15 minutes. Let cool slightly, stirring occasionally to coat the mixture in the syrup. Serve warm.

STEWED GREEN BEANS AND TOMATOES

Originally hailing from Turkey, variations of this flavorful green bean and tomato side dish, called *fasoulia kon tomate*, are also served in Greece, the Balkans, and the Middle East. The beans can be eaten warm or at room temperature, making them a perfect Shabbat dish, and they are also common fare on Sukkot. For a Syrian–inspired variation, stir in a pinch of allspice and ground cinnamon with the paprika.

Serves: 6
Preparation time: 15 minutes
Cooking time: 30 minutes

- ¼ cup (60 ml/2 fl oz) extra-virgin olive oil
- 1 large onion, finely chopped
- 4 garlic cloves, finely chopped
- 1 can (14½ oz/411 g) diced (chopped) tomatoes
- 1 teaspoon sugar
- 1 teaspoon sweet paprika
- 1¼ teaspoons kosher salt, plus more as needed
- ¼ teaspoon freshly ground black pepper
- 2 lb (910 g) green beans, ends trimmed
- Lemon wedges, for serving

In a large Dutch oven (casserole) or other heavy-bottomed pot, heat the oil over medium heat. Add the onion and garlic and cook, stirring occasionally, until softened and browned, about 10 minutes.

Add the tomatoes and their juice, ½ cup (120 ml/4 fl oz) water, the sugar, paprika, salt, and pepper. Bring to a boil, then stir in the beans, reduce the heat to low, cover, and cook until the beans are tender, about 15 minutes. Taste and add more salt, if desired. Serve hot, warm, or at room temperature with lemon wedges alongside for squeezing.

CARROT TSIMMES

This simple take on tsimmes has a bright and surprisingly complex flavor. The apricot preserves spooned in at the end of the cooking process add a hit of tangy sweetness and a glossy sheen.

Serves: 6
Preparation time: 10 minutes
Cooking time: 40 minutes

- 3 tablespoons (45 g) unsalted butter or extra-virgin olive oil
- 2 lb (910 g) carrots, halved lengthwise if thick, and sliced into ½-inch (1.25 cm) pieces
- ¾ cup (175 ml/6 fl oz) orange juice
- 2 tablespoons honey
- 1 teaspoon ground cinnamon
- ½ cup (70 g) golden raisins (sultanas)
- 1 teaspoon kosher salt, plus more as needed
- ½ teaspoon freshly ground black pepper
- 2 tablespoons apricot preserves

In a medium saucepan, melt the butter over medium heat. Add the carrots and cook, stirring occasionally, until crisp-tender, 6–8 minutes.

Stir in the orange juice, honey, cinnamon, golden raisins (sultanas), salt, and pepper. Reduce the heat to medium-low, cover, and cook, stirring occasionally, until the carrots are tender, 25–30 minutes. Uncover and stir in the apricot preserves. Taste and add a little more salt, if desired. Transfer to a serving dish and serve hot.

TSIMMES WITH FLANKEN

Tsimmes made with brisket or flanken is a special treat—a complex mix of sweet (dried prunes, honey, sweet potatoes) and savory (onions, meat) flavors. The dish hails from Eastern Europe, but the Ashkenazi community in Mexico has found ways to incorporate local ingredients linto the traditional recipe. To try the Mexican variation, add 1 teaspoon cinnamon to the braising liquid, and the flesh of 1 mango and 1 dried chiptole chile along with the prunes. This tsimmes tastes even better the second day, making it a great make-ahead dish for entertaining. Store it in the fridge overnight and scoop off the layer of fat congealed on the top before reheating.

Serves: 6–8
Preparation time: 30 minutes
Cooking time: 3 hours

- 2 tablespoons vegetable oil
- 2 lb (910 g) meaty flanken or short ribs, cut into pieces along the bone
- Kosher salt and freshly ground black pepper
- 2 onions, roughly chopped
- 1 lb (455 g) carrots, cut into 2-inch (5 cm) chunks
- 1½ lb (680 g) sweet potatoes, peeled and cut into 2-inch (5 cm) chunks
- 1½ cups (355 ml/12 fl oz) beef or chicken stock
- ¼ cup (85 g) honey
- ½ teaspoon onion powder
- 1 cup (180 g) pitted prunes

Preheat the oven to 300°F (150°C/Gas Mark 2).

In a large Dutch oven (casserole) or other ovenproof pot, heat the oil over medium-high heat. Season the flanken pieces on both sides with salt and pepper. Working in batches if necessary, add the meat to the hot oil and cook, turning once, until seared on both sides, 6–8 minutes.

Remove from the heat and add the onions, carrots, and sweet potatoes. In a medium bowl, whisk together the stock, honey, onion powder, 1½ teaspoons salt, and ½ teaspoon pepper. Pour over the meat and vegetables. Cover the Dutch oven and bake for 1 hour. Remove from the oven and gently stir in the prunes. Re-cover and cook until the meat and vegetables are very tender, about 1 hour. Uncover and continue cooking until the liquid thickens, about 30 minutes.

BRAISED RED CABBAGE AND APPLE

This dish of sweet and tangy braised red cabbage with apples is a particularly welcome and warming during the colder months. German Jews traditionally serve the dish, called *rotkraut* (literally "red cabbage"), on Rosh Hashanah, though it would also perfectly complement Potato Latkes (page 184) on Hanukkah. The low-and-slow cooking process is key to achieving the dish's soft, velvety texture.

Serves: 6–8
Preparation time: 15 minutes
Cooking time: 1 hour

- 3 tablespoons vegetable oil or unsalted butter
- 1 onion, halved through the root and thinly sliced
- 1 small head red cabbage (about 2 lb/910 g), quartered, cored, and thinly shredded
- 1 Granny Smith apple, peeled and chopped
- 1 teaspoon sugar
- 2 teaspoons kosher salt, plus more as needed
- ½ teaspoon freshly ground black pepper, plus more as needed
- ¼ cup (60 ml/2 fl oz) apple cider vinegar
- 1 tablespoon balsamic vinegar

In a Dutch oven (casserole) or other large heavy-bottomed pot, heat the oil over medium heat. Add the onion and cook, stirring occasionally, until just softened, 5–6 minutes. Add the cabbage, apple, sugar, salt, and pepper. Cover, reduce the heat to low, and cook, stirring occasionally, until the cabbage is very tender, 50–60 minutes.

Uncover and stir in the apple cider vinegar and balsamic vinegar. Taste and add more salt or pepper, if desired. Serve hot or warm.

SWEET-AND-SOUR CELERY ROOT

Sephardi Jews from Turkey, Greece, and the Balkans serve this centuries-old recipe, called *apio*, at the Passover seder. The word *apio* simply means "celery" in Ladino, the Judeo-Spanish language, and the dish can be made with either stalks of celery or celery root, as it is here. Either way, it is tart and refreshing.

Serves: 6
Preparation time: 25 minutes
Cooking time: 30 minutes

- 2 lb (910 g) celery root (celeriac), washed well and patted dry
- ½ lb (225 g) carrots, halved lengthwise if thick, and cut into ½-inch (1.25 cm) pieces
- 1 bay leaf
- ¼ cup (60 ml/2 fl oz) vegetable oil
- ¼ cup (60 ml/2 fl oz) fresh lemon juice
- 2 tablespoons honey
- 1 teaspoon kosher salt, plus more as needed
- ¼ teaspoon freshly ground black pepper

Trim off the top and bottom of the celery root (celeriac) and stand the root upright. Using a sharp knife, slice off the peel cutting from top to bottom and following the curve of the vegetable. Cut the peeled root into 1-inch (2.5 cm) pieces.

In a large saucepan, combine the celery root, carrots, 4 cups (950 ml/32 fl oz) water, and bay leaf and bring to a boil over high heat. Reduce the heat to low and cook, partially covered and stirring occasionally, until the vegetables are tender, about 20 minutes. Drain well and set aside to cool.

In the bottom of a large bowl, whisk together the oil, lemon juice, honey, salt, and pepper. Add the celery root and carrots and toss to combine. Let sit 20 minutes before serving, stirring occasionally.

Braised Red Cabbage and Apple

JEWISH-STYLE BRAISED FENNEL

Introduced to southern Italy by traders and merchants from the Middle East and North Africa in the sixteenth century, fennel was originally snubbed by mainstream Italians. Jewish home cooks, meanwhile, embraced the anise-scented vegetable (partly out of necessity, since resources were scarce) and created tempting dishes that eventually helped to usher fennel into widespread use. This dish braises sliced fennel with citrus and honey until it is tender and sweet.

Serves: 6
Preparation time: 10 minutes
Cooking time: 45 minutes

• 3 lb (1.35 kg) fennel bulbs, stems trimmed off
• ¼ cup (60 ml/2 fl oz) extra-virgin olive oil
• 2 large garlic cloves, thinly sliced
• 1½ cups (355 ml/12 fl oz) vegetable stock
• ¾ teaspoon kosher salt, plus more as needed
• ½ teaspoon freshly ground black pepper
• 1 tablespoon honey
• ½ teaspoon finely grated orange zest
• Finely chopped fennel fronds or chopped fresh parsley, for garnish

Cut each fennel bulb in quarters (or eighths if large), removing most of the woody core, but leaving just enough to keep the fennel wedges intact. In a large frying pan, heat the oil over medium heat. Working in batches if necessary, add the fennel pieces in a single layer and cook, turning occasionally, until slightly softened and lightly browned, 8–10 minutes.

Return all of the browned fennel pieces to the pan, add the garlic, and cook, gently stirring, until fragrant, about 1 minute. Add the stock, salt, and pepper. Increase the heat to medium-high and bring to a boil. Cover, reduce the heat to medium-low, and cook until the fennel is tender, 15–20 minutes.

Transfer the fennel pieces to a serving plate. Increase the heat under the pan to medium-high, add the honey and orange zest, and cook, stirring often, until it reduces slightly, 5–10 minutes. Taste and add more salt, if desired. Pour the sauce over the fennel pieces and sprinkle with fennel fronds. Serve hot.

BRAISED CHARD AND CHICKPEAS

Sephardi Jews hailing from Rhodes and Jewish communities from North Africa serve braised chard and chickpeas on Rosh Hashanah—combining two symbolic holiday foods in one dish. The duo can be simmered with stew meat or augmented with meatballs, but it also makes a tasty vegetarian side.

Serves: 6–8
Preparation time: 15 minutes
Cooking time: 25 minutes

• 2 large bunches Swiss chard (about 2 lb/910 g), soaked and drained
• ¼ cup (60 ml/2 fl oz) extra-virgin olive oil
• 1 large onion, halved through the root and thinly sliced
• 4 garlic cloves, thinly sliced
• ¾ teaspoon kosher salt, plus more as needed
• ½ teaspoon onion powder
• ½ teaspoon crushed pepper flakes
• ½ teaspoon freshly ground black pepper
• ½ lb (225 g) tomatoes, cored, seeded, and chopped
• 1 can (15 oz/425 g) chickpeas, rinsed and drained
• 2 tablespoons fresh lemon juice

Remove the chard leaves from their stems. Trim and discard the stems' woody bottoms and cut the remainder into ½-inch (1.25 cm) pieces. Coarsely chop the leaves, setting them aside separately from the stems.

In a large frying pan, heat the oil over medium heat. Add the onion, garlic, and a pinch of salt and cook, stirring occasionally, until softened and lightly browned, 6–8 minutes. Add the chard stems, cover, and cook until the stems are crisp-tender, about 5 minutes. Uncover and stir in the salt, the onion powder, pepper flakes, and black pepper. Then add the chard leaves, tomatoes, and chickpeas. (Add the chard in stages if it doesn't all fit at once.) Cover and cook, stirring occasionally, until the chard is wilted and tender, about 10 minutes. Remove from the heat and stir in the lemon juice. Taste and add a little more salt, if desired. Serve hot or warm.

Jewish-Style Braised Fennel

SWEET-AND-SOUR OKRA WITH TOMATO

Stewed okra dishes, some made with meat and some without, are common throughout Sephardi and Mizrahi Jewish cuisine. The pods are often cooked in tomato sauce that is flavored different ways, depending on where it is being prepared. This sweet-and-sour version, called *bamia*, includes flavors like allspice and tamarind paste that are typical of Syrian kitchens. If fresh okra isn't available, thawed frozen okra works as a substitute.

Serves: 6–8
Preparation time: 10 minutes
Cooking time: 1 hour

- ¼ cup (60 ml/2 fl oz) extra-virgin olive oil
- 1 large onion, finely chopped
- 4 garlic cloves, thinly sliced
- 1½ lb (680 g) small okra pods, stems removed, washed and thoroughly patted dry
- ½ cup (90 g) pitted prunes, roughly chopped
- ¼ cup (45 g) dried apricots, roughly chopped
- 1 tablespoon tomato paste (purée)
- 1 can (28 oz/795 g) diced (chopped) tomatoes
- 2 tablespoons tamarind paste or pomegranate molasses
- 2 tablespoons fresh lemon juice, plus more as needed
- 1 tablespoon honey
- ½ teaspoon ground allspice
- 1½ teaspoons kosher salt, plus more as needed

In a large saucepan, heat the oil over medium heat. Add the onion and garlic and cook, stirring occasionally, until softened and lightly browned, 6–8 minutes. Add the okra and cook, stirring once or twice, until lightly softened, about 5 minutes.

Stir in the prunes, apricots, tomato paste (purée), diced (chopped) tomatoes, tamarind paste, lemon juice, honey, and allspice. Cover, reduce the heat to low, and cook, shaking the pan occasionally, until the okra is tender, 30–40 minutes. Do not stir during cooking.

Uncover and gently stir in the salt. Continue cooking until the sauce thickens slightly, 5–10 minutes. Taste and add more salt and lemon juice, if desired. Remove from the heat and transfer to a serving bowl. Serve hot or warm.

MATZO AND TOMATO SCRAMBLE

Moroccan Jews serve this dish, called *sorda*, as a simple side on the last days of Passover.

Serves: 4–6
Preparation time: 10 minutes
Cooking time: 25 minutes

- 3 tablespoons extra-virgin olive oil
- 1 large onion, finely chopped
- 2 garlic cloves, finely chopped
- 1 teaspoon kosher salt, plus more as needed
- 1 teaspoon sweet paprika
- ½ teaspoon ground turmeric
- ½ teaspoon crushed pepper flakes (optional)
- 1 can (28 oz/795 g) diced (chopped) tomatoes
- Freshly ground black pepper
- 4–5 sheets matzo, broken into 1-inch (2.5 cm) pieces

In a large frying pan, heat the oil over medium heat. Add the onion, garlic, and a pinch of salt and cook, stirring occasionally, until softened and lightly browned, 6–8 minutes. Add the paprika, turmeric, and pepper flakes (if using) and cook, stirring, until fragrant, about 1 minute. Add the tomatoes with their juice, salt, and a generous amount of black pepper and cook, stirring occasionally, until slightly thickened, about 5 minutes.

Add the matzo pieces and stir to coat. Reduce the heat to low, cover, and cook until the matzo is tender and has absorbed some of the sauce, 5–10 minutes. Taste and add more salt and pepper, if desired. Serve hot.

Sweet-and-Sour Okra with Tomato

MARINATED FRIED ZUCCHINI

This ancient fried zucchini (courgette) dish called *concia* employs two techniques favored by Roman Jews—frying in olive oil and marinating. Here, thin planks of zucchini are pan-fried, then steeped in a mix of fresh basil and mint, garlic, and red wine vinegar. The resulting dish is at once sultry and bright, and a wonderful addition to any table. *Concia* isn't complicated to make, but the frying step is time consuming. Speed things up by using two large frying pans—each holding ⅓ cup (75 ml/2½ fl oz) olive oil.

Serves: 4–6
Preparation time: 15 minutes, plus resting
Cooking Time: 1 hour

- ¼ cup (10 g) chiffonade-cut fresh basil
- ¼ cup (10 g) fresh mint leaves, roughly torn
- 3 garlic cloves, finely chopped
- ⅓ cup (75 ml/2½ fl oz) extra-virgin olive oil, plus more as needed
- 3 lb (1.35 kg) zucchini (courgettes), 6–8 medium, ends trimmed and sliced into long planks ¼ inch (6 mm) thick
- ¼ cup (60 ml/2 fl oz) red wine vinegar
- 1 teaspoon kosher salt
- ½ teaspoon freshly ground black pepper

In a small bowl, stir together the basil, mint, and garlic.

In a large frying pan, heat the oil over medium heat. Working in batches, fry the zucchini (courgette) planks, turning once, until softened and lightly browned on both sides, about 5 minutes per side. If the pan begins to look dry, add another tablespoon of oil as needed. Divide the fried zucchini between 2 small baking dishes (not metal). Dividing evenly, sprinkle each with the herb mixture, vinegar, salt, and pepper.

Let sit at room temperature, basting occasionally with the juices in the baking dish, for at least 30 minutes before serving.

ALOO MAKALA

The Jewish community from Calcutta serves these deep-fried potatoes on Shabbat and holidays. The dish's name, a mashup of the Hindi word for "potatoes" (*aloo*) and the Arabic word for "fried" (*makala*) are a testament to the community's Baghdadi roots. The dish is time consuming to prepare, but truly delicious, with crispy, French fry–like outsides and creamy, tender middles. The potatoes make a wonderful companion to a saucy braised dish like Onion and Tamarind Chicken (page 274).

Serves: 6
Preparation time: 30 minutes
Cooking time: 2 hours

- 2 lb (910 g) small waxy (boiling) potatoes, peeled
- 1 tablespoon kosher salt, plus more as needed
- 1 teaspoon ground turmeric
- Vegetable oil, for frying

In a large saucepan, combine the potatoes with water to cover by 1 inch (2.5 cm). Stir in the salt and turmeric and bring to a boil over high heat. Cook for 1 minute, then drain the potatoes and immediately return them to the saucepan (off the heat) to dry in the pan's residual heat. When cool enough to handle, pierce the potatoes in several places with a fork.

Arrange the potatoes in a single layer in a large frying pan over medium-high heat, then add enough oil to cover. Bring to a boil, then reduce the heat to medium-low and cook, uncovered and stirring once or twice, until golden brown, 1–1½ hours. Increase the heat to medium-high and continue cooking until crisp and deep golden brown, 10–15 minutes. Transfer to a large plate lined with paper towels to drain. Transfer the potatoes to a serving dish and sprinkle with a little more salt. Serve hot.

Marinated Fried Zucchini

BRAISED GREENS WITH TOMATOES

Eastern Uganda is home to a small community of Jews (about 2,000 people) called Abayudaya, meaning People of Judah. Their history stretches back to the early twentieth century when a Christian missionary named Semei Kakungulu decided instead to follow the Hebrew Bible and inspired others to do so as well. Abayudaya cuisine largely mirrors that of its Ugandan neighbors. This flavorful braised greens dish, called *sukuma wiki*, is served during the week and also as a side dish at Shabbat dinner. It can be made with meat, but here the untraditional addition of smoked paprika adds savory depth while keeping the dish fully vegan.

Serves: 6
Preparation time: 15 minutes
Cooking time: 30 minutes

- 2 tablespoons peanut (groundnut) oil or vegetable oil
- 1 onion, finely chopped
- 1 tablespoon finely chopped fresh ginger
- 2 large plum tomatoes, finely chopped
- ½ teaspoon ground turmeric
- ½ teaspoon smoked paprika (optional)
- ¼ teaspoon ground coriander
- ¼ teaspoon cayenne pepper
- 1½ teaspoons kosher salt, plus more as needed
- 2 large bunches collard greens or kale, tough stems removed, leaves finely chopped
- 2 tablespoons fresh lemon juice

In a large saucepan, heat the oil over medium heat. Add the onion and ginger and cook, stirring occasionally, until softened and browned, 8–10 minutes. Add the tomatoes, turmeric, smoked paprika (if using), coriander, cayenne, and salt and cook, stirring occasionally, until the tomatoes soften, 2–3 minutes.

Add the collards and ⅓ cup (75 ml/2½ fl oz) water (if the collards don't all fit at once, add half and let them cook down a bit before adding the remainder). Cover and cook, stirring occasionally, until the greens are very tender, 10–15 minutes. Remove from the heat and stir in the lemon juice. Taste and add more salt, if desired. Serve hot.

KASHA VARNISHKES

Roasted buckwheat, called kasha, was a staple of the Eastern European Jewish diet. It was served many ways—plain or with sautéed mushrooms as a side dish, stuffed into knishes (see page 198), and even cooked in milk as a breakfast porridge. But kasha varnishkes, a mix of softened kasha, silky caramelized onions, and chewy bow-tie noodles, is arguably the best known of all kasha preparations. Make sure to use roasted buckwheat, since raw buckwheat groats do not have the right flavor.

Serves: 6–8
Preparation time: 10 minutes
Cooking time: 40 minutes

- Kosher salt
- 12 oz (340 g) farfalle (bow-tie pasta)
- ⅓ cup (75 ml/2½ fl oz) vegetable oil or Schmaltz (page 410), plus more for drizzling
- 2 large red onions, halved through the root and thinly sliced
- 1 teaspoon onion powder
- 1½ cups (355 ml/12 fl oz) vegetable or chicken stock
- ¾ cup (135 g) whole kasha (roasted buckwheat)
- Freshly ground black pepper
- Finely chopped fresh parsley, for serving

Bring a large pot of generously salted water to a boil over high heat. Add the pasta and cook, stirring occasionally, until al dente, about 11 minutes. Drain, transfer to a large bowl, and toss with a drizzle of oil.

Meanwhile, in a large frying pan, heat the oil over medium heat. Add the onions, cover, and cook, stirring occasionally, until softened, about 15 minutes. Uncover, season generously with salt, and continue cooking, stirring occasionally, until the onions are very tender and have reduced in size by about one-third, 10–15 minutes. Stir in the onion powder and remove from the heat.

In a medium saucepan, bring the stock to a boil over high heat. Stir in the kasha, reduce the heat to low, cover, and simmer until kasha is soft and the liquid is absorbed, 12–15 minutes. Remove the pan from the heat and let stand, covered, for 5 minutes. Then add to the pasta along with the cooked onions. Season with salt and pepper to taste, and serve warm, topped with parsley.

Braised Greens with Tomatoes

ROME'S JEWISH GHETTO

In 1555, Pope Paul IV established a walled ghetto for the Jews of Rome. (The first Jewish ghetto had been established about forty years earlier in Venice.) The ghetto was cramped and dark and prone to flooding, and Jews' civil liberties were drastically restricted. But despite the many hardships, Roman Jews endured for more than three hundred years of ghetto life, and their cloistered lifestyle led to an ironic flourishing of culture and cuisine. It is during this time that a true *cucina Ebraica* (Jewish cuisine)

crystallized in Rome—a mixture of the foods of Italkim Jews, who had settled in Rome during ancient times, and the Sephardi Jews who arrived after the Spanish Inquisition. Some of the characteristics of this cuisine included a penchant for frying foods (particularly vegetables and fish) in olive oil, binding pastries with sweet wine, using pine nuts and raisins, and making creative use of anchovies and other small, affordable, and accessible fish.

CARCIOFI ALLA GIUDIA

Unarguably the most iconic dish of Rome's Jewish community, "Jewish-style" deep-fried artichokes can be found in restaurants throughout the city's historic Jewish ghetto, and beyond. The fried thistles are at once addictively crackly and lusciously tender at the heart. They are traditionally fried in olive oil—but a milder oil like safflower or sunflower allows the vegetable's flavor to be the star.

Serves: 4–6
Preparation time: 1 hour
Cooking time: 45 minutes

• 3 lemons, 2 juiced and 1 cut into wedges
• 2 lb (910 g) artichokes (8–10 small)
• Extra-virgin olive oil or vegetable oil, for deep-frying
• Kosher salt, for sprinkling

Fill a large bowl with water and stir in the juice from the two lemons. Working with one artichoke at a time, remove the darker outer leaves. Trim off all but ½ inch (1.25 cm) of the stem and cut ½ inch (1.25 cm) off the top of the artichoke. Add the trimmed artichokes to the lemon water as you work.

Line a large plate with paper towels. Pour about 3 inches (7.5 cm) oil into a large heavy pot, set over medium heat, and bring to 300°F (149°C) on a deep-fry thermometer. Working in batches if necessary, add the artichokes and cook, turning occasionally, until the hearts are tender when pierced with a fork, 10–15 minutes.

Use a slotted spoon to transfer the artichokes to the paper towels to drain and let cool to the touch. Once cool enough to handle, gently pull open each artichoke to expose the center. (It should resemble a flower.) If the artichokes have a hairy choke at the center (larger varieties do, while "baby" artichokes often do not), remove and discard them.

Bring the oil temperature up to 350°F (177°C). Add the fried artichokes back to the oil, blossom side down, and fry until browned and very crispy, 3–5 minutes. Return to the paper towels to drain and sprinkle with salt. Serve immediately, with the remaining lemon wedges on the side for squeezing.

FRITTO MISTO

This dish of battered and fried mixed vegetables (and often meat and seafood, too) enjoys widespread popularity in Italy. But it originated with Roman Jews, who call it *pezzetti fritti* (fried little pieces). The barely-there batter is crisp and ethereally light, allowing the vegetables to shine through. Other vegetables like squash blossoms (courgette flowers), asparagus, thinly sliced sweet potato, fennel, and cauliflower can be substituted.

Serves: 6
Preparation time: 25 minutes, plus resting
Cooking time: 35 minutes

- 1 cup (140 g) all-purpose (plain) flour
- ½ cup (80 g) fine semolina
- 1 egg
- ½ teaspoon kosher salt, plus more as needed
- 1½ cups (355 ml/12 fl oz) seltzer (sparkling water)
- Vegetable oil, for frying
- 2 small zucchini (courgettes), about ½ lb (225 g), ends trimmed and cut lengthwise into 8 wedges
- ½ lb (225 g) cremini (chestnut) mushrooms, stemmed and halved
- ½ lb (225 g) thawed frozen artichoke hearts, thoroughly patted dry
- ½ lb (225 g) green beans, trimmed
- Lemon wedges, for serving

In a large bowl, whisk together the flour, semolina, egg, salt, and seltzer (sparkling water) until smooth and combined. The batter should be slightly thicker than heavy (whipping) cream. Cover the bowl and let rest for 20 minutes while prepping the vegetables.

In a large frying pan, heat ½ inch (1.25 cm) oil over medium heat. Line a large baking sheet with paper towels. Working in batches, drop the vegetables into the batter to coat. Remove with tongs, allowing excess batter to drip off, then fry, flipping once, until lightly golden and crisp on both sides, 2–4 minutes per side. Transfer the fried vegetables to the paper towels to drain.

Transfer the vegetables to a serving plate and sprinkle lightly with salt. Serve immediately, with lemon wedges on the side for squeezing.

MAMALIGA

Mamaliga is to Romanian cooking what pasta is to Italian cooking: central and essential. The rustic cornmeal porridge, which is a close cousin to polenta, is served for breakfast, lunch, and dinner, and for holidays and weekday meals alike. Mamaliga can be eaten straight from the pot, stirred with sour cream and jam, or generously topped with crumbled cheese (feta works well) and black pepper. Sliced, pan-fried leftovers serve as a hearty base for the Romanian vegetable ragout, Guvetch (page 246), or fried eggs.

Serves: 4
Preparation time: 5 minutes
Cooking time: 20 minutes

- 1½ teaspoons kosher salt
- 1 cup (140 g) medium-grind yellow cornmeal
- 3 tablespoons (45 g) unsalted butter, cut into small pieces
- Sour cream and jam, for serving

In a medium saucepan, combine 3 cups (710 ml/24 fl oz) water and the salt and bring to a boil over medium heat. Add the cornmeal in a slow stream, stirring constantly.

Reduce the heat to low, cover, and cook, stirring often, until the liquid is absorbed and the cornmeal thickens, 5–15 minutes. Add the butter pieces and continue stirring until incorporated, 1–2 minutes.

Remove the pan from the heat and serve immediately as a porridge, topped generously with sour cream and jam. Or, transfer the mixture to a lightly greased shallow bowl and let set for 15 minutes. Invert onto a cutting board and slice into wedges.

FRIED CAULIFLOWER

Sephardi Jews serve this delicately crisp, fried cauliflower dish as part of a larger mezze spread. The burst of fresh lemon juice squeezed on at the table brightens the fried florets. They are also delicious drizzled with Tahini Sauce (page 396).

Serves: 4–6
Preparation time: 10 minutes
Cooking time: 35 minutes

- 1 medium head cauliflower (about 2 lb/910 g), cored and cut into 1-inch (2.5 cm) florets
- Vegetable oil, for frying
- 2 cups (280 g) all-purpose (plain) flour
- 1 teaspoon onion powder
- 1 teaspoon garlic powder
- 1 teaspoon kosher salt, plus more for sprinkling
- ¼ teaspoon freshly ground black pepper
- 6 eggs
- Lemon wedges, for serving

Set up a large bowl of equal parts ice and water. Bring a large pot of water to a boil over high heat. Add the cauliflower florets to the boiling water and cook until crisp-tender, 3–5 minutes. Drain and immediately transfer to the ice bath. Drain again and dry thoroughly with paper towels.

In a large, wide saucepan, heat ½ inch (1.25 cm) oil over medium heat until shimmering. Meanwhile, in a shallow dish, whisk together the flour, onion powder, garlic powder, salt, and pepper. Whisk the eggs in a separate bowl.

Working in batches, dip the cauliflower florets in the flour, shaking off excess. Dip in the egg, then again in the flour. Fry, flipping once, until golden and crisp, 3–5 minutes. (If the florets are browning too quickly, reduce the heat slightly.) Use a slotted spoon to transfer the cauliflower to paper towels to drain, and sprinkle with a little more salt. Serve immediately, with lemon wedges on the side for squeezing.

FRIED EGGPLANT WITH SUGAR

Serving fried eggplant (aubergine) drizzled with honey dates back to the Jewish and Moorish communities of pre-Inquisition Spain. This related dish is eaten across several Sephardi communities—some Moroccan families serve it to break the fast after Yom Kippur. The particular mix of sweet and savory flavors may seem unusual to those who haven't tried it, but the dish is unarguably beguiling.

Serves: 6
Preparation time: 10 minutes
Cooking time: 45 minutes

- Vegetable oil, for frying
- 1 cup (140 g) all-purpose (plain) flour
- 2 eggs, beaten
- 2 lb (910 g) eggplant (aubergine), peeled and cut crosswise into ¼-inch (6 mm) rounds
- Kosher salt
- Sugar, for topping

In a large nonstick frying pan, heat about ½ inch (1.25 cm) oil over medium-high heat. Line a large plate or baking sheet with paper towels.

While the oil is heating, spread the flour on a plate and add the eggs to a shallow bowl. Sprinkle the eggplant (aubergine) pieces with a little salt. Dredge them on both sides in the flour, tapping to remove excess, then dip them in the egg, allowing the excess to drip off. Working in batches, fry the coated eggplant slices in oil until softened and lightly browned on both sides, 4–5 minutes per side. Transfer the fried eggplant to the paper towels to drain.

Arrange the eggplant on a dish and sprinkle with sugar to taste, and with a little more salt, if desired. Serve hot.

EYAL SHANI

NORTH ABRAXAS
•
LILIENBLUM STREET 40
TEL AVIV, ISRAEL

MIZNON
•
MULTIPLE LOCATIONS
TEL AVIV, PARIS,
VIENNA, MELBOURNE,
NEW YORK CITY

Eyal Shani, who is one of Israel's best-known chefs, owns several successful restaurants in Tel Aviv, with outposts in Vienna, Paris, Melbourne, and New York City. Whole roasted cauliflower began as a signature offering at his flagship restaurant, North Abraxas. Today, it is also on the menu at his upscale pita chain, Miznon.

WHOLE ROASTED CAULIFLOWER

This tender and gorgeously browned cauliflower dish is as visually striking as it is delicious to eat. Serve it drizzled with tahini sauce and with *s'chug* alongside.

Serves: 2
Preparation time: 25 minutes, plus cooling
Cooking time: 40 minutes

• 1 head cauliflower (1½–2 lb/680–910 g), with leaves
• 6 tablespoons plus 1 teaspoon kosher salt
• 3 tablespoons extra-virgin olive oil
• Tahini Sauce (page 398) and S'chug (page 413), for serving

Trim just the stem of the cauliflower (keeping the leaves intact) so it can sit upright without tipping over. Fill a large pot with about 8 quarts (7.5 liters/2 gal) water. Set over high heat and stir in 6 tablespoons of the salt, until dissolved. Once the water is boiling, carefully add the cauliflower to the pot and place a heatproof ceramic plate on top of the cauliflower to keep it submerged. Boil (the pot should be uncovered) until tender and a fork inserted into the central core of the cauliflower meets no resistance, 12–14 minutes. Using a spider or tongs and a slotted spoon, gently lift the cauliflower from the water and let it drain on a plate.

Position a rack in the center of the oven and preheat to 500°F (260°C/Gas Mark 10).

Meanwhile, place the drained cauliflower, stem side down, on a large sheet pan and let stand until it has cooled slightly and is dry to the touch, about 15 minutes. Using a pastry brush, brush 2 tablespoons of the oil evenly over the surface of the cauliflower and sprinkle the remaining 1 teaspoon salt evenly over the top.

Bake until dark brown, about 25 minutes. Remove from the oven and carefully brush with the remaining 1 tablespoon oil. Serve hot, with tahini and s'chug on the side.

COCONUT RICE

Fragrant with cardamom, ginger, and a triple dose of coconut (coconut oil, coconut milk, and shredded coconut), this rice dish, called *thengha chor*, is truly extraordinary. The robust use of spice is typical of the cuisine of Cochin's historic Indian Jewish community, and the cuisine of the Malabar Coast more broadly. It makes a particularly wonderful side to Chicken Schnitzel (page 280), or Mint and Carrot Chicken (page 276).

Serves: 6–8
Preparation time: 20 minutes, plus soaking
Cooking time: 35 minutes

- 3 tablespoons coconut oil or vegetable oil
- 2 large onions, halved through the root and thinly sliced
- 2 garlic cloves, finely chopped
- 1-inch (2.5 cm) piece fresh ginger, peeled and finely chopped
- 2 cups (400 g) basmati rice, soaked in water for 30 minutes and drained
- ½ cup (40 g) unsweetened shredded (dessicated) coconut
- 2 cinnamon sticks
- 3 cardamom pods, cracked
- ¼ teaspoon ground coriander
- 1¼ teaspoon kosher salt, plus more as needed
- ¼ teaspoon freshly ground black pepper
- 2½ cups (590 ml/20 fl oz) coconut milk

In a large saucepan, heat the oil over medium-high heat. Add the onions, garlic, and ginger and cook, stirring occasionally, until softened and lightly browned, 10–15 minutes. Add the rice, shredded (dessicated) coconut, cinnamon sticks, cardamom pods, coriander, salt, and pepper and cook, stirring, until fragrant, 1–2 minutes.

Stir in the coconut milk and ½ cup water and bring to a boil. Reduce the heat to low, cover, and cook until the rice is tender and has absorbed the liquid, 18–20 minutes. Remove the pan from the heat and let stand, covered, for 10 minutes. Serve hot.

ARROZ KON TOMATE

This homey Turkish tomato and rice pilaf is simple to make and complements virtually any savory meal.

Serves: 6–8
Preparation time: 10 minutes, plus soaking
Cooking time: 35 minutes

- 3 tablespoons extra-virgin olive oil
- 1 onion, finely chopped
- 2 cups (400 g) long-grain white rice, soaked for 10 minutes and drained
- 1 can (14½ oz/411 g) diced (chopped) tomatoes
- 2 tablespoons tomato paste (purée)
- 1½ teaspoons kosher salt

In a large saucepan, heat the oil over medium heat. Add the onion and cook, stirring occasionally, until softened and lightly browned, 6–8 minutes. Stir in the rice, 3 cups (710 ml/24 fl oz) water, tomatoes and their juices, tomato paste (purée), and salt. Increase the heat to medium-high and bring to a low boil.

Reduce the heat to low, cover, and cook until water is absorbed and rice is tender, 20–25 minutes. Remove from the heat and let rest, covered, for 10 minutes. Serve hot.

Coconut Rice

SAFFRON RICE

The golden hue of this saffron-scented rice is festive and celebratory. It is popular throughout the Middle East—Jewish families often serve it on Rosh Hashanah. It is delicious as is, but some cooks stir in golden raisins (sultanas) and sliced almonds or pine nuts to the rice for extra color and crunch.

Serves: 6–8
Preparation time: 10 minutes
Cooking time: 25 minutes

- ½ teaspoon saffron threads, finely crumbled
- 2 tablespoons boiling water
- ¼ cup (60 ml/2 fl oz) extra-virgin olive oil
- 1 large onion, finely chopped
- 2 cups (400 g) basmati rice, rinsed well and drained
- 3 cups (710 ml/24 fl oz) vegetable or chicken stock
- 1 teaspoon kosher salt
- 1 cinnamon stick (optional)

In a small heatproof bowl, stir together saffron and boiling water and set aside.

In a large saucepan, heat the oil over medium heat until shimmering. Add the onion and cook, stirring occasionally, until softened and lightly browned, 6–8 minutes. Add the rice and cook, stirring often, until fragrant, 1–2 minutes.

Stir in the stock, salt, saffron mixture, and cinnamon stick (if using). Increase the heat to medium-high and bring to a boil, then reduce the heat to low, cover, and cook until the water is fully absorbed, 15–18 minutes. Remove the pan from the heat and let stand, covered, for 5 minutes. Fluff the rice with a fork and remove the cinnamon stick, if necessary. Transfer to a serving dish and serve hot.

DILLED RICE WITH LIMA BEANS

This fragrant, vibrantly green rice dish gets folded with a heap of fresh dill and fava beans (broad beans). Persian Jews traditionally serve the dish, called *baghali polo*, on Passover, but it is delicious any time of year.

Serves: 4–6
Preparation time: 10 minutes
Cooking time: 30 minutes

- 3 cups (710 ml/24 fl oz) vegetable or chicken stock
- 2 cups (400 g) basmati rice, rinsed well and drained
- 2 tablespoons extra-virgin olive oil, plus more for drizzling
- 1 large onion, finely chopped
- 2 cups (280 g) thawed frozen fava beans (broad beans) or lima beans (butter beans)
- ½ teaspoon ground turmeric
- ⅛ teaspoon ground cinnamon
- 1 cup (50 g) finely chopped fresh dill
- 3/4 teaspoon kosher salt, plus more as needed
- Freshly ground black pepper

In a medium saucepan, bring the stock to a boil over high heat. Stir in the rice, reduce the heat to low, cover, and cook until the rice is tender, 18–20 minutes. Remove from the heat and let sit, covered, for 10 minutes. Fluff with a fork and set aside.

Meanwhile, in a medium frying pan, heat the oil over medium heat. Add the onion and cook until softened and lightly browned, 6–8 minutes. Add the fava (broad) beans (broad beans) and cook until just tender, about 5 minutes. Stir in the turmeric and cinnamon. Remove from the heat and add the fava bean mixture to the rice along with the dill, salt, a generous amount of pepper, and a drizzle of additional oil. Stir to combine, then taste and adjust the salt and pepper, if desired. Serve hot or warm.

RICE WITH TAHDIG

Rice is highly prized within Persian cuisine, and rice with tahdig—a crusty, golden-brown layer that forms at the bottom of the pot when it is steamed for an extended time—is considered the ultimate expression of rice perfection. Home cooks typically scoop out the tender rice from the pot onto a serving platter, then carefully loosen the tahdig crust, laying it on top like a glorious crown. Tahdig is a technique that can be used on nearly any Persian rice dish. Some recipes layer the bottom of the pot with thinly sliced potatoes. Others mix the rice with yogurt, which helps facilitate a cohesive crust. Whatever the technique, it is important to start with basmati rice, which holds its shape without getting mushy, and to soak it before cooking to help remove any excess starch.

Serves: 6–8
Preparation time: 15 minutes, plus soaking and resting
Cooking time: 1½ hours

- 2½ tablespoons plus ½ teaspoon kosher salt
- 2 cups (400 g) basmati rice, soaked in water for 20 minutes and drained
- 1 cup (50 g) finely chopped fresh dill, parsley, mint, or a combination (optional)
- ¼ cup (60 ml/2 fl oz) vegetable oil or 4 tablespoons (60 g) unsalted butter

In a large saucepan, bring 8 cups (2 liters/2 qt) water and 2½ tablespoons salt to boil over high heat. Add the rice and cook, uncovered and stirring occasionally, until the rice is partly cooked, 5–7 minutes. Drain the rice and immediately rinse with cold water to stop the cooking process. If using the herbs, transfer the drained rice and herbs to a large bowl and toss to combine.

In a large cast-iron skillet, heat the oil over medium heat. Add about 2 cups (270 g) of the cooked rice to the pan and spread into an even layer, pressing down firmly with a spatula to flatten. Mound the remaining rice on top and use a chopstick or the back of a wooden spoon to poke several holes into the rice to help steam escape as the rice cooks. Sprinkle 2 tablespoons water and the remaining ½ teaspoon salt over the rice. Wrap a clean tea towel around the lid of the skillet, securing at the top with a rubber band, then cover the pan. (The towel catches the steam that rises off the rice as it cooks.) Increase the heat to medium-high and cook, undisturbed, for 10 minutes. Reduce the heat to very low and continue cooking, without stirring, for 1 hour 15 minutes. Remove the skillet from the heat and let sit, covered, for 10 minutes.

Uncover the pan and scoop the loose rice onto a serving platter. Using a spatula, carefully nudge under and lift up the crisp tahdig layer, in pieces if necessary, and place on top. Serve hot.

JEWELED RICE

What could be more beautiful and enticing then delicately spiced rice adorned with little jewels of dried fruit and sparkling pomegranate seeds? It is little wonder that Persian Jews traditionally serve large platters of jeweled rice, called *morasa polo*, at weddings and other joyous occasions.

Serves: 8
Preparation time: 15 minutes, plus resting and soaking
Cooking time: 45 minutes

- ¼ cup (30 g) sliced or slivered almonds
- ¼ cup (30 g) unsalted pistachios, roughly chopped
- ½ teaspoon saffron, crumbled
- ¼ cup (60 ml/2 fl oz) boiling water
- 2 cups (400 g) basmati rice, soaked in water for 15 minutes and then drained
- ¼ cup (60 ml/2 fl oz) plus 2 tablespoons vegetable oil
- 1 large onion, finely chopped
- 1½ teaspoons kosher salt
- 1 teaspoon ground cinnamon
- ½ teaspoon ground cumin
- ¼ teaspoon ground allspice
- ¼ teaspoon ground cardamom
- ½ teaspoon freshly ground black pepper
- ½ cup (90 g) dried apricots, very thinly sliced
- ½ cup (70 g) dried cherries or cranberries, roughly chopped
- ½ cup (70 g) golden raisins (sultanas)
- ½ teaspoon finely grated orange zest
- ½ cup (85 g) pomegranate seeds, for serving (optional)

In a small dry frying pan, toast the almonds and pistachios over medium-low heat, shaking the pan occasionally, until fragrant and lightly browned, about 5 minutes. Remove the pan from the heat and let cool. Set aside.

In a small heatproof bowl, stir together the saffron and boiling water. Set aside.

Fill a medium saucepan with water and bring to a boil over high heat. Add the rice and cook, stirring occasionally, until halfway tender, 5–7 minutes. Drain and set aside.

In a medium frying pan, heat 2 tablespoons of the oil over medium heat. Add the onion and cook, stirring occasionally, until softened and lightly browned, 6–8 minutes. Add the salt, cinnamon, cumin, allspice, cardamom, and pepper and cook, stirring, until fragrant, about 1 minute. Stir in the apricots, cherries, golden raisins (sultanas), and orange zest. Remove from the heat and set aside.

In a medium saucepan, heat the remaining ¼ cup (60 ml/ 2 fl oz) oil over medium heat. Spread half of the parboiled rice on the bottom and cover with the onion and fruit mixture, then the remaining rice. Let cook, undisturbed, until fragrant, about 10 minutes. Use the back of a wooden spoon or a chopstick to poke several deep holes in the rice to help steam escape as the rice cooks. Drizzle the saffron-water mixture over the rice. Cover, reduce the heat to low, and cook for 25 minutes. Remove from the heat and let rest, covered, for 10 minutes.

Transfer the rice and onion/dried fruit mixture to a wide serving bowl and gently mix to combine. Use a spatula to carefully remove the bottom crust of rice from the pot and place on top. Serve hot, sprinkled with the toasted nuts and pomegranate seeds (if using).

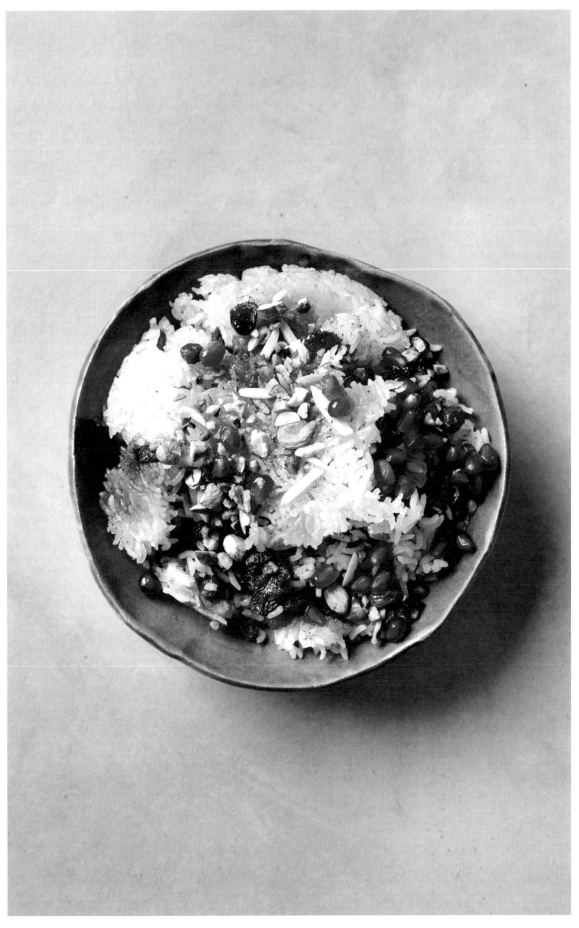

Jeweled Rice

SWEET RICE WITH ORANGE ZEST AND CARROTS

This festive Persian rice dish, called *shirin polo*, is a close cousin to Jeweled Rice (page 174). It comes brimming with sweetened grated carrots and fragrant orange zest. Some cooks add chicken, but it is a delicious vegetarian side dish all on its own. It makes a wonderful addition to the Rosh Hashanah table or any festive fall dinner.

Serves: 8
Preparation time: 30 minutes, plus soaking and resting
Cooking time: 1 hour

- ¼ cup (25 g) sliced almonds
- ½ teaspoon saffron threads, crumbled
- ¼ cup (60 ml/2 fl oz) boiling water
- 2 cups (400 g) basmati rice, soaked in water for 30 minutes and drained
- ¼ cup (60 ml/2 fl oz) plus 2 tablespoons vegetable oil
- 1 lb (455 g) carrots, grated on the large holes of a box grater
- ¼ cup (50 g) sugar
- 1 teaspoon kosher salt
- Finely grated zest of 1 orange
- 1 teaspoon ground cinnamon
- ¼ teaspoon ground cardamom
- ½ cup (70 g) dried currants or barberries

In a small, dry frying pan, toast the almonds over medium-low heat, shaking the pan occasionally, until fragrant and lightly browned, about 5 minutes. Remove the pan from the heat and let cool. Set aside.

In a small heatproof bowl, stir together the saffron and boiling water. Set aside.

Fill a medium saucepan with water and bring to a boil over high heat. Add the rice and cook, stirring occasionally, until halfway tender, 5–7 minutes. Drain and set aside.

In a medium frying pan set, heat 2 tablespoons of the oil over medium-high heat. Add the carrots, sugar, and a small splash of water. Cook, stirring occasionally, until the carrots are tender, 8–10 minutes. Uncover and stir in the salt, orange zest, cinnamon, cardamom, and currants and cook, stirring, until fragrant, about 1 minute.

In a medium saucepan, heat the remaining ¼ cup (60 ml/ 2 fl oz) oil over medium heat. Spread half of the parboiled rice on the bottom and cover with the carrot mixture, then the remaining rice. Let cook, undisturbed, until fragrant, about 10 minutes. Use the back of a wooden spoon or a chopstick to poke several deep holes in the rice to help steam escape as the rice cooks. Drizzle the saffron-water mixture over the rice. Cover, reduce the heat to low, and cook until rice is fully tender, about 25 minutes. Remove from the heat and let rest, covered, for 10 minutes.

Transfer the rice and carrot mixture to a wide serving bowl and gently mix to combine. Use a spatula to carefully remove the bottom crust of rice from the pot and place on top. Serve hot, sprinkled with the toasted almonds.

RICE WITH LENTILS AND DRIED FRUIT

Adas polo is a festive Persian rice dish that is brimming with lentils and dried fruit. It is traditionally served on Shabbat and holidays, and would be appropriate at any festive meal. If desired, substitute an equal amount of Advieh (page 412), the Persian rose petal–based spice mix, for the cardamom and cinnamon.

Serves: 8
Preparation time: 25 minutes, plus soaking and resting
Cooking time: 1 hour 10 minutes

- 1 cup (175 g) brown lentils, rinsed and drained
- 1½ cups (300 g) long-grain white rice (like basmati), soaked in water for 10 minutes and drained
- 1 teaspoon kosher salt, plus more as needed
- ½ cup (120 ml/4 fl oz) vegetable oil
- 2 onions, halved through the root and thinly sliced
- ½ cup (70 g) raisins, barberries, or finely chopped pitted dates
- ½ teaspoon ground cinnamon
- ¼ teaspoon ground cardamom
- ¼ teaspoon ground turmeric
- ¼ teaspoon freshly ground black pepper
- ¼ teaspoon saffron, crumbled
- ¼ cup (60 ml/2 fl oz) boiling water

In a small saucepan, combine the lentils and 2 cups (475 ml/16 fl oz) water and bring to a boil over high heat. Reduce the heat to medium-low, cover, and cook until the lentils are about halfway cooked, about 10 minutes. Drain and set aside.

Meanwhile, in a medium saucepan, combine the rice, a generous pinch of salt, and water to cover 2 inches (5 cm). Bring to a boil over medium-high heat and cook, stirring occasionally, until the is about about halfway tender, 5–7 minutes. Drain and set aside.

In a large Dutch oven (casserole) or other pot, heat ¼ cup (60 ml/2 fl oz) of the oil over medium heat. Add the onions and a pinch of salt and cook, stirring occasionally, until softened and lightly browned, 10–15 minutes. Add the parcooked lentils, raisins, cinnamon, cardamom, turmeric, salt, and pepper and cook, stirring constantly, until fragrant, about 1 minute. Transfer the onion and lentil mixture to a bowl and wipe out the Dutch oven.

In a small heatproof bowl, mix together the saffron and boiling water. Set aside.

Add the remaining ¼ cup (60 ml/2 fl oz) oil to the Dutch oven and set it back over medium heat. Spread about one-third of the parboiled rice on the bottom and cover with the onion and lentil mixture, then top with the remaining rice. Let cook, undisturbed, until fragrant, about 10 minutes. Drizzle the saffron-water mixture over the rice and use the handle of a long, wooden spoon to poke several holes in the rice that reach down to the bottom of the Dutch oven. Cover, reduce the heat to low, and cook for 25 minutes. Remove from the heat and let rest, covered, for 10 minutes.

To serve, scoop out the rice and lentils into a wide serving bowl and gently mix to combine. Using a spatula, carefully remove the bottom crust of rice from the Dutch oven and place on top. Serve hot.

GREEN HERBED RICE WITH MEAT

Heaps of chopped fresh cilantro (coriander) lend a gorgeous, herbal fragrance and flavor to this meaty pilaf. Called *bakhsh*, it is one of the centerpieces of the Bukharian Shabbat table, and pairs beautifully with ground lamb Lyulya Kebabs (page 313). Make sure to start with well-soaked basmati rice, which can hold up to the extended cooking time without getting too soft.

Serves: 6–8
Preparation time: 25 minutes, plus soaking
Cooking time: 1 hour 15 minutes

- 2½ teaspoons kosher salt, plus more as needed
- 2½ cups (500 g) basmati rice, soaked in water for 30 minutes and drained
- ½ cup (120 ml/4 fl oz) plus 1 tablespoon vegetable oil
- 1 lb (455 g) boneless lamb or beef shoulder, cut into ¼-inch (6 mm) pieces
- 2 bunches cilantro (coriander), very finely chopped (stems included)
- 2 bunches scallions (spring onions), thinly sliced
- ½ teaspoon freshly ground black pepper

Fill a large Dutch oven (casserole) or other ovenproof pot with water and a generous pinch of salt and bring to a boil over medium-high heat. Add the rice and cook, stirring occasionally, until just past halfway tender, 5–7 minutes. Drain and let cool slightly.

Preheat the oven to 375°F (°190C/Gas Mark 5). Grease the Dutch oven with 1 tablespoon oil. Return the drained rice to the Dutch oven along with the lamb, cilantro (coriander), and scallions (spring onions). In a medium bowl, whisk together ⅓ cup (75 ml/2½ fl oz) water, the ½ cup (120 ml/4 fl oz) oil, salt, and pepper, then pour over the rice mixure and mix thoroughly. Cover the Dutch oven and bake until the rice is fully tender and the meat is cooked, about 1 hour.

Remove from oven and let stand for 10 minutes before uncovering. Serve hot.

COUSCOUS AU LAIT

Couscous is best known as a savory side dish, but Moroccan Jews also enjoy this sweet, cinnamon-perfumed couscous, which is dotted with raisins and almonds and sometimes served with warm milk. Sweet couscous is served on Purim and, most notably, during Mimouna—the festive Moroccan meal eaten to celebrate the end of Passover.

Serves: 6–8
Preparation time: 5 minutes
Cooking time: 25 minutes

- ½ teaspoon kosher salt
- 2 cups (375 g) couscous
- 6 tablespoons (85 g) unsalted butter, cut into pieces
- ½ cup (70 g) golden raisins (sultanas)
- ½ cup (50 g) sliced almonds
- ¼ cup (45 g) light brown sugar
- 1 teaspoon ground cinnamon, plus more for sprinkling
- 1½ cups (355 ml/12 fl oz) whole milk, for serving

In a medium saucepan, stir together 2½ cups (590 ml/20 fl oz) water and the salt and bring to a boil over high heat. Pour the couscous into the boiling water in a steady stream, stirring constantly. Remove the pan from the heat, cover the saucepan, and let stand for 10 minutes. Fluff with a fork.

Meanwhile, in a medium saucepan, combine the butter, golden raisins (sultanas), and almonds and cook over medium heat, stirring occasionally, until the butter is melted, the raisins are plumped, and the almonds lightly toasted, 4–5 minutes. Remove from the heat and drain the mixture through a fine-mesh sieve directly over the couscous. Stir half of the drained raisin-almond mixture into the couscous and set the remainder aside. Add the brown sugar and cinnamon to the couscous and mix well to combine.

On a serving platter, mound the couscous into a cone shape and sprinkle with lines of cinnamon down the sides. Top the couscous with the reserved raisin-almond mixture. In a small saucepan, heat the milk over medium heat, stirring, until steaming but not boiling. Transfer the warmed milk to a small pitcher and serve alongside the couscous to pour into individual bowls at the table.

Green Herbed Rice with Meat

MEJADRA

This savory jumble of grains (usually rice), lentils, and caramelized onions dates back to at least the thirteenth century and is still widely enjoyed across the Middle East. Perfumed with warming spices and often topped with crisped onions, or in this case shallots, it is comforting and deeply delicious.

Serves: 6
Preparation time: 20 minutes, plus soaking
Cooking time: 1 hour 15 minutes

For the mejadra:
• 1 cup (175 g) brown lentils, rinsed and drained
• ¼ cup (60 ml/2 fl oz) vegetable oil
• 2 large onions, finely chopped
• 1 teaspoon kosher salt, plus more as needed
• ¼ teaspoon freshly ground black pepper, plus more as needed
• 1 teaspoon sugar
• 1 teaspoon ground cinnamon
• 1 teaspoon ground cumin
• ½ teaspoon ground allspice
• ¼ teaspoon ground turmeric
• 1 cup (200 g) long-grain white rice (like basmati), soaked in water for 10 minutes and drained

For the crispy shallots:
• Vegetable oil, for frying
• 6 small shallots, thinly sliced and rings separated
• Kosher salt

For serving:
• Finely chopped fresh parsley
• Labneh or plain whole-milk yogurt (optional)

Make the *mejadra*: In a small saucepan, combine the lentils and 2 cups (475 ml/16 fl oz) water and bring to a boil over high heat. Reduce the heat to medium-low, cover, and cook until the lentils are about halfway cooked, 10–12 minutes. Drain and set aside.

In a large Dutch oven (casserole) or other pot, heat the oil over medium heat. Add the onions, a generous pinch of salt, and 1 tablespoon water and cook, stirring occasionally, until the onions are deep golden brown, 30–35 minutes. Stir in the salt, pepper, sugar, cinnamon, cumin, allspice, and turmeric and cook, stirring constantly, until fragrant, about 1 minute.

Pour 2 cups (475 ml/16 fl oz) water over the browned onions and bring the water to a boil over high heat. Reduce the heat to low and stir in the rice and parcooked lentils. Cover and cook until the liquid is absorbed and the rice and lentils are tender, about 20 minutes. Remove from the heat and let sit, covered, for 10 minutes. Uncover, taste, and stir in additional salt and pepper to taste.

Meanwhile, make the crispy shallots: Line a large plate with paper towels. Pour ¼ inch (6 mm) oil into a medium frying pan. Add the shallots to the cold pan and turn the heat to medium-high. Cook until browned and crispy, 6–8 minutes. (Watch carefully so they do not burn.) Transfer shallots to the paper towels to drain and sprinkle with a little salt.

To serve: Transfer the *mejadra* to a serving platter and top with the crispy shallots. Serve hot or warm, sprinkled with parsley and dolloped with *labneh*, if desired.

PLOV

The Bukharian Jews of Central Asia have ancient Persian roots, so it is no surprise that this layered rice pilaf dish is central to their cuisine. Spiced with coriander and cumin, brimming with beef (or sometimes lamb), shredded carrots, and chickpeas, it is a dish fit for Shabbat dinner or any celebration.

Serves: 8
Preparation time: 35 minutes, plus soaking
Cooking time: 2 hours

- ⅓ cup (75 ml/2½ fl oz) vegetable oil
- 2 medium onions, finely chopped
- 6 garlic cloves, finely chopped
- 2½ lb (1 kg) beef chuck, trimmed of excess fat and cut into ¾-inch (2 cm) pieces
- 1 lb (455 g) carrots, grated on the large holes of a box grater
- 2½ teaspoons kosher salt, plus more as needed
- ¼ teaspoon freshly ground black pepper
- 2 teaspoons ground cumin
- 1 teaspoon ground coriander
- 1 teaspoon sweet paprika
- 2 bay leaves
- 1 can (15 oz/425 g) chickpeas, rinsed and drained
- 2½ cups (500 g) long-grain white rice, soaked in water for 30 minutes and drained
- ⅓ cup (45 g) dried currants or barberries
- Roughly chopped fresh cilantro (coriander) leaves, for serving

In a large Dutch oven (casserole) or other heavy-bottomed pot, heat the oil over medium-high heat. Add the onions and garlic and cook, stirring occasionally, until softened and lightly browned, 6–8 minutes. Add the beef and cook, stirring occasionally, until browned, 7–10 minutes. Add the carrots and cook until just softened, 3–5 minutes. Add 1½ teaspoons salt, pepper, cumin, coriander, paprika, and bay leaves and cook, stirring, until fragrant, about 1 minute.

Stir in 2 cups (475 ml/16 fl oz) water, bring to a simmer, then reduce the heat to low, cover, and cook until the meat is tender, 45–60 minutes. Uncover and stir in the chickpeas.

Sprinkle the rice and the remaining 1 teaspoon salt over the beef mixture (do not stir). Pour 3 cups (710 ml/24 fl oz) water on top and bring to a boil over high heat without stirring. Reduce the heat to medium and cook, uncovered, until the rice begins to swell and most of the water is absorbed (the surface should appear dry), 10–12 minutes.

Poke several deep holes into the mixture with the back of a wooden spoon to facilitate evaporation. Sprinkle the currants on top, reduce the heat to low, and cook, covered, until rice is tender and water is fully absorbed, 15–20 minutes. Remove from the heat and let stand, covered, for 15 minutes, then gently stir to combine. Taste and add more salt, if desired. Serve hot or warm, topped with cilantro (coriander).

FRITTERS & SAVORY
PASTRIES

POTATO LATKES

Potatoes, which are a New World ingredient, did not enjoy widespread use in Eastern Europe until the nineteenth century. once the starchy tubers caught on, they were embraced with gusto, and today these potato fritters, with tender, savory insides and crackly crusts, are the undisputed king of Ashkenazi Hanukkah celebrations.

Serves: 8
Preparation time: 15 minutes
Cooking time: 1 hour

- 4 lb (1.8 kg) russet (baking) potatoes, unpeeled, scrubbed, and patted dry
- 1 medium onion, peeled
- ⅔ cup (95 g) all-purpose (plain) flour
- 4–5 eggs, lightly beaten
- ½ cup (25 g) finely chopped fresh parsley (optional)
- 1 tablespoon kosher salt
- ½ teaspoon freshly ground black pepper
- Vegetable oil, for frying
- Sour cream or Applesauce (page 394), for serving

Line 2 large baking sheets with several layers of paper towels.

Grate the potatoes and onion on the large holes of a box grater. (Alternatively, cut them into quarters and shred on the shredding disc of a food processor.) Working in batches, wrap the shredded potato and onion in a tea towel or several layers of paper towel and squeeze out as much water as possible.

Add the shredded, squeezed potatoes and onion to a large bowl along with the flour, 4 eggs, parsley (if using), salt, and pepper. Mix until the ingredients are fully incorporated. If the mixture looks dry, mix in the remaining egg.

In a large frying pan, heat ¼ inch (6 mm) oil over medium-high heat until shimmering but not smoking. Working in batches of 4–5, drop the batter by the ¼ cup (55 g) into the pan and press gently with a spatula to flatten. Cook, flipping once, until browned on both sides and cooked through, 6–8 minutes. Continue until all of the potato mixture is used up, adding additional oil to the pan if necessary and adjusting the heat if the latkes are browning too quickly or not quickly enough.

Transfer latkes to the paper towels to drain. Serve immediately topped with sour cream, applesauce, or both. Or, let latkes cool and store, tightly wrapped in plastic, in the fridge or freezer. To reheat, arrange the latkes in a single layer on a baking sheet and warm in a 400°F (200°C/Gas Mark 6) oven until crisp and warmed through, about 10 minutes.

Potato Latkes

CURRIED SWEET POTATO LATKES

In America, home cooks have taken many creative liberties with traditional Hanukkah Potato Latkes (page 184), swapping out the usual russet (baking) potatoes for shredded zucchini (courgettes), beets, carrots, parsnips, and, perhaps most commonly, sweet potatoes. This modern take on the latke pairs the bright orange tubers with a fragrant mix of curry powder, ginger, cumin, and a touch of brown sugar. The resulting fritters taste comfortingly familiar and excitingly novel at the same time.

Serves: 8
Preparation time: 25 minutes
Cooking time: 45 minutes

- 3 lb (1.35 kg) sweet potatoes, peeled
- 1 medium onion, peeled
- ⅔ cup (95 g) all-purpose (plain) flour
- 3–4 eggs, lightly beaten
- 1 tablespoon curry powder
- 1 tablespoon light brown sugar
- 1 teaspoon ground ginger
- ¾ teaspoon ground cumin
- 2 teaspoons kosher salt
- ½ teaspoon freshly ground black pepper
- Vegetable oil, for frying
- Sour cream and Applesauce (page 394), for serving

Line 2 large baking sheets with several layers of paper towels.

Grate the sweet potatoes and onion on the large holes of a box grater. (Alternatively, cut them into quarters and shred on the shredding disc of a food processor.) Working in batches, wrap the shredded potato and onion in a clean tea towel or several layers of paper towel and squeeze out as much water as possible.

Add the shredded, squeezed potatoes and onion to a large bowl along with the flour, 3 eggs, curry powder, brown sugar, ginger, cumin, salt, and pepper and mix until the ingredients are fully incorporated. If the mixture looks dry, mix in the remaining egg.

In a large frying pan, heat ¼ inch (6 mm) oil over medium-high heat until shimmering but not smoking. Working in batches of 4–5, drop the batter by the ¼ cup (55 g) into the pan and press gently with a spatula to flatten. Fry, flipping once, until browned on both sides and cooked through, 6–8 minutes. Continue process until all of the potato mixture is used up, adding additional oil to the pan if necessary and adjusting the heat if the latkes are browning too quickly or not quickly enough.

Transfer latkes to the paper towels to drain. Serve immediately, topped with sour cream or applesauce. Or, let latkes cool and store, tightly wrapped in plastic, in the fridge or freezer. To reheat, arrange the latkes in a single layer on a baking sheet and warm in a 400°F (200°C/Gas Mark 6) oven until crisp and warmed through, about 10 minutes.

CHEESE LATKES

Potato Latkes (page 184) are unarguably the best-known Ashkenazi Hanukkah fritter—but they are not the original. That designation goes to *kaese latkes*, a lightly sweetened pancake made from soft-curd cheese that dates back to medieval Italy and that spread geographically over the following centuries. The tender pancakes can be served simply with a sprinkle of cinnamon sugar or extravagantly with a dollop of cool sour cream and jam.

Serves: 4–6
Preparation time: 10 minutes
Cooking time: 15 minutes

- 3 oz (85 g) cream cheese, at room temperature
- 3 eggs
- ¾ cup (105 g) all-purpose (plain) flour
- ¼ cup (50 g) sugar
- ½ teaspoon baking powder
- ½ teaspoon kosher salt
- 1 teaspoon vanilla extract
- 1¾ cups (420 g) ricotta cheese
- Unsalted butter or vegetable oil, for frying
- Sour cream and jam, for serving

In a food processor, combine the cream cheese, eggs, flour, sugar, baking powder, salt, and vanilla and process, scraping down the sides as necessary, until the mixture is completely smooth and the consistency of loose pancake batter. Transfer the mixture to a large bowl and fold in the ricotta until combined.

In a large frying pan, heat about 1 tablespoon of butter over medium heat, swirling the pan to coat. Working in batches of 5–6, drop the batter by the heaping tablespoon into the frying pan, nudging it into a round with the back of a spoon. Fry until golden brown on the bottom, 2–3 minutes. Flip and continue frying until the latkes are cooked all the way through, another 1–2 minutes. Transfer to a plate and serve immediately, with sour cream and jam on the side.

SPINACH FRITTERS

These Sephardi spinach fritters, called *keftes de espinaca*, are bound with mashed potato as well as breadcrumbs, which give them a plush texture. A squeeze of lemon juice elevates them from good to extraordinary.

Serves: 4–6
Preparation time: 15 minutes
Cooking time: 1 hour

- 1 medium russet (baking) potato (about ½ lb/225 g), scrubbed and unpeeled
- Vegetable oil, for frying
- 1 large onion, finely chopped
- 10 oz (285 g) baby spinach
- 2 eggs, lightly beaten
- ¾ cup (45 g) panko breadcrumbs or matzo meal
- 1 teaspoon onion powder
- ⅛ teaspoon ground nutmeg
- 1½ teaspoons kosher salt
- ½ teaspoon freshly ground black pepper
- Lemon wedges, for serving

In a large pot, combine the potato with water to cover by 2 inches (5 cm). Bring to a boil over high heat, cover, then reduce the heat to medium-high and cook until tender all the way through when pierced with a sharp knife, about 30 minutes. Drain and let sit until cool enough to handle, then peel and transfer to a large bowl. Mash with a potato masher until smooth and set aside.

In a large frying pan, heat 2 tablespoons oil over medium heat. Add the onion and cook, stirring occasionally, until softened and lightly browned, 6–8 minutes. Add the spinach (in batches, if it does not all fit at one time) and cook, stirring occasionally, until wilted, about 5 minutes. Remove from the heat and let cool slightly, then add the spinach mixture to the mashed potatoes along with the eggs, panko, onion powder, nutmeg, salt, and pepper. Mix well to combine.

Line a plate with paper towels. In a large frying pan, heat about ⅛ inch (3 mm) oil over medium heat. Scoop out the spinach mixture by the ¼ cup (50 g) and form into round patties, each about ½ inch (1.25 cm) thick. Working in batches of 4–5, fry the patties, flipping once, until golden brown on both sides, 3–4 minutes per side. Transfer to the paper towels to drain. Serve hot, with lemon wedges on the side for squeezing.

CHICKEN, SCALLION, AND GINGER FRITTERS

Calcutta's Jews serve these savory and gently spicy fritters, called *arook tahine*, as a snack or a predinner appetizer. This recipe uses chicken, but they are also commonly made with an equivalent weight of firm fish fillets. The fresh herbs and scallions (spring onions) give the fritters a gorgeous green color.

Serves: 4–6
Preparation time: 20 minutes, plus chilling
Cooking time: 40 minutes

- 1 bunch scallions (spring onions), white and green parts, roughly chopped
- 1 jalapeño, seeded and roughly chopped
- 1-inch (2.5 cm) piece fresh ginger, peeled and roughly chopped
- ½ cup (20 g) roughly chopped fresh cilantro (coriander) or flat-leaf parsley
- 1 lb (455 g) boneless, skinless chicken breasts or firm, skinless fish fillets, roughly chopped
- ¼ cup (35 g) all-purpose (plain) flour
- 2 eggs
- 1½ teaspoons kosher salt
- Vegetable oil, for frying

In a food processor, combine the scallions (spring onions), jalapeño, ginger, and cilantro (coriander) and pulse until very finely chopped. Add the chicken, flour, eggs, and salt and pulse until a wet batter forms—it should be the consistency of thick pancake batter. Transfer to a bowl, cover, and refrigerate for 1 hour.

Line a large plate with paper towels. In a large frying pan, heat about ¼ inch (6 mm) oil over medium heat. Working in batches of 4–5, scoop out the batter by the ¼ cup (60 g) and add to the pan, gently flattening and nudging into rounds. Fry, flipping once, until golden brown on both sides and cooked through, about 8 minutes. Add more oil in between batches, if necessary. Transfer to the paper towels to drain. Serve hot.

MEAT AND HERB FRITTERS

These Syrian meat and herb fritters, called *ijeh b'lahmen*, are deliciously delicate. Serve them drizzled with Tahini Sauce (page 396), either alone or tucked inside of pita.

Serves: 6
Preparation time: 15 minutes
Cooking time: 30 minutes

- 1 lb (455 g) ground (minced) beef
- 4 eggs, lightly beaten
- 1 small onion, grated on the large holes of a box grater
- 2 tablespoons dried breadcrumbs or matzo meal
- 1 small bunch parsley, tough bottom stems removed, leaves finely chopped
- ¾ teaspoon kosher salt
- ½ teaspoon freshly ground black pepper
- ½ teaspoon ground cinnamon
- ¼ teaspoon ground allspice
- Vegetable oil, for frying

In a large bowl, combine the beef, eggs, grated onion, breadcrumbs, parsley, salt, pepper, cinnamon, and allspice and mix thoroughly with your hands until well combined. The batter should feel quite wet.

Line a large plate with paper towels. In a large frying pan, heat about ⅛ inch (3 mm) oil over medium heat. Working in batches of 4–5, drop the batter into the hot oil by the ¼ cup (60 g), pressing gently to flatten. Fry, flipping once, until golden brown on both sides, 5–6 minutes. Add more oil during the cooking process if the pan looks dry. Transfer to the paper towels to drain. Serve hot, warm, or at room temperature.

Chicken, Scallion, and Ginger Fritters

SWEET RICE FRITTERS

These gently sweet rice fritters, called *frittelle de riso*, are a traditional Hanukkah treat for Italian Jews, and have a crunchy outside that gives way to a custardy middle studded with raisins and pine nuts. Serve them sprinkled with sugar or drizzled with a little honey.

Makes: about 2 dozen fritters
Preparation time: 15 minutes
Cooking time: 55 minutes

- 1½ cups (300 g) short-grain white rice
- 1 teaspoon kosher salt
- 6 eggs, lightly beaten
- ¾ cup (105 g) golden raisins (sultanas) or regular raisins, soaked in water for 5 minutes and drained
- ⅓ cup (45 g) pine nuts
- 2 tablespoons sugar, plus more for topping
- 2 teaspoons grated lemon zest
- 1 teaspoon vanilla extract
- Vegetable oil, for frying

In a medium saucepan, bring 3 cups (710 ml/24 fl oz) water to a boil over high heat. Stir in the rice and salt, cover, reduce the heat to low, and cook until the rice is tender and the water is absorbed, 20–25 minutes. Remove from the heat and let the rice cool to the touch.

Transfer the cooked rice to a large bowl and stir in the eggs, golden raisins (sultanas), pine nuts, sugar, lemon zest, and vanilla. Let the mixture rest while heating the oil.

Line a large sheet pan with a few layers of paper towels. In a wide heavy-bottomed saucepan, heat ½ inch (1.25 cm) oil over medium heat. Working in batches, drop the batter by the heaping tablespoon into the oil, pressing gently to flatten. Fry, flipping once, until golden brown on both sides, about 4 minutes. Transfer the fritters to the paper towels to drain. Serve hot, sprinkled with more sugar.

HONEY-SOAKED MATZO FRITTERS

Frying is a central part of Roman Jewish cooking, and Passover is no exception. Roman Jews traditionally serve *pizzarelle con miele*—sweet, airy matzo fritters studded with raisins and pine nuts and drizzled with honey—as a dessert during the weeklong holiday. But they are equally tasty for breakfast.

Serves: 6
Preparation time: 15 minutes
Cooking time: 20 minutes

- 3 eggs, separated
- ½ teaspoon kosher salt
- ⅓ cup (65 g) sugar
- 1 teaspoon finely grated lemon zest
- ¾ cup (95 g) matzo meal
- ⅓ cup (45 g) raisins, soaked in water for 5 minutes and drained
- ¼ cup (30 g) pine nuts
- Vegetable oil, for frying
- Honey, for serving

In a large bowl, whisk together the egg yolks and salt. In a bowl with an electric mixer, beat the egg whites at medium-high speed until fluffy. With the machine running, beat in the sugar 1 tablespoon at a time and continue beating until billowy and holding stiff peaks. Add the egg white mixture to the yolk mixture and gently fold together with a rubber spatula. Fold in the lemon zest, matzo meal, raisins, and pine nuts.

Line a large plate with paper towels. In a large deep frying pan, heat 1 inch (2.5 cm) oil over medium heat. Scoop out rounded tablespoons of the batter and, using moistened hands, form into small oval fritters. Working in batches of 4–5, fry the fritters, flipping once, until golden brown on both sides, about 4 minutes. Transfer the fritters to the paper towels to drain. Serve warm or at room temperature, with a generous drizzle of honey.

LEEK FRITTERS

These crispy leek fritters, called *keftes de prasa*, hail from Turkey and are popular across Sephardi cuisine, where they are traditionally served on Hanukkah and Passover (made with matzo meal instead of breadcrumbs). They taste wonderful with beef, but can also be made vegetarian—simply omit the meat and add a bit of crumbled feta. The dill can also be swapped out for flat-leaf parsley or fresh mint, if desired.

Serves: 4–6
Preparation time: 20 minutes
Cooking time: 30 minutes

- 4 medium leeks, white and light-green parts, thinly sliced, washed, and drained
- ½ lb (225 g) ground (minced) beef
- 3 eggs, lightly beaten
- ½ cup (70 g) dried breadcrumbs or matzo meal
- 4 tablespoons finely chopped fresh dill
- 1 teaspoon kosher salt
- ½ teaspoon Aleppo pepper or ¼ teaspoon crushed pepper flakes
- ¼ teaspoon freshly ground black pepper
- Vegetable oil, for frying
- Lemon wedges, for serving

Bring a medium pot of water to a boil over high heat. Add the leeks and simmer until tender, 8–10 minutes. Drain, rinse with cool water, and drain again, then wrap the leeks in a tea towel and squeeze out all excess water.

In a large bowl, combine the leeks, beef, eggs, breadcrumbs, dill, salt, Aleppo pepper, and black pepper and mix well with your hands to combine.

In a large frying pan, heat ¼ inch (6 mm) oil over medium heat. Working in batches, drop the batter by the heaping tablespoon into the pan and gently press with a spatula to flatten. Fry, flipping once, until browned on both sides and cooked through, 5–6 minutes. Add a little additional oil to the pan as necessary, letting it heat up before continuing to fry. Serve hot or at room temperature, with lemon wedges on the side for squeezing.

CHARD FRITTERS

Delicate and verdantly green, these fritters (*keftes de silka*) have Turkish origins but are eaten throughout the Middle East and North Africa by Sephardi families on Rosh Hashanah. The harissa used here is a distinctly North African touch. You can use any type of chard for this dish and double the recipe when serving a crowd. Made with matzo meal, they are a nice Passover treat.

Serves: 4–6
Preparation time: 10 minutes
Cooking time: 30 minutes

- 1 lb (455 g) Swiss chard
- ½ cup (25 g) chopped fresh parsley
- ½ cup (70 g) dried breadcrumbs or matzo meal
- 2 eggs
- 3 garlic cloves, roughly chopped
- 1 teaspoon dried dill
- 1 teaspoon kosher salt
- ½ teaspoon freshly ground black pepper
- 2 oz (55 g) feta cheese, crumbled (optional)
- 1 teaspoon Harissa (optional; page 409)
- Vegetable oil, for frying
- Lemon wedges, for serving

Trim and discard any woody ends of the chard stems, then coarsely chop the chard. Bring a large pot of water to a boil. Add the chard and cook until slightly wilted, 3–5 minutes. Drain and let cool to the touch, then place in a clean tea towel and squeeze thoroughly to remove all excess water.

Add the chard to a food processor along with the parsley, breadcrumbs, eggs, garlic, dill, salt, and pepper. Pulse until a mostly smooth green batter forms (there should still be some larger pieces). Transfer the mixture to a bowl and stir in the feta and harissa, if using.

Line a large plate with a few layers of paper towel. In a large frying pan, heat ¼ inch (6 mm) oil over medium heat. Working in batches of 4–5, drop the batter by heaping tablespoon into the pan, pressing slightly to flatten. Fry, flipping once, until lightly golden on both sides, 4–5 minutes. Add more oil if the pan begins to look dry. Transfer the cooked fritters to the paper towels to drain. Serve immediately, with lemon wedges on the side for squeezing.

KIBBEH

These torpedo-shaped croquettes have ancient Levantine roots, and were widely adopted by Jews living in Arabic-speaking countries. The shells can be made with rice or semolina, but softened bulgur gives them a particularly delightful crunch once fried. Here, the meat filling is perfumed with mint and the Middle Eastern spice mix, *baharat*, but the seasonings can vary widely depending on where the croquettes are being made.

Makes: about 20 croquettes
Preparation time: 1 hour, plus soaking
Cooking time: 25 minutes

For the bulgur batter:
- 1½ cups (240 g) fine-grain bulgur
- 1 small onion, roughly chopped
- ⅔ cup (95 g) all-purpose (plain) flour
- 1½ teaspoons kosher salt
- ½ teaspoon freshly ground black pepper

For the filling:
- 3 tablespoons vegetable oil
- 1 onion, finely chopped
- ½ lb (225 g) ground (minced) beef
- ¼ cup (30 g) pine nuts
- 1 teaspoon Baharat (page 412)
- ¼ teaspoon dried mint
- ½ teaspoon kosher salt
- ¼ teaspoon freshly ground black pepper

For frying:
- Vegetable oil

Make the bulgur batter: In a large bowl, combine the bulgur with water to cover by 2 inches (5 cm). Let sit 30 minutes, then drain, squeezing out the excess water. In a food processor, pulse the onion until very finely ground. Add the drained bulgur, the flour, salt, and pepper and pulse, scraping down the sides of the bowl as necessary, until a finely textured paste forms. Refrigerate while making the filling.

Make the filling: In a large frying pan, heat the oil over medium heat. Add the onion and cook, stirring occasionally, until softened and lightly browned, 6–8 minutes. Add the beef and pine nuts and cook, breaking up the meat into small pieces with a back of a spoon, until browned, 5–10 minutes. Stir in the *baharat*, dried mint, salt, and pepper and then remove from the heat and let cool to the touch.

Form and fry the *kibbeh*: Scoop out a heaping tablespoon of the bulgur batter and, with moistened hands, roll it into a ball. Use your thumb to create a deep indentation in the center (but not going all the way through), then pinch around the indentation to create a pocket. Fill the pocket with about 2 teaspoons of the meat mixture, then close up the hole around the filling. Gently shape the ball into an oval and gently pinch and taper both ends to form a torpedo. Set aside on a large plate while forming the remaining *kibbeh*.

Line a large plate with paper towels. In a Dutch oven (casserole) or deep heavy pot, heat about 1 inch (2.5 cm) oil over medium heat. Working in batches of 5, add the kibbeh to the hot oil and fry, turning as necessary, until well browned and crispy on all sides, 4–5 minutes. Transfer to the paper towels to drain. Serve hot.

Kibbeh

FALAFEL

This Levantine fritter, which is made from chickpeas—and sometimes fava (broad) beans—is among the most popular Middle Eastern dishes and is enjoyed worldwide. In Israel, it has become ubiquitous street-food fare, and is typically served stuffed into pita, spread with hummus and Tahini Sauce (page 396), and topped with Chopped Tomato and Cucumber Salad (page 78) and pickled vegetables.

Makes: about 30 fritters
Preparation time: 20 minutes, plus soaking
Cooking time: 40 minutes

- 1½ cups (270 g) dried chickpeas
- 2 teaspoons baking soda (bicarbonate of soda)
- 1 small onion, roughly chopped
- 4 garlic cloves, peeled
- ½ cup (25 g) finely chopped fresh flat-leaf parsley
- 3 tablespoons chickpea (gram) flour or all-purpose (plain) flour
- 2 teaspoons ground cumin
- 1 teaspoon ground coriander
- 1½ teaspoons kosher salt
- Vegetable oil, for frying

In a large bowl, combine the chickpeas, baking soda (bicarb), and cold water to cover by at least 2 inches (5 cm). Cover the bowl with a tea towel and let soak overnight at room temperature. Drain, rinse, then drain well again.

Place the soaked chickpeas in a food processor along with the onion, garlic, parsley, chickpea (gram) flour, cumin, coriander, and salt. Pulse until a moist, textured paste forms, scraping down the sides of the bowl as necessary.

Line a large plate with a few layers of paper towels. Pour about 1½ inches (4 cm) oil into a Dutch oven (casserole) or deep heavy-bottomed pot, set over medium heat, and bring to 375°F (190°C) on a deep-fry thermometer.

Meanwhile, moisten your hands, scoop out a heaping tablespoon of the falafel mixture, and use the palms of your hands and fingers to gently squeeze and roll it into a 1-inch (2.5 cm) ball. The falafel batter might seem fragile at this point, but the balls will come together while frying. Set it on a baking sheet and continue with remaining batter.

Working in batches of 5–6, carefully drop the falafel balls into the hot oil and fry until deep golden brown, 4–6 minutes. Remove with a slotted spoon and transfer to the paper towels to drain. Serve hot or warm. Store leftovers, covered, in the fridge or wrapped tightly in the freezer and reheat in a toaster (mini) oven or standard oven at 350°F (180°C/Gas Mark 4) until warmed through, 10–15 minutes.

MEAT-STUFFED PHYLLO CIGARS

These whimsical, crisp-fried parcels are commonly served at festive events. They are traditionally wrapped inside paper-thin rounds of semolina dough called *warka*, but the easier-to-find phyllo makes a good substitute. The cigars are delicious as is, but the meat filling can also be dressed up further with chopped fresh mint, a drizzle of pomegranate molasses, or a pinch of smoked paprika. Alternatively, for a vegetarian version, stuff the dough with the filling for Potato Bourekas (page 212).

Makes: about 30 cigars
Preparation time: 45 minutes
Cooking time: 45 minutes

- 1 lb (455 g) ground (minced) beef
- 1 small onion, grated on the large holes of a box grater
- 1 teaspoon ground cinnamon
- 1 teaspoon sweet paprika
- ½ teaspoon ground cumin
- ⅛ teaspoon cayenne pepper
- 1 teaspoon kosher salt
- 1 package (1 lb/455 g) frozen phyllo dough (13 x 18 inches/33 x 46 cm), thawed
- Vegetable oil, for brushing and frying

In a large bowl, mix together the beef, grated onion (with any juices), cinnamon, paprika, cumin, cayenne, and salt until thoroughly combined.

Unroll the stack of thawed phyllo and cut into 4 long rectangles about 13 × 4½ inches (33 × 11.5 cm) each. Stack the rectangles on top of each other and cover with a damp tea towel to prevent drying out. Working with one piece of trimmed phyllo at a time, scoop out a level tablespoon of the uncooked meat mixture; form into a long, thin sausage; and place it along the short end of the piece phyllo. Starting from the filled end, roll the phyllo around the filling 3–4 times, like a jelly roll (Swiss roll). Turn the ends in to seal in the filling, and continue rolling the rest of the way. Place the cigar, seam side down, on a large plate and brush the top with a little oil. Continue with the remaining phyllo and filling.

Line a large plate with paper towels. In a large frying pan, heat about ½ inch (1.25 cm) oil over medium heat. Working in batches of 6–7, fry, turning as necessary, until golden brown on all sides and cooked through, 8–10 minutes. Transfer to the paper towels to drain. Serve hot.

HERB OMELET FRITTERS

Syrian Jews are particularly partial to these omelet-style fritters, called *ijeh bakdounez*, which come loaded with fresh herbs. They taste wonderful warm and at room temperature, and are typically eaten for lunch or snacks, served inside of sliced pita with tomato and cucumber.

Serves: 4–6
Preparation time: 10 minutes
Cooking time: 15 minutes

- 6 eggs
- 1 teaspoon kosher salt
- ½ teaspoon onion powder
- ¼ teaspoon ground allspice
- 1 small bunch flat-leaf parsley, tough bottom stems removed, leaves finely chopped
- 4 scallions (spring onions), white and green parts, thinly sliced
- 2 tablespoons dried breadcrumbs or matzo meal
- Vegetable oil, for frying

In a large bowl, beat to gether the eggs, salt, onion powder, and allspice. Add the parsley, scallions (spring onions), and breadcrumbs and stir to combine. The batter will look wet.

Line a large plate with paper towels. In a large frying pan, heat about ⅛ inch (3 mm) oil over medium heat. Working in batches, drop the egg mixture by the heaping tablespoon into the hot oil. Fry, flipping once, until puffed and golden brown on both sides, about 4 minutes. Add more oil during the cooking process if the pan begins to look dry. Transfer the fritters to the paper towels to drain. Serve hot, warm, or at room temperature.

TUNA BRIK

Tunisian home cooking includes this delicious fried pastry, made with tuna, eggs, and capers tucked inside ultrathin rounds of semolina dough called *warka*. (The wrappers can be found in Middle Eastern and international food stores, but egg roll wrappers also make a tasty substitute.) Called *brik au thon*, they are often perpared for casual lunches or dinners, when they can be served sizzling from the pan.

Serves: 6
Preparation time: 10 minutes
Cooking time: 15 minutes

• Vegetable oil, for frying
• 6 round brik leaves (warka) or square egg roll wrappers
• 5 oz (140 g) good-quality canned tuna, drained
• ¼ cup (35 g) brine-packed capers, drained
• 2 scallions (spring onions), white and green parts, thinly sliced
• 6 small or medium eggs
• Kosher salt, for sprinkling
• Harissa (page 409), for serving (optional)

Line a baking sheet with paper towels. In a large frying pan, heat about ⅛ inch (3 mm) oil over medium heat.

Working with one wrapper at a time, mound a rounded tablespoon of tuna in the center of the wrapper, followed by a rounded teaspoon of capers and a little scallion (spring onion). Use your fingers to make a small well in the mounded filling and crack 1 of the eggs into it, then sprinkle with a little salt. Fold the wrapper in half and press gently to seal.

Using a spatula and your fingers, carefully slip a filled *brik* into the hot oil (it should sizzle on contact) and cook until browned and crisp, about 1½ minutes. Carefully flip and continue cooking until the egg whites are set and the yolk is still runny, about 1 minute more. Transfer to the paper towels to drain. Continue with the remaining wrappers and filling.

Serve immediately, accompanied by harissa, if desired.

POTATO BRIK

Along with tuna, mashed potato is one of the most common fillings for crisp Tunisian fried turnovers. The mix of fried wrapper, tender potato, salty capers, and runny egg is magnificent. Serve this dish, called *brik bil batata,* with a green salad.

Serves: 6
Preparation time: 15 minutes
Cooking time: 30 minutes

• ¾ lb (340 g) Yukon Gold potato (about 1 large), peeled and cut into chunks
• Kosher salt
• Vegetable oil, for frying
• 6 round brik leaves (warka) or square egg roll wrappers
• ¼ cup (35 g) brine-packed capers, drained
• ¼ cup (10 g) roughly chopped fresh mint or cilantro (coriander) leaves
• 6 small or medium eggs
• Harissa (page 409), for serving (optional)

Bring a small saucepan of water to a boil over high heat. Add the potato chunks and cook until tender, about 15 minutes. Drain well, then season with a little salt and mash with a potato masher until completely smooth. Set aside.

Line a baking sheet with paper towels. In a large frying pan, heat about ⅛ inch (3 mm) oil over medium heat.

Working with one wrapper at a time, mound a rounded tablespoon of mashed potato in the center of the wrapper, followed by a rounded teaspoon of capers and a sprinkle of mint. Use your fingers to make a small well in the mounded filling and crack 1 of the eggs into it and sprinkle with a little salt. Fold the wrapper in half and press gently to seal.

Using a spatula and your fingers, gently slip the filled *brik* into the hot oil and cook until browned and crisp, about 1½ minutes. Carefully flip and continue cooking until the egg whites are set and the yolk is still runny, about 1 minute more. Transfer to the paper towels to drain. Continue with the remaining wrappers and filling.

Serve immediately, accompanied by harissa, if desired.

Tuna Brik

KASHA AND MUSHROOM KNISHES

Softened kasha (roasted buckwheat) mixed with browned onions and mushrooms makes a hearty and flavorful filling for knishes. Served warm from the oven or reheated in a toaster (mini) oven, they are a delicious, portable snack.

Makes: about 1 dozen knishes
Preparation time: 1 hour, plus resting
Cooking time: 45 minutes

For the dough:
- 1½ cups (210 g) all-purpose (plain) flour, plus more for rolling
- 1 cup (140 g) bread flour (strong white flour)
- ½ teaspoon baking powder
- ½ teaspoon kosher salt
- 1 egg
- ½ cup (120 ml/4 fl oz) warm water (110°F/43°C)
- ½ cup (120 ml/4 fl oz) vegetable oil
- 1 teaspoon apple cider vinegar

For the filling:
- 1½ cups (355 ml/12 fl oz) vegetable stock
- ¾ cup (130 g) whole kasha (roasted buckwheat)
- ¼ cup (60 ml/2 fl oz) vegetable oil or 4 tablespoons (60 g) butter
- 1 large onion, finely chopped
- ½ teaspoon kosher salt, plus more as needed
- ¾ lb (340 g) cremini (chestnut) or white button mushrooms, stems discarded, finely chopped
- 1 teaspoon sweet paprika
- Freshly ground black pepper

For assembly and baking:
- Flour, for dusting
- Egg wash: 1 egg beaten with 1 teaspoon water

Make the dough: In a large bowl, whisk together the all-purpose (plain) flour, bread flour (strong white flour), baking powder, and salt. In a small bowl, whisk together the egg, warm water, oil, and vinegar. Make a well in the dry ingredients and pour in the wet. Stir until the dough comes together. (It is okay if the dough feels a little wet.) Knead it a few times in the bowl with the heel of your hand and form it into a ball. Put the ball back into the bowl, cover with plastic wrap (cling film), and let sit at room temperature for 1 hour. (Or, store in the fridge for up to 1 day.)

Meanwhile, make the filling: In a small saucepan, bring the stock to a boil over high heat. Stir in the kasha, reduce the heat to low, cover, and simmer until kasha is tender and the liquid is absorbed, about 15 minutes. Remove the pan from the heat and let stand, covered, for 5 minutes.

In a large frying pan, heat the oil or butter over medium heat. Add the onion and a pinch of salt and cook, stirring occasionally, until softened and lightly browned, 6–8 minutes. Add the mushrooms and cook until tender and most of the liquid has evaporated, about 10 minutes. Stir in the paprika, salt, and a generous amount of pepper, then remove from the heat and stir in the cooked kasha. Set aside to cool slightly.

Assemble and bake the knishes: Preheat the oven to 375°F (°190C/Gas Mark 5). Line a large baking sheet with parchment paper.

Lay a large tea towel or tablecloth on a flat surface and dust generously with flour. Divide the dough in half. Working with one half (keep the other half in the bowl, covered), roll into a large, ⅛-inch (3 mm) thick rectangle. (If you have some rough edges, trim them off.) Take half of the kasha-mushroom mixture and spoon it into a thick line along one of the long edges of the rectangle. Roll the dough around the filling like a jelly roll (Swiss roll). Repeat process with the remaining dough and filling. Trim off the ends of each roll so that they are flush with the filling.

Using the side of your hand (imagine a karate chop motion), make indentations along the log every 3 inches (7.5 cm), then twist the dough at these points. Use a sharp knife to slice the dough at each twist. Working with one knish at a time, pinch one side together to form its base. Flatten the knish a bit between your palms, then pinch together the top, leaving a little of the filling exposed. (It is okay if a little of the filling spills out during the forming process.) Lay the formed knishes on the baking sheet. Brush the tops and sides of each knish with the egg wash (you won't use all of it) and bake, rotating the baking sheet front to back halfway through, until golden brown, about 45 minutes. Set on a wire rack to cool slightly. Serve warm or at room temperature.

Kasha and Mushroom Knishes

MUSHROOM PIROSHKI

These puffed Russian turnovers can be filled with mashed potato, meat, sautéed cabbage, or fruit—but savory sautéed mushrooms are particularly delightful. You can substitute a mix of wild mushrooms in the filling, if desired. Serve them as part of a summery lunch alongside a bowl of Chilled Borscht (page 124) or the sorrel-based soup Schav (page 132).

Makes: about 2 dozen turnovers
Preparation time: 30 minutes, plus rising
Cooking time: 1 hour

For the dough:
- 1 packet (¼ oz/7 g) active dry yeast (2¼ teaspoons)
- 1 tablespoon sugar
- ⅔ cup (150 ml/5 fl oz) warm water (110°F/43°C)
- 3¼–3½ cups (455–490 g) all-purpose (plain) flour
- 1½ teaspoons kosher salt
- ¼ cup (60 ml/2 fl oz) vegetable oil, plus more for greasing the bowl
- 2 eggs

For the filling:
- 1 large russet (baking) potato (about ½ lb/225 g), peeled and cut into 2-inch (5 cm) chunks
- ½ teaspoon kosher salt, plus more as needed
- 2 tablespoons vegetable oil
- 1 large onion, finely chopped
- Kosher salt and freshly ground black pepper
- ½ lb (225 g) cremini (chestnut) or white button mushrooms, stems discarded, finely chopped
- 2 tablespoons mayonnaise
- 2 tablespoons finely chopped fresh dill
- ¼ teaspoon garlic powder
- Freshly ground black pepper

For assembly and baking:
- Flour, for dusting
- Egg wash: 1 egg beaten with 1 teaspoon water

Make the dough: In a large bowl, stir together the yeast, sugar, and water and let sit until bubbling and frothy, 5–10 minutes.

Meanwhile, in a medium bowl, whisk together 3¼ cups (455 g) flour and the salt. Whisk the oil and eggs into the yeast mixture until combined. Add the flour mixture and stir until a shaggy dough begins to form. Turn the dough out onto a lightly floured surface and knead well, adding up to ¼ cup (35 g) additional flour, as necessary, until a supple, elastic dough forms, about 10 minutes. (The kneading can also be done in a stand mixer fitted with a dough hook, 5–7 minutes.) Grease a large bowl with about 1 teaspoon oil, add the dough, and turn to coat. Cover with a tea towel and let sit in a warm place until doubled in size, about 1½ hours.

Meanwhile, make the filling: In a medium saucepan, combine the potato with water to cover by 2 inches (5 cm). Bring to a boil over high heat and cook until the potatoes are tender all the way through when pierced with a sharp knife, 20–30 minutes. Drain well, return to the pot, and mash with a potato masher until smooth.

In a medium frying pan, heat the oil over medium heat. Add the onion and a generous pinch of salt and cook, stirring occasionally, until softened, 6–8 minutes. Add the mushrooms and cook until tender and lightly browned, and any liquid from the mushrooms has evaporated, about 10 minutes.

Add the mushroom mixture to the potatoes along with the mayonnaise, dill, garlic powder, salt, and a generous amount of pepper and mix well. Taste, and add more salt, if desired.

Assemble and bake the piroshki: Line 2 large baking sheets with parchment paper. Pinch off golf ball–size pieces of dough and, on a lightly floured surface, pat and press into 4-inch (10 cm) rounds. (Keep any remaining dough covered, so it does not dry out.) Spoon 1 rounded tablespoon of filling into the center of each round. Bring the sides of the rounds up to meet each other, tucking the filling inside and pinching along the seam to seal. Form the sealed piroshki into ovals and place, seam side down, on the prepared baking sheets, leaving about 1 inch (2.5 cm) of space between them.

Preheat the oven to 375°F (190°C/Gas Mark 5).

Brush the tops of the piroshki with the egg wash (you will not use all of it). Let the piroshki rest and continue rising while the oven preheats.

Bake until golden brown and puffed, about 20 minutes. Transfer the piroshki to wire racks to cool. Serve warm or at room temperature.

EREZ KOMAROVSKY

MINT KITCHEN
•
83 UNIVERSITY PLACE
NEW YORK, NY
USA

Erez Komarovsky runs cooking and baking classes at his beautiful home in the Northern Galilee in Israel. He also partnered with Zeev Sharon and Assaf A. Harlap to open the modern Israeli restaurant, Mint Kitchen, in New York City. Prior to that, the chef, who fell in love with bread baking while working at Acme Bread Company in San Francisco, founded the innovative and influential bakery and café chain Lehem Erez ("Erez's Bread") in Israel.

SAVORY LEEK CAKE

For this savory leek cake, Komarovsky takes a tender yeast dough, fills it with a mix of savory sautéed leeks and sharp cheese, and bakes it into a savory pull-apart cake that would make a gorgeous centerpiece at brunch.

Serves: 8
Preparation time: 30 minutes, plus rising and chilling
Cooking time: 55 minutes

For the pastry:
• 3½ cups (490 g) all-purpose (plain) flour, plus more for rolling
• 1 tablespoon active dry yeast
• 1½ teaspoons kosher salt
• 2 eggs
• ¾ cup (175 ml/6 fl oz) warm water (110°F/43°C)
• 1¼ sticks (5 oz/140 g) unsalted butter, cut into small pieces, at room temperature

For the filling:
• 4 tablespoons extra-virgin olive oil
• 3 large leeks, white and light-green parts only, thinly sliced
• ⅓ cup (45 g) pine nuts
• ½ teaspoon kosher salt
• ¼ teaspoon freshly ground black pepper
• 1 cup (110 g) grated pecorino cheese

For assembly and baking:
• Vegetable oil, for the pan
• Egg wash: 1 egg yolk beaten with 1 teaspoon water

Make the pastry: In a stand mixer fitted with a paddle attachment, combine the flour, yeast, and salt and beat on low speed until combined. Add the eggs, warm water, and a few pieces of the butter and beat on medium speed, scraping down the bowl as necessary, until the dough begins to come together. Switch to the dough hook and with the mixer running, gradually add the remaining butter, a few pieces at a time, allowing the butter to incorporate before adding more, until a supple and sticky dough forms, 5–7 minutes. (The dough will feel very moist. You may feel like you added too much butter at this stage, but resist the urge to add additional flour.) Gather and form the dough into a loose ball and return to the bowl. Cover the bowl and let rise for 30 minutes at room temperature, then refrigerate overnight.

Make the filling: In a large frying pan, heat the oil over medium heat. Add the leeks and cook, stirring occasionally, until softened and lightly browned, about 10 minutes. Add the pine nuts, salt, and pepper and cook until the nuts are lightly browned, 3–5 minutes. Remove from the heat and transfer to a bowl to allow the mixture to cool slightly, then stir in the pecorino.

Assemble and bake the cake: Line the bottom of a 9-inch (23 cm) round springform pan with a round of parchment paper and brush the bottom and sides with a little oil. On a lightly floured work surface, roll out the cold dough into a thin 20 × 12-inch (50 × 30.5 cm) rectangle. Spread the leek filling evenly over the top and, starting with one of the long sides, roll up like a jelly roll (Swiss roll). Slice off either end of the roll so that the dough is flush with the filling. (Discard the scraps.) Cut the roll crosswise into 1-inch (2.5 cm) pieces and arrange the pieces (with one of the filling sides facing up) into a flower shape in the pan. Cover with a towel and let rise for 30 minutes.

Meanwhile, preheat the oven to 350°F (180°C/Gas Mark 4).

Brush the top of the cake with an even layer of egg wash (you will not use all of it) and bake until golden brown and cooked through, 35–40 minutes. (An instant-read thermometer inserted into the center of the cake should register 190°F/88°C.) Set the pan on a wire rack to cool for 15 minutes, then carefully remove the sides of the pan and let the cake continue cooling. Serve warm or at room temperature.

★ STAR RECIPE

CABBAGE STRUDEL

Central European Jews traditionally served cabbage strudel on Sukkot and Purim, when stuffed foods hold special significance. But this delicious savory pastry, with its crackly crust and tender, sweet, and peppery filling, also makes a satisfying snack or *forshpeis* (Yiddish for "before taste," or appetizer). Cabbage strudel tastes most divine when made with butter, but can be made dairy-free by swapping in a neutral vegetable oil like sunflower.

Serves: 6–8
Preparation time: 25 minutes
Cooking time: 50 minutes

- 1½ sticks (6 oz/170 g) unsalted butter or ¾ cup (175 ml/6 fl oz) vegetable oil
- 1 large onion, finely chopped
- 1 lb (455 g) green cabbage, cored and finely shredded
- 1¼ teaspoons kosher salt
- ¼ teaspoon freshly ground black pepper
- 1 teaspoon sugar
- 8 sheets (13 x 18-inch/33 x 46 cm) frozen phyllo dough, thawed
- 8 tablespoons fine dried breadcrumbs

In a large frying pan, melt 3 tablespoons (45 g) butter over medium heat until foaming. Add the onion and cook, stirring occasionally, until softened, 6–8 minutes. Add the shredded cabbage, cover, and cook, stirring occasionally, until tender and lightly browned, 10–15 minutes. Stir in the salt, pepper, and sugar and continue cooking, uncovered, until very tender and lightly browned, 5–7 minutes. If the pan looks dry during cooking, stir in a couple teaspoons water. Remove from the heat and let cool to the touch.

Preheat the oven to 400°F (200°C/Gas Mark 6). Line a large baking sheet with parchment paper.

In a small saucepan or in the microwave (in 20-second intervals), melt the remaining 9 tablespoons (130 g) butter. Lay a piece of parchment paper or a clean tea towel on a flat surface and place 1 sheet of phyllo on top. (Keep the other phyllo sheets covered with a damp cloth so they don't dry out.) Brush the sheet with some of the melted butter and sprinkle evenly with 1 tablespoon breadcrumbs. Repeat the process 7 more times to make a stack of 8 phyllo sheets.

Spoon the cabbage mixture in a thick line along a short side of the phyllo dough, leaving about ½ inch (1.25 cm) of space clear on either side. Use the parchment paper to help roll the dough snugly around the cabbage, tucking the filling inside and ending up with a long, stuffed cylinder. Carefully transfer the strudel to the prepared baking sheet and brush the top with a little more melted butter. Bake until the phyllo is crisp and golden brown, 20–25 minutes. Set the baking sheet on a wire rack to cool slightly. Use a serrated knife to slice the strudel into pieces. Serve warm.

Cabbage Strudel

MINIATURE MEAT PIES

In the realm of savory Sephardi pastries, these miniature, double-crusted meat pies, called *pastelitos,* are relatively labor intensive. But they are tasty and freeze well, so make plenty and save some for another day. Sephardi Jews serve them on Shabbat, but they also make great afternoon snacks.

Makes: about 20 pastries
Preparation time: 1½ hours
Cooking time: 50 minutes

For the dough:
• 4½ cups (630 g) all-purpose (plain) flour
• 1 teaspoon kosher salt
• 1 cup (240 ml/8 fl oz) vegetable oil

For the filling:
• 2 tablespoons vegetable oil
• 1 large onion, finely chopped
• 1 lb (455 g) ground (minced) beef
• 1½ teaspoons sweet paprika
• 1 teaspoon ground cumin
• ½ teaspoon dried mint
• ½ teaspoon cayenne pepper
• ½ teaspoon kosher salt
• ¼ teaspoon freshly ground black pepper

For assembly and baking:
• Egg wash: 1 egg beaten with 1 teaspoon water
• Sesame seeds, for topping

Make the dough: In a food processor, combine the flour, salt, oil, and ¾ cup (175 ml/6 fl oz) cold water and pulse, scraping down the sides of the bowl several times, until the dough comes together. If it looks dry, add a little more water, 1 tablespoon at a time, until it holds together. Gather the dough into a ball and knead a few times with your hands, then place in a large bowl, cover with a clean tea towel, and let rest while making the filling.

Make the filling: In a large frying pan, heat the oil over medium heat. Add the onion and cook, stirring occasionally, until softened and lightly browned, 6–8 minutes. Add the beef, paprika, cumin, mint, cayenne, salt, and black pepper and cook, stirring and using the back of a spoon to break up the meat into small pieces, until well browned, about 10 minutes. Remove from the heat and let cool slightly.

Assemble and bake the pastries: Preheat the oven to 400°F (200°C/Gas Mark 6). Line 2 large baking sheets with parchment paper.

Pinch off a heaping tablespoon of the dough and roll into a ball. Using floured hands, pinch and form the ball into a cup shape about 2½ inches (6.5 cm) wide and almost 1 inch (2.5 cm) deep. Place on one of the prepared baking sheets. Fill the cup with a heaping tablespoon of the meat mixture. Pinch off a slightly smaller piece of dough and roll into a round ⅛ inch (3 mm) thick. Place the round on top of the filled dough cup (like a lid) and press the edges firmly to seal. Continue this process with the remaining dough and filling.

Brush the tops and sides of the filled pastries with a little egg wash (you might not use all of it) and sprinkle with sesame seeds. Bake, rotating the baking sheets halfway through, until golden brown, 30–35 minutes. Transfer to wire racks to cool. Serve warm or at room temperature.

LAHMAJUN

These petite, round flatbreads are popular mezze fare throughout the Middle East, particularly in Syria, Lebanon, and Turkey. Their name stems from a contraction of the Arabic phrase *laham b'ajin* (meat with dough), and they fittingly come topped with fragrantly spiced ground (minced) lamb or beef. *Lahmajun* are delicious served plain, but even better drizzled with tahini and topped with a squeeze of fresh lemon juice.

Serves: 4–6
Preparation time: 25 minutes, plus rising and resting
Cooking time: 25 minutes

For the dough:
• 1 packet (¼ oz/7 g) active dry yeast (2¼ teaspoons)
• 1 teaspoon sugar
• ¾ cup (175 ml/6 fl oz) warm water (110°F/43°C)
• 2 cups (280 g) all-purpose (plain) flour,
  plus more as needed
• 1½ teaspoons kosher salt
• 1 tablespoon plus 1 teaspoon extra-virgin olive oil

For the topping:
• 2 tablespoons extra-virgin olive oil
• 4 garlic cloves, finely chopped
• 1 plum tomato, seeded and finely chopped
• 1 teaspoon kosher salt, plus more as needed
• ½ lb (225 g) ground (minced) lamb or beef
• ½ small onion, grated on the large holes of a box grater
• 1 teaspoon sweet paprika
• ¼ teaspoon crushed pepper flakes
• ½ teaspoon ground cinnamon
• ½ teaspoon ground cumin
• 1 tablespoon tomato paste (purée)
• 1 tablespoon tamarind paste or pomegranate molasses
• ¼ cup (30 g) pine nuts

For serving:
• Chopped fresh flat-leaf parsley, tahini,
  and lemon wedges

Make the dough: In a medium bowl, stir together the yeast, sugar, and warm water. Let sit until foaming, 5–10 minutes.

In a large bowl, stir together the flour and salt. Add 1 tablespoon oil to the yeast mixture, then pour into the flour. Stir until the dough starts to come together, then turn out onto a floured surface and knead, adding a little more flour, if needed, until it is smooth and elastic, but not sticky, 7–8 minutes. (You can also knead it in a standing mixer with the dough hook on medium speed, 5–7 minutes.) Grease a large bowl with 1 teaspoon oil, add the dough, and turn to coat. Cover the bowl with a damp tea towel and leave in a warm place until doubled in size, about 1 hour.

Gently deflate the dough with the palm of your hand. Divide into 4 equal portions and roll each portion into a ball. Transfer the dough balls to a floured baking sheet. Cover with a damp tea towel and let rest until pliable, 30–45 minutes.

Meanwhile, make the topping: In a medium frying pan, heat the olive oil over medium heat. Add the garlic, tomato, and a pinch of salt and cook, stirring occasionally, until softened, 5–7 minutes. Remove from the heat and set aside to cool.

In a large bowl, stir together the lamb, onion, paprika, pepper flakes, cinnamon, cumin, tomato paste (purée), tamarind paste, pine nuts, cooled tomato mixture, and 1 teaspoon salt. Mix together with your hands until well combined.

Preheat the oven to 450°F (230°C/Gas Mark 8). Line 2 large baking sheets with parchment paper.

Lay a piece of parchment paper on a flat work surface. Working with one ball of dough at a time, use a rolling pin to roll dough into an 8-inch (20 cm) round. Lay the dough on a prepared baking sheet, top with one-quarter of the meat mixture, and use your fingers to press it evenly to the edges. Sprinkle with a little salt. Repeat with the remaining dough and meat mixture.

Bake until the dough is golden brown and the topping is cooked through, 15–18 minutes. Let cool slightly before slicing into wedges. Serve warm, sprinkled with parsley, drizzled with tahini, and with lemon wedges on the side.

FRITTERS & SAVORY PASTRIES

BULEMAS

These popular Sephardi pastries are commonly filled with spinach, cheese, eggplant (aubergine), or sweetened pumpkin. The filling is coiled inside an oiled yeast dough that is rolled paper thin, creating a delicate but supple pastry. They are often served for breakfast, or as a snack alongside a glass of the anise-flavored liquor, arak. Sephardi cuisine also includes a pastry called *boyo*, which is essentially the same as bulema, but formed into squares rather than coils.

Makes: 15 pastries
Preparation time: 1 hour, plus rising
Cooking time: 50 minutes

For the dough:
- 1 packet (¼ oz/7 g) active dry yeast (2¼ teaspoons)
- 1 teaspoon sugar
- 1 cup (240 ml/8 fl oz) warm water (110°F/43°C)
- 2½ cups (350 g) bread flour (strong white flour), plus more as needed
- 1½ teaspoons kosher salt
- ⅓ cup (75 ml/2½ fl oz) plus 1 tablespoon vegetable oil

For the filling:
- ⅓ cup (75 ml/2½ fl oz) vegetable oil
- 1 small onion, finely chopped
- Kosher salt
- 1 eggplant (aubergine), about 1 lb (455 g), peeled and cut into ½-inch (1.25 cm) pieces
- 4 oz (115 g) feta cheese, crumbled
- ½ cup (45 g) finely grated parmesan cheese
- Freshly ground black pepper

For assembly and baking:
- Flour, for dusting
- Egg wash: 1 egg beaten with 1 teaspoon water
- Finely grated parmesan cheese

Make the dough: In a medium bowl, stir together the yeast, sugar, and warm water. Let sit until foaming, 5–10 minutes.

In a large bowl, stir together the flour and salt. Add 1 tablespoon oil to the yeast mixture, then pour the mixture into the flour. Stir until the dough starts to come together, then turn out onto a floured surface and knead, adding a little more flour, if needed, until it is smooth and elastic, but not sticky, 8–10 minutes. (You can also knead the dough in a stand mixer with the dough hook on medium speed, 5–8 minutes.)

Pour ⅓ cup (75 ml/2½ fl oz) oil into a large shallow baking dish. Divide the dough into 15 equal portions and roll into balls. Place the balls in the oil and turn to coat, leaving about 1 inch (2.5 cm) space between the balls. Cover the baking dish with a clean tea towel and let stand about 30 minutes.

Meanwhile, make the filling: In a large frying pan, heat the oil over medium heat. Add the onion and a generous pinch of salt and cook, stirring occasionally, until softened and lightly browned, 6–8 minutes. Add the eggplant (aubergine) and cook, stirring often, until very tender, about 10 minutes. Remove from the heat and use a potato masher to mash the eggplant into a chunky paste. Transfer the eggplant mixture to a bowl and stir in the feta, parmesan, and a generous amount of black pepper. Taste and, if desired, stir in a little more salt.

Assemble and bake the pastries: Preheat the oven to 375°F (190°C/Gas Mark 5). Line 2 large baking sheets with parchment paper.

Lay a piece of parchment paper on a flat surface. Working with one ball of dough at a time, on top of the parchment, use your fingertips or a rolling pin to stretch and roll the dough into very thin round about 10 inches (25 cm) in diameter. (The dough should be translucent.) Spread 2 rounded tablespoons of filling in a line along the edge of the dough round. Roll up the dough tightly like a jelly roll (Swiss roll), starting with the filled side. Gently stretch the roll with your fingertips to lengthen slightly and then, starting from one end of the roll, coil it onto itself, tucking the end underneath. Repeat with the remaining dough and filling.

Place the filled coils on the prepared baking sheets and brush with the egg eash. Sprinkle the tops of the *bulemas* with a little parmesan and bake until golden brown, 30–35 minutes. Transfer to wire racks to cool. Serve warm or at room temperature. Store leftovers in an airtight container in the fridge for up to 1 week (or freeze for up to 3 months). Reheat in an oven or toaster (mini) oven.

Bulemas

CHEESE SAMBUSAK

Popular throughout the Middle East, these savory, handheld turnovers get stuffed with a variety of fillings including a mix of sharp and salty cheeses. Traditionally deep-fried (many home cooks today bake them instead), they are commonly served on Shabbat morning and also on Hanukkah, when fried foods are customary. But they are also great for lunch or as a tote-along snack.

Makes: about 2 dozen turnovers
Preparation time: 45 minutes
Cooking time: 35 minutes

For the dough:
• ½ cup (120 ml/4 fl oz) vegetable oil
• 1 egg
• 1½ teaspoons kosher salt
• 2–2½ cups (280–350 g) all-purpose (plain) flour

For the filling:
• 8 oz (225 g) crumbled feta cheese
• 4 oz (115 g) parmesan cheese, grated
• 2 eggs
• ½ teaspoon onion powder (optional)
• ¼ teaspoon kosher salt
• ¼ teaspoon freshly ground black pepper

For assembly:
• Flour, for dusting
• Egg wash: 1 egg beaten with 1 teaspoon water
• Sesame seeds, for topping (optional)

Make the dough: In a large bowl, whisk together the oil, ½ cup (120 ml/4 fl oz) water, egg, and salt until well combined and foamy. Stir in the flour, a little at a time, until a soft dough forms (you might not use the full 2½ cups/350 g). Form the dough into a disc, wrap with plastic wrap (cling film), and let sit at room temperature while making the filling.

Make the filling: In a food processor, combine the feta, parmesan, eggs, onion powder (if using), salt, and pepper and pulse until a thick paste forms.

Assemble the turnovers: Pinch off a walnut-size piece of dough and roll it into a ball. Working on a lightly floured surface, roll it out into a 4-inch (10 cm) round. Place a heaping tablespoon of the filling into the middle of the round. Fold one side of the round over to the other to make a half-moon, pinching it tightly to seal the filling inside. Repeat with the remaining dough and filling.

To bake the *sambusak*, preheat the oven to 350°F (180°C/ Gas Mark 4). Line 2 large baking sheets with parchment paper and dived the turnovers between them. Brush the tops of the turnovers with a little egg wash (you might not use all of it) and sprinkle with sesame seeds (if using). Bake until golden brown, 30–35 minutes. Set the baking sheets on wire racks to cool.

Alternatively, to fry the *sambusak*, line a large plate with two layers of paper towel. In a large saucepan, heat 2 inches (5 cm) vegetable oil over medium heat. Gently slip the turnovers into the hot oil in batches of 4 or 5 and fry until golden brown, flipping once halfway through, 4–5 minutes. Transfer the fried *sambusak* to the paper towels to drain.

Cheese Sambusak

CHICKPEA SAMBUSAK

Iraqi Jews favor these savory turnovers filled with spiced chickpeas on Hanukkah and Purim. They are traditionally fried, but many home cooks today prefer to bake them.

Makes: about 2 dozen turnovers
Preparation time: 45 minutes
Cooking time: 50 minutes

For the dough:
• ½ cup (120 ml/4 fl oz) vegetable oil
• 1 egg
• 1½ teaspoons kosher salt
• 2–2½ cups (280–350 g) all-purpose (plain) flour

For the filling:
• 3 tablespoons extra-virgin olive oil
• 2 medium onions, finely chopped
• ½ teaspoon kosher salt, plus more as needed
• 1 teaspoon ground cinnamon
• 1 teaspoon ground cumin
• 1 teaspoon ground ginger
• ¼ teaspoon cayenne pepper
• 2½ cups (400 g) cooked or canned chickpeas, drained
• ½ teaspoon freshly ground black pepper

For assembly:
• Flour, for dusting
• Egg wash: 1 egg beaten with 1 teaspoon water
• Sesame seeds, for topping (optional)

Make the dough: In a large bowl, whisk together the vegetable oil, ½ cup (120 ml/4 fl oz) water, egg, and salt until well combined and foamy. Stir in the flour, a little at a time, until a soft dough forms (you might not use the full 2½ cups/350 g). Form the dough into a disc, wrap with plastic wrap (cling film), and let sit at room temperature while making the filling.

Make the filling: In a large frying pan, heat the olive oil over medium heat. Add the onions and a generous pinch of salt and cook, stirring occasionally, until softened and lightly browned, 10–15 minutes. Add the cinnamon, cumin, ginger, and cayenne and stir until fragrant, about 30 seconds. Set aside to cool slightly.

In a large bowl, mash the chickpeas with a potato masher until they turn into a thick paste with some bigger pieces. Stir in the cooked onions, salt, and black pepper.

Assemble the turnovers: Pinch off a walnut-size piece of dough and roll it into a ball. Working on a lightly floured surface, roll it out into a 4-inch (10 cm) round. Place a heaping tablespoon of the filling into the middle of the round. Fold one side of the round over to the other to make a half-moon, pinching it tightly to seal the filling inside. Repeat with the remaining dough and filling.

To bake the *sambusak*, preheat the oven to 350°F (180°C/Gas Mark 4). Line 2 large baking sheets with parchment paper and dived the turnovers between them. Brush the tops of the turnovers with a little egg wash (you might not use all of it) and sprinkle with sesame seeds (if using). Bake until golden brown, 30–35 minutes. Set the baking sheets on wire racks to cool.

Alternatively, to fry the *sambusak*, line a large plate with two layers of paper towel. In a large saucepan, heat 2 inches (5 cm) vegetable oil over medium heat. Gently slip the turnovers into the hot oil in batches of 4 or 5 and fry until golden brown, flipping once halfway through, 4–5 minutes. Transfer the fried *sambusak* to the paper towels to drain.

PUMPKIN TURNOVERS

Bukharian Jews serve these stuffed, tricornered turnovers, called *bichak*, as appetizers or comforting snacks. They can be filled with cheese or meat, but the cumin-scented pumpkin version is especially beguiling.

Makes: about 15 turnovers
Preparation time: 45 minutes, plus rising
Cooking time: 50 minutes

For the dough:
- 2 teaspoons active dry yeast
- ½ teaspoon sugar
- 1 cup (240 ml/8 fl oz) warm water (110°F/43°C)
- 2½ cups (350 g) all-purpose (plain) flour, plus more as needed
- 1½ teaspoons kosher salt
- 1 tablespoon plus 1 teaspoon vegetable oil

For the filling:
- 3 tablespoons vegetable oil
- 1 large onion, finely chopped
- 1 small baking pumpkin or butternut squash (about 1½ lb/680 g), peeled, seeded, and cut into ¼-inch (6 mm) dice
- 1 teaspoon sugar
- ¾ teaspoon ground cumin
- 1 teaspoon kosher salt, plus more as needed
- ¼ teaspoon freshly ground black pepper

For assembly and baking:
- Flour, for dusting
- Egg wash: 1 egg beaten with 1 teaspoon water
- Sesame seeds or nigella seeds, for topping

Make the dough: In a medium bowl, stir together the yeast, sugar, and warm water. Let sit until foaming, 5–10 minutes.

In a large bowl, whisk together the flour and salt. Add 1 tablespoon oil to the yeast mixture, then pour into the flour mixture. Stir until the dough starts to come together, then turn out onto a floured surface and knead, adding a little more flour 1 tablespoon at a time, if needed, until it is smooth and supple, 8–10 minutes. (The kneading can also be done in a stand mixer fitted with a dough hook, 5–7 minutes.)

Pour 1 teaspoon of oil into a large bowl. Add the dough and turn to coat. Cover the bowl with plastic wrap (cling film) or a tea towel and leave in a warm place until doubled in size, 1–1½ hours.

Meanwhile, make the filling: In a large frying pan, heat the oil over medium heat. Add the onion and cook, stirring occasionally, until softened and lightly browned, 6–8 minutes. Stir in the pumpkin, sugar, cumin, salt, and pepper. Cover and cook, stirring occasionally, until the pumpkin is tender and lightly browned, 10–15 minutes. Taste and add more salt, if desired. Remove from the heat and let cool to the touch.

Assemble and bake the turnovers: Preheat the oven to 375°F (°190C/Gas Mark 5). Line a large baking sheet with parchment paper.

Gently deflate the dough with the heel of your hand and turn out onto a lightly floured surface. Using a floured rolling pin, roll the dough into a large rectangle ⅛ inch (3 mm) thick rectangle. Using a 3½-inch (4 cm) round biscuit or cookie cutter, cut out as many rounds of dough as possible. Place a rounded teaspoon of the filling in the center of each round, then bring 3 points up and join at the center to make a triangle. Pinch firmly at the seams to close. (Really pinch well, so they do not open in the oven.)

Place the turnovers on the prepared baking sheet. Brush each with a little beaten egg and sprinkle with sesame or nigella seeds. Bake until golden brown, 20–25 minutes. Transfer to wire racks to cool.

POTATO BOUREKAS

With roots in Turkey, variations of these flaky pastry turnovers have become universally loved across Sephardi communities. They are commonly served for breakfast (see Desayuno, page 20) and at special occasions. In Israel, they have become a highly ubiquitous street food, purchased still warm at kiosks and bakeries, and eaten as a portable breakfast or snack. They are traditionally prepared with a flaky homemade dough called *yufka*. But when made with store-bought puff pastry, they are an eminently doable (and satisfying) baking project for home cooks. The cream cheese in this recipe is optional, but makes the filling all the more luscious.

Makes: 18 turnovers
Preparation time: 20 minutes
Cooking time: 1 hour 20 minutes

For the filling:
• 1 head garlic
• 1 teaspoon extra-virgin olive oil
• 1 lb (455 g) russet (baking) potatoes, scrubbed and unpeeled
• 1 egg
• 2 oz (55 g) cream cheese, at room temperature (optional)
• 1 teaspoon onion powder
• 1 teaspoon kosher salt
• ½ teaspoons freshly ground black pepper

For assembly and baking:
• Flour, for dusting
• 2 sheets frozen puff pastry, thawed
• Egg wash: 1 egg beaten with 1 teaspoon water
• Sesame seeds, for sprinkling

Make the filling: Preheat the oven to 400°F (200°C/Gas Mark 6).

Slice the top off the head of garlic, exposing the tips of the cloves. Lay the garlic in a square of foil, drizzle with the oil, and wrap tightly in the foil. Place in a small baking dish and bake until the cloves are soft and golden brown, 30–40 minutes. (Leave the oven on, but reduce the temperature to 350°F/180°C/Gas Mark 4.) Unwrap the garlic and let cool to the touch. Squeeze the cloves out of their skins into a large bowl.

Meanwhile, in a large pot, combine the potatoes with water to cover by 2 inches (5 cm). Bring to a boil over high heat and cook until the potatoes are tender all the way through when pierced with a sharp knife, 20–30 minutes (longer for larger potatoes). Drain and let sit until cool enough to handle.

Peel the potatoes and add to the bowl with the roasted garlic. Mash with a potato masher until smooth. Stir in the egg, cream cheese (if using), onion powder, salt, and pepper until well combined.

Assemble and bake the turnovers: Line 2 large baking sheets with parchment paper. On a lightly floured surface, gently roll out 1 sheet of puff pastry to a 12-inch (30 cm) square, trimming any ragged edges. Cut the square of pastry into nine 4-inch (10 cm) squares. Gently roll each square into a slightly larger rectangle. Spoon a rounded tablespoon of the potato filling along one of the short sides of the rectangle and use your fingers or the back of a spoon to lightly flatten. Starting with the filled edge, roll the pastry up like a jelly roll (Swiss roll), tucking the filling inside. Press firmly along the edges to seal, lightly wetting fingers with water, if necessary. Repeat the process with the second sheet of puff pastry and remaining filling.

Lay the filled *bourekas* on the baking sheets. Brush the tops with the egg wash (you may not use all of it) and sprinkle with sesame seeds. Bake until puffed and golden brown, 20–30 minutes. Set the baking sheets on wire racks to cool. Serve warm or at room temperature.

POTATO KNISHES

Brought over to America by Eastern European immigrants, knishes became a standard menu offering at Jewish delicatessens. These iconic Ashkenazi pastries are mostly commonly found stuffed with mashed potato, but also come filled with ground (minced) beef, curd cheese, grains, or other vegetables, like Sauerkraut (page 102). To try this latter version, just add ½ cup (70 g) drained, roughly chopped sauerkraut to the potato filling. Knishes pair particularly well with hearty soups like Hot Beet Borscht (page 128) or Potato Soup (page 134).

Makes: about 1 dozen knishes
Preparation time: 40 minutes, plus resting
Cooking time: 1 hour 10 minutes

For the dough:
- 1½ cups (210 g) all-purpose (plain) flour
- 1 cup (140 g) bread flour (strong white flour)
- ½ teaspoon baking powder
- ½ teaspoon kosher salt
- 1 egg
- ½ cup (120 ml/4 fl oz) warm water
- ½ cup (120 ml/4 fl oz) vegetable oil
- 1 teaspoon apple cider vinegar

For the filling:
- 1½ lb (680 g) russet (baking) potatoes, peeled and cut into 2-inch (5 cm) chunks
- 4 oz (115 g) cream cheese, at room temperature
- 1 teaspoon kosher salt, plus more as needed
- Freshly ground black pepper
- 2 tablespoons (30 g) unsalted butter or vegetable oil
- 1 medium onion, finely chopped
- 1 teaspoon sugar

For assembly and baking:
- Flour, for dusting
- Egg wash: 1 egg beaten with 1 teaspoon water

Make the dough: In a large bowl, whisk together the all-purpose (plain) flour, bread flour (strong white flour), baking powder, and salt. In a small bowl, whisk together the egg, warm water, oil, and vinegar. Make a well in the dry ingredients and pour in the wet. Stir until the dough comes together. Knead it a few times in the bowl with the heel of your hand and form it into a ball. Put the ball back into the bowl, cover with plastic wrap (cling film), and let sit at room temperature for 1 hour.

Meanwhile, make the filling: In a large saucepan, combine the potatoes with water to cover by 2 inches (5 cm). Bring to a boil over high heat, then reduce the heat to medium and cook until the potatoes are tender, about 15 minutes. Drain and transfer to a bowl. Add the cream cheese, salt, and a generous amount of pepper and mash with a potato masher to combine.

In a medium frying pan, melt the butter over medium heat. Add the onion, sugar, and a generous pinch of salt. Cover and cook until softened, about 10 minutes. Uncover, reduce the heat to medium-low, and continue cooking, stirring occasionally, until the onions are golden brown, 8–10 minutes. Remove from the heat. Fold the onion mixture into the mashed potatoes.

Assemble and bake the knishes: Preheat the oven to 375°F (190°C/Gas Mark 5). Line a large baking sheet with parchment paper.

Lay a large tea towel or tablecloth on a flat surface and dust generously with flour. Divide the dough in half. Working with one half (keep the other half in the bowl, covered), roll into a large, ⅛ inch (3 mm) thick rectangle. (If you have some rough edges, trim them off.) Take half of the potato mixture and form it into a thick roll and lay it along one of the long edges of the rectangle. Roll the dough around the filling like a jelly roll (Swiss roll). Repeat the process with the remaining dough and filling. Trim off the ends of each roll so that they are flush with the filling.

Using the side of your hand (imagine a karate chop motion), make indentations along the log every 3 inches (7.5 cm), then twist the dough at these points. Use a sharp knife to slice the dough at each twist. Working with one knish at a time, pinch one side together to form its base. Flatten the knish a bit between your palms, then pinch together the top, enclosing the filling. Lay the formed knishes on the lined baking sheet and use 2 fingers to press a small indentation into the top of each (this will keep them from opening in the oven).

Brush the tops and sides of each knish with the egg wash (you won't use all of it) and bake, rotating the baking sheet front to back halfway through, until golden brown, about 45 minutes. Allow to cool on a wire rack before eating. Serve warm or at room temperature.

FRITTERS & SAVORY PASTRIES

SHAPING BOUREKAS

Bourekas come in various shapes, ranging from triangular or half-moon turnovers to square and rectangular parcels. In addition to adding beauty to the finished pastries, cooks making several types of *bourekas* at once use the different shapes to indicate what filling is inside each one.

In 2013, the Chief Rabbi Rabbinate of Israel standardized *boureka* shapes to avoid any confusion, for kosher keepers, as to which pastries contained dairy (triangles) and which were parve (rectangles). Meanwhile, home bakers are free to form their *bourekas* in whichever shape they choose.

SPINACH BOUREKAS

When filled with verdant spinach, salty feta, and a hint of dried dill, these Sephardi turnovers are reminiscent of spanakopita. In Seattle, Washington, which is home to a significant population of Sephardi Jews, the two main Sephardi synagogues—Congregation Ezra Bessaroth and Sephardic Bikur Cholim—are home to women's groups that get together and bake on a regular basis. On a given afternoon, the bakers turn out many dozens of *bourekas*—as well as also *bulemas* (page 206), *biscochos* (Sesame Seed Cookie Rings, page 354), and other pastries—to stock community members' freezers and to sell at an annual fundraising bazaar. Together, they keep an ancient tradition alive while fostering local community.

Makes: 18 bourekas
Preparation time: 20 minutes
Cooking time: 40 minutes

For the filling:
• 2 tablespoons vegetable oil
• 1 small onion, finely chopped
• ¼ teaspoon kosher salt, plus more as needed
• 10 oz (285 g) thawed frozen spinach, squeezed dry and roughly chopped
• 1 egg, lightly beaten
• 1 garlic clove, minced or pushed through a press
• ½ teaspoon dried dill
• ½ cup (120 g) ricotta cheese
• 4 oz (115 g) feta cheese, crumbled
• ¼ teaspoon freshly ground black pepper

For assembly and baking:
• Flour, for dusting
• 2 sheets frozen puff pastry, thawed
• Egg wash: 1 egg beaten with 1 teaspoon water
• Sesame seeds, for sprinkling

Make the filling: In a small frying pan, heat the oil over medium heat. Add the onion and a pinch of salt and cook, stirring occasionally, until softened and lightly browned, 6–8 minutes. Remove from the heat and let cool.

Transfer the cooked onion to a bowl and add the spinach, egg, garlic, dill, ricotta, feta, salt, and pepper and mix well.

Assemble and bake the turnovers: Preheat the oven to 350°F (180°C/Gas Mark 4). Line 2 large baking sheets with parchment paper.

On a lightly floured surface, gently roll out 1 sheet of puff pastry into a 12-inch (30 cm) square, trimming any ragged edges. Cut the square of pastry into nine 4-inch (10 cm) squares. Spoon about 2 tablespoons of the spinach filling near one corner of each square and use your fingers or the back of a spoon to lightly flatten. Fold the opposite corner over to meet it, making a triangle and locking the filling inside. Press firmly all along the edges to seal, lightly wetting fingers with water, if necessary. Repeat with the second sheet of puff pastry and remaining filling.

Lay the filled *bourekas* on the baking sheets. Brush the tops with the egg wash (you may not use all of it) and sprinkle with sesame seeds. Bake until puffed and golden brown, 30–35 minutes. Set the baking sheets on wire racks to cool. Serve warm or at room temperature.

Spinach Bourekas

FLAKY CHICKEN AND ALMOND PIE

This rich and flaky Moroccan pie, called *b'stilla*, is a showstopper. It pairs saffron- and spice-scented chicken with sweetened, ground almonds inside crispy phyllo dough. The pie is then dusted with powdered (icing) sugar and cinnamon, creating a pastry that delicately straddles the sweet-savory line. The pie was originally made with squab or pigeon, but is often made with chicken today. It is labor intensive, so typically saved for holidays like Sukkot and Hanukkah, or special occasions like weddings.

Serves: 6–8
Preparation time: 40 minutes
Cooking time: 1 hour 45 minutes

For the chicken layer:
- 3 tablespoons vegetable oil
- 1 large sweet onion, finely chopped
- 2 garlic cloves, finely chopped
- 1 tablespoon Ras el Hanout (page 414)
- ½ teaspoon crushed pepper flakes
- ½ teaspoon saffron threads, crumbled
- 4 lb (1.8 kg) skin-on chicken drumsticks and thighs, patted dry
- 3 cups (710 ml/24 fl oz) chicken stock
- ½ cup (20 g) roughly chopped fresh cilantro (coriander)
- Kosher salt
- 3 eggs

For the almond layer:
- 1 cup (120 g) almond flour (ground almonds)
- 2 tablespoons sugar
- 1 tablespoon vegetable oil
- 1 teaspoon ground cinnamon

For assembly and baking:
- 6 sheets frozen phyllo dough, thawed
- ⅓ cup (75 ml/2½ fl oz) vegetable oil
- Powdered (icing) sugar, for topping
- Ground cinnamon, for topping

Make the chicken layer: In a large pot, heat the oil over medium heat. Add the onion and garlic and cook, stirring occasionally, until softened and lightly browned, 6–8 minutes. Add the *ras el hanout*, pepper flakes, and saffron and cook, stirring, until fragrant, about 1 minute. Add the chicken, stock, and cilantro (coriander). Increase the heat to medium-high and bring to a boil, then reduce the heat to low, cover, and cook until the chicken is tender, about 45 minutes.

Remove the chicken pieces with tongs and transfer to a plate to cool. Strain the cooking liquid through a fine-mesh sieve (discard the solids) and return the liquid to the pot. Set pot over medium-high heat and cook, stirring often, until reduced to about 1 cup (240 ml/8 fl oz) thick gravy, 20–30 minutes. Taste and add salt, if needed (it may not need any salt if the chicken stock used is salted), then remove from the heat and let cool.

Meanwhile, remove the chicken meat from the bones and shred into bite-size pieces (discard the skin and bones).

In a large bowl, whisk the eggs together. Add the cooled reduced cooking liquid and whisk to combine. Set aside.

Make the almond layer: In a bowl, stir together the almond flour, sugar, oil, and cinnamon.

Assemble and bake the pie: Preheat the oven to 400°F (200°C/Gas Mark 6). Lightly grease a 9-inch (23 cm) round cake pan.

Place the phyllo dough on a flat surface and cover with a damp tea towel to avoid drying out. Take one piece of phyllo (leaving the rest covered) and fit it into the bottom and up the sides of the cake pan. (The phyllo will hang over the sides.) Brush the phyllo lightly and evenly with the oil. Repeat with 4 more sheets of phyllo, draping them in different directions. Spread about one-third of the egg mixture into the pan. Mix another one-third with the shredded chicken and spoon into the pan. Spread the remaining one-third egg mixture on top and sprinkle with the almond mixture. Fold the overhanging pastry over the top of the pie and brush with oil. Take the remaining piece of phyllo, fold it in half, and drape it over the top of the pie. Brush it with oil, tucking the edges into the sides of the pan.

Bake until golden brown and set, 20–25 minutes. Let cool for at least 20 minutes before slicing. Just before serving, use a fine-mesh sieve to lightly dust the top of the pie with powdered (icing) sugar, then carefully sprinkle lines of cinnamon in a decorative pattern on top.

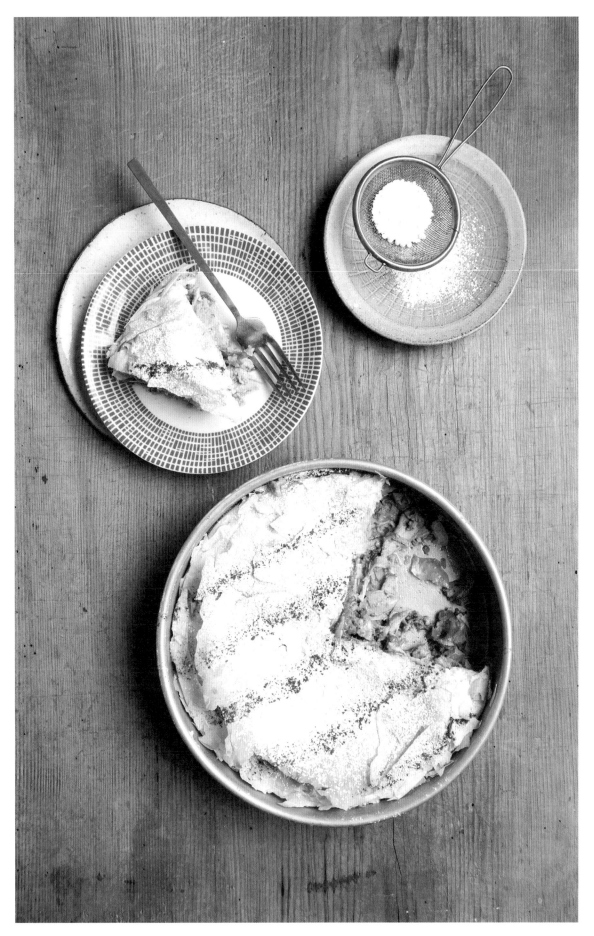

Flaky Chicken and Almond Pie

DUMPLINGS, NOODLES & KUGELS

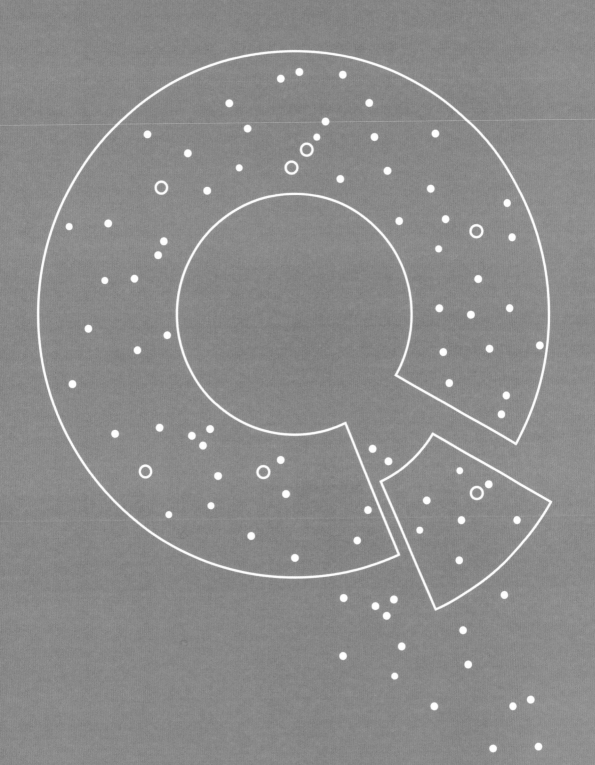

MATZO BALLS

Matzo balls, also called *knaidlach*, are the most popular dumplings within Ashkenazi Jewish cuisine—quite an accomplishment, considering they are made with matzo meal instead of flour. No bowl of Chicken Soup (page 122) served on Passover (and in certain families, Rosh Hashanah) is complete without them. While some people are fond of "sinkers" (dense, heavy matzo balls that tend to sink to the bottom of the soup pot), most prefer them to be light and fluffy in texture. The seltzer (sparkling water) added to the batter gives these matzo balls a bit of extra lift. And a pinch of ground ginger is a distinctly Hungarian twist on this Ashkenazi classic.

Makes: about 15 matzo balls
Preparation time: 10 minutes, plus chilling
Cooking time: 35 minutes

• 4 eggs, lightly beaten
• ¼ cup (60 ml/2 fl oz) vegetable oil or Schmaltz (page 410)
• 1 teaspoon kosher salt, plus more for boiling
• 1 cup (105 g) matzo meal
• 3 tablespoons seltzer (sparkling water)
• Optional add-ins: 1 teaspoon ground ginger or ¼ teaspoon ground nutmeg, ¼ cup (10 g) finely chopped fresh parsley

In a large bowl, mix together the eggs, vegetable oil, salt, matzo meal, seltzer (sparkling water), and any desired add-ins. Cover the bowl and refrigerate for 45 minutes.

Bring a large pot of salted water to a boil over high heat. Reduce the heat to medium-low and keep at a simmer.

Moisten your hands with water, then scoop out a rounded tablespoon of matzo ball batter and roll it into a 1-inch (2.5 cm) ball. Drop into the simmering water, and repeat with remaining batter. Cover and simmer until the matzo balls are tender and puffed, 30–40 minutes. (To check, cut one in half: It should be uniformly pale in color throughout.) Scoop the matzo balls out of the pot with a slotted spoon. Use immediately or let cool to room temperature and store, covered, in the fridge for up to 1 day.

BREAD DUMPLINGS

These rustic, boiled Czech dumplings are made with leftover bread, making them both delicious and thrifty. Called *knedliky*, they are ideal for soaking up the sauce of a flavorful stew like Beef and Paprika Goulash (page 136). Start with a sturdier bread variety like a baguette or ciabatta.

Serves: 6–8
Preparation time: 20 minutes
Cooking time: 35 minutes

• 2 tablespoons vegetable oil
• 1 small onion, finely chopped
• 3 eggs
• 2 teaspoons kosher salt
• 1½ cups (210 g) all-purpose (plain) flour
• 5 cups (175 g) day-old white bread cubes, crusts removed

In a medium frying pan, heat the oil over medium heat. Add the onion and cook, stirring occasionally, until softened and lightly browned, 6–8 minutes. Remove from the heat and let cool slightly.

Bring a large pot of water to a boil over high heat.

Meanwhile, in a large bowl, whisk together the eggs, 2 tablespoons water, and salt until frothy. Add the flour and stir to combine. Place the bread in a medium bowl and cover with water. Let sit for 1 minute, then squeeze the bread dry and crumble into the egg and flour mixture. Stir until a soft batter forms. Add the cooked onion and stir to combine.

Scoop out rounded tablespoons of the batter and using moistened hands, roll into rough balls. Drop the dumplings into the boiling water, using a spoon to loosen them if they stick to the bottom. Cover, reduce the heat to low, and cook until puffed and cooked through, 20–25 minutes. (They will swell in size as they cook.) Use a slotted spoon to transfer to a serving bowl and serve hot.

KISHKE

Kishke is the Slavic word for "intestines." And true to its name, this Ashkenazi "sausage"—a mix of fat (oil or schmaltz), flour or matzo meal, and onions—is traditionally stuffed into a cow intestine casing before being cooked. *Kishke* can be baked in the oven and served, sliced, as a starchy side dish. It makes a lovely companion to Brisket (page 293) and Roast Chicken with Thyme and Honey (page 270). It is also commonly cooked in a batch of Cholent (page 144)—instead of baking, nestle the parchment-wrapped log of *kishke* into the cholent in the slow cooker (just don't forget to unwrap and slice before serving). As the stew enjoys its low-and-slow simmer, the *kishke* firms up and takes on a rich, savory flavor.

Serves: 6–8
Preparation time: 30 minutes
Cooking time: 1 hour 40 minutes

- 5 tablespoons vegetable oil or Schmaltz (page 410)
- 1 large onion, finely chopped
- 2 garlic cloves, finely chopped
- 1 carrot, cut into chunks
- 1 celery stalk, cut into chunks
- 1½ cups (210 g) all-purpose (plain) flour or matzo meal
- 1 teaspoon sweet paprika
- 1¼ teaspoons kosher salt
- ¼ teaspoon freshly ground black pepper

In a medium frying pan, heat the oil over medium heat. Add the onion and garlic and cook, stirring occasionally, until softened and lightly browned, 6–8 minutes. Remove from the heat and let cool slightly.

Transfer the cooled onion mixture (along with any oil left in the pan) to a food processor. Add the carrot and celery and pulse, scraping down the sides of the bowl as necessary, until very finely ground. Add the flour, paprika, salt, and pepper and pulse until a thick paste forms.

Spread a 16-inch (40 cm) length of parchment paper on a work surface. Spoon the vegetable mixture along one of the edges of the parchment and, using moistened hands, roll into a thick log about 8 inches (20 cm) long. Roll the parchment around the log like a jelly roll (Swiss roll), enclosing the filling inside. Twist the ends of the parchment firmly to seal and tuck under the log or tie with kitchen twine.

Preheat the oven to 425°F (220°C/Gas Mark 7).

Place the parchment paper–wrapped log on a baking sheet and bake for 30 minutes. Reduce the oven temperature to 350°F (180°C/Gas Mark 4) and continue cooking until the log is firm and cooked through, 45–60 minutes. Remove from the oven and let cool (it will continue to firm up as it cools), then unwrap the log and slice.

MEAT-STUFFED KREPLACH

Kreplach are to Ashkenazi cuisine what ravioli are to Italian cuisine—delicious parcels of homemade pasta stuffed with meat (or sometimes cheese or vegetables). Kreplach are standard fare on Purim, when foods that conceal their filling are eaten to commemorate how the story's heroine Queen Esther bravely concealed her identity. They are also often served at the meal that precedes Yom Kippur. Serve the boiled version in Chicken Soup (page 122) and the fried version as an appetizer or snack.

Makes: about 2 dozen kreplach
Preparation time: 40 minutes, plus resting
Cooking time: 45 minutes

For the dough:
• 2 cups (280 g) all-purpose (plain) flour, plus more for kneading
• 2 eggs
• 1 teaspoon kosher salt

For the filling:
• 2 tablespoons vegetable oil
• ½ small onion, finely chopped
• 3 garlic cloves, minced or pushed through a press
• ½ teaspoon onion powder
• ½ teaspoon sweet paprika
• ½ lb (225 g) ground (minced) beef or chicken
• ½ cup (25 g) finely chopped fresh flat-leaf parsley
• 1 egg
• ½ teaspoon kosher salt, plus more for boiling
• ¼ teaspoon freshly ground black pepper

Make the dough: In a food processor, combine the flour, eggs, salt, and 5 tablespoons water and pulse until the dough begins to come together in a ball. Transfer to a lightly floured surface and knead until soft and supple, 2–3 minutes. Place the dough in a bowl, cover the bowl with a tea towel, and let rest for 30 minutes.

Meanwhile, make the filling: In a medium frying pan, heat the oil over medium heat. Add the onion and cook, stirring occasionally, until softened and lightly browned, 6–8 minutes. Add the garlic, onion powder, and paprika and cook, stirring, until fragrant, about 1 minute. Remove from the heat and let cool slightly.

In a medium bowl, combine the beef, parsley, cooled onion mixture, egg, salt, and pepper and mix well with your hands. Set aside while rolling out the dough.

On a lightly floured surface, using a lightly floured rolling pin, roll out the dough to less than ⅛ inch (3 mm) thick. (You want it as thin as possible without tearing.) Using a 3-inch (7.5 cm) round biscuit cutter or glass, stamp out as many rounds as possible. Place a rounded teaspoon of the filling in the center of one round. Run a wet finger around the outside edges of the round, then fold in half, enclosing the filling inside and ending up with a half-moon shape. Press the edges firmly to seal. Repeat with the remaining dough and filling.

To boil the kreplach, bring a large pot of salted water to a boil over high heat. Add the kreplach and cook, stirring occasionally, until tender, 15–20 minutes. Drain well.

Alternatively, to fry the kreplach, Line a large plate with paper towels. In a large frying pan, heat ¼ inch (3 mm) vegetable oil over medium heat. Working in batches of 4 or 5, fry the kreplach until golden brown and cooked through, about 3 minutes per side. Transfer to the paper towels to drain.

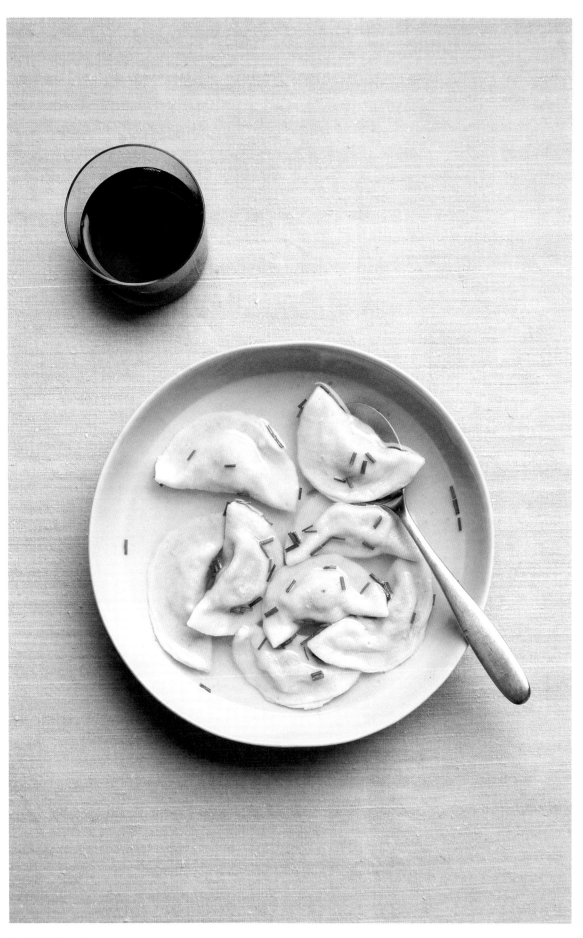

Meat-Stuffed Kreplach

PLUM DUMPLINGS

Hungarian cuisine is replete with different dumplings, but these plum-stuffed dessert dumplings, called *szilvas gombóc*, are especially enchanting. After all, they are made with a tender potato-based dough, rolled in buttery breadcrumbs, and dusted with powdered (icing) sugar. (Czech cuisine has a similar fruit dumpling called *svestkove knedliky* made with an all-flour dough.) These plum dumplings are traditionally made in late summer or early fall, when petite varieties (like Italian prune plums or damsons) are in season and available at farmers' markets. Other times of year, they can be filled with just jam or a quarter or half of a larger plum variety. They are a project to make, so invite a friend over to fill them—and a few more to help eat them.

Makes: 1 dozen dumplings
Preparation time: 45 minutes
Cooking time: 1 hour

For the dough:
- 1½ lb (680 g) russet (baking) potatoes, scrubbed and unpeeled
- 1¾ cups (245 g) all-purpose (plain) flour
- ¼ cup (50 g) sugar
- 1 tablespoon vegetable oil
- 1 teaspoon kosher salt

For the filling:
- ¼ cup (90 g) plum or cherry jam
- ½ teaspoon ground cinnamon
- 12 small plums, halved and pitted

For the coating:
- 6 tablespoons (85 g) unsalted butter or nonhydrogenated margarine
- 1½ cups (90 g) panko breadcrumbs
- Powdered (icing) sugar and sour cream, for serving

Make the dough: In a large pot, combine the potatoes with water to cover by 2 inches (5 cm). Bring to a boil over high heat and cook until potatoes are tender all the way through when pierced with a sharp knife, 20–30 minutes (longer for larger potatoes). Drain and let sit until cool enough to handle.

Peel the cooked potatoes, place in a bowl, and mash with a potato masher until completely smooth. Add the flour, sugar, oil, and salt. Stir until the mixture begins to comes together, then knead with your hands to form into a smooth, pliable dough.

Bring a large pot of water to a boil over high heat.

Make the filling and the dumplings: In a small bowl, stir together the jam and cinnamon. Scoop out ¼ cup (75 g) of the dough and flatten into a round about 5 inches (12.5 cm) in diameter. Spoon about 1 teaspoon jam into the center of a plum half, then top with another plum half to create a whole plum. Place into the center of the dough round and wrap the edges around the filled plum, smoothing it into a round ball. Repeat with the remaining dough, jam, and plums.

Working in batches of 4, gently add the dumplings to the boiling water. Let cook, turning once, until they float and soften, about 8 minutes per batch. Transfer the cooked dumplings to a large plate.

Make the coating: In a large frying pan, heat the butter over medium heat. Add the panko and cook, stirring, until lightly toasted, about 2 minutes. Working in batches, add the dumplings to the pan and shake gently to coat them in breadcrumbs.

Serve immediately sprinkled with powdered (icing) sugar and dolloped with sour cream.

SOUR CHERRY DUMPLINGS

Called *vareniki* in Russian and pierogi in Polish, these filled, pastalike dumplings are typically served boiled and topped with sour cream. They can be filled with mashed potato, mushrooms, cheese, or kasha, but this sour cherry version is a special treat in summer when fresh sour cherries are at their peak—or anytime you can find frozen. Avoid using canned cherries, which do not maintain a great flavor.

Makes: about 30 dumplings
Preparation time: 40 minutes
Cooking time: 30 minutes

For the filling:
• ¾ lb (340 g) fresh or thawed frozen sour cherries, pitted
• ⅓ cup (65 g) sugar
• 1 tablespoon cornstarch (cornflour)

For the dough:
• 2 cups (280 g) all-purpose (plain) flour, plus more for rolling
• 1 teaspoon kosher salt
• ½ cup (120 g) sour cream
• 2 eggs

• Sour cream, for serving

Make the filling: In a medium bowl, mix together the cherries, sugar, and cornstarch (cornflour). Let rest at room temperature while making the dough.

Make the dough: In a food processor, combine the flour, salt, sour cream, and eggs and pulse until a slightly sticky dough comes together. Gather the dough into a ball and divide in half.

Bring a large pot of water to a boil over high heat. Line a large baking sheet with parchment paper.

Meanwhile, working with half of the dough (keeping the rest covered), roll it out on a floured surface with a floured rolling pin to ⅛ inch (3 mm) thick. Using a 3-inch (7.5 cm) round biscuit or cookie cutter, cut out as many rounds of dough as possible. Place 2 cherries in the center of each round and fold in half to make a half-moon, pressing the seams tightly to seal. Gather and reroll the dough scraps, then repeat the rolling and filling process with the remaining dough and cherries.

Working in batches and being careful not to crowd the pot, drop the filled dumplings into the boiling water and cook, stirring occasionally, until tender, about 10 minutes. Scoop out the cooked dumplings with a slotted spoon and let drain. Serve hot, topped with sour cream.

PASSOVER EGG NOODLES

Eastern European Jewish cooks devised an ingenious way to make Passover-friendly noodles. The technique is simple: Whisk up a batter made from eggs, potato starch, and water, then fry the batter into a stack of ultrathin crepes. Rolled up and sliced, the crepes transform into long, tender noodles that are the perfect addition to classic Chicken Soup (page 122) or Vegetarian Chicken Soup (page 125).

Serves: 6–8
Preparation time: 10 minutes
Cooking time: 45 minutes

- ⅔ cup (120 g) potato starch
- 7 eggs
- ½ teaspoon kosher salt
- Vegetable oil, for frying

In a large bowl, whisk together the potato starch and ½ cup (120 ml/4 fl oz) water until the starch is fully dissolved. Add the eggs and salt and beat until a frothy, wet batter forms.

Heat about 1 teaspoon vegetable oil in a 7- to 8-inch (18 to 20 cm) nonstick frying pan over medium heat. Once hot, pour ¼ cup (55 g) of the batter into the pan. Immediately pick up the pan and swirl it in all directions to coat the bottom evenly with a thin layer of batter. Cook until the bottom is golden and the center is just dry, 1–2 minutes. (Do not flip.)

Remove the crepe with a spatula and place it on a piece of parchment paper on the counter to cool slightly. Roll it tightly like a jelly roll (Swiss roll), then slice crosswise at ¼-inch (6 mm) intervals, creating curled up noodles. Continue the frying, rolling, and slicing process with the remaining batter, stirring the egg mixture often to reincorporate any starch that may have settled at the bottom. Serve warm and store leftovers, covered, in the fridge for up to 2 days.

FARFEL

Ashkenazi Jews serve these petite, barley-shaped egg noodles, as a homey and satisfying side dish. Farfel is often toasted, which brings out its nutty flavor, and can be served plain or mixed with sautéed mushrooms and zucchini (courgettes), or dressed up with chopped fresh herbs.

Serves: 6–8
Preparation time: 10 minutes
Cooking time: 20 minutes

- 4 tablespoons vegetable oil
- 12 oz (340 g) egg barley (pasta)
- 1 onion, finely chopped
- 1 medium carrot, finely chopped
- 1 celery stalk, finely chopped
- ½ teaspoon kosher salt, plus more as needed
- ½ teaspoon onion powder
- ½ teaspoon freshly ground black pepper, plus more as needed

Bring a large saucepan of water to a boil.

Meanwhile, in a large frying pan, heat 2 tablespoons of the oil over medium heat. Add the egg barley (pasta) and cook, stirring often, until toasty smelling and lightly browned, 3–5 minutes.

When the water is at a boil, add the toasted egg barley and cook until tender, about 10 minutes (or use the times on the package). Drain well and transfer to a large bowl.

Wipe out the pan used to toast the pasta and heat the remaining 2 tablespoons oil over medium heat. Add the onion, carrot, celery, and a pinch of salt and cook, stirring occasionally, until softened and lightly browned, about 10 minutes. Stir in the onion powder, salt, and pepper.

Remove from the heat and add the cooked onion mixture to the egg barley, stirring well to combine. Taste and add a little more salt or pepper, if desired. Serve hot.

Passover Egg Noodles

SHLISHKES

Hungarian Jews serve these petite potato dumplings, which are coated in sautéed breadcrumbs, as a side for Shabbat dinner. Similar to Italian gnocchi in composition and texture, they pair well with saucy dishes like Chicken Paprikash (page 280) or Beef and Paprika Goulash (page 136).

Serves: 8
Preparation time: 35 minutes
Cooking time: 1 hour

For the shlishkes:
• 2 lb (910 g) russet (baking) potatoes, scrubbed and unpeeled
• 2 tablespoons vegetable oil
• 2 eggs
• 2 teaspoons kosher salt, plus more for the pot
• 2½ cups (350 g) all-purpose (plain) flour, plus more as needed

For the breadcrumb coating:
• 6 tablespoons vegetable oil or unsalted butter
• 1½ cups (210 g) dried breadcrumbs
• ½ teaspoon onion powder
• ½ teaspoon kosher salt
• Sweet paprika, for serving

Make the *shlishkes*: In a large pot, combine the potatoes with water to cover by 2 inches (5 cm). Bring to a boil over high heat, then reduce the heat to medium-high and cook until the potatoes are tender all the way through when pierced with a sharp knife, 20–30 minutes (longer for larger potatoes). Drain and let sit until cool enough to handle.

Peel the cooked potatoes and place in a bowl. Add the oil and mash with a potato masher until smooth. Stir the eggs and salt into the mashed potato mixture, then stir in the flour, a little at at time, to form a soft dough. If the dough feels very sticky, add more flour, a little at a time, until a soft and moist, but not overly sticky, dough forms.

Bring a large pot of well-salted water to a boil.

Meanwhile, using floured hands and a floured surface to avoid sticking, section off handfuls of the dough and roll into ropes about ½ inch (1.25 cm) thick. Cut each rope crosswise into pieces 1 inch (2.5 cm) long.

Working in batches, drop the dough pieces into the boiling water and stir. Let cook until they float to the top and are cooked through and firm, about 5 minutes. Remove with a slotted spoon and transfer to a plate while cooking the remaining batches.

Make the breadcrumb coating: In a large frying pan, heat the oil over medium. Add the breadcrumbs, onion powder, and salt and cook, stirring often, until the breadcrumbs are golden and fragrant, 2–3 minutes.

Remove the breadcrumbs from the heat and add the still-warm shlishkes. Gently stir to coat with the breadcrumbs. Transfer to a serving dish and lightly dust with paprika. Serve hot or warm.

MATZO FARFEL WITH MUSHROOMS

Crumbled matzo, called *matzo farfel,* serves as a starchy, Passover-friendly substitute for the Farfel (page 226) that Ashkenazi Jews serve the remainder of the year. This side dish tosses it with sautéed mushrooms and onion, creating a homey side dish for the seder table. You can serve it right off the stove, or bake it into a kugel—just fold 4 beaten eggs into the finished dish, transfer to an oven-proof dish, and bake at 375°F (190°C/Gas Mark 5) for about 30 minutes. Packaged *matzo farfel* is often available at grocery stores in the weeks leading up to Passover. If you cannot find it, simply begin with full sheets of matzo and crumble them into ½-inch (1.25 cm) pieces.

Serves: 6
Preparation time: 15 minutes
Cooking time: 45 minutes

- ¼ cup (60 ml/2 fl oz) plus 2 tablespoons vegetable oil
- 1 large onion, finely chopped
- 2 celery stalks, finely chopped
- 6 garlic cloves, finely chopped
- 1¼ teaspoons kosher salt, plus more as needed
- 1 lb (455 g) white button or cremini (chestnut) mushrooms, stems discarded, finely chopped
- 5 cups (330 g) matzo farfel
- 2 cups (475 ml/16 fl oz) vegetable or chicken stock
- ¾ teaspoon onion powder
- Freshly ground black pepper
- Chopped fresh parsley, for serving (optional)

In a large frying pan, heat 2 tablespoons of the oil over medium heat. Add the onion, celery, garlic, and a generous pinch of salt. Cook, stirring occasionally, until the vegetables begin to soften, about 8 minutes. Add the mushrooms and continue cooking until the vegetables are very tender and most of the liquid from the mushrooms has evaporated, about 10 minutes. Remove from the heat and set aside.

In large saucepan, heat the remaining ¼ cup (60 ml/2 fl oz) oil over medium-high heat. Add the farfel and cook, stirring often, until toasty smelling, 4–5 minutes. Add the stock, onion powder, salt, and a generous amount of pepper. Bring to a boil, then reduce the heat to low, cover, and cook until the farfel is soft and the stock is fully absorbed, 7–10 minutes. Remove saucepan from the heat and let stand, covered, for at least 10 minutes. (The farfel will continue to steam and any bits stuck to the bottom of the pan will loosen.)

Uncover and stir in the mushroom mixture. Taste and add more salt, if desired. Serve hot or warm, sprinkled with parsley, if desired.

NOODLES WITH CURD CHEESE

Egg noodles stirred with farmer cheese (or cottage cheese) and sour cream, a dish revered by generations of Eastern and Central European Jews as a quick weeknight meal, has fallen by the wayside in recent decades. Served savory with a sprinkle of salt, it is the Ashkenazi answer to macaroni and cheese—pure, delicious comfort. When topped with cinnamon and sugar, it is reminiscent of a deconstructed noodle kugel (see page 236). The lemon zest and chives in this version are not traditional, but help update the dish's Old World flavor for the contemporary palate.

Serves: 4–6
Preparation time: 10 minutes
Cooking time: 10 minutes

- 12 oz (340 g) wide egg noodles
- 2 tablespoons (30 g) unsalted butter, cut into small pieces
- 1½ cups (375 g) pot cheese or large-curd cottage cheese
- ½ cup (120 g) sour cream
- ½ teaspoon packed finely grated lemon zest
- ½ teaspoon kosher salt, plus more for boiling
- Freshly ground black pepper
- Snipped fresh chives, for serving

Bring a large pot of salted water to a boil over high heat. Add the noodles and cook, stirring occasionally, until al dente, about 8 minutes (or follow the times on the package). Drain well and transfer to a large bowl.

Add the butter to the hot noodles and toss until the butter melts and coats the noodles. Stir in the pot cheese, sour cream, lemon zest, salt, and a generous amount of black pepper.

Divide the noodles into bowls and top with a generous amount of chives. Serve warm.

CABBAGE WITH NOODLES

Broad egg noodles mixed with tender, lightly caramelized cabbage is Hungarian comfort food at its finest. This dish, called *kaposztas teszta*, is simple enough to make for a weeknight dinner, and also makes a homey side dish for Shabbat. Some Hungarian Jewish cooks serve cabbage with noodles sprinkled with poppy seeds on Purim.

Serves: 8
Preparation time: 10 minutes
Cooking time: 30 minutes

- ⅓ cup (75 ml/2½ fl oz) plus 1 tablespoon vegetable oil or unsalted butter
- 1 large onion, halved through the root and thinly sliced
- 1½ teaspoons kosher salt, plus more as needed
- 1 small head green cabbage (2–2½ lb), quartered, cored, and very thinly sliced
- 1 teaspoon sugar
- 1 teaspoon onion powder
- ½ teaspoon freshly ground black pepper, plus more as needed
- 12 oz (340 g) wide egg noodles
- Sweet paprika and poppy seeds, for sprinkling (optional)

In a large Dutch oven (casserole) or other heavy-bottomed pot, heat the ⅓ cup (75 ml/2½ fl oz) oil over medium heat. Add the onion and a pinch of salt and cook, stirring occasionally, until soft and translucent, 7–8 minutes. Stir in the cabbage, cover, reduce the heat to medium-low, and cook, stirring occasionally, until the cabbage is very tender, 15–20 minutes.

Stir in the sugar, onion powder, salt, and pepper and continue cooking, uncovered, until lightly browned, about 10 minutes. Remove the pan from the heat.

Meanwhile, bring a large pot of salted water to a boil over high heat. Add the noodles and cook, stirring occasionally, until al dente, about 8 minutes (or follow the times on the package). Drain well, transfer to a large bowl, and add the 1 tablespoon oil, tossing to coat.

Add the cabbage mixture to the noodles and toss until fully combined. Taste and add more salt and pepper, if needed. Transfer to a serving dish. If desired, sprinkle with paprika and poppy seeds. Serve hot.

Noodles with Curd Cheese

SWEET MATZO KUGEL

Romanian and Bulgarian Jews serve this lightly sweetened matzo kugel, called *babanatza*, on Passover as a side dish and sometimes for dessert. Either way, the custardy baked pudding, which is studded with raisins and tender apple, is a treat.

Serves: 6–8
Preparation time: 20 minutes
Cooking time: 45 minutes

- 6 sheets matzo
- 6 eggs, lightly beaten
- ¼ cup (60 ml/2 fl oz) vegetable oil
- ¾ cup (150 g) sugar
- 1 teaspoon ground cinnamon
- ¼ teaspoon kosher salt
- 1 large green apple, peeled and grated on the large holes of a box grater
- ¾ cup (105 g) raisins
- ½ cup (50 g) walnut halves, roughly chopped (optional)

Preheat the oven to 350°F (180°C/Gas Mark 4). Line a 9-inch (23 cm) square baking dish with parchment paper and lightly grease the parchment.

In a shallow container, cover the matzo sheets with warm water and soak for 10 minutes. Then drain and squeeze completely dry.

Meanwhile, in a large bowl, whisk together the eggs, oil, sugar, cinnamon, and salt.

Crumble the soaked matzo into the egg mixture and add the apple, raisins, and walnuts (if using) and stir well to combine. Transfer the mixture to the prepared baking dish and bake until golden brown, about 45 minutes. Let cool slightly before slicing. Serve hot or warm.

SWEET NOODLE KUGEL

In a canon filled with rich, homey dishes, this sweet, cottage cheese and sour cream enriched noodle kugel (called *lokhshen kugel* in Yiddish) is one of the hallmarks of decadent Ashkenazi fare. *Lokshen* kugels are also made dairy-free (see Jam and Poppy Seed Kugel, page 238), which makes them suitable for meat meals. But the dairy version has become a standard of dairy-focused holiday meals. In America, some cooks add drained canned pineapple or chopped apple to the kugel base, or top it with crushed corn cereal for added crunch.

Serves: 8–10
Preparation time: 20 minutes, plus cooling
Cooking time: 1 hour

- 12 oz (340 g) wide or extra-wide egg noodles
- 4 tablespoons (60 g) unsalted butter, melted
- 4 oz (115 g) cream cheese, at room temperature
- 2 cups (480 g) cottage cheese
- 1½ cups (360 g) sour cream
- 5 eggs
- 1 cup (200 g) sugar
- ½ teaspoon kosher salt
- 1½ teaspoons vanilla extract
- ¾ cup (105 g) golden raisins (sultanas) or regular raisins
- Ground cinnamon, for serving

Preheat the oven to 350°F (180°C/Gas Mark 4). Lightly grease a 9 × 13-inch (23 × 33 cm) baking dish.

Bring a medium pot of water to a boil over high heat. Add the noodles and boil until just short of tender, 5–7 minutes. Drain and set aside.

In a stand mixer fitted with the paddle attachment (or using a handheld electric mixer and a large bowl), beat together the melted butter, cream cheese, cottage cheese, sour cream, eggs, sugar, salt, and vanilla at low speed until smooth and combined. Add the cooked noodles and golden raisins (sultanas) and stir to combine.

Pour the mixture into the prepared baking dish and smooth with a spatula. Bake until set, 50–60 minutes. Transfer to a wire rack to cool for about 20 minutes before slicing. Just before serving, use a fine-mesh sieve to dust the kugel with cinnamon. Serve warm or at room temperature.

ZONI
•
PLAC KONESERA 1
WARSAW, POLAND

Aleksander Baron is the owner and chef at Zoni, a Warsaw-based restaurant (housed at the Polish Vodka Museum) that explores contemporary expressions of historical Polish culture and cooking, including many dishes inspired by Jewish Polish cuisine.

CHALLAH KUGEL WITH POPPY SEED SAUCE

This baked kugel is indulgent and rich. Baron serves it for dessert, copiously drizzled with a sweet poppy seed sauce.

Serves: 8
Preparation time: 35 minutes, plus chilling
Cooking time: 1 hour 5 minutes

For the kugel:
- ⅓ cup (30 g) walnut halves, finely chopped
- 6 eggs
- 1¼ cups (300 ml/10 fl oz) heavy (whipping) cream
- 3 tablespoons honey
- ¼ teaspoon kosher salt
- 2 sticks (8 oz/225 g) unsalted butter, melted
- 1 lb (455 g) challah loaf, cut into slices ½ inch (1.25 cm) thick
- ⅓ cup (45 g) golden raisins (sultanas)
- ⅓ cup (60 g) chopped pitted dates

For the poppy seed sauce:
- ½ cup (70 g) poppy seeds
- ¾ cup (175 ml/6 fl oz) whole milk
- 2 tablespoons honey
- 1 cup (240 ml/8 fl oz) heavy (whipping) cream

Make the kugel: In a small frying pan, toast the walnuts over medium-low heat, shaking the pan occasionally, until fragrant and lightly browned, about 5 minutes. Remove from the heat and let cool.

Meanwhile, lightly grease a 9 × 5-inch (23 × 13 cm) loaf pan and set aside.

In a blender, blend the eggs, cream, honey, and salt until fully combined. Pour the melted butter into a shallow dish. Dip one slice of challah on both sides in the melted butter and arrange in the bottom of the loaf pan. Continue adding butter-dipped challah pieces until the bottom of the pan is covered in a single layer. Sprinkle the golden raisins (sultanas) evenly over the top, then add a second layer of butter-dipped challah. Pour about one-quarter of the egg mixture evenly over the top, then evenly sprinkle on the walnuts. Add a third layer of challah, then pour over another one-quarter of the egg mixture and sprinkle with the chopped dates. Add a final layer of challah, then slowly pour the remaining egg mixture over the top. Gently but firmly press the bread down with your hand, cover the pan with plastic wrap (cling film), and refrigerate for 3 hours.

When ready to bake, preheat the oven to 325°F (160°C/ Gas Mark 3).

Remove the plastic wrap from the loaf pan (and discard) and cover the pan with foil. Place the loaf pan in a larger baking dish and fill the dish about one-third of the way with water. Bake for 45 minutes, then uncover and continue baking until golden brown and puffed, about 15 minutes. Remove from the oven and set on a wire rack to cool for 15 minutes before slicing.

Meanwhile, make the poppy seed sauce: Working in batches if necessary, grind the poppy seeds in a spice or coffee grinder until powdery, 15–20 seconds. Transfer the ground poppy seeds to a small saucepan and add the milk. Bring to a simmer over medium heat, then reduce the heat to low and cook, stirring frequently, until the poppy seeds soften and most of the liquid evaporates, about 5 minutes. Add the honey and cream, increase the heat to medium and bring back to a simmer. Reduce the heat to medium-low and continue cooking, stirring often, until the mixture thickens slightly, about 10 minutes. Remove from the heat and let cool slightly.

To serve, slice the warm kugel and divide onto plates. Serve drizzled with poppy seed sauce.

POTATO KUGEL

The potato is a New World vegetable that did not become popular in Eastern Europe until the mid-nineteeenth century. But the starchy tuber caught on quickly, and today, kugels made with shredded potato are among the best known and loved dishes within Ashkenazi cuisine. Crisp on the outside and custardy within, potato kugel is comforting and stick-to-your-ribs hearty. It is commonly served on Shabbat (both for Friday night dinner and Saturday lunch), Passover, and other festive holidays.

Serves: 8–10
Preparation time: 30 minutes
Cooking time: 1½ hours

- 5 lb (2.25 kg) russet (baking) potatoes, scrubbed, peeled, and cut into large chunks
- 2 large onions, quartered
- 8 eggs
- ¼ cup (60 ml/2 fl oz) vegetable oil or Schmaltz (page 410), plus more for the baking dish
- 1 tablespoon kosher salt
- ½ teaspoon onion powder
- ½ teaspoon garlic powder
- ½ teaspoon freshly ground black pepper
- ¼ cup (45 g) potato starch or all-purpose (plain) flour (35 g)

Preheat the oven to 350°F (°180C/Gas Mark 4).

Grate the potatoes and onions on the large holes of a box grater. (Or, working in batches, shred them on the shredding disc of a food processor.) Transfer the shredded potato and onion to a large colander and press to squeeze out most of the water. (It is okay if there is some moisture remaining.)

In a large bowl, whisk together the eggs, oil, salt, onion powder, garlic powder, and pepper. Add the shredded potatoes and onions to the bowl and sprinkle the potato starch on top. Stir well to fully combine.

Grease the bottom and sides of a 9 × 13-inch (23 × 33 cm) baking dish with a couple of tablespoons oil. Place the greased baking dish into the hot oven to heat up for 5 minutes. Carefully remove the baking dish from the oven and spoon in the potato mixture. (It should sizzle on contact.) Return to the oven and bake until the kugel is bubbling and deep golden brown, about 1½ hours.

TOASTED NOODLES

Fried and toasted noodle dishes date back to pre-Inquisition Spain. Today, Sephardi Jews soften the browned noodles in a savory tomato sauce—a dish, called *fideos tostados.*

Serves: 6–8
Preparation time: 5 minutes
Cooking time: 35 minutes

- 12 oz (340 g) vermicelli or angel hair pasta, broken into 1-inch (2.5 cm) pieces
- 3 tablespoons extra-virgin olive oil
- 1 large onion, finely chopped
- 3 cups (710 ml/24 fl oz) vegetable or chicken stock
- 1 can (14½ oz/411 g) diced (chopped) tomatoes
- 2 tablespoons tomato paste (purée)
- 1 teaspoon sugar
- 1 teaspoon kosher salt, plus more as needed
- ½ teaspoon freshly ground black pepper

Preheat the broiler (grill). Place the noodles on a large sheet pan and broil (grill), shaking the pan once or twice and checking often so the noodles don't burn, until they are golden brown and toasty smelling, 2–5 minutes. Set aside.

In a Dutch oven (casserole) or other large saucepan, heat the oil over medium heat. Add the onion and cook, stirring occasionally, until softened and nicely browned, 7–10 minutes.

Stir in the stock, tomatoes with their juice, tomato paste (purée), sugar, salt, and pepper. Increase the heat to medium-high and bring to a boil. Stir in the toasted noodles, reduce the heat to low, cover, and cook, stirring occasionally, until the noodles are tender, 8–10 minutes.

Remove from the heat and let stand with the cover on for 5–10 minutes. (The noodles will continue to steam and absorb the stock while they rest.) Taste and add a little more salt, if desired. Serve warm.

Potato Kugel

KUGELS, SCHALETS, AND BAKED PUDDINGS

Savory and sweet baked puddings made from noodles, potatoes, bread, and other starchy ingredients bound together by eggs, are one of the most widely served Shabbat and holiday foods within Ashkenazi cuisine. The dish's ancestors date back eight centuries to Germany, where cooks originally added small flour dumplings to their long-simmering Shabbat stews. Over time, the dough was placed into small ceramic pots called *kugeltopf* (translating to "ball jar") and steamed over the hot stew, transforming them into a standalone dish. The dish (called either *kugel* or *schalet*) spread from Central to Eastern Europe and took on its own identity. Today, there is a staggering amount of kugel diversity, with everything from rice and egg noodles to sweet potatoes forming the pudding's base.

SWEET POTATO–PECAN KUGEL

This creamy sweet potato–based kugel, which comes topped with a pecan crumble, is representative of how Jewish communities in the American South incorporated local ingredients and flavors into traditional Ashkenazi dishes.

Serves: 6–8
Preparation time: 15 minutes
Cooking time: 1 hour 40 minutes

For the kugel:
• 3 lb (1.35 kg) sweet potatoes (about 3 medium)
• 1 large Granny Smith apple, peeled and grated on the large holes of a box grater
• 2 tablespoons light brown sugar
• 3 eggs, lightly beaten
• ½ cup (70 g) all-purpose (plain) flour
• 1 teaspoon finely grated orange zest
• 1½ teaspoons kosher salt
• ½ teaspoon freshly ground black pepper

For the topping:
• 4 tablespoons (60 g) unsalted butter or coconut oil, melted
• 1½ cups (155 g) pecans, roughly chopped
• ½ cup (90 g) light brown sugar
• 3 tablespoons all-purpose (plain) flour
• ½ teaspoon kosher salt

Make the kugel: Preheat the oven to 400°F (200°C/Gas Mark 6).

Prick the sweet potatoes in several places with a fork and place on a large sheet pan. Roast until the flesh can be easily pierced with a knife, about 1 hour. Remove from the oven, cut in half to facilitate cooling, and let cool to the touch. Scoop the flesh into a large bowl, discarding the skin, and mash well with a potato masher. (This step can be completed up to 1 day in advance.) If making ahead, turn the oven off; if continuing with the recipe, leave the oven on.

Reduce the oven temperature to 350°F (180°C/Gas Mark 4). Grease a 9-inch (23 cm) square baking pan.

To the bowl of mashed sweet potato, add the apple, brown sugar, eggs, flour, orange zest, salt, and pepper and mix well. Spread the mixture into the prepared baking pan.

Make the topping: In a medium bowl, stir together the melted butter, pecans, brown sugar, flour, and salt. Sprinkle evenly over the kugel.

Bake, uncovered, until the kugel sets and lightly browns around the edges, 35–40 minutes.

YERUSHALMI KUGEL

Yerushalmi kugel ("Jerusalem-style kugel") emerged in Jerusalem's ultrareligious neighborhood, Mea Shearim, in the nineteenth century. The inside of the kugel is velvety soft, while the edges brown into candied noodle brittle in the oven. Slices of *Yerushalmi kugel* are served with pickles—an odd-sounding pair that actually delivers a perfect bite of sweet, sour, salty, and bitter flavor. Jerusalem remains the epicenter for this decadent noodle pudding, with observant and secular customers alike flocking to bakeries to buy it on Friday mornings.

Serves: 8–10
Preparation time: 10 minutes
Cooking time: 2 hours

- 12 oz (340 g) fine egg noodles
- ½ cup (120 ml/4 fl oz) vegetable oil, plus more for greasing the pan
- ¾ cup (150 g) sugar
- 5 eggs, lightly beaten
- 3 tablespoons honey
- 2½ teaspoons freshly ground black pepper
- 2½ teaspoons kosher salt

Bring a large pot of water to a boil over high heat. Add the noodles and cook, stirring occasionally, until al dente, 4–8 minutes (or follow the times on the package). Drain well, transfer to a large heatproof bowl, and set aside.

Preheat the oven to 350°F (180°C/Gas Mark 4). Lightly grease a 9-inch (23 cm) round springform pan with oil and line with a round of parchment paper.

In a large frying pan, combine the oil and sugar and cook over medium heat, stirring occasionally, until the sugar turns a deep amber brown, about 15 minutes. (It's okay if the sugar and oil separate during cooking.) Remove the pan from the heat and immediately pour the caramelized sugar and oil mixture over the still-warm noodles, stirring vigorously to combine. (Bits of the caramel may clump, but will melt in the oven.) Let the mixture cool for 10 minutes, then stir in the eggs, honey, pepper, and salt to combine.

Transfer the mixture to the prepared pan and smooth with a rubber spatula. Bake until the kugel is deep brown with a crusty top, 1–1½ hours. Set on a wire rack. If desired, run a knife along the outside of the kugel to loosen, then gently remove it and place on the rack. Slice into wedges and serve hot, warm, or at room temperature.

JAM AND POPPY SEED KUGEL

Hungarians have a particular fondness for poppy seeds, often pairing them with pastries and noodle dishes. Here, the dusky seeds add nutty flavor to a baked *lokshen* (noodle) kugel. The dollops of jam threaded throughout make this kugel equally appropriate as a side dish, a dessert, or the centerpiece for brunch.

Serves: 8–10
Preparation time: 10 minutes
Cooking time: 45 minutes

- 12 oz (340 g) wide egg noodles
- ⅓ cup (75 ml/2½ fl oz) vegetable oil
- 1 cup (225 g) unsweetened applesauce
- 6 eggs
- ¾ cup (150 g) sugar
- 1 teaspoon vanilla extract
- ½ teaspoon kosher salt
- ½ teaspoon ground cinnamon, plus more for dusting
- 1½ tablespoons poppy seeds
- ⅓ cup (110 g) cherry or apricot or jam

Preheat the oven to 350°F (180°C/Gas Mark 4). Lightly grease a 9 × 13-inch (23 × 33 cm) or other 3-quart (3 L) baking dish.

Bring a medium pot of water to a boil over high heat. Add the noodles and cook until just short of tender, 5–7 minutes. Drain and set aside.

In a large bowl, whisk together the oil, applesauce, eggs, sugar, vanilla, salt, and cinnamon until fully combined. Grind the poppy seeds in a spice or coffee grinder until just ground but not powdery (about 10 seconds). Add the ground poppy seeds and the cooked noodles to the egg mixture and stir to fully combine.

Transfer the mixture to the prepared baking dish. Take a teaspoon of the jam and dot it on top of the kugel, using the spoon to nestle it in the noodles. Repeat with the remaining jam, taking care to space the jam out evenly across the kugel. Bake until the kugel is set and golden brown, about 40 minutes. Transfer to a wire rack to cool for about 20 minutes before slicing. Just before serving, use a fine-mesh sieve to lightly dust with cinnamon. Serve warm or at room temperature.

BAKED RICE KUGEL

Sweetened rice kugels were once common on Ashkenazi tables, particularly in Lithuanian and Polish families. Like *lokshen* (noodle) kugels, they can be served as a side dish or dessert, and leftovers are great for breakfast.

Serves: 8–10
Preparation time: 15 minutes
Cooking time: 1 hour 20 minutes

- 2 teaspoons kosher salt
- 2 cups (400 g) long-grain white rice, rinsed and drained
- 6 tablespoons (85 g) unsalted butter, cut into pieces
- 6 eggs
- 1¼ cups (250 g) plus 2 tablespoons sugar
- 1 cup (240 g) sour cream
- ½ cup (120 ml/4 fl oz) half-and-half (single cream)
- 1 teaspoon vanilla extract
- ½ teaspoon finely grated lemon zest
- 1½ teaspoons ground cinnamon
- 1 cup (140 g) regular or golden raisins (sultanas)
- 1 large Gala apple, peeled and cut into ½-inch (1.25 cm) pieces

Lightly grease a 9 × 13-inch (23 × 33 cm) baking dish.

In a large saucepan, bring 4 cups (950 ml/32 fl oz) water and 1½ teaspoons of the salt to a boil over high heat. Stir in the rice, cover, reduce the heat to low, and simmer until the water is fully absorbed, 18–20 minutes. Remove the pan from the heat, add the butter to the hot rice, and stir to melt and combine. Set aside to cool slightly.

Preheat the oven to 350°F (180°C/Gas Mark 4).

In a large bowl, whisk together the eggs and 1¼ cups (250 g) sugar until fully incorporated. Add the sour cream, half-and-half (single cream), vanilla, lemon zest, 1 teaspoon of the cinnamon, and the remaining ½ teaspoon salt and whisk to combine. Fold in the cooked rice, raisins, and apple pieces.

Transfer the rice mixture to the prepared baking pan. In a small bowl, stir together the remaining 2 tablespoons sugar and remaining ½ teaspoon cinnamon. Sprinkle the cinnamon sugar evenly over the kugel and bake, uncovered, until lightly puffed and golden brown, 50–60 minutes. Let rest for at least 10 minutes before serving.

Jam and Poppy Seed Kugel

CARROT RING

This petite Ashkenazi carrot kugel, called *mehren kugel*, is gently sweet with a soft and custardy texture. It is traditionally served as a side dish on Shabbat and Rosh Hashanah, and some families make a variation with matzo meal for Passover.

Serves: 8
Preparation time: 20 minutes
Cooking time: 40 minutes

- 1¼ cups (175 g) all-purpose (plain) flour
- 1 teaspoon baking powder
- ½ teaspoon baking soda (bicarbonate of soda)
- 1½ teaspoons kosher salt
- ½ cup (90 g) light brown sugar
- ½ cup (120 ml/4 fl oz) vegetable oil
- ½ cup (115 g) unsweetened applesauce
- 2 eggs
- 2 teaspoons fresh lemon juice
- 6 medium carrots (about ¾ lb/340 g), grated on the large holes of a box grater

Preheat the oven to 350°F (180°C/Gas Mark 4). Grease a 10-cup Bundt pan.

In a medium bowl, whisk together the flour, baking powder, baking soda (bicarb), and salt.

In a large bowl, whisk together the brown sugar, oil, and applesauce until thoroughly combined. Add the eggs, one at a time, followed by the lemon juice, whisking well after each addition. Add the flour mixture to the wet mixture and whisk to combine, then fold in the carrots.

Pour the batter into the prepared pan and bake until gently puffed and the top springs back when lightly pressed, 35–40 minutes. Set the pan on a wire rack to cool for 30 minutes in the pan. Using a sharp knife, cut along the outer and inner rings of the pan, then gently turn out the carrot ring onto the rack and let cool. Serve warm or at room temperature.

GONDI

These popular Persian Jewish dumplings closely resemble Matzo Balls (page 220)—and indeed, just like matzo balls, they are often eaten on holidays. But instead of matzo meal, the dumpling batter is made from a rich mix of ground chicken and chickpea (gram) flour. *Gondi* are sometimes served as a snack or appetizer, but they are most often added to soup. Serve the tender dumplings in Chicken Soup (page 122). If desired, you can add a ½ teaspoon ground turmeric and a 15-ounce (425 g) can of rinsed and drained chickpeas to the soup as well.

Serves: 6–8
Preparation time: 30 minutes, plus chilling
Cooking time: 1 hour 10 minutes

- 1½ cups (180 g) chickpea (gram) flour
- 1 large onion, quartered
- 1 lb (455 g) ground (minced) chicken
- 1 egg
- 2 tablespoons vegetable oil
- ¾ teaspoon ground cardamom
- ½ teaspoon ground turmeric
- 2 teaspoons kosher salt, plus more for boiling
- ¼ teaspoon freshly ground black pepper

Preheat the oven to 350°F (180°C/Gas Mark 4)

Spread the chickpea (gram) flour in a small baking dish and toast in the oven, shaking the baking dish once or twice, until flour is golden, about 10 minutes. Remove from the oven and let cool.

Meanwhile, in a food processor, pulse the onion until very finely chopped. Pour off any excess liquid from the onion (but do not squeeze) and transfer to a bowl along with the toasted chickpea flour, chicken, egg, oil, cardamom, turmeric, salt, and pepper. Mix thoroughly with your hands, then cover the bowl and refrigerate for 1 hour.

When ready to cook, bring a large soup pot of salted water to a boil over high heat. Reduce the heat to medium-low. Using moistened hands, pinch off rounded tablespoons of the batter and roll into balls. Drop the balls into the water and gently stir to release any dumplings stuck to the bottom of the pot. Cover and cook, undisturbed, until the dumplings are tender, about 1 hour. Remove with a slotted spoon.

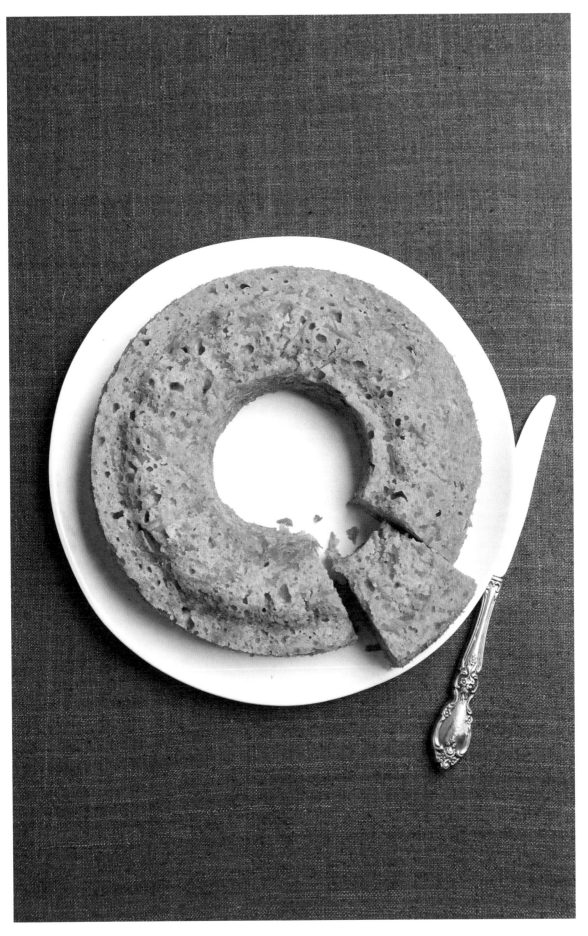

Carrot Ring

APPLE SCHALET

In parts of France and Germany, *schalet* is an interchangeable name for the Shabbat stew, Cholent (page 144). But the word also refers to a sweetened steamed bread pudding, closely related to kugel. *Schalets* are often filled with apple or pear and make a warming side dish or dessert. They can also be prepared with softened matzo meal for Passover.

Serves: 8
Preparation time: 20 minutes
Cooking time: 1 hour 45 minutes

- 2 tablespoons vegetable oil or unsalted butter
- 2 lb (910 g) baking apples, peeled, cored, and cut into ½-inch (1.25 cm) pieces
- ⅓ cup (75 ml/2½ fl oz) dry white wine
- 6 eggs
- ⅔ cup (130 g) sugar
- ½ teaspoon vanilla extract
- ½ teaspoon kosher salt
- 1 lb (455 g) day-old challah, crusts removed and cut into 2-inch (5 cm) pieces
- ½ cup (70 g) golden raisins (sultanas) or regular raisins

Preheat the oven to 350°F (180°C/Gas Mark 4). Lightly grease the bottoms and sides of a large Dutch oven (casserole) or other ovenproof pot with a lid.

In a large frying pan, heat the oil over medium heat. Add the apples and cook, stirring occasionally, until lightly softened, about 5 minutes. Add the white wine, increase the heat to medium-high, and cook, uncovered and stirring occasionally, until most of the liquid has evaporated and the apples are very tender, 5–7 minutes. Remove from the heat and let cool slightly.

Meanwhile, in a large bowl, whisk together the eggs, sugar, vanilla, and salt. In a separate bowl, combine the challah with water to cover. Let sit for a few seconds, then drain and squeeze dry. Add the bread to the egg mixture and stir to combine, then fold in the raisins.

Fold in the cooled apples and transfer the mixture to the prepared Dutch oven. Cover and bake until it is puffed and golden brown, 1–1½ hours. Set the Dutch oven on a wire rack to cool for 20 minutes before serving.

PEAR AND PRUNE KUGEL

In Alsace, France, Jewish families repurposed leftover bread into this beguiling baked pudding, called *birne schalet*, for the Shabbat and holiday table. Flavored with softened onions, fresh autumnal pears, and prunes, it elegantly straddles the sweet-savory divide.

Serves: 6–8
Preparation time: 20 minutes
Cooking time: 1 hour 45 minutes

- 2 tablespoons vegetable oil
- 1 large onion, finely chopped
- 1 teaspoon kosher salt, plus more as needed
- 4 eggs, beaten
- ⅓ cup (75 g) unsalted butter or nonhydrogenated margarine, melted
- ⅓ cup (65 g) sugar
- 1 lb (455 g) loaf sourdough bread, crust removed and torn into 1-inch (2.5 cm) pieces
- 1½ lb (680 g) Bosc pears, peeled and cut into 1-inch (2.5 cm) pieces
- ½ cup (90 g) pitted prunes, roughly chopped, soaked in water 5 minutes, and drained

Preheat the oven to 350°F (180°C/Gas Mark 4). Lightly grease the bottom and sides of a 9-inch (23 cm) round springform or cake pan. Cut out a round of parchment paper and line the bottom of the pan, then lightly grease the parchment.

In a large frying pan, heat the oil over medium heat. Add the onion and a generous pinch of salt and cook, stirring occasionally, until softened and browned, 10–15 minutes. Remove from the heat and let cool slightly.

Meanwhile, in a large bowl, whisk together the eggs, melted butter, sugar, and salt. In a separate bowl, combine the bread pieces with water to cover. Let sit for a few seconds, then drain and squeeze dry. Add the bread to the egg mixture.

Add the cooled browned onion, pears, and prunes to the bowl and stir well to combine. Transfer the mixture to the prepared pan and bake until it is deep golden brown, about 1½ hours. Set the pan on a wire rack to cool for 20 minutes before serving.

Apple Schalet

MAIN DISHES

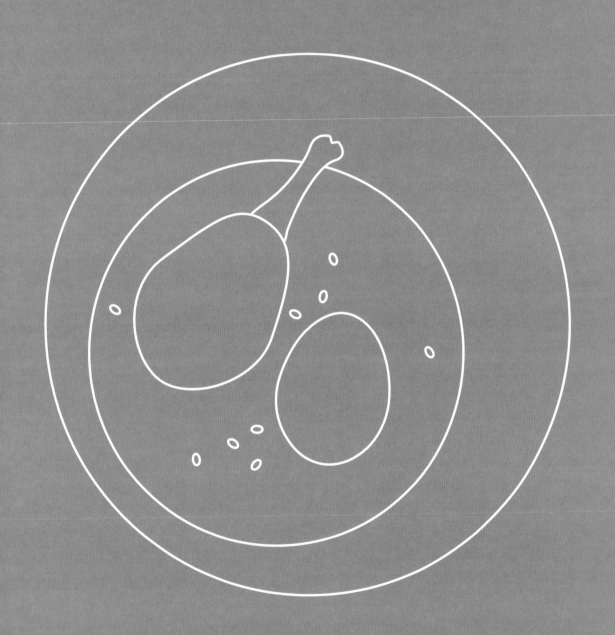

GUVETCH

This ratatouille-like stew gets its name from a *güveç*—the Turkish earthenware pot originally used to prepare it. Endless variations of the dish can be found across the Balkans, employing a wide array of vegetables and sometimes meat. Romanian Jews serve a vegetarian version, typically alongside Mamaliga (page 167). The dish takes some time to prepare, but can be made several days ahead and reheated or served at room temperature.

Serves: 8
Preparation time: 35 minutes
Cooking time: 2 hours

- 6 tablespoons vegetable oil or extra-virgin olive oil
- 2 onions, halved through the root and thinly sliced
- 10 garlic cloves, thinly sliced
- 1½ teaspoons kosher salt, plus more as needed
- 2 large zucchini (courgettes), about 1 lb (455 g), halved lengthwise and sliced into ½-inch (1.25 cm) half-moons
- 1 large red bell pepper, cut into 1-inch (2.5 cm) pieces
- 1 medium carrot, thinly sliced
- ½ lb (225 g) green beans, ends trimmed, halved
- ½ lb (225 g) mushrooms, stems discarded, sliced
- 1 can (28 oz/795 g) whole peeled tomatoes
- ½ cup (120 ml/4 fl oz) vegetable stock or water
- 1 teaspoon sugar
- ½ teaspoon onion powder
- 1 bay leaf
- Freshly ground black pepper
- Finely chopped fresh parsley and crumbled feta, for serving

Preheat the oven to 350°F (180°C/Gas Mark 4).

In a large Dutch oven (casserole) or other ovenproof pot with a lid, heat 4 tablespoons of the oil over medium heat. Add the onions, garlic, and a pinch of salt and cook, stirring occasionally, until softened, 6–8 minutes. Add the zucchini (courgettes), bell pepper, carrot, green beans, and mushrooms and cook, stirring occasionally, until just starting to soften, 8–10 minutes.

Meanwhile, add the tomatoes with their juice to a large bowl and, using your hands, gently squeeze the tomatoes to break them up.

Add the tomatoes and juice to the pot along with the stock, sugar, onion powder, bay leaf, salt, and a generous amount of pepper. Increase the heat to medium-high and bring to a boil. Drizzle the remaining 2 tablespoons oil on top, cover, and transfer to the oven. Bake, stirring once or twice, until the vegetables are very soft, 1–1½ hours.

Remove from the oven, taste, and add more salt and pepper if desired. Discard the bay leaf and serve warm or at room temperature, sprinkled with parsley and feta.

GROUNDNUT STEW

The Abayudaya—a small Jewish community in Eastern Uganda—maintains a largely vegetarian diet. On Shabbat, variations of this saucy peanut stew (groundnut is another name for peanut) are often served as part of the main course alongside a cornmeal porridge called *posho* or a steamed and mashed green banana dish called *matoke*. It is also delicious spooned over rice or slices of roasted or boiled sweet potatoes.

Serves: 4–6
Preparation time: 15 minutes
Cooking time: 55 minutes

- 1½ cups (210 g) unsalted roasted peanuts
- 4 tablespoons peanut (groundnut) oil or vegetable oil
- 2 onions, finely chopped
- 1¼ teaspoons kosher salt, plus more as needed
- 2 large plum tomatoes, finely chopped
- 1½ teaspoons curry powder
- ⅛ teaspoon cayenne pepper

In a food processor, pulse the peanuts, scraping down the sides of the bowl a few times, until very finely ground (but not turning into a paste). Set aside.

In a large saucepan, heat the oil over medium heat. Add the onions and a pinch of salt and cook, stirring occasionally, until softened and browned, 8–10 minutes. Add the tomatoes, curry powder, and cayenne and cook, stirring occasionally, until the tomatoes soften, 2–3 minutes.

Stir in the ground peanuts, 3 cups (710 ml/24 fl oz) water, and salt. Increase the heat to medium-high and bring to a boil. Reduce the heat to low and cook, stirring often, until it thickens into a soupy stew, 35–40 minutes. Taste and add more salt, if desired.

Guvetch

THE SEPHARDI ROSH HASHANAH SEDER

The Rosh Hashanah custom of eating apples dipped in honey as a symbol of one's wishes for a sweet, round year ahead is well documented. Less well known is the Rosh Hashanah "seder." While not formally set like a Passover seder, many Sephardi communities take food imagery to a delicious extreme on Rosh Hashanah, serving and reciting blessings over a variety of foods that hold symbolic significance.

Pomegranates are eaten with the hope that one's good deeds in the coming year will be as numerous as the fruit's seeds. Beet leaves (called *selek* in Hebrew) are eaten to ward off enemies. (*Selek* resembles the word *yistalku*, which means "retreat.") Black-eyed peas (called *rubiyah* in Hebrew and *loubia* in Arabic) are related to the Hebrew word for "increase," and are served with wishes for prosperity. Other common seder foods include dates, Swiss chard, pumpkin or gourds, leeks and scallions (spring onions), and even fish heads, which symbolize a desire to be leaders ("heads"), rather than followers ("tails"), in the coming year.

BLACK-EYED PEA STEW

Jews from Egypt and Syria traditionally eat a stew made from black-eyed peas (called *loubia* in Arabic) on Rosh Hashanah. The peas symbolize one's wishes for success or fertility in the New Year. This stew can be prepared with lamb, but makes a full-flavored vegetarian main dish without any meat.

Serves: 6
Preparation time: 15 minutes, plus soaking
Cooking time: 2 hours 5 minutes

- 2 cups (360 g) dried black-eyed peas (beans)
- 2 teaspoons baking soda (bicarbonate of soda)
- ¼ cup (60 ml/2 fl oz) extra-virgin olive oil, plus more for drizzling
- 1 medium onion, finely chopped
- 2 medium carrots, finely chopped
- 1 celery stalk, finely chopped
- 6 garlic cloves, finely chopped
- 2 teaspoons kosher salt, plus more as needed
- 1 teaspoon ground cumin
- ½ teaspoon onion powder
- 2 teaspoons sugar
- 1 teaspoon smoked paprika
- ½ teaspoon ground ginger
- ¼ teaspoon cayenne pepper
- 1 can (14½ oz/411 g) diced (chopped) tomatoes
- 2 tablespoons tomato paste (purée)
- 3½ cups (830 ml/28 fl oz) vegetable stock, plus more as needed
- ½ teaspoon freshly ground black pepper, plus more as needed
- Chopped fresh cilantro (coriander) or parsley, for serving

In a large bowl, combine the black-eyed peas (beans), baking soda (bicarb), and water to cover by about 2 inches (5 cm). Cover the bowl with a tea towel and soak peas for at least 8 hours or overnight. Drain, rinse, and drain again.

In a large saucepan, heat the oil over medium heat. Add the onion, carrots, celery, garlic, and a generous pinch of salt and cook, stirring occasionally, until the vegetables begin to soften, 8–10 minutes. Add the cumin, onion powder, sugar, smoked paprika, ginger, and cayenne and cook, stirring, until fragrant, 1–2 minutes.

Stir in the diced tomatoes with their juice and the tomato paste (purée). Bring to a simmer and cook, stirring occasionally, until the mixture thickens slightly, about 5 minutes. Add the drained peas, stock, salt, and black pepper. Increase the heat to medium-high and bring the mixture to a simmer, then reduce the heat to medium-low, partially cover, and cook, stirring occasionally, until the peas are tender and creamy, 1½–2 hours. If the pot begins to look dry during cooking, add more stock, ½ cup (120 ml/4 fl oz) at a time. Taste and add more salt and pepper, if desired.

Remove the pan from the heat and let rest for about 10 minutes. Serve hot or warm, drizzled with more oil and sprinkled with chopped cilantro (coriander).

EGGPLANT AND TOMATO STEW

This Persian eggplant (aubergine) and tomato stew, which is flavored with warm spices like cumin, cinnamon, and turmeric, would make a delicious addition to a Sukkot or early-autumn Shabbat table. Called *khoresh bademjan*, it traditionally gets its tangy flavor from pickled sour grapes called *ghooreh*, but pomegranate molasses, which is easier to source, works well, too. Serve the stew over rice and top it with dollops of the Persian *borani esfanaj* (Spinach Yogurt Dip, page 100).

Serves: 6
Preparation time: 25 minutes
Cooking time: 40 minutes

- ¼ cup (60 ml/2 fl oz) plus 2 tablespoons extra-virgin olive oil
- 2 onions, finely chopped
- 3 garlic cloves, thinly sliced
- 2 lb (910 g) eggplant (aubergine), peeled and cut into ½-inch (1.25 cm) pieces
- 1½ teaspoons ground cumin
- 1 teaspoon sweet paprika
- ½ teaspoon ground cinnamon
- ½ teaspoon ground turmeric
- 1 can (28 oz/795 g) whole peeled tomatoes
- 3 tablespoons pomegranate molasses
- 1½ teaspoons kosher salt, plus more as needed
- ¼ teaspoon freshly ground black pepper
- Finely chopped fresh mint and parsley, for serving

In a large saucepan, heat ¼ cup (60 ml/2 fl oz) of the oil over medium heat. Add the onions and garlic and cook, stirring occasionally, until softened and lightly browned, 8–10 minutes. Add the remaining 2 tablespoons oil and the eggplant (aubergine) and cook, stirring occasionally, until the eggplant softens, about 10 minutes. Add the cumin, paprika, cinnamon, and turmeric and cook, stirring, until fragrant, about 1 minute.

Add the tomatoes to a medium bowl and crush with your hands. Add the crushed tomatoes and juice to the saucepan along with the pomegranate molasses, salt, and pepper. Bring to a boil, then reduce the heat to low, cover, and cook, stirring occasionally, until the eggplant is very tender, about 15 minutes. Taste and add more salt, if needed. Serve hot, sprinkled with fresh mint and parsley.

SPICED SPLIT PEA STEW

Ethiopian Jews traditionally serve this savory stew, called *kik wot*, spooned on top of injera, but is also tasty with *dabo* (Spiced Honey Bread, page 50), the sweet bread enjoyed on Shabbat, or over rice.

Serves: 4–6
Preparation time: 10 minutes
Cooking time: 1 hour

- 2 cups (400 g) yellow or green split peas, rinsed and drained
- ⅓ cup (75 ml/2½ fl oz) vegetable oil
- 2 yellow onions, finely chopped
- 4 garlic cloves, minced or pushed through a press
- 1 tablespoon minced or grated fresh ginger
- 1½ teaspoons Berbere (page 414)
- 1 teaspoon onion powder
- 2½ teaspoons kosher salt, plus more as needed

Bring a large saucepan of water (enough to cover the peas by at least 2 inches/5 cm) to a boil over high heat. Add the split peas and cook, stirring occasionally, until very tender and just beginning to break apart, 30–35 minutes. Drain well in a fine-mesh sieve and set aside.

Wipe out the saucepan, then add the oil and set it over medium heat. (Or use a separate saucepan, if desired.) When the oil is hot, add the onions and cook, stirring occasionally, until softened and lightly browned, 6–8 minutes. Add the garlic and ginger and cook, stirring, until fragrant, about 2 minutes. Add the berbere and onion powder and stir until fragrant, about 1 minute.

Stir in the cooked split peas, the salt, and 1½ cups (355 ml/12 fl oz) water. Bring to a simmer, then reduce the heat to low, partially cover, and cook, stirring often, until the stew thickens, about 20 minutes. If the stew looks too dry while cooking, stir in more water, ½ cup (120 ml/4 fl oz) at a time. Taste and add more salt, if needed. Serve hot.

SEVEN-VEGETABLE TAGINE

On Rosh Hashanah, Moroccan Jews serve this produce- and legume-laden stew over steamed couscous. Many of the ingredients—carrots, turnips, zucchini (courgettes), chickpeas, and onions—hold symbolic significance for the Jewish New Year (page 12). Simmered together with sweet and warming spices, they celebrate the bounty of the season. Measure out all of the spices before turning on the heat, so they can be added all at once.

Serves: 6–8
Preparation time: 20 minutes
Cooking time: 55 minutes

- ¼ cup (30 g) slivered almonds
- ¼ cup (60 ml/2 fl oz) extra-virgin olive oil
- 2 onions, halved through the root and thinly sliced
- 4 plum tomatoes (about 1 lb/455 g), seeded and chopped
- 2 garlic cloves, finely chopped
- 1 tablespoon grated fresh ginger
- 1 teaspoon ground cinnamon
- 1 teaspoon sweet paprika
- ½ teaspoon ground coriander
- ½ teaspoon ground cumin
- ½ teaspoon ground turmeric
- 2 teaspoons Harissa (page 409)
- 1 can (15 oz/425 g) chickpeas, rinsed and drained
- 2 zucchini (courgettes), halved lengthwise and sliced crosswise into ½-inch (1.25 cm) half-moons
- 2 cups (280 g) peeled, cubed sweet potato
- 2 medium turnips, peeled and cut into ½-inch (1.25 cm) pieces
- 2 large carrots, halved lengthwise and cut crosswise into ½-inch (1.25 cm) pieces
- ⅓ cup (45 g) golden raisins (sultanas)
- 2½ cups (590 ml/20 fl oz) vegetable stock
- 1 teaspoon kosher salt, plus more as needed
- Freshly ground black pepper
- Chopped fresh parsley, for garnish

In a small, dry frying pan, toast the almonds over medium-low heat, stirring occasionally, until fragrant and lightly browned, 5–7 minutes. Remove from the heat and set aside to cool.

In a medium saucepan, heat the oil over medium-high heat. Add the onions and cook, stirring occasionally, until softened and lightly browned, 8–10 minutes. Add the tomatoes and cook, stirring occasionally, until softened, 3–5 minutes. Add the garlic, ginger, cinnamon, paprika, coriander, cumin, turmeric, and harissa and cook, stirring, until fragrant, 1–2 minutes.

Add the chickpeas, zucchini (courgettes), sweet potato, turnips, carrots, golden raisins (sultanas), stock, salt, and a generous amount of pepper and bring the mixture to a simmer. Reduce the heat to low, cover, and cook until the sweet potato and carrots are tender, about 20 minutes. Uncover and continue cooking, stirring occasionally, until the liquid thickens slightly, 5–10 minutes. Taste and add more salt, if desired. Serve hot, sprinkled with parsley and toasted almonds.

BULGUR WITH CHEESE

Syrian Jews hailing from Aleppo typically serve this comforting mix of bulgur, softened onions, and salty cheese, called *burghol bi jibn*, as a quick Thursday night dinner. The simplicity of the meal allows home cooks to focus on preparing the following night's Shabbat dinner feast. While not traditional, a sprinkle of chopped fresh parsley or mint adds a hint of vibrant flavor to the dish.

Serves: 6
Preparation time: 10 minutes
Cooking time: 20 minutes

- 1½ cups (240 g) medium bulgur
- 1 teaspoon kosher salt, plus more as needed
- 3 cups (710 ml/24 fl oz) boiling water
- 3 tablespoons vegetable oil
- 1 large onion, halved through the root and thinly sliced
- 2 tablespoons (30 g) unsalted butter, cut into pieces
- 8 oz (225 g) Halloumi cheese, cut into small cubes

In a heatproof medium bowl, combine the bulgur, salt, and boiling water and let sit until the bulgur is tender but still chewy, about 15 minutes. Drain well and transfer to a large bowl.

Meanwhile, in a large frying pan, heat the oil over medium heat. Add the onion and a pinch of salt and cook, stirring occasionally, until softened and lightly browned, about 10 minutes. Remove the onion from the heat and immediately add to the warm bulgur along with the butter and about half of the cheese. Stir until the butter melts and the cheese softens. Transfer to a serving dish and top with the remaining cheese.

Seven-Vegetable Tagine

CRUSTLESS SPINACH AND ZUCCHINI QUICHE

Syrian home cooks make *jibn*, essentially a crustless quiche, with all sorts of vegetables including spinach and zucchini (courgettes). Typically, the vegetables appear alone in the dish, but they are especially delicious mixed together. *Jibn* is Arabic for "cheese," and the golden brown, savory quiche always includes a copious amount of salty, melty cheese. Traditionally served as part of the Yom Kippur break-fast meal, *jibn* also makes a tasty weeknight meal paired with a fresh salad and toasted bread or pita. To speed up the preparation, use the shredding disc of a food processor to quickly shred the zucchini and cheddar.

Serves: 6
Preparation time: 25 minutes
Cooking time: 1 hour 10 minutes

- 2 tablespoons plus 1 teaspoon vegetable oil
- 1 medium onion, finely chopped
- ½ teaspoon kosher salt, plus more as needed
- 1 lb (455 g) zucchini (courgettes), peeled and grated on the large holes of a box grater
- 1 package (10 oz/285 g) frozen spinach, thawed and squeezed dry
- 6 eggs, lightly beaten
- 1½ cups (120 g) grated sharp cheddar cheese
- 1½ cups (330 g) full-fat cottage cheese
- ½ teaspoon onion powder
- ½ teaspoon freshly ground black pepper

Preheat the oven to 350°F (180°C/Gas Mark 4). Brush a 9-inch (23 cm) square baking pan with the 1 teaspoon of oil. Line the pan with parchment paper, allowing the parchment to hang over by a couple of inches on two opposite sides.

In a large frying pan, heat the 2 tablespoons oil over medium heat. Add the onion and a pinch of salt and cook, stirring occasionally, until soft and translucent, 5–7 minutes. Increase the heat to medium-high, add the zucchini (courgettes) and spinach, and cook until all of the liquid has evaporated, 7–10 minutes. Remove from the heat and let cool slightly.

Meanwhile, in a large bowl, mix together the eggs, cheddar, cottage cheese, onion powder, salt, and pepper.

Fold the cooled zucchini mixture into the egg-cheese mixture, then transfer to the prepared baking pan. Bake, uncovered, until cooked through and lightly browned on top, 45–55 minutes. Set on a wire rack to cool. Use the overhanging parchment to gently transfer the *jibn* to a cutting board. Slice into squares and serve warm or at room temperature.

MATZO LASAGNA

Lasagna made with sheets of matzo, instead of the traditional wide and flat noodles, has emerged as a popular Passover dish in America in recent decades. While baking, the matzo softens and soaks up the sauce and cheese, yielding a surprisingly convincing facsimile of the Italian casserole.

Serves: 8–10
Preparation time: 30 minutes
Cooking time: 1 hour 25 minutes

• 3 tablespoons extra-virgin olive oil
• 2 large onions, finely chopped
• 1¼ teaspoons kosher salt, plus more as needed
• 1 medium zucchini (courgette), finely chopped
• 1 lb (455 g) cremini (chestnut) mushrooms, finely chopped
• 4 garlic cloves, finely chopped
• 4 cups (960 g) ricotta cheese
• 2 eggs, lightly beaten
• 2 cups (160 g) shredded mozzarella cheese
• 20 basil leaves, sliced into a chiffonade
• 1 teaspoon dried oregano
• ½ teaspoon freshly ground black pepper
• 9 sheets matzo
• 4 cups (950 ml/32 fl oz) good-quality marinara sauce
• ¼ cup (20 g) finely grated parmesan cheese

Preheat the oven to 350°F (180°C/Gas Mark 4).

In a medium frying pan, heat the olive oil over medium heat. Add the onions and a pinch of salt and cook, stirring occasionally, until softened and lightly browned, 5–7 minutes.

Add the zucchini (courgette), mushrooms, and garlic and cook, stirring occasionally, until the vegetables are softened and the liquid has evaporated, 10–15 minutes. Remove from the heat and set aside to cool slightly.

In a medium bowl, stir together the ricotta, eggs, ½ cup (40 g) of the mozzarella, the basil, oregano, salt, and pepper.

Fill a shallow container with warm water. Dip 3 sheets of the matzo in the water and let soften for 1–2 minutes (not longer). Spoon 2 cups (475 ml/16 fl oz) of the marinara into the bottom of a 9 × 13-inch (23 × 33 cm) baking dish. Shake the excess water off the softened matzo pieces and arrange in the baking dish, breaking the sheets as necessary to fit. Top with about half of the ricotta mixture, followed by half of the vegetable mixture. Repeat with another 1 cup (240 ml/8 fl oz) of the marinara, 3 more softened matzos, and the remaining ricotta and vegetable mixture.

Soften the remaining 3 pieces of matzo and arrange on top. Spoon the remaining 1 cup (240 ml/8 fl oz) marinara on top. Sprinkle evenly with the remaining 1½ cups (120 g) mozzarella and the parmesan. Cover with foil and bake until heated through, about 45 minutes. Uncover and continue cooking until the cheese is lightly browned, 10–15 more minutes. Let stand for a few minutes before serving.

TARTE FLAMBÉE

In Alsace, France, a wood-fired flatbread covered with thick cream and fresh cheeses, browned onions, and lardons (pieces of pork fat) is commonly enjoyed on Sunday nights. Jews from Alsace adopted the tradition of *tarte flambée* (sometimes called *flammekueche*, or "flame-cooked"), either omitting the pork entirely, or substituting sautéed mushrooms. Some Jewish families baked *tarte flambée* on Friday afternoons as a quick and filling pre-Shabbat lunch for the family, using extra challah dough as the base. It is delicious and rich as is, but can be further dressed up with a sprinkle of fresh thyme or a touch of grated nutmeg.

Serves: 4
Preparation time: 25 minutes, plus rising
Cooking time: 40 minutes

For the dough:
- 1 packet (¼ oz/7 g) active dry yeast (2¼ teaspoons)
- 1 teaspoon sugar
- 1 cup (240 ml/8 fl oz) warm water (110°F/43°C)
- 2½ cups (350 g) all-purpose (plain) flour, plus more for kneading and rolling
- 1 teaspoon kosher salt
- Vegetable oil, for greasing the bowl

For the topping:
- 3 tablespoons vegetable oil
- 2 medium onions, halved through the root and thinly sliced
- ½ teaspoon kosher salt, plus more as needed
- ½ lb (225 g) cremini (chestnut) mushrooms, stems discarded, thinly sliced
- ¾ cup (180 g) crème fraîche or full-fat sour cream
- ½ cup (120 g) fromage blanc or ricotta cheese
- ½ teaspoon freshly ground black pepper
- Snipped chives, for serving

Make the dough: In a very large bowl, stir together the yeast, sugar, and warm water. Let sit until foaming, 5–10 minutes.

Meanwhile, in a separate large bowl, whisk together the flour and salt.

Add the flour mixture to the yeast mixture and stir until a shaggy dough begins to form. Turn the dough out onto a lightly floured surface and knead well, adding a little more flour, as necessary, until a supple, elastic dough forms, about 10 minutes. (The kneading can also be done in a stand mixer fitted with a dough hook, 5–7 minutes.) Grease a large bowl with about 1 teaspoon of oil, add the dough, and turn to coat. Cover with plastic wrap (cling film) or a tea towel and let sit in a warm place until doubled in size, about 1½ hours.

Meanwhile, make the topping: In large frying pan, heat the vegetable oil over medium heat. Add the onions and a generous pinch of salt. Cook, stirring occasionally, until softened and lightly browned, 10–15 minutes. Add the mushrooms and continue cooking until tender, 5–10 minutes. Remove from the heat and let cool.

Preheat the oven to 450°F (230°C/Gas Mark 8). Line a large sheet pan with parchment paper.

Gently deflate the dough with the heel of your hand and, on a lightly floured surface, roll it into a large rectangle that fits inside the sheet pan. Transfer the dough to the prepared pan.

In a medium bowl, stir together the crème fraîche, fromage blanc, salt, and pepper. Spread over the dough leaving a ½-inch (1.25 cm) border. Top evenly with the mushroom and onions. Bake until browned and bubbling, 15–18 minutes. Let sit for 5 minutes before slicing. Serve hot, with snipped chives sprinkled on top.

Tarte Flambée

KUKU SABZI

This verdant, herb-packed frittata is one of the treasures of Iranian cuisine. Persian Jews traditionally serve it on Shabbat, sliced into small wedges as part of a mezze spread. It makes an equally lovely centerpiece for a light lunch or dinner dolloped with a little yogurt or crème fraîche. To serve it during Passover, substitute matzo meal or potato starch.

Serves: 6–8
Preparation time: 15 minutes
Cooking time: 40 minutes

- ¼ cup (60 ml/2 fl oz) vegetable oil, plus more for greasing the pan
- 2 medium onions, finely chopped
- ¾ teaspoon kosher salt, plus more as needed
- 7 eggs
- 2 tablespoons all-purpose (plain) flour
- 1 teaspoon baking powder
- 2 cups (100 g) finely chopped fresh flat-leaf parsley
- 1 cup (50 g) finely chopped fresh dill
- 2 garlic cloves, minced or pushed through a press
- 1 teaspoon ground turmeric
- ¾ teaspoon onion powder
- ¼ teaspoon crushed pepper flakes
- Freshly ground black pepper
- ¼ cup (35 g) dried currants or barberries (optional)

Preheat the oven to 375°F (190°C/Gas Mark 5). Brush the bottom and sides of a 9-inch (23 cm) springform pan with oil. Line the bottom of the pan with a round of parchment paper, then lightly grease with oil.

In a large frying pan, heat the oil over medium heat. Add the onions, season with a little salt, and cook, stirring occasionally, until softened and lightly browned, 8–10 minutes. Set aside to cool slightly.

In a large bowl, whisk together the eggs, flour, baking powder, parsley, dill, garlic, turmeric, onion powder, pepper flakes, salt, and a generous amount of pepper. Fold in the browned onions and currants (if using).

Pour the mixture into the prepared pan and bake until golden brown and cooked through, 30–35 minutes. Set aside to cool for 15 minutes. Gently remove from the springform pan and slice into wedges or squares.

LEEK AND POTATO FRITTATA

This Sephardi baked egg and vegetable dish has roots in pre-Inquisition Spain, and remains popular on Passover and year-round amongst Jews hailing from Greece, Turkey, and Rhodes. The dish's traditional name, quajado, means "coagulated" in Ladino, the Judeo-Spanish language. While perhaps not the most appetizing descriptor, the dish itself is delicious and makes a tasty side dish for baked fish or a vegetarian main on its own.

Serves: 6–8
Preparation time: 15 minutes
Cooking time: 1 hour 10 minutes

- ½ lb (225 g) Yukon Gold potatoes, peeled and cut into chunks
- 3 tablespoons (45 g) unsalted butter or extra-virgin olive oil
- 5 small leeks, white and light-green parts, thinly sliced
- ½ teaspoon kosher salt, plus more as needed
- 7 eggs, lightly beaten
- 8 oz (225 g) feta cheese, finely crumbled
- 1 cup (90 g) finely grated kashkaval or parmesan cheese
- ½ teaspoon onion powder
- ½ teaspoon crushed pepper flakes
- ½ teaspoon freshly ground black pepper

Bring a large saucepan of water to a boil. Add the potatoes and boil until tender, 15–20 minutes. Drain, mash well with a potato masher, and set aside to cool.

Preheat the oven to 350°F (180°C/Gas Mark 4). Lightly grease a 9-inch (23 cm) round cake pan. Line the bottom of the pan with a round of parchment paper.

In a large frying pan, melt the butter over medium heat. Add the leeks and a generous pinch of salt and cook, until most of the liquid has evaporated, 15–20 minutes. Remove from the heat and let cool.

In a large bowl, whisk the eggs, then stir in the feta, kashkaval, onion powder, pepper flakes, salt, and pepper. Fold the mashed potatoes and leeks into the egg mixture until well combined.

Transfer to the prepared baking dish and bake until puffed and lightly browned, 40–50 minutes. Let cool for 15 minutes before slicing.

VEGETABLE CUTLETS WITH MUSHROOM GRAVY

Long before vegetable burgers were standard menu fare, Jewish dairy restaurants—which, in contrast to the delicatessen, offered no meat dishes—served hearty cutlets made from a variety of vegetables and legumes. The patties were sometimes served with sour cream, but often came decadently topped with savory mushroom gravy (usually labeled as "brown gravy"). The era of the old-school dairy restaurant (page 126) has mostly passed, but these cutlets are too delicious to forget. Softening the vegetables in butter adds wonderful flavor, but those who prefer to go dairy-free can substitute margerine.

Serves: 4–6
Preparation time: 40 minutes, plus cooling
Cooking time: 40 minutes

For the cutlets:
- 1 lb (455 g) russet (baking) potatoes, peeled and cut into chunks
- 3 tablespoons (45 g) unsalted butter or nonhydrogenated margarine
- 1 small onion, finely chopped
- 1 medium carrot, finely chopped
- ½ lb (225 g) white button mushrooms, stems discarded, finely chopped
- 3 eggs, lightly beaten
- 1 cup (120 g) thawed frozen peas
- ½ cup (70 g) dried breadcrumbs
- 1½ teaspoons kosher salt
- ½ teaspoon freshly ground black pepper
- Vegetable oil, for frying

For the mushroom gravy:
- 4 tablespoons (60 g) unsalted butter or nonhydrogenated margarine
- 1 onion, finely chopped
- 1 celery stalk, finely chopped
- 2 garlic cloves, finely chopped
- ½ lb (225 g) white or cremini (chestnut) mushrooms, stems discarded, thinly sliced
- 1 tablespoon tomato paste (purée)
- ½ teaspoon sweet paprika
- ¼ teaspoon dried thyme
- ¾ teaspoon kosher salt, plus more as needed
- ¼ teaspoon freshly ground black pepper
- ¼ cup (35 g) all-purpose (plain) flour
- 2 cups (475 ml/16 fl oz) vegetable stock

Make the cutlets: In a medium pot, combine the potatoes with water to cover by 2 inches (5 cm). Bring to a boil over high heat, then reduce the heat to medium-high and cook until the potatoes are tender, about 20 minutes. Drain, transfer to a large bowl, and mash with a potato masher until smooth.

Meanwhile, in a large frying pan, heat the butter over medium heat. Add the onion and carrot and cook, stirring occasionally, until softened and lightly browned, 6–8 minutes. Add the mushrooms and cook, stirring often, until softened and browned, about 10 minutes. Remove from the heat and let cool slightly.

Add the cooled mushroom mixture to the mashed potatoes along with the eggs, peas, breadcrumbs, salt, and pepper and mix thoroughly to combine. Refrigerate the mixture for 30 minutes to allow it to firm up.

Line a large plate with a few layers of paper towels. In a large frying pan, heat a couple of tablespoons of oil over medium heat. Scoop out ¼ cup (60 g) of the cutlet mixture at a time and form into patties about 3 inches (7.5 cm) wide and ½ inch (1.25 cm) thick. Working in batches of 4–5, add the patties to the oil and cook until browned on one side, about 3 minutes. Flip with a spatula and continue cooking on the other side until golden, 2–3 minutes. Adjust the heat if the patties are browning too quickly or not quickly enough, and add more oil to the pan as it begins to look dry. Transfer the vegetable cutlets to the paper towel–lined plate to drain.

Make the mushroom gravy: In a large frying pan, heat the butter over medium heat. Add the onion, celery, and garlic and cook, stirring occasionally, until softened and lightly browned, 6–8 minutes. Add the mushrooms and cook, stirring often, until softened and browned, about 10 minutes. Stir in the tomato paste (purée), paprika, thyme, salt, and pepper. Sprinkle the flour over and stir to coat the vegetables, then add the stock a little at a time, stirring constantly. Bring the mixture to a simmer and cook until thickened into a gravy, about 5 minutes.

Arrange cutlets on a serving platter. Spoon some of the gravy over the cutlets and serve immediately, with the remaining gravy alongside.

DOUBLE-CRUSTED VEGETABLE PIE

The name for this savory Sephardi pie, *tapada*, comes from the Spanish verb *tapar*, which means "to cover." The dough can be a bit finicky to work with, but makes a tender crust for the mashed eggplant (aubergine) and cheese filling. (*Tapadas* can also be filled with spinach, potatoes, and other vegetables.) Turkish Jews serve *tapadas* on Shavuot, but they also make delightful summer picnic fare.

Serves: 8
Preparation time: 30 minutes
Cooking time: 1 hour 15 minutes

For the filling:
- 2 lb (910 g) eggplant (aubergine), about 2 medium
- 3 tablespoons vegetable oil
- 2 bunches scallions (spring onions), white and green parts, thinly sliced
- 4 oz (115 g) crumbled feta cheese
- ½ cup (45 g) finely grated parmesan or kashkaval cheese
- 2 eggs, beaten
- ¼ teaspoon smoked paprika
- ½ teaspoon kosher salt
- ¼ teaspoon freshly ground black pepper

For the dough:
- 3 cups (420 g) all-purpose (plain) flour, plus more for rolling
- 1½ teaspoons kosher salt
- ½ cup (120 ml/4 fl oz) vegetable oil
- 1 stick (4 oz/115 g) unsalted butter, cut into pieces, at room temperature
- 3 tablespoons dried breadcrumbs
- 1 egg, beaten

Make the filling: Preheat the broiler (grill) and set the rack in the lowest position. Line a large sheet pan with foil.

Prick the eggplants (aubergines) in several places with a fork and lay on the sheet pan. Broil (grill), turning every 5–10 minutes, until the skins burst and the flesh is completely soft, 25–30 minutes. Remove from the oven, carefully slit the eggplants down the center, and place, slit side down, in a colander to cool and drain.

Once cool enough to handle, peel off and discard the skin and place the eggplant pulp in a large bowl. Mash with a potato masher until a chunky paste forms.

In a frying pan, heat the oil over medium heat. Add the scallions (green onions) and cook, stirring often, until wilted and lightly browned, about 10 minutes. Remove from the heat and let cool slightly, then add to the eggplant along with the feta, parmesan, eggs, smoked paprika, salt, and pepper. Mix well to combine and set aside.

Make the dough: In a food processor, combine the flour, salt, oil, butter, and ¼ cup (60 ml/2 fl oz) water and pulse, scraping down the sides of the bowl as needed, until the dough comes together. Turn the dough out onto a lightly floured surface and knead briefly until smooth.

Preheat the oven to 375°F (190°C/Gas Mark 5).

Divide the dough into 2 pieces, one slightly bigger than the other. On a floured surface using a floured rolling pin, roll out the bigger piece of dough into a large, ⅛-inch (3 mm) thick round. Nestle into a 10-inch (25 cm) pie plate, pressing gently to fit it snugly into the sides and bottom, and to repair any cracks. Sprinkle the breadcrumbs evenly into the pie plate, then spoon the filling on top. Roll out the second piece of dough into a large, ⅛-inch (3 mm) thick round and fit on top. (If the dough gets too soft to work with, place it in the refrigerator for 10 minutes to firm up.) Trim off the excess dough and press or crimp the edges to seal. Cut a few slits in the top of the pie and then brush evenly with a thin layer of beaten egg. (You will not use all of it.)

Bake until the crust is golden brown and the filling is set, 40–50 minutes. Set the pie plate on a wire rack to cool. Serve warm.

EGGPLANT GRATIN

Dating back to pre-Inquisition Spain, this Arabic eggplant (aubergine) and cheese casserole, called *almodrote de berenjena*, became a staple of the Spanish Jewish diet. It continues to be a presence on Sephardi tables today.

Serves: 6–8
Preparation time: 15 minutes, plus cooling
Cooking time: 1 hour 15 minutes

• 3 lb (1.35 kg) eggplant (aubergine; about 3 medium)
• 6 eggs, beaten
• 8 oz (225 g) feta cheese, crumbled
• 1½ cups (120 g) shredded mozzarella or Gruyère cheese
• ½ cup (70 g) dried breadcrumbs or matzo meal
• ¾ teaspoon kosher salt
• ¼ teaspoon freshly ground black pepper
• Vegetable oil, for greasing the pan

Preheat the broiler (grill) and set the rack in the lowest position. Line a large sheet pan with foil.

Prick the eggplants (aubergines) in several places with a fork and lay on the prepared sheet pan. Broil (grill), turning every 5–10 minutes, until the skins burst and the flesh is completely soft, 25–30 minutes. Remove from the oven, carefully slit the eggplants down the center, and place, slit side down, in a colander to cool and drain.

Once cool enough to handle, peel off and discard the skin and place the eggplant pulp in a large bowl. Mash with a potato masher until a chunky paste forms. Add the beaten eggs, feta, 1 cup (80 g) of the mozzarella, the breadcrumbs, salt, and pepper.

Preheat the oven to 375°F (190°C/Gas Mark 5). Grease a 9-inch (23 cm) square baking dish with oil.

Spoon the eggplant and cheese mixture into the baking dish and gently smooth the top, then sprinkle with the remaining ½ cup (40 g) mozzarella. Bake until golden brown and cooked through, 35–45 minutes. Let cool slightly before serving.

SABICH

Jews in Iraq typically ate an assortment of cold mezze dishes on Shabbat mornings. In the mid-twentieth century, Iraqi Jewish immigrants to Israel began stuffing these treats into pita and selling them at outdoor kiosks, effectively transforming the traditional Shabbat breakfast into a popular all-day street-food sandwich. To simplify the dish and shorten preparation time, substitute good-quality, store-bought hummus, tahini sauce, and harissa.

Serves: 6
Preparation time: 20 minutes
Cooking time: 35 minutes

• 6 eggs
• Extra-virgin olive oil, for frying
• 2 lb (910 g) eggplant (aubergine), unpeeled and cut into ¼-inch (6 mm) slices
• Kosher salt
• 6 Pitas (page 54), warmed
• Hummus (page 96)
• Chopped Tomato and Cucumber Salad (page 78)
• Tahini Sauce (page 396)
• Sliced Israeli pickles, Harissa (page 409), and amba or mango chutney, for serving

Place the eggs in a medium saucepan and cover with water by 1 inch (2.5 cm). Bring to a boil, uncovered, over high heat. As soon as the water boils, remove from the heat, cover, and let sit for 20 minutes. Drain the eggs and cover with cold water to stop the cooking. Peel the eggs and slice into ¼-inch (6 mm) rounds. Set aside.

Meanwhile, line a large plate with paper towels. In a large frying pan, heat about ¼ inch (6 mm) oil over medium-high heat. Season the eggplant (aubergine) pieces on both sides with salt and, working in batches, add them to the pan and cook, turning once, until golden brown on both sides and very soft, 4–5 minutes per side. Add more oil as necessary. Transfer the fried eggplant to the paper towels to drain.

To assemble, slice the pitas in half and open up their pockets. Spread 1 or 2 tablespoons of hummus in the bottom of each pocket. Add several fried eggplant pieces and egg slices. Top with chopped tomato and cucumber salad, a drizzle of tahini sauce, sliced pickles, and dollops of harissa and *amba*.

POTATO AND EGG STRATA

This layered casserole is comfort food par excellence, and a deeply nostalgic dish for Hungarian Jews. The composed strata, called *rakott krumpli*, includes sliced potatoes and hard-boiled eggs bound with sour cream and sprinkled generously with paprika. Non-Jewish versions of the dish also typically include Hungarian sausage, but even without the meat, it is exceptionally hearty and indulgent.

Serves: 8–10
Preparation time: 20 minutes
Cooking time: 1 hour

• 8 eggs
• 2½ lb (1 kg) medium waxy (boiling) potatoes, scrubbed and unpeeled
• 4 tablespoons vegetable oil
• 2 large sweet onions, halved through the root and thinly sliced
• 1½ teaspoons kosher salt, plus more as needed
• ½ teaspoon freshly ground black pepper
• 2 teaspoons sweet paprika
• 2 cups (480 g) sour cream
• ½ cup (120 ml/4 fl oz) heavy (whipping) cream
• ⅓ cup (45 g) dried breadcrumbs

Place the eggs in a medium saucepan and cover with water by 1 inch (2.5 cm). Bring to a boil, uncovered, over high heat. As soon as the water boils, remove from the heat, cover, and let sit for 20 minutes. Drain the eggs and cover with cold water to stop the cooking process. Peel the eggs and slice them into ½-inch (1.25 cm) rounds.

Meanwhile, in a large pot, combine the potatoes with water to cover by 2 inches (5 cm). Bring to a boil over high heat, then reduce the heat to medium-high and cook until the potatoes are tender all the way through when pierced with a sharp knife, 20–30 minutes. Drain and let sit until cool enough to handle. Peel the cooked potatoes and cut into rounds ½ inch (1.25 cm) thick.

In a large frying pan, heat 3 tablespoons of the oil over medium heat. Add the onions and a generous pinch of salt and cook, stirring occasionally, until very soft and golden brown, 20–25 minutes. Set aside to cool.

Preheat the oven to 350°F (180°C/Gas Mark 4). Grease a 9×13 inch (23×33 cm) baking dish.

Arrange half of the potato rounds in the bottom of the baking dish, followed by all of the egg slices and then all of the sautéed onions. Sprinkle evenly with 1 teaspoon of the salt, pepper, and 1 teaspoon of the paprika. In a small bowl, whisk together the sour cream, heavy (whipping) cream, and the remaining ½ teaspoon salt, then spread the mixture over the onions. Layer the remaining potato rounds on top. In another small bowl, mix the breadcrumbs, the remaining 1 tablespoon oil, and the remaining 1 teaspoon paprika. Sprinkle the breadcrumb mixture evenly on top of the potato layer.

Cover the baking dish with foil and bake for 30 minutes. Uncover and continue baking until lightly browned, about 15 minutes more. Let stand for 15 minutes before serving. Serve hot.

FRICASSÉ

These Tunisian sandwiches are all about the roll—a petite oval of fried dough that tastes something like a savory doughnut. When serving a crowd, lay out these rolls on a platter alongside various fillings on separate plates and let guests fill as they please.

Makes: about 1 dozen sandwiches
Preparation time: 20 minutes, plus rising
Cooking time: 20 minutes

• 1 packet (¼ oz/7g) active dry yeast (2¼ teaspoons)
• 1 teaspoon sugar
• ¾ cup (175 ml/6 fl oz) warm water (110°F/43°C)
• 2–2¼ cups (280–315 g) all-purpose (plain) flour, plus more for kneading
• 1 teaspoon kosher salt
• 2 tablespoons vegetable oil, plus more for frying and greasing the bowl
• Suggested fillings: sliced hard-boiled eggs, drained canned tuna, sliced boiled potatoes, green olives, capers, Harissa (page 409), finely chopped Preserved Lemon (page 116)

In a large bowl, stir together the yeast, sugar, and warm water. Let sit until foaming, 5–10 minutes.

Meanwhile, in a separate bowl, whisk together 2 cups (280 g) flour and the salt.

Add the vegetable oil to the yeast mixture and whisk until combined. Add the flour mixture and stir with a wooden spoon until a shaggy dough begins to form. Turn the dough out onto a lightly floured surface and knead well, adding up to ¼ cup (35 g) additional flour, a little at a time as necessary, until a supple, elastic dough forms, about 10 minutes. You may not need all of the extra flour. (The kneading can also be done in a stand mixer fitted with a dough hook, 5–7 minutes.) Grease a large bowl with about 1 teaspoon of oil, add the dough, and turn to coat. Cover the bowl with plastic wrap (cling film) or a tea towel and let sit in a warm place until doubled in size, 1–2 hours.

Line a large baking sheet with parchment paper. Gently deflate the dough, then pinch off a piece slightly larger than a golf ball (about 1½ oz/42 g) and roll into an oval. Place the oval on the baking sheet and continue with the remaining dough. Let the formed rolls sit, uncovered, while the oil heats.

Line a large sheet pan with paper towels. In a medium frying pan, heat about 1 inch (2.5 cm) oil over medium heat. Working in batches of 3–4, slip the formed ovals into the hot oil and cook, turning once, until golden brown on both sides and cooked through, about 2 minutes per side. If the rolls are browning too quickly, before they have a chance to cook through, nudge down the heat. Transfer the fried rolls to the paper towels to drain.

To serve, use a serrated knife to cut a pocket into the rolls and fill with desired fillings. Serve immediately.

CHRAIME

North African Jews commonly serve fish cooked in a spicy sauce as a first course (see page 118) on Shabbat and Passover—but it also makes a show-stopping standalone main dish. The sauce's components change depending on whether it is being cooked by a Moroccan, Tunisian, or Libyan cook. In Israel, a tomato-based sauce spiced with paprika, cumin, and chilies, has become popular. Measure out the spices before starting to cook so that they can be added all at once. A squeeze of fresh lemon juice at the table elevates the dish's bright flavor.

Serves: 6 as a first course, 4 as a main course
Preparation time: 20 minutes
Cooking time: 40 minutes

• ¼ cup (60 ml/2 fl oz) vegetable oil
• 1 large onion, halved through the root and thinly sliced
• 1 red bell pepper, cut into ½-inch (1.25 cm) pieces
• 8 garlic cloves, thinly sliced
• 2 teaspoons sweet paprika
• 2 teaspoons ground cumin
• 1 teaspoon smoked paprika
• ½ teaspoon ground turmeric
• ½ teaspoon crushed pepper flakes, plus more as needed
• 1 can (14½ oz/411g) diced (chopped) tomatoes
• 4 tablespoons tomato paste (purée)
• 1 teaspoon sugar
• 1 bay leaf
• 1½ teaspoons kosher salt, plus more as needed
• ¼ teaspoon freshly ground black pepper
• 4 salmon, red snapper, or halibut fillets (6 oz/170 g each), patted dry
• Finely chopped fresh cilantro (coriander) and lemon wedges, for serving

In a large, wide frying pan, heat the oil over medium heat. Add the onion, bell pepper, and garlic and cook, stirring occasionally, until softened and lightly browned, 10–15 minutes. Add the sweet paprika, cumin, smoked paprika, turmeric, and pepper flakes and cook, stirring, until fragrant, about 1 minute. Stir in the diced (chopped) tomatoes, 1¼ cups (295 ml/10 fl oz) water, tomato paste (purée), sugar, bay leaf, salt, and black pepper. Increase the heat slightly and bring to a boil. Reduce the heat to medium and cook until slightly thickened, about 5 minutes. Taste and add more salt, if desired.

Nestle the fish fillets in the sauce, spooning sauce on top of the fillets to cover. Reduce the heat to medium-low, cover, and simmer until the fish is cooked through, about 20 minutes. Remove the pan from the heat, discard the bay leaf, and serve directly from the pan. (Or, carefully transfer fillets to a serving platter, then spoon the sauce on top.) Serve hot or warm, topped with cilantro (coriander) and with lemon wedges on the side for squeezing.

Chraime

SALMON CUTLETS

The Jewish community of Manchester, England, has a deep affection for these pan-fried salmon cutlets. Golden brown and delicately flavored, they are delightfully homey. If desired, substitute 15 ounces (425 g) fresh salmon (cooked, then flaked) for the canned.

Serves: 4
Preparation time: 20 minutes, plus resting
Cooking time: 30 minutes

- 2 tablespoons vegetable oil, plus more for frying
- 1 small onion, finely chopped
- 1 teaspoon kosher salt, plus more as needed
- 15 oz (425 g) boneless canned salmon, drained
- 3 eggs, lightly beaten
- ½ cup (70 g) dried breadcrumbs or matzo meal
- 4 garlic cloves, minced or pushed through a press
- 1 teaspoon onion powder
- Freshly ground black pepper
- Lemon wedges, for serving

In a medium frying pan, heat 2 tablespoons oil over medium heat. Add the onion and a generous pinch of salt and cook, stirring occasionally, until softened and lightly browned, 7–10 minutes. Remove from the heat and let cool to the touch.

Add the salmon to a large bowl and flake it with a fork. Add the sautéed onion, eggs, breadcrumbs, garlic, onion powder, salt, and a generous amount of pepper. Stir well to combine and let sit for 15 minutes to allow flavors to meld.

Meanwhile, line a large plate with a few layers of paper towels. In a large frying pan, heat ¼ inch (6 mm) oil over medium heat until shimmering. Scoop out ¼ cup (60 g) of the salmon mixture at a time and form into patties about 3 inches (7.5 cm) wide and ½ inch (1.25 cm) thick.

Working in batches of 4–5, add the patties to the oil and cook until browned on one side, about 3 minutes. Flip with a spatula and continue cooking on the other side until golden, 2–3 minutes. Adjust the heat if the patties are browning too quickly or not quickly enough, and add more oil to the pan if it begins to look dry.

Transfer the fried patties to the paper towels to drain. Serve warm or at room temperature, with lemon wedges for squeezing.

SWEET-AND-SOUR FISH

Italian Jews serve sweet-and-sour fish, called *pesce all'Ebraica* (literally "Jewish-style fish"), on Shabbat, and also to break the Yom Kippur fast. The addition of pine nuts and raisins attest to the influence Arabic cooking has had on Italy's Jewish cuisine, since traders from the Middle East and North Africa originally introduced the Jews of Sicily and southern Italy to these ingredients.

Serves: 6
Preparation time: 25 minutes
Cooking time: 35 minutes

- ½ cup (65 g) pine nuts
- ⅓ cup (75 ml/2.5 fl oz) extra-virgin olive oil
- ⅓ cup (75 ml/2.5 fl oz) red wine vinegar or apple cider vinegar
- 3 tablespoons mild honey
- 1½ teaspoons kosher salt, plus more for sprinkling
- ¼ teaspoon freshly ground black pepper, plus more for sprinkling
- ⅓ cup (45 g) golden raisins (sultanas)
- 6 large shallots, halved and thinly sliced
- 6 garlic cloves, thinly sliced
- 6 firm fish fillets, such as red snapper, sole, or flounder (about 6 oz /170 g each)
- Finely chopped fresh parsley, for serving

Preheat the oven to 400°F (200°C/Gas Mark 6).

In a small, dry frying pan, toast the pine nuts over medium-low heat, shaking the pan occasionally, until fragrant and lightly browned, 5–7 minutes. Remove the pan from the heat and let cool.

In a medium bowl, whisk together the oil, vinegar, honey, salt, and pepper until well combined. Stir in the pine nuts and golden raisins (sultanas). Arrange the shallots and garlic on the bottom of a 9 × 13-inch (23 × 33 cm) baking dish. Drizzle about half of the oil and vinegar mixture on top. Lay the fish in a layer on top of the shallots, sprinkle with a little more salt and the pepper, and drizzle with the remaining oil and vinegar mixture.

Cover the baking dish with foil and roast for 10 minutes. Uncover and continue roasting, basting occasionally with the pan juices, until the fish is tender and cooked through, 10–20 minutes. Serve hot or warm, with pan juices spooned on top and sprinkled with parsley.

FRIED SOLE WITH AGRISTADA

Sephardi Jews from Greece and the Balkans serve fried fish with a creamy egg and lemon sauce called *agristada*. It makes a delicious starter for Shabbat dinner and a simple but special weeknight main dish. The velvety sauce is equally delicious served over steamed artichokes, asparagus, or potatoes.

Serves: 6–8
Preparation time: 20 minutes
Cooking time: 35 minutes

For the egg-lemon sauce:
- 2 egg yolks
- 2 tablespoons fresh lemon juice
- 2 tablespoons cornstarch (cornflour) or potato starch
- ¾ teaspoon kosher salt
- 1½ cups (355 ml/12 fl oz) vegetable stock

For the fish:
- ½ cup (70 g) all-purpose (plain) flour
- 3 eggs
- Vegetable oil, for frying
- 8 sole fillets (4–6 oz/115–170 g each), patted dry with paper towels
- Kosher salt and freshly ground black pepper
- Finely chopped fresh flat-leaf parsley, for serving

Make the egg-lemon sauce: In a small saucepan, whisk together the egg yolks, lemon juice, cornstarch (cornflour), and salt until combined and the cornstarch fully dissolves. Add the stock and set the saucepan over medium heat. Stirring constantly, bring the mixture to a simmer (but do not let it boil) and cook until it thickens into a pourable sauce, about 5 minutes. Remove from the heat and set aside.

Make the fish: Line a large plate with paper towels. Spread the flour onto a plate. Beat the eggs with a splash of water in a wide shallow bowl (like a pie plate or a small baking dish). In a large frying pan, heat about ⅛ inch (3 mm) vegetable oil over medium heat. Season the fillets on both sides with a little salt and pepper. Working in batches, dredge the fillets in flour, tapping off the excess, then dip them in the egg, letting the extra drip off. Slip the coated fish into the hot oil and cook, flipping once, until cooked through and golden brown on both sides, about 3 minutes per side. Transfer the fillets to the paper towels to drain.

Arrange the fish on a serving platter. Serve hot or warm, sprinkled with parsley and egg-lemon sauce on the side.

FISH TAGINE WITH COUSCOUS

A spoonful of the chili-pepper paste harissa adds warmth and complex flavor to this vegetable-packed Tunisian fish stew. Served over couscous, it makes an elegant main dish.

Serves: 6
Preparation time: 30 minutes
Cooking time: 40 minutes

For the fish tagine:
- ¼ cup (60 ml/2 fl oz) extra-virgin olive oil
- 2 onions, halved through the root and thinly sliced
- 2 garlic cloves, thinly sliced
- 1 teaspoon ground cumin
- 1 teaspoon sweet paprika
- ½ teaspoon ground coriander
- ½ teaspoon ground turmeric
- 2 tablespoons tomato paste (purée)
- 1 tablespoon Harissa (page 409)
- 1 can (15 oz/425 g) chickpeas, rinsed and drained
- 2 zucchini (courgettes), halved lengthwise and sliced into ½-inch (1.25 cm) half-moons
- 1 lb (455 g) small waxy (boiling) potatoes, halved
- 2 large carrots, halved lengthwise and cut crosswise into ½-inch (1.25 cm) pieces
- 2 lb (910 g) firm fish fillets (bass, snapper, founder, hake), skinned and cut into 2-inch (5 cm) pieces
- 1½ cups (355 ml/12 fl oz) vegetable stock
- 1 can (14½ oz/411 g) diced (chopped) tomatoes
- 1½ teaspoons kosher salt, plus more as needed
- ¼ teaspoon freshly ground black pepper

For the couscous:
- ½ teaspoon kosher salt
- 2 cups (375 g) couscous

For serving:
- Chopped fresh flat-leaf parsley, for garnish
- Harissa

Make the fish tagine: In a large saucepan, heat the oil over medium-high heat. Add the onions and garlic and cook, stirring occasionally, until softened and lightly browned, 8–10 minutes. Add the cumin, paprika, coriander, turmeric, tomato paste (purée), and harissa and cook, stirring, until fragrant, about 1 minute.

Add the chickpeas, zucchini (courgettes), potatoes, carrots, fish, stock, diced (chopped) tomatoes, salt, and black pepper. Gently stir to combine and bring to a boil. Reduce the heat to low, cover, and cook, stirring once or twice, until the fish is cooked through and the potatoes and carrots are tender, about 20 minutes. (It may look like there is not enough cooking liquid at first, but the zucchini will give off a lot of water as the mixture cooks.) Uncover and continue cooking, stirring occasionally, until the liquid thickens slightly, 5–10 minutes. Taste and add more salt, if desired.

Meanwhile, make the couscous: In a medium saucepan, bring 2½ cups (590 ml/20 fl oz) water and the salt to a boil over high heat. Pour the couscous into the boiling water in a steady stream, stirring constantly. Remove the pan from the heat, cover, and let stand for 10 minutes. Fluff with a fork.

To serve: Mound the couscous on a large serving platter. Make a well in the center and spoon in the fish and vegetables. Spoon a generous amount of the cooking liquid on top and serve hot, topped with parsley and more harissa.

Fish Tagine with Couscous

COUSCOUS AND ISRAELI COUSCOUS

Many people know couscous as a starch that comes in a box and gets rehydrated with boiling water. But few know exactly what it is. True couscous, which has ancient Maghrebi roots and remains a staple starch across North Africa, is technically a type of pasta made from ground semolina and water. The semolina is rolled by hand into small granules, then steamed multiple times in a special pot called a *couscoussier* until it is fluffy and tender—the perfect base for a variety of saucy stews and tagines. Moroccan, Algerian, and Tunisian Jews regularly serve couscous for special occasions. Making couscous by hand is quite labor intensive. Though store-bought couscous makes a decent substitute, if the opportunity arrives to try the handmade version, it should not be missed.

So-called Israeli couscous (called *ptitim* or "little crumbles" in Hebrew) is not actually couscous, but rather a wheat paste that gets extruded by a machine into round, chewy granules and then toasted. *Ptitim* was created by the Osem company in the 1950s when Israel's then–Prime Minister, David Ben Gurion, implored them to create an affordable starch to help feed the new, fledgling state. In Israel, it remains popular as a comfort food, often served simply with browned onions or a basic tomato sauce. The name "Israeli couscous" was born when an expat chef, Mika Sharon, served *ptitim* to her boss at New York City's popular Tribeca Grill. He liked it so much that he put it on the menu, renaming it. Israeli couscous caught on, and now is a favorite in America as well.

FISH CURRY WITH TAMARIND

Fish curries are central to all three of India's primary Jewish communities—the Bene Israel of Mumbai, the Baghdadi Jews of Calcutta, and the Jews of Cochin. This version is scented with coconut, ginger, and cilantro (coriander) and gets its pleasant tanginess from tamarind paste and lime juice. Pomegranate molasses can be substituted for the tamarind paste, if necessary.

Serves: 6
Preparation time: 20 minutes
Cooking time: 35 minutes

- ¼ cup (60 ml/2 fl oz) coconut oil or vegetable oil
- 2 large onions, halved through the root and thinly sliced
- 2 garlic cloves, thinly sliced
- 1-inch (2.5 cm) piece fresh ginger, peeled and finely chopped
- 1 teaspoon kosher salt, plus more as needed
- 1½ teaspoons curry powder
- ½ teaspoon ground turmeric
- ½ teaspoon crushed pepper flakes
- 1 can (14½ oz/411 g) diced (chopped) tomatoes
- ½ cup (120 ml/4 fl oz) vegetable stock
- ½ cup (20 g) roughly chopped fresh cilantro (coriander), plus more for serving
- 2 tablespoons tamarind paste
- 1 tablespoon fresh lime juice, plus quartered limes for serving
- Freshly ground black pepper
- 2 lb (910 g) firm fish fillets (bass, snapper, flounder, hake), skinned and cut into 2-inch (5 cm) pieces

In a medium saucepan, heat the oil over medium heat. Add the onions, garlic, ginger, and a pinch of salt and cook, stirring occasionally, until softened and lightly browned, 10–15 minutes. Add the curry powder, turmeric, and pepper flakes and cook, stirring, until fragrant, about 1 minute.

Stir in the tomatoes with their juice, stock, cilantro (coriander), tamarind, lime juice, salt, and a generous amount of black pepper and cook until slightly thickened, about 5 minutes.

Add the fish, cover, and cook, gently stirring once or twice, until the fish is cooked through, 10–15 minutes. Uncover and continue cooking, spooning the sauce on top, for 5 minutes. Taste and add more salt, if desired. Serve hot, with more chopped cilantro sprinkled on top, and lime wedges on the side for squeezing.

CHICKEN AND QUINCE TAGINE

Quinces, which are related to apples and pears, come into season during the autumn. Not surprisingly then, they show up in dishes served during the High Holidays, particularly Rosh Hashanah. This Algerian tagine uses floral-scented candied quinces to add sweetness to a chicken tagine. When working with quinces, take care to remove the fruit's entire core (which can be quite tough) before cooking.

Serves: 6
Preparation time: 10 minutes
Cooking time: 1 hour 40 minutes

- ⅓ cup (40 g) slivered almonds
- 4 lb (1.8 kg) bone-in, skin-on chicken thighs and drumsticks, patted dry
- Kosher salt and freshly ground black pepper
- ¼ cup (60 ml/2 fl oz) vegetable oil
- 2 large onions, halved through the root and thinly sliced
- 1½ teaspoons ground cinnamon
- ½ teaspoon onion powder
- ½ teaspoon ground turmeric
- ½ cup (120 ml/4 fl oz) chicken stock
- 1 batch Candied Quince (page 402), drained (syrup reserved)
- Chopped fresh parsley, for serving

In a small dry frying pan, toast the almonds over medium-low heat, shaking the pan occasionally, until fragrant and lightly browned, 5–7 minutes. Remove the pan from the heat and let cool.

Sprinkle the chicken pieces with salt and pepper on both sides. In a Dutch oven (casserole) or other large pot, heat the oil over medium-high heat until shimmering. Working in batches, sear the chicken pieces, flipping once, until nicely browned on both sides, 8–10 minutes. Transfer the browned chicken pieces to a large plate.

Reduce the heat under the Dutch oven to medium and add the onions. Cook, stirring often, until softened and golden brown, 7–10 minutes. Stir in the cinnamon, onion powder, and turmeric and cook, stirring, until fragrant, about 1 minute.

Return the chicken pieces to the pot and pour in the chicken stock. Cover, reduce the heat to medium-low, and simmer, stirring occasionally, for 20 minutes. Add the candied quince pieces and drizzle in 2 tablespoons of quince syrup, cover, and simmer until the chicken is tender and cooked through, 20–25 minutes more. Taste and season with additional salt and pepper, if desired.

Transfer the chicken and quince pieces to a serving platter. Continue simmering the liquid in the pot, stirring often, until it thickens slightly, 5–10 minutes. Drizzle the sauce over the chicken and serve hot, sprinkled with toasted almonds and chopped parsley.

ROAST CHICKEN WITH THYME AND HONEY

Roast chicken is one of Ashkenazi cuisine's most iconic Shabbat dinner dishes, and for good reason. It is quick to prepare, homey, and comfortingly delicious. There are infinite ways to dress up plain roast chicken, but a mix of fresh herbs and aromatic vegetables that soak up the drippings as the bird cooks is especially divine.

Serves: 6
Preparation time: 15 minutes
Cooking time: 55 minutes

- 3 medium parsnips, peeled, halved lengthwise, and cut into 1-inch (2.5 cm) pieces
- 3 medium carrots, peeled, halved lengthwise, and cut into 1-inch (2.5 cm) pieces
- 2 small onions, each cut into 8 wedges
- 2 heads garlic, cloves separated and peeled
- 6 sprigs thyme, plus 1 tablespoon finely chopped thyme leaves
- 4 tablespoons extra-virgin olive oil
- Kosher salt and freshly ground black pepper
- 4 lb (1.8 kg) bone-in, skin-on chicken thighs and drumsticks, patted dry
- 1 tablespoon fresh lemon juice
- 2 tablespoons honey

Preheat the oven to 475°F (245°C/Gas Mark 9).

Scatter the parsnips, carrots, onions, garlic, and thyme sprigs in the bottom of a large roasting pan or baking dish. Drizzle the vegetables with 2 tablespoons of the oil and sprinkle generously with salt and pepper.

Lay the chicken pieces on top of the veggies. Drizzle the remaining 2 tablespoons oil over the chicken, rubbing it in to coat all sides, then sprinkle with salt and pepper. Roast for 25 minutes.

Meanwhile, in a small bowl, whisk together the lemon juice, honey, and chopped thyme until combined.

Reduce the oven temperature to 400°F (°200C/Gas Mark 6). Brush the chicken pieces evenly with the lemon-honey mixture, then continue cooking until the skin is browned, the juices run clear, and an instant-read thermometer inserted into the thickest part of a thigh registers 165°F (74°C), 25–30 minutes. Let rest for 10–15 minutes before serving.

CHICKEN SHAWARMA

Preparing authentic *shawarma* at home is next to impossible, as the beloved Middle Eastern street meat is typically cooked on a large, vertical spit. But roasting marinated chicken thighs in a hot oven, then toasting them in a hot pan achieves a convincingly similar flavor and texture. Serve the *shawarma* inside pita, with Chopped Tomato and Cucumber Salad (page 78), and Tahini Sauce (page 396), for drizzling.

Serves: 4–6
Preparation time: 20 minutes, plus marinating
Cooking time: 35 minutes

- 2 lb (910 g) boneless, skinless chicken thighs, each cut into 4 equal pieces
- ¼ cup (60 ml/2 fl oz) plus 2 tablespoons extra-virgin olive oil
- 2 teaspoons ground cumin
- 2 teaspoons sweet paprika
- ½ teaspoon ground cinnamon
- ½ teaspoon ground turmeric
- ½ teaspoon garlic powder
- ¼ teaspoon smoked paprika
- ½ teaspoon kosher salt, plus more as needed
- ¼ teaspoon freshly ground black pepper
- 1 large onion, halved through the root and thinly sliced

Add the chicken pieces to a large zip-top bag. In a medium bowl, whisk together ¼ cup (60 ml/2 fl oz) of the oil, the cumin, sweet paprika, cinnamon, turmeric, garlic powder, smoked paprika, salt, and pepper. Pour the marinade into the bag with the chicken, seal well, and turn to coat the chicken. Refrigerate for at least 1 hour.

Preheat the oven to 425°F (°220C/Gas Mark 7). Grease a large sheet pan with 1 tablespoon of the oil.

Add the onion to the bag with the chicken, reseal, and turn to coat. Transfer the chicken and onion pieces to the prepared sheet pan, spreading them into an even layer. Roast until the chicken is browned and the onion pieces are softened, 25–30 minutes. Transfer the chicken to a carving board, then slice into small pieces.

In a large frying pan, heat the remaining 1 tablespoon oil over medium heat. Add the chicken pieces and onion and cook, stirring often, until crisped around the edges, 3–4 minutes. Taste and add more salt, if desired. Serve hot.

MAIN DISHES

Roast Chicken with Thyme and Honey

CHICKEN SOFRITO

The word *sofrito* is derived from the Spanish word "to lightly fry," and can refer to a variety of browned and braised meat and vegetable dishes. One of the more common variations of *sofrito*, made with chicken and potatoes, has become a staple of Shabbat and Sukkot dinners in Sephardi families. Serve it over rice and with pita alongside for soaking up the flavorful sauce.

Serves: 6–8
Preparation time: 15 minutes
Cooking time: 2 hours 10 minutes

- 3 tablespoons vegetable oil, plus more as needed
- 4 lb (1.8 kg) bone-in, skin-on chicken thighs and drumsticks, patted dry
- Kosher salt and freshly ground black pepper
- 1 lb (455 g) small potatoes (fingerling, creamer, or new), scrubbed
- 1 small sweet potato, peeled and cut into 2-inch (5 cm) pieces
- 1 large onion, halved through the root and thinly sliced
- 2 teaspoons sweet paprika
- ½ teaspoon ground turmeric
- ¼ teaspoon ground cardamom
- ½ teaspoon onion powder
- ½ teaspoon garlic powder
- 1½ cups (355 ml/12 fl oz) chicken stock
- 2 bay leaves

In a large Dutch oven (casserole) or other large heavy pot, heat the oil over medium-high heat. Season the chicken pieces with salt and pepper and, working in batches, brown the chicken, turning once, until browned on both sides, 8–10 minutes. Transfer the browned chicken pieces to a large plate.

If the pan looks dry, add another tablespoon of oil. Working in 2 batches, add the potatoes and sweet potato pieces to the pan and cook, stirring occasionally, until browned and crisp all over, about 10 minutes. The potatoes will not be fully softened at this point. Remove the fried potatoes to a bowl and set aside.

Add the sliced onion and a sprinkle of salt and stir. Cover the pot, reduce the heat to medium, and let the onions cook, stirring occasionally, until softened and browned, 8–10 minutes. Stir in the paprika, turmeric, cardamom, onion powder, garlic powder, ½ teaspoon salt, and ¼ teaspoon pepper and cook until fragrant, about 1 minute.

Return the browned chicken pieces to the pan and add the stock and bay leaves. Cover, reduce the heat to medium-low, and cook, stirring occasionally, until the chicken is tender, 40–50 minutes.

Add the potatoes and sweet potatoes and gently stir to submerge them under the cooking liquid. Increase the heat to medium and cook, uncovered, until the cooking liquid has thickened slightly and the potatoes are fully tender, about 10 minutes. Taste and add more salt or pepper, if desired. Remove the bay leaves and serve hot.

CHICKEN FRICASSEE

There is a lot going on inside a pot of chicken fricassee —braised chicken, tender sautéed mushrooms, and tiny meatballs swimming in a flavorful gravy. Ashkenazi home cooks originally made the dish as a way of repurposing less desirable chicken parts like gizzards, necks, and wings into something delicious. But using a mix of drumsticks and thighs instead makes the dish more compatible with contemporary tastes. Serve it over egg noodles, Farfel (page 226), Matzo Farfel with Mushrooms (page 229), or rice with plenty of Challah (page 46) or matzo to mop up the extra gravy.

Serves: 6–8
Preparation time: 20 minutes
Cooking time: 1 hour 50 minutes

For the chicken:
• 2 tablespoons vegetable oil, plus more as needed
• 3 lb (1.4 kg) skin-on chicken drumsticks and wings
• Kosher salt and freshly ground black pepper
• 2 medium onions, halved through the root and thinly sliced
• 2 medium carrots, finely chopped
• 2 celery stalks, finely chopped
• ½ lb (225 g) white button mushrooms, stems discarded, thinly sliced
• 8 garlic cloves, thinly sliced
• ⅓ cup all-purpose (plain) flour (40 g) or potato starch (60 g)
• ½ cup (120 ml/4 fl oz) dry white wine
• 3 cups (710 ml/24 fl oz) chicken stock
• 1 bay leaf
• 1 tablespoon sweet paprika

For the meatballs:
• ½ lb (225 g) ground (minced) beef
• 1 egg, beaten
• ¼ cup (35 g) dried breadcrumbs or matzo meal
• ½ teaspoon garlic powder
• ½ cup (25 g) finely chopped fresh parsley, plus more for serving
• ½ teaspoon kosher salt

Make the chicken: In a large Dutch oven (casserole) or other large pot with a lid, heat the oil over medium-high heat. Season the chicken with salt and pepper and, working in batches, brown the chicken pieces, turning once, until browned on both sides, 8–10 minutes. If the bottom of the pan begins to look dry, add another 1–2 tablespoons of oil, as needed. Transfer the chicken to a bowl.

Add the onions, carrots, celery, mushrooms, and garlic to the pan and cook, stirring occasionally, until softened and lightly browned, 8–10 minutes. Add the flour and stir to coat the vegetables, then stir in the white wine, scraping up any browned bits from the bottom of the pan, and cook until the liquid evaporates, about 2 minutes. Add the stock, bay leaf, paprika, 1 teaspoon salt, and ½ teaspoon pepper. Increase the heat to medium-high and bring to a boil.

Return the browned chicken pieces to the pan (it is okay if they don't all fit under the liquid). Reduce the heat to low, cover, and cook, stirring occasionally, until the chicken is tender, about 1 hour. The mixture should roll along at a slow, steady bubble. If it isn't bubbling enough, nudge the heat up. If it's bubbling too furiously, nudge it down.

Meanwhile, make the meatballs: In a large bowl, mix together the beef, egg, breadcrumbs, garlic powder, parsley, and salt. Scoop out the mixture by the level tablespoon and form into ½-inch (1.25 cm) meatballs.

After the chicken has cooked for 1 hour, add the meatballs, increase the heat to medium, and continue cooking, covered, until cooked through, about 15 minutes.

Remove from the heat and let stand 10–15 minutes before serving. Serve hot, sprinkled with more chopped parsley. Store leftovers, covered, in the fridge. Reheat on the stove over medium-low heat, until bubbling and warmed through, about 10 minutes.

DORO WOT

Ethiopian Jews serve this fiery chicken stew for special meals. Heaps of onion, garlic, and ginger meld together into a saucy base and get a big boost of flavor from the Ethiopian spice mix, Berbere (page 414).

Serves: 6
Preparation time: 30 minutes
Cooking time: 1 hour 15 minutes

- 6 eggs
- ¼ cup (60 ml/2 fl oz) vegetable oil
- 2 medium onions, finely chopped
- 4 garlic cloves, finely chopped
- 2-inch (2 cm) piece fresh ginger, peeled and finely chopped
- Kosher salt
- ⅓ cup (85 g) tomato paste (purée)
- 1 tablespoon Berbere (page 414)
- 1 teaspoon sweet paprika
- 1 teaspoon ground cumin
- ½ teaspoon ground turmeric
- 4 lb (1.8 kg) skin-on chicken drumsticks, patted dry
- Freshly ground black pepper

Place the eggs in a medium saucepan and cover with water by 1 inch (2.5 cm). Bring to a boil, uncovered, over high heat. As soon as the water boils, remove from the heat, cover, and let sit for 20 minutes. Drain the eggs and cover with cold water. Peel the eggs and set aside.

Meanwhile, in a Dutch oven (casserole), heat the oil over medium heat. Add the onions, garlic, ginger, and a pinch of salt and cook, stirring occasionally, until lightly browned, 8–10 minutes. Add ¼ cup (60 ml/2 fl oz) water, cover, and cook until the onions are very tender, about 5 minutes.

Stir in the tomato paste (purée), berbere, paprika, cumin, and turmeric. Season the chicken on both sides with salt and pepper and add to the Dutch oven along with 2½ cups (590 ml/20 fl oz) water. Increase the heat to medium-high and bring to a simmer. Reduce the heat to medium, cover, and cook, stirring occasionally, until the sauce begins to thicken, 30–35 minutes. If the mixture begins to look dry while cooking, add a little more water.

Add the peeled eggs and ½ teaspoon salt to the pot, cover, and continue cooking until the chicken is very tender, about 20 minutes. Taste and add more salt and pepper, if desired. Serve hot, with the sauce spooned on top.

ONION AND TAMARIND CHICKEN

Jews hailing from Calcutta serve this tamarind-flavored chicken dish, called *chitanee*, for Shabbat and holidays. The dish includes a copious amount of sliced onions, which melt into the tender, tangy sauce.

Serves: 6
Preparation time: 25 minutes
Cooking time: 1 hour 30 minutes

- 3 tablespoons vegetable oil
- 4 medium onions, halved through the root and thinly sliced
- 2-inch (5 cm) piece fresh ginger, peeled and finely chopped
- 2 garlic cloves, finely chopped
- 1 teaspoon kosher salt, plus more as needed
- 1 teaspoon ground cumin
- 1 teaspoon ground coriander
- ½ teaspoon garlic powder
- ½ teaspoon crushed pepper flakes
- 4 lb (1.8 kg) bone-in, skin-on chicken thighs and drumsticks, patted dry
- Freshly ground black pepper
- 2 tablespoons tamarind paste
- 2 tablespoons tomato paste (purée)
- 1 teaspoon sugar

In a large Dutch oven (casserole) or other large pot, heat the oil set over medium-high heat. Add the onions, ginger, garlic, and a pinch of salt and cook, stirring occasionally, until softened and lightly browned, 15–20 minutes. Add the cumin, coriander, garlic powder, and pepper flakes and cook, stirring, until fragrant, about 1 minute.

Season the chicken pieces with a little salt and pepper, then add to the pot. Stir in 1 cup (240 ml/8 fl oz) water, lower heat to medium-low, then cover and cook, stirring occasionally, until the chicken is very tender, 40–45 minutes.

Meanwhile, in a small bowl, stir together the tamarind paste, tomato paste (purée), 1 tablespoon water, the sugar, and salt until combined.

Add the tamarind mixture to the pan, raise the heat to medium, and continue cooking, stirring occasionally, until the sauce thickens, 15–20 minutes. Taste and add more salt and pepper, if desired. Remove from the heat and let stand for 10 minutes. Serve hot with onions and sauce spooned over chicken pieces.

Doro Wot

MINT AND CARROT CHICKEN

The ancient Jewish community of Cochin, India (the majority of whom now reside in Israel), traditionally served this dish on Shabbat and Passover. The combination of carrots, ginger, and fresh mint creates a flavorful sauce for the stovetop-braised chicken.

Serves: 6
Preparation time: 20 minutes
Cooking time: 1 hour 35 minutes

- 4 lb (1.8 kg) bone-in, skin-on chicken thighs and drumsticks, patted dry
- Kosher salt and freshly ground black pepper
- 3 tablespoons vegetable oil
- 2 large onions, halved through the root and thinly sliced
- 6 garlic cloves, thinly sliced
- 2-inch (5 cm) piece fresh ginger, peeled and finely chopped
- 1 jalapeño, seeded and finely chopped
- ½ teaspoon ground turmeric
- 1½ lb (680 g) carrots, halved lengthwise and cut into 1-inch (2.5 cm) pieces
- 2 cups (475 ml/16 fl oz) chicken stock
- 1 cup (50 g) finely chopped fresh mint leaves, plus more for serving

Sprinkle the chicken pieces lightly on both sides with salt and pepper. In a Dutch oven (casserole) or other large pot, heat 2 tablespoons of the oil over medium-high heat until shimmering. Working in batches, sear the chicken pieces, flipping once, until nicely browned on both sides, 8–10 minutes. Transfer the browned chicken to a large plate.

Add the remaining 1 tablespoon oil to the pan. Add the onions, garlic, ginger, and jalapeño and cook, stirring occasionally, until softened and lightly browned, 10–15 minutes. Stir in the turmeric and cook until fragrant, about 1 minute.

Return the chicken to the pan and add the carrots, stock, and ½ teaspoon salt. (It is okay if the chicken is not submerged in the liquid.) Cover and cook, stirring occasionally, until the chicken is tender, about 45 minutes. Uncover, stir in the mint and continue cooking, uncovered, until the sauce thickens, 10–15 minutes. Taste and add more salt, if desired. Serve hot or warm, sprinkled with additional fresh mint.

CHICKEN KOTLETI

Light and flavorful, ground chicken patties are ubiquitous across Russian cuisine, and immigrants from the former Soviet Union introduced their cherished dish to Israel. Serve the patties topped with sautéed mushrooms.

Serves: 6
Preparation time: 15 minutes
Cooking time: 25 minutes

- 1 cup (60 g) panko breadcrumbs
- 1 lb (455 g) ground (minced) chicken
- 1 small onion, grated on the large holes of a box grater
- ¼ cup (60 g) mayonnaise
- 1 egg
- 1½ teaspoons kosher salt
- ½ teaspoon freshly ground black pepper
- 1 teaspoon dried dill
- 1 cup (140 g) all-purpose (plain) flour, for dredging, plus more as needed
- Vegetable oil, for frying

In a large bowl, stir together the panko and ⅓ cup (75 ml/2½ fl oz) cold water and let stand for 5 minutes. Add the chicken, onion, mayonnaise, egg, salt, pepper, and dill and mix well to combine.

Spread the flour onto a plate and line a second large plate with paper towels. Scoop out ¼ cup (60 g) of the chicken mixture and, using moistened hands, form into an oval patty, about ¼ inch (6 mm) thick. The mixture will feel fragile and soft at this point, but will firm up during cooking. Carefully dredge both sides of the patty in the flour, and set aside on a third plate. Repeat with the remaining chicken mixture, adding more flour, as needed.

In a large frying pan, heat about ¼ inch (6 mm) oil over medium heat. Working in batches of 4–5, add the patties, cover, and cook, turning once, until golden brown on both sides, about 8 minutes. Add more oil between batches, if necessary. Transfer the cooked patties to the paper towels to drain. Serve hot.

COCONUT CHICKEN CURRY

Curries made with chicken and flavored with ginger and cilantro (coriander) are a Shabbat dinner staple for India's Bene Israel Jewish community. The use of coconut milk adds a wonderful creaminess.

Serves: 6–8
Preparation time: 30 minutes
Cooking time: 35 minutes

• ¼ cup (60 ml/2 fl oz) plus 3 tablespoons vegetable oil
• 1 large onion, finely chopped
• 2-inch (5 cm) piece fresh ginger, peeled and finely chopped
• 4 garlic cloves, finely chopped
• 1½ teaspoons kosher salt, plus more as needed
• 1 tablespoon mild curry powder
• ⅛ teaspoon cayenne pepper (optional)
• 1 can (14½ oz/411 g) diced (chopped) tomatoes
• 1 large sweet potato (about 1 lb/455 g), peeled and cut into ½-inch (1.25 cm) pieces
• 1 medium red bell pepper, cut into ½-inch (1.25 cm) pieces
• 2 lb (910 g) boneless, skinless chicken thighs, cut into 1-inch (2.5 cm) pieces
• ¼ teaspoon freshly ground black pepper, plus more as needed
• 1 can (14 oz/395 g) coconut milk
• ½ cup (20 g) roughly chopped fresh cilantro (coriander), plus more for serving
• 1 tablespoon cornstarch (cornflour)
• Lime wedges and roughly chopped roasted cashews, for serving

In a large saucepan, heat the ¼ cup (60 ml/2 fl oz) oil over medium heat. Add the onion, ginger, garlic, and a pinch of salt and cook, stirring occasionally, until softened and lightly browned, 6–8 minutes. Add the curry powder and cayenne (if using) and cook, stirring, until fragrant, about 1 minute.

Add the tomatoes with their juice, 1 cup (240 ml/8 fl oz) water, the sweet potato, and bell pepper. (It is okay if the vegetables are not fully submerged.) Increase the heat to medium-high and bring to a boil. Reduce the heat to low, cover, and cook until the vegetables are just short of tender, 8–10 minutes.

Meanwhile, in a medium frying pan, heat the remaining 3 tablespoons oil over medium-high heat. Season the chicken pieces with a generous amount of salt and pepper and cook, stirring occasionally, until lightly browned, about 5 minutes.

Add chicken to the saucepan along with the coconut milk, cilantro (coriander), salt, and black pepper. Increase the heat to medium-high and bring to a simmer, then reduce the heat to medium-low and cook, partially covered, until the chicken is cooked through and the vegetables are fully tender, about 10 minutes.

Add the cornstarch (cornflour) to a small bowl. Measure out about ¼ cup (60 ml/2 fl oz) of the hot cooking liquid and whisk it into the cornstarch until fully dissolved. Add the cornstarch mixture to the saucepan and cook, stirring, until the sauce thickens, 2–3 minutes. Remove from the heat. Taste and add more salt and pepper, if desired. Serve hot, topped with cilantro (coriander) and cashews, with lime wedges on the side for squeezing.

STUFFED TOMATOES WITH CHICKEN

The Jewish cuisine of Calcutta blends Middle Eastern recipes (the community is historically made up of immigrants from Iraq and Syria) with ingredients indigenous to India. Here, Middle Eastern–style stuffed tomatoes, called *mahashas*, are flavored with a generous amount of fresh ginger. Start with tomatoes that are ripe but still a bit firm so they do not completely fall apart during cooking.

Serves: 8
Preparation time: 40 minutes
Cooking time: 1½ hours

For the stuffed tomatoes:
• ½ cup (100 g) long-grain white rice, rinsed and drained
• 12 large firm-ripe tomatoes, rinsed and patted dry
• 2 tablespoons vegetable oil
• 1 onion, finely chopped
• 2-inch (5 cm) piece fresh ginger, peeled and finely chopped
• 4 garlic cloves, finely chopped
• ½ teaspoon dried mint (optional)
• 1 teaspoon kosher salt
• ¼ teaspoon freshly ground black pepper
• 1 lb (455 g) ground (minced) chicken

For the sauce:
• 4 tablespoons tamarind paste or Pomegranate Molasses (page 410)
• 2 tablespoons red wine vinegar
• 2 tablespoons vegetable oil
• ¼ cup (45 g) light brown sugar
• 2 teaspoons kosher salt
• ½ cup (120 ml/4 fl oz) chicken stock or water

Stuff the tomatoes: Bring a small saucepan half filled with water to a boil over high heat. Once boiling, stir in the rice, reduce the heat to medium-high, and cook until halfway softened, 5–10 minutes. Drain and let cool to the touch.

Meanwhile, slice the tops off of each tomato. Using a sharp grapefruit spoon or a serrated knife and a sturdy spoon, hollow out the tomatoes, leaving a ¼-inch (6 mm) shell. (Discard the pulp or reserve for another dish.)

In a medium frying pan, heat the oil over medium heat. Add the onion and cook, stirring occasionally, until softened and lightly browned, 6–8 minutes. Add the ginger, garlic, mint (if using), salt, and pepper and cook until fragrant, about 1 minute. Transfer the onion mixture to a large bowl and let cool slightly. Add the cooked rice and the chicken (uncooked) and mix well to combine, kneading in up to ¼ cup (60 ml/2 fl oz) water as needed, a little at a time, until the meat mixture is soft and pliable.

Preheat the oven to 350°F (180°C/Gas Mark 4). Grease a 9 × 13-inch (23 × 33 cm) baking dish.

Fill each of the tomatoes three-quarters of the way with the chicken and rice mixture, and arrange them, filled side up, in the prepared baking dish. (You may need to squish the tomatoes together a little to fit.) If there is extra meat mixture left over, make 1-inch (2.5 cm) meatballs with the remaining mixture and tuck them into the baking dish.

Make the sauce: In a medium bowl, whisk together the tamarind paste, vinegar, oil, brown sugar, salt, and stock until fully combined. Drizzle about 1 teaspoon of the tamarind mixture into each tomato and pour the remainder around the sides.

Cover the baking dish with foil and bake until the tomatoes are tender, about 1 hour. Uncover and continue baking until the tomatoes begin to collapse on themselves and the liquid in the baking dish reduces by about half, about 30 minutes. Let rest for 15 minutes before serving. Serve hot, spooned with juices from the baking dish.

Stuffed Tomatoes with Chicken

CHICKEN PAPRIKASH

Chicken braised in a rosy paprika-heavy sauce is practically the national dish of Hungary. The Jewish version omits sour cream but is still thick and wonderfully flavorful. Serve with egg noodles, or alongside the Hungarian potato dumplings, Shlishkes (page 228).

Serves: 6
Preparation time: 20 minutes
Cooking time: 1½ hours

- 2 tablespoons sweet paprika (ideally Hungarian)
- 1 teaspoon garlic powder
- ½ teaspoon onion powder
- 1 teaspoon kosher salt, plus more as needed
- ½ teaspoon freshly ground black pepper, plus more as needed
- 4 lb (1.8 kg) bone-in, skin-on chicken thighs and drumsticks, patted dry
- 2 tablespoons vegetable oil
- 1 onion, finely chopped
- 1 red bell pepper, finely chopped
- 2 celery stalks, thinly sliced
- 6 garlic cloves, finely chopped
- 1 can (28 oz/795 g) diced (chopped) tomatoes
- 3 tablespoons tomato paste (purée)
- ½ cup (120 ml/4 fl oz) chicken stock
- 1 bay leaf
- ¼ teaspoon cayenne pepper, plus more as needed
- Chopped fresh parsley, for serving

In a small bowl, stir together the paprika, garlic powder, onion powder, salt, and black pepper. Rub the mixture evenly over the chicken pieces, reserving any excess rub. In a large Dutch oven (casserole) or other large heavy-bottomed pot, heat the oil over medium-high heat until shimmering but not smoking. Working in batches, add the chicken pieces and brown them on both sides, turning once, about 3 minutes per side. Transfer the browned chicken to a plate.

Reduce the heat to medium and add the onion, bell pepper, celery, and garlic and cook, stirring occasionally, until softened and lightly browned, 7–10 minutes. Stir in any remaining paprika rub along with the tomatoes and their juice, tomato paste (purée), stock, bay leaf, and cayenne. Bring the mixture to a low boil, then return the chicken pieces to the pot. Reduce the heat to medium-low, cover, and simmer, stirring occasionally, until the chicken is cooked through and tender, 50–55 minutes.

Remove the chicken pieces with tongs and arrange on a serving platter. Increase the heat to medium-high and allow the sauce to cook down in the pan, stirring often, until it thickens slightly, 5–10 minutes. Taste and season with additional salt, black pepper, and cayenne, if desired. Serve hot, spooning the sauce over the chicken and topping with fresh parsley.

CHICKEN SCHNITZEL

Fried cutlets are common fare across Europe. Central European Jewish cooks prefer their cutlets made with chicken, a dish they brought with them to Israel where it became a national obsession. Serve the cutlets with rice or Israeli couscous, or tuck them inside warm pita spread with hummus and dotted with sliced pickles.

Serves: 6–8
Preparation time: 15 minutes
Cooking time: 30 minutes

- 6 boneless, skinless chicken breasts
- 1 cup (140 g) all-purpose (plain) flour
- 2 teaspoons onion powder
- 2 teaspoons garlic powder
- 4 eggs
- 2 cups (120 g) panko breadcrumbs
- Kosher salt and freshly ground black pepper
- Vegetable oil, for frying
- Lemon wedges, for serving

Using a sharp knife, carefully halve each chicken breast horizontally, then use a meat mallet to gently pound them to a ¼-inch (6 mm) thickness. You should end up with 12 relatively uniform pieces of chicken breast.

In a wide shallow bowl or small baking dish, stir together the flour, onion powder, and garlic powder. Beat the eggs together in a second bowl. Add the panko to a third bowl. Season the chicken pieces on both sides with salt and pepper. Dredge the chicken pieces in the flour mixture on both sides. Dip in the eggs, shaking off the excess, then coat well with the panko.

Line a large plate with paper towels. In a large frying pan, heat ¼ inch (6 mm) oil over medium-high heat until shimmering. Working in batches, add the coated chicken pieces to the hot pan and cook, turning once, until crispy and cooked through, 5–6 minutes. Transfer the chicken to the paper towels to drain. Serve hot, with lemon wedges on the side for squeezing.

CHICKEN AND ALMONDS WITH RED RICE

Iraqi Jews poach chicken in a spiced tomato sauce and then, in a move of culinary thrift and genius, they cook rice in the same flavorful poaching liquid. The resulting rice takes on a lovely red hue and a savory flavor that is complemented by a mix of crunchy slivered almonds and sweet golden raisins. Called *plau b'jeej*, this dish is relatively labor intensive, so is usually reserved for Shabbat, holidays, and other special meals. It reheats well and the flavors blossom overnight in the fridge, so it is an ideal make-ahead dish for company.

Serves: 6
Preparation time: 15 minutes
Cooking time: 1 hour 50 minutes

- ¼ cup (60 ml) plus 2 tablespoons vegetable oil
- 4 lb (1.8 kg) bone-in, skin-on chicken thighs and drumsticks, patted dry
- Kosher salt and freshly ground black pepper
- 1¼ cups (300 g) tomato paste (purée)
- 2 teaspoons sweet paprika
- 1 teaspoon ground cinnamon
- 1 teaspoon ground cumin
- 1 teaspoon ground turmeric
- ½ teaspoon crushed pepper flakes
- 3 large onions, halved through the root and thinly sliced
- ¾ cup (90 g) slivered almonds
- ½ cup (70 g) golden raisins (sultanas)
- 1 tablespoon Baharat (page 412)
- 2 cups (400 g) long-grain white rice, soaked for 20 minutes and drained

In a large Dutch oven (casserole) or other large pot, heat 2 tablespoons of the oil over medium-high heat. Generously season the chicken pieces on both sides with salt and pepper. Working in batches, brown the chicken, turning once, until browned on both sides, 8–10 minutes. Return all the browned chicken pieces to the Dutch oven.

In a medium bowl, whisk together 5 cups (1.2 liters/ 40 fl oz) water, the tomato paste (purée), paprika, cinnamon, cumin, turmeric, and pepper flakes until well combined. Pour over the chicken. Bring to a boil over medium-high heat, then reduce the heat to low, cover, and cook, stirring occasionally, until the chicken is very tender, 1–1½ hours.

Meanwhile, in a large frying pan, heat the remaining ¼ cup (60 ml/2 fl oz) oil over medium heat. Add the onions and a generous pinch of salt and cook, stirring occasionally, until softened and browned, 20–25 minutes. If the onions are browning too quickly, reduce the heat slightly and stir in a couple of teaspoons of water. Add the almonds and golden raisins (sultanas) and continue cooking for 5 minutes. Stir in the *baharat* and cook, until fragrant, 1–2 minutes. Taste, and add more salt, if desired, and remove from the heat.

When the chicken is done, remove the chicken pieces with tongs or a slotted spoon and set aside. Pour the cooking liquid out of the Dutch oven into a bowl. Measure out 3½ cups (830 ml/28 fl oz) of the liquid and return to the Dutch oven (discard the rest). Stir in 1½ teaspoons salt and the rice and bring to a boil. Reduce the heat to low, cover, and simmer until the rice is tender and the liquid has evaporated, 18–20 minutes. Remove the pan from the heat and let stand covered for 5 minutes, then fluff with a fork.

Mound the rice on a large serving platter. Top with the chicken pieces and onion mixture. Serve hot.

CHICKEN AND CHESTNUT OMELET

The cuisine of Azerbaijani Jews (also known as Mountain Jews) is typically quite hearty and satisfying, and closely mirrors the local non-Jewish cuisine. But this baked egg dish, called *hoyagusht*, is specifically linked to the Jews of Baku. There are several variations filled with meat, herbs, or vegetables, particularly eggplant (aubergine). The combination of tender poached chicken and velvety chestnuts is particularly delicious.

Serves: 4–6
Preparation time: 20 minutes
Cooking time: 1 hour 15 minutes

For the chicken and stock:
• 1 lb (455 g) skin-on chicken drumsticks
• 1 onion, roughly chopped
• 2 bay leaves
• 1 teaspoon kosher salt

For the omelet:
• 3 tablespoons vegetable oil
• 1 large onion, halved through the root and thinly sliced
• ¾ teaspoon kosher salt, plus more as needed
• ½ teaspoon ground turmeric
• ½ teaspoon sweet paprika
• ½ cup (100 g) cooked and peeled chestnuts, halved
• 5 eggs
• Freshly ground black pepper

Make the chicken and stock: In a medium pot, combine the chicken, onion, bay leaves, and salt and add cold water to cover the ingredients by 1 inch (2.5 cm). Bring to a boil over high heat, then reduce the heat to medium-low, partially cover, and gently simmer, skimming off any foam that accumulates, until the chicken is tender, 40–45 minutes. Pull out the cooked chicken pieces and set aside to cool to the touch, then remove and shred the meat into bite-size pieces (discard the skin and bones). Strain the stock through a fine-mesh sieve and reserve. (Discard the bay leaves and onion pieces.)

Make the omelet: In a large frying pan, heat the oil over medium heat. Add the onion and a pinch of salt and cook, stirring occasionally, until softened and browned, 10–15 minutes. Add the turmeric and paprika and cook, stirring, until fragrant, about 1 minute.

Stir in 1 cup (240 ml/8 fl oz) of the reserved chicken stock, the shredded chicken, and the chestnuts. Cover the pan and cook for 10 minutes, then uncover and continue cooking until almost all of the liquid has evaporated.

Meanwhile, in a bowl, whisk together the eggs, salt, and a generous amount of pepper.

Add the egg mixture to the pan and let cook undisturbed for 30 seconds. Use a silicone spatula to push the cooked egg from the bottom of the pan in several places, allowing the uncooked egg to spill onto the bottom. Cover the pan and cook until the eggs are just set and no longer runny on top, 5–8 minutes. Remove from the heat and let sit, covered, for 5 minutes before slicing. Serve hot.

Chicken and Chestnut Omelet

FESENJAN

Persian Jews adore this tangy Iranian stew, serving it on Rosh Hashanah, when fresh pomegranates come into season. Many Jewish versions of the recipe include dates, which break down as the sauce cooks and lend extra sweetness to the mix of ground walnuts and pomegranate molasses that coat tender pieces of chicken. If you do not use the rose-petal spice mix Advieh (page 412), substitute ¾ teaspoon ground cinnamon and ¼ teaspoon ground cardamom. Serve the stew over rice.

Serves: 6–8
Preparation time: 20 minutes
Cooking time: 1 hour 10 minutes

- 2½ cups (260 g) walnut halves
- 4 tablespoons vegetable oil
- 2½ lb (1.2 kg) boneless, skinless chicken thighs, cut into 2-inch (5 cm) pieces
- Kosher salt and freshly ground black pepper
- 1 large onion, finely chopped
- 3 cups (710 ml/24 fl oz) chicken stock
- 1 cup (240 ml/8 fl oz) Pomegranate Molasses (page 410)
- 6 Medjool dates, pitted and thinly sliced
- 2 tablespoons honey, plus more as needed
- 1 teaspoon Advieh (page 412)
- ½ teaspoon ground turmeric
- 1 bay leaf
- Pomegranate seeds and chopped fresh parsley, for serving

In a large dry frying pan, toast the walnuts over medium-low heat, stirring occasionally, until fragrant and lightly browned, 5–7 minutes. Remove the pan from the heat and let cool. Add the cooled walnuts to a food processor and pulse until finely ground with a few slightly larger pieces. Set aside.

Meanwhile, in a Dutch oven (casserole) or other large wide pot, heat 3 tablespoons of the oil over medium-high heat. Season the chicken pieces on both sides with salt and pepper. Working in batches, brown the chicken pieces, stirring occasionally, until golden on both sides, 4–5 minutes. Transfer the seared chicken pieces to a plate.

Add the remaining 1 tablespoon oil to the pan along with the onion and a pinch of salt. Cook, stirring occasionally, until softened and lightly browned, 6–8 minutes. Stir in the ground walnuts, stock, pomegranate molasses, dates, honey, *advieh*, turmeric, bay leaf, 1¼ teaspoons salt, and ¼ teaspoon pepper. Bring to a boil, then reduce the heat to medium-low. Return the browned chicken pieces to the pan, cover, and cook, stirring often, until the chicken is cooked through, about 30 minutes. Uncover, increase the heat to medium, and continue cooking, stirring often, until the sauce thickens into a stew, 15–20 minutes.

Remove from the heat, taste, and stir in a little more salt, pepper, or honey, if desired. Remove and discard the bay leaf. Serve hot, with pomegranate seeds and parsley sprinkled on top.

MAIN DISHES

HANUKKAH FRIED CHICKEN

For Italian Jews, fried chicken called *pollo fritto per Hanukka* is a hallmark of the Hanukkah table—an edible commemoration of the winter holiday's "miracle of oil". This version has all the components of great fried chicken: satisfyingly crunchy crust, savory flavor, and tender meat within.

Serves: 4–6
Preparation time: 10 minutes, plus marinating
Cooking time: 1 hour

- 4 lb (1.8 kg) bone-in, skin-on chicken thighs and drumsticks
- Grated zest and juice of 2 lemons (about ¼ cup/ 60 ml/ 2 fl oz juice)
- 4 garlic cloves, minced or pushed through a press
- 1 teaspoon kosher salt, plus more for sprinkling
- ½ teaspoon freshly ground black pepper
- Vegetable oil, for frying
- 1½ cups (210 g) all-purpose (plain) flour
- 2½ teaspoons onion powder
- 2 teaspoons garlic powder
- 4 eggs

In a large nonreactive bowl with a tight-fitting lid, combine the chicken pieces, lemon zest, lemon juice, garlic, salt, and pepper. Cover the bowl and marinate the chicken in the fridge, flipping the bowl occasionally, for at least 1 and up to 2 hours (not longer, or the meat will be tough once cooked). Remove from the fridge to come to room temperature while heating the oil.

Line a large plate with several layers of paper towels. Pour about 1½ inches (4 cm) oil into a large, deep cast-iron skillet, set over medium heat, and bring to 375°F (190°C) on a deep-fry thermometer.

Meanwhile, in a wide shallow bowl, whisk together the flour, onion powder, and garlic powder. Beat the eggs in a separate bowl.

Remove the chicken pieces from the marinade and brush off any visible garlic or lemon zest. Dredge both sides of each piece of chicken in the seasoned flour, tapping off the excess. Dip in the egg to coat, allowing excess to drip off, then dip once more in the flour. Working in batches, add the coated chicken pieces to the hot oil and fry, turning occasionally, until the chicken is golden brown and cooked through, 15–20 minutes. An instant-read thermometer inserted into the deepest part of a thigh should register 165°F (74°C). Add more oil to the pan as necessary.

Transfer the fried chicken to the paper towels to drain. Sprinkle with a little salt. Let rest about 5 minutes before serving.

CHICKEN STUFFED WITH SPICED RICE

Iraqi Jews serve rice-stuffed chicken, called *t'beet*, for Shabbat lunch. Like Cholent (page 144) and Hamin (page 148), the dish is cooked at a very low temperature for many hours (typically overnight) until the chicken is falling off the bone and the spiced tomato rice is deeply infused with savory flavor. It also makes lovely picnic fare.

Serves: 4–6
Preparation time: 15 minutes
Cooking time: 10 hours 25 minutes

- 2 tablespoons plus 1 teaspoon kosher salt, plus more as needed
- 2 cups (400 g) basmati rice
- 5 tablespoons vegetable oil
- 2 tablespoons tomato paste (purée)
- 1½ tablespoons Baharat (page 412)
- ½ teaspoon freshly ground black pepper, plus more as needed
- 1 can (14½ oz/411 g) diced (chopped) tomatoes, drained
- 1 large onion, finely chopped
- 4 garlic cloves, finely chopped
- 1 whole chicken (about 4 lb/1.8 kg), patted dry
- 2 cups (475 ml/16 fl oz) chicken or vegetable stock

Fill a large saucepan with water and 2 tablespoons of the salt. Bring to a boil over high heat, add the rice, and cook, uncovered and stirring occasionally, until the rice is partway cooked, 5–7 minutes. Drain and immediately rinse with cold water to stop the cooking process, then set aside to cool.

In a large bowl, whisk together 2 tablespoons of the oil, the tomato paste (purée), *baharat*, 1 teaspoon salt, and pepper. Add the parboiled rice, drained tomatoes, onion, and garlic and stir to fully combine. Spoon as much of the rice and tomato mixture into the cavity of the chicken as possible, then tie the legs together with kitchen twine. (Some cooks sew up the cavity with a needle and kitchen thread, but that step is not necessary.)

Preheat the oven to 225°F (110°C/Gas Mark ¼).

In a Dutch oven (casserole) or other large ovenproof pot with a lid, heat the remaining 3 tablespoons oil over medium-high heat. Sprinkle the stuffed chicken all over with a little salt and pepper, then add to the Dutch oven and sear, carefully turning as necessary, until browned on all sides, 10–15 minutes. Spoon the remaining rice and tomato mixture around the chicken, pour in the stock, and bring to a boil.

Cover, transfer to the oven, and cook until the chicken is very tender and the rice is beginning to brown, 8–10 hours. Serve hot or warm.

Chicken Stuffed with Spiced Rice

JERUSALEM MIXED GRILL

This classic Israeli street food was born in the late-night food stands of Jerusalem—a savory, spicy mix of grilled chicken (traditionally including the heart, liver, and other innards), lamb, and onion. The jumble, called *me'orav Yerushalmi* in Hebrew, is packed into a pita and topped with tahini, sliced Middle Eastern–style pickles, and the tangy mango pickle condiment *amba*.

Serves: 4
Preparation time: 10 minutes
Cooking time: 20 minutes

- 1 lb (455 g) boneless, skinless chicken thighs, patted dry and cut into 1-inch (2.5 cm) pieces
- ½ lb (225 g) lamb shoulder, patted dry and cut into 1-inch (2.5 cm) pieces
- 2 tablespoons extra-virgin olive oil
- 1 large onion, finely chopped
- 1½ teaspoons ground turmeric
- 1 teaspoon ground cumin
- ½ teaspoon ground allspice
- ½ teaspoon ground cinnamon
- ½ teaspoon kosher salt
- ½ teaspoon freshly ground black pepper
- Pita, chopped pickles, Tahini Sauce (page 396), and amba or mango chutney, for serving

Heat a large grill pan (griddle pan) or frying pan over medium-high heat until very hot. Working in batches if necessary (to not crowd the pan), add the chicken pieces and cook, stirring once or twice, until browned but not fully cooked, 2–3 minutes. Transfer the seared chicken to a bowl. Repeat the process with the lamb pieces.

In a large frying pan, heat the oil over medium-high heat. Add the onion and cook, stirring occasionally, until softened and charred in spots, 4–6 minutes. Add the chicken and lamb along with the turmeric, cumin, allspice, cinnamon, salt, and pepper. Cook, stirring occasionally, until the meat is cooked through, 3–4 minutes.

Remove the pan from the heat. Divide the meat mixture and stuff into pitas. Top with pickles, a drizzle of tahini sauce, and *amba*. Serve hot.

CHICKEN TAGINE WITH PRESERVED LEMON

This bright and tangy tagine, which comes packed with green and Kalamata olives and preserved lemon, is arguably Morocco's best-known chicken dish. Moroccan Jews traditionally serve it for Shabbat dinner and to break the fast on Yom Kippur.

Serves: 6
Preparation time: 10 minutes
Cooking time: 1½ hours

- 3 tablespoons vegetable oil
- 4 lb (1.8 kg) bone-in, skin-on chicken thighs and drumsticks, patted dry
- Kosher salt and freshly ground black pepper
- 1 large onion, halved through the root and thinly sliced
- 4 garlic cloves, thinly sliced
- 2 teaspoons sweet paprika
- 1 teaspoon ground cinnamon
- ½ teaspoon ground cumin
- ½ teaspoon ground ginger
- ½ teaspoon ground turmeric
- 2 cups (475 ml/16 fl oz) chicken or vegetable stock
- 1 small Preserved Lemon (page 116), rinsed and thinly sliced
- ½ cup (80 g) cracked green olives, pitted
- ½ cup (80 g) Kalamata olives, pitted
- 1 tablespoon fresh lemon juice
- 1 tablespoon honey
- Chopped fresh flat-leaf parsley, for serving

In a Dutch oven (casserole) or other large heavy-bottomed pot, heat the oil over medium-high heat. Season the chicken pieces on both sides with salt and pepper and, working in batches, brown the chicken pieces on both sides, turning once with tongs, about 3 minutes per side. Transfer the browned chicken to a plate.

Add the onion to the Dutch oven and cook, stirring occasionally, until softened and lightly browned, 6–8 minutes. Add the garlic, paprika, cinnamon, cumin, ginger, and turmeric and cook, stirring, until fragrant, about 1 minute.

Add the stock and bring to a boil. Arrange the browned chicken in the Dutch oven along with the preserved lemon. Reduce the heat to medium-low, cover, and cook, stirring occasionally, until the chicken is very tender, about 1 hour. Transfer the chicken to a serving platter.

Add the green olives, Kalamata olives, lemon juice, and honey to the cooking liquid left in the Dutch oven. Increase the heat to medium-high and cook, uncovered and stirring occasionally, until slightly thickened, 10–15 minutes. Taste and add more salt and pepper, if needed. Pour the sauce over the chicken, and serve hot, sprinkled with parsley.

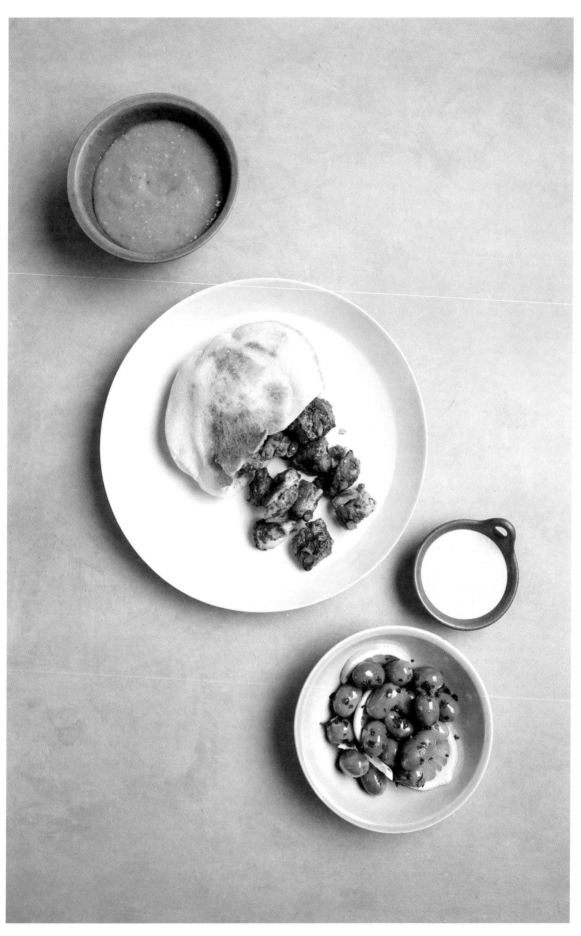

Jerusalem Mixed Grill

SAUERBRATEN

Germany's quintessential pickled pot roast takes serious dedication to prepare—five days of curing in a vinegar-based marinade followed by several hours in the oven. But for a Shabbat, holiday, or other special meal, the tender meat and sweet-meets-tangy sauce is worth the undertaking. Non-Jewish versions of the dish typically contain cream, butter, or both—but this take, scented with a bouquet of spices and sweetened with crumbled gingersnaps (ginger nuts) and raisins, is full of flavor without a hint of dairy. Like Brisket (page 293), sauerbraten tastes best the day after it is made. Let the roast cool, refrigerate it overnight, and then slice the meat and skim off any fat accumulated at the top of the sauce before reheating.

Serves: 6–8
Preparation time: 30 minutes, plus 5 days curing
Cooking time: 3 hours

- 1½ cups (355 ml/12 fl oz) red wine vinegar
- 2½ cups (590 ml/20 fl oz) beef or vegetable stock
- 1 tablespoon honey
- 4 garlic cloves, peeled and smashed
- 6 whole cloves
- 2 bay leaves
- 1 whole star anise
- 2 teaspoons black peppercorns
- 3½–4 lb (1.6–1.8 kg) boneless beef chuck roast (roasting joint)
- Kosher salt and freshly ground black pepper
- 4 large onions, halved through the root and thinly sliced
- 3 tablespoons vegetable oil
- 6 small parve gingersnaps (ginger nuts), crumbled
- ½ cup (70 g) regular or golden raisins (sultanas)

In a medium saucepan, combine the vinegar, stock, honey, garlic, cloves, bay leaves, star anise, and peppercorns. Bring to a boil over medium-high heat, stirring occasionally, then remove from the heat and let cool.

Season all sides of the meat generously with salt and place in a nonreactive baking dish. Add half of the sliced onions to the baking dish, laying some on top of the meat. Pour the cooled marinade on top, cover the baking dish with plastic wrap (cling film), and refrigerate for 5 days. Flip the meat over in the marinade once a day.

On the fifth day, preheat the oven to 325°F (160°C/Gas Mark 3).

Remove the meat from the marinade and thoroughly blot dry with paper towels. Reserving the liquid, strain the marinade through a fine-mesh sieve (discard the solids).

In a large Dutch oven (casserole) or other ovenproof pot with a lid, heat the oil over medium-high heat. Add the meat and sear, turning once, until well browned on both sides, about 12 minutes total. Transfer to a plate.

Add the remaining onions, ½ teaspoon salt, and a generous amount of black pepper to the pan. Cook, stirring often, until softened and lightly browned, about 10 minutes. Return the seared meat to the Dutch oven, pour in the reserved marinade liquid, and bring to a boil.

Cover the Dutch oven, transfer to the oven, and cook for 2 hours. Remove from the oven, flip the meat over, and stir the gingersnaps (ginger nuts) and raisins into the cooking liquid. Continue cooking, covered, until the meat is very tender and the liquid thickens into a sauce, about 1 hour. Transfer the meat to a carving board and let rest for about 30 minutes before slicing. Arrange meat slices on a serving platter and spoon sauce on top.

ANTHONY ROSE

ROSE AND SONS DELI
•
176 DUPONT STREET
TORONTO, ONTARIO
CANADA

FAT PASHA
•
414 DUPONT STREET
TORONTO, ONTARIO
CANADA

SCHMALTZ APPETIZING
•
MULTIPLE LOCATIONS
TORONTO, ONTARIO
CANADA

Anthony Rose is the chef and owner of six Toronto-based restaurants, including several—Rose & Sons Deli, Schmaltz Appetizing, and Fat Pasha—that pay homage to his Jewish Canadian roots.

GRILLED VERSHT AND APRICOTS WITH HONEY AND MUSTARD

This grilled (barbecued) beef salami (*versht* in Yiddish) with charred apricots and jalapeños is a staple at Rose family gatherings and celebrations. It is served with a variety of different honeys and mustards for slathering.

Serves: 6
Preparation time: 20 minutes
Cooking time: 30 minutes

- 6 fresh apricots, halved and pitted
- 1 small red onion, sliced into ¼-inch (6 mm) rounds
- 6 jalapeños, whole
- 3 lb (1.35 kg) all-beef salami, sliced into ¼-inch (6 mm) rounds
- Extra-virgin olive oil, for drizzling
- Kosher salt and freshly ground black pepper
- A variety of honeys, for serving
- A variety of mustards, for serving

Preheat an outdoor grill (barbecue) to medium-hot.

Add the apricots, red onion, jalapeños, and salami to separate bowls. Drizzle each with about 1 tablespoon oil and sprinkle everything but the salami with salt and pepper and gently mix.

Place the apricots on the hot grill, cut side down, and cook, turning once, until softened, about 2 minutes per side. Arrange the apricots on a large serving platter. Add the onion rounds to the grill and grill, turning once, until softened and lightly charred, about 5 minutes per side. Arrange the onions next to the apricots on the platter.

Grill the jalapeños, turning often, until charred all over, about 5 minutes. Transfer to a cutting board and slice into rings, then arrange the jalapeño rings on the platter.

Grill the salami pieces, turning once, until they char and curl up, about 3 minutes per side. Arrange the salami on the serving platter and serve immediately, with honeys and mustards on the side for spreading over top.

SWEET-AND-SOUR BEEF TONGUE

Beef tongue has fallen out of favor in recent decades, but for generations it was considered a thrifty delicacy. In delicatessens, tongue is still generally available, served quite thinly sliced and smeared with mustard. For home cooks, this sweet-and-sour preparation was preferred.

Serves: 6–8
Preparation time: 25 minutes
Cooking time: 9 hours

For the tongue:
- 1 fresh beef tongue (3–4 lb/1.35–1.8 kg)
- 1 teaspoon kosher salt
- ½ teaspoon freshly ground black pepper
- 1 onion, halved through the root and thinly sliced
- 4 garlic cloves, peeled and smashed
- 1 bay leaf

For the sauce:
- 2 tablespoons vegetable oil
- 1 large onion, finely chopped
- 1 can (15 oz/425 g) tomato sauce (seasoned passata)
- 1 tablespoon tomato paste (purée)
- 2 tablespoons red wine vinegar
- ⅓ cup (100 g) apricot jam
- 1 teaspoon kosher salt, plus more to taste
- ½ teaspoon freshly ground black pepper

Prepare the tongue: Season the tongue on both sides with the salt and pepper, then place in a large slow cooker. Add the onion, garlic, bay leaf, and enough water to just cover the ingredients. Cover and cook on low for 8 hours. Transfer the cooked tongue to a carving board and allow to cool to the touch. (Discard the other ingredients.) Carefully peel off the skin and discard, then slice the meat into pieces ¼ inch (6 mm) thick and layer in a baking dish.

Preheat the oven to 350°F (°180C/Gas Mark 4).

Make the sauce: In a Dutch oven (casserole) or large pot, heat the oil over medium heat. Add the onion and cook, stirring occasionally, until softened and lightly browned, 6–8 minutes. Stir in the tomato sauce (seasoned passata), ½ cup (120 ml/4 fl oz) water, tomato paste (purée), vinegar, apricot jam, salt, and pepper. Bring to a simmer, then taste and add more salt, if desired.

Pour the sauce into the baking dish over and around the sliced tongue. Cover the baking dish with foil and bake until the mixture is bubbling, 30–45 minutes.

CORNED BEEF

Along with pastrami (see page 296), corned beef (salt beef) is king of the Jewish delicatessen. But unlike pastrami, which requires a smoker to prepare, any home cook with a little patience can make corned beef and pile it as high as you would like on rye bread slathered with mustard. It goes wonderfully with coleslaw or Health Salad (page 81) and a crunchy kosher dill pickle.

Serves: 6–8
Preparation time: 15 minutes, plus 6 days curing
Cooking time: 4 hours

For the curing:
- 1 cup (160 g) kosher salt
- ½ cup (90 g) light brown sugar
- 2 teaspoons pink curing salt #1
- 5 garlic cloves, peeled and crushed
- 4 bay leaves
- 1 cinnamon stick
- 6 whole cloves
- 2 teaspoons yellow mustard seeds
- 1 teaspoon black peppercorns
- 1 teaspoon coriander seeds
- 4 lb (1.8 kg) brisket

For cooking:
- 1 onion, peeled and halved through the root
- 4 garlic cloves, peeled and smashed
- 1 large carrot, peeled
- 2 celery stalks
- 2 bay leaves
- 1 tablespoon kosher salt

Make the brine and cure the brisket: In a large nonreactive pot, vigorously whisk together 4 quarts (3.8 liters) water, the kosher salt, brown sugar, and curing salt until the sugar and salts fully dissolve. Stir in the garlic, bay leaves, cinnamon, cloves, mustard seeds, peppercorns, and coriander. Add the brisket to the pot, weighing it down with a plate so it stays submerged, if necessary. Refrigerate, turning the brisket over every day, for 6 days.

Cook the brisket: On the sixth day, remove the meat from the brine, rinse it well, and pat it dry with paper towels. In a large pot, combine the onion, garlic, carrot, celery, bay leaves, and salt. Add the brisket, followed by enough water to fully cover the ingredients. Bring to a boil over high heat, then reduce the heat to medium-low, partially cover, and cook until meat is fork-tender, 3–4 hours. Transfer the meat to a carving board and let rest for at least 30 minutes before slicing. (Discard the cooking liquid and vegetables.) Thinly slice the meat against the grain and serve.

BRISKET

Like many Jewish dishes, brisket developed out of necessity. Many Jewish home cooks in Eastern Europe could not afford expensive cuts of meat. So they found ways to transform the tougher, thriftier cuts into something desirable by braising them for extended periods of time until they turned juicy and tender. In twentieth-century America, the dish took on a modern flavor, with cooks adding everything from ketchup and chili sauce to onion soup mix. In the American South, cola became a popular brisket ingredient, with the carbonation contributing to the meat's tender texture, and the syrup adding sweetness. This version keeps things classic and clean, with red wine, tomatoes, garlic, and thyme providing the base of flavor. Brisket takes a while to make, but there is relatively little prep—the majority of the magic happens in the oven. It also tastes even better on the second or third day, the perfect make-ahead dish for any festive dinner.

Serves: 8
Preparation time: 15 minutes
Cooking time: 4½ hours

• 4–5 lb (1.8–2.2 kg) brisket
• Kosher salt and freshly ground black pepper
• 1 tablespoon vegetable oil
• 3 large onions, halved through the root and thinly sliced
• 4 large carrots, halved lengthwise if thick and cut crosswise into 1-inch (2.5 cm) pieces
• 6 sprigs thyme
• 8 garlic cloves, thinly sliced
• 2 bay leaves
• ½ cup (120 ml/4 fl oz) dry red wine
• 3 tablespoons red wine vinegar
• 1 can (15 oz/425 g) can crushed (finely chopped) tomatoes
• 1 cup (240 ml/8 fl oz) beef stock
• ¼ cup (80 g) honey
• 1 teaspoon onion powder
• 1 teaspoon garlic powder

Preheat the oven to 325°F (160°C/Gas Mark 3).

Generously sprinkle both sides of the brisket with salt and pepper. In a large Dutch oven (casserole) or other large pot, heat the oil over medium-high heat. Add the brisket and cook, turning once, until browned on both sides, 8–10 minutes total. (If the brisket does not fit the pan, cut it in half and sear it in two batches.)

Remove the brisket from the pot and set aside. Add the onions, carrots, thyme, garlic, bay leaves, wine, and vinegar. Cook over medium-high heat, stirring often, until the vegetables soften slightly and the mixture is fragrant, about 5 minutes.

In a medium bowl, whisk together the tomatoes, stock, honey, onion powder, garlic powder, and 1 teaspoon salt until fully combined. If you used a Dutch oven: Lay the brisket on top of the onions and carrots and pour the wine-tomato mixture on top. Cover and transfer to the oven. If you used a pot: Transfer the onion and carrot mixture to a roasting pan and top with the brisket, then pour the wine-tomato mixture on top, cover tightly with foil, and transfer to the oven.

Bake for 2 hours. Remove from the oven, uncover, and carefully flip the meat over. Re-cover and continue cooking until the meat is fork-tender, another 1–2 hours.

Transfer the meat to a carving board, cover loosely with foil, and let rest 10–15 minutes before slicing against the grain. Discard the thyme sprigs and bay leaves. Use a slotted spoon to remove the onions and arrange around the brisket. Spoon some pan juices over the brisket before serving.

MAIN DISHES

WINE-BRAISED POT ROAST

Rome's Jews favor their pot roast braised with richly flavored red wine. This saucy version, called *stracotto di manzo*, includes carrots and potatoes, making it a delightful and satisfying one-pot dish.

Serves: 6–8
Preparation time: 10 minutes
Cooking time: 4½ hours

- 3–4 lb (1.35–1.8 kg) boneless beef chuck roast (roasting joint)
- Kosher salt and freshly ground black pepper
- 4 tablespoons extra-virgin olive oil
- 2 large onions, halved through the root and thinly sliced
- 6 garlic cloves, thinly sliced
- 2 bay leaves
- 2 teaspoons onion powder
- ¾ cup (175 ml/6 fl oz) dry red wine
- 1 cup (240 ml/8 fl oz) beef stock
- 1 can (28 oz/795 g) whole peeled tomatoes
- 1 lb (455 g) new potatoes, halved if large
- 2 large carrots, halved lengthwise if thick and cut crosswise into 2-inch (5 cm) pieces

Preheat the oven to 325°F (160°C/Gas Mark 3).

Season both sides of the roast with salt and pepper. In a Dutch oven (casserole) or other large ovenproof pot with a lid, heat 2 tablespoons of the oil over medium-high heat. Add the roast and sear, turning once, until browned on both sides, 8–10 minutes total.

Remove the seared roast and set aside. Add the remaining 2 tablespoons oil to the pan followed by the onions, garlic, and bay leaves and cook, stirring often, until the onions soften, about 10 minutes. Add the onion powder and cook, stirring, until fragrant, about 1 minute.

Add the wine, stock, tomatoes with their juice, and 1½ teaspoons salt. Gently break up the tomatoes with the back of a spoon and bring the mixture to a boil. Nestle the seared meat into the sauce, spooning an ample amount of sauce on top.

Cover, transfer to the oven, and cook for 2 hours. Remove from the oven, uncover, and carefully flip the meat over. Add the potatoes and carrots, tucking them into the sauce. Re-cover and continue cooking until the vegetables are soft and meat is fork-tender, about 2 hours.

Transfer the meat to a carving board, drape loosely with foil, and let rest 10–15 minutes before slicing. Arrange the sliced meat on a serving platter and arrange the potatoes, carrots, and any larger tomato pieces around it. Discard the bay leaves. Set the pan over medium-high heat and boil, stirring occasionally, until reduced by one-third, about 10 minutes. Spoon the sauce over meat and vegetables and serve hot.

Wine-Braised Pot Roast

PASTRAMI, SMOKED MEAT, AND THE JEWISH DELICATESSEN

The delicatessen holds mythical status within Jewish cuisine. Delis are essentially sacred temples of meat—hallowed grounds where sandwiches come thickly piled with juicy cured beef and garlicky salami, where brisket is served smothered in rich gravy, and where chopped liver and pickled beef tongue are revered as icons.

The modern delicatessen that we recognize today formed in New York City—a gift from German sausage makers and butchers who immigrated to America en masse starting in the mid-nineteenth century. Delis began as pushcarts and small shops selling hot dogs, salami, and sausages, primarily on New York's Lower East Side. As an influx of Jewish immigrants from Eastern Europe arrived in the late nineteenth and early twentieth centuries, the deli quickly transformed into something much larger and more established.

Over the decades, delis have spread far beyond New York City and become known for much more than their meaty offerings. The best delicatessens are also reputable places to sample a variety of Ashkenazi home cooking classics, from pillowy knishes (pages 198 and 213) and crispy fried latkes (pages 184–187) and Kasha Varnishkes (page 164). And any deli worth its salt offers a bowl of Kosher Dill Pickles (page 104) and a small saucer of creamy Coleslaw (page 80) in front of customers upon arrival to whet their appetites while they peruse the menu.

And yet, without meat there is no deli—this is particularly true of pastrami (in New York and across America) and smoked meat (in Montreal, Canada, where a smaller, but analogous deli culture emerged at the turn of the twentieth century). Both meats have roots in the Ottoman Empire. Turks cured mutton and fish with salt and spices, creating a jerkylike dish called *basturma*. That technique made its way to the Balkans, where Romanians changed the pronunciation to *pastrama* and used it to cure geese, beef, and other meats.

When Romanian Jews immigrated to New York City in the late nineteenth and early twentieth centuries, they brought *pastrama* with them. There, in the hands of skilled kosher butchers and deli men, it evolved into the heavily spiced, smoked, and steamed brisket-based pastrami people enjoy layered onto sandwiches today. At some point, pastrami methods also took root in Montreal, but the recipe changed again. Montreal smoked meat is rubbed with salt and spices and dry-cured (unlike pastrami, which is wet-brined), then smoked over hardwood, creating a meat that is certainly kin to pastrami, but also entirely its own thing.

Pastrami and smoked meat are unarguably central to delicatessen cuisine, but they are not traditionally dishes people cooked at home. Brisket (page 293), tongue (see Sweet-and-Sour Beef Tongue, page 292), pot roast (Wine-Braised Pot Roast, page 294), and even Corned Beef (page 292) were manageable for home cooks, but pastrami and smoked meat were so time consuming and required such a repertoire of spices and special equipment, people left it to the pros. Everyone else should patronize their local delicatessens as often as possible to help keep these Jewish institutions alive and thriving.

STUFFED CABBAGE

Stuffed cabbage leaf rolls are widespread across both Sephardi and Ashkenazi cuisines, and served spiced and sauced according to local tastes. Russian and Eastern European Jews, who call the dish *holishkes*, tend to prefer a sweet-and-sour sauce—a flavor profile that immigrants from those regions brought with them to America. In the States, home cooks began adding jellied cranberries to the sauce—a decidedly American addition. This version gets its tangy-sweet flavor from vinegar and brown sugar instead, and adds golden raisins (sultanas) for additional jammy sweetness. Tender stuffed cabbage is often eaten on Sukkot, when filled foods help evoke the holiday's themes of harvest and abundance.

Serves: 8–10
Preparation time: 45 minutes
Cooking time: 2 hours

- 1 large head green cabbage (about 4 lb/1.8 kg)
- ½ cup (95 g) long-grain white rice
- 4 cups (970 g) canned crushed (finely chopped) tomatoes
- ⅓ cup (60 g) dark brown sugar
- ¼ cup (60 ml/2 fl oz) red wine vinegar
- 1 teaspoon sweet paprika
- ½ cup (70 g) golden raisins (sultanas)
- 2 teaspoons kosher salt
- 1 lb (455 g) ground (minced) beef
- 1 egg
- 2 large onions, 1 grated on the large holes of a box grater, and 1 thinly sliced
- 1 medium carrot, grated on the large holes of a box grater
- Freshly ground black pepper
- Vegetable oil, for greasing the pan

Bring a large pot filled halfway with water to a boil over high heat. Use a sharp knife to cut out the cabbage core, as deep as you can go without going through to the other side. When the water is boiling, carefully drop in the head of cabbage, core side down, and cover the pot tightly with a lid. Let the cabbage boil for 10 minutes, then remove it to a cutting board. Using a pair of tongs, detach as many outer leaves as possible. When you cannot easily remove more leaves, return the cabbage to the water and boil 10 more minutes. Repeat the process until you have 18 pliable leaves. Use a sharp knife to trim off the bottom of each cabbage leaf's tough inner rib (the leaves should roll easily) and set aside.

Meanwhile, bring a medium saucepan half filled with water to a boil over high heat. Reduce the heat to medium, stir in the rice, and cook until about halfway cooked, about 15 minutes. Drain and set aside.

In another medium saucepan, stir together the crushed tomatoes, brown sugar, vinegar, paprika, golden raisins (sultanas), and 1 teaspoon of the salt. Bring to a boil over medium heat, then remove from the heat. Taste and adjust the seasoning, if desired.

In a large bowl, combine the beef, parcooked rice, egg, grated onion, grated carrot, remaining 1 teaspoon salt, and a generous amount of pepper. Use your hands to combine the mixture.

Preheat the oven to 350°F (180°C/Gas Mark 4). Lightly grease the bottom of a large Dutch oven (casserole) or 9 × 13-inch (23 × 33 cm) baking dish with oil.

Arrange the sliced onion rings evenly across the bottom of the Dutch oven or baking dish.

To form the cabbage rolls, spoon 2 heaping tablespoons of the meat filling ½ inch (1.25 cm) above the bottom edge of a cabbage leaf. Fold that ½ inch (1.25 cm) up over the filling, then fold each side of the leaf toward the center. Roll the cabbage leaf up and away from you, tucking the filling inside a neat package. Place the cabbage roll, seam side down, into the Dutch oven or baking dish. Repeat with the remaining leaves and filling.

Reserving 1 cup (240 ml/8 fl oz) of the tomato sauce, spoon the rest over the rolls. Cover with a tight-fitting lid (or 2 layers of foil if using a baking dish) and bake until the cabbage is tender and the rice is fully cooked, about 1 hour. Uncover and spoon the reserved sauce over everything. Re-cover and bake for an additional 30 minutes. Let rest for 10–15 minutes before serving. Serve hot.

STUFFED VEGETABLES

Jewish cuisine varies dramatically from country to country, but one dish that seems to bind virtually every diasporic community together is stuffed vegetables. Home cooks from Poland, Bulgaria, and Lithuania to Libya, Syria, and India share a deep affection for stuffed vegetables—a cooking technique that transforms a bit of meat or cheese and starch into a soulful, crowd-pleasing meal.

"Stuffed vegetables" can refer to any of three distinct categories of dishes. The first includes vegetables like zucchini (courgettes), tomatoes, and eggplants (aubergines) that get hollowed out (or that have a natural cavity, like bell peppers) and then filled. Then there are "stuffed" leaves (most commonly grape, cabbage, Swiss chard, or spinach) that are rolled burrito-style around a filling. The third category includes recipes that batter and fry the stuffed vegetables before braising them in a flavorful sauce. Some are filled with meat and rice, others with rice, pine nuts, and raisins, and others still with cheese and breadcrumbs. The braising sauces vary, too, soured with tamarind paste, pomegranate molasses, lemon juice, or vinegar. Because they are labor intensive, they are often saved for holidays—particularly Sukkot, when stuffed foods are traditionally eaten to symbolize the abundance of the harvest holiday.

STUFFED BELL PEPPERS

Bell peppers filled with a meat and rice mixture are enjoyed by both Ashkenazi and Sephardi Jews. This version's flavor profile skews Hungarian, thanks to the paprika in the filling and the savory tomato sauce. Look for squat, flat-bottomed bell peppers, which will stand up in the baking dish without tipping over.

Serves: 6
Preparation time: 35 minutes
Cooking time: 1 hour 25 minutes

For the peppers:
- ½ cup (100 g) long-grain white rice
- 1 lb (455 g) ground (minced) beef
- 1 onion, grated on the large holes of a box grater (not squeezed)
- 4 garlic cloves, finely chopped
- ½ cup (25 g) finely chopped fresh flat-leaf parsley, plus more for serving
- 1½ teaspoons sweet paprika
- 1 teaspoon kosher salt
- ¼ teaspoon freshly ground black pepper
- 6 medium bell peppers, tops trimmed off and seeded

For the sauce:
- 1 can (15 oz/425 g) tomato sauce (seasoned passata)
- 2 tablespoons vegetable oil
- 4 tablespoons tomato paste (purée)
- 1 tablespoon honey
- ½ teaspoon garlic powder
- ½ teaspoon onion powder
- 1½ teaspoons kosher salt
- ¼ teaspoon freshly ground black pepper

Preheat the oven to 375°F (190°C/Gas Mark 5).

Stuff the peppers: Bring a small saucepan filled with water to a boil over high heat. Add the rice and cook, stirring occasionally, until the rice is halfway tender, about 10 minutes. Drain well and set aside to cool.

In a large bowl, combine the cooled rice, beef, onion, garlic, parsley, paprika, salt, and pepper. Mix well with your hands, kneading in up to ⅓ cup (75 ml/2½ fl oz) warm water as needed to make a very tender, soft meat mixture. Divide the meat mixture evenly among the bell peppers and place the stuffed peppers, open side up, in a baking dish that holds them snugly.

Make the sauce: In a medium bowl, whisk together the tomato sauce (seasoned passata), 1 cup (240 ml/ 8 fl oz) water, the vegetable oil, tomato paste (purée), honey, garlic powder, onion powder, salt, and pepper until fully combined. Pour a couple of tablespoons of the tomato sauce over and into each filled pepper, then pour the remaining sauce into the dish, around the peppers.

Cover the baking dish tightly with foil and bake until the peppers are tender, about 1 hour. Uncover and continue baking until the sauce thickens, about 15 minutes.

STUFFED ZUCCHINI

Syrian Jews serve these beef- and rice-stuffed zucchini (courgettes), called *kousa mashi*, in a tangy tamarind sauce accented with allspice and cinnamon. It takes a bit of practice and a proper vegetable corer (which are inexpensive and available online) to get the hang of hollowing out the thin-skinned vegetables. But the delectable dish is worth the effort.

Serves: 6
Preparation time: 45 minutes
Cooking time: 2 hours

• ½ cup (100 g) long-grain white rice
• 8 medium zucchini (courgettes),
  about 3 lb (1.35 kg), washed and patted dry
• 1 lb (455 g) ground (minced) beef
• 4 garlic cloves, minced or pushed through a press
• ½ teaspoon ground allspice
• ¼ teaspoon ground cinnamon
• 2 teaspoons kosher salt
• Freshly ground black pepper
• 1 cup (165 g) dried apricots
• 4 tablespoons tamarind paste or
  Pomegranate Molasses (page 410)
• ¼ cup (45 g) light brown sugar
• 3 tablespoons tomato paste (purée)
• 2 tablespoons vegetable oil
• Juice of ½ lemon

Bring a small saucepan half filled with water to a boil over high heat. Once boiling, reduce the heat to medium, stir in the rice, and cook until al dente—softened but with a little bite—about 10 minutes. Drain and set aside to cool to the touch.

Meanwhile, trim the ends off of each zucchini (courgette) and halve them crosswise. Using a vegetable corer, carefully hollow out the zucchini lengths, removing as much of the inside pulp as possible without breaking through the skin. (Reserve the pulp for another use.)

In a medium bowl, combine the beef, parcooked rice, ¼ cup (60 ml/2 fl oz) water, the garlic, allspice, cinnamon, 1 teaspoon of the salt, and a generous amount of pepper. Mix with your hands until just combined. Stuff a couple of tablespoons of the meat mixture into each hollowed-out zucchini. Do not overstuff, as the filling will continue to expand as it cooks.

Preheat the oven to 350°F (180°C/Gas Mark 4).

Scatter the dried apricots on the bottom of a 9 × 13-inch (23 × 33 cm) baking dish and arrange the stuffed zucchini on top. If you have any leftover meat mixture after stuffing, form into small meatballs and tuck into the baking dish alongside the zucchini.

In a medium bowl, whisk together the tamarind paste, brown sugar, ¼ cup (60 ml/2 fl oz) water, the tomato paste (purée), oil, and remaining 1 teaspoon salt. Pour evenly over the top of the stuffed zucchini, followed by 1 cup (240 ml/8 fl oz) water.

Cover the baking dish tightly with foil and bake for 1 hour. Remove from the oven, uncover, and drizzle the lemon juice on top. Continue baking, uncovered, until the zucchini are very tender and beginning to shrivel, another 30 minutes to 1 hour. Serve warm, with apricots and sauce from the baking dish spooned on top.

STUFFED ONIONS

To prepare this Syrian delicacy, called *mashi basal*, whole onions get boiled until their layers separate into individual leaves. The translucent leaves are then filled with beef and rice and rolled tightly before getting simmered in a tamarind-flavored sauce. In other parts of the Middle East, pomegranate molasses is used instead of tamarind. Either way, they are an unparalleled delight—one of the true highlights of Jewish cuisine's canon of stuffed vegetables (see page 298).

Serves: 8
Preparation time: 25 minutes
Cooking time: 2 hours 15 minutes

For the onions:
- 5 large yellow onions, peeled
- ⅓ cup (65 g) long-grain rice, rinsed and drained
- 1 lb (455 g) ground (minced) beef
- 1 teaspoon ground cinnamon
- ½ teaspoon ground allspice
- ½ teaspoon ground cumin
- 1 teaspoon kosher salt
- ¼ teaspoon freshly ground black pepper
- ½ cup (25 g) finely chopped fresh flat-leaf parsley
- 15 pitted prunes

For the sauce:
- ⅓ cup (120 g) tamarind paste or Pomegranate Molasses (page 410)
- ¼ cup (60 ml/2 fl oz) red wine vinegar
- 3 tablespoons vegetable oil
- ¼ cup (45 g) light brown sugar
- 2½ teaspoons kosher salt
- 3 tablespoons tomato paste (purée)
- 1 cup (240 ml/8 fl oz) chicken or beef stock

Stuff the onions: Slice off the ends of each onion. Make a vertical slit into one side of each onion, cutting all the way through to the center of the onion. In a large saucepan, combine the onions and water to cover and bring to a boil over high heat. Reduce the heat to medium and simmer, partially covered, until the onions soften and begin to come apart, 20–30 minutes. Drain and let cool to the touch, then separate the individual layers of the onions and set aside. You will use the onion layers as wrappers, similar to cabbage leaves in stuffed cabbage.

Meanwhile, bring a small saucepan half filled with water to a boil over high heat. Once boiling, reduce the heat to medium, stir in the rice, and cook until al dente—softened but with a little bite—about 10 minutes. Drain and set aside to cool to the touch.

In a large bowl, combine the parcooked rice, the beef, cinnamon, allspice, cumin, salt, pepper, and parsley, mixing well to combine. Knead in up to ⅓ cup (75 ml/2½ fl oz) water as needed, a little at a time, until the meat mixture is soft and pliable.

Preheat the oven to 350°F (180°C/Gas Mark 4).

Spoon a rounded tablespoon of meat mixture into each onion layer and roll tightly to seal. Layer the stuffed onions, seam side down, and the prunes in a large Dutch oven (casserole) or other deep, ovenproof pot with a tight-fitting lid. If there is extra meat mixture left over after all of the onion layers have been used, make 1-inch (2.5 cm) meatballs with the remaining mixture and tuck them into the saucepan.

Make the sauce: In a large bowl, whisk together the tamarind paste, vinegar, oil, brown sugar, salt, tomato paste (purée), and stock until fully combined. Pour over the stuffed onions. It is okay if they are not all submerged.

Cover the pot and cook in the oven, shaking once or twice, until the onions are very tender, about 1½ hours. Let rest for 15 minutes before serving. Serve hot.

Stuffed Onions

STUFFED EGGPLANT WITH CHEESE

Eggplants (aubergines) stuffed with meat and rice or cheese and herbs are popular throughout Sephardi cuisine, from the Middle East to the Balkans. This cheesy version, which is fragrant with mint, oregano, and fresh parsley, is delicious dolloped with Tzatziki (page 396) or *borani esfenaj* (Spinach Yogurt Dip, page 100)

Serves: 8
Preparation time: 35 minutes
Cooking time: 1 hour 25 minutes

- 4 medium eggplants (aubergines), about ¾ lb (340 g) each, stems and ends trimmed, halved lengthwise
- ¼ cup (60 ml/2 fl oz) extra-virgin olive oil, plus more for brushing and drizzling
- 1 large onion, finely chopped
- 1½ teaspoons kosher salt, plus more as needed
- 1 cup (240 g) ricotta cheese
- 1 cup (60 g) panko breadcrumbs
- 1 cup (90 g) finely grated parmesan cheese
- 4 oz (115 g) feta cheese, finely crumbled
- ½ cup (25 g) finely chopped fresh parsley
- 1 egg, lightly beaten
- 1½ teaspoons dried oregano
- ½ teaspoon dried mint
- Freshly ground black pepper

Preheat the broiler (grill) and set the rack in its lowest position.

Using a sturdy spoon, scoop out the eggplant (aubergine) pulp, leaving a shell ½ inch (1.25 cm) thick, reserving the pulp. Arrange the eggplant shells, cut side up, on a large sheet pan and brush each with a little olive oil. Broil (grill), rotating the pan once and checking frequently to avoid burning, until the eggplants are browned and about halfway tender, 10–15 minutes. Remove from the broiler and set aside while making the filling.

In a large frying pan, heat the oil over medium heat. Add the onion and a generous pinch of salt and cook, stirring occasionally, until softened and lightly browned, 6–8 minutes. Chop the reserved eggplant pulp and add to the onions. Cook, stirring often, until softened but not mushy, about 10 minutes. Remove from the heat and transfer the mixture to a large bowl. Let cool slightly.

Preheat the oven to 350°F (180°C/Gas Mark 4).

To the eggplant mixture, add the ricotta, about half of the panko, about half of the parmesan, the feta, parsley, egg, oregano, mint, salt, and a generous amount of pepper and stir until well combined.

Dividing evenly, scoop the eggplant and cheese mixture into the eggplant shells (which should remain on the baking sheet). Mix the remaining panko and parmesan in a small bowl, then sprinkle evenly over the filled eggplants.

Drizzle the tops of each eggplant with a little more oil and bake until the eggplant is fully softened and the filling is golden brown, 35–40 minutes. Let cool slightly before serving hot or warm.

MEAT-STUFFED ARTICHOKES

Like the stuffed potato dish Mafroum (page 304), these spiced beef–stuffed artichoke bottoms, called *t'ajines d'artichauts farcis*, are time consuming to make, but transcendently delicious. Traditionally, Moroccan home cooks laboriously peeled and pared fresh artichokes for the dish, but starting with thawed frozen artichoke bottoms (available at Middle Eastern and international food markets) makes it more manageable without sacrificing the dish's flavor. Some cooks omit the frying step, placing the filled artichokes directly into the sauce.

Serves: 6–8
Preparation time: 45 minutes
Cooking time: 1 hour 50 minutes

For the sauce:
- 2 tablespoons vegetable oil
- 1 red bell pepper, finely chopped
- 4 scallions (spring onions), thinly sliced
- 5 garlic cloves, minced or pushed through a press
- ½ teaspoon red wine vinegar
- ½ teaspoon saffron threads, crumbled
- ½ teaspoon ground cinnamon
- ¼ teaspoon crushed pepper flakes
- 5 canned whole plum tomatoes, drained and chopped
- 1½ teaspoons kosher salt, plus more as needed

For the artichokes:
- 1½ lb (680 g) ground (minced) beef
- 1 large onion, grated on the large holes of a box grater
- ¼ cup (35 g) dried breadcrumbs
- ¼ cup (10 g) finely chopped fresh flat-leaf parsley
- 1½ teaspoons kosher salt
- 1½ teaspoons ground turmeric
- 1 teaspoon freshly ground black pepper
- 1 teaspoon ground coriander
- 1 teaspoon ground mace
- 1 teaspoon onion powder
- ¾ teaspoon ground nutmeg
- ½ teaspoon ground cinnamon
- ½ teaspoon ground cumin
- 3 garlic cloves, minced or pushed through a press
- 16 frozen artichoke bottoms, thawed
- 1 cup (140 g) all-purpose (plain) flour
- 1 tablespoon tomato paste (purée)
- 2 eggs
- Vegetable oil, for frying

Make the sauce: In a very large Dutch oven (casserole) or heavy-bottomed saucepan, heat the oil over medium heat. Add the bell pepper and scallions (spring onions) and cook, stirring occasionally, until softened, 7–8 minutes. Add the garlic, vinegar, saffron, cinnamon, pepper flakes, and tomatoes and cook, mashing the tomatoes with the back of a spoon, until completely tender, about 10 minutes. Add 1 cup (240 ml/8 fl oz) water and the salt, reduce the heat to low, and simmer, stirring occasionally, until slightly thickened, about 15 minutes. Taste and add more salt, if needed. Remove from the heat and set aside.

Make the artichokes: In a large bowl, combine the beef, grated onion, and breadcrumbs. Mix with your hands to combine, adding up to ⅓ cup (75 ml/2½ fl oz) water, until the mixture feels very soft and pliable. Add the parsley, salt, turmeric, black pepper, coriander, mace, onion powder, nutmeg, cinnamon, cumin, and garlic and continue mixing until fully combined.

Take 2 heaping tablespoons of the meat mixture and roll it into a ball. Place the ball in the artichoke's rounded base and use the palm of your hand to gently press it down, creating a mound of meat. Continue with the remaining artichokes and meat mixture. If there is any meat mixture left after the artichoke bottoms are stuffed, make 1-inch (2.5 cm) meatballs with the remainder.

Spread the flour in a shallow bowl. In a separate bowl, whisk together the tomato paste (purée) and 2 teaspoons warm water until the tomato paste dissolves. Add the eggs and whisk until fully combined.

In a large frying pan, heat ¼ inch (6 mm) oil over medium heat. Carefully dip the meat-stuffed side of the artichokes in the flour, shaking off the excess, then dip in the egg. (Dip any meatballs in the flour on all sides, followed by the egg.) Working in batches, gently place the stuffed artichokes, meat side down, along with any meatballs in the pan and fry until browned, 3–4 minutes. Remove the browned artichoke bottoms and meatballs to a plate and let them cool slightly.

Arrange the browned artichokes, meat side up, in a single layer in the Dutch oven on top of the tomato sauce. Tuck any meatballs alongside. Set the pan back over medium heat and add enough water so that the liquid comes halfway up the artichokes. Bring to a simmer, then reduce the heat to low, cover, and cook, occasionally basting the artichokes with the tomato sauce, until completely tender, about 1 hour.

Remove the artichokes to a serving platter. Increase the heat to medium and simmer the sauce, stirring often, until slightly thickened, about 5 minutes. Spoon the sauce over the artichokes and serve hot.

MAFROUM

To make this dish, a vegetable (most often an eggplant/aubergine or potato) is slit almost completely in half to make something akin to a clam shell or pita pocket, then stuffed with spiced ground (minced) beef. From there, it is coated in flour and egg and fried, then braised in a flavorful tomato sauce. The process is laborious, but the resulting dish is nothing short of magical. Libyan Jews serve it for Friday night dinner, but it would be a showstopping main dish at any festive meal.

Serves: 6–8
Preparation time: 45 minutes
Cooking time: 1 hour 45 minutes

For the sauce:
- 3 tablespoons vegetable oil
- 1 large onion, finely chopped
- 4 garlic cloves, minced or pushed through a press
- 1 teaspoon sweet paprika
- 2 cups (475 ml/16 fl oz) chicken or vegetable stock
- 4 tablespoons tomato paste (purée)
- ½ cup (120 ml/4 fl oz) tomato sauce (seasoned passata)
- 1 teaspoon kosher salt
- ½ teaspoon freshly ground black pepper

For the filling:
- 1 lb (455 g) ground (minced) beef
- ½ cup (25 g) finely chopped fresh flat-leaf parsley
- 1 small onion, grated on the large holes of a box grater
- ⅓ cup (45 g) dried breadcrumbs
- 1 teaspoon Baharat (page 412)
- ½ teaspoon garlic powder
- ½ teaspoon kosher salt
- ¼ teaspoon freshly ground black pepper

For the potatoes:
- 6 medium russet (baking) potatoes (about 2 lb/910 g)
- Vegetable oil, for frying
- 1 cup (140 g) all-purpose (plain) flour
- 2 eggs

Make the sauce: In a large Dutch oven (casserole) or a heavy-bottomed pot, heat the oil over medium heat. Add the onion and garlic and cook, stirring occasionally, until softened and lightly browned, 6–8 minutes. Stir in the paprika, stock, tomato paste (purée), tomato sauce (seasoned passata), salt, and pepper. Bring to a boil and cook until slightly thickened, about 5 minutes. Remove from the heat and set aside in the Dutch oven until needed.

Make the filling: In a large bowl, combine the beef, parsley, onion (with any liquid that formed during grating), breadcrumbs, *baharat*, garlic powder, salt, and pepper. Mix with your hands to combine adding up to ⅓ cup (75 ml/2.5 fl oz) warm water, a little at a time, until the mixture feels very soft and pliable.

Prepare the potatoes: Peel the potatoes and slice them into rounds ½ inch (1.25 cm) thick. Using a sharp knife, make a horizontal slit into each potato round, stopping a little past halfway through. (Take care not to go all the way through to the other side.) You should end up with rounds of potato that can open like clams. Take rounded tablespoons of the meat mixture and carefully stuff them into the opening.

In a large frying pan, heat about ½ inch (1.25 cm) oil over medium heat. Spread the flour in a shallow bowl. Beat the eggs in a separate bowl. Dip the stuffed potatoes in the flour on each side, shaking off excess, then dip in the egg, allowing excess to drip off. Working in batches, fry the stuffed potatoes until golden brown on both sides, 3–4 minutes per side. Remove to a large plate to rest while continuing to fry the remaining potatoes.

Arrange the stuffed potatoes in an overlapping single layer in the sauce. If there is remaining meat mixture, roll it into 1-inch (2.5 cm) balls and tuck the meatballs alongside the stuffed potatoes. Set the Dutch oven back over medium heat and bring to a simmer, then reduce the heat to low, cover, and cook, occasionally basting the stuffed potatoes with the sauce, until completely tender, about 1 hour. Serve hot, with sauce spooned over the stuffed potatoes.

Mafroum

LAYERED MEAT AND MATZO PIE

Sephardi Jews' love affair with savory pastries extends into Passover, when several variations of matzo pies are made with greens and cheese, or meat and vegetables. They are popular in communities hailing from Turkey, the Balkans, the Middle East, and North African. This version, called *mina de carne,* layers spiced ground meat and sautéed zucchini (courgettes) between sheets of the softened Passover cracker. It makes a stately main dish for the seder.

Serves: 8–10
Preparation time: 30 minutes
Cooking time: 1 hour 20 minutes

• 3 tablespoons vegetable oil
• 2 large onions, finely chopped
• 4 garlic cloves, finely chopped
• 1 teaspoon kosher salt, plus more as needed
• 2 medium zucchini (courgettes),
  peeled and finely chopped
• 1 lb (455 g) ground (minced) beef or lamb
• 1½ teaspoons ground cinnamon
• 1½ teaspoons ground cumin
• 1 teaspoon sugar
• 1 can (28 oz/795 g) crushed (finely chopped)
  tomatoes
• Freshly ground black pepper
• 5 eggs
• 9 sheets matzo
• Finely chopped fresh flat-leaf parsley, for serving

In a large frying pan, heat the oil over medium heat. Add the onions, garlic, and a pinch of salt and cook, stirring occasionally, until softened and lightly browned, 10–15 minutes. Add the zucchini (courgettes) and cook, stirring often, until softened and any liquid from the zucchini has evaporated, 10–15 minutes. Add the beef and cook, breaking up the meat into small pieces with the back of a spoon, until browned, about 5 minutes.

Carefully pour off any excess fat from the pan, then add the cinnamon, cumin, sugar, tomatoes, salt, and a generous amount of pepper. Cook, stirring occasionally, until slightly thickened, about 5 minutes. Taste and add more salt, if desired. Remove from the heat and let cool to room temperature. Once cool, crack 4 of the eggs into the sauce and stir to fully combine.

Preheat the oven to 350°F (180°C/Gas Mark 4). Grease a 9 × 13-inch (23 × 33 cm) baking dish.

Fill a shallow container with warm water and dip in 3 sheets of matzo. Let the matzo soften until pliable but not falling apart, 2–3 minutes. Shake off the excess water and arrange the matzo sheets in the bottom of the greased baking dish. Break the third matzo, if necessary, to fit it into the dish. Cover with about half of the tomato-meat sauce. Repeat the process with 3 more softened matzo sheets and the remaining tomato-meat sauce.

Soften the remaining 3 sheets of matzo and arrange on top. Whisk the remaining egg in a small bowl and brush generously over the top of the matzo (you will not use all of it). Cover the baking dish with foil and bake until softened and gently puffed, about 35 minutes. Uncover and continue baking until golden brown, 10–15 minutes. Let stand for 10 minutes before cutting. Serve warm or at room temperature, sprinkled with parsley.

SWEET-AND-SOUR POTTED MEATBALLS

Ashkenazi Jews typically serve these meatballs as an appetizer or as hors d'oeuvres at a wedding. But served over rice, they make a lovely weeknight or Shabbat main dish as well. Old World cooks relied on sour salt (citric acid crystals) to give the tomato sauce its mouth-puckering tang, but red wine vinegar makes a fine substitute that is more suited to the contemporary palate.

Serves: 6
Preparation time: 20 minutes
Cooking time: 45 minutes

For the sauce:
• 2 tablespoons vegetable oil
• 1 large onion, finely chopped
• 1 can (15 oz/425 g) tomato sauce (seasoned passata)
• 1 tablespoon tomato paste (purée)
• 2 tablespoons red wine vinegar
• ⅓ cup (60 g) light brown sugar
• 1 teaspoon kosher salt, plus more to taste
• ½ teaspoon freshly ground black pepper

For the meatballs:
• 2 lb (910 g) ground (minced) beef
• 1 medium onion, grated on the large holes of a box grater
• 1 egg, lightly beaten
• ½ cup (70 g) dried breadcrumbs or matzo meal
• ½ teaspoon garlic powder
• 1½ teaspoons kosher salt
• ½ teaspoon freshly ground black pepper

Make the sauce: In a Dutch oven (casserole) or large saucepan, heat the oil over medium heat. Add the onion and cook, stirring occasionally, until softened and lightly browned, 6–8 minutes. Stir in the tomato sauce (seasoned passata), ½ cup (120 ml/4 fl oz) water, the tomato paste (purée), vinegar, brown sugar, salt, and pepper. Bring to a simmer, then taste and add more salt, if desired. Remove from the heat.

Make the meatballs: In a large bowl, combine the beef, onion (with any juices), egg, breadcrumbs, garlic powder, salt, and pepper and mix well to combine.

Place the saucepan back over medium heat. Scoop out rounded tablespoons of the meat mixture, form into balls, and nestle in the sauce. (It is okay if not all of the meatballs fit under the sauce.) Reduce the heat to medium-low, cover, and simmer the meatballs, gently stirring once or twice, until cooked through, 30–35 minutes. Serve the meatballs hot with sauce spooned on top

ALBÓNDIGAS

Meatballs, which are central to the Sephardi kitchen and a mainstay of the Shabbat and holiday table, date back to pre-Inquisition Spain. There, Iberian Jewish and Moorish communities lived and cooked side by side. After the Inquisition, Jews took *albóndigas* with them to North Africa, Turkey, Italy, and other places they settled after being exiled. The dish's name stems from the Arabic word *al-bunduq*, or "hazelnut"—as such, Sephardi meatballs tend to be small and round. For a milder meatball, swap out half of the lamb for beef. When made with matzo meal instead of breadcrumbs, these meatballs make an enticing Passover mezze or main dish.

Serves: 8
Preparation time: 20 minutes
Cooking time: 30 minutes

• 2 lb (910 g) ground (minced) lamb
• 1 teaspoon kosher salt
• 1 tablespoon ground cumin
• 1 teaspoon ground coriander
• ½ teaspoon ground cinnamon
• ¼ teaspoon smoked paprika
• ¼ teaspoon cayenne pepper, plus more to taste
• ½ cup (25 g) finely chopped fresh flat-leaf parsley
• 1 small onion, grated on the large holes of a box grater
• 2 eggs, lightly beaten
• ⅓ cup (45 g) breadcrumbs or matzo meal
• ¼ cup (30 g) pine nuts, minced
• 2 tablespoons vegetable oil, plus more as needed

In a large bowl, combine the ground lamb, salt, cumin, coriander, cinnamon, paprika, cayenne, parsley, onion (with its juice), eggs, breadcrumbs, and pine nuts. Use your hands to mix everything together until well combined.

Scoop out a heaping tablespoon of the lamb mixture and roll it into a 1-inch (2.5 cm) ball. Set it on a baking sheet and continue scooping and rolling with the remaining lamb mixture.

In a large frying pan, heat the oil over medium heat. Working in batches, add the meatballs to the pan and cook, turning occasionally, until browned all over and cooked through, 7–10 minutes. If pan begins to look dry, add a little more oil. Serve hot. Store leftovers, covered, in the fridge for up to 3 days.

MAIN DISHES

MOUSSAKA

Moussaka typically comes topped with a thick layer of béchamel. But observant Greek Jewish home cooks omit the sauce or use a creamy but dairy-free sauce made with stock instead of milk, as this recipe does.

Serves: 8
Preparation time: 25 minutes
Cooking time: 1½ hours

For the base and sauce:
- ¼ cup (60 ml/2 fl oz) plus 6 tablespoons extra-virgin olive oil, plus more for brushing
- 4 small eggplants (aubergines), about 1 lb (455 g) each, peeled
- Kosher salt and freshly ground black pepper
- 2 medium yellow onions, finely chopped
- 1 lb (455 g) ground (minced) lamb or beef
- 6 garlic cloves, minced or pushed through a press
- 1 tablespoon dried oregano
- 1 teaspoon ground cinnamon
- ¼ teaspoon ground allspice
- 1 can (28 oz/795 g) crushed (finely chopped) tomatoes

For the béchamel:
- 6 tablespoons (85 g) nonhydrogenated margarine
- ½ cup (70 g) all-purpose (plain) flour
- 3 cups (710 ml/24 fl oz) chicken stock
- 1 teaspoon kosher salt
- Freshly ground black pepper
- 3 egg yolks

Make the base and sauce: Preheat the oven to 400°F (200°C/Gas Mark 6). Generously grease 2 large sheet pans with 3 tablespoons oil each.

Slice 3 of the peeled eggplants (aubergines) into rounds ½ inch (1.25 cm) thick. Arrange the eggplant slices in a single layer on the pans and brush the tops generously with more oil. Season with salt and pepper. Bake, flipping the eggplant pieces once, until softened and lightly browned, about 25 minutes. Set aside. Leave the oven on, but reduce the temperature to 350°F (180°C/Gas Mark 4).

Meanwhile, cut the remaining eggplant into ½-inch (1.25 cm) cubes. In a large frying pan, Heat the remaining ¼ cup (60 ml/2 fl oz) oil over medium heat. Add the onions and a pinch of salt and cook, stirring occasionally, until soft and translucent, 5–7 minutes.

Add the chopped eggplant and lamb and cook, stirring occasionally and breaking up any large pieces of meat with a spoon, until the meat is browned and the eggplant is softened, 7–10 minutes. Stir in the garlic, oregano, cinnamon, and allspice and cook until fragrant, about 1 minute. Stir in the tomatoes, 1 teaspoon salt, and ¼ teaspoon pepper and simmer until slightly thickened, 5–10 minutes. Taste and season with more salt and pepper, if desired.

Make the béchamel: In a medium saucepan, melt the margarine over medium heat. Add the flour and whisk until fully combined, then gradually whisk in the stock. Bring to a low boil, whisking constantly, until the sauce thickens enough to coat the back of a spoon, 7–10 minutes. Whisk in the salt and a generous amount of pepper. In a separate small bowl, beat the egg yolks. Whisking constantly, slowly drizzle about ½ cup (120 ml/4 fl oz) of the hot béchamel into the beaten eggs. Reduce the heat under the saucepan to medium-low and slowly whisk the tempered egg mixture into the béchamel. Remove from the heat.

To assemble the moussaka, grease the bottom of a 9 × 13-inch (23 × 33 cm) baking dish with a little oil. Layer half of the eggplant slices in the bottom of the baking dish and cover with half of the lamb and eggplant sauce. Layer the remaining eggplant slices into the dish and cover with the remaining sauce. Pour the béchamel evenly on top, smoothing with a rubber spatula. Bake until bubbling and golden brown, 20–25 minutes. Let stand for 15 minutes before serving. Serve hot.

GHORMEH SABZI

Considered one of Iran's national dishes, this robustly flavored, herb-packed stew (*ghormeh* means "stew" in Farsi and *sabzi* means "herbs") is also central to the cuisine of Persian Jews. The stew's bitter-tangy profile, which comes from fenugreek seeds and fragrant dried limes, perfectly offsets the richness of the meat and beans. Both fenugreek and dried limes can be found at Middle Eastern stores or ordered online. This dish tastes best the second day, when the flavors have had a chance to meld.

Serves: 6
Preparation time: 30 minutes
Cooking time: 2½ hours

- ¼ cup (60 ml/2 fl oz) vegetable oil
- 2 lb (910 g) boneless beef chuck, cut into 1-inch (2.5 cm) pieces
- 1 large onion, finely chopped
- ½ teaspoon kosher salt, plus more as needed
- 2 teaspoons fenugreek seeds
- 1½ teaspoons ground turmeric
- 6 scallions (spring onions), white and green parts, thinly sliced
- 2 large bunches flat-leaf parsley, tough bottom stems removed, leaves roughly chopped
- 1 large bunch cilantro (coriander), tough bottom stems removed, leaves roughly chopped
- 4 cups (950 ml/32 fl oz) chicken stock
- 2 dried limes
- 1 can (15 oz/425 g) red kidney beans, rinsed and well drained
- Freshly ground black pepper

In a Dutch oven (casserole) or large pot, heat the oil over medium-high heat. Working in batches, add the beef and cook, stirring occasionally, until lightly browned, about 5 minutes. Transfer the meat to a plate.

Add the onion and a pinch of salt to the Dutch oven and cook, stirring occasionally, until softened and lightly browned, 6–8 minutes. Add the fenugreek, turmeric, scallions (spring onions), parsley, and cilantro (coriander) and cook, stirring, until fragrant and the herbs have wilted, 2–3 minutes.

Add the stock and 2 cups (475 ml/16 fl oz) water. Using a fork, poke a few holes into the limes and add them whole to the Dutch oven. Bring the mixture to a boil, then reduce the heat to medium-low, cover, and cook, stirring occasionally, for 1½ hours.

Stir in the kidney beans, salt, and a generous amount of pepper and continue cooking, covered, until the beef is very tender and the mixture thickens into a stew, 15–30 minutes. Taste and add more salt and pepper, if desired. Discard the limes and serve hot.

GARLICKY BROILED STEAK

Jewish Romanian steakhouses flourished across lower Manhattan in the early and mid-twentieth century. They were classy places with white linen tablecloths and waiters in suits. And obligatory on the menu was broiled steak—a long strip of skirt steak (bavette) that was thickly smeared with garlic paste and broiled (grilled) until glistening. While the era of the Romanian steakhouse has passed (today, Sammy's on the Lower East Side is the lone survivor), the steak itself has timeless appeal.

Serves: 4
Preparation time: 10 minutes
Cooking time: 5 minutes

- 1 lb (455 g) skirt steak (bavette)
- Kosher salt and freshly ground black pepper
- 2 tablespoons extra-virgin olive oil
- 4 garlic cloves, grated on a Microplane

Preheat the broiler (grill). Line a large sheet pan with foil.

Season the meat generously on both sides with salt and pepper and lay on the prepared pan. If the steak is too long, cut it into 2 pieces and lay side by side. Broil (grill) for 3 minutes, then flip and broil another 2–4 minutes, depending on desired doneness. Transfer the meat to a carving board and let rest for 10 minutes.

While the meat is resting, in a small bowl, stir together the oil, grated garlic, and a pinch of salt. Brush the garlic oil evenly on top of the meat. (You might not use all of it.) Slice the steak thinly against the grain and serve hot.

MAKOUD

Tunisian Jews serve this hearty casserole, which is essentially a frittata enriched with beef and mashed potatoes, on the harvest holiday Sukkot.

Serves: 6–8
Preparation time: 20 minutes, plus cooling
Cooking time: 55 minutes

- 8 eggs
- ½ lb (225 g) russet (baking) potatoes, peeled and quartered
- 2 tablespoons vegetable oil
- 1 onion, finely chopped
- 1 lb (455 g) ground (minced) beef
- ¾ teaspoon kosher salt
- ½ teaspoon freshly ground black pepper
- ½ teaspoon onion powder

Place 2 of the eggs in a medium saucepan and cover with water by 1 inch (2.5 cm). Bring to a boil, uncovered, over high heat. As soon as the water boils, remove from the heat, cover, and let sit for 20 minutes. Drain the eggs and cover with cold water to stop the cooking process. Peel the eggs and and chop them.

Meanwhile, in a medium pot, combine the potatoes with water to cover by 2 inches (5 cm). Bring to a boil over high heat, then reduce the heat to medium-high and cook until the potatoes are tender, 15–20 minutes. Drain and mash with a potato masher until smooth.

Preheat the oven to 350°F (180°C/Gas Mark 4). Generously grease a 9-inch (23 cm) round cake pan.

In a medium frying pan, heat the oil over medium heat. Add the onion and cook, stirring occasionally, until softened and lightly browned, 6–8 minutes. Add the beef and cook, breaking up large pieces with the back of a spoon, until just browned, about 5 minutes.

Crack the remaining 6 eggs into a large bowl. Add the mashed potatoes, salt, pepper, and onion powder and stir until fully combined. Add the chopped hard-boiled eggs and the beef-onion mixture and gently fold to combine.

Transfer to the prepared cake pan to the oven and bake until set and golden brown, about 30 minutes.

MICHAEL SOLOMONOV

ZAHAV
•
237 ST. JAMES PLACE
PHILADELPHIA, PA
USA

ABE FISHER
•
1623 SANSOM STREET
PHILADELPHIA, PA
USA

James Beard Award–winning restaurateurs Michael Solomonov and Steven Cook run numerous influential restaurants, including the groundbreaking modern Middle Eastern restaurant Zahav and the artisanal hummus shop Dizengoff, both in Philadelphia. They also partner with chef Yehuda Sichel at Abe Fisher, their small-plates restaurant focused on American Jewish cuisine.

GRILLED RIB-EYE AND BROCCOLI SALAD WITH MANISCHEWITZ STEAK SAUCE

This decadent main dish, which is a fixture of Abe Fisher's menu, pairs grilled steak with a smoky, salami-studded broccoli salad. A drizzle of steak sauce enhanced with sweet kosher wine brings the dish together.

Serves: 4
Preparation time: 30 minutes
Cooking time: 1 hour 15 minutes

For the steak sauce:
• 2 tablespoons soy sauce
• 4 tablespoons sherry vinegar or red wine vinegar
• ⅓ cup (65 g) sugar
• ⅓ cup (75 ml/2½ fl oz) Worcestershire sauce
• 1 cup (240 ml/8 fl oz) beef stock
• 1½ cups (355 ml/12 fl oz) sweet kosher wine
• 1 teaspoon kosher salt

For the steak:
• 2 lb (910 g) bone-in rib-eye steak
• Kosher salt and freshly ground black pepper
• Extra-virgin olive oil, for brushing

For the salad:
• 2 large heads broccoli, cut into 1-inch (2.5 cm) florets
• 3 tablespoons extra-virgin olive oil
• Kosher salt
• ½ lb (225 g) beef salami, cut into small cubes
• 1 red onion, finely chopped
• 1 teaspoon grated fresh ginger
• 1 garlic clove, finely chopped
• 1 teaspoon smoked paprika
• ½ cup (120 g) mayonnaise
• 1 tablespoon sugar
• 1½ tablespoons red wine vinegar
• ½ cup (25 g) chopped fresh cilantro (coriander)
• 1 small bunch scallions (spring onions), white and light-green parts, thinly sliced
• Freshly ground black pepper

Make the steak sauce: In a medium saucepan, combine the soy sauce, vinegar, sugar, Worcestershire sauce, stock, wine, and salt and bring to a boil over medium-high heat. Reduce the heat to medium and cook, stirring occasionally, until the sauce reduces to a syrupy consistency, 35–40 minutes. (It should be thick enough to coat the back of a spoon.) Transfer to a nonreactive bowl and let cool to room temperature. The sauce can be covered and refrigerated for up to 3 days. Bring back to room temperature before using.

Cook the steak: Generously season the steak on both sides with salt and pepper and let sit at room temperature while preheating a grill (barbecue) to medium-high. Brush the grill with olive oil, then grill the steak, flipping once, until it is well charred and reaches an internal temperature of 140°F (60°C) for medium-rare, 6–7 minutes per side. Remove from the grill (but leave the grill on). Let the meat rest for 20 minutes, then remove the bone and slice the steak into ½-inch (1.25 cm) slices.

Make the salad: While the meat is resting, in a large bowl, toss the broccoli florets with 2 tablespoons of the oil and a generous sprinkle of salt, mixing well to coat. Working in batches if necessary, grill the florets, rotating every 2–3 minutes, until charred and just tender. Set aside to cool slightly.

In a medium frying pan, heat the remaining 1 tablespoon oil over medium heat. Add the salami, onion, ginger, and garlic. Cook, stirring occasionally, until the mixture browns, 15–20 minutes. Add the paprika and cook, stirring, until fragrant, about 1 minute.

In the bottom of a large salad bowl, whisk together the mayonnaise, sugar, and vinegar. Add the charred broccoli, the salami mixture, cilantro (coriander), and scallions to the bowl and stir to coat. Taste and add more salt or pepper, if desired.

To serve, divide the broccoli salad between 4 plates. Lay several slices of meat on top of each salad, then generously drizzle the meat with the steak sauce.

✸ STAR RECIPE

LAMB AND DRIED FRUIT TAGINE

This intricately spiced Moroccan tagine, called *tanzeya*, pairs sweet and tender dried fruit with lamb or beef. The saucy dish (which is also sometimes made without meat) is flavored with the robust spice mix *ras el hanout*, and is typically served over couscous on Rosh Hashanah.

Serves: 6
Preparation time: 35 minutes
Cooking time: 2 hours 45 minutes

- ¼ cup (60 ml/2 fl oz) plus 3 tablespoons extra-virgin olive oil
- 2½ lb (1.2 kg) lamb shoulder, cut into 1-inch (2.5 cm) pieces
- 2 onions, halved through the root and thinly sliced
- 6 garlic cloves, thinly sliced
- 1½ tablespoons Ras el Hanout (page 414)
- 1 teaspoon ground cinnamon
- 1 teaspoon ground ginger
- 1¼ teaspoons kosher salt, plus more as needed
- ½ teaspoon freshly ground black pepper
- ¼ teaspoon crushed pepper flakes
- 1 tablespoon tomato paste (purée)
- 1 tablespoon fresh lemon juice
- 4 cups (950 ml/32 fl oz) chicken or vegetable stock
- 2 medium carrots, halved lengthwise and cut crosswise into ½-inch (1.25 cm) half-moons
- 5 dried figs, stems removed, halved lengthwise
- 15 dried apricots, halved
- ½ cup (70 g) raisins
- 1 cup (120 g) slivered almonds
- ¼ cup (85 g) mild honey

In a Dutch oven (casserole) or large pot, heat ¼ cup (60 ml/2 fl oz) of the oil over medium-high heat. Working in two batches, add the lamb pieces and cook, stirring occasionally, until browned, 5–10 minutes. Remove the browned meat to a plate.

Add the onions and garlic to the pan and cook, stirring occasionally, until softened and browned, about 10 minutes. Add the *ras el hanout*, cinnamon, ginger, salt, black pepper, and pepper flakes and cook, stirring, until fragrant, about 1 minute.

Stir in the tomato paste (purée) and lemon juice, followed by the stock. Return the meat to the pan, increase the heat to medium-high, and bring to a boil. Reduce the heat to medium-low, cover, and cook, stirring occasionally, until the meat is tender, about 1½ hours.

Add the carrots, figs, apricots, raisins, about half of the almonds, and the honey and continue cooking, stirring often, until the carrots are fully tender, 30–40 minutes. Taste and add more salt, if necessary.

Meanwhile, in a medium frying pan, heat the remaining 3 tablespoons oil over medium heat. Add the remaining almonds and cook, stirring often, until golden brown and fragrant, 5–7 minutes. Remove from the heat.

Transfer the stew to a serving bowl and sprinkle with the browned almonds. Serve hot.

LYULYA KEBABS

These glistening, minced lamb or beef kebabs are popular throughout Bukharian, Azerbaijani, and Georgian cuisines. Middle Eastern cuisine shares a nearly identical, though differently spiced, dish called *kufta* kebabs. Use flat, metal skewers to make turning the kebabs easier. Serve them alongside Tomato and Onion Salad (page 74).

Serves: 8
Preparation time: 15 minutes, plus chilling
Cooking time: 30 minutes

• 2 lb (910 g) ground (minced) lamb or beef
• 1 onion, grated on the large holes of a box grater
• 2 garlic cloves, minced or pushed through a press
• 1 egg
• 2 tablespoons vegetable oil,
  plus more for brushing the grill
• 2 tablespoons warm water
• 1 teaspoon sweet paprika
• 1½ teaspoons ground cumin
• ½ teaspoon dried mint
• ½ teaspoon garlic powder
• 1½ teaspoons kosher salt
• ½ teaspoon freshly ground black pepper

In a large bowl, combine the lamb, onion, garlic, egg, oil, water, paprika, cumin, mint, garlic powder, salt, and pepper and mix with your hands until combined. Cover the bowl and refrigerate for 30 minutes to firm up the mixture.

Meanwhile, preheat an outoor grill (barbecue) to medium-high. Line a large baking sheet with parchment paper. Scoop out ⅓ cup (70 g) of the meat mixture and gently squeeze the meat around a flat metal skewer, forming a log 1 inch (2.5 cm) thick. Lay the kebab on the prepared baking sheet and continue with additional skewers and the remaining meat mixture.

Brush the heated grill with a little oil. Working in batches if necessary, transfer the kebabs directly to the grill and cook, turning once, until browned and just cooked through, 8–10 minutes. Let sit for 5–10 minutes before serving.

SHASHLIK

A wide variety of grilled, cubed meat kebabs are commonly served throughout Iran, Turkey, the Balkans, and Central Asia, where they are called shashlik and are central to Bukharian and Georgian cuisines. They can be made with beef, lamb, or chicken that gets marinated for many hours and are sometimes served with paper-thin slices of fresh onion draped on top. This basic recipe can be dressed up with paprika, oregano, thyme, dried mint, cumin, or other spices. And don't throw out the onions used to marinate the meat. Sauté them in a bit of oil, with sliced mushrooms if desired, and serve as a side.

Serves: 4
Preparation: 10 minutes, plus marinating
Cooking time: 15 minutes

• 1 medium onion, halved through the root and sliced
• 4 garlic cloves, peeled and smashed
• ¼ cup (60 ml/2 fl oz) red wine vinegar
• ¼ cup (60 ml/2 fl oz) vegetable oil,
  plus more for brushing
• 1 teaspoon kosher salt, plus more as needed
• ½ teaspoon freshly ground black pepper,
  plus more
  as needed
• 2 lb (910 g) beef or lamb cubes, about 2 inches
  (5 cm) each

In a large zip-top bag, combine the onion, garlic, vinegar, oil, salt, and pepper. Add the meat and, using your hands, mix everything together thoroughly. Seal the bag and refrigerate for at least 6 and up to 12 hours, turning occasionally to ensure even distribution of the marinade.

Preheat an outdoor grill (barbecue) to medium-hot. Remove the meat from the marinade and gently pat dry with paper towels, removing any solids. Divide the meat evenly among 6 flat metal skewers. Sprinkle on both sides with a little more salt and pepper. Brush the grates with a little oil, then place the kebabs directly on the grates. Cook, turning with tongs once or twice, until browned on all sides and cooked to desired doneness, about 10 minutes for medium-rare, and 15 minutes for medium. Remove from the heat and let rest for 5 minutes before serving. Serve hot.

CAKES, COOKIES
& SWEET PASTRIES

CINNAMON-WALNUT SPONGE CAKE

For the week of Passover, desserts are traditionally made with finely ground matzo meal (or, as with this cake, potato starch) instead of flour. Like all sponge cakes, this version gets its lift from beaten egg whites. What sets it apart is the coffee cake–like ribbon of cinnamon and walnuts running through the center. It is delicious served with fresh berries, a spoonful of Dried Fruit Compote (page 378), or Strawberry Sauce (page 394).

Serves: 8
Preparation time: 15 minutes
Cooking time: 1 hour

- 1 cup (105 g) walnut halves
- 7 eggs
- 1½ cups (300 g) sugar
- 1 teaspoon grated orange zest
- 2 tablespoons fresh orange juice
- ¾ cup (135 g) potato starch
- ¼ teaspoon kosher salt
- 1¼ teaspoons ground cinnamon

In a small, dry frying pan, toast the walnuts over medium-low heat, shaking the pan occasionally, until fragrant and lightly browned, about 5 minutes. Remove the pan from the heat and let cool, then finely chop.

Preheat the oven to 325°F (160°C/Gas Mark 3). Have ready an ungreased 10-inch (25 cm) tube pan.

Separate 6 of the eggs, placing the yolks in the bowl of a stand mixer or another large bowl, and the whites in a separate bowl. Set the whites aside. Crack the remaining egg into the yolks and, using a stand mixer or handheld electric mixer, beat at medium speed until pale yellow and slightly thickened, 2–3 minutes.

While beating constantly, gradually add 1¼ cups (250 g) of the sugar, followed by the orange zest and orange juice. Switch to low speed and gradually beat in the potato starch, scraping down the sides of the bowl as needed. If using the stand mixer, transfer the batter to a large bowl and thoroughly wash and dry the beaters and bowl.

Add the egg whites and salt to the clean stand mixer or another large bowl and beat at medium-high speed until glossy peaks form, 3–5 minutes. Gently fold the egg whites into the egg yolk batter.

In a small bowl, stir together the chopped walnuts, remaining ¼ cup (50 g) sugar, and cinnamon. Scoop about one-third of the batter into the tube pan and smooth with a spatula, then sprinkle with half of the nut mixture. Spoon in another one-third of the batter, followed by the remaining nut mixture. Top with the remaining batter, smoothing the top gently. Bake—do not open the oven during baking or the cake could fall flat—until the top of the cake springs back when gently pressed, 50–60 minutes.

Remove the cake from the oven and invert the pan over a wire rack. Allow to fully cool in the pan upside down, about 2 hours. Use a sharp serrated knife to gently cut along the outer and inner perimeters of the tube pan. Gently remove the cake and transfer to a serving platter. Slice and serve at room temperature.

CAKES, COOKIES & SWEET PASTRIES

CHOCOLATE MARBLE CAKE

Dual-toned cakes (originally made with molasses and spices instead of chocolate) have German roots, and went on to become a staple of the American Jewish bakery. This cake, called *mamorkuchen* in German, is tender and sweet with chocolate swirling through the batter and a light almond scent. It also tastes best the day after it is made, when the flavors have had a chance to mingle and deepen.

Serves: 8
Preparation time: 40 minutes
Cooking time: 1 hour

For the vanilla batter:
• 2½ cups (350 g) all-purpose (plain) flour
• 2 teaspoons baking powder
• ½ teaspoon kosher salt
• ½ cup (120 ml/4 fl oz) vegetable oil
• ⅓ cup (80 g) unsweetened applesauce
• 1½ cups (300 g) sugar
• 3 eggs
• 2 teaspoons vanilla extract
• ½ teaspoon almond extract
• ½ cup (120 ml/4 fl oz) orange juice

For the chocolate batter:
• 2 oz (55 g) unsweetened (or very dark) baking chocolate, melted
• ¼ cup (20 g) unsweetened cocoa powder
• ¼ cup (50 g) sugar
• ¼ cup (60 ml/2 fl oz) boiling water

Preheat the oven to 350°F (180°C/Gas Mark 4). Line a 9 × 5-inch (23 × 12.5 cm) loaf pan with parchment paper, allowing the parchment to hang over on opposite sides.

Make the vanilla batter: Sift together the flour, baking powder, and salt into a medium bowl.

In a stand mixer (or using a handheld electric mixer and a large bowl), beat together the vegetable oil, applesauce, sugar, eggs, vanilla, and almond extract at medium speed until pale yellow, 2–3 minutes. Beat in half of the orange juice on low speed, followed by half of the flour mixture, scraping down the bowl as necessary. Then beat in the remaining orange juice, followed by the remaining flour, beating on low until combined.

Make the chocolate batter: In a medium bowl, whisk together the melted chocolate, cocoa powder, sugar, and boiling water until smooth and glossy. Add a little less than half of the vanilla batter to the chocolate mixture and gently fold until smooth.

Spoon the 2 batters into the prepared loaf pan in layers, alternating big, about ¼ cup (60 g), spoonfuls of the vanilla and chocolate batters to simulate a checkerboard pattern. The batter will spread, which is okay. When all of the batter is spooned into the loaf pan, use a knife or wooden skewer to run through the batters in a swirling motion, creating the marbling effect.

Bake until a skewer inserted into the center just comes out clean, about 1 hour. If the top of the cake is browning too quickly, loosely drape a piece of foil over the top. Remove from the oven and use the overhanging parchment to gently remove the cake from the loaf pan and transfer to a wire rack to cool.

SOUR CHERRY CAKE

Petite, vibrantly red sour cherries grow abundantly in Hungary in the summer months—and just like their non-Jewish neighbors, Hungarian Jews make the most of the season. This buttery cake, called *meggy lepeny*, is an annual warm-weather favorite. You can use either fresh or frozen cherries, but do not use canned or bottled varieties, which do not have great flavor. If starting with frozen cherries, thaw them completely before using.

Serves: 8
Preparation time: 25 minutes
Cooking time: 45 minutes

- 3 tablespoons dried breadcrumbs
- 2 cups (280 g) all-purpose (plain) flour
- 1½ teaspoons baking powder
- ½ teaspoon kosher salt
- 1½ sticks (6 oz/170 g) unsalted butter, at room temperature
- 1¼ cups (250 g) sugar
- 2 eggs
- 1½ teaspoons vanilla extract
- ½ teaspoon finely grated lemon zest
- ¼ cup (60 ml/2 fl oz) milk
- 1½ cups (285 g) fresh or thawed frozen sour cherries, pitted

Preheat the oven to 350°F (180°C/Gas Mark 4). Lightly grease a 9-inch (23 cm) round cake pan or springform pan and sprinkle evenly with the breadcrumbs.

In a medium bowl, whisk together the flour, baking powder, and salt.

In a stand mixer (or using a handheld electric mixer and a large bowl), beat together the butter and sugar at medium speed until light and fluffy, 2–3 minutes. Add the eggs, one at a time, beating after each addition until incorporated. Beat in the vanilla and lemon zest. Add half of the flour mixture and beat at low speed, scraping down the sides of the bowl as necessary, until just incorporated. Beat in the milk, followed by the remaining flour mixture.

Transfer the batter to the prepared pan and smooth gently with a rubber spatula. Top with the cherries and use a knife to gently poke some of them about halfway down into the batter. Bake until golden brown and a skewer inserted into the center of the cake comes out clean, 40–45 minutes. Transfer the cake pan to a wire rack to cool.

LEKACH

It is difficult to imagine an Ashkenazi Rosh Hashanah celebration without honey cake. The sweet, generously spiced cake has medieval German origins (the name is derived from the German word *lecke*, or "lick"), but today's versions are typically much lighter and more delicate than their predecessors.

Serves: 8
Preparation time: 20 minutes
Cooking time: 45 minutes

- 2¼ cups (315 g) all-purpose (plain) flour
- 1 teaspoon baking powder
- ½ teaspoon baking soda (bicarbonate of soda)
- 1½ teaspoons ground cinnamon
- ½ teaspoon ground allspice
- ⅛ teaspoon ground nutmeg
- ½ teaspoon kosher salt
- ¾ cup (175 ml/6 fl oz) vegetable oil
- ½ cup (120 ml/4 fl oz) strong brewed coffee
- 1 cup (180 g) light brown sugar
- ½ cup (170 g) honey
- 3 eggs
- 1 teaspoon vanilla extract

Preheat the oven to 350°F (180°C/Gas Mark 4). Lightly grease a 9-inch (23 cm) round springform or cake pan. Line the bottom of the pan with a round of parchment paper, then lightly grease the parchment.

In a medium bowl, sift the flour, baking powder, baking soda (bicarb), cinnamon, allspice, nutmeg, and salt.

In a stand mixer, beat the oil, coffee, brown sugar, and honey at medium speed until fully combined. Add the eggs, one at a time, followed by the vanilla, beating to combine after each addition, and scraping down the bowl as necessary. Add the flour mixture in two stages, beating at low speed until just combined.

Pour the batter into the prepared pan and bake until the top gently springs back when you press it with your fingers, and a skewer inserted into the center of the cake comes out clean, 40–45 minutes. Cool the cake in the pan on a wire rack for 10 minutes, then turn the cake out onto the rack to cool completely. Serve at room temperature.

CAKES, COOKIES & SWEET PASTRIES

Sour Cherry Cake

KUGELHOPF

Variations of this majestic bread-cake hybrid are enjoyed across Central Europe, particularly in Austria, Germany, and Alsace, France. With its crusty edges, tender, lemony interior, and heaps of dried fruit threaded throughout, it is no wonder that kugelhopf is so widely loved. The cake gets its name from a special, angled bundt pan. They are easy to find online, inexpensive, and worth the investment to make a kugelhopf with its namesake shape. Alsatian Jews regularly serve kugelhopf on Shabbat, and it is also traditional for Hanukkah and Purim. Slices can be served with whipped cream, or toasted and spread with butter and jam for breakfast or an afternoon snack. Either way, a cup of coffee or tea makes a lovely companion.

Serves: 8
Preparation time: 30 minutes, plus rising
Cooking time: 35–40 minutes

- ½ cup (70 g) raisins
- ½ cup (70 g) dried currants
- ⅓ cup (75 ml/2½ fl oz) sweet red wine or grape juice
- 1 packet (¼ oz/7 g) active dry yeast (2¼ teaspoons)
- ½ cup (100 g) plus 1 teaspoon sugar
- ¼ cup (60 ml/2 fl oz) warm water (110°F/43°C)
- 3¾–4 cups (525–560 g) all-purpose (plain) flour, plus more for kneading and shaping
- ½ teaspoon kosher salt
- ¾ cup (175 ml/6 fl oz) milk
- 2 eggs, lightly beaten
- 1 teaspoon finely grated lemon zest
- 1 stick (4 oz/115 g) unsalted butter, cut into pieces, at room temperature
- Whole blanched almonds, for decorating (optional)
- Powdered (icing) sugar, for dusting

In a small bowl, combine the raisins, currants, and wine and let sit, stirring once or twice, while making the dough.

In a large bowl, stir together the yeast, 1 teaspoon of the sugar, and the warm water. Let sit until foaming, 5–10 minutes.

Meanwhile, in a large bowl, whisk together 3¾ cups (525 g) flour, the remaining 1 cup (100 g) sugar, and the salt.

Whisk the milk, eggs, and lemon zest into the yeast mixture. Add the flour mixture and stir until a wet dough comes together. Turn the dough out onto a floured surface, knead well, adding 6 tablespoons (90 g) of the softened butter, a few pieces at a time, and adding up to ¼ cup (35 g) additional flour as needed, until you have a sticky, supple dough, about 10 minutes. The dough will be quite a bit stickier than babka or challah dough. Dust hands lightly with flour as needed. (The kneading can also be done in a stand mixer with a dough hook, 5–7 minutes.)

Drain the raisins and currants well through a fine-mesh sieve (discard the liquid). Add the dried fruit to the dough and knead thoroughly to incorporate.

Rub the remaining 2 tablespoons (30 g) butter around the bottom and sides of a 10-cup (2.4-liter) nonstick kugelhopf pan. (It will seem like a lot of butter, but use all of it.) If desired, lay one almond in each depression in the bottom of the pan. Using lightly floured hands to reduce sticking, gently stretch the dough into a thick rope, shape it into a ring, and fit into the pan, pressing down gently. Cover the pan with plastic wrap (cling film) or a tea towel and let rise until doubled in size, 1½–2 hours.

Meanwhile, preheat the oven to 375°F (190°C/Gas Mark 5).

Transfer the pan to the oven and bake until puffed, golden brown, and cooked through, 35–40 minutes. If the top is browning too quickly, loosely drape a piece of foil on top. Let cool for 5 minutes in the pan. Invert the cake onto a wire rack and let cool for at least 1 hour. Just before slicing, use a fine-mesh sieve to dust the top with powdered (icing) sugar.

CAKES, COOKIES & SWEET PASTRIES

SOUR CREAM COFFEE CAKE

In Ashkenazi homes, coffee cakes enriched with sour cream were traditionally served on Shabbat morning, for the Yom Kippur break-fast meal, and as a snack —especially with a cup of coffee when unexpected guests dropped by. This cinnamon-perfumed, walnut-studded version gets its plush texture and tender crumb from both sour cream and applesauce. (The latter adds moisture and reduces the overall fat content, although in a cake this decadent it hardly matters.) The chocolate chips are a decidedly American addition to the Eastern European original, but undeniably good.

Serves: 8
Preparation time: 20 minutes
Cooking time: 40 minutes

For the topping:
- 1 cup (180 g) semisweet chocolate chips
- ½ cup (90 g) light brown sugar
- 1 cup (105 g) walnut halves, chopped
- 1 tablespoon ground cinnamon

For the cake:
- 1½ cups (210 g) all-purpose (plain) flour
- ¾ teaspoon baking soda (bicarbonate of soda)
- ¾ teaspoon baking powder
- ½ teaspoon kosher salt
- 1 stick (4 oz/115 g) unsalted butter or nonhydrogenated margarine, at room temperature
- ¾ cup (150 g) sugar
- 2 eggs
- 1 teaspoon vanilla extract
- ½ cup (115 g) unsweetened applesauce
- ½ cup (120 g) sour cream or unsweetened coconut milk yogurt

Preheat the oven to 350°F (180°C/Gas Mark 4). Lightly grease an 8-inch (20 cm) square baking dish, then line the dish with parchment paper, allowing the paper to hang over on two opposite sides.

Make the topping: In a medium bowl, stir together the chocolate chips, brown sugar, walnuts, and cinnamon.

Make the cake: In a medium bowl, whisk together the flour, baking soda (bicarb), baking powder, and salt.

In a stand mixer (or using a handheld electric mixer and a large bowl), beat the butter and sugar at medium speed until pale and fluffy. Add the eggs, one at a time, followed by the vanilla, beating to combine after each addition. Beat in the applesauce and sour cream (it is okay if the batter looks curdled at this stage), then add the flour mixture and beat on low, scraping down the sides of the bowl as necessary, until just combined.

Spread half of the batter evenly into the prepared baking dish. (It will seem like there is not enough batter, but it will fill out while baking.) Top with half of the chocolate-walnut topping. Spread the remaining batter on top and finish with a layer of the remaining topping.

Bake until a skewer inserted into the center comes out just clean, about 40 minutes. If the top is browning too quickly, loosely cover with a layer of foil. Set the baking dish on a wire rack to cool. Using the overhanging parchment, gently lift up the cooled cake and transfer to a serving dish.

PLUM CAKE

This simple German cake, which is known as both *pflaumenkuchen* and *zwetschgenkuchen*, is best enjoyed in the late summer when a wide variety of plums come into peak season. The glossy layer of jam spread on top transforms it from ordinary to extraordinary. Plum cake makes a lovely dessert or snack paired with freshly whipped cream or ice cream, and leftovers are great for breakfast topped with yogurt.

Serves: 6–8
Preparation time: 15 minutes
Cooking time: 35 minutes

- 1 cup (140 g) all-purpose (plain) flour
- ¼ cup (30 g) almond flour (ground almonds)
- 1 teaspoon baking powder
- ½ teaspoon ground cinnamon
- ½ teaspoon kosher salt
- 1 stick (4 oz/115 g) unsalted butter, at room temperature, or ⅓ cup (75 ml/2½ fl oz) vegetable oil
- ½ cup (100 g) sugar
- ⅓ cup (60 g) light brown sugar
- 3 eggs
- 1 teaspoon vanilla extract
- ½ teaspoon almond extract (optional)
- 1 lb (455 g) plums, pitted and halved (or cut into quarters or eighths if large)
- 1 tablespoon cherry or apricot jam

Preheat the oven to 350°F (180°C/Gas Mark 4). Lightly grease a 9-inch (23 cm) round cake pan or springform pan, then line with a round of parchment paper.

In a medium bowl, whisk together the all-purpose (plain) flour, almond flour (ground almonds), baking powder, cinnamon, and salt.

In a stand mixer (or using a handheld electric mixer and a large bowl), beat together the butter, sugar, and brown sugar at medium speed until light and fluffy, 2–3 minutes. Add the eggs, one at a time, beating after each addition until incorporated. Beat in the vanilla and almond extract (if using). Add the flour mixture and beat at low speed, scraping down the sides of the bowl as necessary, until just incorporated.

Transfer the batter to the prepared pan and smooth gently with a rubber spatula. It will look like not enough batter, but the cake will puff up as it bakes. Arrange the plums, cut side down, on top of the batter.

Bake until golden brown and a skewer inserted into the center of the cake comes out clean, 30–35 minutes. Let the cake cool in the pan on a wire rack for 5 minutes. Run a knife around the edges of the pan, carefully remove the cake, and set it on the rack.

In a small microwave-safe bowl, microwave the jam in 20-second intervals, stirring after each, until melted and spreadable. While the cake is still warm, brush the jam evenly on top. Let cool to room temperature before slicing.

FLORENCE KAHN

FLORENCE KAHN BAKERY AND DELICATESSEN

24 RUE DES ÉCOUFFES
PARIS, FRANCE

Florence Kahn is the owner of Florence Kahn Bakery and Delicatessen—an Ashkenazi-inspired pâtisserie and restaurant located in Paris's historic Marais district. She turns out elegant takes on classic dishes, from stuffed cabbage and pastrami to tender challah and sweet fruit strudels.

PISTACHIO CHEESECAKE

Kahn's cheesecake begins with a base of fragrant pistachios and gets topped with a luscious layer of cheese filling. Serve it as is, or decorate the top with whole or finely ground pistachios.

Serves: 8
Preparation time: 20 minutes
Cooking time: 55 minutes

For the pistachio crust:
• 1½ cups (200 g) unsalted pistachios
• ⅓ cup (65 g) sugar
• 6 tablespoons (85 g) unsalted butter, melted

For the filling:
• 16 oz (455 g) cream cheese, at room temperature
• ⅔ cup (160 g) sour cream
• ⅔ cup (130 g) sugar
• 2 eggs
• ¼ teaspoon kosher salt
• 1 teaspoon vanilla extract

Make the pistachio crust: In a small frying pan, toast the pistachios over medium-low heat, shaking the pan occasionally, until fragrant and lightly browned, about 5 minutes. Remove from the heat and let the pistachios cool, then transfer to a food processor and pulse until finely ground with a few larger pieces.

Preheat the oven to 325°F (160°C/Gas Mark 3). Line an 8-inch (20 cm) square baking dish (that is at least 2 inches/ 5 cm deep) with parchment paper, allowing the parchment to hang over on two opposite sides.

Transfer the ground pistachios to a bowl and stir in the sugar and melted butter until combined. Spoon the moistened nut mixture into the baking dish and firmly press into an even layer along the bottom. Refrigerate while making the filling.

Make the filling: In a stand mixer fitted with the paddle attachment, combine the cream cheese, sour cream, and sugar and beat at medium speed until smooth, scraping down the sides of the bowl as necessary. Add the eggs, salt, and vanilla and beat until smooth.

Pour the filling into the crust and smooth the top. Bake until the cake is mostly set with a slightly jiggly center, 45–50 minutes. Remove from the oven and let the cake cool on a wire rack, then cover and refrigerate until chilled, at least 4 hours or overnight. Use the overhanging parchment to carefully transfer the cake to a serving platter. Serve chilled or at room temperature.

CINNAMON–GOLDEN RAISIN BABKA

In South Africa, babka traditionally comes perfumed with cinnamon and orange zest and dotted with golden raisins (sultanas). This babka is ultraplush and tender, and just the right amount of sweet. The syrup painted on top is not traditional, but it adds moisture and a lovely sheen.

Makes: 3 loaves
Preparation time: 40 minutes, plus rising
Cooking time: 40 minutes

For the syrup:
• ½ cup (120 ml/4 fl oz) water
• ½ cup (100 g) sugar

For the dough:
• 1 packet (¼ oz/7g) active dry yeast (2¼ teaspoons)
• ½ cup (100 g) plus 1 teaspoon sugar
• 1 cup (240 ml/8 fl oz) warm water (110°F/43°C)
• 4–5 cups (560–700 g) all-purpose (plain) flour, plus more for kneading
• 1 teaspoon kosher salt
• 2 eggs, lightly beaten
• 1 stick (4 oz/115 g) unsalted butter, cut into pieces, at room temperature
• 1 teaspoon vegetable oil

For the filling:
• 1 cup (105 g) walnut halves
• 1 stick (4 oz/115 g) unsalted butter, cut into pieces, at room temperature
• 1 cup (200 g) sugar
• 2 teaspoons ground cinnamon
• 1 teaspoon vanilla extract
• 1 teaspoon finely grated orange zest
• 1 cup (140 g) golden raisins (sultanas)

Make the syrup: In a small saucepan, bring the water and the sugar to a boil over medium heat, stirring often to dissolve the sugar. Reduce the heat to medium-low and cook until the syrup thickens slightly, 3–5 minutes. Remove from the heat and let cool completely.

Make the dough: In a large bowl, stir together the yeast, 1 teaspoon sugar, and the warm water. Let sit until foaming, 5–10 minutes.

Meanwhile, in a large bowl, whisk together 4 cups (560 g) flour and the salt.

Stir the remaining ½ cup (100 g) sugar and the eggs into the yeast mixture. Add the flour mixture and gently stir until a wet dough comes together. Turn the dough out onto a floured surface and knead well, adding the softened butter pieces a few at a time, and adding up to 1 cup (140 g) additional flour as needed, until you have a supple, slightly tacky dough, about 10 minutes. You might not need all of the flour. (The kneading can also be done in a stand mixer with a dough hook, 5–7 minutes.)

Grease a large bowl with the oil, add the dough, and turn to coat. Cover the bowl with plastic wrap (cling film) or a tea towel and let sit in a warm place until nearly doubled in size, 1–1½ hours.

Meanwhile, make the filling: In a food processor, combine the walnuts, butter, sugar, cinnamon, vanilla, and orange zest and pulse until a smooth paste forms.

Grease three 9 × 5-inch (23 × 12.5 cm) loaf pans.

Gently punch down the dough and turn out onto a lightly floured surface. Divide the dough into 3 equal portions. Working with one piece at a time, roll out the dough into a large rectangle ¼ inch (6 mm) thick.

Evenly spread about one-third of the filling onto dough, leaving a ¼-inch (6 mm) border around the edges. Evenly sprinkle one-third of the golden raisins (sultanas) on top. Starting at one of the short sides, roll the dough up tightly like a jelly roll (Swiss roll). Using a sharp knife, trim ½ inch (1.25 cm) off each end of the roll (and discard). Halve the roll lengthwise. You should now have 2 long strands of dough, with the layers of filling exposed. Twist the strands together and pinch at the top and bottom to seal. Carefully place into one of the prepared loaf pans. Repeat with the remaining pieces of dough and remaining filling and golden raisins. Loosely cover the pans with plastic wrap (cling film) or a tea towel and let rise for 30 minutes.

Meanwhile, preheat the oven to 350°F (180°C/Gas Mark 4).

Bake the babkas, rotating the pans front to back halfway through, until golden brown and just cooked through, 30–35 minutes. Remove the baked babkas from the oven and brush the top of each with 3 coats of sugar syrup (you may not use all of it). Let cool in their pans for 20 minutes, then turn out onto a wire rack to cool completely.

CAKES, COOKIES & SWEET PASTRIES

Cinnamon–Golden Raisin Babka

MEXICAN CHOCOLATE BABKA

Mexico City is home to a sizable community of Jews with Eastern European backgrounds who have found ways to add indigenous and regional Mexican flavors to their traditional dishes. Here, classic chocolate babka gets a spicy-sweet upgrade with the addition of cayenne pepper and cinnamon. For a more classic babka, omit the cayenne, and halve the cinnamon.

Makes: 3 loaves
Preparation time: 40 minutes, plus rising
Cooking time: 40 minutes

For the syrup:
- ½ cup (120 ml/4 fl oz) water
- ½ cup (100 g) sugar
- 2 cinnamon sticks
- ⅛ teaspoon cayenne pepper

For the dough:
- 1 packet (¼ oz/7 g) active dry yeast (2 ¼ teaspoons)
- ½ cup (100 g) plus 1 teaspoon sugar
- 1 cup (240 ml/8 fl oz) warm water (110°F/43°C)
- 4–5 cups (560–700 g) all-purpose (plain) flour, plus more for kneading
- 1 teaspoon kosher salt
- 2 eggs, lightly beaten
- 1 stick (4 oz/115 g) unsalted butter, cut into pieces, at room temperature
- 1 teaspoon vegetable oil

For the filling:
- 1 cup (120 g) unsalted roasted almonds
- ½ cup (40 g) unsweetened cocoa powder
- 1 cup (200 g) sugar
- 2 teaspoons ground cinnamon
- 1 teaspoon instant coffee granules
- ¼ teaspoon cayenne pepper
- ½ teaspoon kosher salt
- ¼ cup (60 ml/2 fl oz) milk
- 1½ teaspoons vanilla extract

Make the syrup: In a small saucepan, combine the water, sugar, cinnamon sticks, and cayenne and bring to a boil over medium heat, stirring often to dissolve the sugar. Reduce the heat to medium-low and cook until the syrup thickens slightly, 3–5 minutes. Remove from the heat and let cool completely.

Make the dough: In a large bowl, stir together the yeast, 1 teaspoon of the sugar, and the warm water. Let sit until foaming, 5–10 minutes.

Meanwhile, in a large bowl, whisk together 4 cups (560 g) flour and the salt.

Stir the remaining ½ cup (100 g) sugar and the eggs into the yeast mixture. Add the flour mixture and gently stir until a wet dough comes together. Turn the dough out onto a floured surface and knead well, adding the softened butter pieces a few at a time, and adding up to 1 cup (140 g) additional flour as needed, until you have a supple, slightly sticky dough, about 10 minutes. You might not need all of the flour. (The kneading can also be done in a stand mixer with a dough hook, 5–7 minutes.)

Grease a large bowl with the vegetable oil, add the dough, and turn to coat. Cover the bowl with plastic wrap (cling film) or a tea towel and let sit in a warm place until nearly doubled in size, 1–1½ hours.

Meanwhile, make the filling: In a food processor, combine the almonds, cocoa powder, sugar, cinnamon, coffee, cayenne, salt, milk, and vanilla and pulse until a paste forms.

Grease three 9 × 5-inch (23 × 12.5 cm) loaf pans.

Gently punch down the dough and turn out onto a lightly floured surface. Divide into 3 equal portions. Working with one piece at a time, roll out the dough into a large rectangle ¼ inch (6 mm) thick. Evenly spread about one-third of the filling onto the dough, leaving a ¼-inch (6 mm) border around the edges. Starting at one of the short side, roll the dough up tightly like a jelly roll (Swiss roll). Using a sharp knife, trim ½-inch (1.25 cm) off each end of the roll (and discard). Halve the roll length-wise. You should now have 2 long strands of dough, with the layers of filling exposed. Twist the strands together and pinch at the top and bottom to seal. Carefully place into one of the prepared loaf pans. Repeat with the remaining pieces of dough and remaining filling. Loosely cover the pans and let rise for 30 minutes.

Meanwhile, preheat the oven to 350°F (180°C/Gas Mark 4).

Bake the babkas, rotating pans front to back halfway through, until golden brown, 30–35 minutes. Remove the baked babkas from the oven and brush the top of each with 3 coats of syrup. Let cool in their pans for 20 minutes, then turn out onto a wire rack to cool completely.

CAKES, COOKIES & SWEET PASTRIES

FLOURLESS CHOCOLATE CAKE

Sometime in the late twentieth century, this dense, fudgy chocolate cake emerged as a staple of the Passover dessert table in America. Serve it topped with freshly whipped cream and berries, or simply dusted with powdered (icing) sugar. It is rich and intensely chocolatey, so a small slice goes a long way.

Serves: 8
Preparation time: 20 minutes
Cooking time: 45 minutes

- 1 stick (4 oz/115 g) unsalted butter or nonhydrogenated margarine, cut into pieces
- 8 oz (225 g) bittersweet chocolate, roughly chopped
- 1 teaspoon vanilla extract
- ¼ teaspoon kosher salt
- 5 eggs
- ½ cup (100 g) sugar

Preheat the oven to 325°F (160°C/Gas Mark 3). Lightly grease a 9-inch (23 cm) round springform or cake pan. Line the bottom of the pan with a round of parchment paper, then lightly grease the parchment.

In a heatproof bowl set over a pan of simmering water, melt the butter and chocolate. Stir in the vanilla and salt.

In a stand mixer, beat together the eggs and sugar at medium-high speed until the mixture is pale yellow and has doubled in volume, about 5 minutes. Pour the chocolate mixture into the egg mixture and gently fold until fully combined.

Pour the batter into the prepared pan and gently smooth the top. Bake until the center of the cake is just set, 35–40 minutes. Set the pan on a wire rack to cool completely. The cake will sink as it cools. Unmold the cake and place on a serving plate. Serve at room temperature.

APPLE STRUDEL

Apple strudel is comfort food par excellence for Central Europeans. Traditionally, a homemade dough is carefully stretched by hand across a tabletop or long board until it is thin enough to read a newspaper through. Fortunately, store-bought phyllo dough makes a worthy substitute without the painstaking process.

Serves: 6–8
Preparation time: 20 minutes
Cooking time: 30 minutes

- 1½ lb (680 g) baking apples, peeled, cored, and cut into
- ½-inch (1.25 cm) pieces
- ⅓ cup (65 g) sugar
- ½ teaspoon finely grated lemon zest
- 2 teaspoons fresh lemon juice
- 1 teaspoon ground cinnamon
- ¼ teaspoon kosher salt
- 7 sheets (13 x 18 inch/33 x 46 cm) frozen phyllo dough, thawed
- 1 stick (4 oz/115 g) unsalted butter, melted, or ½ cup (120 ml/4 fl oz) vegetable oil
- ⅓ cup (45 g) dried breadcrumbs
- Powdered (icing) sugar, for serving

Preheat the oven to 375°F (190°C/Gas Mark 5). Line a large baking sheet with parchment paper.

In a large bowl, combine the apples, sugar, lemon zest, lemon juice, cinnamon, and salt.

Lay a piece of parchment paper on a work surface and place 1 sheet of phyllo on top. (Keep the other phyllo sheets covered with a damp cloth so they don't dry out.) Brush the sheet evenly with melted butter. Repeat the process 6 more times to make a stack of 7 phyllo sheets.

Spread the breadcrumbs evenly over the top of the phyllo, then spoon the apple mixture (leaving the juices in the bowl) in a thick line along one of the short ends of the phyllo dough, leaving about ½ inch (1.25 cm) clear at the sides. Use the parchment paper to help roll the dough around the apples, tucking the filling inside and ending up with a long, stuffed cylinder. Pat down the ends of the phyllo to seal in the filling, and brush the top with a little more melted butter. Carefully transfer the strudel to the prepared baking sheet.

Bake until the phyllo is crisp and golden brown and the fruit is tender, 25–30 minutes. Set the baking sheet on a wire rack to cool for 15 minutes before slicing. Dust the strudel with a little powdered (icing) sugar before serving.

MIMOUNA

For those who observe Passover's eight-day-long dietary restrictions, the return to eating *chametz* (foods made with wheat, rye, spelt, oats, and barley) feels like a party. Moroccan Jews take that festivity especially seriously with a dedicated celebration called Mimouna. Families host feasts starting at nightfall on the last day of Passover and continuing with lavish meals and picnics the following day until sundown.

The focus of Mimouna, aside from returning to floury foods, is peace, brotherhood, and prosperity. Traditionally, Moroccan families would open their homes to the whole community, welcoming Jewish and Muslim visitors alike and wishing one another happiness and good fortune. People would travel from house to house (a practice called "Mimouna hopping"), bringing gifts and partaking in the overflowing tables of crepes and cakes, breads, marzipan and candies, fruit, salads, fish, and couscous dishes.

Morocco's centuries-old post-Passover tradition is continued in Israel today, where many Jews of Moroccan origin settled in the mid-twentieth century. There, the feasts are enjoyed both within and beyond the Moroccan community, with Jews of all backgrounds welcoming the end of Passover with festive meals. There are many dishes traditionally served for Mimouna including, Mofleta (page 372), Sweet Egg Meringue (page 384), Couscous Au Lait (page 178), Candied Eggplant (page 402), and Stuffed Dates with Almond and Rosewater (page 378).

CHOCOLATE-GANACHE MATZO CAKE

Some versions of this Passover-friendly, Napoleon-style icebox cake soak the matzo sheets in sweet wine rather than coffee, so feel free to experiment with both. In either case, use the best-quality chocolate chips possible, since chocolate is the cake's dominant flavor.

Serves: 8
Preparation time: 15 minutes, plus chilling
Cooking time: 5 minutes

• 1 stick (4 oz/115 g) unsalted butter or nonhydrogenated margarine, cut into pieces
• ½ cup (100 g) sugar
• 1 teaspoon vanilla extract
• ¼ teaspoon kosher salt
• 8 oz (225 g) bittersweet or semisweet chocolate chips
• 2 tablespoons milk or almond milk
• 2 cups (475 ml/16 fl oz) strong brewed coffee, warm
• 7 sheets matzo
• 1½ lb (680 g) strawberries, hulled and thinly sliced, plus more for serving

Line a large sheet pan with parchment paper or foil and set aside. In a medium saucepan, combine the butter and sugar and bring to a boil over medium heat, then cook, stirring constantly, until thickened, 1–2 minutes. Remove from the heat and stir in the vanilla and salt, followed by the chocolate. Stir to fully melt the chocolate. Add the milk and stir until a smooth, glossy ganache forms.

Pour the coffee into an 8-inch (20 cm) square container. Dip one sheet of matzo into the coffee and let sit until softened but not falling apart, 1–2 minutes. Remove, and lay on the prepared sheet pan. Spoon a generous amount of the ganache (3–4 tablespoons) on top and use an offset spatula or butter knife to spread all the way to the edges. Soak a second sheet of matzo in the coffee and lay directly on top of the first. Spread with the ganache and layer evenly with strawberries. Continue creating layers with the soaked matzo sheets and ganache, adding strawberries to every other layer, until there are 7 total layers. Top the final sheet of matzo with chocolate, allowing it to spill down the sides.

Refrigerate the cake for 30 minutes to set the ganache, then transfer to a serving plate. Serve chilled or at room temperature, garnished with more strawberries.

COCONUT MACAROONS

In the mid-twentieth century, these sticky-sweet, shredded coconut cookies emerged as America's most popular Passover dessert. (They are an American take on Almond Macaroons, below.) For years store-bought macaroons, which come in a cylindrical tin, were an almost mandatory fixture of the seder table. But in recent years, some families have begun baking their own macaroons at home, yielding much fresher and tastier cookies.

Makes: about 2 dozen cookies
Preparation time: 15 minutes
Cooking time: 25 minutes

- 4 egg whites
- ⅔ cup (141 g) sugar
- 1 teaspoon vanilla extract
- ½ teaspoon kosher salt
- ¾ cup (75 g) finely ground almond flour
- 2¼ cups (185 g) unsweetened shredded (dessicated) coconut

In a medium saucepan, stir together the egg whites, sugar, vanilla, salt, almond flour, and coconut until combined. Set the saucepan over low heat and cook, stirring frequently, until the mixture thickens slightly and turns very sticky, 5–7 minutes. Transfer the mixture to a bowl and let sit, uncovered, for 15 minutes to cool.

Meanwhile, preheat the oven to 325°F (160°C/Gas Mark 3). Line a large baking sheet with parchment paper.

Mound rounded tablespoons of batter onto the prepared baking sheet, moistening hands with water if the mixture is sticking. Bake, rotating the pan front to back halfway through, until the macaroons are lightly golden, 20–25 minutes. (Be careful not to overbake as the cookies will continue to firm up while they cool.) Let cool a few minutes on the pan, then carefully transfer the cookies to wire racks to cool completely.

ALMOND MACAROONS

In America, macaroons made from shredded coconut (see above) have emerged as the most common Passover sweet. This ancient variation, called *marunchinos*, is made with ground almonds and is a classic across Sephardi kitchens. The cookie's predecessors likely date back to pre-Inquisition Spain where Jewish home cooks learned from their Islamic neighbors how to make nut-flour confections. They are dense, chewy, and just the right amount of sweet—colored pale gold when made with blanched almonds, and speckled brown when made with raw (skin-on) almonds.

Makes: about 30 cookies
Preparation time: 25 minutes
Cooking time: 25 minutes

- 2½ cups (310 g) whole almonds (raw or blanched)
- 3 egg whites
- ⅔ cup (130 g) sugar
- ½ teaspoon vanilla extract
- ½ teaspoon finely grated lemon zest

Preheat the oven to 325°F (160°C/Gas Mark 3). Line 2 large baking sheets with parchment paper.

In a food processor, pulse the almonds, until the nuts are very finely ground (but not pasty) with a few slightly bigger pieces. Transfer the ground almonds to a large bowl and add the egg whites, sugar, vanilla, and lemon zest and stir well to combine.

Mound tablespoons of batter onto the prepared baking sheets. Bake, rotating the pans front to back halfway through time, until the macaroons are lightly golden, about 25 minutes. Set the baking sheets on wire racks to cool for 5 minutes. Then transfer the cookies to the racks to cool completely.

CAKES, COOKIES & SWEET PASTRIES

SYRUPY WALNUT CAKE

Syrup-soaked cakes made from semolina, flour, ground nuts, and even matzo meal are ubiquitous throughout Middle Eastern cooking. This version, which has finely ground walnuts and almonds at the base and is perfumed with citrus, is called *tishpishti*. It is traditionally served by Sephardi Jews on Passover or Rosh Hashanah. Top it with whipped cream or plain yogurt.

Serves: 8
Preparation time: 35 minutes, plus cooling
Cooking time: 40 minutes

For the syrup:
• 1½ cups (300 g) sugar
• 2 tablespoons fresh lemon juice
• 2 teaspoons orange blossom water

For the cake:
• 1½ cups (155 g) walnut halves
• ½ cup (60 g) finely ground almond flour
• ½ teaspoon baking powder
• ½ teaspoon kosher salt
• 6 eggs, separated
• ½ cup (90 g) light brown sugar
• 1 teaspoon ground cinnamon
• 1 teaspoon vanilla extract
• ½ teaspoon finely grated orange zest
• ½ teaspoon finely grated lemon zest

Make the syrup: In a small saucepan, combine the sugar and 1 cup (240 ml/8 fl oz) water and bring to a boil over medium-high heat, stirring often to dissolve the sugar. Reduce the heat to medium and cook, stirring occasionally, until the syrup thickens, about 10 minutes. Remove from the heat and stir in the lemon juice and orange blossom water and let cool completely. (The syrup can be covered and refrigerated for up to 2 weeks. Bring to room temperature before using.)

Preheat the oven to 350°F (180°C/Gas Mark 4). Lightly grease the bottom and sides of a 9-inch (23 cm) round or square cake pan. Cut out a round or square of parchment and fit into the bottom of the pan, then lightly grease the parchment.

Make the cake: In a food processor, pulse the walnuts, scraping down the sides of the bowl once or twice, until finely ground with a few slightly larger pieces. (The nuts should not be powdery or pasty.) Transfer the ground walnuts to a medium bowl and whisk in the almond flour, baking powder, and salt.

In a stand mixer (or using a handheld electric mixer and a large bowl), beat the egg yolks at high speed until pale yellow. With the machine running, beat in the brown sugar, 1 tablespoon at a time, beating until the mixture is thick. Add the cinnamon, vanilla, orange zest, and lemon zest and beat until combined. Add the nut mixture and fold in with a rubber spatula until fully combined. (The mixture will feel quite stiff.)

Transfer the nut mixture to a separate bowl and thoroughly wash and dry the stand mixer and beater. Add the egg whites to the clean bowl and beat at medium-high speed until billowy and holding stiff peaks. Add the egg whites to the nut mixture and gently fold in until fully combined, with no remaining white streaks.

Pour the batter into the prepared pan and bake until a skewer inserted in the center comes out clean, about 25 minutes.

Set the pan on a wire rack to cool for 10 minutes. Using a small wooden skewer, poke holes across the entire surface of the cake, about 1 inch (2.5 cm) apart. Pour the cooled syrup evenly over the warm cake and then let the cake cool completely, about 2 hours. It will look like a lot of syrup, but it will absorb into the cake as it cools. Cut the cake into squares or diamonds and serve at room temperature.

ADI DABOUSH

TAVLIN

·

MULTIPLE LOCATIONS
MELBOURNE, VICTORIA
AUSTRALIA

Adi Daboush is the chef and owner of Tavlin, a modern
Middle Eastern restaurant with two locations in Melbourne.

SEMOLINA AND COCONUT CAKE WITH ROSEWATER SYRUP

This cake, which is inspired by Daboush's grandmother
Esther's recipe, is related to a whole genre of syrup-
drenched, semolina-based cakes found throughout the
Middle East, including in Israel. To name a few examples:
In Egypt, these semolina cakes are called *basbousa*; in
Libya, they go by *safra*; in Syria, they are called *namoura*;
and in Lebanon, they are often called *hareesa*. While
some variations are dairy-free, the butter in this cake
gives it a particularly luscious texture. It is equally lovely
for dessert topped with whipped cream or ice cream,
or served at breakfast with a dollop of plain yogurt.

Serves: 6–8
Preparation time: 20 minutes, plus cooling
Cooking time: 45 minutes

For the syrup:
· 1½ cups (300 g) sugar
· 2 teaspoons rose water
· 1 tablespoon fresh lemon juice

For the cake:
· 2½ sticks (10 oz/285 g) unsalted butter or
  nonhydrogenated margarine, at room temperature
· 1 cup (200 g) sugar
· 3 eggs
· 3 cups (480 g) fine semolina
· ⅔ cup (90 g) all-purpose (plain) flour
· ½ cup (40 g) unsweetened shredded
  (desiccated) coconut
· 2 teaspoons baking powder
· ½ teaspoon kosher salt
· 1 cup (240 ml/8 fl oz) fresh orange juice

Make the syrup: In a small saucepan, combine 1 cup
(240 ml/8 fl oz) water and the sugar and bring to a
boil over medium-high heat, stirring often to dissolve
the sugar. Reduce the heat to medium and cook until the
syrup thickens slightly, about 5 minutes. Remove from
the heat and stir in the rose water and lemon juice, then
let cool completely. Set aside until needed, or cover and
refrigerate for up to 1 week.

Make the cake: Preheat the oven to 350°F (180°C/Gas
Mark 4). Grease a 9-inch (23 cm) square cake pan.

In a stand mixer fitted with a paddle attachment, beat the
butter and sugar on medium speed until light and fluffy.
Add the eggs one at a time, beating to incorporate after
each addition and scraping down the sides of the bowl
as necessary.

In a medium bowl, whisk together the semolina, flour,
coconut, baking powder, and salt. Add ½ cup (120 ml/4
fl oz) of the orange juice to the butter-sugar mixture and
beat until just combined. Add half of the semolina mixture
and beat to combine. Repeat with the remaining orange
juice and semolina mixtures.

Spoon the batter into the prepared pan and bake until
the cake is lightly golden, and a skewer inserted into the
center comes out clean, 35–40 minutes. Transfer the
pan to a wire rack and use a very sharp knife to deeply
score diamond- or square-shaped pieces into the still-
warm cake, cutting all the way through to the bottom.

Slowly and evenly pour the cooled syrup over the
hot cake. Let the cake cool to room temperature
before serving.

CINNAMON-SUGAR PULL-APART CAKE

Called *aranygaluska*, this coffee cake lives up to its Hungarian name, which translates to "golden dumpling." This recipe dips nuggets of yeast dough into melted butter and a cinnamon-sugar mixture, tucks them into a pan with dollops of jam, and bakes everything until it puffs into a cake that resembles a cross between doughnut holes and cinnamon rolls. The cake, which is pulled apart at the table, makes a decadent brunch centerpiece.

Serves: 8
Preparation time: 40 minutes, plus rising
Cooking time: 40 minutes

For the dough:
• 1 packet (¼ oz/7 g) active dry yeast (2 ¼ teaspoons)
• ½ cup (100 g) plus 1 teaspoon sugar
• 1 cup (240 ml/8 fl oz) warm water (110°F/43°C)
• 4–4½ cups (560–630 g) all-purpose (plain) flour, plus more for kneading
• 1 teaspoon kosher salt
• 2 eggs, lightly beaten
• 1½ teaspoons vanilla extract
• ½ teaspoon finely grated orange zest
• ½ teaspoon almond extract (optional)
• 1 stick (4 oz/115 g) unsalted butter, cut into pieces, at room temperature
• 1 teaspoon vegetable oil

For the topping:
• 1 stick (4 oz/115 g) unsalted butter
• 1 cup (180 g) light brown sugar
• 1 tablespoon ground cinnamon
• ⅛ teaspoon kosher salt
• ⅓ cup (105 g) apricot jam

Make the dough: In a large bowl, stir together the yeast, 1 teaspoon of the sugar, and the warm water. Let sit until foaming, 5–10 minutes.

Meanwhile, in a large bowl, whisk together 4 cups (560 g) flour and the salt.

Stir the remaining ½ cup (100 g) sugar, the eggs, vanilla, orange zest, and almond extract (if using) into the yeast mixture. Add the flour mixture and gently stir until the dough begins to come together. Turn the dough out onto a floured surface and knead well, adding the softened butter pieces a few at a time, and adding up to ½ cup (70 g) additional flour as needed, until you have a supple, slightly tacky dough, about 10 minutes. You might not need all of the flour. (The kneading can also be done in a stand mixer with a dough hook, 5–7 minutes.)

Grease a large bowl with the vegetable oil, add the dough, and turn to coat. Cover the bowl with a tea towel and let sit in a warm place until nearly doubled in size, 1–1 ½ hours.

Meanwhile, preheat the oven to 350°F (°180C/Gas Mark 4). Generously grease a 9-inch (23 cm) round springform pan.

Make the topping: In a small saucepan, melt the butter over medium-low heat, then transfer to a bowl. In a second bowl, whisk together the brown sugar, cinnamon, and salt.

Gently deflate the dough with the heel of your hand. Pinch off a golf ball–size piece of dough and roll it into a ball. Dip it in the melted butter and then the cinnamon-sugar mixture, making sure all sides are coated, and place it in the prepared pan. Continue this process until the pan is lined with a single layer of dough balls. Evenly dollop the jam on top of and around the dough balls. Repeat the rolling and dipping process until all of the dough is used. If there is any melted butter remaining, drizzle it on top, then sprinkle with any remaining cinnamon-sugar mixture.

Place pan in the oven (if desired, set a parchment paper–lined baking sheet on the rack below the pan to catch any leaks) and bake until the cake is puffed and golden brown, 35–40 minutes. Let the cake cool in the pan on a wire rack to cool for 10–15 minutes, then carefully unmold the cake and transfer to a serving dish. Serve warm.

CAKES, COOKIES & SWEET PASTRIES

CHEESECAKE

Cakes enriched with curd cheese (*kaesekuchen* in Yiddish) have their roots in Central Europe. But cheese-cakes made with cream cheese, as they commonly are today, are an American adaptation. Serve the cheesecake as is, or drizzle it with Strawberry Sauce (page 394) or Blueberry Sauce (page 395).

Serves: 8–10
Preparation time: 15 minutes
Cooking time: 40 minutes

For the crust:
• 1½ cups (150 g) graham cracker (digestive biscuit) crumbs from about 10 full graham crackers
• 3 tablespoons light brown sugar
• 6 tablespoons (85 g) unsalted butter, melted
• ¼ teaspoon kosher salt

For the filling:
• 16 oz (455 g) cream cheese, at room temperature
• ⅓ cup (65 g) sugar
• ¼ cup (45 g) light brown sugar
• 2 eggs
• 1 teaspoon vanilla extract

Preheat the oven to 350°F (180°C/Gas Mark 4).

Make the crust: Pulse about 10 full graham crackers in a food processor, or place them in a plastic bag, seal, and smash with a rolling pin. In a medium bowl, stir together the graham cracker crumbs, brown sugar, melted butter, and salt until combined. Press the moistened crumb mixture into the bottom and sides of a 9-inch (23 cm) pie plate. Place in the freezer while making the filling.

Make the filling: In a stand mixer (or using a handheld electric mixer and a large bowl), beat the cream cheese, granulated sugar, and brown sugar at medium speed until smooth, scraping down the sides as necessary. Add the eggs one at a time, followed by the vanilla, beating until smooth after each addition.

Pour the filling into the crust, then bake until mostly set with a slightly jiggly center, 35–40 minutes. Let cool on a wire rack, then cover and refrigerate at least 4 hours, or overnight. Serve chilled.

RICOTTA CHEESECAKE

In Rome, baked ricotta cheesecakes, called *cassola*, have become a popular Christmas-time dessert. But the confection has roots in Rome's ancient Jewish community. It has a lighter and more custardy texture than a cheese-cake made with cream cheese (see above).

Serves: 8
Preparation time: 15 minutes
Cooking time: 45 minutes

• Vegetable oil, for greasing
• 3 cups (720 g) ricotta cheese
• ¾ cup (150 g) sugar
• 4 eggs
• 1½ teaspoons vanilla extract
• ½ teaspoon kosher salt
• Cocoa powder and fresh raspberries, for serving

Preheat the oven to 400°F (200°C/Gas Mark 6). Lightly grease a 9-inch (23 cm) round springform pan. Cut out a round of parchment paper and line the bottom of the pan, then brush the parchment lightly with oil.

In a food processor, blend the ricotta until completely smooth. Add the sugar, eggs, vanilla, and salt and blend until creamy and combined, about 2 minutes.

Pour the mixture into the prepared pan and bake for 10 minutes. Reduce the oven temperature to 350°F (180°C/Gas Mark 4) and continue baking until lightly golden and still quite wobbly, 30–35 minutes. (Take care not to overbake as the *cassola* will continue to firm up as it cools.) Set the springform pan on a wire rack to cool completely before unmolding and transferring to a serving plate.

Just before serving, use a fine-mesh sieve to generously dust the top of the cake with cocoa powder and garnish with raspberries.

MANDELBROT

Like Italian biscotti, *mandelbrot* ("almond bread" in Yiddish) are baked twice, yielding a crunchy cookie that goes perfectly with tea or coffee. The generous dusting of cinnamon sugar on these nutty cookies makes them irresistible.

Makes: about 40 cookies
Preparation time: 30 minutes
Cooking time: 40 minutes

• 3 cups (420 g) all-purpose (plain) flour
• 1 teaspoon baking powder
• 1 teaspoon baking soda (bicarbonate of soda)
• ½ teaspoon kosher salt
• 2 sticks (8 oz/225 g) unsalted butter or nonhydrogenated margarine, at room temperature
• 2 cups (400 g) sugar
• 4 eggs
• 1 teaspoon vanilla extract
• 1 teaspoon fresh lemon juice
• 1 cup (120 g) finely chopped roasted, unsalted almonds
• 1½ tablespoons ground cinnamon

Preheat the oven to 350°F (180°C/Gas Mark 4). Line 2 large baking sheets with parchment paper.

Sift together the flour, baking powder, baking soda (bicarb), and salt into a medium bowl.

In a stand mixer (or using a handhold electric mixer and a large bowl), beat the butter and 1 cup (200 g) sugar on medium speed, scraping down the bowl as necessary, until pale and creamy, 2–3 minutes. Add the eggs, one at a time, and beat to combine, followed by the vanilla and lemon juice, beating well after each addition. Add the flour mixture in 2 additions and beat on low until just combined, then fold in the almonds with a spatula. The dough should be soft and spreadable.

Divide the dough into 4 portions. Set 2 parts of the dough on one of the prepared baking sheets and use a butter knife or offset spatula to spread each part into a long flat rectangle about 9 × 4 inches (23 × 10 cm) and about ½ inch (1.25 cm) thick, leaving about 2 inches (5 cm) in between. Repeat with the remaining 2 parts of dough and the second baking sheet.

Bake, rotating the pans front to back halfway through, until puffed and lightly browned, about 20 minutes. Remove from oven and let cool slightly (leave the oven on). Meanwhile, in a small bowl, stir together the remaining 1 cup (200 g) sugar and the cinnamon.

Slice the rectangles crosswise into pieces ¾ inch (2 cm) wide. Turn the pieces on their sides and sprinkle generously with half of the cinnamon sugar. Return to the oven and bake 10 more minutes. Remove the pan from the oven, flip the cookies to the other side, and sprinkle with the remaining cinnamonsugar. Return to the oven and bake until firm, another 10 minutes. Set the baking sheets on wire racks to cool for 5 minutes, then transfer the cookies to the racks to cool completely.

ALMOND HORNS

These chewy, chocolate-dipped crescent cookies, which have roots in Central Europe, were ubiquitous in New York's Jewish bakeries in the early and mid-twentieth century. Made from a blend of almond paste and almond flour, and covered in crunchy sliced almonds, they are naturally gluten-free and utterly delicious.

Makes: 18 cookies
Preparation time: 20 minutes
Cooking time: 20 minutes

• 12 oz (340 g) almond paste (not marzipan), broken into small pieces with your fingers
• ½ cup (70 g) almond flour (ground almonds)
• ⅓ cup (65 g) sugar
• 2 egg whites
• ½ teaspoon vanilla extract
• 1½ cups (155 g) sliced almonds
• 4 oz (113 g) bittersweet chocolate, roughly chopped

Preheat the oven to 375°F (190°C/Gas Mark 5). Line a large baking sheet with parchment paper. (You might need two, depending on the size of your baking sheet.)

In a stand mixer (or using a handheld electric mixer and a large bowl), mix the almond paste, almond flour, sugar, 1 of the egg whites, and the vanilla at low speed until a moist dough forms.

Spread the sliced almonds out in a shallow dish. Moisten your hands lightly with water. Divide the dough into 18 equal portions (weigh on a digital kitchen scale for the most accurate results) and roll into balls. Roll and shape one of the balls into a 5-inch (12.5 cm) rope. Press the rope into the almonds on both sides while gently forming it into a U shape, then lay it on the prepared baking sheet. The dough will feel fragile at this stage, but will firm up while baking. Repeat with the remaining dough balls.

In a small bowl, whisk the remaining 1 egg white with about 1 teaspoon water. Gently brush the tops of the cookies with a little of the egg wash (you will not use all of it). Bake, rotating the baking sheet front to back halfway through, until golden, 15–18 minutes. Let cool on the pan for 5 minutes, then carefully transfer to a wire rack to cool completely.

In a heatproof bowl set over a pan of simmering water, melt the chocolate. (Or, melt in the microwave in a micro-wave-safe bowl in 30-second intervals, stirring after each, until fully melted.) Dip the ends of the cookies into the chocolate and place back on baking sheet. Chill in the fridge until the chocolate sets, about 15 minutes. Serve at room temperature.

BLACK AND WHITE COOKIES

Black and white cookies—the cake-textured rounds frosted with white icing on one half and black on the other—were a staple in the New York City Jewish bakery case in the mid-twentieth century. They can still be found in bakeshops today, though many of the commercial options tend to be almost comically large. This version is petite and gently sweet—perfect for dipping into a cup of coffee or tea.

Makes: about 2 dozen cookies
Preparation time: 25 minutes, plus cooling
Cooking time: 15 minutes

For the cookies:
• 1½ cups (210 g) all-purpose (plain) flour, sifted
• ½ teaspoon baking powder
• ½ teaspoon kosher salt
• 6 tablespoons (85 g) unsalted butter, at room temperature
• ⅔ cup (130 g) sugar
• 1 egg plus 1 egg yolk
• ⅓ cup (75 ml/2½ fl oz) milk
• 1 teaspoon vanilla extract
• ¼ teaspoon lemon extract

For the icing:
• 2½ cups (270 g) powdered (icing) sugar, sifted
• 3 tablespoons milk, plus more as needed
• ½ teaspoon vanilla extract
• ¼ teaspoon lemon extract
• 2 tablespoons Dutch-process cocoa powder
• ½ teaspoon instant coffee granules

Preheat the oven to 350°F (180°C/Gas Mark 4). Line 2 large baking sheets with parchment paper.

Make the cookies: In a medium bowl, whisk together the flour, baking powder, and salt.

In a stand mixer (or using a handheld electric mixer and a large bowl), beat together the butter and sugar at medium speed until light and fluffy. Add the whole egg, egg yolk, milk, vanilla, and lemon extract and beat until combined. Don't worry if the batter appears lumpy or curdled at this stage—it will smooth out. Add the flour mixture to the butter mixture in stages, beating briefly on low after each addition and scraping down the sides of the bowl as necessary, to form a soft batter.

Place rounded tablespoons of dough, spaced 2 inches (5 cm) apart, on the prepared baking sheets. Bake, rotating the pans front to back halfway through, until lightly golden around the edges but still pale on top, 12–15 minutes. Carefully transfer the cookies to a wire rack to cool completely.

Make the icing: In a medium bowl, stir together the powdered (icing) sugar, milk, vanilla, and lemon extract. Stir until a thick icing forms. The mixture should be easily spreadable, but not loose or liquid. If necessary, stir in additional milk, 1 teaspoon at a time, until the desired consistency is reached.

Transfer about half of the icing to a separate bowl. Add the cocoa powder and coffee granules and stir to combine. If necessary, add more milk, 1 teaspoon at a time, until the same thick, spreadable icing consistency is reached.

Once the cookies are fully cool, set the wire racks over a piece of parchment paper. Using a butter knife or small offset spatula, carefully glaze one half of the flat (bottom) side of each cookie with the white icing. Repeat on the other half with the black icing. Depending on how thickly the cookies are glazed, there may be some icing left. Set the glazed cookies back on the racks to set for a few minutes before serving.

Black and White Cookies

POPPY SEED COOKIES

Poppy seeds show up in many pastries, often finely ground and cooked with milk and sugar into a thick, spreadable paste. But in these sweet and snappy Eastern European cookies, called *mohn kichlach*, the seeds stay whole, adding a satisfying pop of crunch. They are often cut into rounds, but any shape of cookie cutter will work. They are simple, satisfying, and wonderful with tea. They also freeze beautifully and thaw quickly, so keep a well-sealed bag in the freezer to pull out when company arrives.

Makes: about 50 cookies
Preparation time: 15 minutes, plus chilling
Cooking time: 10 minutes

- 2–2¼ cups (280–315 g) all-purpose (plain) flour, plus more for rolling
- 1 teaspoon baking powder
- ½ teaspoon kosher salt
- 3 tablespoons poppy seeds
- ¾ cup (150 g) sugar
- ½ cup (120 ml/4 fl oz) vegetable oil
- 2 eggs
- 1 teaspoon vanilla extract
- ½ teaspoon finely grated lemon zest (optional)

In a medium bowl, whisk together 2 cups (280 g) flour, the baking powder, salt, and poppy seeds.

In a stand mixer (or using a handheld electric mixer and a large bowl), beat together the sugar, vegetable oil, and eggs at medium-high speed until light and billowy, 3–5 minutes. Beat in the vanilla and lemon zest (if using). Add the flour mixture in two additions, beating on low speed and scraping down the sides of the bowl as necessary, until a firm but pliable dough forms. (It is okay if the dough is still a tiny bit tacky at this stage.) If necessary, add the additional ¼ cup (35 g) flour, 1 tablespoon at a time, to reach the desired consistency. Scrape the dough into a ball and form into a disc. Wrap tightly in plastic wrap (cling film) and refrigerate until firm enough to roll out, 1–2 hours.

Preheat the oven to 350°F (180°C/Gas Mark 4). Line 2 large baking sheets with parchment paper.

Divide the dough in half, keeping one half wrapped in the fridge. On a floured surface using a floured rolling pin, roll the dough into a large rectangle about ⅛ inch (3 mm) thick. Using a 2-inch (5 cm) round biscuit or cookie cutter, cut out as many cookies as possible and transfer them to the prepared baking sheets. (If the cookies are sticking to the surface, run a sharp paring knife underneath the cookie to release.) Gather the scraps, reroll, and cut out more cookies. Repeat the process with the remaining dough.

Bake until gently puffed and just lightly golden, 8–11 minutes. (Watch carefully, as they tend to go from blond to burned rather quickly.) Transfer the cookies to wire racks to cool.

EATING THE ENEMY ON PURIM

On Purim each year, Jewish communities around the world engage in the unusual practice of "eating the enemy." The Purim story celebrates Queen Esther's triumph over her husband's ill-intentioned advisor, Haman, who plotted to destroy ancient Persia's Jewish community. Jews honor Queen Esther's victory by eating a variety of sweets and other baked goods shaped to resemble Haman. The most widely known example, hamantaschen (pages 340–343) are fruit- or poppy seed–filled, tricornered cookies meant to look like Haman's pockets or hat.

In Italy, meanwhile, Jews eat sugar-dusted fried pastries called *orecchie di Aman* (Haman's Ear Fritters, page 367), formed to look like his ears. Moroccan Jews have round loaves of bread with two eggs arranged to symbolize Haman's eyes. And Jews from Greece, Turkey, and Rhodes bake *folares*, bread dough shaped to look like a cage or noose intended to trap the Purim villain.While "eating" one's enemy might seem a bit odd by contemporary standards, for generations it has proven to be a powerful act of sweet, culinary vengeance.

KICHLACH

Kichel simply means "cookie" in Yiddish (*kichlach* is the plural), and the best known is likely this puffed, often sugar-dusted cookie formed into a bow-tie shape. *Kichlach* are crunchy and slightly dry by design—the perfect companion to a cup of coffee, tea, or schnapps. Ashkenazi Jews once served them with slices of pickled herring on Saturday mornings after synagogue services.

Makes: about 4 dozen cookies
Preparation time: 40 minutes
Cooking time: 20 minutes

- 2¼–2½ cups (315–350 g) all-purpose (plain) flour, plus more for rolling
- 1 teaspoon baking powder
- ½ teaspoon kosher salt
- 4 eggs
- ⅓ cup (75 ml/2½ fl oz) vegetable oil
- ½ cup (100 g) plus 2 tablespoons sugar
- 1 teaspoon vanilla extract

Preheat the oven to 350°F (180°C/Gas Mark 4). Line two large baking sheets with parchment paper.

In a medium bowl, whisk together 2¼ cups (315 g) flour, the baking powder, and salt.

In a stand mixer with the paddle attachment, beat together the eggs, oil, 2 tablespoons of the sugar, and the vanilla at medium-high speed until light and frothy, 2–3 minutes. Add the flour mixture and beat on low, scraping down the bowl as necessary, until the dough comes together. Switch to the dough hook and knead the dough, adding up to ¼ cup (35 g) additional flour, 1 tablespoon at a time, until a malleable, slightly sticky dough forms, 5–7 minutes (You may not need all the flour.)

Spread ¼ cup (50 g) of the sugar over a large work surface. Lay the dough on top of the sugar and using a floured rolling pin, roll into a large rectangle ¼ inch (6 mm) thick. Sprinkle the top of the dough evenly with the remaining ¼ cup (50 g) sugar and use your hands to spread it out and very gently press it into the dough. Cut the dough into 3 × 1-inch (7.5 × 2.5 cm) rectangular strips. Lift up a rectangle, twist in the middle to make a bow-tie shape, and place on one of the prepared baking sheets. Repeat with the remaining rectangles.

Bake, rotating the baking sheets front to back halfway through, until the cookies are puffed and lightly browned, 15–18 minutes. Transfer the cookies to wire racks to cool.

HAMANTASCHEN

This sweet, triangular cookie is unarguably the most popular Ashkenazi Purim treat. (They are so popular, kosher cooks devised both dairy and nondairy versions, so the treat could be enjoyed after meat and dairy meals.) The cookie's tricornered shape is meant to evoke the Purim story's notorious villain, Haman. The name *hamantaschen* translates from Yiddish as "Haman's pockets," but the cookies are also colloquially described as Haman's hat or ear. This butter-enriched dough yields tender, full-flavored cookies but requires some chilling time in the refrigerator, so plan ahead. Hamantaschen are traditionally filled with poppy seeds, jam, and chopped nuts, but many contemporary cooks spoon everything from dulce de leche and lemon curd to the chocolate-hazelnut spread Nutella into the cookies' centers. Cuban Jewish cooks sometimes spoon guava paste into their hamantaschen, giving them a deliciously tropical flavor.

Makes: about 3 dozen cookies
Preparation time: 45 minutes, plus chilling
Cooking time: 20 minutes

- 2½ cups (350 g) all-purpose (plain) flour, plus more as needed
- 1 teaspoon baking powder
- ½ teaspoon kosher salt
- 1 stick (4 oz/115 g) unsalted butter, at room temperature
- ¾ cup (150 g) sugar
- 2 eggs
- 1½ teaspoons vanilla extract
- Prune Lekvar (page 408), Apricot Lekvar (page 408), Poppy Seed Filling (page 396), Honey-Walnut Filling (page 400), or other thick jam, for filling

Sift together the flour, baking powder and salt into a medium bowl.

In a stand mixer (or using a handheld electric mixer and a large bowl), beat together the butter and sugar on medium speed until pale and fluffy, about 3 minutes. Add the eggs and vanilla and beat to fully combine. Add the flour mixture to the butter mixture in three additions, beating on low after each addition, and scraping down the sides of the bowl as necessary, until a firm but pliable dough comes together. If the dough looks too dry, add water, 1 teaspoon at a time, until the desired consistency is reached. If it looks too wet, add additional flour, 1 table-spoon at a time. Gather the dough and gently knead it a few times, then form into a flat disc. Wrap tightly in plastic wrap (cling film) and refrigerate for at least 3 hours (or overnight).

Preheat the oven to 350°F (180°C/Gas Mark 4). Line two large baking sheets with parchment paper.

Remove half of the dough from the fridge (keep the other half wrapped and chilled). On a lightly floured surface, using a lightly floured rolling pin, roll the dough to a ¼-inch (6 mm) thickness. Using a 3-inch (7.5 cm) round biscuit cutter or glass, cut out as many rounds as possible and carefully transfer them to the prepared baking sheets. Gather the scraps, reroll, and cut out additional rounds. Spoon 1 rounded teaspoon of the desired filling into the center of each dough round. Fold the left side over on an angle, followed by the right side. Fold the bottom flap up, tucking one end under the side flap to make a pocket (the filling should still be visible in the center). Pinch the corners firmly to seal. Repeat with the remaining dough and filling.

Bake the cookies until lightly golden and browned at the corners, 15–18 minutes. Let the cookies cool on the baking sheets for 5 minutes, then transfer to wire racks to cool completely.

Hamantaschen

YEASTED HAMANTASCHEN

Today, hamantaschen are primarily made with a simple oil- or butter-based cookie dough. But the Purim confection was traditionally made with an enriched yeast dough that yielded a puffed and tender pastry encircling the sweet filling. Yeasted hamantaschen are entirely different than their cookie counterparts, and definitely worth trying.

Makes: about 30 pastries
Preparation time: 35 minutes, plus rising
Cooking time: 20 minutes

• 1 packet (¼ oz/7g) active dry yeast (2¼ teaspoons)
• ½ cup (150 g) plus 1 teaspoon sugar
• ½ cup (120 ml/4 fl oz) warm water (110°F/43°C)
• 2½–3 cups (350–420 g) all-purpose (plain) flour, plus more for rolling
• ½ teaspoon kosher salt
• ¼ cup (60 ml/2 fl oz) vegetable oil or melted butter, plus more for greasing the bowl
• 3 eggs
• 1 teaspoon vanilla extract
• Prune Lekvar (page 408), Apricot Lekvar (page 408), Poppy Seed Filling (page 396), Honey-Walnut Filling (page 400) or other thick jam, for filling

In a large bowl, stir together the yeast, 1 teaspoon of the sugar, and the warm water. Let sit until bubbling and frothy, 5–10 minutes.

Meanwhile, in a medium bowl, whisk together 2½ cups (350 g) flour, the remaining ½ cup (150 g) sugar, and salt.

Whisk the oil, 2 of the eggs, and the vanilla into the yeast mixture until combined. Add the flour mixture and stir until a moist dough forms. Turn the dough out onto a lightly floured surface and knead well, adding up to ½ cup (70 g) additional flour, as necessary, until a supple, elastic dough forms, about 10 minutes. You might not use all of the flour. (The kneading can also be done in a stand mixer fitted with a dough hook, 5–7 minutes.) Grease a large bowl with about 1 teaspoon oil, add the dough, and turn to coat. Cover with a tea towel and let sit in a warm place until doubled in size, about 1½ hours.

Line 2 large baking sheets with parchment paper. Remove half of the dough from the bowl (keep the other half covered). On a lightly floured surface using a lightly floured rolling pin, roll the dough to a ¼-inch (6 mm) thickness. Using a 3-inch (7.5 cm) round biscuit cutter or glass, cut out as many rounds as possible and carefully transfer them to the prepared baking sheets. Gather the scraps, reroll, and cut out additional rounds. Spoon 1 rounded teaspoon of the desired filling into the center of each dough round. Fold the left side over on an angle, followed by the right side. Fold the bottom flap up, tucking one end under the side flap to make a pocket (a little of the filling should still be visible in the center). Pinch the corners firmly to seal. Repeat with the remaining dough and filling. Loosely cover the filled cookies with a tea towel and let rest for 30 minutes.

Meanwhile, preheat the oven to 350°F (180°C/Gas Mark 4).

Whisk the remaining egg in a small bowl. Lightly brush the tops of each cookie with a little of the egg wash (you will not use all of it). Bake the cookies until puffed and golden brown, 18–20 minutes. Transfer the cookies to wire racks to cool.

URI SCHEFT

LEHAMIM BAKERY
·
MULTIPLE LOCATIONS
TEL AVIV, ISRAEL

Uri Scheft is the creative force behind Tel Aviv's beloved and influential Lehamim Bakery, and founder of Breads Bakery in New York City, where his sumptuous take on chocolate babka has reached icon status.

GIANT STRAWBERRY-ALMOND HAMANTASCHEN

These giant hamantaschen, which are more closely akin to a galette than a cookie, are "fork-and-knife" almond shortbread pastries that come brimming with sweet, ruby fruit and are ideal for sharing. The recipe makes more dough than you need. Reroll the scraps, stamp out smaller rounds, and fill with a favorite thick fruit jam.

Makes: 3 large pastries
Preparation time: 1 hour, plus resting and chilling
Cooking time: 30 minutes

For the shortbread:
· 1¼ sticks (5 oz/140 g) unsalted butter,
  at room temperature
· ¾ cup (90 g) powdered (icing) sugar
· ¼ cup (50 g) sugar
· 1 large egg, beaten
· 1¾ cups (245 g) all-purpose (plain) flour,
  plus more for rolling
· ½ cup (60 g) almond flour (ground almonds)
· ¼ teaspoon kosher salt

For the filling:
· 1 lb 6 oz (650 g) small strawberries (about 3 cups),
  hulled (or quartered larger strawberries)
· 1½ cups (300 g) sugar

For assembly:
· ¾ cup (105 g) dried breadcrumbs
· Powdered (icing) sugar, for dusting

Make the shortbread: In a stand mixer fitted with the paddle attachment, beat together the butter, powdered (icing) sugar, and sugar on low speed until combined, about 30 seconds. Add the egg and beat until combined. Add the all-purpose (plain) flour, almond flour (ground almonds), and salt and beat, scraping down the sides of the bowl as necessary, until the dough just comes together. (Be careful not to overmix the dough.) Gather the dough into a ball, flatten into a disc, and wrap in plastic wrap (cling film). Refrigerate for at least 2 hours or up to 3 days.

Make the filling: In a large bowl, gently mix together the strawberries and sugar. Let the mixture stand, covered, at room temperature for 3 hours (or overnight in the refrigerator). Drain the strawberries through a fine-mesh sieve set over a small saucepan to catch the juices and set aside. Set the saucepan of juices over medium-high heat and bring to a boil, then reduce the heat to medium and simmer, stirring often, until the liquid thickens into a loose syrup, about 8 minutes. Remove from the heat and let cool.

To assemble and bake: Line 2 large baking sheets with parchment paper. Place the chilled dough on a lightly floured work surface and lightly flour the top of the dough. Using a floured rolling pin, roll the dough into a 10 × 25-inch (25 × 63 cm) rectangle that is ⅛ inch (3 mm) thick. Stamp out three 8-inch (20 cm) rounds of dough and carefully transfer to the prepared baking sheets. Refrigerate the dough rounds for 10 minutes before filling.

Sprinkle one-third of the breadcrumbs into the center of each dough round, then top each with one-third of the strawberries, leaving a 1-inch (2.5 cm) border around the edges. Using a pastry brush, brush the edges of the dough very lightly with water, then pinch the dough into large triangle shapes, with plenty of the filling showing. Chill the filled cookies for 20 minutes.

Meanwhile, preheat the oven to 325°F (160°C/Gas Mark 3).

Bake the hamantaschen until golden, 20–25 minutes. Remove from the oven and brush a generous amount of the strawberry syrup on top of each cookie's strawberry filling (avoid brushing the dough). Use a fine-mesh sieve to dust powdered (icing) sugar on top and serve warm.

✱ STAR RECIPE

CHOCOLATE RUGELACH

Israeli-style rugelach are noticeably different than those typically enjoyed in America. Instead of a butter and cream cheese dough, they tend to be made from a dairy-free yeasted dough. The baked cookies are also brushed with sugar syrup, giving them a glossy sheen and plush texture. Chocolate and cinnamon are the two standard fillings—here, a thick chocolate paste is amply swirled through the cookie.

Makes: about 2 dozen rugelach
Preparation time: 40 minutes, plus rising
Cooking time: 20 minutes

For the syrup:
- ½ cup (100 g) sugar
- ½ cup (120 ml/4 fl oz) water

For the dough:
- 1½ teaspoons active dry yeast
- ½ cup (50 g) plus 1 teaspoon sugar
- ¾ cup (175 ml/6 fl oz) warm water (110°F/43°C)
- 3–3½ cups (420–490 g) all-purpose (plain) flour, plus more for kneading and rolling
- ½ teaspoon kosher salt
- ¼ cup (60 ml/2 fl oz) vegetable oil, plus more for greasing the bowl
- 2 egg yolks
- 1 teaspoon vanilla extract

For the chocolate filling:
- 1 cup (80 g) cocoa powder, plus more as needed
- ¾ cup (150 g) sugar
- ¼ cup (60 ml/2 fl oz) almond milk or milk, plus more as needed
- ½ teaspoon vanilla extract

Make the syrup: In a small saucepan, combine the water and sugar and bring to a boil over medium-high heat. Reduce the heat to medium and cook until the syrup thickens slightly, about 2 minutes. Remove from the heat and let cool completely. Set aside until needed, or cover and refrigerate for up to 2 weeks.

Make the dough: In a large bowl, stir together the yeast, 1 teaspoon of the sugar, and the warm water. Let sit until foaming, 5–10 minutes.

Meanwhile, in a medium bowl, whisk together 3 cups (420 g) flour, the remaining ½ cup (100 g) sugar, and salt.

Stir the oil, egg yolks, and vanilla into the yeast mixture, followed by the flour mixture, adding it in stages and stirring until the dough begins to come together. Turn the dough out on a lightly floured surface and knead, adding up to ½ cup (70 g) additional flour, a little at a time, until the dough is smooth and supple, 5–10 minutes. You may not need all of the flour. (The kneading can also be done in a stand mixer fitted with a dough hook, 5–7 minutes.) Grease a large bowl with about 1 teaspoon vegetable oil, add the dough, and turn to coat. Cover the bowl with a tea towel and let rise until it has doubled in size, about 1½ hours.

Meanwhile, make the chocolate filling: In a medium bowl, stir together the cocoa powder, sugar, almond milk, and vanilla until a thick but spreadable paste forms. If the mixture is too thick, add a little more almond milk, 1 tablespoon at a time, until the desired consistency is reached. If it is too thin, add a little more cocoa powder, 1 tablespoon at a time, until the desired consistency is reached.

Preheat the oven to 350°F (180°C/Gas Mark 4). Line 2 large baking sheets with parchment paper.

Gently deflate the dough with the heel of your hand and divide into two pieces. Working on a lightly floured surface with 1 piece at a time (keeping the remaining piece covered), roll out the dough into a large rectangle ⅛ inch (3 mm) thick. (Trim off and discard ragged edges.) Spread half of the chocolate filling evenly over the dough, leaving a ¼-inch (6 mm) border. Using a pizza cutter or a sharp knife and starting at one of the long sides, cut out long, thin triangle strips from the dough that are about 2 inches (5 cm) across at the top and taper at the bottom. Starting from the wide end of a triangle, roll up like a jelly roll (Swiss roll) and place on one of the prepared baking sheets. Repeat with the remaining dough and filling.

Bake, rotating the pans front to back halfway through, until puffed and golden brown, 15–18 minutes. Remove from the oven and immediately brush the tops and sides of the rugelach with a generous amount of syrup. Transfer to wire racks to cool.

CAKES, COOKIES & SWEET PASTRIES

Chocolate Rugelach

CINNAMON-NUT RUGELACH

These crescent-shaped cookies have become a darling of traditional Ashkenazi cuisine. But while they have roots in Central Europe (they are preceded by the European pastry, *kipfel*), they are technically a twentieth-century American innovation. The dough, enriched with butter and cream cheese, yields a cookie with almost croissant-like flakiness that is the perfect vehicle for the mixture of jam, dried fruit, nuts, or chocolate that make up a typical filling. Rugelach pair well with tea and coffee and freeze well, making them a wonderful nibble to have on hand when guests drop by.

Makes: 32 rugelach
Preparation time: 45 minutes, plus chilling
Cooking time: 35 minutes

For the dough:
- 2 sticks (8 oz/225 g) unsalted butter, at room temperature
- 8 oz (225 g) cream cheese, at room temperature
- ¼ cup (50 g) sugar
- ½ teaspoon vanilla extract
- ½ teaspoon kosher salt
- 2 cups (280 g) all-purpose (plain) flour, plus more for rolling

For the filling:
- 1 cup (105 g) walnut halves, finely chopped
- ½ cup (50 g) pecan halves, finely chopped
- 3 tablespoons light brown sugar
- 1½ teaspoons ground cinnamon
- 1 cup (320 g) apricot jam

For baking:
- 2 tablespoons sugar
- ½ teaspoon ground cinnamon
- Egg wash: 1 egg beaten with 1 teaspoon water

Make the dough: In a stand mixer (or using a handheld electric mixer and a large bowl), beat together the butter, cream cheese, sugar, vanilla, and salt on medium speed until smooth and creamy, about 2 minutes. Slowly add the flour, beating on low until just incorporated and scraping down the sides of the bowl as necessary until a soft dough forms. Knead the dough a few times in the bowl to bring it together, then divide and form into 2 round discs. Wrap both discs in plastic wrap (cling film) and refrigerate for at least 2 hours, or up to 1 day.

Make the filling: In a medium bowl, stir together the walnuts, pecans, brown sugar, and cinnamon.

Preheat the oven to 350°F (180°C/Gas Mark 4). Line 2 large baking sheets with parchment paper.

Remove one of the dough discs from the fridge and, on a lightly floured surface, roll it into a large round that ⅛ inch (3 mm) thick. Using a ruler as a guide, trim the dough into a round 12 inches (30.5 cm) in diameter. Spread half of the apricot jam evenly over the round, leaving a ½-inch (1.25 cm) border around the edges. Sprinkle with half of the cinnamon-nut mixture and gently press the filling into the dough with your fingers. Using a pizza cutter or sharp knife, cut the dough into 4 equal wedges, then cut each wedge into 4 wedges (ending up with 16 wedges). Starting from the wide edge, roll each wedge in on itself until you reach the point. Place the cookies on the prepared baking sheets. Repeat with the remaining disc of dough and remaining jam and filling.

To bake: In a small bowl, stir together the sugar and cinnamon. Brush the tops of each cookie with a little egg wash and sprinkle with a little cinnamon sugar. Bake, rotating the pans front to back halfway through, until deep golden brown and the tops are crisp like a croissant, 30–35 minutes. Immediately transfer the cookies to wire racks to cool.

NUT CRESCENTS

These delicate, crescent-shaped shortbread cookies, called *nusskipferl*, are enriched with finely ground walnuts. Popular across Hungary, Austria, and Germany, they were brought to America by immigrants from these countries in the nineteenth century.

Makes: about 2 dozen cookies
Preparation time: 25 minutes
Cooking time: 25 minutes

- ¾ cup (70 g) walnut halves
- 4 sticks (1 lb/455 g) unsalted butter, at room temperature
- ½ cup (60 g) powdered (icing) sugar, plus more for dusting
- ½ teaspoon kosher salt
- 1½ teaspoons vanilla extract
- 2 cups (280 g) all-purpose (plain) flour

In a small frying pan, toast the walnuts over medium-low heat, shaking the pan occasionally, until fragrant and lightly browned, 5–7 minutes. Remove the pan from the heat and let the walnuts cool. In a food processor, pulse the toasted walnuts, scraping down the bowl a few times, until finely ground with a few slightly larger pieces.

Preheat the oven to 350°F (180°C/Gas Mark 4). Line 2 large baking sheets with parchment paper.

In a stand mixer (or using a handheld electric mixer and a large bowl), beat together the butter, powdered (icing) sugar, salt, and vanilla at medium speed until light and fluffy. Add the ground walnuts and beat until combined. Add the flour in three additions and beat, scraping down the side of the bowl as necessary, until a firm but pliable dough comes together.

Pinch off rounded tablespoons of dough and roll into 4-inch (10 cm) logs. Place the logs on the prepared baking sheets and shape into crescents. Bake until lightly golden, about 15 minutes. Let the cookies cool on the baking sheets for 5 minutes, then gently transfer to a wire rack to cool completely. When cool, use a fine-mesh sieve to dust the tops of each cookie generously with powdered sugar.

CARDAMOM-BUTTER COOKIES

These cardamom-scented butter cookies are popular throughout Iraq. Called *shakar lama*, they are often served in the afternoon with a cup of tea or coffee.

Makes: about 3 dozen cookies
Preparation time: 20 minutes
Cooking time: 15 minutes

- 1¾ cups (245 g) all-purpose (plain) flour, sifted
- 1 teaspoon ground cardamom
- ½ teaspoon baking powder
- ½ teaspoon kosher salt
- 2 sticks (8 oz/225 g) unsalted butter, at room temperature
- ⅔ cup (130 g) sugar
- 1 teaspoon rose water
- ½ teaspoon vanilla extract
- About 36 sliced almonds

Preheat the oven to 350°F (180°C/Gas Mark 4). Line 2 large baking sheets with parchment paper.

In a medium bowl, whisk together the flour, cardamom, baking powder, and salt.

In a stand mixer (or using a handheld electric mixer and a large bowl), beat together the butter and sugar at medium-high speed until light and fluffy. Add the rose water and vanilla and beat until combined. Add the flour mixture in several additions, beating on low after each addition, and scraping down the sides of the bowl as necessary, until just combined. Refrigerate the dough until it is firm but still pliable, about 10 minutes.

Scoop out level tablespoons of dough and roll into small balls. Place the cookies on the prepared baking sheets and gently flatten with the palm of your hand. Place a sliced almond in the center of each cookie.

Bake, rotating the pans front to back halfway through, until the cookies are pale golden and cooked through, 10–12 minutes. Let cool on the pans for a few minutes, then transfer to wire racks to cool completely.

SWEET CHICKPEA SHORTBREAD

Shortbread cookies made with flour and shortening—and no eggs—are common throughout the Mediterranean, the Middle East, and North Africa. This Tunisian version, called *ghraiba homs*, is especially notable. Made with toasted chickpea (gram) flour, the cookies have a hint of nuttiness and a texture that is at once snappy and chewy. The shortbread cookies are wonderful served with a cup of strong coffee or mint tea.

Makes: about 2 dozen cookies
Preparation time: 20 minutes
Cooking time: 30 minutes

- 1 cup (120 g) chickpea (gram) flour
- 1¼ cups (175 g) all-purpose (plain) flour
- 1 cup (120 g) powdered (icing) sugar
- ½ teaspoon kosher salt
- 1½ sticks (6 oz/170 g) unsalted butter, melted and slightly cooled
- 1½ teaspoons vanilla extract
- Sesame seeds, for sprinkling

Preheat the oven to 350°F (180°C/Gas Mark 4). Line a large baking sheet pan with parchment paper.

Spread the chickpea (gram) flour in a small baking dish and toast in the oven, shaking it once or twice, until golden, about 10 minutes. Remove from the oven and let cool completely.

In a large bowl, whisk together the toasted chickpea flour, all-purpose (plain) flour, powdered (icing) sugar, and salt. Add the melted butter and vanilla and stir with a wooden spoon. Knead the dough briefly with your hands to bring it together. Working with half of the dough at a time, gently squeeze, and roll it into a log 1 inch (2.5 cm) thick. Using a sharp knife, cut slices ½ inch (1.25 cm) thick and place on the prepared baking sheet. Repeat with the remaining dough.

Lightly sprinkle the tops of each cookie with sesame seeds, and bake until gently puffed and lightly golden, 12–15 minutes. Let cool on the baking sheet for 5 minutes, then carefully transfer to wire racks to cool completely.

ALMOND-CARDAMOM COOKIES

Iraqi Jews serve these chewy, cardamom-scented cookies, called *hadgi badah*, as part of a larger table of sweets on Purim.

Makes: about 40 cookies
Preparation time: 15 minutes
Cooking time: 15 minutes

- 2 cups (280 g) all-purpose (plain) flour
- 1½ cups (180 g) almond flour (ground almonds)
- 1 teaspoon ground cardamom
- ½ teaspoon kosher salt
- ½ teaspoon baking powder
- 1½ cups (300 g) sugar
- 3 eggs
- 1 teaspoon almond extract
- ½ teaspoon vanilla extract
- Rose water, for moistening hands
- About 40 whole raw or roasted almonds or salted roasted pistachios, for topping

Preheat the oven to 350°F (180°C/Gas Mark 4). Line 2 large baking sheets with parchment paper.

In a medium bowl, whisk together the all-purpose (plain) flour, almond flour (ground almonds), cardamom, salt, and baking powder.

In a stand mixer (or using a handheld electric mixer and a large bowl), beat together the sugar, eggs, almond extract, and vanilla at medium-high speed until light and creamy, 2–3 minutes. Beat in the flour mixture in a few additions, beating on low after each addition, and scraping down the sides of the bowl as necessary, until just incorporated. The dough should be sticky but not wet.

Moisten hands with rose water. Scoop out level tablespoons of dough and roll into small balls. Place the cookies on the prepared baking sheets and gently press a whole almond into the center of each cookie.

Bake until lightly puffed and golden brown around the edges, 12–15 minutes. Let cool on the pans for about 2 minutes, then transfer to wire racks to cool completely.

CAKES, COOKIES & SWEET PASTRIES

BUTTER COOKIES WITH SPICED ALMONDS

Called *jødekager*, this cookie (the name translates to "Jewish cakes") is the Danish cousin to Holland's *Joodse boterkoek* (Buttery Ginger Cake, 359). It comes topped with a heady mix of cinnamon, cardamom, and chopped almonds. Some versions are made without leavening, yielding a more shortbreadlike texture; here baking powder and baking soda (bicarb) give the cookie a wonderfully supple crumb.

Makes: about 3 dozen cookies
Preparation time: 15 minutes, plus chilling
Cooking time: 10 minutes

- 1½ cups (210 g) all-purpose (plain) flour, plus more for rolling
- ½ teaspoon baking powder
- ½ teaspoon baking soda (bicarbonate of soda)
- ½ teaspoon kosher salt
- 1½ sticks (6 oz/170 g) unsalted butter, at room temperature
- ¾ cup (150 g) sugar
- 1 egg, separated
- 1 teaspoon vanilla extract
- 1 tablespoon ground cinnamon
- ¾ teaspoon ground cardamom
- ¼ cup (40 g) unsalted roasted almonds, finely chopped

In a medium bowl, whisk together the flour, baking powder, baking soda (bicarb), and salt.

In a stand mixer (or using a handheld electric mixer and a large bowl), beat together the butter and ½ cup (100 g) of the sugar at medium speed until light and fluffy, 2–3 min-utes. Add the egg yolk and vanilla and continue beating until combined. Beat in the flour mixture, a little bit at a time, at low speed until a pliable dough forms. Gather the dough into a disc, wrap it in plastic wrap (cling film), and refrigerate for at least 1 hour, or overnight.

Preheat the oven to 375°F (°190C/Gas Mark 5). Line 2 large baking sheets with parchment paper.

Place a sheet of parchment paper on a work surface and sprinkle with flour. Lay the disc of dough on top of the floured parchment and cover with a second piece of parchment. Use a rolling pin to gently roll out the dough in between the parchment until it is ¼ inch (6 mm) thick. If the dough is too hard to roll out, let it soften for 5 minutes and try again. Using a 2-inch (5 cm) round biscuit or cookie cutter, stamp out as many rounds as possible and use a flat spatula to transfer them to the prepared baking sheets. Gather the scraps, reroll, and cut out more rounds up to two more times.

In a small bowl, mix together the remaining ¼ cup (50 g) sugar, the cinnamon, cardamom, and almonds. In another small bowl, whisk together the egg white and 1 teaspoon water. Lightly brush the tops of each cookie with the egg wash, then sprinkle the almond mixture evenly on top (you might not use all of it). Bake until lightly golden, 8–10 minutes. Let cool on the baking sheets for 2–3 minutes, then carefully transfer to wire racks to cool completely. They will continue to firm up as they cool.

MA' AMOUL

These ancient Levantine cookies encase rose water–perfumed nuts or dates (or in this case, both together) inside a tender, buttery shortbread dough. In other words, they are addictively delicious. Muslim communities typically serve *ma'amoul* at the nightly feasts during Ramadan and on other festive holidays. Jews hailing from Syria, Egypt, Lebanon, and other Middle Eastern countries serve them on Rosh Hashanah, Hanukkah, and Purim. *Ma'amoul* are often pressed into elaborately carved wooden molds that imprint ridged patterns on the outside of the cookie. But they can also be simply shaped by hand.

Makes: about 2 dozen cookies
Preparation time: 45 mintues
Cooking time: 20 minutes

For the dough:
- 4 sticks (1 lb/455 g) unsalted butter or nonhydrogenated margarine, at room temperature
- ¾ cup (90 g) powdered (icing) sugar
- ½ teaspoon kosher salt
- 1½ teaspoons vanilla extract
- 2–2¼ cups (280–315 g) all-purpose (plain) flour

For the filling:
- 1½ cups (210 g) Medjool dates, pitted and roughly chopped
- ½ cup (50 g) walnut halves
- 2 tablespoons powdered (icing) sugar
- 1½ tablespoons rose water
- 1½ teaspoons ground cinnamon

- Vegetable oil, for greasing
- Powdered sugar, for dusting

Make the dough: In a stand mixer (or using a handheld electric mixer and a large bowl), beat together the butter, powdered (icing) sugar, salt, and vanilla at medium speed until light and fluffy. Beat in 2 cups (280 g) flour in three additions, scraping down the sides of the bowl as necessary, until a tender, pliable dough comes together. If needed, beat in up to ¼ cup (35 g) additional flour, 1 table-spoon at a time, until the desired consistency is reached. Set the dough aside.

Make the filling: In a food processor, pulse the dates, walnuts, powdered (icing) sugar, rose water, and cinnamon until a thick paste forms.

Preheat the oven to 350°F (180°C/Gas Mark 4). Line a large baking sheet with parchment paper.

Pinch off a tablespoon of the dough and roll into a ball. Using your thumb, make an indentation in the center of the ball, then gently pinch around the sides to make a small cup shape. Spoon a teaspoon of the date-walnut filling into the cup and close the dough over the filling, gently reshaping it into a ball. If the ball feels too thick on any side, gently remove the excess dough. And if the dough gets too soft to work with, place it in the refrigerator for 10 minutes to firm up.

If using a *ma'amoul* mold, lightly grease the mold with oil then lay a filled cookie inside. Gently press the cookie into the mold then tap it out. Repeat with the rest of the cookies.

Lay the shaped cookies on the prepared baking sheet. Bake until lightly golden, 15–20 minutes. Transfer to wire racks to cool. When fully cool, use a fine-mesh sieve to dust the tops of each cookie generously with powdered sugar.

Ma'amoul

SFRATTI

Sfratti are a cookie with a curious history. The word *sfratto* means "eviction" in Italian, and the long, cylindrical cookies are meant to resemble the sticks used by landlords to physically push out Jewish tenants during times of expulsion. Tuscan Jewish bakers found a way to turn that sad legacy on its head, creating a treat that celebrates the Jewish community's perseverance. *Sfratti* are traditionally served on Rosh Hashanah and Purim, but taste wonderful any time of year. The dough and filling can both a bit finicky. For best results, keep the dough cold and the rolling surface well floured.

Serves: 6
Preparation time: 30 minutes, plus chilling
Cooking time: 30 minutes

For the dough:
- 2½ cups (350 g) all-purpose (plain) flour, plus more for rolling
- 1 cup (200 g) sugar
- ½ teaspoon kosher salt
- 1 stick (4 oz/115 g) cold unsalted butter or nonhydrogenated margarine, cut into small pieces
- ⅓ cup (75 ml/2½ fl oz) dry white wine, plus more as needed

For the filling:
- 2 cups (210 g) walnut halves, chopped
- ½ cup (170 g) honey
- ¼ cup (50 g) sugar
- ¼ teaspoon kosher salt
- 1 teaspoon finely grated orange zest
- ½ teaspoon ground ginger
- ⅛ teaspoon freshly ground black pepper

For baking:
- Egg wash: 1 egg beaten with 1 teaspoon water

Make the dough: In a food processor, pulse together the flour, sugar, salt, and butter pieces, scraping down the sides of the bowl as necessary, until the mixture resembles coarse cornmeal. With the motor running, slowly pour in the wine, stopping to scrape down the sides of the bowl several times, until the dough just comes together. If necessary, add a little more wine, 1 tablespoon at a time, until the desired consistency is reached. Gather the dough and knead it a few times on a work surface. Form into a disc, wrap tightly in plastic wrap (cling film), and refrigerate until well chilled, about 2 hours.

Make the filling: In a medium saucepan, combine the walnuts, honey, sugar, and salt and bring to a boil over high heat. Reduce the heat to medium and cook, stirring often, until the honey thickens and turns golden brown, about 5 minutes. Remove from the heat and stir in the orange zest, ginger, and pepper. Let the mixture sit until just cool enough to handle.

Preheat the oven to 375°F (°190C/Gas Mark 5). Line a large baking sheet with parchment paper.

Divide the dough into 4 equal portions. Working with 1 piece at a time (keeping the others refrigerated) and working on a well-floured surface with a floured rolling pin, roll the dough out into a rectangle ¼ inch (6 mm) thick. Trim off the ragged edges (discard the scraps). Spoon a thick line of the honey-nut mixture along one of the long sides of the rectangle, then tightly roll the dough around the filling, tucking it inside. Trim off both ends of the roll until the dough is flush with the filling (discard the scraps). Cut the roll crosswise into 2-inch (5 cm) lengths and place on the prepared baking sheet. Repeat with the remaining dough and filling, sprinkling the board with more flour, as needed.

To bake: Brush the tops and sides of the cookies with a little of the egg wash (you might not use all of it). Bake, rotating the pan front to back halfway through, until golden brown, about 20 minutes. Transfer the cookies to a wire rack to cool. The filling will be very hot, so allow the cookies to cool for at least 20 minutes before serving.

EINAT ADMONY

TAÏM
•
MULTIPLE LOCATIONS
NEW YORK, NY
USA

BALABOOSTA
•
611 HUDSON STREET
NEW YORK, NY
USA

KISH-KASH
•
455 HUDSON STREET
NEW YORK, NY
USA

Einat Admony is an Israeli-born chef and owner of several renowned restaurants in New York City including the artisanal falafel shop Taïm, the imaginative Middle Eastern restaurant Balaboosta, and the North African–inspired Kish-Kash. She is also the author of the cookbook *Balaboosta*, which explores her chef-inflected takes on Jewish home cooking.

FIG AND PISTACHIO BAKLAVA

Admony's take on classic baklava blends jammy dried figs into a pistachio-based filling and paints the confection with syrup perfumed with cardamom, orange zest, and rose water.

Serves: 8
Preparation time: 45 minutes, plus chilling
Cooking time: 50 minutes

For the rose syrup:
- 2 cups (400 g) sugar
- ¼ cup (85 g) honey
- 3-inch (7.5 cm) strip orange zest
- 1 cardamom pod, cracked
- ½ teaspoon rose water

For the baklava:
- 6 tablespoons (85 g) unsalted butter, melted
- 6 tablespoons vegetable oil
- 2 cups (260 g) shelled, unsalted pistachios
- 12 oz (360 g) dried figs, tough stems trimmed, roughly chopped
- ½ cup (60 g) powdered (icing) sugar
- 1 teaspoon rose water
- ½ teaspoon ground cinnamon
- ⅛ teaspoon ground cardamom
- 1 package (16 oz/455 g) frozen phyllo dough, thawed

Make the rose syrup: In a medium saucepan, stir together 1 cup (240 ml/8 fl oz) water, the sugar, honey, orange zest, and cardamom pod. Bring to a simmer over medium heat and cook, stirring often, until the mixture thickens slightly, about 5 minutes. Remove from the heat and stir in the rose water. Discard the orange zest and cardamom pod and let the mixture cool. Transfer the rose syrup to an airtight container and refrigerate until needed. (The rose syrup can be made up to 1 week in advance.)

Make the baklava: Preheat the oven to 350°F (180°C/Gas Mark 4). Line a 9 × 13-inch (23 × 33 cm) baking dish with parchment paper.

In a medium bowl, stir together the melted butter and oil. In a food processor, pulse together the pistachios, figs, powdered (icing) sugar, rose water, cinnamon, and cardamom until finely chopped and combined, but not overly pasty.

Place one sheet of phyllo dough in the baking dish. (Keep the unused sheets of phyllo covered with a damp towel as you work.) Trim off the ends if necessary or fold over to fit the dish. Generously brush the top of the phyllo with the butter-oil mixture. Place another single layer of phyllo on top and brush it again. Repeat the process until you have 8 layers of phyllo dough.

Spread the entire nut mixture on top and firmly pack it down. Place another single layer of phyllo dough on top and brush it with the butter-oil mixture. Repeat the process until you have another 8 layers with the top layer brushed generously with the butter mixture.

Using a very sharp knife, cut the baklava into small (about 2-inch/5 cm) diamonds or squares. Lay a sheet of parchment paper on top and bake for 30 minutes. Remove the parchment paper and continue baking until golden brown, about 15 minutes. Remove from the oven and immediately pour the chilled rose syrup over the baklava, allowing the syrup to flow into all the crevices. Let it cool completely before serving.

SESAME SEED COOKIE RINGS

With roots in pre-Inquisition Spain, these mildly sweet, crisp cookie rings—called *biscochos de susam*, or sometimes just *biscochos*—have become a hallmark of Sephardi cuisine. Middle Eastern Jews bake a similar cookie called *kaak*, which is typically even less sweet and often flavored with anise. The cookie's crunchy texture pairs perfectly with tea or coffee—and indeed, they are often enjoyed at breakfast and for an afternoon snack. *Biscochos* are also served on Rosh Hashanah (the ring shape symbolizes hopes for a full and round year to come), to break the Yom Kippur fast, and as part of a larger sweets platter on Purim.

Makes: about 40 cookies
Preparation time: 45 minutes
Cooking time: 25 minutes

- 2¾–3 cups (385–420 g) all-purpose (plain) flour, plus more for rolling
- 2 teaspoons baking powder
- ¼ teaspoon kosher salt
- 3 eggs
- ½ cup (120 ml/4 fl oz) vegetable oil
- 1 cup (200 g) sugar
- 1 teaspoon vanilla extract
- 1 teaspoon finely grated orange zest
- Sesame seeds, for sprinkling

Preheat the oven to 350°F (°180C/Gas Mark 4). Line 2 large baking sheets with parchment paper.

In a medium bowl, whisk together 2¾ cups (385 g) flour, the baking powder, and salt.

In a stand mixer (or using a handheld electric mixer and a large bowl), beat 2 of the eggs, the oil, sugar, vanilla, and orange zest at medium-high speed until pale and creamy, 2–3 minutes. Add the flour mixture in two additions, beating to incorporate and scraping down the sides of the bowl as necessary, until a firm but pliable dough forms. If the dough is too wet or sticky to handle, add up to ¼ cup (35 g) additional flour, 1 tablespoon at a time as needed, until the desired consistency is reached. (You may not need all of the additional flour.)

Working on a lightly floured surface, pinch off a walnut-size piece of dough and roll it into a rope that is 6 inches (15 cm) long and about ½ inch (1.25 cm) thick. Repeat with several more pieces of dough. Using a sharp knife, score little notches about ¼ inch (6 mm) apart along the length of each of the ropes. With the notched edge facing out, form each rope into a ring, gently pressing the ends together to seal. Place on the prepared baking sheets. Repeat the rolling, scoring, and shaping process until all of the dough is used.

In a small bowl, beat the remaining egg. Brush the rings with a little beaten egg (you may not use all of it) and sprinkle generously with sesame seeds. Bake, rotating the sheets front to back halfway through, until the cookies are gently puffed and golden brown, 20–25 minutes. Transfer the cookies to wire racks to cool. They will continue to firm up as they cool.

Sesame Seed Cookie Rings

PIZZA EBRAICA

This ancient Italian Jewish "pizza" isn't a pizza at all, but rather a bar cookie densely studded with dried fruit and nuts. (In Italian, the word *pizza* is traditionally a catchall term for pie, and *Ebraica* or "Hebraic" denotes the dish's Jewish roots.) The cookies, which are bound with sweet wine, are made by home cooks and can also be found at Pasticceria il Boccione, a tiny kosher bakery that has operated in Rome's Jewish ghetto for more than two hundred years. Boccione's version uses chopped candied citron and glacé cherries, so swap some in for the raisins and dried cherries in this recipe, if desired.

Makes: about 2 dozen cookies
Preparation time: 25 minutes
Cooking time: 25 minutes

- ½ cup (70 g) golden raisins (sultanas) or regular raisins
- ⅓ cup (45 g) dried cherries
- ½ cup (120 ml/4 fl oz) sweet red wine or grape juice
- ⅔ cup (150 ml/5 fl oz) vegetable oil
- 1 cup (200 g) sugar
- 1 teaspoon vanilla extract
- ½ teaspoon kosher salt
- 2½ cups (350 g) all-purpose (plain) flour, plus more for kneading
- ½ cup (70 g) unsalted roasted almonds
- ⅓ cup (45 g) pine nuts

Preheat the oven to 350°F (180°C/Gas Mark 4). Line 2 large baking sheets with parchment paper.

In a small bowl, combine the golden raisins (sultanas), cherries, and wine and let sit for 10 minutes. Reserving the wine, drain the dried fruit.

In a stand mixer (or using a handheld electric mixer and a large bowl), beat together the oil, sugar, vanilla, and salt at medium speed until well combined, 2–3 minutes. Add half of the flour and beat on low speed, scraping down the sides of the bowl as necessary, until incorporated. Beat in ¼ cup (60 ml/2 fl oz) of the reserved wine, followed by the remaining flour and beat until a firm but pliable dough comes together. If the dough looks dry or crumbly, beat in a little more of the wine, 1 tablespoon at a time, until the desired consistency is reached—do not let the dough get too wet. Add the raisins, cherries, almonds, and pine nuts and beat at low speed until combined.

Turn the dough out onto a flat, lightly floured surface and knead with your hands several times to make sure the fruit and nuts are fully incorporated. Pat the dough into a large rectangle ½ inch (1.25 cm) thick. Using a sharp knife, cut into rectangular or square pieces, then use a spatula to transfer them to the prepared baking sheets.

Bake, rotating the pans front to back halfway through, until browned, 20–25 minutes. (They might still feel a bit soft, but will firm up as they cool.) Let the cookies cool on the baking sheets for 5 minutes, then transfer to wire racks to cool completely.

CAKES, COOKIES & SWEET PASTRIES

Pizza Ebraica

FLÓDNI

This deep-dish sweet pie (which in Germany and Alsace, France, is called *fluden* or "flat cake" in German) has ancient roots, and its ancestor was originally filled with sweetened cheese. Today, the dough tends to encase a single or double layer of fruit or nuts. But in Hungary, *flódni* has evolved into a majestic, multilayered pastry filled with tiers of sweetened poppy seeds, ground walnuts, cinnamon-spiced apples, and the prune and apricot jams called *lekvar* (see page 408). One Hungarian pastry chef, Rachel Raj, holds the world record for baking the largest *flódni*—a 72-foot (22 m) pastry that served 1,600 people. This decidedly smaller version makes a festive dessert.

Serves: 10–12
Preparation time: 1 hour, plus chilling and resting
Cooking time: 1 hour

For the dough:
- 4 cups (560 g) all-purpose (plain) flour, plus more for rolling
- ¾ teaspoon kosher salt
- ½ cup (100 g) sugar
- 1¼ sticks (5 oz/140 g) unsalted butter or nonhydrogenated margarine, cut into pieces, at room temperature
- 2 teaspoons finely grated lemon zest
- 3 egg yolks
- ⅔ cup (150 ml/5 fl oz) dry white wine, plus more as needed

For the apple filling:
- 1½ lb (680 g) tart green apples, peeled and finely chopped
- ⅓ cup (65 g) sugar
- 1 tablespoon ground cinnamon
- 1 tablespoon cornstarch (cornflour)

For the walnut filling:
- 3 cups (315 g) walnut halves
- ⅓ cup (75 ml/2½ fl oz) milk
- ½ cup (100 g) sugar

For assembly and baking:
- Poppy Seed Filling (page 397)
- ⅓ cup (110 g) Prune Lekvar (page 408) or Apricot Lekvar (page 408)
- Egg wash: 1 egg beaten with 1 teaspoon water

Make the dough: In a food processor, pulse together the flour, salt, sugar, butter, and lemon zest, scraping down the sides of the bowl as necessary until the mixture resembles coarse cornmeal. Add the egg yolks and wine and pulse until the dough comes together. If necessary, add a little more wine, 1 tablespoon at a time, until the desired consistency is reached. Form the dough into a disc, wrap tightly in plastic wrap (cling film), and refrigerate until chilled, about 2 hours or up to 1 day.

Make the apple filling: In a medium bowl, toss together the apples, sugar, cinnamon, and cornstarch (cornflour). Set aside.

Make the walnut filling: In a food processor, combine the walnuts, milk, and sugar and pulse, scraping down the sides of the bowl as necessary, until a thick paste forms. Set aside.

Assemble and bake: Preheat the oven to 350°F (180°C/Gas Mark 4). Line a 9-inch (23 cm) square baking dish with parchment, allowing the parchment to hang over by a few inches on two opposite sides.

Divide the dough into thirds (keeping 2 pieces refrigerated while working with the remaining piece). On a floured surface using a floured rolling pin, roll out the dough into a large square ⅛ inch (3 mm) thick. Drape the dough into the prepared baking dish, fitting snugly into the sides and bottom. Trim any overhanging edges. Spoon the poppy seed filling into the baking dish and smooth.

Divide a second piece of dough into 2 equal portions. Roll out the first portion into roughly a 9-inch (23 cm) square, trimming off the ragged edges, and place it on top of the poppy seed filling. Spoon the apple filling into the dish. Repeat with the second portion of dough to make a second 9-inch (23 cm) square and place it on top of the apple filling. Spread the walnut filling on top, then dot the surface in several places with the prune *lekvar* and use a butter knife or offset spatula to smooth it.

Roll out the third and final piece of dough to a square ⅛ inch (3 mm) thick and trim to make a 9-inch (23 cm) square. Lay the dough square on top of the walnut filling. Brush the dough evenly with a little egg wash. (You will not use all of it.)

Bake until cooked through and golden brown, about 1 hour. Transfer the baking dish to a wire rack to cool and set for at least 1 hour (ideally longer) before slicing. Serve warm or at room temperature.

BUTTERY GINGER CAKE

The roots of this decadent dessert, *Joodse boterkoek* (the name translates from Dutch to "Jewish butter cake") date back to the Spanish Inquisition when Jews fleeing forced conversion in Spain and Portugal settled in The Netherlands. They brought their baking traditions with them, but traded the olive oil they were accustomed to for butter, which was widely abundant in their new home. Variations of the dessert are still served in Dutch bakeries, and Dutch Jews continue to serve it on Hanukkah and Shavuot.

Serves: 8
Preparation time: 20 minutes
Cooking time: 35 minutes

- 2 sticks (8 oz/225 g) butter, at room temperature
- 1½ cups (300 g) sugar
- 2 eggs
- ½ teaspoon almond extract
- ½ teaspoon kosher salt
- 1½ cups (210 g) all-purpose (plain) flour
- ½ cup (65 g) plus 2 tablespoons finely chopped crystallized ginger
- ¼ cup (25 g) sliced almonds

Preheat the oven to 350°F (180°C/Gas Mark 4). Line the bottom of a 9-inch (23 cm) round cake pan with a round of parchment paper.

In a stand mixer (or using a handheld electric mixer and a large bowl), beat together the butter and sugar at medium-high speed until pale and fluffy, 2–3 minutes. Add 1 of the eggs, the almond extract, and the salt and beat until fully combined.

Add the flour and beat at low speed until just combined. Beat in ½ cup (65 g) of the crystallized ginger, then transfer the dough to the prepared pan and use your fingers or a spatula to press it evenly into the bottom. Beat the remaining egg in a small bowl, then evenly brush the top with a little of the egg (you will not use all of it). Sprinkle the cake with the remaining 2 tablespoons crystallized ginger and the almonds.

Bake until golden brown and set in the middle, about 40 minutes. If the sides are browning too quickly before the center cooks, loosely drape the top of the cake pan with foil. Let the cake cool completely in the pan, then cut into small wedges or squares.

FUDGY PASSOVER BROWNIES

Bakers across the United States and Canada have devised ways to adapt the classic North American dessert for the Passover table. This naturally gluten- and dairy-free version is made with potato starch, yielding sweet, fudge-centered brownies that satisfy during the holiday and year-round.

Makes: 16 brownies
Preparation time: 10 minutes
Cooking time: 25 minutes

- ½ cup (40 g) unsweetened cocoa powder
- ¼ cup (45 g) potato starch
- ½ teaspoon instant coffee granules
- ½ teaspoon kosher salt
- 1 cup (105 g) walnut halves, chopped (optional)
- ½ cup (120 ml/4 fl oz) vegetable oil
- 2 eggs
- 1¼ cups (250 g) sugar
- 1 teaspoon vanilla extract

Preheat the oven to 350°F (180°C/Gas Mark 4). Line the bottom and sides of an 8-inch (20 cm) square pan (not larger) with parchment paper, leaving 1 inch (2.5 cm) of overhang on two opposite sides.

In a medium bowl, whisk together the cocoa powder, potato starch, instant coffee, and salt. Add the walnuts (if using) and toss to coat. In a large bowl, whisk together the oil, eggs, sugar, and vanilla until fully combined. Add the dry mixture to the wet mixture and, using a rubber spatula, fold together until just combined.

Scrape the batter into the prepared pan and bake until a skewer inserted into the center comes out clean, 20–25 minutes. Set the pan on a wire rack to cool. Gently lift up the ends of the parchment and transfer the brownies to a cutting board and cut into 16 pieces.

KOKOSH

The twisted, chocolate-filled loaf cake *kokosh* is sometimes described as the Hungarian take on Mexican Chocolate Babka (page 326)—but the two desserts are not directly related. *Kokosh*'s actual predecessor is *makosh*, a rolled pastry filled with sweetened poppy seeds that is popular in Central Europe. (*Mák* means "poppy seed" in Hungarian; to make *makosh*, spread the dough with Poppy Seed Filling, page 395, instead of chocolate.) The chocolate version developed later and was named *kokosh* as a play on the Hungarian word for cocoa, *kakáo*. The squat, tender, and densely chocolatey loaves can still be found in some Jewish bakeries. But since they are made with a yeasted dough that does not require a rising period, they are also a pleasure to make at home. Serve warm slices of *kokosh* spread with butter and with a cup of coffee or tea alongside.

Makes: 2 loaves
Preparation time: 30 minutes
Cooking time: 40 minutes

For the chocolate filling:
- 1 cup (105 g) walnut halves, very finely chopped
- ½ cup (40 g) unsweetened cocoa powder
- ¾ cup (150 g) sugar
- ½ teaspoon instant coffee granules
- ½ teaspoon kosher salt
- ¼ cup (60 ml/2 fl oz) milk or almond milk
- 1½ teaspoons vanilla extract

For the dough:
- 1 packet (¼ oz/7 g) active dry yeast (2 ¼ teaspoons)
- ¼ cup (50 g) plus 1 teaspoon sugar
- ¼ cup (60 ml/2 fl oz) warm water (110°F/43°C)
- 3 cups (420 g) all-purpose (plain) flour, plus more for kneading
- 1 teaspoon kosher salt
- ⅓ cup (75 ml/2½ fl oz) orange juice
- 3 eggs, 2 whole and 1 separated
- 1 stick (4 oz/115 g) unsalted butter or non-hydrogenated margarine, at room temperature

Make the chocolate filling: In a medium bowl, stir together the walnuts, cocoa powder, sugar, instant coffee, and salt until well combined. Add the milk and vanilla and stir until a spreadable paste forms. Set aside.

Preheat the oven to 350°F (180°F/Gas Mark 4). Line a large baking sheet with parchment paper.

Make the dough: In a small bowl, stir together the yeast, 1 teaspoon of the sugar, and the warm water. Let sit until bubbling and frothy, 5–10 minutes.

Meanwhile, in a stand mixer fitted with the paddle attachment, beat together the flour, remaining ¼ cup (50 g) sugar, salt, orange juice, whole eggs, egg yolk, and butter.

When the yeast mixture is bubbling, pour it into the mixer bowl and mix on low speed until the dough just comes together. Turn the dough out onto a lightly floured surface and knead briefly until the butter is fully dispersed, 2–3 minutes.

Cut the dough into 2 equal portions. Working with 1 piece (keep the other in the bowl, covered), roll out into a large rectangle ⅛ inch (3 mm) thick. Spread half of the chocolate filling evenly over the rectangle, leaving a ½-inch (1.25 cm) border. Brush the border with a little of the egg white to help seal the dough. Starting at one of the short sides, roll up the dough like a jelly roll (Swiss roll), but not too tight, pinch the ends to seal, and place it, seam side down, on the prepared baking sheet. Repeat the filling and rolling process with the remaining dough and filling and place the roll on the baking sheet, leaving 2 inches (5 cm) of space between the two rolls. Brush the tops of each roll with egg white and prick in a few places with a fork to keep it from splitting while it bakes. (Splitting may still occur anyway, but it won't impact the final taste.)

Bake, rotating the pan front to back halfway through, until golden brown and cooked through, 35–40 minutes. Transfer the *kokosh* to wire racks to cool slightly. Serve warm.

BIMUELOS

The word *bimuelos* is a catchall term that refers to a variety of small fritters, pancakes, and doughnuts, both sweet and savory. The doughnut version (also called *bunuelos)* has become the most important Hanukkah treat for Sephardi Jews who celebrate the holiday's "miracle of oil" with these rustic doughnut holes. The honey drizzle is lovely, but *bimuelos* are also delicious simply sprinkled with sugar or cinnamon sugar.

Serves: 6
Preparation time: 15 minutes, plus rising
Cooking time: 30 minutes

For the bimuelos:
• 1 packet (¼ oz/7 g) active dry yeast (2¼ teaspoons)
• ¼ cup (50 g) plus 1 teaspoon sugar
• ¾ cup (175 ml/6 fl oz) warm water (110°F/43°C)
• 3–4 cups (420–560 g) all-purpose (plain) flour, plus more for kneading
• ½ teaspoon kosher salt
• 2 egg yolks
• ¼ cup (60 ml/2 fl oz) milk or almond milk
• ½ teaspoon vanilla extract
• Vegetable oil, for greasing the bowl and frying

For the honey drizzle:
• ½ cup (170 g) honey
• ½ teaspoon finely grated orange zest
• 2 tablespoons fresh orange juice
• 2 teaspoons fresh lemon juice

Make the *bimuelos*: In a large bowl, stir together the yeast, 1 teaspoon of the sugar, and the warm water. Let sit until foaming, 5–10 minutes.

Meanwhile, in a medium bowl, whisk together 3 cups (420 g) flour, the remaining ¼ cup (50 g) sugar, and salt.

Stir the egg yolks, milk, and vanilla into the yeast mixture, followed by the flour mixture, adding it in stages and stirring until the dough begins to come together. Turn the dough out on a lightly floured surface and knead, adding up to 1 cup (140 g) additional flour, a little at a time, until the dough is smooth and supple, 5–10 minutes. You may not need all of the flour. (The kneading can also be done in a stand mixer fitted with a dough hook, 5–7 minutes.) Grease a large bowl with about 1 teaspoon vegetable oil, add the dough, and turn to coat. Cover the bowl with a tea towel and let rise until it has doubled in size, about 1½ hours.

When ready to fry, line a large plate with paper towels. Pour 1½ inches (4 cm) oil into a Dutch oven (casserole) or deep heavy pot, set over medium heat, and bring to 365°F (185°C) on a deep-fry thermometer. Working in batches of 5–6, pinch off walnut-size pieces of dough, roll them into a rough ball shape, and drop them into the hot oil. Fry, flipping once, until puffed, golden, and cooked through, 2–4 minutes. Transfer the *bimuelos* to the paper towels to drain.

Make the honey drizzle: In a medium bowl, whisk together the honey, orange zest, orange juice, and lemon juice. Drizzle a generous amount of the honey mixture over the *bimuelos* and serve immediately.

GULAB JAMUN

India's Bene Israel Jewish community traditionally serves these spherical powdered-milk fritters, which resemble doughnut holes, on Hanukkah. Their gently tangy flavor is sweetened by a long soak in fragrant sugar syrup. The dish's name coarsely translates from Hindi to "rose berries," and points to the inclusion of fragrant rose water in the syrup.

Makes: about 15 fritters
Preparation time: 30 minutes
Cooking time: 20 minutes

For the syrup:
- 1½ cups (300 g) sugar
- 4 cardamom pods, cracked open
- 2 cinnamon sticks
- 1 tablespoon rose water

For the fritters:
- 1 cup (95 g) milk powder
- 3 tablespoons all-purpose (plain) flour
- ½ teaspoon ground cardamom
- ⅛ teaspoon baking soda (bicarbonate of soda)
- ¼ teaspoon kosher salt
- 2 tablespoons plain yogurt (not Greek)
- 2–3 tablespoons milk
- Vegetable oil, for frying

Make the syrup: In a small saucepan, combine 1 cup (240 ml/8 fl oz) water, sugar, cardamom pods, and cinnamon sticks and bring to a boil over medium-high heat, stirring often to dissolve the sugar. Reduce the heat to medium and cook until the syrup thickens slightly, about 5 minutes. Remove from the heat and stir in the rose water. Let cool slightly while making the fritters.

Make the fritters: In a medium bowl, whisk together the milk powder, flour, cardamom, baking soda (bicarb), and salt. Add the yogurt and mix well to combine. Add 2 tablespoons milk and stir to create a smooth, cohesive dough. The mixture may be sticky, but should not feel soggy. If necessary, add up to 1 more tablespoon milk, 1 teaspoon at a time, until the desired consistency is reached. Do not overwork the dough, or the fritters may be tough.

Line a large plate with paper towels. In medium frying pan, heat 2 inches (5 cm) oil over medium heat. While the oil is heating, pinch off small pieces of dough and, using slightly moistened hands, roll into very smooth balls a little larger than a marble (the fritters will seem very small, but will swell in size during frying and while resting in the syrup). Place them on a plate while continuing with the remaining dough.

Working in batches if necessary, add the balls to the hot oil and fry, stirring often, until gently puffed and golden brown on all sides, about 3 minutes. Transfer to the paper towels to drain and cool for 5 minutes.

Meanwhile, strain the syrup through a fine-mesh sieve into a medium bowl (discard the cinnamon sticks and cardamom pods).

Add the fritters to the syrup and let rest, stirring occasionally, until they absorb some of the syrup, about 2 hours. Serve at room temperature in small individual bowls, drizzled with a little extra syrup.

Gulab Jamun

SUFGANIYOT

In Israel, no Hanukkah celebration is complete without *sufganiyot*—puffy yeast doughnuts that are filled with jam. Originally brought to Israel by Polish Jews (who called them *ponchik*), bakeries across the country now overflow with the deep-fried pastries in the weeks leading up to the Festival of Lights. In recent years, *sufganiyot* have also become increasingly popular in America.

Makes: about 15 doughnuts
Preparation time: 20 minutes, plus rising
Cooking time: 15 minutes

- 1 packet (¼ oz/7 g) active dry yeast (2¼ teaspoons)
- ¼ cup (50 g) plus 1 teaspoon sugar
- ½ cup (120 ml/4 fl oz) warm water (110°F/43°C)
- 2½ cups (350 g) all-purpose (plain) flour,
  plus more for kneading and rolling
- ½ teaspoon kosher salt
- 2 egg yolks
- ⅓ cup (75 ml/2½ fl oz) milk
- ½ teaspoon vanilla extract
- 2 tablespoons (30 g) unsalted butter, cut into pieces,
  at room temperature
- Vegetable oil, for greasing the bowl and frying
- Strawberry, raspberry, or apricot jam (not jelly),
  for filling
- Powdered (icing) sugar, for dusting

In a medium bowl, stir together the yeast, 1 teaspoon of the sugar, and the warm water. Let sit until the mixture is bubbling and foaming, about 5 minutes.

Meanwhile, in a large bowl, whisk together the flour and salt.

Add the remaining ¼ cup (50 g) sugar, the egg yolks, milk, and vanilla to the yeast mixture and whisk to combine. Pour the wet mixture into the flour mixture and stir with a wooden spoon until the dough comes together and begins to form a ball.

Transfer the dough to a lightly floured surface. Scatter the butter pieces over the dough and knead, sprinkling with additional flour as necessary, until the butter is fully incorporated and the dough is smooth, shiny, and elastic, about 8 minutes. (The kneading can also be done in a stand mixer fitted with a dough hook, 5–7 minutes.) Grease a large bowl with 1 teaspoon vegetable oil. Form the dough into a ball, place in the bowl, and turn to coat. Cover the bowl with plastic wrap (cling film) or a damp tea towel and let rise in a warm place until doubled in size, 1½–2 hours.

Line a large baking sheet with parchment paper. Fit a wire cooling rack inside a large sheet pan.

Gently deflate the dough with the heel of your hand and transfer it to a lightly floured work surface. Roll out the dough with a rolling pin to a ¼-inch (6 mm) thickness. Using a 3-inch (7.5 cm) round biscuit or cookie cutter, stamp out as many dough rounds as possible and place them on the lined baking sheet. Gather the scraps, reroll, and cut out more rounds. Cover the dough rounds loosely with a damp towel and let rise in a warm place until puffed, about 30 minutes.

Meanwhile, pour 2 inches (5 cm) of oil into a Dutch oven (casserole) or large heavy-bottomed pot, set over medium heat, and bring to 365°F (185°C) on a deep-fry thermometer.

Working in batches of 4, gently add the dough rounds to the hot oil and fry, flipping once, until golden brown on both sides, about 2 minutes. Transfer to the wire rack in the sheet pan. Let cool slightly.

Use a small knife to puncture the side of each doughnut to form a pocket, then use a spoon or piping bag to fill with jam. Place the filled doughnuts back on the wire rack and dust tops with powdered (icing) sugar. Serve immediately.

Sufganiyot

SFENJ

This Moroccan take on the Hanukkah doughnut has a rustic, freeform ring shape. They are delicious drizzled with honey or dusted with more sugar.

Serves: 6
Preparation time: 40 minutes, plus rising
Cooking time: 30 minutes

• 1 packet (¼ oz/7 g) active dry yeast (2¼ teaspoons)
• ¼ cup (50 g) plus 1 teaspoon sugar
• ¾ cup (175 ml/6 fl oz) warm water (110°F/43°C)
• 3–4 cups (420–560 g) all-purpose (plain) flour,
  plus more for kneading
• ½ teaspoon kosher salt
• 2 egg yolks
• ¼ cup (60 ml/2 fl oz) milk or almond milk
• ½ teaspoon vanilla extract
• Vegetable oil, for frying and greasing the bowl
• Honey, for serving

In a large bowl, stir together the yeast, 1 teaspoon of the sugar, and the warm water. Let sit until foaming, 5–10 minutes.

Meanwhile, in a medium bowl, whisk together 3 cups (420 g) flour, the remaining ¼ cup (50 g) sugar, and the salt.

Stir the egg yolks, milk, and vanilla into the yeast mixture, followed by the flour mixture, adding it in stages and stirring until the dough begins to come together. Turn the dough out on a lightly floured surface and knead, adding up to 1 cup (140 g) additional flour, a little at a time, until the dough is smooth and supple, 5–10 minutes. You may not need all of the flour. (The kneading can also be done in a stand mixer fitted with a dough hook, 5–7 minutes.) Grease a large bowl with about 1 teaspoon vegetable oil, add the dough, and turn to coat. Cover the bowl with a tea towel and let rise until it has doubled in size, about 1½ hours.

When ready to fry, line a plate with paper towels and line a second plate with parchment paper. Pour about 2½ inches (6.5 cm) oil into a Dutch oven (casserole) or heavy-bottomed pot, set over medium heat, and bring to 365°F (185°C) on a deep-fry thermometer. Using moistened hands, pinch off a small handful of dough and quickly use two fingers to make a hole in the center and stretch it gently into a ring shape. Place the ring on the parchment-lined plate and repeat 3 more times. Slip all 4 dough rings into the hot oil and fry, flipping once, until puffed, golden, and cooked through, 2–4 minutes. Transfer to the paper towels. Repeat the process, working in batches of 4, until all the dough is used. Transfer the *sfenj* to a serving plate and drizzle with honey to taste. Serve immediately.

HAMAN'S EAR FRITTERS

Italian Jews celebrate Purim with *orecchie di Aman*—crunchy, sugar-dusted fritters shaped like the ear of the holiday's villain, Haman. They are part of a larger tradition of Purim sweets that resemble the infamous man (see page 339), and of which hamantaschen (pages 340–343) are the most widely known. Not surprisingly, *orecchie di Aman* are very closely related to *chiacchiere*—sweet Italian fritters eaten during carnival season, which falls at the same time of year as Purim.

Serves: 6
Preparation time: 30 minutes
Cooking time: 30 minutes

- 2¼–2½ cups (315–350 g) all-purpose (plain) flour, plus more for rolling
- ½ cup (100 g) sugar
- ½ teaspoon kosher salt
- 3 eggs
- 2 tablespoons vegetable oil, plus more for frying
- 2 tablespoons orange juice
- ½ teaspoon finely grated orange zest (optional)
- Powdered (icing) sugar, for dusting

In a medium bowl, whisk together 2¼ cups (315 g) flour, the sugar, and salt in a medium bowl.

In a stand mixer (or using a handheld electric mixer and a large bowl), beat together the eggs, 2 tablespoons oil, orange juice, and orange zest (if using) on medium-high speed until frothy, 2–3 minutes. Add the flour mixture and beat until a supple, slightly sticky dough forms. If necessary, beat in up to ¼ cup (35 g) additional flour, 1 tablespoon at a time, until the desired consistency is reached. Knead the dough in the bowl a couple of times with your hands to bring it together into a ball.

On a large floured surface using a floured rolling pin, roll out the dough into a large rectangle ⅛ inch (3 mm) thick. Using a sharp knife or a pizza cutter, cut out small rectangles about 3 × 4 inches (7.5 × 10 cm). Fold the top two corners of the rectangles to the center, forming a triangle at the top and a sailboat shape overall. Press down gently on the seam so they don't open during frying. (Any scraps of dough can be twisted once or twice to make curls.)

Line a large plate with paper towels. In a large frying pan, heat ½ inch (1.25 cm) oil over medium heat. Working in batches of 3–4, carefully slip the folded pastries into the hot oil and fry, turning once, until golden brown on both sides, 1–2 minutes per side. Transfer to the paper towels to drain. Using a fine-mesh sieve, dust generously with powdered (icing) sugar. Serve immediately.

FRIED PASTRY ROSES

North African Jews celebrate Purim and Hanukkah with these delicate fried pastries, which are coiled into the shape of roses and coated in sweet syrup. The confection goes by various names including *deblas* in Tunisia and *fijuelas* in Morocco. They are rather time consuming to prepare, but worth the fuss.

Serves: 6–8
Preparation time: 40 minutes, plus resting
Cooking time: 1 hour

For the fritters:
• 2 cups (280 g) all-purpose (plain) flour, plus more for rolling and kneading
• ½ teaspoon baking powder
• ¼ teaspoon kosher salt
• 2 eggs
• ¼ cup (60 ml/2 fl oz) vegetable oil, plus more for frying
• 1 teaspoon vanilla extract

For the syrup:
• 1¼ cups (250 g) sugar
• ¼ cup (85 g) honey
• 1 tablespoon fresh lemon juice

Make the fritters: In a food processor, pulse together the flour, baking powder, salt, eggs, oil, vanilla, and 2 tablespoons water, scraping down the sides of the bowl once or twice, until a firm but pliable dough comes together. If necessary, add another tablespoon of water to reach the desired consistency. Form the dough into a ball and transfer to a bowl. Cover the bowl with a tea towel and let rest for 30 minutes.

Line a large plate with paper towels. Pour about 2½ inches (6.5 cm) oil into a small, deep saucepan and set over medium heat.

Divide the dough in half, leaving one half covered. On a floured surface using a floured rolling pin, roll the dough into a very thin rectangle. (It should be almost translucent.) Use a sharp knife or pastry cutter to cut the rectangle into long strips about 1 inch (2.5 cm) wide. When the oil is hot, pick up one of the dough strips and insert the end between the prongs of a fork. Dip the fork and dough into the oil, using the opposite hand to hold the loose end of the dough up and away from the oil. (The oil should bubble vigorously but not violently.) Cook until the dough starts to blister and puff, 5–10 seconds, then rotate the fork, wrapping another layer of dough around the fork, forming a scrolled pastry that resembles a rose. Continue wrapping and frying until the whole strip of dough is crisp and lightly golden. (If the end of the dough is popping up, gently hold the pastry against the side of the saucepan, seam side touching the pan, to help seal.) Transfer the fritter to the paper towels to drain. Continue the rolling, cutting, and frying process with the remaining dough.

Make the syrup: In a small saucepan, combine the sugar, honey, and ¾ cup (175 ml/6 fl oz) water and bring to a boil over medium-high heat, stirring often to dissolve the sugar and honey. Reduce the heat to medium and cook until the syrup thickens slightly, about 5 minutes. Remove from the heat and stir in the lemon juice.

Working in batches of 2–3, add the cooked fritters to the syrup, tilting the pan to cover them entirely, then remove with a slotted spoon and transfer back to the plate. Arrange on a serving plate and serve at room temperature.

CAKES, COOKIES & SWEET PASTRIES

Fried Pastry Roses

TEIGLACH

The roots of this Ashkenazi dessert, which boils nuggets of dough in honey syrup, date back to ancient times. As such, sticky-sweet *teiglach* (the name means "little dough pieces" in Yiddish) can be an acquired taste for the modern palate. Still, they are a beloved treat for many Eastern European Jewish families—particularly on Rosh Hashanah when honey-sweetened foods symbolize wishes for a sweet year ahead.

Serves: 8
Preparation time: 45 minutes, plus resting
Cooking time: 40 minutes

For the dough:
• 1¾ cups (245 g) all-purpose (plain) flour, plus more as needed
• 1 teaspoon baking powder
• ½ teaspoon kosher salt
• 3 eggs
• 2 tablespoons vegetable oil, plus more for greasing
• ½ teaspoon vanilla extract

For the syrup:
• 1 cup (340 g) honey
• ½ cup (100 g) sugar
• 1½ teaspoons ground ginger
• 1 teaspoon finely grated lemon zest
• 1½ cups (190 g) whole almonds or hazelnuts (or a mixture), roughly chopped
• ½ cup (80 g) finely chopped dried apricots or dried cranberries (or a mixture)

Make the dough: In a medium bowl, whisk together flour, baking powder, and salt. In a large bowl, whisk together the eggs, oil, and vanilla until fully combined. Add the flour mixture to the wet ingredients and stir until the dough begins to come together. Transfer to a lightly floured surface and knead, adding a little more flour as needed, until the dough is smooth and supple. Shape the dough into a ball and place back in the bowl. Cover the bowl with a tea towel and let rest for 30 minutes.

Meanwhile, preheat the oven to 350°F (180°C/Gas Mark 4). Line two large baking sheets with parchment paper.

Divide the dough into 4 equal portions. Working with one piece at a time (and keeping the others covered), roll into a long, thin log about ½ inch (1.25 cm) thick. Cut the logs into ½-inch (1.25 cm) pieces and place in a single layer on one of the prepared baking sheets. Repeat with the remaining portions of dough and remaining baking sheet.

Bake until just barely puffed and lightly golden, about 5 minutes. Let cool, gently separating any pieces that fused together during baking.

Make the syrup: In a large saucepan, stir together the honey, sugar, ginger, and lemon zest and bring to a boil over medium-high heat. Reduce the heat to low and simmer, stirring occasionally, until the honey turns a deep golden color, 5–10 minutes.

Add the baked and cooled dough pieces to the simmering honey syrup and cook, stirring occasionally, until the dough begins to take on some color, about 10 minutes. Add the nuts and dried fruit and continue cooking, stirring often, until the mixture is dark brown and very sticky, 5–10 minutes.

Pour the *teiglach* and honey syrup back onto the baking sheet and let cool to the touch. Using wet hands, transfer to a serving plate and shape into a mound. Alternatively, for individual portions of *teiglach*, make smaller mounds 2–3 inches (5–7.5 cm) high and place in cupcake papers (cases). Let cool completely.

ATAYEF

Syrian, Egyptian, and Lebanese Jews all enjoy these silver dollar–size pancakes, which are filled with chopped nuts or soft cheese, fried until crisp, and drenched in syrup. They are tedious to make, so typically reserved for holidays like Hanukkah and Shavuot or special occasions like weddings. (Middle Eastern Muslims, meanwhile, traditionally serve them at the evening feasts during Ramadan.) Once a commitment is made to fill, fry, and repeat, the sweet and crispy confections that emerge from the pan are worth the effort. Orange blossom water can be found at Middle Eastern and international food shops, and online.

Makes: about 30 small filled pancakes
Preparation time: 40 minutes, plus resting
Cooking time: 40 minutes

For the syrup:
- 1½ cups (300 g) sugar
- 1 teaspoon fresh lemon juice
- 1 tablespoon orange blossom water

For the batter:
- 1½ cups (210 g) all-purpose (plain) flour
- 1 teaspoon baking powder
- 1 teaspoon active dry yeast
- 1 tablespoon sugar
- ½ teaspoon kosher salt
- 1 egg, lightly beaten
- 1¾–2 cups (415–475 ml/14–16 fl oz) milk or almond milk

For the filling:
- ¾ cup (100 g) raw pistachios
- ¾ cup (70 g) walnut halves
- 4 Medjool dates, pitted and roughly chopped
- 1 tablespoon sugar
- 1 teaspoon finely grated orange zest
- 1½ teaspoons ground cinnamon

For frying:
- Vegetable oil

Make the syrup: In a small saucepan, combine 1 cup (240 ml/8 fl oz) water and sugar and bring to a boil over medium-high heat, stirring often to dissolve the sugar. Reduce the heat to medium and cook until the syrup thickens, about 10 minutes. Remove from the heat and stir in the lemon juice and orange blossom water, then let cool completely. Set aside until needed, or cover and refrigerate for up to 2 weeks.

Make the batter: In a large bowl, whisk together the flour, baking powder, yeast, sugar, and salt. In a small bowl, whisk together the egg and 1¾ cups (415 ml/ 14 fl oz) milk until fully combined. Add the wet mixture to the flour mixture and whisk until free of lumps. The batter should be just slightly thicker than heavy (whipping) cream. If necessary, add up to another ¼ cup (60 ml) milk, 1 tablespoon at a time, until the desired consistency is reached. Cover the bowl and let rest for 1 hour.

Meanwhile, make the filling: In a food processor, pulse the pistachios, walnuts, dates, sugar, orange zest, and cinnamon, scraping down the sides of the bowl as needed, until a moist, crumbly mixture forms. If you squeeze a bit of the mixture gently in your palm, it should hold together.

For the first frying: Heat a large frying pan over medium heat and lay a large clean tea towel on a flat surface. Once the pan is heated, reduce the heat to medium-low and brush with a little oil. Working in batches of 3–4, pour the batter 2 tablespoons at a time into the pan, letting the batter form small rounds, similar to making pancakes. Cook, undisturbed, until bubbles form on the tops and the surfaces are just short of completely dry, 1–1½ minutes. Do not flip. Immediately transfer the pancakes to the tea towel and fold the towel over to lightly cover (to avoid drying out), while frying the remaining batter. If the bottoms are getting too dark before the top sets, nudge the heat down a little.

For filling and frying: Hold one of the rounds, cooked side down, in your hand and scoop a rounded tablespoon of the filling into the center. Fold one side over to the other to make a half-moon, pressing the edges tightly to seal. Continue with the remaining pancakes and filling.

Line a large plate with paper towels. In a large frying pan, heat ¼ inch (6 mm) oil over medium heat. Working in batches, gently fry the filled pancakes, turning once, until golden and crisp on both sides, 1–2 minutes. (It is okay if they open up a bit during the frying process.) Transfer to the paper towels to drain. Drizzle to taste with syrup and serve immediately.

MOFLETA

Moroccan Jews serve these hand-formed yeasted crepes warm from the pan and spread with butter, honey, jam, or chopped pistachios as part of the post-Passover celebration Mimouna (see page 328).

Makes: about 40 pancakes
Preparation time: 45 minutes, plus rising
Cooking time: 1 hour

- 1 packet (¼ oz/7 g) active dry yeast (2¼ teaspoons)
- 1 tablespoon sugar
- 1½ cups (355 ml/12 fl oz) warm water (110°F/43°C)
- 4 cups (560 g) all-purpose (plain) flour, plus more as needed
- 1½ teaspoons kosher salt
- Vegetable oil, for greasing bowl, dough, and frying
- Optional toppings: salted butter, honey, jam, or finely chopped pistachios

In a large bowl, stir together the yeast, sugar, and warm water. Let sit until foaming, 5–10 minutes.

Meanwhile, in a medium bowl, whisk together the flour and salt.

Add the flour mixture to the yeast mixture and stir until the dough begins to come together. Turn the dough out onto a lightly floured surface and knead well, adding a little additional flour, if needed, 1 tablespoon at a time, until you have a supple, slightly tacky dough, 5–10 minutes. (The kneading can also be done in a stand mixer fitted with a dough hook, 5–7 minutes.) Grease a large bowl with about 1 teaspoon oil, add the dough, and turn to coat. Cover the bowl with a tea towel and let sit in a warm place until almost doubled in size, about 1 hour.

Drizzle a large sheet pan with enough oil to coat the bottom. Pinch off golf ball–size pieces of dough and roll into balls. Place the balls on the baking sheet, turning to coat in the oil, and let rest for 30 minutes.

In a large nonstick frying pan, heat a few teaspoons oil over medium-low heat. While the oil is heating, take one of the dough balls and press it with your fingertips into a very thin round 8–10 inches (20–15 cm) in diameter. (It should be translucent, and it is okay if the dough tears a little.) Gently transfer the dough round to the frying pan and cook, flipping once, until golden brown on both sides, about 1 minute per side. Transfer to a plate.

While the first dough round is frying, flatten the next one. Continue flattening and frying dough rounds in this manner, nudging the heat up or down as needed to avoid burning, until all of the dough balls are fried. As you work, layer the completed crepes on top of one another in a stack. Serve hot or warm with desired toppings.

Mofleta

DESSERT CREPES

Hungarian and Romanian Jews serve these crepes (Hungarians call them *palacsinta*, while Romanians call them *clatite*) both savory and sweet, but the sweet version is particularly beloved. On Shavuot, when dairy dishes are traditional, they are often filled with sweetened curd cheese.

Makes: about 15 crepes
Preparation time: 10 minutes, plus resting
Cooking time: 30 minutes

- 3 eggs
- 1¾ cups (415 ml/14 fl oz) milk
- 2 teaspoons sugar
- ½ teaspoon vanilla extract
- ¼ teaspoon kosher salt
- 1¼ cups (175 g) all-purpose (plain) flour
- About 5 tablespoons (70 g) unsalted butter, for frying
- Jam, finely chopped walnuts, cocoa powder, or filling from Cheese Blintzes (page 30), for filling
- Chocolate sauce, Strawberry Sauce (page 394), Blueberry Sauce (page 395), or powdered (icing) sugar, for topping

In a large bowl, whisk together the eggs, milk, sugar, vanilla, salt, and flour until very smooth and the consistency of heavy (whipping) cream. Cover the bowl with a tea towel and let the batter rest at room temperature for 1 hour.

In a 7- to 8-inch (18 to 20 cm) nonstick frying pan, heat about 1 teaspoon butter over medium heat. Once hot, pour a scant ¼ cup (55 g) batter into the pan. Immediately pick up the pan and swirl it in all directions to coat the bottom evenly with a thin layer of batter. Cook until the bottom is golden brown and the center is dry, about 1 minute. Using a thin spatula, carefully flip the crepe and fry until golden on the reverse side, about 30 seconds. Transfer the crepe to a large plate and continue frying the remaining batter, adding more butter as needed.

To serve, spread the crepes with jam and sprinkle with cocoa powder and ground walnuts, or spread with sweetened cheese filling. Roll up like a jelly roll (Swiss roll) and drizzle with preferred sauce, if desired, or sprinkle with powdered (icing) sugar.

PUMPKIN FRITTERS

These puffed, pancakelike fritters, called *frittelle di zucca*, are a speciality of Venetian Jews. They traditionally get their sunset-orange color from fresh pumpkin that is steamed, roasted, or cooked in milk and then mashed, but good-quality canned pumpkin purée makes a fine substitute. Generously dusted with powdered (icing) sugar, they make a perfect treat for Hanukkah or anytime.

Serves: 6–8
Preparation time: 10 minutes
Cooking time: 45 minutes

- 1½ cups (210 g) all-purpose (plain) flour
- ½ teaspoon baking powder
- ½ teaspoon kosher salt
- 1 cup (250 g) canned unsweetened pumpkin purée
- ½ cup (120 ml/4 fl oz) milk or almond milk
- 2 eggs
- ½ cup (100 g) sugar
- ½ teaspoon finely grated orange zest
- ½ teaspoon ground cinnamon
- Vegetable oil, for frying
- Powdered (icing) sugar, for serving

In a medium bowl, whisk together the flour, baking powder, and salt. In a large bowl, whisk together the pumpkin, milk, eggs, sugar, orange zest, and cinnamon. Add the dry ingredients to the wet and whisk to form a thick, smooth batter.

Line a large plate with paper towels. In a large frying pan, heat ¼ inch (6 mm) oil over medium heat. Working in batches of 4–5, drop the batter by the rounded tablespoon into the hot oil and cook, turning once, until lightly puffed, golden, and cooked through, about 2 minutes per side. Transfer to the paper towels to drain.

Arrange the fritters on a serving plate and dust generously with powdered (icing) sugar. Serve hot.

KANAFEH

Variations of this syrup-soaked pastry, made with shredded phyllo dough called *kadayif*, can be found across the Middle East, Turkey, and the Balkans. (The confection is also called *kadayif* in some regions.) Some versions are filled with chopped nuts, others with thickened cream, and still others with a mix of soft and stretchy cheeses. The shredded phyllo dough can be found in Middle Eastern and international grocery stores. The traditional cheese used is called *ackawi*, but fresh mozzarella makes a worthy substitute. This version is best served hot, when the cheese still has a bit of stretch.

Serves: 6–8
Preparation time: 20 minutes
Cooking time: 1 hour

For the syrup:
- 1½ cups (300 g) sugar
- 1 tablespoon orange blossom water

For the kadayif:
- 2 cups (480 g) ricotta cheese
- 8 oz (225 g) fresh mozzarella cheese, grated on the large holes of a box grater
- 2 tablespoons sugar
- ½ cup (120 ml/4 fl oz) heavy (whipping) cream
- 1 tablespoon cornstarch (cornflour)
- ¼ teaspoon kosher salt
- 1 lb (455 g) frozen kadayif dough, thawed
- 2 sticks (8 oz/225 g) unsalted butter, melted
- Finely chopped pistachios, for topping

Make the syrup: In a small saucepan, combine 1 cup (240 ml/8 fl oz) water and sugar and bring to a boil over medium-high heat, stirring often to dissolve the sugar. Reduce the heat to medium and cook until the syrup thickens slightly, about 10 minutes. Remove from the heat and stir in the orange blossom water, then let cool.

Preheat the oven to 350°F (180°C/Gas Mark 4). Have ready a 9-inch (23 cm) square baking dish.

Make the *kadayif*: In a large bowl, stir together the ricotta, mozzarella, sugar, cream, cornstarch (cornflour), and salt.

Finely crumble the *kadayif* dough into a large bowl. Pour the melted butter on top and use your hands to mix together, making sure the dough is fully coated.

Transfer half of the *kadayif* dough to the baking dish. Pat down firmly with your hands or the flat bottom of a glass. Spoon the cheese mixture on top, spreading it out evenly with a spatula. Top with the remaining *kadayif* dough, gently pressing down.

Bake until golden brown, 40–45 minutes. Remove from the oven and slowly pour the cooled syrup over the hot pastry. Sprinkle the top of the pastry with several small mounds of finely chopped pistachios. Cut into squares and serve hot.

CONFECTIONS
& PUDDINGS

STUFFED DATES WITH ALMOND AND ROSE WATER

Dates stuffed with sweet almond paste or ground nuts are served across North Africa and the Middle East. Jewish families traditionally make them for Purim or festive occasions like bar mitzvahs and weddings. Moroccan Jews also include the confection as part of an extensive sweets and cookie spread during Mimouna (page 328), the celebratory meal held to commemorate the end of Passover.

Serves: 6–8
Preparation time: 25 minutes

• 4 oz (115 g) almond paste (not marzipan)
• 1 teaspoon rose water
• ¼ teaspoon ground cinnamon
• ⅛ teaspoon ground cardamom
• 20 Medjool dates
• 20 salted roasted pistachios

Break the almond paste into small pieces and place in the bowl of a stand mixer. Add the rose water, cinnamon, and cardamom and beat on medium speed until fully combined.

Slice each date lengthwise, taking care not to go through to the other side. Remove and discard the pits. Scoop out 1 teaspoon of the almond paste mixture and roll into an oval. Tuck into one of the sliced dates and top with 1 pistachio, pressing it down gently into the almond paste. Repeat with remaining dates, filling, and pistachios.

DRIED FRUIT COMPOTE

Stewed fruit dishes are a popular dessert among Ashkenazi Jews, particularly on Passover, but also year-round. They can be made with fresh or dried fruit (or a mix of both) and with just a single variety or many. Either way, they make a light and refreshing end to a celebratory meal. Serve this compote in small bowls or dessert glasses, or spoon it over Cinnamon-Walnut Sponge Cake (page 316).

Serves: 6
Preparation time: 10 minutes
Cooking time: 35 minutes

• 2 tart apples, peeled, cored, and thinly sliced
• 1½ cups (270 g) dried apricots
• 1½ cups (270 g) prunes
• 1 cup (180 g) dried figs, stems removed, halved
• ½ cup (70 g) dried cherries or raisins
• ¼ cup (45 g) light brown sugar
• ¾ teaspoon ground cinnamon
• 1½ tablespoons fresh lemon juice

In a large pot, combine the apples, apricots, prunes, figs, cherries, and brown sugar with 4 cups (950 ml/ 32 fl oz) water. Bring to a boil over high heat. Reduce the heat to low, cover, and cook, stirring occasionally, until the fruit is very tender, 25–30 minutes. Uncover and use a slotted spoon to transfer the fruit to a large ceramic or glass bowl. Increase the heat under the pot to high and continue cooking until the liquid reduces by about one-third, about 5 minutes.

Remove the pan from the heat. Stir the cinnamon and lemon juice into the reduced cooking liquid, then pour over the fruit. Let the mixture come to room temperature, then cover and chill for at least 2 hours (or overnight) before serving. The mixture will continue to sweeten as it chills.

Stuffed Dates with Almond and Rose Water

BAKLAVA

Baklava is so central to Greek Jewish cuisine, they developed a version made with matzo so they would not have to go without on Passover. The crisp-topped phyllo pastry dessert, which comes layered with finely chopped nuts and soaked in sugar syrup, is also popular throughout the Middle East and the Balkans. Jewish families serve it on Rosh Hashanah, when sweet foods are paramount, and also on happy occasions like weddings. It pairs wonderfully with very strong black coffee.

Serves: 10–12
Preparation: 45 minutes, plus resting
Cooking time: 35 minutes

For the baklava:
• ½ lb (225 g) walnut halves
• ½ lb (225 g) unsalted pistachios
• 1½ teaspoons ground cinnamon
• ½ teaspoon ground cardamom
• 2 tablespoons light brown sugar
• ¼ teaspoon kosher salt
• 1 package (1 lb/455 g) frozen phyllo dough, thawed
• 2 sticks (8 oz/225 g) unsalted butter, melted, or 1 cup (240 ml/8 fl oz) melted coconut oil or vegetable oil

For the syrup:
• 1¼ cups (250 g) sugar
• ¼ cup (85 g) honey
• 1 cinnamon stick
• 5 cardamom pods, cracked (optional)
• 2 tablespoons fresh lemon juice

Preheat the oven to 350°F (180°C/Gas Mark 4). Lightly grease a 9 × 13-inch (23 × 33 cm) baking dish.

Make the baklava: In a food processor, combine the walnuts, pistachios, cinnamon, cardamom, brown sugar, and salt and process until the nuts are finely ground.

If necessary, trim the stack of the phyllo dough to fit the bottom of the baking dish, then cover with a damp towel so the sheets don't dry out as you work. Fit one sheet of phyllo in the bottom of the baking dish and generously brush with melted butter. Repeat 7 times, brushing with butter after each addition and ending up with a stack of 8 phyllo sheets. Spoon in half of the nut mixture and spread evenly. Repeat the process with 4 more phyllo sheets, brushing with butter between each addition. Spread the remaining nut mixture on top, and repeat the process with 8 more phyllo sheets. Bake until the top is lightly golden and crisp, 30–35 minutes. Let cool for 5 minutes, then use a sharp knife to cut the baklava into squares or diamonds in the pan.

Meanwhile, make the syrup: In a medium saucepan, stir together the sugar, honey, cinnamon stick, cardamom pods, if using, and ¾ cup (175 ml/6 fl oz) water and bring to a boil over medium-high heat. Reduce the heat to medium-low and cook, stirring often, until the syrup thickens slightly, about 5 minutes. Remove from the heat and stir in the lemon juice. Strain the mixture through a fine-mesh sieve into a bowl (discard the cinnamon stick and cardamom pods).

Carefully and evenly spoon the syrup over the slightly cooled and cut baklava. Let sit for at least 2 hours before serving to allow the syrup to soften the filling. Serve at room temperature.

THE SEVEN BIBLICAL SPECIES

The Old Testament names seven agricultural products that hold special, almost sacred significance within the Land of Israel. These species—wheat, barley, dates (and date honey), grapes, figs, pomegranates, and olives—grew locally and were widely consumed by ancient Israelites and their neighbors. The first fruits from each growing season were brought as offerings to the Holy Temple in Jerusalem.

Today, the Jewish people maintain an ancient connection to the land and to agriculture, and these fruits and grains remain central to the Jewish diet. Grapes and wheat are consumed every week on Shabbat in the form of wine and challah, and foods made with the seven species are enjoyed on the holiday of Tu Bishvat (see page 13). They can also be found in abundance throughout Jewish recipes.

POPPYSEED CANDY

Packed with nutty, blue-black poppy seeds, these sticky-crunchy confections, called *mohnlach,* are part of a larger family of Ashkenazi candies called *pletzlach*. Make sure to have a stack of small wax (greaseproof) paper squares on hand (similar to the ones used to package caramel) to individually wrap the cooled candies.

Makes: about 5 dozen candies
Preparation time: 40 minutes
Cooking time: 20 minutes

- 1 cup (200 g) sugar
- 1½ cups (510 g) honey
- 2 cups (280 g) poppy seeds
- 1 cup (50 g) walnut halves, finely chopped
- 1 teaspoon ground ginger

Line a large sheet pan with parchment paper.

In a medium saucepan, stir together the sugar and honey and cook, stirring often, over medium-low heat until the sugar fully dissolves, 5–10 minutes. (When the sugar is dissolved, the mixture will no longer feel gritty.)

Add the poppy seeds, walnuts, and ginger and continue cooking, stirring often, until the mixture thickens and a candy thermometer registers 280°F (138°C). Be careful not to let the mixture get any hotter or it will turn brittle as it cools.

Pour or spoon the mixture into the prepared sheet pan and use a spatula or knife to spread it to a ¼-inch (6 mm) thickness. Let cool until just firm, about 15 minutes, then use a sharp knife to cut the candy into small squares or rectangles. If the mixture is sticking, dip the knife in hot water and proceed.

Allow the mixture to cool completely, then use a spatula to remove the candies from the parchment. If they are sticking together, use a sharp pair of kitchen shears to separate them. Wrap the candies individually in wax (greaseproof) paper and store at room temperature or in the fridge.

SESAME HALVA

While halva is typically associated with Sephardi or Mizrahi cuisines, Romanian Jews were introduced to sesame halva while Romania was under Ottoman rule. Halva is delicious just as it is, but can also be dressed up by mixing in sesame seeds, chopped pistachios, almonds, chocolate, cinnamon, crystallized ginger, or other desired flavorings along with the sugar syrup. It is simple to make, but does require a candy thermometer to ensure the proper texture. Timing is everything, so have all the ingredients prepped before getting started.

Serves: 8
Preparation time: 10 minutes
Cooking time: 15 minutes

• 2 cups (400 g) sugar
• ½ cup (120 ml/4 fl oz) water
• 1½ cups (330 g) tahini
• ⅛ teaspoon kosher salt

Line an 8-inch (20 cm) square baking pan with parchment paper, allowing the parchment to hang over on two opposite sides.

In a medium saucepan, stir together the sugar and water. Set over medium-high heat, bring to a simmer without stirring, and cook until it registers at 248°F (120°C) on a candy thermometer.

While the sugar mixture is simmering, add the tahini and salt to the bowl of a stand mixer fitted with the paddle attachment.

When the sugar mixture hits 248°F (120°C), turn the mixer to medium and slowly pour the sugar mixture in. Mix until the mixture begins to pull away from the sides of the bowl, about 30 seconds. (Do not overmix, or the halva will be too crumbly.)

Working quickly, transfer the mixture to the lined baking pan. Place another piece of parchment on top and use hands to smooth. Cool completely and slice into squares.

APPLE-CRANBERRY CRISP

This quintessential New England sweet has been adopted by American Jews as a dessert for autumnal meals. Some families refer to the dish as a "kugel" and also serve it as a side dish during the meal, despite its decidedly sweet nature.

Serves: 8–10
Preparation time: 25 minutes
Cooking time: 50 minutes

For the topping:
• 1 cup (140 g) all-purpose (plain) flour
• 1 cup (80 g) rolled oats
• ¾ cup (135 g) light brown sugar
• 1½ teaspoons ground cinnamon
• ½ teaspoon kosher salt
• 1½ sticks (6 oz/170 g) unsalted butter or nonhydrogenated margarine, at room temperature

For the filling:
• 5 lb (2.25 kg) baking apples, peeled, cored, and cut into ½-inch (1.25 cm) cubes
• 2 cups (215 g) fresh or thawed frozen cranberries
• ½ cup (100 g) sugar
• 3 tablespoons cornstarch (cornflour)

Preheat the oven to 350°F (180°C/Gas Mark 4). Have ready a 9 × 13-inch (23 × 33 cm) baking dish.

Make the topping: In a stand mixer fitted with the paddle attachment, combine the flour, oats, brown sugar, cinnamon, salt, and butter and beat at low speed until a moist crumble forms. (Or place all ingredients in a bowl and mix together with your hands until the desired consistency is reached.)

Make the filling: In a large bowl, combine the apples, cranberries, sugar, and cornstarch (cornflour) and mix until fruit is fully coated.

Transfer the fruit mixture to the baking dish and top evenly with the topping mixture. Bake until the fruit is bubbling and the top is browned, 45–50 minutes. Let rest for 10 to 15 minutes before serving.

GINGER AND MATZO FARFEL CANDY

These sticky, Passover-friendly candies are part of a larger family of homemade Ashkenazi candies called *pletzlach*. Bound with boiled honey, the satisfyingly chewy confections can be made from a base of chopped nuts, poppy seeds (see Mohnlach, page 000), finely shredded carrots, or, as they are here, *matzo farfel*. When ground ginger is added, they are called *ingberlach* (*ingber* is Yiddish for "ginger"). If you do not have *matzo farfel* on hand, substitute sheets of matzo crumbled into ½-inch (1.25 cm) pieces.

Makes: about 3 dozen candies
Preparation time: 30 minutes, plus cooling
Cooking time: 30 minutes

1 cup (200 g) sugar
1½ cups (510 g) honey
2 cups (100 g) matzo farfel
1½ cups (155 g) walnut halves, finely chopped
1 teaspoon ground ginger
Vegetable oil, for forming the candies

Line a large sheet pan with parchment paper.

In a medium saucepan, stir together the sugar and honey and cook, stirring often, over medium-low heat until the sugar fully dissolves, 5–10 minutes. (When the sugar is dissolved, the mixture will no longer feel gritty.)

Add the matzo farfel, walnuts, and ginger and continue cooking, stirring often, until the mixture thickens and a candy thermometer registers 280°F (138°C). Be careful not to let the mixture get any hotter or it will turn brittle as it cools.

Pour or spoon the mixture into the prepared sheet pan and let cool until just enough to handle, but not firm, 20–30 minutes. Using lightly oiled hands, pinch off pieces of the candy and roll into 1-inch (2.5 cm) balls. Store in single layers, with parchment paper between each row, in an airtight container for up to 2 weeks.

BAKED APPLES WITH RAISINS AND WALNUTS

Apples cored and filled with a comforting chop of walnuts, raisins, and brown sugar were once a common aftermeal sweet served in Ashkenazi households. They have since fallen out of favor, as tastes for more elaborate desserts have emerged, but they continue to shine at breakfast, served with a dollop of plain yogurt.

Serves: 6
Preparation time: 20 minutes
Cooking time: 35 minutes

- 6 large firm baking apples
- ⅓ cup (60 g) light brown sugar
- ½ cup (50 g) chopped walnuts
- ¼ cup (35 g) raisins
- 1 teaspoon ground cinnamon
- ⅛ teaspoon ground nutmeg
- ½ teaspoon finely grated lemon zest
- ⅛ teaspoon kosher salt
- 6 teaspoons apricot jam
- 2 tablespoons (30 g) cold, unsalted butter or nonhydrogenated margarine, cut into small pieces
- 1 cup (240 ml/8 fl oz) apple cider (cloudy apple juice) or apple juice

Preheat the oven to 375°F (190°C/Gas Mark 5).

Using a sharp paring knife, cut out each apple stem. Use a spoon or melon baller to scoop out the cores and some of the flesh, leaving the bottom ½ inch (1.25 cm) of the apples intact. The holes left in the apples should be about 1 inch (2.5 cm) wide.

In a medium bowl, stir together the brown sugar, walnuts, raisins, cinnamon, nutmeg, lemon zest, and salt. Place 1 teaspoon of jam in the bottom of each apple, then stuff the apples with the nut and raisin mixture, mounding it on the top. Place the stuffed apples in a baking dish and top each apple with a few pieces of butter.

In a small saucepan, warm the apple cider or juice over medium heat until just simmering, but not boiling. Pour the warm cider in the bottom of the baking dish.

Bake, basting once or twice with juices from the dish, until the apples are tender and beginning to collapse, but not mushy, 25–35 minutes. Set aside to cool. Serve warm or at room temperature.

SWEET EGG MERINGUE

Moroccan Jews serve this billowy, soft-meringue pudding (called *jaban* or *zaban*) at the post-Passover feast, Mimouna (page 000). It is typically served in a large bowl, and guests spoon cloudlike dollops onto their plates. Note that the eggs are not cooked in this recipe.

Serves: 4–6
Preparation time: 10 minutes
Cooking time: 5 minutes

- ⅓ cup (35 g) sliced almonds, walnut halves, or shelled pistachios, chopped
- 4 egg whites
- ½ teaspoon cream of tartar
- ½ teaspoon vanilla extract
- 4 tablespoons sugar

In a small frying pan, toast the nuts over medium-low heat, shaking the pan occasionally, until fragrant and lightly browned, 5–7 minutes. Remove the pan from the heat and let cool. Set aside.

In a stand mixer fitted with the whisk attachment, beat the egg whites and cream of tartar at medium-high speed until foamy and beginning to increase in volume, 1–2 minutes. With the mixer running, add the vanilla followed by the sugar, 1 tablespoon at a time, until thick and billowy, and holding stiff peaks, 3–5 minutes.

Transfer the egg white mixture to a serving bowl, cover with plastic wrap (cling film), and refrigerate until cold, at least 2 hours. Serve chilled, decorated with toasted nuts.

CHOCOLATE MATZO TOFFEE

In the 1980s, Canadian baker and cookbook author Marcy Goldman invented this Passover-friendly confection, inspired by a similar sweet made with saltine crackers. Today, the dessert, which goes by the names caramel matzo crunch, matzo toffee, matzo brickle, matzo brittle, matzo bark, and matzo crack (for its addictive nature), has become ubiquitous on Passover dessert tables across Canada and America. For a dairy-free version, you can use nonhydrogenated margarine. Eat it as is, or sprinkle the top with chopped nuts or dried fruit, flaky sea salt, shredded coconut, or ground cinnamon or cayenne.

Serves: 6
Preparation time: 10 minutes
Cooking time: 20 minutes

- 4–6 sheets matzo
- 2 sticks (8 oz/225 g) unsalted butter
- 1 cup (180 g) light brown sugar
- 1 teaspoon vanilla extract
- ½ teaspoon kosher salt
- 1 cup (225 g) semisweet chocolate chips

Preheat the oven to 350°F (180°C/Gas Mark 4). Line a large sheet pan with foil, then top with parchment.

Arrange as many matzo sheets as needed to make a single layer over the surface of the sheet pan, breaking pieces in half to fit, if necessary.

In a medium saucepan, combine the butter and brown sugar and bring to a boil, stirring often, over medium heat. Cook, stirring constantly, until it begins to thicken into a caramel, 2–3 minutes. Remove the pan from the heat and stir in the vanilla and salt, then immediately pour the caramel over the matzo, spreading it with a spatula to cover completely. Transfer the sheet pan to the oven and bake until bubbling and dark brown (watching carefully so it does not burn), about 15 minutes.

Remove from the oven and immediately cover with the chocolate chips. Let stand until the chocolate melts, about 5 minutes, then spread the chocolate evenly over the top. Transfer the pan to the refrigerator and chill until the chocolate sets, then break into pieces. Serve chilled or at room temperature.

Sweet Egg Meringue

SAHLAB

Hot-chocolate aficionados should try this warm, drinkable pudding that is beloved throughout the Middle East. It is traditionally thickened with powder made from ground orchid roots, but cornstarch (cornflour) makes a fine substitute. Delicate, sweet, and scented with rose water, it is particularly comforting during the colder winter months.

Serves: 2
Preparation time: 5 minutes
Cooking time: 10 minutes

• 3 tablespoons cornstarch (cornflour)
• 2 cups (475 ml/16 fl oz) milk
• 3 tablespoons sugar
• ½ teaspoon vanilla extract
• ½ teaspoon rose water
• Ground cinnamon and finely chopped pistachios, for topping

In a small bowl, whisk together the cornstarch (cornflour) and ¼ cup (60 ml/2 fl oz) of the milk until the cornstarch is completely dissolved. Transfer the cornstarch mixture to a small saucepan and add the remaining 1¾ cups (415 ml/14 fl oz) milk and the sugar. Cook over medium heat, stirring often, until the mixture comes to a gentle boil. Allow to boil, stirring constantly, until the mixture thickens, 1–2 minutes. (It should be a drinkable consistency, less thick than pudding.)

Remove from the heat and stir in the vanilla and rose water. Let the mixture cool, stirring occasionally, for 5 minutes.

Divide between 2 glasses and top with cinnamon and pistachios. Serve warm.

SAFFRON RICE PUDDING

This creamy rice pudding, called *kheer*, is fragrant with cardamom and saffron. Mumbai's Bene Israel Jewish community serves it to break the fast after Yom Kippur, but it also makes a delicious and light dessert. To make it dairy-free, substitute canned coconut milk for the milk, and use coconut cream (skimmed from the top of the can) for the heavy cream.

Serves: 6–8
Preparation time: 5 minutes, plus cooling
Cooking time: 35 minutes

• ½ cup (100 g) basmati rice, rinsed and drained
• 6 cardamom pods, cracked open
• ⅛ teaspoon kosher salt
• 5 cups (1.2 liters/40 fl oz) milk
• Generous pinch of saffron threads, crumbled
• ¼ cup (60 ml/2 fl oz) heavy (whipping) cream
• ½ cup (90 g) light brown sugar
• Golden raisins (sultanas) and finely chopped pistachios, for serving

In a large saucepan, stir together the rice, 1 cup (240 ml/8 fl oz) water, cardamom pods, and salt and bring to a boil over medium-high heat. Stir, reduce the heat to low, cover, and cook until the rice is tender and the water is absorbed, about 15 minutes.

Stir in the milk, increase the heat to medium-high, and bring to a simmer. Reduce the heat back to medium and cook, uncovered and stirring frequently, until the mixture thickens into a soupy porridge, 20–25 minutes. If it bubbles too quickly, nudge the heat down a little.

Meanwhile, crumble the saffron threads into a powder between your fingers and place in a small bowl. Stir in 1 tablespoon warm water and let sit 5 minutes. In a medium bowl, whisk together the heavy (whipping) cream, brown sugar, and steeped saffron, with its liquid.

Pour the saffron-cream mixture mixture into the pudding and stir until sugar dissolves, 1–2 minutes. Remove the pan from the heat and let the pudding cool for 15 minutes, stirring occasionally.

Remove the cardamom pods and serve warm, sprinkled with golden raisins (sultanas) and pistachios. Or, continue cooling until room temperature, cover, and refrigerate until chilled, 3–4 hours. The pudding will continue to thicken as it chills.

Sahlab

MALABI

In Israel, this creamy rose water–scented custard (which is a popular dessert throughout the Middle East) is sold everywhere—from kiosks, at beachside cafes, and even in fine-dining restaurants. It is also simple to prepare at home. *Malabi* is typically served drizzled with raspberry sauce and sprinkled with chopped nuts or shredded coconut.

Serves: 6
Preparation time: 5 minutes
Cooking time: 20 minutes

• 4 cups (950 ml/1 qt) milk or coconut milk
• ½ cup (70 g) cornstarch (cornflour) or potato starch
• ½ cup (100 g) sugar
• 1 tablespoon rose water
• Raspberry preserves and chopped,
  salted pistachios or shredded coconut, for serving

In a small bowl, whisk together 1 cup (240 ml/8 fl oz) of the milk and the cornstarch (cornflour) until the cornstarch fully dissolves. Set aside.

In a medium saucepan, combine the remaining 3 cups (710 ml/24 fl oz) milk and the sugar and bring to a simmer over medium heat, whisking often. Add the cornstarch-milk mixture and cook, whisking constantly, until the mixture thickens into a loose pudding consistency, 3–5 minutes. Remove from the heat and whisk in the rose water.

Divide the mixture evenly among 6 small serving bowls, let cool to room temperature, then cover with plastic wrap (cling film) and refrigerate until cold, at least 4 hours. Serve chilled, topped with a drizzle of raspberry preserves and chopped pistachios.

RICE FLOUR PUDDING

Sephardi cuisine includes two categories of rice pudding—a textured version called *arroz con leche*, which is made with whole rice grains, and a smooth and creamy version called *sutlach*, which is thickened with rice flour. Versions of the dish are beloved across Turkey, the Balkan region, and the Middle East. The pudding is mildly sweet when served warm from the pot, with a flavor that deepens and blossoms as it chills.

Serves: 4–6
Preparation time: 5 minutes
Cooking time: 30 minutes

• ⅓ cup (45 g) rice flour
• ⅓ cup (65 g) sugar
• 4 cups (950 ml/32 fl oz) milk
• ½ teaspoon vanilla extract
• 1 teaspoon rose water
• Ground cinnamon, ground cardamom,
  and chopped pistachios or almonds, for serving

In a large saucepan, combine the rice flour and sugar. Whisk in a little of the milk to dissolve the rice flour. Set the pan over medium heat and gradually whisk in the remaining milk. Bring to a boil, stirring constantly, then reduce the heat to low and cook, stirring constantly, until the pudding thickens and turns creamy, 15–20 minutes.

Remove the pan from the heat and stir in the vanilla and rose water. Divide the pudding into 4–6 small serving cups. Serve warm, sprinkled with cinnamon, cardamom, and pistachios. Or, to serve chilled, cover the serving cups and place in the refrigerator for at least 4 hours or overnight. The pudding will continue to thicken and sweeten as it cools.

SWEET BULGUR PORRIDGE

The Jewish holiday of Tu Bishvat, colloquially called the New Year of the Trees, does not have a lot of specific recipes associated with it. Instead, it is customary to eat fruit grown on trees. But some Sephardi Jews have a custom of serving this sweet bulgur porridge, called *prehito,* as part of the celebration. It is also commonly served on the harvest holiday of Sukkot. *Prehito* can be served room temperature or chilled, and is also delicious warm from the pot.

Serves: 6–8
Preparation time: 5 minutes
Cooking time: 35 minutes

- 1 cup (185 g) fine or medium bulgur
- 2 cups (475 ml/16 fl oz) milk or almond milk
- ½ teaspoon kosher salt
- 2 tablespoons sugar
- 2 tablespoons honey
- 2 teaspoons ground cinnamon
- 1 cup (150 g) unsalted roasted almonds, chopped

In a large saucepan, combine the bulgur, 2 cups (475 ml/ 16 fl oz) water, the milk, and salt and bring to a boil over medium-high heat. Reduce the heat to medium-low and cook, stirring often to prevent a skin from forming, until the bulgur is tender and nearly all of the liquid is absorbed, about 30 minutes. Add the sugar and continue cooking, stirring constantly, until the sugar is fully combined, 3–5 minutes.

Remove from the heat and stir in the honey, cinnamon, and about half of the almonds. Serve warm, spooned into bowls and sprinkled with the remaining almonds.

To serve chilled: Lightly grease an 8-inch (20 cm) square baking dish. Pour in the bulgur mixture, smooth with a spatula, and sprinkle with the remaining almonds. Cover and chill in the refrigerator until cold, at least 2 hours. Slice into squares and transfer to a serving plate.

MALIDA

India's Bene Israel Jews created an edible ceremony in his honor of the prophet Elijah that echoes deity offerings found in Hinduism. At the center is *malida,* a sweetened porridge made from flattened rice called *poha* that gets decorated with fresh and dried fruit, flowers, nuts, and coconut. The *malida* ceremony is held at births, engagements, graduations, or any other auspicious occasion.

Serves: 8
Preparation time: 15 minutes

- 4 cups (400 g) thin poha
- Boiling water
- 1 cup (80 g) unsweetened shredded (desiccated) coconut
- ⅓ cup (60 g) light brown sugar, plus more as needed
- 1 teaspoon ground cinnamon
- ½ teaspoon ground cardamom
- ½ cup (50 g) sliced almonds
- ½ cup (70 g) raisins
- 6 dried dates, pitted and thinly sliced
- Sliced strawberries, bananas, oranges, grapes, and pears, for serving

Place the *poha* in a large heatproof bowl and cover with boiling water. Stir and let sit until the *poha* softens, about 1 minute. Drain in a fine-mesh sieve and return the *poha* to the bowl. Stir in the shredded coconut, sugar, cinnamon, cardamom, almonds, raisins, and dates. Taste and add more brown sugar, if desired.

To serve, spread the mixture on a large serving platter. Arrange desired fruits around and on top of the *poha*.

CARROT HALWA

This creamy, cardamom-scented carrot pudding is widely enjoyed during Diwali, a central Hindu festival celebrated in India. But for Indian Jews, it is also a popular Passover sweet.

Serves: 6–8
Preparation time: 25 minutes
Cooking time: 55 minutes

- 6 tablespoons (85 g) unsalted butter, cut into chunks
- 1 lb (455 g) carrots, grated on the large holes of a box grater
- ¼ teaspoon kosher salt
- 3 cups (710 ml/24 fl oz) milk
- ½ cup (100 g) sugar
- ⅓ cup (45 g) golden raisins (sultanas)
- ½ teaspoon ground cardamom
- ½ teaspoon ground cinnamon, plus more for serving
- Finely chopped pistachios and toasted coconut, for topping

In a medium saucepan, melt the butter over medium heat. Add the carrots and salt and cook, stirring occasionally, until the carrots start to soften, about 5 minutes. Add the milk, increase the heat to medium-high, and bring to a boil. Reduce the heat to medium-low and cook, stirring often, until the carrots are completely soft and the mixture thickens into a pudding, 40–45 minutes.

Stir in the sugar, golden raisins (sultanas), cardamom, and cinnamon and cook, stirring, until the sugar dissolves and the mixture thickens, about 5 minutes. Remove from the heat and let cool to room temperature before serving. Spoon into small bowls and sprinkle with pistachios, toasted coconut, and a little more cinnamon.

COCONUT HALWA

India's Bene Israel community serves this sliceable pudding on Rosh Hashanah. It is traditionally thickened with wheat starch, but when India's Jews immigrated en masse to Israel starting in the mid-twentieth century, cornstarch (cornflour) became a common substitute. Enriched with butter and perfumed with coconut and cardamom, it makes a sweet start to the Jewish New Year.

Serves: 8
Preparation time: 5 minutes, plus chilling
Cooking time: 15 minutes

- 3 cups (710 ml/24 fl oz) milk
- 1 can (13½ oz/383 g) coconut milk
- ¾ cup (150 g) sugar
- ¾ cup (105 g) cornstarch (cornflour)
- ⅛ teaspoon kosher salt
- 4 tablespoons (60 g) unsalted butter, cut into pieces
- ½ teaspoon ground cardamom
- ½ teaspoon ground cinnamon
- ⅓ cup (45 g) roughy chopped pistachios

Grease a 9-inch (23 cm) square baking dish.

In a large saucepan, whisk together the milk, coconut milk, sugar, cornstarch (cornflour), and salt and bring to a simmer over medium heat, whisking constantly to dissolve the cornstarch and break up any lumps, about 10 minutes. Add the butter, cardamom, and cinnamon and continue cooking, whisking vigorously, until the mixture turns very thick, 3–5 minutes.

Immediately pour the mixture into the prepared baking dish. Sprinkle the top evenly with pistachios. Let cool to room temperature, then cover the dish and refrigerate until chilled and set, 2–3 hours. Slice into diamonds or squares and serve. Store leftovers, covered, in the fridge for up to 3 days.

Carrot Halwa

CHILLED APPLES WITH ROSE WATER

For some Persian Jewish families, breaking the Yom Kippur fast begins with *faloodeh sib*—a mixture of chilled grated apples flavored with rose water and sugar. The dish is a holiday-specific variation of a popular Iranian confection, which is made with thin vermicelli noodles instead of apples. Cold, sweet, and fragrant, it also makes a light and refreshing dessert after a summer meal.

Serves: 4–6
Preparation time: 15 minutes, plus chilling

- 3 large apples, peeled and grated on the large holes of a box grater
- 3 tablespoons sugar
- 2 tablespoons rose water
- 1 tablespoon fresh lemon juice

In a large bowl, stir together the apples, sugar, rose water, and lemon juice. Cover and refrigerate until fully chilled, at least 2 hours or up to 1 day.

Just before serving, add 1 cup (240 ml/8 fl oz) chilled water, mix gently, and divide into small bowls. Serve immediately.

ORANGE-SCENTED FLAN

Sephardi Jews make a dairy-free variation of the classic Spanish custard tart. Topped with caramel and brightly flavored with citrus, it is delicious and also completely free of flour, which makes it a great dessert for the Passover seder.

Serves: 8
Preparation time: 15 minutes, plus cooling and chilling
Cooking time: 1 hour

- 2 cups (400 g) sugar
- 5 eggs
- 3 egg yolks
- ¾ cup (175 ml/6 fl oz) unsweetened almond milk
- 2 teaspoons finely grated orange zest
- ¼ cup (60 ml/2 fl oz) fresh orange juice
- 1 teaspoon vanilla extract

Preheat the oven to 350°F (180°C/Gas Mark 4). Have ready an 8-inch (20 cm) round nonstick cake pan.

In a small saucepan, combine 1 cup (200 g) of the sugar and ¼ cup (60 ml/2 fl oz) water and bring to a boil over medium heat without stirring. Continue cooking (do not stir, but swirl the pan once or twice) until the mixture turns a deep golden color, about 10 minutes. (Watch carefully so it does not burn.) Pour the caramel into the cake pan and swirl to coat the bottom. It is okay if the caramel sets at this stage.

In a large bowl, whisk together the whole eggs, egg yolks, and remaining 1 cup (200 g) sugar until fully combined. Add the almond milk, orange zest, orange juice, and vanilla and whisk to combine. Pour the mixture into the pan, on top of the caramel.

Place the cake pan into a larger baking dish and pour hot water into the baking dish until it comes halfway up the sides of the cake pan. Cover the entire baking dish with foil and bake until the custard is just set, 40–50 minutes. Remove pan from the oven (and water bath) and allow the flan to cool, then refrigerate until completely chilled, at least 2 hours. Just before serving, dip the bottom of the cake pan briefly in hot water. Invert onto a serving plate and serve immediately.

Chilled Apples with Rose Water

CONDIMENTS, SPICES & DRINKS

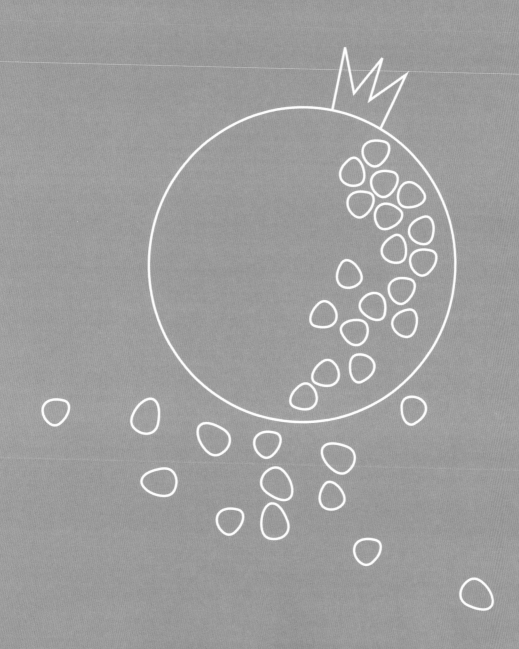

APPLESAUCE

Fried Potato Latkes (page 184) topped with applesauce is a classic Hanukkah pairing in Ashkenazi households. The sweet-tart flavor of the sauce brightens the oil-crisped pancakes. It is no accident that potatoes and apples became central to the winter holiday in Eastern Europe. Both ingredients store well in cold weather, when little other fresh produce was available. This simple version of the Hanukkah condiment is made from unpeeled red baking apples, imparting a rosy blush and velvety texture to the sauce.

Serves: 8
Preparation time: 15 minutes
Cooking time: 20 minutes

• 3 lb (1.35 kg) red baking apples, unpeeled, cored, and cut into eighths
• ½–¾ cup (100–150 g) sugar
• 1½ teaspoons ground cinnamon

In a large pot or saucepan, combine the apples and ⅓ cup (75 ml/2½ fl oz) water. Cover and cook over medium heat, stirring occasionally, until the apples are very soft, 15–20 minutes. Remove from the heat and let cool about 5 minutes. If there is excess liquid in the pot, pour off all but a tablespoon or two.

Transfer the cooked apples to a food processor and process, scraping down the sides of the bowl as necessary, until smooth. Transfer the applesauce to a large bowl and stir in ½ cup (100 g) sugar and the cinnamon while it is still warm. Taste and, if desired, stir in up to an additional ¼ cup (50 g) sugar. Serve immediately or store, covered, in the fridge for up to to 5 days, or in the freezer for up to 3 months.

STRAWBERRY SAUCE

Blintzes (pages 30 and 32), Cheesecake (page 333), Cinnamon-Walnut Sponge Cake (page 316), and yogurt or ice cream all benefit from a hearty dollop of this vibrantly red, sweet-tart sauce.

Serves: 6
Preparation time: 5 minutes, plus cooling
Cooking time: 10 minutes

• 2 cups (260 g) hulled and quartered strawberries
• ½ cup (100 g) sugar
• ⅛ teaspoon kosher salt
• ½ teaspoon finely grated lemon zest
• 1 tablespoon fresh lemon juice
• 2 teaspoons cornstarch (cornflour)

In a medium saucepan, combine the strawberries, sugar, and salt. In a small bowl, whisk together the lemon zest, lemon juice, and cornstarch (cornflour) until the cornstarch dissolves. Stir the cornstarch mixture into the strawberry mixture.

Set the pan over medium-low heat, bring to a simmer, and cook, stirring occasionally, until the berries release their juices and the mixture thickens slightly, 8–10 minutes. If desired, mash the berries a little with a potato masher during cooking. Remove from the heat and set aside to cool completely, then refrigerate until needed, or up to 5 days.

BLUEBERRY SAUCE

This simple sauce, made from either fresh or frozen blueberries, makes a bright, fruit-forward topping for Cheese Blintzes (page 30), Cheesecake (page 333), or Cinnamon-Walnut Sponge Cake (page 316). It is also delicious spooned into yogurt or ice cream, and can be used to fill Blueberry Buns (page 37).

Serves: 6
Preparation time: 5 minutes, plus cooling
Cooking time: 10 minutes

- 2 cups (280 g) fresh or thawed frozen blueberries
- ½ cup (100 g) sugar
- ⅛ teaspoon kosher salt
- ½ teaspoon finely grated lemon zest
- 1 tablespoon fresh lemon juice
- 1 teaspoon cornstarch (cornflour)

In a medium saucepan, combine the blueberries, sugar, and salt. In a small bowl, whisk together the lemon zest, lemon juice, and cornstarch (cornflour) until the cornstarch dissolves. Stir the cornstarch mixture into the blueberry mixture.

Set the pan over medium-low heat, bring to a simmer, and cook, stirring often, until the berries release their juices and the mixture thickens slightly, about 10 minutes. Remove from the heat and set aside to cool completely, then refrigerate until needed, or up to 5 days.

POPPY SEED FILLING

This sweet pastry filling is called *mohn* after the Yiddish word for poppy seeds. In Ashkenazi cuisine, *mohn* refers specifically to the nutty, blue-black confection. Try spooning it into Hamantaschen (pages 340–343) on Purim, or spread it into the decadent, trilayered Hungarian dessert, Flódni (page 358).

Makes: about 1½ cups (435 g)
Preparation time: 10 minutes
Cooking time: 15 minutes

- 1 cup (140 g) poppy seeds
- 1 cup (240 ml/8 fl oz) milk or almond milk
- ½ cup (100 g) sugar
- ⅓ cup (60 g) finely chopped dried apricots
- 1 tablespoon orange juice
- ½ teaspoon finely grated lemon zest
- 1 tablespoon fresh lemon juice
- 1 tablespoon (15 g) unsalted butter or vegetable oil
- 1½ teaspoons vanilla extract

Grind the poppy seeds in a spice or coffee grinder, working in batches if necessary, until powdery, 15–20 seconds. In a small saucepan, combine the ground poppy seeds, milk, sugar, and apricots and bring to a simmer over medium heat. Reduce the heat to low and cook, stirring frequently, until the mixture thickens and nearly all of the liquid is absorbed, 7–10 minutes.

Stir in the orange juice, lemon zest, lemon juice, butter, and vanilla and continue cooking until absorbed and the mixture is very thick, 3–5 minutes. Remove the pan from the heat and let cool completely. It will continue to thicken as it cools. Store, covered, in the fridge for up to 2 weeks. Let the mixture come back to room temperature before using.

TAHINI SAUCE

This bright and creamy sauce, which is made from ground sesame seed paste and flavored with lemon juice and garlic, is among the most popular condiments in the Middle East, including in Israel. A dollop of tahini sauce can enliven all sorts of savory dishes from roasted vegetables to grilled meat or fish, but is most commonly used as a topping for pita-based sandwiches such as Falafel (page 194), Sabich (page 259), and Jerusalem Mixed Grill (page 288).

Serves: 6–8
Preparation time: 10 minutes

- 4 garlic cloves, peeled
- ¼ cup (60 ml/2 fl oz) fresh lemon juice
- ¾ teaspoon kosher salt
- ¾ cup (180 g) tahini

In a food processor, combine the garlic, lemon juice, and salt and process until the garlic is minced. Add the tahini and process to combine. With the motor running, slowly drizzle in ½–1 cup (120–240 ml/4–8 fl oz) warm water, as needed, to achieve a smooth sauce. Transfer to an airtight container and store, covered, in the fridge for up to 2 days. Bring to room temperature before serving.

TZATZIKI

Yogurt and cucumber sauces are popular throughout Greece, Turkey, Lebanon, Armenia, and Iran, among other places. Sephardi Jews traditionally use it as a sauce for Fried Eggplant Slices (page 108) or fish, or serve it as a dip with pita. It can also be thinned with ice cold water and eaten as a chilled soup.

Serves: 6–8
Preparation time: 20 minutes, plus chilling

- 1½ cups (300 g) Greek yogurt
- ½ cup (100 g) sour cream
- 2 tablespoons extra-virgin olive oil, plus more for drizzling
- ¼ teaspoon grated lemon zest
- 1 tablespoon fresh lemon juice
- 1 teaspoon apple cider vinegar
- 1 large garlic clove, minced or pushed through a press
- 2 teaspoons dried dill
- 1 tablespoon finely chopped fresh mint leaves
- ½ teaspoon kosher salt, plus more as needed
- Freshly ground black pepper
- 5 Persian (mini) cucumbers or Kirby (pickling) cucumbers (about ¾ lb/340 g), peeled and grated on the large holes of a box grater

In a medium bowl, stir together the yogurt, sour cream, oil, lemon zest, lemon juice, vinegar, garlic, dried dill, fresh mint, salt, and a generous amount of pepper.

Place the grated cucumbers in the center of a clean tea towel and squeeze out as much liquid as possible. Fold the cucumbers into the yogurt mixture. Cover and refrigerate for at least 1 hour (or overnight) to let flavors meld. Before serving, taste and add a little more salt if desired. Serve chilled, drizzled with more oil.

ALON SHAYA

SABA
•
5757 MAGAZINE STREET
NEW ORLEANS, LA
USA

SAFTA
•
3330 BRIGHTON
BOULEVARD
DENVER, CO
USA

Alon Shaya is a James Beard Award–winning chef who was born in Israel, raised in Philadelphia, and now lives in New Orleans. He was formerly the executive chef and partner of three celebrated restaurants: Domenica, Pizza Domenica, and Shaya in New Orleans. In 2017, he founded Pomegranate Hospitality and currently helms two inventive Middle Eastern eateries: Saba, in New Orleans, and Safta, in Denver.

ROSE TAHINI

Shaya's rose tahini, which is sweet and intricately spiced, is delicious drizzled on toasted challah (he adds a slab of foie gras as well) or spooned over pancakes.

Serves: 6–8
Preparation time: 15 minutes, plus cooling
Cooking time: 10 minutes

• 6 dried rosebuds (about 1 heaping tablespoon)
• 6 allspice berries
• 3 cardamom pods
• 1 teaspoon pink peppercorns
• 1 teaspoon coriander seeds
• ¼ teaspoon grated dried Persian lime
• ⅛ teaspoon caraway seeds
• ¾ cup (150 g) sugar
• ½ teaspoon kosher salt
• ½ teaspoon rose water
• ¾ cup (180 g) tahini

With a mortar and pestle, lightly crush the rosebuds, allspice, cardamom, pink peppercorns, coriander, dried lime, and caraway seeds. Add the ground spices to a small saucepan along with 1 cup (240 ml/8 fl oz) water, the sugar, salt, and rose water and bring to a boil over high heat. Cook for 2 minutes, stirring often, until the mixture thickens slightly. Remove from the heat and let the syrup cool completely, then strain through a fine-mesh sieve. (Discard any solids.)

Add the syrup and the tahini to a large bowl and whisk well to combine. Use immediately or store, covered, in the fridge for up to 1 week.

✱ STAR RECIPE

CHERMOULA

Moroccan, Tunisian, Algerian, and Libyan home cooks typically use this simple, vibrant sauce made of herbs, spices, and chilies to dress up roasted fish—but it is equally delicious paired with chicken, steak, and vegetable dishes. Change up the flavor by swapping out half of the parsley for equal parts fresh cilantro (coriander).

Serves: 6
Preparation time: 10 minutes
Cooking time: 5 minutes

- 1½ teaspoons cumin seeds
- 1 teaspoon coriander seeds
- 4 cups (120 g) packed fresh parsley, tough bottom stems removed
- 2 medium garlic cloves, roughly chopped
- 1 tablespoon finely chopped peel and 1 tablespoon brine (plus more as needed) from Preserved Lemons (page 116)
- 1 teaspoon sweet paprika
- ¼ teaspoon cayenne pepper
- ¼ teaspoon kosher salt
- ½ cup (120 ml/4 fl oz) extra-virgin olive oil

In a small dry frying pan, toast the cumin seeds and coriander seeds over medium heat, shaking the pan occasionally, until they smell fragrant, 2–3 minutes. Remove from the heat and let cool.

Add the cooled seeds to a food processor and pulse until coarsely ground. Add the parsley, garlic, preserved lemon peel and brine, paprika, cayenne, and salt and pulse, scraping down the bowl as necessary, until finely chopped.

With the motor running, drizzle in the oil until smooth. Taste, and if a more acidic flavor is desired, add another drizzle of preserved lemon brine. Use immediately, or store in an airtight container in the fridge for up to 1 week.

CHRAIN

This ruby-colored, spicy-sweet horseradish relish is most often dolloped onto Gefilte Fish (page 114), but also tastes great on roast chicken or meat. The sweetness and vinegar levels can be adjusted to taste.

Serves: 6–8
Preparation time: 15 minutes
Cooking time: 45 minutes

- 2 medium beets, scrubbed and tops trimmed off
- 4-inch (10 cm) piece fresh horseradish root, peeled and roughly chopped
- 2 tablespoons apple cider vinegar or red wine vinegar
- 1 teaspoon kosher salt, plus more as needed
- 1½ teaspoons sugar or honey

In a large saucepan, combine the beets and water to cover by 2 inches (5 cm). Bring to a boil over high heat and cook until beets are fully tender, 30–45 minutes. Drain the beets and set aside until cool enough to touch, then peel and coarsely chop.

In a food processor, pulse the horseradish until finely ground. Add the cooked beets, vinegar, salt, and sugar and pulse, scraping down the sides of the bowl as necessary, until a textured paste forms. Taste and add more salt, if desired. Transfer to an airtight container and store in the fridge for up to 1 week.

Chermoula

HONEY-WALNUT FILLING

Romanian Jews fill hamantaschen (pages 340–343) with a mixture of honey and walnuts. The nuts are cooked in the honey until caramelized, then pieces of the sticky confection are pinched off and rolled into small balls that get tucked into the tricornered Purim cookie. A bit of lemon zest brightens up the filling's rich honey flavor.

Makes: about 1½ cups (375 g)
Preparation time: 5 minutes, plus cooling
Cooking time: 5 minutes

- 1½ cups (155 g) walnut halves, chopped
- ½ cup (170 g) honey
- ¼ cup (50 g) sugar
- ½ teaspoon kosher salt
- ½ teaspoon finely grated lemon zest

In a medium saucepan, combine the walnuts, honey, sugar, ½ cup (120 ml/4 fl oz) water, and the salt and bring to a boil over high heat. Reduce the heat to medium and cook, stirring often, until the honey thickens and turns golden brown, about 5 minutes.

Remove from the heat and stir in the lemon zest. Let cool to the touch, stirring occasionally. If desired, transfer to a container and store covered in the fridge, for up to 1 week. Let the mixture come back to room temperature before using.

BEET EINGEMACHT

Eingemacht is a German and Yiddish word for fruit or vegetable preserves cooked with sugar. Beet *eingemacht* was traditionally served on Passover because very little fresh produce was available in Eastern Europe in early spring. Instead, home cooks turned to the cellar, finding ways to enliven whatever storage crops were left over from fall. The sweet-vegetal taste is a bit unusual to modern tastebuds, but delicious. Spread it on matzo or serve it as part of a cheese plate.

Serves: 8
Preparation time: 20 minutes
Cooking time: 30 minutes

- 2 lb (910 g) beets, peeled and grated on the large holes of a box grater
- 1½ cups (300 g) sugar
- Grated zest of 1 lemon
- 3 tablespoons fresh lemon juice
- 1 tablespoon grated fresh ginger
- ¼ teaspoon kosher salt
- ¾ cup (105 g) whole almonds, chopped

In a large saucepan, stir together the beets, sugar, lemon zest, lemon juice, ginger, and salt. Bring to a boil over medium-high heat, then reduce the heat to medium and cook, stirring often and being careful not to burn, until the beets are very tender and the liquid has evaporated, 20–30 minutes.

Remove from the heat and let cool slightly. Using a hand blender, blend the mixture a couple of times until a chunky jam forms. (It should be textured, not fully smooth.) Stir in the almonds and allow the mixture to cool in the pan (it will continue to thicken as it cools), then transfer to a large glass jar or other airtight container, cover, and store in the fridge for up to 2 weeks.

APPLE MURABBA

Calcutta's Jewish community serves apples cooked in a rose water–perfumed syrup on Rosh Hashanah. The fragrant confiture evokes wishes for a sweet year ahead. Start with sweet-tart apples that hold their shape well during cooking.

Serves: 6
Preparation time: 10 minutes, plus cooling
Cooking time: 15 minutes

• 1 cup (200 g) sugar
• 6 medium apples, peeled, cored, and halved or quartered
• 1 teaspoon whole cloves
• 1 cinnamon stick
• 2 teaspoons fresh lemon juice
• 1 teaspoon rose water

In a medium saucepan, combine ¾ cup (175 ml/6 fl oz) water and the sugar and cook over medium heat, stirring occasionally, until the sugar dissolves, about 2 minutes. Add the apples, cloves, and the cinnamon stick. Increase the heat to medium-high and bring to a boil. Reduce the heat to low, cover, and cook until the apples are soft but still mostly retain their shape, 10–15 minutes.

Remove the pan from the heat and stir in the lemon juice and rose water. Let cool to room temperature (the mixture will sweeten as it cools), then remove and discard the cloves and cinnamon stick. Store, covered, in the fridge, for up to 2 weeks. Serve cold or at room temperature.

PUMPKIN JAM

Sephardi Jews in Iraq, Tunisia, and elsewhere serve this autumnal preserve, called *m'rabah ab kra*, on Rosh Hashanah when eating foods made from pumpkin or squash hold symbolic meaning (see page 248). Spoon the vibrant orange jam over yogurt or spread it on Challah (page 46).

Makes: about 1½ cups (500 g)
Preparation time: 20 minutes
Cooking time: 45 minutes

• 1½ lb (680 g) baking pumpkin or butternut squash, peeled, seeded, and cut into 1-inch (2.5 cm) pieces
• 1½ cups (300 g) sugar
• ⅛ teaspoon kosher salt
• ½ teaspoon ground cinnamon
• 1 tablespoon fresh lemon juice
• 2 teaspoons rose water or orange blossom water (optional)

In a medium saucepan, stir together the pumpkin, sugar, 2 tablespoons water, and the salt. Bring to a boil over medium heat, stirring occasionally, then reduce the heat to medium-low and cook, stirring often (almost constantly near the end to avoid burning) until the mixture is thick and jammy with some visible pieces of pumpkin remaining, 35–45 minutes.

Remove the pan from the heat and stir in the cinnamon, lemon juice, and rose water (if using). Allow to cool, then transfer to an airtight container and store in the fridge for up to 1 month.

CANDIED EGGPLANT

Syrian and Moroccan Jews serve these sweet preserved eggplants (aubergines) as a dessert, sometimes stuffed with nuts. But they are also delicious used as a condiment on top of grilled or roasted meat dishes and would make a magnificent addition to a cheese plate. Start with a miniature variety of eggplants.

Serves: 6
Preparation time: 5 minutes, plus cooling
Cooking time: 1 hour

- 15 miniature eggplants (aubergines), 2–3 inches (5–7.5 cm) long, pricked in a few places with a fork
- 3 cups (600 g) sugar
- 1½ teaspoons whole cloves
- 2 cinnamon sticks
- ¼ cup (60 ml/2 fl oz) fresh lemon juice

Bring a large saucepan filled with water to a boil over high heat. Add the eggplants (aubergines) and cook until slightly softened, about 5 minutes. Drain the eggplants in a colander and let cool to the touch. When cool, give each eggplant a gentle squeeze to push out some of the water inside.

Meanwhile, in the same saucepan, combine the sugar, 1 cup (240 ml/8 fl oz) water, cloves, and cinnamon sticks and bring to a low boil over medium heat, stirring to dissolve the sugar. Reduce the heat to low and cook, stirring often, until the mixture thickens into a rich syrup, 15–20 minutes.

Add the eggplants and lemon juice, reduce the heat to medium-low, and cook, stirring occasionally, until the eggplants are very soft, 35–40 minutes. Remove from the heat and let stand until cool. Transfer the eggplants and any syrup to a glass jar. Store, covered, in the fridge for up to 2 weeks.

CANDIED QUINCE

Quinces are prized across Sephardi and Mizrahi cuisines, showing up in meaty stews and braises (like Chicken and Quince Tagine, page 269), and poached or stewed into compote. Since quince comes into season in the fall, it is commonly served on Rosh Hashanah and Sukkot, as well as at Shabbat meals throughout autumn. These candied quinces are tender and fragrant—a perfect addition to a cheese plate or spooned over ice cream or yogurt. To make a quick, spreadable quince jam, mash the candied fruits with a potato masher or purée them in the food processor with a tablespoon of their cooking liquid.

Serves: 4–6
Preparation time: 15 minutes, plus cooling
Cooking time: 45 minutes

- 2 quinces
- 1½ cups (300 g) sugar
- 1 tablespoon fresh lemon juice

Rinse and dry the quinces. Peel and quarter them, removing the cores and seeds, and then slice each quarter into three pieces. Wrap the peels, cores, and seeds in cheesecloth and tie with kitchen twine.

In a heavy-bottomed medium saucepan, combine the sugar, quince slices, cheesecloth bundle, and 2 cups (475 ml/16 fl oz) water. Bring to a simmer over medium heat, then reduce the heat to medium-low, cover, and cook, gently stirring once or twice, until the quinces soften, about 20 minutes.

Uncover and continue cooking until the syrup thickens, about 25 minutes. Stir in the lemon juice and continue cooking for another minute. Remove the pan from the heat and let the quinces cool to room temperature—they will turn deep golden as they cool. Discard the cheesecloth bundle and transfer the quinces and syrup to a covered container. Store in the refrigerator for up to 2 weeks.

Candied Eggplant

ASHKENAZI CHAROSET

Charoset is a core part of the Passover seder plate—a chunky fruit relish or spread meant to symbolize the mortar used by Israelites while enslaved as builders in ancient Egypt. Ashkenazi versions of charoset tend to be chopped apples mixed with walnuts, cinnamon, and a drizzle of sweet red wine. In this version, honey and fresh orange juice add extra depth of flavor.

Serves: 8
Preparation time: 25 minutes

- 2 cups (210 g) walnut halves
- 4 large apples (about 2 lb/910 g), peeled, cored, and finely chopped
- 2½ teaspoons ground cinnamon
- 2 tablespoons fresh orange juice
- 2 tablespoons honey, plus more as needed
- ¼ cup (60 ml/2 fl oz) sweet red wine, plus more as needed

In a small dry frying pan, toast the walnuts over medium-low heat, stirring occasionally, until fragrant and lightly browned, about 5 minutes. Remove the pan from the heat and let cool, then finely chop with a knife or pulse in a food processor.

In a large bowl, combine the walnuts, apples, cinnamon, orange juice, and honey. Stir in the wine. Taste and add a little more wine and honey, about 1 teaspoon at a time, until the desired flavor is reached. Cover and refrigerate until ready to serve.

GREEK CHAROSET

Greek charoset often contains dried currants, a sweet-tart addition that sets it apart from other versions. For an extra hint of flavor, add a small pinch of cloves.

Serves: 8
Preparation time: 10 minutes

- 1 cup (140 g) dried currants
- 1 cup (140 g) raisins
- 1 cup (140 g) dates, pitted and roughly chopped
- 1 cup (140 g) blanched almonds
- ½ teaspoon ground cinnamon
- ½ cup (120 ml/4 fl oz) sweet red wine or grape juice, plus more as needed

In a food processor, combine the currants, raisins, dates, almonds, cinnamon, and wine and pulse, scraping down the sides as necessary, until a thick, textured paste forms. If needed, drizzle in a little more wine, pulsing until the desired consistency is reached. Store, covered, in the fridge, for up to 1 week.

KURDISH CHAROSET

Kurdish charoset, called *halich*, tends to be quite thick and is often served rolled into small balls.

Serves: 8
Preparation time: 20 minutes

- 1 cup (90 g) walnut halves
- 1 cup (130 g) unsalted roasted hazelnuts
- ½ cup (70 g) unsalted roasted almonds
- ½ cup (65 g) pistachios
- 1 cup (140 g) golden raisins (sultanas)
- 1 cup (140 g) raisins
- 5 large dates, pitted and roughly chopped
- 2 teaspoons ground cinnamon
- ½ teaspoon ground cardamom
- ½ teaspoon ground ginger
- ¼ teaspoon kosher salt
- 2–3 tablespoons dry or sweet red wine

In a food processor, combine the currants, raisins, dates, almonds, cinnamon, and wine and pulse, scraping down the sides as necessary, until a thick, textured paste forms. If needed, drizzle in a little more wine, pulsing until the desired consistency is reached. Store, covered, in the fridge, for up to 1 week.

Ashkenazi Charoset (top), Greek Charoset (middle), and Kurdish Charoset (bottom)

ITALIAN CHAROSET

There are multiple versions of Italian charoset, but most include roasted chestnuts—an addition that gives the sweet spread a distinctly earthy flavor.

Serves: 8
Preparation time: 15 minutes
Cooking time: 15 minutes

• ¾ cup (110 g) roasted, peeled chestnuts, finely chopped
• 2 large apples, peeled and finely chopped
• 1 cup (170 g) Medjool dates, pitted and roughly chopped
• 1 cup (140 g) golden raisins (sultanas)
• 1 cup (240 ml/8 fl oz) sweet red wine or grape juice
• ¼ cup (60 ml/2 fl oz) orange juice
• ½ teaspoon ground cinnamon
• ½ cup (50 g) walnuts, finely chopped
• 1–2 tablespoons honey (optional)

In a medium saucepan, combine the chestnuts, apples, dates, raisins, wine, orange juice, and cinnamon and bring to a boil over medium-high heat. Reduce the heat to low, cover, and simmer, stirring occasionally, until the fruit is very tender and most of the liquid has evaporated, about 15 minutes. If the mixture still looks wet, uncover and continue simmering for another 5 minutes. Remove from the heat and let cool.

Transfer to a serving bowl and stir in the walnuts. Taste and, if desired, add 1–2 tablespoons honey to sweeten. Cover and refrigerate until needed, or up to 3 days. Allow mixture to come to room temperature before serving.

INDIAN CHAROSET

Calcutta's traditional charoset, a Middle Eastern transplant called *halek*, is a delicious mix of date syrup and walnuts. It is more time consuming to make than other charosets, but the combination of sticky-sweet flavor and silky-meets-crunchy texture is entirely worth it. A little *halek* spooned over matzo goes a long way, and the syrup is also wonderful drizzled over ice cream or cake. For a quicker version, high-quality bottled date syrup (often called *silan*) is available at many Middle Eastern and international food stores, and online.

Serves: 6
Preparation time: 10 minutes, plus cooling
Cooking time: 40 minutes

• 1 lb (455 g) Medjool dates, pitted and roughly chopped
• ⅓ cup (30 g) walnut halves, roughly chopped

In a medium saucepan combine the dates and 5 cups (1.2 liters/40 fl oz) water and bring to a boil over high heat. Reduce the heat to medium and cook for 5 minutes. Remove from the heat and let the mixture cool completely.

Set a fine-mesh sieve over a large bowl. Pour in the date mixture, pressing down on the softened dates with a spatula to press through as much liquid as possible into the bowl. (Discard the date pulp, or reserve for another use.)

Pour the date liquid into a small saucepan and bring to a boil over high heat. Reduce the heat to medium and cook until it reduces into a syrup slightly thicker than maple syrup, 20–30 minutes. (Do not overcook; it will continue to thicken as it cools.) Remove from the heat and let cool completely.

To serve, stir the walnuts into the mixture and transfer to a serving bowl. Store leftovers covered in the refrigerator for up to 1 month.

THE WORLD OF CHAROSET

One of the central components of the Passover seder plate is charoset—a mix of finely chopped fruit, nuts, and sweet wine (sometimes cooked, other times raw) that is meant to resemble the mud and mortar used by the Israelites to build structures when they were enslaved in ancient Egypt. Like everything on the seder plate, charoset serves as both an edible reminder of a painful memory, and as a form of symbolic redemption from it.

Jews across the world eat charoset (sometimes called *halek* or *halich*) on Passover, but the dish is far from uniform. Instead, different communities incorporate local ingredients that give the dish distinctly regional identities. The traditional Ashkenazi Charoset (page 404) combines apples, walnuts, and cinnamon and is bound by sweet wine. Italian Charoset (page 406) often includes roasted chestnuts, while Greek Charoset (page 404) often features dried currants. Sesame seeds are commonly included in Yemenite Charoset (below), while Indian Charoset (page 406) simply mixes date syrup and chopped walnuts.

The different charosets in this cookbook are just a sampling of many dozens of global recipes. But together, they give a good representation of the dish's diversity.

YEMENITE CHAROSET

Yemenite charoset's use of dried figs and dates is typical for the region. But this charoset is set apart by the addition of sesame seeds and unexpected spices like coriander and black pepper. It is definitely worth trying, either for the Passover seder, or as a companion for cheese throughout the year.

Serves: 6
Preparation time: 15 minutes

- ½ cup (50 g) walnut halves
- ¼ cup (35 g) sesame seeds
- ½ cup (70 g) raisins
- 8 large dates, pitted and chopped
- 6 large dried figs, stems removed, chopped
- 1 medium red apple, unpeeled and chopped
- 1½ teaspoons ground ginger
- ½ teaspoon ground cardamom
- ½ teaspoon ground cinnamon
- ¼ teaspoon ground coriander
- ⅛ teaspoon freshly ground black pepper
- ¼ cup (60 ml/2 fl oz) sweet red wine

In a small dry frying pan, toast the walnuts and sesame seeds over medium-low heat, shaking the pan occasionally, until fragrant and lightly browned, about 5 minutes. Remove the pan from the heat and let cool.

Transfer the toasted walnuts and sesame seeds to a food processor and add the raisins, dates, figs, apple, ginger, cardamom, cinnamon, coriander, pepper, and wine. Process, scraping down the sides of the bowl as necessary, until a spreadable paste forms. Transfer to a serving dish, cover, and refrigerate until needed, or up to 2 days.

CONDIMENTS, SPICES & DRINKS

PRUNE LEKVAR

Hamantaschen (page 340–343), Flódni (page 358), and a wide variety of other baked goods across Central and Eastern Europe are traditionally filled with *lekvar*—a thick fruit butter made from prunes, apricots, peaches, and other jammy fruits. *Lekvar* is also delicious spread on dark bread or spooned over yogurt.

Makes: 1½ cups (435 g)
Preparation time: 10 minutes
Cooking time: 30 minutes

• 2 cups (300 g) pitted prunes
• ½ cup (120 ml/4 fl oz) apple juice
• 4 tablespoons sugar
• ⅛ teaspoon kosher salt
• 1 tablespoon honey
• ½ teaspoon ground cinnamon

In a small saucepan, stir together the prunes, ¾ cup (175 ml/6 fl oz) water, the apple juice, sugar, and salt. Bring to a low boil over medium-high heat, then reduce the heat to medium-low, cover, and cook, stirring occasionally, until the prunes are very soft and most of the liquid is absorbed, 25–30 minutes.

Remove the pan from the heat, and use a hand blender to blend the fruit into a chunky puree. (Or, transfer to a food processor and process until the desired consistency is reached.) Transfer to a bowl and stir in the honey and cinnamon until fully combined. Let cool completely then store, covered, in the fridge.

APRICOT LEKVAR

Aside from prunes, sweet-tart apricots are the most common fruit used to make this jammy Central and Eastern European fruit butter.

Makes: about 1¼ cups (400 g)
Preparation time: 10 minutes
Cooking time: 30 minutes

• 1½ cups (270 g) dried apricots, roughly chopped
• ⅓ cup (65 g) sugar
• 1 teaspoon grated orange zest
• 1 tablespoon fresh orange juice
• Kosher salt

In a small saucepan, stir together the apricots, 1 cup (240 ml/8 fl oz) water, the sugar, orange zest, orange juice, and a pinch of salt. Bring to a boil over medium-high heat, then reduce the heat to medium-low, cover, and cook, stirring occasionally, until fruit is very soft and nearly all of the liquid has absorbed, 25–30 minutes.

Remove the pan from the heat and use a hand blender to blend the fruit into a chunky puree. (Or, transfer to a food processor and process until the desired consistency is reached.) Let cool completely then store, covered, in the fridge for up to 2 weeks.

HARISSA

This popular North African condiment blends dried chilies, spices, and olive oil into a fiery, richly flavored paste. Harissa is used to flavor tagines, couscous dishes, salads, and stews, and is dolloped over pita sandwiches like Sabich (page 259). Other varieties of chilies like chipotle and pasilla can also be used.

Makes: about 1 cup (150 g)
Preparation time: 35 minutes, plus soaking

- 1½ oz ancho peppers
- 1½ oz guajillo peppers
- Boiling water
- 3 garlic cloves, roughly chopped
- ¾ teaspoon ground cumin
- ½ teaspoon crushed pepper flakes
- ½ teaspoon ground coriander
- ½ teaspoon dried mint
- 1½ teaspoons kosher salt, plus more as needed
- 1½ tablespoons apple cider vinegar, plus more as needed
- ½ cup (120 ml/4 fl oz) extra-virgin olive oil

In a heatproof bowl, combine the ancho and guajillo peppers with boiling water to cover. Cover the bowl and let peppers steep for 1 hour. Drain well then, using gloved hands, remove and discard the peppers' stems and seeds.

Place the peppers in a food processor along with the garlic, cumin, pepper flakes, coriander, mint, salt, and vinegar. Pulse, scraping down the sides of the bowl as necessary, until a chunky paste forms. With the motor running, slowly drizzle in the oil and pulse until the mixture smoothens out.

Place a fine-mesh sieve over a large bowl and add the harissa mixture. Using a rubber spatula, press it through the sieve. Discard the solids and transfer the smooth harissa to a glass jar. Cover and store in the fridge for up to 2 weeks.

HILBEH

When soaked overnight in water, fragrant fenugreek seeds swell considerably in size and take on a gelatinous consistency. Blended with lemon juice, tomato, and the fiery chili paste *s'chug*, they create a piquant relish that Yemenite Jews serve with nearly everything. The Jews of Calcutta (many of whom have Middle Eastern roots) brought their beloved condiment with them to India, adding in local ingredients like fresh cilantro (coriander) leaves and ginger. To try this variation, called *hulba*, add ½ cup (10 g) cilantro (coriander) leaves and 1 tablespoon finely grated fresh ginger with the lemon and tomato before blending.

Makes: about 1½ cups (315 g)
Preparation time: 15 minutes, plus soaking

- 3 tablespoons fenugreek seeds
- 1 large plum tomato, roughly chopped
- 2 garlic cloves, roughly chopped
- 2 tablespoons fresh lemon juice, plus more as needed
- 1 teaspoon S'chug (page 411)
- ¼ teaspoon ground cumin
- ½ teaspoon kosher salt, plus more as needed

In a medium bowl, combine the fenugreek seeds with water to cover by about 2 inches (5 cm). Cover the bowl with a tea towel and let soak at least 8 hours, or overnight.

Drain the soaked fenugreek seeds and transfer to a food processor. Pulse until a gelatinous paste forms. Add the tomato, garlic, lemon juice, *s'chug*, cumin, and salt and pulse until a thick paste the consistency of mayonnaise forms. Taste and add more lemon juice and salt, if desired. Store, covered, in the fridge, for up to 1 week.

CONDIMENTS, SPICES & DRINKS

SCHMALTZ AND GRIBENES

Rendered poultry fat is used in many Ashkenazi dishes from Matzo Balls (page 220) to Chopped Chicken Liver (page 94). In Eastern and Central Europe, Jews translated their neighbors' practice of frying foods in lard, finding a kosher-friendly substitute in goose and chicken fat. The cracklings (*gribenes*) left in the pan after the fat renders make a delicious treat for the cook.

Makes: ½ cup (120 g) schmaltz
Preparation time: 30 minutes
Cooking time: 35 minutes

- 1 lb (455 g) chicken fat and skin, rinsed and patted dry
- ½ teaspoon kosher salt, plus more as needed
- 1 large onion, halved and thinly sliced

Using a very sharp knife or a pair of scissors, cut the chicken fat and skin into ¼-inch (6 mm) pieces. Place the fat and skin in a large nonstick frying pan set over medium-low heat and sprinkle with 1 teaspoon water and the salt. Cook, uncovered, and stirring often, until the fat melts and pools at the bottom of the pan and the skin darkens and begins to curl up at the edges, 20–30 minutes. Add the onion slices and cook for 5 minutes. Remove the pan from the heat and strain the fat through a fine-mesh sieve into a glass jar. (For *gribenes*, see below, reserve the skin and onion slices.) Let the schmaltz cool completely then cover and refrigerate or freeze.

To make the *gribenes*: Return the skin and onion to the frying pan and season with additional salt. Set the pan over medium heat and continue cooking, stirring often, until the skin and onions are deeply browned and crispy, 15–25 minutes. (Watch carefully so they do not burn.) Transfer the *gribenes* to paper towels to drain and serve immediately.

POMEGRANATE MOLASSES

When pomegranate juice gets boiled down, it turns into a thick, concentrated syrup that is widely used throughout Middle Eastern cooking. Bottles of store-bought pomegranate molasses (sometimes called pomegranate syrup) are available in specialty food stores and online, but it is also simple to make at home. The addition of sugar helps to thicken the juice quickly and evenly, while the lemon juice helps balance the sweet-tart flavor.

Makes: about 1 cup (240 ml/8 fl oz)
Preparation time: 5 minutes, plus cooling
Cooking time: 1½ hours

- 4 cups (950 ml/32 fl oz) unsweetened pomegranate juice (not from concentrate)
- ½ cup (100 g) sugar
- 2 tablespoons fresh lemon juice

In a small saucepan, stir together the pomegranate juice, sugar, and lemon juice and bring to a boil over medium heat. Reduce the heat to medium-low and cook, stirring often, until the juice thickens into a syrup that lightly coats the back of a spoon, 1 hour 10 minutes to 1 hour 20 minutes. (Don't overcook, as it will continue to thicken as it cools.)

Remove the pan from the heat and let the syrup cool for 20 minutes. Pour into an airtight glass container and store in the fridge until needed, up to 3 months.

GRATED TOMATO RELISH

This fresh tomato relish is traditionally served as a condiment for Yemenite breads like Malawach (page 18), Kubaneh (page 48), and Jachnun (page 41). The bright combination of tomato and salt perfectly complements the pastries' richness. It also tastes wonderful with the overnight eggs, Huevos Haminados (page 16). *S'chug*, the fiery cilantro (coriander) and chili paste, is sometimes served separately from the tomato dip, but it can also be mixed directly into it, as here, for a touch of tingling heat.

Serves: 6–8
Preparation time: 5 minutes

• 1 lb (455 g) ripe plum tomatoes, washed and dried
• 1 small garlic clove, grated or pushed through a press
• ½ teaspoon kosher salt, plus more as needed
• ¼ teaspoon S'chug (below), plus more as needed

Grate the tomatoes on the large holes of a box grater and transfer the pulp to a medium bowl (discard the skin). Stir in the garlic, salt, and *s'chug*. Taste and adjust seasonings as desired.

S'CHUG

This fresh and fiery relish, which is made from a mix of hot chili peppers, garlic, and cilantro (coriander), is arguably the most defining flavor of Yemenite cuisine. It is dolloped into meaty stews like *marak temani* (Beef and Cilantro Soup, page 140), and spooned over Jachnun (page 41), Malawach (page 48), and other Yemenite breads and pastries. And a bowl of *s'chug* is a permanent fixture on most Yemenite tables. This version is already rather spicy, but true heat seekers can leave the seeds in one or more of the peppers.

Serves: 6–8
Preparation time: 10 minutes

• ½ teaspoon cumin seeds
• ¼ teaspoon ground cardamom
• 4 garlic cloves, roughly chopped
• 3 fresh jalapeños, seeded and roughly chopped
• 3 dried chiles de árbol, seeded and roughly chopped
• 2 cups (60 g) packed fresh cilantro (coriander) leaves (stems okay)
• ¾ teaspoon kosher salt, plus more as needed
• ½ cup (120 ml/4 fl oz) extra-virgin olive oil

In a food processor, combine the cumin seeds, cardamom, garlic, jalapeños, chiles de árbol, cilantro (coriander), and salt and pulse, scraping down the sides of the bowl as necessary, until a smooth paste forms.

With the motor running, drizzle in the oil until combined. Taste and add more salt, if desired. Transfer to an airtight container and store in the refrigerator for up to 2 weeks.

ADVIEH

Persian Jewish cooks turn to a blend of cinnamon, cardamom, and dried rose petals to flavor dishes both savory (like pilafs and stews) and sweet (like rice pudding and charoset). Some variations also include ginger, while others incorporate more traditionally savory spices like cumin and coriander. Petite dried rosebuds can be purchased at Middle Eastern and specialty stores, or online.

Makes: about ½ cup (30 g)
Preparation time: 5 minutes

• ½ cup (20 g) dried rosebuds, stems removed
• 1½ tablespoons ground cinnamon
• 1 teaspoon ground cardamom

Grind the rosebuds in a spice grinder or coffee grinder until fine and powdery. Add the ground rosebuds, cinnamon, and cardamom to a small container with a tight-fitting lid. Shake or stir to combine. Store, covered, for up to 3 months.

BAHARAT

Baharat is a multipurpose spice blend used across the Middle East, including in Israel, to flavor meat, vegetable, and rice dishes, as well as soups and stews. Like most blends, the recipe for *baharat* varies from cook to cook, but typically includes some combination of black pepper, cardamom, cinnamon, cumin, and coriander.

Makes: ½ cup (50 g)
Preparation time: 5 minutes

• 2 tablespoons sweet paprika
• 1½ tablespoons ground cumin
• 1 tablespoon ground cinnamon
• 1 tablespoon ground coriander
• 1½ teaspoons ground allspice
• 1 teaspoon ground cardamom
• 1 teaspoon freshly ground black pepper
• ½ teaspoon ground cloves
• ½ teaspoon ground nutmeg

In a container with a tight-fitting lid, combine the paprika, cumin, cinnamon, coriander, allspice, cardamom, black pepper, cloves, and nutmeg and shake or stir to combine. Store, covered, for up to 3 months.

Advieh

RAS EL HANOUT

With a name that translates to "top of the shop," this regal and complex spice mix traditionally featured the best-quality spices a merchant had to offer. The recipe changes widely from shop to shop, but typically includes some combination of ginger, cardamom, turmeric, cumin, black peppercorns, and fennel. It is used to flavor tagines and couscous dishes or as a dry rub for meat.

Makes: about ⅓ cup (20 g)
Preparation time: 10 minutes
Cooking time: 5 minutes

• 2 tablespoons coriander seeds
• 2 tablespoons cumin seeds
• 1 teaspoon fennel seeds
• 1 tablespoon ground cinnamon
• 1 tablespoon sweet paprika
• 1 teaspoon ground ginger
• ¾ teaspoon ground cardamom
• ½ teaspoon crushed pepper flakes
• ½ teaspoon ground turmeric
• ½ teaspoon freshly ground black pepper

In a small dry frying pan, toast the coriander seeds, cumin seeds, and fennel seeds over medium heat, stirring frequently, until fragrant, 2–3 minutes. Remove the pan from the heat and let seeds cool, then add to a spice grinder and pulse until finely ground.

In a container with a tight-fitting lid, combine the ground toasted spices, the cinnamon, paprika, ginger, cardamom, pepper flakes, turmeric, and black pepper. Shake or stir to combine. Store, covered, for up to 3 months.

BERBERE

This spice blend sits the heart of the Ethiopian pantry. Made with dried chili peppers and a lengthy list of other spices, it is both quite fiery and also complexly flavored. In Israel, Ethiopian home cooks often keep several large jars of homemade berbere in the cupboard or refrigerator to have on hand when making the chicken and egg stew, Doro Wot (page 274), *kik wot* (Spiced Split Pea Stew, page 249), or many other traditional dishes.

Makes: about ½ cup (35 g)
Preparation time: 15 minutes

• 6 dried chiles de árbol, stemmed and seeded
• ½ teaspoon black peppercorns
• ½ teaspoon fenugreek seeds
• 3 tablespoons sweet paprika
• 1 teaspoon ground ginger
• 1 teaspoon onion powder
• ½ teaspoon kosher salt
• ½ teaspoon ground coriander
• ½ teaspoon garlic powder
• ¼ teaspoon ground cardamom
• ¼ teaspoon ground cinnamon
• ¼ teaspoon ground nutmeg
• ⅛ teaspoon ground allspice

Add the chilies, peppercorns, and fenugreek seeds to a spice grinder and pulse until finely ground. In a container with a tight-fitting lid, combine the ground spices with the paprika, ginger, onion powder, salt, coriander, garlic powder, cardamom, cinnamon, nutmeg, and allspice. Shake or stir to combine. Store, covered, for up to 3 months.

CONDIMENTS, SPICES & DRINKS

HAWAIJ FOR SOUP

Yemenite Jews flavor a number of stews, soups—like *marak temani* (Beef and Cilantro Soup, page 140)—and other savory dishes with this turmeric-based spice mix.

Makes: about ⅓ cup (20 g)
Preparation time: 5 minutes

• 2 tablespoons ground cumin
• 2 tablespoons ground turmeric
• 1 tablespoon ground coriander
• 1 teaspoon ground cardamom
• 1 teaspoon freshly ground black pepper
• ½ teaspoon kosher salt
• ¼ teaspoon ground cloves

In a small container with a tight-fitting lid, combine the cumin, turmeric, coriander, cardamom, pepper, salt, and cloves and shake or stir to combine. Store, covered, for up to 3 months.

HAWAIJ FOR COFFEE

Yemenite Jews flavor coffee with this mix of sweet and warming spices. A small pinch can be added to the coffee pot to infuse the grounds while they brew, or sprinkled directly over the mug.

Makes: about ½ cup (30 g)
Preparation time: 5 minutes

• 4 tablespoons ground cardamom
• 4 tablespoons ground ginger
• 1½ tablespoons ground cinnamon
• ½ teaspoon ground cloves

In a small container with a tight-fitting, combine the cardamom, ginger, cinnamon, and cloves and shake or stir to combine. Store, covered, for up to 3 months.

TURKISH COFFEE

Turkish cooks are particularly renowned for their thick, intensely flavored coffee, which is prepared in a metal coffee pot with an elongated handle called a *cezve*. The coffee beans must be very finely ground and the coffee is sweetened in the pot, rather than at the table. Cardamom is often added, giving the coffee a heady perfume. A pinch of the rose petal spice *advieh*, or the Yemenite spice blend *hawaij* are also delicious additions. Serve Turkish-style coffee alongside *tishpishti* (Syrupy Walnut Cake, page 330), or slices of Baklava (page 380).

Serves: 2
Preparation time: 5 minutes
Cooking time: 10 minutes

• 1½ tablespoons Turkish coffee grounds
• 1–2 teaspoons sugar
• ⅛ teaspoon ground cardamom, Advieh (page 414), or Hawaij for Coffee (above)

Add 1 cup (240 ml/8 fl oz) cold water to a *cezve* or very small saucepan. Set over medium heat and bring to a boil. Remove from the heat and stir in the coffee grounds, sugar, and cardamom. Return to the heat and allow to boil again. Remove from the heat and pour into 2 small cups. Let the coffee rest for a few minutes before serving, which allows the grounds to settle.

EVERYTHING BAGEL SPICE MIX

"Everything" bagels, which are topped with a fragrant, crunchy mix of poppy and sesame seeds, dehydrated garlic and onion, and salt, are a relatively new addition to the Jewish culinary canon. As the story goes, they were invented in New York City in the 1980s by a bagel baker who had a stroke of genius while sweeping up the rainbow of excess seeds and toppings that had fallen to the floor. This spice mix makes a wonderful topping for bagels (pages 58–60), of course, but is also delicious sprinkled on popcorn, roasted vegetables, pasta, dips, or anything else that could benefit from a hit of salty-savory flavor.

Makes: about ½ cup (30 g)
Preparation time: 5 minutes

- 2 tablespoons poppy seeds
- 2 tablespoons sesame seeds
- 2 tablespoons dehydrated garlic flakes
- 2 tablespoons dehydrated onion flakes
- 1 tablespoon kosher salt

In a small container with a tight-fitting lid, stir together the poppy seeds, sesame seeds, dehydrated garlic, dehydrated onion, and salt. Store in an airtight container for up to 3 months.

DUKKAH

In Egypt, this fragrant blend of nuts, seeds, and spices (sometimes spelled *duqqa*) is most often served alongside olive oil as a dip for crusty bread and pita. But it is also delicious as a topping for fish, eggs, salads, or roasted vegetables. Here, toasted hazelnuts and sesame seeds provide the foundation, but other versions use peanuts and pistachios.

Makes: about 1 cup (130 g)
Preparation time: 10 minutes
Cooking time: 20 minutes

- ¾ cup (95 g) hazelnuts
- 2 tablespoons coriander seeds
- 1½ tablespoons cumin seeds
- ½ cup (70 g) toasted sesame seeds
- 1 teaspoon freshly ground black pepper
- ¾ teaspoon kosher salt, plus more as needed

Preheat the oven to 350°F (180°C/Gas Mark 4).

Spread the hazelnuts in a small baking dish and toast in the oven, shaking the dish occasionally, until the skins have darkened and blistered, 10–15 minutes.

Meanwhile, in a small dry frying pan, toast the coriander seeds and cumin seeds over medium heat, stirring frequently, until fragrant, 2–3 minutes. Add the toasted spices to a spice grinder and pulse until finely ground. Transfer to a medium bowl.

Remove the hazelnuts from the oven and wrap them in a clean tea towel. Let rest for 1 minute, then rub the nuts in the towel to remove the loose skins. (It is okay if not all of the skins come off.) Set the hazelnuts aside to cool, then pulse in a food processor until coarsely ground.

Add the ground hazelnuts to the toasted spices in the bowl and add the sesame seeds, pepper, and salt. Mix well to combine. Taste and add more salt, if desired. Store in an airtight container in the fridge for up to 2 weeks.

Everything Bagel Spice Mix

From the late nineteenth through mid-twentieth centuries, carbonated water, called seltzer, was the reigning king of Jewish drinks in America. The bubbly water was spritzed into glasses at soda fountains and candy shops and mixed with syrups into refreshing tonics and sodas. The drink was brought over to America with Jewish immigrants from Germany, who named the drink after Niederselters, the town that first sold it.

For many decades, seltzer peddlers delivered siphon-topped glass bottles of the drink to customers' doors. The pressurized bottles delivered powerful streams of carbonated water and refreshed generations of New Yorkers. According to connoisseurs, today's seltzer is not as fizzy as spritzes from generations past, but for those looking to mix up a classic soda fountain drink, it is fortunately still widely available.

CELERY SODA

For New Yorkers of a certain age, celery soda tastes like nostalgia in a glass. It hearkens back to the nineteenth century, when carbonated celery tonics were given to patients with everything from indigestion to anxiety. The drink is also an essential part of the Jewish delicatessen experience, pairing perfectly with a pastrami sandwich and a potato knish.

Serves: 4–6
Preparation time: 5 minutes, plus cooling
Cooking time: 5 minutes

• 1½ tablespoons celery seeds
• 1 cup (200 g) sugar
• Seltzer (sparkling water) and ice, for serving

Pulse the celery seeds in a spice grinder a couple of times (or grind in a mortar and pestle until coarsely ground). In a small saucepan, combine the seeds, sugar, and 1 cup (240 ml/8 fl oz) water and bring to a boil over medium heat. Cook, stirring occasionally, until the sugar is dissolved and the mixture begins to thicken slightly, 4–5 minutes. Remove the pan from the heat and let infuse at room temperature for 1–2 hours (depending on desired strength). Strain through a fine-mesh sieve into a jar.

To serve, add 1–2 tablespoons of the syrup to a glass. Add seltzer (sparkling water) and ice to taste.

CHOCOLATE EGG CREAM

This effervescent drink was a fixture of New York Jewish life in the early twentieth century. People would gather at the corner candy store to drink a frothy egg cream while catching up on the latest gossip. Egg creams taste best made with fresh seltzer pumped from a soda fountain or a pressurized glass seltzer bottle, but store-bought seltzer works, too.

Serves: 1
Preparation time: 5 minutes

• 2 tablespoons chocolate syrup (ideally Fox's U-Bet)
• 3 tablespoons whole milk, chilled
• Seltzer (sparkling water), chilled
• 1 pretzel rod, for serving

Add the chocolate syrup and milk to a tall glass. Add seltzer (sparkling water) to taste, beginning with about ½ cup (120 ml/4 fl oz). Use a long spoon to vigorously stir in the chocolate and create a foamy head on top of the egg cream. Serve immediately, with a pretzel rod.

Celery Soda

SPIRITS

The Jewish culinary repertoire does not include a wide variety of drink recipes. But Jews across the world share a fondness for spirits. Eastern and Central European Jews tend to sip Scotch or fruit brandies like plum-based *slivovitz*, cherry-based kirsch, or Hungarian *pálinka*, which can be made with apricots, pear, peaches, or a wide variety of other fruits. Despite being fruit based, these brandies tend to be bracing rather than sweet. They are typically served on Shabbat morning after synagogue, or as an aftermeal digestif.

Spirits are also important to Sephardi and Mizrahi Jews. Moroccan Jews favor *mahia*, which is distilled from figs or dates. In New York's Hudson Valley, Morocco native David Nahmias and his wife, Dorit, distill *mahia* (using an heirloom family recipe) under the name Nahmias et Fils. Theirs is the only commercial *mahia* distillery in the United States. Meanwhile, across the Mediterranean and Middle East, variations of arak (also called raki and ouzo, depending on who is making it)—the clear, anise-flavored spirit that turns milky-white when diluted with water and ice—are central. Arak is traditionally served as part of the mezze course.

LIMONANA

When the mercury spikes in the summer, people across the Middle East turn to a deeply refreshing mixture of sweet-tart lemonade and bright fresh mint. (The name is a mashup of the Hebrew and Arabic words for "lemon"—*limon*—and "mint"—*nana*.) In Israel, kiosks and cafes do brisk business in the drink, which can be served straight up or swirled into an icy frappé.

Serves: 2
Preparation time: 10 minutes

- ⅓ cup (75 ml/2½ fl oz) fresh lemon juice (from 2–3 lemons)
- ⅓ cup (65 g) sugar
- ¼ cup (5 g) loosely packed mint leaves (no stems), plus more for garnish
- 2 cups (about 10) ice cubes

In a high-powdered blender, combine the lemon juice, ¾ cup (175 ml/6 fl oz) water, sugar, mint leaves, and ice cubes and blend until frothy. Divide into glasses and serve immediately, garnished with additional mint leaves.

NIKI RUSS FEDERMAN AND JOSH RUSS TUPPER

RUSS & DAUGHTERS
•
179 EAST HOUSTON
STREET
NEW YORK, NY
USA

**RUSS & DAUGHTERS AT
THE BROOKLYN NAVY
YARD**
•
141 FLUSHING AVENUE
BROOKLYN, NY
USA

**RUSS & DAUGHTERS
CAFE**
•
127 ORCHARD STREET
NEW YORK, NY
USA

**RUSS & DAUGHTERS AT
THE JEWISH MUSEUM**
•
1109 FIFTH AVENUE
NEW YORK, NY
USA

Niki Russ Federman and Josh Russ Tupper are the fourth-generation owners of Russ & Daughters, the historic (and truly iconic) appetizing shop on New York's Lower East Side. In addition to the shop, they run Russ & Daughters Cafe, serving traditional, Ashkenazi-inspired fare, and a bakery and appetizing counter in Brooklyn. They are best known for their wide array of lox, herring, smoked salmon, and sable—and the delicious bagel sandwiches made with these cured and smoked fish.

BEET AND LEMON SHRUB

Russ & Daughters' expertise goes far beyond bagels, lox, and cream cheese. In this recipe, a refreshing and effervescent beet tonic brings Old World flavor into the twenty-first century. Try it straight up or mixed into a cocktail.

Makes: 7¼ cups (1.7 liters/58 fl oz)
Preparation time: 20 minutes, plus chilling

• 1 cup (240 ml/8 fl oz) fresh beet juice
• 1 cup (240 ml/8 fl oz) fresh lemon juice
• 2 tablespoons distilled white vinegar
• ½ cup (100 g) sugar
• Ice and lemon wedges, for serving

In a large pitcher, whisk together the beet juice, lemon juice, vinegar, and sugar until the sugar dissolves. Add 5 cups (1.2 liters/40 fl oz) water and mix well to combine. Cover and refrigerate for 48 hours before serving. To serve, fill a glass with ice and pour the shrub over top. Top with a lemon wedge.

BEET AND LEMON SHRUB COCKTAIL

Serves: 12

• 6½ cups (1.5 liters/52 fl oz) Beet and Lemon Shrub (above)
• 12 oz (355 ml) vodka
• Ice
• Seltzer (sparkling water)
• Wedges of Pickled Green Tomato (page 411), for garnish

In a large pitcher, mix together the shrub and vodka. Fill twelve 8-ounce (240 ml) glasses with ice and fill each two-thirds of the way with the shrub mixture. Top off each glass with seltzer (sparkling water) and garnish with a wedge of pickled green tomato.

INDEX

Note: Page references in *italics* indicate photographs.

A

aash-e reshteh, 138
Abayuda community, 11, 164
Abe Fisher (Philadelphia), 311
achik chuchuk, 74
adafina, 147
adas polo, 177
adjaruli khachapuri, 64, *65*
Admony, Einat, 353
advieh, 414, *415*
albóndigas, 307
Aleppo pepper
   schmaltzy corn bread with Aleppo pepper, 57
   turmeric-pickled cauliflower, 107
almodrote de berenjena, 259
almonds
   almond-cardamom cookies, 348
   almond horns, 335
   almond macaroons, 329
   beet *eingemacht*, 402
   butter cookies with spiced almonds, 349
   buttery ginger cake, 359
   cardamom-butter cookies, 347
   chicken and almonds with red rice, 281
   chremslach, 26
   couscous au lait, 178
   crème d'amandes challah perdu, 33
   flaky chicken and almond pie, 216, *217*
   giant strawberry-almond hamantaschen, 343
   Greek charoset, 406, *407*
   jeweled rice, 174, *175*
   Kurdish charoset, 406, *407*
   lamb and dried fruit tagine, 312
   malida, 389
   mandelbrot, 334
   Mexican chocolate babka, 326
   pizza *Ebraica*, 356, *357*
   seven-vegetable tagine, 250, *251*
   stuffed dates with almond and rose water, 378, *379*
   sweet and spicy fennel, orange, and olive salad, 91
   sweet bulgur porridge, 389
   sweet egg meringue, 384, *385*
   sweet rice with orange zest and carrots, 176
   teiglach, 370
aloo makala, 162
apio, 156
appetizing shops, 26
apples
   apple-cranberry crisp, 382
   apple murabba, 403
   applesauce, 396
   apple *schalet*, 242, *243*
   apple strudel, 327
   Ashkenazi charoset, 406, *407*
   baked apples with raisins and walnuts, 383
   baked rice kugel, 238
   braised red cabbage and apple, 156, *157*
   chilled apples with rose water, 392, *393*
   chopped herring pâté, 89
   Danish herring salad, 88
   dried fruit compote, 378
   flódni, 358
   Italian charoset, 408
   sweet matzo kugel, 232
   Yemenite charoset, 409
applesauce, 396
apricots
   apricot *lekvar*, 410
   cinnamon-nut rugelach, 346
   dried fruit compote, 378
   flódni, 358
   grilled *versht* and apricots with honey and mustard, 291
   jeweled rice, 174, *175*
   lamb and dried fruit tagine, 312
   poppy seed filling, 397
   stuffed zucchini, 299
   sweet-and-sour okra with tomato, 160, *161*
   teiglach, 370

tsimmes, 154
aranygaluska, 332
arbes, 111
Ardinast, James and David, 125
arook tahine, 188
arroz kon tomate, 170
artichokes
   carciofi alla giudia, 166
   fritto misto, 167
   meat-stuffed artichokes, 303
Ashkenazi charoset, 406, *407*
Ashkenazi Jews, 10, 11
atayef, 371
avgolemono, 126, *127*
avocado and egg dip, 90

B

baba ghanouj, 72
babanatza, 252
babka
   cinnamon–golden raisin babka, 324, *325*
   Mexican chocolate babka, 326
bagelach, 42
bagels
   Baltic rye bagel, 63
   cheese bagels, 42, *43*
   Jerusalem bagels, 60, *61*
   Montreal-style bagels, 59
   New York–style bagels, 58
baghali polo, 172
baharat, 414
baked apples with raisins and walnuts, 383
baked rice kugel, 238
baked salmon salad, 86, *87*
bakhsh, 178
baklava, 380
baklava, fig and pistachio, 353
Balaboosta (NYC), 353
Baltic rye bagel, 63
bamia, 160
Barbary (London), 91
barley
   cholent, 144, *145*
   mushroom and barley soup, 130
   vegetarian cholent, 144
Barney Greengrass (NYC), 26
Baron, Aleksander, 11, 233
basbousa, 331
baygaleh, 211
bazargan, 82, *83*
beans. *See also* chickpeas; green beans; lentils
   bean, herb, and noodle stew, 138, *139*
   black-eyed pea salad, 86
   black-eyed pea stew, 248
   cholent, 144, *145*
   dilled rice with lima beans, 172
   ghormeh sabzi, 309
   hummus with fava beans, 97
   kidney bean–filled bread, 66
   rice, lamb, and dried fruit stew, 140
   stewed fava beans, 21
   tangy white bean salad, 85
   vegetarian cholent, 144
   white bean and meatball stew, 150, *151*
Beckerman, Leo, 27, 103
beef. *See also* pastrami; salami
   beef and cilantro soup, 140
   beef and paprika goulash, 136
   beef and spelt stew, 141
   beef-stuffed grape leaves in spiced tomato sauce, 109
   brisket, 293
   chicken fricassee, 273
   cholent, 144, *145*
   corned beef, 292
   garlicky broiled steak, 310
   ghormeh sabzi, 309
   green herbed rice with meat, 178, *179*
   grilled rib-eye and broccoli salad with Manischewitz steak sauce, 311
   hamin, 148
   hot beet borscht, 128
   hummus with spiced meat, 98, *99*
   kharcho, 142, *143*
   kibbeh, 192, *193*
   lagman soup, 146
   lahmajun, 205
   layered meat and matzo pie, 306
   leek fritters, 191

lyulya kebabs, 313
mafroum, 304, *305*
makoud, 310
meat and herb fritters, 188
meat-stuffed artichokes, 303
meat-stuffed kreplach, 222, *223*
meat-stuffed phyllo cigars, 195
miniature meat pies, 204
moussaka, 308
plov, 181
sauerbraten, 290
shashlik, 313
semolina dumplings in beet soup, 123
stuffed bell peppers, 298
stuffed cabbage, 297
stuffed onions, 300, *301*
stuffed zucchini, 299
sweet-and-sour beef tongue, 292
sweet-and-sour cabbage soup, 128, *129*
sweet-and-sour potted meatballs, 307
tsimmes with flanken, 155
white bean and meatball stew, 150, *151*
wine-braised pot roast, 294, *295*
Yemeni oxtail soup, 137
beets
   beet and lemon shrub, 423
   beet and lemon shrub cocktail, 423
   beet and red onion salad, 77
   beet *eingemacht*, 402
   beet-pickled turnips, 107
   beets with sour cream, 77
   chilled borscht, 124
   chrain, 400
   hot beet borscht, 128
   semolina dumplings in beet soup, 123
Bene Israeli Jews of Mumbai, 11
berbere, 416
berches, 49
berenjena frita, 108
Beta Israeli Jews of Ethiopia, 11
beverages
   beet and lemon shrub, 423
   beet and lemon shrub cocktail, 423
   celery soda, 420, *421*
   chocolate egg cream, 420
   limonana, 422
   Turkish coffee, 417
bialys, 62
bialystoker kuchen, 62
bichak, 211
bimuelos, 361
birne schalet, 242
biscochos de susam, 354
black and white cookies, 336, *337*
black-eyed pea salad, 86
black-eyed pea stew, 248
black radish and onion relish, 72
blintzes
   cheese blintzes, 30, *31*
   Passover blintzes, 32
Bloom, Ari, 27, 103
Bloom, Evan, 27, 103
blueberries
   blueberry buns, 37
   blueberry sauce, 397
borani esfanaj, 100
borscht
   chilled borscht, 124
   hot beet borscht, 128
bourekas
   potato *bourekas*, 212
   shaping, 214
   spinach *bourekas*, 214, *215*
braised chard and chickpeas, 158
braised greens with tomatoes, 164, *165*
braised red cabbage and apple, 156, *157*
brandied chicken bouillon with lemon-ginger matzo balls, 125
bread dumplings, 220
bread pudding
   apple *schalet*, 242, *243*
   pear and prune kugel, 242
breads. *See also* bagels; challah
   adjaruli khachapuri, 64, *65*
   bialys, 62
   cinnamon–golden raisin babka, 324, *325*
   kidney bean–filled bread, 66
   kubaneh, 48
   kugelhopf, 320

malawach, 18
Mexican chocolate babka, 326
onion and poppy seed pletzel, 67
pita, 54
rye bread, 56
schmaltzy corn bread with Aleppo pepper, 57
sour cream biscuits, 54, *55*
spiced honey bread, 50
toasted pita and scrambled eggs, 20
yeasted pumpkin bread, 52, *53*
breakfast
   blueberry buns, 37
   challah French toast, 34
   cheese bagels, 42, *43*
   cheese blintzes, 30, *31*
   cheese Danish, 36
   chremslach, 26
   coiled cinnamon buns, 40
   crème d'amandes challah perdu, 33
   everything onion bread, 27
   huevos haminados, 16, *17*
   jachnun, 41
   lox, 24
   lox, eggs, and onions, 22
   malawach, 18
   matzo brei, 21
   matzo brei with *ikura* and crème fraîche, 23
   matzo coffee, 32
   matzo meal pancakes, 34, *35*
   Passover blintzes, 32
   pastrami hash, 24, *25*
   pastrami lox, 28, *29*
   salami and eggs, 22
   schnecken, 38, *39*
   shakshuka, 18, *19*
   stewed fava beans, 21
   toasted pita and scrambled eggs, 20
   tomato scrambled eggs, 16
brik
   potato *brik*, 196
   tuna *brik*, 196, *197*
brik au thon, 196
brik bil batata, 196
brisket, 293
broccoli and grilled rib-eye salad with Manischewitz steak sauce, 311
brownies, fudgy Passover, 359
b'silla, 216
bubaleh, 34
bulemas, 206, *207*
bulgur
   bazargan, 82, *83*
   bulgur with cheese, 250
   kibbeh, 192, *193*
   sweet bulgur porridge, 389
   tabbouleh, 82
burghol bi jibn, 250
Butcher & Bee (Charleston and Nashville), 51, 73
butter cookies with spiced almonds, 349

C

cabbage
   braised red cabbage and apple, 156, *157*
   cabbage strudel, 202, *203*
   cabbage with noodles, 230
   coleslaw, 80
   health salad, 81
   hot beet borscht, 128
   sauerkraut, 102
   stuffed cabbage, 297
   sweet-and-sour cabbage soup, 128, *129*
cakes
   buttery ginger cake, 359
   chocolate-ganache matzo cake, 328
   chocolate marble cake, 317
   cinnamon-sugar pull-apart cake, 332
   cinnamon-walnut sponge cake, 316
   flourless chocolate cake, 327
   kokosh, 360
   kugelhopf, 320
   lekach, 318
   plum cake, 322
   savory leek cake, 201
   semolina and coconut cake with rose-water syrup, 331
   sour cherry cake, 318, *319*
   sour cream coffee cake, 321
   syrupy walnut cake, 330

calves' feet, 112
candied eggplant, 404, *405*
candied quince, 404
candy
  chocolate matzo toffee, 384
  ginger and *matzo farfel* candy, 383
  poppyseed candy, 381
  sesame halva, 382
capers
  potato *brik*, 196
  tuna *brik*, 196, *197*
caponata *alla giudia*, 116
caraway seeds
  Baltic rye bagel, 63
  everything onion dip, 27
  rye bread, 56
carciofi alla giudia, 166
cardamom
  almond-cardamom cookies, 348
  cardamom-butter cookies, 347
  gulab jamun, 362, *363*
  hawaij for coffee, 417
carrots
  carrot halwa, 390, *391*
  carrot ring, 240, *241*
  carrot salad with cumin, 78
  carrot tsimmes, 155
  cholent, 144, *145*
  coleslaw, 80
  hamin, 148
  health salad, 81
  mint and carrot chicken, 276
  orange soup, 134, *135*
  plov, 181
  roast chicken with thyme and honey, 270, *271*
  seven-vegetable tagine, 250, *251*
  sweet-and-sour celery root, 156
  sweet rice with orange zest and carrots, 176
  tsimmes, 154
  tsimmes with flanken, 155
  wine-braised pot roast, 294, *295*
cassola, 333
cauliflower
  fried cauliflower, 168
  turmeric-pickled cauliflower, 107
  whole roasted cauliflower, 169
celery root, sweet-and-sour, 156
celery soda, 420, *421*
challah, 46
  challah French toast, 34
  challah kugel with poppy seed sauce, 233
  potato challah, 49
  rice challah, 51
  for the Shabbat table, 47
  shaping into braids, spirals, and rolls, 47
chard
  braised chard and chickpeas, 158
  chard fritters, 191
charoset
  Ashkenazi charoset, 406, *407*
  Greek charoset, 406, *407*
  Indian charoset, 408
  Italian charoset, 408
  Kurdish charoset, 406, *407*
  regional variations, 409
  Yemenite charoset, 409
cheese. *See also* cream cheese
  adjaruli khachapuri, 64, *65*
  bulemas, 206, *207*
  bulgur with cheese, 250
  cheese bagels, 42, *43*
  cheese blintzes, 30, *31*
  cheese latkes, 187
  cheese *sambusak*, 208, *209*
  crustless spinach and zucchini quiche, 252
  double-crusted vegetable pie, 258
  eggplant gratin, 259
  fried Halloumi, 111
  kanafeh, 375
  leek and potato frittata, 256
  matzo lasagna, 253
  noodles with curd cheese, 230, *231*
  ricotta cheesecake, 333
  savory leek cake, 201
  spinach *bourekas*, 214, *215*
  stuffed eggplant with cheese, 302
  sweet noodle kugel, 232

cheesecake, 333
  pistachio cheesecake, 323
  ricotta cheesecake, 333
chefs and nouveau Jewish cuisine, 11
chermoula, 400, *401*
cherries
  jeweled rice, 174, *175*
  pizza *Ebraica*, 356, *357*
  sour cherry cake, 318, *319*
  sour cherry dumplings, 225
  sour cherry soup, 132, *133*
chestnuts
  chicken and chestnut omelet, 282, *283*
  Italian charoset, 408
chicken
  brandied chicken bouillon with lemon-ginger matzo balls, 125
  chicken and almonds with red rice, 281
  chicken and chestnut omelet, 282, *283*
  chicken and quince tagine, 269
  chicken fricassee, 273
  chicken *hamin* with bucatini, 148, *149*
  chicken kotleti, 276
  chicken paprikash, 280
  chicken, scallion, and ginger fritters, 188, *189*
  chicken schnitzel, 280
  chicken *shawarma*, 270
  chicken *sofrito*, 272
  chicken soup, 122
  chicken stuffed with spiced rice, 286, *287*
  chicken tagine with preserved lemon, 288
  chopped chicken liver, 94
  coconut chicken curry, 277
  fesenjan, 284
  flaky chicken and almond pie, 216, *217*
  gondi, 240
  Hanukkah fried chicken, 285
  Jerusalem mixed grill, 288, *289*
  meat-stuffed kreplach, 222, *223*
  Mexican chicken soup, 122
  mint and carrot chicken, 276
  onion and tamarind chicken, 274
  roast chicken with thyme and honey, 270, *271*
  stuffed tomatoes with chicken, 278, *279*
chickpeas
  bean, herb, and noodle stew, 138, *139*
  braised chard and chickpeas, 158
  chickpea salad, 84
  chickpea *sambusak*, 210
  falafel, 194
  fish tagine with couscous, 266, *267*
  hamin, 148
  harira, 131
  hummus, 96
  hummus with fava beans, 97
  hummus with spiced meat, 98, *99*
  plov, 181
  salt-and-pepper chickpeas, 111
  seven-vegetable tagine, 250, *251*
  sweet chickpea shortbread, 348
Chief Rabbi Rabbinate, 214
chile peppers
  berbere, 416
  harissa, 411
  s'chug, 413
chilled apples with rose water, 392, *393*
chilled borscht, 124
chitanee, 274
chocolate
  almond horns, 335
  chocolate egg cream, 420
  chocolate-ganache matzo cake, 328
  chocolate marble cake, 317
  chocolate matzo toffee, 384
  chocolate rugelach, 344, *345*
  flourless chocolate cake, 327
  fudgy Passover brownies, 359
  kokosh, 360
  Mexican chocolate babka, 326
  sour cream coffee cake, 321
cholent, 144, *145*
  for Shabbat lunch, 147
  vegetarian cholent, 144
chopped egg and onion, 92, *93*
chopped herring pâté, 89
chopped tomato and cucumber salad, 78, *79*

chraime, 262, *263*
chrain, 400
cilantro
  beef and cilantro soup, 140
  beef-stuffed grape leaves in spiced tomato sauce, 109
  fried fish with cilantro-garlic sauce, 117
  ghormeh sabzi, 309
  green herbed rice with meat, 178, *179*
  pipirrana salad, 95
  s'chug, 413
  spinach and walnut pâté, 102
  tabbouleh, 82
  Yemeni oxtail soup, 137
cinnamon
  advieh, 414, *415*
  cinnamon–golden raisin babka, 324, *325*
  cinnamon-nut rugelach, 346
  cinnamon-sugar pull-apart cake, 332
  cinnamon-walnut sponge cake, 316
  coiled cinnamon buns, 40
  Mexican chocolate babka, 326
  sour cream coffee cake, 321
clatite, 374
Coal Office (London), 91
coconut
  coconut chicken curry, 277
  coconut halwa, 390
  coconut macaroons, 329
  coconut rice, 170, *171*
  malida, 389
  semolina and coconut cake with rose-water syrup, 331
coffee
  matzo coffee, 32
  Turkish coffee, 417
coiled cinnamon buns, 40
coleslaw, 80
concia, 162
cookies
  almond-cardamom cookies, 348
  almond horns, 335
  almond macaroons, 329
  black and white cookies, 336, *337*
  butter cookies with spiced almonds, 349
  cardamom-butter cookies, 347
  chocolate rugelach, 344, *345*
  cinnamon-nut rugelach, 346
  coconut macaroons, 329
  hamantaschen, 340, *341*
  kichlach, 339
  ma'amoul, 350, *351*
  mandelbrot, 334
  nut crescents, 347
  pizza *Ebraica*, 356, *357*
  poppy seed cookies, 338
  sesame seed cookie rings, 354, *355*
  sfratti, 352
  sweet chickpea shortbread, 348
corn bread, schmaltzy, with Aleppo pepper, 57
corned beef, 292
cornmeal
  mamaliga, 167
  schmaltzy corn bread with Aleppo pepper, 57
couscous
  about, 268
  couscous au lait, 178
  fish tagine with couscous, 266, *267*
cranberry-apple crisp, 382
cream cheese
  cheese blintzes, 30, *31*
  cheesecake, 333
  cheese Danish, 36
  cheese latkes, 187
  cinnamon-nut rugelach, 346
  lox spread, 89
  paprika cheese spread, 92
  pistachio cheesecake, 323
  potato *bourekas*, 212
  potato knishes, 213
  sweet noodle kugel, 232
crème d'amandes challah perdu, 33
crème fraîche and *ikura*, matzo brei with, 23
crepes, dessert, 374
crustless spinach and zucchini quiche, 252

cucumbers
  chickpea salad, 84
  chopped tomato and cucumber salad, 78, *79*
  dilled potato salad, 84
  fattoush, 80
  health salad, 81
  kosher dill pickles, 104, *105*
  lox spread, 89
  pickled cucumber salad, 81
  pipirrana salad, 95
  tabbouleh, 82
  tzatziki, 398
cumin
  carrot salad with cumin, 78
  hawaij for soup, 417
currants
  Greek charoset, 406, *407*
  kugelhopf, 320
  kuku sabzi, 256
  plov, 181
  schnecken, 38, *39*
  stuffed grape leaves, 110
  sweet rice with orange zest and carrots, 176
curried fish balls, 118, *119*
curried sweet potato latkes, 186
curries
  coconut chicken curry, 277
  fish curry with tamarind, 268

D
Daboush, Adi, 331
dairy recipes, 13
dairy restaurants, 90
dates
  atayef, 371
  challah kugel with poppy seed sauce, 233
  Greek charoset, 406, *407*
  Indian charoset, 408
  Italian charoset, 408
  ma'amoul, 350, *351*
  malida, 389
  stuffed dates with almond and rose water, 378, *379*
  Yemenite charoset, 409
deblas, 368
delicatessen cuisine, 296
desayuno meals, 20
dessert crepes, 374
Diaspora, 10
dill
  dilled potato salad, 84
  dilled rice with lima beans, 172
  kosher dill pickles, 104, *105*
  kuku sabzi, 256
  stuffed grape leaves, 110
dips and spreads
  baba ghanouj, 72
  baked salmon salad, 86, *87*
  black radish and onion relish, 72
  caponata *alla giudia*, 116
  chopped chicken liver, 94
  chopped egg and onion, 92, *93*
  chopped herring pâté, 89
  egg and avocado dip, 90
  egg salad, 93
  everything onion dip, 27
  hummus, 96
  hummus with fava beans, 97
  hummus with spiced meat, 98, *99*
  lox spread, 89
  mashed eggplant salad, 70
  matbucha, 71
  mock chopped liver, 98
  muhammara, 100
  paprika cheese spread, 92
  red pepper and tomato ragout, 71
  smoked whitefish salad, 88
  smoked whitefish tartine with pickled mustard seeds, 103
  spiced squash dip, 96
  spinach and walnut pâté, 102
  spinach yogurt dip, 100, *101*
  tuna salad, 85
dobo, 50
dolmades, 108, 110
doro wot, 274, *275*
double-crusted vegetable pie, 258
doughnuts
  bimuelos, 361

sfenj, 366
sufganiyot, 364, *365*
dried fruit compote, 378
dukkah, 418
dumplings
  bread dumplings, 220
  gondi, 240
  matzo balls, 220
  meat-stuffed kreplach, 222, *223*
  plum dumplings, 224
  semolina dumplings in beet soup, 123
  shlishkes, 228
  sour cherry dumplings, 225

E
eggplant
  baba ghanouj, 72
  bulemas, 206, *207*
  candied eggplant, 404, *405*
  caponata *alla giudia*, 116
  double-crusted vegetable pie, 258
  eggplant and tomato stew, 249
  eggplant gratin, 259
  fried eggplant slices, 108
  fried eggplant with sugar, 168
  mashed eggplant salad, 70
  matbucha, 71
  moussaka, 308
  roasted eggplant with tahini and
    pomegranate, 113
  sabich, 259
  spicy eggplant and harissa salad, 73
  stuffed eggplant with cheese, 302
eggs
  avgolemono, 126, *127*
  chicken and chestnut omelet, 282, *283*
  chicken *hamin* with bucatini, 148, *149*
  chopped chicken liver, 94
  chopped egg and onion, 92, *93*
  chopped herring pâté, 89
  doro wot, 274, *275*
  egg and avocado dip, 90
  egg salad, 93
  grilled vegetable salad, 74
  hamin, 148
  herb omelet fritters, 195
  huevos haminados, 16, *17*
  jachnun, 41
  kuku sabzi, 256
  leek and potato frittata, 256
  lox, eggs, and onions, 22
  makoud, 310
  matzo brei, 21
  matzo brei with *ikura* and crème
    fraîche, 23
  mock chopped liver, 98
  potato and egg strata, 260
  potato *brik*, 196
  rice, lamb, and dried fruit stew, 140
  sabich, 259
  salami and eggs, 22
  schav, 132
  shakshuka, 18, *19*
  stewed fava beans, 21
  sweet-and-sour eggs, 112
  tangy white bean salad, 85
  toasted pita and scrambled eggs, 20
  tomato scrambled eggs, 16
  tuna *brik*, 196, *197*
everything bagel spice mix, 418, *419*
everything onion dip, 27

F
falafel, 194
faloodeh sib, 392
farfel, 226
  farfel kugel, 229
  matzo farfel with mushrooms, 229
fasoulia kon tomate, 154
fatoot samneh, 20
Fat Pasha (Toronto), 291
fattoush, 80
Federman, Niki Russ, 423
fennel
  fennel and black olive salad, 76
  Jewish-style braised fennel, 158, *159*
  sweet and spicy fennel, orange, and
    olive salad, 91
fesenjan, 284
fideos tostados, 234
figs
  dried fruit compote, 378

fig and pistachio baklava, 353
lamb and dried fruit tagine, 312
Yemenite charoset, 409
fijuelas, 368
Fine Bagels (Berlin), 33, 63
fish. *See also* salmon
  chopped herring pâté, 89
  chraime, 262, *263*
  curried fish balls, 118, *119*
  Danish herring salad, 88
  fish curry with tamarind, 268
  fish tagine with couscous, 266, *267*
  fried fish with cilantro-garlic
    sauce, 117
  fried gefilte fish, 114
  fried sole with *agristada*, 265
  gefilte fish, 114, *115*
  gefilte fish, about, 117
  gefilte fish quenelles, 114
  grilled vegetable salad, 74
  salmon cutlets, 264
  served as first course, 118
  smoked whitefish salad, 88
  smoked whitefish tartine with pickled
    mustard seeds, 103
  sweet-and-sour fish, 265
  tuna *brik*, 196, *197*
  tuna salad, 85
flaky chicken and almond pie, 216, *217*
flammekueche, 254
flan, orange-scented, 392
flódni, 358
Florence Kahn Bakery and Delicatessen
  (Paris), 323
flourless chocolate cake, 327
folares, 339
forshmak, 89
forshpeis, 112
freekeh
  pipirrana salad, 95
French toast
  challah French toast, 34
  crème d'amandes challah perdu, 33
  matzo brei, 21
fricassée, 261
fried cauliflower, 168
fried eggplant slices, 108
fried eggplant with sugar, 168
fried fish with cilantro-garlic sauce, 117
fried gefilte fish, 114
fried Halloumi, 111
fried pastry roses, 368, *369*
fried sole with *agristada*, 265
frittatas
  kuku sabzi, 256
  leek and potato frittata, 256
frittelle di riso, 190
frittelle di zucca, 374
fritters. *See also* latkes
  chard fritters, 191
  chicken, scallion, and ginger
    fritters, 188, *189*
  chremslach, 26
  falafel, 194
  gulab jamun, 362, *363*
  Haman's ear fritters, 367
  herb omelet fritters, 195
  honey-soaked matzo fritters, 190
  leek fritters, 191
  meat and herb fritters, 188
  pumpkin fritters, 374
  spinach fritters, 187
  sweet rice fritters, 190
fritto misto, 167
fruit. *See also specific fruits*
  dried fruit compote, 378
fudgy Passover brownies, 359

G
Garden Cafeteria (NYC), 90
garlic
  everything bagel spice mix, 418, *419*
  fried fish with cilantro-garlic
    sauce, 117
  garlicky broiled steak, 310
  potato *bourekas*, 212
  Yemeni oxtail soup, 137
gefilte fish, 114, *115*
  about, 117
  fried gefilte fish, 114
  gefilte fish quenelles, 114
gehakte leber, 94

ghormeh sabzi, 309
ghraiba homs, 348
giant strawberry-almond
  hamantaschen, 343
ginger
  buttery ginger cake, 359
  chicken, scallion, and ginger fritters,
    188, *189*
  ginger and *matzo farfel* candy, 383
  hawaij for coffee, 417
goldene yoykh, 122
gondi, 240
goulash, beef and paprika, 136
grains. *See specific grains*
Granit, Assaf, 91
grape leaves
  beef-stuffed grape leaves in spiced
    tomato sauce, 109
  stuffed grape leaves, 110
grated tomato relish, 413
green beans
  fritto misto, 167
  guvetch, 246, *247*
  stewed green beans and tomatoes, 154
green herbed rice with meat, 178, *179*
greens. *See also* cabbage
  braised chard and chickpeas, 158
  braised greens with tomatoes, 164, *165*
  chard fritters, 191
  crustless spinach and zucchini
    quiche, 252
  spinach and walnut pâté, 102
  spinach *bourekas*, 214, *215*
  spinach fritters, 187
  spinach yogurt dip, 100, *101*
gribenes, schmaltz and, 412
grilled rib-eye and broccoli salad with
  Manischewitz steak sauce, 311
grilled vegetable salad, 74
grilled *versht* and apricots with honey
  and mustard, 291
groundnut stew, 246
gulab jamun, 362, *363*
guvetch, 246, *247*

H
hadgi badah, 348
halek, 408
halich, 406
halva, sesame, 382
halwa
  carrot halwa, 390, *391*
  coconut halwa, 390
Haman's ear fritters, 367
hamantaschen, 340, *341*
  giant strawberry-almond
    hamantaschen, 343
  yeasted hamantaschen, 342
hamin
  chicken *hamin* with bucatini, 148, *149*
  for Shabbat lunch, 147
  hamin macaroni, 148
Hanukkah, 13
Hanukkah fried chicken, 285
hareesa, 331
harira, 131
harissa, 411
  spicy eggplant and harissa salad, 73
hash, pastrami, 24, *25*
hawaij
  hawaij for coffee, 417
  hawaij for soup, 417
hazelnuts
  dukkah, 418
  Kurdish charoset, 406, *407*
health salad, 81
herbs. *See also specific herbs*
  herb omelet fritters, 195
herring
  chopped herring pâté, 89
  Danish herring salad, 88
hilbeh, 411
holishkes, 297
honey
  bimuelos, 361
  honey-soaked matzo fritters, 190
  honey-walnut filling, 402
  lekach, 318
  spiced honey bread, 50
  teiglach, 370
horseradish
  chrain, 400

hot beet borscht, 128
hoyagusht, 282
huevos haminados, 16, *17*
hulba, 411
hummus, 96
  hummus with fava beans, 97
  hummus with spiced meat, 98, *99*
  hummus ful, 97
  hummus im basar, 98

I
ijeh bakdounez, 195
ijeh b'lahmen, 188
ikura and crème fraîche,
  matzo brei with, 23
ingberlach, 383
Israel, Aaron, 23
Israeli couscous, about, 268

J
jaban, 384
jachnun, 41
jam
  jam and poppy seed kugel, 238, *239*
  pumpkin jam, 403
Jerusalem bagels, 60, *61*
Jerusalem mixed grill, 288, *289*
jeweled rice, 174, *175*
Jewish cuisine
  collecting and cataloging, 11–12
  contemporary, 11
  definitions of, 10
  history of, 10–11
Jewish Diaspora, 10
Jewish dietary laws, 13, 90
Jewish holidays and food traditions,
  12–13
Jewish-style braised fennel, 158, *159*
jibn, 252
jødekager, 349
joodse boterkoek, 359

K
kadayif, 375
kaesekuchen, 333
kaese latkes, 187
Kahn, Florence, 323
kanafeh, 375
kaposztas teszta, 230
kartofl zup, 134
kasha
  kasha and mushroom knishes, 198, *199*
  kasha varnishkes, 164
kaskarikas, 108
keftes de espinaca, 187
keftes de prasa, 191
keftes de silka, 191
kharcho, 142, *143*
kheer, 386
khoresh bademjan, 249
kibbeh, 192, *193*
kichlach, 339
kidney bean–filled bread, 66
kik wot, 249
kipfel, 346
Kish-Kash (NYC), 353
kishke, 221
knaidlach, 220
knedliky, 220
knishes
  kasha and mushroom knishes, 198, *199*
  potato knishes, 213
kokosh, 360
Komarovsky, Erez, 201
körözött, 92
kosher delicatessens, 26
kosher dill pickles, 104, *105*
kosher traditions, 13, 90
kousa mashi, 299
Kratochvila, Laurel, 33, 63
krautsuppe, 128
kreplach, meat-stuffed, 222, *223*
krupnik, 130
kubaneh, 48
Kubeh (NYC), 113
kugel
  baked rice kugel, 238
  carrot ring, 240, *241*
  challah kugel with poppy seed
    sauce, 233
  farfel kugel, 229
  jam and poppy seed kugel, 238, *239*

pear and prune kugel, 242
potato kugel, 234, *235*
sweet matzo kugel, 232
sweet noodle kugel, 232
sweet potato–pecan kugel, 236
types of, 236
Yerushalmi kugel, 237
kugelhopf, 320
kugeltopf (ceramic pots), 236
kuku sabzi, 256

L
lagman soup, 146
lahmajun, 205
lamb
  albóndigas, 307
  green herbed rice with meat, 178, *179*
  Jerusalem mixed grill, 288, *289*
  lagman soup, 146
  lahmajun, 205
  lamb and dried fruit tagine, 312
  lamb and pea soup, 136
  layered meat and matzo pie, 306
  lyulya kebabs, 313
  moussaka, 308
  rice, lamb, and dried fruit stew, 140
  shashlik, 313
lasagna, matzo, 253
latkes
  cheese latkes, 187
  curried sweet potato latkes, 186
  potato latkes, 184, *185*
La Vara (Brooklyn), 95
layered meat and matzo pie, 306
lecsó, 71
leeks
  leek and potato frittata, 256
  leek fritters, 191
  savory leek cake, 201
Lehamim Bakery (Tel Aviv), 343
lekach, 318
lekvar
  apricot *lekvar*, 410
  prune *lekvar*, 410
lemons
  avgolemono, 126, *127*
  beet and lemon shrub, 423
  beet and lemon shrub cocktail, 423
  chicken tagine with preserved
    lemon, 288
  limonana, 422
  preserved lemons, 116
lentils
  bean, herb, and noodle stew, 138, *139*
  harira, 131
  lentil soup, 130
  mejadra, 180
  mock chopped liver, 98
  rice with lentils and dried fruit, 177
limonana, 422
linzen, 130
liptauer, 92
liver, chicken, chopped, 94
lobiani, 66
lokshen kugel, 232
lox, 24
  lox, eggs, and onions, 22
  lox spread, 89
  pastrami lox, 28, *29*
lyulya kebabs, 313

M
ma'amoul, 350, *351*
macaroons
  almond macaroons, 329
  coconut macaroons, 329
mafroum, 304, *305*
mahashas, 278
makoud, 310
malabi, 388
malawach, 18
malida, 389
mamaliga, 167
mamorkuchen, 317
mandelbrot, 334
marak katom, 134
marak kubbeh adom, 123
marak temani, 140
marinated fried zucchini, 162, *163*
marunchinos, 329
mashed eggplant salad, 70
mashi basal, 300

matbucha, 71
matzo
  chocolate-ganache matzo cake, 328
  chocolate matzo toffee, 384
  chremslach, 26
  layered meat and matzo pie, 306
  matzo and tomato scramble, 160
  matzo brei, 21
  matzo brei with *ikura* and crème
    fraîche, 23
  matzo coffee, 32
  matzo lasagna, 253
  sweet matzo kugel, 232
matzo farfel
  ginger and *matzo farfel* candy, 383
  matzo farfel with mushrooms, 229
matzo meal
  brandied chicken bouillon with
    lemon-ginger matzo balls, 125
  honey-soaked matzo fritters, 190
  kishke, 221
  matzo balls, 220
  matzo meal pancakes, 34, *35*
Maxie Eisen (Frankfurt), 11, 125
meat. *See also* beef; lamb
  meat-stuffed artichokes, 303
  meat-stuffed kreplach, 222, *223*
  meat-stuffed phyllo cigars, 195
meatballs
  albóndigas, 307
  sweet-and-sour potted meatballs, 307
  white bean and meatball stew, 150, *151*
meat (versus dairy) recipes, 13
mechouia, 74
meggy lepeny, 318
meggy leves, 132, *133*
mehren kugel, 240
mejadra, 180
menemen, 16
me'orav Yerushalmi, 288
meringue, sweet egg, 384, *385*
Mimouna celebration, 328
mina de carne, 306
miniature meat pies, 204
mint
  bean, herb, and noodle stew, 138, *139*
  beet and red onion salad, 77
  limonana, 422
  marinated fried zucchini, 162, *163*
  mint and carrot chicken, 276
  stuffed grape leaves, 110
  tabbouleh, 82
Mint Kitchen (NYC), 201
Miznon (multiple locations), 169
Mizrahi Jews, 10–11
mock chopped liver, 98
mofleta, 372, *373*
mohibir'yon, 117
mohn, 397
mohn kichlach, 338
mohnlach, 381
Montreal-style bagels, 59
morasa polo, 174
moussaka, 308
m'rabah ab kra, 403
muhammara, 100
murabba, apple, 403
mushrooms
  chicken fricassee, 273
  fritto misto, 167
  guvetch, 246, *247*
  kasha and mushroom knishes, 198, *199*
  matzo farfel with mushrooms, 229
  matzo lasagna, 253
  mushroom and barley soup, 130
  mushroom piroshki, 200
  pickled mushrooms, *105*, 106
  tarte flambée, 254, *255*
  vegetable cutlets with mushroom
    gravy, 257
mustard seeds, pickled, smoked
  whitefish tartine with, 103

N
nahit, 111
namoura, 331
New York–style bagels, 58
noodles
  bean, herb, and noodle stew, 138, *139*
  cabbage with noodles, 230
  farfel, 226
  lagman soup, 146

noodles with curd cheese, 230, *231*
  Passover egg noodles, 226, *227*
  sweet noodle kugel, 232
  toasted noodles, 234
  Yerushalmi kugel, 237
North Abraxas (Tel Aviv), 169
nusskipferl, 347
nuts. *See also specific nuts*
  nut crescents, 347

O
Okochi, Sawako, 23
okra, sweet-and-sour, with tomato,
  160, *161*
olives
  caponata *alla giudia*, 116
  chicken tagine with preserved
    lemon, 288
  fennel and black olive salad, 76
  grilled vegetable salad, 74
  orange and olive salad, 76
  sweet and spicy fennel, orange, and
    olive salad, 91
omelet, chicken and chestnut, 282, *283*
onions
  bean, herb, and noodle stew, 138, *139*
  beet and red onion salad, 77
  bialys, 62
  black radish and onion relish, 72
  chopped chicken liver, 94
  chopped egg and onion, 92, *93*
  everything bagel spice mix, 418, *419*
  everything onion dip, 27
  grilled vegetable salad, 74
  huevos haminados, 16, *17*
  kasha varnishkes, 164
  lox, eggs, and onions, 22
  onion and poppy seed pletzel, 67
  onion and tamarind chicken, 274
  stuffed onions, 300, *301*
  sweet-and-sour eggs, 112
  tarte flambée, 254, *255*
  tomato and onion salad, 74, *75*
orange blossom water
  atayef, 371
  kanafeh, 375
oranges
  orange and olive salad, 76
  orange-scented flan, 392
  sweet and spicy fennel, orange, and
    olive salad, 91
  sweet rice with orange zest and
    carrots, 176
orange soup, 134, *135*
orecchie di Aman, 367
oshi savo, 140
Ottolenghi (London), 11, 137
Ottolenghi, Yotam, 11, 137

P
palacsinta, 374
Palomar (London), 91
pancakes
  atayef, 371
  matzo meal pancakes, 34, *35*
  mofleta, 372, *373*
pan de calabaza, 52
paprika
  beef and paprika goulash, 136
  paprika cheese spread, 92
parsley
  bazargan, 82, *83*
  beef-stuffed grape leaves in spiced
    tomato sauce, 109
  chermoula, 400, *401*
  ghormeh sabzi, 309
  herb omelet fritters, 195
  kuku sabzi, 256
  meat and herb fritters, 188
  spinach and walnut pâté, 102
  tabbouleh, 82
  Yemeni oxtail soup, 137
parve recipes, 13
Passover, 13
Passover blintzes, 32
Passover egg noodles, 226, *227*
pasta. *See also* couscous; noodles
  chicken *hamin* with bucatini, 148, *149*
  farfel, 226
  harira, 131
  kasha varnishkes, 164
pastelitos, 204

pastrami
  history of, 296
  pastrami hash, 24, *25*
  pastrami lox, 28, *29*
pastries
  blueberry buns, 37
  bulemas, 206, *207*
  cabbage strudel, 202, *203*
  cheese bagels, 42, *43*
  cheese Danish, 36
  coiled cinnamon buns, 40
  fried pastry roses, 368, *369*
  giant strawberry-almond
    hamantaschen, 343
  jachnun, 41
  kanafeh, 375
  miniature meat pies, 204
  potato *brik*, 196
  potato knishes, 213
  schnecken, 38, *39*
  tuna *brik*, 196, *197*
  yeasted hamantaschen, 342
pastry fillings
  apricot *lekvar*, 410
  honey-walnut filling, 402
  poppy seed filling, 397
  prune *lekvar*, 410
pâté, chopped herring, 89
peanuts
  groundnut stew, 246
pear and prune kugel, 242
peas
  black-eyed pea salad, 86
  black-eyed pea stew, 248
  lamb and pea soup, 136
  spiced split pea soup, 249
  vegetable cutlets with mushroom
    gravy, 257
pecans
  cinnamon-nut rugelach, 346
  schnecken, 38, *39*
  sweet potato–pecan kugel, 236
peppers. *See also* chile peppers
  black-eyed pea salad, 86
  chickpea salad, 84
  grilled vegetable salad, 74
  guvetch, 246, *247*
  health salad, 81
  matbucha, 71
  muhammara, 100
  pipirrana salad, 95
  red pepper and tomato ragout, 71
  roasted red pepper salad, 70
  shakshuka, 18, *19*
  stuffed bell peppers, 298
  tangy white bean salad, 85
pesce all'Ebraica, 265
pezzetti fritti, 167
pflaumenkuchen, 322
phyllo-based pastries
  apple strudel, 327
  baklava, 380
  cabbage strudel, 202, *203*
  fig and pistachio baklava, 353
  flaky chicken and almond pie, 216, *217*
  kanafeh, 375
  meat-stuffed phyllo cigars, 195
pickled cucumber salad, 81
pickles
  beet-pickled turnips, 107
  kosher dill pickles, 104, *105*
  pickled green tomatoes, 104, *105*
  pickled mushrooms, *105*, 106
  turmeric-pickled cauliflower, 107
pickling and preserving, 106
pierogi, 225
pies
  double-crusted vegetable pie, 258
  flaky chicken and almond pie, 216, *217*
  flódni, 358
  layered meat and matzo pie, 306
  miniature meat pies, 204
piments rotis, 70
pine nuts
  bazargan, 82, *83*
  beef-stuffed grape leaves in spiced
    tomato sauce, 109
  caponata *alla giudia*, 116
  honey-soaked matzo fritters, 190
  hummus with spiced meat, 98, *99*
  kibbeh, 192, *193*
  lahmajun, 205

pizza *Ebraica*, 356, *357*
savory leek cake, 201
stuffed grape leaves, 110
sweet-and-sour fish, 265
sweet rice fritters, 190
pipirrana salad, 95
piroshki, mushroom, 200
pistachios
  atayef, 371
  baklava, 380
  coconut halwa, 390
  fig and pistachio baklava, 353
  jeweled rice, 174, *175*
  Kurdish charoset, 406, *407*
  pistachio cheesecake, 323
  sahlab, 386, *387*
  stuffed dates with almond and rose
    water, 378, *379*
  sweet egg meringue, 304, *385*
pita, 54
  toasted pita and scrambled eggs, 20
piyaz, 85
pizza *Ebraica*, 356, *357*
pizzarelle con miele, 190
pkhali, 102
plau b'jeej, 281
pletzel, onion and poppy seed, 67
plov, 181
plums
  plum cake, 322
  plum dumplings, 224
pollo fritto per Hanukah, 285
pomegranate molasses, 412
pomegranate seeds
  jeweled rice, 174, *175*
  roasted eggplant with tahini and
    pomegranate, 113
poppy seeds
  bialys, 62
  challah kugel with poppy seed
    sauce, 233
  everything bagel spice mix, 418, *419*
  everything onion dip, 27
  flódni, 358
  jam and poppy seed kugel, 238, *239*
  Montreal-style bagels, 59
  onion and poppy seed pletzel, 67
  poppyseed candy, 381
  poppy seed cookies, 338
  poppy seed filling, 397
porridge
  malida, 389
  sweet bulgur porridge, 389
potatoes. *See also* sweet potatoes
  aloo makala, 162
  beef and cilantro soup, 140
  beef and paprika goulash, 136
  chicken *sofrito*, 272
  cholent, 144, *145*
  dilled potato salad, 84
  fish tagine with couscous, 266, *267*
  hamin, 148
  leek and potato frittata, 256
  mafroum, 304, *305*
  makoud, 310
  pastrami hash, 24, *25*
  plum dumplings, 224
  potato and egg strata, 260
  potato *bourekas*, 212
  potato brik, 196
  potato challah, 49
  potato knishes, 213
  potato kugel, 234, *235*
  potato latkes, 184, *185*
  potato soup, 134
  rice, lamb, and dried fruit stew, 140
  schav, 132
  shlishkes, 228
  vegetable cutlets with mushroom
    gravy, 257
  vegetarian cholent, 144
  wine-braised pot roast, 294, *295*
  Yemeni oxtail soup, 137
prehito, 389
preserved lemons, 116
preserving and pickling, 106
prunes
  dried fruit compote, 378
  flódni, 358
  pear and prune kugel, 242
  prune lekvar, 410
  rice, lamb, and dried fruit stew, 140

stuffed onions, 300, *301*
sweet-and-sour okra with tomato,
  160, *161*
tsimmes, 154
tsimmes with flanken, 155
p'tcha, 112
pudding
  carrot halwa, 390, *391*
  rice flour pudding, 388
  saffron rice pudding, 386
  sahlab, 386, *387*
  sweet egg meringue, 384, *385*
puff pastry–based dishes
  potato *bourekas*, 212
  spinach *bourekas*, 214, *215*
pumpkin
  pumpkin fritters, 374
  pumpkin jam, 403
  pumpkin turnovers, 211
  yeasted pumpkin bread, 52, *53*
Purim, 13, 339

Q
quajado, 256
quenelles, gefilte fish, 114
quiche, crustless spinach and
  zucchini, 252
quince
  candied quince, 404
  chicken and quince tagine, 269

R
radish, black, and onion relish, 72
Raij, Alex, 95
raisins
  apple *schalet*, 242, *243*
  baked apples with raisins and
    walnuts, 383
  baked rice kugel, 238
  Baltic rye bagel, 63
  caponata *alla giudia*, 116
  carrot halwa, 390, *391*
  carrot tsimmes, 155
  challah, 46
  challah kugel with poppy seed
    sauce, 233
  chicken and almonds with red rice, 281
  chremslach, 26
  cinnamon–golden raisin babka,
    324, *325*
  couscous au lait, 178
  Greek charoset, 406, *407*
  honey-soaked matzo fritters, 190
  Italian charoset, 408
  jeweled rice, 174, *175*
  kugelhopf, 320
  Kurdish charoset, 406, *407*
  lamb and dried fruit tagine, 312
  malida, 389
  pizza *Ebraica*, 356, *357*
  rice with lentils and dried fruit, 177
  sauerbraten, 290
  schnecken, 38, *39*
  seven-vegetable tagine, 250, *251*
  stuffed cabbage, 297
  sweet-and-sour eggs, 112
  sweet-and-sour fish, 265
  sweet matzo kugel, 232
  sweet noodle kugel, 232
  sweet rice fritters, 190
  Yemenite charoset, 409
rakott krumpli, 260
Rappaport's (NYC), 90
ras el hanout, 416
Ratner's (NYC), 90
red pepper and tomato ragout, 71
relish
  black radish and onion relish, 72
  chrain, 400
  grated tomato relish, 413
  hilbeh, 411
  s'chug, 413
retach mit schmaltz, 72
rice
  arroz kon tomate, 170
  avgolemono, 126, *127*
  baked rice kugel, 238
  chicken and almonds with red rice, 281
  chicken stuffed with spiced rice,
    286, *287*
  coconut rice, 170, *171*
  dilled rice with lima beans, 172

green herbed rice with meat, 178, *179*
jeweled rice, 174, *175*
kharcho, 142, *143*
mejadra, 180
plov, 181
rice challah, 51
rice flour pudding, 388
rice, lamb, and dried fruit stew, 140
rice with lentils and dried fruit, 177
rice with tahdig, 173
saffron rice, 172
saffron rice pudding, 386
stuffed bell peppers, 298
stuffed cabbage, 297
stuffed grape leaves, 110
stuffed onions, 300, *301*
stuffed tomatoes with chicken,
  270, *279*
stuffed zucchini, 299
sweet rice fritters, 190
sweet rice with orange zest and
  carrots, 176
ricotta cheesecake, 333
roast chicken with thyme and honey,
  270, *271*
roasted eggplant with tahini and
  pomegranate, 113
roasted red pepper salad, 70
Roman Jews, 10–11
Rose, Anthony, 291
rosebuds
  advieh, 414, *415*
Rose & Sons Deli (Toronto), 291
rose water
  apple murabba, 403
  cardamom-butter cookies, 347
  chilled apples with rose water,
    392, *393*
  fig and pistachio baklava, 353
  gulab jamun, 362, *363*
  ma'amoul, 350, *351*
  malabi, 388
  rice flour pudding, 388
  rose tahini, 399
  sahlab, 386, *387*
  semolina and coconut cake with
    rose-water syrup, 331
  stuffed dates with almond and rose
    water, 378, *379*
Rosh Hashanah, 12, 248
rotkraut, 156
rugelach
  chocolate rugelach, 344, *345*
  cinnamon-nut rugelach, 346
Russ & Daughters (NYC), 11, 26, 423
rye
  Baltic rye bagel, 63
  rye bread, 56

S
Saba (New Orleans), 57, 399
sabich, 259
saffron
  flaky chicken and almond pie, 216, *217*
  jeweled rice, 174, *175*
  rice with lentils and dried fruit, 177
  saffron rice, 172
  saffron rice pudding, 386
  sweet rice with orange zest and
    carrots, 176
safra, 331
Safta (Denver), 11, 57, 399
sahlab, 386, *387*
salads
  baked salmon salad, 86, *87*
  bazargan, 82, *83*
  beet and red onion salad, 77
  beets with sour cream, 77
  black-eyed pea salad, 86
  carrot salad with cumin, 78
  chickpea salad, 84
  chopped egg and onion, 92, *93*
  chopped tomato and cucumber
    salad, 78, *79*
  coleslaw, 80
  Danish herring salad, 88
  dilled potato salad, 84
  egg salad, 93
  fattoush, 80
  fennel and black olive salad, 76
  grilled rib-eye and broccoli salad with
    Manischewitz steak sauce, 311

grilled vegetable salad, 74
health salad, 81
mashed eggplant salad, 70
orange and olive salad, 76
pickled cucumber salad, 81
pipirrana salad, 95
roasted red pepper salad, 70
smoked whitefish salad, 88
smoked whitefish tartine with pickled
  mustard seeds, 103
spicy eggplant and harissa salad, 73
sweet and spicy fennel, orange, and
  olive salad, 91
tabbouleh, 82
tangy white bean salad, 85
tomato and onion salad, 74, *75*
tuna salad, 85
salami
  grilled rib-eye and broccoli salad with
    Manischewitz steak sauce, 311
  grilled versht and apricots with honey
    and mustard, 291
  salami and eggs, 22
salata loubia, 86
salatat albisbas, 76
salmon
  baked salmon salad, 86, *87*
  chraime, 262, *263*
  lox, 24
  lox, eggs, and onions, 22
  lox spread, 89
  pastrami lox, 28, *29*
  salmon cutlets, 264
salt-and-pepper chickpeas, 111
sambusak
  cheese sambusak, 208, *209*
  chickpea sambusak, 210
sandwiches
  fricassé, 261
  smoked whitefish tartine with pickled
    mustard seeds, 103
sauces
  applesauce, 396
  blueberry sauce, 397
  chermoula, 400, *401*
  rose tahini, 399
  strawberry sauce, 396
  tahini sauce, 398
  tzatziki, 398
sauerbraten, 290
sauerkraut, 102
sautéed zucchini peels, 108
savory leek cake, 201
scallions
  chicken, scallion, and ginger fritters,
    188, *189*
  double-crusted vegetable pie, 258
  green herbed rice with meat, 178, *179*
schalet
  apple *schalet*, 242, *243*
  history of, 236
  pear and prune kugel, 242
schav, 132
Scheft, Uri, 11, 343
Schildkraut's (NYC), 90
schmaltz and gribenes, 412
Schmaltz Appetizing (Toronto), 26, 291
schmaltzy corn bread with Aleppo
  pepper, 57
schnecken, 38, *39*
s'chug, 413
Seder, Sephardi Rosh Hashanah, 248
seltzer, history, 420
semolina
  semolina and coconut cake with rose-
    water syrup, 331
  semolina dumplings in beet soup, 123
Sephardi Jews, 10, 11, 20
sesame halva, 382
sesame seeds. *See also* tahini
  dukkah, 418
  everything bagel spice mix, 418, *419*
  everything onion dip, 27
  Jerusalem bagels, 60, *61*
  Montreal-style bagels, 59
  sesame seed cookie rings, 354, *355*
  Yemenite charoset, 409
Seven Biblical Species, 381
seven-vegetable tagine, 250, *251*
sfenj, 366
sfratti, 352
Shabbat, 12, 47

Shabbat lunch dishes, 147
shakar lama, 347
shakshuka, 18, *19*
Shalom Japan (Brooklyn), 23
Shani, Eyal, 11, 169
shashlik, 313
Shaya, Alon, 57, 399
Shelsky's (Brooklyn), 26
Shemtov, Michael, 51, 73
shirin polo, 176
shlishkes, 228
shortbread, sweet chickpea, 348
shrub, beet and lemon, 423
Shurka, Melanie, 113
Sichel, Yehuda, 311
slaws
    coleslaw, 80
    health salad, 81
smirkás, 92
smoked meats, history of, 296
smoked whitefish salad, 88
smoked whitefish tartine with pickled
    mustard seeds, 103
sole, fried, with *agristada*, 265
Solomonov, Michael, 311
sorda, 160
sorrel
    schav, 132
soups
    avgolemono, 126, *127*
    beef and cilantro soup, 140
    brandied chicken bouillon with
        lemon-ginger matzo balls, 125
    chicken soup, 122
    chilled borscht, 124
    harira, 131
    hot beet borscht, 128
    kharcho, 142, *143*
    lagman soup, 146
    lamb and pea soup, 136
    lentil soup, 130
    Mexican chicken soup, 122
    mushroom and barley soup, 130
    orange soup, 134, *135*
    potato soup, 134
    schav, 132
    semolina dumplings in beet soup, 123
    sour cherry soup, 132, *133*
    sweet-and-sour cabbage soup, 128, *129*
    vegetarian chicken soup, 124
    Yemeni oxtail soup, 137
sour cherries
    sour cherry cake, 318, *319*
    sour cherry dumplings, 225
    sour cherry soup, 132, *133*
sour cream
    beets with sour cream, 77
    everything onion dip, 27
    sour cream biscuits, 54, *55*
    sour cream coffee cake, 321
spelt and beef stew, 141
spice blends
    advieh, 414, *415*
    baharat, 414
    berbere, 416
    dukkah, 418
    everything bagel spice mix, 418, *419*
    hawaij for coffee, 417
    hawaij for soup, 417
    ras el hanout, 416
spiced honey bread, 50
spiced split pea soup, 249
spiced squash dip, 96
spicy eggplant and harissa salad, 73
spinach
    crustless spinach and zucchini
        quiche, 252
    spinach and walnut pâté, 102
    spinach *bourekas*, 214, *215*
    spinach fritters, 187
    spinach yogurt dip, 100, *101*
spirits, 422
squash. *See also* pumpkin; zucchini
    orange soup, 134, *135*
    pumpkin fritters, 374
    pumpkin jam, 403
    spiced squash dip, 96
stewed fava beans, 21
stewed green beans and tomatoes, 154
stews
    bean, herb, and noodle stew, 138, *139*

beef and paprika goulash, 136
beef and spelt stew, 141
black-eyed pea stew, 248
carrot tsimmes, 155
chicken and quince tagine, 269
chicken *hamin* with bucatini, 148, *149*
cholent, 144, *145*
doro wot, 274, *275*
eggplant and tomato stew, 249
fesenjan, 284
fish tagine with couscous, 266, *267*
ghormeh sabzi, 309
groundnut stew, 246
guvetch, 246, *247*
hamin, 148
rice, lamb, and dried fruit stew, 140
    for Shabbat lunch, 147
spiced split pea soup, 249
tsimmes, 154
tsimmes with flanken, 155
vegetarian cholent, 144
white bean and meatball stew, 150, *151*
stracotto di manzo, 294
strawberries
    chocolate-ganache matzo cake, 328
    giant strawberry-almond
        hamantaschen, 343
    strawberry sauce, 396
strudel
    apple strudel, 327
    cabbage strudel, 202, *203*
stuffed bell peppers, 298
stuffed cabbage, 297
stuffed dates with almond and rose
    water, 378, *379*
stuffed eggplant with cheese, 302
stuffed grape leaves, 110
stuffed onions, 300, *301*
stuffed tomatoes with chicken, 278, *279*
stuffed zucchini, 299
sufganiyot, 364, *365*
Sukkot, 12
sukuma wiki, 164
sumac
    fattoush, 80
    tangy white bean salad, 85
sutlach, 388
sweet-and-sour beef tongue, 292
sweet-and-sour cabbage soup, 128, *129*
sweet-and-sour celery root, 156
sweet-and-sour eggs, 112
sweet-and-sour fish, 265
sweet-and-sour okra with tomato,
    160, *161*
sweet-and-sour potted meatballs, 307
sweet and spicy fennel, orange, and
    olive salad, 91
sweet bulgur porridge, 389
sweet chickpea shortbread, 348
sweet egg meringue, 384, *385*
sweet matzo kugel, 232
sweet noodle kugel, 232
sweet potatoes
    cholent, 144, *145*
    curried sweet potato latkes, 186
    orange soup, 134, *135*
    seven-vegetable tagine, 250, *251*
    sweet potato–pecan kugel, 236
    tsimmes, 154
    tsimmes with flanken, 155
    vegetarian cholent, 144
sweet rice fritters, 190
sweet rice with orange zest and
    carrots, 176
syrupy walnut cake, 330
szilvas gombóc, 224

T
tabbouleh, 82
tagines
    chicken and quince tagine, 269
    chicken tagine with preserved
        lemon, 288
    fish tagine with couscous, 266, *267*
    lamb and dried fruit tagine, 312
    seven-vegetable tagine, 250, *251*
tahdig, rice with, 173
tahini
    baba ghanouj, 72
    hummus, 96
    hummus with fava beans, 97
    pipirrana salad, 95

roasted eggplant with tahini and
    pomegranate, 113
rose tahini, 399
sesame halva, 382
tahini sauce, 398
Taïm (NYC), 353
t'ajines d'artichauts farcis, 303
tamarind
    fish curry with tamarind, 268
    onion and tamarind chicken, 274
tangy white bean salad, 85
tanzeya, 312
tapada, 258
tarte flambée, 254, *255*
tartine, smoked whitefish, with pickled
    mustard seeds, 103
Tavlin (Melbourne), 331
t'beet, 286
teiglach, 370
t'fina pakaila, 150, *151*
thengha chor, 170
tishpishti, 330
toasted noodles, 234
toasted pita and scrambled eggs, 20
toffee, chocolate matzo, 384
tomatoes
    arroz kon tomate, 170
    beef-stuffed grape leaves in spiced
        tomato sauce, 109
    black-eyed pea salad, 86
    braised greens with tomatoes,
        164, *165*
    caponata *alla giudia*, 116
    chicken paprikash, 280
    chopped tomato and cucumber
        salad, 78, *79*
    chraime, 262, *263*
    eggplant and tomato stew, 249
    fattoush, 80
    grated tomato relish, 413
    grilled vegetable salad, 74
    groundnut stew, 246
    guvetch, 246, *247*
    hilbeh, 411
    layered meat and matzo pie, 306
    matbucha, 71
    matzo and tomato scramble, 160
    pickled green tomatoes, 104, *105*
    red pepper and tomato ragout, 71
    shakshuka, 18, *19*
    stewed green beans and tomatoes, 154
    stuffed cabbage, 297
    stuffed tomatoes with chicken,
        278, *279*
    sweet-and-sour cabbage soup,
        128, *129*
    sweet-and-sour okra with tomato,
        160, *161*
    tabbouleh, 82
    tangy white bean salad, 85
    toasted noodles, 234
    tomato and onion salad, 74, *75*
    tomato scrambled eggs, 16
tongue, sweet-and-sour beef, 292
tsimmes, 154
    carrot tsimmes, 155
    tsimmes with flanken, 155
Tu Bishvat, 13
tuna
    grilled vegetable salad, 74
    tuna *brik*, 196, *197*
    tuna salad, 85
Tupper, Josh Russ, 423
turmeric
    hawaij for soup, 417
    turmeric-pickled cauliflower, 107
turnips
    beet-pickled turnips, 107
    seven-vegetable tagine, 250, *251*
turnovers
    cheese *sambusak*, 208, *209*
    chickpea *sambusak*, 210
    mushroom piroshki, 200
    potato *bourekas*, 212
    pumpkin turnovers, 211
turshi left, 107
tzatziki, 398

V
vareniki, 225
varnishkes, kasha, 164
vasser challah, 49

vegetables. *See also specific vegetables*
    double-crusted vegetable pie, 258
    grilled vegetable salad, 74
    seven-vegetable tagine, 250, *251*
    stuffed, types of, 298
    vegetable cutlets with mushroom
        gravy, 257
    vegetarian chicken soup, 124
vegetarian chicken soup, 124
vegetarian cholent, 144
vegetarian restaurants, 90

W
walnuts
    Ashkenazi charoset, 406, *407*
    atayef, 371
    baked apples with raisins and
        walnuts, 383
    baklava, 380
    bazargan, 82, *83*
    challah kugel with poppy seed
        sauce, 233
    cinnamon–golden raisin babka,
        324, *325*
    cinnamon-nut rugelach, 346
    cinnamon-walnut sponge cake, 316
    fesenjan, 284
    flódni, 358
    ginger and *matzo farfel* candy, 383
    honey-walnut filling, 402
    Indian charoset, 408
    Italian charoset, 408
    kharcho, 142, *143*
    kokosh, 360
    Kurdish charoset, 406, *407*
    ma'amoul, 350, *351*
    mock chopped liver, 98
    muhammara, 100
    nut crescents, 347
    poppyseed candy, 381
    sfratti, 352
    sour cream coffee cake, 321
    spinach and walnut pâté, 102
    sweet matzo kugel, 232
    syrupy walnut cake, 330
    Yemenite charoset, 409
Wexler, Micah, 109
Wexler's Deli (LA), 11, 109
wheat berries
    hamin, 148
white bean and meatball stew, 150, *151*
whitefish
    gefilte fish, 114, *115*
    smoked whitefish salad, 88
    smoked whitefish tartine with pickled
        mustard seeds, 103
whole roasted cauliflower, 169
wine-braised pot roast, 294, *295*
Wise Sons Jewish Delicatessen, 11,
    27, 103

Y
yeasted hamantaschen, 342
yeasted pumpkin bread, 52, *53*
Yerushalmi kugel, 237
yogurt
    everything onion dip, 27
    pipirrana salad, 95
    spinach yogurt dip, 100, *101*
    tzatziki, 398
Yom Kippur, 12

Z
zaban, 384
Zahav (Philadelphia), 11
zeeuwse bolussen, 40
Zoni (Krakow), 11
Zoni (Warsaw), 233
zucchini
    crustless spinach and zucchini
        quiche, 252
    fish tagine with couscous, 266, *267*
    fritto misto, 167
    guvetch, 246, *247*
    layered meat and matzo pie, 306
    marinated fried zucchini, 162, *163*
    matzo lasagna, 253
    sautéed zucchini peels, 108
    semolina dumplings in beet soup, 123
    seven-vegetable tagine, 250, *251*
    stuffed zucchini, 299
zwetschgenkuchen, 322

AUTHOR ACKNOWLEDGMENTS

This book is dedicated to cookbook author, Jewish food historian, and all-around mensch, Gil Marks, of blessed memory. Without you, nothing.

I am also indebted to many other cookbook writers and Jewish culinary legends including Poopa Dweck, Maggie Glezer, Marcy Goldman, Joyce Goldstein, Joan Nathan, Claudia Roden, Arthur Schwartz, Edda Servi Machlin, Flower Silliman, and Bonnie Stern, among others. I am grateful for and in awe of your scholarship and passion.

Meanwhile, endless thanks to my "Jew food crew" for having my back and for being such inspirations. I am so thankful for the supportive and collaborative community we have created together: Elizabeth Alpern, Mitchell Davis, Devra Ferst, Gabriella Gershenson, Naama Shefi, Adeena Sussman, and Jeff Yoskowitz.

To all of the generous people who opened up their recipe boxes and invited me into their kitchens (or cooked with me in mine), who shared cooking techniques and priceless family food memories, and who served as a sounding board or geographic guide as I researched, developed recipes, and wrote—thank you:
Arlene Abitan, Rachel Almeleh, Sousan Aminfard, Ron and Leetal Arazi, Adam Baldachin, Eylem Basaldi, Dasee Berkowitz, Mitchell Davis, Julie Dawson, Aliza Donath, Tova du Plessis, Devra Ferst, Hilda Fine, Sharon Freudenstein, Rena Fruchter, Anna Gershenson, Norene Gilletz, Lisa Goldberg and the Monday Morning Cooking Club, Elissa Goldstein, Sonya Gropman, Anna Hanau, Mindy Harris, Yoni Kaston, Debbie Kaufman, Carol Koenig, Jeanette Klein, Naomi Kramer, Sabrina Malach, Penina Meghnagi Solomon, John Ment, Sarah Meyer, Rachman Nachman, Micaela Pavoncello, Kat Romanow, Amy Rosen, Gabrielle Rossmer Gropman, Nina Sabnani, Tannaz Sassooni, Nigel Savage, David Sax, Flower Silliman, Emily Socolov, Vafa Shayani, Beth Shulman, Nili Simhai, Marlene Souriano-Vinikoor, Adina Steiman, Bonnie Stern, Edith Stevenson, Giovanni Terracina, Esther Werdiger, Itta Werdiger Roth, Michael Wex, Rabbi Ari Witkin, Tamás Wormser, and Hillary Zana.

For everyone who took one or more of the recipes in this cookbook into their own kitchens, gave them a spin, and provided critical feedback—thank you:
Miriam Bader, Judith Belasco, Abby Bellows, Idan Cohen, Erin Corber, Julie Dawson, Alex Elinson, Elizabeth Fisher, Rabbi Karen Fox, Benjy Fox-Rosen, Tyla Fowler, Amy Freeman, Ora Fruchter, Temim Fruchter, Dana Gerschel, Abi Goodman, Stacy Hadley, Jessica Halfin, Ahuva Hanau, Anna Hanau, Chad Hawthorne, Marjorie Ingall, Stephen Klein, Shira Kline, Shira Koch Epstein, Carol Koenig, Debbie Koenig, Naomi Kramer, Laurel Kratochvila, Jenny Levison, Devorah Lev-Tov, Beth Lipoff, Olga Massov, Lisa Mayer, Debra Nussbaum Cohen, Gilda Outremont, Lindsey Paige, Emily Paster, Deena Prichep, Lara Rabinovitch, Jesse Rabinowitz, Marti Reinfeld, Jamie Reynolds, Shannon Sarna, David Schlitt, Tal and Eric Schulmiller, Ellen Smith Ahern, Beth Shulman, Lorin Sklamberg, Rachel Spurrier, Gayle Squires, Eve Stoller, Aleza Summit, Alix Wall, Rachel Weston, Itiya Hanau Wolman, Molly Yeh, Daniel Zana, and Sarah Zarrow.

Thank you to Temim Fruchter and Carol Koenig for giving second and third eyes to the manuscript, raising important questions, and catching some very amusing typos.

Enormous gratitude to all of the chefs around the world who took the time to contribute recipes. Your culinary visions make this book—and Jewish food in general—more vibrant. And special thanks to Laurel Kratochvila of Fine Bagels for contributing recipes and also for connecting me with so many wonderful chefs in Europe.

Thanks to everyone at Phaidon, as well as the photography team, including Emily Takoudes, Anne Goldberg, Evan Sung, Mira Evnine, Martha Bernabe, Stacy La, Kate Slate, and Julia Hasting.

As always, thank you to my Koenig and Fruchter families for your endless support.

Bountiful love and thanks to my husband and kids: Yoshie Fruchter, Max Fruchter, and Beatrice Fruchter.

ABOUT THE AUTHOR

Leah Koenig has dedicated the last decade of her professional life to chronicling the countless fascinating stories and recipes that make up global Jewish cuisine. She began the journey as editor of *The Jew & The Carrot*, the food and sustainability blog founded by the Jewish environmental organization, Hazon. She is the author of six cookbooks, including *Modern Jewish Cooking*, and her writing and recipes have appeared in the *New York Times*, the *Wall Street Journal*, and *Saveur*, and on Food52, Epicurious, Taste, and Tablet Magazine, among other publications. Leah leads cooking classes and demonstrations across North America and further afield. She lives in Brooklyn, New York, with her family.

RECIPE NOTES

Milk is always whole.
Cream is always heavy (whipping).
Eggs are always large (US)/medium (UK) unless otherwise indicated.
Herbs, unless indicated otherwise, are always fresh, and parsley is always flat-leaf.
Butter is always unsalted, unless specified otherwise.
Salt is always kosher salt. If substituting a different kind of salt, start with slightly less than the recipe calls for and add to taste.

Cooking and preparation times are for guidance only, as individual equipment may vary. If using a fan (convection) oven, follow the manufacturer's instructions concerning oven temperatures.

To test whether your deep-frying oil is hot enough, add a cube of stale bread. If it browns in 30 seconds, the temperature is [350–375°F / 180–190°C], about right for most frying. Exercise a high level of caution when following recipes involving any potentially hazardous activity, including the use of high temperature and open flames. In particular, when deep-frying, add the food carefully to avoid splashing, wear long sleeves, and never leave the pan unattended.

Some recipes include raw or very lightly cooked eggs. These should be avoided by the elderly, infants, pregnant women, convalescents, and anyone with an impaired immune system.

Both metric and imperial measures are used in this book. Follow one set of measurements throughout, not a mixture, as they are not interchangeable.

All spoon measurements are level.

When no quantity is specified, for example of oils, salts, and herbs used for finishing dishes, quantities are discretionary and flexible.

Exercise caution when making fermented products, ensuring all equipment is spotlessly clean, and seek expert advice if in any doubt.

All herbs, shoots, flowers, and leaves should be picked fresh from a clean source. Exercise caution when foraging for ingredients; any foraged ingredients should only be eaten if an expert has deemed them safe to eat. Mushrooms should be wiped clean.

Phaidon Press Limited
Regent's Wharf
All Saints Street
London N1 9PA

Phaidon Press Inc.
65 Bleecker Street
New York, NY 10012

phaidon.com

First published 2019
© 2019 Phaidon Press Limited

ISBN 978 0 7148 7933 8

A CIP catalogue record for this book is available from
the British Library and the Library of Congress.

Commissioning Editor: Emily Takoudes
Project Editor: Anne Goldberg
Production Controller: Nerissa Vales
Design: Julia Hasting
Illustrations: Julia Hasting
Typesetting: Luisa Martelo
Photography: Evan Sung
Printed in China

The publisher would like to thank Kate Slate, Ellen
Cavalli, Elizabeth Parson, Kat Craddock, Jane Hornby,
Mira Evnine, Martha Bernabe, and Stacy La for their
contributions to the book.